A Companion to Contemporary
Political Philosophy

Blackwell Companions to Philosophy

This outstanding student reference series offers a comprehensive and authoritative survey of philosophy as a whole. Written by today's leading philosophers, each volume provides lucid and engaging coverage of the key figures, terms, topics, and problems of the field. Taken together, the volumes provide the ideal basis for course use, representing an unparalleled work of reference for students and specialists alike.

Already published

Forthcoming

Blackwell
Companions to
Philosophy

A Companion to Contemporary Political Philosophy

Edited by

ROBERT E. GOODIN

and

PHILIP PETTIT

Copyright © Blackwell Publishers Ltd, 1993,1995
Editorial organization © Robert E. Goodin and Philip Pettit 1993, 1995

First published 1993
First published in USA 1993
First published in paperback 1995
Reprinted 1996 (twice), 1997 (twice), 1998, 1999

Blackwell Publishers Ltd
108 Cowley Road
Oxford OX4 1JF, UK

Blackwell Publishers Inc.
350 Main Street
Malden, Massachusetts 02148, USA

British Library Cataloguing in Publication Data
A CIP catalogue record for this book is available from the British Library

Library of Congress Cataloging in Publication Data
A Companion to contemporary political philosophy/edited by Robert E. Goodin and
Philip Pettit.
p. cm. – (Blackwell companions to philosophy)
Includes bibliographical references and index.
ISBN 0–631–17993–3 (Hbk) (alk paper) — ISBN 0–631–19951–9 (Pbk) (alk paper)
1. Political science – Philosophy. I. Goodin, Robert E.
II. Pettit, Philip, 1945–. III. Series
JA71.C565   1993   92–41450
320'.01–dc20   CIP

Typeset in 10.5 on 12.5pt Photina by Alden Multimedia
Printed and bound in Great Britain by MPG Books Ltd, Bodmin, Cornwall

This book is printed on acid-free paper

Contents

CONTENTS

vi

CONTENTS

Preface

This *Companion* – like the series of *Blackwell Companions to Philosophy* more generally – has come about through the initiative of Stephan Chambers and Alyn Shipton who, together with Richard Beatty, have been sources of sound advice and encouragement. We should record, first and foremost, our debt – and the profession's – to them.

In commissioning pieces for the present volume, our first priority has of course always been academic excellence. But excellence takes many forms. Within that broad constraint, we were always also striving for a good blend of younger and more established scholars, representing a fair mix of disciplinary affiliations, national origins and intellectual styles. We are pleased with our contributors' handiwork; each, in his or her own very different way, has made a strong statement of how to do political philosophy in that particular mode. We would also like to think that, without any heavy-handed attempt on our part at imposing uniformity on what is by its nature a disparate academic community, our contributors have managed among themselves to produce a genuinely coherent synopsis of the 'state of play' in contemporary political philosophy worldwide.

This *Companion* owes something of its character and stance to the simultaneous development of the *Journal of Political Philosophy*. It, too, is published by Blackwell and edited from Canberra by a team which is strongly represented in the *Companion*: Robert Goodin and Chandran Kukathas are the Editors of the *Journal*; its Associate Editors include Geoffrey Brennan, Tom Campbell, Barry Hindess, Philip Pettit, Andrew Reeve and Jeremy Waldron. We hope that one of the many purposes the *Companion* might serve is as something of an indication of where the *Journal* is coming from and where it is heading.

The editing of this *Companion* (and that new *Journal*) was made much easier by the many political philosophers who are now based in Canberra. Joining long-time denizens of the Australian National University like John Passmore, Eugene Kamenka, Robert Brown and Richard Sylvan, and well-established ones like Philip Pettit, Geoffrey Brennan and Knud Haakonssen, are a spate of fairly recent arrivals including Robert Goodin from Essex, Tom Campbell from Glasgow, Peter Self from the LSE, Barry Hindess and David West from Liverpool and, on an Adjunct Professor basis, Brian Barry from the LSE and Carole Pateman from UCLA. Many other *Companion* contributors (among them, Russell Hardin, Alan Ryan, Gerald Dworkin and Alan Hamlin) are frequent visitors to the ANU.

The form of a reference book precludes authors of individual chapters from acknowledging assistance, as several would have wished. Editors operate under no such constraint. And there is much assistance to be acknowledged. Valuable suggestions regarding the shape of the book as a whole (including possible topics and contributors) have come from Russell Hardin, Chandran Kukathas and John Passmore, as well as from our Blackwell editors. Peter Singer, as editor of a sister volume, provided useful advice on the perils and pitfalls of such an enterprise. Canberra-based contributors benefited from comments of colleagues at a pair of one-day workshops (focusing primarily on Parts I and II of the *Companion*) held at the Australian National University in September 1991.

ROBERT E. GOODIN *and* PHILIP PETTIT
Canberra, Australia
May 1992

Contributors

Richard Arneson: Professor of Philosophy, University of California at San Diego, La Jolla, Calif., USA.

Terence Ball: Professor of Political Science, University of Minnesota, Minneapolis, Minn., USA.

Geoffrey Brennan: Professor of Economics and Director, Research School of Social Sciences, Australian National University, Canberra, ACT, Australia.

Chris Brown: Senior Lecturer in International Relations, Faculty of Social Sciences, University of Kent, Canterbury.

Robert Brown: History of Ideas, Research School of Social Sciences, Australian National University, Canberra, ACT, Australia.

Allen Buchanan: Professor of Philosophy, University of Arizona, Tucson, Ariz., USA.

Tom Campbell: Professor of Law, Australian National University, Canberra, ACT, Australia.

C. A. J. Coady: Professor of Philosophy and Director, Centre for Philosophy and Public Issues, University of Melbourne, Parkville, Vic., Australia.

Patrick Dunleavy: Professor of Government, London School of Economics, London.

John Dunn: Professor of Political Theory, University of Cambridge, and Fellow, King's College, Cambridge.

Gerald Dworkin: Professor of Philosophy, University of Illinois at Chicago, Chicago, Ill., USA.

Richard E. Flathman: George Armstrong Kelly Memorial Professor of Political Science, Johns Hopkins University, Baltimore, Md., USA.

Allan Gibbard: Richard B. Brandt Professor of Philosophy, University of Michigan, Ann Arbor, Mich., USA.

Robert E. Goodin: Professor of Philosophy, Research School of Social Sciences, Australian National University, Canberra, ACT, Australia.

Amy Gutmann: Professor of Politics, Laurance S. Rockefeller University, and Director of the University Center for Human Values, Princeton University, Princeton, NJ, USA.

Knud Haakonssen: Senior Research Fellow in the History of Ideas, Director's Unit, Research School of Social Sciences, Australian National University, Canberra, ACT, Australia.

Alan Hamlin: Reader in Economics, University of Southampton, Southampton.

Jean Hampton: Professor of Philosophy, Department of Philosophy, University of Arizona, Tucson, Ariz., USA.

Russell Hardin: Professor of Political Science and Philosophy, University of Chicago, Chicago, Ill., USA.

Barry Hindess: Professor of Political Science, Research School of Social Sciences, Australian National University, Canberra, ACT, Australia.

Bob Jessop: Professor of Sociology, University of Lancaster, Lancaster.

Eugene Kamenka: Professor of the History of Ideas, Research School of Social Sciences, Australian National University, Canberra, ACT, Australia.

Serge-Christophe Kolm: Professor, Ecole des Hautes Etudes en Sciences Sociales, Paris, France.

Chandran Kukathas: Senior Lecturer in Politics, Australian Defence Force Academy (University of New South Wales), Canberra, ACT, Australia.

Will Kymlicka: Adjunct Professor, Department of Philosophy, University of Ottawa, Ottawa, Canada.

Ernesto Laclau: Professor of Government, University of Essex, Colchester.

Stephen Macedo: Associate Professor of Government, Harvard University, Cambridge, Mass., USA.

Jane J. Mansbridge: Jane W. Long Professor of the Arts and Sciences, Department of Political Science, Northwestern University, Evanston, Ill., USA.

Susan Moller Okin: Professor of Political Science, Stanford University, Stanford, Calif., USA.

John Passmore: Emeritus Professor of Philosophy, History of Ideas, Research School of Social Sciences, Australian National University, Canberra, ACT, Australia.

Philip Pettit: Professor of Social and Political Theory, Research School of Social Sciences, Australian National University, Canberra, ACT, Australia.

Anthony Quinton (Lord Quinton): Sometime Fellow, New College, Oxford, and President, Trinity College, Oxford.

Andrew Reeve: Senior Lecturer in Politics and International Studies, University of Warwick, Coventry.

William H. Riker: Wilson Professor of Political Science, University of Rochester, Rochester, NY, USA.

Alan Ryan: Professor of Politics, Princeton University, Princeton, NJ, USA.

Peter Self: Emeritus Professor, University of London, and Visiting Fellow in Political Science and Urban Research, Research School of Social Sciences, Australian National University, Canberra, ACT, Australia.

Michael Slote: Professor of Philosophy, University of Maryland, College Park, Md., USA.

Richard Sylvan: Research School of Social Sciences, Australian National University, Canberra, ACT, Australia.

C. L. Ten: Reader in Philosophy, Monash University, Clayton, Vic., Australia, and Visiting Professor of Philosophy, National University of Singapore, Singapore.

Richard Tuck: University Lecturer in History, University of Cambridge, and Fellow, Jesus College, Cambridge.

Jeremy Waldron: Professor of Law, Jurisprudence and Social Policy Program, Boalt Hall School of Law, University of California, Berkeley, Calif., USA.

David West: Lecturer in Political Science, Australian National University, Canberra, ACT, Australia.

Introduction

A 'companion' is not a dictionary or an encyclopedia or a literature review. Unlike a dictionary, it is not primarily intended to provide an explication or a history of technical concepts; it is meant to offer substantive commentary on the work pursued in the relevant field of study. Unlike an encyclopedia, it is not committed to the systematic perspective of the official record; it is designed to be a practical guide for someone who wants to find their way through the relevant field. And unlike a literature review, it is not directed only at professionals in the area; it is also written with a view to those who come fresh and unseasoned to the topics discussed.

So much for the distinctive viewpoint of a companion. What now of the terrain on which it is trained? What is encompassed in *Contemporary Political Philosophy?*

Instead of *philosophy* we might well have said 'theory', for political theory is often taken to coincide with what we have in mind as political philosophy. If we have chosen the word 'philosophy', that is to mark, unambiguously, the fact that our interest is in normative thinking. Political theory sometimes connotes empirical as well as normative thought, thought that bears primarily on how to explain rather than on how to evaluate; another Blackwell Dictionary takes those topics as its focus (Outhwaite and Bottomore, 1993). Political philosophy, in contrast, is unequivocally concerned with matters of evaluation.

But though our interest is in normative or evaluative thought, we should stress that we take a broad view about the range of issues that are normatively relevant to political philosophy. Thus we suppose that questions about what can feasibly be achieved in a certain area are just as central to normative concerns as questions about what is desirable in that area. We understand political philosophy in such a way that it does not belong to the narrow coterie of those who would just contemplate or analyse the values they treasure. It should come as no surprise that we look to a range of disciplines in charting contributions to political philosophy. We look, not just to philosophy – analytical or continental – but also to economics, history, law, political science and sociology.

What does it mean to say that our concern is with *political* philosophy? Moral philosophy – if you like, ethics – is concerned with normative thinking about how in general various agents, individual or indeed institutional, should behave. So what is the concern of political philosophy? Primarily, it is a concern to identify the sorts of political institution that we should have, at least given the background sort of culture or society that we enjoy. To take the view that we should have certain political institutions will imply that if such institutions are in place, then, other things being equal, agents should not act so as to undermine them. But in general the connections between moral and political philosophy are quite weak. Thus, our political philosophy may not tell us how agents should behave in the imperfect world where the ideal institutions are lacking or where the ideal institutions are abused by those who run them. It may not give us much guidance on issues related to what used to be described as the problem of political obligation.

But if political philosophy is concerned with which political institutions we ought to have, what institutions count as political? On a narrow construal, political institutions would mean the institutions associated with political process such as the voting system, the parliamentary system, the system for choosing the executive, and so on: the sorts of thing surveyed in the parallel *Blackwell Encyclopedia of Political Institutions* (Bogdanor, 1987). On a broader construal, political institutions would include not just those procedural devices but also any substantive institutions associated, as we might say, with the political product: any institutions that can be affected by those who assume power under the political process. Political institutions in this sense would include the major legal and economic and even cultural institutions, in addition to the arrangements of government. We understand political institutions in this broader way, as indeed do most political philosophers. Political philosophy, as we conceive of it, is not just interested in the routines that govern politics but also in the various systems which politics may be used to shape. It is concerned with all the institutions that help to determine what John Rawls (1971, sec. 2) describes as the 'basic structure' of a society.

Finally, what is connoted by our focus on *contemporary* political philosophy? Within the analytical tradition of thought, as that affects both philosophy and other disciplines, political philosophy has become an active and central area of research in the past two or three decades; it had enjoyed a similar status in the nineteenth century but had slipped to the margins for much of the twentieth. In directing the *Companion* to contemporary political philosophy, we mean to focus on this recent work. (For other anthologies and surveys, see for example: Quinton, 1967; Ionescu, 1980; Hamlin and Pettit, 1989; Miller, 1990; Held, 1991.) In many cases discussion of recent work requires some commentary on earlier literature, but here we do only as much of that as is strictly necessary to understand the contemporary scene and anyone wanting full background ought to look elsewhere (for example, Miller, 1987).

Within non-analytical traditions, in particular, it is not so clear what is to count as contemporary; but here too our general focus has been on work in the last two or three decades. Often, however, non-analytical thought is intimately tied up with figures from the past – history has a different presence here – and we have been happy in these cases to have our contributors give more attention to such figures. For example, it would be impossible to understand the French wave of deconstructionist thought without some understanding of Nietzsche, for deconstructionists focus on this nineteenth-century German thinker as though he were a prophet of their perspective.

Because it is a companion to contemporary political philosophy, and not a reference work of a more standard kind, we have decided to organize the material in an unusual manner. The book is divided into three broad parts, with long discussions in Part I of the contributions of different disciplines to the subject area; somewhat shorter discussions, in Part II, of the major ideologies which have cast their shadow across the territory; and shorter treatments still, in Part III, of various topics of special interest.

The distinctive and exciting thing about contemporary political philosophy is that it has involved the work of practitioners in a variety of disciplines, or at least the use of work done by people in a variety of disciplines. Rawls in analytical philosophy, Habermas in continental philosophy, Sen in economics, Dworkin in law, Skinner in history, Barry in political science: all of these are names that would figure in any account of what is happening in contemporary political philosophy. But while the researchers involved in different disciplines focus on questions that are treated across an interdisciplinary front, and while most of them maintain a working knowledge of what is happening in disciplines besides their own, the disciplinary dispersion of the subject does create many problems.

It is with these problems in mind that we decided to open the *Companion* with a section devoted to long introductions to the contributions made by each of these relevant disciplines to contemporary political philosophy. Each article is meant to familiarize the reader with the sorts of issue in political philosophy that have particularly concerned those in the discipline in question and with the techniques and models developed in an attempt to cope with them. We hope that the articles will serve as a whole to enable the relative newcomer to look at the different avenues on which political philosophy is pursued, and that it will make it possible for the relative expert in any one discipline to get a picture of what is happening elsewhere.

It is a striking feature of political philosophy, hardly surprising in virtue of the practical relevance of the subject, that apart from divisions on disciplinary lines, it also displays divisions on ideological dimensions. In selecting the ideologies to be covered in the second part, we tried to identify those principled world-views that have a substantial impact in contemporary public life as well as an impact on philosophical thinking.

Environmentalism and internationalism figure in Part III, rather than here, on the grounds that they do not really represent complete world-views, at least for most of those espousing them. Nationalism – still less racism, sexism or ageism – does not figure, on the grounds that it hardly counts as a principled way of thinking about things. And republicanism does not get in, because while the rediscovery of republican thought has influenced a number of theorists, it has not had a substantial impact on public life. Yet other ideologies – like theism, monarchism, fascism – are omitted on the grounds that, whatever impact they once had on public life, they would seem to play only a marginal role in the contemporary world.

The ideologies that we do include in Part II are of such importance, both as social movements and as traditions of thinking, that someone unacquainted with any one of them would be seriously compromised in their ability to understand what is happening in contemporary political philosophy. And since our interest in them is essentially as systems of ideas, we organize discussions of them along the lines of their theoretical self-descriptions rather than in terms of their institutional instantiations: 'Marxism' rather than 'communism', 'socialism' rather than 'social democracy', and so on.

We believe that Parts I and II cover much of the ground that is relevant to contemporary political philosophy, and enable us to see that ground from different angles. But there are a number of important topics which receive too little attention in those parts: usually they are topics which it would be impossible to deal with adequately in the course of an overview treatment of a discipline or an ideology. Part III identifies a range of such topics and includes shorter discussions of them. The *Companion* would not approach the ideal of being a more or less complete guide to contemporary political philosophy unless it gave this level of attention to the matters involved.

How to use this volume? We hope that readers will find the different articles more or less self-sufficient discussions of the subjects they treat. The treatment in each case is distinctive, reflecting the viewpoint of the author. But in no case is the treatment idiosyncratic; in no case does it warp the topics covered to fit with the angle taken. We would like to believe that the volume represents an attractive way of getting a perspective on contemporary political philosophy and an accessible way of getting into particular areas of interest.

But the volume is not just an integrated set of introductions to different aspects of contemporary political philosophy. It should also serve as a useful reference work. Here we think that the index is of primary importance. We have designed the index to cover the concepts that someone looking for a reference work in political philosophy would be likely to want to explore. We think that in the articles which the volume contains there is material sufficient to elucidate those concepts, and often to elucidate them from different angles: from the viewpoint, now of this discipline, now of that; in the context, now of one ideology, now of another; with the focus, now of a contextualized treatment, now of a specialized discussion. The index is designed to enable someone to access relevant material easily and to use the volume effectively as a work of reference.

References

Bogdanor, V., ed.: *The Blackwell Encyclopedia of Political Institutions* (Oxford: Blackwell, 1987).

Hamlin, A. and Pettit, P., eds: *The Good Polity* (Oxford: Blackwell, 1989).

Held, D., ed.: *Political Theory Today* (Oxford: Polity, 1991).

Ionescu, G., ed.: 'A generation of political thought', *Government & Opposition*, 15 (1980), 261–566.

Miller, D., ed.: *The Blackwell Encyclopedia of Political Thought* (Oxford: Blackwell, 1987).

————'The resurgence of political theory', *Political Studies*, 38 (1990), 421–37.

Outhwaite, W. and Bottomore, T., eds: *The Blackwell Dictionary of Twentieth-century Social Thought* (Oxford: Blackwell, 1993).

Quinton, A., ed.: *Political Philosophy* (Oxford: Oxford University Press, 1967).

Rawls, J.: *A Theory of Justice* (Cambridge, Mass.: Harvard University Press, 1971).

PART I
DISCIPLINARY CONTRIBUTIONS

I

The contribution of analytical philosophy

PHILIP PETTIT

I shall assume that we are agreed on what philosophy is. After all, we must begin somewhere. So what, then, is analytical philosophy? It is philosophy, I shall take it, in the mainstream tradition of the Enlightenment. Specifically, it is philosophy pursued in the manner of Hume and Kant, Bentham and Frege, Mill and Russell. What binds analytical figures together is that they endorse, or at least take seriously, the distinctive assumptions of the Enlightenment. These assumptions go, roughly, as follows:

1 There is a reality independent of human knowledge of which we human beings are part.
2 Reason and method, particularly as exemplified in science, offer us the proper way to explore that reality and our relationship to it.
3 In this exploration traditional preconceptions – in particular, traditional evaluative preconceptions – should be suspended and the facts allowed to speak for themselves.

With these assumptions in place, analytical philosophers see their job in one of two ways. Either they see themselves as pursuing the Enlightenment project of methodical investigation, carving out areas of philosophical inquiry and methods of philosophical argument; or they see themselves as methodologically charting the pursuit of that project elsewhere, providing a perspective on the nature of scientific and other approaches to knowledge. Either way the key word is 'method'. In this focus on method, and in their broader affiliations, analytical philosophers distinguish themselves from the counter-Enlightenment or continental tradition. They take their distance from more or less romantic figures like Rousseau, Herder, Hegel and the early Marx, and from disciplinary approaches – say, in sociology or anthropology – that are heavily influenced by such thinkers. They distance themselves equally from philosophers of a more sceptical and anti-systematic cast like Kierkegaard and Nietzsche and from the many later thinkers, philosophical and non-philosophical, who identify with them. And, finally, they reject styles of philosophical thought that are distinctively shaped by certain traditions of religious, cultural or political commitment.

While I cannot defend this account of analytical philosophy here, I should remark that it is controversial. Sometimes analytical philosophy is demarcated by reference to substantive assumptions, as the style of philosophy pursued in the heyday of logical atomism, logical positivism and linguistic analysis, under the influence of figures like Moore and Russell, Carnap and Ayer, Austin and Ryle. Sometimes it is demarcated geographically as the style of philosophy pursued, in the main, among English-speaking philosophers, or at least among English-speaking philosophers this century. My account of analytical philosophy fits well with the geographical approach, for most English-speaking philosophy is methodologically driven or methodologically focused in the Enlightenment manner and most continental thinking is not: the most striking contemporary exception is Jürgen Habermas, but even he belongs to a school, critical theory, which is deeply connected with the early, more or less romantic Marx. Both approaches score over the substantive mode of demarcation, for this would not allow us to count even figures like John Rawls and Ronald Dworkin in the analytical camp.

My concern here is with the contribution that analytical philosophers, in particular recent analytical philosophers, have made to political philosophy: that is, to normative thinking about the sorts of institutions that we ought politically to try to establish. It will be convenient to discuss this contribution in two different phases. First, I will offer an overview of the history of analytical political philosophy in recent decades. Then I will look at the legacy of assumptions, often assumptions unnoticed and unannounced, which analytical philosophers have tended to intrude, for good or ill, into political thinking.

Analytical political philosophy: the history

The long silence

One of the most striking features of analytical philosophy is that its major practitioners have often neglected politics in their active agenda of research and publication. Political philosophy was a focus of analytical concern and activity in nineteenth-century Britain, when the main figures were Jeremy Bentham, John Stuart Mill and Henry Sidgwick. These thinkers established a broad utilitarian consensus, according to which the yardstick in assessing political institutions – in assessing institutions that are politically variable – is the happiness of the people affected by those institutions, in particular the happiness of the people who live under the institutions. They all acknowledged other values, in particular the value of liberty, but they argued that such values were important only for their effect on happiness.

But the utilitarian bustle of the nineteenth century soon died down. From late in the century to about the 1950s political philosophy ceased to be an area of active exploration. There was lots done on the history of the subject, and of course this often reflected a more or less widely accepted set of assumptions. But there was little or nothing of significance published in political philosophy itself. Peter Laslett summed up the situation in 1956 when he wrote: 'For the moment, anyway, political philosophy is dead' (Laslett, 1956, p. vii).

This all changed within a decade of Laslett's pronouncement. In 1959 Stanley Benn and Richard Peters published *Social Principles and the Democratic State*, in 1961 H. L. A. Hart published *The Concept of Law* and in 1965 Brian Barry published *Political Argument*. Benn and Peters argued, in a fashion that would have cheered many of their nineteenth-century forebears, that most of the principles we find attractive in politics reflect a utilitarian disposition. The books by Hart and Barry were considerably more revolutionary. Each used techniques associated with current analytical philosophy to resume the sort of discussion of grand themes which had been the hallmark of the nineteenth century. And each developed a novel perspective on the matters that it treated. Hart used contemporary techniques to defend a positivist view of law against the view that law was the command of the sovereign; that view had been defended by the nineteenth-century utilitarian jurisprude, John Austin. Barry used such techniques to try, among other things, to make a pluralism about values intellectually respectable; this pluralism was directly opposed to the utilitarian tradition in which everything had been reduced to the value of utility.

Why had there been such a silence in political philosophy through the first half of this century? A number of factors may have made a contribution. There were methodological reasons why political philosophy may not have seemed to be an attractive area to analytical philosophers during that period. But there was also a substantive reason why it should have failed to engage them. I will look at the methodological reasons first, and then at the substantive consideration.

Analytical philosophy became methodologically more and more self-conscious in the early part of the century, with the development of formal logic in the work of Frege and Russell. Two propositions emerged as orthodoxy and were incorporated into the logical positivist picture of the world which swept the tradition in the 1920s and 1930s (Ayer, 1936). One of these propositions was that evaluative or normative assertions did not serve, or at least did not serve primarily, to essay a belief as to how things are; their main job was to express emotion or approval/disapproval, much in the manner of an exclamation like 'Wow!' or 'Ugh!' The other proposition was that among assertions that do express belief, there is a fairly exact divide between empirical claims that are vulnerable to evidential checks and analytical or *a priori* claims, such as mathematical propositions, that are true in virtue of the meaning of their terms.

These two propositions would have given pause to any analytical philosophers bent on doing political philosophy. They would have suggested that since philosophy is not an empirical discipline, and since there are few *a priori* truths on offer in the political arena, its only task in politics can be to explicate the feelings or emotions we are disposed to express in our normative political judgements. But that job may not have seemed very promising to many philosophers. If you are possessed of the Enlightenment urge to advance the frontiers of knowledge, or to map the advances that occur elsewhere, then trying to articulate non-cognitive feelings may look like small beer. The best-known logical positivist tract on political philosophy is T. D. Weldon's *The Vocabulary of Politics*, published in 1953, and while it left room for this task of articulation, its main contribution was to pour cold water on the aspiration of political philosophy to say something important.

The propositions dividing the factual from the evaluative and the *a priori* from the empirical did not bulk large in the alternative to logical positivism, and to theoretical philosophy generally, which was developed by Ludwig Wittgenstein from the 1930s through to the 1950s. But the propositions still retained a place in this post-positivist variety of analytical philosophy and, in any case, the Wittgensteinian development introduced extra methodological reasons why political philosophy should not have seemed a promising area of research. The development brought strains of counter-Enlightenment thought into analytical philosophy, emphasizing that the job of the philosopher is to dispel the false images of reality which theorizing can generate – images like that of logical positivism – and to restore us to the ease and quiet of unexamined language-use. If philosophy is cast in this therapeutic role, then, once again, it is not obvious why political philosophy should be an attractive research area. Whatever the problems in politics, they do not look like problems of the sort that any kind of therapy could resolve.

Some figures who are associated loosely with the later Wittgenstein, in particular J. L. Austin and Gilbert Ryle, did not embrace his therapeutic view of philosophy. But these thinkers also nurtured a picture of philosophy in which political philosophy would not have been represented as a fetching or challenging activity. Both of them thought of the main task of philosophy as charting and systematizing distinctions and habits of thought that are marked in ordinary language but that are often overlooked in crude theorizing, in particular theorizing about mind and its relation to the world. This conceptualization of the task of philosophy does as badly as the Wittgensteinian by political philosophy. It leaves political philosophy, at best, in a marginal position.

We can see, then, that there were methodological reasons why political philosophy may have come off the analytical research agenda in the first half of this century. But, as Brian Barry (1990) has argued, such reasons may not be sufficient to explain why it disappeared so dramatically. Consistently with thinking that normative judgements express feeling, one may believe that there is still an important task for reason in sorting out the different commitments that can be consistently made. The point would have been clear to most philosophers from the influential work of C. L. Stevenson (1944) or R. M. Hare (1952) in ethics. Again, consistently with thinking that the main job of philosophy is to carry forward the sort of programme described by Wittgenstein or Ryle or Austin, one may believe that a subsidiary job is to sort out the commitments that can rationally be sustained. So is there any other reason why political philosophy should have been neglected by analytical thinkers in the first half of the century?

Apart from methodological considerations, there is a substantive reason why the subject may not have engaged the best minds in this period. There was probably little puzzlement in the minds of Western philosophers in the early part of the century as to what are the rational commitments in regard to political values. Continental refugees like Popper may have felt that they had something to establish, for they would have had a greater sense of the attractions of totalitarian government; Popper was one of the very few analytical philosophers to contribute, however historically and indirectly, to political theory (Popper, 1945; 1957). But the majority of analytical philosophers lived in a world where such values as liberty and equality and democracy held unchallenged sway. There were debates, of course, about the best means, socialist or otherwise, of advancing those values. But such debates would have seemed to most analytical philosophers to belong to the empirical social sciences. Hence those philosophers may not have seen any issues worth pursuing in the realm of political philosophy itself.

One qualification. There would have been an issue as to how unquestioned values like liberty and equality should be weighted against each other. But many would have seen that question as theoretically irresoluble and intellectually uninteresting. And of those who found it resoluble most would have adopted the utilitarian view that the different values involved all reflect different aspects of utility, however that is to be understood, in which case the question becomes equally uninteresting. Brian Barry (1990, p. xxxv) suggests that utilitarianism was the prevalent attitude over the period and that this made the enterprise of political philosophy look unfetching. Under utilitarianism exact political prescription depends entirely on facts about circumstances and so it lies beyond the particular expertise of the philosopher.

If these observations on the political silence of analytical philosophy are correct, then analytical philosophers in the mid-century would have been inhibited from tackling political matters by two factors. They had a sense, on the one side, that there was little useful work to be done on questions specifically related to values and, on the other, that questions related to facts were properly left to empirical disciplines. With these considerations in mind, we can understand why a book like Barry's *Political Argument* should have made such an impact when it appeared in 1965.

Barry rejected utilitarianism in favour of a value pluralism; here he was influenced by Isaiah Berlin's 1958 lecture on 'Two Concepts of Liberty' (Barry, 1990, p. xxiv). But he introduced the apparatus of indifference curves from economics to show that there is still interesting intellectual work to be done, even if you are a pluralist about values: even if you acknowledge different values, like liberty and equality and democracy, and believe that they do not resolve into a single value like the utilitarian's notion of happiness. There is work to be done in looking at the different possible trade-offs between the values involved and at their different institutional implications. This feature of Barry's work meant that he showed the way beyond the inhibition about discussing values.

He also showed the way beyond the inhibition about trespassing on empirical disciplines. Barry may have maintained a traditional notion of the demarcation between philosophy and the empirical disciplines. But, if he did, he still had no hesitation about advocating a union between philosophy and, for example, an economic way of modelling political problems, when considering how to match various packages of values with social institutions. His programme for pursuing this task was conceived in 'the marriage of two modern techniques: analytical philosophy and analytical politics' (Barry, 1965, p. 290).

Barry's book is reasonably identified as marking the end of the long political silence of analytical philosophy. While Hart's *Concept of Law* (1961) had also made a great impact, and while it retains the status of a classic, it was easily seen as a contribution to jurisprudence rather than philosophy, and it did not open up new ways of thinking about politics. But Barry's book was itself superseded less than a decade later when John Rawls published *A Theory of Justice* in 1971. Barry (1990, p. lxix) generously acknowledges the fact: '*Political Argument* belongs to the pre-Rawlsian world while the world we live in is post-Rawlsian . . . *A Theory of Justice* is the watershed that divides the past from the present.'

A Theory of Justice

Rawls' book resembles Barry's in two salient respects. Like Barry, he is a pluralist about values, but finds this no obstacle to the intellectual discussion of how the different values that are relevant in politics ought to be weighted against each other; the point is discussed below. And, like Barry, he is happy about contaminating pure philosophical analysis with materials from the empirical disciplines in developing a picture of how to institutionalize his preferred package of values and in considering whether the institutions recommended are likely to be stable. Rawls does not acknowledge the clear distinction that logical positivists postulated between the empirical and the *a priori*. He writes, more or less consciously, in the tradition associated with the work of his Harvard colleague, W. V. O. Quine. For Quine (1960) all claims are vulnerable to experience, though some claims may be relatively costly to revise, and therefore relatively deeply entrenched in our web of belief: if you like, relatively *a priori*. This pragmatic attitude may explain how Rawls can comfortably import material from economics and psychology and other disciplines into his discussion.

So much for continuities between Rawls and Barry. The largest methodological break between the two writers comes in their different views of what the intellectual discussion of values involves. In Barry, the project is one of looking at principles that are actually endorsed in political life – specifically, in the politics of Britain, the United States and some similar countries after 1945 (Barry, 1965, p. xvii) – and then exploring the different possibilities of trade-offs between the values involved. In Rawls, the project gets to be much more engaged, in the way in which nineteenth-century utilitarianism had been engaged. He is interested, not in the different beliefs we actually hold about what is politically right, but in what beliefs we ought to hold about what is politically right.

Rawls restricts himself to the question of what makes for justice, of what makes for the proper political balancing of competing claims and interests (Rawls, 1971, pp. 3–6); he believes that justice in this sense, justice as fairness, is the main right-making feature of political institutions (ibid., pp. 3–4). But Rawls is not interested just in distinguishing different, internally coherent conceptions of justice and in looking at what they institutionally require, as Barry is interested in different packages of values and their institutional requirements. He is concerned, in the first place, with what is the appropriate conception of justice to have and what, therefore, are the right institutions to establish.

The aspiration to identify the appropriate conception of justice is tempered in Rawls' later work, where he explicates his aim as one of identifying the appropriate conception for people who share the commitments 'latent in the public political culture of a democratic society' (Rawls, 1988, p. 252). But whether or not it is tempered in this way, the aspiration raises a question of method. How is the political philosopher to identify the appropriate conception of justice? It is significant that Rawls' first publication, 'Outline for a decision procedure for ethics' (1951), offers an answer to this question to which he remains broadly faithful in his later work. The method he proposes, in the language of *A Theory of Justice*, is the method of reflective equilibrium (Rawls, 1971, pp. 46–53).

Consider a discipline like logic or linguistics. To develop a logic, in the sense in which logic is supposed to explicate deductive or inductive habits of reasoning, is to identify principles such that conforming to those principles leads to inferences that are intuitively valid: valid on reflective consideration, if not at first sight. Again, to develop a theory of grammar is to find principles that fit in a similar fashion with our intuitions of grammaticality as distinct from validity. Rawls' proposal is that to develop a political theory, in particular a theory of justice, is to identify general principles such that their application supports intuitively sound judgements as to what ought to happen in particular cases. It is to identify abstract principles that are in equilibrium with our concrete, political judgements.

It may seem that under this proposal, political theory is going to be nothing more than an attempt to reconstruct our political prejudices systematically, finding principles that underpin them. But that would be a mistake. The judgements with which the principles are required to be in equilibrium are considered judgements: judgements reached after due consideration, free from the influence of special interests and other disturbing factors. Moreover, the equilibrium sought under Rawls' approach is a reflective equilibrium. It is very likely when we try to systematize our sense of justice that we will find certain considered judgements which refuse to fall under principles that elsewhere fit perfectly well. The reflective qualification means that in such a case we should focus, not on the principles, but on the recalcitrant judgements themselves, with a view to seeing whether they may not prove disposable in the light of the disequilibrium that they generate.

The method of reflective equilibrium is a method of justification in political philosophy, and in normative thinking generally. But Rawls does better still in answering the question as to how we are to determine the appropriate conception of justice. In *A Theory of Justice* he directs us to a method of discovery for political philosophy as well as a method of justification. We want to know which principles for the ordering of society are just. Well then, he says, what we should do is each to ask after what principles we would want to establish for the ordering of society if we had to make our choice under ignorance about our characteristics and under ignorance, therefore, about which position we are likely to reach in that society. We should pursue a contractual method of exploration in seeking out the principles of justice, resorting later to the test of reflective equilibrium in checking whether the principles identified are satisfactory.

Why use the contractual method, rather than some other heuristic, in seeking to identify appropriate principles of justice? The idea of asking what would be chosen under a veil of ignorance is attractive to Rawls because, intuitively, any principles chosen in that sort of situation – the original position, he calls it – will be fair. The idea had already been urged by the utilitarian economist-cum-philosopher, John Harsanyi (1953; 1955). But the device of the original position, and the associated contract, also serves to dramatize something that is very important in Rawls' thought: that the principles to be chosen should play a public role in the life of the society, being treated like a founding constitution or covenant (Kukathas and Pettit, 1990, ch. 3). The principles are to be general in form, not mentioning particular persons; they are to be universal in application, applying potentially to everyone; and, most important, they are to be publicly recognized as the final court of appeal for resolving people's conflicting claims (Rawls, 1971, pp. 1430–6).

Rawls thinks that as we do political philosophy, in particular as we seek out an appropriate conception of justice, we should move back and forth between the promptings of the contractual method and the requirements of the method of reflective equilibrium. We take a certain specification of the original position and consider what principles it would lead us to endorse as principles of justice. If we find a match or equilibrium between those principles and our considered judgements, then that is fine. If we do not, then we must think again. We must look to see whether it may be appropriate to alter the specification of the original position in some way, so that different principles are endorsed, or whether it may rather be required of us to rethink the considered judgements with which the principles conflict. We carry on with this process of derivation, testing and amendment until finally, if ever, we achieve a reflective equilibrium of judgement. At that point we will have done the best that can be done by way of establishing an appropriate conception of the principles of justice that ought to govern our institutions.

In outlining this method of doing political philosophy, Rawls made contact with earlier traditions of thought. The contractual method connects explicitly with the seventeenth- and eighteenth-century tradition of contemplating a fictional state of nature prior to social or political life and considering the contract which people must have made, or perhaps ought to have made, in such a position (Lessnoff, 1986). Rawls uses the notion of contract only in a hypothetical fashion, where his predecessors gave it an historical or quasi-historical significance, but he clearly means to forge a connection with that earlier, contractual mode of thought. The method of reflective equilibrium, on the other hand, connects with a long tradition of ethical theory, at least according to Rawls (1971, p. 51). He suggests in particular that it was well articulated by the nineteenth-century utilitarian, Henry Sidgwick, in his monumental study *The Methods of Ethics* (but see Singer, 1974).

I have drawn attention to two features of Rawls' work. Like Barry in *Political Argument* he finds room for the intellectual discussion of matters of value and, like Barry, he is willing to mix traditional philosophical discussion with a variety of contributions from more empirical disciplines. But in the intellectual discussion of values, he makes a decisive break with Barry. He sets the realm of value as an area worthy of intellectual exploration, not just in the spirit of the cultural analyst or critic, but in the spirit of someone seeking to determine the right political commitments; he justifies this stance by appeal to the test of reflective equilibrium and the heuristic of contractualist thinking.

But *A Theory of Justice* was influential for substantive as well as methodological reasons. It developed a distinctive and widely discussed view of the appropriate principles of justice and it sketched the way to develop those principles in more concrete institutions. Rawls argued that in the original position, where we are ignorant of our chances of success in any social arrangement chosen, each of us would be led rationally to make a conservative choice, opting for a basic social structure which at its worst – though not necessarily at its best and not necessarily on average – would do better for someone than alternatives. He argued, in short, that the parties in the original position would maximin: they would choose the alternative with the highest low point, the maximal minimum. Given that the parties would maximin, he then went on to argue that this strategy would lead them to choose, among salient alternatives, a basic structure characterized by two principles of justice.

The two principles defended by Rawls are first, 'Each person is to have an equal right to the most extensive total system of equal basic liberties compatible with a similar system of liberty for all' (Rawls, 1971, p. 250); and second, 'Social and economic inequalities are to be arranged so that they are both (a) to the greatest benefit of the least advantaged and (b) attached to all under conditions of fair equality of opportunity' (Rawls, 1971, p. 83; see too p. 302). The first principle expresses a concern for liberty; the second, which is known as the difference principle, expresses a presumption in favour of material equality, a presumption which is to be defeated only for the sake of raising the lot of the worst-off in the society. The principles are to be applied, according to Rawls (1971, pp. 302–3), under two priority rules; these rules give him a way of handling the plurality of values represented by the principles.

The first priority rule is that under normal, non-starvation conditions the first principle should never be compromised in the name of the second: its lesser fulfilment is never justified by the greater satisfaction of the second principle; more intuitively, no interference with the system of liberties, whether in respect of extensiveness or equality, is compensated for by an increase in anyone's socio-economic advantage. The second rule of priority is mainly concerned with the relationship between the two parts of the second principle, ordaining that fair equality of opportunity should never be restricted out of consideration for the greatest benefit of the least advantaged. Both of these rules are lexicographic forms of ordering, being of a kind with the rule that dictates the position of words in a dictionary. In each case the second element comes into play in ordering alternatives, only when the first element has made its contribution, as the second letter of a word comes into play in the ordering of a dictionary, only when the first letter has had its effect.

So much for the methodological and substantive novelties of *A Theory of Justice*. The developments that have characterized analytical political philosophy since the appearance of that book – and many of the developments that have characterized political theory more generally – can be represented as reactions of different sorts. We are now living, as Barry puts it, in a post-Rawlsian world.

There has been a great deal of work since *A Theory of Justice*, including work by Rawls himself, on the more or less detailed discussion and critique of the approach in that book (Daniels, 1978; Pogge, 1989; Kukathas and Pettit, 1990). Again, there has been a lot of work, inspired by the framework if not always the vision of the book, on matters which are identified as important there but are not treated in any detail. There has been a growing amount of research on issues of international justice, for example (Beitz, 1979), inter-generational justice (Parfit, l984) and criminal justice (Braithwaite and Pettit, 1990). Pre-eminent among such studies is the extended work by Joel Feinberg on *The Moral Limits of the Criminal Law* (1988).

Rejection

But the period since *A Theory of Justice* has been dominated by two more dramatic sorts of reaction to the book: on the one hand, reactions of rejection; on the other, reactions of radicalization. The reactions of rejection come in two varieties. The reactions in the first category represent positions on matters of political philosophy that remain broadly analytical in character and connection. Usually they argue that the sort of ideal depicted in *A Theory of Justice* is undesirable; it is not the sort of thing we ought to be after in designing our institutions. The reactions in the second category connect, on the whole, with non-philosophical or at least non-analytical traditions of thought. They argue that the enterprise of *A Theory of Justice* is infeasible in some way; its methods or its ideals are just not capable of being followed through.

Among reactions of the first kind, Robert Nozick's *Anarchy, State and Utopia* (1974) is outstanding (see Paul, 1981). Nozick points out that Rawls' conception of justice is primarily non-historical. He means that how things are to be distributed among people in a society is to be determined, under the theory, not by reference to where the things originated – not by reference to who made them, who exchanged them, and so on – but rather by reference to the aggregate patterns which different distributions represent: in particular, by reference to which distribution will do best by the worst-off in the society. As against this, he makes two main points. First, he argues that Rawls' conception is unrealistic in treating the goods to be distributed as if they were manna from heaven: 'Isn't it implausible that how holdings are produced and come to exist has no effect at all on who should own what?' (Nozick, 1974, p. 155). And he argues, second, that enforcing Rawls' two principles, like enforcing a socialist regime, would require constant monitoring of the exchanges between people and constant interference and adjustment: 'The socialist society would have to forbid capitalist acts between consenting adults' (ibid., p. 163).

Largely in reaction to Rawls' vision, as indeed he admits, Nozick elaborates a libertarian alternative to the two-principles theory. He begins by postulating certain rights, roughly of a kind with the rights recognized by Locke in the seventeenth century, and he then looks into what sort of state is compatible with those rights: 'Individuals have rights and there are things no person or group may do to them (without violating their rights)' (Nozick, 1974, p. ix). Each right is a constraint on how others, in particular the state, may treat the bearer: it constrains others not to treat the bearer in fashion X – say, not to interfere with his or her freedom of movement or association or speech – even if treating the bearer in that way would reduce the level of X-treatment of others by others. Each right is a more or less absolute constraint, in the sense that short of catastrophic horror, it cannot be infringed for the sake of promoting some social good like equality or welfare. And each right is a fundamental constraint, in the sense that the satisfaction of the right is a good in itself, not something that is good in virtue of promoting an independent goal.

This libertarian assertion of Lockean rights naturally generates a different, and more distinctively historical, conception of justice in holdings from that which Rawls defends. It means that the justice of holdings will depend on who had the things in question in the first place and on how they were transferred to others (Nozick, 1974, pp. 150–3). But a traditional problem with the libertarian assertion of rights is that it may seem to rule out the moral permissibility of a state of any kind. Every state must tax and coerce, claiming a monopoly of legitimate force, and so apparently it is bound to offend against libertarian rights. Nozick's book may remain important, not so much for its criticisms of Rawls – these depend on some questionable representation (Kukathas and Pettit, 1990) – but for the resolution which it offers for this long-standing difficulty.

Nozick presents an ingenious, though not wholly conclusive, argument that if people were committed to respecting rights, and if they were disposed to act in their rational self-interest, then in the absence of a state they would take steps which, little by little, would lead to the establishment of a certain sort of state: 'Out of anarchy, pressed by spontaneous groupings, mutual protection associations, division of labour, market pressures, economies of scale, and rational self-interest, there arises something very much resembling a minimal state or a group of geographically distinct minimal states' (Nozick, 1974, pp. 16–17). Given this argument, Nozick holds that libertarians can endorse the minimal state: the state which is limited in function to the protection of its citizens against violence, theft, fraud, and the like. And absent any parallel argument for the more than minimal state – say, the redistributive state envisaged by Rawls – he holds that this is all that libertarians can endorse.

I mentioned Nozick as the outstanding example of a reaction of rejection to Rawls which remains tied to analytical philosophy. The Nozickian reaction is centred on the idea of rights, to which he gave a new currency among analytical and other thinkers (Lomasky, 1987; see too Waldron, 1984; Frey, 1985). Other negative reactions to Rawls, which stay within the analytical camp, are organized around different but still more or less familiar ideas (see Miller, 1976). The idea of utility has remained a rallying point for well-known figures like R. M. Hare, John Harsanyi, and Richard Brandt, and it has provided a starting point for a number of newer studies (Griffin, 1986; Hardin, 1988; see too Sen and Williams, 1982). The idea of deserts has focused a further variety of opposition (Sadurski, 1985; Sher, 1987; Campbell, 1988). The idea of autonomy or self-determination, itself a theme in Rawls, has been widely explored, with different lessons derived from it (Lindley 1986; Raz 1986; Young 1986; Dworkin, G., 1988.) And the idea of needs has served as yet another focus of opposition (Wiggins, 1987; Braybrook, 1987). Finally, and perhaps most importantly, the idea of equality has been reworked in different ways by a number of thinkers, all of whom distance themselves in some measure from the Rawlsian orthodoxy (Dworkin, R. M., 1978; Sen, 1985; Cohen, 1989; Kymlicka, 1990; Nagel, 1991). This work has included work displaying a decidedly socialist or Marxist stamp (Roemer, 1988; Miller, 1989).

So much for reactions of rejection that stay within the analytical camp. There have also been reactions to *A Theory of Justice* which point beyond the analytical way of thinking and which have served to connect with other traditions of political theory. These reactions have not served to question the desirability of the two-principles ideal but, more fundamentally, the feasibility of any such theory of justice. One reaction of this kind is associated with the economist, F. A. von Hayek (1982), who argues that implementing a Rawlsian view of justice, or indeed any redistributive conception, would require a sort of information that is never going to be available to central government (Barry, N., 1979; Gray, 1986; Kukathas, 1989). Another reaction in the same vein is the more recently voiced complaint that a Rawlsian theory is of little or no relevance in a world where states are deeply enmeshed in international networks of commerce and law and administration (Held, 1991). But the reactions of this kind that have made the greatest impact are associated with feminism and with communitarianism.

There are two feminist challenges, which have been particularly emphasized in the literature since *A Theory of Justice*. One is that while a theory like Rawls' seeks to deal even-handedly with men and women, while it envisages a state that is gender-blind, the ideal projected in such a theory is bound to fail in practice: it is bound to prove infeasible. The reason invoked for this inevitable failure is that the sociology which implicitly informs the theory – for example, the assumptions as to what it is reasonable to expect of public office-holders and committed citizens – systematically favours males: 'Men's physiology defines most sports, their needs define auto and health insurance coverage, their socially-designed biographies define workplace expectations and successful career patterns, their perspectives and concerns define quality in scholarship, their experiences and obsessions define merit' (MacKinnon, 1987, p. 36).

The other challenge which feminists have often brought against Rawlsian theory rests on the claim that it assumes that there is a clear distinction between the public and the domestic arenas and that the business of the state is restricted to the public sphere: 'The assumption that a clear and simple distinction can be drawn between the political and the personal, the public and the domestic, has been basic to liberal theory at least since Locke, and remains as a foundation of much political theory today' (Okin, 1991, p. 90). The challenge issued on the basis of this claim is that by neglecting the domestic sphere a theory like Rawls' is bound to fail in its own aspiration to articulate what justice requires; it is bound to overlook the subordination and the exploitation of women in the domestic sphere (Pateman, 1983). The personal is the political, so it is alleged, and any theory that fails to appreciate that fact cannot articulate a feasible ideal of justice.

Communitarians do two things. They argue for the desirability of community, social involvement and political participation (Buchanan, 1989). And, more importantly, they offer critiques of the sort of political philosophy which Rawls is taken to epitomize. For communitarians Rawlsian political philosophy exemplifies, above all, a type of approach which abstains from asserting the inherent superiority or inferiority of any particular conception of the good life (Rawls, 1971, pp. 447–8). The sort of state it countenances is recommended in abstraction from any particular view of the good life, so Rawls claims, and the sort of state endorsed is meant to operate without favouring such a view. Communitarian challenges are usually cast as challenges to any theory which resembles Rawls' in this normative abstraction, this ethical neutrality. Such neutral theories are often described, in recent usage, as liberal theories of politics (Barry, B., 1990, p. li; Kymlicka, 1990, pp. 233–4). Communitarians prefer a theory of politics in which the state endorses the conception of the good life which is tied up with the community's practices and traditions. They prefer a politics of the common good, as it is sometimes put, to a politics of neutrality.

There are three broadly communitarian critiques that I will mention (for a survey, see Gutmann, 1985; Buchanan, 1989; Kymlicka, 1990; Walzer, 1990). One argues that effective political debate has to be conducted in the currency of meanings, in particular evaluative meanings, which exists in the local society, and that any theory that tries to abstract from such meanings, as a neutral theory must allegedly do, will not yield a feasible ideal of the state: an ideal that can be expected to command the allegiance of ordinary folk (Walzer, 1983). Under the meanings shared in our society, it might be argued, it is fine for ordinary goods and chattels to be distributed on market principles but not intuitively all right for emergency medical care to be made available on that basis; the culturally given categories embody normative expectations of a kind that any credible and workable political philosophy must respect.

A second communitarian challenge is directed to the ideal of autonomy implicit in the neutral, liberal image of the state: the ideal of a self which chooses the sort of person to be, picking from among the options which are made available under the meticulously neutral framework provided by the state. The claim is that this ideal is empty and unrealizable and, once again, that a political philosophy which is built around such an ideal cannot effect a grip on people's imagination, The fact is, so the argument goes, that moral choice is always a matter of self-discovery, in which the self unearths the culturally given commitments that define and constitute it. Only a political philosophy which identifies and reinforces those sorts of commitments can have a hope of being workable (MacIntyre, 1981; Sandel, 1982).

The third communitarian challenge endorses a version of the liberal ideal of the self-determining subject. It argues, first, that in order to achieve such autonomy, people need to be culturally provided with appropriate concepts and ideals, or that they need to have the opportunity for public debate about such matters, or whatever; and second, that the neutral, liberal state is constitutionally incapable of furnishing such resources, so that it makes the very ideal it fosters unreachable (Taylor, 1985; Raz, 1986). There are many variations on this argument, as there are on the other communitarian claims, but the general idea should be clear: the realization of the liberal ideal is not possible under the neutral, liberal state; it requires a state that is prepared to be assertive about the conception or conceptions of the good life which are allegedly associated with the given community and culture.

Feminist and communitarian challenges allege that Rawlsian theory, and any theory in its general image, is sociologically uninformed and, consequently, that its prescriptions are infeasible; they may do for the ciphers conjured up in the philosophical armchair but they will not work for ordinary, culturally situated human beings. Such approaches would lead us away from how analytical philosophers do political philosophy and into the richer pastures seeded by this or that sociological theory. Analytical philosophers have not been hugely disturbed, it must be said, by these attacks. The general line has been that if good points are made in some of the criticisms offered, they are points which can be taken aboard without giving up on the enterprise of analytical political philosophy, Rawlsian or otherwise (Larmore, 1987; Buchanan, 1989; Macedo, 1990; Kymlicka, 1990, chs 6 and 7; Kukathas and Pettit, 1990, ch. 5).

Radicalization

I have discussed the reactions of rejection to *A Theory of Justice*. In order to complete this historical sketch I need also to mention the category of responses that I describe as reactions of radicalization. There are two methodological novelties in *A Theory of*

Justice, associated respectively with the method of reflective equilibrium and the contractual method. The method of reflective equilibrium has attracted a good deal of support and has sometimes been consciously extended in ways that go beyond Rawls. One sort of extension is the method of argument – we might call it the method of dialectical equilibrium – whereby a thinker establishes firm intuitions about what is right in a given area and then shows that in consistency they should also apply, however surprising the results, in areas that are somewhat removed from the original one (Nozick, 1974; Goodin, 1985). That type of extension can be seen as a radicalization of the Rawlsian approach. But radicalization of the Rawlsian approach has been pursued much more widely and systematically in relation to the other methodological novelty in *A Theory of Justice*: the use of the contractual method. A great deal of the political philosophy pursued in analytical circles since the publication of that book has been contractualist in character.

I said above that for Rawls the contractual method is a method of discovery which complements the method of justification by reflective equilibrium. Rawls is interested in identifying just or fair institutions; he argues that such institutions are the ones that would be chosen in a just or fair procedure and he then constructs the original position contract as a procedure with a good claim to be fair. The fact that the two principles would be chosen in the original position, as he thinks they would, is as good an indication as we are going to get that the principles are fair; it shows, for all relevant purposes, that they are fair: 'The fairness of the circumstances transfers to fairness of the principles adopted' (Rawls, 1971, p. 159).

The radicalization of Rawls' contractual method casts a hypothetical contract of the kind instantiated in the Rawlsian approach in a more radical role than that which is strictly envisaged in *A Theory of Justice*. Consider the contractarian property of a set of institutions or principles, which consists in the hypothetical fact that they would be chosen under appropriate circumstances. The fact that the two principles possess that property is a sign that they are fair, under Rawls' way of thinking, but it is not of their essence: fairness or rightness is not defined by that property, at least not to begin with (Rawls, 1971, p. 111); fairness or rightness is independently defined as the target we want to track and the contractarian property is identified as a useful tracker. The radicalizations of Rawls resist this merely heuristic construal of the contractual method. They say that the very notion of what it is to be politically right is, or ought to be, nothing more than the notion of what would be contractually chosen in appropriate circumstances. They claim that the contractarian property constitutes rightness rather than merely tracking it.

In Plato's *Euthyphro*, Socrates asks whether something is holy because the gods love it or whether the gods love it because it is holy. Take that question to be an inquiry as to whether or not the criterion of holiness is love by the gods; ignore the causal reading of the question as an inquiry after the sources of the gods' love (Pettit, 1992, p. 209). The issue between Rawls – or at least Rawls of *A Theory of Justice* – and more radical contractarians has to do with a parallel, criterial issue (Pettit, 1982). If a set of institutions or principles is contractually eligible, if it is such as would be chosen in a suitable contract, is that because they are right – is that because they satisfy some independent criterion of rightness – as in the Rawlsian, heuristic view? Or are they right because they would be the object of contract, as in the view that takes rightness to be constituted by contractual eligibility?

The radical contractarians who have dominated political philosophy since the publication of Rawls' book divide, broadly, into two camps. The one camp casts the contract in an economic image, as a procedure of striking a bargain; the other takes it in a more political way, as a process of reaching deliberative conviction and consensus (Kukathas and Pettit, 1990, p. 32; see too Barry, B., 1989, p. 371; Hamlin, 1989). Under the economic interpretation, the upshot of the contract is treated as something which is to the mutual advantage of parties whose relevant beliefs and desires are formed prior to exchange with one another; the contract represents a reciprocal adjustment that is in everyone's interest, not an exchange in which anyone tries to influence the minds or hearts of others. Under the political interpretation, the upshot of the contract is treated as a more or less commanding conclusion: as something which each is led to endorse under reasoning – say, reasoning about common interests – that survives political discussion, collective or otherwise, and that elicits general allegiance.

Something like the economic version of contractarianism had been explored prior to *A Theory of Justice* by two economists, James Buchanan and Gordon Tullock (1962). They argued, roughly, that the right set of principles for a society is the set which would be unanimously preferred. This approach operationalizes a static criterion of what is to the mutual advantage of parties, and in recent discussions it has been eclipsed by the sort of economic contractarianism developed in the work of David Gauthier (1986). Under Gauthier's approach, the right principles for ordering a society are those on which rational bargainers would converge under circumstances that it would be rational of them to accept as a starting point for bargaining. Gauthier develops a theory of rational bargaining in the course of advancing his contractarian vision and, applying that theory, he is led to argue for a more or less minimal state. In exploring this approach he claims to resolve a type of bargaining problem which Rawls had described as 'hopelessly complicated': 'Even if theoretically a solution were to exist, we would not, at present anyway, be able to determine it' (Rawls, 1971, p. 140).

There are traces of economic contractarianism in *A Theory of Justice* and the book undoubtedly served as a stimulus for people like Gauthier. But the political reading of the contractual method is probably more in the spirit of Rawls. The parties involved in a bargain take their own reasons for preferring one or another outcome as given and they are impervious to any reasons which others may offer for rethinking their preferences. They have no care for what other parties believe or want, and are disposed, if let, to impose their own wishes on others; when they settle for anything less, that is because that is the best they can squeeze out of their fellow-bargainers. Under the political version of contractarianism, the parties are cast in a very different light. They are conceptualized as persons who each wish to find a structure on which all can agree, seeking out the intellectually most compelling candidate.

A political version of contractarianism is to be found in the work of the continental thinker, Jürgen Habermas (1973); he argues that the best structure for society is that which would be supported by people involved in collective debate under ideal conditions of speech, where all are equal, each has the chance to speak and each has the opportunity to question the assertions of others. In analytical circles, the most influential contributions have come from Bruce Ackerman (1980) and Thomas Scanlon (1982). The general approach has also been endorsed by Brian Barry (1989), and it will undoubtedly be a focus of attention in future research.

Ackerman (1980) suggests that the best sort of state, the best social structure, is by definition the kind of arrangement that would be supported in neutral dialogue: in dialogue where no one is allowed to assert either that their conception of the good is better than that asserted by others or that they are intrinsically superior to any of their fellows. Scanlon (1982, p. 110) argues that the best basic structure will be characterized, at least in part, by 'rules for the general regulation of behaviour which no one could reasonably reject as a basis for informed, unforced general agreement'. These formulae are each meant to catch a guiding idea for further exploration and argument.

We have discussed the long silence of analytical political philosophy in the early part of the century; the break in that silence with the books published by Benn and Peters (1959), Hart (1961) and especially Brian Barry (1965); the new era introduced with Rawls' publication of *A Theory of Justice* in 1971; the reactions of rejection to that book, analytical and non-analytical: in particular, communitarian and feminist; and the reactions of radicalization which the book occasioned, with new developments in contractual thinking, economic and political. This gives us an image of the recent history of analytical political philosophy and I would now like to turn to more speculative and controversial matters. I want to offer a picture of the most important assumptions which analytical philosophy has bequeathed, for good or ill, to normative political thinking.

Analytical political philosophy: the legacy

There are two distinct areas where normative questions arise, according to the lore of analytical philosophers: in the theory of the good, as it is called, and in the theory of the right. The theory of the good is the theory in which we are instructed on what properties, in particular what universal properties, make one state of the world better than another; we are instructed on what properties constitute values, specifically impersonal values that do not refer to any particular individuals or indeed any other particular entities. Utilitarianism offers a theory of the good according to which the only property that matters in the ranking of states of the world is the happiness of sentient creatures, The theory of the right, on the other hand, is the theory in which we are told what makes one option right and another wrong, among the options in any choice; the choice may be a personal decision among different acts, or a social decision among different basic structures. Utilitarianism is a theory of the right to the extent that it identifies the right option in any choice as that which suitably promotes happiness: that which suitably promotes the good.

The analytical tradition of thinking bequeaths distinctive assumptions in both of these areas, assumptions that bear intimately on political matters. In the theory of the good it has tended, more or less unquestioningly, to support certain substantive constraints on the sorts of properties that can be countenanced as political values. And in the theory of the right it has generated a set of distinctions around which to taxonomize different possible approaches to questions about what institutions to prefer. I will deal first of all with assumptions in the theory of the good and then with assumptions in the theory of the right. As will become clear, I think that the contribution of analytical philosophy to political thinking is rather different in the two areas. The received analytical theory of the good is a contribution of dubious worth, at least in one respect, serving to constrain political thought rather than liberate it. The analytical theory of the right is a contribution of positive merit and political thought is the better for taking the relevant analytical distinctions on board.

Theory of the good

There are two elements in the received analytical assumptions about the theory of the political good. The first is a universalist form of personalism, as I shall describe it, and the second a valuational solipsism. Personalism is a plausible working assumption in political philosophy but it has often been distorted by association with the solipsist thesis.

Personalism is the assumption that whatever is good or bad about a set of institutions is something that is good or bad for the people whom they affect. The fact that a set of institutions is allegedly in accordance with God's will; the fact that it is the set which best preserves a certain culture or language; the fact that it is the set of institutions which puts least strain on the natural environment: these features allegedly count for nothing, except so far as they are associated with a benefit to individuals, It will be important that the institutions fit with allegedly divine decrees if that means that people will benefit from a consequent harmony of doctrine; it will be important that they preserve a culture or language if this means that people will enjoy a consequent solidarity of association or a plurality of options; it will be important that they reduce the strain on nature if people are likely to benefit in some way, at some stage, from the enhanced environment. But, considerations of this kind apart, political philosophy need not look to how institutions would answer on these counts.

Personalism is not likely to be resisted on the grounds that it challenges theocentric visions of politics. It may well be resisted on environmental grounds, but here the conflict is either of minor practical import or it can be accommodated by a slight shift of commitments. Many environmental measures that are likely to be prized independently of their impact on human beings – measures to do with preserving other species or preserving wildernesses – are arguably for the good of people, though perhaps only in the very long term. And if there are attractive measures for which this does not hold, then they can be accommodated by stretching personalism to encompass the good of the members of certain other species.

Personalism is primarily designed, not as a form of opposition to environmentalism, or even to theocentrism, but to the belief that nations or cultures or states or societies, or corporate entities of any kind, have interests that transcend the interests of individuals. According to such a belief, such an institutional anti-personalism, it may be right to introduce a political measure, even when that measure does not make any people better off, even indeed when it makes some people worse off. Specifically, it

23

may be right to do this, because of how the measure affects some supra-personal, corporate entity.

Personalism rejects such institutionalism, arguing instead that the only interests that are relevant in the assessment of politically variable arrangements are the interests of those present or future people who may be affected by the arrangements; it is usually assumed that the dead do not have interests, or that their interests do not count. Imagine two societies in which the interests of individuals are equally well served but where certain corporate entities fare differently – if that is possible. The personalist claims that there is no ground for ranking the arrangements in either of those societies above the other; if affected individuals fare equally well – however that is judged – then the arrangements have to count as equally good. Perhaps one set of arrangements is aesthetically more attractive than the other, and perhaps it is ranked above the other on those grounds. But that sort of ranking, so the personalist will claim, is not strictly a ranking in political philosophy. From the point of view of political philosophy, the only considerations that should be taken into account are considerations about how individuals fare.

Jeremy Bentham (1843, p. 321) sums up the personalist credo nicely: 'Individual interests are the only real interests. Take care of individuals; never injure them, or suffer them to be injured, and you will have done well enough for the public.' The thesis is also to be found, more or less explicitly, in *A Theory of Justice*: 'Let us assume, to fix ideas, that a society is a more or less self-sufficient association of persons who in their relations to one another recognise certain rules of conduct as binding and who for the most part act in accordance with them. Suppose further that these rules specify a system of cooperation designed to advance the good of those taking part in it' (Rawls, 1971, p. 4). Given this view of society, Rawls naturally thinks that the normative question with a basic structure is how well it answers to those individuals whose good it is supposed to advance. The personalist assumption has been explicitly noted by a number of authors but it generally goes without saying in analytical circles (see Raz, 1986; Hamlin and Pettit, 1989; Broome, 1990; 1991, ch. 8).

In ascribing personalism to the broad tradition of analytical philosophy, we need to be clear that the personalism ascribed is universalist in character. It holds that not only are persons the only entities that ultimately matter in politics, all persons matter equally. Consistently with personalism, strictly formulated, we might have said that the good of the King or Queen or the good of individuals in some class or caste is all that matters. But the universalist twist blocks this possibility. The commitment is nicely caught in a slogan also attributed to Bentham: 'Everybody to count for one, nobody for more than one' (Mill, 1969, p. 267).

If personalism has been systematically challenged, at least in its anti-institutionalism guise, that has probably occurred only within the more or less Hegelian tradition of continental thinking. But isn't personalism opposed, less dramatically, to the sort of communitarianism which argues that a state ought to endorse and further the conception of a good life associated with the local culture? At the least, isn't it opposed to the sort of communitarian doctrine which argues that communal solidarity and rootedness is itself a good that ought to be furthered by the state? More generally, indeed, isn't it opposed by any theory which argues that what the state ought to value and advance is a property, not of individuals, but of aggregates of individuals?

Personalism is not opposed, despite appearances, to doctrines of these kinds. The personalist assumption is that if institutions are good or bad, then they are good or bad for individuals. Even if a conception of the good life is associated with a received culture, and is not endorsed by all individuals, it may be a personalist conception; it may represent the way of life as good, because of the alleged good it does for individuals. For example, a traditional, religious conception of the good life may represent a certain way of life as good for the salvation of individuals. Again, even if the valued properties which a state promotes are properties of groups rather than individuals – properties like solidarity – they may be valued for the good which their realization involves for individuals. Solidarity may not be prized in itself, as it were, but on the grounds that it is good for individuals to belong to a solidaristic community.

I said that the personalism of the analytical tradition usually goes without saying. No one makes much of it, since it is taken to be more or less obvious. But there is one exception to this theme that is worth mentioning in passing. Ronald Dworkin draws attention to the personalist commitment, in arguing that all plausible, modern political theories have in mind the same ultimate value, equality (Dworkin, 1978, pp. 179–83; see too Miller, 1990). For what Dworkin means is not that each theory argues for the equal treatment of individuals, but only, as he puts it, that every theory claims to treat all individuals as equals. No one is to count for less than one, and no one for more than one.

Dworkin's claim is sustained by the Benthamite observations which I have mentioned – it has a personalist core – but it goes considerably further than those observations. Dworkin holds, in effect, that every plausible political theory countenances the same value and, more specifically, the same fundamental right: the right of each individual to be treated as an equal with others. This claim would be of great interest, for it suggests that there is more unity than first appears in the variety of contemporary political theories: it suggests that they are all egalitarian philosophies. The observation would be of methodological significance. If it holds, then all political theories can be assessed in a common egalitarian currency for how well they do in interpreting the demand to treat individuals as equals (Kymlicka, 1990, p. 4).

This is not the place to explore the claim that there is a methodologically significant unity among contemporary political theories. Suffice it to mention that, at the least, the claim requires substantive vindication. By our account of personalism, contemporary analytical theories are certainly committed to thinking that whatever is of value in political institutions, it is something which is of value from the point of view of the persons affected, and, moreover, from a point of view that does not necessarily privilege any particular individuals over others; it is something which we can countenance as a good consistently with treating individuals as equals. But so far, this constraint leaves it open as to whether what is of value is utility or fairness or opportunity or whatever. The constraint requires that the good which is countenanced is consistent with it, but it does not entail anything more positive. It does not entail that the good must be seen as an interpretation of what it is to meet the constraint, of what it is to treat individuals as equals. And certainly it does not entail that the good must be such that when the state advances it, then it can be adequately and usefully characterized as honouring the right of individuals to be treated as equals.

Personalism is a plausible and harmless working assumption in political philosophy. Or so it seems to me. But the analytical tradition has also bequeathed a second, more specific assumption to the theory of the political good and this proposition is anything but harmless. Until very recent times it has had a massive, warping impact on analytical thinking about politics: in effect, on the English-speaking, political-theoretic tradition of the past couple of hundred years. I describe this second assumption as one of valuational solipsism.

The word 'solipsism' derives from *solus ipse*, the lone self. The assumption of valuational solipsism is the assumption that any property that can serve as an ultimate political value, any property that can be regarded as a yardstick of political assessment, has to be capable of instantiation by the socially isolated person, by the solitary individual. It is the assumption that the ultimate criteria of political judgement – the reserve funds of political debate – are provided by non-social as distinct from social values. A value will be social just in case its realization requires that there are a number of people who are intentionally active in certain ways: in effect, that there are a number of people who are intentionally involved with one another. A value will be non-social just in case it can be enjoyed by the wholly isolated individual, even by the lone occupant of a world.

There are a great variety of social values which are invoked in discussions of politics. They cover the goods enjoyed by people in intimate relations and the goods that they enjoy in the public forum. Such goods include family and friendship, fraternity and citizenship, status and power, protection and equitable treatment and participation. Social values also include goods that do not inhere in individuals, but in the institutions that individuals constitute; the personalist can countenance such values too, as we have seen, for their realization will have an impact on the well-being of persons. These sorts of social value include cultural harmony, social order, political stability and the rule of law.

There are also a variety of non-social values which are invoked in discussions of politics. Material welfare is an obvious example, since it is clear that the isolated individual may logically enjoy that sort of good without any involvement with other people. Another example is happiness or utility, in the sense in which this is associated, as it is in the utilitarian tradition, with the balance of pleasure over pain or the absence of frustrated preferences and desires. A third example is liberty in the sense in which this requires just the absence of intentional interference by others; the isolated individual is likely to score particularly well on this count, since there won't be any others intentionally involved with her as potential interferers. And a final example is liberty in the more positive sense in which it requires, not just the absence of interference by others, but also a high degree of autonomy or self-rule.

Apart from clearly social and clearly non-social values, there are also some values invoked in political discussion which can be interpreted either way. A good example here is the value of equality. This may be understood as an active sort of equality which presupposes that people are intentionally involved with one another and which requires that they recognize one another as equals in certain ways: say, as equals before the law. Alternatively, it may be taken in a purely passive mode, as a comparative value which someone may enjoy relative to others with whom she has no dealings whatsoever and, therefore, as a value which someone may enjoy in total isolation; she is equal – say, equal in material respects – with the other human beings who happen to exist, or exist in a certain region; but that is a brute fact about her, as it were, not a fact that has social significance.

Analytical political philosophy has been traditionally committed, not only to personalism, but also to solipsism. Among the many different strands of radical political thought which emerged within that tradition in the last century, all of them tended to emphasize distinctively non-social values as the ultimate criteria of judgement. Most appealed to utility as the basic good of individuals, taking utility to be determined by the balance of pleasure or the absence of frustrated desire. Failing that, they appealed to the enjoyment of non-interference, to the realization of a degree of personal autonomy, and to the attainment of a certain level of material welfare or a passive sort of material equality. This is a particularly striking feature in the tradition, given that there were many factors that might have been expected to lead the tradition towards the articulation of certain social values as the basic terms of political evaluation.

Democracy became a rallying point for many radicals in the tradition, for example, yet few of them thought of democratic participation or the democratic resolution of differences – the achievement of public deliberation – as a fundamental criterion of political assessment: democracy was valuable, if at all, for its effects in promoting utility or liberty or whatever. Again, the rule of law was hailed by all as one of the great features of English common law institutions, but no one advanced the rule of law as an ultimate value by which to judge a system; on the contrary, the fashion among radicals like Bentham was to see law as a mixed good, as a form of interference that was justified, if at all, by the other forms of interference that it inhibited. Finally, while the Chartist and trade union movements emphasized the importance of solidarity and comradeship, none of the theorists of those movements ever really argued that whether such a value would be realized was a basic test to administer in assessing a proposed political arrangement. Socialism may have pushed many thinkers in that direction, but mostly the push was resisted.

Consider how different were the approaches to politics that emerged in the same period in continental circles. Think of Rousseau on the general will and on the value of democractic deliberation. Think of Herder on the cultivation of the self in relation to the *Volksgeist*. Think of Kant on the kingdom of ends or Hegel on the realization of *Geist* in the world. Think of juridical ideals like that of the *Rechtstaat*, or sociological ideals like the overcoming of *anomie*. In all of these cases we see a spontaneous tendency to assume that the basic values for the assessment of political structures are essentially social in nature. There is no evidence of the imperative that ruled English-speaking, analytical circles: the imperative to go back to properties that could be enjoyed even by a solitary individual in the search for basic political criteria.

There continue to be strains of solipsism in analytical political philosophy today, as communitarians and others often complain (Black 1991, pp. 366–7). But it must be said that a number of recent developments have put solipsistic prejudices under pressure. Communitarian critics have undoubtedly had an impact on analytical thought and they have stressed the importance of the social goods associated with the enjoyment of community. Other non-analytical critics who may have had an anti-solipsistic influence include adherents of radical or strong democracy, who think of the deliberative, democratic resolution of various issues as a good in itself (Cohen and Rogers, 1983; Barber, 1984). But the tendency away from solipsism has also been nurtured from within analytical circles. The contractualist way of thinking, especially in the radical form in which the property of contractual eligibility becomes constitutive of political rightness, has also provided an impetus away from solipsism. Thus the political version of contractarianism has tended to hail the social value of public justification as the ultimate yardstick of political acceptability: this is the value involved in an institution's being publicly justifiable and justified (Gaus, 1990).

Why should the analytical tradition have proved so resistant, over such a long period, to the idea that social values might offer the basic terms of political assessment? Why should it have tended to endorse, not just personalism, but solipsism? The main reason, I suggest, has to do with the social atomism which has characterized the tradition from its earliest days (Pettit, 1992).

The social atomist holds that the solitary individual – the agent who is and always has been isolated from others – is nevertheless capable, in principle, of displaying all distinctive human capacities. The anti-atomist or holist denies this, arguing that there is an intimate, non-causal tie between enjoying social relations with others and exercising certain distinctive human capacities: 'The claim is that living in society is a necessary condition of the development of rationality, in some sense of this property, or of becoming a moral agent in the full sense of the term, or of becoming a fully responsible, autonomous being' (Taylor, 1985, p. 191).

The issue between social atomism and holism turns around the issue of how far people depend – that is, non-causally or constitutively depend – on their relations with one another for the enjoyment of proper human capacities; we may describe this as a horizontal issue, as the relations in question are collateral, horizontal relations between people. The issue should be distinguished from the question that divides social individualism and collectivism, as I call the doctrines. That issue is a vertical question rather than a horizontal one. It bears on how far people's autonomy is compromised from above by aggregate social forces and regularities: individualists deny that there is any compromise, whereas collectivists say that human beings are controlled or constrained in a way that diminishes their agency. Atomists and holists may agree that people are more or less autonomous subjects – that they conform to the image which we project in our ordinary psychological thinking about one another – while arguing about the extent to which their capacities as human subjects require social relations. I mention this point, as the philosophical tradition, analytical and otherwise, has tended to confuse atomism with individualism and holism with collectivism (Pettit, 1993).

Social atomism appeared for perhaps the first time in the seventeenth century, with the notion that political and social order, if it were legitimate, had to be the product of some tacit contract between pre-social individuals. Social atomism was forced on many thinkers by the espousal of such a radical contractarian vision, at least in the contractarianism of a thinker like Thomas Hobbes; the vision only made sense if human beings did not depend on society for their status as human beings and therefore as potential contractors (Hobbes, [1651] 1968).

Such an atomistic picture was almost certainly encouraged by the discoveries of people who seemed to many Europeans to live more or less in the wild. Those discoveries nurtured the view that actual society must have evolved from a contract made by individuals in a state of nature. It may be no great accident that, in Charles Taylor's words, 'the great classical theorists of atomism also held to some strange views about the historicity of a state of nature in which men lived without society' (Taylor, 1985, p. 190).

The long tradition of philosophy from Aristotle had stressed that human beings are essentially social animals but holism only became a prominent philosophical doctrine as a reaction to atomism, among seventeenth- and eighteenth-century forerunners of German Romanticism, like Vico and Rousseau and Herder (Berlin, 1976). These were all thinkers who were familiar with the atomistic vision of individuals and society, and they self-consciously emphasized a thesis that challenged such atomism. They held that people were dependent on language for the capacity to think and that the language on which they were dependent was essentially a social creation (Wells, 1987). They maintained that people depended on one another's presence in society to be able individually to realize what is perhaps the most distinctive human ability.

In stressing the dependence of thought on language and of language on society, these thinkers were taking issue directly with Hobbes. For someone like Rousseau it was self-evident that language, which he assumed to be social, was required for thinking. This is what created for him the famous chicken-and-egg problem: 'which was most necessary, the existence of society to the invention of language, or the invention of language to the establishment of society?' (Rousseau, [1762] 1973, p. 63; Wokler, 1987, ch. 4). But where Rousseau thought that language – and therefore society – was essential in the development of thought, Hobbes saw it as something that was only of instrumental value, albeit of enormous instrumental value; it served a crucial mnemonic and communicative role (Hobbes, [1651] 1968, pp. 101, 111; see Hampton, 1986, ch. 1). Thus Hobbes could write: 'besides Sense, and Thoughts, and the Trayne of thoughts, the mind of man has no other motion; though by the help of Speech and Method, the same Facultyes may he improved to such a height, as to distinguish men from all other living Creatures' (Hobbes, [1651] 1968, p. 99).

The romantic thesis – that thought is dependent on language and that language is an essentially social creation – came to fruition, perhaps over-ripened, in Hegel's notion of the *Volksgeist*: 'the spirit of a people, whose ideas are expressed in their common institutions, by which they define their identity' (Taylor, 1975, p. 387). It came thereby to influence a variety of thinkers, from Marx to Durkheim to F. H. Bradley, who all stressed the social constitution of the individual. They claimed that the individual's relations with her fellows were not entirely contingent or external; some of those relations were internal or essential, being required for the individual to count as a full person. As Bradley (1962, p. 173) puts it: 'I am myself by sharing with others, by including in my essence relations to them, the relations of the social state.'

The analytical tradition of philosophy has remained predominantly atomistic right down to the present day, and this atomism, in my view, is the principal reason why the tradition should have favoured valuational solipsism (Pettit, 1993). Anyone who is an atomist is bound to take the possibility of the isolated individual to be a relevant alternative in radical political evaluation: in evaluation that covers all conceivable alternatives. It may be enough in casual political discussion to argue for the superiority of an arrangement over the status quo, and over the more salient alternatives, but in radical political thought the arrangement must also be shown to be superior to the lot of the isolated individual; otherwise, as the atomist sees things, the business of political evaluation will not be logically complete. It is unsurprising, then, that the many thinkers in the atomist tradition, which goes back to Hobbes, have emphasized that the isolated individual gives us a relevant perspective on political arrangements. They have implicitly or explicitly assumed that we should judge the attraction of political arrangements, at least in part, from the point of view of that individual: from the point of view, as it is often articulated, of a state of nature in which isolation is the norm. They have assumed, to put the matter otherwise, that part of the job of supporting any political arrangement is to show what there is in it for individuals who could logically have enjoyed a solitary existence instead: what there is about that arrangement that makes it superior to a solitary existence for such individuals.

Suppose, then, that the atomist takes the possibility of the solitary individual as a relevant scenario and thinks that the task of political evaluation is to rank various social arrangements, not just against one another, but also against the scenario where individuals remain isolated. It follows that the terms of evaluation which he uses in the course of this ranking must be terms that apply, not just under different social arrangements, but also in the condition of the isolated individual. The values which serve as his ultimate criteria of assessment must be capable of being realized, not just in the social alternatives assessed, but also in that more or less solipsistic condition. This is to say that the values that serve as evaluative primes for the atomist must all be non-social values, for only such values can be realized in the circumstances of the solitary individual as well as under social arrangements. And so we reach the conclusion that atomism forces the political theorist to restrict his attention to non-social values: it forces him to be a valuational solipsist.

This line of reasoning may be evaded by the atomist who chooses to regard the scenario of the isolated individual as politically irrelevant; such an atomist will resist the aspiration to the radical form of political evaluation which would bear on that possibility as well as on more familiar arrangements. What the reasoning establishes is that if the isolated individual is allowed to figure among the alternatives to be evaluated in political theory, as it has traditionally figured, then atomism filters social values out of the set of ultimate political criteria; it drives the theorist to countenance only non-social values as the ultimate terms of political assessment.

Theory of the right

I have been discussing the legacy of the analytical tradition for thinking about the theory of the political good. It is time, finally, to consider the legacy of the tradition for thought about what is politically right. To have views about the politically good is to identify one or another property or set of properties as desirable in political institutions: in institutions which are susceptible to political shaping. It is to prize liberty or

30

democracy or equality or whatever. But having such views is not yet enough to enable one to decide which institutions represent the right option for a given society; a theory of the good is not sufficient, on its own, to yield a theory of the right. The point becomes obvious in light of the now well-established analytical distinction between consequentialist and deontological theories of the right.

Suppose you think that the main or unique political good is that of individual, negative liberty: the good enjoyed by people, as the standard tradition has it, when they do not suffer interference from others in the pursuit of independent activities (Pettit, 1989). What institutions ought you to regard, then, as politically right for a society? The consequentialist answer is, roughly, those institutions whose presence would mean that there is more liberty enjoyed in the society than would otherwise be the case: those institutions which do best at promoting liberty. The answer is rough, because this formula does not yet say whether promoting a property like liberty means maximizing its actual or expected realization and, if the latter, whether the probabilities that should determine the expectation are subject to any checks. But we need not worry about such details here. The general point should be clear: that for a consequentialist whose only concern is liberty, the right institutions will be those with consequences that are best for liberty.

At first blush, it may seem that consequentialism is the only possible theory of the right. But a little thought will show that this is not so. Suppose that the society with which the consequentialist is concerned is one that contains a minority group of fanatical traditionalists, whose aspiration is to install an authoritarian government under which the values of a certain religion would be imposed, at whatever cost in bloodshed, on everyone in the community. Suppose that this means that the institutions that will best promote liberty must ban the meetings and activities of that group; otherwise the chances are too high that the group will grow in stature and eventually seize power. Suppose, in other words, that the consequentialist theory of the right will commit someone who prizes liberty above all else to the repression of a certain religious group. Does it still remain obvious in such a case that consequentialism is the proper theory of the right?

Many will say that for someone who prizes liberty above all else, the right institutions are not those that promote liberty, and are not therefore those that would ban the minority group, but rather are the institutions that would testify suitably to the value of liberty. They are the institutions that would promote liberty, but only by means that do not themselves involve interference with liberty. They are the institutions, in a word, that would honour liberty rather than promote it. To honour liberty under ideal conditions – under conditions where there are no recalcitrant agents like the minority fanatics – will be to promote it there. But in the real world where other agents and agencies are bent on undermining liberty, honouring the value may mean failing to promote it: heroically failing to promote it, as it were.

The distinction applies to individual agents as well as to agencies like institutions, and it also applies with a variety of values. Consider, for example, the difference between the consequentialist and the deontological pacifist. The consequentialist will want to do things, and to have others do things, which mean that in the long run the consequences will be best for peace; this may involve being prepared to wage or condone a war, provided that the war looks essential for the promotion of peace. The deontological pacifist, on the other hand, will want to pursue only peaceful activities and will want others to pursue only such activities; thus he will not be prepared to wage or condone any war, even a 'war to end all wars'. He will want to honour peace, not promote it: not promote it, that is, by any means.

The distinction between promoting and honouring a value is a version of the analytical distinction between having a consequentialist and a deontological attitude towards the value (Pettit, 1991; see Scheffler, 1988). That distinction has been carefully elaborated in analytical moral philosophy but it applies in political philosophy as well. It is a different distinction, it should be noticed, from that which John Rawls (1971, pp. 446–52) assumes when he argues for the priority of the right over the good. Rawls is anxious, not to stake out a deontological position, but rather to emphasize that the basic structure should be capable of neutral justification, without reference to the particular conceptions of the good life entertained among the population (Kymlicka, 1990). It is unfortunate that he should use the terminology of the right and the good to make this point.

The distinction between the consequentialist and the deontological theory of the right, in particular the political right, applies across the full spectrum of political values. With any value whatsoever we can distinguish between the consequentialist strategy of designing institutions so that the value is promoted by them and designing institutions so that the value is honoured by them. Take a personal value like equality or fairness or welfare; take a more communal value like democracy or the rule of law or public justification; take the value which is allegedly associated with the satisfaction of certain rights; or take even the contractarian value of a set of institutions which consists in the fact that it would be chosen under certain circumstances. With any such value – or with any weighted mix of such values – we can in principle distinguish between institutionally promoting the value and institutionally honouring it. We can identify the right institutions as those that give consequentialist countenance to the value or we can identify them with those that give it deontological countenance.

This point is well worth stressing, as it is a lesson of analytical thought which is often lost in political theory. For example, many political theorists hail certain rights as being of great political importance, without making it clear whether the rights are to be honoured – whether, in Nozick's term, they are to be treated properly as constraints – or whether their satisfaction is to be promoted, if necessary by violation of the rights in certain cases (Nozick, 1974, p. 28). Again many political theorists invoke 'just deserts' as the main concern of the state in criminal justice, without saying whether the criminal justice system is to honour just deserts or to promote them. If the idea is to promote the delivery of just deserts then this may call for the occasional exemplary sentence; if the idea is to honour that value then no such sentence will ever be permitted (Braithwaite and Pettit, 1990).

But not only does political theory often ignore the distinction between the institutional promotion and honouring of a value. It also often misconstrues what is involved in having institutions which promote a value, and on this point too analytical philosophy has an important lesson to teach. The lesson was well expressed in an article by John Rawls on 'Two concepts of rules' (1955), but it was implicit in much earlier writing and it has been reworked in many different forms over the past couple of decades (Brandt, 1979; Hare, 1982; Scheffler, 1982; Parfit, 1984; Railton, 1984; Johnson, 1985; Pettit and Brennan, 1986).

What Rawls brought out in his article is that if certain institutions are designed to promote a value, that does not necessarily mean that the agents of the institutions will be authorized to take the value into consideration in their various deliberations and to act in the way that promises to promote it best, by their lights. Consider a value like utility. It is not necessarily the case, as Rawls made clear, that the institutions which will best promote utility are those in which the agents make their decisions in a calculating, utilitarian way. For example, the criminal justice system that best promotes utility is not likely to be the one within which each judge acts in that way; it is more likely to be the ordinary sort of system under which each judge acts according to a specified brief: a brief that prohibits, or at least limits, utilitarian reasoning.

This point has been generally acknowledged within analytical, political philosophy, but it does leave a problem in its wake, which has not been given due attention: this is the problem of the zealous agent, as we might call it (Lyons, 1982; Braithwaite and Pettit, 1990). Suppose that a set of institutions is designed to promote a certain value X and that the agents of the institutions internalize that value and are zealously concerned about its promotion. Such agents will undoubtedly come across situations where, by their own lights, the best way to promote the value will be by going beyond their allotted brief. So what is there to restrain them from doing this? More generally, what is there to prevent zealous agents from undermining any institutions that seek to promote a certain goal and that seek to do so, in particular, without letting the agents of the institutions calculate in regard to those goals? The question requires careful consideration by consequentialists (Braithwaite and Pettit, 1990).

If my line of argument is correct, then all salient political theories fall into one of two categories: they are deontological theories, which recommend the honouring of certain values, or they are consequentialist theories, which recommend the promotion of certain values. But the line of argument needs defence on two fronts. First, it needs to be defended against those who would say that the deontologist does not recognize values at all; he identifies what is right independently of any concern with what is good (Foot, 1985). And second, it needs to be defended against the influential view which Ronald Dworkin (1978) has put forward, that political theories divide rather into three categories: the goal-based, the duty-based and the right-based. I will conclude with some remarks on each of these challenges.

The account given of the distinction between consequentialists and deontologists presupposes that in every decision there is a value at issue: specifically, a neutral value that does not inherently involve any particular individual or circumstance. It represents the doctrines as rival theories as to how the relevant value or values determine the right option: the one says that the value should be promoted, the other that it should be honoured. So how should we respond, if someone says that for the deontologist, value – that is, the value of independent states of affairs – plays no role: that whereas the consequentialist holds that the right choice is that which promotes relevant values, the deontologist identifies the right choice without any reference to values? The deontologist may be thought to identify that choice on the basis of intuition or by reference to a formula of some kind: say, the Kantian formula according to which a choice is right just in case the implicit maxim can be willed as a general law.

The response to this objection is to ask whether the deontologist who claims to identify a right choice without reference to values is prepared to universalize his prescription (Hare, 1982). Is he ready to say that the choice is right, not just for the agent or agency in question, and not just for the situation and society under discussion, but for any similar agency in similar circumstances? I presume that any reasonable thinker will be prepared to universalize in that way, since otherwise he must seem to be making too much of the particularities on hand. But if the deontologist does universalize, then he is committed to recognizing a certain value. He is committed to believing that it is good that any agent or agency of the relevant kind makes the sort of choice recommended in relevant sorts of circumstances; he is committed to thinking that the world will be better off for the obtaining of this sort of state of affairs. With regard to that value, indeed, he holds that the particular agent or agency in question should honour it rather than promote it; our account of the deontological position fits nicely with the posture that he adopts.

There is a natural salience about the division of political theories suggested by Ronald Dworkin (1978, pp. 172–3): 'Such a theory might be *goal-based*, in which case it would take some goal, like improving the general welfare, as fundamental; it might be *right-based*, taking some right, like the right of all men to the greatest possible overall liberty, as fundamental; or it might be *duty-based*, taking some duty, like the duty to obey God's will as set forth in the Ten Commandments, as fundamental. It is easy to find examples of pure, or nearly pure, cases of each of these types of theory. Utilitarianism is, as my example suggested, a goal-based theory; Kant's categorical imperatives compose a duty-based theory; and Tom Paine's theory of revolution is right-based.' So how does our division into consequentialist and deontological theories measure up to this taxonomy? Consequentialist theories correspond to Dworkin's goal-based theories, so there is no problem of match there. But what is the connection between deontological theories and theories that are duty-based and right-based?

The connection is fairly straightforward. All deontological theories involve the recognition of obligations. If we say that a structure should be judged for how it honours a value like liberty or equality or respect, then we say that there is a set of response-types, which are obligatory for any basic structure; there are certain intrinsically binding obligations, which have to be countenanced by every such structure. This makes an important point of contrast with the consequentialist way of thinking, for on that approach the only matter of obligation is to promote the relevant goal and this may select one set of response-types in this society, a different set in another, and so on; there may be no intrinsically binding types of obligation.

The distinction between duty-based and right-based theories is a distinction between those deontological, obligation-involving theories which make the obligation primitive and those theories that hold that the obligations obtain because of the pre-existing rights of relevant individuals. The natural law tradition is probably the longest established school of thought within which obligations are represented

34

as primitive (d'Entreves, 1970; Finnis, 1980). The tradition of natural rights, which developed in the seventeenth century, is the best-known school of thought to postulate rights as the source of all relevant obligations (Tuck, 1979). Rights get conceived of in that tradition as moral controls which individuals can exercise, activating obligations on the part of the state to respond appropriately to them.

In this last section I have distinguished between the theory of the political good and the theory of the political right and I have tried to identify the legacy of the analytical-philosophical way of thinking in each area. The theory of the good, with its combination of personalism and solipsism, is a mixed bag, but the theory of the right, with the important distinctions between consequentialist and deontological stances, is of the greatest importance. Political theory is emerging rapidly as an independent teaching discipline and an independent area of research. Whatever the connection it maintains with the tradition of analytical philosophy, it would do well to retain the habits of intellectual precision manifested in such distinctions.

See also 2 CONTINENTAL PHILOSOPHY; 5 ECONOMICS; 11 LIBERALISM; 15 COMMUNITY; 16 CONTRACT AND CONSENT; 19 DEMOCRACY; 22 DISTRIBUTIVE JUSTICE; 25 EQUALITY; 29 LIBERTY; 32 REPUBLICANISM; 33 RIGHTS

References

Ackerman, B.: *Social Justice in the Liberal State* (New Haven, Conn.: Yale University Press, 1980).
Arneson, R. J., ed.: 'Symposium on Rawlsian theory of justice: recent developments', *Ethics*, 99 (1989), 695–944.
Ayer, A. J.: *Language, Truth, and Logic* (London: Gollancz, 1936).
Barber, B.: *Strong Democracy* (Berkeley, Calif.: Berkeley University Press, 1984).
Barry, B.: *Political Argument* (London: Routledge, 1965).
————: *The Liberal Theory of Justice: A Critical Examination of the Principal Doctrines in a 'Theory of Justice' by John Rawls* (Oxford: Oxford University Press, 1973).
————: *Theories of Justice* (Hemel Hempstead: Harvester Wheatsheaf, 1989).
————: *Political Argument: A Reissue* (Hemel Hempstead: Wheatsheaf, 1990).
Barry, N.: *Hayek's Economic and Social Philosophy* (London: Macmillan, 1979).
Beitz, C.: *Political Theory and International Relations* (Princeton, NJ: Princeton University Press, 1979).
Benn, S. I.: *A Theory of Freedom* (Cambridge: Cambridge University Press, 1988).
———— and Peters, R. S.: *Social Principles and the Democratic State* (London: Allen & Unwin, 1959).
Bentham, J.: *The Works of Jeremy Bentham*, vol. 1 (Edinburgh: William Tait, 1843).
Berlin, I.: *Two Concepts of Liberty* (Oxford: Oxford University Press, 1958).
————: *Vico and Herder* (London: Hogarth Press, 1976).
Black, S.: 'Individualism at an impasse', *Canadian Journal of Philosophy*, 21 (1991), 347–78.
Bradley, F. H.: *Ethical Studies*, 2nd edn (London: Oxford University Press, 1962).
Braithwaite, J. and Pettit, P.: *Not Just Deserts: A Republican Theory of Criminal Justice* (Oxford: Oxford University Press, 1990).
Brandt, R. B.: *A Theory of the Good and the Right* (Oxford: Oxford University Press, 1979).
Braybrooke, D.: *Meeting Needs* (Princeton, NJ: Princeton University Press, 1987).

Broome, J.: 'Irreducibly social goods', in G. Brennan and C. Walsh, eds, *Rationality, Individualism and Public Policy* (Canberra: Anutech, 1990).

————: *Weighing Goods* (Oxford: Blackwell, 1991).

Buchanan, A. E.: 'Assessing the communitarian critique of liberalism', *Ethics*, 99 (1989), 852–82.

Buchanan, J. M. and Tullock, G.: *The Calculus of Consent* (Ann Arbor, Mich.: University of Michigan Press, 1962).

Campbell, T.: *Justice* (London: Macmillan, 1988).

Cohen, G. A.: 'On the currency of egalitarian justice', *Ethics*, 99 (1989), 906–44.

Cohen, J. and Rogers, J.: *On Democracy* (Harmondsworth: Penguin Books, 1983).

Daniels, N., ed.: *Reading Rawls* (Oxford: Blackwell, 1978).

d'Entreves, A. P.: *Natural Law*, revised edn (London: 1970).

Dworkin, G.: *The Theory and Practice of Autonomy* (Cambridge: Cambridge University Press, 1988).

Dworkin, R. M.: *Taking Rights Seriously* (1977), 2nd impression (London: Duckworth, 1978).

Feinberg, J.: *Doing and Deserving: Essays in the Theory of Responsibility* (Princeton, NJ: Princeton University Press, 1970).

————: *The Moral Limits of the Criminal Law*, 4 vols (Oxford: Oxford University Press, 1988).

Finnis, J.: *Natural Law and Natural Rights* (Oxford: Oxford University Press, 1980).

Foot, P.: 'Utilitarianism and the virtues', *Mind*, 94 (1985), 196–209.

Frey, R. G., ed.: *Utility and Rights* (Oxford: Blackwell, 1985).

Gaus, G. F.: *Value and Justification* (Cambridge: Cambridge University Press, 1990).

Gauthier, D.: *Morals by Agreement* (Oxford: Oxford University Press, 1986).

Goodin, R. E.: *Protecting the Vulnerable* (Chicago: Chicago University Press, 1985).

Gray, J. N.: *Hayek on Liberty*, 2nd edn (Oxford: Oxford University Press, 1986).

Griffin, J.: *Wellbeing: Its Meaning, Measurement, and Moral Importance* (Oxford: Oxford University Press, 1986).

Gutmann, A.: 'Communitarian critics of liberalism', *Philosophy and Public Affairs*, 14 (1985).

Habermas, J.: 'Wahrheitstheorien', in *Wirklichkeit und Reflexion: Walter Schulz zum 60 Geburtstag* (Pfullingen: Neske, 1973).

Hamlin, A.: 'Liberty, contract and the state', in A. Hamlin and P. Pettit, eds, *The Good Polity* (Oxford: Blackwell, 1989).

———— and Pettit, P.: 'The normative analysis of the state', in A. Hamlin and P. Pettit, eds, *The Good Polity* (Oxford: Blackwell, 1989).

Hampton, J.: *Hobbes and the Social Contract of Tradition* (Cambridge: Cambridge University Press, 1986).

Hardin, R.: *Morality within the Limits of Reason* (Chicago: University of Chicago Press, 1988).

Hare, R. M.: *The Language of Morals* (Oxford: Oxford University Press, 1952).

————: *Moral Thinking* (Oxford: Oxford University Press, 1982).

Harsanyi, J. C.: 'Cardinal utility in welfare economics and in the theory of risk-taking', *Journal of Political Economy* (1953).

————: 'Cardinal welfare, individualistic ethics, and interpersonal comparisons of utility', *Journal of Political Economy* (1955).

Hart, H. L. A.: *The Concept of Law* (Oxford: Oxford University Press, 1961).

Hayek, F. A. von: *Law, Legislation and Liberty: A New Statement of the Liberal Principles of Justice and Political Economy*, 3 vols (London: Routledge, 1982).

Held, D., ed.: *Political Theory Today* (Stanford, Calif.: Stanford University Press, 1991).

Hobbes, T.: *Leviathan* (1651), ed. C. B. MacPherson (Harmondsworth: Penguin Books, 1968).

Johnson, C. D.: 'The authority of the moral agent', *Journal of Philosophy*, 82 (1985), 391–413.

Kukathas, C.: *Hayek and Modern Liberalism* (Oxford: Oxford University Press, 1989).

———— and Pettit, P.: *Rawls: A Theory of Justice and its Critics* (Cambridge: Polity Press, 1990).

Kymlicka, W.: *Contemporary Political Philosophy: An Introduction* (Oxford: Oxford University Press, 1990).

Larmore, C.: *Patterns of Moral Complexity* (Cambridge: Cambridge University Press, 1987).

Laslett, Peter, ed.: *Philosophy Politics and Society*, series 1 (Oxford: Blackwell, 1956).

Lessnoff, M.: *Social Contract* (London: Macmillan, 1986).

Lindley, R.: *Autonomy* (London, Macmillan, 1986).

Lloyd Thomas, D. A.: *In Defence of Liberalism* (Oxford, Blackwell, 1988).

Lomasky, L.: *Persons, Rights and the Moral Community* (Oxford: Oxford University Press, 1987).

Lyons, David: 'Utility and rights', *Nomos*, 24 (1982), 107–38.

Macedo, S.: *Liberal Virtues* (New York: Oxford University Press, 1990).

MacIntyre, A.: *After Virtue: A Study in Moral Theory* (London: Duckworth, 1981).

MacKinnon, C.: *Feminism Unmodified: Discourses on Life and Law* (Cambridge, Mass.: Harvard University Press, 1987).

Mill, J. S.: *Essays on Ethics, Religion and Society, Collected Works*, vol. 10 (London: Routledge, 1969).

Miller, D.: *Social Justice* (Oxford: Oxford University Press, 1976).

————: *Market, State, and Community: Theoretical Foundations of Market Socialism* (Oxford: Oxford University Press, 1989).

————: 'Equality', in K. Hunt, ed., *Philosophy and Politics* (Cambridge: Cambridge University Press, 1990).

Nagel, T.: *Equality and Partiality* (New York: Oxford University Press, 1991).

Nozick, R.: *Anarchy, State and Utopia* (Oxford: Blackwell, 1974).

Okin, S. M.: 'Gender, the public and the private', in D. Held, ed., *Political Theory Today* (Stanford, Calif.: Stanford University Press, 1991).

Parfit, D.: *Reasons and Persons* (Oxford: Oxford University Press, 1984).

Pateman, C.: 'Feminist critiques of the public–private dichotomy', in S. I. Benn and G. F. Gaus, eds, *Public and Private and Social Life* (London: Croom Helm, 1983).

Paul, J., ed.: *Reading Nozick: Essays on Anarchy, State and Utopia* (Oxford: Blackwell, 1981).

Pettit, P.: *Judging Justice: An Introduction to Contemporary Political Philosophy* (London: Routledge, 1980).

————: 'Habermas on truth and justice', in G. H. R. Parkinson, ed., *Marx and Marxisms* (Cambridge: Cambridge University Press, 1982).

————: 'A definition of negative liberty', *Ratio*, NS2 (1989), 153–68.

————: 'Consequentialism', in P. Singer, ed., *A Companion to Ethics* (Oxford: Blackwell, 1991).

————: *The Common Mind: An Essay on Psychology, Society and Politics* (New York: Oxford University Press, 1993).

———— and Brennan, G.: 'Restrictive consequentialism', *Australasian Journal of Philosophy*, 64 (1986).

Pogge, T. W.: *Realizing Rawls* (Ithaca, NY: Cornell University Press, 1989).

Popper, K.: *The Open Society and Its Enemies* (London: Routledge, 1945).

————: *The Poverty of Historicism* (London: Routledge, 1957).

Quine, W. V. O.: *Word and Object* (Cambridge, Mass.: MIT Press, 1960).

Railton, P.: 'Alienation, consequentialism and morality', *Philosophy and Public Affairs*, 13 (1984).

Rawls, J.: 'Outline of a decision procedure for ethics', *Philosophical Review*, 60 (1951), 177–97.
————: 'Two concepts of rules', *Philosophical Review*, 64 (1955), 3–32.
————: *A Theory of Justice* (Oxford, Oxford University Press, 1971).
————: 'The priority of right and ideas of the good', *Philosophy and Public Affairs*, 17 (1988), 251–76.
Raz, J.: *The Morality of Freedom* (Oxford: Oxford University Press, 1986).
Roemer, J.: *Free to Lose: An Introduction to Marxist Economic Philosophy* (Cambridge, Mass.: Harvard University Press, 1988).
Rousseau, J.-J.: *The Social Contract and Discourses* (1762); (London: J. M. Dent, 1973).
Sadurski, W.: *Giving Desert its Due: Social Justice and Legal Theory* (Dordrecht: Reidel, 1985).
Sandel, M.: *Liberalism and the Limits of Justice* (Cambridge: Cambridge University Press, 1982).
Scanlon, T. M.: 'Contractualism and utilitarianism', in A. Sen and B. Williams, eds, *Utilitarianism and Beyond* (Cambridge: Cambridge University Press, 1982).
Scheffler, S.: *The Rejection of Consequentialism* (Oxford: Oxford University Press, 1982).
————: ed.: *Consequentialism and its Critics* (Oxford: Oxford University Press, 1988).
Sen, A.: *Commodities and Capabilities* (Amsterdam: North-Holland, 1985).
———— and Williams, B., eds: *Utilitarianism and Beyond* (Cambridge: Cambridge University Press, 1982).
Sher, G.: *Desert* (Princeton, NJ: Princeton University Press, 1987).
Sidgwick, H.: *The Methods of Ethics* (London: Macmillan, 1962).
Singer, P.: 'Sidgwick and reflective equilibrium', *The Monist*, 58 (1974).
Stevenson, C. L.: *Ethics and Language* (New Haven, Conn.: Yale University Press, 1944).
Taylor, C.: *Hegel* (Cambridge: Cambridge University Press, 1975).
————: *Philosophy and the Human Sciences: Philosophical Papers*, vol. 2 (Cambridge: Cambridge University Press, 1985).
Tuck, R.: *Natural Rights Theories* (Cambridge: Cambridge University Press, 1979).
Waldron, J., ed.: *Theories of Rights* (Oxford: Oxford University Press, 1984).
Walzer, M.: *Spheres of Justice: A Defence of Pluralism and Equality* (Oxford: Blackwell, 1983).
————: 'A critique of philosophical conversation', *The Philosophical Forum*, 21 (1989–90), 182–196.
————: 'The communitarian critique of liberalism', *Political Theory*, 18 (1990), 6–23.
Weldon, T. D.: *The Vocabulary of Politics* (Harmondsworth: Penguin Books, 1953).
Wells, G. A.: *The Origin of Language* (La Salle, Ill.: Open Court, 1987).
Wiggins, D.: *Needs, Values, Truth* (Oxford: Blackwell, 1987).
Wokler, R.: *Rousseau on Society, Politics, Music and Language* (New York: Garland, 1987).
Wolff, R. P.: *Understanding Rawls* (Princeton, NJ: Princeton University Press, 1977).
Young, R.: *Personal Autonomy: Beyond Negative and Positive Liberty* (London: Croom Helm, 1986).

Further reading

Brown, A.: *Modern Political Philosophy: Theories of the Justice Society* (Harmondsworth: Penguin Books, 1986).
Horton, J.: 'Weight or lightness? Political philosophy and its prospects', in A. Leftwich, ed., *New Developments in Political Science* (Aldershot: Gower, 1990).
Sterba, J.: *How to Make People Just: A Practical Reconciliation of Alternative Conceptions of Justice* (Totowa, NJ: Rowman & Littlefield, 1988).
Walzer, M., ed.: *The State of Political Theory*, Special Issue *Dissent* (Summer 1989).

2

The contribution of continental philosophy

DAVID WEST

The continental tradition

The opposition between analytical and continental philosophy has something in common with that other, more worldly and now obsolete opposition between East and West. The observer of politics quickly realizes that 'East' and 'West' are ideological rather than geographical terms. The West is free and prosperous and celebrates human rights and the American way; the East has been totalitarian, stagnant and oppressive. Japan and Australia are for most purposes in the West, Cuba and, until recently, Nicaragua in the East. Similar anomalies beset our more philosophical dichotomy. There are obvious difficulties in the path of any straightforwardly geographical interpretation. Frege played a seminal role in the development of analytical philosophy despite being German; so did the Vienna Circle and Wittgenstein. On the other hand, there are obvious affinities between such British idealists as Bradley, Collingwood and Oakeshott and their colleagues across the Channel. Even John Stuart Mill was deeply influenced by the ideas of German Romanticism. Contemporary figures like Richard Rorty, Alasdair MacIntyre and Charles Taylor self-consciously develop 'continental' themes in an idiom more congenial to analytical philosophy. Again, there are growing schools of analytical philosophy in contemporary France and Germany as well as recurrent waves of a neo-Kantianism which, in its fundamental claims, is not so very different.

The contemporary discovery of continental philosophy in the English-speaking countries is actually quite recent. Only about fifteen years ago a course in philosophy that failed to mention Hegel or Nietzsche, Husserl, Heidegger or Sartre was not considered deficient. But as the anomalies in the geographical definition show, this 'discovery' is in fact more akin to the remission, perhaps temporary, of a more active process of forgetting and exclusion. The anomalies testify to the frequent waves of influence which have occurred between the camps in the past. Hegel, German idealism and Romanticism already had an enthusiastic following in Britain and America in the nineteenth century. Indeed, students of analytical philosophy will perhaps recall the triumphant blows dealt at the turn of the century by Russell, Whitehead and Moore against what was in Britain an overwhelmingly Hegelian and idealist philosophical establishment. The ascendancy of analytical philosophy in its contemporary guise dates from this time, with *Principia Mathematica* as a symbolic watershed (Whitehead and Russell, 1903). Skirmishes persist, with the diatribes of logical positivism against the 'senseless' utterances of 'metaphysics' and the continuing though abating concern to demarcate 'science' from 'nonsense'. When A. J Ayer reiterated the Humean repudiation of metaphysics as consisting neither of verifiable statements of fact nor of analytical or logical truths, he found it natural to choose Heidegger as a principal target (Ayer, [1946] 1971, pp. 59–61).

A second symptom of a real opposition between continental thought and philosophical analysis is what seems like an equally active process of misunderstanding. Admittedly, works of continental philosophy often present stylistic difficulties. In part these result from the sheer weight of allusion, born of the conviction that the philosophical tradition is more than a comedy of errors. The reader accustomed to analytical clarity is unlikely to be surprised or disturbed at the claim that the propositions of Heidegger's *Being and Time* (1967) are senseless, and she is liable to be relieved to be told that 'metaphysics' can safely be ignored by the clear-headed philosopher of empirical bent. The allusive and occasionally opaque style of philosophy in the continental mode is taken to define continental philosophy as the 'other' of analytical clarity and rigour. But the suspicion that this incomprehension is a symptom more of active rejection than a passive inability is reinforced, once the obscurities of much analytical philosophy are recalled. G. E. Moore's indefatigably common-sense reflections on perception are scarcely less impenetrable than Hegel's equally conscientious explorations of 'sensuous certainty'. The crystalline prose of Wittgenstein's *Tractatus Logico-Philosophicus* is no less difficult than the *Logical Investigations* of Husserl (Wittgenstein, 1961; Husserl, 1970).

There is, then, something arbitrary and artificial about the attempt to distinguish two opposed and mutually isolated traditions in Western philosophy. The geographical basis for such a division is neither obvious nor philosophically interesting. On the other hand, there is evidence of an active hostility between philosophical camps, a process of forgetting, exclusion and misunderstanding, which points to a real opposition, a suppressed dialectic perhaps. The approach taken here traces a distinctively continental tradition in philosophy back to the critique of Enlightenment which, initiated by Herder and Rousseau, found its first most systematic expression in Hegel's reaction to Kant. Subsequent contributors to the tradition are 'post-Hegelians', in the sense that they develop or react against Hegel, but never simply ignore him. Their ideas bear the marks of the Hegelian system even when they most vigorously oppose it. The tradition so defined includes Marx, Kierkegaard, Nietzsche, Husserl and Heidegger. It also comprises the existentialisms of Sartre, Camus and de Beauvoir, the neo-Marxism of the Frankfurt School and Habermas, the schools of phenomenology, structuralism, post-structuralism, deconstruction and postmodernism. This avowedly historical approach to the identification of a continental tradition reflects its most important and distinctive features. It is sceptical of the timeless rationalisms of an Enlightenment overly impressed by natural science. It has a deepened awareness of the cultural and historical constitution of thought, so that even philosophy must orient its enterprise in terms of a particular context and a particular history. In this sense, to seek to identify a *tradition* of thought is itself an aim more congenial to the continental critics of Enlightenment.

Critics of Enlightenment

The term 'Enlightenment' refers to a period of social and cultural transformation self-consciously illuminated by reason. A decisive assault on the strongholds of medieval thought was encouraged by the scientific achievements of 'natural philosophers' like Newton and Galileo in the seventeenth century. The predominantly Aristotelian and Christian world-view of the Middle Ages unravelled, as philosophers and political theorists cast doubt on religious belief and traditional authority and searched for more rational foundations for moral beliefs and the political order. Humanity should live solely by the lights of its own reason. Kant saw Enlightenment as the transition from 'immaturity' and dependence to the 'spirit of freedom' and autonomy, the ability 'to use one's understanding without guidance from another' (Kant, [1784] 1983, p. 41). At the same time, great social and economic changes occurred with the rise of capitalism. Overall, a profound transformation of the social, cultural and intellectual life of Europe moulded the contours of modernity.

What were the main features of this transformation? In the first place, the Enlightenment dissolved the Aristotelian and medieval view of the world as a cosmos. The modern world is no longer 'a meaningful order' but 'a world of ultimately contingent correlations to be patiently mapped by empirical observation' (Taylor, 1975, p. 4). Hume ridiculed the attempt to understand nature as a teleological system of entities propelled by some inner necessity to fulfil their essential natures. Even if they existed, we could never have knowledge of these essences or of the necessary connections between events which they implied. Knowledge of this world is, secondly, attributed to a redefined subject of experience. The self is no longer constrained and defined by an essential purpose, moved to realize its intrinsic nature, whether as human animal or *zoon politikon*. The characteristic self of the Enlightenment is the Cartesian subject of consciousness. Descartes' methodical doubt leads him to the conclusion that the only thing that is certain is that 'I am, I exist', and therefore what I am essentially is a thing which thinks: 'I am not more than a thing which thinks, that is to say a mind or a soul, or an understanding, or a reason' (Descartes, 1931, pp, 151–2). The primary relation between self and world so defined is epistemological; the self is above all a knowing subject. But knowledge, finally, is also understood differently. Its goal is no longer to decipher the cosmos in order to realize God's will or to live more in harmony with nature. Rather, our ever-increasing knowledge of objects in the world makes our lives more certain, our experience more predictable and increases our mastery of nature. The value and purpose of knowledge is principally instrumental.

Some Enlightenment thinkers still professed faith in God, whether out of genuine conviction or cautious expediency. Descartes not only provided a proof of the existence of God, but avoided radical scepticism only with its help (Descartes, 1931). Other thinkers assumed the compatibility of faith and reason or, like Bacon, the validity of religious 'wisdom' as opposed to mere 'learning' (Bacon, [1605] 1973). Still, the world of the Enlightenment is significantly disenchanted. The divinely ordered cosmos is no longer replete with moral and religious significance. The causal regularities uncovered by science are of no moral or ethical significance; empirical knowledge cannot support evaluative conclusions. Hume's classic statement of the distinction between facts and values announces that 'virtue is not founded merely on the relations of objects' (Hume, [1739–40] 1888, p. 470). Hume also provides a devastating challenge to all attempts to base religious belief on our experience of events in the world, however miraculous ([1777] 1902, section X; [1779] 1990). Moral, political or aesthetic value can only be something injected into or projected on to the world by subjects of experience, 'self-defining' subjects who must seek moral guidance from within (Taylor, 1975). Value, which had previously shone from every facet of a meaningful world, must now be justified. whether as impressions of a 'moral sense' (Hume), as the decrees of self-legislating rational beings (Kant), as projections of human desire or manifestations of the capacity for pleasure and suffering (utilitarianism), or as the unchallengeable expressions of a capricious will (subjectivism).

The contours of the Enlightenment world-view are still recognizable in analytical philosophy. The continental tradition, on the other hand, constitutes a sustained attempt to surpass or transcend this position. An important inspiration is the conviction, against the more atomist assumptions of Enlightenment thinkers, that individuals are constituted within societies and cultures. Herder (1744–1803) argues that language is the essential medium of our humanity ([1770] 1967). The powers of memory and anticipation implicit in 'reflection' or 'consciousness' are only possible through language. They are what compensate the human animal for the relative paucity and weakness of its instincts, substituting both freedom and an enhanced ability to co-operate, more useful in a changing environment, for the fixity and certainty of the animal's instinctual responses. Language is not just a vehicle for the expression of thoughts or ideas which could exist without it, but the essential medium for human thought and consciousness. Different languages reflect and imply different ways of thinking and feeling, with the result that it is not always possible to translate easily from one language to another. The languages of different peoples correspond to differences of culture and sensibility which, for Herder, define distinct nationalities. By the same token, because there can be no universal human essence, whether natural, intellectual or spiritual, independent of the particular conditions of language and culture, the universal programmes of the Enlightenment's 'free thinkers' are called into question.

Herder's insight into the social nature of human consciousness was in tune with the political thought of his near contemporary, Jean-Jacques Rousseau (1712–78). Rousseau is associated with the view that humanity is naturally good; he is seen as a source of Romanticism and the 'return to nature'. According to the first sentence of Rousseau's Èmile: 'God makes all things good; man meddles with them and they become evil' (Rousseau, [1762] 1974, p. 35). More accurately, Rousseau refuses to posit any universal human nature existing prior to society, whether good or bad, altruistic or selfish. Rousseau denies, for example, that it makes sense to justify political authority in terms of the rational choices of individuals in a 'state of nature'. Hobbes's belief, that selfish individuals would, out of fear, accept the sovereign authority of the Leviathan, is as unfounded as the more optimistic belief of an anarchist like Godwin, for whom natural individuals, untainted by civilization or authority, would live in uncontentious harmony without the legislative and coercive apparatus of the state. For Rousseau individuals only exist within societies. Nor is the political will of these individuals simply equivalent to the 'will of all' or the sum of particular wills. Rousseau's 'general will' is only reached after a process of negotiation and deliberation and should reflect the common interest of the social body. It does not leave unchanged the wills of the particular individuals who contribute to it. Equally, the sacrifices these individuals make for its sake are ambivalent. What the individual loses in 'natural liberty', she gains in 'civil' and 'moral liberty':

The passage from the state of nature to the civil state produces a very remarkable change in man, by substituting for instinct in his conduct, and giving his actions the morality they had formerly lacked. Then only, when the voice of duty takes the place of physical impulses and right of appetite, does man, who so far had considered only himself, find that he is forced to act on different principles and consult his reason before listening to his inclinations. (Rousseau, [1762] 1973, pp. 177–8)

Although this transition involves the loss of 'some advantages which he got from nature', in society the individual is compensated by a stimulation and extension of his faculties, an ennobling of feeling and an uplifting of the soul. It is this 'moral liberty' which 'alone makes him truly master of himself; for the mere impulse of appetite is slavery, while obedience to a law which we prescribe to ourselves is liberty' (ibid., p. 178). This equation of liberty with subjection to law and society has been seen as a first approach to totalitarianism, a licence for the tyrannical view that individuals can be 'forced to be free'. But a valuable insight remains: that, whatever the defects of existing societies, it is only within society that individuals exist as rational, purposive, moral beings with access to a range of values, interests and forms of life incomparably richer than the meagre repertoire of our instinctual responses and biological needs. On John Keane's more sympathetic interpretation, Rousseau describes 'an individualism of cooperation and uniqueness (*Einzigkeit*) compared with that of mere singleness (*Einzelheit*)' (Keane, 1984, p. 254).

Hegel (1770–1831) was inspired by both Rousseau and Herder, but it is the overwhelming synthetic power of his system which inaugurates a genuinely distinct tradition of continental philosophy. His critique of the Enlightenment is all-encompassing, but it can be understood most pointedly in terms of his reaction to Kant's moral and political philosophy and the French Revolution. In contrast to Kant, Hegel is sceptical of the possibility of deriving concrete moral judgements, the principles of a full ethical life, from the commitment to universality alone. Simply universalizing the maxims of one's actions, as Kant recommends, will never generate a determinate moral content. Nothing rules out the possibility that the autonomous self might be consistently and indiscriminately evil. Indeed, Hegel's account of the French Revolution implies that this is the most likely outcome. Hegel describes how, when 'each individual consciousness rises out of the sphere assigned to it' and 'grasps itself as the notion of will', it finds that 'its purpose is the universal purpose, its language universal law, its work universal achievement' ([1807] 1967, pp. 601–2). But universal consciousness finds itself unable to produce any positive achievement or deed and 'there is left for it only negative action: it is merely the rage and fury of destruction' which aims only for death (ibid., p. 604). On this account, the French Revolutionary Terror is a characteristic manifestation of the 'absolute freedom' and abstract universality of Kantian autonomy.

Hegel's arguments suggest that the universalization of a 'monological' process of deliberation – a process that can in principle be performed by the reasoning subject in isolation – does not sufficiently reconstruct the concrete intersubjectivity essential for 'ethical life'. In Hegel's terms, Kant's categorical imperative is a reconstruction of universal 'morality' (*Moralität*), but cannot ground the full intersubjectivity of ethical life (*Sittlichkeit*). For Hegel, as for Rousseau, ethical life can only be sustained through involvement with a concrete community and its culture, values and forms of life. By the same token, the moral or rational will is not simply opposed to the natural inclinations of the biological individual, as it is for Kant, but is rather the result of a rationalizing of these inclinations. Whereas the particular impulses of the human organism simply ignore the universal demands of society, the socially constituted interests of the individual already reflect the requirements of the community, even when they are not in harmony. The will, as opposed to mere impulse, is 'particularity reflected into itself and so brought back to universality, i.e. it is individuality' (Hegel, [1821] 1952, p. 23). The individual is a product rather than a premiss of the social order.

Other aspects of Hegel's system unfold from this basic point of view. If individuals must always be understood as members of a concrete community and culture, then, since cultures change over time, individuals must also be conceived in terms of a particular history. It would seem to follow that, without universal moral or political principles, we must be indifferent to the apparently repugnant values of a different culture or time. Hegel avoids relativism, however, by ordering alternative cultural forms in terms of a process of development. His philosophy of history portrays the diversity of cultural forms as moments in an unfolding 'dialectic'. Like the Socratic dialogue, the dialectic advances through the conflict of opposing points of view, the contradiction between 'thesis' and 'antithesis' leading to a higher 'synthesis'. In the same way, the tensions implicit in one cultural form or world-view – one particular manifestation of 'spirit' (*Geist*), in Hegel's terms – are resolved or 'transcended' (*aufgehoben*) in the transition to a higher form. Thus a given society can be understood as both dialectically transcending previous social forms, incorporating their positive features while overcoming their contradictions, and as itself destined to be succeeded by other, more developed forms. In these terms Hegel magisterially accounts not only for world history but also for the entire development of cultural and intellectual life. Furthermore, for Hegel the outcome of this spirally ascending dialectic can be known in advance. Through the dialectic, 'spirit' becomes increasingly rational and self-conscious. The dialectic culminates in the attainment of the 'Absolute', the self-reflective appropriation of the whole process of dialectical development in art and religion. In the dialectical philosophy itself, finally, 'spirit' becomes fully and most rationally self-conscious.

In his earlier writings Hegel saw the need to rescue the rational kernel of a dogmatic religion which had been largely discredited by the Enlightenment. Arguably this aim is implicit in modified form throughout his mature writings. Hegel's system aims to distinguish 'reason' (*Vernunft*), as the only sound basis for a full ethical life, from mere 'understanding' (*Verstand*). He wishes to preserve evaluative discourse of all kinds from the reductive analytical grasp of the Enlightenment, but without relinquishing claims to rationality. Hegel foresaw the threat, already apparent in the excesses of the French Revolution, of an increasingly tyrannical reign of limited and one-sided rationality. However, the Hegelian synthesis was to prove unstable. The overweening ambition and speculative bravura of a philosophy of the Absolute could not be sustained. Nevertheless, from the dissolution of the Hegelian system there have emerged a further array of responses to the one-sided rationality of the Enlightenment, which together constitute a distinctively continental tradition in philosophy.

After Marx: the Frankfurt School and Habermas

The most famous continuation of Hegel is, perhaps, that represented by Karl Marx (1818–83) and the Marxist philosophy constructed in his name. Marx declared his intention of 'putting Hegel back on his feet' by replacing Hegel's dialectic of spirit with a materialist dialectic located within the economic sphere. History is driven not by the contradictions within particular world-views, but by the development of 'productive forces' and the resulting contradictions between forces and 'relations of production'. Marx was also a 'left Hegelian'. For Hegel, apparently, the dialectic comes to an end with the Prussian state of his own time, and his own philosophy corresponds to the last stage of the dialectic of spirit, the final achievement of the Absolute. 'Right Hegelians' accepted this interpretation, with its conservative implication that no further transformation of society or philosophy need be anticipated. According to Marx and the left Hegelians, on the other hand, present society and philosophy correspond to only the latest stage of the dialectic, destined to be overcome in yet another spiral turn. For Marx this final step is the transition from capitalism to socialism and then communism. However, the Marxist project has been beset with difficulties, in particular the non-occurrence of revolution in the West and the degeneration and now collapse of socialist revolution in the East. More orthodox Marxists have attempted to retain the framework of historical materialism and explain these failures in terms of merely contingent factors, such as the imperfection of leaders or unfavourable historical circumstance. However, according to a significant tradition of 'critical Marxists' these failures reflect inadequacies in the project itself. They have proposed a thoroughgoing renewal of Marxist theory, inspired by Marx's own Hegelian insight into the historically situated nature of all theory. In its revision of Marxist assumptions, and against the materialist suspicion of philosophy, this tradition has also reclaimed an important role for a specifically philosophical critique and, in the process, resumed the Hegelian critique of Enlightenment.

Members of the 'Frankfurt School', the Institute for Social Research founded in Frankfurt in 1923, are inspired by Marx's famous 'Theses on Feuerbach', that whereas until now 'philosophers have only *interpreted* the world, in various ways; the point is to *change* it' (Marx, 1975, p. 423). Philosophers should construct a 'critical theory' of society, which both provides a diagnosis of the faults of existing society and contributes to the struggle for its transformation in the interests of the oppressed and exploited. However, although the self-styled critical theorists of the Frankfurt School see Marxism as a prototype for this kind of theory, they also recognize an urgent need to revise some of its most basic assumptions. In this sense, they take advantage of Lukács' view that the orthodox Marxist is committed only to the

Marxist method, not to its content (Lukács, 1971, p. 1). The dogmatic commitment to historical materialism, the systematization of Marx's ideas bequeathed to the socialist movement by Engels, contradicts the Hegelian and materialist insight into the social and historical constitution of all knowledge. A critical theory should develop and change, just as capitalist society has undergone important transformations since the time of Marx and Engels. A critical theory should also be self-critical. This return to the more Hegelian insights of the early Marx, at the expense of the more self-consciously scientific economic theory of the later Marx, was reinforced by the belated publication in 1932 of Marx's *Economic and Philosophical Manuscripts* of 1844 (Marx, [1932] 1975).

The return to Hegel and the early Marx also informs the specific criticisms levelled at historical materialism. A particular object of critique is the 'scientism' of this theory. The notion that a rigorous science of society could identify 'iron laws' of capitalism, provide a complete explanation of social evolution and even predict the inevitable collapse of capitalism and its eventual replacement by communism, is identified as the source of the defects of both Stalinism in the East and revolutionary communism in the West (Marcuse, 1971). The pretensions of 'scientific socialism' serve to justify the doctrine of 'democratic centralism', the ultimate authority of the Party's intellectuals and leaders as experts in the theory, paving the way for bureaucratic authoritarianism. Cruder versions of the primacy of the economic in the explanation of social evolution encourage the 'economistic' belief in the centrality and sufficiency of struggles at the 'site of production' and an indifference towards more directly moral or political activism as merely 'utopian'. A scientifically certified revolutionary optimism may even encourage apathy, because eventual victory is assured. Expedient violations of 'bourgeois morality' are excused, because the inevitable advance towards communist utopia could never be diverted by the corruption of the revolutionary movement (see Lukes, 1987). In more voluntaristic style, Leninism appeals to the scientific authority of the revolutionary activist in an energetically political but none the less authoritarian vanguardism.

Generalizing these criticisms of the historical materialism of orthodox Marxism, members of the Frankfurt School develop a wide-ranging critique of 'positivism'. Positivists view natural science as the model for all valid knowledge and, therefore, tend to regard other forms of discourse, for example moral or aesthetic, as invalid or inferior. Already Hume had advocated the 'application of experimental philosophy to moral subjects' in order to lay the 'science of man' on the 'solid foundation' of 'experience and observation' ([1739–40] 1888, p. xx). Hume's positivist heirs either share or unconsciously reinforce his conservative convictions by theorizing alterable social relations as a 'second nature'. In applying the methods of natural science to uncover the laws of economy or society, positivist social theorists portray the regularities of capitalist societies as facts which can only be accepted. For Marx too the 'vulgar economists' of his day were ideological, because they described capitalism as a natural system, obscuring its contingent historical origins and veiling its exploitative relations. As a result they hindered the advance towards a more rational and less unjust society. The Frankfurt School recognize parallel tendencies in contemporary sociology, in so far as it is modelled on the methods and assumptions of natural science. They see it as a species of what Horkheimer calls 'traditional theory' (Horkheimer, 1937; Adorno et al., 1976). A genuinely critical theory, on the other hand, should uncover the 'negative' dimension of existing reality; it should identify suppressed human potentialities, the possibility of a more just and less oppressed society. In bourgeois society, the utopian possibilities suppressed by positivist social science are expressed in politically innocent form as works of art or idealist philosophy, as romanticism or the ideal of beauty. Only if phantasy becomes an integral part of social science, can theory fulfil its emancipatory potential: 'Without phantasy, all philosophical knowledge remains in the grip of the present or the past and severed from the future, which is the only link between philosophy and the real history of mankind' (Marcuse, 1968b, p. 155).

Frankfurt School theorists also incorporate features of German sociology after Marx, in particular Weber's less reductionist explanation of social action and his influential account of the rationalization of society. In contrast to historical materialism, Max Weber's (1864–1920) study of the role of the 'Protestant ethic' in the rise of capitalism places greater emphasis on the 'superstructural' factor of religion in the revolutionary transition from feudalism to capitalism (Weber, 1930). Weber also saw capitalism as just one instance of a more general process of 'rationalization' characteristic of 'modern' civilization. Rationalization was evident in Roman law as well as in the increasingly bureaucratic organization of the state. However, both bureaucracy and capitalism represent only a one-sided form of rationality. They rationalize society only in the sense of 'formal' or 'instrumental' rationality, which organizes efficient means for a given end. They do nothing to further the 'substantive' rationality of ends, the moral or practical reason capable of evaluating the ultimate goals of human activity. In fact, the formal rationalization of state or economy is compatible with the occurrence of substantively irrational outcomes. The state can be efficiently organized to realize undesirable or even obnoxious ends – a possibility most strikingly confirmed by fascism. Equally, this limited rationalization of society increasingly confines human beings to an alienated and disenchanted 'iron cage', a bureaucratically organized existence without meaning.

The analysis of the Frankfurt School is deeply influenced by this account of the rationalization of modern societies. However, whereas Weber saw this process as inevitable, they continue to search for an escape from the iron cage of instrumental rationality, despite their experience of the failures of Marxism and the barbarities of fascism. Horkheimer and Adorno propose a revised 'dialectic of Enlightenment' (Horkheimer and Adorno, 1972). They return to the story of Odysseus for the 'primal history of a subjectivity that wrests itself free from the power of mythic forces' (Habermas, 1987, p. 108). The victory of instrumental rationality over superstition and myth is only partial and is won at a cost. Although science liberates us from the animistic terrors and uncertainties of nature, it offers us only a diminished, one-sided understanding of nature as an object to be manipulated and controlled. Furthermore, the ascendancy of scientific reason comes at the cost of an 'introversion of sacrifice', a corresponding loss of our humanity. An instrumental logic initially applied to a world of objects is extended to relations between persons. As a result, these relations are impoverished and our access to a full, subjective life is impaired. As Habermas puts it: 'The permanent sign of enlightenment is domination over an objectified external nature and a repressed internal nature' (Habermas, 1987, p. 110). There is a further dialectical sting to this analysis. Suppressed 'internal nature' threatens to erupt destructively into modern life, a possibility once again exemplified by fascism. In similar vein Marcuse, influenced by Freud's (1856–1939) psychology of the unconscious, charts the psychic costs of modern society (Marcuse, 1969a). Fixed, like the neurotic, in patterns of behaviour more appropriate to the scarcities of the past, Western society imposes a level of self-denial, a curtailing of the 'polymorphous perversity' of the pleasure principle, no longer necessary in an era of unprecedented productive potential. Marcuse's account of the sacrifice of 'Eros' for the sake of 'civilization' holds out the promise of an eventual release from the 'surplus repression' imposed by society. Written in the conformist 1950s, this analysis would be taken up with enthusiasm in the 'permissive' decade of sexual revolution.

However, other studies of the Frankfurt School are more pessimistic. From one point of view the return to a broader agenda of aesthetic, cultural, psychological and sociological studies promises to enrich the Marxist critique of ideology and, perhaps, provide a better explanation of the disasters of twentieth-century history. Freudian psychoanalysis complicates the historical drama, in part transposing it to the internal stage of Oedipus complex, repression and sublimation, Eros and Thanatos. The technological revolution in mass media (radio, sound reproduction, film) inspires analyses of the 'culture industry', conceived as an extension of industrial techniques to the cultural domain (Benjamin, 1968). The origins of the authoritarian personality are explored with the techniques of social psychology (Adorno et al., 1950). But this inventory of the subtlety and all-pervasiveness of the mechanisms of power harbours more worrying implications. The more the conformity of contemporary society is explained, the more any sudden upsurge of revolutionary enthusiasm seems unlikely. In the end, Adorno's aphoristic excursions into the darker recesses of contemporary culture, his 'minima moralia' or 'reflections from a damaged life', suggest few avenues of escape (Adorno, [1951] 1974). Marcuse's similarly bleak but more systematic portrayal of the 'one-dimensionality' of contemporary existence offers little hope. With the seamless mediocrity of mass-produced entertainment, with the overfed complacency of the affluent society, with its positivistically disarmed sociology and philosophy, contemporary western society either stifles or marginalizes genuine opposition, all but eliminates the negative dimension of critical thought (Marcuse, 1968a). Even the liberties of the one-dimensional society defuse resistance by their 'repressive tolerance', only entrenching a more effectively totalitarian control.

The mood of pessimism haunting the Frankfurt School's account of contemporary society is, then, not incidental. The tendency to reinforce apathy rather than stiffen resistance is exacerbated by a relatively undifferentiated treatment of intersubjectivity and domination. In the *Dialectic of Enlightenment* nature is confronted by a generalized humanity. Marcuse's account of the totalitarian expansion of instrumental rationality suggests a society of uninterrupted manipulation and control. Marcuse only finds likely agents of revolution in those whose existence lies essentially outside of the totalitarian system, in 'the substratum of the outcasts and outsiders, the exploited and persecuted of other races and other colours, the unemployed and the unemployable'. Significantly, these groups can bring about revolution, only if they are led by the radical students and youth, who represent 'the most advanced consciousness of humanity' (1968, pp. 199–200). But a critical theory which discovers seeds of opposition only in the bearers of the critical theory itself surely risks encouraging the voluntarism and elitism of another revolutionary vanguard. There are, in Paul Connerton's phrase, no 'structural gaps within the system of repressive rationality' (Connerton, 1980, p. 102). Losing sight of the relations of domination operating between social groups, the Frankfurt School's neo-Marxism has had a largely apolitical outcome.

More recently, the neo-Marxism of the Frankfurt School has been renewed by the wide-ranging and ambitious project of Jürgen Habermas. In his earlier work Habermas produces an ambitious synthesis of some of the main insights of the Frankfurt School tradition of critical theory. The critique of positivism is reworked on the basis of a modified pragmatism. The achievements of natural science and technology are understood as developments of the logic of instrumental or 'purposive-rational' action, which Habermas also terms 'work' or 'labour'. Technological development – and indeed instrumental rationality more generally – 'follows a logic that corresponds to the structure of purposive-rational action regulated by its own results, which is in fact the structure of work' (1971, p. 87). However, a form of rationality more relevant to our moral or practical concerns is understood in terms of a different pragmatic context, what Habermas calls 'interaction' or 'communication according to consensual norms'. Interaction corresponds to the context of interpersonal relations, the relationship between subjects seeking mutual understanding as opposed to the instrumental relationship between subject and object in work or labour. Work and interaction are the pragmatic contexts for very different forms of knowledge. 'Empirical-analytic sciences', like the natural sciences, are grounded in labour or work and fulfil a technical interest in the control of external reality. 'Historical-hermeneutic sciences' (including history, anthropology and disciplines concerned with the interpretation of texts) find the basis of their objectivity in interaction or communication and serve an interest in mutual understanding, providing 'interpretations that make possible the orientation of action within common traditions' (1972, p. 313).

In *Knowledge and Human Interests* Habermas identifies a third kind of knowledge, critical theory itself, which is grounded in a further pragmatic context, what Habermas calls 'self-reflection'. Even hermeneutic knowledge, though it does not imply a manipulative or instrumental relationship with its object, fails to uncover ideological consciousness. It is blind to forms of false consciousness which reflect the workings of power or domination – what Habermas calls 'distorted communication'. Again, although the identification of law-like correlations between social phenomena is a legitimate component of social theory, critical social science must go beyond this 'to determine when theoretical statements grasp invariant regularities of social action as such and when they express ideologically frozen relations of dependence that can in principle be transformed' (1972, p. 310). Marx's critique of bourgeois economics is the prototype of a critical theory in this sense: it uncovers and helps to dissolve the 'frozen' regularities of capitalism, revealing supposedly natural relations of dependence as socially instituted and alterable. In a similar way, psychoanalysis can lead to

49

the recognition and dissolution of neurotic symptoms as obsolete defence mechanisms inhibiting the individual's 'internal communication'. Critical theories, in other words, serve an interest in emancipation.

Habermas also reformulates the Frankfurt School's diagnosis of modernity, with its 'iron cage' of rationalization. Increasingly, science and technology serve an ideological purpose, justifying the technocratic rule of experts, veiling moral or political (i.e. 'practical') issues from public discussion. Traditional and dogmatic supports of authority are undermined, only to be replaced by an ideology of scientism (Habermas 1971, ch. 6). In the preferred language of his later work, the 'lifeworld', corresponding to the domain of communication or interaction, is 'colonized' by the 'systems' or 'steering mechanisms', the rationalized state and economy, of modernized Western societies. In this context, the welfare state and Keynesian economics of advanced capitalist societies represent a further expansion of the state into the lifeworld, bureaucratically defining and administering needs and desires previously moulded by authoritarian processes of socialization. Resistance to this colonization is blunted by the prevalence of the one-sided, instrumental rationality of 'work' in both positivist sociology and orthodox Marxism. However, Habermas also holds out the possibility of a more progressive, emancipatory rationalization of the lifeworld. The authoritarian features of the lifeworld of traditional societies (for example, the patriarchal family and dogmatic religion), which are erased by modernity, may be replaced by a 'universalistic discourse ethics' permitting a genuinely discursive will formation beyond the constraints of conventional morality. 'New social movements' of women and 'greens' potentially 'put reformed lifestyles into practice' in the spirit of the 'rationalized lifeworld' of open communication, universal values and post-conventional morality (Habermas, 1981; 1984a).

The outlines of a 'universalistic discourse ethics' are implicit in Habermas's attempt to provide more adequate evaluative foundations for the practice of critique. In the spirit of the return to Hegel, previous members of the Frankfurt School had advocated an 'immanent critique' of society. Society would be transformed by rendering explicit the tensions and contradictions within it, by turning its own values and principles against it, just as Marx had castigated the sham universality of bourgeois justice. Critique in this sense is specific to a particular historical period and relies on prevailing standards of right or justice. Habermas, on the other hand, believes that the whole enterprise of immanent critique is endangered within contemporary cultures, because universalistic bourgeois values have in fact retreated before the prevailing technocratic ideology of value-freedom. Bourgeois consciousness has become 'cynical', and its immanent critique can no longer be expected to lead to social transformation (1976, p. 10–11). Habermas seeks instead to base critical theory on values presumed to be implicit in the pragmatics of language. As McCarthy puts it, Habermas's argument is 'that the goal of critical theory – a form of life free from unnecessary domination in all its forms – is inherent in the notion of truth; it is anticipated in every act of communication' (1978, p. 7).

Habermas's 'linguistic turn', paralleled by much of this century's philosophy, inspires an exploration of the evaluative presuppositions of communication. Every act of communication involves an implicit raising of 'validity claims':

The speaker has to select a *comprehensible* expression in order that the speaker and hearer can *understand one another*: the speaker has to have the intention of communicating a *true* propositional content in order that the hearer can *share the knowledge* of the speaker; the speaker has to want to express his intentions *truthfully* in order that the hearer can *believe* in the speaker's utterance (can trust him); finally, the speaker has to select an utterance that is *right* in the light of existing norms and values in order that the hearer can accept the utterance, so that both speaker and hearer can *agree with one another* in the utterance concerning a recognised normative background. (Habermas, quoted by McCarthy, 1978, p. 288)

The four validity claims reflect the relation of language (comprehensibility) to a realm of intersubjectivity or society (rightness), to external reality or nature (truth) and to the 'internal nature' of the speaker's own feelings, beliefs and intentions (truthfulness or sincerity). According to Habermas, our communicative competence – our ability to engage in communication with other subjects – includes 'mastery of these values, the basis of our ideas of truth, freedom and justice' (1970, p. 17, my translation). A fuller account of these values is given by Habermas's consensus theories of theoretical and practical truth. Challenges to particular utterances are often met with appeals to authority (for example, priests, oracles or sacred texts) or the use of force (e.g. the Inquisition); indeed, in some cultures and in some regions and periods of Western culture these responses are regarded as perfectly legitimate. However, Habermas believes that a more rational response is not only to be preferred but, in some sense, also implicitly anticipated whenever people enter into communication (see McCarthy, 1978). This more rational response consists in the attempt to construct an 'ideal speech situation', a 'discourse' free of relations of domination and undogmatically committed to the consideration of alternative conceptual schemes.

   Habermas's universal pragmatics has been criticized as a new transcendentalism in the spirit of Kant, a return to the doomed Enlightenment project of providing timeless and universal foundations for morality. Some even see Habermas's idealized, anticipatory commitment to consensus as constraining and potentially oppressive (see pp. 65–6). Most critics have been sceptical of the universal status accorded to 'discourse ethics' (see McCarthy, 1978; Thompson and Held, 1982; Benhabib and Dallmayr, 1990). How can we suppose that members of every culture, whatever its norms governing communication, have always implicitly raised precisely those validity claims, discursively redeemable, which Habermas describes? Recognizing the difficulties of his quasi-transcendental enterprise, Habermas has more recently qualified its claims. In the terms of Hegel's distinction, Habermas now explicitly limits its scope to the validation of universalistic norms of 'morality' (*Moralität*) as opposed to the values and forms of life of 'ethical life' (*Sittlichkeit*). He admits that the universalistic rationality of a morality which is still essentially Kantian is unable to adjudicate between life-forms and customs inextricably bound to particular human communities (Habermas, 1983; 1984b; Dews, 1986).

Existentialism

Hegel's systematic philosophy attempts to rescue the underlying truths of religion and morality from an over-hasty Enlightenment critique. Hegel believed, in Peter Rohde's words, 'that it was possible to unite faith and thought and create an all-comprehending synthesis in which all oppositions could be reconciled' (Rohde, 1959, p. 31). In this sense, Hegel stands in the tradition of a humanist theology seeking to reconcile human reason with faith. If faith does not survive in a recognizably religious form, then this is the price that dogmatic religion has to pay for its escape from the sceptical onslaught of the Enlightenment. In Hegel's speculative idealism the truths of religion and morality are recovered in a higher, more rational form, 'transcended' in the higher synthesis of 'Absolute Spirit'. In rejecting the Hegelian solution, Søren Kierkegaard (1813–55) founds a second post-Hegelian strand of continental philosophy, a strand which can be seen to lead to existentialism. Kierkegaard denies that reality can be completely captured by any systematic philosophy. The disinterested, contemplative knowledge of *theoria*, championed by the Enlightenment and then deployed against it with such ingenuity and persistence by Hegel, is unsuited for an understanding of the inner life or 'existence' of the human individual. The one-sided, merely abstract knowledge championed by the Western philosophical tradition fails to illuminate the subjective experience of human beings. The attempt to weave the truths of morality and religion into a theoretical account of the world, however sophisticated and dialectical, can only falsify them. Rather, the proper object of thought is the 'personal existence', the distinctively ethical reality of the individual. In Blackham's words, 'The individual cannot be defined; he can be known only from within' (Blackham, 1961, p. 8).

Kierkegaard's exploration of subjective truth is concerned primarily with religious experience. Renewing the religious tradition which includes St Augustine, Meister Eckhart and Luther and in opposition to a more humanist theology seeking to reconcile faith and reason, Kierkegaard regards faith as something apart from, and beyond, human reason. Religious truth is something which would be diminished rather than reinforced by its reduction to the principles of a merely human reason. In effect, Kierkegaard takes seriously the ironic taunt of David Hume who, after demolishing all rational grounds for a belief in miracles, remarks that anyone who still has faith 'is conscious of a continued miracle in his own person, which subverts all the principles of his understanding, and gives him a determination to believe what is most contrary to custom and experience' (Hume, [1777] 1902, p. 131). In response, Kierkegaard seeks to found religious belief on the subjective truth of personal experience. His claim is that, through faith, a truth can be approached which is far more important for our lives than either the theoretical truths of science or the speculative systems of philosophy.

However, in order to ground religious faith in this way Kierkegaard provides a more general account of the human condition. The primary fact of existence is the need to decide, the need to make a choice about how we shall live. What is more, faced with the impossibility of any rationally certified moral system, we are forced to choose under conditions of uncertainty and, as a result, we are prey to feelings of 'dread' or 'anxiety'. More positively, this anxiety is in fact the inevitable counterpart of human freedom. Anxiety is, in Rohde's words, 'the state of mind which precedes the act of freedom' (1959, p. 102), it points 'towards the possibility of freedom and spiritual realization' (ibid., p. 66). Anxiety reflects the tremendous responsibility borne by the individual aware of her freedom to decide what she will do with her life. If we are indecisive, existence is empty and drifting, comprising only the disconnected and ultimately meaningless pleasures of the hedonistic or 'aesthetic' life. By contrast, 'The thinker gives himself stable ethical reality by forming and renewing himself in critical decisions which are a total inward commitment (decisions, for example, as to vocation, marriage, faith)' (Blackham, 1961, p. 9). These decisions cannot be deduced by purely rational means from self-evident moral premisses; if they could, our freedom would be illusory. They can only be informed by experience, by an understanding of the different spheres of existence or approaches to life which are available to us. Beyond the aesthetic or hedonistic sphere, Kierkegaard identifies two other spheres, the 'ethical' and the religious. The second part of *Either/Or*, Kierkegaard's first major work, provides a somewhat unappealing account of the 'ethical' sphere, the socially responsible life of duty, as represented by marriage (Kierkegaard, 1987). But even this 'election of a definite calling' is ultimately inadequate. Only the religious life is fully satisfactory, though it is by no means an easy choice. God's will may, as in the case of His command to Abraham to kill his son Isaac, violate not only our wishes but also the moral demands of the community (Kierkegaard, 1960). For Kierkegaard we must believe even though religious faith violates our rationality and our morality. True faith is only attained with a commitment which persists despite our intellectual and moral reservations, In the phrase adapted from Tertullian, '*credo quia impossibile*' – 'I believe, because it is impossible.' An influential tradition of existentialist theology, which includes such figures as Martin Buber and Gabriel Marcel, has drawn inspiration from this approach.

Other thinkers have developed a more atheistic but still recognizably existentialist philosophy. Friedrich Nietzsche (1844–1900) was virulently anti-Christian (though he sometimes praises Christ himself as a great individual), describing Pascal's somewhat Kierkegaardian faith as 'a continuous suicide of reason' (Nietzsche, 1973, p. 57). Still, though religion is no longer seen as the solution to existence, Nietzsche recognizes more clearly than the Enlightenment's 'free thinkers' the nihilistic implications of the 'death of God'. However, Nietzsche rejects not only the self-denying, other-worldliness of Christianity but also the historical eschatology of Hegel and Marx. He sees Hegel's dialectical system as itself little more than the pursuit of religion by other means (see Deleuze, 1983, ch. 5). The problem of existence is deferred rather than solved by a philosophy of history that values the present only as a step towards the foreordained future of 'Absolute Spirit' or communism. Nor is what comes later necessarily better; the process of history is not necessarily a tale of progress. Rather, the point of existence must lie in the immediacy of present experience. Nietzsche is drawn to the ideal of the 'supra-historical' man 'who does not envisage salvation in the process but for whom the world is finished in every single moment and its end attained' (quoted by Kaufmann, 1974, p. 147): 'No, the goal of humanity cannot lie in its end but only in its highest exemplars' (Nietzsche, 1983, p. 111). Value lies in cultural, intellectual or personal achievements whenever they occur, and these achievements are more likely to be realized through the lives of exceptional individuals like Goethe or Spinoza than by the collective political agents of the world-historical process.

The supra-historical powers 'lead the eye away from becoming towards that which bestows upon existence the character of the eternal and stable, towards art and religion' (Nietzsche, 1983, p. 120). The doctrine of the 'eternal return' can also be interpreted as an affirmation of existence in this sense. The joy of the 'overman' is expressed in *'amor fati'*, the 'love of fate' which craves the eternal recurrence of the present moment. This existentialist emphasis on individual life and the present moment implies a relatively distanced relationship with politics. As Kaufmann puts it, Nietzsche develops 'the theme of the antipolitical individual who seeks self-perfection far from the modern world' (Kaufmann, 1974, p. 418). Certainly, only a distorted reading of Nietzsche could blame him for the rise of fascism. He is contemptuous of both German nationalism and anti-Semitism. His 'master race' is conceived as 'a future, internationally mixed race of philosophers and artists who cultivate iron self-control' (Kaufmann, 1974, p. 303), hardly the self-indulgent gangsters of national socialism. On the other hand, to derive a more constructive politics from Nietzsche's avowedly elitist, even anti-social ethic is no easy task (see Ansell-Pearson, 1991).

Heidegger's earlier philosophy has also been recognized as an important contribution to existentialism. In *Being and Time* Heidegger attempts to 'break away from the traditional domination of Western thought by the category of substance (thinghood)' (Macquarrie, 1968, p. 5; Heidegger, 1967). The 'category of substance' is associated with the temper of natural science and technology. In other words, his diagnosis has analogies both with the Frankfurt School's critique of instrumental reason and with Kierkegaard's espousal of subjective truth against contemplative theory. Heidegger's original approach sets him on the quest for an alternative understanding of 'Being'. Crucial to this approach is his belief that the 'question of Being', the question of what it means to be, can best be explored through the existence of the questioner – that being for whom Being is a question. In contrast to other beings, man 'not only *is*, but has some understanding of and some responsibility for who he is' (Macquarrie, 1968, p. 8). Heidegger's first soundings of Being take the form of sensitive descriptions of 'Being-in-the-world' and 'Being-with-others'. A fundamental theme of his account is the temporality of existence. Human projects are aimed at the future, but we are also limited by the 'facticity' of the situation we inherit from the past. Authentic existence is an arduous state possible only through an intense awareness of the ever-present possibility of death.

It is with Jean-Paul Sartre (1905–80), whose *Being and Nothingness* (Sartre, 1958) was deeply influenced by the early Heidegger, that existentialism makes its most explicit contribution to political thought. Sartre differs from both Kierkegaard and Nietzsche in the privileged status he accords to political experience and action, as opposed to either the religious or aesthetic domains. In his famous essay on *Existentialism and Humanism* Sartre defends existentialism from the reproach of a morbid and individualistic celebration of despair and anxiety which must inevitably lead to either political quietism or nihilism. Rather, the fundamental existentialist principle, that for human beings 'existence comes before essence', implies the individual's absolute responsibility for her own life. To be constrained by custom, ideas of human nature or divine will, or any other notion of human essence, is to live inauthentically or in 'bad faith'. Our existence defines our essence in the sense that we are free to create our own lives and values, we are 'condemned to liberty' (Sartre, 1972, pp. 28–9). What is more, our choices inevitably have political implications as well, because an individual's decision is at the same time tantamount to a proposal for humanity in general. What remains unclear is why the seemingly arbitrary choices of the individual, unconstrained by convention or pre-existing moral norms, should carry such universal moral weight, how humanity's creation of values can avoid 'bad faith' without being completely arbitrary. Sartre's existentialist reformulation of the categorical imperative faces similar problems to Kant's.

Sartre's early political involvement came during the Second World War with the French resistance to the German occupation. After the war he embarked on a long and tortuous relationship with Marxism and the French Communist Party. He was prominent as an 'engaged' intellectual in opposition both to American 'imperialism and genocide' in Vietnam and France's rearguard colonialism in Algeria (Sartre, 1974; and see Elliott, 1987). In his novels and plays Sartre explored various aspects of political practice and experience, for example, the dilemmas facing the political terrorist in *Les Mains sales* (Sartre, 1961) and the formation of a fascist sympathizer in his short story, 'L'Enfance d'un chef' (Sartre, 1969). In his later work Sartre proposes an ambitious synthesis of the insights of existentialism and Marxism, but now at the level of social action rather than individual engagement (Sartre, 1976). His suggestive but problematic 'critique of dialectical reason' seeks to theorize human society and history according to the principle that 'men make history'. He explores the various mediations between the individual and the social totality such as families and nations as well as classes. He holds out the optimistic promise that, in Poster's words, 'human beings can attain freedom through the recognition of freedom in the other and in the consequent action of solidary groups pursuing this freedom' (Poster, 1979, p. 43). Particularly interesting is his analysis of different kinds of collective: the alienated, 'serial' interaction between individuals relating to one another as things, as for example in a bus queue; the 'indirect gathering' of the passive and isolated listeners to the radio broadcast; and the 'impotent bond' of individuals buying and selling in a free market (Sartre, 1976, pp. 256–342). This analysis helps to pose the problem of genuinely collective action in an acute way, namely how to explain the occasional and often unexpected eruption of solidary action in what Sartre calls the 'fused group', the sudden 'upsurge of mutual recognition in the context of daily life' which constitutes freedom (Poster, 1979, p. 86).

Albert Camus (1913–60) provides an alternative account of the politics of existentialism (see Cruickshank, 1960; O'Brien, 1970). In a dramatic allusion to Descartes, Camus seeks to derive collective solidarity from individual action in a way analogous to Sartre's existential modulation of the categorical imperative. The individual's only defensible response to the absurdity of existence is revolt. But for Camus, 'Je me révolte, donc nous sommes' – 'I revolt, therefore we are' (Camus, 1954, p. 36). His ethic of revolt, an uncompromising honesty in the face of the absurdities and cruelties of existence, encounters its most obvious enemies in the stifling atmosphere of conventional bourgeois morality and, more dramatically, in totalitarianism, terror and the concentration camp. Attacked by Sartre for keeping clean hands at the expense of engagement on the side of the exploited, his reputation also suffered from his support for his former compatriots, the French colonists, in the Algerian war of independence.

In another significant contribution to the politics of existentialism, Simone de Beauvoir applied the categories of Sartre's existentialism to woman as the 'perpetual Other', the 'second sex' (de Beauvoir, 1972). However, de Beauvoir's feminism is unduly influenced by Sartre's derogatory view of femininity and the female body. In *Being and Nothingness* Sartre explicitly associates woman with the 'sliminess' of the 'in-itself', the self reduced to the status of a thing, with its tendency to engulf the transcendent subjectivity of the 'for-itself', the freedom of untrammelled subjectivity: 'Slime is the revenge of the in-itself. A sickly-sweet, feminine revenge . . . a soft yielding action, a moist and feminine sucking . . .' (quoted by Gatens, 1991, p. 56). As Gatens comments, 'Femininity is here associated with that which threatens to engulf transcendence and degrade it to the level of mere "sticky existence".' What is worse, de Beauvoir 'shares this view of femininity as "the Other" that threatens the free consciousness with its cloying and "appealing" nature'. As a result, the historically recent opportunity of women to participate more fully in social and intellectual life is thought to require the sacrifice of her 'Otherness': 'women's participation in [the] fraternity is predicated on her repudiation of the female body and femininity. A symmetrical repudiation of the male body and masculinity is not in evidence in the case of men's participation' (ibid., pp. 56–7).

Overall the contribution of existentialism to social and political thought has been ambivalent. Camus has been more influential as a novelist and philosopher of the absurd than for his more overtly political writings. Sartre moved away from existentialism as he developed a more articulated political theory in the *Critique of Dialectical Reason*. Theorists associated with the Frankfurt School have criticized existentialism for the abstractness of its concept of human freedom (Marcuse, 1972). For the Sartre of *Being and Nothingness* authenticity – the free subjectivity of the 'for-itself' (*pour-soi*) – does not depend on social and political conditions. To allow oneself to be determined by either social conditioning or genetic inheritance is an instance of bad faith. Freedom is founded on a basic 'lack', a tendency to frustration, which is ontologically rather than socially or politically grounded. As a result, Marcuse sees existentialism as an apolitical and ultimately futile attempt to resolve the problems of 'concrete existence' with the abstract and transcendental resources of philosophy rather than a 'theory of society' (Marcuse, 1973, p. 174). Like the Stoic's withdrawal into a subjective stance beyond the reach of social and political realities, the ontological-existential definition of freedom may have conservative or, at best, apolitical implications.

The anti-humanist critique of the subject

An alternative reaction to the Hegelian synthesis leads to what might be called the 'anti-humanist critique of the subject'. Both the origins and some of the themes of this critique are similar to those of existentialism. There are echoes of Kierkegaard's rejection of the systematic philosophy of Hegel. Nietzsche is again a significant source and so is Heidegger. However, through a series of intellectual transitions and external influences a very different strand of post-Hegelian thought can be traced. The major impact of these changes serves to undermine the privileged philosophical and political status accorded to the subject. The Cartesian ego or consciousness is no longer conceived as the privileged subject of knowledge. The political agent – whether in the guise of the responsible 'bourgeois' individual of liberalism and republicanism or the collective, self-conscious proletariat of Marxism – can no longer be regarded unproblematically as the subject of political practice. Even the subjective truth and authentic engagement of the existentialist individual is compromised. In these theoretical developments both the later thought of Heidegger and the linguistics of Saussure have played a central role.

The anti-humanism of Heidegger and Saussure reflects tendencies already apparent in the human and social sciences. A series of developments had already effected a significant 'decentring' of the subject of experience and action. The Marxist theory of ideology implies that our consciousness is determined primarily by class location and conflicts within the prevailing mode of production. Our beliefs and attitudes, even our most deeply held moral values, may reflect our social origins more than reality or what is right (Marx, 1977). On another front, Freudian psychoanalysis probes the unconscious causes of our mental states. The reasons we give for our actions may be no more than rationalizations. The real causes may be neurotic remnants of childhood trauma or unresolved emotional conflict. Neurotic symptoms and obsessions, jokes and apparently accidental slips of the tongue, the forgetting of names or appointments, our dreams and fantasies, are all interpreted as expressions of the unconscious mind (Freud, 1938; 1976). Again, 'hermeneutic' disciplines, concerned with the interpretation and criticism of texts, place greater emphasis on the social and linguistic context than on the 'literal meaning' of words or the author's conscious intentions. Interpretation need not be restricted by the 'surface' meaning of the text. Nevertheless, all of these theoretical approaches retain a qualified role for the subject (Bubner, 1981). By virtue of its class location the proletariat is destined to achieve true consciousness and bring about the revolutionary overthrow of capitalism. Through psychoanalysis the self can come to understand the unconscious springs of its conscious states and remove the barriers to a free 'internal communication' (Habermas, 1972, ch. 10). The practice of hermeneutics promises a never-ending but always improving understanding of the text.

A more radical decentring of the subject occurs with Heidegger's famous 'turn' or 'Kehre' and the associated attack on Sartre's humanism. In Heidegger's later writings his earlier, apparently existentialist account of individual existence – as 'anxious' or 'caring', 'authentic' or 'fallen' – gives way to a more impersonal preoccupation with Being. Heidegger wishes to divert our 'thinking' from its individualistic concerns towards a greater 'attentiveness to Being'. Only by transcending the limited perspective of the Cartesian subject, 'who may deign to release the beingness of beings into an all too loudly bruited "objectivity"', can 'thinking' 'realize the proper dignity of man' as 'the shepherd of Being'. Accompanying this change of emphasis, there is in Heidegger's later writings an overriding concern with language as 'the house of Being' (Heidegger, [1947] 1977, pp. 210, 193). Language discloses Being or 'brings it into the open':

language alone brings beings as beings into the open for the first time. Where there is not language, as in the Being of stone, plant, and animal, there is also no openness of beings, and consequently no openness either of nonbeing and of the empty. (Heidegger, [1936] 1977, p. 185)

Crucially, language is something which transcends individual consciousness or existence. The shift of emphasis from existence to language therefore serves to undermine the privileged position accorded to the subject by humanism. It casts doubt both on the freely choosing, authentic subject of existentialism and the collective political subjects of Marxism and critical theory. In the 'Letter on Humanism' of 1947, Heidegger explicitly responds to Sartre's claim that existentialism is also a humanism (see pp. 54–5). Heidegger is particularly hostile to Sartre's Cartesian claim that 'one must take subjectivity as his point of departure' (Sartre, 1977, p. 17.). Heidegger's anti-humanism leads instead to 'thinking' as the 'letting-be' of transcendent Being. Although for Heidegger this attitude 'can be theistic as little as atheistic' ([1947] 1977, p. 230), it undoubtedly represents a rejection of the anthropocentrism of the Enlightenment for the sake of more mystical qualities.

Heidegger's confidence in the distance between anti-humanism and the 'affirmation of inhumanity' seems puzzling and even disingenuous, in view of his own associations with national socialism and his subsequent tardiness in disowning them (see Lacoue-Labarthe, 1990; Lyotard, 1990). The almost mystical injunction to be attentive to Being, like the call to obey the will of God, seems compatible with almost any conceivable political stance. What is worse, the evident difficulty of 'thinking' in its full Heideggerian sense surely encourages authoritarian claims, since only the initiate or the more adept is able to achieve the appropriate relationship to Being. It may well be that when Heidegger speaks of 'the internal truth and the greatness of the movement', he is not speaking of the Nazi Party. As Lyotard points out:

'those people [who] were far too limited in their thinking' (Heidegger, VII, 280) could only mask and mislead the authentic anxiety that Heidegger thinks he recognises in the desperate search (the 1930s) which, at that time, projects the Volk towards a decision, a resolution that may be in accord with what is 'peculiar' to it. The movement that derives from the unbearable anxiety of being thrown before nothingness, Heidegger believes, needs 'knowledge' in order to guide and resolve itself to a decision . . . (Lyotard, 1990, p. 64)

Nevertheless, a knowledge so shrouded in obscurity is surely at least more amenable to the claims of the charismatic despot. On the other hand, humanist philosophies have their own share of historical guilt, as Althusser's discussion of Stalinism as a form of humanism implies (Althusser, 1976). Heidegger's claim, that humanism is not the only philosophy capable of inspiring humane relations between people, must at least be taken seriously.

Language is at the heart of another source of the anti-humanist strand, namely the structural linguistics of Saussure. Saussure focused on the distinction between 'langue', or language as a system of forms or signs, and 'parole' in the sense of 'actual speech, the speech acts which are made possible by the language' (Culler, 1976, p. 29; Saussure, [1916] 1959). Saussure's emphasis on 'langue' undermines the notion that words are related to meanings, either through conscious acts of intending on the part of the subject or through some kind of mental association. Rather, particular utterances depend on the pre-existing system of signs. When language is considered in this way, it becomes obvious that the association between a particular 'signifier' (a word considered as sound or inscription) and its 'signified' (or meaning) is arbitrary. Different languages employ different signifiers for the same signified. They embody different conceptual distinctions, with the result that translation between languages is rarely straightforward and is sometimes impossible. Words change their meaning as languages evolve. Rather, meanings depend on the differential relations which exist between the system of forms or signs which make up a *langue* at a particular time: 'Since the sign has no necessary core which must persist, it must be defined as a relational entity, in its relations to other signs' (Culler, 1976, p. 36). The only essential feature of a language or code is that it is possible to distinguish between its elements. The implication of Saussure's analysis is that the speaking subject – and by extension also the subject of knowledge and consciousness – is removed from its central position in the constitution of meaning.

Heidegger and Saussure's radical 'decentring' of the subject is paralleled in an array of approaches in the social and human sciences, themselves often inspired by structural linguistics. According to these 'structuralist' approaches, social structures more generally should not be considered as the intentional products of human subjects, but as complex systems existing prior to these subjects and unfolding according to their own specific rules, whether as modes of production, kinship systems, or elements of the unconscious (see Piaget, 1971; Pettit, 1975). Perhaps most famously, the structural anthropology of Lévi-Strauss has inspired a generation of social scientists. Typical of the structuralist approach more generally, his analyses of society and culture as systems of differentially related elements depend neither on the attribution of particular intentions to social agents nor on some overarching philosophy of history. Acknowledging his debt to Saussure and Jakobson, Lévi-Strauss claims that 'anthropology draws its originality from the unconscious nature of collective phenomena' (Lévi-Strauss, 1968, p. 18; and see 1969). Like the rules of a language, customs and rituals are usually followed without being explicitly understood or chosen. Althusser's structuralist Marxism is another well-known and explicitly anti-humanist product of this current of thought (see Anderson, 1983, ch. 2).

Michel Foucault (1926–84) is responsible for one of the most influential contributions to anti-humanist thought. Although never straightforwardly a structuralist himself – influenced more directly by Nietzsche, Heidegger, Canguilhem and Dumézil – Foucault's work also implies a radical critique of the subject. In a series of historical studies Foucault charts the ascendancy of a form of reason he sees as original to Western culture. In *Madness and Civilization*, for example, Foucault describes the emergence of a new understanding and treatment of madness as the 'other' of reason. He explores the interrelationships between values, new ways of dealing with the insane (e.g. confinement in the asylum, medical treatment, mechanical procedures of purification, immersion or restriction of movement) and novel forms of knowledge or 'discourse'. The culmination of these developments is psychiatry, conceived as 'a certain moral tactic contemporary with the end of the eighteenth century, preserved in the rites of asylum life, and overlaid by the myths of positivism' (Foucault, 1971, p. 276). Foucault has described a series of parallel transformations characteristic of modernity. Medicine develops alongside the birth of the clinic (Foucault, 1973). Criminology emerges as the scientific face of the prison (Foucault, 1977a). In each case, the 'human sciences' are implicated in the unprecedented expansion of the 'disciplinary' powers deployed by both state and non-state institutions. Disciplinary power 'produces subjected and practised bodies, "docile" bodies' (1977, p, 138). An 'architectural figure' of disciplinary power is Bentham's 'panopticon', a building designed to ensure the permanent visibility of the prisoners to the warder without allowing them to see one another. The panopticon is a way of 'arranging spatial unities' in order 'to induce in the inmate a state of conscious and permanent visibility that assures the automatic functioning of power' (1977, p. 200–1). Discipline may take the form of an 'exceptional discipline' with the negative functions of 'arresting evil, breaking communications, suspending time' (1977, p. 209). However, after the 'Classical Age' of the eighteenth century, disciplinary power assumes more and more the form of a 'generalized surveillance', which strives for more positive effects throughout society in order to increase the productivity of populations.

Foucault's account of the emergence of modern reason, with the associated institutions and practices of disciplinary power, has analogies both with Weber's account of the irreversible rationalization of society and the Frankfurt School's fateful dialectic of Enlightenment. Foucault's originality lies in his anti-humanism. He proposes to chart the discontinuities and ruptures of 'discursive formations', while dispensing with the humanist conceptions infecting the human sciences. The subject, which is taken as given by humanist or 'bourgeois' social theory, must itself be explained. He aims at 'an analysis which can account for the constitution of the subject within the historical texture . . . a form of knowledge which accounts for the constitution of knowledge [savoirs], discourses, domains of objects, etc., without having to refer to the subject, (1979, p. 35). This approach is essential, because, as his more detailed accounts of the characteristic institutions of modernity imply, the subject and its projects are a tainted, 'subjected' product of the strategies of an increasingly productive power. However, Foucault also seeks to dispense with the 'macro' subjects of Hegelian or Marxist philosophies of history. Even in his early methodological writings Foucault emphasizes the discontinuities and ruptures of historical transformation, rather than traditions, influence, development or evolution. He refers approvingly to the model of Nietzsche's 'genealogy' of morality (Foucault, 1976, Introduction). The genealogist traces institutions and discourses to 'naked struggles of power'. It is Nietzschean 'will to power', rather than any ultimate purpose or goal, which underlies the confusion of historical change. Genealogical history should 'record the singularity of events outside of any monotonous finality', the genealogist must 'maintain passing events in their proper dispersion' (Foucault, 1984, pp. 76, 81).

Any theoretical approach like Marxism, which seeks to subsume the diversity of historical events under a single explanatory framework, is an example of what Foucault calls a 'totalizing theory' (Foucault, 1977b). Totalizing theories are typically an excuse for domination. To theorize the manifold variety of life as an organized totality is a strategy of power which, even in the hands of critical intellectuals or socialist militants, inevitably contributes to the reproduction of power. As the experience of bureaucratic state socialism demonstrates, experts exploit totalizing theories both to legitimate their authority and as an instrument for its exercise. Foucault and his collaborator Gilles Deleuze propose instead a less authoritarian role for theory. Social and political theory should be a 'local and regional practice'. Rather than a single 'master' theory, there should be a plurality of theories. The role of the intellectual should also be different:

The intellectual's role is no longer to place himself 'somewhat ahead and to the side' in order to express the stifled truth of the collectivity; rather it is to struggle against the forms of power that transform him into its object and instrument in the sphere of 'knowledge', 'truth', 'consciousness', and 'discourse'. (Foucault, 1977b, p. 208)

Intellectuals should not put themselves forward as representatives of the people or vanguard of the proletariat. They should avoid 'the indignity of speaking for others' (Deleuze, in Foucault, 1977b, p. 209).

Perhaps closer in spirit to the later Heidegger is the work of Jacques Derrida (1930–) and, in particular, his advocacy of a critical 'deconstruction' of the forms of discourse characteristic of Western rationality (see Norris, 1987). His major impact on the philosophical scene dates from 1967, with the publication of three major works: *Speech and Phenomena* (1973), *Of Grammatology* (1976) and *Writing and Difference* (1978). Derrida's notion of deconstruction can be understood in terms of his critical encounter with Husserlian phenomenology. Husserl's (1859–1938) project was also directed against the reductive reason of the Enlightenment. Husserl hopes, in Peter Dews's words, that:

the unprejudiced description of the essential structures of experience will constitute a new, rigorously scientific philosophy which will place the empirical sciences themselves on an apodictic basis while at the same time . . . preventing the 'objectivist' impetus of the sciences from leading to a culturally disastrous obliteration of awareness of the constituting role of subjectivity. (Dews, 1987, p. 6)

The 'phenomenological' method aims to describe the contents of consciousness in abstraction from the question of the empirical existence of their object. Through this 'epoché', or 'bracketing', of the vulnerable claim that experience reflects reality, Husserl supposes that in all experience 'it is possible to distinguish *what* is presented from *the fact that* it is presented, the essential from the empirical' (Dews, 1987, p. 5). Derrida approves of Husserl's transcendental riposte to the pretensions of positivistic science, but recognizes the difficulties facing the project in its original form (see also Pivcevic, 1970, ch. 14). In a series of arguments, many with parallels in Wittgenstein's more analytical philosophy of language, Derrida transforms phenomenology with the help of the conceptual insights of structuralism. In following the structuralist path from meaning to sign, from the subject of *parole* to the anonymous system of *langue*, Derrida also carries anti-humanism to the heart of metaphysics.

A prime target is what Derrida calls the 'metaphysics of presence'. Husserl's phenomenology is an example of a metaphysics of presence, in the sense that meanings or the contents of consciousness are understood as essentially independent of their embodiment in language. Language is regarded simply as a medium for the expression or communication of meanings. The 'acts of meaning-intention', and the pure meanings intended or introspected, are what is essential; the sign (*qua* signifier) is simply the incidental vehicle of thought. According to Derrida, however, this approach ignores the quasi-transcendental role of the signifier. This lapse occurs because, in tune with the 'phonocentrism' of the Western philosophical tradition, Husserl privileges the immediacy and presence of speech over writing. With speech the 'fleeting transparency of the voice promotes the assimilation of the word to the expressed meaning' (Habermas, 1987, p. 176 – I am indebted to Habermas for much of the following account). Against Husserl's 'Platonizing' of meaning, Derrida 'wants to bring out the indissoluble interweave of the intelligible with the sign-substrate of its expression', the 'transcendental primacy of the sign as against the meaning' (Habermas, 1987, p. 171). In contrast to the immediacy of speech, 'the written form detaches any given text from the context in which it arose' (Habermas, 1987, p. 165). Writing makes it obvious that meaning need not – and indeed, cannot – be guaranteed by the 'living presence' of the subject, but rather is generated by the system of oppositions between signs, the *langue* which Saussure had identified as the basis of meaning. However, once these characteristics of writing are identified, they can be recognized in other forms of thought and discourse. Every use of language involves representation and is, therefore, an instance of 'writing' in Derrida's general sense.

Derrida's account of representation has further, more radical implications. According to Derrida, all acts of representation involve a recognition of sameness and difference which necessarily refers to a temporal context. Derrida describes this aspect of representation in terms of an irreducible interdependence of 'difference' and 'deferral':

The experience that is present 'at the moment' is indebted to an act of representation, perception is indebted to a reproducing recognition, such that the difference of a temporal interval and thus also an element of otherness is inherent in the spontaneity of the living moment . . . at the very source of this apparently absolute presence, a temporal difference and otherness looms on the horizon, which Derrida characterizes both as a *passive difference* and as a *deferral that produces difference*. (Habermas, 1987, pp. 174–5)

Derrida refers neologistically to this 'difference' and 'deferral' at the heart of all representation as 'différance' (where, appropriately enough, although 'différance' and 'différence' are written differently, they are pronounced the same). Because of these fundamental features of representation, 'writing' cannot be tied to a single, univocal meaning; it cannot, in particular, be referred to the originary meaning intended by either author or speaker. The interpreter cannot even hope for the endlessly improving approximations of hermeneutic interpretation. Rather, the interpretation of texts depends on a potentially infinite array of possible contexts and interpreters, and so leads to what Derrida calls 'dissemination', the endless dispersion and multiplication of meanings. Dissemination 'marks an irreducible and *generative* multiplicity' (Derrida, 1981, p. 45). It undermines all fixities of interpretation, proliferates rather than reduces instances of ambiguity. As McCarthy puts it: 'our meaning always escapes any unitary conscious grasp we may have of it, for language, as "writing", inevitably harbors the possibility of an endless "dissemination" of sense, an indefinite multiplicity of recontextualizations and reinterpretations' (McCarthy, 1989–90, p. 148).

Derrida's account of the the 'différance' implicit in all thought informs the critical practice he terms 'deconstruction'. Deconstruction is turned against the metaphysics of presence – it is 'a means of carrying out this going beyond being, beyond being as presence, at least' (Derrida, in Mortley, 1991, p. 97). In deconstruction 'différance' is put to explicitly anti-Hegelian purposes: 'If there were a definition of différance, it would be precisely the limit, the interruption, the destruction of the Hegelian *relève* wherever it operates' (Derrida, 1981, pp. 40–1; *relève* is Derrida's translation of Hegel's notion of transcendence or '*Aufhebung*'). The Hegelian dialectic tries to absorb and neutralize contradictions in a higher synthesis which, according to Derrida, is always unstable. By contrast, Derrida refuses to deny the tensions inherent in the basic conceptual oppositions of Western metaphysical and political thought. These oppositions are always 'violent hierarchies', in the sense that one term is invariably conceived as superior to or dominant over the other. Typical are the oppositions of mind and body, masculine and feminine, reason and emotion, sameness and difference. These fundamental dichotomies are, therefore, the object of a dual strategy, complementary tactics of what McCarthy terms 'internal' and 'external' critique:

the first does not 'change terrain' but turns 'what is implicit in the founding concepts and the original problematic' against those very concepts and problematic; the second involves a 'discontinuous' change of terrain, 'placing oneself outside' of, and 'affirming an absolute break' with, those concepts and problematic. (McCarthy, 1989–90, p. 149, quoting Derrida)

Derrida acknowledges that an absolute break with the dichotomies of Western metaphysics is impossible. Nor can there be any stable Hegelian synthesis. Rather deconstruction demands an 'interminable analysis', if it is 'to avoid both simply *neutralizing* the binary oppositions of metaphysics and simply *residing* within the closed field of those oppositions, thereby confirming it' (Derrida, 1981, p. 41–2).

The deconstruction of the 'violent hierarchies' of Western metaphysics is also claimed to have fundamental implications for Western political thought:

deconstruction counteracts the 'politics of language' which conceals practices of exclusion, repression, marginalization, and assimilation behind the apparent neutrality of 'purely theoretical' discourses. Its effects, however, are not confined to language, but 'touch all the social institutions . . . More generally, it touches everything, quite simply everything.' (McCarthy, 1989–90, p. 153, quoting Derrida)

Deconstruction bears witness 'to the other of Western rationalism', counteracts the associated 'repression of the other in nature, in ourselves, in other persons and other peoples . . . [it] speaks on behalf of what does not fit into our schemes and patiently advocates letting the other be in its otherness' (McCarthy, 1989–90, pp. 153–4). Derridean manoeuvres have influenced a wide range of other theorists, particularly those associated with postmodernism and French feminism (see pp. 64 ff.). Michael Ryan has recruited the resources of Derridean deconstruction for an anti-authoritarian socialism to be 'worked out, as a texture and not as a punctual instance of power', and for which unity does not imply an organised and authoritarian movement but 'the articulation of a diverse, differentiated plurality' (Ryan, 1982, pp. 219 and 215). Derrida himself sees the refusal of the 'longing for an impossible truth' as politically radical

(Dews, 1987, p. 34). He has written with admiration of the role of Nelson Mandela in the resistance to apartheid (Derrida, 1987). He has also made plain both his opposition to neo-colonialism and his support for feminism. However, Derrida does little to develop a constructive political stance. Indeed, he is constrained in that task by his own stringently critical attitude to all systematic theorizing. Where he has made overtly political comments, they are often undercut by irony or the claim that 'all of our political codes and terminologies still remain fundamentally metaphysical' (Derrida, quoted by McCarthy, 1989–90, p. 157). On McCarthy's analysis Derrida resists the perspective of the participant in social life, who is forced to adopt a position and assume certain values (ibid. p. 156). But, as McCarthy points out, to confine one-self to the sceptical role of the observer as critic would, in the end, be tantamount to acceptance of the status quo (see also Boyne, 1990).

Postmodernism and the flight from Western history

In its most radical form the anti-humanist critique of the subject undermines the fundamental categories of Western political thought and practice. And it is not just the prevailing forms of power and rationality, the capitalist rationalization of production or the bureaucratic rationalization of the state, which are deconstructed. Major sources of opposition to these social and political formations are also called into question. Both Marxism and existentialism are undermined as varieties of humanism. The Enlightenment tradition as well as some of its most virulent critics are implicated in the shameful events of recent European history, from imperialist genocide to the gulag and the holocaust. Only an even more radical critique seems to offer release from a modernist project, which can no longer hide its guilty secrets. This 'postmodernist' response to the débâcle of Western civilization holds, in effect, that every possible move in the Enlightenment game has been played. Postmodernism proposes a last desperate leap from the fateful complex of Western history. Anti-humanism, with its critique of the subject and genealogical history, has shaken the pillars of Western political thought. Heidegger's 'dismantling' of metaphysics and Derrida's deconstruction carry the corrosion of critique to the fundamental conceptual foundations of modernity.

Jean-François Lyotard is perhaps the clearest exponent of the postmodernist case. During his career Lyotard has held a variety of political positions, from neo-Marxism and 'spontaneist' anarchism to a scepticism, which, for some, is tantamount to conservatism. His more recent concern with justice is articulated in a short but influential description of the *Postmodern Condition*. Characteristic of modernity, according to Lyotard, is its reliance on 'metanarratives' for the legitimation of both science and the state. This reliance is intrinsic to 'the choice called the Occident' (Lyotard, 1984, p. 8). Metanarratives can take a variety of forms, 'such as the dialectics of Spirit, the hermeneutics of meaning, the emancipation of the rational or working subject, or the creation of wealth' (ibid., p. xxiii). However, Lyotard isolates two basic types, representative of both of the main strands of post-Enlightenment thought: the 'narrative of emancipation', implicit both in modern science and in the politics of the French revolution; and the 'speculative narrative' of Hegelianism (ibid., p. 37).

According to Lyotard, our faith in these metanarratives has been shaken by far-reaching developments in both society and culture. He adopts the notion of 'postindustrial' society to refer to a society dominated by a mode of production in which knowledge and information technology play the central role. The cultural and intellectual counterpart of this social form is a postmodern culture, characterized by 'incredulity toward meta-narratives' (ibid., p. xxiv). Ironically, the nihilistic delegitimation of modern reason in postmodern culture is a result of modernity's own novel demand for legitimation.

The political conclusions Lyotard draws from this discussion are largely sceptical and anti-authoritarian. Society can no longer be artificially homogenized or unified according to some grand theory. We should recognize society as a 'heterogeneity of language games' or 'institutions in patches'. Far from resembling some application of Newtonian mechanics, society consists of 'clouds of sociality' more amenable to a 'pragmatics of language particles' (ibid., pp. xxiv–xxv). Even the consensus theory of Habermas is an attempt to reduce heterogeneity to an oppressive unity, because it ignores the diversity of language games. 'Consensus has become an outmoded and suspect value' (ibid., p. 66). Only the diversity and heterogeneity of social and cultural forms offers some resistance to the 'spirit of performativity', the attempt to reduce society to an efficient system guaranteeing 'the best possible input/output equation' (ibid., pp. 45–6). Only temporary and local consensus is desirable, only provisional contracts should be sought. The price to be paid for any residue of nostalgia for totalizing theory is 'terror', 'the efficiency gained by eliminating, or threatening to eliminate, a player from the language game one shares with him' (ibid., p. 64). Artistic modernism is an ally in this 'war on totality', but only if it is understood as a constantly renewed challenge to the rules of image and narration, even the rules instituted by earlier modernisms: 'Postmodernism thus understood is not modernism at its end but in the nascent state, and this state is constant' (ibid., p. 79).

The postmodern diagnosis has a clear critical edge. It can be seen as one more response to the catastrophes of twentieth-century history. For postmodernists, totalitarianism demonstrates the dangers of totalizing political theory, any attempt to bring the whole of society into harmony with some wish of the '*Volk*' or the goal of socialist utopia. Postmodernists seek to disrupt all forms of discourse, and particularly forms of political discourse, which might encourage the totalitarian suppression of diversity. They seek to entrench a multiplicity of 'subject positions' (Laclau and Mouffe, 1985). They are suspicious of the claims of all leaders, particularly leaders who claim to be experts or intellectuals. They are even suspicious of intellectuals who claim to be authorities on the democratic process or the conditions of democratic will formation. They are opposed to the rationalistic reduction of the 'other' to sameness, any suppression of the other as a threat to the coherence of our identity. More difficult to discern is the constructive political thought and practice implied by postmodernism. Certainly, Lyotard claims that 'justice as a value is neither outmoded nor suspect' (Lyotard, 1984, p. 66). However, his first positive steps towards an idea of justice – his commitment to difference and diversity as well as to the local and the provisional – do not take us very far. Other writers have done more to develop a distinctively postmodernist politics. Iris Marion Young presents an acute challenge to the ideal of community

in socialist and feminist thought. The desire for 'mutual identification in social relations' is a desire she associates with sectarianism, chauvinism and even racism. The
desire for unity and wholeness 'generates borders, dichotomies, and exclusions'
(Young, 1990a, p. 301; see also Young, 1990b). The celebration of otherness and
difference has also influenced the feminisms of Julia Kristeva, Jane Flax and Alice
Jardine, as well as the anti-racism of Edward Said, Gayatri Spivak and Homi Bhabha
(see Connor, 1989, ch. 9). Baudrillard's 'political economy of the sign' reproduces
themes from the situationist analysis of the 'society of the spectacle', though, once
again, it is difficult to extract a constructive politics from his writings (see Baudrillard, 1988).

Also questionable is the extent to which the insights of postmodernism are really
incompatible with universal categories like oppression or exploitation, or universal
ideals of liberation, equality or community. More specifically, Lyotard's case against
critical theory and, in particular, Habermas's contribution do not seem decisive.
The claim that only local and provisional consensus should be sought is hardly incompatible with Habermas's account. For Habermas, genuine consensus is a state which
can only be *anticipated*, and which could only be achieved in an ideal discourse free
from the distortions of power through the 'unforced force' of the better argument.
Even if it were possible, Habermas acknowledges that we could never know that
such an idealized discourse had been achieved. Actual agreements are always provisional and subject to revision. Indeed, if Habermas is correct, the unrealizable anticipation of genuine consensus is the basis for any concept of truth, and therefore is
necessary for any challenge to a distorted or imposed consensus (Bernstein, 1985;
Habermas, 1987; and see above, pp. 49–51).

In the end, the implications of postmodernism appear largely negative. The commitment to a heterogeneity of cultures and lifestyles surely implies a framework of values
to protect them. Postmodernists seem, in any case, to have a detectable moral or evaluative framework, an implicit theory of justice. But how can postmodernists provide
an account of justice without violating their own austere, critical principles? In the
absence of sustainable discursive warrants for political practice, we are left with few
options. We might be politically engaged on behalf of those we like, our friends, but
then we forget the postmodernist commitment to the 'other', to what is not friendly
or familiar or like us in some way. On the other hand, if we simply relapse into political scepticism or apathy, this choice is surely tantamount to conservatism. To see no
good reason for active political engagement is inevitably to accept the status quo. After
all, Michael Oakeshott also directed his critique of 'rationalism in politics' against both
of the main parties of modernity. He attacks not only the liberal advocates of universal
human rights and liberties, but also all the left Hegelian protagonists of the 'upstart'
classes (Oakeshott, 1962). Even Oakeshott's advice to listen to the 'intimations of the
tradition' is not so very different from Heidegger's 'attentiveness to Being'.

At the risk of insisting too strongly on a certain narrative coherence and finality
(not a happy ending, perhaps, but at least an ending), the dispute between critical
Marxism and postmodernism can be seen as perhaps the central argument of the contemporary debate within the continental tradition. To seek to resolve this dispute is
obviously beyond the scope of this essay. In any case, to hope for the eventual recon-

ciliation of the critical insights of postmodernism with the other major traditions of post-Enlightenment thought is, no doubt, to theorize the quarrels between modernists and postmodernists in terms more amenable to a critical theory of Marxist provenance. It seems we are left with an uncomfortable dilemma. There is surely a continuing need for principles of political engagement and critique, if only for the sake of those who have not even begun to benefit from the political values of modernity. On the other hand, postmodernists may also be right in thinking that politics as a faith is no longer plausible. The benefits of political practice have been too meagre, the disasters too calamitous. Political engagement may still be unavoidable, but its efficacy is surely in serious doubt.

See also I ANALYTICAL PHILOSOPHY; 3 HISTORY; 9 CONSERVATISM; II LIBERALISM; I2 MARXISM; I3 SOCIALISM; I4 AUTONOMY; I5 COMMUNITY; I8 CORPORATISM AND SYNDICALISM; 2I DISCOURSE; 34 SECESSION AND NATIONALISM

References

Adorno, T. W.: *Minima Moralia* (Frankfurt: Suhrkamp, 1951); trans. E. F. N. Jephcott, *Minima Moralia* (London: New Left Books, 1974).

——, Frenkel-Brunswik, E., Levinson, D. J., and Sanford, R. N.: *The Authoritarian Personality* (New York: Harper & Row, 1950).

—— et al.: *The Positivist Dispute in German Sociology*, trans. G. Adey and D. Frisby (London: Heinemann, 1976).

Althusser, L.: 'Marxism and humanism', in *For Marx*, trans. B. Brewster (London: Allen Lane, 1969).

——: *Essays in Self-criticism*, trans. G. Lock (London: New Left Books, 1976).

Anderson, P.: *In the Tracks of Historical Materialism* (London: Verso, 1983).

Ansell-Pearson, K.: *Nietzsche contra Rousseau* (Cambridge: Cambridge University Press, 1991).

Ayer, A. J.: *Language, Truth, and Logic* (1936); (Harmondsworth: Penguin Books, 1971).

Bacon, F.: *The Advancement of Learning* (1605), ed. G. W. Kitchin (London: Dent, 1973).

Baudrillard, J.: *Selected Writings*, ed. and trans. M. Poster (Cambridge: Polity Press, 1988).

Beauvoir, S. de: *The Second Sex*, trans. H. M. Parshley (Harmondsworth: Penguin Books, 1972).

Benhabib, S. and Dallmayr, F.: *The Communicative Ethics Controversy* (Cambridge, Mass. and London: MIT Press, 1990).

Benjamin, W.: 'The work of art in the age of mechanical reproduction', in *Illuminations*, ed. H. Arendt, trans. H. Zohn (London: Fontana/Collins, 1968).

Bernstein, R. J., ed.: *Habermas and Modernity* (Cambridge: Polity Press, 1985).

Blackham, H. J.: *Six Existentialist Thinkers* (London: Routledge & Kegan Paul, 1961).

Boyne, R.: *Foucault and Derrida* (London and Boston: Unwin Hyman, 1990).

Bubner, R.: *Modern German Philosophy*, trans. E. Matthews (Cambridge and New York: Cambridge University Press, 1981).

Camus, A.: *The Rebel*, trans. A Bower (New York: Alfred Knopf, 1954).

Connerton, P.: *The Tragedy of Enlightenment* (Cambridge and New York: Cambridge University Press, 1980).

Connor, S.: *Postmodernist Culture* (Oxford and Cambridge, Mass.: Basil Blackwell, 1989).

Cruickshank, J.: *Albert Camus and the Literature of Revolt* (Oxford: Oxford University Press, 1960).

Culler, J.: *Saussure* (London: Fontana/Collins, 1976).

Deleuze, G.: *Nietzsche and Philosophy*, trans. H. Tomlinson (London: Athlone Press, 1983).

Derrida, J.: *Speech and Phenomena*, trans. D. B. Allison (Evanston, Ill.: Northwestern University Press, 1973).

————: *Of Grammatology*, trans. G. C. Spivak (Baltimore and London: Johns Hopkins University Press, 1976).

————: *Writing and Difference*, trans. A. Bass (London: Routledge & Kegan Paul, 1978; Chicago: Chicago University Press, 1978).

————: *Positions*, trans. A. Bass (Chicago: Chicago University Press, 1981).

————: 'The laws of reflection: Nelson Mandela, in admiration', in *For Nelson Mandela*, ed. J. Derrida and M. Tlili (New York: Seaver, 1987).

Descartes, R.: 'Meditations on first philosophy', in *The Philosophical Works of Descartes*, 2 vols. Vol. 1, trans. E. S. Haldane and G. R. T. Ross (London and New York: Dover, 1931).

Dews, P.: 'Introduction' to Habermas, J.: *Autonomy and Solidarity*, ed. P. Dews (London: Verso, 1986).

————: *Logics of Disintegration* (London and New York: Verso, 1987).

Elliott, G.: 'Further adventures of the dialectic', in *Contemporary French Philosophy*, ed. A. Phillips Griffiths (Cambridge and New York: Cambridge University Press, 1987).

Foucault, M.: *Madness and Civilization*, trans. T. Howard (London: Tavistock Publications, 1971).

————: *Birth of the Clinic*, trans. A. M. Sheridan Smith (New York: Random House, 1973).

————: *The Archaeology of Knowledge*, trans. A. M. Sheridan Smith (London: Tavistock Publications, 1976).

————: *Discipline and Punish*, trans. A. Sheridan (Harmondsworth: Penguin Books, 1977a).

————: 'Intellectuals and power: interview with Gilles Deleuze', in *Language, Counter-Memory, Practice*, ed. D. F. Bouchard, trans. D. F. Bouchard and S. Simon (New York: Cornell University Press, 1977b).

————: 'Truth and power', in *Michel Foucault: Power, Truth, Strategy*, ed. M. Morris and P. Patton (Sydney: Feral Publications, 1979).

————: 'Nietzsche, genealogy, history', in *The Foucault Reader*, ed. P. Rabinow (New York: Pantheon Books, 1984).

Freud, S.: *The Psychopathology of Everyday Life*, trans. A. A. Brill (Harmondsworth: Penguin Books, 1938).

————: *The Interpretation of Dreams*, trans. J. Strachey (Harmondsworth: Penguin Books, 1976).

Gatens, M.: *Feminism and Philosophy* (Cambridge: Polity Press, 1991).

Habermas, J.: *Über Sprachtheorie – Vorbereitende Bemerkungen zu einer Theorie der kommunikativen Kompetenz* (Vienna: Handblume Edition, 1970).

————: 'Technology and science as "ideology" ', in *Towards a Rational Society*, trans. J. J. Shapiro (London: Heinemann, 1971).

————: *Knowledge and Human Interests*, trans. J. J. Shapiro (London: Heinemann, 1972).

————: *Zur Rekonstruktion des Historischen Materialismus* (Frankfurt: Suhrkamp, 1976).

————: 'New social movements', *Telos*, 49 (1981), 33–7.

————: 'Diskursethik – Notizen zu einem Begründungsprogramm', in *Moralbewusstsein und kommunikatives Handeln* (Frankfurt: Suhrkamp, 1983).

————: *The Theory of Communicative Action*, 2 vols, trans. T. McCarthy (Boston: Beacon Press, 1984a).

————: 'Über Moralität und Sittlichkeit – was macht eine Lebensform "rational"?', in *Rationalität*, ed. H. Schnädelbach (Frankfurt: Suhrkamp, 1984b).

————: *The Philosophical Discourse of Modernity*, trans. F. G. Lawrence (Cambridge: Polity Press, 1987).

Hegel, G. W. F.: *The Phenomenology of Mind* (1807), trans. J. B. Baillie (New York and London: Harper & Row, 1967).

————: *The Philosophy of Right* (1821), trans. T. M. Knox (Oxford and New York: Oxford University Press, 1952).

Heidegger, M.: 'The origin of the work of art' (1936), in *Basic Writings*, ed. D. F. Krell (New York: Harper Collins, 1977).

————: 'Letter on humanism' (1947), in *Basic Writings*, ed. D. F. Krell (New York: Harper Collins, 1977).

————: *Being and Time*, trans. J. Macquarrie and E. Robinson (Oxford: Blackwell, 1967).

Herder, J. G.: 'Essay on the origin of language' (1770), in *On the Origin of Language*, ed. J. H. Moran (New York: F. Ungar, 1967).

Horkheimer, M.: 'Traditionelle und kritische Theorie', *Zeitschrift für Sozialforschung*, 6 (1937).

———— and Adorno, T. W.: *The Dialectic of Enlightenment*, trans. J. Cumming (London: Allen Lane, 1972).

Hume, D.: *A Treatise of Human Nature* (1739–40), ed. L. A. Selby-Bigge (Oxford: Clarendon Press, 1888).

————: *Enquiries Concerning the Human Understanding and Concerning the Principles of Morals*, (1777), ed. L. A. Selby-Bigge (Oxford: Clarendon Press, 1902).

————: *Dialogues Concerning Natural Religion* (1779), ed. M. Bell (London and New York: Penguin Books, 1990).

Husserl, E.: *Logical Investigations*, trans. J. N. Findlay (London: Routledge & Kegan Paul, 1970).

Kant, I.: 'An answer to the question: What is Enlightenment?' (1784), in *Perpetual Peace and Other Essays*, trans. T. Humphrey (Indianapolis and Cambridge: Hackett Publishing Company, 1983).

Kaufmann, W.: *Nietzsche* (Princeton, NJ: Princeton University Press, 1974).

Keane, J.: *Public Life and Late Capitalism* (Cambridge and New York: Cambridge University Press, 1984).

Kierkegaard, S.: 'Fear and trembling', in *Selections from the Writings of Kierkegaard*, trans. L. M. Hollander (New York: Anchor Books, 1960).

————: *Either-Or*, trans. H. V. Kong and E. H. Kong (Princeton, NJ: Princeton University Press, 1987).

Laclau, E. and Mouffe, C.: *Hegemony and Socialist Strategy* (London: Verso, 1985).

Lacoue-Labarthe, P.: *Heidegger: Art and Politics* (Oxford: Blackwell, 1990).

Lévi-Strauss, C.: *Structural Anthropology*, trans. C. Jacobson and B. G. Schoepf (Harmondsworth: Penguin Books, 1968).

————: *The Elementary Structures of Kinship*, trans. J. H. Bell, J. R. von Sturmer and R. Needham (London: Eyre & Spottiswoode, 1969).

Lukács, G.: 'What is orthodox Marxism?', in *History and Class Consciousness*, trans. R. Livingstone (London: Merlin Press, 1971).

Lukes, S.: *Marxism and Morality* (Oxford: Oxford University Press, 1987).

Lyotard, J.-F.: *The Postmodern Condition*, trans. G. Bennington and B. Massumi (Manchester: Manchester University Press, 1984).

————: *Heidegger and 'the Jews'*, trans. A. Michel and M. S. Roberts (Minneapolis: University of Minnesota Press, 1990).

McCarthy, T.: *The Critical Theory of Jürgen Habermas* (London: Hutchinson, 1978).

————: 'The politics of the ineffable: Derrida's deconstructionism', *Philosophical Forum*, 21 (1989–90), 146–68.

Macquarrie, J.: *Martin Heidegger* (London: Lutterworth Press, 1968; Richmond, Va.: John Knox Press, 1968).

Marcuse, H.: *One-Dimensional Man* (London: Sphere Books, 1968a).

————: 'Philosophy and critical theory', in *Negations* (Harmondsworth: Penguin Books, 1968b).

————: *Eros and Civilization* (London: Sphere Books, 1969a).

————: 'On revolution', in *Student Power*, ed. A. Cockburn and R. Blackburn (Harmondsworth: Penguin Books, 1969b).

————: *Soviet Marxism* (Harmondsworth: Penguin Books, 1971).

————: 'Sartre's existentialism', in *Studies in Critical Philosophy* (London: New Left Books, 1972; Boston: Beacon Press, 1973).

Marx, K.: 'Economic and philosophical manuscripts' (1932), in *Early Writings*, trans. R. Livingstone and G. Benton (Harmondsworth: Penguin Books, 1975).

————: 'Theses on Feuerbach', in *Early Writings*, trans. R. Livingstone and G. Benton (Harmondsworth: Penguin Books, 1975).

————: *The German Ideology*, ed. C. J. Arthur (London: Lawrence & Wishart, 1977).

Mortley, R.: *French Philosophers in Conversation* (London and New York: Routledge, 1991).

Nietzsche, F.: *Beyond Good and Evil*, trans. R. J. Hollingdale (Harmondsworth: Penguin Books, 1973).

————: *Untimely Meditations*, trans. R. J. Hollingdale (Cambridge and New York: Cambridge University Press, 1983).

Norris, C.: *Derrida* (London: Fontana/Collins, 1987).

Oakeshott, M.: *Rationalism in Politics* (London: Methuen, 1962).

O'Brien, C. C.: *Camus* (London: Fontana/Collins, 1970).

Pettit, P.: *The Concept of Structuralism* (Berkeley: University of California Press, 1975).

Piaget, J.: *Structuralism*, trans. C. Maschler (London: Routledge & Kegan Paul, 1971).

Pivcevic, E.: *Husserl and Phenomenology* (London: Hutchinson, 1970).

Poster, M.: *Sartre's Marxism* (London: Pluto Press, 1979).

Rabinow, P., ed.: *The Foucault Reader* (New York: Pantheon Books, 1984).

Rohde, P.: *Kierkegaard* (London: Allen & Unwin, 1959).

Rousseau, J.-J.: *The Social Contract and Discourses* (1762), trans. G. D. H. Cole (London: Dent, 1973).

————: *Emile* (1762), trans. B. Foxley (London: Dent, 1974).

Ryan, M.: *Marxism and Deconstruction* (Baltimore and London: Johns Hopkins University Press, 1982).

Sartre, J.-P.: *Being and Nothingness*, trans. H. E. Barnes (London: Methuen, 1958).

————: *Les Mains sales* (London: Methuen, 1961).

————: *The Wall: Intimacy*, trans. L. Alexander (New York: New Directions, 1969).

————: 'Vietnam: imperialism and genocide', in *Between Existentialism and Marxism*, trans. J. Matthews (London: New Left Books, 1974).

————: *Critique of Dialectical Reason*, 2 vols. Vol. 1, *Theory of Practical Ensembles*, trans. A. Sheridan-Smith (London: New Left Books, 1976).

————: *Existentialism and Humanism* (New York: Haskell, 1977).

Saussure, F. de: *Course in General Linguistics* (1916), ed. C. Bally and A. Sechehaye, trans. W. Baskin (New York and London: McGraw-Hill, 1959).

Taylor, C.: *Hegel* (Cambridge and New York: Cambridge University Press, 1975).

Thompson, J. B. and Held, D., eds: *Habermas: Critical Debates* (London and New York: Macmillan, 1982).

Weber, M.: *The Protestant Ethic and the Rise of Capitalism*, trans. T. Parsons (London: Unwin University Books, 1930).

Whitehead, A. N. and Russell, B.: *Principia Mathematica* (1903), 3 vols (Cambridge: Cambridge University Press, 1950).

Wittgenstein, L.: *Tractatus Logico-Philosophicus*, trans. D. F. Pears and B. F. McGuinness (London: Routledge & Kegan Paul, 1961).

Young, I. M.: 'The ideal of community and the politics of difference', in *Feminism/Postmodernism*, ed. L. J. Nicholson (London and New York: Routledge, 1990a).

————: *Justice and the Politics of Difference* (Princeton, NJ: Princeton University Press, 1990b).

Further reading

Bubner, R.: *Modern German Philosophy*, trans. E. Matthews (Cambridge and New York: Cambridge University Press, 1981).

Connor, S.: *Postmodernist Culture* (Oxford and Cambridge, Mass.: Blackwell, 1989).

Descombes, V.: *Modern French Philosophy*, trans. L. Scott-Fox and J. M. Harding (Cambridge and New York: Cambridge University Press, 1980).

Dews, P.: *Logics of Disintegration* (London and New York: Verso, 1987).

Held, D.: *Introduction to Critical Theory* (London: Hutchinson, 1980).

McCarthy, T.: *The Critical Theory of Jürgen Habermas* (London: Hutchinson, 1978).

Macquarrie, J.: *Martin Heidegger* (London: Lutterworth Press, 1968; Richmond, Va.: John Knox Press, 1968).

————: *Existentialism* (Harmondsworth and New York: Penguin Books, 1972).

Singer, P.: *Hegel* (Oxford and New York: Oxford University Press, 1985).

Skinner, Q., ed.: *The Return of Grand Theory* (Cambridge and New York: Cambridge University Press, 1985).

Taylor, C.: *Hegel* (Cambridge and New York: Cambridge University Press, 1975).

3

The contribution of history

RICHARD TUCK

The relationship between the history of political thought and modern political philosophy since the late 1960s has been marked by an apparent paradox. On the one hand, a number of leading historians of political theory, such as Quentin Skinner, John Pocock and John Dunn, have at various times expressly asserted that their subject should have very little relevance for modern theory; on the other hand, many of the same historians have also been distinguished contributors to discussions among political philosophers about issues such as republicanism, democracy or justice. Moreover, these assertions have failed to discourage the philosophers, many of whom have continued the ancient practice of pillaging the classics in search of ideas and styles to be revived for their own time. (Obvious examples would be Nozick's use of Locke (1974), Kavka's use of Hobbes (1986), and maybe even Rawls' use of Kant (1971).) Some philosophers – notably Macintyre and Taylor – have gone so far as to argue that we cannot disentangle ourselves from the complex histories of our own culture, and that unhistorical political theory is both conceptually barren and morally hazardous. It would not have been surprising if the practitioners of positivist political science, of the kind which was widely accepted earlier in this century, had disclaimed any interest in the history of political thought; but what is disconcerting is that the positivist generation seems to have been more enthusiastic in principle about the modern relevance of studying the history of theories than the anti-positivist generation of the period since 1960. So I will begin this paper by trying to explain the character of the methodological debate on the history of political thought which began in the 1960s, and how far the historians were really opposed to any modern exploitation of the classic texts of political theory.

The period from 1870 to 1970 was a very strange one in the history of thinking about politics in the Anglo-American world (and, to a lesser extent, on the Continent also). There are a number of alternative ways of characterizing its strangeness. One is to point to the absence of major works on political philosophy, of a more or less familiar kind, between Sidgwick and Rawls, something that immediately struck the first reviewers of *A Theory of Justice*. Another is to remind ourselves that serious commentators in the 1950s could believe that 'for the moment . . . political philosophy is dead' (Laslett, 1956, p. vii). Yet another, and my own preferred way, is to observe that some of the major themes of traditional political thought – questions about the right way in which commodities should be produced and distributed – had been handed over to a guild of scholars who displayed little interest in the rest of what had been taken to be political thought. Adam Smith, James Mill, John Stuart Mill, Sidgwick or Marx had not solely been economists: their work on the production and distribution of commodities was integrated into their own original moral philosophies. But the late nineteenth and early twentieth centuries saw no such figures; even Keynes was much more of a technical and specialized economist than most of the 'classical' writers had been. Since these questions were naturally enough the central issues for government to consider, political thought (in so far as there was any) came to be excessively detached from the real business of politics.

How had this state of affairs come about? In some ways, the goal of a value-free science of human conduct had been central to European culture since the Enlightenment; but what was distinctive about the later nineneenth century was this fracturing of intellectual enquiry into human behaviour between a set of technical, allegedly value-free disciplines devoted to particular aspects of social life, and a high-level and rather detached attitude to moral philosophy. Clearly, Kant's influence was important in this development, for Kant had set out the argument for just such a fracture between ethics and the human sciences. The practical implication of this distinction (though this might have disconcerted Kant himself) was that 'objective' human science came to carry more weight in thinking about human conduct than did ethics: for it was embodied in difficult, systematic and impressive works which required intellectual resources on a different scale from those devoted to moral philosophy. Thus the first generation of Kant's followers in Germany was the generation that discovered modern British political economy and turned it into a Kantian science, much to the alarm and disgust of critics such as Hegel and Marx, whose deep hostility to Kantianism rested primarily on their hostility to such a science, and on their awareness that Smithian political economy could not reasonably qualify as one.

But the influence of Kant is not enough to explain the great change that came over political theory in the late nineteenth century, particularly as that influence was not brought to bear in a steady or persistent manner. England was obviously not very open to Kantian influences as long as utilitarianism, even of a Millian sort, reigned supreme; while on the Continent the mid-century was the period of the Hegelians and other critics of Kant. Some exogenous development was needed to allow Kantianism to be adopted or re-adopted as the theoretical foundation for the human sciences, and that development is most plausibly seen as the increasing sense in the 1860s that a new kind of political economy could, after all, be the first clear example of a genuinely value-free human science.

In England, the roots of this are to be found in the mid-nineteenth-century criticisms of utilitarianism, and in particular the attack launched by philosophers such as John Grote on the idea that one can make interpersonal comparisons of utility. In his posthumously published *An Examination of the Utilitarian Philosophy*, Grote argued primarily against the well-known argument in Mill's *Utilitarianism* about 'higher' and 'lower' pleasures:

the fact is, two pleasures cannot be tasted with a view to the comparison of them, as a chemist may taste two fluids: the utilitarian is led astray by his language, talking as he does about

73

pleasures as if they were separate entities, independent of the mind of the enjoyer of them: the pleasures are always mixed with something from ourselves, which prevents us speaking, with any philosophically good result, of this sort of independent comparability among them . . .

As a matter of fact we do not look upon pleasures as independent things to be thus compared with each other, but as interwoven with the rest of life, as having their history and their reasons, as involving different kinds of enjoyment in such a manner that our being able to enter into one kind is accompanied with a horror of another kind, which would entirely prevent the comparison of the one with the other as pleasures. Besides this, it must be remembered that, in the interval between the one pleasure and the other, the mind is changed: you have no permanent touchstone, no currency to be the medium of comparison. Supposing a man whose youth has been grossly vicious, whose mature age is most deeply devout: according to disposition, the view as to past life in this case will probably much differ: but most commonly I think the man will wonder that he was ever able to find pleasure at all in what he once found pleasure in. Earnestness in the later frame of mind, whatever it is, would only preclude the possibility of a cool comparison of it, as to pleasure, with the earlier one . . .

We have, most of us, our own pleasures, and other people's pleasure often seem to us none at all. I cannot understand a happiness for everybody, after we have gone beyond our universal wants of meat, drink, and shelter, and till we arrive at a sphere where pleasure may be of a temper and nature which at present we cannot enter into. (Grote, 1870, pp. 53–5)

Sidgwick said the same in his *The Methods of Ethics*: 'the represented pleasantness of different feelings fluctuates and varies indefinitely with changes in the actual condition of the representing mind (or minds, in so far as we elect to be guided by others)' (Sidgwick, 1874, p. 129). (His whole discussion at this point is directly modelled on that of Grote.)

As the example of Sidgwick notoriously shows, these critics were much more effective in their arguments against utilitarianism than they were in putting forward any substantive alternative. Both Grote and Sidgwick were ostensibly committed to some modified and better founded version of utilitarianism (Grote was a close personal friend of J. S. Mill), but neither was able in the end to advance a moral theory that commanded much support. Sidgwick revealingly remarked *à propos* of any utilitarian theory (including his own) that:

the assumption is involved that all pleasures are capable of being compared quantitatively with one another and with all pains . . . This assumption is involved in the very notion of Maximum Happiness: as the attempt to make 'as great as possible' a sum of elements not quantitatively commensurable would be a mathematical absurdity. Therefore whatever weight is to be attached to the objections brought against this assumption (which was discussed in c.3 of Book II [from which the sentence quoted earlier was taken]) must of course tell against the present method. (1874, p. 384)

Nowhere in *The Methods of Ethics* did he give any grounds for supposing that these objections were *not* to be taken seriously. Indeed, Sidgwick is reported to have remarked gloomily just after the appearance of the first edition (of which it is true) that 'the first word of my book is "Ethics", the last word is "failure"' (Hayward, 1901, p. xix).

However, these criticisms had made it clear that any serious account of human conduct now had to eschew interpersonal comparisons of utility. Smithian or 'classical' political economy was full of such comparisons: not only were the comparably diminishing marginal utilities of different individuals widely used in the Benthamite tradition to justify an egalitarian distribution of goods, but the labour theory of value itself was arguably based on an interpersonal comparison of utility. Labour, to Smith and his followers, was by definition disutility; and a fair exchange of commodities between two people meant that the pain one person had incurred in producing the first commodity ought to be equivalent to the pain incurred by the other person in producing the second commodity. On the face of it, therefore, the impossibility of interpersonal comparison should have led to a general scepticism about political economy; but in the 1860s a number of economists independently realized that the subject could be transformed and rescued from these difficulties.

The full story of that rescue is too long to tell here, but essentially, it fell into two phases. The first, represented by the pioneering work of Jevons, Walras and Menger, involved the explicit repudiation of interpersonal comparison. As Jevons said:

The reader will find . . . that there is never, in any single instance, an attempt made to compare the amount of feeling in one mind with that in another. I see no means by which such comparison can be accomplished. The susceptibility of one mind may, for what we know, be a thousand times greater than that of another. But, provided that the susceptibility was different in a like ratio in all directions, we should never be able to discover the difference. Every mind is thus inscrutable to every other mind, and no common denominator of feeling seems possible. ([1871] 1888, p. 14)

Correspondingly, the labour theory disappeared from their work, to be replaced by the modern notion that a 'fair' exchange is one in which each party does better in terms of their own utility scales than they would in any possible alternative arrangement. Ironically, this new theory appeared at almost the same moment as Marx's *Capital*: the political economy whose internal contradictions Marx exposed had been replaced by one that was impervious to that critique. It is this fact, above all others, that explains the peculiar history of Marxism, and its failure to capture the highest ground inside the societies that gave birth to it.

In the work of the first generation of the new economists, there was no systematic account of *social* choice based on these principles (there is only the barest hint of such a thing, in Walras' *Elements of Pure Economics* (1954, pp. 143, 511)). Jevons admired Sidgwick, a feeling that was reciprocated, and the new political economy was seen by both men (albeit inconsistently) as something that could be fitted inside Sidgwickian utilitarianism. But it was not long before it occurred to economists that a minimalist social choice principle was possible, in the form of the famous Pareto principle put forward by Vilfredo Pareto in 1897. Essentially, Pareto simply generalized the operational definition of exchange value found in Jevons or Walras: a social arrangement of any kind was 'optimal' or 'efficient' if no alternative arrangement existed which would be judged no worse by all the participants, and better by at least one of them. The importance of the Pareto principle is that it avoids interpersonal comparisons of utility, for the social states are to be judged by the participants according to their own, incommensurable standards of utility. On the face of it, however, it should precisely for this reason be a relatively useless principle: for what social choice is likely to be possible on the basis of such a principle? As it happened, one important social choice did turn out to be vindicated (apparently) by the Pareto principle: it was the choice of an allocation of goods in a society by a perfectly competitive market rather than by the decisions of monopolistic or oligopolistic producers. Although the rigorous demonstration of this took a great deal of intellectual effort, and was not fully achieved until the 1950s (see Debreu, 1959), the basic idea was the simple one, familiar since at least the eighteenth century, that a fully competitive economy produces more commodities than a monopolistic one, and that there must therefore exist some allocation of those commodities, which benefits everyone as much as or more than any allocation arrived at in a monopolistic economy.

Pareto himself argued that modern socialism should recognize this fact and strive to produce by social fiat the kind of allocation that would be arrived at by perfect competition; indeed, the principal defence of socialism which he put forward was precisely that it might be more effective at generating such an allocation than a real market system with its attendant failures and corruption (1971, pp. 267–9). It should not be forgotten that right across the industrialized world the late nineteenth and early twentieth centuries were the heyday of monopolistic trusts and cartels, with the newly powerful German industries in particular being deliberately and successfully organized on the basis of cartels. A politically unregulated economy was obviously very different from a perfectly competitive one. In the 1930s and 1940s, Pareto's ideas were turned against those critics of socialism and communism, such as Mises (1920), who had argued that centralized planning procedures could never work efficiently. Writers like Abram Bergson (1938; 1949) and Oscar Lange (1942) tried to wrongfoot the conservatives by accepting a Pareto optimum as the goal of social planning, and arguing that it was as easy to achieve it through the centralized distribution of goods as through a fallible capitalist mechanism. To some extent, the actual practice of certain Eastern European regimes after the Second World War followed these guidelines, though never with the success that Bergson hoped for (and in retrospect it is hard not to believe that Mises had the best of the argument). But this view of the socialist project at least had the advantage that it made sense in modern terms, and rescued socialists from the technical difficulties of authentic Marxism.

The new economics represented by Pareto and his successors was a formidable intellectual construct, a human science based on what seemed to be the most plausible candidate to date for a genuinely universal principle of morality. The Pareto principle is hard to reject as at least one component in any conceivable moral outlook; to this extent, its use as the foundation of a human science resembles the use made 250 years earlier of the principle of self-preservation. The founders of the 'science of morality' in the seventeenth century thought that they had detected a fundamental principle underpinning all possible ethical and legal systems, namely that an individual has the right to preserve himself. They then proceeded to construct elaborate accounts of the laws of nature based, as far as possible, on that principle alone, in the expectation that their accounts would prove compelling to any reader, whatever the rest of his moral theories might be. For a hundred years or more, this 'science' was as dominant in the universities of Europe as modern economics has been; its subsequent fate illustrates how unfounded any claim may prove in the end to provide a scientific account of human conduct.

By 'scientific', both theories really meant 'universal'; although many of the modern economists have claimed that the Pareto principle is in some sense 'value-neutral', this is of course not so. At the very least, it requires that we prefer a state of affairs in which other people are better off than in the alternative, while we ourselves remain no worse off, and this presupposes that we *care* about other people's welfare when our own is not involved. Some influential moral theorists (notably Hobbes) have claimed that all altruistic sentiments are concealed egotism; if they are right, then the Pareto principle could not make sense, since if it were strictly the case that on the basis of our own welfare we were indifferent between two outcomes, we could have no good reason for preferring one to the other. To be a Paretian is to take up a determinate moral position. But it is true that it is an extremely exiguous position, and that we would be unlikely in practice to encounter many people possessing anything resembling a moral viewpoint who did not subscribe to it. The same, incidentally, might still be said about the principle of self-defence.

Nevertheless, the universality of the principles on which they were basing their subject encouraged late nineteenth- and early twentieth-century economists, and their admiring colleagues in the schools of political and social science, to suppose that it was now possible to talk about an 'objective science' of man. An extremely revealing example of this comes from the dominant economics textbook of the later twentieth century, Paul Samuelson's *Economics*. In it, he wrote:

'Beauty is in the eye of the beholder' is an aphorism reminding us that judgements of better or worse involve *subjective* valuations. But this does not deny that one person's nose may be *objectively* shorter than another's. Similarly, there are elements of valid reality in a given economic situation, however hard it may be to recognize and isolate them. There is not one theory of economics for Republicans and one for Democrats, one for workers and one for employers, one for the Russians and still another for the Chinese. On many basic principles concerning prices and employment, most – not all! – economists are in fairly close agreement.

This statement does not mean that economists agree closely in the *policy* field. Economist A may be for full employment at any cost. Economist B may not consider it of as vital importance as price stability. Basic questions concerning right and wrong goals to be pursued cannot be settled by mere science as such. They belong in the realm of ethics and 'value judgements.' The citizenry must ultimately decide such issues. What the expert can do is point out the feasible alternatives and the true costs that may be involved in the different decisions. But still the mind must render to the heart that which is in the heart's domain. For, as Pascal said, the heart has reasons that reason will never know. (1976, pp. 7–8. This textbook was largely composed in the 1950s and 1960s)

This extract from Samuelson's *Economics* is revealing in a number of different ways. First, it shows how 'fairly close agreement' among economists was treated as evidence for 'elements of a valid reality', and how intersubjectivity was confounded in practice with objectivity. Second, it illustrates the role that ethics of a more traditional kind continued to play in the general scheme of even as 'scientific' a student of humanity as Samuelson (whose collected essays were called his *Collected Scientific Papers*). What he called 'value-judgements' were still recognized as possessing force, and to an extent he might be regarded as a kind of Kantian; but value-judgements were not to be derived from accurate thinking about the categorical imperative. Instead, they were matters of 'the heart' which 'the citizenry' must decide.

These two themes – that value-judgements are not the product of systematic, rational thought, and that it is necessary in a modern society for citizens to make decisions about the moral basis of public policy – dominated the study of the history of political theory in North America (and, though characteristically to a less extreme degree, in Britain also) during the first half of the twentieth century. The study of a body of classic texts was treated, it might be said, as a way in which the motions of the heart might be regulated and future citizens exposed to a range of values which they could subsequently employ in their decision-making. As an example of this, we can take what was easily the influential textbook on the history of political thought in the middle years of this century (a book which has never been out of print since it was first published), George Sabine's *History of Political Theory* (1937). In the preface to the first edition, Sabine duly registered his own firm allegiance to the Humean claim that 'neither logic nor fact implies a value':

Taken as a whole a political theory can hardly be said to be true. It contains among its elements certain judgements of fact, or estimates of probability, which time proves perhaps to be objectively right or wrong. It involves also certain questions of logical compatibility respecting the elements which it tries to combine. Invariably, however, it also includes valuations and predilections, personal or collective, which distort the perception of fact, the estimate of probability, and the weighing of compatibilities . . . (Sabine, [1937] 1963, p. v.)

And Sabine honestly described his point of view as a 'sort of social relativism' (ibid., p. vi.). A similar combination of interest in the history of the subject together with a confidence in the truth of the fact/value distinction, and in the possibility of an objective political science, is to be found in many other writers of this generation; another good example would be the Englishman George Catlin, who wrote some extraordinarily positivist works on political science in the 1930s, and followed them up with *A History of the Political Philosophers* in 1950.

In its essentials, this sub-Kantian (or, perhaps, sub-Humean) alliance between the sciences of man and the history of political theory held together until the 1960s, though its avowed relativism led to some strains in the 1950s. David Easton, in an influential article in 1951, attacked the practices of the historians of political theory in the politics departments of his time, accusing them of living parasitically on past ideas and failing to deliver either a truly empirical political science or an adequate 'valuational frame of reference'. (He himself, it should be said, regarded the former as the prime goal of political theory.) Partly in response to attacks from the more narrow positivists such as this, and partly driven by an older fear of modern relativism, some distinguished historians of political thought in postwar North America emerged as sages who saw some eternal truths embodied in their subject. Hannah Arendt, Eric Voegelin and, above all, Leo Strauss talked about the tradition represented by the classic texts of Western political thought as containing – albeit often in a fractured and deceptive form – some ancient wisdom which was not accessible to modern political science. For them as much as for Easton, Sabine's belief that no political theory can really be said to be 'true' was anathema.

However, it was also in the 1950s that the theoretical foundations of the standard view of political science came to appear much less secure. In part, this was the result of a tradition of post-Wittgensteinian scepticism about the possibility of that kind of human science (a scepticism voiced for example by Peter Winch in 1958 in his *The Idea of a Social Science*). But as important were developments within the citadel of political science itself. Historically speaking, this may have been the most important role of Kenneth Arrow's famous 'Impossibility Theorem' of 1951: for what Arrow showed, with as much rigour as any human scientist could conceivably demand, was that the programme of an educated citizenry deciding social values – the picture rather vaguely assumed by Samuelson and the others – did not make sense. Arrow accepted the fundamental premises of early twentieth-century economics, in particular its refusal to make interpersonal comparisons and its reliance on the Pareto principle as the fundamental principle of social choice. But he denied that around this core 'science' there could be put the socially agreed set of values which the older writers had relied on, since there could be no method of reaching a coherent social ordering of the individual citizen's values which did not breach at least one of a number of very reasonable and eminently liberal conditions. It took a long time for Arrow's message to sink in (maybe not until the late 1960s, when writers such as Amartya Sen carried it to a wider audience), but his 'Theorem' made it impossible for the old trust to be placed in such an unexamined fashion in the citizenry deciding social values.

At the same time, the core 'science' became a much more politically controversial matter. As we saw earlier, it was possible for socialists in the first half of the century to be neo-classical economists, even if a strictly Marxian approach was impossible for a neo-classicist. To this extent, it was true that, as Samuelson claimed, there was one economics for both capitalist and socialist. But the socialism of Bergson or Lerner rested on a confidence that a bureaucracy could in principle allocate resources to mimic the allocations produced by a perfectly competitive market, and that the same bureaucracy could alter the allocations as necessary in order to promote some general social ends. The bureaucracy, they thought, could draw on information about the utility scales of the individual citizens and could construct a 'social welfare function', based on some commonly agreed principles, which would be sensitive to changes in individual utility functions.

The idea that a central agency could possibly either have access to or handle the amount of information that this would require was always implausible; but a fundamental blow was dealt to the picture by a number of writers on public finance in the 1950s, including Samuelson himself, as it happens (see Samuelson, 1954). They pointed out that it was in principle impossible for a bureaucracy to have accurate information of this kind in the area of public goods – that is, goods that are not acquired for individual consumption – since people would never give accurate information about the value to them of a public good if by doing so they laid themselves open to a tax in order to pay for it. Samuelson also observed that the same would be true for any industry with decreasing costs (Samuelson, 1958). Since most important services under socialism would be public goods, or would have something of their character (such as a heavily-subsidized public transport system), these observations represented a formidable new objection to the socialist programme.

The result of this was that many economists were made aware of the very peculiar properties of an actual competitive market, and this new awareness may be reckoned the basis of the strongly conservative movements such as the Chicago School, who argues that our inability to solve these social computational problems meant that we should not even try to do so, but should leave our social decision-making as far as possible to the workings of a market which was artificially kept in perfectly competitive working order (something which Samuelson, it should be said, was not particularly keen on). Theorists who continued to favour the social provision of public goods, such as Mancur Olson in his justly famous *The Logic of Collective Action* (1965), were forced to recognize that the provision of public goods might require various techniques of coercion (such as closed shops enforced by trades unions in order to compel members to pay their dues). These developments had the unwelcome consequence that neo-classical economics ceased to appear as a politically-neutral science, but rather as a challenge to the fundamental assumptions of socialism.

It was against this background of uncertainty over the orthodox political sciences that modern political philosophy emerged. In the later 1960s philosophers such as John Rawls began to believe that it was possible to provide a new set of *rational* grounds for holding various political principles, and that our political theory was not dependent on either the narrow core of universally held beliefs (such as the Pareto principle) or the wider periphery of the historically given culture of our particular society. It should of course be said that, strictly speaking, Rawls has always argued that the liberal theory of justice embodied in his work is in some sense properly to be understood as rooted in our culture; but for him it is present at such a deep level that the old project of using the historical texts of political and moral theory to develop our values is clearly unnecessary. Rawls' famous 'Kantianism' helped to give him this aloofness from the wide and complicated historical culture; it also had the great merit of helping to fit him into the story of twentieth-century political science, in which, as we have seen, the distinction between the objective science and the subjective account of value had been foundational.

Modern political philosophy thus challenged the old practice of the history of political thought. If the domain of value was amenable to rational analysis, then the traditional point of reading the classics of the genre had been removed. They could linger on as labels attached to modern views (as Locke does in Nozick's work, or Kant himself in Rawls'), but the idea that one would get one's values by actually reading and engaging with the specific text had been radically weakened.

Historians responded appropriately, and this was the beginning of the famous argument over the methodology of the history of ideas which has persisted down to our time. By general consent, the two most important manifestos for a new kind of history of political thought appeared in the late 1960s, John Dunn's 'The Identity of the History of Ideas' (1968), and Quentin Skinner, 'Meaning and Understanding in the History of Ideas' (1969). Skinner's was the longer and more comprehensive of the two, and has attracted most subsequent discussion; one of its advantages was that he clearly located his targets among modern political scientists and (in a rare unguarded moment) drew the most explicit conclusion about the relationship between history and theory:

I turn first to consider the methodology dictated by the claim that the *text* itself should form the self-sufficient object of inquiry and understanding. For it is this assumption which continues to govern the largest number of studies, to raise the widest philosophical issues, and to give rise to the largest number of confusions. This approach itself is logically tied, in the history of ideas no less than in more strictly literary studies, to a particular form of justification for conducting the study itself. The whole point, it is characteristically said, of studying past works of philosophy (or literature) must be that they contain (in a favoured phrase) 'timeless elements', in the form of 'universal ideas', even a 'dateless wisdom' with 'universal application'.

   Now the historian who adopts such a view has already committed himself, in effect, on the question of how best to gain an understanding of such 'classic texts'. For if the whole point of such a study is conceived in terms of recovering the 'timeless questions and answers' posed in the 'great books', and so of demonstrating their continuing 'relevance', it must be not merely possible, but essential, for the historian to concentrate simply on what each of the classic writers has *said* about each of these 'fundamental concepts' and 'abiding questions'. The aim, in short, must be to provide a 're-appraisal of the classic writings, quite apart from the context of histor-ical development, as perennially important attempts to set down universal propositions about political reality'. For to suggest instead that a knowledge of the social context is a necessary condition for an understanding of the classic texts is equivalent to denying that they do contain any elements of timeless and perennial interest, and is thus equivalent to removing the whole point of studying what they said. ([1969] 1988, p. 30)

In the footnotes to this passage, a mixture of conventional political scientists such as Catlin and critics of political science such as Leo Strauss were listed as the figures Skinner had in mind. Later in the article, Skinner drew the principal conclusion about the consequence of treating the classic texts as historically-specific *actions*:

All I wish to insist is that whenever it is claimed that the point of the historical study of such questions is that we may learn directly from the *answers*, it will be found that what *counts* as an answer will usually look, in a different culture or period, so different in itself that it can hardly be in the least useful even to go on thinking of the relevant questions as being 'the same' in the required sense at all. More crudely: we must learn to do our own thinking for our-selves. (ibid., p. 66)

   It is clear that Dunn had the same kind of idea in mind when in the previous year he had complained that:

few branches of the history of ideas have been written as the history of an *activity*. Complicated structures of ideas, arranged in a manner approximating as close as may be (frequently closer than the evidence permits) to deductive systems have been examined at different points in time or their morphology traced over the centuries. Reified reconstructions of a great man's more accessible notions have been compared with those of other great men; hence the weird ten-dency of much writing, in the history of political thought more especially, to be made up of what propositions in what great books remind the author of what propositions in what other great books . . . ([1968] 1980, p. 15)

Moreover he produced in these years a clear and comprehensive example of a new methodology, in his famous book *The Political Thought of John Locke* (1969), in which

81

he vastly extended the insights of Peter Laslett (see below) into the historical specificity of Locke's ideas. The book contains the equivalent of Skinner's 'crude' claim that 'we must learn to do our own thinking for ourselves' in what Dunn was later to call the 'peculiarly ill-considered' sentence, 'I simply cannot conceive of constructing an analysis of any issue in contemporary political theory around the affirmation or negation of anything which Locke says about political matters.' At the same time, Skinner produced some prolegomena to a similar entirely historical investigation of a classic author, in a series of articles locating Hobbes in the context of the pamphlet warfare of the English revolution, and in particular the arguments over the 'Engagement' to obey the new republic of 1649 (Skinner, 1964; 1965; 1966; 1974).

These manifestos of the late 1960s could draw on some predecessors as examples of the kind of historical approach they had in mind. For Skinner, the foremost example was Collingwood, who represented in English dress the German tradition stemming at least from Dilthey, that had always seen utterances (including complex philosophical texts) as part of the history of action; but for both Skinner and Dunn there were more recent and more local exemplars. One was Peter Laslett, who in 1960 had produced a famous edition of Locke's *Two Treatises of Government*. In the introduction he argued that no distinction should be made between Locke's intentions in the First Treatise and those in the Second: it had always been recognized that the First was a polemical tract with a specific historical target, namely Sir Robert Filmer, and Laslett argued (with a wealth of close scholarship) that Filmer was equally the target of the Second Treatise. Locke's role in some putative history of liberal values, and in particular his supposed refutation of Hobbes, was thereby called into question. (It might incidentally be remarked that Laslett's views about the relationship of the First and Second Treatises have recently been questioned by Professor Ashcraft (1987), while the Second Treatise has been claimed by both Professor Tully and myself to have a much wider objective than the refutation of Filmer (Tully, 1980; my own views are contained in my 1991 Carlyle Lectures, to appear shortly) – the first and in many ways the best example of the new method appears much shakier than it once did.)

The other more recent example was John Pocock. He had achieved fame through the publication in 1957 of a remarkable work, *The Ancient Constitution and the Feudal Law*, in which he studied the constitutional conflicts of seventeenth-century England through a close examination of the rather technical historical scholarship produced by seventeenth-century antiquaries. The book was highly unusual in the care and intelligence which Pocock devoted to a whole group of writers who on no stretch of the imagination could be fitted into the standard array of classic authors, but whose activities were shown to be historically more significant in many ways than that of the great theorists.

In the following years, Pocock developed a general theory to vindicate this approach, expressed most clearly in an essay of 1962. In this essay, he urged historians of ideas to take seriously as the material to be understood and explained the whole set of writing or other products on politics available from a particular society – what he called the 'stereotypes' and 'languages', and what he has subsequently termed 'paradigms'. Even the major political philosophers, he argued, could only be read against a rather minutely specified and historically particular background of linguistic practices. It was true, he acknowledged, that:

as the lanuage employed in political discussion comes to be of increasing theoretical generality, so the persuasive success of the thinker's arguments comes to rest less on his success in invoking traditional symbols than on the rational coherence of the statements he is taken to be making in some field of political discourse where statements of wide theoretical generality are taken to be possible. Here, sooner or later, our historian must abandon his role of a student of thought as the language of a society, and become a student of thought as philosophy – i.e. in its capacity for making intelligible general statements . . . [But because the historian had approached his philosopher *via* a study of the wider language, he] can now consider the level of abstraction on which the thinker's language tends to make him operate, and the level of abstraction on which the thinker's preoccupations tend to make him use his language. He can now give some precision of meaning to the vague phrase – every thinker operates within a tradition; he can study the demands which thinker and tradition make upon each other. (Pocock, 1962, pp. 200–1)

Skinner's work on Hobbes and the Engagers a few years later was seen by both men as a fine example of this kind of approach.

It is important to stress that to see philosophical reflection as in its essence a kind of historical activity, no different from other actions by historical agents (such as cutting off King Charles' head or running the Counter-Reformation Catholic Church) is not *eo ipso* to deny its significance from the point of view of modern theory. But it is to concede its significance in the same way as the rest of our history is significant. This is an issue which much of the methodological argument of the last twenty years has been somewhat evasive about, largely because it raises a number of very fundamental questions about the extent to which the historically-given character of modern ideas is relevant to a proper understanding of them. Marxists, of course, have never had any trouble about this: they have straightforwardly believed that many of the values which govern modern society are ideological, and formed by the exigencies of the economic history of the human race. An understanding of that economic history (broadly defined) would then be vital to a proper apprehension of those values – such as why certain puzzling things (e.g. the labour theory of value and the legitimacy of capitalist profit) go together.

But many non-Marxists have taken a similar view (for example, Weber), though with a much less single-minded approach to the past. They have believed that many different kinds of historical action, not just the construction of new modes of production, had some causal relation to the kinds of values which our current society seems to espouse, and that understanding that history might dissolve some of the puzzles about the values. Part of that history will be economic, part will be political or constitutional (e.g. the impact on all subsequent Western societies of the actual institutional story of the Reformation or the French Revolution) and part might be intellectual, to do with the theoretical resources readily available to the agents at any particular time. The history of political thought, treated as part of historical enquiry in general rather than as some privileged and special means of understanding our values, would fall readily into this last category.

The attack on the notion that we will get our political values from a simple scrutiny of the great texts could thus go in two quite different directions. One was towards support for the analyical enterprise of modern political philosophy, with the history of political thought treated as a quite separate study (the position apparently adumbrated in Dunn and Skinner's early pronouncements). The other was towards support for an historical criticism of modern theories, in which their inconsistencies and puzzles were to be resolved not by abstract thinking but by laying bare their historical origins, including (though not exclusively) their origins in the history of theory. In their actual practice as historians, both Dunn and Skinner and their pupils and followers have often been inclined towards the latter approach; though it would (I think) be fair to say that none of them have given a wholly convincing or comprehensive account of *how* historical enquiry solves conceptual puzzles, preferring instead to offer examples of the process. But as the enterprise of modern political philosophy has faltered, and as the possibility of 'doing our thinking ourselves' has become more remote, this second approach has seemed increasingly attractive.

A particularly good example of it has been the resurrection of something like a classical theory of republicanism. For the last couple of decades, Skinner has been working on the political thought of Machiavelli (see e.g. Skinner, 1978; 1981; 1983; 1988; 1990a and b). Initially (it might be fair to say) his interest in Machiavelli was as an example of the misunderstandings to which historians of political thought are liable if they ignore the actual context of a writer's work – in Machiavelli's case, the context of Renaissance Ciceronian political theory. But in some of his more recent essays, Skinner has felt able to use Machiavelli in a rather different way, as an example of a 'republican' theorist of liberty whose writings might (with appropriate qualifications) help us to recover a 'republican vision of politics'. His argument in these essays starts from the famous distinction made by Isaiah Berlin between 'positive' and 'negative' liberty. As is well known, by 'positive' liberty Berlin meant an idea of human freedom in which – paradoxically – we must be constrained in various ways in order to be led along the paths which represent our real interests (a view associated allegedly with Rousseau or Marx); while 'negative' liberty is the coventional liberal notion of free individuals pursuing the ends which they assign to themselves in a framework which maximizes their general ability to do so. Skinner has argued forcefully that this dichotomy is implausible, at least if it is taken to be the basis upon which a sharp distinction must be drawn between (in modern terms) 'communitarian' and 'rights' theories:

Contemporary liberalism, especially in its so-called libertarian form, is in danger of sweeping the public arena bare of any concepts save those of self-interest and individual rights. Moralists who have protested against this impoverishment – such as Hannah Arendt, and more recently Charles Taylor, Alasdair MacIntyre and others – have generally assumed in turn that the only alternative is to adopt an 'exercise' concept of liberty [a term which Taylor uses to make the point that we are only in full possession of our liberty if we actually exercise our principal human capacities], or else to seek by some unexplained means to slip back into the womb of the polis. I have tried to show that the dichotomy here – either a theory of rights or an 'exercise' theory of liberty – is a false one. (Skinner, 1990b, p. 308)

Instead, Skinner has insisted that the tradition of classical republicanism embodied the claim that *in order* to protect our individual liberty, understood in a 'negative' sense, we should live a relatively strenuous life of republican involvement, in which our duties as citizens might be quite extensive, and might include many of the actual practices which the supposed 'positive' theorists took to be necessary – including for example, the kind of republican activitism which Rousseau pleaded for. (Skinner has not made Rousseau a central figure in his story, and seems in the most recent statement to treat him as essentially a theorist of a 'positive' kind, though it may well in fact be possible to align him more closely to Skinner's negative republicans.) A republican life of this kind is necessary, these theorists are held to have argued, since without it political institutions will become corrupt, and the citizens will lose their independence either through internal domination by a party or single ruler, or through external domination by an imperial power. So although a conceptual distinction between positive and negative liberty might be justified, the negative concept can in practice underpin a much less exclusively right-based political regime. Skinner has drawn the contemporary moral clearly enough:

It will be objected that this attempt to enlist the traditions of Machiavellian republicanism as a third force amounts to nothing more than nostalgic anti-modernism. We have no realistic prospect of taking active control of the political processes in any modern democracy committed to the technical complexities and obsessional secrecies of present-day government. But the objection is too crudely formulated. There are many areas of public life, short of directly controlling the actual executive process, where increased public participation might well serve to improve the accountability of our *soi disant* representatives. Even if the objection is valid, however, it misses the point. The reason for wishing to bring the republican vision of politics back into view is not that it tells us how to construct a genuine democracy, one in which government is for the people as a result of being by the people. That is for us to work out. It is simply because it conveys a warning which, while it may be unduly pessimistic, we can hardly afford to ignore: that unless we place our duties before our rights, we must expect to find our rights themselves undermined. (1990, pp. 308–9)

I do not want to consider here how far this is a convincing historical reconstruction of Machiavelli's views. There have been some criticisms of it, and it may be the case that Skinner has overestimated the liberal basis for any pre-Rousseauian theory of republicanism. Both ancient and Renaissance republicans, for example, were pretty sure that sharp distinctions of social capacity, including (usually) slavery, were necessary to protect the liberty of the free citizens, and they were after all repudiated by the liberal rights theorists for precisely that reason. But the point I want to stress is that this use of a classic text is not a repudiation of the methodology originally called for at the end of the 1960s. Instead, it offers an example of using an historical enquiry to resolve or at least illuminate a modern theoretical puzzle – the puzzle in this case being the stark and unconvincing antagonism between communitarians and liberals.

Another example from very recent writing would be Dunn's explicit repudiation of his youthful and extravagant claim that there is nothing alive in Locke's political thought. In an essay directly addressing the question ' What is Living and What is Dead in John Locke?', Dunn continued his long-standing attack on the popular notion that modern rights theories can reasonably be located in Locke's actual political writings, pointing (as he had always done) to the explicitly theistic foundation upon which Locke based his account of natural rights. But Dunn was now prepared to concede that 'the main set of categories which he elaborated to interpret the *role* of men and women within God's history can in large measure stand free of that setting and serve still to interpret their political fate when left severely on their own' (Dunn, 1990a, p. 22). These categories, he argued, were three in number: the conception of an agent's responsibility for his own actions, the conception of a human society as 'the unintended consequence of a vast array of past human contrivances' (ibid., p. 23), and the conception of *trust* as the foundation of any worthwhile and persisting social relationship. This last feature was the most important and distinctive feature of Locke's political vision, and Dunn has written persuasively elsewhere about its continued salience in modern politics (e.g. Dunn, 1990b). But he observed about Locke that what was distinctive was the measured way in which all three of these categories were employed together:

> Even this conjunction, of course, has nothing magical about it. It ends no arguments and grounds no conclusive claims to authority. But that is its virtue, not its weakness: the index of its sober realism . . . Locke's view of the political project still has a huge distance to go. But it is a view which captures – and captures most evocatively – what politics is still like: captures it without superstition but also without despair.
>
> Locke saw politics this way; and I do not know of any other modern thinker who quite contrived to do so. And because he saw it this way and because this is the way it still is and is always likely to remain, we *do*, I think, have good reason to nerve ourselves for the full unfamiliarity of his vision – its unblinking historical distance – and to use it in all its integrity and imaginative force to help us to think again.
>
> And what could be more alive than that? (Dunn, 1990a, p. 25)

Yet another example of historians using their enquiries into past political theories to illuminate present arguments would be the increasing array of investigations into linguistic changes of various sorts. In so far as modern philosophers have at various times retreated to appeals to what a certain key term 'means', as part of their exposition of a particular theory, they have laid themselves open to the simple observation that terms do not necessarily have meanings that are stable over a relevant period or within a relevant group. My own book on *Natural Rights Theories* (Tuck, 1979) offered some thoughts about the complicated history of rights terminology, though it also tried to extract from the principal early-modern rights theorists a liberal political theory with many illuminatingly paradoxical elements (e.g. the constant association of natural rights with voluntary slavery), in an attempt to address directly the kinds of liberal theories which modern philosophers have put forward. In a much more systematic way, the essays in a volume such as *Political Innovation and Conceptual Change* (Ball, Farr and Hanson, 1989) (let alone the German enterprise edited and inspired by Professors Brunner, Conze and Koselleck, the *Geschictliche Grundbegriffe*) offer a much better example of how a kind of etymological analysis can influence modern theory.

But, as I said earlier, these are all *examples* of an historical investigation put to the service of philosophical reflection. We still lack a fully developed and coherent account of *why* historical enquiry should matter. In part, it might be said, the very absence of such a thing is testimony to its redundancy: there is an obviousness about the need for us to think at least partly in historical terms which is rooted in very deep facts about our psychology. It is often said, albeit somewhat glibly, that a society which did not have an intense interest in its own history would be rather like an individual without a memory; the analogy is trite, and it obviously needs unpacking with care, since the directly functional advantages of a memory for an individual are not straightforwardly there for a society. On the other hand, it *is* true that the political and social institutions which we inhabit have never, even in the most revolutionary society, been invented completely *de novo* (and this would be true of the institution of 'revolution' itself, one of the more self-consciously historical practices of modern society). In so far as philosophers are going to reflect on the value and coherence of these institutions, including such fundamental things as private property, the state and the family, they are going to have to take into account the fact that the institutions as we have them were the product of historical development, and that their character was often given to them as a result of a particular history of *ideas*. That history may now be implicit in their operation, but recovering it can suddenly illuminate the point of an otherwise inscrutable set of habits and assumptions.

The question which this prompts is then, what difference did the methodological arguments of the 1960s in fact make? Has the actual practice of the historians concerned, driven (as we have seen) by perfectly consistent motives, turned out to be radically different from that of their predecessors? To answer this question, we need to recall what I argued in the first half of this paper, that the 'old' history of political thought was primarily concerned to survey the classics of the genre in a search for the values expressed in their philosophies, which were taken to be applicable with relatively little difficulty to any society. On this account, Plato, Locke and Hegel all had (for example) competing theories of the state, and it was up to the reader to choose the most plausible (in practice, he was usually nudged towards Locke's). The fundamental idea of the 'new' history is that what matters is the combination of social and political history – the history of our actual institutions or languages – and the history of ideas. The state was not a given entity with an independent existence, about which philosophers could think: it is something with a history formed in part by practical exigencies, in part by the low-grade theoretical reflection of a wide variety of agents, and in part by the clear and distinct ideas of great philosophers.

It is this which has led the 'new' historians to incorporate into their writings accounts of a wide variety of lesser figures alongside the traditional canon (often, it should be said, to the point of self-parody), and which has led Pocock into being in many ways the most consistent practitioner of the new history, constantly subverting the orthodox subject-matter of his discipline. Clearly, much that was written about the classics of political theory in the past will still be relevant to our historical investigations today; equally clearly, the high-level philosophical reflections of the classic writers will sometimes be more historically important than other elements in the history of our institutions, since they are the elements to which continued attention has been paid by our society. So the superficial difference between 'old' and 'new' history will often not be very great. But the wider contexts in which each operates are very different; and one of the things which the historian can illuminate is precisely the change in the contexts, and how the theoretical world which political philosophers inhabit today is fundamentally different from that of the earlier twentieth century.

See also I ANALYTICAL PHILOSOPHY; 5 ECONOMICS; 6 POLITICAL SCIENCE; 9 CONSERVATISM; I2 MARXISM; I7 CONSTITUTIONALISM AND THE RULE OF LAW; 22 DISTRIBUTIVE JUSTICE; 25 EQUALITY; 28 LEGITIMACY; 29 LIBERTY; 30 POWER; 32 REPUBLICANISM; 33 RIGHTS; 39 TRUST; 4I WELFARE

References

Arrow, K. J.: *Social Choice and Individual Values* (New York: Wiley, 1951; 2nd edn 1963).

Ashcraft, A.: *Locke's Two Treatises of Government* (London: Allen & Unwin, 1987).

Ball, T., Farr, J. and Hanson R. L., eds: *Political Innovation and Conceptual Change* (New York: Cambridge University Press, 1989).

Bergson, A.: 'A reformulation of certain aspects of welfare economics', *Quarterly Journal of Economics*, 52 (1938), 310–34.

————: 'Socialist economics', in *A Survey of Contemporary Economics*, ed. H. S. Ellis (Philadelphia: Blakiston Co., 1949), pp. 412–48.

Brunner, O., Conze, W. and Koselleck, R.: *Geschictliche Grundbegriffe: Historisches Lexicon zur politisch-sozialen Sprache in Deutschland* (Stuttgart: Ernst Klett Verlag, 1972)

Catlin, G.: *A History of the Political Philosophers* (London: Allen & Unwin, 1950).

Debreu, G.: *Theory of Value* (New York: Wiley, 1959).

Dunn, J.: *The Political Thought of John Locke* (Cambridge: Cambridge University Press, 1969).

————: 'The identity of the history of ideas' (1968), in *Political Obligation in its Historical Context* (Cambridge: Cambridge University Press, 1980), pp. 13–28.

————: 'What is living and what is dead in the political theory of John Locke?', *Interpreting Political Responsibility* (Cambridge: Cambridge University Press, 1990), pp. 9–25.

————: 'Trust and political agency', *Interpreting Political Responsibility* (Cambridge: Cambridge University Press, 1990), pp. 26–44.

Easton, D.: 'The decline of modern political theory', *Journal of Politics*, 13 (1951), 36–58.

Grote, J.: *An Examination of the Utilitarian Philosophy* (London: Drichton Bell, 1870).

Hayward, F.: *The Ethical Philosophy of Sidgwick* (London, 1901).

Jevons, W. S.: *The Theory of Political Economy* (1871), 3rd edn (London: Macmillan, 1988)

Kavka, G. S.: *Hobbesian Moral and Political Theory* (Princeton, NJ: Princeton University Press, 1986).

Lange, O.: 'The foundations of welfare economics', *Econometrica*, 10 (1942), 215–28.

Laslett, P., ed.: *Philosophy, Politics and Society* (Oxford: Blackwell, 1956).

————: *John Locke, Two Treatises of Government* (1960); (Cambridge: Cambridge University Press, 1988).

Mises, L.: 'Die Wirtschaftsrechnung im sozialistischen Gemeinwesen', *Archiv für Sozialwissenschaften*, 47 (1920), 86–121.

Nozick, R.: *Anarchy, State and Utopia* (Oxford: Blackwell, 1974).

Olson, M.: *The Logic of Collective Action* (Cambridge, Mass.: Harvard University Press, 1965).

Pareto, V.: *Manual of Political Economy* (1909); trans. A. S. Schwier (London: Macmillan 1972).

Pocock, J. G. A.: *The Ancient Constitution and the Feudal Law* (Cambridge: Cambridge University Press, 1957).

————: 'The history of political thought: a methodological enquiry', *Philosophy, Politics and Society*, Series II, ed. P. Laslett and W. G. Runciman (Oxford: Blackwell, 1962), pp. 183–202.

Rawls, J.: *A Theory of Justice* (Cambridge, Mass.: Harvard University Press, 1971).

Sabine, G. H.: *A History of Political Theory* (1937); 3rd edn (London: Harrap, 1963).

Samuelson, P. A.: 'The pure theory of public expenditure', *The Review of Economics and Statistics*, 36 (1954), 387–9.

————: 'Aspects of public expenditure theories', *The Review of Economics and Statistics*, 40 (1958), 332–8.

————: *Economics*, 10th edn (Tokyo: McGraw-Hill, 1976).

Sidgwick, H.: *Methods of Ethics* (London: Macmillan, 1874).

Skinner, Q. R. D.: 'Hobbes's *Leviathan*', *Historical Journal*, 7 (1964), 321–33.

————: 'History and ideology in the English revolution', *Historical Journal*, 8 (1965), 151–78.

————: 'The ideological context of Hobbes's political thought', *Historical Journal*, 9 (1966), 286–317.

————: 'Conquest and consent: Thomas Hobbes and the Engagement controversy', *The Interregnum*, ed. G. E. Aylmer (London: Macmillan, 1974), pp. 79–98.

————: 'Meaning and understanding in the history of ideas', *History and Theory*, 8 (1969), 199–215: *Meaning and Context: Quentin Skinner and his Critics*, ed. J. Tully (Cambridge: Polity Press, 1988), pp. 29–67.

————: 'Machiavelli's *Discorsi* and the pre-humanist origins of republican ideas', *Machiavelli and Republicanism*, ed. G. Bock, Q. R. D. Skinner and M. Viroli (Cambridge: Cambridge University Press, 1990), pp. 121–42.

————: 'The republican ideal of political liberty', *Machiavelli and Republicanism*, ed. G. Bock, Q. R. D. Skinner and M. Viroli (Cambridge: Cambridge University Press, 1990), pp. 293–309.

Tuck, R. F.: *Natural Rights Theories* (Cambridge: Cambridge University Press, 1979).

Tully, J. H.: *A Discourse on Property* (Cambridge: Cambridge University Press, 1980).

Walras, L.: *Elements of Pure Economics* (1874), trans. W. Jaffe (London: Allen & Unwin, 1954).

Winch, P.: *The Idea of a Social Science* (London: Routledge & Kegan Paul, 1958).

Further reading

Ball, T., Farr, J. and Hanson, R. L., eds: *Political Innovation and Conceptual Change* (Cambridge: Cambridge University Press, 1987).

Brunner, O., Conze, W. and Koselleck, R.: *Geschictliche Grundbegriffe: Historisches Lexicon zur politisch–sozialen Sprache in Deutschland* (Stuttgart: Ernst Klett Verlag, 1972).

Condren, C.: *The Status and Appraisal of Classic Texts* (Princeton, NJ: Princeton University Press, 1985).

Dunn, J.: *Political Obligation in its Historical Context* (Cambridge: Cambridge University Press, 1980).

————: *Interpreting Political Responsibility* (Cambridge: Cambridge University Press, 1990).

Gunnell, J.: *Political Theory: Tradition and Interpretation* (Cambridge, Mass.: Harvard University Press, 1979).

Pocock, J. G. A.: 'The history of political thought: a methodological enquiry', *Philosophy, Politics and Society*, Series II, ed. P. Laslett and W. G. Runciman (Oxford: Blackwell, 1962), pp. 183–202.

Skinner, Q. R. D.: 'The republican ideal of political liberty', *Machiavelli and Republicanism*, ed. G. Bock, Q. R. D. Skinner and M. Viroli (Cambridge: Cambridge University Press, 1990), pp. 293–309.

Tuck, R. F.: 'History of political thought', *New Perspectives on Historical Writing*, ed. P. Burke (Cambridge: Cambridge University Press, 1991), pp. 193–205.

Tully, J. H. ed.: *Meaning and Context: Quentin Skinner and his Critics*, ed. J. Tully (Cambridge: Polity Press, 1988).

4

The contribution of sociology

ROBERT BROWN

From sociology to political philosophy

Well into the nineteenth century economic and sociological commentaries were familiar features of the work of political philosophers. From Plato to John Stuart Mill there is hardly a major political philosopher who does not comment on the social institutions, processes and structure of actual societies. In the past, if a philosopher had put forward a political theory that was philosophically based but gave no sign of being applicable in practice, he would have been thought to be imposing on the good will and patience of his audience. Even the most reckless of the utopian writers took their imaginary societies to embody political principles that human beings should, and therefore could, adopt. Feasibility, taken broadly, was what distinguished earthly utopias from the political arrangements devised for the Aliens of outer space. Thus the sociological contribution to political philosophy has been, until quite recently, that of one element, sociology, in a system, that of political theory. Whatever the value of this sociological component, its contribution to political philosophy has been that of part to whole and not that of one discipline to another. For the latter relationship, we must look to the consequences of the attempt throughout the nineteenth century by such thinkers as Saint-Simon, Comte, Mill and Spencer to develop a separate science of society, a science whose character, it was hoped, would be similar to that of such empirical natural sciences as chemistry or physics – and thus distinct from mere philosophical speculation, especially that concerning human society. Only after sociology had become an independent discipline with substantial results to exhibit could the question of its usefulness to political philosophy arise. Late in the century that question did arise in the work of two men: that of the founder of empirical French sociology, Emile Durkheim (1858–1917), and that of his German contemporary, the sociological and historical economist, Max Weber (1864–1920).

Since the question 'How has sociology contributed to political philosophy?', and its converse, 'How has political philosophy contributed to sociology?', can be answered in many different ways, a choice has to be made among them. An obvious procedure, and the one adopted here, is to begin where modern sociology began – with the problems and solutions devised by Durkheim and Weber. Their thought is still highly valued and has perhaps never been more widely discussed. They stand pre-eminent in their field. Both men had explicit and well-developed views concerning a number of the topics of political philosophy and their relationship to sociological ideas. Each man was familiar with at least part of the other's work and took it into account when producing his own judgements on issues in political theory. Both Durkheim and Weber were deeply interested in what sort of discipline sociology could become, what its connections with history, psychology and economics might be, what methods were appropriate to a genuine science of human society. All these facts taken together make it both natural and useful for us to devote the first part of our discussion to the views of Durkheim and Weber. For after they had helped to establish modern 'scientific' sociology, the question of the contribution made by that kind of sociology to political philosophy changed. The question then invited answers rather different from those given by earlier thinkers, thinkers for whom sociology was still in process of emerging from the intersection of political philosophy, psychology, economics and history. Some examples of these later contributions will be discussed below.

Durkheim: society as a moral system

The hopes held for the emerging discipline of a social science are illustrated by the ideas put forward in 1813 by the social reformer and herald of a new scientific revolution, Henri Saint-Simon (1760–1825), in his dedication to Napoleon of *Travail sur la gravitation universelle*: 'Sire, the progress of the human mind has reached the point where the most important reasoning on politics can and must be deduced directly from the knowledge acquired in the high sciences and the physical sciences' (Saint-Simon, [1813] 1975, p. 124) The high sciences were physiology and psychology. Based on them, such fields as morals, politics and philosophy would jointly form part of an emerging and unified science of man. From this science, founded as it was on biological knowledge, political conclusions for the organization of human society could, and should, be drawn. After Saint-Simon's death his former assistant and collaborator, Auguste Comte (1798–1857), produced a modified version of this ambitious but inchoate programme. According to it the laws of sociology – those concerning the relationships of people to one another – are basic in that they cannot be reduced to psychological laws about individual persons. Furthermore, psychology is itself merely a branch of physiology since every mental state is produced by a state of the brain. With psychology eliminated as a factor for explaining social life, only sociological premises are needed to explain human behaviour in society. Because Comte did not distinguish explicitly between description and prescription, between questions of fact and questions of value, he drew a conclusion of a kind that has been debated ever since. The conclusion is that most political principles and policies, that is, political recommendations and prescriptions which incorporate value-judgements, are logically deducible from purely sociological descriptions. Hence on Comte's view, what sociology can contribute to political philosophy is almost everything. This is the view with which as a student Durkheim became familiar, and from which his own methodological beliefs took their origin.

Durkheim defined 'political society' as 'one formed by the union of a large number of secondary social groups that are subject to a single authority not itself under the jurisdiction of any other properly constituted superior authority' (Durkheim, [1950] 1983, p. 45; Lukes, 1975, p. 268). The state itself is for Durkheim the 'organ of social thought' and consists of a group of legislative and executive officials whose function is to produce ideas and take decisions concerning matters that affect the entire society. These officials deliberate and plan, and they guide collective conduct. But if we then go on to ask, in the traditional fashion, 'What is the aim or goal of the state as a collective agency?' Durkheim replies by first recasting the question so as to evoke an answer that is in part sociological and in part philosophical: 'what end', he asks, 'does the State normally pursue and therefore should it pursue, in the social conditions of the present day?' (Durkheim, [1950] 1983, p. 51). The answer to the first, factual question is 'many ends – and increasingly many in the course of political history'. The more complex and highly developed a nation's economy, legal system, cultural life and administrative system become, the more functions the state must perform, and hence the more ends it must and should pursue. This is the answer to the second, or normative, question. In consequence, it is misguided to urge that the role of the state be kept to a minimum, that it confine itself to protecting each person's rights and not attempt to confer additional benefits on its people. The growth of the state cannot be reversed without also dismantling the structure of civilized life and relinquishing the values that are embedded in it.

Similarly, the cultivation of the private individual has become irreversible. The individual is no longer 'lost in the depths of the social mass' and is no longer wholly absorbed in the collective beliefs, aspirations, and practices of a dominating community. 'The scope of the individual life', says Durkheim, 'expands and becomes the exalted object of moral respect. The individual comes to acquire ever wider rights over his own person and over the possessions to which he has title; he also comes to form ideas about the world that seem to him most fitting and to develop his essential qualities without hindrance' (Durkheim, [1950] 1983, p. 56). Given this historical process, Durkheim concludes that these gains in personal dignity cannot now be annulled: 'We cannot undo the individual having become what he is' and submerge him once more in the life of the social mass (ibid., p. 57). That submersion, according to Durkheim, was the answer offered by Hegel. He argued 'that every society has an aim superior to individual aims and unrelated to them'. The task of the state is to carry out this aim for which the individual is a mere 'instrument'. His only reward for working to make the society great and wealthy is to receive some of the 'reflected rays of its glory'. But Durkheim replies that such a radical depreciation of the social position of the individual would he in direct conflict with the powerful tendency in modern societies to raise the value and esteem in which individual lives are held. How could we force people who have been treated as ends in themselves to become mere means and instruments for achieving some completely independent goals of the state? (Durkheim, [1950] 1983, pp. 54, 56).

There is a further consideration, says Durkheim. The rights that the individual possesses in a society are given and maintained by the power of its state: 'the stronger the State, the more the individual is respected'. The growth of moral individualism has proceeded in tandem with the expansion of the state. Where the state is weak it can neither protect individual rights nor lead the society to develop new forms of freedom. Nor can the state then shield the individual from the coercive moral authority of smaller social groups within the society. Secondary groups, such as those of occupation, religion and education, are often small enough to exert close supervision and surveillance of their members, and if unregulated by the state tend to suppress dissent and liberty of action. On the other hand, such groups are necessary to prevent the state apparatus from becoming either so powerful as to be repressive and tyrannical or so impotent in its leadership as to be unable to organize its citizens for common action except by threatening them with force. In general, the state is remote from the life of the ordinary citizen, and hence is incapable of dealing by itself with the complexities of group behaviour. The relation of the state to its citizens, writes Durkheim, is 'too external and intermittent to penetrate deeply into individual consciences and socialize them within'. Durkheim goes on to issue a caution and prescribe this remedy:

Where the State is the only environment in which men can live communal lives, they inevitably lose contact, become detached, and thus society disintegrates. A nation can be maintained only if, between the State and the individual, there is intercalated a whole series of secondary groups near enough to the individuals to attract them strongly in their sphere of action and drag them, in this way, into the general torrent of social life. (Durkheim, [1893] 1964, p. 28)

Having described what he takes to be the chief aspirations and value-judgements now held by the people of advanced nations concerning social life, Durkheim turns to the second and philosophical part of his question – the part that asks what end the modern state ought to pursue. Its aim, he suggests, should be twofold: first, the state should continue to protect individual citizens from being oppressed and dominated by their secondary groups: for in the past it was the state that freed the child from absolute control by its family, the craftsman from his guild, and the labourer from his feudal lord (Durkheim, [1950] 1983, pp. 62–4). Second, the state should aim to provide the conditions and institutions that will encourage the individual to 'realize himself more fully'. For this, the 'collective apparatus' needs to 'bear less hard on the individual'. In addition, there needs to be both a reliable and friendly exchange of 'goods and services' and widespread co-operation towards the fulfilment of a common ideal (Durkheim, [1950] 1983, p. 71).

Durkheim argued that there are two features which, by the degree to which they are present, distinguish the various forms of government from each other. One feature is the range and depth of attention the government gives to public affairs, including its self-critical grasp of its own operations. The other feature is the ease and extent of communication between the government and the public. In a democracy these features can be most fully developed because of all forms of government democratic political institutions best provide for deliberation, self-criticism, and reflection. The ever-increasing pace and complexity of social change in modern societies make it necessary that a government be able to alter its policies and procedures rapidly and rationally. A democracy is especially well placed to do this – to find new solutions to new problems – for the thoroughness of communication between citizens and their state officials distributes information and comment very widely; it also weakens resistance to change when that resistance is based merely on habit and tradition rather than on critical scrutiny (Durkheim, [1950] 1983, pp. 88–90). Because a democratic system requires citizens to deliberate and reflect on public affairs, it fits best with the value that we now place on freedom of thought and action for the individual person. A democratic country's citizens are not confined to being mere passive observers of the government's behaviour. They can be active and intelligent participants in many of its activities. As a result, they can come to understand and accept the limits of its possible action. Thus their lives become intertwined with the life of the state. All this, Durkheim concludes, 'gives democracy a moral superiority' over other forms of government since it best ensures the fulfilment of the moral, and chief, task of the state: the development of the autonomy, understanding, and knowledge possessed by individual citizens (Durkheim, [1950] 1983, pp. 89–91).

Durkheim under scrutiny

We can set aside as unimportant the looseness of Durkheim's definition of 'political society'. Unions of secondary social groups are formed for many different kinds of activities, and some of these unions, such as the international Mafia or certain multinational corporations, are subject completely to managerial authorities, which are independent of any political jurisdiction or control. Unions of this kind meet Durkheim's specifications but are neither full societies nor political. Often they are economic leagues owing allegiance to no state. Moreover, Durkheim argues that we need to preserve secondary social groups in modern society as a barrier against the possible misuse of power by the officials of the state. But if the secondary groups of a society can be largely eliminated by an authoritarian regime, as Durkheim is suggesting, then the union of such groups cannot be used as a requirement of a political society – unless, of course, a regime without secondary groups is not to be classified as a political one. But to do that would be to make the presence of secondary groups, a non-political feature, into a necessary condition of the society being treated as a political organization. Yet what purpose could such a distinction serve in Durkheim's discussion?

What we ought not to set aside is the correct view that different nations instantiate the notions of political society and the state in different respects and to varying degrees. There are many countries in Southeast Asia, South America and Africa, for example, in which political control of outlying areas and of distinct tribal populations is either absent or minimal. In those countries there may be an elaborate state administration in the capital and a few ineffective soldiers and officials in the countryside. The state apparatus may be strong where it holds sway, but its domain uncertain beyond the suburb. In such cases the secondary work and residential groups – labour unions, village councils, football clubs – may perform the tasks and pursue the aims elsewhere taken up by the state. In fact, its role as the 'organ of social thought' may be limited to just that: to surveys, plans, and recommendations for a population whose size or composition will vary with the willingness and ability of various secondary groups to carry out the policies of the state officials. In countries where the state apparatus depends upon, but gives little protection against, the powers exercised by secondary groups, the answer to the question, 'What ends should the state pursue?' cannot be simply projected from a knowledge of what aims the state in question usually seeks to achieve. If the state does very little, we can, on Durkheim's view, still give the same answer as before, namely protection of the individual against secondary groups and an opportunity for citizens to undertake self-development. We cannot, however, support this conclusion by claiming that it describes the government's usual policy and actions, for the government has no such aims.

It is a further and more general question how far Durkheim was justified in taking a state's usual goals to be an indication, or perhaps a model, of those it should pursue. The increasing complexity of a nation's economy and social organization does not in itself ensure that the state must perform more functions. They may be performed by secondary groups, or dealt with privately, or simply be neglected. These alternatives are familiar enough to have become enshrined everywhere in the programmes of competing political parties. It may be true, as Durkheim asserted, that all attempts to restrain, in any major way, the growth of the state will destroy the benefits and values characteristic of a modern society. However, the truth of this claim largely rests, for Durkheim, on his view that a strong state is necessary for the continued development of moral individualism, a development that he thinks is both inherently valuable and irreversible. But this need for a strong state, the value of the moral individualism that it supposedly produces, and the irreversibility of this process, have often been denied.

The notion of moral individualism or self-realization has been attacked as useless. For sometimes the qualities to be cultivated as valuable are left unspecified and hence cannot be judged. At other times the qualities that should be fostered are identified; but this still leaves unanswered the question whether they are worthy of moral respect, and thus whether the lives that display them should be highly valued and esteemed. In itself, the approving use of the terms 'moral individualism' and 'self-realization' merely marks the fact that the qualities of individual lives are being more highly valued than those of group life. 'The group', wrote Durkheim, 'no longer seems to have value in itself and for itself: it is only a means of fulfilling and developing human nature to the point demanded by the current ideals' (Durkheim, [1950] 1983, p. 112). The question whether these ideals are satisfactory is not answered. Instead, it is transformed by Durkheim into two other questions: 'How did they arise?' and 'Are they permanent changes?' To the first query he answers that various factors, such as the increasing density of population and the division of labour, have weakened 'certain collective sentiments'. The diversity thus produced among a society's members has left them with less in common; but they still share the qualities of their common human nature. It is these qualities that are the subject of the new ideals.

Durkheim's negative reply to the question concerning the reversibility of moral individualism is based, as we saw earlier, on his belief that moral individualism is deeply and widely connected with many other features of contemporary life. To eradicate the former would both greatly disturb the latter and require their replacement by new collective sentiments. Neither change, he thinks, could be forced on to what would be an unwilling population. But here recent political events tell against Durkheim's conclusion. Much of the appeal of such regimes as Stalin's Russia, Hitler's Germany, Mao's China, and of innumerable socialist countries elsewhere, has sprung from their populations' willingness to adopt collectivist values. The same is true of the religious fundamentalists who struggled to political power in Iran and came close to success in other countries. All have attempted to submerge the individual once again in the 'social mass', to raise the values of collective life above those of the individual personality, and to call for the recognition that the highest value the individual citizen can pursue is an increase in the welfare and glory of the state. The fact that the socialist variety of collectivism is now everywhere in retreat does not ensure that the religious variety will soon follow. In some nations the latter may simply replace the former. The fact that so many countries have reverted, even for the short term, to reliance on collective sentiments – religious, political and economic – is enough to cast doubt on the irreversibility of self-realization as the dominant value.

It may well be that under specifiable conditions a strong state is necessary to protect the growth of moral individualism. A strong state, however, as Durkheim himself said, need not do so. It may try to destroy secondary groups and thus expose individual citizens to the direct and unimpeded power of the state apparatus. In that case moral individualism will suffer as much, if not more, as it would have in the total absence of support from the state. In itself, the increasing strength of the state is not sufficient to assure either the maintenance or the growth of moral individualism. A strong state may promote collective values instead. As part of this programme the state can try to improve the material condition of its people, using the citizen's right to good health, housing, work and a pension as both an inducement to, and a reward for, loyal service in achieving the aims of the government. While these benefits may indirectly encourage moral individualism, any direct encouragement of civil rights and political democracy can be suppressed. With them can be suppressed the tendency to moral individualism that political democracy makes possible, and in many cases powerfully stimulates – stimulates because the ability to make free political choices is itself one of the ways in which a person can come to have wider rights over his or her person and possessions, and to develop in Durkheim's words, 'essential qualities without hindrance'.

For Durkheim, the phrase 'moral individualism' refers to a specific kind of moral system, one in which the self-cultivation of a person's character, and the pursuit of personal goals, are not often subjugated to the competing interests of the social group to which the person belongs. Thus for Durkheim the increasing adoption of individualist values in recent years is simply a confirming instance of his generalization that 'all moral systems practised by peoples are a function of the social organization of these peoples, are bound to their social structures and vary with them' (Durkheim, [1924] 1974, p. 56). Each society is for him 'the centre of a moral life'. Its proper function is to direct people towards an ideal that embodies the best that a society of that particular kind can produce. Societies are responsible for improving both the material and moral welfare of their members. Because every distinct moral system is so closely connected to the particular society that gave it birth, the sociological study of that society's structure will help us greatly to understand, judge, and improve its moral rules. Often, however, these rules outlive the social conditions from which they sprang. In such cases we can use our sociological information to account for the mismatch, and to describe the new features of social life for which moral rules are required. The increasing division of labour in advanced societies, for example, creates new duties and rights which link people together in new ways and thus increase their dependence upon each other. We have to produce moral rules to regulate these relations; but if we do not use scientifically adequate means of keeping ourselves informed about such changes and their consequences, we cannot know what moral rules we should be considering for adoption. Nor can we know what moral rules we should be rebelling against because they no longer fit in with, and adequately govern, our social relations. From sociological investigation we can learn, for instance, that in advanced societies 'the ties which bind the individual to his family, to his native soil, to traditions which the past has given to him, to collective group usages, become loose'. This increase of the individual's mobility and independence weakens the moral control of the group over him. However, it can be replaced by that of his work group. He can form new ties with it, and 'from it come the forces which keep him in check and restrain him' (Durkheim, [1893] 1964, pp. 400–1). Having by sociological means learned of the existence of these forces, we can then rationally encourage and support their development.

The exact nature of Durkheim's basic claim – the claim that the moral system of a society is a function of its social organization – is by no means clear. Many societies, perhaps most industrialized ones, have a number of competing moral systems with overlapping rules. The strength of these systems rises and falls over time, as does that of individual rules. This variation may well be in sympathy with some local conditions, but if so the same moral system often seems to be equally compatible with a succession of different social structures. Conversely, the same social structure often seems to be equally compatible with different moral systems. The abolition of legal slavery in the United States did not in itself seem to alter greatly, for the next hundred years, the moral views of the southern white population directly affected. Nor, despite major changes in Australian moral views concerning women, marriage and children, did the social organization of Australia between 1945 and 1990 show a corresponding alteration. There is the further, and troublesome, problem, of course, as to how we are to decide which rules belong to a particular moral system of a society. If it is a necessary condition of membership that each rule individually be a function of, or influenced by, the social structure, then that is a much stronger claim than that only the moral system as a whole need be influenced and that at least some individual rules need not. In neither case will such influence be sufficient to determine membership. For many kinds of non-moral rules – for example, those of games, etiquette, industry and commerce – are also affected by social organization. The mere survival of outmoded moral rules tells against there being a close temporal fit between morality and social structure. That often the two systems influence each other is not seriously in doubt; but which system exerts the greater effect upon the other can be a serious question. Some moral rules are tenaciously held because they are thought to be of central importance in the life of a society. In such a case they can certainly affect the social organization at least as much as it can affect them. However, in some cases no individual element of either system may impinge directly on an element of the other even when, as sometimes happens, the two systems themselves have a systemic connection.

Yet however complicated or loose or indirect the connections between a specific moral system and the social organization of a given society turn out to be, that need not be, for Durkheim, an argument against the state providing moral leadership. The looseness of connection between the two systems would simply make the task of the state rather different. For even if there were no influence exerted by one system upon the other, Durkheim could still maintain that societies ought to encourage their peoples to pursue certain moral ideals. Of course, the social organization of a society would not help to shape or constrain the kind of moral values its people adopted. Societies with very different forms of social organization could have the same moral system. It might, however, be accepted for many sorts of reasons – historical, economic, sociological, religious or philosophical – which varied from one society to another. The understanding of these reasons would have to replace the study of social organization recommended by Durkheim for comprehending, judging and improving the moral rules of a society. Both his original view and its replacement would have to deal with the crucial and unavoidable question of precisely how empirical information about a society could, and would, bear upon its moral improvement. Nevertheless, Durkheim left that question largely unanswered although he was certainly familiar with its long history in the writings of such earlier authors as Machiavelli, Bodin and Montesquieu. The belief that the appropriate characterisation of a society would somehow be sufficient to indicate how its moral health could be improved was both old and popular. The difficulty, equally old, has been to show that the belief can be made precise enough for its truth to be tested.

Weber: The bureaucratization of social life

Max Weber, the German contemporary of Durkheim, was also much concerned with the relationship between morality and social structure; but Weber expressed their common problem in a more general fashion. The problem, he thought, was an instance of the logical relationship, or lack of it, between matters of fact and judgements of value, between 'is' and 'ought', or between description and prescription. Weber distinguished sharply, as Durkheim did not, between the members of each of these pairs: statements of fact and judgements of value are logically distinct, he thought. Hence the soundness of scientific hypotheses, for example, cannot be affected by moral principles. Any given 'religious, political, aesthetic or moral persuasion is compatible with anything which empirical science may disclose because, and only because, such persuasions derive from premises which are logically independent of those which underlie empirical sciences' (Runciman, 1972, p. 57). It follows 'that wholly irreconcilable values are compatible with the acceptance of the same set of facts' (ibid.). It also follows, of course, that the same set of values is compatible with different sets of facts. For Weber, the results of an empirical study of a society cannot by themselves be sufficient to entail the adoption of a particular moral system or set of value-judgements. The fact – if it turns out to be a fact – that certain kinds of moral systems are functions of specific forms of social organization does not by itself logically compel us to leave such connections undisturbed. We can, if we wish, change either one of the systems and then deal with the consequent changes in the other.

In 'The Meaning of "Ethical Neutrality" in Sociology and Economics' (1917), Weber wrote:

The fact that one investigates the influence of certain ethical or religious convictions on economic life and estimates it to be large under certain circumstances does not, for instance, imply the necessity of sharing or even esteeming those causally very significant convictions.

Likewise, the imputation of a highly positive value to an ethical or religious phenomenon tells us nothing at all about whether its consequences are also to be positively valued to the same extent.

Weber went on to remark that he certainly did not agree that 'the analysis of the influence which the ethical evaluation of a group of people have on their other conditions of life and of the influences which the latter, in their turn, exert on the former, can produce an "ethics" which will be able to say anything about what *should* happen' (Weber, 1949, p. 13). What, then, can an historical and psychological scrutiny of the social conditions under which particular evaluations arise, and are maintained, actually give us? It can give us, says Weber, an *'understanding explanation'*, one that helps us to understand which value-judgements are actually present in someone's views, why the person holds those judgements, and what our own view ought to be (Weber, 1949, p. 14). So while value-judgements cannot be extracted from information about trends and tendencies in social life, people who value the achievement of their ideals will use new facts to readjust the means they employ to reveal side-effects, and to reconsider the desirability of their goals. Nevertheless, Weber concludes that 'whether this readjustment *should* take place and what *should* be the practical conclusions to be drawn therefrom is not answerable by empirical science' (ibid., p. 23). For some people believe that the intrinsic value of their intentions and consequent actions outweighs the certain failure of those actions to bring about the goals to which they are directed (ibid., p. 24).

Weber's views are not incompatible, of course, with Durkheim's policy that the state should provide moral leadership. It is simply that such a policy does not follow, according to Weber, from any causal connection between the moral system of a society and its social organization. If there turns out to be such a connection in particular cases, then an additional moral judgement is needed to decide whether or not the state should assume the role of moral leadership. Some states obviously do no such thing: they either refuse to take on the role or else pursue the merely personal interests of state officials and power-holders at the expense of the general population. In the latter case the result is often institutionalized immorality. However, neither Durkheim nor Weber defined the state as an organization that pursued moral ends. In fact, Weber said in *Economy and Society* (1922) that it is not possible to define the state 'in terms of the end to which its action is devoted'. Every end has been pursued by political organizations and no end has been pursued by all of them (Weber, 1968, p. 55). So Weber makes this stipulation:

A 'ruling organization' will be called 'political' insofar as its existence and order is continuously safeguarded within a given *territorial* area by the threat and application of physical force on the part of the administrative staff. A compulsory political organization with continuous operations [*politischer Anstaltsbetrieb*] will be called a 'state' insofar as its administrative staff successfully upholds the claim to the *monopoly* of the *legitimate* use of the physical force in the enforcement of its order. (ibid., p. 54)

Several decades earlier in his lectures on civic morals, Durkheim had criticized the suggestion that a group's occupation of a specific territory be used as a defining property of the state. Occupation of a given area is also true of the family in some societies because in them the family is inseparable from its domain. It was the patrimony of the landed estate, for example, 'that made its unity and continuity and it was about this focus that domestic life revolved. Nowhere, in any political society, has political territory had a status to compare with this in importance.' Moreover, the importance of political territory is recent. Some of the large nomad societies of the past were states, and so were those groups of organized conquerers who settled 'in the country vanquished, without thereby losing their own cohesion or their political identity' (Durkheim, [1950] 1983, p. 43). It is not, says Durkheim, possession of a limited territory that distinguishes the state, modern or ancient, but the subjection of a considerable number of secondary social groups to one supreme authority. On Durkheim's view, Weber's definition is only half-correct. Hence it is somewhat misleading to assert, as Anthony Giddens does, that while 'Weber emphasises above all the capacity of the state to claim, through the use of force, a defined territorial area', such writers as Durkheim 'regarded the modern nation-state primarily as a moral institution' (Giddens, 1972, p. 34). This contrast is skewed, for Durkheim agreed with Weber in not taking moral leadership to be a defining feature of the state. The two men agreed also that in practice some states try to set moral ideals for their peoples. What the two disagreed on was whether the statements of such ideals were the conclusions of a valid argument whose premises were social descriptions.

Now it may be pointed out, and perhaps should be, that much of the discussion generated by Durkheim's and Weber's views is philosophical rather than sociological. The distinction between fact and value, the tasks which the state should bear, the nature of moral individualism, the definition of 'moral system' – all these are topics in moral and political philosophy, not in sociology. How, then, can such issues help us to understand the influence of the latter upon the former? The shortest and most general answer is this: our understanding of social processes is indispensable to our learning which conditions in a society are necessary for the existence and survival of specific political ideals and the policies that embody them. But this understanding requires us to be clear about the nature of our political ideals and policies. Otherwise we shall not know to what task our social understanding is to be devoted. If we exclude philosophical topics from consideration, how are we to decide, for example, whether the role of the state should be large or small? How to decide whether moral individualism should be encouraged or checked? How to discover what bearing, if any, a particular description of social structure has on our political recommendations for that society? Even the closest attention to sociological information alone will not help us unless it entails, or is somehow connected to, prescriptive consequences; and that question is one of those under discussion.

Weber was, of course, primarily an historically-minded sociologist and dealt with philosophical questions only as they arose in the course of his empirical work. However, one of the best known of his sociological contributions – his account of the rise, significance and irreversibility of bureaucratization – has had consequences in political theory. For according to Weber, in the end the expansion of a specialized and centralized administration gravely hinders the advance of political democracy. This occurs despite the fact that, in Weber's words, 'bureaucracy inevitably accompanies modern mass democracy'. The democrats' insistence upon 'equality before the law', their rejection of privilege, of differing decisions from case to case, and of economic or social misuse of administrative position, has increased social equality at the cost of centralizing, and thus strengthening, the powers of the governmental bureaucracy (Weber, 1968, p. 983). Directly opposed to such an increase of power are the policies derived by the democrats from their belief in the equal rights of those being governed. Weber lists two of these policies: (1) 'prevention of the development of a closed status group of officials in the interest of a universal accessibility of office, and (2) minimization of the authority of officialdom in the interest of expanding the sphere of influence of "public opinion" as far as practicable'. To these Weber adds that 'wherever possible, political democracy strives to shorten the term of office through election and recall, and to be relieved from a limitation to candidates with special expert qualifications'. The upshot is an unavoidable conflict between democratic tendencies toward self-realization and the 'iron cage' of bureaucratic specialization in which so many people are confined. What is decisive here, Weber writes, 'is the *leveling of the governed* in face of the governing and bureaucratically articulated group, which in its turn may occupy a quite autocratic position, both in fact and in form' (ibid., p. 985).

Weber believed that a well-established bureaucracy is an almost indestructible 'system of domination' – indestructible because of the conditions that it creates both for the administrators and the governed. For the bureaucrat, these conditions are summarized in the fact that 'In the great majority of cases he is only a small cog in a ceaselessly moving mechanism which prescribes to him an essentially fixed route of march.' His specialized training and tasks, his mastery of a limited field, the rationally organized apparatus into which he fits, all ensure that he cannot start or stop 'the mechanism'. That can only be done by the most senior officials. 'The individual bureaucrat is, above all, forged to the common interest of all the functionaries in the perpetuation of the apparatus and the persistence of its rationally organized domination.' Nor can those being governed simply refuse to cooperate with the bureaucrats. 'If the apparatus stops working', says Weber, 'chaos results, which it is difficult to master by improvised replacements from among the governed.' Hence their material well-being is increasingly dependent 'upon the continuous and correct functioning of the ever more bureaucratic organizations of private capitalism, and the idea of eliminating them becomes more and more utopian'. The results are twofold: (1) the bureaucratic apparatus 'is easily made to work for anybody who knows how to gain control over it', for only the highest officials need to be replaced; (2) the imposition by force of a revolution – 'the forceful creation of entirely new formations of authority' – becomes less and less feasible. Not only does the bureaucracy control all the means of communication between the government and the public, but the rational organization of the work of the bureaucracy's officials will prove technically superior to any alternative form, and thus be found indispensable. Revolutions will be replaced by *coups d'état*, which seize control of the chief bureaucracies, both public and private (Weber, 1968, pp. 987–9).

What bureaucratic organization offers to any government is administrative stability, reliability, precision, calculability of outcome, wide scope of applications and firmness of discipline. Its benefits arise, on the one hand, from the technical knowledge that the organization can bring to bear on request and, on the other hand, from its access to a store of restricted information that has been accumulated as a result of administrative experience over a long period of time. So while at different periods the bureaucratic apparatus may be officially controlled by politicians with widely different policies, their influence is constrained by their lack of specialized technical knowledge. 'Generally speaking', writes Weber, 'the highest-ranking career official is more likely to get his way in the long run than his nominal superior, the cabinet minister, who is not a specialist.' The more duties and tasks are given to the government bureaucracy the more powerful it becomes. Hence it does not matter 'whether the economic system is organized on a capitalistic or socialistic basis. Indeed, if in the latter case a comparable level of technical efficiency were to be achieved, it would mean a tremendous increase in the importance of professional bureaucrats' (Weber, 1968, pp. 223–5). Under socialism, state ownership and regulation of such services as transport, communication and housing, state control of mining, agriculture and banking, the expansion of welfare, and the restrictions on market forces, would all lead to an unprecedented growth in central bureaucratic authority and its regulative procedures. There would be a corresponding decrease in the ability of politicians and other outsiders to check this growth. As Giddens puts it, on Weber's view the socialist effort to encourage self-realization and political participation 'will in fact further reduce the political autonomy of the mass of the population' (Giddens, 1971, p. 182).

What can, and does, simultaneously check bureaucratic expansion, and provide the political leadership that the bureaucracy cannot supply, is the presence of the charismatic leader of a political party. According to Weber, charisma is

a certain quality of an individual personality by virtue of which he is considered extraordinary and treated as endowed with supernatural, superhuman, or at least specifically exceptional powers or qualities. These are such as are not accessible to the ordinary person, but are regarded as of divine origin or as exemplary, and on the basis of them the individual concerned is treated as a 'leader'. (Weber, 1968, p. 241)

Charisma can be displayed by a diverse group: by prophets, heroes, saviours, political leaders, swindlers and by people of maniacal passion. The possessor of charisma lays claim to 'complete personal devotion' on the part of those who recognize their duty to trust and follow that person's leadership. But if the leader remains unsuccessful and the promises are not fulfilled. the devotion is unlikely to continue (ibid., pp. 241–2). It is only charismatic political leaders who have the 'capacity to set new goals and to open new paths in societies hampered by political stagnation and bureaucratic routine' (Mommsen, 1974, p. 93). Mass democracy in a parliamentary system consists in a competitive struggle between demagogues for the votes of the people. The successful leader, with the aid of the party machine, maintains a parliamentary majority that in turn exercises a moderating influence on political decisions. In addition, parliament trains new leaders and prevents the bureaucracy from imposing its rule-bound procedures on political life in general. If such rigidity is to be avoided, then means must be found to allow charismatic leaders to rise to positions of power, 'to realize their personal political conceptions with the techniques of both a "positive" demagogy and efficient party machines' (ibid., p. 94). Only a parliamentary democracy with demagogues and party machines – the system called by Weber 'plebiscitary democracy' because the leader is elected by the party organization – can deal successfully both with the need for political innovation and the danger of bureaucratic torpor.

Weber criticized: the social world of moral emotivism

Weber's characterization of charisma, and of its political uses in democracies present and future, has been often criticized. It has been claimed that in his anxiety to employ charismatic leadership against bureaucratic lethargy Weber overlooked a basic distinction, that between beneficent and malevolent charisma. The fact that someone with the required abilities can persuade people in significant numbers to follow unreservedly his or her leadership does not make the outcome democratic. The charismatic leaders best known in our century have been avowedly anti-democratic, for much of their appeal has come from their success in identifying, and then attacking, suitable scapegoats. Once these foreign, and potentially critical, elements have been removed from the society, there is no need for true believers to consider the merits of rivals, and hence no need for democratic procedures designed to guarantee the existence of alternative candidates and policies. In defence of Weber it has been said that he thought bureaucratic 'stagnation and ossification the real dangers of his age, rather than charismatic breakthroughs', and that he did not foresee the rise of those combinations of charismatic leadership and bureaucratic techniques that we now call 'totalitarian regimes' (Mommsen, 1974, pp. 92–3). That Weber took administrative torpor to be the chief danger is certainly true. But his own reflections on the problem of succession – the 'routinization of charisma' – should have prepared him for the possibility that the accession to power of a charismatic leader could be followed by a process of administrative legalization of the new authority. Weber himself spoke of this process as 'the transformation of the charismatic mission into an office . . . of a bureaucratic character' (Weber, 1968, p. 251). Charisma and bureaucracy need not be contrasted, then, as complete innovation versus complete stagnation. There are degrees of each that can coexist and interact.

Because of his belief that all successful leaders require charismatic qualities, Weber also thought that the maintenance and steady performance of a law-governed bureaucracy demanded that high political offices be open to such people. They could devise novel aims whereas the bureaucrats could only administer the existing regulations. However, these claims do not seem to be true of any bureaucracy except Weber's highly artificial model. In actual bureaucratic systems the senior officers often suggest and design new policies for which they think they can obtain the approval of their political masters. The officers also alter and revise the plans sent to them by the ministers whom they serve, consider the administrative and financial feasibility of such proposals, and are often able either to promote, or to frustrate, the intentions of politicians. Sometimes the latter are the captives rather than the rulers of their administrative staff. Nor are all effective leaders charismatic ones. There are leaders in many fields, including politics, who succeed by cajolery, blackmail, bribery, exchange of favours, kindness, goodwill, appeals to self-interest or rational argument. These are not exceptional powers that command complete trust and devotion, but qualities and procedures that are often used to organize a substantial following for a new programme. So unless we are prepared to call every successful leader 'charismatic', it is not true to assert, as Weber does, that only someone with charismatic appeal can become a political leader in a bureaucratic society. Some political leaders, such as Coolidge and Truman in the United States, or Fraser in Australia, or Mulrooney in Canada, are elected because they appear to the voters to be quite ordinary people with familiar virtues and manageable vices. The appeal of such politicians often lies in their policies or parties rather than in their personalities.

Again, there is no evidence that political, social or economic innovation is confined to the programmes of charismatic leaders because of the resistance offered to it by bureaucracies. Many new goals have been set and achieved by non-charismatic prime ministers and presidents in North America, Europe, Australia and New Zealand. Clement Attlee, British prime minister from 1945 to 1951, presided over the nationalization of the iron and steel, coal, electricity and gas industries, the Bank of England, and the railways. His government also introduced the National Health Insurance Act. These were extraordinary political events but no one has ever thought that Attlee was a charismatic leader who forced through these changes against the opposition of a stagnant bureaucracy. In fact, the expansion of welfare services and the nationalization of industries were favoured by many bureaucrats because their numbers and powers were greatly increased. This effect was the very one that Weber had used earlier as an argument against the adoption of the socialist programme. Actually, much the clearest examples of anti-bureaucratic innovation are the various freedom of information acts now operating in many democratic countries. Although these statutes have been opposed by bureaucrats and hedged about with restrictions, it did not require charismatic leaders to introduce them. The statutes were introduced by quite ordinary politicians. Nor has the power of government bureaucracies been sufficient to have the acts repealed or rendered useless. In any case, the information made available by the acts has proven to be at least as dangerous to government politicians as to their bureaucratic staff. What such varied and unexpected outcomes show is that neither the politicians in power nor the government bureaucracies are able to predict with any accuracy the full results of their major innovations. Hence, generally speaking, it is a mistake for either group to stake a great deal on outcomes that are so uncertain; and it is a mistake of some sociologists to believe that members of these groups do not sometimes realize this. Bureaucracies do not always resist social change and charismatic leaders do not always seek it.

Weber, as we have seen, answers 'yes' to the question whether the path to high political office must be left open for charismatic personalities. His reason is that otherwise new goals and proposals cannot overcome bureaucratic opposition. But once we reject this unqualified answer, we can ask whether there are other, and better, formulations, or perhaps additional reasons. One reply that embraces both these queries is this: the problem of providing political opportunities for those gifted with charisma is no different from that of providing suitable careers for gifted people in general. Not to do for them what we can is to leave the society's chief resource unused and to embitter its possessors. The consequences of such reckless negligence are almost certain to threaten the future of the social system, for they amount to protecting the mediocre from competition by the talented. So the best reason for making high political office open to those gifted with charisma is not that only they can conquer bureaucratic hostility to change. It is that like other talented people the charismatic should be offered the chance to show what benefits they can contribute to social life. To fail to do so would endanger social stability by creating a pool of able but disaffected people; and it would ensure that desirable social change was left in the hands of those least capable of bringing it about.

Is charismatic leadership compatible, as Weber believed, with plebiscitary democracy – with democratic government based on mass elections? Weber thought so because he took a popularly supported government to be one that needs its demagogic leader to rely on the formal consent of the governed. Examples of such leaders, he said, were Gracchus, Cromwell, Robespierre and Napoleon. The willingness of charismatic leaders to resort to a plebiscite, and in later periods to work with a parliament, shows their confidence that they have the devotion, trust and support of the masses. Weber suggested that the consolidation of this power quite commonly leads to rational routinization: to efforts to form an efficient administrative staff, to the abolition of traditional privileges and powers. to material rewards for supporters by the improvement of economic activity, and to reorganization of the legal system (Weber, 1968, pp. 268–9). These changes, often desirable, need not take place, but they do so often enough for Weber to count them as common features of plebiscitary democracy. Nevertheless, there is an obvious conflict between the demagogue's personal support by the masses and the constitutional limits within which that support is supposed to be confined. How does the charismatic leader weigh the supporters' demands for rapid and radical change against constitutional requirements for just and careful procedures? Weber himself wrote that 'Every parliamentary democracy eagerly seeks to eliminate, as dangerous to parliament's power, the plebiscitary methods of leadership selection' (ibid., p. 1452). However, the alternative system was even worse. A democracy without a charismatic leader chosen by direct popular election would lead to rule by professional politicians who could offer no new policies, and leaderless democracy would rely on the government bureaucrats to a dangerous degree. This warning by Weber assumed that elected leaders would usually be charismatic figures, an assumption not borne out by experience any more than was the correlative assumption that leaders chosen by parliament would not be charismatic. In any event, charismatic dictators, not bureaucratic torpor, have proven to be the greatest threat to constitutional democracy during most of the twentieth century.

Weber's views on the role of bureaucracies in modern states have been attacked from a rather different quarter by Alasdair MacIntyre in his book *After Virtue* (1981, 2nd edn 1984). He begins by remarking that in ethics Weber was avowedly an emotivist, a person who believes that value-judgements simply express the attitudes and feelings of their supporters. No genuine appeal to 'impersonal criteria' is possible, for they do not exist: 'I may think that I so appeal and others may think that I so appeal, but these thoughts will always be mistakes. The sole reality of distinctively moral discourse is the attempt of one will to align the attitudes, feelings, preference and choices of another with its own. Others are always means, never ends' (MacIntyre, 1984, p. 24). The result is 'that emotivism entails the obliteration of any genuine distinction between manipulative and non-manipulative social relations' (ibid., p. 23). Successful bureaucratic power and bureaucratic authority are identical because all value-judgements are non-rational, and there is no rational method of choosing one rather than another. All are equally subjective so that moral debate is impossible. The only rational appeal, according to emotivism, is not to the differing value of ends but to the differing effectiveness of means. What justifies the existence of bureaucracy is simply its efficiency; what justifies the manipulation of the public by managerial bureaucrats is the effectiveness with which they carry out the government's policies. Hence if that effectiveness is an illusion, says MacIntyre, then so is the justification of bureaucratic systems (ibid., pp. 74–5).

There are two good reasons, according to MacIntyre, why claims to 'managerial expertise' in controlling social life are clearly false. The first reason is that there is no realm of 'morally neutral fact' in which the manager can use his expertise. All facts are states of affairs that are perceived or observed or identified by means of theoretical interpretations: that is, by the application of theory-laden concepts. In the case of the description and explanation of human action, these concepts include ineliminable reference to people's moral beliefs, intentions and emotions about their goals (ibid., pp. 77–84). The second reason is that the managerial expert, despite his pretensions, has no supply of dependable generalizations on which to base useful forecasts and explanations of organizational behaviour. Lacking both a realm of neutral facts and a set of reliable generalizations, the managerial project of a bureaucratically controlled society must be still-born (ibid., pp. 88–9). Moreover, studies of effective large organizations have shown that their 'need to allow for individual initiative, a flexible response to changes in knowledge, the multiplication of centres of problem-solving and decision-making', requires that they 'tolerate a high degree of unpredictability' within themselves. MacIntyre writes: 'Since organizational success and organizational predictability exclude one another, the project of creating a wholly or largely predictable organization committed to creating a wholly or largely predictable society is doomed and doomed by the facts about social life.' There is, and can be, then, no class of successful manipulative managers in control of an all-conquering bureaucratic machine. There is only the pretence of successful manipulation – of 'scientifically managed social control' – for our social system is not under anyone's control. 'No one is or could be in charge' (ibid., pp. 106–7).

However, these various criticisms of Weber, even if they were wholly correct, would tell against only a portion of his argument. They would show, at best, that the operation of bureaucracies was not technically superior to that of every competitor, and that it was false that if a bureaucracy stopped working, then chaos would occur because no other form of organization could be equally efficient. So MacIntyre's comments help only a little with the two problems that Weber thought were most pressing in this area: the stagnation of bureaucratic procedures in the life of large organizations; and the conflict between the bureaucratic specialization of labour and such qualities of individualism as moral independence, spontaneity and creativity The fact, if it is one, that manipulative managers and their techniques are not actually effective often makes these two problems worse. For lack of managerial control can produce mindless adherence by officials to familiar procedures, and thus increase organizational stagnation. This adherence will reduce the administrative risks taken by staff, reduce their exposure to external criticism, and of course also decrease their readiness to engage spontaneously in creative and independent work. Their effort to enlarge the area of predictable behaviour will, according to the view held by MacIntyre's sources, make the organization even less effective than when its managers claimed to be in control of it. Weber thought that it was the nature of bureaucracies to be engines of mechanical administration. If managers do not actually exert much influence on their operation, then Weber's description of bureaucratic 'routinization' is strongly supported by MacIntyre's conclusion. What it does not support – in fact opposes – is Weber's belief that bureaucracies are the most efficient kind of large organization.

But here we have to distinguish between different kinds of organizations, and hence the various sorts of tasks for which they are appropriate. Weber might well argue that the routine administrative tasks that his bureaucracies were devised to do could not be done better by a more creative and adventurous form of organization. Individual initiative, flexibility of response, the ability to solve problems and take difficult decisions are needed, Weber might say, only under certain conditions – conditions not met in the work of most bureaucracies. Therefore, to compare bureaucratic organizations with those of a very different type, such as entrepreneurial, research or investment companies, is simply a mistake. These organizations have widely different functions, and thus widely different features, that enable them to perform their distinctive kinds of work. For this reason MacIntyre's criticism of managerial pretensions, Weber might conclude, has little to contribute on the dangers, or advantages, of bureaucracies themselves.

From political philosophy to sociology

Since both Durkheim and Weber were sociologists, a considerable proportion of their discussion of issues in political philosophy was explicitly based on sociological conclusions. They believed, and asserted, that sociological procedure, and the information obtained by its use, could contribute directly to the description of various philosophical alternatives. Whether sociological information could, or should, do more than that – by providing a decisive reason for choosing a particular alternative – was, they thought, a different question. Durkheim believed that sociology could supply us with such value-judgements, whereas Weber claimed that it could not legitimately do so. That it could be done illegitimately – by smuggling disguised value-judgements into sociological propositions – Weber never denied. Nor did he ever deny that the history of European social thought was in large part a history of eminent thinkers who often mistook their own value-judgements for empirical discoveries concerning the operation of human societies. It was against the unacknowledged influence of this tendency that the creators of 'scientific' sociology rebelled.

One of the most prominent of these critics was Ferdinand Tönnies (1855–1936), the German scholar of Hobbes' thought, the chief expositor of the distinction between two kinds of society and behaviour, *Gemeinschaft* (community) and *Gesellschaft* (association), and the author of a wide variety of work, some theoretical, some empirical, on such topics as law, custom, morality, socialism and politics. Another sociologist and economist whose influence continues was his American contemporary, Thorstein Veblen (1857–1929), author not only of *The Theory of the Leisure Class* (1899) and *The Theory of Business Enterprise* (1904), but of the equally savage attack on a different aspect of commercial civilization in *The Higher Learning in America: A Memorandum on the Conduct of Universities by Business Men* (1918). For our purposes here, what two such different men have in common is a permanent interest in monitoring the process of commercialization and industrialization in their societies, ones that had recently been small, self-contained, traditional and rural. Both men paid much attention to the psychological and social problems created by this process of massive and rapid change; both men were representatives of a widespread concern in their societies about the effects of this change. In American universities there were, for many years, courses offered in rural as against urban sociology, and this was a distinction thought to hold between the two different forms of social life encapsulated by the two ideal types of *Gemeinschaft*, or community of face-to-face relationships, and *Gesellschaft*, or association of impersonal economic agents. No actual society, Tönnies emphasized, ever fully possessed all the features of either type, and as a social scientist he claimed no preference for one rather than the other. Veblen was less circumspect. Unwilling to favour the traditional community with its technological stagnation, Veblen also disliked the capitalist financial structure which supported the use of advanced technical processes. In consequence, he belaboured the practices of modern business and commerce without approving of the rural life offered by folk societies.

Tönnies and Veblen were merely two of the innumerable social commentators whose work, in the late nineteenth and early twentieth centuries, charted the urbanization of Western societies. It was these scholars and investigators who, in Western Europe and North America, recognized the importance of the economic, social and political transformation taking place in their midst. They included Le Play in France, the Webbs, Charles Booth and Hobhouse in Britain, Lester Ward and Albion Small in America. As a result of their work, they and many others discovered both a need to explain what was occurring and an opportunity to develop political beliefs and programmes that would be compatible with their sociological accounts. From that need and opportunity grew an interaction between social reformers and political activists, sociological investigators and political philosophers. The second pair provided intellectual support and justification for the first pair. In the case of Durkheim and Weber this support was openly maintained and acknowledged, for there was no reason to do otherwise. However, with the increasing professionalization of sociology and its conversion into a field of technical practice, with a great mass of information, there has developed the practice of political philosophers relying on sociology as a ready source of useful examples and empirically-based lessons. But since political philosophers are not usually sociologists and must borrow what they need of this material, it plays a subordinate, often merely illustrative, role in the course of their general arguments. When not simply used in that way, sociological propositions are commonly treated as inexplicit premises: that is, are taken as implicit assumptions or presuppositions in philosophical arguments.

In recent years considerable attention has been devoted to revealing and evaluating implicit assumptions. If we now examine their use in one of the most important controversies of recent years, that on the nature of community, we can introduce a set of interrelated issues that are the modern descendants of Tönnies' concern with *Gemeinschaft* and *Gesellschaft*, and of Durkheim's with his corresponding pair of ideal types, societies with mechanical solidarity and those with organic solidarity. These issues are, first, the problem of irreducibly social goods; second, the value-neutrality of the liberal state; third, natural sociability and the sense of community; fourth, the connection between that sociability and political liberalism; and, finally, the interaction between tendencies and values. Although all of them are connected with the others, we can conveniently consider each of them in the order just given.

Irreducibly social goods

According to Charles Taylor, the question at issue concerning irreducibly social goods is whether the states of affairs that people find satisfying – those states that they find good – are found good only because they satisfy individual agents. That is, are there sources of group satisfactions, so-called public goods, that are necessarily not reducible or decomposable into the sources of the satisfactions given to individual people? Taylor believes that there are non-reducible sources and he attacks methodological individualism for denying their existence (Taylor, 1990, p. 47). He takes methodological individualism to be the view that since societies are simply groups of interacting individual people, 'the events and states which are the subject of study in society are ultimately made up of events and states of the component individuals. In the end, only individuals choose and act.' It is they who by their thoughts and actions produce laws, customs, rules, offices and institutions. Hence to understand the nature of a society we need, in the end, only to understand the acts and thoughts of its individual members. Within the society there are no additional and independent sources of collective features and group properties – features and properties that require explanation (Taylor, 1990, pp. 47–8).

Taylor argues, or at least asserts, that methodological individualism is mistaken because it completely neglects the existence in every society of background beliefs and practices. These are presupposed, for example, as norms in the utterance of every individual act of speech. Without our knowledge of such norms the individual speaker's utterance cannot be understood by us. Of course, over time modifications in these speech-acts change the background norms, and the latter in turn influence the former. Both are necessary, for they exemplify 'the ongoing interchanges of our social life'. The same kind of process occurs in every sector of social life. Background practice cannot be reduced to the thoughts and actions of individual people, Taylor says, because practices, customs, institutions and ways of living within a particular society are based on the common understanding of its members. The common understanding is a feature that belongs to the entire society and not simply to individual members. For although they create and maintain that common understanding, it is not a mere 'compound of individual states'. It is a new property of the group as a whole (Taylor, 1990, pp. 51–4; 1985, II, pp. 45–6).

The irreducibility of background understanding provides us with Taylor's explanation of why we must agree that there are irreducibly social goods. There are, he says, two ways of identifying them. The first requires us to realize that the experiences, outcomes and works of art that we cherish are valuable only 'because of the background understanding which has developed in our culture'. In the absence of this understanding our evaluations will be very different. So if we wish 'to maximize these goods', then we 'must want to preserve and strengthen' the culture that is necessary to their existence – a culture that is an irreducible property of the whole society. The second method of identification is to notice that some good things, such as friendship or love or equality, require the participants to have a common understanding that they do in fact value these things. Thus the relationship of love needs the lovers' recognition that they cherish the relationship in common. This common recognition is not reducible, Taylor concludes, to any kind of recognition by the lovers separately, or to the understanding produced by adding together their separate responses (Taylor, 1990, pp. 54–7). The importance of this point, and hence of the irreducibility of social goods in general, is that as long as we believe that all goods must be individual goods we exclude all genuine social goods from consideration. In discussing the question of which things are good we simply ignore the whole class of irreducibly social goods and ignore, also, the problem of determining their value in the production of human welfare (ibid., p. 63).

Most of Taylor's claims have not lacked for critics. His main thesis, that on irreducibility, has been under detailed attack for the many errors that it is said to include, and thus for leaving its targets unaffected. According to Robert Goodin (1990, p. 64), a basic, although preliminary, error arises from Taylor 'seemingly forgetting that what is "intrinsically good" is good by reason of something intrinsic to its *own* nature, not by reason of any facts about the society in which it is set'. What, then, remains of the irreducibly *social* value of the goods whose character is at issue? For the claim that Taylor disputes is that the value of those social goods 'is decomposable into the value derived from them by the individuals constituting the collectivity' – that is, that the value of the social goods cannot be given an exhaustive analysis in terms of their value to each person in the group (Goodin, 1990, p. 68). Yet Taylor gives us no reason, says Goodin, to accept this view. All Taylor's examples – speech-acts, background norms and culture, social institutions and the common understanding embodied in personal relations – are irreducibly social only in being impossible to produce and use outside a society. They can take place only within a group of interacting members who create and maintain them. But this truth does nothing to show that once they exist their value is not simply their value for the individual members of the group, but arises from a new property of the group itself; and it is this claim that Taylor has failed to establish. In any case, what difference would it make in practice if there were goods of irreducibly social value? Very little, Goodin replies. They would simply become part of the class of ordinary public or social goods such as highways, dams, parks, friendship and voting. All these are products of social procedures and not of isolated private agents. The benefits to society of goods with irreducible value would be no different from the benefits arising from goods of reducible value. The method of calculating those benefits would be the same in both cases. Only their sources would differ (Goodin, 1990, pp. 73–6). The method of calculation, as John Broome has emphasized, would require that social goods such as culture and friendship be of benefit to at least some of the individual participants. Otherwise there would not be much point in having those goods. But if that is so, then their value is not irreducibly social (Broome, 1990, pp. 84–5).

Taylor's thesis about social goods embodies the sociological assumption that human social life exhibits emergent group properties that have been largely unrecognized as such, and hence unvalued. The counter-argument has been that while lack of recognition may be true of some properties of groups – equality and respect, for example – nothing about their value follows from the mere existence of such properties. In particular, nothing follows concerning the reducibility of their value to the value obtained from the properties of non-social goods. This is to claim that Taylor's sociological assumption does not have the philosophical consequences that he took it to have. One of those supposed consequences is that methodological individualism is correct, and that the only way we have of identifying social goods and making sure of their existence is by first doing so for the individual goods to which they are reducible. However, not only is the reduction of goods a different problem from that of the reduction of their value, but the existence of group properties does not entail either the correctness or falsity of methodological individualism – does not tell us how those group properties should be analysed. What discussion of Taylor's thesis does reveal is that some goods usually treated as individual and private are in fact dependent, either causally or logically, upon a social context.

Natural sociability and community: Sandel on Rawls

There are many familiar sociological assumptions and generalizations embedded in the problems characteristic of political philosophy. Some of these assumptions are of interest only because the process of their dismissal helps to clarify the state of discussion. If Taylor's critics are correct, that is the chief contribution of his advocacy of the existence of irreducibly social goods. Some sociological examples, however, are so common and well-entrenched that their removal would produce grave disorder in the political theories that they support. One case of this type arises from the notion of 'liberal neutrality' that John Rawls makes use of in *A Theory of Justice* (1971), Liberal neutrality is 'the view that the state should not reward or penalize particular conceptions of the good life but, rather, should provide a neutral framework within which different and potentially conflicting conceptions of the good can be pursued' (Kymlicka, 1989, p. 883). The question then becomes 'What counts as neutrality and how is it to be exercised?' For the state can either attempt to equalize the material and intellectual resources of the competing parties or it can try to remain aloof from their debates. Both policies have been objected to on the ground that social conditions and causes are always present. In the words of Michael Sandel, 'liberalism is wrong because neutrality is impossible', for 'try as we might we can never wholly escape the effects of our conditioning. All political orders thus embody *some* values; the question is *whose* values prevail, and who gains and loses as a result' (Sandel, 1982, p. 11).

This objection to the neutrality of the state is oddly misdirected. What the liberals such as Rawls have advocated is that the state provide a 'neutral framework' within which competing advocates can plead their cases. Whether the institutional framework provides a neutral arena has nothing to do with the various conditioning processes that the advocates have undergone. The claim that the framework must 'embody *some* values' and political views is undisputed. Otherwise it could be neither neutral towards the participants – since neutrality is itself a policy that embodies certain values – nor an institution dependent for its maintenance upon a political view of a specific kind. Nevertheless, the fact that neutrality incorporates some of the values and beliefs that have brought it into existence hardly shows that neutrality is impossible. To be neutral is to be non-aligned and unengaged only under certain conditions, and only concerning specifiable claims, people or attitudes. Thus a referee, umpire or field judge, if reliable, is neutral only with respect to the application of the rules relevant to the contenders within a particular sphere of authority. As long as a referee is impartial in demanding adherence to the appropriate rules within that sphere the referee's background is irrelevant. Similarly, an institutional framework that sets, and enforces, the same rules for all participants is neutral towards them whatever its history and whatever the values and beliefs of its creators. Their sympathies and preferences may incline them towards one contender, but as long as these are not expressed in partiality of rules and their administration, neutrality can be preserved.

Supporters of the opposing view must solve some intractable problems. The first of these is for the state authorities to find a technique for ranking, in the state's order of preference, various conceptions of the good life. It is not clear how this is to be done or what part agreement by the public is to have in the process. Unless public agreement is obtained by some morally acceptable means, liberalism will have been rejected in favour of authoritarianism; and if conceptions are not identified and ranked, nothing will have been gained over a policy of neutrality. After the favoured conceptions are identified, there is the subsequent problem of influencing the public to adopt them because they are the best, and not for some other reason such as fear of penalties or hope of material reward. We owe both these observations to Will Kymlicka (1989, p. 902, fn) Moreover, what happens to the remaining conceptions of the good life that may be clung to by subordinate minorities? Are they to be required, on pain of punishment, to justify their preferred ways of living? If so, we need to be told what kinds of reason will be acceptable parts of a justification.

Underlying this debate on liberal neutrality is another and more general one. It concerns the natural sociability of human beings, and hence the extent to which political institutions proper, as distinct from merely social ones, are needed in order to ensure that people join together in their search for a good life. Kymlicka puts the controversy in this way:

It is commonly alleged that liberals fail to recognize that people are naturally social or communal beings. Liberals supposedly think that society rests on an artificial social contract, and that a coercive state apparatus is needed to keep naturally asocial people together in society. But there is a sense in which the opposite is true – liberals believe that people naturally form and join social relations and forums in which they come to understand and pursue the good. The state is not needed to provide that communal context and is likely to distort the normal processes of collective deliberations and cultural development. It is communitarians who seem to think that individuals will drift into anomic and detached isolation without the state actively bringing them together to collectively evaluate and pursue the good. (Kymlicka, 1989, p. 904)

The question at issue here concerning the natural sociability of people is obviously not specific enough for it to be given a useful answer. People are 'naturally social or communal beings' in that children require adults to rear them, and most adults require at least one partner, whether permanent or a member of a series. For much of the year, hunting and gathering groups often consisted of only one extended family. Many of these groups had no political organization, although during certain seasons they met in larger numbers for ceremonial and other social purposes. To that extent human beings are naturally sociable. For long periods of human history there were neither political organizations nor states, and the latter were far outnumbered by stateless societies. Does this show that without the efforts of a 'coercive state apparatus' human beings 'will drift into anomic and detached isolation'? Or that unless forced to by the state, people will not take part in collective discussions? All available evidence is against these views. On the other hand, similar evidence tells against the claim that people, unless prevented, will naturally form large groups and even larger political organizations. Whether they do so will depend on needs recognized by them and on propitious circumstances of time and place. The natural sociability of people is an empirical issue and subject, therefore, to the qualifications and restrictions necessary for it to be a testable view. In the form given to the issue by the liberals and communitarians in Kymlicka's report the issue has no clear answer. From such an assumption not much that is reliable or worth using can follow.

There is a natural extension of the debate on the natural sociability of people, an extension that Sandel develops in order to criticize one of Rawls' sociological assumptions in his theory of justice. The assumption is about Rawls' conception of the individual person or self, and thus about his notion of community. According to Sandel, the Rawlsian self is described in such a way as to make it impervious to any change in its own notion of the good life: in its plans, purposes, commitments, or in its attitudes and values, such as new forms of self-understanding. The characteristics, and hence identity, of this kind of self or person are permanently fixed and are unaffected by later experience. One result is to rule out all possibility of 'a plurality of selves within a single, individual human being, as when we account for inner deliberation in terms of the pull of competing identities'. It is to assume 'that every individual consists of one and only one system of desires', and that there is no serious problem of alternating, confused, or conflicting desires within one individual – to assume that one person never has, for certain periods and purposes, a number of selves (Sandel, 1982, pp. 62–3). Rawls' conception of the self also rules out, says Sandel, the possible effect of multiple selves on the sense of community held by its members. Their aims do not, for Rawls, affect their sense of community. He does not treat that sense as a constituent element of a good society, but as a merely contingent property both of it and of the members' own identity (ibid., p. 64).

This conclusion, Sandel argues, should be rejected for two reasons. The first is that people's sense of community is in fact a constituent part of their identity and of a good society. The second is that in writing about social union, Rawls himself accepts this view, and thus contradicts his previous assumption of the existence of changeless independent agents. Sandel notes that Rawls has written, for example, that 'The social nature of mankind is best seen by contrast with the conception of private society. Thus human beings have in fact shared ends and they value their common institutions and activities as good in themselves' Rawls, 1971, p. 522). Rawls has also written:

it is through social union founded upon the needs and potentialities of its members that each person can participate in the sum total of the realized natural assets of the others. We are led to the notion of the community of humankind the members of which enjoy one another's excellences and individuality elicited by free institutions, and they recognize the good of each as an element in the complete activity the whole scheme of which is consented to and gives pleasure to all. (Rawls, 1971, p. 523)

The contributions made by any individual member of a group, association, company, club, or some other kind of social union, become part of the collective action of a still larger community that is a 'social union of social unions'. In a truly just society everyone's private activity becomes 'a plan within a plan, this superordinate plan being realized in the public institutions of society. But this larger plan does not establish a dominant end, such as that of religious unity . . . to which the aims of all individuals and associations are subordinate.' Instead, says Rawls, the superordinate plan is a 'just constitutional order' that supplies a 'framework' of principles within which individuals and smaller social unions can flourish (ibid., p. 528)

Let us begin with Sandel's second criticism of Rawls – that Rawls' later view of the self contradicts his earlier one. This criticism has been answered by Chandran Kukathas and Philip Pettit in the following way. According to Sandel, it is a mistake for Rawls to claim that the independent agents that he describes have no special moral values or social policies; and that therefore Rawls is also mistaken in believing that the principles of justice these agents produce in their considerations are uninfluenced by particular values and policies. However, this complaint is misguided. By the time that Sandel made it, Rawls had already agreed in his Dewey lectures (1980) that his aim was 'not to supply a universal standard of justice but to discover those moral principles which might best serve his own society, with all its particular concerns. The starting point of this philosophical inquiry is . . . the prevailing moral beliefs and intuitions of modern liberal democratic societies.' Rawls' goal is not to 'construct the good society from scratch', but to refine and systematize 'the moral principles of his own society' (Kukathas and Pettit, 1990, pp. 107, 115). Hence, there was never any assumption by Rawls of the existence of changeless independent agents who formulated universal principles of justice. So in writing later of the social nature of people, Rawls did not contradict himself. That social nature was never excluded by his original description.

Sandel's other criticism of Rawls, that concerning his treatment of people's sense of community, has also been attacked by Kukathas and Pettit. It is an exaggeration, they say, for Sandel to claim that a sense of community must be a constituent part of a person's identity, or that a person's identity is provided entirely by the social context. At most, the self is 'only partly constituted by its context and its goals or ends, and is quite capable of participating in the determination of its identity'. It can choose which of the possible goals it will try to reach. Thus Arthur, ignorant of his ancestry and reared by a foster-father, was identified as a villager whose father was Ector. When Arthur learned that he was King of the Britons he was forced to choose between two ways of life, between two different identities. The fact that he could choose to change indicates that 'a self constituted by its ends can nonetheless be reconstituted'. Clearly, there is much more to a person's self than is provided by the social context (Kukathas and Pettit, 1990, p. 108). To these remarks we can add that for all Sandel's argument shows, a person's sense of community can be a merely contingent property of the person's identity and not an indispensable part of it. To identify with a community, and to be identified by having a role in it, need not be a permanent feature of a person's self. Moreover, if a person can have different selves for different purposes and periods, as Sandel claims, then he or she can also have different senses of community at different times or even at the same time. So for a sense of community to be a constituent element of a person's identity amounts, in the end, to a property that is not very dissimilar to a contingent one.

Communitarian arguments against liberalism

We have been observing that one of the basic complaints made of liberal thought by communitarians is that it takes people to be independent agents who need not rely on the social context for the development and support of their capacities. Liberal theory, then, emphasizes individual rights at the expense of the claims of society, and does so because it neglects the traditions, practices and roles that actually form the character of the individual. This mistake is important because social identity, including the inheritance of traditions, practices and obligations, strongly affects people's conception of the good life and thus of the political policies and actions needed to realize it. However, this comment has little force unless a person's social identity or social role – Australian middle-class business executive of Protestant Scotch-Irish ancestry, for example – allows us to identify the goal towards which the person is directing his or her efforts. Otherwise, we have no grounds for asserting that someone's social role or identity exerts a strong influence on the ends that person pursues. Yet it is obvious that most contemporary social roles carry a number of aims, and so the roles do not allow us to infer from each of them one desirable end that the agent is pursuing. In addition, as Amy Gutmann points out, 'Even if there is a single good attached to some social roles (as caring for the sick is to the role of a nurse . . . let us suppose), we cannot accurately say that our roles determine our good without adding that we often choose our roles because of the good that is attached to them' (Gutmann, 1985, p. 316).

It is easy to slide from emphasizing the importance to people of a sense of social community to emphasizing the need for people to have a sense of political community. This transition has been made, either wittingly or unwittingly, by some advocates of communitarianism. There are three communitarian theses that Allen Buchanan has suggested should be kept distinct. One is that 'community is a fundamental human good' in which commitments and values are shared by members of a group. Another is that for all people a good life must include 'participation in a political community'. The third is that the good life requires 'communal participation' in a political organization of the widest scope, such as the nation-state. Buchanan thinks that the first thesis is 'relatively uncontroversial', the second 'more controversial, but still rather plausible', and the third bold, unsupported, and perhaps unsupportable (Buchanan, 1989, p. 859). Although Buchanan takes the first thesis to be common ground for the communitarians and the liberals, it is not clear whether a small isolated band of a few families is to count, for this purpose, as a community. If it is, the question arises as to what communitarian benefits the band supplies that a family lacks. If the band is not to count, the question becomes 'why not?' What community benefits do neighbourhood associations such as tennis clubs, children's nurseries, rural firefighters and village councils offer that hunting and gathering bands cannot provide to their members? Similar questions arise from the second thesis. According to it, the best life demands abilities that can only be developed by our exercising authority over our equals who, in their turn, come to have authority over us. Yet even if we manage to single out those abilities, what reason have we to believe that they can be acquired only in that way? Not only are there leaderless groups that operate successfully by consensus alone, but the desirable abilities that they use and encourage do not seem to be very different from those developed by participation in hierarchical groups. Responsibility for other people, for example, is different from having authority over them. Nevertheless, much the same set of abilities may be called for in the two cases.

The third thesis is an extreme version of the second, and thus even less plausible. Buchanan believes that unless participation in political organizations of wide scope is supported by some theory of objective good, the third thesis is 'sheer dogmatism'. The communitarians, he says, have still to produce such a theory. However, the thesis must also be in part a sociological claim concerning the growth of specific abilities under specific conditions. It then requires a separate argument of a philosophical kind to show that those abilities are demanded by the best life for human beings. Since sociological claims are subject to test by evidence, it is worth asking which are the abilities that are developed only by participation in political communities of a large scale. It is also worth asking how we can establish the truth of the assertion that political participation of this kind develops these abilities. Neither question seems to have an obvious answer. The first question asks us to distinguish between the abilities produced in large as against small scale communities. But how are such differences, if they exist, supposed to bear on communitarian aims? Can the best life only be lived in a modern nation-state – or better yet, in a superpower? Do their traditions, practices and social roles offer such a superior array of communitarian benefits, and so few disadvantages, that smaller political communities cannot compete? If responding to the claims of the nation-state is the most effective way of restoring our lost sense of community, then it is clear that restoration is a potentially hazardous procedure, which may terminate in an unwanted goal, that of the totalitarian society. Of course, until we know which abilities are to be developed or restored, we cannot say how the existence of those processes is to be established. Hence in its present state the third thesis, like the other two, neither clarifies nor advances the communitarian argument to any useful degree.

One response to the communitarian complaint about the liberal emphasis on individual rather than group rights is to argue, as Buchanan does, that communities are strengthened, and the sense of community fostered, by the enforcement of individual rights. For political liberalism, participation in group activity, he suggests, can be an indispensable element of a good life (Buchanan, 1989, p. 858). Buchanan gives four reasons why strengthening the rights of the individual also strengthens communal life. Because these reasons are sociological generalizations, they illustrate how arguments in political philosophy rely upon, and are thus intertwined with, the truth of empirical propositions. The first reason is this:

individual rights to freedom of religion, thought, expression, and association facilitate rational, nonviolent change in existing communities as well as the rational, nonviolent formation of new communities. Individual rights do this by allowing individuals who are dissatisfied with current forms of community to advocate and to try to develop alternatives even when the majority of their fellow members (or the official leaders of the community) do not share their views.

Buchanan adds that if these rights belonged to groups instead of to individuals – a change advocated by some communitarians – the rights would not protect individuals or minorities who tried to organize new communities or to alter existing ones. The individuals and minorities would have no right to association except as voting members of the established community (ibid., p. 862)

The second reason is that individual rights permit cheaper, easier and readier appeals in defence of the community. In order for an appeal to be lodged, only one person's rights need to be infringed. Violation of a group right, on the other hand, would have to be met by a group response which might well be cumbersome to organize (ibid., p. 863). In any event, the mistreatment given one member might not arouse the remainder of the group to collective action if it were troublesome to initiate, or if the member was unimportant and perhaps disliked. Similarly, the third and fourth reasons concern the difficulties of exercising a group right as compared to the simplicity of maintaining an individual one. With the former, there is the likelihood of conflict of interest between ordinary members and a hierarchy of administrators who may have their own reasons for either not exercising the right when asked to do so or for exercising it to their own advantage. The fourth reason is that an individual holder of a right controls its exercise and is not dependent upon the decision of anyone else. There is no benefit to the general community in having unnecessary delegation of this power (ibid., p. 863). All four reasons assert that assigning rights to individuals strengthens rather than weakens communal life. Since this assertion is open to evidence and testing, it would be reasonable to expect some investigation to have been made into the truth of the four claims. But it is not obvious that any inquiry has been thought appropriate. Is it true, for instance, that 'individual rights to freedom of religion, thought, expression, and association facilitate rational, non-violent change' by allowing the dissatisfied to develop without hindrance alternative forms of communal life? If it is true, does this process strengthen the original community? Neither claim need go unchallenged. Change without hindrance will be non-violent by definition, but must it be rational? Splinter groups often arise for strange causes, and leave the parent body for motives, such as ambition and greed, irrelevant to the general aims of any of the participating groups. Sometimes the effect is to weaken the parent body whereas the use of preventive force may preserve it. Depending on the circumstances prevailing at the time, unhindered change by the dissatisfied may or may not enhance the other members' sense of community.

There is more than one reason, communitarian critics of liberalism have argued, why liberals undervalue the fundamental importance of social and political community in the good life. But one common reason is that liberals hold too shallow a view of what genuine community requires. Sandel writes:

to ask whether a particular society is a community is not simply to ask whether a large number of its members happen to have among their various desires the desire to associate with others or to promote communitarian aims – although this may be one feature of a community – but whether the society is itself a society of a certain kind, ordered in a certain way, such that community describes its basic structure and not merely the dispositions of persons within the structure. For a society to be a community in this strong sense, community must be constitutive of the shared self-understandings of the participants and embodied in their institutional arrangements, not simply an attribute of certain of the participants' plans of life. (Sandel, 1982, p. 173)

On this view, members of a genuine community have common values and goals that belong to the group as a whole and are not merely the joint outcome of parallel private activity. Some examples are families, clans and other kin groups, hunting bands and hamlets. They are to be contrasted with single-purpose associations, economic units and multi-cultural assemblages, none of which embodies in its institutions the sense of a shared form of living. The liberals, because they believe in a neutral framework for a society's pursuit of a good life, are unable to appreciate this contrast between genuine communities and mere associations.

Now the point of reverting to this claim once again is that it reveals how completely the communitarian thesis, when applied on any given occasion, relies upon the truth of a sociological proposition, namely that a particular society has basic institutional arrangements of a collectivist kind. Without them, that society is not to be classified as a community. The procedure for determining whether they are present can only be empirical investigation. So what sociology contributes to this discussion is a means of discovering whether there are existing instances to which the phrase 'genuine community' can be properly applied. If there are not, the communitarians, given their enthusiasm for community, can be invited to explain the absence of examples. This question of the existence of genuine communities is of some importance to the communitarian argument. For as Buchanan puts it, 'The claim that community is a fundamental good for human beings may be understood in two ways, either as a descriptive psychological generalization that human beings strongly desire community, or at least find it deeply satisfying or fulfilling when they achieve it, or as a normative claim that community is an important objective good for human beings. Communitarians are often unclear as to whether they are advancing the psychological thesis, the normative thesis, or both' (Buchanan, 1989, p. 857).

We are concerned here only with the psychological interpretation, and since its truth is a matter of evidence the existence of genuine communities can be used as a confirmatory fact. Anyone who disputed the psychological interpretation would have to account for the existence of these communities in some other, and more plausible, manner. If there were no such communities, the explanation of their absence would also have to tell us what other reasons there are for believing that people in general strongly desire to join and maintain them – that is, for believing in the psychological interpretation.

Tendency statements and value-judgements

Whatever value we place on community life and people's desire for it, there are, in-escapably, other values and goals with which that desire must compete. When we give reasons for choosing one political policy or programme, or for making one value-judgement, rather than another, some of those reasons – but only some – commonly refer to matters that are subject to empirical investigation. Often these are matters of presumed fact about individual events, but more often they are generalizations about human social behaviour. For example, Gutmann quotes Sandel to the effect that 'communitarians would be more likely than liberals to allow a town to ban porno-graphic bookstores, on the grounds that pornography offends its way of life and the values that sustain it'. Sandel's reply to the liberal view, the view 'that such a policy opens the door to intolerance in the name of communal standards, is that "intolerance flourishes most where forms of life are dislocated, roots unsettled, traditions undone"' (Gutmann, 1985, p. 318), But this generalization, Gutmann then argues, has no basis in history. The Salem Puritans of the seventeenth century were intolerant enough to hunt witches; the American Moral Majority of this century hunts down homosexuals. Gutmann obviously believes that neither the Puritans nor the Moral Majority is a group with dislocated roots and undone traditions; but, nevertheless, they are groups, she thinks, in which intolerance has flourished (Gutmann, 1985, p. 319). From this point the argument might proceed in various directions: Sandel could revise his generalization so that it included apparent threats to a community's way of life, and Gutmann could then challenge Sandel to frame a criterion for distinguish-ing between apparent and genuine threats; or Gutmann could ask why every form of social life should be protected against threats to its moral standards unless other, and more serious, social damage was likely. At each step there might well be empirical considerations even though the original generalization was no longer held. The inter-play between these attempts to describe people's actual behaviour and the attempts to describe how they ought to behave could continue throughout the discussion.

However, arising from such exchanges is a common observation: that there appear to be no true lawlike statements concerning social life, only false ones, and that there-fore no reliance can be placed on them for the purposes of political philosophy. On the other hand, social generalizations of some kind seem to be indispensable in political debates if we are to learn from experience and prepare for the future. How is this con-flict to be resolved? A favourite solution is to begin by identifying the reasons why there do not appear to be, and in fact are not, any laws of social behaviour. MacIn-tyre, for instance, identifies four sources of difficulty: (1) necessarily unpredictable inventions, discoveries and innovations; (2) the unpredictable effect of an agent's own unpredictable future actions upon those of other agents; (3) the need of agents to withhold information from other agents; and (4) accidents and chance events. All four conditions operate strongly against successful generalization. There are, how-ever, countervailing factors, and MacIntyre lists four of these. The first is the regularity of our social practices, a regularity that arises from our need to arrange and co-ordi-nate our social activities. The second is the statistical regularities that appear as un-intended consequences of social life. The third and fourth factors are the genuine causal regularities of nature and society respectively (MacIntyre, 1984, pp. 93–103). The latter differ from genuine laws in being true only of specific times and places, and thus in being culture-bound. The former can be genuine laws but they are laws of nature, not of society. The effect of all these conflicting factors is to make social generalizations into tendency statements that admit of a steady stream of counter-examples. This weakens the usefulness of the generalizations without destroying it.

To rely on a tendency statement in an argument is to believe that the statement will be true in many, or perhaps most, instances yet capable of being false in any given case. Conversely, to ban pornographic bookstores in a particular town because they offend its way of life is not necessarily to believe in a tendency statement – to believe that most other towns will find them offensive. For there may be conditions believed to be peculiar to the town in question that make banning appropriate. But when a statement of a social tendency is knowingly relied upon, its mere public expression may help to generate counter-examples to itself. A burglar may learn that most burglaries in his area take place in mid-morning and that the police patrols at that period have been increased. It is then possible for the burglar, and others like him, to change their hours of work; and thus for the change in police surveillance to produce so many counter-examples to the original tendency statement that it will no longer be true. Hence in political arguments to rely on statements of social tendencies is both essential, for commonly there is nothing better available, and fraught with risk – the risk that making them public will make today's tendencies obsolete tomorrow. Of course, innumerable other factors can alter a social tendency. The simplest of them is a change in belief. The tendency for hospital staff to avoid physical contact, when feasible, with patients who are HIV positive would probably change if the staff came to believe that they were in no danger of contracting AIDS as a result of non-sexual contact.

In political philosophy, many changes in tendency statements are produced by the changes of belief that are expressed in alterations to value-judgements and political theories. If a prominent Catholic churchman announces his conversion to Islam, or a senior communist official embraces Western democracy, or a leading communitarian becomes a liberal, various tendencies may be transformed, or perhaps vanish. The strong tendency of Catholics, communists and communitarians to attend to, agree with and give support to, their remaining representatives may be greatly weakened and schisms may develop; the tendency of the public to take the three movements seriously may be affected; and the tendency of the leaders of similar organizations to remain loyal may change. When social tendencies alter in this way as a result of people modifying their value-judgements and the political policies based on them, the arguments in which the truth of the relevant tendency statements is relied upon must also change. Sometimes merely stating in public an argument in which the existence of some tendency is relied upon is sufficient to begin the process of changing it. For example, a legislator might argue in a parliamentary bill that because of the tendency of many people to drive on public roads when drunk, there should be mandatory confiscation of the vehicles whose drivers are found guilty of that offence. It might then turn out that in those circumstances the bare threat to pass such a bill was enough to reduce the amount of drunken driving. We should not forget, of course, that the process of modification is reciprocal: that the discovery of tendencies often changes our value-judgements. In learning that a tendency to neglect children is both common and harmful in its effects, we may be moved to judge its perpetrators more harshly than before. In turn, this judgement may help to change the tendency. Thus the sociologists' contribution to political philosophy is reciprocated by the political philosophers' contribution to sociology; and in this fashion the constant influence of each field upon the other can continue indefinitely.

See also 2 CONTINENTAL PHILOSOPHY; 3 HISTORY; 5 ECONOMICS; 6 POLITICAL SCIENCE; 7 LEGAL STUDIES; 9 CONSERVATISM; 11 LIBERALISM; 12 MARXISM; 13 SOCIALISM; 14 AUTONOMY; 15 COMMUNITY; 17 CONSTITUTIONALISM AND THE RULE OF LAW; 18 CORPORATISM AND SYNDICALISM; 22 DISTRIBUTIVE JUS-TICE; 23 EFFICIENCY; 28 LEGITIMACY; 30 POWER; 34 SECESSION AND NATIONALISM; 35 SOCIO-BIOLOGY; 36 STATE; 37 TOLERATION AND FUNDAMENTALISM; 38 TOTALITARIANISM; 39 TRUST; 40 VIRTUE

References

Brennan, G. and Walsh, C., eds: *Rationality, Individualism and Public Policy* (Canberra: Australian National University, 1990).

Broome, J.: 'Irreducibly social goods – comment II', in *Rationality, Individualism and Public Policy*, ed. G. Brennan and C. Walsh (Canberra: Australian National University, 1990).

Buchanan, A.: 'Assessing the communitarian critique of liberalism', *Ethics*, 99 (1989), 852–82.

Durkheim, E.: *The Division of Labor in Society* (1893), trans. George Simpson (New York: Free Press, 1964).

——: *Sociology and Philosophy* (1924), trans. D. F. Pocock (New York: Free Press, 1974).

——: *Professional Ethics and Civic Morals* (1950), trans. Cornelia Brookfield (Westport, Conn.: Greenwood Press, 1983).

Giddens, A.: *Capitalism and Modern Social Theory* (Cambridge: Cambridge University Press, 1971).

Goodin, R. E.: 'Irreducibly social goods – comment I', in *Rationality, Individualism and Public Policy*, ed. G. Brennan and C. Walsh (Canberra: Australian National University, 1990).

Gutmann, A.: 'Communitarian critics of liberalism', *Philosophy and Public Affairs*, 14 (1985), 308–22.

Kukathas, C. and Pettit, P.: *Rawls* (Cambridge: Polity Press, 1990).

Kymlicka, W.: 'Liberal individualism and liberal neutrality', *Ethics*, 99 (1989), 883–905.

Lukes, S.: *Emile Durkheim, His Life and Work* (Harmondsworth: Penguin Books, 1975).

MacIntyre, A.: *After Virtue*, 2nd edn (Notre Dame, Ind.: University of Notre Dame Press, 1984).

Mommsen, W. J.: *The Age of Bureaucracy* (Oxford: Basil Blackwell, 1974).

Rawls, J.: *A Theory of Justice* (Cambridge, Mass.: Harvard University Press, 1971).

——: 'Kantian constructivism in moral theory', *The Journal of Philosophy*, 88 (1980), 515–72.

Runciman, W. G.: *A Critique of Max Weber's Philosophy of Social Science* (Cambridge: Cambridge University Press, 1972).

Saint-Simon, H.: *Selected Writings*, trans. and ed. Keith Taylor (London: Croom Helm, 1975).

Sandel, M.: *Liberalism and the Limits of Justice* (Cambridge: Cambridge University Press, 1982).

Taylor, C.: *Philosophical Papers*, 2 vols (Cambridge: Cambridge University Press, 1985).

——: 'Irreducibly social goods', in *Rationality, Individualism and Public Policy*, ed. G. Brennan and C. Walsh (Canberra: Australian National University, 1990).

Tönnies, F.: *Gemeinschaft und Gesellschaft* (1887); translated as *Community and Association*, trans. C. P. Loomis (London: Routledge & Kegan Paul, 1955).

Veblen, T.: *The Theory of the Leisure Class* (1899), reprint (London: Unwin Books, 1970).

————: *The Theory of Business Enterprise* (1904), reprint (New Brunswick, NJ: Transaction Books, 1978).

————: *The Higher Learning in America* (1918), reprint (New York: Viking Press, 1935).

Weber, M.: *The Methodology of the Social Sciences*, trans. E. A. Shills and H. A. Finch (New York: Free Press, 1949).

————: *Economy and Society*, eds G. Roth and C. Wittich, 3 vols (New York: Bedminster Press, 1968).

Further reading

Bernstein, R. J.: 'One step forward, two steps backward', *Political Theory*, 15 (1987), 538–63.

Broome, J.: *Weighing Goods* (Oxford: Basil Blackwell, 1991).

Champlin, T. S.: 'Tendencies', *Proceedings of the Aristotelian Society*, 90 (1990–1), 119–33.

Collini, S.: *Liberalism and Sociology* (Cambridge: Cambridge University Press, 1979).

Freund, J.: *The Sociology of Max Weber* (Harmondsworth: Penguin Books, 1972).

Giddens, A: *Politics and Sociology in the Thought of Max Weber* (London: Macmillan, 1972).

Hamlin, A. and Pettit, P., eds: *The Good Polity* (Oxford: Basil Blackwell, 1989).

Holmes, S.: 'The permanent structure of antiliberal thought', in *Liberalism and The Moral Life*, ed. N. L. Rosenblum (Cambridge, Mass.: Harvard University Press, 1989).

Kamenka, E., ed.: *Community as a Social Ideal* (London: Edward Arnold, 1982).

Kymlicka, W.: *Liberalism, Community, and Culture* (Oxford: Clarendon Press, 1989).

Runciman, W. G.: 'Sociological evidence and political theory', in *Philosophy, Politics and Society*, 2nd Series, ed. P. Laslett and W. G. Runciman (Oxford: Basil Blackwell, 1962).

Tönnies, F.: *On Sociology: Pure, Applied, and Empirical*, ed. and trans. W. J. Cahnman and R. Heberle (Chicago: University of Chicago Press, 1971).

Wallach, J. R.: 'Liberals,communitarians, and the tasks of political theory', *Political Theory*, 15 (1987), 581–611.

Walzer, M.: 'The communitarian critique of liberalism', *Political Theory*, 18 (1990), 6–23.

5

The contribution of economics

GEOFFREY BRENNAN

Introduction

Some understanding of what 'political philosophy' and 'economics' are is presupposed by the title to this article. It is useful to begin by briefly setting out what those understandings will be. Political philosophy for my purposes here will be taken as equivalent to normative social theory. Political philosophy's concerns may be *centred* on the institutions and actions of the state – on politics more narrowly construed – but I shall include *all* forms of social organization, including specifically decentralized ones like anarchy and the market, within the scope of political philosophy as here understood. This understanding of political philosophy may be rather broader than that adopted in other contributions to this volume, but given the nature of economists' preoccupations within political theory the greater breadth is necessary.

The situation in defining economics itself is more complicated. Economics can be understood either in terms of its subject matter (incomes, prices, production, industrial organization, etc.) or in terms of its intellectual method. The understandings are not equivalent: the economy can be examined by reference to methods that no economist would own; and much of current journal space in economics is taken up with non-traditional subject-matter (the 'economics' of politics; the economics of law; the economics of crime and punishment, and so on). I here explicitly take the latter line: economics will be defined by reference to its distinctive 'way of thinking' (as Paul Heyne (1973) puts it in his admirable introductory textbook). This way of thinking has several characteristic features – its individualist methodology; its assumptions about agent rationality; its abstract, deductive style; its attention to relative prices and changes in them in explaining social phenomena; its exploitation of the average–marginal distinction; and so on. We shall examine briefly how this intellectual method has been applied to the analysis of political processes specifically; that application will turn up as a matter of course in discussing the economist's theory of the state (pp. 143–53).

At this point, however, I want to draw attention to a more general aspect of 'the economic way of thinking', namely, the economist's characteristic style of normative theorizing. This style is not necessarily unique to economists: in broad terms, it is shared by utilitarians and indeed most other kinds of consequentialists. But in the economistic incarnation, there are certain features that are in other incarnations less severely drawn. Two features, in particular, are notable:

1 The radical separation of 'purely positive' from 'purely normative' elements in normative social theory;
2 The concentration of analytical firepower on the former 'positive' element.

The positive/normative separation at stake here is not primarily an epistemological one. Its major effect is to conceptualize normative social theory in terms more or less analogous to the standard model of individual consumer choice. In that latter model, the consumer is conceived as scanning the set of feasible options and choosing that option which is of highest value to her; the analysis presupposes a radical dichotomy between 'opportunity sets' and 'preferences', between demand and supply. In the case of normative analysis, there is a corresponding scanning of the feasible set, to isolate that element that is best according to the ethical norm used – a corresponding confrontation of the feasible with the desirable. And just as the consumer who misspecifies the feasible set will, in general, choose a less preferred bundle, so the ethical observer who misspecifies the feasible set will typically make moral mistakes. Taking feasibility considerations seriously is on this account a critical aspect of proper normative theorizing, and it is in providing a proper sense of what *is* feasible that the economist's contribution lies. Moreover, it is the failure to isolate feasibility considerations in this self-conscious way and to focus appropriately on them – the failure, in short, to take feasibility seriously – that the economist identifies as the primary weakness of traditional political philosophy.

Now, the requirement that due account be taken of the feasible is an unambitious one and ought to be uncontentious. Moreover, it is (or ought to be) the claim of any social scientist and not just the economist. After all, if there is anything at all to the idea of social science, it must hang on the possibility that not all imaginable worlds are feasible: the acceptance of causal links that 'explain' why the social order is as it is (or why particular aspects of the social order are as they are) carries with it the implication that, given those causal factors, the social order could not have been otherwise, or could have been otherwise only by virtue of the intervention of unusual factors. The social scientist, whatever the particular mode of analysis brought to bear and whatever the causal factors perceived to be relevant, will therefore want to insist on a form of normative analysis that takes feasibility seriously in my sense.

None of this would serve, though, to justify a disproportionate attention to feasibility considerations. Desirability and feasibility are, within this scheme, equal partners – equally indispensable blades of the normative scissors (exactly analogous to 'demand' and 'supply' in the determination of price, or preferences and opportunity sets in the standard analysis of consumer choice). How then can the economist's focus on the feasible be justified?

In considerable measure, the economist's focus simply reflects an appropriate division of intellectual labour. The economist/social scientist has (or ought to have) a special expertise in matters of feasibility that she does not possess in matters of desirability. Nevertheless, economists have wanted to say *something* about desirability, and this for two reasons. First, for some purposes in ethical theorizing, the abstract, technical, deductive orientation of economic theory turns out to be extremely useful. For example, Arrow's (1951) famous impossibility theorem (which we discuss briefly below, pp. 137–8); Harsanyi's work in utilitarianism and uncertainty (Harsanyi, 1955; 1976); Buchanan's (1962; 1977) exposition of one important strand of contractarianism; and the writings of Amartya Sen (1977; 1979; 1982) and John Broome (1978; 1991) all represent contributions to ethical theory by persons who were originally trained and now practise as economists. This work involves the application of logic and sometimes mathematical technique to questions in moral philosophy without the intrusion of any social constraints as such in the analysis. To the extent that this literature simply demonstrates the power of logic, it will not be of any further concern in this discussion. (Hamlin (1986) provides a useful survey treatment.) However, there is a second reason for the economist's interest in purely ethical questions, and this aspect will be of concern here. The reason is this: the conception of normative social theory as the confrontation of the feasible with the desirable has implications for how desirability is conceived and formulated. If there is to be a major role for feasibility analysis in political philosophy, not just any old conception of desirability will do. Moreover, feasibility considerations may bite more deeply into the definition of desirability than might at first appear. I shall examine two particular areas where economists have used feasibility considerations to make an assault directly on conceptions of the desirable (pp. 133–42). One of these involves the collapse of utilitarianism as the central paradigm in welfare economics. The second revolves around the constraints imposed by 'fallen' human nature – and the way in which feasibility in the area of human motivations colours the way in which the notion of desirability is formulated. That discussion forms a suitable point of departure for the discussion of the economist's 'theory of the state' (see pp. 143–53).

Before we get to that point, however, it will be useful to lay out the economist' s conception of desirability, to connect it to more familiar utilitarian notions and to explain how that conception fits within an overall normative scheme in which feasibility considerations are to play a major, and perhaps predominant, independent role. This task occupies pp. 126–32. A brief conclusion is offered at pp. 153–5.

General normative theory: the economist's picture

An economist's picture of desirability

The predominant conception of desirability used in economics is based on the Paretian family of concepts. The Pareto criterion states that a state of the world, X, is better than another state, Y, if no one is worse off in Y than in X, and that at least one person is better off in X. A movement from one state to another which satisfies the Pareto criterion is said to be 'Pareto-desirable'. Three characteristics of this norm are worth noting. First, it is consequentialist in the sense that the immediate objects of evaluation are alternative states of the world. The question of whether an action or policy or institutional arrangement (which is appropriate is a question we pursue below) is desirable derives from that action/policy/institution's influence on how the world lies as a result of its implementation. Second, the Pareto criterion is 'personal' in the sense that the moral desirability of alternative states of the world is exhausted by the well-offness of *persons*: any 'moral goodness' is moral goodness *for someone*. Third, the goodness of persons is a matter of their preference-satisfaction: an individual is 'better off' if she enjoys more preference-satisfaction.

These three features are shared with utilitarianism – at least the variant of utilitarianism that is most familiar in economics. Where utilitarianism is distinctive is that utilitarianism ranks states of the world according to the aggregate sum of preference satisfaction across persons, whereas the Pareto criterion ranks only those states of the world in which everyone's preference satisfaction is higher (or no less). One implication is that whereas utilitarianism provides a complete ranking of all possible states of the world, the Pareto criterion does not. Comparisons between states of the world in which some individuals are better off and some worse off are not possible under the Pareto criterion.

Since virtually any action or policy or institutional change is almost certain to make someone worse off, the test of Pareto-desirability does not seem to be of much use as a guide to practical action. Two kinds of responses to this difficulty can be found in the welfare economics literature. One begins with the notion of 'Pareto optimality'. A Pareto optimum is a position from which no Pareto-desirable moves are feasible. This strand then attempts to measure the 'distance' from Pareto optimality associated with particular states of the world, and recommends moves 'closer' to Pareto optimality. This is the strategy of the so-called 'new welfare economics' of Hicks (1940), Kaldor (1939), Scitovsky (1941–2), and is most familiar from the techniques of modern cost-benefit analysis. Head (1974) provides a useful, article-length survey of this literature. One object in this conception of the Pareto norm has been to leave scope for the application of distributional considerations. Greater 'efficiency' (closeness to a Pareto optimum) may have to be weighed against greater 'equity' (normally conceived as reducing the variance or some similar measure of dispersion in the income distribution). The clear object here is to be able to proffer normatively defensible advice on matters of day-to-day policy. (A classic application of this approach is to be found in Musgrave, 1959.)

The other response to the failure of the Pareto criterion to deliver decisive moral advice is to restrict the application of the Pareto criterion to the 'constitutional' level, at which the basic rules of the socio-politico-economic game are chosen. That is, instead of applying the Pareto criterion to particular policies, the analyst applies it to the rules under which policies are determined. The claim here is that, at this more abstract level of evaluation, agreement is most likely to be secured – both because, on an argument akin to Rawls' defence of the veil of ignorance, individuals will be more prone to look to aggregate interests, and because we are likely to know more about the normative properties of institutional arrangements than about those of particular policies. The chief exponent of this second, 'institutional' interpretation of the Pareto test is Buchanan (1962; 1977) both individually and in various collaborations (Buchanan and Tullock, 1962; Brennan and Buchanan, 1985).

The institutional focus characteristic of the Buchanan approach draws some of its force from the fact that important propositions in welfare economics (that part of economics that deals explicitly with normative issues) relate specifically to the institution of the competitive market. These propositions are referred to as the 'fundamental theorems' of welfare economics. The first theorem states that perfect competition, in an environment of complete markets, yields an outcome that is Pareto optimal. The second theorem states that every possible Pareto optimum can be achieved under perfect competition, with the appropriate set of lump-sum transfers. The classic modern treatment is Arrow and Hahn (1971). Analogously, the most familiar exercise in welfare economics involves the comparison of perfect competition with monopoly (showing the departure from Pareto optimality that the monopoly structure involves). Buchanan's particular ambition has been to expand the range of such institutional comparisons so as to include not only alternative forms of market organization but also, specifically, alternative *political* arrangements.

Three properties of 'desirability', economist-style

With this rather spare description as background, I want to turn to the question as to why the Paretian framework has commended itself to economists. This question has two parts: first, why the Paretian framework has been preferred over ordinary utilitarianism; and second, the more general question as to what properties the conception of the desirable will have to exhibit if matters of feasibility are to occupy a central place in normative theory. The former question is postponed (see pp. 133–8). The latter I turn to immediately.

I want to argue briefly three propositions in this connection: first, that a concern with feasibility requires 'continuity' in ethical norms – that is, norms must specify what it means to be 'closer to' or further away from the ideal – a requirement that utilitarianism and its cognates fulfil; second, that to make room for feasibility concerns, the ultimately valued ends must be an appropriate analytical distance away from the objects of choice (actions, policies, institutional arrangements, etc.), something that is true of utilitarianism and most forms of consequentialism and is less likely to be true of deontological accounts of desirability; and third, that feasibility concerns are antipathetic to certain kinds of ethical idealism (kinds that tend to be common in much standard moral philosophy).

Continuity of norms If feasibility is a relevant issue, it is so because any independently specified 'ideal' (in whatever terms that ideal is specified) may turn out, on investigation, to be infeasible. Accordingly, if specifying that independent ideal is to do any real normative work, the normative framework must contain a notion of being closer to or further from that ideal, at least within the relevant range. This requirement does not necessarily involve the norm in specifying a complete ranking of all imaginable states of the world – or even a complete ranking of all *feasible* states though clearly either would be *sufficient* conditions for relevance). All that is required is that within any set of feasible states, the norm will isolate that which is best. Which among the others is second and which third best is in itself irrelevant. However, in the absence of independent knowledge as to what the feasible set is, or in the face of possible changes in that feasible set which may eliminate a previous best, some form of 'continuity' in the norm will be required if that norm is to be capable of speaking.

Note that the Pareto criterion will not, in general, serve to isolate a *unique* 'best': all states of the world that are Pareto desirable *vis-à-vis* some status quo state are equally superior, and there will typically be many such. But the requirement of continuity in the sense used here is fulfilled by the Pareto criterion: in any feasible set, the Pareto criterion will always isolate a subset of ideal points.

The problem of non-continuity can best be captured by an illustration. Consider the concept, widely used in normative tax analysis, of 'horizontal equity'. This concept specifies that taxes (or more appropriately, the total tax system) should be such as to 'treat equals equally', normally interpreted to mean that identical tax burdens should be imposed on those with identical capacity to pay. Almost all the debate in public finance theory has revolved around how 'capacity to pay' should be defined. However all *feasible* tax systems will violate that norm to some extent, almost independently of how capacity to pay is understood. It is not enough therefore to define the horizontal equity ideal; comparison of rival tax systems requires some suitable measure of the 'degree of horizontal inequality'. It is, moreover, important to specify such a measure explicitly. We need to be sure that such a measure satisfies our disciplined intuitions, and that policies taken to 'improve' horizontal equity do indeed do so. (The small literature in public finance theory on this matter – Johnson and Mayer (1962); White and White (1965); Brennan (1971; 1972) and Plotnick (1982) – reveals a considerable amount of controversy over aspects that have quite major tax policy implications.)

There are, in fact, quite general dangers in being intuitionist about nearness to a well-specified ideal. These dangers are the subject-matter of the so-called 'theory of the second-best' in welfare economics, and it is useful to discuss this theory briefly at this point. The basic issue in the theory of the 'second-best' is that of isolating the (first) best arrangement in a context where a well-specified conceptual ideal is infeasible. Thus, the theory of the 'second' best is really the theory of the *feasible* best when all relevant constraints are fully specified. The *point* of the theory, however, is to emphasize that the ostensible character of that feasible best may differ markedly from the character of the ideal. The original formulation of the second-best theorem (Lipsey and Lancaster, 1956–7) relates to a circumstance in which the conceptual ideal is specified in terms of the simultaneous application of three interrelated conditions: the theorem states that if there is a constraint that prevents satisfying one of these conditions, then the feasible best (feasible *given* that constraint) will in general involve violating all three conditions. To take a well-worked economic example, it is ideally efficient that a goods and services tax should impose identical tax rates on all objects of agent satisfaction (supposing that distributional objectives can be attended to via other instruments of policy). But suppose that some good *cannot* be taxed (the 'good' in question is often taken to be leisure). Then in general it will not be best to tax all taxable goods at uniform rates: goods should be taxed at different rates according to their degree of substitutability with the tax-exempt good (leisure) (see Atkinson and Stiglitz, 1980, Lecture 12). An analogous theorem can be derived for the case in which horizontal equity rather than efficiency is the tax goal: if some good or income-source cannot be (fully) taxed, then it will increase horizontal equity to tax remaining goods/income sources at appropriately differential rates.

The general argument here is, then, that taking proper account of feasibility requires one to formulate the desirable in appropriately continuous form: in general, specifying the desirable by reference to some independently derived 'ideal' will not in itself be enough.

The abstract conception of the desirability   If there is to be scope for feasibility analysis, there must be an appropriate gap between the objects of ultimate value and the objects of choice: it is in that gap that feasibility analysis bites. To appeal to a mechanistic analogy, the objects of choice can be construed as levers to the social machine from which the valued output emerges. The role of social analysis is to explain how that machine works – how action on levers translates into output. If the machine is simple, or if there is no engine at all – if, for example, the lever is itself the object of ultimate value – there is no room for social analysis to do relevant work.

It may seem at first blush that the requirement commits us to some form of consequentialism – to something like the utilitarianism or modified utilitarianism that has played such a major role in economics, for example – against any form of deontology. But the consequentialism/deontology issue is logically independent of the issue at hand. Consider, for example, a deontological norm of the Kantian-imperative kind. Here, each person is required to act in a way (according to some *rule* of conduct, perhaps) that would, if universalized, lead to the social ideal. Deriving what action is implied by this requirement (whether the notion is mediated by a rule or not) will often require much in the way of social analysis. Obversely, a consequentialist scheme may specify as the relevant consequence something which is pretty much directly under the agent's control. Suppose, for example, that the relevant norm is maximal truth-telling. Here, to be sure, the agent has to be concerned in principle with the possibility that her truth-telling in a particular case may lead to *less* truth-telling overall. But the force of that concern in all but special cases is surely negligible: in practice, the agent can simply go ahead and tell the truth. There seems to be little scope here for social analysis of the elaborate kind that economics represents. There is no need to 'take feasibility seriously'.

What is at stake here may be clarified by a relevant example. So, consider 'democracy'. It is self-evident that in order to evaluate democracy as an alternative to other forms of political organization, democracy itself cannot figure as an ethical prime. To point out that democracy is, after all, democracy provides in itself no reason for supporting it – except perhaps to the extent that multiple meanings of the term are in play (in which case proper argument is aided by suppressing the ambiguity). To describe some regime or policy or action as 'undemocratic or 'anti-democratic' can only have normative force when democracy is already taken as a 'good': the description can invite questions of classification (is the regime really undemocratic?) or definition (what characteristics would determine whether it is democratic or not?) but it cannot operate to show how or why democratic regimes/policies, etc. are superior. One way or another, any justificatory argument (as opposed to mere assertion) must make appeal to more primal values which democracy is seen to promote in some way.

Now, it is customary to distinguish two ways in which those more primal values might be promoted: democracy may 'express' those values; or democracy may produce social outcomes that are superior by reference to those values. Suppose for argument's sake that the primary value here is 'equality' (appropriately specified). Then we might say that democracy promotes equality either

1 by exhibiting equality directly – say, via universal franchise;

or 2 by establishing a more egalitarian sentiment generally in the population;

or 3 by producing, through democratic procedures, a more equal distribution of income or wealth.

In the latter two cases at least, there seems to be considerable scope for social analysis – in the one case, how values come to be established within the community and what the influence of choice of different political institutions on the relevant value-creation processes are; in the other case, how democracy works to produce particular policies that have distributive impact and how those policies actually affect the income distribution. The contrast is with the first case in which democracy is evaluated by reference to an intrinsic property: here there is no analytical gap between democracy and equality in which the social theorist can work. But even here it is the *directness* rather than the notion of instantiation/expression/exhibition that bears. If equality were seen to be exhibited not directly via universal franchise but indirectly via the 'equal' pattern of representation to which democratic institutions are supposed to give rise, then scope for analysis reappears. The question of whether universal franchise on a one-person-one-vote basis does reliably generate an accurate pattern of representation is on its face a complex one; and the possibility that some appropriately unequal pattern of voting rights might generate a more accurate pattern of representation cannot be ruled out on *a priori* grounds.

We should perhaps also note that it is by no means self-evident that democratic institutions will have egalitarian effects on the distribution of income. Economists may not have focussed much on this question (though see Brennan and Buchanan, 1985, ch. 8), but it does seem to be important. If income equality matters and if greater such equality is seen to be part of the reason for democratic processes, then whether greater income equality is *feasible* and whether and to what extent democracy promotes such equality are questions that naturally arise. My point here is not to argue one position or another on these questions. The point is rather that those questions and others like them must be on the agenda if economists (or social analysts more generally) are to have anything to contribute. Whether those questions *are* on the agenda or not depends on how much logical distance there is between the object of control and the object of evaluation. What the objects of evaluation are is one critical aspect of that issue. Those economists who believe that they have something to contribute to political philosophy will therefore be those who hold to an appropriately abstract account of 'the desirable'. Utilitarianism or something like it is an obvious contender, but as I have been at pains to point out, it is not the only possibility.

The comparative mode: the best vs the good When one starts normative analysis from the feasibility end, with a conception of moral evaluation as an act of *choice*, one is almost by necessity forced into a comparative mode of thinking: the relevant exercise is to compare the ethical properties of *alternative feasible* possibilities (whether these possibilities be actions or states of the world or institutional arrangements or whatever). Any such possibility *chosen* clearly involves another forgone – that is what it means for the (feasible) possibilities to be alternatives. If the possibilities are not alternatives – if one can have one's cake and eat it too – then it is not clear how feasibility constraints bite at all. The forgone options necessarily involved in any choice must obtrude into any proper moral evaluation of that choice.

This requirement is an assault on our natural repertoire of moral responses. We are often outraged at some aspect of what we see. Sometimes we are delighted at some aspect of what we see and naturally want to lend it support. But this procedure of giving an observed situation an ethical ranking in isolation from relevant alternatives, or based on some intuitive comparison with a notional ethical ideal, violates the requirement of proper comparative analysis. After all, anyone with a little moral imagination will have no difficulty in conceiving a world better than the one we currently inhabit – where wars are made to cease in all the world; where the lion and lamb lie down together, where the desert rejoices and blossoms as a rose; where all eat and are satisfied. The question is whether such better worlds are really feasible. Put another way, feasibility analysis points up as a critical part of the moral enterprise the identification of 'real' problems (those for which some remedy exists) as opposed to spurious ones (those that are a creature of humans' excessively fertile moral imaginations). For the economist, identifying 'real' problems so defined is a central part of the economist's own art. As Frank Knight used to remark, to call a situation hopeless is to recognize it as optimal. This then is one sense in which the best may be the enemy of the good. The feasible best may not be 'good' at all. However, if all feasible alternatives are even worse – if what we see is indeed the *best* – then the quest for better options can only lead to deterioration.

There is another sense in which the good and the best may be at odds. Suppose you have focused your attention on a particular action or policy, and suppose you have good reason for believing this action/policy to have good consequences, and that this action or policy is something you *can* bring about. Nevertheless, the moral case is inadequate. There may be some other action/policy, also feasible, that is ruled out by undertaking the first – perhaps, in the policy case, because fiscal dollars are limited, or the parliamentary agenda can only accommodate one more bill, or in the action case because one can't be in two places at once. Then the first action/policy should make way for the better one. What economists refer to as the 'opportunity cost' (the value of what is forgone) of the first action/policy is too high. This then is a second way in which the good may be the enemy of the best.

Both manifestations of the comparative mode may appear deeply conservative: on the one hand, doing nothing while we wait around to be sure that some manifest improvement does not preclude an even greater improvement; and on the other, suppressing natural outrage at elements in the status quo (or suppressing natural enthusiasm for promoting some other elements) on the grounds that bad may be best. But the alleged conservatism involves a mistake. Feasibility analysis does not establish a case for absence of change in policy or institutional arrangements, where there is a presumption that such changes would lead to improvement. All that is demanded is that the changes in question must be *specified*, so that their likely effects can be analysed and compared. What is ruled out is merely the argument that because something is 'wrong', anything would be better.

Finessing desirability questions

So far in this section, I have described what conceptions of desirability economists have in fact been inclined to use, and have tried to show how these conceptions fit with a view of political philosophy (normative social analysis) that leaves considerable room for feasibility analysis. Within that view of political philosophy, feasibility considerations are 'trumps': actions undertaken or policy proposals implemented on the basis of false theories, and specifically theories that misperceive what is feasible, will not achieve desired improvements and will sometimes have extremely undesirable consequences. But desirability considerations are no less trumps in this sense: actions/policies/institutions recommended on the basis of a false perception of desirability are no less likely to have undesirable consequences.

Nevertheless, economists – particularly those most interested in the traditional concerns of political philosophy – have been inclined to assign a kind of priority to matters of feasibility. A medical metaphor to the effect that diagnosis is necessary *before* prescription of treatment is often wheeled in, as if its applicability were self-evident. But that medical metaphor is far from innocent, and it is worth unpacking it a little. In the medical case, there is a presumption that what constitutes 'good health' is self-evident. There is also an implication that false diagnosis will lead to treatments that are likely to do more harm than good. Do these presumptions carry over to the social case? It is by no means obvious that they do. What is, however, clear is that economists have been attracted to formulations of desirability that are as undemanding as possible. The attraction of the Pareto criterion and of consensus-based norms may well lie partly in this: that no one would, or on pain of self-contradiction could, deny the desirability of a move that she herself preferred. Who, after all, would support a move that made everyone in the normatively relevant community *worse* off (for that is what refraining from making a Pareto-desirable move involves)? Economists may not be able to get as much out of such a weak normative apparatus as they might out of a richer ethical framework, but what they can get out of it will have strong claims to be compelling. It is clearly an attraction for the economist to avoid being dragged back continually into the niceties of moral philosophy. If some simple, tolerably unexceptionable conception of desirability can be found, the way is clear to focus all the analytic firepower on matters of feasibility, and for the economist to get on with the job.

Feasibility analysis at work: two extended examples

In this section, I want to deal with two particular applications of feasibility analysis. These applications are interesting because they show how the conception of desirability itself is constrained by feasibility considerations. The first example deals with the overthrow of utilitarianism as the prevailing paradigm in normative economics, and its replacement by the Paretian framework. The central argument in that overthrowal revolved around the claim that utilitarianism is infeasible because the information necessary to make it operational is unavailable. The argument is not that utilitarianism is *ethically* deficient, but rather that is infeasible.

The second application of feasibility analysis bites at quite a different level, but is in its own way every bit as important. It deals with the issue of human motivation and specifically with the role of morality in motivating action. Economics, following Mandeville and Smith and the American 'founding fathers', is deeply sceptical about human moral capacities and grounds its conception of normative social theorizing in that scepticism. It is that scepticism in particular that explains economists' interests in 'invisible hand' mechanisms and the 'incentive effects' implied by particular institutional arrangements. On one reading (in my view a perceptive one) economists are interested, perhaps even preoccupied, with realism about *virtue*: they are concerned, that is, with the *feasibility* of any arrangement that makes too extensive a demand on people's preparedness to behave 'morally'. As I shall argue, this particular feasibility concern deeply influences the economist's view of the world and in particular the economist's view of what prospects for improvement in the world are worth taking seriously. But first, the economist's attack on utilitarianism.

Is utilitarianism feasible?

It is no secret that utilitarianism has played a special role in the development of economics – and this not merely in its normative strand. From its origins in Hume and Smith through John Stuart Mill up until the 1930s, the overwhelmingly predominant formulation of 'the desirable' in economics was utilitarian in character

It is also no secret that in the 1930s utilitarianism, at least in its standard form, was more or less decisively overturned in economics, in favour of some variant of the Paretian framework. The critical move in this overthrow was delivered by Lionel Robbins' influential book *The Nature and Significance of Economic Science*. Robbins' book coincided and was loosely linked with the ordinalist revolution in economics more generally and Robbins' arguments doubtless borrowed some authority from those more general ordinalist arguments. Robbins' purposes were however distinct. Ordinalists of the standard kind were concerned to generalize the mainstream Marshallian formulation of demand analysis which assumed cardinal measurability of utility by showing that cardinalism was a hypothesis that could be dispensed with. Their object was to show that the full array of propositions in demand theory could be derived merely on the basis of individual preference rankings, without any utility measure attached. Ordinalists of this stripe did not need to argue that cardinal utility measures were *impossible* – merely that they were unnecessary. The application of Occam's razor, on the basis of which ordinalism was justified, would also shave off any argument to the effect that cardinality was strictly *infeasible* because no such argument was logically necessary.

Robbins' object was to show something else – namely, that arguments advanced by Mill, Edgeworth and Pigou on utilitarian foundations in favour of a radical egalitarian income distribution programme depended on 'value-judgements' and further that these value-judgements had no place in 'economic science'. The Mill/Edgeworth/ Pigou argument was that, given diminishing marginal utility of income to individuals, and given that individuals' capacities for income enjoyment were identical, maximizing total utility required complete income equalization. Taking a dollar from one who has more dollars and giving it to one who has fewer must impose a utility loss on the first less than the utility gain to the second if marginal utility declines with income. Hence, egalitarian redistribution will add to total utility until all incomes are equalized, unless the process of redistribution itself is costly. Of course, it might be expected that a programme of income equalization would have enormous disincentive effects; individuals would all get average post-tax-transfer income whatever they did, and would be expected to 'free-ride' on each other's effort. Clearly such disincentive effects would weigh in any proper utilitarian calculus. When the relevant calculations are made, the utility-maximizing degree of income redistribution turns out to fall well short of equalization – for plausible values of the relevant parameters, the utility-maximizing redistributive scheme would involve an equal flat grant paid to all persons financed by a 25 per cent income tax (see Stern, 1976; Atkinson and Stiglitz, 1980). Allowing for disincentive effects of equalizing redistributions is, then, one way in which feasibility considerations might work to moderate the extreme requirements of an unconstrained application of ethical norms. However, these disincentive effects were not Robbins' concern. Robbins' line involved a much more wholesale epistemological challenge to the feasibility of the utilitarian programme. How, Robbins asked, could one *know* that transferring a dollar from A to B would make B better off than it made A worse off? In particular, what 'scientific' evidence – what observations of behaviour of the kind economists are inclined to regard as decisive elsewhere – could be adduced in favour of any such proposition? In other words, Robbins was not offering the view that value-judgements are unnecessary in drawing normative conclusions; he was arguing rather that the object of maximizing aggregate utility requires information to which we do not and cannot normally have access.

With a small number of exceptions (most notably Little, 1957; and, ingeniously, Lerner, 1944), Robbins' challenge was taken to be unanswerable, and the welfare economics programme of the utilitarians was replaced by the Pareto framework for which interpersonal utility comparisons were seen not to be required. Robbins appealed to a contrast between market *exchange* where both parties could be recognized as better off (at least, in the relevant *expected* sense) and state-managed income transfers where one party was made better off at the expense of another.

One conspicuous feature of the Robbins argument is its strong behaviourist orientation. Only information about preferences revealed in actual behaviour is to be accepted as authoritative; information gleaned from introspection, discussion, questionnaires, etc. is regarded as hopelessly unreliable or otherwise 'unscientific'. Robbins believed perhaps that the latter kind of information, coloured as it would apparently be by interests in redistribution in one's own direction, would be systematically unreliable. There is some connection here with the Austrian critique of 'socialist calculation': a central element in the arguments of Hayek (1975; 1988) and Mises (1922) is the radical inaccessibility of information from which the 'optimal' social plan could be devised. Hayek argues that even the individuals themselves cannot articulate their utility functions or their productive capacities independent of the context for action that the market-place supplies. At least a critical part of the knowledge required to simulate the market via planning he argued to be either inarticulable

(Hayek prefers the term 'tacit') or actually unknown by the individuals themselves. It is worth noting that Hayek's critique of socialist calculation is not the 'public choice' one that socialist planners would not have the *incentive* to establish the optimal plan or workers the incentives to implement their part in that plan. Hayek is prepared for the purposes of the argument to allow all agents to be appropriately motivated. Hayek's point seems to be that even in that case the information required will not be forthcoming and the co-ordination of that information into an appropriate set of rules of conduct for each agent will be impossible. Hayek's argument is that agents need the market system (and its price signals specifically) to discern what the 'public interest' requires. Robbins' arguments and Hayek's deal with rather different questions and pose rather different informational demands (of which more below). But they are of the same general kind: they both pose the challenge as to how the ethical observer is to obtain the information required to make the ethical system *feasible.*

Of course, one might well ask whether, in Robbins' case, the Paretian framework he recommends is really any less informationally demanding than the utilitarian scheme. How, after all, are we to know that a policy makes someone better off and no one worse off? Or whether a policy moves citizens closer to some notional 'frontier' in which all possible mutual gains have been appropriated by citizens? With a few notable exceptions, such questions do not seem to have much worried welfare economists.

The most notable exception is James Buchanan (1962; 1977; for example) together with those influenced by his work. Buchanan's case for the unanimity criterion as the ultimate basis for all normative claims rests in large part on a Robbins-like argument: without the explicit unanimity test, the analyst simply has no adequate grounds for believing that the Pareto criterion has been satisfied. If the utilitarian scheme of Pigou and Edgeworth is informationally infeasible, then so will be those variants of the Paretian framework that cannot be grounded in some 'scientific test'.

At this point, I want to note three things about seeing voluntary exchange in the market place as such a test. First, we should note that what is at stake in such a test is the 'revealed preference' tradition in economics – the assertion that whatever is revealed in action accurately reflects the agent's welfare. This assertion goes with a collapse of categories of taste, preference and value to a single category – that which is revealed in action. If we imagine values to be at war with inclinations (an image that is hardly a novel one in ethics), then the market test carries the assumption that action invariably involves an optimal reconciliation of the competing claims. If that assumption is taken seriously, then agents' actions seem to be exempt from ethical scrutiny: ethics cannot constitute an independent point of evaluation for human action because agents' actions are in accord with their values by assumption. The charge that no one 'should' behave any differently from the way they actually behave surely spells the death of ethics. Equally, if ethics is to have a voice, something other than mere observation of behaviour must be available as a source of information: some access to the human mind via what the agent *says* (or otherwise) must be presumed.

The second thing we should note about the market test involves foreshadowing arguments that I will discuss later about 'market failure' (pp. 144–8). Market failure deals with those cases in which the pursuit of their own values by all agents leads each to fail to achieve her maximal feasible value. The circumstances under which this may occur will preoccupy us later, but (in one form or another) they have been the focus of welfare economics for the entire history of the subject. One thing can, however, be noted – that the market test itself cannot tell us whether or not such circumstances apply. And yet the question of whether those circumstances apply or not is the critical one for almost all normative economics. (Buchanan's claim is that only the explicit unanimity test can tell us whether such circumstances apply. On this reading, the market test is appropriate only if there is prior unanimous agreement in favour of the market as the appropriate institutional arrangement: otherwise, the market test is arbitrary.)

None of this is to deny that agent behaviour provides some information about agent values: it is simply to deny that behaviour is the sole source of such information. In fact, although few economists seem to have accepted the implication, Robbins' claims about the epistemological arbitrariness of interpersonal comparisons seem to lead to an extreme ethical nihilism.

One notable demonstration of this nihilism, at least on my interpretation, lies in Kenneth Arrow's famous impossibility theorem (Arrow, 1951). There is an enormous literature on this theorem (and variants of it) in both economics and philosophy, and I shall not attempt to survey that literature here. Rather, I will offer a statement of the theorem and my own interpretation. Arrow's theorem asserts that there is no way, in general, in which an ordering of social states can be derived from the individual orderings of those states without violating some apparently simple and unexceptional norms. Specifically, given that the individual orderings are themselves unconstrained there exists no social ordering that exhibits all of the following properties:

1 Pareto dominance: If at least one person prefers x to y and no one prefers y to x, then the social ordering will rank x above y.
2 Transitivity: If the social ordering ranks x above y, and y above z, it must rank x above z.
3 Independence of irrelevant alternatives: The social ranking between x and y is unaffected by the introduction of any third option w.
4 Non-dictatorship: There is no individual whose preferences match the social ordering (i.e. if 'society' ranks y if and only if some individual i does, then i is a dictator in Arrow's sense; and Arrow requires that no such i exists).

Strategic restrictions on the individual orderings (the inputs to the social ranking) can be devised so that Arrow's result can be avoided; but 'in general', the theorem assures us, no 'decent' social ordering can be derived (with decency defined by reference to the specified criteria).

One way of interpreting Arrow's theorem (the way I prefer) is to conceive it as showing that, in general, in order to make any reasonable sense of the notion of the 'public interest' or 'community welfare' one requires interpersonal utility comparisons. In all those cases where the individual rankings differ, there is no way of generating a composite ranking that is transitive, non-dictatorial and Paretian other than by appeal to a cardinal weighting of the different preferences, and some form of aggregation (which violates the independence of irrelevant alternatives axiom).

It is, I believe, a mistake to see the Arrow theorem as a proposition about the potential for intransitivity in electoral decision-making specifically (and hence a theorem about majoritarian cycling in public choice, about which more below, p. 151). It is a mistake to see the Arrow theorem in this way because although democratic politics confronts the problem of aggregating individual preferences into a 'social ordering' in the absence of a numeraire, there are institutional possibilities that might prevent intransitivities emerging (see Hammond and Miller, 1987, for example), as well as the possibility that voters may vote stochastically in ways that would suppress majoritarian instability (Coughlin, 1982). The problem is not that of securing an electoral equilibrium; it is rather one of securing an equilibrium for which a plausible ethical defence can be made. Arrow's theorem assures us that this latter task cannot be performed without interpersonal utility comparisons.

It is an interesting fact that, although moral philosophers have offered a variety of arguments against utilitarianism (of varying degrees of persuasiveness), the line that has proven decisive within economics is a distinctively economistic one. The economist's line has been that utilitarianism is *infeasible* because it requires information that is inaccessible. As I have emphasized here, if one accepts that view, one may well be committed to a great deal more in the way of ethical nihilism than economists have seemed to realize. But my interest here has been as much on the nature of the argument as its substance. The argument is an *economist's* argument in that it attempts to bring feasibility considerations to bear in the exercise of specifying 'the desirable'. My claim is that, in the economist's world, feasibility is the central test. The overthrow of utilitarianism within economics in the 1930s is a classic instance of the application of that test.

Realism about virtue

One particular dimension of feasibility that has played a critical role in the development of normative economics (and in Enlightenment social theory more generally) revolves around human moral imperfections. Virtually any social analysis entails some account of human nature: and in normative social analysis, it is perhaps natural to suppose that a moral theory will, if correct, prove compelling to the agents who accept its correctness. But within the economist's scheme, establishing what it is that virtue (or justice or whatever) *requires* by way of action (or social policy or whatever) is not enough: it is also necessary to show how agents will be induced to *take* the relevant action. Compliance with a morality, even one that agents regard as 'true', simply cannot be taken for granted. 'If men were angels', the economist is inclined to argue, things might be different; but in the real world we must determinedly set aside heroic conceptions of human nature and deal with human behaviour as it is, warts and all. To do so commits the economist to a particular interest in institutions, which, as economists often put it, 'economize' on virtue (see Robertson, 1956; and for a critical view, Hirschman, 1985).

The predominant model of human behaviour in economics is the *homo economicus* model. This conception of human nature involves, in most applications, two assumptions – that people are 'rational' (that their actions are those that, given their beliefs, best fulfil their desires) and that they are predominantly egoistic (that their desires are oriented towards themselves as subject). Exactly what these assumptions amount to in particular cases is a somewhat complicated matter which need not be engaged here. Different applications will focus on the rationality and egoistic aspects, and for some purposes the assumptions can be weakened considerably. In particular, to make 'economizing on virtue' a relevant ambition, all that is necessary is the assumption that actors will often enough *not* act in the public interest . To make the economist's remedies to this problem relevant, all that is necessary is the assumption that private interest is a significant motive in human action.

Both assumptions are, economists believe, unexceptionable. Attention is therefore directed towards the question of how arrangements might be made to bend private interests to the service of the public interest – to secure benign consequences from human interactions, despite the impaired motivations of the participants. Clearly, the archetypal example is Adam Smith's 'invisible hand'; the fact that we do not depend on the benevolence of our butchers and bakers to secure our dinner is the notable feature of the free-market order (Smith's 'system of natural liberty'). It is that feature that enables us to economize on (scarce) benevolence. But invisible hand mechanisms are not necessarily restricted to market interactions. The quest for analogous mechanisms in the political arena was, for example, the driving ambition of the American Constitutional framers, and indeed of political theorists in the Enlightenment tradition down to the present day. Bolingbroke (1730) believed that 'governments may be so formed, or laws so framed, as will necessarily produce virtue and make good ministers even of bad men'. Hamilton (1788) argued that . . . 'the best security for the fidelity of mankind is to make their interest coincide with their duty'; more generally, the object of the institutions discussed in the Federalist Papers was to ensure that, as far as possible, interest and duty do coincide.

The 'virtue–parsimony' characteristic of this tradition is, at least these days, pretty much a distinctive economistic contribution. Within mainstream economics, the notion is formalized within the so-called 'principal–agent' literature. A general characterization of principal–agent problems would involve a 'principal', who specifies some goal, to be implemented by some 'agent', who is strategically placed to secure that goal but who has independent ends which he seeks to pursue. The divergence between the objectives of principal and agent is clearly critical to the problem: if the agent fully internalizes the principal's goal, then the problem is simply assumed away. The challenge for the principal is to design arrangements that will provide the agent with incentives to use his (the agent's) strategic superiority in the principal's interest. In conventional economic settings, such problems are conceptualized 'in the small': for example, what commission arrangements will maximally induce the real estate agent, with her special knowledge and skills, to secure the best price for your house when her interests lie more in securing a quick sale at little effort (or perhaps selling to herself through an intermediary)? However, the principal–agent *approach* is clearly generalizable to a larger scope: let the principal's object be the achievement of some general moral end, and let the agent(s) be those whose actions are to produce that moral end; then the same general principal–agent apparatus can be directly applied. Thus, the central problem in politics is to ensure that those entrusted with political power will indeed reliably use that power in the interests of citizens. Specifically, the central problem for democracy is whether, and to what extent, the institutions of democracy – periodic elections under conditions of majority rule, most notably – serve so to constrain the use of political power that the public interest is served. Examination of that problem represents the main agenda of normative public choice theory. The presumptions underlying this formulation are precisely those of the principal–agent problem – viz. that principals (citizens) have interests, with whose pursuit political agents are entrusted; and that those political agents have independent interests that are, at the relevant margin, in conflict with those of citizens. The central analytic question then becomes whether the institutions of democracy represent a solution to the principal–agent problem so formulated.

It is worth emphasizing that this formulation of the central issue in normative political theory presupposes that the normative ends to be served are connected to the preferences/interests/values of the citizens. 'Virtue' on the part of political agents collapses more or less to a disciplined benevolence – the capacity to recognize the citizens' interest and the inclination to act accordingly. Conceptions of the 'good', independent of the citizens' interests, that might be held by political agents (or their philosopher advisors) can have no special place here; indeed, such conceptions are simply one possible manifestation of agents' particularized 'interests'. Within the principal–agent formulation, politics is assigned an *agency* role; normative considerations are exhausted by the question of how well political institutions fulfil that role.

Aspects of the argument here can usefully be elaborated by appeal to the prisoners' dilemma interaction. The prisoners' dilemma is in fact a central concept of normative economics: it is the economist's version of the fallacy of composition and it will reappear in the subsequent discussion of the economist's theory of the state. The original version of the prisoners' dilemma (attributed to A. W. Tucker) involves two suspects who are believed to have co-operated in a particular crime. They are captured, and the prosecutor places them in separate cells, and confronts both with the following set of 'pay-offs':

If both confess, eight years each.
If neither confesses, one year each on a minor charge.
If one confesses and the other does not, the confessor goes free and the non-confessor gets ten years.

The question facing each prisoner is whether to confess or not. The structure of the interaction here can be illustrated by a standard matrix in which the entries in each cell of the matrix are a number pair showing the number of prison-years prisoner I receives as the first number in each pair and the number of prison-years prisoner II receives as the second. This matrix is shown as Figure 5.1. Prisoner I chooses the row; prisoner II the column.

The critical feature of the prisoners' dilemma interaction is that, while the prison-minimizing outcome for the two prisoners considered together is for both *not* to confess, each will be led to confess if each acts independently to minimize his own prison sentence. To see this, consider player I's calculus. There are two contingencies that player I can reckon with: player II confesses; or player II does not confess. Whichever contingency applies, it minimizes I's own sentence to confess; for if II also confesses, I

		Prisoner II	
		Confess	Don't confess
Prisoner I	Confess	8 yrs, 8 yrs	free, 10 yrs
	Don't confess	10 yrs, free	1 yr, 1yr

Figure 5.1
The prisoner's dilemma

gets eight years for confessing and ten years for not, and if II does not confess, I gets off free for confessing and one year if he does not. So whatever II does, it is best for I to confess. And whatever I does, it is best for II to confess. Individually rational action requires each to confess, even though the outcome in which both confess is worse for both than the outcome in which neither confesses. The 'equilibrium' outcome (both confess) is Pareto-dominated by another outcome (neither confesses).

Now, in the particular example offered by Tucker, the prosecutor is presumed to know, independently, that the prisoners are guilty and so the (confess, confess) outcome is morally defensible. The prosecutor engages in a piece of 'institutional design', in which an unambiguously desirable outcome is secured by a strategic manipulation of the context within which the prisoners choose. But of course, the prisoners are led to confess whether they are guilty or not. And one might equally well take it that the prisoners are innocent and the prosecutor either mistaken or simply anxious to increase his convictions score for the month. The intrusion of the prosecutor's motives are, in fact, a distraction from what is surely the point of the story – namely, that the prisoners are led under independent action to choose an outcome that both would prefer not to prevail. If we conceive of the public interest solely in terms of the interests of the participants (the prisoners in this case), then the problem exposed by the prisoners' dilemma is the tension between private and public interest. Clearly, an appropriate degree of benevolence or 'public spiritedness' by the participants would remove that tension: if each prisoner weighs the cost imposed on the other by his own confession sufficiently heavily, he will not confess. Here, then, we *require* virtue: in its absence, the jointly preferred outcome does not prevail.

Recall, however, that the dilemma is to some extent an artifact of the district attorney's ambitions (moral or otherwise). And just as the prisoners' dilemma is in this case artificially constructed, so perhaps it may be *avoided* by strategic design of the rules of interaction. For example, it is often argued by economists, following G. Hardin (1968), that the English common constituted a prisoners' dilemma interaction in that each villager had an incentive to over-graze; and that the dilemma could be solved by creating private title in the land. Private ownership in this case economizes on virtue, and is therefore to be preferred.

(There is now a vast literature on the prisoners' dilemma, both in its two-person and

		Player B	
		b_1	b_2
Player A	a_1	0, 0	2, 1
	a_2	1, 2	3, 3

Figure 5.2
Invisible hand

n-person forms, and both in one-off and iterated plays. An accessible treatment is Luce and Raiffa (1957, ch. 5), which despite its age remains remarkably modern and vigorous. Martin Shubik (1982) provides a more recent survey of attempts to apply simple game theory to social contexts. At a less technical and much more inductive level, the various applications by Schelling (1960; 1978) make fascinating and instructive reading.)

The invisible hand mechanism can also be illustrated by a two-person interaction, with an analogous matrix depiction, shown as Figure 5.2. In this interaction, each actor again has two actions, denoted a_1 and a_2 for player A and b_1 and b_2 for player B. The pay-off associated with each 'outcome' is again shown as a number pair, with the first entry showing the pay-off to A and the second entry showing the pay-off to B. Clearly, (a_2, b_2) is the equilibrium outcome involving the pay-off (3, 3). This equilibrium is, however, utterly benign, unlike the prisoners' dilemma case. Moreover, this interaction has the feature that the action of each player serves as much to promote the interests of the other as to promote his own. The invisible hand economizes virtue/benevolence/public spirit in this simple sense. And again, to the extent that institutional arrangements can be so ordered that the interactions between agents are of the 'invisible hand' type, they should be. Everyone has an interest in promoting institutional arrangements of this kind – whether by acting to preserve them when they spontaneously evolve, or by establishing them where they can be established.

A sense of such institutional possibilities – of so ordering social life that invisible hands are encouraged and prisoners' dilemmas suppressed – colours the economist's approach to normative social theory. Indeed, on one reading (say, Buchanan, 1977), this is precisely the normative agenda. And it is worth noting what is presupposed by this conception of normative social theory – namely, that the limits to human benevolence, to civic virtue, are a fundamental constraint in the pursuit of normatively desirable ends. Moral reasoning on its own can never be taken to be compelling for action: any normative social theory that simply *assumes* compliance is therefore seriously incomplete at best and at worst can encourage action that is perverse in its consequences. Misspecifying the constraint of human moral frailty is no less an error than misspecifying other kinds of constraints, but it is an error to which economists see traditional political theory as particularly prone.

The economist's theory of the state

Market 'success'

The point of departure for the economist's theory of the state is a set of propositions about 'market success'. In their modern welfare economics variant, these propositions revolve around the claim that perfectly competitive markets generate a Pareto optimal outcome – an outcome, that is, where all the possible mutual benefits from exchange are fully exploited. It is common for economists to identify a direct intellectual line in such reasoning from Adam Smith, through David Ricardo, to the formal theorems of the Arrow–Debreu general equilibrium models; but there are some subtle shifts of emphasis in that development. Smith's view of market success involved an ever-increasing elaboration of specialization and the division of labour: Smith believed, for example, that doubling the size of the market would more than double the wealth generated. This 'increasing returns' aspect of Smith's account has been effectively obliterated in the static, constant returns context of formal welfare economics. Moreover, Smith's claim is that the market order, the 'system of natural liberty', leads to an increase in the *wealth* of nations, and it is on the plutological dimension that Smith focuses. Given the emphasis in Smith's 'psychology' on the role of popular illusions (e.g. the illusion that higher wealth for an individual leads to more prestige and happiness), the connection between the wealth of nations and their happiness remains complex and somewhat under-argued. Such issues are finessed by the Pareto criterion: preference satisfaction is the measure of desirability and individuals can be left to themselves to choose among wealth and other desired 'goods'. In Smith's view, however, as in the more modern welfare economics variant, the market system should be let alone to do its work: once one recognizes an 'invisible hand' in operation, the best rule for action is *laissez-faire*.

It is worth emphasizing. however, that the market order (or commercial society) is not sustained by the absence of government *altogether*. Smith's view of the market as clockwork, even a spontaneously evolved clockwork, does not collapse to a naive anarchism. There is a critical role for government (the wise sovereign in Smith) in assisting the invisible hand to work. After all, the market only works to the extent that property rights, including rights of persons in themselves, are well understood and respected, and to the extent that arrangements for the exchange of such rights and for the enforcement of complex contracts are in place. The state, with its statutory monopoly in the use of coercive power, has a critical 'constitutional' role in sustaining the institutions of the free-market order, and this role is potentially extensive. It includes, specifically, the provision of courts to decide cases and of police to enforce those decisions. In the absence of such legal institutions, fraud will be rife, contracts broken, property unsafe: the enormous gains from specialization and division of labour will remain unappropriated because the requisite institutional environment will not be in place. Following Buchanan's line in *The Limits of Liberty* (1975), most economists have seen no logical connection between arguments for market success and romantic anarchism. If anything, economists tend to take a Hobbesian view of anarchy, while remaining essentially supportive of market institutions (at least in those arenas where markets can be shown to work tolerably well).

Economists – even enthusiasts for the 'free market order', like Milton Friedman – have also been inclined to allow a role for government in redistributional matters. Theorems about market success do not include propositions to the effect that the market will generate an ideal *income distribution* – merely an ideal arrangement of individuals' productive activities based on some natural distribution of talents and abilities. Whether that natural distribution of talents and abilities will satisfy independently derived norms of distributive justice must be an open question. In fact, Smith himself does have an argument to the effect that commercial society will generate a natural distribution 'almost identical to that one might have chosen on independent grounds'; this is one of only three explicit references to an invisible hand mechanism in Smith's entire corpus. But this argument has never commended itself much to modern economists – even those who are acquainted with it.

There is, indeed, widespread acceptance of the proposition that arguments for market success in mobilizing gains from trade (or in increasing total wealth) are distinct from and much more compelling than arguments for market success (or otherwise) in *distributing* those gains. There is also widespread agreement that redistributive activities by the state (or by other large-scale charitable agencies), whether in directions required by distributive justice or otherwise, tend to upset the capacity of the market system to mobilize gains from exchange; hence, the 'efficiency–equity trade-off'. The existence of any such trade-off implies that the pursuit of distributive justice will be *constrained*: any normative ideal will have to take account of the efficiency cost of any additional achievements in the area of distributive justice or collective charity. In the simple utilitarian case, as we have mentioned, the disincentive effects of tax-transfer schemes greatly restrict the amount of redistribution required for total utility maximization. Of course, it could be argued independently that utilitarianism fails to take proper (indeed any) account of the special claims of the poor *per se*; the poor only get special treatment to the extent that the utility of an extra dollar to a poor person exceeds that of an extra dollar to a richer one.

To summarize, the virtues of the market order can be seen as 'economizing' virtues. First, the market order by relying minimally on the *benevolence of* participants relaxes the limits imposed by human moral frailty. And second, the market order provides signals to agents about how to act in the public interest – a public interest that they could never identify in the absence of those signals. Simply put, the market provides agents with both the information they need to act in others' interests and the motivation to act in the way required. The role for the state in this idealized free market order has two strands: first, to provide the institutional framework (one might say, the 'regulatory apparatus') required to allow the market to work well; and second, to adjust the income distribution 'optimally' in the light of independently derived norms of distributive justice. There is in this picture, however, no 'productive' role for the state – no need for the state to provide any goods and services, merely to act as umpire and to redistribute in the minimally distorting way.

The productive state – market failure

The foregoing picture is, however, question-begging in at least two ways. First, if the market can reliably produce those goods and services for which there is effective demand, why can it not produce its own institutional apparatus and its own institutions of enforcement? And if it cannot, do the reasons for such failure not generalize to other goods and services? Second, if there is a demand for *redistribution* why is *that* not able to be articulated appropriately in the market? And if there is no such demand and yet redistribution is held independently to be normatively desirable, why is it that such independent ethical norms do not obtrude more generally? In short, is the normative ideal, whether defined narrowly in terms of preference satisfaction or more broadly, really *feasible* in freely operating market contexts?

The economic theory of the productive state represents a negative answer to that question. That theory is essentially a theory of market failure, and was contrived precisely as such by its architects. Thus, Samuelson (1954; 1955) in his seminal contribution begins by posing the question as to what model of public expenditure the scholar should set against the classical Smithian account of market success. Smith actually foreshadows the public goods argument in Book V of *The Wealth of Nations* in his discussion of public activities, and David Hume has a clear account of the free-rider problem in *The Treatise*. Relevant early continental literature is provided in English translation in Musgrave and Peacock (1967): the excerpts from Mazola, Sax, Lindahl and Wicksell are particularly apposite.

A brief sketch of the Samuelsonian line may be useful here. Samuelson's strategy is first to *define* a pure 'public good' then to derive optimality conditions for the public good (to be contrasted with the analogous conditions for a 'private' good); and then to show that in the free market the optimum so defined will not be sustained. Samuelson takes from Lindahl and Wieksell the concept of a 'public good', a good which is equally and totally consumed by all members of a relevantly large group in such a way that no single consumer can be excluded from the benefits. Standard examples include outdoor fireworks displays, bushfire prevention, nuclear deterrence and ozone layer protection: more ozone layer protection for me is more for you and more for each current inhabitant of the earth. Such goods will be 'optimally' produced when the last unit of 'output' is valued at its opportunity cost – but the value in question must be the sum of the values placed on that unit by all the relevant consumers. Unlike private goods, where an additional unit (orange, ice-cream, loaf of bread) can be consumed *either* by you or me but not both, the extra unit of public good is consumed by all and hence the values that all place upon it are relevant. Samuelson formally derives the optimal conditions of production for the public good (the requirement that the sum of individual marginal valuations should equal marginal cost) and then proceeds to show that, if this optimal output happened to prevail in the market, it could not be sustained. At optimality, the last unit of output is valued by each at less than its cost; hence, no rational individual will contribute voluntarily at that level of output. Rather, each will have an incentive to 'free-ride' on the contributions of others. Samuelson does not formally derive market *equilibrium* conditions, but it is clear that in market equilibrium any person who contributes anything to the public good must receive a dollar's worth of benefit for the marginal dollar's contribution and this equilibrium condition is inconsistent with optimality (except in very special cases).

There is a substantial literature in economics dealing with public goods. (Olson

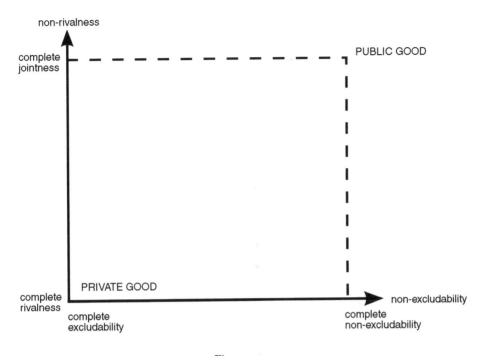

Figure 5.3
Map of possibilities

(1965) and R. Hardin (1982) provide discussions that are familiar outside economics as well as within.) The central theme in this literature has been to generalize the public goods concept and to trace market failure to various 'root causes'. Clearly, the pure public good is a kind of limiting case – as Samuelson puts it, a polar extreme. There are however *two* poles at stake, two properties that public goods exhibit in extreme form: one is 'non-excludability', which means that non-contributors cannot be excluded from consumption; the other is 'jointness in consumption' (or 'non-rivalness'), which involves the property that any consumers admitted can consume the entire output without reducing the consumption of other consumers. These properties are independent: the 'tragedy of the commons' (e.g. over-fishing the sea) is an example of non-excludability without jointness (see G. Hardin, 1968); theatrical performances (the indoor as opposed to outdoor circus) are an example of non-rivalness with full excludability. Both properties can be present in greater or lesser degree; exclusion may be more or less costly; non-rivalness can extend up to a certain number of consumers and then congestion may set in, or consumption may vary among consumers according to location (e.g. proximity to the source). One might on this basis conceptualize a two-dimensional map of possibilities, with two spectra – one running from complete excludability to total non-excludability; the other running from complete rivalness to complete non-rivalness. Such a map is offered as Figure 5.3. The two rival polar extremes of public and private goods are shown as the corners of the conceptual square; the task is to match each point in the square with some notional 'degree of market failure', measured conceptually by the value of unconsummated gains (supposing these gains could be recognized and valued), with the limiting case of zero failure at the private goods origin. Moreover, related concepts in the welfare economics literature (external economies, decreasing costs, etc.) can be located within this map and connected up to the corresponding level of market failure. All such market failure is ultimately attributable to n-person versions of the prisoners' dilemma interaction – the failure of decentralized action to produce preferred outcomes, or better put, the failure of market arrangements to motivate appropriate individual actions and to coordinate those individual actions to achieve desirable results. In all cases of market failure, it is not that markets do not send signals or provide incentives but the signals sent and the incentives provided are significantly distorted: in the pure public goods case, the distortions are extreme.

The moral of the Samuelsonian account is clear enough: whereas the market will reliably generate Pareto optimal qualities of private goods, there will be gross under-provision of public goods. Any normative presumption in favour of the market in the public goods case is thereby removed: if optimality in public goods supply is to be secured, state action will be required. Accordingly, the theory of public goods provides an in-principle answer to two of the central questions in any normative theory of state activity: first, what activities should government pursue? and second, on what scale should those activities be pursued (i.e. how large a share of GDP should the fisc appropriate)? Clearly, the second of these questions cannot be answered without reasonably detailed information about individuals' preferences (of a kind that the normative framework denies is available, apart from (necessarily distorted) market behaviour). But one apparent virtue of the Samuelsonian formulation is that no such detailed information is required to answer the first question. After all, public goods are defined by reference to their technical characteristics: lighthouses, defence, environmental protection, certain public health programmes (e.g. draining malarial swamps) are the classic examples. We may not know exactly how much environmental protection to provide, but we know that the market is not going to provide it in appropriate amounts. Happily, the implied domain of state activity includes many of the things that historical practice and our intuitions suggest *ought* to be the things government provides. And it is clear that the provision of the institutional apparatus of the market itself has significant public goods characteristics: the courts, the police, the relevant laws, all exhibit non-rivalness and non-excludability to an appreciable degree. The theory of the *productive* state is therefore appropriately connected analytically to the theory of the market-constitutional state.

But what of redistribution? Can the requirements of distributive justice be plausibly subsumed under the public goods rubric? To some extent, surely so. The responsibility that persons may feel to look after the poor in their community, the desire to pre-empt civil unrest, the preference for clean cities – these are all public goods of a kind: in each case, citizens may rationally contribute if their doing so ensures that large numbers of others will, but if each gives unilaterally then each will have a rational incentive to *under*-contribute. It is not by any means clear, however, that the moral demands of distributive justice are exhausted by 'internalizing' all the relevant 'external' effects. Persons may accept that they have moral obligations to the poor – accept, that is, that they have compelling reasons to act in a charitable manner, and yet not be at all inclined to act in the way required. If so, it is the way in which action is connected to (compelling, *tout court*) *reasons* for action that is defective – the very 'rationality' of the agent is open to question.

Musgrave, in his influential public economics treatise, baptized the term 'merit goods' to deal with such generalized failures of 'rationality'. For Musgrave, merit goods were to sit alongside public goods in his generalized 'economic theory of the state', although his own treatment of merit goods was sketchy and somewhat apologetic. Nor have merit goods achieved much currency in economics circles. Appeals to irrationality, multiple selves or possible paradoxes of preference endogeneity have not generally been recognized by economists as grounds for public intervention in market processes – perhaps because such appeals seemed to allow excessive scope for authoritarian governments, or because it was felt that decentralized action could in various ways handle such problems, or because the possibility of irrationality was simply ruled out by assumption.

Hence, the grammar of economist's reasoning in normative debate has a distinctive cast. In looking at a policy or programme or possible world, the economist will ask not whether that policy/programme or the world that results from it are themselves good or bad, but rather: *où sont les externalités?* Where are the elements of non-excludability and non-rivalry that would lead to 'market failure'? Unfortunately, in a large number of cases, the kind of information about individuals' preferences required to answer such a question will be difficult to acquire and may be inaccessible: the Robbins' critique of utilitarianism clearly bears here. Consequently, even if political agents were perfectly motivated to pursue the normative ideal that the economist's framework offers, it is by no means clear that those political agents would be able to deliver. For purely informational reasons, the identification of relevant externalities may be infeasible.

The constrained state – the 'public choice' challenge

Any normative theory of the state should attempt to answer questions about what government should do. And it is natural perhaps, that any deficiency observed in the social order should be an occasion for the remark that 'government should do something about it'. But this line is to cast government as *deus ex machina* in normative argument – and neither the *deus* nor the *ex machina* elements sit comfortably with the economic approach. As public choice theorists have continuously argued, the public goods account of the role of government makes appeal to a 'benevolent despot' model of government that is hopelessly at odds with assumptions made elsewhere in economics about human motivations and social institutions.

In the first place, if it *were* appropriate to assume that government could be treated as a single decision-making agent, then that agent ought to be assumed to be motivated in exactly the same way as all other agents: that is, to have purposes and interests of his own and in particular purposes distinct from and independent of those of (other) citizens. But, in the second place, government (even autocracy) cannot be plausibly modelled as a single independent decision-maker. There are always constraints – threat of coup or popular uprising, people to be bought off, etc. – that require that some account be taken of others' interests. And of course in democratic settings, what stands for government is the whole network of political institutions. Given that conception of 'government' as *political process*, the idea of those political processes *directly* choosing a social outcome according to some independent ethical norm appears as an absurdity. The relevant question is rather whether democratic institutions offer a solution to the principal–agent problem – whether democratic political process has 'invisible hand' properties analogous to those of the idealized market, which might reliably produce public goods in roughly optimal quantities. For if *not*, then market failure is not sufficient grounds for state action – politics cannot be expected not to 'fail' also. Pareto optimality in public goods supply is not only infeasible though markets, it may be infeasible *simpliciter*.

The investigation of possible 'invisible hand' properties of democratic political process is the central item on the agenda of normative public choice scholarship (sometimes called 'constitutional political economy'). Because the major issue in this investigation is the comparison of political processes with idealized markets, it is natural that public choice economists should seek to appraise political processes using the same analytic techniques, the same assumptions about human motivation, the same general intellectual apparatus as they use in the analysis of markets. To do otherwise is to run the risk of introducing bias into the politics/market comparison. Accordingly, while some scholars may be attracted to public choice analysis because it offers a theoretical structure to political science, or because it offers a set of predictions about behaviour that seems to have worked tolerably well in other settings, or because they happen to believe that the basic premisses of economics are TRUE, 'constitutional political economists' are attracted to public choice analysis for *methodological* reasons. The analyst makes identical behavioural assumptions and exposes institutions to the same normative tests because that is what proper comparative institutional analysis requires.

Given the intellectual history as I have outlined it, public choice scholarship has naturally focused on the question of what the proper domain of the productive state should be. This question, although a central one for political philosophy, certainly does not exhaust political philosophers' concerns. Nevertheless, the economist would insist that feasibility questions are central to any of those wider concerns: a purely descriptive understanding of the workings of political processes must underpin any authoritative normative claims. And what the modern economist would accept as a suitable 'descriptive understanding' will include extensive reliance on formal deductive models, producing hypotheses that the data do not decisively reject.

Predictably, public choice economists have concentrated on those pieces of political apparatus that seem most significant in constraining the behaviour of political agents. And within democratic contexts, the primary such piece is electoral competition. As public choice scholars see it, the requirement that candidates/parties and the policies they stand for must submit to periodic popular elections is the primary mechanism (and perhaps ultimately the only one) ensuring that those candidates/parties have a derived interest in the interests of citizens. To the economist's eye, all other possible pieces of democratic apparatus – freedom of the press; bicameralist legislatures; even the separation of powers, or the rule of law – are either of second-order significance or parasitic upon electoral constraints. In this sense at least, public choice economists are democrats to the core. That is, the presence of electoral constraints, with full freedom of entry into electoral races, is a characteristic feature of democracy – and without those constraints, the likelihood that citizens' interests would figure in the conduct of politics is seen to be minimal. Hence, although public choice scholarship has been critical of democratic political process in terms of its capacity to achieve Pareto optimality, and critical of democratic politics *vis-à-vis* the market place in those cases where goods are 'private', democracy is nevertheless seen to be the best form of political organization. Or at least democracy will be best to the extent that electoral 'constraints' *do* constrain. And it is that question – the constraining properties of electoral competition in ensuring outcomes in accord with those that citizens want – that has been the main item on the public choice agenda.

It is not possible here to give much more than a sketch of the central results that emerge from that agenda. But not much more than a sketch is necessary (see Mueller, 1990, for an extensive treatment). The natural point of departure is the so-called 'median-voter theorem' – the proposition that, provided voters' ideal political positions can be laid out along a single spectrum, electoral competition between two parties will ensure an outcome at or close to the median position of that spectrum (i.e. the 'ideal' of the median voter). The force of the proposition can be seen by supposing that a party/candidate were to locate somewhere else: such a candidate could always be beaten by a rival who locates closer to the median, provided that all voters vote for outcomes closer to their ideal (an assumption that sits comfortably with standard preference theory). Take the public goods case specifically, and suppose that the tax system is such that each voter can recognize the (marginal) cost in private goods forgone of an additional dollar of public goods spending. Then, assuming that each voter reliably votes for the party/candidate who offers a level of public goods 'closer' to her ideal, electoral competition will push candidates/parties towards the ideal of the median voter. (I say 'push towards' because parties may not know voters' preferences, or they may be constrained by pre-selection by requirements or other considerations.) The result here is a direct application of spatial competition models, originally addressed (by Hotelling, 1929) to the issue of firms locating along a road. The normative implications of this model are encouraging for democracy. Although full optimality will be achieved only in special circumstances, the level of public goods supply generated will be, in general, not too far from the optimal level (as specified by the Samuelsonian conditions). Of course, the median outcome takes no account of different individuals' intensity of preference: for example, every voter bar one (the median) could reduce her demand for the public good and there would be no response in the political outcome, provided that the median *ex ante* remained the median *ex post*. This observation is sufficient to sustain the conclusion that the median voter outcome is not in general Pareto optimal: optimality would require that the outcome respond to changes in any one citizen's demand, other things equal.

Within that median voter model, electoral competition constrains the behaviour of politicians completely; political candidates/parties become mere ciphers for the median voter. One can, of course, loosen the bounds of electoral constraints (for example, by allowing uncertainty about the median voter's location along the policy dimension, or by assigning major parties some natural advantage over new entrants in the electoral stakes) but in this simple model, policies *are* pretty much constrained by citizen preferences over them: one can have tolerable confidence in political processes, provided the median voter result obtains (Downs, 1957, provides the classic early treatment).

However, the public choice literature reveals just how fragile that median voter result is. For example, once we move from a one-dimensional issue space to a two- or higher dimensional one, the median voter rule collapses into a chaos of perpetual instability. The reason for this is clear. In the single dimension case, the scope for construction of a majority is severely limited: in particular, there is no possible coalition involving the extremes that could defeat a centrist policy. In the two-dimensional case, there is no such restriction, in general. The high demanders of one public good (defence, say) can form a coalition with the high demanders of another (welfare spending, say) or with the low demanders of welfare spending – and equally, the low demanders of defence can bid to form competitive coalitions. The two- (and higher) dimensional case is analogous to the problem of dividing up a fixed amount of money among n-voters; there is clearly no way of dividing 100 dollars among three persons in such a way that there is no other division that will not leave two of those persons better off. The general theorem here is McKelvey's (1976): that, in general, there exists a path of majority approved moves (pair-wise comparisons) which will lead from any starting point in policy space to any finishing point. Strictly speaking, there is no majority equilibrium. And more to the point there is no position in policy space that cannot be ruled out under majority rule, however little it accords with what citizens want. McKelvey interprets the result as implying that a strategic agenda-setter can always secure the outcome she herself wants. In that sense, majority rule does not ultimately constrain political agents at all: as a solution to the principal–agent problem, democratic processes (and electoral competition specifically) fail.

The restrictions on individual preferences required to avoid this problem of majoritarian instability seem on their face to be so severe that any optimism attaching to democratic process (whether grounded in the median-voter theorem or elsewhere) seems illusory. The issue space is almost necessarily n-dimensional, for once governments have the power to redistribute (whether directly through taxes and transfers or indirectly via regulations, tariff protection, production subsidies and the like), the general indeterminacy of dividing the cake so that a majority approves instantly appears. All that is required for this instability result is the apparently innocuous assumption that voters vote for whatever makes them better off.

Public choice theorists have then generally seen the central problem of democratic politics to be that of majoritarian instability – not because stability is an end in itself but because the instability knows no logical bounds. We seem to confront either a random walk through policy space in which no policy however bad can be excluded, or a stable outcome that reflects the preferences of the strategic agenda-setter. Or at least we would do so unless some further institutional apparatus can be set in place that would limit the prospects for such instability. Various possibilities have been discussed in this connection – presidential veto (Hammond and Miller, 1989); bicameralism (Hammond and Miller, 1989; Brennan and Hamlin, 1992);

the Congressional committee system (Shepsle and Weingast, 1981), and so on. In all such cases, however, the analysis is predicated on a particular diagnosis of 'the problem of democracy': in all cases, the aim is to suppress natural majoritarian instability in such a manner that the cure is not worse than the disease.

Brennan and Lomasky (1992) have argued that this diagnosis of 'the problem' is itself somewhat defective. Certainly those whose interpretations of democratic process are not informed by public choice analysis have difficulty in identifying the kinds of radical instability in policy outcomes that public choice theory implies ought to characterize the world we observe. If anything, we seem to confront rather a policy inertia – enormous reluctance to depart from existing policy arrangements except via marginal adjustments. Some significant changes are, of course, occasionally observed but they are rarely reversed in short order or followed by a set of other changes in some very different direction. Moreover, any claim that politicians are not significantly constrained by electoral considerations seems to be belied by the extraordinary attention those politicians pay to the media and the opinion polls.

The Brennan–Lomasky thesis is that majoritarian cycling is not the salient problem that public choice orthodoxy makes out because voters do not systematically vote for outcomes that leave them better off. Voting is, on our view, more like cheering at a football match than like choosing an asset portfolio, because in voting the 'expression of preference' by any individual voter is crucially divorced from the electoral outcome. The one-to-one connection between action and outcome characteristic of individual choice in market settings and on which the 'revealed preference' logic of consumer theory depends is absent in the electoral context One implication is that ethical and ideological factors are likely to play a disproportionately large role in politics: the cost to voters of expressing ethical or ideological convictions is almost negligible compared with that cost in arenas like the market-place where the chooser is decisive. The individual's reasons for acting according to the dictates of 'interest' (however exactly interests are defined) are virtually absent at the ballot box. Accordingly, in the simple 'divide-the-cake' example, individuals are much more likely to be led by affective considerations (such as the claims of justice) than by their own particular pay-off: the expected difference to a voter of a personal pay-off of, say, $10,000 and a personal pay-off of zero is almost certainly only a matter of a few cents, once that voter takes account of the likelihood that his vote will exercise an influence on the outcome.

If, however, this 'veil of insignificance' afflicting the individual voter is likely to suppress majoritarian instability and cycling problems, the absence of a connection between votes and interests must be an occasion for anxiety of a different kind. Specifically, there is nothing in the logic of voter choice to prevent the electoral process from securing electoral outcomes that *no* voter would choose if decisive. Voters may vote according to ethical or ideological convictions – but they may equally vote according to candidates' looks or party loyalty or whim or from hatred of the 'other side' or a whole host of other factors that have little connection with the public interest, almost however the 'public interest' is conceived. Political representatives might be constrained by electoral considerations, but those electoral considerations bear no necessary connection to community or majority interests. The simple median voter model might, for example, be applicable in a wide range of cases, but the normative implications of that model are utterly ambiguous unless the median voter (and other voters) reliably vote their interests, or more heroically their conceptions of the public good.

The general message of all this is an appropriately dismal one. Pareto optimality (and for that matter distributive equity) is feasible neither through decentralized market institutions, because of public goods problems arising in a significant range of cases, nor via centralized collective action. Political arrangements are prone both to majoritarian instability problems and to problems of electoral perversity. In the latter case, there is much scope for the intrusion of moral argument in political process itself – but the kinds of morality that are likely to dominate are those of the demagogue, those that will induce voters to cheer, rather than those associated with the philosophic temperament. On this reading, 'morality' plays a positive rather than normative role: only that moral reasoning that is politically effective will be analytically relevant – not the morality that is compelling in the quieter setting of the political philosophy seminar.

In the specific public goods case, it must remain a somewhat open question as to whether 'state intervention' in the market is desirable or not. The market failure literature surely indicates that the argument for state intervention is strongest for pure public goods, but whether that argument is strong enough must be a matter for conjecture. Moreover, here as elsewhere, feasibility considerations bite. For if decisions on the domain of state activity are taken as a matter of in-period politics itself, then those decisions too are to be analysed by appeal to a descriptive rather than purely prescriptive model of politics. In the Brennan–Lomasky 'expressive voting' model, for example, the domain of public activity will tend to be decided according to whether voters find an activity 'cheerable' or not rather than because of the non-rivalness and non-excludability properties of the good in question. Many voters may of course 'cheer' much of the time for what they perceive as the 'public interest', and if prevailing conceptions of the public interest are informed by market failure theory then the argument that the public sector should provide 'public goods' will predictably exercise some influence. This possibility, however, hardly represents a robust rehabilitation of welfare economics as positive politics. Welfare economics may isolate an appropriate conception of the desirable – including a detailed specification of what goods government ought to provide, and in what quantities. But welfare economics in itself cannot tell us how to *achieve* the desirable, and the message from public choice theory, a message from *within* economics, does not encourage much optimism in this regard.

Implications, conclusions and misgivings

By way of conclusion, let me offer a brief summary. First I tried to give an account of the economist's contribution to political philosophy as a matter of taking feasibility considerations seriously (p. 125). I then tried to show what that ambition might imply for the style of normative theorizing adopted and for the conception of the desirable itself (pp. 126–33). I next directed attention to two instances of 'feasibility-thinking' which have been important for economics – Robbins' epistomological attack on simple utilitarianism; and the assumptions about human nature that dominate economic thinking (pp. 133–42). Finally, I tried to give an account – albeit a sketchy and somewhat personal one – of the economist's theory of the state, in both its 'normative' and positive aspects (pp. 143–53). I place quotation marks around 'normative' here because in my view the public choice claim that public goods theory is inadequate as an account of what government 'should do' is totally unexceptionable. The theory of public goods should be seen simply as an account of 'market failure' with the 'failure' understood by reference to an idealized market benchmark (and not by inference to the implied institutional alternative). A proper normative theory of the state must include some analogous account of 'political failure', and that account must be grounded in a purely positive theory of how political process actually works. In developing such a theory, public choice economists have focused largely on the issue of the proper domain of democratic political activity and in particular on the comparison of centralized (political) with decentralized decision-making processes. However, public choice analysis can also be (and occasionally is) used to evaluate particular political arrangements – including such institutions as bicameralism, super-majoritarian voting rules, the committee system, the secret ballot, and so on.

One aspect of the economic approach that is conspicuous here is its emphasis on institutions. On at least one influential view (Buchanan, 1977), institutions are the uniquely proper domain of the economist's concern. There are three reasons for taking that line: first, that normative analysis of particular policies or actions (as opposed to the institutional setting in which those policy/actions are determined) requires information about individual preferences that is not normally available; second, that the analytic techniques of economics are particularly oriented towards institutional study; and third, that because (on an argument similar to Rawls') institutions aggregate instances of choice in which participants play a variety of roles, each rational individual is likely to take a more enlightened view than would be taken in each instance – uncertainty about roles to be played over the indefinite future life of the institution washes out narrow self-interest, simply by making it unidentifiable. Isolating the circumstances under which particular institutional arrangements (decentralized market arrangements or centralized collective ones) are likely to work better is the core of the economist's theory of the state and of the economic contribution to normative social theory more generally.

Let me conclude with a proviso and a misgiving. The proviso is that the emphasis on feasibility, and the constraints imposed by the real world, carry a false impression of confidence in social analysis. After all, an outcome is either feasible or it is not. Yet economic analysis (and social science more generally) is not capable of determining the 'feasible set' with any degree of specificity. Determining what is feasible depends on an enormous range of assumptions about the way the social world is and the complex connections between the various bits of it – assumptions that are sometimes controversial and that are, by the nature of the beast, rarely able to be conclusively rejected on the basis of the available evidence. To acknowledge this fact is not to concede that anything goes: it is rather to accept that feasibility claims are, properly understood, ones about what is more (and less) likely. Taking feasibility seriously is mainly a matter of rejecting implausible assumptions rather than producing incontrovertible 'laws' of social organization.

And finally a misgiving about the anti-idealist thrust of the economist's style of normative theorising. We are nowadays utterly familiar with the notion that the act of observation may alter that which is being observed. The dimensions of interconnectedness between observer and observed (and indeed between behaviour and theory about behaviour) are, however, much richer and more complex in social life than in modern physics. As the aphorism goes, nothing is so implausible that thinking cannot make it so. In the particular context here, unheroic theories of human behaviour may enter popular discourse and colour the behaviour those theories are meant to describe. More particularly still, institutions chosen to deal with worst case scenarios or even most likely ones, may be embodying particular assumptions about human nature which encourage that behaviour and undermine the virtue or heroism that helps those institutions to work well. Anxieties of this kind are not new: the concept of the 'noble lie' is a Platonic one. Nor is the anxiety decisive: the predicted feedback effects of institutional choice on behaviour ought to be included in proper normative analysis but they surely do not *exhaust it.* Nevertheless, the anxiety is one that is especially notable in commentary on economics (usually by non-economists) and more especially still in commentary on public choice theory (S. Kelman, 1987 and M. Kelman, 1988 provide notable examples). The dismal science may, whatever its 'purely scientific' virtues, serve to make life more dismal – and that is a cost to be reckoned with.

See also 1 ANALYTICAL PHILOSOPHY; 3 HISTORY; 4 SOCIOLOGY; 6 POLITICAL SCIENCE; 11 LIBERALISM; 13 SOCIALISM; 14 AUTONOMY; 16 CONTRACT AND CONSENT; 17 CONSTITUTIONALISM AND THE RULE OF LAW; 18 CORPORATISM AND SYNDICALISM; 19 DEMOCRACY; 22 DISTRIBUTIVE JUSTICE; 23 EFFICIENCY; 25 EQUALITY; 29 LIBERTY; 30 POWER; 31 PROPERTY; 36 STATE; 38 TOTALITARIANISM; 41 WELFARE

References

Arrow, K.: *Social Choice and Individual Values* (New York: Wiley, 1951).

———— and Hahn, F.: *General Competitive Analysis* (Edinburgh: Oliver & Boyd, 1971).

Atkinson, A. B. and Stiglitz, J.: *Lectures on Public Economics* (New York: McGraw-Hill, 1980).

Becker, G. and Stigler, G.: 'De gustibus non est disputandum', *American Economic Review*, 67, 2 (March 1977), 76–90.

Bolingbroke, Viscount: In *The Craftsman*, 28 February 1730.

Brennan, G.: 'Horizontal equity: an extension', *Public Finance/Finances Publiques*, 26, 3 (1971), 437–56.

————: 'Second-best aspects of horizontal equity questions', *Public Finance/Finances Publiques*, 27, 3 (1972), 282–91.

———— and Buchanan, J.: *The Reason of Rules* (New York: Cambridge University Press, 1985).

———— and Hamlin, A.: 'Bi-cameralism and stability', *Public Choice* (1992).

———— and Lomasky, L.: *Democracy and Decision* (New York: Cambridge University Press, 1992).

Broome, J.: 'Rational choice and value in economics', *Oxford Economic Papers*, 30 (1978), 313–33.

————: *Weighing Goods* (Oxford: Basil Blackwell, 1991).

Buchanan, J.: 'The relevance of Pareto optimality', *Journal of Conflict Resolution*, 6 (1962), 341–54.

————: *The Limits of Liberty* (Chicago: University of Chicago Press, 1975).

————: *Freedom in Constitutional Contract* (College Station: Texas A & M University Press, 1977).

———— and Tullock, G.: *The Calculus of Consent* (Chapel Hill, NC: University of North Carolina Press, 1962).

Coughlin, P.: 'Pareto optimality of policy proposals with probabilistic voting', *Public Choice*, 39 (1982), 427–34.

Downs, A.: *An Economic Theory of Democracy* (New York: Harper & Row, 1957).

Hamilton, A.: *Federalist Papers*, No. 72 (21 March 1988).

Hamlin, A.: *Ethics, Economics and the State* (Brighton: Wheatsheaf Books, 1986).

Hammond, T. and Miller, G.: 'The core of the constitution', *American Political Science Review*, 81, 4 (1987), 1155–74.

Hardin, G.: 'The tragedy of the commons', *Science*, 162 (1968), 1243–8.

Hardin, R.: *Collective Action* (Baltimore, Md.: Johns Hopkins University Press, 1982).

Hayek, F., ed.: *Collectivist Economic Planning: Critical Studies on the Possibilities of Socialism* (London: Routledge, 1975).

————: *The Fatal Conceit: The Errors of Socialism* (Chicago: University of Chicago Press, 1988).

Harsanyi, J.: 'Cardinal welfare, individualistic ethics and inter-personal comparisons of utility', *Journal of Political Economy*, 63 (1955), 309–21.

————: *Essays in Ethics, Social Behaviour and Scientific Explanation* (Dordrecht: D. Reidel, 1976).

Head, J.: *Public Goods and Public Welfare* (Durham, NC: Duke University Press, 1974).

Heyne, P.: *The Economic Way of Thinking* (London: Macmillan, 1973).

Hicks, J.: 'The valuation of social income', *Economica*, 7 (1940), 105–24.

Hirschman, A.: 'Against parsimony', *Economics and Philosophy*, 1 (1985), 7–22.

Hotelling, H.: 'Stability in competition', *Economic Journal*, 39 (1929), 41–57.

Johnson, S. and Mayer, T.: 'An extension of Sidgwick's equity principle', *Quarterly Journal of Economics*, 76 (1962), 454–63.

Kaldor, N.: 'Welfare propositions of economics and interpersonal comparisons of utility', *Economic Journal*, 49 (1939), 549–52.

Kelman, M.: 'On democracy bashing', *Virginia Law Review*, 74, 2 (1988), 199–273.

Kelman, S.: 'Public choice and public spirit', *Public Interest*, 80 (1987), 80–94.

Lerner, A.: *The Economics of Control* (New York: Macmillan, 1944).

Lipsey, R. and Lancaster, K.: 'The general theory of second-best', *Review of Economic Studies*, 24 (1956–7), 11–32.

Little, I. M. D.: *A Critique of Welfare Economics* (Oxford: Oxford University Press, 1957).

Luce, D. and Raiffa, H.: *Games and Decisions* (New York: John Wiley & Sons, 1957).

McKelvey, R.: 'Intransitivities in multi-dimensional voting models and some implications for agenda control', *Journal of Economic Theory*, 12 (1976), 472–82.

Mises, Ludwig von: *Socialism* (1922); (Indianapolis: Liberty Classics, 1981).

Musgrave, R.: *The Theory of Public Finance* (New York: McGraw-Hill, 1959).

———— and Peacock, A.: *Classics in the Theory of Public Finance* (London: Macmillan, 1967).

Olson, M.: *The Logic of Collective Action* (Cambridge, Mass.: Harvard University Press, 1965).

Plotnick, R.: 'The concept and measurement of horizontal inequity', *Journal of Public Economics*, 17, 3 (1982), 373–92.

Robbins, L.: *The Nature and Significance of Economic Science* (London: Macmillan, 1932).

Robertson, D.: 'What do economists economize?', in *Economic Commentaries* (London: Staples Press, 1956).

Samuelson, P.: 'The pure theory of public expenditure', *Review of Economics and Statistics*, 36 (1954), 387–9.

——: 'Diagrammatic exposition of a theory of public expenditure', *Review of Economics and Statistics*, 37 (1955), 350–6.

Schelling, T.: *The Strategy of Conflict* (Cambridge, Mass.: Harvard University Press, 1960).

——: *Micromotives and Macrobehaviour* (New York: W. W. Norton, 1978).

Scitovsky, T.: 'A note on welfare propositions in economics', *Review of Economic Studies*, 9 (1941–2), 77–88.

Sen, A.: 'Rational fools: a critique of the behavioral foundations of economic theory', *Philosophy and Public Affairs*, 6 (1977), 314–44.

——: 'Utilitarianism and welfarism', *Journal of Philosophy*, 76 (1979), 463–89.

——: 'Rights and agency', *Philosophy and Public Affairs*, 11 (1982), 3–39.

Shepsle, K. A.: 'Institutional arrangements and equilibrium in multi-dimensional voting models', *American Journal of Political Science*, 23 (1979), 27–60.

—— and Weingast, B. R.: 'Structure induced equilibrium and legislative choice', *Public Choice*, 36 (1981), 221–37.

Shubik, M.: *Game Theory in the Social Sciences* (Cambridge, Mass.: The MIT Press, 1982).

Stern, N.: 'On the specification of models of optimum income taxation', *Journal of Public Economics*, 6 (1976), 123–62.

White, M. and White, A.: 'Horizontal inequity in the federal income tax treatment of homeowners and tenants', *National Tax Journal*, 18 (1965), 225–39.

6

The contribution of political science

ROBERT E. GOODIN

Within modern moral philosophy there has been a recent shift away from questions of personal rectitude and towards questions of public values (Schneewind, 1991, pp. 155–6). Within modern political philosophy, we are on the verge of a similar shift. The shift here in view is away from a narrow focus on questions of what values ought to be pursued publicly and more towards questions of how values can and ought to be embodied institutionally.

One of the central lessons of contemporary social science for contemporary political philosophy is that we cannot propound any values we like, confident that an institutional shell can be found for pursuing all of them simultaneously. Indeed, sometimes we cannot even find satisfactory institutions for pursuing each of them separately. Take something as presumably straightforward as economic redistribution: it turns out that notionally progressive income taxes are actually mildly regressive in their real incidence (Pechman, 1974); and notionally egalitarian social services freely available to all actually benefit the middle classes marginally more than the poor (Goodin et al., 1987).

Social reformers necessarily proceed, after the fashion of Rousseau ([1762] 1973, Book 1), 'taking men as they are and laws as they can be'. But the lessons of the behavioural revolution are that taking people 'as they are' may be more constraining than we ever imagined. The lessons of the policy sciences are that there are far fewer ways that institutions 'can be' than we ever supposed. All told, the constraints might be so severe that it would make more sense to start with the limited number of institutional options, rather than with a value-driven wish list and searching for institutions that might more or less fill that bill.

It is not all a matter of constraints, though. Putting politics first in this way might reveal new values, as well. When working down from first principles, the social centrality of a principle of 'protecting the vulnerable' might not immediately strike us; but it certainly does working from the other end, reflecting upon the fair distribution of radiological risks from nuclear power plants (Goodin, 1982a, p. 214; 1985). Similarly, principles of just war must be adapted in light of new technologies of mass destruction: harms to noncombatants that are clearly foreseen but not intended might have been tolerable when military hardware was such that civilian fatalities occurred only occasionally and were kept within modest proportions; they are far less so when the weaponry is such that it necessarily kills everyone for miles around, inevitably including a great many innocent civilians.

In this chapter, I shall concentrate upon the contribution to political philosophy from mainstream, empirically-oriented political science and its ancillary subdisciplines. Despite its roots among nineteenth-century British social reformers (Collini, Winch and Burrows, 1983), political science as presently practised is essentially a postwar and predominantly a North American discipline (Lipset, 1969). A survey such as this cannot help but reflect that fact, although I shall allude to as diverse a set of locales as the literature permits.

In concentrating on the contribution of empirical political science, I do not mean to denigrate the role of normative political theory. That remains a thriving subdiscipline within political science, and one whose contributions to contemporary political philosophy can safely be ignored in this chapter precisely because they so thoroughly permeate so many of the others. The contributions of the more empirical sides of the discipline, although less obvious, can be no less substantial. That certainly is so where empirical enquiries are explicitly guided by genuinely normative concerns; there may even be certain empirical facts touching on political philosophy almost however it is conceived and almost whatever one's normative stance.

According to the self-conception of the discipline of empirical political science, its distinctive focus is on 'power' – its distribution and its distributional consequences. Politics, in Harold Lasswell's (1950) famous phrase, is the study of 'who gets what, when, how'. The question of 'how' is to be answered by studying the distribution and interplay of power and influence in all their myriad forms. Therein lies the essence of 'modern political analysis' (Dahl, 1976).

That disciplinary self-conception fixes our initial focus upon the intentional actions of particularly powerful individual agents. Power is first and foremost the 'production of intended effects'. But intentions ossify into structures. These artefacts come to have a life all their own and, in a way, even to exercise power (or at least constrain others in their attempts to exercise power) all on their own. For one famous example, Robert Moses intentionally built the underpasses on the Long Island Expressway too low to allow passage of buses, which might carry poor blacks to prosperous white suburbs: the structures and consequent constraints on movement of bus-riding New Yorkers remain, even after Moses was long in his grave (Winner, 1980, pp. 22–3; Ward, 1987, p. 604–5). Political scientists are divided over whether the study of individual agents or of social structures is the most fruitful path to the understanding of social power distributions (Skocpol, 1979; Wendt, 1987). Much can be learnt from studying the internal logic of certain social structures, abstracting from any individuals' intentions. Given the problems to which Wittfogel's (1957) 'hydraulic society' constitutes a solution – problems of governing water supply in arid regions – 'oriental despotism' is arguably the inevitable consequence. Given the way military technology unfolded in the early modern age, the modern state was arguably the inevitable consequence (Mann, 1986). And – for the most famous claim of this sort – the socio-legal and political superstructure of a society is arguably fully determined by the economic base and the fundamental technological mode of production contained within it (Cohen, 1978, ch. 6).

There is, of course, a raging dispute surrounding each of those claims, not least the last. Many doubt that the liberal democratic state constitutes the 'perfect shell' for capitalism and that it predominates for that reason (Jessop, 1990). Still, it is tolerably clear how this broad style of argument might plausibly work. Given all the rest of the surrounding institutional structure, a niche of a very particular shape is created for any particular social institution (Ollman, 1971, pp. 249–54). Some such jigsaw-fitting analogy constitutes the essence of the structuralist claim. Still, even in the most structurally determined of theories, there remains considerable scope for the exercise of human agency. The work of the 'analytical Marxists' – of Jon Elster (1985) and John Roemer (1982; 1986), most especially – show just how many of the central Marxian tenets derive from collective action problems and bargaining among people with unequal resources. Those very individualistic tools of neoclassical micro-economics explain much that might otherwise be put down, in off-hand fashion, to the play of purely structural forces.

There is the further question of whence the structures themselves arose. Some constraints on human action (the laws of physics, and so forth) are truly independent of human agency. But social structures are the creation of social action, which in the last analysis arguably always comes down to the actions and interactions of natural individuals. (See chapter 1 above.) That is not to imply intentionality in the outcome: on the contrary, many social structures and outcomes are unintended, the accidental effects of various agents pulling in their own directions and for their own reasons (Merton, 1936). And at least sometimes those individual actions themselves might not be 'purposive' in any strong, goal-seeking sense. Be all that as it may, it seems a fair general characterization of the subject to say that politics is all about agency working through structures, which are themselves just the embodiments of past power-plays.

The operation of democracy

For all its official macro-sociological concern with the distribution of power and its influence on the patterning of social benefits and burdens, postwar political science has concentrated heavily on individual-level behaviour. Furthermore, the focus has been on behaviour in one particular (electoral) setting, which may or may not bear much relation to overall social power or distributional consequences. I shall follow the profession itself in focusing first on voting behaviour, but I shall soon open that out into a larger discussion of the operation of democracy more generally.

Empirical results: voting

There is a certain populist view of democracy, easily parodied and possibly never actually embraced in precisely that form. Still, it remains influential. According to this populist view, political power is supposed to be dispersed to voters who, reflecting deeply upon the issues at stake, form their reasoned, independent judgements of what ought be done; and all those judgements are then aggregated impartially into an overall social decision (Berelson, Lazarsfeld and McPhee, 1954, ch. 14; cf. Duncan and Lukes, 1963).

If that is what democracy requires, there is little chance of realizing that ideal – at least according to the standard interpretation of the results of modern sample surveys of political attitudes and behaviour (Thompson, 1970; cf. Pateman, 1970; 1971). Whereas that model posits reasoned reflection on the issues, surveys find that only a tiny proportion of voters say they are taking any principled stand on the issues (Converse, 1964, p. 218). Whereas that model posits independent, rational agents, survey researchers standardly claim to find people voting in knee-jerk response either to unexamined group or class loyalties (Berelson, Lazarsfeld and McPhee, 1954) or to their early childhood socialization experiences – the best correlate of the vote, it is often said, is the voter's party identification, the best correlate of which in turn is the parents' party identification (Campbell et al., 1960, ch. 7). Whereas the model of populist democracy requires the impartial aggregation of votes – and a corresponding willingness to weigh all opinions equally and to count everyone else's vote as equal to one's own – survey research shows voters to be intolerant, even of some of the most fundamental prerequisites of democratic politics including free expression itself (McCloskey, 1964). All this evidence seems to suggest that ordinary people were unfit to discharge their civil functions responsibly – so unfit, indeed, that many commentators took to saying that the stability of democratic institutions presupposes not mass participation, but rather mass apathy (Almond and Verba, 1963).

Such conclusions depend crucially on imposing a heavily social-psychological interpretation upon the evidence, however. Sociologists themselves began reacting against such an 'oversocialized conception of man' (Wrong, 1961) and mounting pleas to 'bring men back in' (Homans, 1964) at just about the time political scientists were themselves buying heavily into that model. In recent years, political scientists have come increasingly to share such reservations.

It has long been recognized that there are various other ways of interpreting the central findings that gave rise to models of political socialization in the first place. V. O. Key (1966) argued, in defence of *The Responsible Electorate*, that people vote the same way as their parents, not as automata responding unthinkingly to early childhood programming, but simply because they inherited the same socio-economic lot as their parents: rational reflection on their interests would lead them to the same party political conclusions as their parents. Or again, higher levels of political participation among people of higher socio-economic status need not be explained in terms of their greater 'ego strength' (cf. Verba and Nie, 1972; Verba, Nie and Kim, 1978): it might just be that people with more social resources rationally suppose that they stand a better chance of changing social outcomes (Pateman, 1971; 1989, ch. 7; Goodin and Dryzek, 1980).

The most systematic re-analysis to date of the survey data on which that sociological interpretation of voting was based leads to the compelling conclusion that, far from being socially or psychologically programmed, voters are rational agents trying the best they can – under decidedly non-ideal conditions – to choose candidates whose policy preferences most nearly match their own (Popkin et al., 1976; Page and Shapiro, 1992). The non-ideal conditions in view derive primarily from the fact that it is perfectly rational for any one voter, given how little chance her own vote has of changing the outcome, not to invest heavily in information to enable her to choose precisely the right candidate. A certain measure of voter ignorance is therefore perfectly rational. In those circumstances, various shortcuts prove rational, among them fixating on party labels as cues to likely policy positions (Downs, 1957, ch. 7) and voting retrospectively on the basis of experience with a party in power rather than cuing on mere promises (Downs, 1957, ch. 3; Fiorina, 1981).

Flattering though this may be to the rationality of voters, it still leaves them largely unfit to govern directly in the ways that the populist parody prescribes. But it does at least go some way towards underwriting, normatively, the democratic component within models of democratic elitism, canvassed below (pp. 162–5). Voters are at least capable of making reasoned, independent decisions on issues of broad policy. They are capable of – indeed, they are inclined towards – genuine political deliberation and judgement, at least within limits.

Note well that in saying that voters are rationally choosing candidates nearest to their own policy preferences, the basis for those policy preferences is left open. There is, specifically, no presumption that voters are egoistically maximizing material benefits for themselves or their families. There is considerable evidence of 'symbolic' voting (Sears et al., 1980) on the one hand, and of genuinely public-spirited voting on the other (Sen, 1977a; Mansbridge, 1990).

In what is still the most telling demonstration of the latter, Kiewiet (1983) re-analysed the familiar fact that voters tend to re-elect governments they perceive to have managed the economy well. The natural, cynical interpretation of that fact is that people vote for their own financial interests, on the assumption that the better the economy is doing overall the better people would be doing individually. Disaggregating the responses, however, Kiewiet finds that the strongest correlate with pro-incumbent voting is not one's own economic fate over the last few years but rather one's perception of the national economy as a whole; so even those who have themselves suffered economic hardships are none the less willing to reward parties that have been good for the country as a whole. Voters were thus casting their ballots in a public-spirited fashion, all along.

Power and elites

The findings of modern political science thus drive us away from populist models and toward models of 'democratic elitism'. Instead of dictating the micro-management of particular policies, or even putting together the policy packages themselves, voters are – according to Schumpeter's (1950, ch. 12) model, which remains the most compelling of its kind – asked to choose between competing elites offering distinctive policy packages of their own devising. Voters in this way set the broad outlines of policy, which is what social surveys suggest they might be competent to do, while leaving the detailed development and implementation of those policies to elected officials and their advisers. Periodic opportunities to ratify or revoke a government's authority to continue ruling in this way makes the scheme tolerably democratic. Entrusting day-to-day management of policy to elected officials (and civil servants responsible to them) makes it elitist, in the way that any political system evidently has to be (Self, 1977).

While the name 'democratic elitism' is novel and possibly provocative, the basic idea is familiar to the point of being trite. Arguments for representative versus direct democracy, and for representatives regarding themselves as trustees rather than as mere delegates, ultimately have always been couched in just such terms. So too has the parallel distinction, found even in Rousseau ([1762] 1973, Book 3), between politics and administration – between the basic choice of policy directions and the day-to-day management of those policy initiatives. It has long been conceded by virtually everyone writing on the topic that we will need 'elites' of at least this latter, purely bureaucratic sort; and it has widely been thought that we will need ones of the former, more political sort, as well.

The fear of elites that has long bedevilled the so-called 'community power' debate is fear of a rather different sort of power holder. This elite is literally policy-making, rather than merely policy-proposing or policy-implementing in character. The fear is that there might be some small number of citizens who – because of their economic power or social status – might be in a position to dictate all or almost all policy outcomes within the community. The preferences of the masses would then literally not matter, thereby compromising any claim that the polity is democratic in any important sense of being systematically responsive to the preferences of the people as a whole.

There have been many studies, conducted in many modes, trying to settle the empirical question of whether any such elites actually exist in modern Western societies. Some are quite bold in their conception, exploring for example the extent of interlocking directorates among major US and UK firms and the political consequences of such concentrations of power (Useem, 1984). Most, however, have focused upon the politics of cities (and of cities in America, at that). Localism is arguably justifiable, though at the national level, peak associations consolidating the preferences of many constituent individuals and organizations inevitably will, and arguably should, have substantial influence. If we are to find power being widely dispersed anywhere, we would naturally expect it to be in local rather than national-level politics.

In the initial studies of this sort, sociologists and political scientists tended to talk past one another. The former asked people 'who has power around here', and concluded it was a small elite when the same small number of names kept cropping up (Hunter, 1953). The latter observed what actually happened in city council debates, and inferred 'pluralism' (or at least multiple, competing centres of power) from the fact that different people were central on different issues (Dahl, 1961). But the sociologists had a point, in that 'a reputation for power is power', as Hobbes (1651, ch. 10) himself had observed. People simply do not bother raising issues knowing that they would lose, pursuing instead their objectives politically only where they have reason to hope that those more powerful than themselves might stand aside. And, on at least some sociological accounts, power might even be exercised – intentionally or otherwise – by and through structures of social values and rules of political discourse which differentially favour status quo distributions of social resources (Lukes, 1974).

If these sorts of power imbalances worry us – if we think they are sufficiently pervasive and exercised sufficiently often to be truly pernicious – it is the mechanisms by which they are exercised to which we must look, with a view to denying those devices their power to pervert democratic processes. The illegitimate interpenetration of economic power into the political realm is discussed below (pp. 171–2). But that is not the only form such power plays may take. The devious manipulation of language, symbols and social ritual can also play a role (Therborn, 1978) – though, happily, one that is moderately easily defeasible (Goodin, 1980).

There is one semi-structural sense in which certain people inevitably have more power than others in a democracy. Assuming a fair procedure for aggregating votes, the median voter should always get her way, precisely because she sits at the strategically central point in the spectrum of political opinion. There being, by definition, as many voters to one side of her as to the other, the party that captures her vote wins the election (on certain empirical assumptions, primarily that voters vote for parties offering policies nearest their own preferences). This leads, in the two-party case, to Anthony Downs' (1957, ch. 8) famous model of 'Tweedledee–Tweedledum' politics, with both parties converging towards the centre.

Even in multi-party contests, where parties naturally spread themselves more evenly over the policy space, something similar happens, though. It just happens later, when the time comes to form a coalition government. Assuming parties are likewise policy-interested and always prefer to coalesce with parties nearer to them in policy terms, the party at the centre of the political spectrum (the one that has captured the median voter) must always be included in any majority coalition; and given the strategic power which that fact carries, that party is also in a position pretty much to dictate terms to would-be coalition partners.

There are questions of empirical validity to be raised with such models, which are necessarily highly stylized. But the empirical results are broadly supportive (Taylor and Laver, 1973; Page, 1978). The larger question from the present perspective is simply whether any of this really matters, normatively. True, the median voter is, directly or indirectly, in a position of great power – a position of 'structural power', one might even say, since it derives from the structure of preferences among the electorate at large. But the 'median voter' refers to a place on the spectrum of opinion, not to any particular, named person. She cannot exercise power in the strong sense that the owner of a company town can: the latter can dictate outcomes, in the sense that if he changes his mind he can use his power to impose his new preference upon all others; if the median voter changes her mind, in contrast, she just loses her position of power, her opinion no longer falling at the strategically central median point in the opinion distribution.

Other sources of structural power matter more. Consider the economic relationships between centres and peripheries, both domestically (Lipset and Rokkan, 1967, esp. ch. 1; Hechter, 1975) and internationally (Wallerstein, 1974). It is the structural centrality of the centre – economically, sociologically, geographically – that allows it to systematically thrive, at the expense of its associated peripheries. The most striking example, perhaps, was the way in which the United States under Reagan was able to run up massive foreign debts that would immediately have led the International Monetary Fund to crack down on virtually any other country in the world. The United States could do what others could not because of the centrality of America in the world economy and, more specifically, because of the role of the US dollar as the reserve currency of choice for much of the world. While the United States is no longer the hegemonic force it once was, either militarily or economically, it is precisely because no new hegemon has emerged that other states cling so tenaciously to practices developed when it was, for fear of slipping into international anarchy (Keohane, 1984). But that is simply to say that America's position of power – and genuine power, it is – is explicable. It is not to say that it is ethically justifiable.

Party competition

The model of democratic elitism just adumbrated presupposes, among other things, parties offering electors real choices. It further presupposes that parties will implement their promised policies to the best of their ability. Cynics might query both propositions.

The 'convergence towards the centre' just mentioned suggests that parties might not be offering voters real choices at all, at least in the two-party case. As I said, there is substantial evidence in support of that proposition. But there is also, evidently, a limit to the phenomenon. Competing parties, like retailers, must differentiate their products from those of competitors if consumers are to have any reason to opt for their wares. They must do so in the face of inevitably (and rationally) ignorant voters, who are largely insensitive to nuances of policy detail. The conjunction of those facts gives parties a real motive for spreading themselves apart a fair bit, rather than assuming policy positions literally adjacent to one another, even in a two-party world, and of course with three or more parties everyone agrees that parties should spread themselves out across the entire policy space (Downs, 1957, ch. 8).

The same pair of propositions may also explain the fascinating finding that parties, in effect, 'own' issues (Budge, Robertson and Hearl, 1987). Whenever unemployment, for example, becomes 'the' issue of the election that inevitably works to the advantage of parties of the left, whatever parties of the right say on the topic; conversely, whenever economic management becomes 'the' issue of the election, that always benefits parties of the right. Such phenomena might reflect yet another information-economizing device, akin to cuing on party labels rather than investigating details of policy proposals, which would appeal to rationally ignorant voters economizing on information costs.

The question of whether, once elected, parties do as promised is trickier. The promises are inevitably imprecise and they are inevitably implemented in circumstances which were at least partly unforeseeable at the time they were made. So it is no straightforward matter to specify what ought be counted as acting in good faith to discharge manifesto promises. Still, it seems that parties at least try to do something to implement most of their promises most of the time (Pomper, 1968; Budge and Hofferbert, 1990).

Collective action in politics

Problems with respect to collective action to provide public goods, in general, are canvassed in chapter 5. The problem, in a nutshell, is that the benefits will accrue to people whether or not they contribute to the costs of their production, so everyone would rationally wait for others to contribute – which, being equally rational, they would not. The upshot is that public goods will be systematically underprovided through voluntary efforts among rational actors.

The point to notice, in the present context, is that political parties and interest groups provide public goods in precisely that sense. They shape public policies which will affect whole broad classes of people, whether or not those people have themselves borne the costs of helping to shape those policies. So unless (almost *per impossible*) someone has reason to suppose that her own contribution would make all the difference between provision and non-provision of the policy goods – or unless (far less implausibly) she expects some private perquisite like office or official favours – no one would have any rational reason to contribute to political campaigns, at all.

Political scientists have energetically risen to the challenge of economists, most notably Olson (1965), on this score. They have gone to great lengths to show that in repeated interactions among the same people, time and again, co-operative 'tit-for-tat' norms naturally emerge. Each contributes, on condition that others do likewise (Hardin, 1982; Axelrod, 1984; 1986; Taylor, 1987). As long as the group is small enough and stable enough in its composition, this mechanism evokes a very substantial measure of voluntary contribution to public goods – political activity among them.

Such norms seem to work quite well in ensuring co-operative behaviour among parliamentarians and political elites more generally, so long as their membership is not too fluctuating (Weingast and Marshall, 1988; cf. Uslaner, 1991). They seem to work quite well in organizing the potential anarchy of international relations (Oye, 1986), again precisely because there we find the same two hundred or so national governments and non-governmental organizations facing off time and again. They similarly serve to motivate industries with a few big players to organize powerful trade associations to lobby governments (Useem, 1984) and indeed governments to consolidate multiple claimants into routinized policy networks (Heclo and Wildavsky, 1974; Rhodes, 1988).

The preconditions that such mechanisms require – small, stable groups – are less well satisfied in cases where the interests involved are those of the public at large, however. Of course, there are genuine public-interest movements lobbying government. But the evidence suggests that their members either are acting on a very partial subset of 'public' interests (McFarland, 1976) or else they are driven more by expressive than by instrumental concerns (Hardin, 1982, ch. 7)

All told, this tit-for-tat analysis of collective action is probably most useful, therefore, as an account of the differential formation of interest groups. It seems safe to assume that the costs of organizing an interest group increase with size, if only because tit-for-tat is harder to monitor and enforce in such circumstances. If so, however, small and concentrated interests will always be overrepresented relative to large and diffuse ones in the councils of state (Goodin, 1982b; McFarland, 1987). Empirical studies of the causes of the inegalitarian impact of US government tax and spending policies bear out these theoretical speculations (Page, 1983).

The more interesting question in institutional design is how to shift public discourse out of this preference-cum-interest logic altogether. In so far as people have public preferences as distinct from private ones, preferences for the public good rather than personal advantage, those are the ones that we – and presumably they, as well – would prefer to evoke, politically. But that in turn requires structuring politics as an arena for 'deliberation' rather than 'contestation', evoking judgements which can be challenged and revised rather than just votes to be counted (March and Olsen, 1986; Wilson, 1990). Free-form debates within the relatively undisciplined American congressional parties, especially in the specialist committees of Congress, compare favourably in this regard to the performance of parliamentary parties, where the government whips invariably have the votes even if the other party has all the arguments.

Social choice theory

A final requirement of democratic theory is that individuals' preferences be aggregated impartially into some determinate collective choice. But as has long been known, majority rule may well be indeterminate. The structure of people's preferences may be such that any option can beat any other option by a majority vote. Where we stop – what we settle upon as 'the' democratic outcome – is, then highly arbitrary.

In the simplest three-voter, three-issue case, suppose preferences are distributed as follows:

Voter A prefers Option Z to Y to X;
Voter B prefers Option X to Z to Y;
Voter C prefers Option Y to X to Z.

Then majority rule leads us around in circles. Option Y beats X (by the votes of A and C), option Z beats Y (by the votes of A and B), but option X beats Z (by the votes of B and C). In cases such as this, majority voting yields no determinate answer to the question of which option is socially preferred.

Condorcet first noticed this danger in the eighteenth century. A vast literature has now grown up in and around mathematical economics trying – largely unsuccessfully (Sen, 1977b; Ordeshook, 1986, ch. 2) – to find a way out of the general impossibility result that Arrow (1963) constructed upon those foundations. (See chapter 5, this volume, for further details on this topic.) Under some really very rather weak assumptions, it is apparently always possible via a finite sequence of majority votes to cycle from anywhere to (or, more precisely, 'to arbitrarily near') anywhere else in the policy space (Schofield, 1976; McKelvey, 1979). A parallel literature, in the same spirit, has grown up demonstrating that there is no decision rule – majority rule or any other – that is 'strategy proof', in the sense that it would never pay to misrepresent your preferences (Gibbard, 1973; Satterthwaite, 1975). Yet that, too, is contrary to the democratic ethos: it is surely people's true preferences that democratic theory would have us aggregate.

Happily, there prove to be certain political solutions to these dilemmas which economists find so mathematically intractable. One is a new voting procedure. The Condorcet/Arrow paradox emerges only in connection with pairwise comparisons, pitting option X against option Y and then the winner of that round against option Z. There would be no scope for going around in circles among those options if the voters' task were conceived, instead, as picking which option they favoured from among the trio {X,Y,Z}. A variation on that theme, which evades the Condorcet/Arrow paradox in similar fashion, is the institution of 'approval voting': voters are merely asked to vote for all options (as many as they like) that they prefer to the status quo, with the winner being that option getting the most positive votes (Brams and Fishburn, 1978).

A second solution to the Condorcet/Arrow paradox works at the level of individuals' preferences. If people's preferences are 'single-peaked', that too defeats the Condorcet paradox (Black, 1958). Colloquially single-peakedness amounts to no more than a requirement that people not jump all over the place in their preference orderings: if their first preference is on the far left of the political spectrum, their second preference should be on the left too rather than on the far right. More technically, single-peakedness amounts to a requirement that everyone sees political space in the same way, with the same basic options being arrayed alone the same dimensions in the same order. It is not unrealistic to suppose that such a condition might often be satisfied. Public debate, whatever else it does, should surely serve to synchronize people's perceptions of what is at issue in political disputes.

This trick works, of course, by constraining what preference orderings people might have – specifically, by requiring them to rank alternatives along some generally accepted dimension or dimensions of political cleavage within their society. Some, following Arrow (1963) or Habermas (1975), may deem this an intolerable interference with people's preference orderings. But others would see it as almost akin to a prerequisite for the existence of a 'community' sufficiently cohesive for the notion of a collective choice to have meaning.

Aggregating people's preferences into a collective choice only makes sense under certain special conditions, after all. Minimally, participants in the process must be agreed that they are one 'people', for whom a single collective choice ought to be binding (Rustow, 1970). They must be further agreed that collective choice ought somehow to be systematically responsive to their individual preferences. We might in like fashion also add that the whole idea of making a collective choice further presupposes a community of people agreed on the basic dimensions of political discourse. That thought – which seems independently attractive – would incidentally help us to evade the Condorcet/Arrow challenge.

A third political solution to that paradox lies in the structure of political institutions themselves. Even if the structure of people's preferences is such that they risk going around in circles, the rules of political life might not allow them to do so. In direct democracies, popular petitions or legislative edicts succeed in putting only a small subset of all possible options on a referendum ballot; and among such a small subset of options, there is much less risk of a voting cycle emerging. Similarly, representative assemblies have rules requiring that legislative proposals be voted upon in a certain order or come to the floor via certain committees (each of which has a peculiar character, unrepresentative of the assembly as a whole). Those facts of legislative life likewise constrain the number and kinds and ordering of options that appear before legislators – once again reducing the risk of a Condorcet cycle (Shepsle and Weingast, 1981; 1984; 1987; Ordeshook, 1986, ch. 6; Weingast and Marshall, 1988; Baron and Ferejohn, 1989). The constitutional constraints characteristic of liberal democracies further limit what options appear, and hence the chance of a voting cycle (Riker, 1983).

In all these ways, political scientists have found devices, if not always necessarily for ensuring, at least for greatly increasing the likelihood of 'structure-induced' equilibria (Shepsle and Weingast, 1981; 1984). With the spectres of Condorcet and Arrow thus ceasing to haunt them, political scientists and philosophers may now begin to reflect in earnest upon the various and interestingly political lessons that the study of public choice in the micro-economic mode might hold.

Bureaucracy and democracy: organization theory

Such an 'institutionalist' solution to the Condorcet/Arrow paradox forces political scientists back to their roots. Throughout the interwar years, the study of governmental structures and processes was the bread and butter of the study of 'government' (as political science was then called). Sociologists, too, have always known that social structures and political institutions mattered. 'Bringing the state back in' is only the latest rallying cry in a long campaign against their insistently political scientific brethren on this front (Evans et al., 1985).

At some level, political scientists always appreciated the way in which institutional rules and practices shaped political outcomes. This is especially true of electoral law, for example (Rae, 1967). It obviously makes a great difference to the outcome whether the rules stipulate single-member districts with victory going to whoever enjoys a plurality of votes, or whether the rules stipulate multiple-member constituencies with seats being awarded according to (any of the several forms of) proportional representation (which can themselves yield radically different outcomes).

The 'new institutionalism' goes well beyond that, however, to study the particular details of political organization at all levels and their consequences for policy choice. Once relegated to a backwater of public administration, questions of organizational form and function have once again come to be central to the discipline as a whole (March and Olsen, 1984; 1989). Organization structures create communities of interest, both within the organization and among those dependent upon the organizations. They direct the flow of information. Some say they even shape preferences themselves. Be that as it may, how authority is structured within an organization and where within it veto points are located certainly do matter to policy outcomes (Wilson, 1989; Immergut, 1990) – although, of course, not always in the ways intended by institutional designers themselves.

Indeed, one of the first things one notices in studying organizational function is dysfunction. In one recent period it was commonplace to complain that public bureaucracies were 'overloaded', asked to do too much with too few resources (King, 1975; Rose and Peters, 1978). Various reforms are suggested, inspired by advances in artificial intelligence, for organizing this level of social complexity and rendering it administratively tractable for beleaguered bureaucrats (La Porte, 1975; Simon, 1981). But one suspects that they are always going to be forced to settle for solutions that are 'good enough' rather than the 'very best' (Simon, 1954; 1985) and that they will always start searching for them in the vicinity of the status quo – thus leading to incremental rather than radical responses to new policy puzzles, however fallacious incremental thinking may be in the circumstances (Lindblom, 1959; cf. Goodin, 1982a, ch. 2).

Another source of organizational dysfunction might lie in the behaviour of public personnel themselves. The 'new economics of organization' (Moe, 1984), highlight the 'principal-agent' problem, canvassed in chapter 5. That analysis warns that civil servants are not necessarily selfless ciphers eager to serve the public interest: instead they are agents with interests of their own, which do not always overlap the public interest and which will sometimes contradict it (Arrow, 1974; Williamson, 1975; Lipsky, 1980).

Evidence of this phenomenon is arguably found in studies showing the very imperfect implementation of public policies, enacted by people with one set of priorities but then entrusted to ones with quite another (Bardach, 1977; Brewer and de Leon, 1983, chs 9 and 10). But what the political science findings seem to suggest, rather more strongly, is that bureaucrats are keen to pursue their 'institutional interests'. As the slogan goes, 'Where you stand depends upon where you sit' (Allison, 1971, p. 176). Representatives of Treasury internalize that agency's priorities and process them in intramural bargaining with other agencies; representatives of Defence, that agency's; and so on (Niskanen, 1971; cf. Goodin, 1982b; Dunleavy, 1991).

This form of partisanship is obviously less problematic than simply lining one's own pockets, as in the classic principal–agent case. Such bargaining may even lead to socially optimal results, on a certain idealized model of inter-agency bargaining – one wherein all aspects of the public interest find some agency to champion them, with power proportional to that cause's importance to the public interest itself (Lindblom, 1965).

But that model is, of course, highly idealized. Not all aspects of the public interest find institutional advocates; and the balance of power among those which do bears no necessary relation to the public interest. Which agencies exist, and what power they have, is largely a historical accident. Thereafter, government organizations tend to be 'immortal' – to survive long after their original purpose has passed (Kaufman, 1977). Policy-making is more characterized by a swirling mix of problems looking for solutions, pet solutions seeking problems, and temporarily idle people looking for something to do next (Olsen, 1972).

One consequence is a familiar pattern of 'policy succession'. In policy terms, one intervention leads 'naturally' to another, along certain predetermined lines (Hogwood and Peters, 1983). For perfectly understandable reasons connected to the logic of organization, there is all too little attempt to step back and consider whether we were on the right basic track, in the first place.

Power and distributional regimes

There are many different ways of organizing the distribution of the benefits and burdens of social co-operation. At root, all are arguably variations on two basic alternative – markets and planning. Each has its own characteristic strengths and weaknesses and its own characteristic consequences for the distribution of social power (Dahl and Lindblom, 1953; Lindblom, 1977; Wolf, 1988).

Politics and markets

Even in a fundamentally market-based social system, there are reasons for the state to supplant the market in the distribution of valued resources. One, canvassed in chapter 5 and pp. 165–6 above, is that the market underproduces public goods and positive externalities more generally (and, conversely, overproduces negative ones). That might be called an 'efficiency-based' rationale for state action. How strong a rationale it is depends upon the extent to which political action to correct the market failures might be blocked by the self-same collective action reasons as caused the market failure in the first place.

A second reason for state action supplanting the market, at least in certain realms, is that people respond differently to the same question when it is asked in different contexts. Asked their market preferences, they will usually give a more private, self-interested response than when asked their public policy preferences. There, as noted above (p. 162) they are apt to respond in a more public-spirited way. Call this the 'virtue-based' rationale (Goodin and Roberts, 1975; Benn, 1979; Brennan and Lomasky, 1985).

Finally and historically most centrally is a 'power-based' rationale. The market-based distribution results from a certain distribution of power (which may lead to literal inefficiencies, as well). We may be happy to let that power distribution dictate distribution of most goods and services – or perhaps we simply see no realistic way of preventing it from so doing. Still, there are certain things we think ought be distributed more equally than money and social resources more generally. Among the disparate goods that fall into this category are basic necessities (food, shelter, medical care), on the one hand, and symbols of citizenship (voting rights, military and jury duty), on the other. Insisting that these particular goods be distributed equally, when little else is, has come to be known as 'specific egalitarianism' – an attitude of egalitarianism which people apply to specific commodities but do not extend to all commodities in general (Tobin, 1970).

Whichever the rationale, the basic idea in all cases is to allocate certain items politically, according to very different rules than would govern market distributions. The fundamental question is then whether the two currencies – one political, the other economic – can really be kept as separate as that requires (Lindblom, 1977). In part, this is a question of the extent to which monied interests can directly bribe public officials. In part it is a question of indirect bribery – monied interests subsidizing (or threatening to withhold subsidies from) increasingly expensive election campaigns (Alexander, 1980; Jacobson, 1980; Berry, 1994, ch. 8). In part it is merely a matter of the political power of private capital to threaten to migrate out of the political jurisdiction in question unless it is given preferential treatment (Finer, 1955–6).

By whatever precise mechanisms, the democratic path to social equality thus seems decisively blocked. This is confirmed by a large body of research on social welfare expenditures, which shows that the growth of public expenditure on such activities is driven almost entirely by economics and demographics. Once those influences are factored out, political variables such as democratic participation, competitiveness or the strength of leftist parties seem to have no effects on levels of expenditure on social welfare programmes (Wilensky, 1975; Jackman, 1975), although such political variables do shape important characteristics of those programmes (Esping-Andersen, 1990, ch. 5).

The upshot seems to be that our polity cannot be very much more democratic than is our economy itself. If so, there are two possible responses. One is to accept that our polity inevitably is going to be much less democratic than we would like. The other is to insist that our economy be more democratic than we might otherwise be inclined.

Seepage from the economic to the political is not the only source of non-democratic influences, however. There is no reason to believe that simply replacing the economic market with a political 'markets in votes' would necessarily lead to egalitarian outcomes. True, everyone has one vote and no one has more than one. But then again, there is no reason for the governing coalition to take equal note of everyone's preference. It needs to secure the support of only just enough to win office comfortably and to govern. A classic conclusion of modern coalition theory – revised subsequently only at the margins – is that coalitions will squeeze out superfluous members, defined as ones whose votes are not required for them to win and hold office (Riker, 1962; Taylor and Laver, 1973). So within politics just as in economics, we ought naturally to expect that some ('the many', in Aristotelian terms) will exploit others ('the few').

We can only hope that the tables turn often enough that these effects even out in the end – or that anticipation of tables turning may prevent them from occurring at all. There are, however, reasons to expect systematic biases here in favour of some groups and against others. Those who are systematically advantaged include, most conspicuously, the middle classes: they, presumably, are the all-powerful median voters, at least on distributional questions (Stigler, 1970). Those who are systematically disadvantaged include the working classes: on one persuasive account, the electoral pursuit of socialism is doomed by the inexorable need for working-class parties to craft their programmes so as to attract sufficient non-working-class votes to win an electoral majority; the working classes must forsake socialism, and hence their own interests, if they are to win power in a democracy at all (Przeworski and Sprague, 1986).

These systematic biases are especially apparent at the international level. Given patterns of resource distribution, and hence trade, certain nations are necessarily peripheral. Precisely because no one needs them, economically or politically, they are eminently exploitable. Furthermore, they are particularly prey to the influence of capital from abroad, both public and private – and they are particularly at the mercy of strings being attached to the provision of such funds by multinational corporations or national or international lenders (Cassen et al., 1986, ch. 4).

Politics and planning

The conventional alternative to a market economy is a socially-planned, command economy. Halfway measures include 'market socialism', wherein there is an initially egalitarian distribution of social capital but all thereafter is left to the market (Lange, 1936–7; Elster and Moene, 1989). None of these alternatives has been tested in sufficiently propitious circumstances to ascertain their real viability, though.

The principal reason for politicians to take command of the economy in this way is, presumably, resentment at the maldistribution of previously private capital. So, on the face of it, it would seem likely that command economies – whatever their economic inefficiencies – would at least enjoy much more egalitarian distributions of income and wealth.

That presumption is too quick, though. One problem is that planners have great difficulty in planning anything to any degree of precision (Wildavsky, 1973); and that includes social distributions just as surely as it does material production. Another problem derives from the disjunction between ownership and control of nationalized assets; and insofar as it is control over resources rather than the right to buy and sell them that creates social inequities, taking private capital into public hands simply replaces private owners with public functionaries in positions of authority within the command economy (Dahrendorf, 1959). These problems are not just theoretical but real. Those who have lived under such regimes complain bitterly of a 'new class' (Djilas, 1957) enjoying perquisites denied to ordinary citizens. Djilas's term was originally a reference to the *nomenklatura* – the favoured members of the ruling party – but it can in light of subsequent experience also be extended to those who benefit from black markets or with access to hard currency.

It may well be, despite all this, that distributions within planned economies are none the less more equal than in market societies. Perhaps, although a gap remains between the top and bottom, it is smaller in planned economies than in market economies; or perhaps, despite the fact that positions of privilege remain, there are far fewer people in such privileged positions in planned economies than in market ones. Still, 'more equal' might not be good enough. The inequality may rankle all the more, precisely because those politically responsible for ensuring equality are among its prime beneficiaries (Parkin, 1971, chs 5 and 6). The 'moral collapse of communism' throughout Eastern Europe has plausibly been traced to resentment of precisely this fact (Clark and Wildavsky, 1990).

Equality is not the only reason for instituting a command economy, however. There is also an urge to secure 'popular control' of the economy, to make it democratically responsive to popular demands. It is an open question how best to accomplish that goal. On its face, a command economy would seem more responsive to political (which, under certain idealized conditions, equates to popular) will. But politicians' commands are filtered through layers of imperfectly responsive bureaucrats; so even if the politicians are themselves highly responsive to popular demands, the economy which they command might not be (Wolf, 1988). It might, on balance, turn out that even very imperfectly responsive markets (where people's preferences are weighted according to wealth and stifled by the operation of market power) might none the less he more responsive than bureaucratically sticky planned economies.

Constitutional regimes: rights and liberties

Normative theorists unhesitatingly commend schemes of 'universal' human rights, constitutional constraints on political rule, and so forth. But it is worth recalling just how sociologically contingent such political constraints have historically been.

At a purely political level, respect for human rights and constitutional constraints has always been contingent upon which elites come to rule. Nor is this purely a matter of whether democrats or tyrants take power. Even among those who would count as clearly 'democratic' elites, there is substantial variation in their commitment to 'basic' democratic values – more variation, in fact, than among the 'mass public' itself. Recent evidence suggests that, however undemocratic the mass public might be, it is actually more supportive of certain fundamental principles of democracy than are the elites within parties of the right (Sniderman et al., 1991).

At a more macro-sociological level, the very existence in any given polity of constitutional democracy depended upon a peculiar constellation of historical circumstances. Liberal democracy (and allied notions of rule of law and constitutional rights and liberties) are the products of a political 'stand-off' during the crucially formative era. Where the balance of power was different – where the crown was stronger, or the clergy more dominant, or the gentry less assertive, or the urban bourgeoisie less powerful – the social bases for liberal democracy would simply have been lacking (Moore, 1967).

Of course, once pioneered in one place such institutions can, with greater or lesser success, be transplanted elsewhere. When, as often happens, the transplant does not take it is unclear what to infer. Some count that as a criticism of rights theorists for trying to transpose such notions to settings that are less apt. Others count it as a criticism of the social situation that rights cannot thrive there.

Both responses have merit. If we have good moral reasons for wanting to give robust rights to everyone worldwide, and if that course of action requires a certain mixed social milieu, then we are thereby provided with good grounds for favouring those social circumstances – for trying to create such social circumstances wherever we can, for criticizing situations where they are absent as being morally deficient, and so on.

Still, the aphorism that 'ought implies can' ought itself to give moralists pause. It suggests that they ought to think twice about making their 'oughts' so demanding as to be almost everywhere irrelevant. While strong rights might be better, they might often be socially infeasible, especially in much of the developing world. We ought not set our standards so high as to exempt rulers from pursuing such modest accomplishments as are genuinely within their grasp. It is better that there should be no arbitrary arrests, even if there remain a few executions; it is better that the social rights of indigenous cultures be respected, even if disease and starvation remain endemic (Geertz, 1977).

By the same token, we ought not assume too easily the necessity of sacrifice. There is a fallacy – associated with the slogan 'no free lunch' – which holds that no two good things can ever be obtained simultaneously. Such thinking leads, all too often, to sacrifices that are utterly gratuitous. This is nowhere more true that in the ostensibly necessary trade-off between economic development on the one hand, and human rights and civil liberties on the other. Philosophers as distinguished as Rawls (1971, section 82) sometimes write as though the one can come only at some substantial cost to the other. But in truth there is no good reason in theory (Goodin, 1979) – and no good evidence in cross-national data (Frohoch and Sylvan, 1983) – for supposing that violating rights systematically enhances economic growth.

Politics and civil society

Finally, there is a theory afoot that democracy presupposes certain broad bases of agreement within the larger civil society. Some see this as a manifestation of more general and more radical claims, built around notions of 'hegemony' (Gramsci, 1971; Laclau and Mouffe, 1985). Others would offer a less sinister and more straightforwardly political account of the relationship between politics and civil society, with much the same practical consequences (Rustow, 1970; O'Donnell et al., 1986, part 4, ch. 5; Przeworski, 1991).

The basic idea, in either case, is just this. In order to govern any moderately diverse plural community at all there must be 'agreement' of a certain sort across all the disparate subgroups constituting that society. What is needed is agreement, not necessarily on substantive issues, but at least on the basic procedures by which substantive disagreements are to be resolved. In a democracy, that agreement must be on the basic procedures of democracy itself.

Political scientists report that some such agreement is indeed at work within the best-functioning, most stable democracies (Prothro and Grigg, 1960; Almond and Verba, 1963; 1980; Eckstein, 1966; Budge, 1970). Where such agreement is lacking, so too is political stability. The intractable ungovernability of places like Northern Ireland is standardly taken to be dramatic proof of that latter proposition (Rose, 1971).

Such arguments turn out to be suspect, both logically (Barry, 1970) and sociologically (Pateman, 1971; 1989, ch. 7). Re-analysis of the evidence leads careful sociologists to conclude that, even in the best-functioning and most stable democracies, a value consensus exists only among the rulers; among the underclasses, consent is more pragmatic, situationally determined and hence shaky (Mann, 1970; Abercrombie, Hill and Turner, 1980). So as a positive explanation of democratic stability, value consensus probably will not suffice; and perhaps we ought talk about 'bargains' which, however grand their titles ('the historical compromise', 'the post-war settlement'), are actually of a perfectly ordinary divide-the-spoils sort (Kirchheimer, 1969; O'Donnel, Schmitter and Whitehead, 1986, part 4, chs 4 and 5; Przeworski, 1991).

Still, as a normative ideal, the notion of a 'value consensus' of some sort or another retains its charm. Rawls (1987), in his later work, seems to want to rest the social contract on an 'overlapping consensus' of a broadly similar sort. The root idea is that there may remain some deeper social-cum-political principles upon which we can all agree, whatever our other differences. Similar aspirations recur throughout the older literature on 'nation-building' in the politics of the developing areas (Geertz, 1963; Huntington, 1968; O'Donnell, Schmitter and Whitehead, 1986, part 4, chs 4 and 5); and one suspects that postmodernist literature on the 'politics of difference' (Minow, 1990; Young, 1990) will be drawn back to this model, however much it strives to escape from it.

Much in the experience of literally 'divided societies' seems to support such a model. Many societies with deep religious, ethnic or other sociological divisions practise a 'politics of accommodation' which, without for a moment trying to fudge those differences, none the less prevents those differences from leading to civil strife. Obviously, though, the trick will work at all only in so far as the accommodation of differences is a 'fundamental rule' upon which all agree. In such societies, the political style is no longer democratic in a narrowly majoritarian sense: instead we see the politics of consultation or pillorization (consociationalism, co-option, corporatism). But as long as those rules are broadly respected the society can function politically, with virtually nothing else being contained in a socially overlapping consensus (Lijphart, 1968; 1975; 1977; Rogowski, 1974; Steiner and Dorff, 1980; Barry, 1989, chs 4 and 5).

One other thing also needs to be agreed. That is where the boundaries of politics lie. The reference is, in the first instance, to the national boundary in the most literal sense: where does one political community end and another begin? Geography aside, there remain fundamental sociological questions of inclusion and exclusion: who is to be regarded as a proper claimant on which among our social resources (Minow, 1990)? That in turn leads to the further question of which resources ought be up for grabs politically: what rights attach to social citizenship (Marshall, 1949; King and Waldron, 1988), how should we delimit the spheres of the public and private (Okin, 1989; Pateman 1989, ch. 6), and so on?

There are various political equivalents of strong and weak forces of nature at work binding together political unions. The composition of political communities can no longer be taken for granted; and that is no longer just a matter of the unravelling of colonial empires. Centripetal forces of politics increasingly lead to outright secession or to enfeebled confederations. With each such weakening of the claims that each group has on the others, those centripetal forces are further exacerbated. Perhaps practices of 'politics by accommodation' are doomed once such possibilities are so such as broached at all. That, arguably, is the lesson of Ulster (Rose, 1971; Lijphart, 1975) and the unnatural unions of central Europe, ranging from the Yugoslav to the Soviet.

Conclusion: political possibilities

Politics, it is standardly said, is 'the art of the possible' – the study of constrained pursuit of moral ideals in the public sphere. Those constraints take various familiar forms. Between them they are often thought so severely to delimit our practical socio-politico-economic options as to leave little if any room for the play of our higher ideals. If there is only a handful of closely adjacent options feasible, then the pretence of value-driven choice among them is largely a fraud.

The upshot of this survey is that the familiar forms of constraint may not be so very constraining, after all. Economic constraints, for example, may make the pursuit of certain ideals hard. But typically they do not make it impossible. We have to look for a way to meet basic needs without drastically handicapping a poor nation's prospects for economic growth, perhaps – but look and we will find. The same is broadly true of social and psychological constraints. They too may make moral ideals harder to realize, politically – but not impossibly so. The transformation of capitalist maximizers into socialist citizens, for example, was once thought psychologically next to impossible because of the very different incentives to which people would be required to respond under the two systems. Upon closer inspection, however, it seems that late capitalist societies are already inculcating the psychological prerequisites for socialist citizens into people: a large proportion of people's rewards there come in the form of social esteem, already (Lane, 1978; 1991).

The main constraint on achieving political ideals is possibly not any of those more familiar economic, sociological or psychological ones. Rather, it may be the availability of *political* ideas themselves: the policy techniques/mechanisms/solutions available to solve tricky equations. From the study of public policy-making we know that there are strikingly few 'solutions' – strikingly few well-worked-out policy options – on offer at any given moment (Olsen, 1972). Weapons systems designed for one purpose are knocking around forever until they finally find a problem to which they might plausibly constitute a solution (Levine, 1972). So too, perhaps, with technologies to solve ethical problems.

If this speculation has merit, then what it suggests is the following pair of conclusions. First, normative theorists ought shift attention, at least for a while, from values to mechanisms for implementing them. There is no point in fine-tuning desiderata when there are only a few and very rough-grained choices presently among our policy options for satisfying them.

Second, in looking with a normative eye for other empirical policy options, we ought not be too tightly constrained by 'realism'. Much in the literature on policy choice testifies to the sorts of artificial blinkers that 'cognitive models', 'conceptual lenses' or 'frames of reference' impose upon us (Allison, 1971; March, 1972). What we need is instead to think – at least for a time – in more free-form fashion, 'trying on' outrageous propositions.

In the real world of politics, revolutions and crises function as 'moments of madness' in just this constructive way (Zolberg, 1972). Precisely because constraints that once seemed insurmountable have been overcome, one assumes that anything might be possible. Much is not, of course; but the illusion helps us to see what is. And that may be why it takes a profound political 'crisis' to initiate a perfectly predictable, progressive 'sequence' of political development (Binder, 1971). Seen in this light, the periodic 'crises' proclaimed within political philosophy itself might be no bad things.

See also 5 ECONOMICS; 7 LEGAL STUDIES; 8 ANARCHISM; 11 LIBERALISM; 12 MARXISM; 13 SOCIALISM; 15 COMMUNITY; 17 CONSTITUTIONALISM AND THE RULE OF LAW; 18 CORPORATISM AND SYNDICALISM; 19 DEMOCRACY; 22 DISTRIBUTIVE JUSTICE; 23 EFFICIENCY; 26 FEDERALISM; 27 INTERNATIONAL AFFAIRS; 28 LEGITIMACY; 30 POWER; 34 SECESSION AND NATIONALISM; 36 STATE; 38 TOTALITARIANISM; 41 WELFARE

References

Abercrombie, N., Hill, S. and Turner, B. S.: *The Dominant Ideology Thesis* (London: Allen & Unwin 1980).

Alexander, H.: *Financing Politics* (Washington, DC: Congressional Quarterly Press, 1976; 2nd edn, 1980).

Allison, G. T.: *Essence of Decision* (Boston, Mass.: Little, Brown, 1971).

Almond, G. and Verba, S.: *The Civic Culture* (Boston, Mass.: Little, Brown, 1963).

———— and Verba, S., eds: *The Civic Culture Revisited* (Boston, Mass.: Little, Brown, 1980).

Arrow, K. J.: *Social Choice and Individual Values* (New Haven, Conn.: Yale University Press, 1951; 2nd edn, 1963).

————: *The Limits of Organization* (New York: Norton, 1974).

Axelrod, R.: *The Evolution of Cooperation* (New York: Basic Books, 1984).

————: 'An evolutionary approach to norms', *American Political Science Review*, 80 (1986), 1095–112.

Bardach, E.: *The Implementation Game* (Cambridge, Mass.: MIT Press, 1977).

Baron, D. P. and Ferejohn, J. A.: 'Bargaining in legislatures', *American Political Science Review*, 83 (1989), 1181–206.

Barry, B.: *Sociologists, Economists and Democracy* (London: Collier-Macmillan, 1970).

————: *Democracy, Power and Justice* (Oxford: Clarendon Press, 1989).

Benn, S. I.: 'The problematic rationality of political participation', *Philosophy, Politics and Society*, 5th series, ed. P. Laslett and J. Fishkin (Oxford: Blackwell, 1979), pp. 291–312.

Berelson, B. R., Lazarsfeld, P. F. and McPhee, W. N.: *Voting* (Chicago: University of Chicago Press, 1954).

Berry, J. M.: *The Interest Group Society* (Boston, Mass.: Little, Brown, 1984).

Binder, L. et al.: *Crises and Sequences in Political Development* (Princeton, NJ: Princeton University Press, 1971).

Black, D.: *The Theory of Committees and Elections* (Cambridge: Cambridge University Press, 1958).

Brams, S. J. and Fishburn, P. C.: 'Approval voting', *American Political Science Review*, 72 (1978), 831–47.

Brennan, G. and Lomasky, L.: 'The impartial spectator goes to Washington', *Economics and Philosophy*, 1 (1985), 189–211.

Brewer, G. D. and de Leon, P.: *The Foundations of Policy Analysis* (Homewood, Ill.: Dorsey, 1983).

Budge, I.: *Agreement and the Stability of Democracy* (Chicago: Markham, 1970).

———— and Hofferbert, R. I.: 'Mandates and policy outputs: U.S. party platforms and federal expenditures', *American Political Science Review*, 84 (1990), 111–31.

————, Robertson, D. and Hearl, D., eds: *Ideology, Strategy and Party Change* (Cambridge: Cambridge University Press, 1987).

Campbell, A., Converse, P. E., Miller, W. A. and Stokes, D.: *The American Voter* (New York: Wiley, 1960).

Cassen, R. et. al.: *Does Aid Work?* (Oxford: Clarendon Press, 1986).

Clark, J. and Wildavsky, A.: *The Moral Collapse of Communism* (San Francisco, Calif.: ICS Press, 1990).

Cohen, G. A.: *Karl Marx's Theory of History* (Oxford: Clarendon Press, 1978).

Collini, S., Winch, D. and Burrows, J.: *That Noble Science of Politics* (Cambridge: Cambridge University Press, 1983).

Converse, P.: 'The nature of belief systems in mass publics', *Ideology and Discontent*, ed. D. Apter (New York: Free Press, 1964), pp. 206–61.

Dahl, R. A.: *Who Governs?* (New Haven, Conn.: Yale University Press, 1961).

————: *Modern Political Analysis* (Englewood Cliffs, NJ: Prentice-Hall, 1963; 3rd edn, 1976).

————: *A Preface to Economic Democracy* (Berkeley, Calif.: University of California Press, 1985).

Dahrendorf, R.: *Class and Class Conflict in Industrial Society* (Stanford, Calif.: Stanford University Press, 1959).

Djilas, M.: *The New Class* (New York: Praeger, 1957).

Downs, A.: *An Economic Theory of Democracy* (New York: Harper, 1957).

Duncan, G. and Lukes, S.: 'The new democracy', *Political Studies*, 11 (1963), 156–77.

Dunleavy, P.: *Democracy, Bureaucracy and Public Choice* (Hemel Hempstead: Harvester Wheatsheaf, 1991).

Eckstein, H.: *Division and Cohesion in Democracy* (Princeton, NJ: Princeton University Press, 1966).

Elster, J.: 'Marxism, functionalism, and game theory', *Theory and Decision*, 11 (1982), 453–82.

————: *Making Sense of Marx* (Cambridge: Cambridge University Press, 1985).

———— and Moene, K. O., eds: *Alternatives to Capitalism* (Cambridge: Cambridge University Press, 1989).

Esping-Andersen, G.: *The Three Worlds of Welfare Capitalism* (Princeton, NJ: Princeton University Press, 1990).

Evans, P. B., Rueschemeyer, D. and Skocpol, T., eds: *Bringing the State Back In* (New York: Cambridge University Press, 1985).

Finer, S. E.: 'The political power of private capital', *Sociological Review*, 3 (1955), 279–94 and 4 (1956), 5–30.

Fiorina, M. P.: *Retrospective Voting in American National Elections* (New Haven, Conn.: Yale University Press, 1981).

Frohock, F. M. and Sylvan, D. J.: 'Liberty, economics and evidence', *Political Studies*, 31 (1983), 541–55.

Geertz, C., ed.: *Old Societies and New States* (New York: Free Press, 1963).

————: 'The judging of nations', *Archives Européenes de Sociologie*, 18 (1977), 245–61.

Gibbard, A.: 'Manipulation of voting schemes: a general result', *Econometrica*, 41 (1973), 587–601.

Goodin, R. E.: 'The development–rights trade-off', *Universal Human Rights* [now *Human Rights Quarterly*], 1 (1979), 31–42.

————: *Manipulatory Politics* (New Haven, Conn.: Yale University Press, 1980).

————: *Political Theory and Public Policy* (Chicago: University of Chicago Press, 1982a).

————: 'Rational politicians and rational bureaucrats in Washington and Whitehall', *Public Administration*, 60 (1982b), 23–41.

————: *Protecting the Vulnerable* (Chicago: University of Chicago Press, 1985).

———— and Dryzek, J.: 'Rational participation: the politics of relative power', *British Journal of Political Science*, 10 (1980), 273–92.

———— et al.: *Not Only the Poor* (London: Allen & Unwin, 1987).

———— and Roberts, K. W. S.: 'The ethical voter', *American Political Science Review*, 69 (1975), 926–9.

Gramsci, A.: *Selections from the Prison Notebooks*, ed. and trans. Q. Hoare and G. Nowell Smith (London: Lawrence & Wishart, 1971).

Habermas, J.: *Legitimation Crisis*, ed. T. McCarthy (Boston: Beacon, 1975).

Hardin, R.: *Collective Action* (Baltimore, Md.: Johns Hopkins University Press, 1982).

Hechter, M.: *Internal Colonialism*(London: Routledge & Kegan Paul, 1975).

Heclo, H. and Wildavsky, A.: *The Private Government of Public Money* (London: Macmillan, 1974).

Hobbes, T.: *Leviathan* (London: Andrew Crooke, 1651).

Hogwood, B. W. and Peters, B. G.: *Policy Dynamics* (New York: St Martin's, 1983).

Homans, G. C.: 'Bringing men back in', *American Sociological Review*, 29 (1964), 809–18.

Hunter, F.: *Community Power Structures* (Chapel Hill, NC: University of North Carolina Press, 1953).

Huntington, S. P.: *Political Order in Changing Societies* (New Haven, Conn.: Yale University Press, 1968).

Immergut, E. M.: 'Institutions, veto points and policy results: a comparative analysis of health care', *Journal of Public Policy*, 10 (1990), 391–416.

Jacobson, G. C.: *Money in Congressional Elections* (New Haven, Conn.: Yale University Press, 1980).

Jessop, B.: *State Theory* (Cambridge: Polity Press, 1990).

Kaufman, H.: *Are Government Organizations Immortal?* (Washington, DC: Brookings Institution, 1977).

Keohane, R. O.: *After Hegemony* (Princeton, NJ: Princeton University Press, 1984).

Key, V. O., Jr: *The Responsible Electorate* (Cambridge, Mass.: Harvard University Press, 1966).

Kiewiet, D. R.: *Micropolitics and Macroeconomics* (Chicago: University of Chicago Press, 1983).

King, A.: 'Overload', *Political Studies*, 23 (1975), 284–96.

King, D. S. and Waldron, J.: 'Citizenship, social citizenship and the defence of welfare provision', *British Journal of Political Science*, 18 (1988), 415–44.

Kirchheimer, O.: 'Changes in the structure of political compromise', *Politics, Law and Social Change*, ed. F. S. Burin and K. L. Shell (New York: Columbia University Press, 1969), pp. 131–59.

La Porte, T. R., ed.: *Organized Social Complexity* (Princeton, NJ: Princeton University Press, 1975).

Laclau, R. and Mouffe, C.: *Hegemony and Socialist Strategy* (London: Verso, 1985).

Lane, R. E.: 'Waiting for lefty: the capitalist genesis of socialist man', *Theory & Society*, 6 (1978), 1–28.

————: *The Market Experience* (Cambridge: Cambridge University Press, 1991).

Lange, O.: 'On the economic theory of socialism', *Review of Economic Studies*, 4 (1936–7), 53–71 and 123–42.

Lasswell, H. D.: *Politics: Who Gets What, When, How?* (New York: P. Smith, 1950).

Levine, H. D.: 'Some things to all men: the politics of cruise missile development', *Public Policy*, 7 (1972), 117–68.

Lijphart, A.: *The Politics of Accommodation* (Berkeley, Calif.: University of California Press, 1968; 2nd edn 1975).

————: 'The Northern Ireland problem', *British Journal of Political Science*, 5 (1975), 83–106.

————: *Democracy in Plural Societies* (New Haven, Conn.: Yale University Press, 1977).

Landblom, C. E.: 'The science of muddling through', *Public Administration Review*, 19 (1959), 79–88.

————: *The Intelligence of Democracy* (New York: Free Press, 1965).

————: *Politics and Markets* (New York: Basic Books, 1977).

Lipset, S. M., ed.: *Politics and the Social Sciences* (New York: Oxford University Press, 1969).

———— and Rokkan, S., eds: *Party Systems and Voter Alignments* (New York: Free Press, 1967).

Lipsky, M.: *Street Level Bureaucracy* (New York: Russell Sage, 1980).

Lukes, S.: *Power: A Radical View* (London: Macmillan, 1974).

McCloskey, H. A.: 'Consensus and ideology in American politics', *American Political Science Review*, 58 (1964), 361–82.

McFarland, A. S.: *Public Interest Lobbies* (Washington, DC: American Enterprise Institute, 1976).

————: 'Interest groups and theories of power in America', *British Journal of Political Science*, 17 (1987), 129–48.

McKelvey, R. D.: 'General conditions for global intransitivities in formal voting models', *Econometrica*, 47 (1979), 1085–112.

Mann, M.: 'The social cohesion of liberal democracy', *American Sociological Review*, 35 (1970), 423–39.

————: *The Sources of Social Power* (Cambridge: Cambridge University Press, 1986).

Mansbridge, J. J., ed.: *Beyond Self-interest* (Chicago: University of Chicago Press, 1990).

March, J. G.: 'Model bias in social action', *Review of Educational Research*, 42 (1972), 413–29.

———— and Olsen, J. P.: 'The new institutionalism: organizational factors in political life', *American Political Science Review*, 78 (1984), 734–49.

———— and Olsen, J. P.: 'Popular sovereignty and the search for appropriate insitutions', *Journal of Public Policy*, 6 (1986), 341–70.

———— and Olsen., J. P.: *Rediscovering Institutions* (New York: Free Press, 1989).

Marshall, T. H.: 'Citizenship and social class' (1949), *Class, Citizenship and Social Development* (Chicago: University of Chicago Press, 1963), pp. 70–134.

Merton, R. K.: 'The unintended consequences of purposive social action', *American Sociological Review*, 1 (1936), 894–904.

Minow, M.: *Making All the Difference: Inclusion, Exclusion and American Law* (Ithaca, NY: Cornell University Press, 1990).

Moe, T.: 'The new economics of organization', *American Journal of Political Science*, 28 (1984), 739–77.

Moore, B., Jr.: *Social Origins of Dictatorship and Democracy* (Harmondsworth: Penguin, 1967).

Niskanen, W. A.: *Bureaucracy and Representative Government* (Chicago: Aldine-Atherton, 1971).

O'Donnell, G., Schmitter, P. C. and Whitehead, L., eds: *Transitions from Authoritarian Rule: Prospects for Democracy* (Baltimore, Md.: Johns Hopkins University Press, 1986).

Okin, S. M.: *Justice, Gender and the Family* (New York: Basic Books, 1989).

Ollman, B.: *Alienation* (Cambridge: Cambridge University Press, 1971).

Olsen, J. P.: 'Public policy-making and theories of organizational choice', *Scandinavian Political Studies*, 7 (1972), 45–62.

Olson, M., Jr: *The Logic of Collective Action* (Cambridge, Mass.: Harvard University Press, 1965).

Ordeshook, P. C.: *Game Theory and Political Theory* (Cambridge: Cambridge University Press, 1986).

Oye, K. A., ed.: *Cooperation under Anarchy* (Princeton, NJ: Princeton University Press, 1986).

Page, B. I.: *Choices and Echoes in Presidential Elections* (Chicago: University of Chicago Press, 1978).

————: *Who Gets What from Government?* (Berkeley: University of California Press, 1983).

———— and Shapiro, R. Y.: *The Rational Public* (Chicago: University of Chicago Press, 1992).

Parkin, F.: *Class Inequality and Political Power* (London: MacGibbon & Kee, 1971).

Pateman, C.: *Participation and Democratic Theory* (Cambridge: Cambridge University Press, 1970).

————: 'Political culture, political structure and political change', *British Journal of Political Science*, 1 (1971), 291–305.

————: *The Disorder of Women* (Oxford: Polity Press, 1989).

Pechman, J. A.: *Who Bears the Tax Burden?* (Washington, DC: Brookings Institution, 1974).

Polsby, N. W.: *Community Power and Political Theory*, 2nd edn (New Haven, Conn.: Yale University Press, 1980).

Pomper, G.: *Elections in America* (New York: Dodd, Mead, 1968).

Popkin, S. et al.: 'What have you done for me lately?', *American Political Science Review*, 70 (1976), 779–805.

Prothro, J. W. and Grieg, C. W.: 'Fundamental principles of democracy: bases of agreement and disagreement', *Journal of Politics*, 22 (1960), 276–94.

Przeworski, A.: *Democracy and the Market* (Cambridge: Cambridge University Press, 1991).

———— and Sprague, J.: *Paper Stones: A History of Electoral Socialism* (Chicago: University of Chicago Press, 1986).

Rae, D. W.: *The Political Consequences of Electoral Laws* (New Haven, Conn.: Yale University Press, 1967).

Rawls, J.: *A Theory of Justice* (Cambridge, Mass.: Harvard University Press, 1971).

————: 'The idea of an overlapping consensus', *Oxford Journal of Legal Studies*, 7 (1987), 1–25.

Rhodes, R. A. W.: *Beyond Westminster and Whitehall* (London: Unwin Hyman, 1988).

Riker, W. H.: *Theory of Political Coalitions* (New Haven, Conn.: Yale University Press, 1962).

————: *Liberalism against Populism* (San Francisco, Calif.: W. Freeman, 1983).

Roemer, J.: *A General Theory of Exploitation and Class* (Cambridge, Mass.: Harvard University Press, 1982).

———— ed.: *Analytical Marxism* (Cambridge: Cambridge University Press, 1986).

Rogowski, R.: *Rational Legitimacy* (Princeton, NJ: Princeton University Press, 1974).

Rose, R.: *Governing Without Consensus* (London: Faber & Faber, 1971).

———— and Peters, B. G.: *Can Government Go Bankrupt?* (New York: Free Press, 1978).

Rousseau, J.-J.: *The Social Contract* (1762), trans. G. D. H. Cole (London: Dent, 1973).

Rustow, D. A.: 'Transitions to democracy', *Comparative Politics*, 2 (1970), 337–63.

Satterthwaite, M. A.: 'Strategy-proofness and Arrow's conditions', *Journal of Economic Theory*, 10 (1975), 187–217.

Schneewind, J. B.: 'Modern moral philosophy', *A Companion to Ethics*, ed. P. Singer (Oxford: Blackwell, 1991), pp. 147–57.

Schofield, N.: 'Instability of simple dynamic games', *Review of Economic Studies*, 45 (1976), 575–94.

Schumpeter, J. A.: *Capitalism, Socialism & Democracy*, 3rd edn (New York: Harper & Row, 1950).

Sears, D. O., Lau, R. R., Tyler, T. R., Allen, H. M., Jr.: 'Self-interest vs. symbolic politics in policy attitudes and presidential voting', *American Political Science Review*, 74 (1980), 670–84.

Self, P.: *Administrative Theories and Politics* (London: Allen & Unwin, 1972; 2nd edn, 1977).

Sen, A. K.: 'Rational fools', *Philosophy & Public Affairs*, 6 (1977a), 317–44.

————: 'Social choice theory: a re-examination', *Econometrica*, 45 (1977b), 53–89.

Shepsle, K. and Weingast, B.: 'Structure induced equilibrium and legislative choice', *Public Choice*, 37 (1981), 593–19.

———— and Weingast, B.: 'Political solutions to market problems', *American Political Science Review*, 78 (1984), 417–34.

———— and Weingast, B.: 'The institutional foundations of committee power', *American Political Science Review*, 81 (1987), 85–104.

Simon, H. A.: 'A behavioral theory of rational choice', *Quarterly Journal of Economics*, 69 (1954), 99–118.

————: *The Sciences of the Artificial* (Cambridge, Mass.: MIT Press, 1969; 2nd edn, 1981).

————: 'Human nature is politics: the dialogue of psychology and political science', *American Political Science Review*, 79 (1985), 293–304.

Skocpol, T.: *States and Social Revolutions* (Cambridge: Cambridge University Press, 1979).

Sniderman, P. M., Fletcher, J. F., Russell, P. H., Tetlock, P. E. and Gaines, B. J.: 'The fallacy of democratic elitism: elite competition and commitment to civil liberties', *British Journal of Political Science*, 21 (1991), 349–70.

Steiner, J. and Dorff, R. H.: *A Theory of Political Decision Modes* (Chapel Hill, NC: University of North Carolina Press, 1980).

Stigler, G. J.: 'Director's law of public income redistribution', *Journal of Law and Economics*, 13 (1970), 1–10.

Taylor, M.: *The Possibility of Cooperation* (Cambridge: Cambridge University Press, 1987).

———— and Laver, M.: 'Government coalitions in Western Europe', *European Journal of Political Research*, 1 (1973), 205–48.

Therborn, G.: *What Does the Ruling Class Do When it Rules?* (London: New Left Books, 1978).

Thompson, D. F.: *The Democratic Citizen* (Cambridge: Cambridge University Press, 1970).

Tobin, J.: 'On limiting the domain of inequality', *Journal of Law and Economics*, 13 (1970), 363–78.

Useem, M.: *The Inner Circle* (New York: Oxford University Press, 1984).

Uslaner, E. M.: 'Comity in context', *British Journal of Political Science*, 21 (1991), 45–78.

Verba, S. and Nie, N. H.: *Participation in America* (New York: Harper & Row, 1972).

————, Nie, N. H. and Kim, J.-O.: *Participation and Political Equality: A Seven-Nation Comparison* (Cambridge: Cambridge University Press, 1978).

Wallerstein, I.: *The Modern World-System* (New York: Academic Press, 1974).

Ward, H.: 'Structural power – a contradiction in terms?', *Political Studies*, 35 (1987), 593–610.

Weingast, B. R. and Marshall, W.: 'The industrial organization of Congress; or, why legislatures, like firms, are not organized as markets', *Journal of Political Economy*, 96 (1988), 132–63.

Wendt, A. E.: 'The agent-structure problem in international relations theory', *International Organization*, 41 (1987), 335–70.

Wildavsky, A.: 'If planning is everything, maybe it's nothing', *Policy Sciences*, 4 (1973), 127–53.

Wilensky, H. L.: *The Welfare State and Equality* (Berkeley: University of California Press, 1975).

Williamson, O. E.: *Markets and Hierarchies* (New York: Free Press, 1975).

Wilson, J. Q.: *Bureaucracy: What Government Agencies Do and Why They Do It* (New York: Basic Books, 1989).

————: 'Interests and deliberation in the American republic', *PS: Political Science & Politics*, 23 (1990), 558–62.

Winner, L.: 'Do artifacts have politics?', *Daedalus*, 109 (Winter 1980), 121–36.

Wittfogel, K. A.: *Oriental Despotism* (New Haven, Conn.: Yale University Press, 1957).

Wolf, C., Jr: *Markets or Governments* (Cambridge, Mass.: MIT Press, 1988).

Wrong, D.: 'The oversocialized conception of man in modern sociology', *American Sociological Review*, 26 (1961), 184–93.

Young, I. M.: *Justice and the Politics of Difference* (Princeton, NJ: Princeton University Press, 1990).

Zolberg, A.: 'Moments of madness', *Politics & Society*, 2 (1972), 183–208.

Further reading

Butler, D., Penniman, H. and Ranney, A., eds: *Democracy at the Polls* (Washington, DC: American Enterprise Institute, 1981).

Greenstein, F. I. and Polsby, N. W., eds: *Handbook of Political Science*, 8 vols (Reading, Mass.: Addison-Wesley, 1975).

Hennessy, B.: *Public Opinion* (Monterey, Calif.: Wadsworth, 1965; 5th edn, 1985).

Hogwood, B. W. and Peters, B. G.: *The Pathology of Public Policy* ((Oxford: Clarendon Press, 1985).

Mackenzie, W. J. M.: *Politics and Social Sciences* (Harmondsworth: Penguin, 1967).

7

The contribution of legal studies

TOM D. CAMPBELL

The studies of politics and law are closely related in that both deal with the use of coercive power in society, yet the two disciplines are often curiously isolated from each other. Political theorists are rarely concerned with the specific content and application of the legislation which they regard as one of the main outputs of a political system, while legal academics are, traditionally at least, noted for their general indifference to the political and economic context of the rules and procedures which they seek to explain and systemize.

Increasingly, however, the academic discipline of law is influenced and, indeed, revitalized by the application of information and ideas derived from political science and political philosophy. The flow of intellectual stimuli in the reverse direction is not as pronounced, but, as we shall see, it is not insignificant. Moreover, it seems clear that the study of politics and, in particular, political philosophy, could be further enriched by a deeper awareness of what is going on within the discipline of law. It is this perspective that has governed the choice and presentation of the highly selective account of contemporary legal studies which follows.

One explanation for the gap between the disciplines of law and politics is that the study of law is more closely integrated into the sphere with which it deals than is the case with political science and philosophy. Legal academics tend to be lawyers, whereas political scientists and philosophers are only rarely politicians. Much academic legal work involves the investigation and presentation of the substantive and procedural rules and principles which are regarded as authoritative within the jurisdiction in question. This work may be described as 'doctrinal' or 'black letter' in that it seeks to exhibit and give legal authority for the basic principles and rules of each area of law. The norms in question are selected on the basis of their legal validity and the consequent analysis and explanation is carried out from a point of view which is internal to the process of law and intended largely for the consumption of legal officials and other practitioners, present and future.

The discipline of politics, on the other hand, is more empirically and theoretically-based and seeks principally to describe and explain political behaviour, and – in its more philosophical and prescriptive aspects – to criticize or justify political systems or political outcomes. Political science and philosophy are external accounts, explanations and justifications of social and political phenomena such as social class, pressure groups, individual preferences and democratic procedures; the discipline of law is more of an insider's view of distinctively legal phenomena, such as statutes, cases, precedents, interpretation and court procedures.

There are, however, three areas of the discipline of law to which such juxtapositions do not apply. The first is the study of law and society; the second is the study of 'jurisprudence' or legal philosophy; the third takes the form of commentary on the reasonings and decisions of the Supreme Court of the United States.

In contrast to the doctrinal approach mentioned above, there is a growing body of work done in the style of social science which seeks to give an account of 'law in context', focusing on the forces which shape the content and processes of law and examining the observable effects of legal process on other social phenomena. These studies involve the self-conscious application of the methods of the social sciences to law as a social phenomenon. I draw attention later in the chapter to some of this work which is of particular significance for political philosophy.

The second area of legal studies that is cognate to legal philosophy is the philosophy of law. The old-style 'jurisprudence' which, following the path set by the first professor of that title, John Austin (1790–1859), deals with the analysis of basic concepts – such as obligation, rights and sanctions – which were assumed to be common to all 'developed' legal systems (Austin, 1885, Lecture V), has all but given way to an altogether more philosophical approach to the interpretation of fundamental legal concepts. Contemporary legal philosophy takes in the examination and evaluation of the role of law within different types of society in a thoroughly philosophical manner. In so far as this work deals with the 'principles of legislation', that is the elaboration and critique of principles which set standards for substantively good or acceptable law, legal philosophy is in much the same business as a great deal of political philosophy. There is a similar overlap when legal philosophers consider the nature and legitimacy of states as a source of valid law.

However, the most distinctive concern of legal philosophers is the nature of legal process itself, and in particular the analysis and criticism of legal argumentation as it is manifest in the selection, interpretation and application of laws, principally in the setting of the court room. This central aspect of legal philosophy has important implications for political philosophy in that it raises issues about the institutional and philosophical presuppositions of the idea of the rule of law, one of the principal ideological foundations of liberal politics and the theory of democracy. For this reason competing philosophies of legal argumentation feature centrally in this exposition of those aspects of the discipline of law which are of evident relevance to political philosophy.

In the United States a great deal of politically relevant legal studies arises from the constitutional role of the Supreme Court in the exercise of its extensive powers of judicial review. The legal arguments used to justify decisions on alleged violations of constitutional rights provide a focus for much debate on issues of political moment. More specifically, the extensive body of commentary on the rationales and critiques of Supreme Court decisions includes much straight political philosophy, while the political twists and turns reflected in the past and present decisions of the Supreme Court are a standard part of the subject matter of political science. This material represents the third area of legal studies which is atypically close to the work of political philosophers.

The disciplinary separation of law and politics is an institutional fact with considerable ideological overtones. For many lawyers, law is respectable and politics is not. To some of these the very idea that law is a manifestation or type of politics seems almost offensive. Within legal academia, however, the most eye-catching of contemporary work rests on precisely such a claim: there is no science of law independent of or isolated from politics. This is, for instance, one of the main contentions of the 'Critical Legal Studies' movement and most versions of 'Feminist Jurisprudence' as the theoretical wing of legal feminism is sometimes called. Similarly, although the increasingly influential 'Economic Analysis of Law' approach to legal studies has very different political content and is overtly about economics rather than politics, its practitioners share the assumption that law is not an autonomous social phenomenon.

Because of their evident political relevance and relative novelty it is tempting to begin with and to concentrate on these distinctive trends in current legal studies. However, a great deal of these contemporary legal critiques is best understood against the background of the more formalistic legal positivism, which represents the traditional liberal position from which they take their disrespectful departure. For this reason, I commence the substantive discussion in this chapter with the work of Herbert Hart, the most widely read of all contemporary legal philosophers and a sophisticated exponent of modern legal positivism, that is, the doctrine that all law is made or 'posited' in a way which can be identified by social observation.

Herbert Hart's *Concept of Law*

In the late 1950s and through the 1960s when contemporary political philosophy was re-emerging from a period of inactivity, not to say academic disrepute, and political science was just beginning to gain acceptance as an independent subject, the discipline of law was not considered as an important model to be adopted, despite the fact that many university courses on 'government' emerged from a background of public law teaching. Interestingly, it was the school of linguistic, or 'ordinary language' philosophy, which had done so much to discredit the intellectual status of theorists who sought to commend substantive moral and political views, that gave birth to perhaps the most important legal philosopher of the modern period, Herbert Hart. Hart, a one-time practising barrister and war-time civil servant, and subsequently Professor of Jurisprudence at Oxford University, published, in 1961, *The Concept of Law*, a book which set out in a lucid and straightforward manner a theory of law which restated in modern guise the legal positivist's doctrine on the separation of law and morals in a way which enabled the political philosophy of the time to pursue its own concerns with scant regard for the details of law and legal systems.

Hart's legal philosophy represents a typically British view of law and politics in that he allocates to the realm of politics the articulation and defence of moral rights and community conceptions of justice, leaving law with the humbler role of identifying and applying, in a politically neutral manner, existing legal rules. Legal positivism, as the theory that all law has its origins in human acts and contrivances (rather than, for instance, the natural law contention that law is essentially related to pre-existing moral ideals), conveys precisely such assumptions. The thesis that there is no necessary connection between the existence of a law and its moral justification

(Hart, 1961, ch. IX) fits well with the assumption that law can be identified by its distinguishing social features and interpreted by reference to its intelligible content alone. In this respect, at least, Hart carries on the tradition stemming from John Austin's insistence that 'the existence of a law is one thing, its merit or demerit another' (Austin, 1885, p. 174). Where Hart departs from Austin is in his revision of the latter's contentions that all laws are the generalized commands of a sovereign and that all positive law (or 'law properly so-called') is the command of a human sovereign, that is of a person or body who is habitually obeyed by all members of a given society and who does not habitually obey any other person or body.

Despite the parochial nature of some of Hart's assumptions, *The Concept of Law* represents the working assumptions about law of most political philosophy, namely that a legal system is a system of rules, which emanate in large measure from the political process via legislatures, but are routinely applied by a separate body of officials, the judiciary and supporting legal practitioners, in a manner which is in itself politically neutral and therefore politically uninteresting. In this regard the US Supreme Court is seen as atypical in that it has been able to adopt an overtly political role through its interpretation of vaguely worded constitutional rights and their application to social circumstances far removed from those in which the rights originated. However, in the world of ordinary law, at least, the model of judicial duty has, as its paradigm of legal process, the application of those rules which can be shown to be legally valid within the system in question to facts as they are established through procedures designed to arrive at the truth about the circumstances at issue. This is believed to give an appropriately neutral role to non-elected officials, thus safeguarding the liberty of the individual against the arbitrary intrusions of government.

While endorsing Austin's general positivistic line, Hart seeks to distance himself from the imperatival aspects of Austin's analysis, particularly in so far as the concept of a command is cashed out in terms of liability to (in the sense of the statistical likelihood of) the infliction of a sanction if the alleged commander's wish is not complied with. This model, Hart considers, may fit well enough with the criminal law, but it does not begin to explain the legal nature of the civil law, with its emphasis on contracts and tort where the law enforces agreements or requires compensation for injuries without imposing anything comparable to a punishment. Instead, Hart fills the role of the sovereign in providing unity for a legal system (as the unitary source of all laws) with the idea of a 'rule of recognition' which, by stating the requirements for acceptance as valid law of ordinary legal rules (which lay down an obligation or permit the exercise of a legal power), enables the officials charged with the task of applying the law to recognize a rule of their legal system when they come across one (Hart, 1961, ch. 6). The task of specifying which rules are legal rules, involves not a passage from rules to rulers but an elaboration of the concept of a rule by distinguishing between what he calls primary rules of conduct, rules which require or enable individuals to act or refrain from acting in certain ways, and secondary rules, or rules about rules, which are followed in the adoption, alternation and application of primary rules. A legal system is a combination of primary and secondary rules whose systematic unity depends on the existence of a particular secondary rule, the 'rule of recognition', which states those properties which a primary rule must possess to be 'recognized' by those charged with the application of such rules as a 'valid' rule of the system.

Precisely what the criteria for acceptance as valid law are is left largely unspecified. It may be that such rules must have been enacted by a particular institutional body, such as a legislature; it may be that the rules in question have been applied in the past in the courts; it may be that the rules are to be found in a particular book. In practice it is likely that there is a hierarchically ordered combination of such criteria. All that is excluded is that the utilization of the criteria involves the exercise of personal value judgements as to the content of the putative rules. In this sense all valid law must have a social origin which judges can recognize from its social source rather than from the understanding or evaluation of its contents alone.

Paradoxically, perhaps, for a legal positivist intent on marking the logical distinction between law and morals, Hart is keen to assert the similarity of many of the features of both legal and moral obligations: both render certain conducts mandatory, both involve the idea of potential criticism and blame for non-compliance, both relate to matters of some social importance (Hart, 1961, pp. 79–88). As a linguistic philosopher, Hart is happy to point to the overlapping vocabulary of law and morals (rights, duties, fault, etc.), relying on the existence of a set of officials united in the deployment of a single rule of recognition to mark off positive law from the positive morality of the community and the personal or critical morality of the individual. Almost all that remains of Austin at this point is that the rules identified and applied by these officials are 'efficacious' in that they are generally obeyed within a given territory.

Several features of Hart's model of law facilitate political analysis. In particular the content of differing rules of recognition can be used to characterize different types of political systems, democratic and non-democratic, constitutional and traditional. The same analysis gives us a framework for discussing political revolutions in terms of the changing content of a system's rule of recognition. However, more significantly for our purposes, it is a model that enables a working division of labour between legal and political studies which mirrors the analytical distinction within Hart's theory. Legal studies can concentrate on the processes of law application, leaving political science to study the processes leading up to legislation, and political philosophy to deal with the normative principles which determine what is 'good' law. Thus Hart himself enunciates and defends a version of Mill's 'harm' principle relating to the extent of legitimate government intervention (modified by an allowance for a measure of paternalism) which has had some influence in legal philosophy (see Feinberg, 1985–8).

The most serious difficulty for Hart's theory is its method for identifying the accepted rule of recognition within a given political community. Hart himself simply notes that the rule of recognition is a sociological fact to be ascertained by observing the activities of judges, a method which does little to account for either the normative force or the origins of such rules. From the point of view of political analysis, it is not clear that we will readily be able to identify which rule of recognition is in force, given that it is of the nature of rules which govern conduct that they are not always followed by those to whom they apply. Simple generalization from the judicial activities of individual persons will hardly suffice. Further, since judges do not explicitly formulate a rule of recognition as they go along, it may be difficult to divine what rule they are following, or failing to follow, or if indeed their behaviour is rule governed at all. Certainly, it seems no more than an article of faith that all judges in the same system are following the same rule of recognition.

This problem is simply a particular form of a general difficulty that we encounter when it comes to the further element of positivistic theories, such as Hart's, namely the idea that once a rule is recognized as a valid law, then our problems in separating law and politics are over, a claim that seems to ignore the fact that any form of words, or any series of legal decisions, can be taken in a variety of ways, and that the decision which way to take them is in itself, at least potentially, a political act. This is particularly so when, as is often the case, the rules in question are stated in a highly general form (such as that goods must be 'of merchantable quality' or conduct must be 'reasonable') which invites moral interpretation.

Although in the British context it is relatively easy to go along with the contention that laws are rules whose application at least in normal cases has difficulty only with respect to determinations of fact, even at the time Hart's views did not square with the developing consensus in the United States that the 'legal realists' must be right about the fact that it is judges not rules who decide cases and that rules can be no more than general guides to the making of what are essentially political decisions about who is to get what, where, when and how. Hart's own response to American legal realism is to assert that it is feasible, if not always attained, to have rules which are capable of relatively straightforward application in terms of their obvious meanings. Problems do emerge in marginal cases where general terms are applied at the limits of their normal applications or where gaps in the law require that existing rules be stretched beyond their normal contexts, but these are not typical law in its normal everyday operations. He argues that, as a matter of sociological fact, most words have a core of certainty in their meanings about which there is no reasonable doubt, and at the same time a 'penumbra of doubt' where we cannot be sure how they are to be taken. In other words, there are lot of paradigm cases and not very many borderline judgements in the application of most sensibly formulated rules. Further, such 'open texture' as there is in the meaning of legal rules permits the judiciary to exercise a useful degree of discretion, thus enabling law to adapt to changing circumstances (Hart, 1961, pp. 138–44).

This may seem a sensible mediating position between the extreme 'rule sceptics' who take any decision to be compatible with any rule, and those formalists who hold that – potentially at least – all law can be reduced to rules with uncontroversial meanings. Yet, if the number of legal rules which fit the model of applicable clarity, and/or the number of fact situations which fall within clear rules turns out to be relatively small, and if, worst still, there are ways in which even an ostensibly clear rule can be rendered obscure so that 'easy' cases become 'hard' ones, Hart's theory may turn out to be a highly misleading model on which to posit a working relationship between legal and political studies. More seriously from the point of view of political philosophy, we may have to accept that there is a major objection to the traditional idea of the separation of judicial and legislative powers under the model of the rule of law.

Given the plurality of jurisdictions within the United States and the overtly political role of its Supreme Court, both of which contribute to making legal realism such a plausible view, it is not surprising that Hart's strongest early critics came from the ranks of US legal theorists. Ironically, however, the critics in question may readily be interpreted as developing variants on Hartian positivism. The first, Lon Fuller, echoes, although in a formulation with which he could not agree, Hart's recognition of the moral value of the rule of law, while the second, Ronald Dworkin, presents a method through which Hart's alleged gaps and obscurities in positive law may be overcome without recourse to the exercise of judicial discretion.

Lon Fuller's 'inner morality of law'

In some ways the objections raised by Lon Fuller against Hart's positivism is a domestic jurisprudential dispute without immediate political relevance. Both agree with the idea that laws should be clear, prospective (in that they do not apply to conduct which occurred before the laws existed), general (in that they are not *ad hoc* commands to named individuals or groups), practicable (in that those affected are able to fulfil their legal obligations), stable (in that they are not liable to constant change), consistent (in that they do not require a person both to do and not to do the same actions) and public (in that they can be known by those to whom they apply) (Fuller, 1969, pp. 35–7). Further, both agree that these properties of 'good' law have instrumental value in that, by enabling citizens to know in advance precisely how they stand in relation to the legal effects of their conduct, it enlarges human freedom and individual responsibility (see Hart, 1968). Their disagreement arises over Fuller's further claim that the virtues of formally proper law produce a necessary connection between law and morality, in that it is no accident that those systems which are committed to the rule of law are those which also have substantively the best laws. This is the basis of his theory of 'procedural natural law' according to which aspiration towards perfect legality provides some sort of protection for fundamental substantive rights. For instance, retrospective legislation is 'absurd' because it could not have been followed by those who are retrospectively affected by it, but it is also 'brutal and oppressive' precisely because those burdened in this way do not have the opportunity to avoid their fate.

Hart seems to have the best of the dispute when he points out that the clearest, most prospective and most stable rules may serve the most awful purposes (Hart, 1983, pp. 347–53). Fuller's rejoinder, to the effect that the use of general, prospective rules, cannot but to some extent respect human freedom more than particular retrospective commands seems too flimsy a base on which to build his more expansive claims about the internal morality of law. The politically interesting aspect of the dispute centres on whether Fuller's position tends to support an unduly complacent view of the benefits of lawfulness as such. His theory might be thought to give encouragement to the belief that by striving for all procedural perfections we are thereby contributing to the furtherance of rules which are acceptable in their content. Hart offers no such comfort to the conscience of the legal officials engaged in their administrative and judicial functions.

However, Fuller, in carrying on the American realist position that courts may properly look to the purpose of legislation and judicial precedent in their interpretations and decisions, points to a method which may avoid the abstract formalism which Hart's 'clear meaning' can engender. In particular, appeals to the purpose of legislation is a device which is often called into play when the meaning of a rule is disputed. This is, however, a two-edged sword for Fuller and other rule of law theorists who see law as a defence against arbitrary political power, since resort to the purposes of legislators is one of the sources of abuse which the rule of law ideal is intended to curb by limiting the discretion of officials to tailor their decisions to the immediate requirements set by policy objectives. There is no defence for the citizen against arbitrary political authority if rules are treated as flexible instruments to secure purposes which override their immediately evident implications.

Nevertheless, when purposive interpretation is adopted, it creates an interesting legal role for the political scientist who may be asked to provide an answer to the impossible question. what is the purpose which lies behind a particular piece of legislation, or a particular clause in a legislative act. Political philosophers, however, may reasonably ask whether it makes sense to ask for the purpose or intention of a legislative body, or worse still, of an electorate, given that legislation is the outcome of a complex process of pressure group activity, bargaining, economic power and plain chance.

Ronald Dworkin's principles

Hart's second American critic, Ronald Dworkin, provides a much more detailed and apparently far reaching assault on the legal positivist's model of law as a corpus of rules. Dworkin, one of the most charismatic and innovative contemporary legal philosophers, has a theoretical approach which licenses him to merge legal and political theory without denying the distinctiveness of legal argumentation. In the end his position may be seen as naively American as Hart's is British, and to have the added disadvantage that it matches Hart's low-keyed common sense approach with an extravaganza of impracticalities. So much so that one recent commentator notes that 'Dworkin's theory was and remains quite bizarre' (Alexander, 1987, p. 419). Along the way, however, Dworkin provides us with suggestive insights and important distinctions of evident interest to political philosophers.

Dworkin's initial objection to Hart is that he over- emphasizes the role of rules in law (Dworkin, 1977, pp. 14–80). He does not deny that there are rules, that is specific legal permissions or requirements that have an either/or effect in establishing or denying the existence of legal obligations and rights. His point is that law contains other norms, such as principles, which are not, as is usually believed, simply more general than rules. Indeed, principles may be more specific than rules. What is important, for Dworkin, is that principles have a very different function from rules in that they state more fundamental considerations which may be used to override the immediate implications of rules in favour of the background values of the legal system. Thus the principle that 'no one shall be permitted to profit from his own fraud, or to take advantage of his own wrong' may he used to set aside an otherwise valid will (Dworkin, 1977, p. 23), or the background value that 'the courts will not permit themselves to be used as instruments of inequity and injustice' may be used to extend the liability of motor manufacturers for defective products (ibid., p. 24). Principles are different in kind from rules, in that they have 'weight' which has to be put in the balance with other possibly competing principles, and may override established legal rules. This is because principles represent underlying justificatory values embodied in the legal system in question.

Dworkin develops a model of legal reasoning according to which a legally all-knowing and intellectually faultless judge ('Hercules') works out *the* right answer to every legal dispute. The Herculean judge determines the actual pre-existent rights of the parties involved by reaching an answer which is consistent with or 'fits' all existing principles and rules in so far as they are not set aside by the principles in question. In his judgements, even in hard cases, Hercules pursues 'integrity', by which Dworkin means a decision which coheres with the legal tradition in question, and does so on the interpretation which adopts the most justifiable reading of that tradition (Dworkin, 1986, pp. 176–275). For, while there may be many answers which cohere with the tradition, only one of these represents a coherence of the best interpretation of the tradition, a conception which he derives from efforts in literary criticism to justify the priority of a specific interpretation as giving the best literary or aesthetic result. In the case of Hercules the standards applied are those of contemporary political community. Dworkin speaks of a 'constructivist interpretation' of law that involves asserting the most acceptable political justification of the tradition in question as it is embodied in the inherited legal material (ibid., pp. 52–3).

Ready sense can be made of Dworkin's approach by considering the role of the US Supreme Court in its activist phases. The background principles and rights to which Dworkin has such easy recourse can be identified with the relevant provisions of the US constitution which are routinely used by the Supreme Court to override the decisions of lower courts. Indeed Dworkin's theory can be seen as a legitimation of the role of the Supreme Court, for he is able to argue that while the court should have no role in overruling on utilitarian grounds the policies which have been arrived at by duly constituted legislatures, it is its task to veto such proposals which conflict with the rights embodied in the constitutional principles that the courts are there to defend. This presupposes the very bold and important claim that all political issues can be distinguished into those which are within the majoritarian democratic process, because they have to do with the maximization of preferences, and those which are also within the legal process because they deal with the fundamental rights of the individual. Moreover rights, in Dworkin's well-known phrase, are 'trumps', so that, within this sphere, at least, courts dominate over the current electoral political process. All this is of a piece with liberal views on the role of the Supreme Court (see Michelman, 1986).

Writing within a tradition that has come to accept that the mass of judicial decisions is a jumble of incoherent findings dependent on numerous extrajudicial factors, Dworkin's radical claims about 'right answers' have been greeted with some scepticism both as a description of judicial practice and as a feasible ideal. Quite apart from the fact that there are no judges of Herculean capacities to be found, the whole enterprise seems inherently unreal in so far as it requires the judge to exercise a judgement as to which interpretations are best in relation to principles which are so general as to admit of an endless variety of determinations. It thus turns out that Dworkin's critique of Hart, which was designed to show that judicial discretion is neither required nor desirable, makes its extensive use inevitable in practice since every legal argument is open to challenge through the introduction of highly elastic general norms.

Dworkin himself goes some way towards suggesting an appropriate objective methodology for moral-cum-legal argument through his elucidation of the most basic principle of all, that of 'equal concern and respect' (Dworkin, 1977, p. 275). He interprets this principle as requiring us to give equal weight to the preferences of all individuals but only in so far as they relate to their own welfare and interests, thus excluding those 'external preferences' which relate to the lives of other people, preferences which can provide an easy entrance for racialism and other inegalitarian prejudices.

There is no doubt that, given a morally passable senior judiciary, a legal system which managed to follow out some such principle as Dworkin's 'equal concern and respect' could avoid some of the evils which come from democratic oppression of minorities, but the principle is so vague as to be compatible with as many enormities as could coexist with a commitment to Fuller's procedural principles. Dworkin in the end has to believe that 'equal concern and respect' can be unpacked to provide the political content of the presently fading left liberalism of contemporary US politics. His many endeavours to demonstrate that this is the case with respect to current constitutional issues, such as free speech, racialism and pornography, are formidable and clever but invariably in the end somewhat *ad hoc* and unconvincing.

Thus, despite its trappings of modern literary theory, if Dworkin's theory is to be of more than dubious local (i.e. US) application, it seems to require a more substantive theory of natural law. For some, this requirement may be met by John Finnis' refurbished presentation of traditional Thomism (Finnis, 1980). Certainly, without some such underpinning Dworkin's theory lacks the epistemological basis for controlling the power of unelected judicial officers who are in effect licensed to deploy unspecific principles to complicated political conflicts.

Economic analysis of law

The debate between Fuller and Hart, and the positivistic revisionism of Dworkin, have been overtaken by a more bitter and overtly political struggle between two products of the American Legal Realists, those who practise the Economic Analysis of Law (EAL) and those who take EAL to embody an evidently ideological stance on the nature and purpose of law, a view that is held particularly strongly by those within the Critical Legal Studies movement (CLS).

The intellectual roots of EAL are to be found largely outside legal studies, at least in the modern period, although it has to be remembered that Adam Smith taught law as well as economics as part of his course in 'moral philosophy' at Glasgow University. It is the Chicago-based free market economic theory of Milton Friedman and others that provides the inspiration of Richard Posner and other practitioners of EAL. However, the application of classical libertarian economics to law has developed a degree of sophistication and originality which makes it more than a mere reflection of general economic theory. In particular, argument that the common law as developed by judges over long periods of time is inherently efficient while state legislation tends to inefficiency is argued with a conceptual subtlety and empirical grounding which make EAL, potentially at least, an important contributor to the analysis of the role of law in contemporary political systems.

Political philosophers who read Posner will find that his position has many similarities to those of Robert Nozick in its endorsement of the private ownership of productive resources and the free exchange of goods without governmental intervention (Nozick, 1974). However, Posner goes beyond the unargued assertion of certain basic rights and argues, on consequentialist grounds, for positive rights to life, liberty and property as the best institutional means to promote economic 'efficiency', by which he means 'exploiting economic resources in such a way that human satisfaction as measured by aggregate willingness to pay for goods and services is maximized' (Posner, 1977, p.4). Law is then shown to have its part to play in an essentially economic system, not simply because judges, like everyone else, behave in accordance with classic economic assumptions of self-interested rationality, but because they determine cases which come before them in the most economically efficient way. This is achieved (whether consciously or not) by adopting the allocation for rights and liabilities, which would be the result of free individual bargaining in a world in which there are no 'transaction costs', that is the costs of gaining relevant information and setting up the most rational agreements. In this way the law ensures that rights are possessed by those who, given an ideal market, would pay most for them, thus maximising their value.

According to EAL, the law of torts, for instance, ensures the efficient distribution of the costs of accidents, taking into account the losses involved in the accidents themselves, the costs of preventing accidents and the costs of administering a system of allocating liabilities for accidents. The contention is that the party who can most cheaply adopt the precautions which would most effectively reduce or prevent those accidents of which the cost is greater than the precautions which would prevent them is the party who is to be liable for the losses incurred when such accidents occur. The standard illustration of this approach is the judgment of Judge Learned Hand in *US v Carroll Towing* (1947) where negligence is defined as the failure to take care when the cost of the care is less than the probability of the accident, multiplied by the loss if the accident occurs. This principle gives incentives to take efficient precautions, to which rational economic agents will respond in a way which prevents those accidents worth preventing, at least cost. On the same basis property rights are defended as giving individuals exclusive rights over things which can be alienated only by voluntary transfer, so that material good are in the hands of those who are able to make the most productive use of them (Posner, 1977, ch. 3). Similar arguments are deployed to vindicate the basic principles of existing Anglo-American common law.

The proponents of EAL do not suggest that the actual market could take the place of the common law, for the significance of law, beyond setting a framework for free exchange, is largely that it enables actual markets to become more like the markets without the imperfections of transaction costs. Rather, the common law seeks to 'mimic' a transaction costless market, that is a market where there is no cost in the gathering of information, making the necessary communications between parties and in arriving at a voluntary and informed agreement (Posner, 1977, p. 138).

Posner's position on the efficiency of the common law is derived from the work of the recent Nobel laureate Ronald H. Coase, whose article 'The Problem of Social Cost' (1960) must represent one of the most influential contributions of legal studies to political philosophy. There Coase argues that, where transaction costs are low, it is immaterial for efficiency which party in a dispute has the legal right in dispute since the party who values that right most highly will purchase it from whomsoever is the current right-holder. Eventually all rights will be then possessions of those who are able and willing to pay most for them (see Ellikson, 1989–90).

Posner himself goes further than this by arguing that the efficient outcomes mimicked by common law rules and principles are also just. He achieves this remarkable result by interpreting the maximization of wealth as the maximization of preferences and adopting an essentially utilitarian standard of justice, adding, in Nozickian terms, that the market also maximizes liberty since all transactions are freely entered into. While it is clear that, at least in relation to those liberties, such as freedom of contract, which are integral to the free market, liberty is an entrenched value, it turns out that wealth-maximization is ultimately fundamental since it is used to justify limitations on liberty, as in prohibitions of those monopoly economic powers which do not maximize wealth.

Posner does not extend his favourable analysis of the law's efficiency beyond the Anglo-American common law system. In fact, the activities of legislatures, because their interventions in the market are typically in the interests of particular groups and do not have the results that are intended, are said to be grossly inefficient. In other respects, however, his analyses echoes the work of Jeremy Bentham. Thus, for instance, Posner follows a Benthamite analysis of criminal law, although with more stress on the costs of preventing crime than on the suffering caused by the prohibited acts. In Posner's view, the strategy of criminal law is to 'increase the costs of unlawful conduct where the conventional damage remedies are insufficient' (Posner, 1977, p. 164) so that, for the potential offender, the costs exceed the benefits, discounting for the chances of being caught. The costs include the outlays required to carry out a crime and the criminal's opportunity costs as well as the associated punishment, while the benefits include the psychological satisfaction of perpetrating a crime as well as material benefits. Thus crime levels can be reduced by increasing employment (thus increasing opportunity costs), by varying the penalties, or by increasing detection rates. And, of course, if the benefit to the criminal exceeds the losses of the victim(s) then the crime is 'justified', i.e. the actions in question should be decriminalized, bearing in mind that we are not dealing with isolated actions of, for instance, theft, but a pattern of activity with long term implications for wealth creation, and that the imposition of sanctions is itself a very costly business.

The limitations of EAL, particularly when it is extended beyond the sphere of property and commerce, are the limitations of libertarian economic philosophy in general: the failure to consider the initial distribution of rights as a matter of justice beyond the calculation of maximization; the need to provide a basis of what is essentially a crude utilitarianism of wealth; and the factual implausibility of many of its assumptions about instrumental rationality (see Baker, 1975; Coleman, 1988). Moreover there is now plenty of evidence to cast doubt on the specific claim of EAL relating to the relative efficiency of the common law as against government regulation (see Sunstein, 1990). It cannot be denied, however, that the persistent pursuit of economic analysis throughout the common law has increased the credibility of EAL to the point where it is considered to be about the only theory which can purport to provide sub- ✓ stantive guidelines for understanding and making the legal decisions which are so widely assumed to be underdetermined by formal rules. Political philosophers should note that in some jurisdictions there is a conscious effort to utilize the principle of EAL in the courtroom and that, whatever the theoretical deficiencies of EAL, the use of its methods in actual judicial process is a fact of some political significance.

Critical legal studies

The Economic Analysis of Law epitomises the sort of liberal certainties which the Critical Legal Studies movement is committed to destabilizing. Given that its origin in the early 1970s coincided with the political emergence of the New Right, CLS is a surprisingly leftist movement to emerge from the elite law schools of North America. Sociologically, the movement may be viewed as a reaction against the populist libertarianism of Middle America and the less than attractive part that American lawyers played in the enrichment of those who benefited most from the entrepreneurial opportunities of the period. Philosophically its proponents have been characterised as 'a diverse group . . . generally marked by a commitment to a more egalitarian society and a dissatisfaction with current legal scholarship' (Boyle, 1992, p. 3).

CLS is no mere external commentary on unjustified pretensions and tainted performance of courts and lawyers. True it is a community tenet of the CLS movement that its members should be active in community politics. But the prime force of much CLS work is to condemn existing forms of legal education and research for the way in which they perpetuate and even promote the formalist myths which legitimate the high status of law and lawyers, and the rights-based constitution so revered in the political culture of the United States (see Kennedy, 1982).

Nor does CLS work turn its attention away from law to the alleged 'real' determinants of political change. Rather, the prime focus of CLS work is directed to the detailed scrutiny of law in its traditional manifestations: statutes, law reports, court decisions, etc. CLS writing centres on understanding the legal house and setting it in order, or, rather, disorder, through intense and sustained scholarly attention to legal history and the ways in which rules are handled and decisions justified in the legal realm.

In some ways the CLS movement is not particularly novel either in legal or in philosophical terms. Its central presupposition and refrain that rules and hence laws are irretrievably 'indeterminate' in that they can be construed in an elastic and open-ended variety of ways is largely a reassertion of the influential thesis of the American legal realists (such as Jerome Frank, 1949; Karl Llewellyn, 1960) to the effect that judges not rules decide cases and that judges are influenced by a variety of competing factors and adopt a variety of interpretative styles with radically different results.

The 'critical' element in CLS could be regarded as little more than a deployment of postmodernist anti-essentialism to open up a left-wing analysis of law and the state (see Unger, 1975). The postmodernism lies in the thesis, derived from Wittgenstein, Foucault, Derrida and Lacan, that all meanings are constructed in that no text has a correct or essential meaning. In consequence, there can be little weight attached to the idea of the 'core meanings' of words, which is so central to the model of legal reasoning presented by modern legal positivists, such as H. L. A. Hart (see Boyle, 1985).

The left-wing, or neo-Marxist, content of CLS is two-fold. First, that actual legal process involves inherent 'contradictions' between incompatible elements which reflect the conflicts inherent in social relationships. Without being committed to historical materialism, the CLS development of American realist contentions concerning the political tensions within and without the legal realm are at the very least reminiscent of Marx's critique of the 'contradictions' of capitalism, such as the incompatibility of social production and individual appropriation.

Another quasi-Marxist theme is the exposure of objectified or reified social forms as legitimations of existing power relationships (see Gabel, 1979). For CLS the paradigm of reification is apparent in the 'formalist' view that law is a process whereby clear rules are applied by impartial adjudicators. The implied division of powers between those who make law and those who apply it and the associated tenet that the judicial function is limited to the accurate application of pre-existing rules and principles makes up the 'rule of law' ideology that serves to cloak and rationalise legally mediated oppression. The echoes of Marxian theories of ideology and false consciousness are audible, albeit without the full trappings of economic class analysis (see Gabel and Harris, 1982–3).

Critical Legal Studies may thus be viewed as an appropriation of pre-existing political philosophy rather than a source of novel insights. This is, however, an ignorant oversimplification of the CLS themes and substantially underestimates the significance of the detailed work done by CLS scholars in the analysis of law and legal systems (see, for instance, Horwitz, 1977; Tushnet, 1981). Influential among this work have been the writings of Duncan Kennedy whose approach to the analysis of legal thought is manifest in the claim that the underlying structure of the common law legal tradition is a constant and unrecognized tension between the self and others, or between individualism and collectivism. This tension represents a reality inherent in human relationships which involves a clash between the desire to assert the priority of our individual choices and the recognition of our dependence on and need for the assistance of others. This genuine social phenomenon is, however, masked in the legal realm which serves to deny the dichotomy in a way which legitimates the status quo, making present (oppressive) social structures appear inevitable and natural. Thus the 'fundamental contradictions' which underlie all legal doctrines represent a 'single dilemma of the degree of collective as opposed to individual self-determination that is appropriate'. At the same time, law itself is simply a 'mechanism for denying contradictions' in a manner which enables the stabilisation of existing social hierarchies (Kennedy, 1979, p. 213).

Kennedy seeks to show that this mystifying and legitimating process is to be found in the organisation of the classic liberal statement of the common law, Blackstone's *Commentaries on the Law of England* (1765–9). His analysis demonstrates a rare familiarity with a text that may be considered the leading authority in traditional jurisprudence. He follows this through in his examination of the underlying structure of current law, pointing, for instance, to the way in which contract law both insists on the imposition of the wills of the parties (thus respecting the self) and also allows for recognition of the necessary altruism of social life in that its standards enable the courts to set aside 'unconscionable' bargains and agreements not entered into in good faith (thus respecting others) (Kennedy, 1976). While some of his contentions, such as the claim that *the* contradiction is between egoism and altruism, or the view that individualism is expressed in precise rules while altruism comes in via more general standards, are vulnerable to criticism (see Kelman, 1987), the general theme that the law is a mess of incompatible maxims from which the judiciary can draw such conclusions as they will, is less easily controverted.

Crucially, if CLS claims are even roughly accurate, then the traditional focus of political philosophy on the activities leading up to the legislative moment must be seen as hopelessly limited, and the standardly unargued use of the imagery of the 'rule of law' in the justification of democratic process totally discredited. Further the emphasis of legal philosophy on inputs to the legislative process as distinct from the supposedly 'adjudicative' branch of government must he misplaced and misleading.

In assessing the contribution of CLS, it is best to keep a firm distinction between the postmodernist thesis in the philosophy of language according to which there can be no firm interpersonal or consensus meaning, and the neo-Marxist use of this notion of linguistic indeterminacy to expose the underlying inconsistencies of apparently coherent language systems which serve to bolster existing power relationships. Uncovering contradictions does not require that these be obfuscated by linguistic flexibilities, and the actual indeterminacy of meaning may mask nothing more than underlying confusion and chaos. Indeed, it seems evident that if law were entirely open and indeterminate, then it would not be possible to show that it is consistently contradictory. It may therefore be necessary to moderate Klare's claim that 'legal reasoning is a texture of openness, indeterminacy, and contradiction' (Klare, 1982, p. 34). At the risk of losing touch with the characteristic CLS theme that oppressors protect their legitimacy by exploiting indeterminacy to hide their privileged positions, I shall examine these elements separately.

As far as the rule of law is concerned it is the indeterminacy thesis that is initially the more alarming theme, for it implies that there is ultimately no distinction between government by individual whim and government via the enactment and enforcement of general rules. The interesting question for our purposes is not whether the indeterminacy thesis is correct or incorrect in its basic philosophical underpinnings, but whether the study of law has contributed to, rather than simply plundered, this debate. Here, the main focus seems to be on the legally typical (but not legally unique) process of applying general terms to particular circumstances, since routinely, law consists of prescriptions and permissions containing a number of general terms of varying degrees of abstraction with a paucity of proper names and other particularities. This generality of law is part of its vaunted political impartiality.

Jeremy Waldron provides a good example which highlights both the issue of indeterminacy and the 'intrusion' of political values into adjudicative process. He cites the case of the Greater London Council (GLC) which had its policy of subsidized transport declared illegal (or *ultra vires*) by the House of Lords on the grounds that the GLC is by statute required 'to promote the provision of integrated, efficient and economic transport facilities and services in Greater London' (Waldron, 1990, ch. 6). Backed by an electorally approved manifesto which pledged them to a policy of subsidized transport, and taking 'economic' to mean 'cost-effective' or giving 'value for money', the GLC were amazed to be confronted by what appeared to be a straight political overruling of their policy by the House of Lords, which, in accordance with the spirit of the times, took 'economic' to mean 'breaking even' (*R. v London Transport Executive, ex parte* GLC [1983] 2 All ERT 129). Waldron's discussion goes on to show how no plausible theory of statutory interpretations can require that one reading of 'economic' is to be preferred to another except in terms of judicial policy-making, and suggests that, in such cases, judges should simply make the political aspect of their decisions openly. On the other hand, it is clearly not the case either that 'economic' can be taken to mean just anything simply because it means different things in different contexts and to different social groups, or that it is not capable of more precise legislative definition in a manner that favours one decision over another. What is clearly established, is that there is often scope for interpretative disagreements with evident political implications and that it is nonsense to pretend that one interpretation is to be preferred purely on account of the meanings of the terms involved.

In this arena the multiplication of legal examples of decisions which involve choices about the scope of general terms which are conceptually arbitrary but are presented as linguistically required does serve to give some inductive plausibility to the contention that rules do not constrain decisions in particular cases. It is clear, however, that judges do not always proceed along this formalist model rather than admitting ambiguities and deciding along one or other of the permitted interpretative devices, such as investigating legislative intent or seeking parallels in analogous legal rulings. Nor is it evident that any number of illustrations can prove the universal claim that rules cannot limit judicial discretion. The move whereby any clear case can be turned into a 'hard' case by pointing to possible alternative interpretations does not establish that some interpretations are not much more plausible than others.

Here there is confusion between the claim that, if the local conventions on meanings were different, then the case would be no longer evident, and the claim that there are no local conventions on which agreement can ever be reached. This latter contention in its extreme form is, of course, unarguable since it can be used self-referentially to make nonsense of the critical thesis. If words cannot be used to communicate, they certainly cannot be used to criticize. In its weaker form it becomes a matter of the degree to which there is consensus on the meanings of words or success in establishing agreed criteria for the use of technical language. The mere possibility that any such consensus can be undermined by a clever lawyer, a scheming tyrant, a prejudiced judge or an oppressor class does not establish the incoherence of such communicative objectives.

Once the indeterminacy debate becomes a matter of the degree to which there is or is not agreement on meanings and the extent to which the lack of agreement is utilized to perpetrate hierarchy, then it is no longer a philosophical dogma which negates the very idea of the rule of law and becomes no more than one of the many factors which can intervene to negate efforts to establish the rule of law. CLS may be descriptively correct as to its factual claims about actual legal systems, but the view that all legal systems must be this way remains an unprovable if sometimes plausible dogma which does not undermine the rule of law as a partially realizable ideal. It may seem intuitively and experientially correct that liberals are mistaken to claim that law is both an instrument of the state and a means of limiting state power, but it remains an open question whether or not law is an essential part of any set up which seeks to solve this central Hobbesian paradox of politics.

While it is not to be expected that the answer to such profound questions in the philosophy of language will emerge from legal scholarship, CLS has made a sufficiently plausible claim for the weaker version of legal indeterminacy to make the judicial process a prime site for political analysis and a central concern for the political philosopher.

Feminist jurisprudence

In this chapter I pick out those areas of legal study which can be shown to have gone beyond absorbing materials from other disciplines and provide significant new ideas and impetus worthy of note beyond the sphere of law itself. Nowhere is this better illustrated than in the area of women's studies in law, which have been transformed from the cataloguing and critique of women's oppression through law and the study of laws as a mechanism for combating sexism to the articulation of a distinctively feminist view of law as such and a genuine theoretical endeavour to identify the core of gender-based domination. 'Feminist jurisprudence' in its most contemporary phase offers powerful arguments to the effect that law itself is a masculine enterprise and that the study of male domination through law reveals the sexual core of male violence and gender hierarchy.

The most recent phase of feminist legal studies manifests an ambivalent attitude towards law. There is little desire to decry the importance of the legally-oriented victories which have been attained by the women's movement. The long and hard battles to remove legally enforced gender disqualifications in the spheres of politics and employment; the moves to counter male prejudice by requiring formal equality of opportunity and permitting or requiring 'preference' to be given to women in competitive employment situations through 'affirmative action'; the efforts to bring the domestic sphere more fully into the arenas of civil and criminal law; all these achievements are celebrated and defended with more or less enthusiasm.

On the other hand, the realities of continuing gender inequality in employment, economic well-being and political power, together with the general ineffectiveness of legal remedies for matters of most concern to women, such as domestic violence, rape and employment discrimination, generates a deal of scepticism about the power and relevance of law to the lot of women in modern society. Thus Smart, noting the persistence of gender inequalities, is led to wonder 'why law is so resistant to the challenge of feminist knowledge and critique' (1989, p. 2). Drawing on Foucault's insight into the connections between the authoritative sources of knowledge and societal power, Smart identifies the 'malevolence' of law in its congruence with masculine culture, a culture which uses law to define social categories and behavioural norms in ways which delegitimize women's perspectives. This is illustrated in various legal processes: by decreeing that certain matters are outside the law it is made to appear that law is neutral on matters such as prostitution which involve the exploitation of women; by defining relevance in ways which, for instance, admit in evidence the victim's sexual history but not the accused's, the whole adjudicative procedure is biased against women in rape trials; and by requiring that legal argument be presented in terms of case analysis ensures that if the interests of particular women caught up in the legal process are to be protected, then it is necessary to utilize precedents which embody gender prejudiced outlooks, so that the practising lawyer has a choice between being a good lawyer or a good feminist. For such reasons feminists are urged to be suspicious of law and seek other avenues for reform. In Smart's terminology, law is to be 'decentred' so that at least this one epistemological source of male domination can be bypassed.

Not all feminists take such a negative view of the law's potential, and continue to seek radical reform in such matters as redrawing the boundaries between 'public' and 'private' and thus between law and non-law so that women can be protected more effectively in their sexual and economic relationships; or proposing various devices for replacing a male with a female or gender-neutral perspective on legally relevant categories, such as what counts as 'work' for the purposes of compensation. However, the more exciting, if also the more speculative, line is that such objectives are bound to be illusory because of the masculine nature of law itself. On this view, it is not simply that men have captured law as an ideological weapon for male supremacy, but that the idea of law expresses a masculine frame of mind. This view can be traced to Gilligan's (1982) findings that the tendency to see disputes in terms of rights and rules rather than in terms of interconnections and accommodations is essentially a male phenomenon. In a return to something akin to the much criticized stereotypes of woman as caring and man as combative, Gilligan's thesis concerning the non-individualistic even loving approach to problems of human interaction has been taken up and developed into the thesis that a Fuller-style characterization of law as the 'enterprise of subjecting human conduct to the governance of rules' (Fuller, 1969, p. 96) is a male venture that seeks solutions through dividing lines, creating dichotomies and giving simplistic yes/no answers to complex problems. In Rifkin's words: 'law is a paradigm for maleness' (1980, p. 85), 'the historical image of maleness – objective, rational and public – is the dominant image of law' (ibid., p. 92)

Rifkin's own contribution to this line of thought is an historical one in that she traces women's exclusion from the public sphere in the capitalist world as something that was achieved in the past through the manipulation of developing contract law to express male authority and exclude women from trade and commerce. In the event she seeks to undermine the male paradigm of law as power rather than law itself. Similarly, other theorists look to law adopting a feminist method which will avoid abstract universals and concentration on the observable similarities and different classes of persons and behaviours. Such abstractions, it is argued, have little to offer in seeking a solution to concrete social inequalities. Thus to have a gender-neutral law which prevents employers discriminating against women with pre-school age children but allows job selection to exclude those who have the duty of caring for such children, simply perpetuates the inequality which stems from the social fact that it is women who in practice are the predominant childcarers. Such questions should, it is argued, be solved on the basis of standards which use abstractions only as a method of uncovering the underlying moral issues at stake in legal disputes. In the example cited, the standard commended will be oriented towards eliminating disadvantage. This will enable legislators and judges to see past the abstract concerns about similarity and difference to the social situation which requires women to be compensated for the unfair distribution of the burdens of childcare (Scales, 1980, pp. 1395ff.).

It is perhaps a terminological matter whether such methods are characteristically 'legal', although they certainly do not fit the rigid rule-based model of some liberal positivists. On the other hand, if mandatory decisions are made by courts on the basis of generalized standards, then we may be said to have another form of law rather than an alternative to law. Which method is most open to abuse by powerful social groups is clearly a matter for investigation, since generalized standards can be manipulated for hierarchical ends and specific rules can be exclusionary of oppressed group interests. However, when enforceable decision procedures are replaced by entirely voluntary conciliation processes we have clearly left the sphere of law, but such methods are entirely unrealistic where there are entrenched social inequalities that inevitably render such 'voluntary' processes *de facto* coercive.

Many of the criticisms of law as individualistic, abstract and rights-centred are readily detachable from feminist critique and, indeed, represent long-standing socialist and communitarian responses to the law of liberal capitalism. There is a flourishing literature on this subject (see Sypnowich, 1990). We need to know whether, in addition to exposing the ideological role of modern law with respect to the promotion of liberal individualism, the feminist approach offers a compelling alternative or supplementary theory to explain the force and success of this ruling paradigm.

Here we must note the most powerful law-centred feminist theory articulated by Catharine MacKinnon. MacKinnon is deeply suspicious of Gilligan's line on women's 'different voice', if this implies a biological or other female essence. MacKinnon views Gilligan's data as evidence of socially constructed responses which exhibit women as adopting and expressing male views as to what women should say and be. For MacKinnon the language of altruism, for all its attractions, is the language of submission and, as such, likely to be completely ignored by the forces of male dominance.

In the pursuit of a thoroughly explanatory social theory to account for male oppression which is of sufficient power and scope to rival socialist theories of class exploitation, MacKinnon goes straight to the phenomenon of male sexuality as the underlying cause of gender-related inequality. Her claim is, quite simply, that power is gendered. This does not mean that all power relations are in the end sexual ones, but that all power relations have an important sexual element. Moreover, this sexual element is determined by the dominance and violence within male sexuality. The converse of this thesis is that male–female relationships are essentially political in that they involve a coercive element. The state itself is male with respect to its methods and objectives: 'the liberal state coercively and authoritatively constitutes the social order in the interests of men as a gender – through its legitimating norms, forms, relation to society, and substantive policies' (MacKinnon, 1989, p. 62).

Although MacKinnon presents a general theory of male oppression, her work is centrally about law. Her starting point is the study of such matters as the law of incest, abortion, harassment, male violence and pornography (MacKinnon, 1989, pp. 111ff). The nature of the theory is particularly clear in her analysis of rape. Here we have a criminal law which appears to protect women but in fact serves to legitimize routine male coerciveness within and beyond specifically sexual relationships. Not only are the rules and procedure such that even prosecution and certainly conviction for rape is rare. The very fact of identifying certain acts of sexual intercourse as non-consensual and therefore wrong implies that 'normal' sexual intercourse is unproblematic, when in fact women's 'consent' in an inegalitarian society is standardly not consent at all, but simply a more indirect form of involuntary submission. In this sense 'normal' men can be rapists in normal situations.

MacKinnon's theory is difficult to categorize. She is hostile to Gilliganesque stereotyping, while clearly endorsing altruist values; she is at one with CLS in undermining the hierarchical constructs of liberal law, but takes issue with the indeterminacy thesis if this involves asserting unpredictability since, to her eyes, law looks highly predictable once the underlying sexual-political forces are known (MacKinnon, 1990, p. 170); she agrees that gender differences are socially constructed, but sees sexuality as fundamental to the construction of dominance: 'sexuality is the linchpin of gender inequality' (MacKinnon, p. 113); she is critical of existing law as male law, but is still committed to using law as a means of mitigating oppression. Thus MacKinnon is, famously, at the forefront of the movement to ban pornography as a glorification and encouragement of male sexual violence and dominance. And, while she is unswervingly critical of the male assumption that there is a universal truth that law can reflect and implement, her hope is that together women can come to a common consciousness of their situation which will produce a superior perspective to the present methodology of disinterested observation (see Littleton, 1987).

MacKinnon's work comes up against the general problems of the reformative-minded postmodernist who seeks to provide anything more than an *ad hoc* reaction to currently perceived wrongs. She can dismiss some of the testimony of women (e.g. that they enjoy submissive sex) because this is the expression of a male voice in a female body, but she still holds to the prospect of consciousness-raising to the point where it can express an authentic and female outlook which is evidently preferable to the violent dominance of men and the world view that it engenders. At this point we may feel that we have passed from lawyer's to philosopher's work, but this is to ignore the claims of a methodology that seeks to base itself on awarenesses which are brought into sharp focus in specifically legal experience. No male epistemologist, it is contended, can counter the shared experience of women in rape and its legal aftermath and how it echoes women's constant experience of being treated as an object of male sexuality (see MacKinnon, 1989, ch. 5; Smart, 1990, pp. 79ff.). In this respect her legally-centred approach has general applications for political philosophy.

Law and society

MacKinnon's theory is bolstered, although not established, by the extensive empirical evidence as to how women are treated in male-dominated legal processes. This points us in the direction of a mass of legal studies which relate to the evident failures of the rule of law, even in its own liberal terms, and the general ineffectiveness of many legal provisions in relation to their apparent objectives.

It is not possible to mention here all the various empirical studies of law and its social causes and effects which have potential impact on political philosophy, but it is worth noting just some of the material that is most prone to spark off conceptual and justificatory debates about the political system as a whole.

First there is the continuing saga of criminological research, much of which is, of course, state-financed and directed to immediate policy issues within the confines of 'law and order'. Here the incompatibility of deterrence philosophies of punishment with the confirmed data on the ineffectual nature of threatened punishment is well known; so much so that officially-oriented criminologists have welcomed the resurgence of retributivist theories, such as that of von Hirsch (1976), as a basis for justifying current penal practices, while political philosophers have called on the retributivist tradition to limit the potentially draconian implications of preventive (and deterrent) utilitarian policies by arguing that no one should be punished beyond the extent that their degree of moral guilt warrants.

Now, while retributivism does not seem to have the same vulnerability to empirical falsification, at least its feasibility as an operative policy can be brought into question. The idea that any legal system can be trusted to get anywhere near convicting the guilty and acquitting the innocent, even if we take it that criminal laws do correlate to some extent with immoral behaviour, seems incompatible with the limited data that is available about the routine operation of the summary justice which represents by far the greatest quantum of criminal cases. The dominant characteristics of mainstream criminal justice is that it is 'fast, easy and cheap' rather than fair, open and adversarial (McBarnet, 1981, p. 153). Deference to police evidence, pre-trial bargaining, coerced guilty pleas, selective policing, inadequate counsel – all these factors lead us to conceptualize standard criminal process as a crude form of ineffective behaviour control with little pretence at any ideal of arriving at punishment in proportion to moral ill-desert. This sort of evidence is reflected in the lively debate in the philosophy of criminal law between the 'crime control' theorists, who concentrate on the objective of reducing the incidence of undesirable behaviour, and the 'due process' theorists, who concentrate on the protection of the rights of the accused (see Fletcher, 1972).

An example of the way in which such criminological work can spark off original political philosophizing is the use which has been made of John Braithwaite's analysis of the shaming element in criminal process and punishment, which he and Philip Pettit have used as the basis for the development of a 'republican' consequentialist

203

theory of criminal justice, which presents the criminal law as protecting negative liberty through an effective system of rights and duties of which citizens are aware and in which they have confidence, thus contributing to a social ideal embodying equality, dignity and fraternity (Braithwaite and Pettit, 1990). They contrast their approach to that adopted by some modern retributivists who can draw on the extensive literature on the place of the victim in the criminal process, to develop a general theory of justice in terms of a fair balance between benefits and burdens which has implications far beyond the confines of law (see Sadurski, 1985).

Similarly in the civil courts it appears clear from such studies as that conducted by Galanter (1974) that the law is no neutral adjudicator between equal parties, but is primarily a mechanism whereby those with the money and the material interests use the courts to process, for instance, their debt collection in a very one-sided battle between those with experience and resources on the one hand and those with neither on the other.

More alarming perhaps for political theorists who look to legislation as an index of political change and achievement is the empirical evidence about the ineffectiveness of laws in relation to their ostensible objectives. To some extent these failures can be put down to the false societal assumptions which lie behind much legislation, but it is worth noting the evidence of the extent to which implementation depends on the activities and interests of the regulatory bureaucracies that are charged with their enforcement and the ability of powerful groups with clear and substantial interests at stake to affect the processes of implementation. The most evident examples of this are environmental and occupational health and safety laws which, while they may be assumed to be merely symbolic at the outset, can often be shown to be easily subvertible by those who are likely to be adversely affected by them (see Gunningham, 1984; Rose-Ackerman, 1988).

To a large extent, of course, these data are simply an extension of the familiar interest group and public choice theories of politics, but theorists must be interested in the implementation studies which show just how various and effective are the means whereby rules made are only rarely rules enforced, and rules enforced usually do not have the results intended, although, as Sunstein has shown, this is by no means always the case (Sunstein, 1990).

This work is not unambiguous in its political implications. For a start it is by no means easy to identify the purpose of any piece of legislation, making it impossible to make a clear judgement on its effectiveness in relation to that purpose. It is particularly easy to confuse the direct effects of legislation on the target subjects and immediate implementors with the indirect effects on consequent results which are desired. A change in the law may produce more prompt tax returns without thereby increasing total tax revenue (see Griffiths, 1979). Further, laws may have effects quite independent of either their direct or indirect effects, such as promoting a political party's image, or providing for greater social solidarity according to a Durkheimian functionalist schema whereby criminalizing conduct, such as taking 'dangerous drugs', leads to a unity-enhancing feeling of communal virtue.

However, the more that empirical studies reveal the ways in which implementation of law can be affected, intentionally or unintentionally, by the actors and agencies involved, the greater scope is given to theories which can suggest ways of combating such inefficiencies. If health and safety standards are not enforced because inspectors are recruited from the ranks of the managers whose performance they are intended to monitor, then the way to ensure better enforcement via more energetic inspection and prosecution seems clear (see Grabosky and Braithwaite, 1986).

All this material suggests that the fact that law in practice does not conform to the formalist model presupposed by the rule of law ideal may be explicable by factors other than the alleged indeterminacy of rules and their cognitive open-endedness. To this extent the sociological explanations for disagreement about law contain the materials for the refurnishment of formalism at least as a partially realizable ideal.

Legal research and political principles

In this concluding section I deal with just a few of the many political elements and implications of some particular legal studies to illustrate the way in which law can be an instigator and participant in first order political philosophizing.

Theory in legal studies is not confined to specialist and abstract studies but pervades the best work in specific areas of law. While there are still plenty of 'black letter' doctrinal legal textbooks, areas such as contracts and torts are replete with competing theoretical analyses. Thus, the philosophical foundations of contract law are vicariously said to lie in the moral obligation to keep promises (Fried, 1981), the idea of reciprocation or reliance (Atiyah, 1978; 1979); and the requirement of economic efficiency (Posner, 1973). The first approach fits best with the practice of awarding damages for breach of contract in terms of the expectations of the wronged party in relation to the completion of the contract ('expectation damages'); the second fits best with the tendency to take into account the actual losses incurred by those who take action in reliance on the existence of an agreement ('reliance damages'); while the third fits best with the observation that different measures of contract damages are used in different economic contexts.

It is a source of annoyance to philosophers that legal theorists wish to argue that their theories best describe the actual history and content of law, while it is quite evident that the main thrust of their theories is often directed towards prescriptive conclusions relating to what the law ought to be like. It is not hard, however, to deconstruct the usually overt ambitious historical claims and construe the competing theories as rival evaluations of what is the proper model for contract law to follow.

A distinctive feature of such controversies within legal theory is that they so often lead back to arguments about interpretation which tie in with our earlier discussion of formalism and realism. Thus, in considering defences bearing on breach of contract, theorists such as Kronman (1980) argue that in seeking to determine the proper limits of such defences as 'duress' or 'necessity', it is not possible to read off an answer from a consideration of the idea of what it is to enter 'freely' into an agreement or to be 'forced' to resile from a contractual arrangement. There are no literal meanings to these terms which are, therefore, always to be viewed in the context of what is considered to be justified or reasonable behaviour. In other words, a formalist approach is unavailing. His suggestion is that the lines between duress and non-duress and between necessity and non-necessity are to be seen purely in policy terms, and he advocates a Rawlsian policy which benefits the weaker and more vulnerable party. Other theorists can, of course, step in and argue for other policy objectives, leaving it to the moral rights theorists to insist that there is independent meaning to be given to concepts such as consent and duress. On the other hand, feminists, for instance, can claim that these disputes demonstrate the inappropriateness of either/or solutions to complex problems of human relationships. Many of these themes are familiar enough to political philosophers in their discussions of political obligation and hierarchy, but the concrete material provided by legal cases adds substance and interest to the development of these themes.

Similar debates take place in the context of tort law, which deals with the allocation of liability to pay compensation for the damage caused by accidents or other harms which may be related to the conduct of others. This literature contains lively exchanges between those who take the utilitarian consequentialist line familiar in the work of Posner (1974) and Calabresi (1970) and those who have sought to reassert the significance of being fair to the individuals involved, such as Fletcher (1983), Epstein (1973) and Weinrib (1989). Parts of this debate are predictable in that the deontological theorists such as Fletcher, Epstein and Weinrib are concerned to see that tort laws should be confined to those instances where individuals have caused harm to others, but the picture is much more confused when it comes to the issue of whether liability should require that there be 'fault' on the part of the person who caused the harm, thus permitting excuses such as compulsion and ignorance, or whether liability should be 'strict' in being attributed on the basis of the causal relationship alone. It might be thought that consequentialists such as Posner would support strict liability as the most effective means of maximising deterrent effects, while those who stress individual responsibility would place more emphasis on the element of fault. In fact, the position is reversed to some extent, in that Posner's study of the specifics of law leads him to suggest the efficiency of the fault principle, while Epstein takes the line that the standard excuses simply undermine the necessary rigour of a free market system.

In the development of this controversy it becomes clear that the notion of 'cause' in law is by no means without its association with notions of responsibility in the sense of blameworthiness, so that the two positions are not so sharply juxtaposed. This is pointed out by Perry (1988), following Hart and Honoré's (1985) analysis, which pointed to the particular role which causal attribution has in specifically legal contexts in selecting out as 'the cause' the factor which is considered abnormal or unacceptable rather than manifesting a scientific conception of cause. This is an interesting debate which has implications for the understanding of all *ex post facto* analyses of significant historical events, but the message which political philosophers are likely to draw is the pervasive influence of individualism in all mainstream legal modes of thought and the consequent inability of traditional legal remedies to cope with the major ways in which harm arises and is distributed within societies.

More direct political imports of legal studies are evident in US constitutional law which, on non-formalist interpretations in particular, may properly be regarded as a branch of politics. In the opening words of the most impressive recent work on the subject:

There was a time not long ago when constitutional law seemed in danger of becoming essentially anecdotal and fragmentary . . . Lately constitutional law seems in equal danger of being submerged in political and legal and even literary theory. (Tribe, 1988, p. 1)

This theme is well illustrated in the debates about rights of communication and expression which centre on the first amendment: 'Congress shall make no law respecting an establishment of religion, or prohibiting the exercise thereof; or abridging freedom of speech, or of the press; or the right of the people peaceably to assemble, and to petition the Government for a redress of grievances.' Modern protections for the right of freedom of communication have been extensively developed in the United States on the basis of the first amendment since Oliver Wendell Holmes' dissenting judgement in *Abrams* v *U.S.* (1919).

What is it to abridge freedom of speech, and what is speech anyway? Does 'no law' really mean no law? If speech may sometimes be restricted, what reasons must be given and how must they be established? Does the prohibition apply to state as well as federal governments? These are just a few of the legal questions which pass into philosophical realms.

It is clear that not any utterance is beyond abridgment, as the exceptions of defamation and 'fighting talk' make clear. Immediately, therefore, we require a theory about the purpose of the protection of free speech if we are to be able to define and circumscribe it in a principled manner. From the modern jurisprudence of the Supreme Court a variety of themes emerge for theoretical development, many of which are variations on the classic statement by John Stuart Mill that freedom of expression is a necessary means for reaching and being justified in knowledge of the truth in a democratic society (Mill, 1859). The Millian theme has been taken in a variety of directions.

Thus, the pioneering work of Alexander Meiklejohn (1965) to the effect that freedom of speech has to do with protecting and furthering the preconditions of self-government and democracy, has been followed by arguments to the effect that freedom of speech is a civilized and civilizing response to the realities of human intolerance (Bollinger, 1986). These basically instrumental views are strongly countered by those who argue that freedom of expression is a deontologically grounded right, an essential ingredient of individual and group autonomy (see Tucker, 1985). Freedom of communication cannot therefore be restricted to political expression (as Meiklejohn argued) or limited by the potential dangerousness of the views or emotions being expressed, unless the speech is in effect directly causing immediate harm, or balanced against competing utilitarian considerations.

These general approaches to freedom of communication can in themselves claim to be legal inputs to political philosophy. Further, the proliferation of interesting and morally relevant distinctions arising from the hard choices that call to be made in the Supreme Court over different attempted restrictions on freedom of expression often provoke philosophical reflection. Thus the distinctions between the different types of speech: political, economic, etc. (Tribe, 1988, pp. 890–904), and the different degrees of protection that may be afforded to them (see Schauer, 1982); the distinction between direct prohibitions of free speech ('communicative impact') and laws which only indirectly affect the flow of ideas (Scanlon, 1972); the shifting line between speech and conduct (Ely, 1975).

Also noteworthy is the move beyond the restrictions which may be imposed of obscene material, that is, material which has the tendency to deprave and corrupt its recipients, to restrictions on 'pornography', on the grounds that sexually explicit material which represents male domination of women harms women collectively. This argument is derived from the work of Catharine MacKinnon (1984; 1986). Such restrictions have been robustly rejected by the appellate courts because of their broad terms and unproven causal connections with the well-being of groups and also because they are said to single out for prohibition communications with a specific viewpoint, however objectionable it may be. The short shrift which the jurisprudence of the first amendment has given to what many people will see as a valid demand of emerging feminist political movements, together with its failure to deal with the problems of racial vilification, serves to indicate the weakness of traditional liberal rights to deal with the pernicious effects of much modern communication.

Freedom to communicate is just one of the civil rights which are both illuminated and obscured by the decisions of the US Supreme Court and its commentators. The historical judgement in *Roe* v *Wade* (1973), which gave American women a limited right to choose to have an abortion on the grounds that this right is implicit in the (judicially developed) constitutional right to 'privacy' can be seen both as an exemplar of judicial recognition of an autonomy right and as an unhappy example of the use of the idea of privacy to place in a separate category matters of sexual and reproductive behaviour (see Rubenfeld, 1989; Tribe, 1990). Similarly, the tortuous history of judgements on affirmative action on racial grounds demonstrates the horrendous difficulties faced by a tradition which is basically individualistic when seeking to give expression to the fourteenth amendment, the due process clause of the constitution, one of those passed after the Civil War to give some protection to the newly-freed black slaves but couched in terms of individual not group rights and therefore usable to prohibit state intervention to benefit underprivileged groups rather than to enhance the interests of such groups (see Fiss, 1976; Tribe, 1988, pp. 1521–53; Krenshaw, 1988).

Many more examples of incipient and fully-fledged political philosophizing can be drawn from every area of legal study. I have chosen to dwell on just some of those topics which have a special bearing on the disputed conceptual boundaries between law and politics, particularly where the material has potential application beyond the sphere of law itself. From this survey it seems clear that the discipline of law has much to contribute to the development of political philosophy, particularly when it serves to demonstrate the unresponsiveness of law to contemporary political requirements. As we have seen, many empirical legal studies highlight the ineffectual nature of legal regulation. Whether this is because of the practical difficulties of implementing laws which are unwelcome to those affected by them or run contrary to the interests of powerful groups, or whether it is in the nature of general rules that they cannot be interpreted or applied to achieve specific social purposes, remains the central issue which legal studies raise for the political theorist to consider. What is at stake here is not just the viability of the ideal of the rule of law and its halo of legal virtues which are intended to protect the interests of individuals and minorities, but the very idea that changing laws is ever a particularly sensible political objective. Of course, the same material can, in a more positive vein, often prompt reflection as to how existing legal structures might be rebuilt to overcome at least some of the defects exposed in the process of legal studies. One way or the other, it seems clear that there is much in the discipline of law by way of material, some raw and some at least partially cooked, which political philosophers may find digestible and even sustaining.

See also 1 ANALYTICAL PHILOSOPHY; 2 CONTINENTAL PHILOSOPHY; 5 ECONOMICS; 10 FEMINISM; 16 CONTRACT AND CONSENT; 17 CONSTITUTIONALISM AND THE RULE OF LAW; 25 EQUALITY; 28 LEGITIMACY; 31 PROPERTY; 33 RIGHTS; 36 STATE; 37 TOLERATION AND FUNDAMENTALISM; 38 TOTALITARIANISM; 39 TRUST

References

Alexander, L.: 'Striking back at the empire: a brief survey of problems in Dworkin's theory of law', *Law and Philosophy*, 6 (1987), 419.

Altman, A.: *Critical Legal Studies, A Liberal Critique* (Princeton, NJ: Princeton University Press, 1990).

Atiyah, P.: 'Contracts, promises and the law of obligations', *Law Quarterly Review*, 94 (1978), 193.

————: *The Rise and Fall of Freedom of Contract* (Oxford: Oxford University Press, 1979).

Austin, J.: *The Province of Jurisprudence Determined*, 5th edn, ed. Robert Campbell, 2 vols (1885).

Baker, C. E.: 'The ideology of the economic analysis of law', *Philosophy and Public Affairs*, 5 (1975), 15.

Bollinger, L. C.: 'The tolerant society', *Freedom of Speech and Extremist Speech in America* (New York: Oxford University Press, 1986).

Boyle, J.: 'The politics of reason: critical legal studies and local social thought', *University of Pennsylvania Law Review*, 133 (1985), 685.

———— ed.: *Critical Legal Studies* (Aldershot: Dartmouth, 1992).

Braithwaite, J. and Pettit, P.: *Not Just Deserts* (Oxford: Clarendon Press, 1990).

Calabresi, G.: *The Cost of Accidents: A Legal and Economic Analysis* (New Haven, Conn.: Yale University Press, 1970).

Coase, R. H.: 'The problem of social cost', *Journal of Law and Economics*, 3 (1960), 1–30.

Coleman, J.: *Markets, Morals and the Law* (Cambridge: Cambridge University Press, 1988).

Dworkin, R.: *Law's Empire* (London: Fontana, 1986).

————: *Taking Rights Seriously* (London: Duckworth, 1977).

Ellikson, R. C.: 'The case of Coase and against "Coaseanism"', *Yale Law Journal*, 99 (1989–90), 610.

Ely, J. H.: 'Flag discretion: a case study in the roles of categorization and balancing in a first amendment analysis', *Harvard Law Review*, 88 (1975), 1482.

————: *Democracy and Distrust: A Theory of Judicial Review* (Cambridge, Mass.: Harvard University Press, 1980).

Epstein, R.: 'A theory of strict liability', *Journal of Legal Studies*, 2 (1973), 151.

Feinberg, J.: *The Moral Limits of the Law*, 4 vols (Oxford: Oxford University Press, 1985–8).

Finnis, J.: *Natural Law and Natural Right* (Oxford: Clarendon Press, 1980).

Fiss, O.: 'Groups and the equal protection clause', *Philosophy and Public Affairs*, 5 (1976), 107.

————: 'Why the state?', *Harvard Law Review*, 100 (1987), 781.

Fletcher, G. P.: 'Fairness and utility in torts', *Harvard Law Review*, 85 (1972), 537.

————: *Rethinking Criminal Law* (Boston: Little, Brown, 1976).

————: 'The search for synthesis in tort theory', *Journal of Law and Philosophy*, 2 (1983), 63.

Frank, J.: *Law and the Modern Mind* (London: Stevens, 1949).

Fried, C.: *Contract as Promise* (Cambridge, Mass.: Harvard University Press, 1981).

Fuller, L.: *The Morality of Law* (New Haven, Conn.: Yale University Press, 1969).

Gabel, P.: 'Reification in legal reasoning', *Research in Law and Sociology*, 3 (1979), 25.

———— and Harris, P.: 'Building power and breaking images: CLS theory and practice of law', *Review of Social Change*, 11 (1982–3), 25.

Galanter, M.: 'Why the "haves" come out ahead: speculations on the limits of social change', *Law and Society Review*, 9 (1974), 95.

Gilligan, C.: *In a Different Voice* (Cambridge, Mass.: Harvard University Press, 1982).

Grabosky, P. and Braithwaite, J.: *Of Manners Gentle: Enforcement Strategies of Australian Regulatory Agencies* (Oxford: Oxford University Press, 1986).

Griffiths, J.: 'Is law important?', *New York University Law Review*, 53 (1979), 339.

Gunningham, N.: *Safeguarding the Worker: the Role of Law* (Sydney: Law Book Company, 1984).

Hart, H. L. A.: *The Concept of Law* (Oxford: Clarendon Press, 1961).

————: *Punishment and Responsibility* (Oxford: Clarendon Press, 1968).

————: *Essays in Jurisprudence and Philosophy* (Oxford: Clarendon Press, 1983).

———— and Honoré, A.: *Causation and the Law* (Oxford: Oxford University Press, 1985).

Hirsch, A. von: *Doing Justice: The Choice of Punishments* (Boston: Hill and Wang, 1976).

Horwitz, M.: *The Transformation of American Law 1780–1860* (Cambridge, Mass.: Harvard University Press, 1977).

Kelman, M.: *A Guide to Critical Legal Studies* (Cambridge, Mass.: Harvard University Press, 1987).

Kennedy, D.: 'Form and substance in private law adjudication', *Harvard Law Review*, 89 (1976), 1685.

————: 'The structure of Blackstone's commentaries', *Buffalo Law Review*, 28 (1979), 209.

————: 'Legal education as training for hierarchy', in D. Kairys, ed., *The Politics of Law: A Progression Technique* (New York: Pantheon, 1982).

Klare, K.: 'The law school curriculum in the 1980s: what's left?', *Journal of Legal Education*, 32 (1982), 34.

Krenshaw, K. W.: 'Race, reform and retrenchment: transformation and legitimation in antidiscrimination law', *Harvard Law Review*, 101 (1988), 1331.

Kronman, A. T.: 'Contract law and distributive justice', *Yale Law Journal*, 89 (1980), 472.

Littleton, C.: 'Reconstructing sexual inequality', *University of California Law Review*, 75 (1987), 1279.

Llewellyn, K.: *The Common Law Tradition: Deciding Appeals* (Boston: Little, Brown, 1960).

MacKinnon, C.: 'Not a moral issue', *Yale Law and Policy Review*, 2 (1984), 321.

————: *Toward a Feminist Theory of the State* (Cambridge, Mass.: Harvard University Press, 1989).

McBarnet, D.: *Conviction: Law, the State and the Construction of Justice* (London: Macmillan, 1981).

Meiklejohn, A.: *Political Freedom: The Constitutional Powers of the People* (New York: Oxford University Press, 1965).

Michelman, F.: 'Traces of self-government', *Harvard Law Review*, 100 (1986), 4.

Mill, J. S.: 'On Liberty' (1859), in J. S. Mill, *Utilitarianism, Liberty and Representative Government* (London: Dent, 1910).

Nozick, R.: *Anarchy, State and Utopia* (New York: Basic Books, 1974).

Packer, H.: *The Limits of the Criminal Sanction* (Stanford, Calif.: Stanford University Press, 1918).

Perry, S. R.: 'The impossibility of general strict liability', *Canadian Journal of Law and Jurisprudence*, 147 (1988), 1.

Posner, R.: *Economic Analysis of Law*, 2nd edn (Boston: Little, Brown, 1977).

Rifkin, J.: 'Toward a feminist jurisprudence', *Harvard Women's Law Journal*, 3 (1980), 83–95.

Rose-Ackerman, S.: 'Progressive law and economics', *Yale Law Journal*, 98 (1988), 341.

Rubenfeld, J.: 'The right of privacy', *Harvard Law Review*, 137 (1989), 102.

Sadurski, W.: *Giving Desert its Due* (Dordrecht: Reidel, 1985).

Scales, A.: 'Towards a feminist jurisprudence', *Indiana Law Journal*, 56 (1980), 375–444.

Scanlon, T.: 'A theory of freedom of expression', *Philosophy and Public Affairs*, 204 (1972), 1.

Schauer, F.: *Freedom of Speech: A Philosophical Enquiry* (Cambridge: Cambridge University Press, 1982).

Smart, C.: *Feminism and the Power of Law* (London: Routledge, 1989).

Sunstein, C. R.: 'Pornography and the first amendment', *Duke Law Journal* (1986), 589.

————: *After the Rights Revolution: Reconceiving the Regulatory State* (Cambridge, Mass.: Harvard University Press, 1990).

Sypnowich, C.: *The Concept of Socialist Law* (Oxford: Clarendon Press, 1990).

Tribe, L. H.: *American Constitutional Law*, 2nd edn (Mineola, NY: The Foundation Press, 1988).

————: *Abortion: The Clash of Absolutes* (New York: Norton, 1990).

Tucker, D. F. B.: *Law, Liberalism and Free Speech* (Totowa, NJ: Rowman and Allanheld, 1985).

Tushnet, M.: *The American Law of Slavery* (Princeton, NJ: Princeton University Press, 1981).

Unger, R.: *Law in Modern Society* (New York: Free Press, 1975).

Waldron, J.: *The Law* (London: Routledge, 1990).

Weinrib, E.: 'The special morality of tort law', *Yale Law Journal*, 97 (1989), 949–1016.

Further reading

Ackerman, B. A.: *Social Justice in the Liberal State* (New Haven, Conn.: Yale University Press, 1980).

Coleman, J. L.: *Markets, Morals and the Law* (Cambridge: Cambridge University Press, 1988).

Dworkin, R. M., ed.: *The Philosophy of Law* (Oxford: Oxford University Press, 1977).

Goodrich, P.: *Legal Discourse* (London: Macmillan, 1987).

Guest, A. G., ed.: *Oxford Essays in Jurisprudence* (Oxford: Clarendon Press, 1961).

Hacker, P. M. S. and Raz, J., eds: *Law, Morality and Society* (Oxford: Clarendon Press, 1977).

Hart, H. L. A.: *Essays in Jurisprudence and Philosophy* (Oxford: Clarendon Press, 1983).

Hirst, P. Q.: *Law, Socialism and Democracy* (London: Allen & Unwin, 1986).

Honoré, T.: *Making Law Bind* (Oxford: Clarendon Press, 1987).

Kairys, D.: *The Politics of Law* (New York: Pantheon Books, 1982).

MacCormick, N.: *Legal Right and Social Democracy* (Oxford: Clarendon Press, 1982).

Peczenik, A.: *On Law and Reason* (The Hague: Kluwer, 1989).

Raz, J.: *The Morality of Freedom* (Oxford: Clarendon Press, 1986).

Simpson, A. W. B., ed.: *Oxford Essays in Jurisprudence*, 2nd series (Oxford: Clarendon Press, 1973).

Summers, R. S., ed.: *Essays in Legal Philosophy* (Berkeley: University of California Press, 1968).

Waldron, J.: *The Right to Private Property* (Oxford: Clarendon Press, 1988).

PART II
MAJOR IDEOLOGIES

8

Anarchism

RICHARD SYLVAN

Most of the seminal and interesting work on anarchism has come from outside universities and standard intellectual circles. Academics have contributed histories (e.g. Ritter, 1969), surveys (e.g. Woodcock, 1962) and (usually not so sympathetic) criticisms (e.g. Miller, 1984). With a very few exceptions, however, they have contributed little original anarchist thought.

Academics seem ideologically stuck with the state: 'Most political philosophers in the past few generation have what the psychoanalysts might call a "state fixation"' (Mitrany, 1975, p. 98). 'The idea of abolishing the state entirely must', they say, 'strike us as utopian' (Miller, 1984, p. 182); anarchists, of course, would regard it as 'eutopian'. It is easy to speculate on reasons for these attitudes, reasons connected with academics being part of the expensive state scene. While anarchism has vanished from the mainstream academic scene, it is again becoming prominent in alternative, especially green politics (e.g. Bookchin, 1989), and in work of disaffected academics with green affiliations.

Anarchism is considered essentially a modern ideology, arising after and in opposition to the modern state. Though there are significant anticipations of anarchism in earlier philosophy (notably in Stoicism and Taoism), and while there are worthwhile examples of early anarchistic societies, the main intellectual work begins only in the late eighteenth century with the outbreak of the French Revolution. Originally, 'the word "anarchist" . . . was used pejoratively to indicate one who denies all law and wishes to promote chaos. It was used in this sense against the Levellers during the English Civil War and during the French Revolution by most parties in criticizing those who stood to the left of them along the political spectrum' (Woodcock, 1962, p. 111). It was first prominently used in an approbatory way in Proudhon's *What is Property?* (1840), where he describes himself 'as an anarchist because he believed that political organization based on authority should be replaced by social and economic organization based on voluntary contractual agreement' (Woodcock, 1962, p. 111; cf. Lehning, 1968, p. 71). Since then there have been waves of anarchistic output of varying strength, most recently in the late 1960s.

Explication

Philosophically, anarchism is the theory, principles or practice of anarchy. It refers, according to the dictionaries, to the 'lack of coercive government', the 'absence of a political state', the 'want of authoritarian political heads or leaders, institutions or organizations'. In its normal political form, the term is applied to societies or communities, territories or countries. Politically there are three key structural components: authority, coercion and, normally comprehending both, the state. The notion has recently been extended beyond political arrangements to apply to other institutional forms, such as the church, science and law, to mean alternative forms lacking authoritarian structure and coercive methods. Thus appear such varieties as epistemological anarchism and philosophical anarchism. Although it is political anarchism upon which this essay focuses, those other far-reaching analogies should not be lost sight of: they matter. Anarchism is to political authority as atheism is to religious authority, and rather as scepticism is to scientific authority.

Principles, central and otherwise

Although the conditions specified for anarchy are normally taken as conjoined, it is possible to construe them disjointly, yielding what could be called 'diluted' anarchism. One diluted form which has obtained a little exposure is an anarchism appropriately opposed to the state but prepared to endorse carefully controlled coercive authorities. A differently diluted form is a *de facto* anarchism, which is opposed to all prevailing states because of some serious (but in principle removable) defect in each and every one of these states. This sort of anarchism is not opposed to the very idea of an ideal state or to a new wonderful order of states; it is not, so to say, a principled anarchism. It is sometimes difficult to ascertain whether historic anarchists are principled anarchists or merely *de facto* ones. There are limits, however, to how far definitional dilution should be allowed to proceed: a theory, such as Nozick's (1974) libertarianism, postulating a minimal coercive centralized state exceeds acceptable bounds of dilution.

In place of awkward locutions involving notions like 'absence', 'lack', 'want', anarchy can be better characterized in contrast to what it rejects: 'archy', or centralized coercive forms. That simpler formulation, anarchy as the rejection of archy, isolates the principle at work beneath arguments for anarchism. In so doing, it makes it immediately evident that much of what might vulgarly pass for essential features of anarchism actually are not.

First, a variety of political arrangements and organization, including governments of *certain sorts*, are entirely compatible with anarchy. All that is required is that these arrangements not include authoritarian or coercive elements. Certainly, it is true that territory without government, and therefore lacking an archist government, is anarchistic, but the popular converse fails: an anarchistic system may well have a small, smooth-running public administration, free of authoritarian elements (as did, for example, several societies substantially destroyed by European conquest). It may also be true, as dictionaries assert, that an anarchist would 'oppose all existing systems of government', but this is not a matter of meaning: it is crucially contingent upon the character of prevailing state systems (cf. Clark, 1984, pp. 118ff).

Nor are prevailing political forms everywhere so far removed from anarchistic alternatives, as a partial example indicates. When traffic police stop work, traffic keeps on going much as before. It is irrelevant to object that such anarchistic periods are mere interludes, presupposing surrounding authoritarian structures (somewhat as anarchistic end-states of Marxism are premissed on preceding super-productive authoritarian states). The point of such thought experiments is simply to demonstrate the error in the common assumption that anarchism is utterly remote from the political practice of complex modern states.

Such arrangements may be realizable as more than an interlude only in restricted or anomalous circumstances. The stronger anarchist theme is that there is never any need at all for authoritarian or coercive regulation – so such forms can be rejected universally. Universal anarchism encounters many problems (such as how to rectify especially degenerate or evil societies) which do not trouble less ambitious particular anarchisms such as those to be advanced here.

An attempt is sometimes made to render all anarchism universal, through the connecting thesis that for anarchism to succeed anywhere it must succeed everywhere (perhaps because otherwise it will be destroyed by ruthless or greedy states). The connecting thesis, though popular with critics, is implausible, however.

Just as it is mistaken to assume that anarchism is incompatible with government, even well-regulated government, so too is it erroneous to assume that anarchism is incompatible with organization, with regulation, with a positive non-coercive 'law', with order. Likewise mistaken, therefore, are the widespread assumptions that anarchism entails disorganization, disorder, confusion, lawlessness, chaos. Yet all these negative associations have been incorporated into degenerate popular meanings of anarchism. It is the same with related assumptions that anarchism implies violence, paramilitary activity or terrorism. A popular picture of the anarchist, encouraged by authors like Conrad, is the excitable fictional character with a bomb in his pocket – not a Tolstoy or a Thoreau. These too are assumptions and pictures, with little basis either in semantics or in general anarchist theory or practice, promulgated by an unsympathetic opposition generally comfortable in present political systems or unaware of alternatives. Much of what is popularly and journalistically associated with anarchism consists of optional extras which are neither necessary nor even typical features of it. This is true not only of negative characterizations but also of other more benign features widely taken to characterize anarchism, Included here are attempts to tie anarchism to individualism, voluntarism, spontaneity or socialism.

With anarchy as with many other valuable terms, there has been a concerted effort at confusion or destruction of meanings – part of an extensive terminological vandalism in human intellectual affairs. Rather than reconciling ourselves to sacrifice of the damaged term 'anarchism', let us salvage the term explicitly for the pristine notion, isolating the conventional associations under the term 'degenerate anarchism'. Most of the fictional anarchists depicted by authors supportive of the present state system are degenerate and thus unrepresentative of real anarchists. There are many anarchists who are not terrorists, few who are; there are many who are not dangerous troublemakers bent upon violently upsetting local settled order; increasingly there are many anarchists within peace and environmental movements. While organization and government are entirely compatible with anarchism, that most conspicuous modern institution – the state – is not. It is the paradigmatic archist form. Nor are ancient power formations such as the empire and the kingdom really compatible with anarchism, owing not only to their authoritarian character and their extensive use of coercion and violence but also to their central organisation. But it is wrong literally to define anarchism in terms of 'hostility to the state' (as in Miller, 1984, p. 5), Again, that is not a feature of anarchism but rather a contingent and consequential one, derived from the conjunction of anarchism's defining features together with a particular standard theoretical characterization of 'the state'. Under a standard (though strong – stronger than necessary for anything that follows) characterization, the state is:

a *distinct* and *sovereign* body [:] . . . it claims complete authority to define the rights of its subjects . . . . Second, the state is a *compulsory* body, in the sense that everyone born into a given society is forced to recognise obligations to the state that govern that society. Third, the state is a *monopolistic* body: it claims a monopoly of force in its territorial area, allowing no competitor to exist alongside it. (Miller, 1984, p. 5)

It also normally claims other monopolies, such as on legal tender. It is virtually inevitable that such a state is a centralized authoritarian institution with extensive coercive powers. So it is that anarchism is often epitomized as directed at the dissolution of what is widely seen as *the* major political problem, the state. (As to why it is such a problem, anarchist critiques of the state, sketched below, will reveal.) With anarchism in a place, there is an end to any institution that is recognizably a state of that form.

A refinement

Early English uses of 'anarchism' emphasized the corrupt, drunk-and-disorderly side of the notion, contrasting disorder with splendid state order: that was what (in defiance of the original Greek meaning) 'anarchy' and ' anarchism' were introduced to mean (see the *Oxford English Dictionary* citations from the sixteenth and seventeenth centuries). Thus the early usage, which persists, contradicts what is here presented as the refined usage.

In technical presentations, this problem might easily be sliced through by coining a term to mean what 'anarchy' as refined means ('anakyrie' and 'anacracy' are such terms). Here, however, we shall simply persist with the refinement of the prevailing term – and in the course of giving it etymological justification over the early corrupt uses, further refine. But the justification for refinement is not only etymological. What we need is not yet another term for disorder but, rather, a term to help break the false dichotomy between 'the state', on the one hand, and 'political disorder', on the other. Such a dichotomy falsely suggests that there are no further alternatives (like stateless orders of various kinds) and that without the state there is no political theory, merely untheorizable confusion.

Etymologically 'anarchism' derives from the ancient Greek 'an-archos', meaning 'without a chief or head' or 'without a top authority'. Of course, what the form derives from, though often indicative, does not determine what it now means. (Anarchism was not, after all, a distinguished ancient political theory; under familiar classifications, it is in fact the most recent and novel of major political ideologies.) Here, however, it is worth drawing out the etymological meaning because it is revealing.

What it appears to exclude are political arrangements structured with a top element of any of the familiar authoritarian sorts (a monarch, a prince, a ruler, a leader, a president, a prime minister) and shifting from individual to group forms (a party, a clique, a ruling elite, etc.).

There are, analysis reveals, two interacting foci: (1) a top or centre; and (2) control or dominance flowing from this top, by what are adjudged inadmissible (in particular, authoritarian or coercive) means. A chief both stands at the top of a power hierarchy and exercises authoritarian control from there. Under this elliptical double-foci refinement, anarchy entails structure or organization without inadmissible top-down or centralized means. Let us look at the foci in turn, beginning with the more independent one: the top.

Topologically, 'without a top' amounts to 'without a centre', because by topological transformations ('bending') what is a top transforms to a centre, and vice versa. Thus, in excluding top-down relations, anarchism also excludes arrangements structured with a controlling centre, such as a ruling central government. Anarchism thus implies decentralization, but in a precise sense. Eliminating the centre does not thereby also remove all structure. It leaves available the possibility of a rich variety of structures, including network arrangements with no centres or with multiple 'centres' (federal structures, and such like).

Remarkably, the main features adduced are mirrored in logic, which can serve as a structural guide. It is striking, as well as technically advantageous, that logical and political predictions converge. Mainstream ('non-relevant') logics have algebraic structures with top elements, Boolean algebras in the case of classical logics. By contrast 'relevant' logics, which now challenge the classical logical paradigm, do not; their corresponding algebras need include no top element (Dunn, 1986). A plurality of local 'centres', regional nodes, induces no paradox.

Technical comparisons now reach much further than logic alone. Intelligent organisation without top or central elements may abound both in nature (for instance, in insect cerebral organization and in vertebrate brain structure) and in many future artificial intelligence applications. Logic and computing technology demonstrate what is widely appreciated outside political theory: that topless is feasible. There is thus both scope and need for twenty-first-century anarchism to be highly techno-logically sophisticated.

There is, however, more to anarchism than lateral structuring, more than political structure without an operative top or head or centre. That more, the residue of the rejection of archy, is bound up with the operation of the active top, with the control it exercises, the power it exerts. Anarchists, generically, insist that it not operate 'by unacceptable means'; but as to what count as unacceptable means, different types of anarchists would offer different specifications. These include force, coercion, authoritarianism (and systems implying any or all of those, such as totalitarianism). More controversially, they might be said to include any means that are non-voluntary, non-individualistic, socialist or communist. As in the dictionaries, only coercive and authoritarian elements will here be ruled unacceptable in terms of undiluted anarchism. Holistic and tribal means are anarchistically admissible, as are utterly individualistic ones.

The two features are connected through the anarchist's response to the obvious question, 'If there is no head, top or centre, how are political affairs structured?' A standard anarchist response – not essential for mathematical structure, but incorporated in the modern definition of anarchism – goes as follows. There should be organization, of course, but that organization should be by acceptable means. That entails non-coercive, non-authoritarian organization; and that, in turn, is typically (though, again, by no means necessarily) taken to involve voluntary and co-operative organization.

Elaboration

There are many anarchist theories. For an anarchist theory is just *any* laterally structured theory which duly conforms to the principle of rejecting political authority and coercion. While received anarchist theories often try to restrict anarchism to certain more specific forms, 'pluralistic' anarchism does not. Plural anarchism not only admits plurality, but takes social advantage of it.

Not all of these anarchisms are of equal merit, however. Some forms (like those terroristic, violent or chaotic varieties of journalistic imagination) are decidedly undesirable, in much the same way in which the nasty states of modern history which anarchism opposes are undesirable. While standard anarchisms have been located in the more desirable or even eutopian end-range of anarchist systems, they by no means exhaust the satisfactory, or even the most promising, forms (see pp. 233–4). Indeed, in important respects the desirable range is significantly open for further elaboration of newer (and greener) forms.

As varieties of anarchy diverge widely, so too, correspondingly, do motivations and justifications for these divergent forms. These motivations range from entirely theoretical (conceding the warranted force of political scepticism) to practical (changing the local world); from personal and perhaps selfish (getting the state off one's back, or out of one's business and one's till) to other-directed (eliminating a state oppressing its people) to environmental (disestablishing another vandalistic state). Common motivations trace back to the common character of anarchism: repulsion by or opposition to oppression and domination, perhaps generalized from the state to all its variants and institutions, perhaps generalizing still further to all gross power relations. Indeed, it is sometimes suggested – correctly as regards gentler anarchisms – that what anarchy is really all about is gross power relations, their reduction and removal; the coercive and authoritarian powers of the state are but paradigmatic of such domination relations. There are other liberal democratic motives, further varying this theme: a yearning for removal of constraints and for more extensive freedom; or a desire for more extensive equality, which would, of course, diminish those inequalities which power delivers. Such motivations, too, have illicitly worked their way into variant characterizations of anarchism.

Many anarchists are joined by opposition to all naked authority or coercion. Indeed 'behind the anarchist attack on the state and other coercive institutions, there has often stood a fundamental critique of the idea of authority itself' (Miller, 1984, p. 15). An important, though certainly not invariant, motivating reason for anarchism does derive from a more sweeping anti-authoritarianism: the theme that no person or

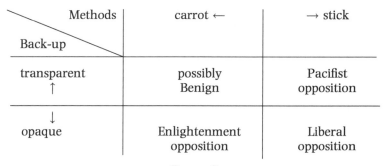

Methods / Back-up	carrot ←	→ stick
transparent ↑	possibly Benign	Pacifist opposition
↓ opaque	Enlightenment opposition	Liberal opposition

Figure 8.1
Matrix of authority relations

organization can ever rightfully exercise authority (of a political cast) over another. Picturesquely, it is the theme that no authority is justified: no one, state or other, has a right to push another around. Such general opposition to the principle of authority is dubbed 'philosophical anarchism' by Wolff (1970), terminology which is unfortunate in light of Feyerabend's (1975) different challenge to much in philosophical theory and practice going by the same name. Here some further classification helps. A *principled* anarchism takes exception on principled, characteristically ethical, grounds to objectionable authority or to coercion. Both grounds merit consideration .

There are many types of authority relations, not all of which are objectionable. Consider, for example, the relation of a student to an authority in some field of knowledge, who can in turn back up expert judgements by appeal to a further range of assessable evidence. Such an authority might be called 'transparent' (or 'open'), because anyone with time and some skill can proceed past the authority to assess claims made. Contrasted with these are 'opaque' (or 'closed') authorities, who simply stand on their position or station; such authority is objectionable in part because of its dogmatic character. Closely allied is the category of 'substantially opaque' authorities, who appeal to a conventional rule or procedure ('that is how things are done' or 'have always been done') without being willing or able to step beyond some rule book. Rule-book authorities are commonplace in bureaucracies, which often encourage such practice in lower level officials. With 'indirectly opaque' authorities, the justificatory procedure stops a step further back: there is a set of rules, which has been enacted (for reasons not open to, or bearing, examination) by a further substantially opaque authority.

Other authority relations are objectionable because of the way in which (or the means by which) they are backed up. There is nothing objectionable in the authority figure which exercises authority through the power of example, where what it exemplifies is in its turn satisfactory. Not so relations backed by coercive means, by violence or threats of violence: big stick authority relations. For instance, pacifists, being opposed to violence, condemn such relations on moral grounds, whereas they would not lodge any similar objections to non-violent and 'carrot' methods of trying to get things done. The overlay of this dimension on the other is represented in Figure 8.1.

It will be evident that the objections to non-benign authority relations – to what in clear cases may be presented as 'authoritarianism' – can be of significantly different sorts. To more opaque authority relations, there are objections of 'Enlightenment' cast: reason is lacking for what an authority requires, proposes or asserts, as was the case in the authoritarian religious and political practice against which the Enlightenment was primarily targeted. (A significant stand of anarchism, a more theoretical anarchism, is a descendant: undisclosed 'reasons of state' are not adequate reasons.) To more coercive authority relations, there are objections from 'pacifist' devotees of non-violence. To both there may be a kind of 'liberal' opposition: the party subject to authority is being denied, in one way or another and for unacceptable reasons, a certain freedom sometimes explicated as autonomy (Wolff, 1970, following Kant). Naturally, then, 'liberation' movements are directed at breaking down authoritarian power relations, domination relations: masters over slaves, humans over animals, men over women, adults over children, and so on. On a par with that is the authoritarian power of states over citizens. Thus, a comprehensive civil liberties movement would merge with anarchist movements.

There are objections to closed authority, quite independently of the generally regressive methods usually deployed to back it up. First, by virtue of its very character, it is without ethical justification. Secondly, it is incompatible with other perhaps absolute desiderata, most notably autonomy. Because the state operates as a closed authority, the point permits nice development into an argument, from autonomy, to anarchism (thus Wolff, 1970; many archist critics have tried to bury Wolff).

There is a range of analogous objections to, what is very different, coercion and coercive methods. These are generally recognized to be ethically undesirable, if not outright impermissible (cf. Dahl, 1989, p. 42).

Arguments against and for the state

Beyond the theoretical arguments for principled anarchism, the main argument for anarchism can be concentrated in a detailed critique of the state, and therewith of state-like institutions. Anarchist critiques of the state assert that states and state-like institutions are without satisfactory justification; such institutions are not required for organizational purposes; such institutions have most inharmonious consequences, bringing a whole series of social and environmental bungles or evils in their train. In brief, they are unnecessary, unjustified evils.

The anarchist critique of the state does not end there, however. It typically includes further themes, such as: states are devices for channelling privilege and wealth to certain minorities with inside linkages to state power; and societies are not ineluctably saddled with states but, rather, states can be displaced or even decay (though they are unlikely to just wither away).

A corollary is that political obligation lapses. In so far as political obligation is obligation with respect to the state, political obligation vanishes with the exposure of the state for what it is and as without due justification.

The state is undesirable, or even downright evil

Anarchists maintain that states entrench inequities, domination and exploitation.

States are devices for the protection of wealth, property and privilege; they redistribute upwards, and often concentrate, wealth and privilege. A minor but popular illustration is offered by the expensive conferences and other junkets that state employees or party officials organize for themselves and manage to bill to state revenue, in turn sucked up from inequitable taxation. Certainly, a main historical outcome of the state has been domination or exploitation of certain segments of society by others, and some see its main, and barely concealed, purpose as just that: domination and exploitation. States are typically corrupt. There are enquiries presently in train in many states in Australia, for example, which have revealed considerable corruption; there are *prima facie* cases for similar enquiries in most of the remainder. Nor is this a new phenomenon: these revelations often resemble older or ongoing scandals.

States are enormously expensive and constitute a heavy drain upon regional resources and accordingly on local environments. In poorer regions they are not merely a heavy burden but a main cause of impoverishment. One reason for their voracious appetite is an excess of over-remunerated and often under-productive state employees. Another connected reason is that many state operations are far from lean and efficient; instead, they incorporate many duplications, drag factors and dead weight. Under anarchisms of all varieties, these heavy cost burdens, weighing down subservient populaces, would be shed. Costs of organization would be very significantly reduced. States have excessive power and are continually accumulating or trying to accumulate more, through more centralization, further controls, additional licences, and so on. Obvious responses to excessive power are separation of powers, achieved by decoupling and some fragmentation, limitation of powers. Modern separations of church from state, and executive from administration from judiciary, illustrate broad separation procedures. Functional decomposition, breaking powers down to specific functions, carries that separation further, and continues it with sharp limitations of the powers of resulting departments. It can be combined (as will appear) with earlier anarchism which aimed to curtail power through institutional excision, decentralisation and federation.

States are major impositions on everyday life. They are intrusive and demanding. Never has this been more forcefully expressed than in Proudhon's famous denouncement of state government:

To be GOVERNED is to be at every operation, at every transaction, noted, registered, enrolled, taxed, stamped, measured, numbered, assessed, licensed, authorized, admonished, forbidden, reformed, corrected, punished. It is, under pretext of public utility, and in the name of the general interest, to be placed under contribution, trained, ransomed, exploited, monopolized, extorted, squeezed, mystified, robbed; then, at the slightest resistance, the first word of complaint, to be repressed, fined, despised, harassed, tracked, abused, clubbed, disarmed, choked, imprisoned, judged, condemned, shot, deported, sacrificed, sold, betrayed; and, to crown all, mocked, ridiculed, outraged, dishonoured. That is government; that is its justice; that is its morality. (Proudhon, 1923, p. 294)

As a result, there are constant demands for the reduction of the cancerous state, for removing parts of it through deregulation, for selling off state enterprises and so on. There are two troubles with such demands from anarchist standpoints. First, they never go far enough, to the complete reduction of state activities to zero: they characteristically retain parts supportive of bigger business. Second, they proceed in the wrong way: they strip away social safety nets, rather than ripping off business support nets (such as limited liability, strike-limiting legislation, and so on).

States, for all that they have been promoted as delivering public goods, are mostly dismal news for environmental protection and health and for social justice. Furthermore they are liable to impose substantial hazards or risks upon subservient populations – not merely through military and like activities but, more insidiously, through support and promotion of dangerous industries, such as nuclear and giant chemical industries.

States usually exert a heavy pressure to uniformity, they tend to eliminate plurality and cultural differences. These pressures are exercised by a state in the alleged interests of national unity against its enemies, external and internal. Even the most liberal of states tend to make the lives of minorities more difficult in times of stress, such as war. They are always espousing national values, state interests and commonly assimilation and adoption of state values. Such exercises are conspicuous, not only in citizenship ceremonies and other state rituals such as national sporting and religious events; more importantly, they are virtually ubiquitous in elementary education.

States are a major source of wars, and the major source of major wars, which are undoubted evils, however supposedly inevitable. They are major sources and suppliers of military technology and weapons, the means of war. Roughly, the more powerful and 'advanced' a state, the further it is engaged in weapon production and export. Without states it is doubtful that there would be any nuclear weapons, and accordingly, without weapons with which to fight them, there would be no prospect of nuclear wars.

States are in other respects too, a serious drag on a more satisfactory international order. That there are not more, and more satisfactory, international regulatory organizations 'is mainly a matter of the reluctance of nation states to surrender their powers and the dangers of their being dominated by very powerful states. If only nation states would be dissolved into specialized [departments] there is every reason to believe that most world problems could be handled by appropriate specialized [organizations]' (Burnheim, 1986, p. 221).

Two corollaries emerge. First, states cannot be justified merely historically, by virtue of being in place or having evolved. Unsatisfactory items in place, like man-made or natural disasters, lack justification and sometimes permissibility Nor, second, can they be given a straightforward utilitarian justification. For states appear far from a good bargain on a preliminary consideration of costs. That is especially true of bad states (far from uncommon) which engage in politically motivated incarceration or torture of their citizens, and so on. Where are the compensating benefits? Would we really be significantly worse off without these bad states, or even the better cases? Apparently not, especially given that we can get along without them (allowing for alternative non-statist arrangements which states have precluded or systems they have usurped). But arguments for states are not usually so directly utilitarian, or simply historical, in character. Such arguments would make it look as if we might well opt out of state organization, and often be better off doing so. No, it is contended that, contrary to appearances, we cannot get along without state cossetting: states are necessary.

The state lacks adequate justification

The state is not a self-justifying object. But none of the justificatory arguments to the state is cogent. A familiar theme concedes that the state is problematic but claims that it is a necessary evil. But the contrary seems more nearly correct: states, though generally evil, are hardly necessary. It needs stressing, furthermore, how weak the necessity claimed has to be. For it is becoming increasingly easy, with the advances in logical modellings and computer simulations of other worlds (involving 'virtual states', and the like) to envisage accessible worlds organized without modern states.

No doubt, then, the necessity has to be of some more *pragmatic* sort – a 'social human necessity', for example, appealing to emergent features of humans, kinks of human nature, obtruding in unfavourable situations of high concentrations and extensive scarcity. (These are, of course, situations which states themselves have helped contrive.) Remarkably, none of the extant arguments leading to the state makes it plain that such a weak pragmatic 'necessity' is involved, though they would hardly establish more. And they do make strong, implausible assumptions about the invariably brutal situation outside states (in 'states-of-nature', and so on) and about human motivation and practice (its utterly selfish, self-interested, acquisitive and frequently debased character).

Mostly, little serious effort is any longer made, outside a few abstruse texts, to justify the state. Within contemporary institutional arrangement the state (like Big Science) is simply taken for granted: as axiomatic, as God was under medieval arrangements. But unlike God – who was Good personified and therefore had a large problem with the extent of evil in the world – the state is acknowledged as problematic and far from unimplicated in the evil of the world. Such a problematic object cannot stand up as merely postulated. Nor is there any argument for the state, corresponding to the ontological argument for God, as that organizational structure than which nothing more perfect can exist. Outside the flawed imagination of German idealists there is no such Super State: all actual states are manifestly highly imperfect; all humanly realizable ones are likely similar.

As a result of the institutionalization of the state itself as a received and central part of modern political arrangements, the onus of proof has become curiously inverted. Efforts to justify the state have become fairly ideal and academic, no longer a serious issue; and the onus has thus been transferred to anarchists to demonstrate that human social life could proceed well and smoothly (as it now does, of course) without states.

While anarchists are not absolved from offering some account of operations of good social lives without states (for except in fairy tales it does not all just emerge, unplanned, in the new stateless setting), neither are statists absolved from justification of *de facto* statist arrangements, beginning with the state itself. In so far as efforts to justify the state as pragmatically necessary are attempted, these generally take one of the following forms.

Ideal reconstructions

Justifications for the state sometimes rely upon ideal reconstructions or political thought-experiments, which relate the mythological development of the state from an imaginary pre-state situation. The most notorious of these constructions are the social contract theories (of Hobbes, Rousseau, recently Rawls), whereby individual members of a society fictitiously enter into an enforceable contract, inescapably for themselves and all their descendants, setting up the state, primarily as a security arrangement. (Gough (1936) investigates 2000 years of such justificatory attempts, concluding that none such succeeds.) In later versions there is much negotiating and bargaining in contrived situations, where humans lose many of their distinctive features and accoutrements in an effort to ensure some initial fairness (Rawls, 1971).

A variant on contract theories, which justify some sort of state arrangements *as if* they arose in an ideal way, is retro-justification of the state as naturally arising as a sort of super-insurance agency from (suitably contrived) pre-state arrangements. For example, the minimal state evolves from a competing set of state-like security agencies one of which somehow, through some 'invisible hand', gains a monopoly, and is retro-justified through insurance arguments concerning risk and compensation (Nozick, 1974).

Now, modern states did not arise in any such 'natural' or contractual way. Often they were imposed by conquest or through colonialization, and (with a few exceptions) using military means rather than by offering much sweetness and light and choice. Nor do the ideal constructions or mythic histories offer much justification for these resulting state power configurations. For the states so delivered are very different from those most people presently toil under.

In any case, the arguments involved do not succeed. They are extraordinarily full of gaps, by the standards of contemporary logic; and they depend upon some utterly implausible assumptions (for example, as to how vile conditions are in extra-state situations, as to how property is distributed there, and so on). No doubt some of the gaps could be plugged by further (furthermore, contestable) assumptions; but such analytic work remains to be attempted and assessed. Meanwhile the state continues to operate, unjustified.

In any case, such arguments characteristically exhibit unlikely and even paradoxical features. For example, in consenting to a political state for security purposes, participants proceed to establish an institution which is far more dangerous to them than the power of others taken distributively. Presumably those smart enough to enter into a social contract for a state would be smart enough to foresee the problems of hiring a monster – and to avoid states in consequence.

Finally, these arguments, even if somehow repaired, would not establish an institution with anything approaching the power and complexity of the modern state. Arguments leading to the state typically establish only a rather minimal state, with certain protective and regulatory powers. Such a minimal state would not deliver many of the goods which economists, still less socialists, have come to expect of the state. The arguments certainly do not establish anything like the oppressive paternal state with a panoply of powers to which many citizens are forcibly subject – powers that states have accumulated by their own unjustified predatory activity. In this respect too, arguments for the state resemble arguments for God (Routley and Routley, 1982). Deistic arguments characteristically establish (in so far as they establish anything) only a quite minimal 'that which': a first cause, a most perfect object, a universal designer, 'clockmaker', or the like. They do nothing to establish many of the powers or properties ascribed to God.

Unavoidable state functions

A second approach in trying to justify the state is couched in terms of the functions which the state discharges. The state is necessary *for* this or that. In particular, it is necessary for the optimal provision of public goods (including, but not limited to, pre-servation of public order).

Notice that this important type of argument need not presume to establish necessity. It is obvious, from the operation of nastier states, that societies can function not only without optimal provision of public goods, but indeed with very little *state* provision of any such goods. It would, moreover, be a rash archist who pretended that modern states deliver anything remotely approaching optimal allocations of public goods. Two things follow. First, justificatory exercises which (like those drawing on game theory) assume optimal assignments fail as entirely unrealistic. Second, anarchistic alternatives need not ensure optimal allocations to defeat their statist competitors; indeed, it may only be a matter of exceeding the state's rather poor provision of public goods.

Most of the arguments attempting to justify the state in terms of its role in the provision of public goods depend further upon a false private/public dichotomy, flowing from individualism, in which the private is delivered by individuals or individual firms and the public is delivered by the state. In between, however, lie many social groupings: clubs, communities, unions, societies, clans, tribes, and so on (Buchanan, 1965; Pauley, 1967; McGuire, 1974). Such groups, too, can deliver social goods of a broadly public sort.

As the modern state developed more or less at the time of the rise of individualism in its exuberant modern forms, it is unremarkable that there is a heavy individualistic setting presumed in most arguments to the state. A central group of these arguments comprise variations upon Prisoners' Dilemma situations, including therewith the 'Tragedy of the Commons' (Hardin, 1982; cf. Taylor, 1987). These arguments take the following broad form. Individuals operating on their own, in certain prearranged (game-theoretical) settings which involve but limited relations to other individuals also operating independently, will sometimes make seriously sub-optimal decisions or follow sub-optimal practices – unless brought into line by an outside influence, too swiftly presumed to be a surrogate of the state. Even on their own ground these arguments are inconclusive (as Taylor, 1982, shows).

It should be evident, even without going into any details of these important arguments, that the state is neither necessary nor sufficient for resolution of the problems that issue from independent individual operations and from individual competition. It is not sufficient because tragedies of the commons (such as the overexploitation of commons' resources by competing fishermen, farmers or firms) can proceed apace in the presence of the state, and may even be encouraged through state activity. It is not necessary because the relations of interdependence among individuals in dilemma or tragedy situations can be exposed, and restored, in a variety of ways into which the state (possibly of no help) does not enter – for example, by establishing communication linkages, by social activity, conciliation and arbitration through engaged organizations, and so on. (Commonly, such relations are, in any case, evident in analogous real-life situations before the state becomes involved, or can be got involved.) That also shows how anarchism can resolve such dilemmas as need to be resolved in the absence of the state: namely, by having alternative arrangements, structure and organisation in place which will serve instead.

One of the major deceits of modern political theory lies concealed in the persistent theme that the state, with a centralized monopoly on coercion, is necessary in order to assure adequate public goods, including public order. For the most that appears required, the most that arguments would deliver, are specific organizations that look after specific kinds of goods, those necessary for this or that. There is no inherent reason why societies should not institute and regulate specialized bodies co-ordinated among themselves (by negotiations or, failing that, by recognized arbitrators) to ensure the adequate maintenance or production of various types of public goods, including control of damaging crime. Each such institution could gain community standing from its support base, for instance through achieving democratically generated recognition. Such an institution would aim to secure execution of its recommendations and decisions by sanctions and like admissible means, and in doing this it could mobilize in co-operation with other recognized institutions (Burnheim, 1986, p. 221).

There are many examples of such bodies operating successfully internationally. Those for postal and communication arrangements were among Kropotkin's favourite examples (see Baldwin, 1970), and much in the modern academic literature on international relations now confirms the rich opportunities for 'co-operation under anarchy' (Oye, 1986). Another example considered by Burnheim (1986, p. 221) concerns the case of international sport. As he remarks, each major sport has its international body that regulates a variety of matters, ranging from the rules of the game to the administration of competitions. While such bodies are, of course, open to schisms and rivalries, these are seldom a major problem. Moreover their organization generally succeeds despite the fact that they have few sanctions to ensure compliance other than, for instance, excluding competitors from participation in the events they organize.

An anarchism viable for other than small communities appears to presuppose some such alternative organizational and social arrangements. If such a system is to persist, then its prospects are exceedingly poor if it is nothing more than a do-nothing set of arrangements spontaneously arising out of a revolution. But the state, as it grows, tends to undermine or eliminate such alternative arrangements. Correspondingly, people come more and more to expect the government to what they might formerly have done, or have banded together to do, themselves. The state again proceeds, like other persistent systems and ecosystems, to establish conditions for its own survival; to become needed for social and even for individual activities and functions.

Core state functions: public order and defence

Now that the state is established, many of these social substitutes are under threat of withdrawal. Under ideological pressure from economic rationalism, pliant states have been attempting to corporatize, privatize or relinquish more and more of what had become regarded as necessary state functions, including some necessary to meeting basic health and shelter needs of citizens. But curiously, given the magic capabilities of the market, a few core state functions remain sacrosanct, such as taxation and money supply, defence and public order. While it is not particularly difficult to see how financial organization could devolve from state control, to social, community or private management (as historically), the issues of public order, property security and defence are regarded as essentially state functions; these are the functions of leaner minimal states, particularly recalcitrant to state excision. It was not always so (state police forces are a recent retrograde development), and it need not be so.

Another apparently powerful argument for the state, deriving from similar (mixed game and choice theoretical) sources, asserts that the state is required for these essential functions, for instance in order to control and to limit such social evils as crime and corruption. Observe, however, that it is not supposed these features of life are eliminated under the state; so questions arise about tolerable levels, cost-benefit ratios of varying levels of controls (down to the point of any controls at all), and so on. Observe again that the typical state, so far from limiting corruption and crime, is itself a major source of them. The state structure, by virtue of its power, expanse and character, induces much of the evil it is supposed to remove, such as crime.

There are several different reasons for this. For one, the state tends to become the guardian of a partisan morality and tries to prosecute what, outside a 'moral minority', are not offences at all but are instead victimless 'crimes'; thus arise a range of medical, sexual and drug 'offences'. For another, the state acts to protect its questionable monopolies: whence a range of banking, gambling, gaming and other offences. For yet another, the state supports social outcomes involving gross inequalities and privatization of wealth and resources: whence property crime.

Anarchists all agree that the major background source of these crimes – the state and its legion of 'law and order' officers – should be removed. They differ over what, if anything, replaces this extensive apparatus. Different types of anarchism are bound to offer different suggestions. Under communist forms, where an extensive institution of private property vanishes, property crimes will therewith disappear also; under individualistic forms which sanction unlimited accumulation of property, some procedures for safeguarding property will need to be provided. Again, however, there are many and much less demanding ways of achieving the requisite protection of property than a resort to the state. One is that which effectively operates in many places that also waste their finances paying for ineffectual police protection: namely, insurance. Another is social, neighbourhood or community security.

As with security of property, so with other kinds of security, including territorial defence: different types of anarchism will propose and experiment with different compatible forms. Social and individualistic types will both operate defence through institutional arrangements, social types through functional bodies geared just to defence of

relevant territory, individual types through a set of defence firms. Each sort of arrangement allows for various kinds and levels of defence (individualistic types depending
upon what is purchased). In particular social arrangements allow for social defence,
a kind that is stable, highly compatible with gentler anarchism, and invulnerable to
the severe political problems generated by standing armies (Sharp, 1990).

There is really no practical alternative

This is more an excuse for the state than a justification of it, of course. Advocates of the
state none the less rely upon it heavily. Anarchism, they insist, has not worked in
practice; it is, they infer, therefore unworkable. Neither is true. Before the modern
era of states, it seemed to work well enough in some places, for instance in parts of
the Americas and of the Pacific. Since the modern advent of states, it has been
afforded but little opportunity to work at the national level, but it remains strikingly
operative at the transnational level (Luard, 1979, p. 163).

According to a condescending pragmatic argument, simple primitive societies may
have been able to struggle along without state structure or organization, but it is
entirely out of the question for the practical operation of modern industrial societies. No recent anarchist societies have worked. A short response is again that few
have had an opportunity to succeed. There is extraordinarily little room for social
experiment in modern state-dominated societies. Moreover, where anarchist societies
have had some chance to flourish (as, briefly, in Spain before they were suppressed),
some of them appear to have functioned moderately well.

At the international level, anarchy has operated for many generations. The
arrangements *work*: in this sense they are successful, though hardly ideal. The international order is anarchistic, because there is no coercive government or authoritative
political body with authority backed by enforcing power. International order is instead
a prime example of anarchy. (While it is not a wonderful example, neither are many
states terrific examples of archy.) It affords a conspicuous standing counterexample to
stock arguments, like that of Hobbes, to some sort of well-ordering authority, such as
the state (Oye, 1986).

Granted, international order leaves much to be desired. There are, accordingly,
repeated calls for new world orders of one sort or another. But it has been persuasively argued (through a sort of top-down argument against states) that international
order is as bad as it is because of the power and intransigence of states. The standard
recommendation for an improved world order is through stronger international institutions. But an alternative recommendation, which would follow equally well from
the diagnosis of the problem of world order, is an anarchist prescription calling for
the erosion of states and diminution of state sovereignty.

As for real testing in practice, there is now no experimental space outside states.
There used to be some room in the world for sizeable political experimentation, for
testing different arrangements. We are now locked into large, overpopulated states
with little room to move, let alone to experiment without states. There is, however,
space *within* more liberal states for limited experimentation, and there is increasing
scope for simulation and modellings as computer power and versatility grow. Most
of the experimentation has been with small commune arrangements. What practice

has shown – about all it has shown, negatively – is that *communistic* arrangements do not tend to work well for long with present humans, unless they are committed to a strong ideology. Various other sorts of arrangements can work well enough given opportunities (as the well-established commune movement in Australia demonstrates).

'With the state removed', it is said, 'the system has no ultimate guarantor.' So it used to be said in favour of God. But who guarantees the guarantor? A state may underwrite a social insurance scheme or a bank: but a state itself can fail, despite support of other states, despite states all the way down. There is no ultimate guarantor.

There is the further matter of the character of the guarantor. In theology, a further, illicit stipulation serves to ensure that God has the right features. In the case of the state, nothing guarantees that an 'ultimate guarantor' is not (rather like most states) corrupt, unfair, heavy-handed and incompetent. If in social relations a guarantee cannot be obtained without coercive authoritarianism, it is unlikely that a satisfactory one will be obtained with it. So even if an ultimate guarantee was needed, none of satisfactory character could be guaranteed.

Lesser assurances without the state can none the less be offered. A bank's books can be opened to public scrutiny and assessment, so that it can be seen that it is trading in a responsible and viable fashion. It is better that a person's healthy state be assured by observation that the person is functioning well than by intrusive interventions, treating the person as a closed system and relying on a doctor's guarantee of the person's health. So too with the social structures the state purports to guarantee.

Varieties and options within anarchism

There are several recognized varieties of anarchism, among them: individualistic anarchisms, anarcho-capitalisms, anarcho-communisms, mutualisms, anarcho-syndicalisms, libertarian socialisms, social anarchisms and now eco-anarchisms. These varieties are not particularly well characterized. They are by no means at all mutually exclusive. So far even a satisfactory classification is lacking. Usually something of a ragbag is offered. Textbooks single out a very few varieties for scrutiny, invariably leaving out others that are as important.

Still, it is not difficult to discern some of the more independent dimensions along which variation occurs and which, accordingly, are relevant to an improved multidimensional tabular classification. (Some of these 'dimensions', it ought be noted, are not strictly linear, but that they are not, and that they are not fully independent, does not impede a much-improved classification none the less.) Some main dimensions are presented in figure 8.2.

The 'part–whole' dimension (figure 8.2.A) is a significant dimension of variation for organizational arrangements for analysis (see Routley and Routley, 1980). It helps to account for a major bifurcation between European anarchisms, which tend to be socially-oriented, and American anarchisms, which (except for religious communities, which are usually European transplants anyway) are typically highly individualistic. For markedly holistic arrangements to persist, some strong ideological glue appears required, such as an immersing spiritual ideology; not so for more relaxed community arrangements.

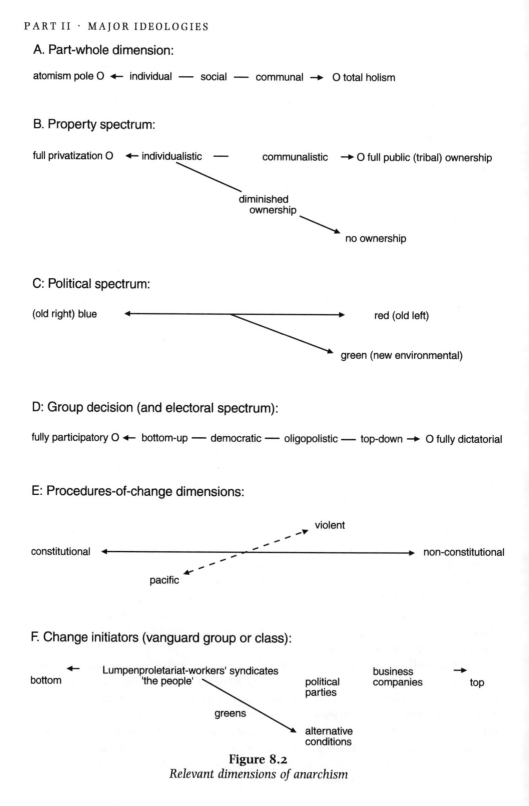

A. Part-whole dimension:

atomism pole O ← individual — social — communal → O total holism

B. Property spectrum:

full privatization O ← individualistic —   communalistic → O full public (tribal) ownership

diminished
ownership

no ownership

C: Political spectrum:

(old right) blue ←   red (old left)

green (new environmental)

D: Group decision (and electoral spectrum):

fully participatory O ← bottom-up — democratic — oligopolistic — top-down → O fully dictatorial

E: Procedures-of-change dimensions:

violent

constitutional ←   → non-constitutional

pacific

F. Change initiators (vanguard group or class):

← Lumpenproletariat-workers' syndicates   business →
bottom   'the people'   political   companies   top
                          parties

greens

alternative
conditions

Figure 8.2
Relevant dimensions of anarchism

There are other dimensions, relevant for the bifurcation as well. One such is the 'property spectrum'. Although it can be compressed into two-dimensional form, it is better presented three-dimensionally, as in figure 8.2.B. This spectrum evidently connects with the preceding holistic dimension. Both contribute to what was the old right–left division (a sort of crude superposition) and to what should be seen as superseding it, which is a three-colour political spectrum (figure 8.2.C). This relates in turn to differences in ways of comprehending group decisions (figure 8.2.D), of procedures for effecting social change (figure 8.2.E) and for agents of change (figure 8.2.F).

The schemata presented are clearly far from exhaustive. Nothing has been directly included concerning distribution methods (market versus command, open versus closed storehouses, and so on), there is nothing on admissible technology, nothing so far on work–leisure arrangements – to take three important examples. More pieces will be picked up as we proceed, and some of the rather schematic sketches ventured above will receive some development in what follows.

Once the relevant (n) dimensions are duly elaborated 'an' anarchism can be located and classified (pigeon-holed in n-space) by placement in each dimension. For instance, a type of anarchism advocated elsewhere is located as follows; it is social (with a significantly qualified communistic safety-net, to each according to her or his basic needs); it is market-oriented but non-capitalistic, with diminished ownership; it is democratic but without politicians and with alternative electoral arrangements; it is pacific but not bound by 'constitutional' procedures; it utilizes modest safe technologies and so on (Routley and Routley, 1980).

Thus there are many anarchisms, a rich variety of different types, some of them scarcely investigated or known. That anarchism composes such a plurality has proved puzzling to those who assume it must be a single ideology, either individual or collective. Indeed, the pluralist character of anarchism has led even apparently sympathetic critics to 'wonder whether anarchism is really an ideology at all, or merely a jumble of beliefs . . .' (Miller, 1984, p. 3). Of course, the impression that anarchism 'is amorphous and full of paradoxes and contradictions' is marvellously assisted by conflating 'degenerate anarchism' and 'diluted anarchisms' with unadulterated anarchisms, chaos with order, individualistic anarchisms with socialistic with holistic ones, and so on.

By properly regarding anarchism under a standard model for pluralism as a sheaf of overlapping types assembled around a core characterization (that of the refined explication above), the problematic elements of anarchism as an ideology disappear. No doubt it is not an ideology like Marxism, but then Marxism is atypical in its set of paradigmatic texts, concentrated in the works of the master. Other ideologies such as liberalism or environmentalism afford better comparisons. While anarchism is an ideology (in both good and bad senses), it is not really a movement. There is not, anywhere really, such a movement, in the way there have been a succession of liberation movements or there is a peace or a green movement (on obtaining a movement, however, see pp. 240–2).

Such pluralism as anarchism unproblematically exhibits does not enjoy an impressive historic track-record, and it does not go unopposed either outside anarchism (e.g. because it makes refutation so much more difficult) or within. Standard anarchist positions have tended to shy away from pluralism in the direction of rigid monistic forms and toward insistence upon particular structure, organization and distributional methods – leading to much intense and often fruitless discussion and friction between anarchists committed to different arrangements. True, there was a doctrine of spontaneity, according to which the masses would, in the course of the revolution overthrowing the state (in the very heat of that revolution!), spontaneously decide upon new arrangements. That made it appear that nothing anarchist was excluded, any structures at all were open for consideration. But it was also assumed that certain arrangements would be selected, towards which active (and likely doctrinaire) anarchists in a vanguard would provide guidance.

Anarchists – over-attracted, like others, to monistic schemes – have regularly attempted to advance their own schemes by introducing many further postulates that reach far beyond anything that flows simply from the basic characterization of anarchism. Some examples of optional, and rejectable, extras from a recent anarchist manifesto include: '. . . direct democracy, destruction of all hierarchies, maximization of freedom, total Revolution, no ends–means distinction, no leaders, optimism about an anarchist future . . .' (most of this Australian student manifesto may be sourced not only in classic anarchism but in recent work, e.g. Bookchin, 1989). But genuine anarchists are not bound by any of that.

Because of the expansive pluralism of anarchism, it overlaps many other ideologies. Indeed, it overlaps all that do not include, as a theme, unmitigated commitment to a state or like central coercive authority. Thus, while anarchism excludes fascism and is incompatible with state capitalism, anarchism overlaps liberalism, democracy and even Marxism (since Marxism affords a future anarchism). There has been much confusion about these interrelations.

Take democracy. Anarchism does not entail democracy, as is sometimes claimed: advice of a select minority or of a sage could regularly be adopted, though the advice did not reflect the will of the people and its source was not elected or appointed by the people. Nor does anarchism entail the negation of democracy (as Dahl, 1989, p. 50 erroneously supposes); it does not entail undemocratic procedures. There are, in the plurality of anarchisms, forms that are democratic, in various ways, and others that are undemocratic. Democratic forms may well enjoy a better prospect of enabling genuine democracy than life under the state. For as some have argued, 'both the nation state and electoral democracy are inadequate as vehicles for democracy under modern conditions' (Burnheim, 1986, p. 218).

Is its goal individual freedom or communal solidarity? Sometimes one, sometimes the other, sometimes neither, sometimes both. A pluralist anarchism offers several different sorts of communities, not just one kind: independent individuals, families or firms, perhaps interrelated and organized through markets and contracts; solidaristic groups working freely together and sharing according to need; and various attractive intermediaries, where there may be more individual-oriented market arrangements but there are also safety nets ensuring distribution according to basic needs.

It is not difficult, in theory, to devise structures that allow a wide variety of kinds. In simple cases, this can be accomplished through regional patterning, with different varieties of anarchism in different places. (Such a modelling for political pluralism is further elaborated in Sylvan and Bennett, 1990.) The brief interlude of anarchism in Spain afforded a small-scale example of such a regional patterning, with different varieties of anarchism at work.

The different kinds of anarchistic societies are bound to be of very variable quality, both theoretically and in practice. Some will only work with rather special sorts of people (or instance, with members with strong religious or ideological commitments); some will not succeed at all. Some verge on incoherence, such as those genuinely against coercive organizations which approve of terrorist tactics. But while some kinds of anarchism are entangled in serious problems, others are not. Anarchists generally have no obligation to defend defective kinds. Yet many criticisms of anarchism are directed at just such defective forms.

Although there is a rich variety of anarchistic end-states (virtually uninstantiated possibilities), there are common organizational and structural features. Such cluster features are what hold the plurality together. These include non-coercive versions of those arrangements essential to a functioning society: for instance, broad features of arrangements for production and distribution, for arbitration and reconciliation, and so on. Though there are many different strands that can be interwoven through the pluralistic out-fall from the basic characterization of anarchism, there are some broad tendencies common to virtually all anarchistic arrangements. These include:

- Reliance on self-regulatory methods of organization that require little or no intervention, as opposed to highly regulated procedures, perhaps tending towards centralism or paternalism. (This is one reason why markets are often favoured, but analogues of centralized control and coercive legal systems are rarely considered except in diluted forms.)
- Emphasis on voluntary methods, in place of imposed methods. (Coercive methods are of course excluded by virtue of basic characterization; *de facto* power may remain, of course, but it will be without justification.)
- Favouring of decentralization and deconcentration, rather than centralized or concentrated structures. (That does not imply there can be no downward relations: of course, under federal arrangements there will be, and natural sideways relations as well, amounting to a full control system.)
- Discouragement of empowerment, encouragement of depowerment, with opposition to oppression and domination as a corollary.

But although each type of anarchist society will have such organizational features, they will differ in detail. A main distributional feature of a simple communist society may comprise a common storehouse from which members take according to need, whereas in a simple individualist society distribution will typically proceed through some sort of market exchange. More generally, different types of anarchism will offer different economic theories. Those with stronger individualistic component will tend to rely not merely upon market or allied exchange arrangements, but upon capitalistic organization; thus anarcho-capitalisms, logical end-points when libertarianism and economic rationalism are really driven to state minimalization. These types of anarchism, whose small home base is the United States, propose several, often ingenious uses of private and market means to substitute for social and state functions

(Friedman, 1973; Rothbard, 1977). But they provide no satisfactory resolution of ubiquitous market failure, which becomes even more widespread and severe without the state, and accordingly they remain unacceptable for environmental and other progressive social movements (Dryzek, 1987, p. 86). The types of anarchism favoured here avoid these fatal flaws by striking an intermediate route: regulated markets without capitalism.

How is such complex organization to be achieved without a state? Does not such organization and government require a state? To remove that familiar assumption and associated blockages – encouraged by too much life under states and too little experience of alternatives – take a wider look around. Look at how many activities and procedures are organized without states or any essential participation of states: by voluntary arrangements. Prominent examples are sporting organizations, churches, labour unions and business corporations of various sorts. In short, organization can be accomplished through a range of appropriate institutions .

Such examples also provide the appropriate key to how more extensive organization can be achieved in the absence of the state: namely, through appropriate institutions. The state dissolves into functioning components, a set of appropriate institutions, and at bottom into its relevant minimization. It fragments into compartments, in two interconnected ways: into regional parts and into capacities, or functional parts.

There are other valuable clues to stateless reorganization. What happens within the more self-regulating state can also happen without it. As Gramsci emphasized:

the ability to govern without overt coercion depends largely on the ability of those in power to exploit systems of belief that the larger population shares. The nature of that system of belief is to some extent determinable by policy makers, since in the modern state they possess a significant ability to propagandize for their view. Yet . . . (Gramsci, 1971, p. 63)

Recent empirical investigations tend to yield allied results. People tend to follow rules and obey laws they regard as substantively moral or otherwise satisfactory and procedurally fair (Tyler, 1990, p. 178). There are important messages here for anarchistic organization, for arrangements without coercion, overt or otherwise. Anarchistic rules will try to go with the prevailing flow, and will only vary (as over vindictive punishment, which still remains popular) where an evidently satisfactory justification can be given. More generally, smarter anarchistic arrangements will aim to include desirable self-regulating systems, such as fair small-scale markets.

As there are too many alternatives in the pluralistic cluster to list examine all of them, let us consider only some with preferred features. Anarchistic societies of any complexity, including cities, will typically consist of a network of decentralized organizations, or of federations of these. Most organizations will thus be regional, but beyond that set up according to issue, role or function. So they will conform to an *eco-regional functionalism* (a mixture of political functionalism with ecological bioregionalism; on which see Mitrany, 1975, and Sale, 1980, respectively). Many of the stock features of decentralized political functionalism will accordingly recur: separation of powers, tailoring of administration to needs, and so on. The organizations will furthermore be non-coercive; no individual or group will be forced to join. Typically, they will be voluntary arrangements.

A critical question is how these organizations substituting for the operation of state and its bureaucracies are to be controlled, regulated, and so on. In much-favoured democratic structures, such as electoral bureaucracies, control is usually weak and remarkably indirect. A populace weakly selects a central parliament, which through other bureaucratic bodies exercises some control of state organizations. A genuine anarchism is obliged to dissolve or provide substitutes for central parliaments. It has an obvious option, namely direct democratic control of state-substituting organizations (such as replacements for present departments of local, regional and federal governments).

A simple way of achieving this is through sortition. There the membership of the governing component of each organization is chosen randomly from those qualified of the regional community who volunteer to be on it. In some cases volunteers may require accessible qualifications, such as having served before at a lower local or federal level. ('Levels', note, which stack up in flat-topped pyramidal arrays, do not imply any vicious hierarchy.) Furthermore, some volunteers might be disqualified on the basis of their past record. Where the community decides that certain categories of people (disabled, minorities, and so forth) should be represented, then it is a matter of arranging random selection of the required fraction of group numbers from these categories. This style of statistical democracy dates back at least to original democracies of Greek city-states where public officials were sometimes selected by lot (it is discussed under democracy in Aristotle's *Politics*). Nowadays it is called 'demarchy' (Burnheim (1985), from whom main details of administrative arrangements can be drawn), a term with unfortunate prior meanings. Here in its anarchistic form it will be alluded to under the neologism 'demanarchy'.

Such demanarchy has the immediate virtue of removing a most expensive duplication: namely, between elected government ministers and their appointed counterparts in the civil Service (between the Chancellor of the Exchequer and Permanent Secretary of Treasury, for example). Indeed, the whole charade of central parliamentary government, ministers and hordes of minders, governments and replicating opposition teams, is duly removed – inevitably under non-centralization. Such top-down parliamentary centres are eliminated. In so far as anything replaces them, it is the dispersed community, having no centre, which is linked directly to functional organiziation.

Gone or seriously reduced with the demise of the centre are several stock political worries, directed against anarchism, such as those of coup, takeover, insurrection or invasion. These usually involve capturing the centre and its command structure, no longer there to capture; there is no command or control structure that could be taken by an invader or through internal insurrection. Community defence is thereby rendered much easier. The stock problem of who controls the controllers is also largely removed, partly because control is so diffused and partly because a main controller is the federated communities (which is one of the advantages of more direct democracy).

Appropriate functional institutions take care, then, of the day-to-day running of community affairs, of standard administration. But what of major policy, big-issue decisions, resolution of conflict, changes of political direction or structure? Where necessary these can be accomplished from the bottom, through referendums, propositions, and the like (with public assessment organized through a suitably independent electoral college), rather than in present top-down, inflexible fashion. (Some of these methods, of which there is worthwhile experience in parts of Europe, are sketchily investigated in Wolff, 1970; with recent rapid improvements in communicational technology, such participatory methods can be much sophisticated, on which see McLean, 1989.)

The outline offered invites many questions and criticisms. How is such a stateless structure is to be financed without coercive mechanisms available? Observe that unless the target is being pursued for other reasons (such as criminal or political activities), coercive means are very rarely resorted to in order to obtain revenue payments from wealthier corporations, firms or individuals – from where in a more equitable community much of the funding would derive (by contrast with most present states). Note, too, that very much less public revenue would be required to support anarchistic systems, because several most expensive, most wasteful and least productive components of state have been excised. These include the whole apparatus of central government and electoral politics and the associated system of coercion (standard military forces and defence establishment, espionage framework, and police forces, prison establishment and expensive adversarial courts).

None the less there remain many institutions to finance, including smaller substitutes for some of the abolished structures (such as social defence arrangements). There are several parts to a satisfactory answer as to how to finance these institutions.

- Many institutions can be largely or entirely self-financing through fair user-pays principles or because (like customs and import organizations) they collect revenue. Reasonable returns taken can be channelled to an independent revenue office with no outside spending or redistribution powers.
- Much, if not all, further social revenue could be raised through resources taxation (adequate royalties, and the like), through rental taxes on property or leases, through gift and gains taxes and through auctions (of goods that would previously have been inherited). How this would work depends upon community arrangements.

Consider, for instance, anarchistic arrangements where that most problematic item, private property, has not been instituted or has been weakened or abolished (as again under main proposals of European anarchism, by contrast with North American forms). After all, full private property, like the state, manages to stand, without satisfactory justification (Carter, 1989, p. 126). While small items may be held, valuable durables – roughly, any durable worth stealing for re-sale in present systems – will be rented instead of bought. Leasehold systems can be operated very like private property (as the land system in the Australian Capital Territory reveals) facilitating market operations; but they offer significantly better environmental controls, they enable the social component of generated wealth to be reflected through a rental charge, they can be of finite term and of such a form as to exclude excessive accumulation and transfer by inheritance. In place of the customary 'land titles office' a 'durables office' with subdivisions for types of durables would be instituted, with each durable being indelibly marked or described. (Here as with referendums modern computing facilities remove many previous obstacles to such developments: anarchist organization can move with newer technologies.)

Leasehold arrangements are readily applied to prevent the accumulation of scarce property resources, such as urban land, which is a major feature of capitalism. Leases of scarce commodities can be allocated according to need and ability to use, not merely through an historically rooted market distribution, as with private property. It is private property, not a market-extended system of distribution, that is really distinctive of capitalism. It is that which not only provides a place to park and increase capital but also it enables transmission of accumulated wealth (within a family or dynasty, for example) and control of the means of production. It is that which a social anarchism opposes and would dissolve.

A frequent criticism, intended to demolish not just social anarchism but all types, is that no form of anarchism has developed an adequate economic theory. Now, a cynic might well observe in response that no strand of capitalism or of socialism has either. But theories there no doubt are, in certain narrow reaches, in abundance.

Anarchism, it is true, commonly assumes the benefits of autonomous market operations. Indeed 'the individualistic ideal is one of personal sovereignty in the market place'; but then 'is not the state an indispensable prerequisite for a successfully functioning economy?' (Miller, 1984, p. 169). There are two parts to a response. First, markets functioned before states and function outside states, for example internationally. States are inessential. Second, whatever institutions are required for the operation of markets can be supplied regionally under anarchistic fragmentation of the state. Problems remain only for individualistic forms, which have to locate (available) privatized replacements for social structures.

How much background structure do markets depend upon, and how much of it might presuppose the apparatus of a state? A market has a place of transactions (which can be common or waste ground) and a supply of goods or services, to be exchanged there for other goods or services (barter) or for currency (in a money economy). Buyers and sellers enter the market to effect exchanges. No doubt there are certain things presupposed by markets: at least limited entitlement (leasehold or property rights), so a seller is entitled to transfer to a new user what is offered for sale; contractual arrangements; and, in a money economy, some recognized currency. Also normally presumed, where markets operate, are certain levels of security against invasion, assault and theft; but these are normal expectations for much of social life, even for conducting a conversation. As for the rest, except perhaps for currency, it is a mere pretence that a state is required for their assurance: customs or tribal arrangements will ensure both property in transportable goods and recognition of verbal contracts or undertakings; modern stateless organization can also. An appropriate currency too can develop in the absence of states, as exemplified in the shell currencies of Melanesia and the bank notes of early America. Bank notes are not fully public goods; for a bank which can profit from their circulation or issue has an incentive to supply them (Hayek, 1976). And banks themselves do not require a sponsoring state, even if sometimes that helps, as in bailing them out.

It is also said, against anarchism, that 'a central agency seems necessary to maintain any society-wide distribution of resources' (Miller, 1984, p. 172). Which resources? Where markets operate, many resources will be distributed without any role for a central agency, which would often serve as a serious blockage.

What distribution? What is intended in the charge is surely 'a just distribution of resources', so that the blatant inequalities now observed in even the wealthiest societies are mitigated and the conditions of the worst off are alleviated. But that is simply drawing upon experience of capitalism: anarchism would not start out from such an invidious position. Furthermore, it is again assumed that there are only two ways of righting such (capitalistic) maldistribution: through purely private means or by a centralized state means. So presented it represents a false dichotomy – private or state. In that dichotomy, society is either equated with the state or else drops out, and all other public means disappear.

For socially inclined anarchists there is no disputing that there need to be safety-nets in place for the poor and disadvantaged. What is in question is how those nets are placed and administered, and whether the state has an essential role or whether it is instead an inefficient and officious nuisance. There are many stateless alternatives. One option canvassed redistributes some funds collected from resource sales and leases. Another option is a socially instituted tithing system, where members of society are offered a choice of schemes to contribute to, and expected to contribute to these, and encouraged to make their contribution open to public inspection. Those who tried to evade contribution and closed their books would be subject to a range of social pressures (Taylor, 1982).

It is further claimed that while smaller anarchist communities (especially those of a collectivistic or communistic bent) may be able to resolve inequitable distribution problems, 'there are major difficulties' in attempting to realize some distributive ideal 'between communities' (Miller, 1984, p. 173). There are major difficulties, now. But that is scarcely an argument for a central authority. Some redistribution and a small transfer of wealth already occurs, deliberately undertaken through non-state organizations, without any central authority involvement. There is no decisive evidence that central authorities help facilitate global redistributions; it may well be, as many suspect, that they make matters worse.

Roads to anarchy: old routes and new inputs

Anarchism, even though theoretically viable, is undoubtedly hard to obtain, for states are now extremely well entrenched, and form a club of their own. None the less, opportunities arise for overthrowing them. Periods of crises, in particular, afford opportunities – which should be seized, as they may not arise often. A well-prepared anarchist group will organize, then, when the moment arrives, pounce. But such opportunities and risky revolutionary routes are only one way to change. As there is a plurality of anarchistic positions and end-states, so too there is a plurality of routes to anarchism, but not in any directly corresponding way. Figure 8.3 provides a survey of the larger possibility field.

Pluralistic anarchism is not obliged to dismiss political and constitutional routes to anarchism or to anarchist objectives, including therein more congenial state arrangements. A state may be, or become, more congenial as regards how decently it treats its peoples, environments and neighbours: it may also be more benign in that it does not significantly impede anarchist political activity or render paths significantly more

Ways	Evolutionary	Revolutionary
Intra-state: within state setting	1. Typically slow or incremental operations through received political channels	2. Typically rapid operations circuiting established channels: coups, insurrections, etc.
Extra-state	3. Operations establishing alternative organizations bypassing or substituting for statist arrangements	4. Operations comprising external interference or intervention: by negotiation, military means, sanctions, examples, etc.

Figure 8.3
Ways to change

difficult. Overlapping that, more benign, less domineering states may leave substantial room for significant anarchist practice, both in lifestyle and in building organizational structures and (as it were) alternatives to archist arrangements (such as 'people's banks' and 'time stores'). What are in important respects anarchist communities can operate within, and be modelled within, less intrusive states. (The limits to this quasi-anarchism, elaborated in Nozick, 1974, are explained in Sylvan and Bennett, 1990). States that better meet anarchist (and green-socialist) criteria for benignness can conveniently be distinguished as more 'sympatico' states. A committed anarchist can quite well also be committed, as an intermediate goal among others, to achieving more sympatico states. That, in turn, may involve political activity, conventional or unconventional.

Main anarchist routes to change lie, however, outside conventional politics. They comprise, first, *substitution* for the operations and functions of the state, through alternative arrangements set up within the territory determined by the state (e.g. the succession model in Routley and Routley, 1982; the utopian framework of Nozick, 1974). Except in utopian circumstances, successful substitution is bound to lead to confrontation with the state. Other main routes lead more directly to confrontation and to revolutionary means, routes through *direct action*, against state activities and practices.

Goal-directed change through forms of direct action – in significant respects a contemporary upgrading of former anarchist ideas of actions through deeds and propaganda by deeds – requires both some planning and a movement to carry through planned operations. Planning and organization of anarchist action is certainly not excluded, in revolutionary operation or elsewhere. The rival 'spontaneity' view, still fashionable in many anarchist circles, depends upon the unpromising idea of directly igniting the radically dissatisfied masses (and is ideologically underpinned by a confused picture of freedom). Furthermore, it issues in bad decision-making, choice deliberately uninformed by available information, for instance as to more desirable ends and means. Naturally, however, planning is not and cannot be total, and it should not be too inflexible.

Unfortunately, it is hard to find anywhere, even in the worst of states, much anarchist planning, and there is little visible evidence of constructive anarchist movements any more; what gets exhibited in on-going crises of states is degenerate anarchism. There is undoubtedly much scope for anarchism proper to become involved in those crisis situations, for instance by influencing and organizing active dissatisfied groups, and for it to flourish.

What are also now conspicuously exhibited are extensive movements, making considerable use of direct action techniques, substantial parts of which have heavy (but often under-appreciated) anarchist commitments: notably environmental and peace movements, which are highly compatible with social anarchism (Martin, 1980; Routley and Routley, 1980; Dobson, 1990). A main contemporary chance for social anarchism lies in mobilizing these movements, activating their latent anarchism. That is the great hope for the future (Callenbach, 1992).

See also 6 POLITICAL SCIENCE; 12 MARXISM; 13 SOCIALISM; 14 AUTONOMY; 15 COMMUNITY; 16 CONTRACT AND CONSENT; 18 CORPORATISM AND SYNDICALISM; 19 DEMOCRACY; 24 ENVIRONMENTALISM; 26 FEDERALISM; 27 INTERNATIONAL AFFAIRS; 28 LEGITIMACY; 29 LIBERTY; 30 POWER; 31 PROPERTY; 34 SECESSION AND NATIONALISM; 36 STATE; 38 TOTALITARIANISM

References

Baldwin, R. N., ed.: *Kropotkin's Revolutionary Pamphlets* (New York: Dover, 1970).

Bookchin, M.: *Remaking Society* (Boston: South End Press, 1989).

Buchanan, J. M.: 'An economic theory of clubs', *Economica*, 32 (1965), 1–14.

Burnheim, J.: *Is Democracy Possible?* (Cambridge: Polity Press, 1985).

————: 'Democracy, nation states and the world system', *New Forms of Democracy*, ed. D. Held and C. Pollitt (London: Sage, 1986), pp. 218–39.

Callenbach, E.: *Ecotopia Emerging* (New York: Bantam New Age, 1982).

Carter, A.: *The Philosophical Foundations of Property Rights* (Brighton: Harvester Wheatsheaf, 1989).

Clark, J.: *The Anarchist Movement* (Montreal: Black Rose Books, 1984).

Dahl, R.: *Democracy and its Critics* (New Haven, Conn.: Yale University Press, 1989).

Dobson, A.: *Green Political Thought* (London: Unwin Hyman, 1990).

Dryzek, J. S.: *Rational Ecology* (Oxford: Blackwell, 1987).

Dunn, J. M.: 'Relevance logic and entailment', *Handbook of Philosophical Logic*, vol. 3, ed. D. Gabbay and D. Guenther (Dordrecht: Reidel, 1986), pp. 117–224.

Feyerabend, P.: *Against Method* (London: NLB, 1975).

Friedman, D.: *The Machinery of Freedom* (New York: Harper, 1973).

Gough, J. W.: *The Social Contract: A Critical Study of its Development* (Oxford: Clarendon Press, 1936).

Gramsci, A.: 'The intellectuals' and 'The modern prison', in *Selections from the Prison Notebooks*, ed. Q. Hoare and G. N. Smith (New York: International Publishers, 1971).

Hardin, R.: *Collective Action* (Baltimore, Md.: Resources for the Future, 1982).

Hayek, F. A.: *Denationalization of Money* (London: Institute of Economic Affairs, 1976).

Held, D. and Pollitt, C.: *New Forms of Democracy* (London: Sage, 1986).

Holterman, T. and van Moorseveen, eds: *Law and Anarchism* (Montreal: Black Rose, 1984).

Lehning, A.: 'Anarchism', *Dictionary of the History of Ideas*, ed. P. P. Weiner (New York: Charles Scribner's Sons, 1968), pp. 70–6.

Luard, E.: *Socialism without the State* (London: Macmillan, 1979).

Mannison, D. et al., eds: *Environmental Philosophy* (Canberra: Research School of Social Sciences, Australian National University, 1980).

Martin, B.: *Changing the Cogs* (Canberra: Friends of the Earth, 1980).

McGuire, M.: 'Group segregation and optimal jurisdictions', *Journal of Political Economy*, 82 (1974), 112–32.

McLean, I.: *Democracy and New Technology* (Cambridge: Polity Press, 1989).

Miller, D.: *Anarchism* (London: Dent, 1984).

Mitrany, D.: *The Functional Theory of Politics* (London: Martin Robertson, 1975).

Naess, A. et al.: *Democracy, Ideology and Objectivity* (Oslo: Oslo University Press, 1956).

Nozick, R.: *Anarchy, State and Utopia* (Oxford: Blackwell, 1974).

Oye, K., ed.: *Cooperation under Anarchy* (Princeton, N.J.: Princeton University Press, 1986).

Pauley, M. V.: 'Clubs, commonality and the core: an integration of game theory and the theory of public goods', *Economica*, 35 (1967), 314–24.

Proudhon, P. J.: *Qu'est-ce-que la propriété?* [What is Property?] (Paris, 1840).

————: *General Idea of the Revolution in the Nineteenth Century*, trans J. B. Robinson (London: Freedom Press, 1923).

Ritter, A.: *The Political Thought of Pierre-Joseph Proudhon* (Princeton, NJ: Princeton University Press, 1969).

————: *Anarchism: A Theoretical Analysis* (Cambridge: Cambridge University Press, 1980).

Rothbard, M. N.: *Power and Market – Government and the Economy* (Kansas City: Sheed Andrews and McMeel, 1977).

Routley, R. and Routley, V.: 'Social theories, self-management and environmental problems', in *Environmental Philosophy*, ed. D. Mannison et al. (Canberra: Research School of Social Sciences, Australian National University, 1980).

———— and Routley, V.: 'The irrefutability of anarchism', *Social Alternatives*, 2(3) (1982), 21–9.

Sale, K.: *Human Scale* (New York: Coward, Cann & Geoghegan, 1980).

Sharp, G.: *Civilian-Based Defense* (Princeton, NJ: Princeton University Press, 1990).

Spretnak, C. and Capra, F.: *Green Politics* (Santa Fé, N.Mex.: Bear & Co., 1984; rev. edn, 1986).

Sylvan, R.: *Universal Purpose, Terrestrial Greenhouse and Biological Evolution*, Research Series in the Fashionable Philosophy No. 4 (Canberra: Research School of Social Sciences, Australian National University, 1990).

———— and Bennett, D.: *On Utopias, Tao and Deep Ecology*, Discussion Papers in Environmental Philosophy No. 19 (Canberra: Research School of Social Sciences, Australian National University, 1990).

Taylor, M. J.: *Community, Equality and Liberty* (Cambridge: Cambridge University Press, 1982).

————: *Anarchy and Cooperation* (London: Wiley, 1976); 2nd edn as *The Possibility of Cooperation* (Cambridge: Cambridge University Press, 1987).

Tyler, T. R.: *Why People Obey the Law* (New Haven, Conn.: Yale University Press, 1990).

Wolff, R. P.: *In Defense of Anarchism* (New York: Harper & Row, 1970).

Woodcock, G.: *Anarchism* (Harmondsworth: Penguin Books, 1962).

9

Conservatism

ANTHONY QUINTON

Preliminaries

The boundaries of an idea

Conservatism is the only body of right-wing opinion represented in the part of this *Companion* dedicated to ideologies. Of the other five, four are leftist and the fifth, liberalism, straddles the centre, having a right-wing version – classical, individualistic liberalism – and a leftish one – the interventionist liberalism, which emerged in the later part of the nineteenth century. Further to the right of conservatism there are the ideologies of fascism, authoritarianism and elitism, as well as a number of political attitudes which are not articulate enough to amount to ideologies. I shall argue that the former are quite distinct from conservatism and that the latter are, at any rate, not identical with it.

This way of proceeding has two things to recommend it. In the first place it allows for a greater comprehensiveness of treatment. Second, it makes it possible to demarcate conservatism more precisely by distinguishing it from other bodies of opinion with which it is commonly confused. Since the late nineteenth century and the emergence of socialism as the politically effective ideology of the newly enfranchised proletariat, conservative parties have absorbed so many right-wing liberals in alliance against a common enemy, that at times the truly conservative element in them has been almost overwhelmed by liberal individualism.

The confusion of conservatism with the ideologies of the extreme right is more a matter of rhetoric, although it has some basis in political practice. Conservatives in a time of crisis have allied themselves with parties animated by other, more ferocious right-wing ideologies.

What I shall identify as conservatism is a long-lasting body of political doctrine which is seldom nowadays represented by a single party. It is, above all, the political doctrine of Burke. But it goes much further back in English history, at least to Hooker, and, in the world as a whole, perhaps to Aristotle. Since Burke it has taken the form of a continuous tradition, culminating for the time being in Oakeshott.

The central doctrines

This main tradition of conservative thought derives from three central doctrines which are themselves connected. The first and most obvious of them is traditionalism, which supports continuity in politics, the maintenance of existing institutions

244

and practices and is suspicious of change, particularly of large and sudden change, and above all of violent and systematic revolutionary change. At its most rudimentary this is simply a widespread human disposition, present to some extent in everyone, though by no means universally predominant, to love the familiar and to fear the unknown. Suspicion of change is not the same thing as rigid opposition to it. But, for the conservative, if there is to be change it should be gradual, with each step carefully considered, as though one were venturing on to ice.

The chief intellectual, rather than emotional, support for traditionalism is a sceptical view about political knowledge. Political wisdom for the conservative is embodied, first of all, in the inherited fabric of established laws and institutions. This is seen as the deposit of a great historical accumulation of small adjustments to the political order, made by experienced political practitioners, acting under the pressure of a clearly recognized need and in a cautious, prudent way. It follows that the management of public affairs is best remitted to those with extensive direct political experience and not to theorists with their privately fabricated abstract systems. What is needed for successful political practice is skill or know-how. Even less welcome to conservatives than abstract principles, such as doctrines of universally applicable natural or human rights, are utopias, systematic proposals for comprehensive social transformation.

Political scepticism in its turn rests on the third central doctrine of conservatism, the conception of human beings and society as being organically or internally related. Individual human beings are not fully formed, except in their basic biological aspect, independently of the social institutions and practices within which they grow up. There is, therefore, no universal human nature. People's needs and desires and expectations differ, from time to time and from place to place. Social institutions generally, and the state and its laws, in particular, should not be thought of as appliances, like a bicycle or a toothbrush, selected for an already formed purpose. Such an organic conception of the relations between individual and society does not have to take a Hegelian, metaphysical form. It does not claim that a socially undetermined individual is somehow logically inconceivable, although that could be argued for in contemporary terms on the grounds that language is essentially social and that it is language which makes human beings human, and not just primates that walk upright. It is enough that it is a matter of fact.

Since individual and society are organically, internally related, it follows that their activities are not susceptible of the kind of abstract theorization that is characteristic of the natural sciences. Just as there can be no literal science of poetic composition or friendship, there can be no literal science of politics, from which a technology of statecraft can be derived.

The non-conservative right

Right-wing political doctrines that are different from conservatism, but are often confusedly run together with it, are of two kinds. First, there are some fully-fledged ideologies, which have achieved a measure of intellectual articulation, and which are, if examined closely, really quite distinct from conservatism, at least in the traditional and central sense in which I have taken it. Second, there are some recurrent or persistent right-wing political attitudes, not intellectually elaborated enough to count as ideologies, which are not identical with conservatism and not even an essential part of it, but are nevertheless often to be found among conservatives. The non-conservative ideologies are right-wing *alternatives* to conservatism, while the less articulate attitudes are rather possible *variants* of it.

Fascism is the right-wing ideology that, because of its dramatic and destructive role in the history of the twentieth century, first comes to mind. It is non-conservative in a number of obvious respects. It is radical, and even revolutionary, to start with, calling for a wholesale replacement of existing institutions and an immense enlargement of the functions of government. It has no respect whatever for customary law, for constitutions and, indeed, for the rule of law in general. The inspired leaders it calls for are self-taught political virtuosi, from the remote margins of ordinary political life. In Weber's terms, the fascist leader claims charismatic authority, where the authority of the conservative ruler is traditional.

Authoritarianism has been just as common a feature of the political experience of the twentieth century, if less conspicuous than the fascism to which it is sometimes allied, sometimes hostile. Perhaps the most usual form is military dictatorship, as with Primo de Rivera and Franco in Spain or Pilsudski and Jaruzelski in Poland. But civilians, such as Dollfuss and Salazar, have also ruled as authoritarians. Like fascism it endorses emergency measures, prescriptive rules which dispense with tradition. But it is not totalitarian. It does not see the penetration by the state of every aspect of human life as required for the preservation of order which is its overriding political value. But it is not a form of conservatism either, because of its readiness to dispense with laws and constitutions.

Elitism, with its Platonic ancestry, is perhaps the oldest political ideology. It is non-conservative in respect of all three of conservatism's central doctrines. It does not take human beings and the societies they compose to be theoretically impenetrable. It contends that the best elite is an intellectual one, composed of those who are particularly qualified by abilities and training to understand the workings of society. It can accord respect to tradition, but not reverence, seeing tradition as the surviving residue of the work of past elites. Unlike most conservatives, the elitist attaches little importance to people's inherited position.

To the left of conservatism, but still of the right rather than the left, is classic, individualistic liberalism. Practically allied with conservatives against the common enemy, socialism, liberals of this kind have been continuously recruited to conservative parties since the late nineteenth century. Sometimes, nowadays, parties calling themselves conservative are dominated by liberal individualists. The leading twentieth-century exponent of classical liberalism, Hayek, ends his major treatise, *The Constitution of Liberty* (1960), with a chapter called, without irony, 'Why I am not a conservative'.

Classic liberals favour change, admittedly in the economy and society at large, rather than the state, at least where liberal institutions prevail. They favour theory, above all classical economics, with its apparent implication that an unfettered market will lead to the greatest possible satisfaction of human needs and desires and the most productive use of resources. They are more suspicious than conservatives of all but the most minimal government.

Finally, there are the inarticulate political attitudes, which, although often associated with conservatism, are no essential part of it. A conservative is not a reactionary, though he may be. But only to a limited extent. If the reaction envisaged is a large one, to a long past state of affairs, it is unconservatively revolutionary, even if only negatively so.

A conservative does not have to be an immobilist, an unwavering and absolute opponent of change, although he may be, again within certain limits. Conservatives accept change as required by changing circumstances, but they insist that, to minimize its dangers, it should be continuous and gradual.

A conservative will not be an absolutist, except to the extent that the tradition of his society is an absolute one. But absolutism, the idea that the sovereign is free from all constraints of the law, perhaps by reason of a supposed divine right to rule, is at odds with conservative respect for the impersonal wisdom embodied in laws and the constitution.

Conservatism as an ideology

There is a difficulty about treating conservatism as an ideology which should be confronted as soon as possible. Conservatism is distrustful of, or hostile to, theory. An ideology is a kind of theory. Therefore conservatism would not wish to see itself, or to be seen, as an ideology. There can be no doubt that an ideology is, or essentially comprises, a theory. That is what differentiates it from mere political prescriptions, convictions or opinions, even from political principles and from systematic political ideals or utopias. An ideology derives political prescriptions or principles, even sometimes utopias, from theories about human nature and society.

Central to conservatism, I have said, is an organic theory of human nature and society which implies a sceptical theory of abstractly theoretical political knowledge. These are taken to imply, in their turn, attachment to tradition, reluctance to change and a preference for politically experienced rulers. The crucial question is: does the theory which conservatism rejects self-destructively include the kind of theory which, in its developed form as something more than an emotional disposition, it itself embodies?

The conservative answer is that conservatism does not depend on a substantive theory about universal human nature, issuing in universal political principles, such as lists of the rights of man. No doubt it has been confused, both by supporters and opponents, as such a theory of which, for example, a monarch, a hereditary aristocracy of landowners and an established church are ingredients. But the desirability of such institutions for a conservative is relative to the circumstances of a particular time and place, one in which they are historically established. (In modern Britain, for instance, they are largely, if not wholly, formal and vestigial.) As an ideology conservatism is, then, procedural or methodological rather than substantive. It prescribes no principles or ideals or institutions universally and so falls outside the scope of its own rejection of abstract theory.

The notion that conservatism is not an ideology, but only a disposition, or, more reductively, an expression of the self-interest of those who benefit from the status quo, is also assisted by its lack of an appropriately theoretical classic text. Liberalism

247

has Locke's *Treatises of Government* and Mill's *On Liberty*; socialism has *The Communist Manifesto*; elitism has Plato's *Republic*. The nearest thing to a classic text it possesses is Burke's *Reflections on the Revolution in France*. But that, like all Burke's mature political writing, is an occasional work, evoked by and principally concerned with the particular event mentioned in its title. The great bulk of it is taken up with polemic, expressed with a measure of rhetorical excess, about attitudes to that event. The ideology has to be separated out from the highly concrete matter in which it is immersed. But it is unquestionably to be found there.

Historical survey

The prehistory of conservatism

Plato and Aristotle, from whom all later political thought derives, were both men of the right. In the Greece of their time the kind of revolutionary turmoil that evokes explicit conservative thinking as a reaction was vehement and uninterrupted, although to be extinguished by the authoritarian imperial order imposed by Aristotle's pupil, Alexander the Great. Plato was not, however, a conservative but an elitist, who devised a utopia to arrest all change. In his *Republic* there is no place for law as conservatives understand it. The state was to be run by a non-hereditary caste of intellectually gifted experts. Nor did he confine his proposals to a particular community, but went to the tyrant of Syracuse in an attempt to export them there.

Aristotle, on the other hand, if not exactly conservative, was certainly of a conservative temperament. He favoured the rule of impersonal laws over the rule of individual men and saw constitutional states as healthy, and despotic states as perverted. Always concerned with the practically possible, he was critical of Plato's utopia, especially in its elimination for the ruling class of the great traditional institutions of the family and private property. He believed that the best available constitution for a community depended on its nature and circumstances. He intimated an organic theory of human nature and society in his fundamental thesis that man is a political animal, who can realize his human potential only in a state. All the main conservative notes are sounded in his work, even if, under Plato's influence, he still saw it as the business of the political philosopher to outline an ideal state. His own outline remained amorphous and unfinished.

Cicero was a Stoic and a believer in natural law and the essential equality of men in all times and places. But he was conservative in practice, upholding the traditions of the Roman republic against the new imperial authoritarianism of Augustus, who had him killed.

In the Middle Ages, after the translation of Aristotle's *Politics* into Latin around 1260, the Christian political theory of passive obedience was theoretically articulated by Thomas Aquinas. The principal theme of political reflection in this period was that of the proper relation between church and state. Orthodox conformism saw the state as a divinely ordained remedy for human sinfulness, in need of guidance and endorsement from the church. The political secularism that was to emerge in the Renaissance

248

was foreshadowed in the theories of the state as means for the satisfaction of earthly human ends by Occam and Monsiglio of Padua.

From the Reformation to Burke

There had been palace revolutions in medieval England and brief, popular risings, which governments firmly repressed. But the first major challenge to the established order came in the sixteenth century with the Protestant Reformation. The position of subjects whose faith differed from that of their rulers led to warfare in Europe – the French Wars of Religion in the late sixteenth century and the Thirty Years War in Germany in the early seventeenth. In England there was violence but no open warfare.

The opposing sides justified themselves either by appealing to a supposed divine right of kings, by which religion was subject to the state, or some more or less theocratic principles such as those, for example, advanced by Calvin. The Elizabethan church settlement established the royal supremacy over the church and the exclusion of the Pope, but retained much of Catholic ritual and the institution of the episcopacy. Hooker's *The Laws of Ecclesiastical Policy* was produced as a defence of that settlement, but turned out to be much more, perhaps the first truly conservative theory. He rejected both the competing absolutisms of the age: the divine right theory and the Puritan belief that all truth is to be found in the Bible, which says nothing of bishops and royal supremacy. Against the former he argues that the monarch must uphold the customary law; against the latter that circumstances have fundamentally changed. The idea of the historically developed complexity of the social order is everywhere in the background of his thinking.

Although he argues that we have in reason a capacity to apprehend natural law, he develops this rationalist theme in a conservative way. Natural law is broad and schematic; it does not imply any specific political arrangements. Similarly, some general references to the need for consent if government is to be legitimized, on which Locke seized for his own, more radical purposes, takes consent to be mediated through custom and established laws.

Hooker was influenced by his contemporary Jean Bodin, who is the first French conservative thinker of note, although an uncharacteristically moderate and pacific one. He was the chief intellectual voice of the *politiques* who tried to alleviate the bellicosity of the warring religious factions. Bodin is best known for his defence of religious toleration and his theory that an ultimately sovereign power is needed to constitute a well-ordered state. The absolutist appearance of that doctrine of sovereignty is deceptive. Bodin insists that the sovereign source of law is himself subject both to the laws of God and nature and to what he calls *leges imperii*, constitutional rules definitive of sovereignty, which require him to respect the property of citizens, who may not be taxed without their consent.

The ups and downs of English political life between the mid-seventeenth and mid-eighteenth centuries gave a series of active politicans the opportunity, when out of office or in exile, to reflect on politics in general terms. Clarendon, Halifax and Bolingbroke all spent part of their careers at or near the centre of power at pol'.ically crucial moments. Clarendon, chief minister of Charles II in the early part of his reign and historian of the Great Rebellion, developed ideas about the limits of political knowledge by way of an elaborate criticism of the secular, purportedly scientific absolutism of Hobbes, and used the idea of the 'ancient constitution', the traditional basic law of the community, to limit the pretensions of the crown.

Halifax, a more brilliant, but more occasional, aphoristic writer, is the first truly secular conservative thinker. For him religious dogmatism was the main cause of social instability and of the violence and cruelty that accompanied it. He preferred 'natural reason of state', the fruit of practical, historically inherited experience of actual political life, to abstract ratiocination about 'fundamentals'.

Bolingbroke is a more ambiguous figure. A talented and copious writer, he has been neglected in a morally disapproving way on account of his Alcibiades-like duplicity and, perhaps, his dissoluteness. There is certainly nothing conservative about his best-known book, *The Idea of a Patriot King*, where he pins his hopes for good government on a virtuous, properly educated monarch. Elsewhere, more thoughtfully, he supports a conservative, empirical version of natural law, as indeterminate and variable in its application as Hooker's. He takes man to be naturally sociable and the rule of some over others to be as natural outside the family as in it. The state is an historical growth, not a mechanical contrivance. He endorses constitutionally traditional mixed government and is hostile to the increasing power of the moneyed interest, as encouraged by his enemy, Walpole. Montesquieu, the most conservative of the *philosophes*, may have acquired the idea of the separation of powers from Bolingbroke, rather than, as used to be thought, from a misreading of Locke. A conservative view of Montesquieu's is that good political systems are relative to the particular characteristics – climate, population, and so forth – of the communities involved.

David Hume was a Tory in his practical political allegiance and even more hostile, at any rate more openly hostile, to religion than Bolingbroke. As the first thoroughgoing utilitarian, he rejected the whole Lockean apparatus of natural rights and a social contract which has generally underlain the more high-minded sort of liberalism. But that rejection is entirely compatible with liberalism as the example of Bentham shows. Hume respected custom but more because it is familiar than because it is wise. Despite his scepticism, he thought a science of politics is possible. A much truer and less marginal conservative is his great disapproving contemporary, Samuel Johnson.

Burke and English conservatism

If conservatism has something of a prehistory, and an early history from Hooker to Bolingbroke and Johnson, it reaches its maturity only with Edmund Burke's tumultuous response to the French Revolution. He began his career as a Whig and called himself a 'new Whig' after he had broken with the old Whigs about the revolution. In the early part of his career he adopted what might appear to be a liberal attitude to the claims of the American colonists and to the right of Britain's Indian subjects to good government. In fact, both positions can more properly be seen as applications of his basic conservatism. In supporting the American colonists he was not appealing to the abstract rights of man but to the colonists' traditional rights as Englishmen. Similarly, in the case of India, he was moved by the consideration that India had a long historic civilization of its own.

Burke's subscription to what I have called the three central doctrines of conservatism may be briefly illustrated by quotations. As a traditionalist he saw the constitution as something historic and continuous, not as a contrivance. We are its 'renters and temporary possessors' not its outright owners. Prescription, he affirms, is the most solid of titles. As a political sceptic he says that 'the science of constructing a commonwealth, or renovating it, or reforming it is . . . not to be taught *a priori*.' It 'recognizes experience, and even more experience than a person can gain in his whole life'. As an organicist, he holds that the wise legislator 'has to study the effects of those habits which are communicated by the circumstances of civil life'. 'The operation of this second nature on the first', he goes on, brings about 'many diversities among men' so as to make them 'as it were, so many different species of animals'. There is no universally applicable political ideal or set of abstract human rights.

Morality, as divinely authorized and revealed, may be universal, but politics is circumstantial, a matter of expediency, the prudent pursuit of the advantage of a particular community. But prudence is not the mechanical selection of means to such a simple, universal end as self-interest.

Coleridge in his early years was an adherent of the purest radical of the revolutionary period, William Godwin, and meditated setting up an ideal community of an anarchistic kind in America. But with the passage of time he moved, like his collaborator Wordsworth, to the right, and to the conservative right. 'In Mr. Burke's writings', he proclaimed, 'the germs of almost all political truths are to be found.' In his *Constitution of Church and State* he sketches what looks at first like a utopia, but is, in fact, a romantic idealization of the traditional British political order, in which the permanent interest of land is in harmonious balance with the progressive, urban interest of commerce and industry. Two original contributions are his conception of the national church as having primary responsibility for the maintenance of culture, particularly by way of its control of education and his strong concern with the social consequences of industrialization.

Newman was hardly a political theorist, but he picked out liberalism as the main enemy to be resisted, identifying it with 'false liberty of thought', that is to say, with an optimistic view of the capacity of abstract reason to ensure progress. In state as well as church, although there is, inevitably, change, it should be a continuous development.

Where he, in his spiritual, introspective fashion, was detached from the social problems that had burst out in Victorian Britain, that was what two reflective conservative prime ministers, Disraeli and Salisbury, brought into relation with the fundamental conservative creed. Disraeli, lauding Bolingbroke and taking over ideas from Burke wholesale, believed that the solution to the social problem was a compound of ameliorative legislation to control industry and a call to the new property-owners to assume the kind of traditional responsibilities for welfare that had been attached to property. By Salisbury's time, with the Conservative Party transformed into the party of all substantial owners of property by the inclusion in it of the right-wing liberals who broke with Gladstone, conservatism was reduced to a desolate call for resistance to the passion and ignorance of the masses.

A comparable limitation is to be found in the short but influential treatise of his son,

Lord Hugh Cecil, half of which is devoted to exploration of the familiar basic principles, the rest to more or less ingenious defences of limited taxation, the maintenance of the British Empire and other, fairly contingent, elements of the platform of the Edwardian Conservative Party. There is quite as evident a conflation of the essential and the accidental in the lively but all too inclusive treatise of Lord Hailsham, *The Case for Conservatism*.

The only impressively new development in conservative thinking in twentieth-century Britain is that to be found in the writings of Michael Oakeshott, who, unlike his predecessors back to Disraeli, was a pure theorist, not a political practitioner. His attack on rationalism in politics is the most thorough and sophisticated assault on the treatment of politics as a technical activity of aiming scientifically at means for clearly determinate ends.

Conservatism in France, Germany and America

Outside Britain before the French Revolution, conservatism, or more precisely the authoritarianism of dynastic absolute monarchies, was so overwhelming in practice, that there was no occasion for conservative doctrine. The only French political thinker of any importance in the seventeenth century, Bossuet, was an authoritarian defender of the divine right of kings, rather than a conservative proper. Even the imported, and sharpened, liberalism of the eighteenth-century *philosophes* did not evoke an articulate conservative response.

The revolution gave an occasion for doctrine, and Burke a powerful and widely followed example. Both de Maistre in France and Möser and Adam Müller in Germany looked up to and imitated him. But French and German conservatives differed from British ones in their extremism. Where Britain had been largely stable for a century and a half, France had undergone a major revolution prolonged, through the Napoleonic era, for a quarter of a century, while Germany had experienced crushing defeats at the hands of the French. In both countries conservative thinkers took these catastrophes to be God's vengeance for impious ratiocination in the one case, for the crushing of the nobility by the Prussian monarchy in the other.

French conservatism, as well as being comparatively extreme, is also clear-cut and principled. De Maistre used reason to deny the claims of reason in human affairs and to exalt instinct, particularly the instinct to adhere to the customary, which he saw as divinely implanted. British conservatism had often had a diffuse religious background; in de Maistre and Bonald, an outright theocrat, throne and altar are indissolubly connected as the proper objects of unquestioning and reverent obedience. There was a distant echo of Coleridge, and even Bolingbroke, in their hostility to industry as enthroning self-interest above communal loyalty and patriotism.

Their German contemporaries were more romantic and sentimentally backward-looking, seeing in the feudal organization of the Middle Ages the historic framework within which the German spirit had developed. The state is not a machine for the protection of natural rights or the furtherance of individual interests. They followed Herder in supposing each nation to have its own unique character and needs and repudiated Kant's abstract liberalism, which sought to transcend national boundaries and outlaw war.

The conservative reaction to the second major revolutionary upsurge in 1848 takes on a different form. *Ancien régime* legitimism had been discredited by the follies of the restored Bourbons. Nationalism, having begun as a liberal repudiation of the dynastic principle, was taken over by conservatives, first in Germany in the skilful practice of Bismarck and the theory of Treitschke, later in France, after the débâcle of 1870, by Barrès, Maurras and the Action Française.

Before historical misfortune had excited that brand of aggressive nationalism in France for which the nation was all, the army and the church its vital protection, there had been a more moderate strain of secular conservatism, inspired by Comte's positivism, and detached from much of his speculative and utopian extravagance by Renan and Taine. Renan argued for an elite of scientifically intelligent (and artistically gifted) people but, more conservatively, said 'hereditary prejudice is but unconscious reason'.

In the early nineteenth century European conservatives expressed hostility to industry, railways and large towns as disturbers of social harmony and order. But the irresistible strength of industrial capitalism eventually had to be acknowledged. Both Napoleon III and Bismarck associated authoritarian conservatism with economic modernization, forging an alliance parallel to that developing in Britain between conservatives proper, the agricultural interest, and right-wing liberalism, the political expression of industry. Doctrine found this harder to digest than political practice.

America has always found a place for some kind of conservatism. The American revolution was widely construed as conservative in nature, being an enforcement of the traditional rights of Britons in America. The Federalists believing in centralization, aimed to limit states' rights and to mitigate democracy in the interests of stability. Southern conservatism, as in Randolph and Calhoun, was altogether more traditional. Both strands of conservatism have persisted up to the present day; one in the form of a combative preference for an unfettered market for individual enterprise to prosper in, the other, more nostalgically, and, perhaps, unrealistically, looking back to a traditional hierarchical order which had only the most fitful and marginal existence.

The central doctrines defended

Traditionalism

There are three main arguments – or families of arguments – against change, one direct, another, more important one, indirect and a third empirical.

The direct argument is that change is generally upsetting or distressing, all the more so if it is large and sudden. Stated at that level of generality it can be countered with the objection that surprises are often agreeable, at worst a relief in a time of tedium and monotony, at best an exciting transformation into a better state of things. An answer to that objection is that, for the most part, the changes we find most agreeable or acceptable are usually on a small, comparatively personal scale. Changes of a large, remote and imponderable nature are likely to inspire fear and anxiety. A new car, a promotion, a rearrangement of the living room furniture are welcome because they can be controlled and even reversed. But large political change, heavy with unpredictable results, is a very different matter, like a volcanic eruption.

The strongest case in general terms for resistance to large and sudden change is, however, indirect. It rests on the great number of unintended and unpredicted consequences that will emerge from change of that kind. The prevailing political system influences numerous and various aspects of life. If it is suddenly or violently transformed, a host of stabilities which provide a background of regularity within which life can be rationally and prudently led are jeopardized. A change of tailor will affect one's clothing but will have few other substantial results and, if they are objectionable, the change can easily be reversed. A change of political system is likely to influence the whole social environment. It is not only that large political changes have many unintended results that are unwelcome. They also frequently fail to achieve their intended results or achieve opposite ones.

It may be thought that this line of reasoning assumes that most change is for the worse, or, at any rate, that most unintended and unexpected change has bad results. Are these unplanned by-products of change never bonuses, never changes for the better? In the abstract, is not unplanned change as likely to be good as bad? The formation and running of a state is more like walking on a girder high above the ground or driving a car along a narrow, winding road than like tossing a coin. There are innumerable ways in which it is possible to go wrong, indeed disastrously wrong, but only a very tightly restricted number of ways in which you can go right, apart from the simple policy of staying where you are.

Conservative traditionalism does not rule out change. As Burke said in his *Reflections*, 'A state without the means of some change is without the means of its conservation'. But change should be in response both to a change in extra-political circumstances – increase in population, of the proportion of the population that is literate, a new balance between agriculture and industry – and to a widely-felt need arising from it, and it should be gradual so that unplanned detrimental side-effects be counteracted. A particular reason for hostility to revolutionary change is that revolutions, when serious and not of the palace variety, bring about a large transfer of power and, naturally, of wealth and status. The resentment of the newly deprived is likely to be violent. The ensuing civil war is likely to divert the revolutionaries from their original intentions.

The third argument, from historical experience of large and sudden political change, reinforces the argument from bad unplanned consequences with specific examples. The English civil war led not to the rule of the saints but to a military dictatorship. Most of what it managed to achieve was undone at the Restoration and the democratic movement was driven underground for a century or more. The French Revolution quickly degenerated into a brutal, if mercifully brief, despotism, followed by a military dictatorship that was at least glamorous. The Commune of 1871 was rapidly extinguished by the violent reaction it provoked. About the more or less disgusting consequences of the Russian and Chinese Revolutions of 1917 and 1947 it is hardly necessary to go into detail. Parliamentary control of the crown and the extension of the franchise in Britain were attained piecemeal by a long sequence of comparatively small steps.

Scepticism

The theoretical pretensions of revolutionaries and radical reformers which conservatives seek to undermine are not those of political science but rather those of abstract political theory. Political science as an organized form of inquiry is comparatively modern, although anticipated from time to time, for example in much of Aristotle's *Politics*, in various essays of Hume, in the writings of de Tocqueville and Bagehot. Abstract political theory starts from certain propositions about ends, typically about the universal rights of man or the supreme political values, and proposes, usually in a fairly simple-minded way, means to those ends. A utopia is a conception of society in which those ends are fully realized. A system of natural rights may be presented either as something whose guaranteeing is a necessary condition of political obligation or as an ideal which should guide policy. If the former then a state which does not provide the required guarantee should be overthrown by revolution. In the latter case there should be consistent pressure for reform in the desired direction.

There are several objections to the non-conservative conception of political ends. In the first place the rights or the supreme political values they subserve are thoroughly indefinite and, therefore, endlessly contestable. Liberty, the ability to do what one wants to do, is, of course *prima facie*, a good. But freedoms conflict and which ones are to be endorsed? Should freedom of expression extend to sedition, slander, provocative utterance dangerous to public order? Justice is even more amorphous. Is it equality, whatever precisely that may be, or distribution according to needs or to desert, that is to say, for services rendered.

Conservatives would agree that there are political ends but they would maintain, first, that there are a considerable number of them. Besides the liberty and equality exalted by the two main kinds of reformer – liberal and socialist – they endorse security, both internal, the preservation of public order, and external, the defence of the community from enemies outside, and also prosperity, the general economic well-being of the community and its members. (Authoritarians make a fetish of security, free enterprise libertarians of prosperity.) For the conservative, none of these is supreme, in the sense that it wholly overrides all the others. But security is, to a certain extent, primary, as being a condition of the effective realisation of the others (as also, up to a point, is prosperity). Since there is an irreducible plurality of political values, none is an inalienable right, none should be pursued at the expense of all the rest.

Ends, then, are contestable and plural. This plurality raises the question of the extent to which changes designed to augment the realization of any one of them are likely to undermine the realization of the others. The experience of revolution suggests that they are extremely likely to do so. The French Revolution, directed to the enlargement of liberty and equality led, first, to the brutal but mercifully short-lived despotism of the Jacobin elite and then to the more efficient and more comprehensive despotism of Napoleon, with a brand new aristocracy of adventurers taking the place of that of the *ancien régime*. The Russian Revolution maximized the diametrical opposite of its intended ends; carrying exploitation to undreamed-of heights.

A conservative need not dispute the intellectual legitimacy of genuine political science which, unconcerned with ends as such, takes no one, prejudicially defined end as axiomatic. Its concern will be with the way in which political institutions actually work, the way they act on and are acted on by the rest of society, and it will be conscious of the variety and complexity of these interactions. It is more calculated to endorse Burke's recommendation of a cautious prudence than the excited elimination of the existing order of things.

Here too the conservative position can draw on abundant empirical support and not merely from massive revolutionary catastrophes like the collectivization of Russian agriculture under Stalin. The replacement of slums by tower blocks rather than their rehabilitation, the attempt to eliminate drunkenness by Prohibition in the United States, which as well as having the opposite effect, gave an enormous boost to organized crime, are bleak examples of localized totalitarianism.

Oakeshott has argued that the distinction between means and ends, taken for granted here, is not applicable to political activity, arguing that it is its own end, like friendship or recreational fishing. Skill here certainly does not require the study of Dale Carnegie-like manuals. But many successful and constructive politicians have been serious students of history in which the rational consideration of politics has largely been found until recent times. Even Oakeshott distinguishes, in effect, between political activity strictly so called, the business of government, and the preservation of conditions in which people can flourish by safely and freely going about their own affairs.

Organicism

The best argument for the view that human beings and the societies of which they are members are organically interrelated is empirical. There are cultures and, in particular, there are national cultures, typically if not quite universally, defined by language. (Where linguistic unity is missing its place can be supplied by a long and continuous history of nationhood, as in Switzerland. In other cases, such as Canada, there hardly is a national culture.) Another way of putting the point is to insist that there is such a thing as national character. People are not, in general, easily exportable like bicycles, which function just as well in Denmark as in Thailand. The pains of exile are deep-seated, not just a matter of missing certain familiar conveniences and objects of affection.

It is language that humanizes human beings, differentiates them from the rest of the primates, many of which use tools, live in societies, teach their young how to do things. But different languages are only within limits translatable. The way in which an adult immigrant comes to speak the language of his new home is different from that of the natives and carries echoes of his original social setting.

Nations differ from one another in the physical facts of environment and climate, in the balance of occupations within them, in the style of their family life, in type of religion, in degree of technological development. Their citizens differ in what, with varying amounts of illusion, they suppose the distinguishing characteristics of people of their nationality to be. The political and legal system, whatever detached outsiders may think of it, is part of this personality-forming social context, contributing to the settled desires and expectations of those who live under it. That does not mean it is incapable of improvement, only that ramifying and probably undesirable consequences will result from changing it suddenly and systematically. The fact of distinct national cultures as determining the human nature of their members explains both the complexity of any given society, since so many factors in the society have an influence, and the irreducible variousness of those cultures.

It follows that political and social science ought to be carried on in a comparative, not an abstractly generalizing, way. Nations need not be so unique as to defeat all generalization. There can be interesting truths about Colombia and Uruguay, but much less of interest is true about both Cambodia and Sweden.

A more direct empirical support for organicism is the failure of attempts to export the political institutions of advanced Western nations to other parts of the world. In the Victorian heyday of Eurocentrism, when liberals believed in the essential unity of mankind and the supreme excellence of liberal parliamentary democracy, that scheme of institutions was exported to Latin America and prepared for its twentieth-century transmission to Africa with both ludicrous and tragic results.

A feature of the last century has been a large-scale technological convergence of the world, so that every nation tries to take on as much of what may be called the material culture of the advanced Western nations as it can: large-scale mechanical industry, financial institutions, public utilities, scientific medicine, and so on. But this, as the case of Japan, the most brilliantly successful importer of Western technology, shows, does not imply the incorporation of the rest of the culture of the West. It may lead gently in that direction, but it does not automatically bring it about.

To consider society as an organism is implicitly to compare it to the human body. The parts of the latter cannot really flourish except in their places as parts of the whole. Conservatives would not, like metaphysical authoritarians of a Hegelian kind, press the analogy to the point of saying that the whole significance of the parts is exhausted by the functional service they give to the whole. In the social case it is the parts that are of primary importance even if they essentially require a social whole to be, or have been, part of. But conservatives would agree that where something is recognized to be wrong with the whole it is best to create conditions in which it can get better on its own, rather than to try to cure it by force. But in statecraft as in medical treatment, there are no absolutes; emergencies can arise in which drastic measures are inescapable (an invasion, a revolution, a large natural catastrophe in the political case). Emergencies, however, are, by definition, exceptional.

Implications: real and supposed

So far the discussion has been confined to the three rather general doctrines, which have been picked out as central to conservatism. But there are a number of associated doctrines of a more substantive nature which have been closely associated with historical conservatism to such an extent that they have some claim to be essentially constituents of it. The main purpose of this section will be to consider whether such claims are correct, whether these associated doctrines are really implied by the central ones.

Religion

Religion occupies a large place in the greater part of conservative writing: in Hooker, Coleridge and in the French and German conservative thinkers of the early nineteenth century. Burke's references to the divinely ordained character of the state play little part in his essential argument, but are not merely rhetorical; they express his sincere religious faith.

In general terms conservatives have seen the church as an indispensable support to the state in ensuring social order and stability. They have favoured an established church in some shape or form, indeed, in the cases of Hooker and Coleridge, they have seen it as an aspect of the state, even as identical with it, being the state itself considered from a particular point of view.

For better or worse it is hard not to see this as an anachronism. Two sorts of religious division have taken place which have to be taken into account. One is between adherents of the established church and other sects: dissenters and Catholics in Britain, for example. The second is between Christians and non-Christians or, going even further, between believers and those with no religious belief.

The hard political core of establishment is the relegation of those outside it to an inferior form of citizenship, in which only restricted civil rights are enjoyed, of, say, occupation or residence, and the rights to vote and to hold public office are withheld. Tolerance and, in a broad sense, enfranchisement of those outside the established church has been a long and consequently gradual process, usually fiercely resisted by conservatives at every step. It has been accompanied by a steady attenuation of the social functions of the church in education and social welfare. In the contemporary world churches are voluntary societies, of which an individual may attach himself to any or to none.

Although there were conservatives in the past without much or any religious faith – Halifax, Bolingbroke, Hume, probably Disraeli – they still supported the view that there should be an established church. But with the historic transformation of religion it is entirely consistent for a conservative to adjust to changes he would, at the time, have opposed, as Burke absorbed the reduction of royal power brought about by the minimally revolutionary revolution of 1688. Today, to the extent that it is politically active, the church is dominated by left-wing dissidence.

Property and the family

Conservative parties certainly represent the interests of substantial property owners. But, unlike right-wing liberals, individualists and libertarians, conservatives do not follow Locke in taking the right to property to be absolute and indefeasible. Their ideal of property-ownership is agricultural, even feudal. Property is a trust rather than a matter of absolute right of use and disposal. Its possession carries with it responsibilities as well as rights. That is the theme of much past conservative criticism of industrialization and of unfettered free enterprise. Furthermore, property is defended and protected by the state, so the state must be allowed to tax it to pursue the indispensable social purposes it serves. Convinced that public security, from enemies outside or inside, is the prime object of state action, they favour a strong and, therefore, adequately supported state.

Conservatives cannot easily accommodate themselves to the idea of a true proletariat, a class without significant property that makes up the greater part of the population. They see it as the unhappy by-product of generally enriching economic changes. In the nineteenth century, it is worth noticing, it was conservatives like Shaftesbury and Disraeli who worked for the relief of distress and the improvement of conditions at work and in the home.

The positive virtue of widely diffused property is that it enhances independence and self-reliance. The indiscriminate and bureaucratically wasteful distribution of welfare doles, by contrast, encourages passivity and inertness.

Property, furthermore, strengthens the family by increasing its ability to fend for itself and, through the institution of inheritance, by linking its generations through time. If any society is natural it is the family, and conservatives regard its increasing fragility and loss of functions with deep suspicion. There is no plausible alternative to it as the primary means by which children are turned into truly social beings. It is, generally, a socially stabilizing institution. Both property and the family are continuing arrangements which develop in their owners and members a sense of the community as something historically extended and persisting, not a bare arena for the pursuit of immediate satisfaction.

The nation and imperialism

For conservatives the primary object of political loyalty is the nation and not, as for the liberal, mankind in the abstract, or for the socialist, a particular class (theoretically in every country). Both of the other two ideologies are internationalist, at any rate in principle. So far the conservative is a nationalist. He sees it as the chief task of government to pursue the national interest, by, particularly, warding off attack from outside and seeking its prosperity. It was consistent for Victorian conservatives in Britain to support protectionism and is consistent today for many conservatives to be hostile to large-scale Europeanization.

But conservative nationalism is not aggressive. First, it is not essentially imperialistic, even if the Victorian enlargement of the British Empire was supported by conservatives and resisted by liberal adherents of Little England. The original eighteenth-century British Empire was a Whig invention and was deplored by Bolingbroke. Going back further, Cromwell was the chief British empire-builder of earlier times. But once, by whatever means, an empire has been acquired, where its members are of quite different nationality and culture, conservatives would aim to govern them with their own laws and in the light of their own customs.

Secondly, it is not interfering. It is no part of the proper business of one state to improve the conduct of another. Only in defence of a clear national interest is it a responsible act for a government to become involved with the internal conflicts of another nation or with conflicts between other nations.

Law and the constitution

Law for the conservative is the politically authorized part of custom and custom, as an historical accumulation, deserves our respect. The alternative to the rule of law is discretionary rule and to that he is inevitably opposed. As developed and amended through time, properly applied laws are the outcome of manifold adjustments and on that account to be preferred to the sudden decisions of a single ruler or a small group. Their persistence also ensures that they will have entered into the formation of those affected by them, if only as creating expectations whose disappointment will be upsetting. Just as law is generally to be preferred to discretion, so new legislation should not be so copious as to overwhelm the law as already established.

Of all parts of law the constitution, the law that determines what is the making of a law, is that which should be changed least often and least rapidly. British conservatives, because there is no written British constitution, oppose such a thing, where Americans, with the opposite historical experience, revere it. From a generally conservative point of view, both are right. The British have the monarch in parliament, the Americans have their written constitution. A conservative would reject the idea of either exchanging constitutional arrangements with the other.

Liberty, equality and democracy

Conservatism does not take any single political ideal, value or alleged 'natural right' to be supreme and to override all the others, although it accords a certain primacy to security, whose preservation it regards as the main task of government.

It does not concern itself with liberty in general or liberty in the abstract. But it does uphold traditional, customary, established liberties. It is opposed to the according of absolute power to government and therefore endorses the preservation of a large area for the private activities of individuals and of the non-governmental associations or institutions in which they are involved. It is unimpressed with the credentials as lovers of liberty of those professed liberals who wish to prevent buying a drink from anyone prepared to sell you one, smoking in public places or the reading by children of *Little Black Sambo*.

Conservatism does not identify equality with justice and, in view of the massive and massively varied differences between people, does not admit any initial presumption in favour of equality of condition. Justice, for the conservative, is, in the first instance, procedural, the impartial application of the law. Substantively, justice is a matter of guaranteeing the enjoyment of customary and established rights. It may often be reasonable and proper to extend the enjoyment of certain rights from some people to others, but that is not to say that such extensions are requirements of justice.

Democracy, as embodying a particular form of equality, is thus not seen as a good in itself. But representative parliamentary institutions, continuously developed in parallel with the political maturity of the population, is, in advanced Western societies, an historically established mode of proceeding and, therefore, worthy of preservation. That does not make it a universal political panacea, as the melancholy history of almost universal lip-service to it makes clear.

Criticisms

A mask for self-interest

Because conservative doctrine has usually been embedded in detailed polemical responses to particular situations and has no recognized or authoritative general formulation, criticism of it has been spasmodic and, perhaps understandably, superficial. Even where conservative doctrine is identified and tackled directly, its purported refutation serves as a preliminary for the more agreeable business of unmasking the interests in preserving the status quo which, it is held, really determine its adoption.

All ideologies lend themselves to some particular interest, but it is unrealistic to suppose that they are no more than a discreet camouflage behind which the bearers of those interests can self-deceivingly cover their selfishness. It is certainly not a unique feature of conservatism to answer pre-eminently to a particular interest. If conservatism appeals to those who want to hold on to what they have got, socialism appeals to those who want to deprive them of it by force of law, liberal individualism to those who want to acquire it by unrestricted competition.

It is obviously the case that not all support of ideologies is provided by those whose interests would be conspicuously served by the realization of their ideals or policies. Many with inherited and with earned wealth are socialists. Many more who are without significant property are conservatives. It may be argued that that is because of 'false consciousness', because, in the case of the working-class conservatives, they are deluded about their real interests. It is not clear that the impoverishment of the rich will actually enrich the poor. But, in any case, there is nothing irrational or deluded about having other interests than strictly economic ones.

Against traditionalists

There are two main lines of argument against traditionalism. The first is that it is so vague that it is hardly possible to disagree with and that consequently it does not have any substantial content. The conservative is not opposed to change as such and absolutely, but rather to large and sudden or violent change. But how great does a change have to be to be unacceptably large? Again, conservatives admit that large political changes may be needed to cope with large changes of social or natural circumstances. The same vagueness, it may be argued, is present here.

This is an objection which conservatives should meet by agreeing with it, rather than seeking to rebut it. The vagueness complained of, the conservative could reply, is inevitable, the future course of events cannot be predicted and so cannot be prepared for in specific and detailed terms. The conservative response to novelty must be a matter of judgement, based on experience, not a business of the application of a set of rigid principles.

The critic could argue further that circumstantial changes, for the most part the outcome of technological progress, have very greatly increased in magnitude in recent times, as shown by huge increases in population, in the destructiveness of weapons, in damaging pressure on resources and the natural environment. This is harder for the conservative to deal with, suggesting as it does the anachronistic character of inherited political wisdom. But he could reply that the conservative method of dealing with change, by continuous, gradual steps, is better than confronting it with vast speculative schemes.

The other main argument against conservative traditionalism is that it is inconsistent since it now endorses political and legal arrangements which it strenuously resisted when they were first proposed – the emancipation of Catholics and Jews, the enlargement of the franchise to the unpropertied and women, the reduction of the monarchy to a merely ceremonial status and the political marginalization of the House of Lords, to take only British examples.

The conservative could reply that there is no inconsistency, the high social cost of absorbing these political innovations, which would not have been called for if they had been introduced more gradually, has now been paid. They are now themselves a part of the customary, established political fabric. But one may wonder if they would ever have come about at all if they had not been forced through against conservative opposition.

Against scepticism

The political scepticism of the conservative is in conflict with the whole tradition of the philosophical theory of knowledge as it has developed since Descartes first brought that discipline into the central position in philosophical studies. Cartesian rationalism regards knowledge as an individual acquisition, in which logic is applied, in a conscious and explicit fashion, to the deliverances of personal, indeed usually private, experience. The social aspect of knowledge is fleetingly acknowledged in casual references to testimony as a source of knowledge, ignoring the fact that most of any individual person's knowledge is derived from others.

Cartesian theorists of knowledge would admit that their picture of the growth of individual knowledge as an explicit, conscious operation is an idealized one. But they would hold that the idealization is an innocent one since, even if incorrect as an account of the way in which beliefs are actually formed, it makes clear what has to be provided for a belief if it is to be justified.

The conservative view of political knowledge as experienced judgement rather than abstract theory denies both the need for and the possibility of explicit, inferential justification of the beliefs involved in it. That does not mean they are just 'intuitions', that is to say a sort of inarticulate guesswork. There is an alternative theory of unreasoned, but not unreasonable, belief to be found in Pascal's *ésprit de finesse*, in Newman's 'illative sense' and, in a less rarefied form, in Ryle's doctrine of the priority of knowing-how to knowing-that.

The natural objection to make to political scepticism about conscious and explicit reason is that, fallible as it may be, it is all we really have, if we are not to fall back on guesses, hunches and prejudices. But to say that is to ignore both the social and the primarily implicit nature of practical knowledge. The conservative would argue that far from being undermined by Cartesian epistemology, his doctrine supplies one of many bodies of evidence against it.

Against organicism

A good deal of intellectual energy has been directed against the metaphysical, Hegelian version of the organic principle that human beings derive their characteristically human properties, their language, culture and critical rationality, for example, from their interaction with the other human beings who make up the society in which they have grown to maturity. In that overweening form organicism is presented as a logical necessity, the conception of a solitary but fully human individual as a self-contradiction. The extravagance of this has tended to cast doubt on the more reasonable contention that organicism is a pervasive fact about human life, like gravity in nature.

A substantial specific objection to the version of organicism required by the conservative is that although human beings are indeed formed by society or, more accurately, the great variety of distinct social relationships into which they enter, that does not prove any special dependence on the state. Family, school, local community, working group are far more influential.

The objection clearly had some force, although less in the modern world of nation-states than it once had, since nations are real cultural unities, not just administrative contraptions. In modern circumstances, then, the state is one of the major formative, humanizing influences. But the point at issue is the complexity of the web of social relations in which human beings are accustomed to live. It is not the primacy of the state which the conservative relies on organicism to establish, but the liability of state action to have harmful effects on the whole social system when it pursues some end that is in itself expectably beneficial.

Anther criticism is that the organic view implicitly denies creative originality to individuals by seeing their nature and achievements as social products. Wherever there is progress there is creativity emerging from a background of tradition. The scientist is not a pure virtuoso, but science stagnates without virtuosi. The same principle informs Western, although not Eastern, art. The crucial distinguishing feature between politics and those other domains of human activity is that revolutionary innovations do no harm in the latter. In science, as Popper has said, we let our theories die for us. Social experiments tend to kill human beings. Some large historical figures – 'great heroes' – look like artists whose raw material is human beings, but no conservative would wish to be one or be ruled by one.

Idealogies of the non-conservative right

Authoritarianism

Authoritarianism is the modern version of absolutism, the operating ideology of most governments in the history of the world, and, in particular, of European monarchies between the seventeenth and nineteenth centuries. The underlying support of the old absolutism was the doctrine of the divine right of kings. In its more legalistic version that doctrine was legitimist, insisting on rights of royal inheritance, literally interpreted, as with the Jacobite adherents of the Stuart house in Britain and the partisans of the Bourbons in France. In a more practical version the mark of divine authorization is power. Embellished with the contractual apparatus that was the prevailing explanatory convention of its age, Hobbes' *Leviathan* argues for the rationality of submission to a ruler, whose authority lasts as long as his power to enforce it and his power to protect his subjects from one another. The fact that the first of these powers does not have to be conjoined with the power, or, at any rate, the willingness, to maintain the subjects' security is one he fails to confront adequately.

In the modern world authoritarianism usually, as was said earlier, taking the form of military dictatorship, does not go in for the development of articulated ideology. The leader's speeches, largely composed of patriotic rhetoric, are likely to be all that is available. In general, authoritarianism defends itself negatively, as a responsible alternative to the inefficiency and corruption of parliamentary democracy. In the countries where it has prevailed that charge has often been of considerable force.

The military dictatorships of the 1930s were not, for the most part, even allied with the fascists and those of Pilsudski in Poland and Metaxas in Greece fought bravely against Hitler. Franco worked with the fascists of Spain during the civil war, but subsequently discarded them.

Authoritarianism gives the highest place among political values to security: Hobbes' first 'law of nature' was to seek peace. It is an understandable response to circumstances in which security is seriously menaced, whether from outside or from within.

Fascism

Fascism is the youngest of ideologies and of ideologies that have had large political consequences it is the most intellectually inarticulate. It has nothing to offer on the scale of Bossuet's or Hobbes' political writings. It combines an intense nationalism, which is both militarily aggressive and resolved to subdue all aspects of public and private life, to the pursuit of national greatness. It asserts that a supreme leader is indispensable, a heroic figure in whom the national spirit is incarnated. It seeks to organize society along military lines, conceiving war as the fullest expression of the national will as brought to consciousness in the leader. It sees the nation not primarily as a cultural entity, defined by a common language, traditional customs, perhaps a shared religion, a history of heroes and great events, but also in questionably biological terms.

It was anticipated in some details by Fichte's nationalism and emphasis on the will, by Carlyle's doctrine of heroes and by Nietzsche's idea of the superman (an idea which had no political implication for Nietzsche, who was neither a nationalist nor a racist). It began in a comparatively trashy, theatrical way with Mussolini in Italy, but achieved its fullest development with Hitler. His atrocities have excluded it from any serious consideration except of a pathological nature.

Where authoritarianism is primarily defensive, fascism is aggressive and militant. Authoritarianism does not seek to mobilize the community and to exercise total control over every aspect of human life; fascism is totalitarian without qualification. Both see the mass of the population as incapable of contributing to the state except through obedience, and fascism calls for active, self-sacrificing obedience. Fascism has no theory as to how leaders should be selected or how leadership should be transferred from one leader to another. Leaders are presumably to emerge as victors in the struggle for power within the ruling party.

In less ferocious hands than Hitler's, such as those of Mosley, it is a kind of elitism of the resolute, taken to be made necessary by the weakness of will of the public in general, including democratic politicians. It makes little appeal to personal self-interest, except to the extent that the political strength of the nation enhances its economic vigour. It attracts those ready to submerge their individuality in the fact of their being members of a particular nation. The organicist doctrine can be called on to justify that submersion when it is taken, as it is not by conservatives, to imply that the whole *raison d'être* of the individual is the service of the state, in the way that the function of a particular organ is to contribute to the well-being of the body of which it is a part.

Elitism

The elitism of Plato's *Republic* is strictly intellectual. The rulers should be the most intelligent, who will become the wisest if given the right kind of education. The idea that the wisest should rule has an obvious attraction. If there is to be government at all, there must be a ruling minority which makes laws and determines policy, and a ruled majority which obeys it.

A version of this point of view of some elaboration is to be found in Fitzjames Stephen's *Liberty, Equality and Fraternity*, his polemic reply to Mill in which he sets out a kind of administrative elitism, nourished by his experiences as a judge in India, on a utilitarian basis, as best calculated to satisfy the more deep-rooted desires, or, at any rate, to meet the serious needs, of the public at large.

It is encumbered with two main difficulties. One is theoretical, that of deciding what wisdom, the wisdom required of rulers, actually is. The other is practical, that of identifying its possessors and installing them in positions of power. The institution of the Chinese mandarinate supplies an answer, of sorts, to both questions. Wisdom is what is revealed by doing well in examinations. Government posts are open only to those who have done well. Nineteenth-century reforms in the mode of recruitment of the British civil service, where examinations selected those prepared in Jowett's Oxford, created a form of mandarinate operating in association with a hereditary aristocracy and an elected chamber. The graduates of the *grandes écoles*, particularly the Ecole Nationale d'Administration, in France form a comparable group of, partially, ruling experts.

The most notable writings in this century about the rule of an elite are sociological rather than explicitly ideological. Pareto, Mosca and Michels all subscribed to the 'iron law of oligarchy' proclaimed by the last named, which holds that every organization must develop a ruling elite. All, particularly Pareto, convinced of the limited political rationality of the bulk of the public, examined the techniques of deception by means of which elites preserve themselves in power. Those who suppose elites to be inevitable might be expected to address the question of what constitutes a good one and the associated question of how to secure it.

There is an implicitly prescriptive element in what has been called Schumpeter's theory of 'democratic elitism'. Ostensibly he offers an account of the actual workings of representative democracy. It is not a device for the expression and realization of any kind of general will. It is rather a competition between different groups in the politically active minority to secure the permission of the voting public to run the government. In holding direct democracy in the manner of Rousseau to be impossible, he is really saying that it would lead to intolerable results. In democracy as he sees it, the public's influence on the process of government is tailored to their capacity to contribute to it.

Each of these three non-conservative right-wing ideologies differs from conservatism in its own way. Authoritarianism endorses unlimited government, free from constitutional restraint and attaching no great importance to the rule of law. Fascism is a revolutionary creed, taking what conservatism regards as crisis to be the healthiest condition of the state. Elitism is rationalistic and locates political wisdom in the intelligent living rather than their experienced ancestors. What all have in common is a higher valuation of security than any of the ideologies to the left of them.

See also 3 HISTORY; 8 ANARCHISM; 15 COMMUNITY; 17 CONSTITUTIONALISM AND THE RULE OF LAW; 19 DEMOCRACY; 31 PROPERTY; 34 SECESSION AND NATIONALISM; 36 STATE; 37 TOLERATION AND FUNDAMENTALISM; 38 TOTALITARIANISM; 39 TRUST; 40 VIRTUE

References

Aquinas, St T.: *De Regimine Principium*, trans. G. B. Phelan, *On Kingship, to the King of Cyprus* (Toronto: Pontifical Institute of Medieval Studies, 1949).

Aristotle: *Politics*, trans. Ernest Barker (Oxford: Clarendon Press, 1946).

Bagehot, W.: *Physics and Politics* (London: H. S. King, 1872).

Barrès, M.: *Le Roman de l'énergie nationale* (Paris: Bibliothèque-Charpentier, 1897–1911).

Bodin, J.: *Six Books of the Commonwealth*, trans. M. J. Tooley (Oxford: Blackwell, 1953).

Bolingbroke, H. St J. (Viscount Bolingbroke): *Works*, ed. D. Mallett (London, 1754); (Hildesheim: G. Olma, 1968).

Bonald, L. G. A. (Vicomte de): *Théorie de pouvoir politique et religieux* (1796); (Paris: Bloud et Barral, 1988).

Bossuet, J.-B.: *Politique tirée des propres paroles de l'écriture sainte* (1709), ed. J. le Brun (Genève: Librairie Dioz, 1967).

Calhoun, J. C.: *A Disquisition on Government* (1853), ed. R. K. Cralle (New York: P. Smith, 1943).

Carlyle, T.: *On Heroes, Hero-worship and the Heroic in History* (London: Chapman, 1840).

Cecil, H.: *Conservatism* (London: Williams & Norgate, 1912).

Cicero: *De Republica*, trans. G. H. Sabine and S. B. Smith (Columbus, Ohio: Merrill, 1929).

Clarendon, E. (Earl of): *A Brief View of Leviathan* (Oxford: The Theatre, 1676).

Coleridge, S. T.: *On the Constitution of Church and State*, ed. J. Colmer (London: Routledge & Kegan Paul, 1976).

Disraeli, B.: 'Vindication of the English constitution', in *Of Whigs and Whiggism*, ed. W. Hutcheon (London: J. Murray, 1913).

Fichte, J. G.: *Reden an die deutsche Nation; Addresses to the German Nation*, trans. R. F. Jones and G. H. Turnbull (Chicago: Open Court, 1922).

Halifax, G. S. (Marquis of): *Works*, ed. Walter Raleigh (Oxford: Clarendon Press, 1912).

Hamilton, A., Madison, J. and Jay, J.: *The Federalist* (1787–8), ed. J. E. Cooke (Middletown, Conn.: Wesleyan University Press, 1961).

Hayek, F. A.: *The Constitution of Liberty* (London: Routledge & Kegan Paul, 1960).

Herder, J. G.: *Ideen zur philosophie der Geschichte der Menschheit* (1800), trans. F. E. Manuel, *Reflections on the Philosophy of the History of Man* (Chicago: University of Chicago Press, 1988).

Hitler, A.: *Mein Kampf* (1933), trans. and ed. R. Manheim (London: Hutchinson, 1972).

Hobbes, T.: *Leviathan* (1651), ed. R. Tuck (Cambridge: Cambridge University Press, 1991).

Hogg, Q. (Lord Hailsham): *The Conservative Case* (Harmondsworth: Penguin Books, 1948).

Hooker, R.: *The Laws of Ecclesiastical Polity* (1593–7), ed. A. S. McGrade (Cambridge: Cambridge University Press, 1989).

Hume, D.: *Treatise of Human Nature* (London: John Noon, 1739).

————: *Essays: Moral, Political and Literary* (1777), ed. E. F. Miller (Indianapolis, Ind.: Liberty Classics, 1985).

Johnson, S.: *Works*, ed. A. Murphy (London: F. C. & J. Rivington, 1823).

Maistre, J. M. (Comte de): *Works*, ed. J. Lively (London: Allen & Unwin, 1965).

Maurras, C.: *Enquête sur la monarchie* (1900), 2nd edn (Paris: Nouvelle Librairie Nationale, 1924).

Michels, R.: *Political Parties*, trans. E. and C. Paul (Glencoe, Ill.: Free Press, 1949).

Montesquieu, C.-L. de S.: *The Spirit of the Laws*, ed. F. Neumann, trans. T. Nugent (New York: Hafner, 1949).

Mosca, G.: *The Ruling Class*, ed. A. Livingstone, trans. H. D. Kahn (New York: McGraw-Hill, 1939).

Mosley, O.: *The Greater Britain* (London: British Union of Fascists, 1932).

Müller, A. H. R. v. N.: *Die Elemente der Staatskunst* (1809); (Wien: Wiener Literarische Anstalt, 1922).

Newman, J. H.: 'Appendix', *Apologia Pro Vita Sua* (1864), ed. D. J. DeLaura (New York: Norton, 1968).

————: *A Grammar of Assent*, ed. T. I. Ker (Oxford: Clarendon Press, 1985).

Nietzsche, F. W.: *Beyond Good and Evil*, trans. R. J. Hollingdale (Harmondsworth: Penguin, 1973).

————: *The Genealogy of Morals*, trans. W. Kaufman (New York: Random House, 1989).

Oakeshott, M.: *Rationalism in Politics* (London: Methuen, 1962).

Pareto, V.: *The Mind and Society*, ed. A. Livingstone, trans. A. Bongiorno and A. Livingstone (London: Cape, 1935).

Pascal, B.: *De l'espirit géométrique*, in *Oeuvres Complètes*, ed. J. Chevalier (Paris: Gallimard, 1954).

Plato: *Republic*, trans. A. D. Lindsay (London: Dent, 1939).

Popper, K. R.: *The Open Society and Its Enemies* (London: Routledge & Kegan Paul, 1945).

Renan, E.: *La Réforme intellectuelle et morale* (1871), ed. P. E. Charvet (Cambridge: Cambridge University Press, 1950).

Ryle, G.: *The Concept of Mind* (London: Hutchinson, 1949).

Salisbury, R. A. T. G.-C. (Marquess of): *Lord Salisbury on Politics*, ed. P. Smith (Cambridge: Cambridge University Press, 1972).

Schumpeter, J. A.: *Capitalism, Socialism and Democracy*, 3rd edn (New York: Harper & Row, 1950).

Stephen, J. F.: *Liberty, Equality and Fraternity* (London: Smith, Elder, 1873).

Taine, H.: *Les Origines de la France contemporaine* (1876–85); (Paris: Hachette, 1947).

Tocqueville, A. de: *Democracy in America* (1835), trans. G. Lawrence, ed. J. P. Mayer and M. Lerner (New York: Harper, 1966).

Treitschke, H. von: *Politics*, trans. B. Dugdale and T. de Bille (London: Constable, 1916).

Further reading

Allison, L.: *Right Principles* (Oxford: Blackwell, 1984).

Aris, R.: *History of Political Thought in Germany 1789–1815* (London: Allen & Unwin, 1936).

Covell, C.: *The Redefinition of Conservatism* (New York: St Martin's, 1986).

Cowling, M., ed.: *Conservative Essays* (London: Cassell, 1978).

Gilmour, I.: *Inside Right* (London: Hutchinson, 1977).

Hearnshaw, F. J. C.: *Conservatism in England* (London: Macmillan, 1933).

Honderich, T.: *Conservatism* (London: H. Hamilton, 1990).

Huntington, S. P.: 'Conservatism as an ideology', *American Political Science Review*, 51 (1957), 454–73.

Kirk, R.: *The Conservative Mind* (London: Faber, 1954).

Mannheim, K.: 'Conservative thought', in *Essays in Sociology and Social Psychology*, ed. P. Kecskemeti (London: Routledge & Kegan Paul, 1953).

O'Sullivan, N.: *Conservatism* (New York: St Martin's, 1976).

Quinton, A.: *The Politics of Imperfection* (London: Faber & Faber, 1978).

Santayana, G.: *Dominations and Powers* (London: Constable, 1951).

Scruton, R.: *The Meaning of Conservatism* (London: Macmillan, 1980; 2nd edn, 1984).

Soltau, R. H.: *French Political Thought in the Nineteenth Century* (London: E. Benn, 1935).

Viereck, R. E.: *Conservatism* (Princeton, NJ: D. van Nostrand, 1956).

Weiss, J.: *Conservatism in Europe, 1770–1945* (London: Thames & Hudson, 1977).

IO

Feminism

JANE MANSBRIDGE AND SUSAN MOLLER OKIN

Feminism as a political movement

Feminism is a political stance more than a systematic theory. Political life forms its base; its goal is to change the world. Like Marxism, or any other movement aimed at political change, its thought is inextricably mingled with action. Unlike Marxism, an ideology initiated by a single man, feminism is essentially plural. It is thought derived implicitly from the experience of every woman who has resisted or tried to resist domination.

Three points follow. First, feminism privileges experience. A direct report of the way one perceives one's own experience has great weight with feminists trying to make sense of their world. Much of feminist theory is thus inductive, proceeding from the particular to the general. Second, feminism is not easily systematized. Its experiential plurality, proceeding from different experiences differently perceived, constantly undoes attempts to derive a full theory from a single point, or make all pieces fit a coherent whole. Finally, feminism makes the personal political. Real experiences of gender domination cut across the formal lines that divide the public from the private sphere. They require for their explanation a political theory that assumes the interpenetration of these spheres.

Throughout its plurality, feminism has one obvious, simple and overarching goal – to end men's systematic domination of women. Feminist theory also has one overarching goal – to understand, explain and challenge that domination, in order to help end it. As feminist theorists carry out this project, their conclusions often illuminate political philosophy more broadly. The central ideas of great Western thinkers appear differently after feminist critiques. Familiar political concepts take on new or additional meanings in the light of women's experiences. Feminist theories, based on women's experiences, support a different, or differently nuanced, view of the relation of self and other from those traditionally central in Western philosophy. Women's experiences of sexual violation bring power and the effects of system-wide domination into the most private aspects of interpersonal relations.

Differences among feminist theorists stem both from intellectual differences in interpretation and from differences in experience. An early classification scheme in the United States divided feminists into 'liberal feminists', 'radical feminists', 'Marxist feminists' and 'socialist feminists' (Jaggar, 1983), in a way that accurately demarcated important lines of intellectual difference but also indicated the intellectual and experiential milieux from which those feminists usually had come. In the same

269

way, different experiences and intellectual milieux have produced 'cultural feminism' (usually used pejoratively, e.g. Echols, 1989), 'French psychoanalytic feminism' (e.g. Irigaray, [1977] 1985), 'lesbian ethics' (e.g. Hoagland, 1988), 'eco-feminism' (e.g. Diamond and Orenstein, 1990) and 'black feminism' (e.g. Collins, 1990) or, in Alice Walker's (1983) term, 'womanism'. Other experiences will undoubtedly produce other forms, particularly as women in countries with traditions different from those in the West develop their own theoretical understandings.

In the United States it has been hard for white feminists to recognize that the experiences they had categorized simply as 'women's' experiences were shot through with assumptions that did not apply to the experiences of many women of colour. The differences in experience were often so stark that hearing experiences antithetical to their own described simply as 'women's' felt to many black women and others like an active act of exclusion. But many feminists who are not white or middle-class have now won a significant space in the public dialogue. And many white feminists who still dominate that dialogue are beginning the process of understanding and assimilation required to do some justice to a perspective not fully their own. Questions of policy continue to divide feminists, over both ends and means. In the United States, although feminists presented a relatively united front during the suffrage struggle, afterwards they divided on whether or not to support an Equal Rights Amendment, which would have eliminated many of the special protections for women that the Left had achieved in part as a substitute for the more far-reaching protections European labour had been able to secure for both men and women workers. They divided on whether or not to support the prohibition of alcohol, which many correctly saw as a major cause of wife and child battering. They divided on whether or not to support world peace by advocating disarmament and draft resistance.

In the 'second wave' of the women's movement in the United States, the movement divided on tactics (whether to focus on the Equal Rights Amendment or other issues, whether to work through government or direct action, whether to work with men or without them, whether or not one could commit oneself to women's causes while engaging in a heterosexual relationship) and on the analysis of root causes (class or race versus sexual oppression). More recent divisions have pitted opponents of pornography against those who make free speech an absolute right, and proponents of special protections for women against the proponents of formal equality. In the academy, postmodern feminists stress differences between women and the unsettled, relative quality of all thought, while others stress concurrences in women's experiences and the need for some relatively settled understandings of rights or justice in order to better the conditions of women. In the Near East and Africa, feminists divide on opposition to specific practices, such as clitoral excision and infibulation, or the veil. Muslim feminists divide on whether or not some aspects of their religion support feminist principles. In Latin American (and some African) countries marked by 'motherist' resistances to militarism, feminists divide on whether or not women can bring purity into political life through their essence or experience as mothers. In developing nations, feminists divide on whether to stress 'strategic' gender interests, which explicitly try to change the relations between the sexes (for example, by creating all-women police stations for reporting violence to women), or 'immediate' gender interests, in which women organize as women to get goods in a way that does not directly challenge gender relations (for example, organizing as women to get water for a village). In countries where the state is military and not benign (such as Brazil, Argentina and Turkey have been), feminists divided on the advisability of working with the state to achieve their ends. In many countries, women and women's groups are divided by religion, ethnicity, political affiliation, allegiance to a particular leader or organization, social class and structural position (Nelson and Chowdhury, 1993; see also Mohanty, Russo and Torres, 1991).

Georg Simmel ([1908] 1955) once observed that similarity often generates hostility, thus provoking in any large-scale movement the tendency to split into warring sects. This tendency seems less exacerbated within the feminist movement than within most past progressive movements, perhaps because of the weight feminists give to voices speaking from their own experience. Because many advances in feminist thought have come from women collectively talking with one another and trying to make sense of their experiences, differences in those experiences are somewhat more likely than in other movements to be taken as food for thought rather than as attacks on a tightly held previous position. Some of the best feminist research on anti-feminism proceeds from a genuine desire to understand the anti-feminists' own perspective as women (e.g. Luker, 1978). In the United States today, affiliating with 'feminism' is almost as respectable as affiliating with either of the mainstream political parties. In a 1989 survey representing the population of the United States, almost one-third of the women responded affirmatively to the question, 'Do you consider yourself a feminist?' Only slightly more responded affirmatively to the question, 'Do you consider yourself a Republican?' or to the question, 'Do you consider yourself a Democrat?' (Mansbridge and Tate, 1992). This political situation requires a broad definition of feminism, bounded by the single goal of equality between men and women. The meaning of feminism in political philosophy is almost as broad.

Feminist critiques of the canon

Three central questions drive feminist social science and political philosophy: 'How did male domination arise?' 'Why was it so widely accepted?' and 'What are its consequences?' How, until recently, have men managed with a semblance of legitimacy to exclude women from formal politics in almost every tribe, state and civilization on the globe? And what are the current implications of this history for women, for human relations, for philosophy and for politics?

The collective understandings that justified the universal exclusion of women from politics – with occasional exceptions, as for orderly succession in a ruling family – must have been extraordinarily powerful. Not yet recognized in all their force, they continue to work unperceived on our ways of interpreting reality, particularly political reality. Because no one can think without incorporating some of these understandings, it is a major task of feminist political philosophy to uncover and open them to conscious, public scrutiny.

A few examples from the feminist critique suggest the extent to which recognizing the assumptions about gender of major Western political thinkers sets in relief the foundations of their thought, clarifying the problematically close connections between that which is liberatory and that which is harmful today for women and for men.

Take the moment that launched political philosophy as a separate branch of Western philosophy, when Aristotle enshrined the *polis* as the most sovereign, final and perfect of associations, directed to the most sovereign good, a good life. This moment coincided with and depended on his definition of the household as 'other'. The subsequent enterprise of political philosophy, which looked to the 'political' for the culmination of human development, continued to define the political in explicit contradistinction to the realm of women. An understanding of the 'political' as both 'supreme good' and 'not-household/not-woman' continued to undermine women's contributions to political thought long after most people rejected Aristotle's conclusion that women were naturally inferior to men.

Take the famous sentence that introduces Rousseau's *The Social Contract*: 'Man is born free, but everywhere he is in chains.' Women's experience, expressed in feminist thought, makes that sentence seem presumptuous nonsense. Human beings are born to mothers and fathers who are not morally free to abandon them (as Rousseau did his children) any more than the children are physically free to live on their own. Some chains are there, for both parties, at birth.

Take Rousseau's enduring goal, which feminists have reworked to mean that with and through others people should, as they grow, begin to give to themselves the laws that bind them. To realize this goal, feminists can borrow carefully from Rousseau's ideas on development and his own hated experience with submission, but must attend even more carefully to the way his 'will' is often intertwined with power. In *Emile*, the first text in progressive education and the book that would launch the Romantic Movement, Rousseau educated young Emile to natural honesty, an uncorrupt appreciation of natural virtue, and a capacity to give the law to himself. He educated young Sophie to be Emile's wife, that is, to obey. Rousseau, the egalitarian radical, argued in this pre-romantic text for the relatively new idea that sex ought to require the woman's 'consent'. How should the powerful determine this consent? Sophie should be taught, when she means 'yes', to say a modest 'no', and Emile taught to read not her words but her body movements for her answer. On the grounds that nature gave women enough strength to resist whenever it pleased them to do so, Rousseau concluded that in the ordinary case no 'real' rape was possible. As elsewhere in his philosophy he considered explicit consent less important than the underlying 'will', which in this case men, not the women themselves, would interpret (see Pateman, 1989).

Take again Rousseau's appealing strictures on the falseness of court and salon. These, we now see, were aimed particularly at women. His words stripped legitimacy from the women who, barred from any formal political role, had come by force of intellect, political skill and birth to influence public thought and action in Paris and Versailles. In their place the Rousseauian post-revolutionary 'Republican mother' stayed at home to prepare her sons for republican virtue rather than contaminating the public stage. The faction and intrigue that Rousseau deplored (so much as to suggest that collective decisions would be better if citizens had no communication with one another) seems to have had a distinctly gendered cast (Landes, 1988; Manin, 1987).

Take Kant's contribution to moral theory that only duty, based on reason, has 'true moral worth'. We now see that idea underpinned by a misogyny that facilitated the elision of the dichotomies 'reason/emotion' and 'male/female' (and implicitly 'public/private'). Kant contended that although many minds are 'so sympathetically constituted that . . . they find pleasure in spreading joy around them', their actions, while amiable, proper, and deserving of 'praise and encouragement', do not deserve 'esteem' ([1785] 1949, pp. 15–16). Women, he had decided earlier, 'will avoid the wicked not because it is unright but only because it is ugly . . . Nothing of duty, nothing of compulsion, nothing of obligation! . . . They do something only because it pleases them . . . I hardly believe the fair sex is capable of principles' ([1763] 1960, 81). The gender-coding of the constellations duty/obligation/reason versus sympathy/impulse/emotion facilitated a philosophical understanding that dichotomized the sources of moral action, dubbing the one of 'true moral worth', the other not worthy of esteem (Gould, 1976, p. 18; Blum, 1982; Grimshaw, 1986, pp. 42–4; Lloyd, 1983, on Kant and Hegel).

John Stuart Mill was more aware than any man in his time of the great, damaging limits on women's liberty and self-development of established relations between men and women. He questioned the naturalness of differences between men and women in a way that was then astonishingly radical. Yet Mill in one book defended democracy on the grounds that participation in public affairs enlarges the self and hence the polity, while in another he assumed that most women would choose freely a domestic life in which such participation was sharply curtailed. Although thinking about democracy led him to advocate the vote for women, and thinking about liberty led him to see the constraints in development imposed by social convention, even Mill could not combine these insights to understand how the relations he categorized as fundamentally private could deeply influence political life (Pateman, 1988; 1989).

Take John Rawls' vision of a community bonded by public principles of justice, arrived at by free, equal beings who are rational, self-interested, and know no particulars about themselves. Rawls realizes eventually that such a community must depend on families that give their members the emotional basis for empathy and the daily experience of domestic justice. But he cannot integrate that realization with his traditional philosophical reliance on the public/rational side of the gender-coded dichotomy (Okin, 1989).

Take Robert Nozick's counter to Rawls – a justice based on who produced a good, rather than who benefits most from it or what all parties would agree to if they did not know who would get what. Nozick's justice assumes that we own what we produce. Women, who as childbearers and childrearers work hard to produce what they never expect to own, make nonsense of Nozick's assumption, as they do of Rousseau's. Production is and ought to be only one factor in the complex social construction of 'ownership' (Okin, 1989).

The sharp, repeatedly reinforced dichotomy between the domestic and the public, in which the public and male sphere defines morality and politics, is dangerous both for women and for the larger polity. To draw for politics from all the conceptual and experiential resources available to us as human beings, we cannot afford to slice off and discard the household.

The personal is political

To challenge the traditional dichotomies is not to deny all difference between public and private. When a woman first spoke the words 'the personal is political', and a hundred thousand others took up those words, realizing that what they had thought was their own individual, domestic, private problem was in fact structural, public and shared, their insights would have had no force if the words on either side of 'is' had exactly the same meaning.

Challenging the dichotomy of public and private does not mean denying any distinction between the meanings of the words, demeaning the value of privacy, or making all behaviour similarly subject to state action. It does not repudiate the increasingly legitimate pressure, as one moves from individual to collective decision, to take the good of the whole into account. It does not mean arguing that the virtues appropriate for good action in private life, such as motherhood, are exactly the same as those appropriate for a sphere that deals primarily with partial strangers. The challenge does, however, mean seeing every action as potentially infused with public meaning. It means recognizing that the power which constitutes much of politics reaches into and begins with the smallest gesture of interpersonal domination, and that the reason which constitutes much of public persuasion is not so universal as to be untouched by assumptions, emotional connotations and linguistic patterns formed in the most private of relations.

Challenging the public/private dichotomy means insisting on the non-triviality, the non-exclusion from central public debate, of intimate, domestic concerns. It means insisting that what goes on between a man and a woman in their home, even in their bedroom, is created by and in turn creates what goes on in legislatures and on battlefields.

The causal arrow runs in both directions. The very existence of the private sphere, its acknowledged extent and limits, and the kinds of behaviour acceptable within it result from decisions made formally and informally in public, in legislatures, courts, bureaucracies, in print and on the airwaves. Public decisions create domestic inequalities of power. Private actions, in turn, create public inequalities of power. The people who make decisions in formal politics, from voters to legislators, develop their first political selves in private, domestic, familial settings. The domestic division of labour, which makes the care of children a woman's job, underlies the public inequalities between men and women. Acts of heterosexual courting encode patterns of domination, do some traditional acts of heterosexual intercourse itself (on private/public, see Elshtain, 1981; Dietz, 1985; Benhabib, 1988; Young, 1987; MacKinnon, 1989, p. 120; Okin, 1989; on courting, see Brownmiller, 1984; on intercourse, see Dworkin, 1987; MacKinnon, 1987).

Stretching and breaching the boundaries of the traditionally political, feminists find allies among economic democrats who take as 'political' decisions in the workplace and the corporation, and with scholars in comparative politics who take as 'political' acts of informal resistance to established power. Marxist scholars have pointed out that boundaries between the public and private, and the law that frequently enforces those boundaries, benefit capital far more than labour. Feminist scholars point out that similar boundaries, and the law that reinforces them, benefit men far more than women.

Rethinking concepts

Feminist thought brings into Western political discourse women's perspectives from the domestic sphere. Two such perspectives, in some tension with one another, have so far produced important reformulations of Western liberal political concepts. The first builds on the experience of familial connection, challenging the central assumption in liberal political theory that the individual is essentially separate from, and in conflict with, others. The second builds from the experience of sexual domination, revealing that political and economic domination has roots in the most private of sexual relations.

Connection

From the earliest beginnings of feminism, many women have been unwilling to discard, in order to claim full equality, the special virtues men have accorded women in the Western tradition. They have instead rejected gender-based dichotomies, calling on men to assume the 'female' virtues along with the 'male' in their individual characters and political ideals.

In the late 1970s, feminist thinkers in the psychoanalytic tradition rooted certain traditional women's virtues in the experiences of early childhood. Nancy Chodorow (1978) attributed 'women's relatedness and men's denial of relation' to the male child's need to create a separate, oppositional, identity by differentiating himself from his mother, a need the female child did not experience to so great a degree (see also Dinnerstein, 1977). Carol Gilligan's psychological study of moral development adopted much of Chodorow's analysis, arguing that 'since masculinity is defined through separation while femininity is defined through attachment, male gender identity is threatened by intimacy while female gender identity is threatened by separation. Thus males tend to have difficulty with relationships, while females tend to have problems with individuation' (Gilligan, p. 8).

Gilligan's empirical investigations of women's responses to moral dilemmas suggest that highly educated American women are more likely to define themselves 'in a context of human relationship' and less likely to adopt a 'rights' orientation to moral questions than highly educated men. These women are not lower in a scale of moral development, as Lawrence Kohlberg's (1981) work suggested, but rather have developed, along with some men, a different approach to morality, one that emphasizes maintaining and enhancing relationships rather than rights. Gilligan's recent work (Gilligan et al., 1988) points out that many individuals take both approaches, with many being able to see a question from the other perspective when asked, 'Is there another way you could look at this?' Conceptually, 'rights' and 'relationships' approaches are not mutually contradictory (Flanagan and Jackson, 1987; Sher, 1987; Okin, 1990; see also Tronto, 1987).

The finding of Gilligan and her students (1988) that moral orientations can differ by gender appears primarily, perhaps only, among the most highly educated groups in

275

American society. It may also appear most strongly when an interview facilitates the assumption of traditional gender roles. In the study of empathy, which both Chodorow and Gilligan link with women's deeper attachment to relationships, researchers find no physiological differences between men and women in situations that might provoke empathy (such as heart rate on hearing a newborn cry), but do find that the more the individual studied knows that empathy is being measured, the older the individual is, and the more attached the individual is to gender stereotypes, the stronger the relationship appears between gender and empathy (Eisenberg and Lennon, 1983). Studies of 'connection' more broadly may follow the same pattern.

While these studies may not demonstrate any large difference between the actual behaviour or even the normative orientations of most men and women even in American society, they do draw attention to the deeply gender-coded nature in that society of the dichotomy 'separation versus connection'. The researchers who cannot duplicate Gilligan's findings still find differences in the way most Americans code the two approaches, with both men and women rating Gilligan's 'care' or 'relationships' orientation as more feminine and the 'rights' orientation as more masculine (Ford and Lowery, 1986). These ratings are consonant with the typical coding of women as 'emotional' and men as 'rational' in English-speaking countries and to a lesser degree in most other countries (Williams and Best, 1982). In the United States the 'feminine' sex role includes being 'understanding', 'sensitive to the needs of others', and 'compassionate' (Bem, 1974; Markus et al., 1982). The 'communal' goals of 'selflessness, concern with others and a desire to be at one with others' are also associated with the household, and therefore with women more than with men. American students rate 'male homemakers' higher on these communal goals than 'female office workers' (Eagly and Steffen, 1984).

Feminists who emphasize 'connection', and thus women's 'difference' from men, refuse to relinquish the virtues associated with intimate connection simply because they have been coded as female. Their strategy is, instead, to draw attention to the deep gender-coding of philosophical concepts, and to use their gendered familiarity with intimate connection – as daughters, mothers, and women friends – to reformulate central concepts in Western democratic theory.

Autonomy in classic liberal theory is achieved by 'erecting a wall (of rights) between the individual and those around him' (Nedelsky, 1989, p. 12). The experience of familial connection suggests a contrasting model of autonomy, in which the capacity to act for oneself and give law to oneself is nurtured through relationships with others. In this feminist reconceptualization of autonomy, the boundaries of the self are permeable, with others an inevitable part of self (Nedelsky, 1989; see also Chodorow, 1989; di Stefano, 1990).

Obligation in the liberal tradition is voluntarily assumed. The experience of mothering suggests that many obligations begin as given, part of the embedded fabric of established mutual relationships, and are subsequently negotiated to provide space for separation, as needs, capacities and preferences change (Hirschmann, 1989; Mansbridge, 1993).

Similarly, negative freedom in the liberal tradition is primordial, the starting place. Liberal interaction begins with a negative, the absence of impediments to motion, and stresses processes, such as contract, that create connection out of separation while retaining as much as possible of the original valued independence. The experience of mothering begins with connection and stresses processes, such as personal growth and negotiation, that create negative freedom out of connection while retaining as much as possible of the original valued relationship (Hirschmann, 1989; Held, 1990; Benhabib, 1986. See also Brown, 1988 and O'Brien, 1981 against conceiving freedom as freedom from the physical, the body, and the demands of everyday life).

Power in the liberal tradition means getting others to do something through the threat of sanction or through force, assuming conflicting interests (Lukes, 1974). Feminists in the 'first wave' of feminism in the United States drew from their domestic experience to stress, in addition, a politics of persuasion – getting others to do something through an appeal to long-run self-interest, duty and empathy, assuming that on some issues common interests exist or can be created (e.g. Hannah Mather Crocker, in Kraditor, 1971). Feminists in the early 'second wave' redefined power not only as coercion but also as 'energy, strength and effective interaction', as they designed their small collectives on the principles of friendship (Carroll, 1972; Hartstock, 1981; 1983. See also Gould, 1976; Mansbridge, 1983; Ferguson, 1984; Held, 1990).

Domination

The domestic realm, as we have seen, provides experiences of commonality which the liberal tradition finds hard to reconcile with politics. It also provides experiences of deep conflict which that tradition rules off limits to political scrutiny.

Some of these conflicts are sexual. Through 'compulsory heterosexuality' (Rich, 1980), women are rewarded for defining their own needs in ways that please men and are punished for resistance. Sex itself is defined as leading to male climax. Catharine MacKinnon (1989, p. 113) argues that because men's dominance of women is sexualized, it is not possible to separate gender roles from sexuality: 'Sexuality is gendered as gender is sexualized. Male and female are created through the erotization of dominance and submission. The man/woman difference and the dominance/submission dynamic define each other.'

Male power affects, in blatant and in subtle ways, almost every form of male/female relations, including the most private relations that enter into the everyday making of oneself. Feminist analysis of this power can be inspired by Karl Marx's recognition that the ideas of a culture are the ideas of its ruling class, Antonio Gramsci's concept of hegemony, Bachrach and Baratz's (1963) 'non-decisions', which set the intellectual agenda by ruling out the contemplation of alternatives, and Michel Foucault's (1980) capillary power, which runs through the smallest veins of the system. Feminist analysis takes power even deeper, into the creation of self. 'No woman escapes the meaning of being a woman within a social system that defines one according to gender' (MacKinnon, 1989, p. 38).

Black feminists in the United States have done much to develop the feminist understanding of how external power suffuses one's own construction of one's self. Early in feminism's second wave, white feminists realized that the pieces of themselves that

277

they saw in a mirror, pieces that male attention had made salient, were often in their own eyes either inadequate or prized only because men set those values on them. Black feminists have revealed further how in a racist society gender is intertwined inextricably with race. While the images of a slender ankle or tiny foot arched into a high-heeled shoe do not oppress differentially by race, most 'feminine' attributes have in the United States a racial component as well: fair skin, blue eyes, blond hair. As Michele Wallace wrote of childhood games she played with her sister, 'Being feminine *meant* being white to us' (Wallace, 1990, p. 18; also Collins, 1990; Harris, 1990). Particularly in the American South, femininity meant white, pale, weakness, delicate frailty, having to be helped from a chair or through a door, in contrast to the black woman slave, valued for doing the work of a man (Carby, 1987). The images black women had to scrape from their souls – the mammy, Jezebel or Sapphire – were not the images white feminists needed to fight (Collins, 1990). Post-colonial writers have both preceded and reinforced the feminist realization that political oppressions infiltrate and help define the self (Lionnet, 1989).

These manifestations of power respect no public/private boundary. They appear in the bed, in the home or streets, where women are raped and battered, and in the halls of Parliament. Resistance to such power, accordingly, also appears in the smallest and most private of acts.

As Simone de Beauvoir (1989) pointed out, women's most pervasive struggle must be against the category of Other, defined by the dominant class to marginalize the subordinate. Capping a long-standing feminist recognition that men form the automatic norm (Austin, 1932, cited in Cott, 1986; also later Minow, 1987, pp. 32ff), MacKinnon writes,

Men's physiology defines most sports, their needs define auto and health insurance coverage, their socially designed biographies define workplace expectations and successful career patterns, their perspectives, and concerns define quality in scholarship, their experiences and obsessions define merit, their objectification of life defines art, their military service defines citizenship, their presence defines family, their inability to get along with each another – their wars and rulerships – defines history, their image defines god, and their genitals define sex. (1987, p. 36)

Among English speakers, language itself encodes the message of male as norm and female as other. The communitarian philosopher Michael Sandel writes that the kind of community that constitutes the self is marked by 'a common vocabulary of discourse and a background of implicit practices and understandings' (Sandel, 1982, pp. 172–3). Charles Taylor writes that the norms, ends, institutions and practices of a community function 'as a kind of language', both creating and requiring mutual understanding (1979, p. 89). Feminists point out that the 'common vocabulary' is not neutral among those who use it.

Feminist sensitivity to the structuring of political and social worlds around the dichotomy of self and other generates the recognition that any word implies (as words must) the dominant or majority subcategory within the category covered by that word, thereby excluding by implication the less powerful or the minority. Thus, the use of 'man' to mean 'human being' theoretically includes women – except that the word 'man' has connotations and establishes expectations that exclude women.

Similarly, as black feminists have pointed out, the word 'women' theoretically includes African-American women – except that because white women in the United States comprise the great majority of women, the word in that context has connotations that exclude many experiences of the majority of African-American women. In the same way, the phrase 'African-American women' implies 'heterosexual African-American women', and the phrase 'heterosexual African-American women' implies 'able-bodied heterosexual African-American women'. Each category, conjuring up its dominant or majority referent, implicitly excludes those whose experiences differ from that majority (Bartlett, 1990, p. 848; cf. Spelman, 1988). Because we must use words, and cannot maintain in consciousness the potentially infinite regress of the implicitly unincluded, we need to recognize that all communication encodes power, and be sensitive both to the worst abuses and to those who legitimately bring that power to the surface for conscious criticism.

The act of speech, which creates or precludes political possibility, is also gendered. In the United States, for instance, women are more likely to adopt linguistic usages that connote uncertainty. Men are more likely to interrupt. Women speak less than men when men are present, both in private and in public, and much less often than men in democratic public assemblies. Even women legislators speak less often than their male counterparts. The 'higher register' of women's voices seems, in addition, to generate an automatic discounting of their substantive meaning. But in spite of women's curtailed and discounted speech, throughout the world proverbs discipline women for talking too much: 'the tongue is the sword of a woman, and she never lets it become rusty' (Lakoff, 1975; Zimmerman and West, 1975; Henley, 1977; Haas, 1979; Mansbridge, 1983; Epstein, 1988; Kathlene, 1990).

The feminist recognition of pervasive male domination has produced a rethinking of liberal concepts that sometimes conflicts with reconceptualizations derived from intimate connection. Rethinking consent from this perspective means, for example, ideally taking consent as given only when power is absent. Because power is rarely if ever absent, consent can never in practice play the fully voluntary role that liberal democratic theory demands.

Rethinking justice from this perspective means rethinking impartiality. Impartiality, unexamined, will code dominant experiences as the norm, excluding or discriminating against individuals whose experiences are not encompassed by that norm. Universality, unexamined, will not accept or accommodate difference. A concept of justice that addresses these problems focuses less on ideal distribution than on eliminating institutionalized domination (Benhabib, 1987; Minow, 1987; Young, 1987; 1990; Friedman, 1991).

Rethinking autonomy from this perspective means discarding the concept of a 'true' or 'authentic' self that is revealed when interference (in the liberal tradition) or 'false consciousness' (in the Marxist tradition) is removed. If the self is a constructed, changing entity, which is identifiable as a subject and author of its own narrative only by living in it and with it, autonomy cannot be gained simply by shedding adverse socialization. Autonomy must be not a state, but a practice, embedded in existing power relations. Autonomy must be the exercise of a competency, a 'repertoire of coordinated skills' that makes possible a personal integration tested in the context of different levels and kinds of power, trying out possibilities that one sees others have achieved and say are achievable (Meyers, 1989; di Stefano, 1990).

The significance of 'difference'

Feminists have taken three approaches to the issue of women's differences from men. One approach stresses the 'sameness' of the subordinate to the dominant group. This approach challenges assumptions of natural difference leading to different spheres. In other respects, however, its stress on the similarities between men and women works against the conclusion that women's different experiences provide alternatives to standard male understandings of key philosophical concepts. As we have seen, a second approach, celebrating the subordinate's 'difference' from the dominant group, has produced the feminist reconceptualizations that focus on 'connection.' A third approach, stressing the effects of 'dominance' on the subordinate group, has produced the feminist reconceptualizations that focus on domination.

Feminist philosophy needs all three approaches. In gender domination, as in most other forms of domination, it is in the interest of the dominant group to exaggerate the differences between it and subordinate groups, deprecate the attributes associated with the subordinates, and obfuscate the effects of its own domination. In response, the subordinates need to emphasize sameness, lay claim to those attributes associated with their different experiences that their own lives reveal to be permanently valuable, and unmask the effects of domination. Each task is necessary. But the three tasks often work against one another, creating important splits in feminist philosophical thought.

Sameness

Most cultures prescribe strikingly different behaviour patterns for the two sexes, with rare exceptions, for example among the Hausa in the mid-twentieth century, only men prepared skins and only women milked, while among the Rwala only women milked and only men prepared skins (Murdoch and Provost, 1973). Among the inhabitants of the United States in the same era, with rare exceptions, only men filled cars with fuel and only women taught in kindergarten. Cultures prescribe different work, clothing, rituals, language and human nature for men and for women, thereby creating, enlarging, and making more salient various aspects of male–female difference. Because in all cultures gender is highly salient, people code a great deal of information into the prevailing gender schema and remember information through that schema. Our written memory is also biased, because, as with other differences in the social sciences, journals publish studies that show a difference between men and women more than studies that show no difference (Maccoby and Jacklin, 1974; Fausto-Sterling, 1985; Epstein, 1988).

Yet the deeper the chasm between the genders, the more unthinkable it is for women to lay claim to male privilege. Feminist social scientists and philosophers must accordingly continue to draw attention to the accumulating evidence that shows no difference between men and women on many of the traits on which the two have traditionally been thought to differ (Maccoby and Jacklin, 1974; Hyde, 1990).

The task of stressing sameness is complicated by our present ignorance of the exact extent or import of biological differences between men and women. Most philosophers no longer give biological differences between men and women, or between one race and another, the importance that earlier generations attributed to them. That an impulse is 'natural' does not make it either good or ineradicable; to meet social ideals societies usefully spend a great deal of effort modifying natural impulses, such as the impulse to defecate spontaneously. The demonstration that hormones and similar biological mechanisms can be deeply affected by the social environment also removes some of the aura of immutable primacy previously attributed to biology (McClintock, 1981; Madsen, 1986). Technological changes in production and reproduction have made it possible for men and women to do almost all of one another's traditional work, so that productive efficiency has now become an argument against traditional divisions of labour. Finally, several decades of psychological research have proved unfounded many previous convictions regarding differences in men's and women's abilities. If there are some biologically-based aptitudes for, say, childrearing which differentiate on the average between men and women, we need to find out what these aptitudes are, in what contexts they have important effects, and how they can be measured directly rather than by using gender as a proxy. Although the experience of many men raising children without noticeable ill effects suggests that such differences as may exist are probably small; we do not yet know enough to be more than agnostic about the full effects of biology, or more generally what differences between the sexes might remain in a feminist world.

Difference

When the dynamics of dominance and subordination cleave the salient experiences of a culture into two, widening the chasm between them, some valuable human experiences will be thrust into the subordinate side of the cleavage and derogated accordingly. Even if the cultures were genuinely separate but equal, an abstract contemplation of human experience that drew on only one side of the divide would be deprived of insight. 'Difference feminists', who draw philosophical lessons from women's experiences with intimate connection, seek both to redress the traditional derogation of ways of being or thinking associated with women and to add experiences from 'women's sphere' to the pool from which abstract thought can draw.

Anglophone feminists who mine for insight into women's differences from men rarely contend that women's virtues have a biological base (for partial exceptions, see Rossi, 1977; Griffin, 1978; Wolgast, 1980; and implications in West, 1988). French feminists in the psychoanalytic tradition are more likely to root their theories in bodily differences, seeing women as more fluid, less separate from their bodies, more interrelational. Their understanding of the body, however, is more symbolic than biological. Luce Irigaray (1985a, pp. 24ff), for example, makes women's genitals, their 'two lips', the basis of 'parler femme', speaking (as) woman, a way of speaking and thinking that, in opposition to Lacan's 'phallus', captures both-at-once, plurality, limitlessness, and activity-with-passivity. Irigaray widens the differences between women and men, making masculine and feminine 'syntaxes' 'irreducible in their strangeness and eccentricity one to the other' (Irigaray, 1985b, p. 139). Accordingly, even feminists who agree with her stress on the problems inherent in speaking as woman in a man's world have attacked her 'essentialism', that is, the assumption that there is one way of being 'woman', singular, which is closely linked to, if not founded in, biology (see Fuss, 1989, esp. pp. 62–4; also Gross, 1986; Brennan, 1989; Flax, 1990; Berg, 1991).

Yet even without a biological base, stressing difference works against the need to stress sameness. The stress on difference derives from and cannot avoid reinforcing the very gaps that are created by and serve to rationalize traditional patterns of domination.

Dominance

Catharine MacKinnon, arguing against any celebration of women's 'difference' from men, points out that in societies permeated by men's dominance of women any differ- ence already encodes dominance: 'When difference means dominance as it does with gender, for women to affirm differences is to affirm the qualities and characteristics of powerlessness' (MacKinnon, 1989, p. 51).

There are distinct dangers in affirming qualities that have been associated for gen- erations with powerlessness and that often derive from powerlessness itself. A greater familiarity with intimate relations derives largely from exclusion from public relations; a preference for persuasion derives largely from exclusion from power. 'Caring' gener- ates moral claims in the absence of rights. 'Intuition' and 'empathy' are the protective sensitivities of those who cannot exercise their will directly. Recognizing these and many other differences between men and women, the 'dominance' perspective warns that they are suffused with hierarchical power.

In this controversy, feminists who wish to adopt features of the sameness, difference and dominance perspectives face a delicate task. They must, at the same time, demon- strate how the dominant culture widens perceived differences, draw distinctive insights from women's side of the divide (on the grounds that roots in subordination do not automatically invalidate an insight), and, while struggling against power inequalities embedded in existing differences, find new tools, drawn from the process of struggle itself, to fight the male domination that permeates women's lives.

Legal theory and public policy

Debates among feminist legal theorists in the United States play out some of these controversies in the arena of law and public policy. During the decade of the 1970s in the United States, most feminist jurists argued that the law should be completely sex-blind, recognizing no differences between the sexes. Proponents of this kind of 'formal equality' continue to oppose, for example, state-mandated pregnancy leaves when the state does not mandate leaves for any other form of disability. Mandating or allowing legal distinctions between men and women, they argue, will undermine gender equality in the long run by reinforcing traditions of special treatment (e.g. Kaminer, 1990; see also Brown et al., 1971). 'Difference' and 'dominance' theorists contend to the contrary that because women are at this historical juncture situated differently from men, making their lives in a world designed primarily by and for men, the law must recognize the needs that their different situations create. Domi- nance theorists focus particularly on ending the domination inherent in rape, battering, incest, sexual harassment, and pornography (Becker, 1987; MacKinnon, 1987; 1989; for discussion see Okin, 1991).

The debates between 'sameness' and 'difference' jurists reflect different guesses in an uncertain situation about what is best for women in the short and long run. If the law recognized gender differences only when such a recognition would be likely to reduce sex-based disparities in political, economic or social power (Rhode, 1989), it would still be hard to know in practice when legal differentiations based on gender would reduce such disparities. In a society that held women more responsible than men for childcare, women might on the average take more days of leave from work than men even under gender-neutral laws providing disability leave for all forms of inability to work and childcare leave for both parents. Mandating such leaves might cause employers to choose and promote men over women on the margin. The depth of the expectation that only women will care for children (and older adults) is so great in every society that it is highly unlikely in the near future either that norms will change dramatically so that men voluntarily take as much responsibility for children and the elderly as women and develop the skills and dispositions to care for them, and/or that states will pass legislation requiring rather than permitting both parents to take childcare leaves in the first months of a child's birth. In the context of these larger social expectations, Swedish laws making parental leave and half-time employment easily available, although adding considerably to the welfare of women and children, seem at the same time to have helped perpetuate traditional gender stereotypes in that country (Rosenfeld and Kalleberg, 1991).

Differences among women

The philosophical and legal debate over differences between men and women has a parallel in the current debate within feminist theory over differences among women. Feminist theories that make claims about and in the name of 'women' often reveal under closer inspection that they are based on the experiences of only some women, usually women much like the theorist herself. French feminists particularly, reacting against Enlightenment reifications of 'man' and essentialist visions of 'woman', have provided a language and critique that stresses 'difference'. Influenced by postmodernism, they consider the category 'woman' as illegitimate as any other generalization. 'The belief that "one is a woman"', writes Julia Kristeva, 'is almost as absurd and obscurantist as the belief that "one is a man"' ([1974] 1981a; see also [1979] 1981b).

We propose that the assumption that 'there is a generalizable, identifiable and collectively shared experience of womanhood' (Benhabib and Cornell, 1988, p. 13) be treated as contested, historical and subject to changing perceptions. Women of different cultures and historical situations are currently adopting feminist perspectives tentatively to see whether an analysis of their lives as subject to male domination makes sense to them. Under that general rubric, what is salient to some individuals may differ from what is salient to others. Certain laws and norms will harm differently women who are lesbian and heterosexual, poor and aristocratic, urban and rural, Christian and Moslem, with and without children, or in other ways differently situated in individual and social history. These differences will lead to differences in political priorities, and, because collectives often have to focus on a limited number of issues, to political struggle over those priorities.

We hazard, however, that in the midst of this diversity, there will emerge one universal, though general, definition of feminism – the rejection of male domination. We also hazard that there will emerge several predictable loci of contestation with existing male-dominated arrangements: sexual domination, through incest, battering, rape and other violence against women; sickness and death, for in many societies females are aborted, badly fed and given worse medical treatment than males; household power, reinforced by legal and bureaucratic procedures that treat the household as a single unit represented by its head, very often a man; unequal economic opportunity, including not only unequal legal access to work and social discrimination against women in every craft and profession, but also unequal access to education, credit, and other sources of economic power; and, finally, unequal political opportunity, including the unequal economic and cultural bases for political power and deliberation (Okin, 1989).

At least in the United States, some of the paths to equality for women seem obvious. The reduction of violence against women, whether sexual or not, whether in the streets or in more private settings, must take high priority. Women's rights to control their reproductive lives must be not only preserved but enhanced. And public policy should focus on breaking women's 'cycle of vulnerability', a cycle that results from women having far greater responsibility than men for domestic work – including the care of the young, the sick and the old – then being further disadvantaged in the (male-centred) paid workplace by direct discrimination and the indirect discrimination that results from greater domestic responsibilities, then having this workplace disadvantage in turn render them less powerful at home. How can this cycle be broken? In part by greater vigilance against direct workplace discrimination, and in part by restructuring the workplace – including its hours and benefits – to suit better the needs of mothers and of those still rare fathers who participate equally in raising their children. Breaking the cycle will also require subsidized day care, because society, not just women, should share the responsibilities of raising the next generation. Reforms in divorce and family law can help ensure that women who choose to live with women, and women who choose more traditional lives as homemakers, are not thereby rendered vulnerable, economically and socially.

Some public policies will work to the advantage of all or almost all women in a society. Others will hurt some while helping others. Many will be contested. The feminist philosophical concern with difference should help undermine the political certainty that any particular reform is unequivocally good for 'women.'

Feminism as an ideology

If we think of an 'ideology' as an organizing tool for understanding the universe, a tool that necessarily affects perception but does not necessarily serve the dominant power, feminism is distinguished by the view that 'gender is a problem: that what exists now is not equality between the sexes' (MacKinnon, 1989, p. 38; see also le Doeuff, 1990, p. 29).

Such a definition of feminism does not require deriving it from a single root, such as the domination inherent in erotic heterosexuality. (For arguments to the contrary, see MacKinnon, 1989; O'Brien, 1981). In our analysis, desire for control over reproduction also plays an independent role in gender domination, as does, probably, the simple desire of the stronger to exploit the weaker, perhaps facilitated by early historical patterns of childbearing and lactation, or even by early effects on power of the relatively small differences between men and women in size and upper body strength. For most feminists it is too early to settle on one root cause of all gender oppression.

Emphasizing the constructed and self-constructing character of the forms of domination links feminist analysis to postmodernism and post-structuralism. Feminist sensitivity to power and to binary opposition creates links with Foucault and Derrida. Yet unlike many forms of postmodernism and post-structuralism, feminism is rooted in politics. In spite of caution derived from understanding the constructed and biased character of all actual administrations and conceptions of justice, feminism must be committed to some sense of justice and rights that transcends any one society. In spite of caution derived from understanding the processes of false consciousness, feminism must be committed to crediting women's experience. In spite of caution derived from understanding that any set of settled relations creates imbalances of power and that any form of coercion diminishes freedom, feminism must be committed, in order to accomplish change, to creating and partaking in the legitimate coercion embodied in law. In these ways feminism differs necessarily from the thrust of important implications in Foucault, Derrida and other post-structuralists.

Because feminism is based in women's experiences, we expect it to ally partially with, and borrow partially from, new philosophical initiatives, both progressive and conservative, that themselves have some tie to experience. Feminists learn both from reaction and from appropriation. When Alasdair MacIntyre (1984) explores the way human beings are constituted by traditions, feminists learn about the depth of our socialization from our sharp reaction, 'whose traditions?' Women appear in MacIntyre's traditions as wolves or stepmothers; mostly they do not appear at all (Okin, 1989). But feminists can also appropriate and extend MacIntyre's insight that we construct ourselves in part through the narratives we create about our lives.

These different borrowings and alliances, combined with real differences in experience, lead us to expect in feminism a series of productive wars. Like the social movement from which it is derived, feminist philosophy will be many-headed. It will be a quilt as much as a tapestry. Some forms of feminism will even incorporate elements antithetical to the broader struggle against domination in all its forms. Several early suffragist leaders in the United States, and undoubtedly many of their followers, were white racist feminists – a combination of feminism with a moral evil, but not a contradiction in terms.

As an ideology, a way of seeing and making sense of things, we expect feminism, as it spreads across the globe, to take forms not easily predictable from Western experience. In Western political philosophy, a central task now is to penetrate the public/private dichotomy, reveal its intimate connection with gender, and loosen its grip on both philosophy and policy. Feminists in other countries and cultures may find themselves challenging, in the philosophies that constitute and derive from their own social arrangements, the binary oppositions of purity/impurity, war/maternity, spirituality/ animality, and other dichotomies now occluded with gender. The gendering of politically relevant concepts is deep and pervasive in every culture. It is the task of feminist philosophy to unmask the effects on power of these categories of thought, revealing the conscious and unconscious gender valence of central philosophical and political ideas. As feminists work through public policy to change the political, economic and social structures that perpetuate male domination, the obstacles they meet and the relations they unearth will in turn influence feminist philosophy. The interaction of women's experiences, feminist politics and a feminist philosophy that sees the personal as political will produce, in continual evolution, feminism as an ideology.

See also 1 ANALYTICAL PHILOSOPHY; 2 CONTINENTAL PHILOSOPHY; 4 SOCIOLOGY; 7 LEGAL STUDIES; 11 LIBERALISM; 15 COMMUNITY; 16 CONTRACT AND CONSENT; 19 DEMOCRACY; 22 DISTRIBUTIVE JUSTICE; 25 EQUALITY; 30 POWER; 31 PROPERTY; 33 RIGHTS; 36 STATE; 37 TOLERATION AND FUNDAMENTALISM; 39 TRUST; 40 VIRTUE

References

Arendt, H.: 'Reflections on violence', *Journal of International Affairs*, 23 (1969), 1–35.
Bachrach, P. and Baratz, M.: 'Decisions and non-decisions: an analytic framework', *American Political Science Review*, 57 (1963), 632–44.
Bartlett, K. T.: 'Feminist legal methods', *Harvard Law Review*, 103 (1990), 829–88.
Becker, M.: 'Prince Charming: abstract equality', *The Supreme Court Review*, 5 (1987), 201–47.
Bem, S. L.: 'The measurement of psychological androgyny', *Journal of Consulting and Clinical Psychology*, 42 (1974), 155–62.
Benhabib, S.: *Critique, Norm, Utopia: A Study of the Foundations of Critical Theory* (New York: Columbia University Press, 1986).
————: 'The generalized and concrete other' (1987), in *Feminism as Critique*, ed. S. Benhabib and
D. Cornell (Minneapolis: University of Minnesota Press, 1988).
Berg, M.: 'Luce Irigaray's "Contradictions": poststructuralism and feminism', *Signs*, 17 (1991), 50–70.
Blum, L. A.: 'Kant and Hegel's moral rationalism: a feminist perspective', *Canadian Journal of Philosophy*, 12 (1982), 287–302.
Brennan, T.: 'Introduction', in *Between Feminism and Psychoanalysis*, ed. Teresa Brennan (London: Routledge, 1989).
Brown, B. A., Emerson, T. I., Falk, G. and Freedman, A. E.: 'The equal rights amendment', *Yale Law Journal*, 80 (1971), 955–62.
Brown, W.: *Manhood and Politics* (Totowa, NJ: Rowman & Littlefield, 1988).
Brownmiller, S.: *Femininity* (New York: Fawcett Columbine, 1984).
Carby, H.: *Reconstructing Womanhood: The Emergence of the Afro-American Novelist* (Oxford: Oxford University Press, 1987).
Carroll, B.: 'Peace research: the cult of power', *Journal of Conflict Resolution*, 4 (1972), 585–616.
Chodorow, N.: *The Reproduction of Mothering: Psychoanalysis and the Sociology of Gender* (Berkeley: University of California Press, 1978).
————: 'Gender, relation and difference in psychoanalytic perspective' (1979), in *Feminism and Psychoanalytic Theory* (New Haven, Conn.: Yale University Press, 1989).

Collins, P. H.: *Black Feminist Thought* (London: Allen & Unwin, 1990).

Cott, N.: 'Feminist theory and feminist movements', in *What is Feminism?*, ed. J. Mitchell and A. Oakley (New York: Pantheon, 1986).

de Beauvoir, S.: *The Second Sex* (1949); (New York: Vintage Books, 1989).

Diamond, I. and Orenstein, G. F., eds: *Reweaving the World: The Emergence of Ecofeminism* (San Francisco: Sierra Club Books, 1990).

Dietz, M. G.: 'Citizenship with a feminist face: the problem with maternal thinking', *Political Theory*, 13 (1985), 19–37.

Dinnerstein, D.: *The Mermaid and the Minotaur: Sexual Arrangements and Human Malaise* (New York: Harper Colophon, 1977).

di Stefano, C.: 'Rethinking autonomy', paper delivered at the 1990 meeting of the American Political Science Association.

Dworkin, A.: *Intercourse* (New York: Free Press, 1987).

Eagly, A. H. and Steffen, V. J.: 'Gender stereotypes stem from the distribution of women and men into social roles', *Journal of Personality and Social Psychology*, 46 (1984), 735–54.

Echols, A.: *Daring to be Bad: Radical Feminism in America 1967–1975* (Minneapolis: University of Minnesota Press, 1989).

Eisenberg, N. and Lennon, R.: 'Sex differences in empathy and related capacities', *Psychological Bulletin*, 94 (1983), 100–31.

Elshtain, J. B.: *Public Man, Private Woman: Women in Social and Political Thought* (Princeton, NJ: Princeton University Press, 1981).

Epstein, C. F.: *Deceptive Distinctions: Sex, Gender and the Social Order* (New Haven, Conn.: Yale University Press and Russell Sage Foundation, 1988).

Fausto-Sterling, A.: *Myths of Gender: Biological Theories about Women and Men* (New York: Basic Books, 1985).

Ferguson, K.: *The Feminist Case Against Bureaucracy* (Philadelphia, Pa.: Temple University Press, 1984).

Fishman, P. M.: 'Interaction: the work women do', *Social Problems*, 25 (1978), 397–406.

Flanagan, O. and Jackson, K.: 'Justice, care and gender: the Kohlberg–Gilligan debate revisted', *Ethics*, 97 (1987), 622–37.

Flax, J.: *Thinking Fragments: Psychoanalysis, Feminism and Postmodernism in the Contemporary West* (Berkeley: University of California Press, 1990).

Ford, M. R. and Lowery, C. R.: 'Gender differences in moral reasoning: a comparison of the use of justice and care orientations', *Journal of Personality and Social Psychology*, 50 (1986), 777–83.

Foucault, M.: 'Prison talk' (1975), in *Power/Knowledge*, ed. Colin Gordon (New York: Pantheon, 1980).

Friedman, M.: 'The practice of partiality', *Ethics*, 101 (1991), 818–35.

Fuss, D.: *Essentially Speaking: Feminism, Nature & Difference* (New York: Routledge, 1989).

Gilligan, C.: *In a Different Voice* (Cambridge, Mass.: Harvard University Press, 1982).

———— et al.: *Mapping the Moral Domain: A Contribution of Women's Thinking to Psychological Theory and Education* (Cambridge, Mass.: Harvard University Press, 1988).

Gould, C.: 'The woman question: philosophy of liberation and the liberation of philosophy', *Women and Philosophy: Toward a Theory of Liberation*, ed. C. Gould and M. W. Wartofsky (New York: G. P. Putnam's Sons, 1976), pp. 5–44.

Griffin, S.: *Woman and Nature: The Roaring Inside Her* (New York: Harper & Row, 1978).

Grimshaw, J.: *Philosophy and Feminist Thinking* (Minneapolis: University of Minnesota Press, 1986).

Gross, E.: 'Philosophy, subjectivity and the body: Kristeva and Irigaray', in *Feminist Challenges: Social and Political Theory*, ed. C. Pateman and E. Gross (Boston, Mass.: Northeastern University Press, 1986).

Haas, A.: 'Male and female spoken language differences: stereotypes and evidence', *Psychological Bulletin*, 96 (1979), 616–26.

Harris, A.: 'Race and essentialism in legal theory', *Stanford Law Review*, 42 (1990), 581–616.

Hartsock, N.: 'Political change: two perspectives on power' (1974), in *Building Feminist Theory: Essays from Quest*, ed. C. Bunch (New York: Longman, 1981).

————: *Money, Sex, and Power: Toward a Feminist Historical Materialism* (New York: Longman, 1983).

Held, V.: 'Mothering versus contract', *Beyond Self-Interest*, ed. J. J. Mansbridge (Chicago: University of Chicago Press, 1990), pp. 287–304.

Henley, N.: *Body Politics* (Englewood Cliffs, NJ: Prentice-Hall, 1977).

Hirschmann, N. J.: 'Freedom, recognition and obligation: a feminist approach to political theory', *American Political Science Review*, 83 (1989), 1227–44.

Hoagland, S. L.: *Lesbian Ethics* (Palo Alto: Institute of Lesbian Studies, 1988).

Hyde, J. S.: 'Meta-analysis and the psychology of gender differences', *Signs*, 16 (1990), 5–73.

Irigaray, L.: *This Sex Which is Not One* (1977), trans. C. Porter with C. Burke (Ithaca, NY: Cornell University Press, 1985a).

————: *Speculum of the Other Woman* (1974), trans. L. C. Gill (Ithaca, NY: Cornell University Press, 1985b).

————: 'Gesture in psychoanalysis', in *Between Feminism and Psychoanalysis*, ed. T. Brennan (London: Routledge, 1989).

Jaggar, A. M.: *Feminist Politics and Human Nature* (Totowa, NJ: Rowman and Allanheld, 1983).

Kaminer, W.: *A Fearful Freedom: Women's Flight from Equality* (Reading, Mass.: Addison-Wesley, 1990).

Kant, I.: *Fundamental Principles of the Metaphysic of Morals* (1785), trans. Thomas K. Abbott (Indianapolis: Bobbs-Merrill, 1949).

————: *Observations on the Feeling of the Beautiful and the Sublime* (1763), trans. John Goldthwait (Berkeley: University of California Press, 1960).

Kathlene, L.: 'The impact of gender on the legislative process: a study of the Colorado state legislature', *Feminist Research Methods*, ed. J. McC. Nielsen (Boulder, Col.: Westview, 1990), pp. 246–7.

Kohlberg, L.: *The Philosophy of Moral Development* (San Francisco: Harper & Row, 1981).

Kraditor, A.: *The Ideas of the Woman Suffrage Movement* (Garden City, NY: Doubleday, 1971).

Kristeva, J.: 'Woman can never be defined' (1974), trans. M. A. August, in E. Marks and I. de Courtiveron, eds, *New French Feminisms* (New York: Schoken, 1981a).

————: 'Women's time' (1979), trans. Alice Jardine and Harry Blake, *Signs*, 7 (1981b), 13–35.

Lakoff, R.: *Language and Woman's Place* (New York: Harper & Row, 1975).

Landes, J. B.: *Women and the Public Sphere in the Age of the French Revolution* (Ithaca, NY: Cornell University Press, 1988).

le Doeuff, M.: *Hipparchia's Choice* (1989), trans. Trista Selous (Oxford: Blackwell, 1990).

Lionnet, F.: *Autobiographical Voices: Race, Gender, Self-Portraiture* (Ithaca, NY: Cornell University Press, 1989).

Lloyd, G.: 'Reason, gender and morality in the history of philosophy', *Social Research*, 50 (1983), 491–513.

Luker, K.: *Taking Chances: Abortion and the Decision Not to Contracept* (Berkeley, Calif.: University of California Press, 1978).

Lukes, S.: *Power: A Radical View* (London: Macmillan, 1974).

Maccoby, E. E. and Jacklin, C. J.: *The Psychology of Sex Differences* (Stanford, Calif.: Stanford University Press, 1974).

MacKinnon, C. A.: *Feminism Unmodified* (Cambridge, Mass.: Harvard University Press, 1987).

————: *Toward a Feminist Theory of the State* (Cambridge, Mass.: Harvard University Press, 1989).

MacIntyre, A.: *After Virtue* (Notre Dame, Ind.: Notre Dame University Press, 1984).

Madsen, D.: 'Power seekers are different: further biochemical evidence', *American Political Science Review*, 80 (1986), 261–70.

Manin, B.: 'On legitimacy and political deliberation', trans. E. Stein and J. J. Mansbridge. *Political Theory*, 15 (1987).

Mansbridge, J. J.: *Beyond Adversary Democracy* (Chicago: University of Chicago Press, 1983).

————: 'Feminism and democratic community', in J. W. Chapman and I. Shapiro, eds, *Democratic Community: Nomos XXXV* (New York: New York University Press, 1993).

———— and Tate, K.: 'Race trumps gender: the Thomas nomination in the Black community', *PS: Political Science and Politics*, 25 (1992), 488–92.

Markus, H., Crane, M., Bernstein, S. and Siladi, M.: 'Self-schemas and gender', *Journal of Personality and Social Psychology*, 42 (1982), 38–50.

McClintock, M.: 'Social control of the ovarian cycle', *American Zoologist*, 21 (1981), 243–56.

Meyers, D. T.: *Self-Society, and Personal Choice* (New York: Columbia University Press, 1989).

Minow, M.: 'Justice engendered: foreword to the Supreme Court 1986 term', *Harvard Law Review*, 101 (1987), 10–95.

Mohanty, C. T., Russo, A. and Torres, L., eds: *Third World Women and the Politics of Feminism* (Bloomington, Ind.: Indiana University Press, 1991).

Murdock, G. P. and Provost, C.: 'Factors in the division of labour by sex', *Ethnology*, 12 (1973), 203–25.

Nedelsky, J.: 'Reconceiving autonomy', *Yale Journal of Law and Feminism*, 1 (1989), 7–36.

Nelson, B. and Chowdhury, N., eds: *Women and Politics Worldwide* (New Haven, Conn.: Yale University Press, 1993).

O'Brien, M.: *The Politics of Reproduction* (London: Routledge & Kegan Paul, 1981).

Okin, S. M.: *Justice, Gender and the Family* (New York: Basic Books, 1989).

————: 'Thinking like a woman', in Deborah L. Rhode, ed., *Theoretical Perspectives on Sexual Difference* (New Haven, Conn.: Yale University Press, 1990).

————: 'Sexual difference, feminism, and the law', *Law and Social Inquiry*, 16 (1991), 553–73.

Pateman, C.: *The Sexual Contract* (Stanford, Calif.: Stanford University Press, 1988).

————: *The Disorder of Women* (Stanford, Calif.: Stanford University Press, 1989).

Rhode, D. L.: *Justice and Gender* (Cambridge, Mass.: Harvard University Press, 1989).

Rich, A.: 'Compulsory heterosexuality and lesbian existence', *Signs*, 5 (1980), 631–60.

Rosenfeld, R. and Kalleberg, A.: 'Gender inequality in the labor market', *Acta Sociologica*, 34 (1991), 207–25.

Rossi, A.: 'A biosocial perspective on parenting', *Daedelus*, 106 (1977), 1–3.

Sandel, M.: *Liberalism and the Limits of Justice* (Cambridge: Cambridge University Press, 1982).

Sher, G.: 'Other voices, other rooms? Women's psychology and moral theory', in *Women and Moral Theory*, ed. E. F. Kittay and D. T. Meyers (Totowa, NJ: Rowman & Littlefield, 1987).

Simmel, G.: *Conflict* (1908), trans. K. H. Wolff (New York: Free Press, 1955).

Spelman, E.: *Inessential Woman: Problems of Exclusion in Feminist Thought* (Boston: Beacon Press, 1988).

Taylor, C.: *Hegel and Modern Society* (Cambridge: Cambridge University Press, 1979).

Tronto, J. C.: 'Beyond gender difference to a theory of care', *Signs*, 12 (1987), 644–63.

Walker, A.: *In Search of Our Mothers' Gardens* (San Diego, Calif.: Harcourt, Brace, Jovanovich, 1983).

Wallace, M.: 'Anger in isolation: a black feminist's search for sisterhood' (1975), in *Invisibility Blues* (New York: Verso, 1990).

West, R.: 'Jurisprudence and gender', *University of Chicago Law Review*, 55 (1988), 1–72.

Williams, J. E. and Best, D. L.: *Measuring Sex Stereotypes* (Beverley Hills, Calif.: Sage, 1982).

Wolgast, E. H.: *Equality and the Rights of Women* (Ithaca, NY: Cornell University Press, 1980).

Young, I. M.: 'Impartiality and the civic public', in *Feminism as Critique: On the Politics of Gender*, ed. Seyla Benhabib and Drucilla Cornell (Minneapolis: University of Minnesota Press, 1987).

————: *Justice and the Politics of Difference* (Princeton, NJ: Princeton University Press, 1990).

Zimmerman, D. H. and West, C.: 'Sex roles, interruptions and silence in conversation', in *Language and Sex*, ed. Barry Thorne and Nancy Henley (Rowley: Newbury House, 1975).

Further reading

Bartlett, K. T. and Kennedy, R., eds: *Feminist Legal Theory* (Boulder, Colo.: Westview, 1991).

Benhabib, S. and Cornell, D., eds: *Feminism as Critique* (Minneapolis: University of Minnesota Press, 1987).

Bono, P. and Kemp, S., eds: *Italian Feminist Thought* (Oxford: Blackwell, 1991).

Clark, L. and Lange, L., eds: *The Sexism of Social and Political Theory* (Toronto: University of Toronto Press, 1979).

Fraser, N. and Bartky, S. L., eds: *Revaluing French Feminism* (Bloomington, Ind.: Indiana University, 1992).

Frazer, E., Hornsby, J. and Loviband, S., eds: *Ethics: A Feminist Reader* (Oxford: Blackwell, 1992).

Gould, C. C., ed.: *Beyond Domination: New Perspectives on Women and Philosophy* (Totowa, NJ: Rowan and Allenheld, 1983).

Hanen, M. and Nielsen, K., eds: *Science, Morality and Feminist Theory* (Calgary, Alberta: University of Calgary Press, 1987).

Hirsch, M. and Keller, E. F., eds: *Conflicts in Feminism* (London: Routledge, 1990).

Keohane, N., Rosaldo, M. Z. and Gelpi, B. C., eds: *Feminist Theory: A Critique of Ideology* (Chicago: University of Chicago Press, 1982).

Kittay, E. F. and Meyers, D. T., eds: *Women and Moral Theory* (Totowa, NJ: Rowman and Littlefield, 1987).

Lovell, T., ed.: *British Feminist Thought* (Oxford: Blackwell, 1990).

Marks, E. and de Courtivron, I., eds: *New French Feminisms* (Amherst: University of Massachusetts Press, 1980).

Moi, T., ed.: *French Feminist Thought* (Oxford: Blackwell, 1987).

Pateman, C. and Gross, E., eds: *Feminist Challenges: Social and Political Theory* (Boston: Northeastern University Press, 1986).

Phillips, A. and Barrett, M., eds: *Destabilizing Theory: Contemporary Feminist Debates* (Stanford, Calif.: Stanford University Press, 1992).

Rhode, D. L., ed.: *Theoretical Perspectives on Sexual Difference* (New Haven, Conn.: Yale University Press, 1990).

Shanley, M. L. and Pateman, C., eds: *Feminist Interpretations and Political Theory* (University Park, Penn.: Pennsylvania State University Press, 1991).

Sunstein, C., ed.: *Feminism and Political Theory* (Chicago: University of Chicago Press, 1990).

I I

Liberalism

ALAN RYAN

What is liberalism?

Anyone trying to give a brief account of liberalism is immediately faced with an embarrassing question: are we dealing with liberalism or with liberalisms? It is easy to list famous liberals; it is harder to say what they have in common. John Locke, Adam Smith, Montesquieu, Thomas Jefferson, John Stuart Mill, Lord Acton, T. H. Green, John Dewey and contemporaries such as Isaiah Berlin and John Rawls are certainly liberals – but they do not agree about the boundaries of toleration, the legitimacy of the welfare state, and the virtues of democracy, to take three rather central political issues. They do not even agree on the nature of the liberty they think liberals ought to seek (Berlin, 1969, pp. 122–34).

It is a familiar complaint in writing about politics generally that key terms are undefined or indefinable; the boundaries between 'political' and 'non-political' behaviour and institutions are disputed, the defining characteristics of statehood, the necessary and sufficient conditions of legitimacy are incessantly debated. Liberalism may be no worse off than its ideological competitors, of course. In everyday political practice, all the 'isms' seem to be in the same condition; liberals, conservatives and socialists can be identified only issue by issue, and their stand on one issue offers little clue to their stand on another. The conservative who opposes railway nationalization supports government subsidies of defence contractors, while the liberal who applauds the establishment of an ethics committee to investigate the financial dealings of politicians will deplore the establishment of a committee to investigate the ethics of school teachers.

However, even if conservatism and socialism are in the same plight one is still inclined to ask, is liberalism one thing or many? Is liberalism determinately describable at all (Dworkin, 1985, pp. 183–203)? The observation that the terms of political discourse are not easily brought to an agreed definition is not new. More than three hundred years ago, Thomas Hobbes remarked that if anyone had stood to profit from a similar confusion in geometry, mankind would still be waiting for Euclid. While Hobbes' remark suggests that it is the self-interest of priests, intellectuals and politicians that explains this lack of precise definitions, twentieth-century writers have suggested another reason, that political concepts are 'essentially contested' (Gallie, 1955–6, pp. 167–98; Gray, 1983, pp. 75–101). A third explanation, and one more relevant to liberalism in particular, is that liberals' political concerns have altered over the past three centuries. All three kinds of explanation suggest, however, that we should be seeking to understand liberalisms rather than liberalism.

One reason for the indefinability of political terms, or the systematic slipperiness of our concepts of the state, the political, or, as here, liberalism, is the use of these terms as terms of praise or obloquy in the political struggle; this is a modern version of Hobbes' view that disputed definitions are the result of competing interests. Since the 1970s for instance, there has been an intellectual and political movement known as 'communitarianism' whose main defining feature is hostility to liberalism (Sandel, 1982). Communitarians emphasize the innumerable ways in which individuals are indebted to the societies in which they are reared; liberals, they say, write as if human beings come into the world with no social ties, owning no allegiances, and one way and another entirely detached from the societies they in some fashion inhabit. So described, liberalism is unattractive, built on sociological falsehoods and moral autism. Self-described liberals have naturally said that this is a parody of their views (Rawls, 1985, pp. 233; Rorty, 1991, pp. 179ff).

Liberals themselves have sometimes tried to define liberalism in such a way that only the very deluded or the very wicked could fail to be liberals. At the height of the Cold War, it was easy to present the alternatives as liberal-democracy on the one hand, and assorted forms of one-party totalitarianism on the other. This attempt to narrow the range of political options was itself resisted. *Social*-democrats who opposed both the one-party state and uncontrolled capitalism believed their disbelief in the legitimacy of private property in the means of production distinguished them from *liberal*-democrats. American conservatives distinguished themselves from liberals by according state and central governments a greater role in preserving national identity and some form of traditional moral consensus than liberals accept or else by advocating a more *laissez-faire* economy and a reduced role for government (Rossiter, 1982, pp. 235ff). Their critics retorted that they were none the less doomed by American history to remain liberals (Hartz, 1955, pp. 145–9).

The attempt to produce a clear-cut definition of a political stance is not always part of a hostile campaign to present the doctrines in question as incoherent or malign. Many political movements have devoted much effort to establishing a creed to which members must swear allegiance. Lenin spent as much time denouncing his Marxist allies for their misunderstanding of scientific socialism as attacking the Czarist regime. He thought a revolutionary movement must know exactly what it thought and hoped to achieve. If the faint-hearted or intellectually unorganized were driven out, so be it; as one essay proclaimed: 'Better Fewer but Better'. Of all political creeds, liberalism is the least likely to behave like this. Whatever liberalism involves, it certainly includes toleration and an antipathy to closing ranks around any system of beliefs. All the same, liberals have often asked themselves what they have in common, where the boundaries lie between themselves and, say, socialists on the one side, and conservatives on the other.

Another explanation of the difficulty of defining political terms is that they are 'essentially contested' terms, terms whose meaning and reference are perennially open to debate. If we define liberalism as the belief that the freedom of the individual is the highest political value, and that institutions and practices are to be judged by their success in promoting it – perhaps the most plausible brief definition – this only invites further argument. What is liberty? Is it positive or negative? How does the liberty of a whole nation relate to the liberty of its members? Nor is liberty the only concept to invite such scrutiny. Who are the individuals in question? Do they include children? Do they include the senile and the mentally ill? Do they include resident aliens or the inhabitants of colonial dependencies? This might be thought to be unsurprising; any definition opens up discussion of the terms in which the definition is proffered. The sting in the claim that these are essentially contested concepts is the thought that any elaboration will provoke further argument (Gallie, 1956, pp. 175ff).

There is a clear direction in which any elaboration of the definition of a chair, say, must go, and a clear line beyond which discussion is merely captious. This seems not to be true of the discussion of political doctrines. Whether the view that there are 'essentially contested concepts' is entirely coherent is another question. Unless some substantial portion of the meaning of a concept is uncontested, it is hard to see how the concept could be identified in the first place. There must be a central uncontested core of meaning to terms like 'liberty' if arguments about the contested penumbra are to make sense. A man in jail is paradigmatically not free; a man threatened with punishment if he writes a book is paradigmatically less free to write it than the man not so threatened (Berlin, 1969, pp. 122ff). Even so, we may agree that political terms are constantly being endowed with new meanings, in much the way the terms of the law are endowed with new meanings in the course of legal argument. If liberalism is distinct enough to be identifiable, it still changes over time.

Varieties of liberalism – classical vs modern

To agree that liberalism may have a variety of institutional manifestations, while resting on one moral basis – Locke's claim that men are born 'in a state of perfect freedom, to order their actions and dispose of their possessions, and persons, as they see fit . . . a state also of equality . . . ' (Locke, 1967, p. 287), for instance – does not mean that all doubts about the porosity of liberalism have been laid to rest. One argument that has taken on the status of a commonplace is that there have been two kinds of liberalism, one 'classical', limited in its aims, cautious about its metaphysical basis, and political in its orientation, the other 'modern', unlimited, incautious, global in its aims and a threat to the achievements of 'classical liberalism'. Classical liberalism is associated with John Locke ([1690] 1967), Adam Smith ([1755] 1976), Alexis de Tocqueville ([1835] 1964) and Friedrich von Hayek (1973–9). It focuses on the idea of limited government, the maintenance of the rule of law, the avoidance of arbitrary and discretionary power, the sanctity of private property and freely made contracts, and the responsibility of individuals for their own fates.

It is not necessarily a democratic doctrine, for there is nothing in the bare idea of majority rule to show that majorities will always respect the rights of property or maintain the rule of law (Madison, 1987, X, pp. 122–5); it is not always a progressive doctrine, for many classical liberals are sceptical about the average human being's ability to make useful advances in morality and culture, for instance. It is hostile to the welfare state; welfare states violate the principle that each individual ought to look to their own welfare, and frequently couch their claims in terms of the achievement of social justice, an ideal to which classical liberals attach little meaning (Hayek, 1976). More importantly, perhaps, welfare states confer large discretionary powers upon their politicians and bureaucrats, and thus reduce to dependency their clients, and those who depend upon the state for their prosperity.

Modern adherents of classical liberalism often ground their defence of minimal government on what they take to be a minimal moral basis. Minimal government may, for instance, be justified by the prosperity that economies deliver when they are not interfered with by governments; this argument has been current from Adam Smith's *Wealth of Nations* defence of 'the simple system of natural liberty' (Smith, [1775] 1976, p. 687) down to von Hayek's in our own time. It is not morally contentious to claim that prosperity is better than misery, and it has been given greater credibility than ever by the collapse of the communist regimes of Eastern Europe and the discrediting of military and authoritarian governments elsewhere.

An equally minimalist defence of liberalism as minimal government is provided by pointing to the nastiness of government coercion, and the contrast between the negative effects of mere brute force and prohibition compared with the benign effects of uncoerced co-operation. No classical liberal denies the need for law; coercive law represses force and fraud, and the non-coercive civil law allows people to make contracts and engage in any kind of economic activity. Still every classical liberal holds that all the forces that make for imagination, invention and growth come from the voluntary sector of the social order.

Classical liberals are not unanimous about the relationship between minimal government and the cultural and moral order, and this is perhaps the most important point about their moral views. Unlike 'modern' liberals, they do not display any particular attachment to the ideal of moral and cultural progress. David Hume was more of a political conservative than Adam Smith, but was more inclined than Smith to admire the 'brisk march of the spirits' typical of a flourishing commercial society. De Tocqueville was doubtful whether liberty could survive in the absence of strong religious sentiment, thinking that the self-reliance and self-restraint that he admired was not natural to modern man (de Tocqueville, 1964, pp. 310–25), and von Hayek is inclined to think that political liberalism rests upon cultural conservatism (Gray, 1984, pp. 129–31).

Contemporary defenders of 'classical' liberalism think it threatened by 'modern' liberalism. Modern liberalism, on this view, reverses the ambitions and restraints of classical liberalism, and in the process threatens the gains that classical liberals achieved when they replaced the tyranny of kings and courtiers with constitutional regimes. Modern liberalism is exemplified by John Stuart Mill's *On Liberty*, with its appeal to 'man as a progressive being' and its romantic appeal to an individuality which should be allowed to develop itself in all its 'manifold diversity' (Mill, [1861] 1974, pp. 120–2). Philosophically, it is exemplified equally by the liberalism of the English Idealists and 'new liberals' such as L. T. Hobhouse (1911).

In practice, it is exemplified by the assault on freedom of contract and on the sanctity of property rights represented by the welfare legislation of the Liberal government before World War I, by Roosevelt's New Deal between the wars, and by the explosion of welfare state activity after World War II. Modern liberalism is usually (but not always) agreed even by its critics to be a form of liberalism, for its underlying moral basis is couched in terms of freedom. Negatively, the aim is to emancipate individuals from the fear of hunger, unemployment, ill-health and a miserable old-age, and positively, to attempt to help members of modern industrial societies to flourish in the way Mill and von Humboldt wanted them to.

It is liberal, too, because it does not share the antipathies and hopes of a socialist defence of the modern welfare state. Although some defenders of the rights of property claim that almost any restriction on the absolute liberty of owners to dispose of their own as they choose amounts to confiscation (Epstein, 1985), modern liberalism has no confiscatory ambitions. In as much as the ideals of the welfare state cannot be achieved without a good deal of government control of the economy, modern liberalism cannot treat property as sacrosanct, and cannot limit government to the repression of force and fraud; but distinguished modern liberals such as John Rawls argue that personal property is a necessary element in individual self-expression, especially by means of freedom of choice in careers, even if vast shareholdings are not (Rawls, 1971, pp. 272–4). Critics of modern liberalism usually insist that it is liberalism but a dangerous variety.

The fear that modern liberalism is inimical to the spirit of classical liberalism and will in practice threaten the latter's gains, rests on two things. The first is the thought that modern liberalism is ideologically or metaphysically overcommitted. Mill's vision of man as a progressive being, with its demand that everyone should constantly rethink her opinions on every conceivable subject, is one with at best a minority appeal. To found one's politics on a view of human nature that most people find implausible is to found one's politics on quicksand. There is no need to appeal to such a vision of human nature to support classical liberalism; conversely, it is not clear that the kind of independent and imaginative personalities by which Mill set such store are best produced in a liberal society. History suggests that many of them have flourished by resisting an illiberal and conservative environment (Berlin, 1969, p. 172).

The second is the thought that modern liberalism makes everyone an unrealizable promise of a degree of personal fulfilment that the welfare state cannot deliver, and that its efforts to deliver will inevitably frustrate. For one thing, people resent being forced to part with their hard-earned income to provide the resources that supply jobs, education and the various social services that modern liberalism employs to create its conception of individual freedom for other people. This creates a hostility between more and less favoured groups of citizens that is wholly at odds with what modern liberals desire.

Moreover, the welfare state must employ an extensive bureaucracy whose members are granted discretionary powers and charged by law to use those powers for the welfare of their clients. This means that the classical liberals' concern for the rule of law, and the curtailing of arbitrary discretion is ignored, as bureaucrats have been given resources to disburse to their clients, and meanwhile the allegiance of the citizenry has been undermined, as the state has failed to produce the good things it has been asked to provide. The liberation the welfare state promises – liberation from anxiety, poverty and the cramped circumstances of working-class existence – is easily obtained by the educated middle class and is impossible to achieve for most others. There is thus a grave risk of disillusionment with liberalism in general as the result of its failure when it over-extends itself. Some writers suppose that the world-wide popularity of conservative governments during the 1980s is explained by this consideration.

Varieties of liberalism: libertarianism and liberalism

There is a closely related but not identical divide within liberal theory, between liberalism and libertarianism. Just as in the case of the conflict between classical and modern forms of liberalism, there is a tendency for the partisans of one side or the other to claim that their version of liberalism is true liberalism and the alternative something else entirely. Contemporary libertarians often claim that they are classical liberals. This is not wholly true. There is at least one strand of libertarian thought represented by Robert Nozick's *Anarchy, State and Utopia* that advocates the decriminalization of 'victimless crimes' such as prostitution, drug-taking and unorthodox sexual activities (Nozick, 1974, pp. 58–9). There is nothing of that in John Locke or Adam Smith.

The line between liberal and libertarian theories is not easy to draw. Both are committed to the promotion of individual liberty; both rest most happily on a theory of human rights according to which individuals enter the world with a right to the free disposal of themselves and their resources. The line of cleavage lies between the libertarian view that government is not a necessary evil but a largely (and for so called 'anarchocapitalists' a wholly) unnecessary evil, and the liberal view that government power is to be treated with caution, but like any other instrument may be used to achieve good ends. Perhaps the most important point of difference is that libertarians see our rights as a form of private property, what Nozick has called 'entitlements' (Nozick, 1974, pp. 150ff). The individual is the owner of his or her person and abilities; so viewed, our rights have two sources only – our initial ownership of our own selves and capacities, and the claims on whatever resources and abilities other people have freely agreed to transfer to us. The state, if legitimate at all, may do no more than secure these rights. It has no resources of its own and cannot engage either in the redistributive activities of modern welfare states or in the quasi-charitable activities of such states. Nobody has the right to deprive anyone else of their property by force – if they have committed no crime – and neither does the state.

This is in sharp contrast to the most famous recent account of welfare state liberalism, John Rawls' *A Theory of Justice*. In Rawls' account, we arrive at an understanding of what rights we possess, and of how far our liberty extends, by asking ourselves a hypothetical question – 'what rights would we all demand for ourselves and acknowledge in others if we were to establish a social and political system *de novo*, knowing nothing about our particular abilities and tastes, and therefore being forced to strike a fair bargain with everyone else?' (Rawls, 1971, pp. 11–17). Rawls' claim is that we should acknowledge two rights: the right to the most extensive liberty consistent with the same liberty for everyone, and a right to just treatment enshrined in the thought that inequalities are justified only to the extent that they improve the situation of the least advantaged (Rawls, 1971, pp. 60–1).

This second principle is often called the maximin theory of justice, since it explains social justice as *max*imizing the size of the *min*imum holding of social resources. This principle is clearly inimical to any account of the state that restricts it to the defence of property rights. The introduction of a conception of social justice into the defence of a liberal political theory rests on the idea that individuals have a right to self-development, and therefore on the kind of theory of individual development that underpins Mill's *On Liberty* and alienates defenders of 'classical' liberalism.

All dualisms ride roughshod over a complicated world. There are forms of liberalism that are non-libertarian, but also more nearly 'classical' than 'modern liberalism'. Locke's *Two Treatises* is on the face of it more kindly to private property than the views of Rawls or Mill, and yet Locke shows none of the hostility to the state that libertarians do. The state is obliged to act according to the rule '*salus populi suprema lex*' – 'the good of the people is the highest law' – and there is no suggestion that this is only a matter of repressing force and fraud (Locke, [1690] 1967, p. 391). On the other hand, there is also no suggestion that the least advantaged members of society have a right to do as well as possible. Locke suggests that they have to do well enough to make membership of civil society a good bargain – otherwise, they might as well emigrate to some unoccupied part of the world and start again – but he does not suggest that they have any claim beyond that (Locke, [1690] 1967, pp. 314–15). Certainly, Locke's individualism treats each person as responsible for his or her own welfare, but, Locke's concern with our *moral* welfare rather *economic* well-being means that he was more concerned with religious toleration than with 'health and human services'.

Liberal antipathies

Because we are tempted to acknowledge that we are faced with liberalism*s* rather than liberalism, and also inclined to say that they are all versions of one liberalism, it is tempting also to suggest that liberalism is best understood in terms of what it *rejects*. Nor would it be surprising to come to such a conclusion. Conservatism is no easier to define than liberalism, and it is not infrequently observed that what conservatives believe is a matter of what they want to conserve and who threatens it. Indeed, Louis Hartz's *The Liberal Tradition in America* argued that conservatives in the United States as opposed to their counterparts in Britain and Europe were in a bad way because the society and political system they want to conserve has always been a liberal one; temperamental conservatives are thus forced to be ideological liberals (Hartz, 1955, pp. 145–54). However that may be, it is not implausible to argue that liberalism is well defined in negative terms. Its central commitment, liberty, is in general a negative notion – to be free is to be *not* in jail, *not* bound to a particular occupation, *not* excluded from the franchise) and so on – and the history of liberalism is a history of opposition to assorted tyrannies.

Anti-absolutism

One way of understanding the continuity of liberal history in this light is to see liberalism as a perennial protest against all forms of absolute authority. It is notoriously difficult to suggest a starting date for liberal political theory, or, rather, it is notoriously easy to suggest all sorts of starting dates, running from the pre-Socratics onwards, but notoriously difficult to find any kind of consensus on one of them. In British politics, for instance, it was only in the 1860s that the more radical members of the Whigs called themselves the Liberal Party. Yet it would be odd not to count Locke among early liberals, just as it would be absurd to call Hobbes a liberal even while one might want to acknowledge that he supplied many of the ingredients for a liberal theory of politics in the course of himself defending absolute and arbitrary authority as the only alternative to the anarchy of the state of nature and the war of all against all.

Whatever liberalism has been concerned with, it has been concerned with avoiding absolute and arbitrary power. It is not alone in this. English constitutional theory had for several centuries an aversion to anything that smacked of confiding absolute power to anyone whatever. Neither parliament, nor the judiciary, nor the king was entitled to a monopoly of political authority. The imagery of the body politic was called upon to suggest that the elements in the political system had to co-operate with one another for the body to function coherently. What makes *liberal* hostility to absolute rule liberal rather than merely constitutionalist is the liberal claim that absolute rule violates the personality or the rights of those over whom it is exercised (Locke, [1690] 1967, pp. 342–8).

This argument connects Locke's *Second Treatise*, with its claim that absolute and arbitrary authority were so inconsistent with civil society that they could not be considered a form of government at all, with the twentieth-century liberal's contempt for the totalitarian regimes of Nazi Germany and Stalinist Russia. Liberals have disagreed about just which sorts of absolute authority are intolerable. Locke agreed that a general needed absolute authority over his soldiers in battle, and might shoot deserters out of hand. But this was not arbitrary authority – generals might shoot deserters, but not take sixpence from their pockets (Locke, [1690] 1967, pp. 379–80).

J. S. Mill thought the principles of *On Liberty* did not apply to people who could not benefit from rational discussion (Mill, [1861] 1974, pp. 69–70). Elizabeth and Peter the Great had rightly exercised unaccountable power over sixteenth-century Britain and eighteenth-century Russia, respectively, and the despotic power of the East India Company over its Indian subjects was legitimate. The nineteenth-century British working class, on the other hand, was entitled to full civil and political rights, and women of all classes as much as men. Other liberals have been rather less ready to describe entire populations as 'childish', and have thought absolute authority over colonial possessions as indefensible as any other absolute power.

The thought behind liberal opposition to absolute power is not complex, although it has several strands. One is the idea that political authority exists for purely secular ends, towards which we should adopt a rational, scientific attitude, adjusting our political institutions and our policies in an instrumentally efficient way. Negatively, this means that liberals do not see authority as conferred either by the voice of God, as in theories of divine right or charismatic authority, or by the dictates of history as in Marxist theory, or by racial destiny as in Nazi theory. Authority exists only to enable a society to achieve those limited goals which a political order enables us to achieve – the security of life, property and the pursuit of happiness (Locke, [1689] 1956, pp. 128–9).

It follows that nobody can claim absolute power, since their title to exercise power rests on their ability to pursue these limited goals in an efficient fashion. A second idea that reinforces the first is that the content of these limited goals can only be set by attending to the opinions of all the people under that authority, or at least all those who have not shown themselves to be anti-social or a menace to the political order. To exclude anyone's views is to devalue them; it is also to deny what liberalism relies on for its effect as a moral argument, the claim that we are born free and equal (Dworkin, 1985, pp. 191ff). As free, we must be persuaded to give our allegiance, and as equal, we must be obliged on the same terms as everyone else. This means that government must listen to the people, and cannot therefore take to itself any kind of absolute power (Rawls, 1971, pp. 221–3).

A third element provides much of the anti-totalitarian energy of modern liberalism. Free and equal individuals must be so recognized in the legal system as well as in the political system narrowly conceived. They must be free to form associations for their own purposes, and to engage in varied social, commercial and intellectual activities. Absolute authority is inimical to, and unwilling to share control over the lives of the citizenry with the leaders of other, secondary groups. The history of twentieth-century totalitarian states indeed shows that such states have always destroyed the independent authority of all other associations they could lay hands on. Liberals believe that the energy and liveliness of a society comes from these secondary allegiances, and therefore that absolute power is both an affront to the moral personality of individuals and destructive of the life of society at large (Dworkin, 1985, pp. 193–200).

Anti-theocracy

The opposition to absolutism, which links Locke to Mill and both of them to Rawls, Dworkin and contemporary liberal thinkers, had its origins in another issue. This was the liberal hostility to the confusion of secular and religious authority, and the liberal obsession with the rights of conscience. It has often been pointed out that the first usage of the term 'liberal' in a political context was in the context of European anticlerical politics in the nineteenth century. For many Roman Catholics the term 'liberal' was, except when used to qualify 'education', a term of abuse. Voltaire was not a whole-hearted liberal, but the cry of '*écrasez l'infame*' with which he attacked the repressive and brutal power of the Catholic church in eighteenth-century France became a rallying cry of anti-clerical liberals all over Europe.

Liberalism was associated with the nineteenth-century movement of European ideas that was concerned to drive a wedge between church and state and to make the Catholic Church no more influential in the politics of Catholic countries than the various Protestant churches were in the countries where they flourished. In essence, the argument was an argument in favour of religious toleration and against any kind of religious monopoly.

It is sometimes thought that toleration arises when people are convinced that there is no way of knowing what the truth is in matters of religion, and that toleration is the fruit of scepticism. But this is quite wrong. Hobbes was a sceptic, but he was also deeply hostile to supposed *rights* to toleration. It is this that marks him as a non-liberal. The advocacy or denial of toleration as a matter of right divides the liberal and the non-liberal more sharply than anything else. For Hobbes, religious doctrines were too important to be left to private men to pick and choose; even if those doctrines were intellectually quite absurd, they stirred up the passions and so threatened the peace. It was thus the task of the sovereign to regulate what might and might not be said in public on all such matters; if the sovereign failed in this duty, the peace would be broken, exactly the outcome which the sovereign existed to prevent (Hobbes, [1651] 1991, pp. 124–5).

Locke put forward the modern doctrine of toleration some thirty years after Hobbes. In Locke's eyes, there were two distinct realms, the sacred and the secular. Locke thought the first much more important than the second, but he also thought that secular authority was quite impotent to achieve anything useful in that realm. The political realm dealt with what Locke termed *bona civilia*, the goods of earthly peace and security, which he otherwise characterized as life, liberty, property and physical well-being (Locke, [1689] 1956, p. 128). A sovereign who tried to dictate how we practised our religion was overstepping the proper bounds of his authority. Conversely, a church that tried to dictate the secular law was overstepping the bounds of its authority. The state was essentially a non-voluntary organization, and one to which we owed obedience willy-nilly; churches were essentially voluntary, and probably plural.

Locke was, as Hobbes was not, a devout Christian, who thought a great deal about religion as religion, rather than from a sociological perspective. It was this that made Locke a passionate defender of toleration. One of the arguments in favour of toleration and against the mingling of church and state was precisely that human beings – especially late seventeenth-century human beings of a Protestant persuasion – were extremely tender about matters of conscience. To force someone to assert a belief he did not really hold was to outrage his deepest nature.

Where Hobbes had suggested that men quarrelled over matters of conscience because there was next to nothing to be known about religion by the light of reason alone, and therefore ought to be made to assert something in common, simply for the sake of peace, Locke was committed to the view that God required a willing assent and a real faith, so that whatever kind of forced assent the state might induce us to make was an insult to God as well as an outrage upon the individual (Hobbes, [1651] 1991, pp. 26off; Locke, [1689] 1956, pp. 132–3).

Conversely, true religion can make no demands upon the state. This is a view that modern readers find harder to accept. Locke thought it impossible that there might be a valid religious reason for a group to do anything that might come into conflict with the ordinary criminal law. Thus he would have differed with most liberals of today over the case in 1990, in which the US Supreme Court found that the First Amendment guarantees of religious liberty did not entitle Native Americans to use the hallucinogenic drug peyote in their religious rituals once the state of Oregon had banned the consumption of peyote.

Locke would have sided with the Court, but many contemporary liberals thought the demands of any religion should weigh more heavily than that. Locke also confined toleration to opinions that did not threaten the political order; modern readers are often shocked to find that neither Roman Catholics nor atheists would be tolerated in any society that followed Locke's prescriptions. In both cases, the argument was that they were *politically* dangerous; atheists lacked motives to keep their promises and behave decently, while Catholics professed earthly loyalty to the Pope and so could not be relied on by the rulers of whatever state they happened to belong to (Locke, [1689] 1956, pp. 157–8).

This reflected Locke's sharp distinction between those matters over which secular authority might be exercised and those over which it must not. Locke argued that earthly governments existed for certain simple tasks and no others, an argument that depended very heavily on the idea that it is obvious what the function of earthly government is, and that it does not include saving men's souls. Mill's *On Liberty* took a different route to much the same conclusion, not by arguing that it was obvious what the function of government was, but by showing that a consistent utilitarian who believed in the importance of individuality and moral progress must agree that coercion, especially the organized coercion exerted by governments, was legitimate only to defend certain this-worldly interests – our own liberty and security above all else (Mill, [1861] 1974, pp. 119ff; Gray, 1983).

Mill's argument is no more conclusive than Locke's. An enthusiast for the mixing of church and state may set no value on individuality for its own sake, and believe that an enlarged freedom would lead to depravity rather than moral progress. It is on this basis that s/he demands the union of spiritual and secular authority. In the second half of the twentieth century, liberals have generally taken a less rhetorical, more practical line than Locke and Mill. Totalitarian regimes, the lineal descendants of confessional states, have two great drawbacks. The first is that they employ a distasteful amount of force in securing their goals. Because it is so difficult to tell whether one's subjects are really saved or really loyal to the Nazi Party, or whatever, the temptation is to pile on the penalties for dissent, and to engage in acts of exemplary brutal punishment, which does little to secure a real loyalty to the regime and much to make its rulers insecure when they contemplate the hatred of the population they have intimidated (Arendt, 1968).

The second is that such regimes are inefficient; they may be effective when fighting a real, all-out war, but they are economically less efficient than liberal societies in which the division of labour between the sacred and the profane is respected in approximately the form Locke laid down. Whether this practical argument captures the liberals' deepest beliefs is doubtful. It is hard not to suspect that liberals feel more passionately than that about the wickedness of totalitarian regimes and for that matter about the wickedness of authoritarian clerical regimes of the kind typified by the Spain of General Franco. When they feel passionately about such regimes, it is in much the same way as Locke, for modern notions of the violation of personality reflect in a secularized fashion, Locke's view that the imposition of belief on any individual was an affront to that individual and God their creator (Rawls, 1971, pp. 205–11).

Anti-capitalism

The history of hatred for despotism, theocracy and the modern union of the two that is reflected in totalitarianism is a long history. The third of liberalism's antipathies has a shorter history. From the middle of the nineteenth century until today, one strand of liberalism has regarded capitalism as an enemy of liberty (Mill, [1848] 1965, pp. 766–9; Dewey, 1931). This marked a great reversal in the history of liberalism. It is not a large over-simplification to say that until the early nineteenth century there was no question of opposing liberalism to capitalism. The movement of ideas and institutions that emancipated individuals from tradition, that insisted on their natural rights, and demanded that 'careers should be open to talent' rather than birth, was a seamless whole.

Just as a man must think for himself, so he must work for himself; just as society would progress only if each person took responsibility for their own ideas and moral convictions, so it would flourish economically only if everyone stood on their own two feet. How far this was an articulate defence of capitalism as such is debatable; the term 'capitalism' itself did not come into general use until the late nineteenth century, and it is difficult to decide how appropriate it is to characterize as capitalist societies which possessed nothing one could call a proletariat, where the great majority still lived in the countryside and worked on the land, and which thought of themselves as 'commercial societies' rather than 'capitalist economies' (Smith, [1775] 1976, pp. 399–403).

Moreover, many of the rights to dispose of property just as one wished, to work for anyone willing to employ one, and to contract with anyone for any purpose not obviously damaging to the security and good morals of the commonwealth, had been established by successive decisions made by judges appealing to the English common law rather than by legislation of a self-consciously liberal kind. Still, there is an obvious affinity between liberalism and the rule of private property and freedom of contract. The liberal view that the individual is by natural right, or by something tantamount to it, sovereign over himself, his talents and his property is at once the basis of limited government, the rule of law, individual liberty and a capitalist economy.

But it was apparent from the beginning that property might be employed oppressively as well as harmlessly or beneficially. Apart from the conflict between the rights of property-owners and the traditional claims of rural workers – such as customary claims to gather wood or to glean in the fields or to take small game – there was a more general conflict between the liberty of the large property-owner to do what he chose with his property and the impossibility of his workers or competitors striking anything like a fair bargain with him. Throughout the nineteenth century, the sentiment grew that if it had once been necessary to liberate the entrepreneur from misguided or oppressive government, it was now necessary to liberate the worker and consumer from the tyranny of the capitalist (Hobhouse, [1911] 1964, pp. 22–4, 82–4; Green, 1892, pp. 366–70).

Mill observed that the modern wage labourer had as little real choice of occupation as a slave had in antiquity. In that spirit, he defended the right of working people to organize into trade unions to redress the balance of power a little. T. H. Green and L. T. Hobhouse went further, suggesting that capitalism exerted a kind of moral tyranny over the ordinary person, as exemplified by the spread of drinking establishments that destroyed both the health and the self-respect of their victims (Green,

1892, pp. 380–5). 'New Liberalism', exemplified in Britain by the social policy of the Asquith government of 1908–16, and in the United States by the demands of the Progressives and the practice of the Democratic Party after the election of Franklin D. Roosevelt in 1932, had many positive ambitions but one negative assumption was that the working man needed to be freed from the power of the capitalist. It is this that explains the seeming paradox that late twentieth-century conservatives are often characterized as 'neo-liberals'. The contemporary defence of property rights is not, as it was two centuries ago, the defence of landed property against commercial and industrial capital, but the defence of nineteenth-century *laissez-faire* and the property rights of commercial and industrial capital against modern reformers.

Liberal prescriptions

The tidiness of a definition of liberalism couched in terms of its oppositions is only apparent. Certainly, liberalism is anti-despotic, anti-clerical and hostile to twentieth-century manifestations of those evils, including the perverted manifestations of totalitarianism. But, just as there is a tension between classical and modern liberalisms, the same tension reappears between pro- and anti-capitalist liberalisms. And just as most liberals would not wish to pursue the goals of the welfare state to the lengths of threatening the survival of limited, lawful government, so they would not wish to restrain the operations of a capitalist economy to the point where it turned into a command economy. Whether we start from liberal enthusiasms or liberal antipathies, we find the same controversies.

The wish to find a position that is intellectually attractive and politically responsible exposes liberals to accusations of not knowing their own minds or of being 'wishy-washy'. Liberals have retorted that it is not their fault that the world is a complicated place that requires nuanced handling. One way of underpinning that reply is to provide the positive liberal theory that explains both why liberalism is hostile to the threats to freedom that it encounters and why these threats have varied over time.

A theory for individuals

In spite of the suggestion that liberalism should confine its attention to political institutions, liberalism is best understood as a theory of the good life for individuals linked to a theory of the social, economic and political arrangements within which they may lead that life. John Rawls' *Theory of Justice* provides some persuasive arguments for the view that we should build a liberal theory for institutional design without committing ourselves to any particular view of 'the good life', and its eventual failure to convince tells us a lot about why a broader theory is needed.

Rawls argues that the search for a consensus in favour of liberal political and economic institutions will go more smoothly if we seek foundations that are neutral with respect to the great, but sharply contested, issues of religion and personal ethics (Rawls, 1989, pp. 233–8). Critics have noted, however, that Rawls' minimalist assumptions about 'the good life' remain decidedly liberal – he takes it for granted that slavery is an unspeakable evil, that the suppression of conscientious belief is so intolerable that no rational person could trade the chance of being in command of the Inquisition for the risk of being one of its victims, and that freedom of choice in career and lifestyle is essential for life to have any meaning.

The same critics have also pointed out that the principles of justice proposed by Rawls are not suited to absolutely anyone but especially to persons holding a late twentieth-century conception of themselves and the meaning of their lives. The thinness of the premisses about human nature and the human good that Rawls builds on do not reflect scepticism or a lack of moral conviction so much as the eminently liberal thought that each person is in command of his or her own moral destiny, and that it is not for others to dictate it, as Rawls has subsequently tended to agree (Rawls, 1975).

At all events, liberalism viewed as a doctrine for individuals can be understood in terms one might borrow from Immanuel Kant, Wilhelm von Humboldt, J. S. Mill, Bertrand Russell or John Dewey, since a variety of formulations seize on the same points. The essence is that individuals are self-creating, that no single good defines successful self-creation, and that taking responsibility for one's own life and making of it what one can is itself part of the good life as understood by liberals. Dewey labelled this experimentalism, Kant defined it as the spirit of the enlightenment; Mill borrowed from von Humboldt to argue that the fundamental aim is to develop human nature in all its diversity (Mill, [1861] 1974, pp. 121–2; Dewey, [1931] 1984, pp. 114–20; Kant, 1991, pp. 53–4).

Its positive attractions become clearer when they are contrasted with pre-liberal or anti-liberal views. *Self*-discipline is a great good, because nobody can conduct 'experiments in living' without the self-control that allows them to stand back and assess their success or failure; submission to discipline, as praised by many Christian writers, and before them by Plato, is not a good in itself (Plato, *Republic*, pp. 127–40). Attachment to one's country and fellow citizens is a great good, because few human virtues flourish except against a background of loyalty and strong fellow feeling; 'my country right or wrong' is an illiberal sentiment, suggesting an immersion in patriotic sentiment inconsistent with the ideals of individual autonomy.

Plato condemned democratic Athens for its attachment to diversity and variety; liberals condemn Athens for being insufficiently hospitable to diversity and variety as good in themselves. Pericles' famous funeral oration praises the Athenians for their willingness to allow others to live as they pleased, but suggests no positive enthusiasm for variety as a human good, denies that women have any place in public life and ranks politics higher than any private good. Liberals generally praise public spirit, and most at any rate would agree that in time of crisis we are obliged to put aside our private concerns and do what we can for our country, but they would also see this as a sacrifice of one good for another, while Pericles was true to the classical ideal in ranking the goods of private life much lower than the goods of public life (Thucydides, *Peloponnesian War*, pp. 143–51).

It is true that liberalism has no single positive picture of 'the good life for man'. It is true because liberals have commonly been empiricists, and inclined to believe that only experience can reveal what really conduces to individual flourishing, and also because liberals have often been pluralists and have thought that autonomous individuals might choose a great variety of very different, but equally good lives (Berlin, 1969, pp. 172–4). It is not, as critics often maintain, that liberals elevate choice to the only absolute good; no liberal would applaud a life of crime merely because the criminal had chosen it. It is, however, true that most liberals have thought that the kind of autonomous individual they have admired can only become a fully autonomous being by exercising his or her powers of choice. Some people may strike lucky and find what suits them without very much exploration of alternatives; others may need to search much longer. But a person incapable of making a choice and sticking to it will have little chance of leading a happy life.

This vision is not uncontroversial, and it is unattractive to many critics. It is unsympathetic to a vision of an orderly universe in which the best lay down the rule of life to the rest of us; it is anti-aristocratic, at odds with a belief in Platonic guardians, Aristotelian aristocrats and the Catholic Christian tradition's claim to know what we must do to be saved. Conversely, it is too strenuous for anyone who thinks most people do well enough by thoughtlessly following the habits and customs of their fellows. It is too optimistic for anyone who believes in the essential depravity of the human race. Liberals look for improvement, not merely to prevent our worse natures getting out of hand. Writers like Joseph de Maistre and Georges Sorel have not unpersuasively ridiculed this outlook.

Looked at from the other side, it can be criticized as insufficiently serious about its own premises. Nietzsche claimed that liberals did not take choice seriously, since they assumed that everyone would share their ideas about what constituted good choices and good reasons for choosing one way rather than other. His successors in the existentialist tradition made essentially the same point. As observed before, liberals are uncomfortably aware that they can seem equivocal at worst or wishy-washy at best in their attempts to steer a tidy course between the critics who complain that they overestimate the value of autonomy and critics who complain that they have not understood that human freedom is a curse and a source of anguish rather than an achievement. It is too late in the day to rely on Aristotle's claim that the truth in these matters is to be found in the mean between extremes, but the liberal can at any rate reply that there is no more reason to suppose that it lies in the extremes than in the ground between them that liberalism occupies.

A theory for society

It is a common complaint against liberalism that it undervalues the role of community. Over the past fifteen years this has been a constant refrain, but it replicates the complaints made by critics of philosophical radicalism in the early 1800s and by philosophical idealists in the late 1800s (Sandel, 1982, passim). One response to the complaint might be to list those liberals who took the role of the community entirely seriously – they include de Tocqueville, Mill, T. H. Green, L.T. Hobhouse, Emile Durkheim, William James and John Dewey. This is only the starting point for an answer to the question whether liberalism has or even can have a liberal theory of society. The answer is plainly that it can and indeed that it does. In fact, one might argue that it is only because liberals are so impressed by the ways in which society moulds and shapes the lives of its members that liberals are so eager to ensure that society does not also cramp and distort those lives.

Sociologists used to claim that their opponents were attached to a contractual account of society, and by this they meant that their opponents believed that society literally had its origins in some kind of agreement. Although it is plain that no contemporary liberal would think anything of the sort, it is true that liberals find it illuminating to think of society as if it involved a sort of contract. The authority of the group over the individual is not absolute, but extends only to the hypothetical terms of a bargain by which individuals agree to accept that authority (Nagel, 1991, pp. 33ff). The terms of the bargain are what remain in dispute. In his essay *On Liberty* Mill essentially treated it as a compact for self-protection. Society was as it were a device for lending individuals the force of the whole group in fending off attacks on their persons and property (Mill, [1861] 1974, pp. 119–22).

This only covered the coercive authority of society. A more elusive topic was what a liberal society would look like, going beyond the question of what rules it might properly enforce on its members. Just as in the case of its account of the values that give point to an individual existence, liberalism is to some extent hampered in giving a very rich account by its attachment to the value of choice. Once we have said that a society full of liberals would be replete with voluntary associations devoted to enhancing the existences of all their members, there is little more to say. We may agree that a liberal would think it desirable that stamp collectors should get together and discuss their enthusiasms, exchange stamps, circulate journals about their hobby and all the rest, but it defies the imagination to offer a liberal theory of philately.

Liberals would object strongly to any regime which made philately difficult – it would be a pointless interference with liberty – and would divide on the question whether a government might properly assist philatelic societies to get started by a temporary subsidy, as liberals have always divided in their attitudes to government assistance for art, education, and high culture. Beyond that, the liberal answer to the question of what a society attached to liberal principles would actually look like is that the answer is a matter for the society in question. It might have many churches or none, a multitude of different schooling systems or one, an effective public transport system or not; what would matter would be that the human rights or individual liberty of its members were respected in the process of reaching these outcomes. In particular, liberalism is agnostic about what the implementation of the vision of a society of free individuals entails for the economic arrangements it embraces. Certainly, too many state controls threaten liberty, a state monopoly of employment threatens liberty (Rawls, 1971, pp. 377ff). So does a capitalism that allows rich men to buy politicians. Where the best feasible regime lies is a matter for experiment.

A theory for the state

What applies to society does not apply in the same way to the state. Society is the realm of both informal and formal associations, a realm in which public opinion plays some coercive role, but there is much scope for voluntary association; in a manner of speaking society is a plurality of smaller societies. The state is essentially the realm of coercively sanctioned co-ordination, and its essence is that it has no competitors or alternatives. That a liberal state must operate according to the rule of law goes without saying; that it must employ as little coercion as possible in its dealings with its citizens also goes without saying. What is more hotly contested is whether liberalism dictates any particular form of government.

Liberals have historically thought at one time that liberalism was threatened by democracy, and at another that liberalism entailed democracy. What liberalism is always committed to is constitutional government. Save in emergencies, where the preservation of a liberal regime may force governments to take powers that would otherwise be intolerable, the requirements of the rule of law extend to the ways in which governments acquire power and exercise it. How this is achieved has no fixed answer. It is an ongoing argument whether the British view that governments are kept liberal by public opinion and fear of the voter is more or less plausible than the American view that a written constitution and a formal Bill of Rights are uniquely effective. It is more than plausible that such institutional devices as an independent judiciary, a diverse and free press, and a great variety of watchdog organizations such as the US Council for Civil Liberties are all of them useful, and that one needs both the formal protections of American constitutionalism and a liberal-minded citzenry that makes them more than parchment barriers to oppression (Madison, 1987, Paper 48, p. 309).

This leaves the connection between liberalism and democracy for further analysis. If democracy is just a matter of majority rule, it is a contingent matter whether the majority will generally subscribe to liberal views. If they do, there will be a liberal democracy, if not, not. Various devices may be set up to restrain the majority, such as an entrenched Bill of Rights, but all such devices favour liberty by restricting democracy. They are intrinsically undemocratic in so far as they restrict the authority of the majority. On the whole, this view was the view of Jefferson, de Tocqueville and Mill, who were correspondingly anxious to educate the fledgling democracy of their day in order that democracy should not be majority tyranny (Mill, 1974, pp. 62ff; de Tocqueville, [1835] 1964, pp. 269ff).

The alternative view is that liberalism is committed to democracy, and that illiberal democracy is not democracy at all. Each individual has a right to take part in the decisions that affect his or her society. Nobody ought to be governed without their voice being heard, for that is a violation of their human rights, or of their right to be treated as a free and equal member of their society (Dworkin, 1985, pp. 193ff). To the objection that majority rule may be inconsistent with liberty, the sophisticated reply is essentially that the authority, as distinct from the power, of the majority is intrinsically self-limiting. We cannot claim the right to vote, for instance, on terms that violate others' rights. On this view, a Bill of Rights does not limit the majority's authority so much as spell out what its authority is. Liberal democracy is not something one may realize if one is lucky; the only legitimate democracy is liberal democracy.

However we decide between these two conceptualizations, liberal government must be limited government. Freedom of conscience, freedom of occupational choice, privacy and family rights all place limits on what governments may do. Limited government may none the less be active government; securing these rights will keep government busy. More to the point, liberal governments will inherit many illiberal arrangements from their predecessors. Abolishing racial and sexual discrimination in the United States has been neither quick nor easy. Reducing the effects of inherited privilege in the United Kingdom has hardly begun. A government that takes liberalism seriously will be a busy government, especially since it will also have to be ingenious in pursuing its goals through lawful channels.

On this point, defenders of 'classical' and 'modern' forms of liberalism can agree. Both deplore the advantages of monopolists; sexual and racial discrimination, and the advantages of inherited position, share in the wickedness of monopolies, for they give undeserved advantages to their beneficiaries and undeserved handicaps to their victims. It may be that 'classical' liberals suppose that once a 'level playing field' has been achieved, it will remain level, while modern liberals suppose that it will need constant attention. It is certainly true that modern liberals emphasize the 'equal' in equal opportunity, where their predecessors perhaps stress 'opportunity', and have no particular liking for equality of any other kind. Still, the point remains that limited governments need not be inactive or lazy governments.

Success or Failure?

It is a task of some delicacy to sum up the successes and failures of the liberal project. In the terminology of practising politicians, it has been avowed conservatives who have prospered in the Western democracies over the past two decades, though they have often been at odds among themselves as to whether they were conservatives *tout court* or 'neo-liberals', trying to revive the political and economic ideals of the early nineteenth century. 'Roosevelt liberals', on the other hand, enthusiasts for an expansive welfare state and for an energetic egalitarianism in social and economic policy, have done rather badly. Here, too, however, it is an open question whether the voting public in the Western democracies have turned against the liberal welfare state, or have merely decided that they are grateful for what they have received and are sceptical about the chances of going much further.

One success for the liberal project is the striking collapse of Marxist regimes worldwide. Since Marxist governments drew their legitimacy from the supposed superiority of Marxian socialism over its liberal alternatives, the wholesale failure of Marxist regimes in all possible respects – their failure as economic systems, their inability to secure the political loyalties of their subjects, their failure to secure the human rights of the citizenry, and so on – in effect amounts to a practical demonstration that liberalism of some kind has won.

In this contest, it is liberalism only in the very broadest sense that has triumphed – that is, a liberalism that stresses human rights, economic opportunity and the values of the open society, rather than one with narrower party political attachments. This liberalism has triumphed, not only over Marxism, but also over the illiberalism of nationalistic military regimes of the kind that once held power all over Latin America. It has, up to a point, triumphed over the apartheid regime of South Africa. Whether a narrower liberalism is particularly popular is another matter entirely, as is the prospect of any kind of liberalism making inroads into military dictatorship in Asia and most of Africa.

That it is only liberalism in the broadest, non-party political sense that has triumphed is obvious enough. Western conservatives do not support theocratic absolutism, or government by divine right, but would still reject the liberal label as a description of their politics. Liberalism has been equally criticized for the past forty years or so from another direction for its lack of interest in political participation and the development of an active citizenry. Writers who take their cue from classical republicanism think, as do the communitarians, that the liberal view of the individual is of someone essentially cut off from public life, concerned with affairs that are private in the sense of being jealously protected from everyone else. This, they argue, makes for a less healthy politics than the participatory politics described by Aristotle, Machiavelli and other republican writers.

On the republican view, there is certainly a place for the negative liberty – immunity from oppression by the government or any other powerful organization or individual – that liberalism puts at the front of its political demands. But this liberty cannot be preserved unless the citizenry is active in preserving it. In effect, one republican complaint is that liberalism is unable to offer a coherent story about how liberal goals are to be secured, while the other is that liberalism in action tends to turn individuals in on themselves, encourages them to quit the public stage and concentrate only on domestic, or economic goals. To this, many liberals reply that the French Revolution of 1789 is a sufficient warning about the dangers of trying to make ancient republicans out of modern Frenchmen, and by the same token, out of modern Americans, Australians or Englishmen, too – as Benjamin Constant's 'Essay on the liberty of the ancients compared with that of the moderns' pointed out in 1818 (Constant, 1990, pp. 309–12). Having said so, however, they are as quick as anyone to lament the failure of public spirit and political engagement that seems to afflict the Western world at the end of the twentieth century.

The liberalism that has triumphed, then, is not an intellectually rigorous system, manifested in its only possible institutional form. It is an awkward and intellectually insecure system, committed to democracy tempered by the rule of law, to a private enterprise economy supervised and controlled by government, to equal opportunity so far as it can be maintained without too much interference with the liberty of employers, schools, and families. It by no means embraces *laissez-faire* with the same fervour that Marxism brought to its attack on property and its passion for rational, central control of economic activity, a point made eloquently by Daniel Bell (1961, pp. 393–407). Moreover, the inhabitants of liberal democracies are deeply, and properly, conscious of the shortcomings of their societies, and certainly feel their 'success' is an equivocal one.

To know how permanent the success of liberalism is, or how complete it is, one would need a crystal ball rather than the resources of philosophy or political science. In any case, a liberal society can never be more than a partial 'success' by its own standards; its aspirations for the individual, for society and for the conduct of government guarantee that its ambitions will always exceed its performance. On the other hand, its members may, under most circumstances, feel that their failures are only partial and temporary, and that the way in which liberalism institutionalizes self-criticism is itself a guarantee of some progress even if it is also a guarantee of permanent dissatisfaction.

See also 5 ECONOMICS; 7 LEGAL STUDIES; 14 AUTONOMY; 16 CONTRACT AND CONSENT; 17 CONSTI-
TUTIONALISM AND THE RULE OF LAW; 19 DEMOCRACY; 22 DISTRIBUTIVE JUSTICE; 25 EQUALITY; 28
LEGITIMACY; 29 LIBERTY; 31 PROPERTY; 32 REPUBLICANISM; 33 RIGHTS; 36 STATE; 37 TOLERATION AND
FUNDAMENTALISM; 38 TOTALITARIANISM; 39 TRUST

References

Arendt, H.: *Totalitarianism* (1951); (New York: Harcourt, Brace and World, 1968).
Bell, D.: *The End of Ideology* (New York: The Free Press, 1961).
Berlin, I.: *Four Essays on Liberty* (Oxford: Oxford University Press, 1969).
Constant, B.: *Political Writings*, ed. B. Fontana (Cambridge: Cambridge University Press, 1990).
Dewey, J.: *Individualism Old and New* (1931); (Carbondale: Southern Illinois University Press, 1984).
Dworkin, R.: 'Liberalism', *A Matter of Principle* (Cambridge, Mass.: Harvard University Press, 1985), pp. 181–204.
Epstein, R.: *Takings: Private Property and the Power of Eminent Domain* (Cambridge, Mass.: Harvard University Press, 1985).
Gallie, W. B.: 'Essentially contested concepts', *Proceedings of the Aristotelian Society*, 56 (1956), 167–98.
Gray, J.: *Mill on Liberty: A Defence* (London: Routledge & Kegan Paul, 1983).
————: *Hayek on Liberty* (Oxford: Blackwell, 1984).
————: *Liberalism* (Milton Keynes: Open University Press, 1986).
Green, T. H.: 'Liberal legislation and freedom of contract' (1874), in *Collected Works* (London: Macmillan, 1892).
Hartz, L.: *The Liberal Tradition in America* (New York: Harcourt, Brace and World, 1955).
Hayek, F. von: *Law, Liberty and Legislation*, 3 vols (London, Routledge & Kegan Paul, 1973–9).
————: *The Mirage of Social Justice* (London: Routledge & Kegan Paul, 1976) (vol. II of the above).
Hobbes, T.: *Leviathan* (1651); (Cambridge: Cambridge University Press, 1991).
Hobhouse, L. T.: *Liberalism* (1911); (New York: Oxford University Press, 1964).
Kant, I.: *Political Writings*, ed. Hans Reiss (Cambridge: Cambridge University Press, 1991).
Locke, J.: *A Letter on Toleration*, in *Second Treatise on Government* (1689), ed. J. M. Gough (Oxford: Blackwell, 1956).
————: *Two Treatises on Civil Government* (1690), ed. Peter Laslett (Cambridge: Cambridge University Press, 1967).
Madison, J. et al.: *The Federalist* (Harmondsworth: Penguin Books, 1987).
Mill, J. S.: *On Liberty* (1861); (Harmondsworth: Penguin Books, 1974).
————: *Principles of Political Economy* (1848); (Toronto: University of Toronto Press, 1965).
Nagel, T.: *Equality and Partiality* (Oxford: Oxford University Press, 1991).
Nozick, R.: *Anarchy, State and Utopia* (New York: Basic Books, 1974).
Plato: *The Republic*, trans. and ed. Francis Cornford (Oxford: The Clarendon Press, 1941).
Rawls, J.: *A Theory of Justice* (Cambridge, Mass.: Harvard University Press, 1971).
————: 'Justice as fairness: political not metaphysical', *Philosophy and Public Affairs*, 14 (3) (summer 1985), 221–56.
————: 'The domain of the political and overlapping consensus', *New York University Law Review*, 64 (1989), 233–55.

Rorty, R.: 'The priority of democracy to philosophy', *Philosophical Papers* (Cambridge: Cambridge University Press, 1991), pp. 175–96.
Rossiter, C.: *Conservatism in America* (Cambridge, Mass.: Harvard University Press, 1982).
Sandel, M.: *Liberalism and the Limits of Justice* (Cambridge: Cambridge University Press, 1982).
Smith, A.: *The Wealth of Nations* (1775); (Oxford: The Clarendon Press, 1976).
Thucydides: *The Peloponnesian War* (Harmondsworth: Penguin Books, 1972).
Tocqueville, A. de, *Democracy in America* (1835); (New York: Random House, 1964).

Further reading

Historical

Green, T. H.: *Lectures on Political Obligation* (Cambridge: Cambridge University Press, 1986).
Montesquieu, Baron de: *The Spirit of the Laws* (Cambridge: Cambridge University Press, 1986).
Russell, B.: *Principles of Social Reconstruction* (London: Allen & Unwin, 1916).
Spencer, H.: *The Man versus the State* (Indianapolis: Liberty Classics, 1981).

Commentary

Arblaster, A.: *The Rise and Decline of Western Liberalism* (Oxford: Blackwell, 1984).
Rosenblum, N.: *Another Liberalism* (Cambridge, Mass.: Harvard University Press, 1989).
Ruggiero, G. de: *The History of European Liberalism*, trans. R. G. Collingwood (Oxford: Clarendon Press, 1924).

Contemporary

Ackerman, B.: *Social Justice in the Liberal State* (New Haven, Conn.: Yale University Press, 1980).
Flathman, R.: *Toward a Liberalism* (Ithaca, NY: Cornell University Press, 1989).
Galston, W.: *Liberal Purposes* (Cambridge: Cambridge University Press, 1991).
Macedo, S.: *Liberal Virtues* (Oxford: Clarendon Press, 1990).
Raz, J.: *The Morality of Freedom* (Oxford: Clarendon Press, 1986).
Rosenblum, N., ed.: *Liberalism and the Moral Life* (New York: Cambridge University Press, 1990).
Spitz, D.: *The Real World of Liberalism* (Chicago: Chicago University Press, 1982).
Taylor, C.: *Sources of the Self* (Cambridge, Mass.: Harvard University Press, 1990).

I2

Marxism

BARRY HINDESS

The idea that 'Marxism' exists in the form of a codified body of thought is largely an invention of the period following shortly after Marx's death in 1883. Attempts to systematize his and Engels' ideas, and then to popularize the result, began with Engels' *Anti-Dühring* in 1878 and were continued by the socialist parties of the Second International. The largest and most influential of these parties was in Germany, and it is there that the first significant Marxist orthodoxy was established. Almost from the beginning, Marxist orthodoxy was disputed by revisionists – that is, by Marxists and Marxist sympathizers who denied the very possibility of constructing an orthodoxy in an approach to the study of history that was thought to be to be scientific and therefore open to revision. Bernstein's *Evolutionary Socialism* (Bernstein, [1899] 1961) is the best-known early example. Competing orthodoxies emerged, the most influential being communism, under the leadership (later disputed by other parties) of the Communist Party of the Soviet Union, and the many varieties of Trotskyism (named after the refugee communist anti-pope of the Stalin era).

Lenin once described Marx's 'doctrine . . . as the direct and immediate continuation of the teachings of the greatest representatives of philosophy, political economy and socialism' (Lenin, [1913] 1964, p. 23), and that judgement would not be disputed by representatives of other orthodoxies or by revisionists. The various Marxisms have invariably regarded themselves as being political and highly theoretical – and most of them have claimed to be scientific. They have also hoped to be severely practical. Where communist or Trotskyist movements have been strong, they have tried to offer appropriately tailored versions of their science to different sections of their real or potential supporters. Some of the versions on offer have been remarkably crude, but others have been relatively sophisticated. In the West, where attempted revolutions have been defeated or where would-be revolutionary parties were too weak even to make the attempt, Marxist discussion has often developed in contexts somewhat remote from direct political involvement. Many commentators have suggested that this remoteness from the stimulus of effective political action, and from the constraints imposed by party leaderships, accounts for some of the distinctive features of Western Marxism (Anderson, 1976). However, even in these cases, the assumption that there is or should be an intimate link between theory and practical politics has meant that theoretical differences have often been interpreted as having great political importance. Conversely, political differences have frequently been understood as resulting from theoretical errors or deviations.

The existence of competing Marxist orthodoxies and of various revisionisms ensures that Marxism presents a very different image from the inside than it does to an outsider. From within, Marxism has usually been perceived as if it were a relatively coherent body of thought, in which certain issues could be regarded as matters of legitimate disagreement while others marked the boundaries between Marxism on the one side and its intellectual/political opponents (including Marxist renegades) on the other. From without, the image of an overall coherence is less than compelling. Instead, the observer is likely to be impressed by the sheer diversity of activities that have been able to describe themselves as Marxist. In this respect – and in spite of its apparent derivation from the thought of one man – Marxism is not unlike the other great 'isms' of contemporary politics.

More appropriate, perhaps, than the image of a relatively coherent body of thought is that of a collection of Marxisms held together by family resemblances – a collection in which distinctive features recur, sometimes with startling variations, but few are universal. The image of the family has other advantages: it suggests the great variety of feelings – ranging from genuine closeness, through respectful distance to outright hatred – which different family members might have for one another, and it suggests that while family histories are likely to privilege certain lines of descent, there will also be recurrent features that suggest affinity with other families, to such an extent at times that the paternity of some members of the Marxist family may be open to dispute.

The most familiar recurrent features in the Marxist family are the following:

1 A teleological theory of history in which ideas of class struggle and of the primacy of the economy play a major explanatory role.
2 The claim to provide a critical analysis of society, with the fundamental rider set out in Marx's last thesis on Feuerbach that 'the philosophers have only *interpreted* the world . . . the point however, is to *change* it' (Marx, [1845] 1968, p. 30). Marxism presents itself both as a theory of society and as a socialist political project.
3 The claim that, unlike many competing socialisms, both Marxist theory and its political project are scientific.

These features are considerably more prominent in some cases than they are in others – and, like phenotypical features of other kinds, they each bring together a number of disparate elements.

Following a short discussion of these features in the first part of this chapter, the second part considers their appearances in influential contemporary branches of the Marxist family.

Familial features

In *The Communist Manifesto* (1848), Marx and Engels insist that 'history is the history of class struggle'. In other words, classes and conflicts between them have been central features of social life throughout recorded history, and they are among the most important sources of social change. This treatment of class struggle as an important feature of many societies is by no means peculiar to Marxism. Marx himself admitted that he had taken the idea from the work of bourgeois historians, and it is still widely employed by non-Marxist sociologists. What is distinctively Marxist in this respect is largely a result of its attempts to integrate class analysis into a general theory of history involving a three-level model of society in which the economy plays the most important part. These attempts normally define classes by reference to the positions that individuals occupy within the economy, and they treat the existence of classes as an *objective* feature of the society in question – meaning that the existence of a class does not depend on any subjective awareness or commitment on the part of its members.

In effect, Marxism brings an account of class as a set of individuals who share a common economic location together with an understanding of class as an active social force, as required by the claim that history is the history of class struggle. The combination is not an easy one. On the one hand, the mere fact of their objective membership of a class will not necessarily bring together as a collective actor those who happen to belong to that class. On the other hand, the forces that engage in social conflict are more or less organized collectivities and agencies – armies, police, trades unions, parties and religious organizations, riotous mobs – but not classes as such. It is one thing to say that social conflict is a central feature of human history, and quite another to say that *classes* are the basic forces involved in that conflict.

Marxists have not been unaware of the difficulties here, and they have tended to approach them from one or both of two directions (Hindess, 1987). One is to treat classes, and the conflicts between them, as the key to understanding the variety of agencies and forces at work in any given society. It is from this perspective that Marxists routinely interpret the activities of state agencies, political parties and other organizations – and sometimes even the theoretical work of intellectuals – as *representing*, perhaps unconsciously, the interests of one or more classes. The alternative approach is to regard the formation of a class as an effective collective actor – essentially through the development of an appropriate level of class consciousness among the individual members of that class – as a political achievement that must be secured if the class in question is to pursue its interests with any hope of success. This problem has been addressed with varying degrees of rigour, ranging from Lukács' classic *History and Class Consciousness* (Lukács, 1922) to numerous Trotskyist attempts to come to terms with the absence of successful socialist revolutions in the West; and also, more recently, in 'analytical Marxism', which I discuss below.

Now consider the primacy of the economy. In the Preface to his *Contribution to the Critique of Political Economy* Marx (1872) sketches a view of societies as consisting of an economic foundation, 'upon which rises' a political and legal superstructure, and 'to which correspond . . . forms of social thought'. While there is a strong implication that the economy plays a fundamental role, the character of the relationships suggested by the quoted phrases is far from clear. Following Engels' lead, Marxists have generally tried to have things both ways: insisting on the real autonomy of the superstructures in some contexts, while in other contexts maintaining that 'in the last instance' the economy plays the most important part.

Except for this notoriously ambiguous doctrine of 'the last instance' and for the analysis of the economy itself in terms of relations of production and productive forces, there is little in this general view of societies that is peculiar to Marxism. The suggestion that societies consist of economic, political, legal and cultural (or ideological) components is a commonplace of Western social thought in the modern period. So too, is the teleological ranking of human societies which identifies the societies of the modern West as the most advanced to date.

However, the closely related idea that societies – together with economies and other parts within them – have a reality and a life of their own, subject to their own particular laws of motion, requires some further comment. It has been disputed from the standpoint of methodological individualism, a Marxist variant of which is considered below, but what concerns us at this point is the form in which the idea itself emerged in seventeenth- and eighteenth-century European thought.

Notice first that the modern understanding of the economy (and the science of political economy which aimed to investigate its behaviour) developed out of, and in opposition to, an understanding of relations between a ruler and the wealth at his command that was conceived on the model of the management of a household or estate (Tribe, 1978). Where both understandings concerned themselves with the provision of advice to government, political economy (and its successor, economics) insisted that government action should take account of the laws governing the natural development of the economy itself. With notable exceptions (such as Malthus) the general presumption was that, left to itself, there was a natural tendency for the wealth of the community to grow, although that tendency might be inhibited by the ignorance and superstition of the people, and, of course, by the misguided actions of their rulers. As faithful children of the Enlightenment, the political economists tended to believe that the most damaging effects of ignorance and superstition among the population at large were on the way to being dispelled – at least in their own societies. This belief left government as the most important single obstacle to continued economic development. Government intervention might still be justified, however, if only to clear away other obstacles to economic growth, including the effects of earlier governmental interventions.

The assumption that there is a natural tendency towards economic growth provides Marxism with the underlying mechanism for its teleology of history. Most Marxist orthodoxies have followed the view set out in Marx's Preface (and strongly defended in Cohen, 1978) that this natural tendency – which may in some cases be blocked by countervailing pressures – will generate revolutions as one type of economy is replaced by another. However, the Marxist analysis of politics in class terms implies an attitude towards government which is very different from that of political economy. Marxism has regarded governmental intervention in capitalist societies as being essentially linked to class interests. Rather than the provision of supposedly disinterested advice in the name of economic growth, it has concerned itself with the transformation of society by means of class struggle. Eventually, Marxist orthodoxies suggest, economic development will lead to communism. This is a type of society based on forms of co-operative economic organization which are more productive even than capitalism, in which there is no place for class divisions. For that reason, Marxism maintains that it will also be a society in which there is no state. The ideal society then, is seen by Marxism – as it is by many liberals – as one in which economic activity has been purged of all political interference.

315

A second respect in which society has been thought to have a life of its own relates to the view that social theory is or should be a form of critique. In fact, Marxism has understood the idea of social theory as critique in at least two different senses. One understanding can be regarded as relatively straightforward, at least for the purposes of the present discussion. It is a version of the critique of ideology – derived in Marx's case, from Feuerbach and the Young Hegelians – and it involves the claim that society itself generates forms of perception that are essentially illusory. An example would be Marx's argument that the commodity forms of capitalist society promote categories of thought which lead people to treat relations between persons as if they were relations between things. In such cases, scientific analysis could be said to perform a critical function by exposing reality for what it is. Much of Marx's own work was clearly intended to be critical in that sense, although, as his 'Theses on Feuerbach' indicate, Marx also thought that it was necessary to move beyond criticism into action.

However, the understanding of social theory as critique that most concerns us at this point is the sense in which it is regarded as a moral critique of political power. To see what is at stake here it may be helpful to take a detour through the history of the idea of civil society, conceived of as a realm of social interaction independent of direct control by government and other extraneous social forces. An early version of this idea (but not the term itself, which has a rather different provenance; see Keane, 1988) appears in Locke's *Essay Concerning Human Understanding*, which argues that our sense of what is morally right and morally wrong is largely the result of the pleasures and pains that follow from our interaction with laws – the most effective of which in the actual regulation of human behaviour belong to 'the Law of Opinion and Reputation'. This Law develops in and through the expressions of approval and disapproval that occur in our interactions with our fellows. It depends on no central authority, either for its enunciation or its enforcement, and it is one from which only the hermit can ever hope to escape. Not only does it regulate behaviour in the immediate sense but also, through the repeated experiences of pleasure and pain that it occasions, it forms the internal standards by which we each regulate our own behaviour. Locke suggests that this Law has governed the greater part of human behaviour throughout history.

What matters for present purposes is not so much what Locke himself made of this idea, but rather the manner in which it was taken up in the absolutist regimes of continental Europe, and, in a rather different fashion, in the North American colonies. Together with the Lockean account of the legitimacy of government, it provided the foundations for a powerful critique of political power that was elaborated throughout the eighteenth century both in the writings of Enlightenment philosophers and in the activities of such groups as the Freemasons, the Illuminati and the Republic of Letters (Koselleck, 1988). The idea of a morality that arises out of the life of society itself appeared to provide the moral foundations of the relation of trust that the Lockean account of legitimacy tells us should obtain between the people and their government. Conversely, where that relation of trust failed to obtain, civil society seemed to provide the foundations on which the moral critique of government could be developed.

If civil society is to be able to perform this role it must satisfy two conditions. First, it must remain relatively free from direct government control if the morality which it generates is to provide an independent basis from which to assess the character and behaviour of government. Secondly, it must consist of rational, autonomous individuals since, on the Lockean account of legitimacy, these are the only persons capable of giving or of refusing to give their rational consent to government. On the one hand, then, individuals are seen as malleable creatures, whose moral character and other attributes are formed by the civil society in which they live. On the other hand, those same individuals must be regarded as autonomous.

Both understandings of the individual – and therefore of the civil society in which it lives – have played an important part in Western social thought, and in Marxism in particular. To the idea that much of morality and other habits of thought emerge out of the interactions that take place within civil society, Marxism has added the claim that civil society is invariably structured by the effects of class conflict. This implies that the habits of thought of individuals will themselves be infected through the impact of class relations on civil society. In this way class power can affect the thoughts and desires of its victims without them being aware of it. This view of civil society also suggests that morality in a class society should be regarded as a matter of class struggle – of their morality and ours, as Trotsky once put it (Trotsky, 1938). Where Rawls treats the morality that prevails in Western societies as providing the independent basis from which we can evaluate the actions of government and others, Marxism tends to regard it as serving the interests of the ruling class.

Marxists, then, can hardly be expected to treat existing civil society as if it could perform the functions which the earlier tradition of critical thought had assigned to it. Nevertheless, as we shall see in the second part of this chapter, Marxists of the Frankfurt School of critical theory, and many of their post-Marxist successors, have taken up the ideal of a civil society inhabited by rational, autonomous individuals and unaffected by the impact of class power as the basis on which to erect a normative critique of modern societies. This is the second sense in which Marxism offers a critical theory of society.

Consider, finally, the claim that Marxism offers a socialism that is scientific. At the simplest level what is at stake here is the claim that Marxism provides the scientific knowledge of society which is a necessary condition of rational action in the field of politics. This desire to base political action on the best available knowledge is no more – and certainly no less – problematic in the case of Marxism than it is in the case of other would-be rational modes of politics. What is distinctive rather is first, the specific content of the science that Marxism claims to offer, and second, its understanding of what it is to be scientific. The first need not detain us further, except to note that few contemporary non-Marxist conceptions of science would countenance the unashamedly teleological view of human history presented by most forms of Marxism. However, it would hardly be reasonable to single Marxism out for special attention in this respect: if there is a problem here for Marxism, it is a problem that has affected the greater part of Western social thought throughout the modern period. As for the second, Marxists have generally tried to base their own accounts of Marxism as a science on the best available contemporary knowledge, while at the same time remaining faithful to the essentials of Marxism – sometimes including earlier Marxist, or Marx's own, understandings of science. There are conflicting accounts of each of these desiderata, and of the relative weight to be accorded to each of them. Those who have placed greater weight on the first have generally also argued for revision of the second.

Three varieties of Western Marxism

In the years between the Second World War and the late 1980s, Western academic Marxism flourished, producing substantial bodies of work in economics, history and the social sciences. In philosophy, and in political and social theory more generally, Marxism was more influential in Western Europe than in Britain or North America: critical theory was re-established in German academic life in the 1950's; Merleau-Ponty, Sartre and other French intellectuals entered into a sustained critical encounter with communism (Lichtheim, 1966), and Sartre (1960) later attempted a major reconstruction of Marxist theory; and a lively Marxist intellectual culture emerged in Italy, inspired in part by the work of Gramsci. Much of this work was made available to an English-language audience through such journals as *New Left Review* and *New German Critique*. Rather than attempt to survey this considerable volume of material, the remainder of this chapter concentrates on three varieties of Marxist social theory. The first is critical theory, which has been perhaps the single most influential tradition of academic Marxism in the West. It continues today, notably in the work of Habermas. The second is Marxist anti-humanism, most strongly represented in the work of Althusser and his associates in France during the 1960s. In his Preface to the first German edition of *Capital*, Marx insists that

here individuals are dealt with only in so far as they are the personification of economic categories, embodiments of particular class relations and class interests. My standpoint . . . can less than any other make the individual responsible for relations whose creature he socially remains, however much he may subjectively raise himself above them (Marx, [1867] 1967, pp. 20–1)

The great distinction of Althusser's Marxism lies in his sustained attempt to develop the sense of these remarks into an anti-humanist manifesto – in spite of the difficulty posed by Marx's final phrase. The failure of the Althusserian project cleared the way for the influence of a non-Marxist anti-humanism in France – and also for the emergence of a distinctive kind of Marxist humanism in Britain and North America. This last is our final topic. Analytical Marxism is a comparatively new development, which tries to pursue Marxist questions using analytical tools developed primarily in Anglo-American philosophy and social science.

Critical Theory

The term 'critical theory' is now usually taken to refer to a tradition of thought originating in the work of the Institute for Social Research, established in Frankfurt in 1923 and later, after a period of exile during the Nazi period, re-established there in 1950. The work of the original members of the Institute (comprehensively surveyed in Jay, 1973) is often referred to as the 'Frankfurt School'. In the areas of philosophy and political theory the names of Horkheimer, Adorno and Marcuse are perhaps the best known, although Kirchheimer and Neumann made important contributions to the analysis of the total state and of the political conditions required for the survival of pluralist politics in democratic societies. Many commentators insist that the work of Habermas, Offe and Wellmer represents another, quite distinct branch of critical theory, which takes its inspiration mainly from Habermas' attempts to reconstruct the Frankfurt School's understanding of critical theory (Held, 1980). Following a short discussion of what the Frankfurt School and the later generation of critical theorists share, this section concludes with an examination of the distinctive character of Habermas' more recent contribution.

Perhaps the single most important common feature is the aim of developing a theory of society that is *critical* in a number of what the critical theorists clearly regard as intimately related respects: first, taking the idea of critique in something like its Kantian sense, as involving an overriding concern with the conditions of possibility of knowledge and of reason; second, as a reflection on the development of Reason, now conceived as the subject of history, somewhat in the manner of an Hegelian spirit; third, in the sense of the critique of ideology, as unmasking the distorting images that conceal and legitimate the realities of power in modern societies; and finally, in the sense of a moral critique of political power based on the ideal of a society of rational and autonomous individuals. Together these imply that critical theory will promote enlightenment and emancipation: on the one hand, enabling individuals and collectivities to determine what their true interests are, and on the other, releasing them from those forms of coercion that depend on the mystifications of ideology.

Since critical theory regards itself as a study of society it offers a positive content. In that respect it is like the natural sciences. But it also regards itself as having a moral and aesthetic aspect, inducing self-reflection and self-improvement among those who are exposed to it. At a somewhat more general level, critical theory represents itself as a form in which Reason reflects upon its own condition. In these respects, critical theory invariably claims to offer not only an objective knowledge of the kind provided by the natural sciences but also something more. Although it is critical, and in that respect partisan, it represents itself as none the less capable of objectivity. While critical theorists acknowledge an important sense in which all knowledge is historically conditioned, they have also insisted that truth claims can be rationally adjudicated in a way that is independent of particular class or other interests.

In effect, critical theory insists that social investigation should aim to provide knowledge of society that is at once truthful and critical. For this reason, critical theorists have always been particularly opposed to 'positivism', which they interpret as the view that all cognition has the 'objectifying' structure of the natural sciences. Positivism denies the cognitive content of the critical or reflective aspects of the knowledge that critical theory claims to provide. Critical theory regards positivism as a mistaken epistemological doctrine. More seriously, however, since positivism denies the legitimacy of the critical enterprise, it is also seen as a serious threat to one of the most important contemporary vehicles of human emancipation. The controversies surrounding this view of the nature and objectives of social enquiry are well illustrated in *The Positivism Dispute in German Sociology* (Adorno et al., 1976).

Its self-consciously reflective character and its concern with the prospects for emancipation have meant that critical theory has always disputed the more deterministic interpretations of Marxism – for their 'positivism' as much as for their neglect of the independent significance of non-economic factors in human social development. While insisting on the fundamental importance of Marx's work for our understanding of modern society, critical theory also regarded the rise of fascism and the development of Stalinism in the East and of large public and private bureaucracies in the West as indicating that Marxism was seriously incomplete. The development of bureaucracies suggested that Marx's analysis of economic activity in terms of the unfettered development of market relations was unsatisfactory. It also demonstrated the importance of the characteristically Weberian concern with the development of instrumental reason, spreading like a plague to infect all institutional areas of modern life. The fragmentation of work within large-scale organizations and the impersonal character of bureaucratic rule within them and in the larger society induces reification and a sense of loss of control. Domination continues to exist, but it becomes increasingly anonymous and difficult to pin down.

While these developments present the individual with an external world that is difficult to comprehend, related developments affecting the character of the individual make it less likely that he or she will be able to develop a critical perspective on that world. One such development concerns the commercialization of popular culture. In their *Dialectic of Enlightenment* (Adorno and Horkheimer, 1972), for example, Horkheimer and Adorno argue that the great art of the modern period retains a certain autonomy from class and other social interests. While it often represents the established order in its content, it does so in a way that has critical and often subversive implications. By the middle of the twentieth century, however, culture had become an industry. Cultural artefacts had a standardized form often disguised by marginal product differentiation, and they were promoted and distributed in a similar manner to other commodities. Far from demanding a critical perspective from their audiences, the products of the culture industry offer only distraction and relaxation.

Laments about the quality of popular culture are common features of the modern world. What is distinctive about critical theory is the effort to integrate its lament into an account of socialization and social control. The development of the culture industry, and especially the mass marketing of its products, has resulted in the extensive manipulation of the leisure activities of most individuals, with consequent effects on their socialization. In effect, the culture industry and the media superimpose false needs, with the result that we act freely on the basis of thoughts and desires that come to us from without. However, what makes the impact of these external forces so significant is the fact that the individual's capacity for autonomous action has also been undermined by changes affecting the earliest stages of childhood socialization. Bringing psychoanalytic concepts into their treatment of bureaucratization and rationalization, critical theorists argued that the family was becoming less important as an independent source of personality formation. On the one hand, the helplessness of the individual in the face of modern systems of domination undermined the legitimacy of the father's authority within the family – thereby leaving the male child more vulnerable to the appeal of powerful images projected by the culture industry, the media, or political propaganda (Adorno et al., 1950). On the other hand, many of the socializing functions once performed by the family have now been taken over by outside agencies – by social workers and other welfare professionals, and by the media.

In the first part of this chapter I referred to the importance of an earlier critical tradition which regarded civil society both as regulating the behaviour and habits of thought of individuals and as providing moral foundations for an assessment of the legitimacy or otherwise of political power. The Frankfurt School of critical theory addresses a similar set of concerns and it retains the normative ideal of a society of autonomous rational individuals. It uses ideas derived from Marx, Weber and Freud to evaluate the civil societies that exist in the modern world, and it finds them all to be remarkably wanting. Civil society hardly existed in the East, and in the West it was dominated by forces that imposed false needs and desires on individuals, with the result that what they experienced as freedom was not genuine autonomy. A civil society of that kind could not provide the foundations for an independent moral critique of political power. In one of the most influential elaborations of this argument, Marcuse insists that freedom therefore demands repression 'of the heteronomous needs and satisfactions which organize life in this society' (Marcuse, 1972, p. 192).

The pessimism of this conclusion reflects a deeper pessimism about enlightenment itself. In effect, the Frankfurt theorists shared many of Weber's reservations about the consequences of rationalization, treating it as resulting at one level in a loss of meaning and at another level in the subordination of the individual to the requirements of bureaucracy. Their commitment to enlightenment and to reason was therefore deeply ambivalent. In that respect there are significant parallels between the later work of the Frankfurt School and the arguments of Foucault, Derrida and other 'postmodernists'.

This point brings us to Habermas' attempts to provide critical theory with more secure foundations. His earliest major work, only recently translated into English (Habermas, [1962] 1989), is a study of the emergence and development of a public sphere (i.e. civil society) in the seventeenth and eighteenth centuries, and of its later distortion and disintegration. In many respects, this study may be regarded as elaborating on some of the central concerns of the earlier generation of critical theorists. However, Habermas has been increasingly critical of that earlier generation's treatment of rationality. His attempts to provide the critical project with more secure intellectual foundations has gone through several stages, culminating in the two-volume, *The Theory of Communicative Action* (Habermas, 1984; 1987a). In his view the major figures of the earlier generation were too prone to treat questions concerning the conditions of reason and of knowledge as if they were about the situation of the individual subject. They therefore paid insufficient attention to the intersubjective conditions of rationality and of the formation of the individual in the course of interaction with others. Negative features which they attributed to rationalization should rather, in Habermas' opinion, be seen as consequences of the social conditions in which rationalization has taken place.

In place of the earlier critical theorists' 'philosophy of the subject', Habermas proposes an intersubjective account of rationality, making extensive use of phenomenological sociology, symbolic interactionism, and analytical philosophy. His focus is less on the situation of the individual subject than it is on the character of the lifeworld that individuals share with others. For that reason, language and its place in intersubjective relations are central to Habermas' argument. Not only does the use of language presuppose some degree of mutual understanding but also, in Habermas' view, the 'orientation to reaching understanding is the *original* mode of language use' (Habermas, 1984, p. 288). Other uses of language are predicated on that original orientation. In particular, then, instrumental rationality is parasitic upon a more fundamental *communicative* rationality.

This account of language provides the foundations for two rather different lines of argument in Habermas' work. First, he suggests that the original orientation to reaching understanding involves assumptions – about the rationality of other participants and about the process of communication between them – which are shared, if not always acknowledged, by anyone who attempts to engage in communication with others. These shared assumptions define a bedrock of agreement, independent of class or other interests, for the adjudication of aesthetic, cognitive and normative disputes. Habermas' concept of an ideal speech situation refers to a situation in which communication is in fact organized around the attempt to reach rationally motivated agreement. Where the Frankfurt theorists made use of the normative ideal of a society of autonomous individuals, Habermas posits an idealized lifeworld, oriented to the requirements of an ideal speech situation, to serve as a standpoint from which the present organization of society can be judged and found wanting.

Unfortunately – and this is Habermas' second line of argument – the character of the existing lifeworld may distort the communication that takes place within it. On the one hand, following Weber's account of the world views characteristic of non-Western societies, he suggests that the development of rationality may be blocked by tradition. In such cases, the orientation towards understanding will be satisfied by a reliance on traditionally certified interpretations that are not themselves regarded as being open to criticism. The extensive rationalization of life in the West however has resulted in a lifeworld in which the need for achieving understanding is now more likely to be met by the attempt at rationally motivated agreement. An important part of that process of rationalization was the emergence of a 'political public sphere . . . which, as a medium for permanent criticism, alters the conditions for the legitimation of political domination' (ibid., p. 341). On the other hand, Habermas also argues that the emergent rationality of the lifeworld has been distorted by the impact of extraneous factors. Power and money in particular 'work back upon contexts of communicative action and set their own imperatives against the marginalized lifeworld' (ibid.). Their intrusion into intersubjective relations results in forms of communication that are structured, not around the attempt to reach rationally motivated agreement, but rather by deference, fear and insecurity. The effect, in other words, is to undermine rationality.

I noted above that Habermas makes this case in relation to the public sphere in his first major work (Habermas, 1962). The argument is that, far from being a realm of free and open discussion, the public sphere has been distorted as a result of its development within capitalist society. His more recent work has retained the critical concerns of this earlier argument while moving away from the Marxist terms in which it is elaborated. Instead, he now makes use of the systems approaches of Parsons and Luhman to develop an analysis of rationality involving both a systems and a lifeworld perspective. The process of rationalization has certainly overcome the most debilitating effects of tradition within the lifeworld, but it has also provided conditions in which power and money could develop as societal media. To say that they are societal media is to say that power and money should be conceived of as generalized social mechanisms performing functions for the system, and not simply as serving the interests of those who possess them (compare the treatment of power in Parsons, 1963). The distortions of the lifeworld induced by these media are not, in Habermas's view, effects of the media as such. Rather, they should be seen as consequences of a pathological 'uncoupling of system and lifeworld' in which 'the mediatization of the lifeworld turns into its colonization' (Habermas, 1987, p. 318). In particular, the negative features which Weber and the Frankfurt theorists attributed to rationalization itself should really be regarded as consequences of the unfortunate conditions in which rationalization has developed.

Habermas' reworking of the foundations of critical theory appears, then, to immunize it from the worst effects of the Weberian ambivalence about rationality. In place of the doubts of the earlier generation of critical theorists, Habermas now regards himself as the unequivocal champion of enlightenment – and it is in that role that he presents himself as a persistent critic of conservatism on the one hand and of 'postmodernism' on the other (Habermas, 1987b; 1989). How far Habermas' reconstruction succeeds even in its own terms remains a matter of considerable debate (Honneth and Joas, 1991). In spite of his disagreements with the Frankfurt theorists, Habermas shares much of their critical orientation and especially its foundations in the utopian vision of an idealized civil society (Geuss, 1981; Lyotard, 1984, pp. 71–84).

Althusser

Althusser was a professional philosopher and an active member of the French Communist Party. His most influential works *For Marx* and *Reading Capital* were published in Paris in the mid-1960s – that is, before the events of May 1968 – and some years later in English translation (Althusser, 1969; Althusser and Balibar, 1970). His later retraction of some of his most important theses (Althusser, 1976) took the form of a partial reassertion of Marxist orthodoxy, and it will not be considered here. The influence of Althusser's ideas in France had declined by the early 1970s. Among English-speaking Marxists they remained significant throughout the 1970s, either directly or indirectly through the related work of Balibar, Pecheaux and Poulantzas and the early work of Hindess and Hirst (1985).

Perhaps the most distinctive features of Althusser's Marxism derive from his explicit refusal of what, in a usage not unlike that of Heidegger, he calls 'humanism' – that is, 'a problematic of human nature (or the essence of man)' (Althusser, 1969, p. 227). Whilst Althusser's anti-humanist strictures were most obviously directed against the humanistic Marxism of Sartre and others in France, they could equally well have been detected against the tradition of critical theory considered above. Its theoretical anti-humanism accounts for much of the hostility with which the Althusserian project has been greeted (for example, in Thompson, 1978), as it does to similar responses to the anti-humanism of Derrida and other 'left' Heideggerians. These latter authors follow Heidegger's lead in viewing humanism both as something to be wary of and as an inescapable feature of Western thought. In contrast, Althusser claims to present us with a Marxism that has finally escaped the intellectual shackles of humanism, thereby developing into a fully-fledged science. 'It is impossible', he insists, 'to *know* anything about men except on the condition that the philosophical (theoretical) myth of man is reduced to ashes' (Althusser, 1969, p. 229). The clearest manifestations of Althusser's anti-humanism occur first in his critique of 'the empiricist conception of knowledge' and his account of science and ideology as distinct forms of knowledge, and second, in his reworking of the traditional three-level model of society.

Althusser uses the phrase 'the empiricist conception of knowledge' to refer to the understanding of knowledge in terms of a relation between a knowing subject (an empirical or transcendental human individual, a scientific community, or whatever) on the one hand, and an object of knowledge on the other. The circularity of this conception of knowledge has often been noted – for example, in the Introduction to Hegel's *Phenomenology* – and in that respect Althusser merely reiterates a well-known theme in the history of philosophy. What is unusual about Althusser's discussion is that he makes no attempt to save empiricism by recasting it in a different form. Instead, he proposes an alternative conception in which knowledge is regarded as the outcome of a practice – that is, of a labour of transformation 'which sets to work, in a specific structure, men, means, and a technical method of utilizing the means' (ibid., pp. 166–7). On this view the central issues for the theory of knowledge concern that 'specific structure', and certainly not the men who work within it or the foundations on which knowledge is often supposed to rest. By analogy with Marx's analysis of manufacturing, Althusser describes science as a distinctive mode of production of knowledge in which the process of production itself is not governed by the intentions of individual scientists, but rather by the problematic (the system of concepts and relations between concepts) with which they work. The problematic determines the questions to be posed, the difficulties that are seen or not seen, and the kinds of evidence to be gathered, much as an assembly-line determines the tasks to be performed by the individuals who work on it. Following Bachelard (1938), Althusser maintains that, in so far as there are protocols for scientific practice, they cannot be derived from any extra-scientific (or philosophical) epistemology. There is no such thing as *the* scientific method, only scientific methods, each of which is determined by the problematic of the science in question.

Ideological knowledge, on the other hand, is not governed by problematics in the same way as the sciences. Althusser defines ideology in terms of the 'lived' relation between individuals and the social conditions of their existence – a relation that exists in the realm of the Lacanian imaginary. In a sense then, ideology does conform to empiricism as Althusser describes it, but the knowledge it produces is not a knowledge of the real. Theoretical ideologies (for example, Aristotelian physics, pre-Darwinian biology, and the non-Marxist social sciences) are reflected and elaborated forms of these lived relationships. Like the sciences, they are each governed by a problematic, by a specific system of concepts and relations between concepts. But, quite unlike the sciences, these problematics are themselves governed by the forms of consciousness of human subjects, and therefore by whatever determines those forms.

In Althusser's view then, theoretical ideology differs from science in two fundamental respects: first, theoretical ideology is always a kind of empiricism, whereas each science has its own distinct problematic; second, ideology is subject to the play of class interests whereas each scientific problematic has its own autonomous dynamic.

Unfortunately, this attempted demarcation between theoretical ideology on the one hand, and the sciences (including Marxism) on the other, is less successful than Althusser's argument requires. There are two major problems here. One concerns the arbitrariness of the demarcation itself. Theoretical ideology, we are told, is incurably empiricist. It operates with extra-theoretical elements that appear to be given; but they are given to theoretical discourse by ideology, not by the real as such. It is in these terms that Althusser, in *Reading Capital* (1970, Part II, ch. 7), investigates the discourse of political economy and finds it wanting. For all its theoretical sophistication the evidence of ideology can be seen throughout its foundations.

So much the worse, it seems, for political economy. The difficulty for Althusser's analysis is that Marx's *Capital* too appears to exhibit many of the empiricist symptoms of ideology. The reason for this unfortunate state of affairs, we are told, is that a science is created as the outcome of an epistemological break, a revolutionary reconstruction of the mode of production of knowledge in which one kind of problematic is replaced by another. Althusser maintains that such an epistemological break can be identified in Marx's own work, separating the humanist writings of his youth from the scientific texts of his maturity. This account of the emergence of the sciences suggests that they are not born in all their purity – and also that they remain forever threatened by ideological encroachments. Marx, for example, had little choice but to construct his arguments making use of elements taken over from the theoretical ideology in opposition to which he was laboriously attempting to construct his new science. *Capital* then should be read as a scientific text that is heavily contaminated by ideological remains. It has to be purged of these remains through what Althusser describes as a 'symptomatic reading'. Althusser takes this argument to its conclusion in *Lenin and Philosophy* (Althusser, 1971), which insists that the principal task of philosophy is precisely to defend the sciences against ideological encroachment. The task of Marxist philosophy in particular is to conduct the class struggle in the realm of theory.

It seems, then, that we should read political economy for evidence of its ideological character while reading *Capital* and other texts of Marxist theory for the science that we know is buried within them. The reading establishes the demarcation between the discourses of theoretical ideology and those of the sciences, and that demarcation tells us how the discourses are to be read. The evident circularity of this procedure together with the curious suggestion that the sciences need to be defended undermines the plausibility of Althusser's claim that the sciences are indeed autonomous, and not subject to the economic determinism that ultimately governs theoretical ideology.

This point brings us to the second major difficulty with Althusser's account of science, namely, the claim that each science has an *autonomous* dynamic governed by its own distinctive problematic. Notice first, that the analogy with manufacturing is a curious one. While it is true that workers on an assembly-line are assigned tasks by their position in the process itself, it is surely misleading to suggest that they function merely as the bearers of that process. The more serious point, though, is that the production process itself is subject to the commanding will of an individual labourer or of a capitalist or manager who directs the labour of others. There is no place for such a commanding intelligence in Althusser's anti-humanist conception of science. Instead, we have to imagine that, in their scientific endeavours, scientists are creatures of their problematic, while, in other contexts, these same individuals are creatures of the social formation (society) in which they live. This brings us to the problem of structural determination to which we now turn.

In the first part of this chapter I suggested that Marxists have always had difficulty with the idea that the economy plays a fundamental role, if only in the last instance, and with the correlative idea that law, politics and ideology are autonomous, but only relatively so. Althusser elaborates his own attempt to combine autonomy and deter-mination in terms of the concept of structural causality, which he develops in opposi-tion to the 'Hegelian' (mis)interpretations of Marxism to be found in most Marxist orthodoxies and in Lukács' classic *History and Class Consciousness* (1922). In Althus-ser's view Hegelian Marxism analyses societies in terms of an 'expressive' causality which allows law, politics and ideology to be read as expressions of an essence located elsewhere – ultimately in the functional requirements of the relations of production or else in the competing class interests established by those relations.

'Structural causality' refers to a relationship between a structure and its parts such that the parts provide the conditions of existence of the structure while the structure itself provides the conditions of existence of the parts. According to Althusser's account, it differs from the expressive causality of 'Hegelian' Marxism in two respects. First, the economy plays a double role: while it determines what relation-ships hold between the levels of the structure it is also present as a level in the pattern of relationships it establishes. It is determining on the one hand, but it may also be affected by the political-legal or the ideological levels on the other. In practice, this account is not much more than a sophisticated version of the traditional Marxist attempt to have and to eat the cake of economic determinism. The second difference from the Hegelian model is that the Althusserian structure does not contain the prin-ciple of its own destruction. On the contrary, the continued existence of the structure is logically entailed by its existence; and it is for this reason that Althusser refers to the structure as 'eternity in Spinoza's sense' (Althusser and Balibar, 1970, p. 107). This position is difficult to reconcile with traditional Marxist accounts of class struggle – or indeed, with its claim, which Althusser supports in other contexts, to provide a theory of historical development.

However, the main interest of Althusser's attempt to rework the traditional three-level model of society lies in its apparent anti-humanism. If, as the notion of structural causality suggests, the conditions of existence of the structure are secured by the actions of the structure itself then the behaviour of human individuals must also be determined by the structure to which they belong. Individuals, in other words, are merely bearers of functions that arise from their structural location. If Althusser had never existed, methodological individualism would have had to invent him.

Althusser's most influential discussion of the implications of structural causality for our understanding of the human individual can be found in 'Ideology and Ideological

State Apparatuses' (in Althusser, 1971), where he poses the problem of how the reproduction of capitalist relations of production is secured. His answer is that individuals are distributed to places in the social division of labour and they are endowed with an ideological formation appropriate to the position they are destined to occupy. Althusser suggests that the educational system plays a central role in both respects. In modern capitalist societies the differentiation of the labor force is achieved through the development of specialized capacities in individuals. These capacities include both technical skills and an appreciation of 'the "rules" of good behaviour, i.e. the attitude that should be observed by every agent in the division of labour, according to the job he is "destined" for' (1971, p. 127).

Althusser's argument here displays a surprising faith in the efficacy of the educational system, but the more interesting issue that it raises concerns his understanding of ideology as involving a distinct level of the social formation. This level is the site of ideological practice which works on the consciousnesses of human individuals by constituting representations of their imaginary relationships to their social conditions of existence. Ideology constitutes their consciousnesses, and they live in ideology in the sense that all acts of consciousness are necessarily ideological. Ideology constitutes individuals as subjects who experience themselves as free: 'the individual is interpolated as a (free) subject in order that he shall submit freely to the commandments of the Subject . . . i.e. in order that he shall make the gestures and actions of his subjection "all by himself"' (ibid., p. 169). The intention of Althusser's argument here is clear enough – even if he does undermine its force by insisting (in an epilogue) on the importance of class struggle and, especially in relation to education, on those teachers who fight against their duly allotted role. The intention is to show that social relations are reproduced in and through the formation of individuals with consciousness appropriate to the tasks they are required to perform.

Perhaps the most obvious point to notice about this argument is that it turns all behaviour into an effect of the structure. In that respect it reproduces precisely that expressive causality that Althusser is so concerned to castigate in the work of other Marxists. The more serious point is that the mechanisms Althusser invokes to account for the reproduction of relations of production can at most account only for the formation of individuals as subjects of a certain type, endowed with attributes, desires and habits of thought appropriate to their stations in life. But that is by no means sufficient to determine their behaviour, since what they do will also depend on the circumstances in which they find themselves. Althusser's account of the formation of individuals does not also account for those circumstances. Still less does it ensure that those circumstances are of a kind that will provoke an unambiguous response.

Notice, finally, that Althusser treats his subjects as endowed with a faculty of experience which allows them to interiorize the forms of subjectivity they are destined to occupy in the structure. Far from accounting for the formation of human individuals as subjects, Althusser's treatment of the mechanisms of ideology must suppose that they are already constituted as subjects. In this respect, Althusser's structural determinism rests on an implicit view of human nature. Rather than a systematic antihumanism, Althusser in fact provides us with an inverted image of the humanism

327

he tries so hard to avoid. People are born free in the imaginary, but in reality they are in chains. This point brings us to analytical Marxism.

Analytical Marxism

Analytical Marxism offers a particularly striking counterpoint to the Marxism of the Althusserian project. Where the latter views individuals as the bearers of functions that arise from their structural location, the former proposes to analyse social life in terms of an uncompromising methodological individualism. In his Introduction to *Analytical Marxism* Roemer suggests, somewhat disingenuously, that 'its practitioners are largely inspired by Marxian questions, which they pursue with contemporary tools of logic, mathematics, and model-building . . . These writers are, self-consciously, products of both the Marxian and non-Marxian traditions' (Roemer, 1986, p. 1).

In fact, Marxists have always claimed to make use of the best available contemporary knowledge, but there have been conflicting accounts of where that knowledge is to be found. What is distinctive, then, about analytical Marxism is not its use of non-Marxist ideas, but rather the particular non-Marxist ideas which it finds valuable: especially analytical philosophy and economics. Analytical Marxism, as its name suggests, is a Marxism in the tradition of analytical philosophy and, like so much of that tradition, it has little time for its continental counterparts.

Analytical Marxism is more a style of work than it is a body of doctrine. There are fundamental disagreements amongst its practitioners, many of which are represented in Roemer's 1986 collection. Cohen, for example, argues that historical materialism involves a defensible type of functional explanation and that the natural development of productive forces is the motor of historical development. Elster denounces the first of these positions, arguing that functional explanation invariably presupposes a causal mechanism, and that no such mechanism is available in the social case. Brenner disputes the second, insisting that the development of the productive forces depends on prior transformations in property relations. If there is a motor of historical development then Brenner locates it in class struggle, not in the development of the productive forces. Such differences notwithstanding, the practitioners of analytical Marxism do share a commitment to methodological individualism, understood in the manner of contemporary economics as a matter of providing the micro-foundations of historical explanation. The suggestion is that, at least in principle, the explanation of historical change must be based on the rational behaviour of individuals.

In the areas of philosophy and political theory perhaps the most interesting product of analytical Marxism has been the wholesale reconstruction of Marx's social theory attempted, in rather different ways, by Elster and Przeworsky. In *Making Sense of Marx*, Elster maintains that the causal explanation of aggregate phenomena in terms of the individual actions that go into them 'is the specifically Marxist contribution to the methodology of the social sciences' (Elster, 1985, p. 4). He also insists that whatever is worth retaining in Marx's work can be understood in those terms. The remainder should be discarded: Marx's theory of value and much of his economic analysis, his functional and teleological arguments, and especially his methodological collectivism. Marx's methodolodical collectivism, exemplified in the passage quoted earlier from the Preface to the first German edition of *Capital*, assumes that 'there are supra-individual entities that are prior to the individual in the explanatory order' (ibid., p. 6). It therefore leaves little scope for the intentional analysis of human action. Where Althusser treats the humanist elements in Marx's mature works as ideological residues that should be excised, Elster sees them as containing the core of Marx's contribution, namely, his moral critique of exploitation and alienation and his methodological individualism.

This last point in particular marks a radical departure from received accounts of Marxism and it not immediately clear how it can be reconciled with the structural analyses of capitalist economic life that appear to play such an important part in Marx's mature work. In order to show that much of this structural analysis is not inconsistent with methodological individualism Elster refers us to Marx's pioneering explanations in terms of the unintended consequences of human action. Such consequences arise, for example, 'when agents entertain beliefs about each other that exemplify the fallacy of composition' (ibid., p. 48) – and it is this that Elster describes as Marx's central contribution. Imagine an economy in which one capitalist enterprise induces its workers to accept lower wages while other enterprises continue as before. Its profits will increase. However, if all enterprises were to act on the assumption that each of them could improve profits by reducing wages, then the general level of wages and the general level of profits would both fall. In this example, what seems to be rational action for each individual enterprise turns out to be irrational in the aggregate. Elster suggests, in effect, that 'structural' tendencies in the economy can be explained as the unintended consequences of numerous individually rational decisions. Indeed: 'this mechanism generates social change not only in capitalism, but in any society in which economic decisions suffer from lack of coordination' (ibid., p. 26). Plans often go awry, and they do so no matter what beliefs actors entertain about each other. The fact that the aggregate consequences of numerous individually rational actions were not intended carries little explanatory weight in any particular case. What accounts for the 'structural' tendency in Elster's example is the assumption that capitalist enterprises act to reduce wages by virtue of their rationality and of how they perceive their situation – which is in turn a function of their social location as capitalists. In other words, the weight of explanation is carried by the 'structural' assumption that significant features of actors' perceptions were determined by their social location as members of a particular class.

Where Elster insists that Marx's methodological collectivism should be abandoned, Przeworski's challenges the standard socialist assumption that the workers' pursuit of their material interests will lead to socialism. Przeworski's does not deny that socialism would be more successful than capitalism at satisfying workers' material interests. Even if that were the case, he argues, it might not be rational for workers in a capitalist society to opt for socialism. First, the period of transition to a socialist society could well involve a decline in living conditions. Second, it may well be possible for the working class to establish a *modus vivendi* with the ruling class in which a relatively low level of industrial militancy was exchanged for high and reliable levels of capitalist investment. Under such conditions workers would be irrational to pursue the goal of a socialist society.

329

I noted in the first part of this chapter that there was a tension in Marxist thought between the understanding of class as a set of individuals who share a common economic location and the understanding of class as an active social force: it is exacerbated in Przeworski's argument by his uncompromising methodological individualism. He insists that classes should not be regarded as objective structures given by the character of property relations. Rather, they are formed 'as effects of struggles; as classes struggle they transform the conditions under which classes are formed' (Przeworski, 1985, p. 92).

There are two rather different issues to notice here. First, if classes are not collective actors, they can hardly engage in struggle. Second, while the suggestion that agencies of collective action are formed in part by collective action is uncontentious it is less clear why we should regard the agencies that are formed in that way as if they were *classes*. In effect, and in spite of his insistence on the formation of classes in struggle, Przeworski's continues to treat class interests as if they were objectively given in the structure of property relations. Individuals who are forced to sell their labour power in return for wages share 'interests defined in terms of a number of secondary characteristics, particularly of a distributional nature [which] leads to the notion of the working people' (ibid., p. 91). It is in this sense that Przeworski and Sprague write of workers 'as the only potential proponent of the class organisation of politics – when no political forces seek to mobilize workers as a class, separately from and in opposition to all other classes, class is absent altogether as a principle of political organization' (Przeworski and Sprague, 1986, p. 11).

In other words, Przeworski takes class interests to be objective features of society and he treats collective action in pursuit of those interests as a contingent product of political struggle. Once interests are identified as objectively given in this way, then the choices of *rational* individuals are also given – by those interests and by the conditions of action they confront. Przeworski's reconstruction of Marxist theory in terms of methodological individualism depends, like that of Elster, on a surreptitious structural determination.

At the beginning of this section I suggested that analytical Marxism offers an interesting counterpoint to Althusser's project of a systematic anti-humanism. On the one side is a model of the individual as a rational agent, pursuing its interests to the best of its ability under conditions that are themselves the outcome of numerous individual actions. On the other is the model of the individual as the bearer of functions given by the structure of social relations in which it is embedded. In fact, for all their apparent opposition, these views of the individual have a great deal in common. Both treat individuals as creatures of their social location: in the one case because they pursue the most rational course of action given the situation in which they find themselves, and in the other because they have internalized the appropriate norms and act on them. The mechanisms by which individuals are subordinated to their situations may be different in the two cases but the overall result is much the same.

See also 2 CONTINENTAL PHILOSOPHY; 3 HISTORY; 4 SOCIOLOGY; 5 ECONOMICS; 13 SOCIALISM; 18 CORPORATISM AND SYNDICALISM; 21 DISCOURSE; 30 POWER; 31 PROPERTY; 36 STATE; 38 TOTALITARIANISM

References

Adorno, T. and Horkheimer, M.: *Dialectic of Enlightenment* (New York: Herder & Herder, 1972).

———: Fenkel-Brunswick, E., Levinson, D. J. and Nevitt, R.: *The Authoritarian Personality* (New York: Harper, 1950).

———: Albert, H., Dahrendorf, R., Habermas, J., Pilot, H. and Popper, K. R.: *The Positivism Dispute in German Sociology* (London: Heinemann, 1976).

Althusser, L.: *For Marx* (London: Allen Lane, 1969).

———: *Lenin and Philosophy* (London: New Left Books, 1971).

———: *Essays in Self-Criticism* (London: New Left Books, 1976).

——— and Balibar, E.: *Reading Capital* (London: New Left Books, 1970).

Anderson, P.: *Considerations on Western Marxism* (London: New Left Books, 1976).

Bachelard, G.: *La Formation de l'esprit scientifique* (Paris: Vrin, 1938).

Bernstein, E.: *Evolutionary Socialism* (1899); (New York: Schocken, 1961).

Cohen, G. A.: *Marx's Theory of History: A Defence* (Oxford: Oxford University Press, 1978).

Elster, J.: *Making Sense of Marx* (Cambridge: Cambridge University Press, 1985).

Geuss, R.: *The Idea of a Critical Theory* (Cambridge: Cambridge University Press, 1981).

Habermas, J.: *The Theory of Communicative Action.* Vol. 1: *Reason and the Rationalization of Society* (Boston: Beacon Press, 1984).

———: *The Theory of Communicative Action.* Vol. 2: *The Critique of Functionalist Reason* (Boston: Beacon Press, 1987a).

———: *The Philosophical Discourse of Modernity. Studies in Contemporary German Social Thought* (Cambridge, Mass.: MIT Press, 1987b).

———: *The New Conservatism* (Cambridge, Mass.: MIT Press, 1989).

———: *The Structural Transformation of the Public Sphere* (1962); (Oxford: Polity Press, 1989).

Held, D.: *Introduction to Critical Theory* (London: Hutchinson, 1980).

Hindess, B.: *Politics and Class Analysis* (Oxford: Blackwell, 1987).

——— and Hirst, P. Q.: *Pre-Capitalist Modes of Production* (London: Routledge, 1985).

Honneth, A. and Joas, H.: *Communicative Action: Essays on Jürgen Habermas' The Theory of Communicative Action* (Oxford: Polity Press, 1991).

Jay, M.: *The Dialectical Imagination* (Boston: Little, Brown, 1973).

Keane, J.: *Democracy and Civil Society* (London: Verso, 1988).

Koselleck, R.: *Critique and Crisis. Enlightenment and the Pathogenesis of Modern Society* (Oxford/ New York/Hamburg: Berg, 1988).

Lenin, V. I.: 'The three sources and three component parts of Marxism' (1913); *Collected Works*, vol. 19 (London: Lawrence & Wishart, 1964), pp. 23–8.

Lichtheim, G.: *Marxism in Modern France* (New York: Columbia University Press, 1966).

Lukács, G.: *History and Class Consciousness: Studies in Marxist Dialectics* (1922); (London: Merlin, 1971).

Lyotard, J.-F.: *The Postmodern Condition: A Report on Knowledge* (Minneapolis: University of Minnesota Press, 1984).

Marcuse, H.: *One Dimensional Man* (London: Abacus, 1972).

Marx, K.: *Capital* (1867); (London: Lawrence & Wishart, 1967).

———: 'Theses on Feuerbach' (1845); Marx and Engels, *Selected Works* (one-volume edition) (London: Lawrence & Wishart, 1968), pp. 28–30.

———: Preface to *A Contribution to the Critique of Political Economy* (1859); Marx and Engels, *Selected Works* (one-volume edition) (London: Lawrence & Wishart, 1968), pp. 181–5.

——— and Engels, F.: *The Communist Manifesto* (1848); Marx and Engels, *Selected Works* (one-volume edition) (London: Lawrence & Wishart, 1968), pp. 31–61.

Parsons, T.: 'On the concept of political power', *Proceedings of the American Philosophical Society*, 107 (1963), 232–62.

Przeworski, A.: *Capitalism and Social Democracy* (Cambridge: Cambridge University Press, 1985).

———— and Sprague, J.: *Paper Stones* (Chicago: Chicago University Press, 1986).

Roemer, J., ed.: *Analytical Marxism* (Cambridge: Cambridge University Press, 1986).

Sartre, J.-P.: *Critique of Dialectical Reason* (1960); (London: New Left Books, 1976).

Thompson, E. P.: *The Poverty of Theory* (London: Merlin, 1978).

Tribe, K.: *Land, Labour and Economic Discourse* (London: Routledge, 1978).

Trotsky, L.: *Their Morals and Ours* (1938); (London: New Park, 1974).

Further reading

Benton, E.: *The Rise and Fall of Structural Marxism* (London: Macmillan, 1984).

Bottomore, T., ed.: *Modern Interpretations of Marx* (Oxford: Blackwell, 1981).

———— ed.: *A Dictionary of Marxist Thought* (Oxford: Blackwell, 1983; 2nd edn, 1991).

Buchanan, A. E.: *Marx and Justice* (Totowa, NJ: Rowman & Allenheld, 1982).

Cohen, M., Nagel, T. and Scanlon, T., eds: *Marx, Justice and History* (Princeton, NJ: Princeton University Press, 1980).

Cutler, A. J., Hindess, B., Hirst, P. Q. and Hussain, A.: *Marx's Capital and Capitalism Today* (London: Routledge & Kegan Paul, 1977, 1978).

Elliott, G.: *Althusser: The Detour of Theory* (London: Verso, 1987).

Fisk, M.: 'Ethics and society', in *A Marxist Interpretation of Value* (Brighton: Harvester, 1980).

Kolowkowski, L.: *Main Currents of Marxism*, 3 vols (Oxford: Oxford University Press, 1978).

Lukes, S.: *Marxism and Morality* (Oxford: Oxford University Press, 1987).

Miller, R. W.: *Analyzing Marx: Morality, Power and History* (Princeton, NJ: Princeton University Press, 1984).

Pennock, J. R. and Chapman, J. W., eds: *Nomos XXVI: Marxism* (New York: New York University Press, 1983).

White, S.: *The Recent Work of Jürgen Habermas* (Cambridge: Cambridge University Press, 1988).

Wolff, R. P.: *Understanding Marx* (Princeton, NJ: Princeton University Press, 1984).

Wood, A.: *Karl Marx* (London: Routledge & Kegan Paul, 1981).

13

Socialism

PETER SELF

The Marxist legacy

Socialism grew up in opposition to capitalism, just as liberalism developed in reaction to feudalism. Both liberalism and socialism combined potent critiques of the existing socio-economic order with blueprints for a desirable future society. However, liberalism provides a rather more coherent body of thought than does socialism, and its theories are linked with the emergence of a dominant system combining capitalism and liberal democracy. By contrast, no widespread socio-economic order has as yet emerged which can be confidently or closely associated with the ideas of socialism. In both cases the relationship between theories and actual systems is a contestable one, but it has been particularly problematic in the history of socialism.

Liberalism preached a doctrine of free competition and exchange between isolated individuals, policed by an impartial state but unfettered by aristocratic rights and privileges. Liberalism took many centuries to overcome feudalism with its 'old conservative' doctrine of a stable system of hierarchical classes and hereditary rule. As late as 1914 the feudal order remained dominant in Prussia, Austria and Russia, while as Schumpeter (1943) noted, modern capitalism continued to be nursed within the decaying fabric of a more glamorous aristocratic shell. Moreover, the gradual triumph of liberal democracy involved a very considerable dilution and for a time indeed a reversal of the individualist basis of liberalism. The resurgence of an individualistic liberal philosophy in recent decades can be seen either as a culminating assertion of liberalism within a now mature international capitalist system, or as the last gasp of an increasingly ill-matched blend of theory and practice.

Socialism also has taken a long time to develop. Writing mainly in the first half of the nineteenth century, the early socialist theorists displayed a certain ambivalence towards the growth of industrialism, sometimes seeking to harness it to the welfare of the impoverished masses, sometimes turning their backs upon the new order. Their ideas struck chords which were to redound from later socialist movements. Saint-Simon's vision of a technocratically planned and controlled industrial society was presented by him largely as the alternative to an effete and functionless feudal order, but it prefigured later theories (such as those of the early Fabians) of the superiority of state planning over the wastes and inefficiencies of the capitalist system. Robert Owen's advocacy of self-governing workers' co-operatives anticipated guild socialism as the way through which industrial workers could control their own destinies. Fourier's local communities (*phalanstères*), based on diverse and freely chosen forms of work, set the stage for many socialist experiments in communitarian living down to our own day. Writing somewhat later, Proudhon's egalitarianism and strong belief in individual liberty led him to be regarded, possibly a little erroneously, as the father of socialist anarchism. (For a brief survey, see Crick, 1987, ch. 3.)

These early thinkers combined a passionate interest in social justice with diverse proposals for economic reform. They introduced key themes, such as the dignity of work and the value of workers' co-operation, and also key conflicts, such as that between central planning and industrial self-government, which have marked and sometimes plagued socialist discourse from the start.

However, the influence of these early 'utopians', as Marx regarded them, was overshadowed by the gigantic impact of Marxism which first emerged, dramatically and brilliantly, in *The Communist Manifesto* of 1848. Any account of modern socialist ideology has to come to terms with the legacy of Marxism, even though much (but by no means all) that Marx and Engels proclaimed in the second half of the last century has now to be discarded as false or no longer relevant.

The strength of Marxism stemmed from its providing both a science and a religion to light the path of the labour movement. To note first its enduring elements, Marx and Engels provided a strong empirical critique of the extreme inequalities and instability of capitalism, and of its capacity to enlist the support of the state in 'liberal' societies. This critical tradition of analysis has retained enormous vitality as the contours of capitalism have changed over the years. Thus in the early twentieth century J. A. Hobson (1902) analysed the ways in which colonies were exploited in the search for new markets and profits, so that British workers (for example) could be co-opted into the system with a share of the spoils. Following a post-1945 period in which state planning and welfare seemed to be taming and controlling capitalism, a fresh impetus of international capitalism developed, linking the whole world into a sophisticated system of mobile capital and financial speculation. It is surely no accident that from the 1960s on there was also a new explosion of 'neo-Marxist' critiques, explaining the features of 'neo-colonialism' in the Third World, suggesting causes for the 'fiscal crisis' of the state (O'Connor, 1973), or analysing the ways in which urban development and planning has been turned into a fruitful arena for capitalist profits (Harvey, 1973).

However, the trenchant critiques of capitalism by Marx and Engels and their numerous later disciples were (and still often are) accompanied by an allegedly scientific theory of growing class conflict and polarization, followed by inevitable capitalist collapse, which has proved untrue. The ingenuity of neo-Marxists in explaining how the state has been co-opted to buy off revolt by the workers cannot explain the increasing differentiation and complexity of social classes, although developments within capitalism that were unforeseen by Marx can help to explain this development. More fundamentally, Marxism has been vitiated by its 'laws' of economic determinism, which simplify history excessively, underrate the independent influence of politics, and present an improbable future of a classless, conflict-free society. On the other hand, the 'economism' of Marx did represent a significant advance in realistic social thought, and is indeed the mirror image of modern economic individualism, while Marx himself was by no means so consistent or dogmatic about economic laws as most of his disciples.

The religious element in Marxism found its expression in the workers' prospect of liberation from oppression, alienation and poverty in a future classless society, while his 'scientific' theory further assured the proletariat that their eventual victory was certain, since capitalism would destroy itself through its internal contradictions. Marx's picture of this future classless society was a highly humanist one that managed to combine the economic progress achieved by capitalism (which he recognized) with the transition to a freely chosen and abundant life for all individuals. Once class oppression was gone, there should be no problem over reconciling individual freedom with social solidarity and equality. This Marxist vision, never adequately spelled out, was in truth a lot more utopian than the alleged utopianism of the early socialists; yet the Marxist mixture of science and idealism, laced in practice with a burning sense of social injustice, provided a powerful ideology to back the political struggles of the new industrial working class and its leaders.

Marxism did much to provide the emerging socialist parties of Western Europe with a general philosophy and a final goal in the shape of the 'common ownership of all means of production and distribution'. This goal could incorporate the various socialist beliefs in workers' co-operation and self-management without specifying clearly how a socialist society would actually operate. The First International (1864–76) and Second International (1889–1914) were attempts to incorporate Western labour movements into an international organization based upon Marxist philosophy and the common interests of workers everywhere. These attempts won some success, especially in France and Germany, and up to 1914 it seemed that the emerging ideas of democratic socialism could be reconciled with and partly based on Marxist ideology.

Socialism, however, remained too diffuse and varied a creed to be confined within any one political doctrine or interpretation. British and still more American labour movements were unresponsive to the dogmatic and revolutionary elements in Marxism, preferring peaceful democratic evolution towards a vaguely defined goal, while the English Fabian Society (founded in 1883) struck out on its pragmatic path towards benevolent state planning and welfare. German social democrats were the strongest and most Marxist socialist party, yet here too Bernstein's (1899) 'revisionism' argued that Marx's diagnosis of the course of capitalism was flawed and that its bad features were being gradually overcome through democratic means.

During this period, and to some extent subsequently, socialist anarchism was also a powerful force. Anarchists were often prepared to use violence to destroy the existing political order, but not to use political power in order to remake society. The reconstruction of society was to proceed from the bottom upwards on a basis of individual liberty and free co-operation. The First International was destroyed by the conflicts between Marxists and Anarchists. Anarchism was particularly prevalent in repressive quasi-feudal societies such as Russia and Spain. The same idealistic belief in a moral regeneration of society also existed in a more peaceful and evolutionary form in countries like England, for example in the thought of the Christian Socialists.

The First World War and the Russian Revolution transformed socialism and created an enduring split between its communist and democratic forms. The Bolshevik Revolution was the product of a disciplined elite not a mass proletarian movement, and occurring also in an economically backward country was very doubtfully related to Marx's theories and expectations. However its evolution did show up the weakness of Marxist political theory, which viewed government simply as coercion by a dominant economic class and not as a separate or independent source of power. Stalin demonstrated how overwhelmingly tyrannical a complete union of political and economic power could be. The growth of new privileged classes and police tyranny far exceeded any plausible hypothesis about the need for a 'temporary' dictatorship of the proletariat. The communist experiment in Eastern Europe proved finally to be a shattering deadend for one version of socialist ideology which put its faith in the uncontrolled domination of a revolutionary party.

Democratic socialism received body blows in the First World War, first from the complete failure of industrial workers to unite in opposing the war, and then from the intellectual hegemony achieved by the successful Russian Revolution. The international brotherhood of workers as a united class could never again resume its central place in socialist ideology, and increasingly it came to be recognized that socialism might take different paths in different countries, although the new international thrust of capitalism (and the consequent weakness of economic planning by individual states) has revived the need to pursue socialism at the international level. In the period between the two world wars, victorious Soviet communism and its pliant tool, the Third International, undermined the growth of Western democratic socialism. Communist antagonism was a prime cause of the collapse of democratic socialism in Germany and Italy, while the example of Russia – as a supposedly successful socialist society – exerted a hypnotic effect upon many Western socialist intellectuals such as Shaw and the Webbs (1935).

Democratic socialism took a long while to recover from the frequent association of socialism with authoritarian communist regimes. Indeed, thanks to the critics of socialism, this disengagement is still not complete. Yet while communism deteriorated and eventually foundered on the rocks, democratic socialist parties managed gradually to win power in Scandinavia and Western Europe, and even Western communist parties showed a democratic face with the advent of Eurocommunism. The biggest change came with the 1959 Godesberg programme of the German Social Democrats, which rejected completely the party's strong Marxist traditions and opted for piecemeal democratic reforms. However, in embracing democracy, socialism makes the feasibility of its final ends dependent upon that of its democratic means and thereby has given a large hostage to fortune. A democratic temper is not only incompatible with the dogmatism and authoritarianism of communism, but also requires large concessions to the exigencies of practical politics as well as toleration of the many diverse traditions and beliefs within the socialist movement itself.

Consequently, the elaboration of a distinctive socialist ideology has been and remains a hazardous enterprise. Embodied in Western political parties, socialism has shown the same pragmatic traits as parties professing liberalism or conservatism; but to claim that this pragmatism has destroyed socialist ideals once and for all would be as false as to refute Conservative Party policies because they do not follow the principles of Edmund Burke or Michael Oakeshott; yet there is the significant difference that socialism remains essentially on the defensive against the capitalist

336

system and its supporting liberal philosophy of 'possessive individualism' (MacPherson, 1962).

Labour parties and trade unions have reached many pragmatic accommodations with capitalist interests. Unions are often concerned primarily with differentials whereas socialism is about equality. In prosperous times Labour parties have been more concerned to 'milk the capitalist cow' than to transform society, until bad times reveal the continuing dominance of capitalism. The effective co-option of Labour leaders by the ruling establishment is a familiar theme of novelists and critics. In the present world some Labour parties have become so accepting of the capitalist market system as to reduce their policies to a very weak form of 'welfarism'.

These trends tread along the fine line between 'democratic socialism' and 'social democracy'. What remains distinctively socialist? Marxism remains relevant for its critique of capitalism but the economic fate of the communist states has given a sharp warning of the bureaucratic and other problems that are inherent in comprehensive state management of economic resources. The goal of 'public ownership of the means of production and distribution' was always for democratic Labour parties a final aspiration, and was only very partially and unsatisfactorily implemented when they gained power. Now it has largely dropped out of the vocabulary of party politics. This does not mean that this goal has become irrelevant, but that socialists must give it a more limited and acceptable meaning and relate it to other elements of a coherent philosophy.

At least the 1980s witnessed a revival of socialist thought. Democratic socialism has trod a long hard road, lessons have been learned (especially over the limits of Marxism and the fate of Communism) and its emerging philosophy is groping for a new synthesis of principles and their possible applications.

First we are now dealing with 'socialisms' (Wright, 1986). The rich heritage of socialist thought, submerged for a time by simple-minded panaceas, is being rediscovered. The idea that there are different possible forms of socialism, suitable for different times and places, is congruent with a new belief in freedom, diversity and experiment, but in itself would be thin and muddled were it not for a second return to traditional beliefs.

This is the rediscovery of 'ethical socialism', the belief that socialism must be founded upon and reflect the acceptable moral principles of a good society. Marxism had rejected and ridiculed this belief, despite drawing freely in practice on moral indignation about the evils of capitalism, but now it is the Marxist vision of a classless society – not the appeal to moral principles – which can be seen as utopian. Moral purpose is an essential ingredient of all successful causes, including the world religions.

Abstract moral principles are also inadequate. They must be capable of realization, which implies the need for an effective theory of social transformation. Socialists are still struggling to meet this need by developing theories of the economy, the state and social change, which draw on the socialist heritage but which recognize how much the world has changed from the one known to their predecessors. The remainder of this essay will outline these efforts and some of the puzzles which they present.

337

Ethical socialism

Socialism has a more optimistic and positive view of human nature than does conservatism or liberalism. One guiding belief is in the equal moral worth of each individual. This idea reflects a long Christian and humanist tradition, notably expressed in the moral philosophy of Immanuel Kant ([1785] 1948). Kant held that every person should be treated as an end in him or herself, and that moral equality and individual autonomy reflected the two great features of the universe – 'the starry heavens above and the moral law within'.

The belief in 'equal moral worth', 'equal moral capacity' and consequently 'equal entitlement to consideration' is not, of course, confined to socialists. The difference is that socialists take its implications seriously. Conservatives accept a hierarchical order of privilege or talent. Liberals accept the gross inequalities of the market system. Socialism is nothing if it does not struggle to carry the implications of 'equal worth' into the social and economic realms.

Socialists also have a strong preference for social co-operation over competition. Democratic socialists want this co-operation to be based upon a free moral choice rather than upon economic or physical coercion. This hope is often linked with a somewhat Pelagian belief in the *potential* (not necessarily actual) goodness of human beings. (Pelagianism was a Christian heresy which believed in the natural goodness of humans.) The socialist tendency is towards the assumption of 'moral man in immoral society' rather than its reverse, and consequently carries the expectation that basic institutional reform can release beneficial human energies.

It is easy to criticize these beliefs as unrealistic. Certainly, it was natural for socialists, speaking for the poor or exploited, to suppose that good would prevail if what they saw as an evil system were destroyed (Marx shared this view). The fate of many attempted 'ideal communities' shows how easily a belief in natural goodness can be undermined. Yet surely this belief is at least as tenable an aspiration, and much more conducive to human improvement, as modern versions of 'original sin' which assume, for example, with the liberal public choice theorists, that every individual is a 'rational egoist', mechanically calculating his material advantage in every situation – in politics as much as in the market (Self, 1985, pp. 48–69).

Ethical socialism draws strongly upon Christian and humanitarian traditions, so that Morgan Phillips (then Secretary of the British Labour Party) once perceptively remarked that his party owed more to Methodism than to Marx. Tawney was the leading figure of English ethical socialism, and the revival of his thought by the 1980s is clearly evidenced in a recent collection of Fabian Essays (Pimlott, 1984). Tawney foresaw no easy route for socialism, which requires both 'a demanding code of personal conduct and of social organisation, appealing to the same principles of fellowship' (Dennis and Halsey, 1988, p. 240). In his view, individuals would have to strive unselfishly to build up the social norms, and bring about the institutional reforms, upon which the slow progress towards a more co-operative, equal and 'decent' society depends; and just as these norms could be built up so they could be run down by lazy or selfish socialists as well as by their opponents. Thus the release of co-operative energies and individual capacities is indeed possible and not utopian, but it is a slow process hinging upon a real sense of 'fellowship'.

The rallying cry of the French Revolution – equality, liberty and fraternity – now constitute essential socialist values. It would be foolish to deny conflicts between interpretations of these values, more especially between liberty and the other two, which causes modern socialist leaders to stress their concern with the freedom value. However, the point is that the values must not just be taken separately but related within a coherent socialist philosophy.

The egalitarian value is undeniably the most exclusively socialist one and, following some disillusionment with state ownership of industry, it became elevated for a time into the key objective of socialism (Crosland, 1956). Absolute equality is a chimerical and undesirable goal; Bernard Shaw's proposition that the state should give everyone £1000 a year (at pre-inflation prices), and as a necessary condition make sure that he earned it, gives the game away. Extreme equality overlooks the diversity of individual talents, tastes and needs, and save in a utopian society of unselfish individuals would entail strong coercion; but even short of this goal, there is the problem of giving reasonable recognition to different individual needs, tastes (for work or leisure) and talents. It is true therefore that beyond some point the pursuit of equality runs into controversial or contradictory criteria of need or merit.

What then is the socialist goal? One approach is to start with a strong presumption in favour of equality, and to insist upon cogent reasons being given for treating individuals differentially. The problem is that defenders of inequality can give reasons for their position, even for a system such as apartheid. Thus one must further require that the reasons are acceptable moral ones which recognize that most basic individual wants and aspirations are common to all (Rees, 1971, pp. 91–125). But this is no more than to return to the socialist's starting point; either the factor of our common humanity is seen or it is not. One cannot make the blind see.

For practical purposes the socialist has an answer to these problems. Economic inequalities are so enormous in the modern capitalist world that substantial progress over reducing them should be practicable without running into the sands of detailed judgements about differential claims. In allegedly affluent countries, such as the United States or the United Kingdom, the top 10 per cent command over nine times the income (even after tax) of the bottom group, and completely dominate the ownership of wealth. Increasing numbers of millionaires or billionaires coexist with a sixth of the population living below the official poverty line (for a survey, see Hoover and Plant, 1989). The contrast between rich and poor countries is still more glaring with two-thirds of the world still locked in hunger (and increasingly so in many countries), while the affluent are titillated with ever more sophisticated – and often environmentally destructive – consumer goods (Harrington, 1989, ch. 6). Thus the pursuit of equality can be seen as essentially an onslaught upon gross inequalities which contradict the very idea of the dignity and worth of the individual. As Tawney (1931, p. 27) said, when a more decent and humane society has been brought about, it will become more practicable to arbitrate the more detailed issues of differential needs and claims.

The pursuit of equality has been badly fudged by its assumed or declared dependence upon continuous economic growth. The ethical case for equality does not hinge upon any particular level of economic development, but simply requires that the wealth of the community – whatever it may be – should be fairly shared. Indeed, the moral injunction to do this is greater not less in hard times, while the assumption that more affluence brings more fellow feeling has proved far from true.

In socialist eyes the value of individual liberty has been perversely appropriated by liberals. Isaiah Berlin's (1969) well-known distinction between 'negative' and 'positive' liberty has been perverted by extreme liberals ('libertarians') into the argument that only the negative form of liberty is real and that it should be restrictively interpreted as the absence of direct coercion. 'Positive' liberty in the sense of the exercise of free will or of moral autonomy is possible even for a slave and, as Berlin says, no amount of favourable conditions will necessarily bring individuals to exercise positive liberty. However, as he also recognizes, the scope for personal development or for the responsible exercise of citizenship does depend a lot upon the individual's social and economic circumstances. Thus the enjoyment of liberty can be broadly said to depend on the range of opportunities open to each individual, and upon the extent to which she or he is in a position to make a free choice of career and way of life (Ryan, 1984).

Restrictive coercions upon individual freedom will always exist and come variously from the state, the economic system and, as J. S. Mill stressed, the sanctions of public opinion, but these sources can also provide beneficent opportunities. The critical questions are how to trade off the diverse pattern of restrictions and opportunities which surround the individual. Libertarians insist on regarding the state as the sole agent of coercion, and it is true enough that the state has a unique power of direct coercion which has produced the worst tyrannies. Vigilance against excessive state power is as necessary for a socialist as anyone else. Yet it is surely perverse to ignore the enormous indirect power of the capitalist system over individual lives and opportunities, exercised with the necessary support of the state over the making and enforcement of laws of property and contract, and supported by the substantial political influence of wealth.

Berlin himself does not make this error, since he fully recognizes that 'the blood-stained story of economic individualism' has led to 'brutal violations of negative liberty', and that 'the case for intervention, by the state or other effective agencies, to secure conditions for both positive, and at least a minimum degree of negative, liberty for individuals, is overwhelmingly strong' (Berlin, 1969, xlv-xlvi). The curious point is that as recently as 1969 Berlin thought that capitalism had been tamed and curbed by the state, without foreseeing the rapid explosion of a new libertarianism. Socialism has to return to propounding a concept of liberty grounded in human experience and not in an obsession with property rights.

Thus it is natural for socialists to bring in the state, not only to combat gross inequalities but to diffuse and modify economic power and to enlarge the opportunities open to individuals, more particularly the poor and disadvantaged. Free men and women cannot accept the Hayekian thesis that an admittedly amoral (or immoral) economic system must not be interfered with because of the latent danger of an unacceptable degree of state coercion. That is an appeal to Hobbesian fears, not this time of anarchy but of its opposite. In considering the balances of coercion and freedom one has to ask the old question; is the rich man more restricted by having to pay a high tax rate or the poor family by being unable to keep their children healthy or send them to a decent school?

T. H. Green, a liberal before the great split between liberals who believed in welfare (and often became socialists) and those who stuck with *laissez-faire*, described the role of the state as 'removing obstacles to the good life' (Green, 1890). Ethical socialism has an Aristotelian belief in the promotion of individual capacities for self-development and personal fulfilment. There is a difference here from the agnostic liberal view that the 'good life' is a wholly subjective matter of personal opinion and choice (Dworkin, 1978), or that alternatively, as Bentham put it 'quantity of pleasure being equal, pushpin is as good as poetry'.

The belief of earlier socialists in the great value of education and cultural development generally, exemplified by such bodies as the Workers' Educational Association, seems to have faded away in the modern world of the mass media and capitalist 'bread and circuses', yet this belief in the capacity of individuals to pursue 'higher goals', according to their special capacities and tastes, still needs to remain basic to socialist goals. It is a necessary condition of responsible citizenship, without which a socialist world can never be democratically created. It extends not only to the enrichment of leisure, but to the transformation of the work system so that William Morris's ideal of 'honourable and fitting work' for all in 'decent surroundings' should become a possibility, not (as in the capitalist society) an irrelevance. Within this context, monopoly ownership and trivialization of the mass media, and the perversion of education to meet solely market demands not personal development, are especially offensive to socialists.

Fraternity, and/or as Crick (1987, pp. 98–106) prefers 'sisterhood', is the third socialist value, standing alongside equality and liberty and functioning as an essential solvent for their realization and reconciliation. Tawney regarded it as the basic value and termed it 'fellowship', meaning a free acceptance by individuals of a mutual obligation to care for each other. In the past fraternity was the right word, because this sentiment was largely confined within a male industrial working class, especially workers in heavy industry. The mutual co-operation among workers, both informal and formal, through friendly societies, unions, workers' clubs and cultural events like Welsh eisteddfods, warmed socialist hearts with its contrast from the chilly individualism or occasional calculated charity of the bourgeoisie. However, this fraternity was limited by a narrow reference group and male chauvinism, so that modern socialists need to cope with the barriers to fellowship caused by differences of sex and ethnicity as well as between rich and poor countries (Phillips, 1984).

It would be impossible to sweep away these barriers quickly so socialism has to proceed through a gradual extension of sympathy and consideration for the needs of different and remote groups, and through a search for institutional means of reducing group tensions. More than this, universal benevolence has a chilly character unless associated with the personal practice of face-to-face fellowship. The revived socialist concern with the value of local community may be seen partly as a tactical retreat from broader horizons, but also as renewing in an appropriate modern way the socialist legacy of direct fellowship.

The greatest moral problem for socialism has always been the tendency for the pursuit of fraternity to end up as its opposite. This is especially the problem of revolutionary socialism where in the worst case of Stalinism, 'socialism achieved its apogee in the period of the destruction of social bonds' (Nowak, 1983, p. xvi). In much milder form democratic socialism has always had the problem of reconciling its ideal of voluntary co-operation with an extensive use of state powers. Socialists can argue that the coercive impact of the state turns not simply or even primarily upon the number of its acts but upon their methods and acceptability. The coercive defence of property rights under conditions of inequality and instability can and has led to more repressive acts than democratic socialism need necessarily require.

All the same socialism has difficulty in coming to terms with the coercive powers of the state. The important anarchist tradition, now muted, had no use for the state. Many socialist idealists looked forward to a time when conditions of abundance would have solved the 'economic problem' and individuals could lead a free life of voluntarily chosen work and leisure, in which both individual freedom and free fellowship could flourish. Marx himself subscribed to this vision, as did such utopian socialists as Oscar Wilde.

Short of such utopian beliefs, many socialists have believed – and still believe – in what Martin Buber (1950) called the gradual transformation of political power into social power. The project here is one of a peaceful revolution from below, whereby co-operative cells are formed at the grassroots which spread and transform society from within. This was the essence of G. D. H. Cole's (1917) concept of 'guild socialism' which favoured the creation of a system of worker's self-management permeating the operations of industry from the base upwards. Such proposals could build upon the early success of friendly societies, consumers' co-operatives and other forms of self-help in new industrial societies, and some socialists deplore the way that these earlier initiatives have been overtaken by massive, top-down measures of state planning and welfare. For some socialists this is a retreat from a true concept of fellowship and co-operation.

There has been a long conflict within socialism between the arguments for centralized planning (geared to equality and efficiency) and grassroots socialism (geared to liberty and fellowship). Outstanding examples concern the balance to be struck between the powers of central and local government and the choice to be made between public corporations and guild socialism as devices of common ownership. In the past the centralizers have won most of these arguments. As a movement seeking radical social change, socialism has always been understandably disposed to want to make sweeping changes from the top downwards. Considering their goals, democratic socialist governments have been surprisingly circumspect in their use of state powers, but a belief in strong centralized planning has certainly dominated. Today, the balance is swinging in the other direction, but centralized powers are still needed to establish or promote local forms of democratic socialism.

Socialists have often been reproved with having anything but fraternal feelings for each other. Individuals who believe passionately in a cause are bound to find mutual toleration difficult, and there have always been passionate differences over both ends and means within the socialist camp. These are the conditions which can spawn intolerance of dissenting opinions among colleagues as well as opponents. A genuinely moral and democratic concept of fellowship needs the safeguard of open dissent, and the best, perhaps only real, protection against excessive use of state powers is citizens who think for themselves.

There are many possible definitions of socialism, ranging from empirical statements about planning or public ownership to highly idealistic visions of a future society (see Wright, 1986, p. 20). A definition which joins equality and liberty is Bottomore's:

> the creation of a social order in which there is the maximum feasible equality of access, for all human beings, to economic resources, to knowledge, and to political power, and the minimum possible domination exercised by any individual or social group over any others. (Bottomore, 1984, p. 190)

Interestingly, this definition stresses the very diffusion of power within society which market liberalism claims so unconvincingly actually to produce. It stresses the very limited nature of political rights if these are accompanied and influenced by highly unequal economic power, and the limitations of democracy if it has no scope in the workplace and the boardroom. It ties in with T. H. Marshall's (1963) hopeful but as yet unrealized extension of modern citizenship into the spheres of social and economic rights. All this is a long way removed from much traditional socialism and its pursuit depends upon translating the third value of fellowship into its political context of responsible citizenship.

The socialist economy

Socialism is basically about human welfare. Socialists have always wanted to put 'first things first', to attend to the basic requirements of a good or at least decent life for all before satisfying the luxuries of the affluent. Today this concern necessarily extends (in view of environmental crises) to the basic needs of future generations and to the general quality of life for all (the affluent included). Moreover *democratic* socialism is dedicated to the promotion of individual autonomy and responsible participation in social and political life. Socialism seeks to broaden the political concepts of both social welfare and democratic procedures.

Viewing the modern world, socialists cannot but see a gross neglect of these basic priorities. The traditional socialist criticism of capitalism as wasteful and inefficient gains new force from the irresponsibility of 'casino capitalism', from the human tragedies of massive unemployment, from the instability of a system which places local communities in bondage to financial decisions made in distant boardrooms, and from the rapid exploitation of natural resources and its dire environmental effects. Surely, the socialist will exclaim, we can do better than this!

Capitalism has the seeming advantage of a coherent economic theory which argues the generally beneficial outcome of voluntary exchanges in competitive markets. However the modern capitalist system is far removed from its supposedly theoretical basis. Not only is the system pervaded throughout by inequalities of bargaining power between individuals and groups, but it is dominated by giant citadels of economic power; what exactly, for example, is the relationship between the theory of perfect competition and (in many countries) the dominance of the media by a few proprietors? (Yet the media is a vital channel of information and education to all citizens, not – as it is now widely regarded – just another industry.) As Heilbroner (1985) concludes, neo-classical market theory is a convenient rationalization of the interests of the dominant social formation (capitalism) which pursues its own special dynamism of extending the opportunities for private profit.

This capitalist dynamism can be claimed to have raised the material standard of living in Western societies in such matters as food, clothes and household equipment. Writers such as Hayek and Friedman assume that the same dynamic will continue to deliver large increments of human welfare because their eyes are fixed upon the past and an abstract theory, not upon actual social and institutional change. Inevitably among the affluent, increments of market goods yield diminishing returns; plastic dolls and visits to distant beaches (often polluted) may be welcome but they do not yield the solid satisfaction of a square meal or a warm overcoat. The growth of 'positional goods' (Hirsch, 1976), meaning goods which are necessarily elitist or in limited supply, bids up competition for a limited range of positions or causes environmental damage through the multiplication of cars, yachts, second homes and other private goods. The diversion of economic growth into positional goods widens inequality and reduces public access to basic resources of land and water. Capitalism uses technology to produce increasingly sophisticated goods by a diminishing proportion of the labour force, while functions vital for human welfare – such as environmental conservation, the renewal of urban infrastructure, many social services and houses for the homeless – are left very short of resources even in many rich countries.

Socialism is admittedly stronger in its critique of capitalism than in its design of a coherent alternative. Some socialists seized on Keynesianism as offering an alternative economic blueprint. Keynes' own concern was with the mismatch between savings and investment, the consequent unemployment and need for a public investment programme (Keynes, 1936), a diagnosis that retains its basic validity. However, in the Keynesian postwar period of high employment, a different kind of institutional 'stickiness' developed in the form of wage and price inflation. Traditional market theorists and right-wing politicians could now argue that if one particular market 'distortion' (wages) were pushed downward to their 'natural' level, the system would work efficiently even at the cost of high if allegedly temporary unemployment.

This conclusion was quite unjustified because what Keynesianism actually helps to reveal is that the whole economic system (and not just wages) is pervaded with institutional rigidities and inequalities. If the cure for inadequate or misdirected investment is corrective action by the state, so also should the cure for inflation take the form of a statutory incomes and prices policy, not the debilitating medicine of low wages and unemployment. This possible socialist interpretation of Keynes stands in contrast to the 'neo-classical synthesis' which reconciles Keynes with orthodox market theory (Eatwell and Green, 1984); yet the socialist interpretation, valid as it may be, still amounts to a series of institutional corrections rather than the full design of a new order.

Even an extended form of Keynesianism would retain the capitalist system, although it would greatly modify its operations. For many socialists, this approach amounts to mere empty 'reformism', to supping with the enemy. For example,

Adam Przeworski (1985, p. 243) says, 'if socialism consists of full employment, equality and efficiency, the Swedish Social Democrats are reasonably close to this goal, especially if they also socialise much of industry.' He concedes that such reformism may be excellent and necessary, but claims that it is not socialism. Similarly, John Dunn (1984) defines 'true socialism' in terms of a drastic cultural change in all human relationships which, however appealing, is utopian because socialists offer no realistic blueprint of how it could be realized. These writers are but echoing the long utopian socialist tradition that is strong on ideals but feeble on effective action; yet such critiques point also to a real issue: to what extent do socialists still believe in 'common ownership', and can or should democratic socialism have any truck with capitalism?

Before trying (briefly) to tackle this question, it is as well to point out that the Swedish achievements, as listed above, did represent progress towards all three socialist values of equality, liberty and fellowship. Full employment policy preserves the dignity and worth of the worker and enlarges his liberty; Swedish wage policy entails sacrifices by the more skilled workers to help the less skilled, an example of both fellowship and equality; and the high level and comprehensiveness of Swedish welfare services increases not only equality but the opportunities for disadvantaged individuals to lead a reasonable life. Comprehensive state welfare is often claimed to weaken family and local ties with baleful effect upon 'fellowship', but Ringen (1987) concludes that it has strengthened amity and companionship within families. Possibly there may be effects both ways.

Another major step forward that could be possible within the capitalist system is much stronger participation by workers in the details of work organisation. Such measures enhance both fellowship in working life and give some room for individual autonomy – for example, technology can often be used either to deskill the worker or to increase the independence and interest of his or her work. Hodgson (1984, pp. 129–52) quotes plenty of evidence that workers' participation often increases their productivity as well, but is often resisted by managers (and sometimes union officials) defensive of their command or bargaining roles. Harrington (1989, pp. 188–217) notes the opportunities which advanced technology offers for more autonomous forms of work, but adds that management may prefer technology which restricts the workers' role and skills.

'Economic democracy' is not exclusively a socialist creed, for example it is warmly endorsed by a liberal pluralist such as Dahl (1985). However, the empowerment of workers through such means as workers' co-operatives would further advance the distinctive socialist values, and is now generally the preferred way of promoting the traditional socialist goal of 'common ownership'. The theory corresponds to the socialization of production caused by its modern dependence upon multiple skills and accumulated resources of research and education; but because of the complex social choices to be made between alternative forms of technology and organization, it does not amount to a full blueprint for the management of industry.

A vigorous debate has emerged about the desirability of 'market socialism'. The phrase may be an unhappy one if it suggests that socialism would accord markets, even played according to different rules, the dominant place in its desired system. Many socialists, perhaps understandably, equate markets with capitalism. However, the price signals given by competitive markets do provide an efficient way of meeting consumer preferences for those goods which are not better collectivized. Consumer markets seem to play an essential role in any system, and attempts to separate production from consumption decisions (as in the Soviet Union) have been anything but successful. Some socialists cannot accept any system which retains some role for profits; however, if production were largely in the hands of workers' co-operatives, and their entitlement to profits was limited, profits would be more equitably shared as well as playing a smaller social role.

A socialist economy would entail not only a widespread development of economic democracy, but a considerable redirection of investment so as to meet social and environmental priorities. There would need to be a plan for steering surplus labour into socially valuable but not strictly profitable tasks. Many functions might need to form an intermediate sector between tax-supported social services and profitable enterprises. There would be basic economic and social entitlements which in hard times would have priority over additions to private consumption. These various activities would not necessarily be directly operated by the state but government would certainly need to orchestrate and facilitate them.

A socialist economy would need to modify and transform the capitalist market system quite drastically in order to cure its abuses and introduce significant social values that are absent or trampled on. It could also, however, aim to preserve the competitive and allocative functions of markets. For example, David Miller's (1989) version of 'market socialism' envisages a system of market competition between self-governing workers' co-operatives who would get their capital from publicly owned or controlled investment banks. Thus capital would be socialized and ownership of productive facilities diffused (as far as proved praticable) among workers, but the system would still be motivated by prices and profits. Indeed, Miller would control the allocation of capital in order to maintain maximum competition, a policy which would also protect small firms as offering the most fruitful opportunities for workers' self-government. Capital funds would also be allocated for such purposes as regional development and environmental conservation.

Any such plan poses problems over issues such as the effective management of the investment banks and the maintenance of small workers' co-operatives under modern technological conditions. The biggest problems would appear to be political, in the double sense of achieving a successful transition to a radically new system and of managing well and without abuses the substantial new public powers which the system would entail. It can very plausibly be argued, however, that some such version of the 'new socialism' would increase the freedom and autonomy of workers without necessarily hurting the interests of consumers.

Plans of this type go well beyond the bounds of mere 'reformism', of tinkering with the capitalist system. The radicalism of their goals can be seen from the conflicts with capitalism that have arisen over plans for workers' ownership in the relatively benign environment of Sweden. It is often claimed that if workers wanted to create co-operatives, they could do so perfectly well under capitalist institutions, but in fact the large accumulations of acquisitive market power which these institutions produce are inimical to the smaller size and different incentives which prevail in workers' co-operatives.

346

Where the economic climate can be made more benign, and a suitable investment bank created, workers' co-operatives function well, as is shown by the Mondragon co-operatives in the Basque region of Spain (Thomas and Logan, 1982).

Many socialist idealists dislike any such concept of 'feasible socialism' (Nove, 1983) because it retains scope for markets, profits and competition. However an ideal of purely voluntary co-operation requires conditions of economic abundance which simply do not exist in the modern world. In the visionary socialist ideal, the problem of production has been solved and the individual is free to choose a life of personal self-fulfilment. From Marx onwards, socialists have favoured economic development which brings that day nearer. This goal remains highly relevant so far as it concerns the provision of decent material conditions for all citizens, but that goal is still distant.

Beyond that point, modern socialists have considerable sympathy with the values of a post-materialist society. They accept the need for environmental conservation and protection; they share the concern for quality of life as opposed to the mere multiplication of new consumer goods; and they would like to enhance the dignity and autonomy of work, which suggests restrictions upon the size and direction of economic enterprises and the exclusion of many dubious commercial practices. The difficult challenges before socialism are to ensure that the costs of limiting economic growth are equitably shared, that priority is given to basic material needs, and that the opportunities of a post-material society are widely shared and not confined to the tastes of middle-class radicals. Such ideas actually look back as well as forward, to socialist ideals of a simpler but more satisfying life, in which the accumulation of possessions counts for less and the cultivation of personal capacities and of community life for a great deal more.

The design of a workable socialist economy is inevitably difficult simply because the modern capitalist world is so very far removed from ultimate socialist ideals. Indeed this world, with its towering concentrations of international finance and its urgent 'Third World' and environmental problems, is also a long way removed from conditions in which it made some sense to talk of 'socialism in one country'. On the other hand, the failure of capitalism to solve problems of unemployment and inequality, or to cope adequately with quality of life concerns, offers hope for some movement towards socialist ideals across a broad front of nations. Such a movement may inevitably use new forms of the 'mixed economy', but that need not matter if ground can be genuinely gained for the future.

To gain such ground, it is necessary for socialists to rebut the association of capitalism with a beneficent form of 'economic growth'; and to show that capitalism, even when prosperous, leads to a distorted form of growth which has many adverse features and omits many urgent social needs. There is now a plentiful literature and evidence to support a critique of this kind. The problem for socialism is to develop and popularize a theory of human welfare which shows how a wider range of goals can be specified, evaluated and effectively pursued.

The design of a workable socialist economy is therefore an untidy, controversial and pragmatic affair. There are no easy answers to the balances to be struck between central planning and local initiatives, between various forms of economic organization and the relations between them, or over the various uses of taxes, subsidies and regulations. As Nove says (1983, p. 213), socialists cannot neglect the economic problems of efficient allocation, calculation and valuation, although they will apply different values from capitalism to these measurements. Socialism does not have the luxury of a comprehensive economic theory, but the apparent advantage of capitalism in this respect rests in large part upon a methodological illusion. Neo-classical economics gains its elegant coherence through its abstraction from social and institutional conditions. Any theory which depends upon purposeful collective action is necessarily more pragmatic and institutional. It need not be the worse for that fact. There can be no determinate theory of collective action, since the results depend upon motives and means and upon the ultimate capacity of human societies to shape their own destiny.

The socialist state and society

The picture of a too powerful, oppressive and bureaucratic state has become the bogeyman of anti-socialist argument. A crude contrast is drawn, following the much earlier theories of Mises (1922) and his disciple Hayek (1944), between the beneficial outcomes of 'free markets' and the oppressive features of 'centralized planning'. This argument has gained impetus from the collapse of allegedly the only actual examples of socialist systems, those of Eastern Europe. This comparison is quite untenable in the modern world. Not only is organized capitalism far from the free market theory and deeply entangled with the supportive role of the state, but democratic socialists see progress towards their values as having occurred in some Western European countries and certainly not within the Eastern bloc.

However, modern democratic socialists are willing, perhaps too willing for a coherent philosophy as opposed to political tactics, to join in heavy criticism of the state. Socialism cannot in fact dispense with a strong and effective use of political power. Such power is the only way of changing the economic system and more immediately of checking the present abuses of capitalist power. In some respects, socialists have to argue that modern Western states are not too strong but too weak, too dependent upon the special market forces and interests of organized capitalism, especially in relation to its enormous international range and impact.

Moreover socialists see many uses of political power as being not oppressive but enabling. They should be used, for example, to help individuals to achieve a decent material sufficiency and to have real opportunities for personal growth; to protect them from the appalling impacts (now and in the future) of environmental degradation; and to remove the curse of unemployment by the development of new opportunities for socially useful and intrinsically satisfying forms of work. All these aims require a more positive use of powers which states already exercise in such fields as regulation, taxation, subsidies, incentives, research, education and technical advice – only redirected to other and better ends.

Socialists also believe in the collective provision of at least some basic services such as health and education. They see a positive value of 'fellowship' in the joint sharing of basic risks and opportunities, and in the promotion of a civilized 'public estate' (of streets, parks, cultural and recreational facilities, public transport and an attractive

348

environment) in place of the waste, ugliness and inequalities of a society dominated by private consumption. As Barry (1989) says, this belief need not imply an 'organic' or idealistic theory of the state itself or a denial of the value of individual choice. There is no such thing as unstructured individual choice; the state's role is to change the parameters within which such choices are made – for example, by changing the balance of advantage between the uses of public transport and the private car – and to promote the common interests of a shared civilization in place of the entrenched rights to property and its unlimited acquisition.

The critical question for democratic socialists is how far a transformation of society will be voluntarily accepted and seen as good by individual citizens. Socialism in the past has certainly been prone to try to impose its goals from the top downwards, but so – and arguably to a greater extent – have right-wing governments. The new feature in Western socialism is its stress upon the desirability of democratic forms of participation and control at all levels within the state and the economy. Socialists have come to believe in decentralization in such forms as workers' co-operatives and participation in industrial decisions; a broader and more discretionary role for local governments; and direct participation by clients in the running of such services as health and education.

These new beliefs represent a remarkable *bouleversement* in the history of socialist thought. There must be reservations, however, as to how far the concept of decentralization can be taken under the actual conditions of the modern world. For one thing the freedom for local governments, workers' co-operatives or local school boards could lead to the re-emergence of substantial inequalities; some framework for controlling and redistributing resources has to be kept. More significantly many economic or environmental goals can only be effectively pursued by higher levels of government – increasingly indeed at an international level. Thus Luard, in his *Socialism without the State* (1979), ends up quite realistically by allocating as many new functions to the international as to the local level. Socialist political power needs, at least for the time being, to match the realities of economic power, and to move to such wider forums as the European Community.

There is a possible answer to this problem of overcentralization through the ultimate development of socialism. Thus socialism could seek to redesign the economic system and to utilize the marvellous flexibility and inventiveness of modern technology so as to create relatively smaller and more self-sufficient political communities, linked in ways which accept but reduce their mutual dependence. Such a vision borrows from the ideas of Schumacher (1974) and other believers in 'small is beautiful' to create communities with greater stability and autonomy (hence more scope for fellowship), and having systems of work and leisure that reflect both individual creativity and proper care for the environment. Some losses of technical productivity and gains from trade might be willingly accepted in such societies as being less important than the realisation of human values. This is an authentic socialist vision, not so different from the earlier ideas of Kropotkin (1901), which could realize the old ideals of individual creativity and voluntary co-operation far better than a world of large controlling organizations; yet it must be admitted that, save for particular community experiments, it is a long distance away from present realities.

Democratic socialism, notably in the English Fabian tradition of the Webbs but also in the German tradition, has tended towards a favourable view of bureaucracy, viewed as a strong, essential and rational element for transforming society. The newer stress upon democracy as well as much practical disillusionment has heavily qualified this attitude; yet bureaucracy remains essential to socialist goals not only for the efficient and impartial administration of laws (as Etzioni-Halévy (1983) rightly says, democracy needs bureaucracy to guard against the ever-present dangers of political patronage), but also for its technical resources, since one of socialism's strongest assets is the attraction of public service for talented and idealistic individuals. Socialism therefore needs to promote a creative bureaucracy, skilled enough to help resolve the many technical problems of policy implementation and independent enough to apply those policies without fear or favour.

The creation of such a bureaucracy represents a formidable challenge for socialism. The dangers of 'technocracy' are now widely understood and feared, not least by many socialists. However if socialism is to strive for a society which places much more stress upon basic needs and less upon profit-making, and which enlists technology positively to overcome pressing environmental dangers and to design a more creative system of work, skilled advice and support has to be assembled for these purposes and given the encouragement to produce fertile ideas. Such results cannot be expected so long as the thinking of bureaucracy is governed by a narrow economic orthodoxy, independent thought is discouraged and much policy work is farmed out to private consultants. In line with socialist ideas, the dehumanizing secrecy of bureaucratic opinion needs to be ended, and open, creative debate encouraged among official experts and advisers, while leaving final decisions to the politicians. Conversely, impartiality and incorruptibility are more necessary than ever in the actual administration of the laws, given the many obstructions and financial temptations which capitalist institutions can use to block socialist reforms. However much decentralization in introduced, the revival of a distinctive sense of public service and the 'public interest' is an essential step forward for democratic socialism.

Socialism has much difficulty over finding any theory of social transformation which could replace the failed Marxist belief in the victory of the proletariat as an emergent dominant class representing society as a whole. Not only have classes become more fragmented but the very concept of 'class consciousness' has taken some hard knocks. The underclass of modern capitalism consists of a fragmented set of disadvantaged groups who show (as yet anyhow) little capacity for cohesion or effective action. The working class, while much diminished (but possibly growing again as automation cuts into clerical work and a new army of low-paid, often female workers emerges), is still a possible basis of socialist change. The enlarged middle and professional class can be regarded either as effectively co-opted by capitalism or as a possible reservoir for radical action (Bottomore, 1984, pp. 143-4).

Political parties have replaced the concept of the proletariat as the carriers of socialism. Socialist parties can hope to enlist support from new social movements such as environmentalism, feminism and sometimes ethnic or regional groups. However these movements have an independent momentum, and environmentalism in particular has replaced socialism in many countries as the cause of idealistic youth. This is a sobering situation for socialism. It can seek common ground in its critique of capitalism and in embracing up to a point environmental goals, but any such loose alliance is faced by the more clearly defined and entrenched interests of the defenders of the existing system. Disillusionment with capitalism can certainly bring about the victory of nominally socialist parties, but the conditions of political competition easily draw those parties into sectional and opportunistic policies or into retreat in the face of a hostile economic environment. Moreover, in placing democratic consent in the forefront of their principles, socialists have a heavy task over gaining the support of public opinion for radical measures.

Democracy must be seen as the 'wild card' in modern socialist theory. Attachment to democratic pluralism has become the conventional wisdom of political theory, not just a new belief of socialism. Socialism claims to take the concept more seriously by extending it into economic life and by seeking greater economic and social equality so as to 'empower' individuals more effectively, but as Durbin (1940) warned, an increase in equality does not necessarily produce more democracy. Mass opinion can be tyrannical, lazy or apathetic. Socialism by its own choice can now be built only upon a basis of responsible citizenship, as being necessary for both the widespread popular participation which socialism now seeks and for developing the firm public support needed to withstand the certainty of strong, hostile counter-attacks.

The 'responsible citizen' that socialism needs is far removed from the apathetic individual absorbed in private consumption and pleasure who is so willingly tolerated and indeed preferred by dominant interests in Western societies; he or she is a long way too from the calculating egoist assumed and even admired by much liberal thought. The responsible citizen actually takes politics seriously and has social ideals. Socialists therefore have to give priority, not just afterthoughts, to educational goals and to the reform of the media so as to achieve greater diversity of opinion, more and more reliable information and fuller treatment of social issues.

Perhaps the best hope for a socialist transformation lies in Connolly's 'interpretive' theory of political change, based upon his view of society as 'a porous set of institutional interdependencies in which participants retain some capacity for reflexivity' (Connolly, 1981, p. 43). On this view the existing system has the powerful support of confining debate within a given set of individual opportunities and expectations, as well as of the need of most individuals to accept and feel at home in their society. However, there is not complete structural determinism, since individuals are also capable of gradually perceiving too wide a gap between the ideology of the existing system and their actual experience.

This description fits surprisingly well the almost spontaneous dissolution of Eastern communist regimes. The gap there between ideology and actual experience became simply too great. Ironically, as the dissonance between market theory and capitalist outcomes also grows greater, the same diagnosis could apply to the capitalist democracies. Their systems are more sophisticated, and include the safety valves of free opinion and political choice, but these devices are weakened by public apathy where political choice seems too limited or narrow as it increasingly does in capitalist societies. Schumpeter's belief that capitalism will be destroyed through its increasing lack of credibility could still in a way prove right.

Modern socialism has to reject both historical or structural determinism and the weak 'psychologism' of liberal individualism which abstracts the exercise of choice from its social context. Socialism has to rally to its banner all those who are disadvantaged and dissatisfied with the 'possessive individualism' of the existing order, since it can no longer ground its appeal upon the collective interests of a homogeneous proletariat. Socialism is said to have changed from being an idea in search of a constituency to a constituency in search of an idea (Wright, 1986, pp. 115–16).

The problem for socialism is not that it has no attractive ideas to offer this potential constituency. It has good and appealing ideas in abundance, even if their integration is a difficult task. Its problem is much more one of persuading the somewhat politically disillusioned or apathetic citizens of Western societies that it could deliver its promises without succumbing to the dangers of political turmoil or corruption and bureaucratic inefficiency.

Socialism therefore has to re-establish the potentiality of politics for creating the framework of a better life in place of the dominant liberal view of politics as wholly an arena of competing interests and self-regarding individuals. To do this it has to stress the moral basis of citizenship itself instead of appealing simply to the material interests of political supporters. A society made up of rational egoists pursuing exclusively their private interests in both economic and political life, is found to continue its downhill route. Socialism can be seen as struggling within a crippled world (Hampton, 1981), because the impulse to fellowship, which is the necessary basis for a decent society, is confined to particular groups and retains little vitality at the civic or political level. The limitations and difficulties of extending 'fellowship' into politics has of course always been a stumbling block for socialist ideals, but they can tap the dismay which many people feel at the decline of community values in the modern world under the influence of economic individualism.

Socialists also have to prove their practical capacity to design new political institutions which express their goals effectively. This also is not easy because of the tensions that are bound to exist between their adherence to extending the scope of democracy and their need to establish new institutions for supervising market operations. The most beneficent socialist reforms, if they are to be effective, are bound to awaken old anxieties about the uses of state powers. Socialists have to stress the truth that politics, whatever its appearances, settles either positively or by abnegation the framework of society. It must be a socialist belief that, whatever the political risks and dangers, a good society can only be built upon sound political foundations, not the internal logic of a particular market system.

While socialism is intrinsically optimistic about the potentialities of human nature, it can no longer countenance facile utopian hopes. Every advance towards socialism involves a forward step in the social norms of co-operation and understanding, and each advance can easily be reversed. Socialism has changed dramatically from being the prophet of proletarian revolt to becoming the standard-bearer for new meanings of democracy and community. Its adherents can only live up to that role if they eschew political opportunism and advance clear moral arguments. There are no shortcuts to socialism.

Thus as Bernstein (1899) recognized long ago, socialism is a movement, not a set of finite goals. It must be tested by the congruence of its immediate direction with its basic moral yardsticks, as well as by the practical efficacy of each step in facilitating further progress. The mistaken and partisan identification of democratic socialism with authoritarian communism must finally be buried, and credit not cynicism awarded for the modest but genuine steps towards socialism achieved in some democratic countries. Bernstein and at a later stage Tawney (1935) recognized progress towards socialism in the politics of their societies; as events have shown they were too sanguine, but ground lost is capable of being regained. Socialism needs its visionaries and can absorb a catholicity of interpretations about the final goals of society. It was ever thus, but socialist philosophy will always rest upon a positive view of the capacities of ordinary people to shape their collective destiny.

See also 2 CONTINENTAL PHILOSOPHY; 4 SOCIOLOGY; 5 ECONOMICS; 6 POLITICAL SCIENCE; 8 ANARCHISM; 11 LIBERALISM; 12 MARXISM; 14 AUTONOMY; 15 COMMUNITY; 18 CORPORATISM AND SYNDICALISM; 19 DEMOCRACY; 22 DISTRIBUTIVE JUSTICE; 25 EQUALITY; 29 LIBERTY; 30 POWER; 31 PROPERTY; 36 STATE; 37 TOLERATION AND FUNDAMENTALISM; 38 TOTALITARIANISM; 39 TRUST; 41 WELFARE

References

Barry, B.: *Does Society Exist? The Case for Socialism* (London: Fabian Society Tract 536, 1989).

Berlin, I.: 'Two concepts of liberty', in *Four Essays on Liberty* (Oxford: Oxford University Press, 1969).

Bernstein, E.: *Evolutionary Socialism* (1899); (New York: Schocken Books, 1961).

Bottomore, T.: *Sociology and Socialism* (Brighton: Harvester Press, 1984).

Buber, M.: 'Marx and the renewal of society', *Paths in Utopia* (1950); reprinted in *Essential Works of Socialism*, ed. I. Howe, 2nd edn (New Haven, Conn.: Yale University Press, 1976).

Cole, G. D. H.: *Self-Government in Industry* (London: Bell, 1917).

Connolly, W.: *Appearance and Reality in Politics* (Cambridge: Cambridge University Press, 1981).

Crick, B.: *Socialism* (Milton Keynes: Open University Press, 1987).

Crosland, C. A. R.: *The Future of Socialism* (London: Jonathan Cape, 1956).

Dahl, R. A.: *A Preface to Economic Democracy* (Berkeley: University of California Press, 1985).

Dennis, N. and Halsey, A. H.: *English Ethical Socialism* (Oxford: Clarendon Press, 1988).

Dunn, J.: *The Politics of Socialism* (Cambridge: Cambridge University Press, 1984).

Durbin, E.: *The Politics of Democratic Socialism* (London: Routledge, 1940).

Dworkin, R.: 'Liberalism', in *Public and Private Morality*, ed. S. Hampshire (Cambridge: Cambridge University Press, 1978).

Eatwell, J. and Green, R.: 'Economic theory and political power', in *Fabian Essays in Socialist Thought*, ed. B. Pimlott (London: Heinemann, 1984).

Etzioni-Halévy, E.: *Bureaucracy and Democracy* (London: Routledge & Kegan Paul, 1983).

Green, T. H.: *Lectures on the Principles of Political Obligation* (1879); reprinted in *Collected Works*, ed. R. Nettleship (London: Longmans Green, 1890), vol. 2.

Hampton, C.: *Socialism in a Crippled World* (Harmondsworth: Penguin Books, 1981).

Harrington, M.: *Socialism Past and Future* (New York: Arcade Publishing, 1989).

Harvey, D.: *Social Justice and the City* (London: Edward Arnold, 1973).

Hayek, F. A.: *The Road to Serfdom* (London: Routledge & Kegan Paul, 1944).

Heilbroner, R.: *The Nature and Logic of Capitalism* (New York: W. W. Norton, 1985).

Hirsch, F.: *Social Limits to Growth* (Cambridge, Mass.: Harvard University Press, 1976).

Hobson, J. A.: *Imperialism* (1902); 3rd edn (London: Allen & Unwin, 1938).

Hodgson, G.: *The Democratic Economy* (Harmondsworth: Penguin Books, 1984).

Hoover, K. and Plant, R.: *Conservative Capitalism in Britain and the US* (London: Routledge, 1989).

Kant, I.: *The Moral Law* (1785); ed. H. J. Paton (London: Hutchinson, 1948).

Keynes, J. M.: *The General Theory of Employment, Interest and Money* (London: Macmillan, 1936).

Kropotkin, P.: *Fields, Factories and Workshops* (New York: G. P. Putnam, 1901).

Lichtheim, G.: *A Short History of Socialism* (London: Weidenfeld & Nicolson, 1970).

Luard, E.: *Socialism Without the State* (London: Macmillan, 1979).

MacPherson, C. B.: *The Political Theory of Possessive Individualism* (London: Oxford University Press, 1962).

Marshall, T. H.: 'Citizenship and social class', in *Sociology at the Crossroads* (London: Heinemann, 1963).

Miller, D.: *Market, State and Community* (Oxford: Clarendon Press, 1989).

Mises, L. von: *Socialism* (1922); (Indianapolis, Ind.: Liberty Classics, 1981).

Nove, A.: *The Economics of Feasible Socialism* (London: Allen & Unwin, 1983).

Nowak, L.: *Property and Power* (Dordrecht: D. Reidel, 1983).

O'Connor, J.: *The Fiscal Crisis of the State* (New York: St Martin's Press, 1973).

Phillips, A.: 'Fraternity', in *Fabian Essays in Socialist Thought*, ed. B. Pimlott (London: Heinemann, 1984).

Pimlott, B., ed.: *Fabian Essays in Socialist Thought* (London: Heinemann, 1984).

Przeworski, A.: *Capitalism and Social Democracy* (Cambridge: Cambridge University Press, 1985).

Rees, J.: *Equality* (London: Macmillan, 1971).

Ringen, S.: *The Possibility of Politics* (Oxford: Oxford University Press, 1987).

Ryan, A.: 'Liberty and socialism', in *Fabian Essays in Socialist Thought*, ed. B. Pimlott (London: Heinemann, 1984).

Schumacher, E. F.: *Small is Beautiful* (London: Abacus, 1974).

Schumpeter, J.: *Capitalism, Socialism and Democracy* (1943); 5th edn (London: Allen & Unwin, 1976).

Self, P.: *Political Theories of Modern Government* (London: Allen & Unwin, 1985).

Tawney, R. H.: *Equality* (1935); (London: Allen & Unwin, 1964).

Thomas, H. and Logan, C.: *Mondragon: An Economic Analysis* (London: Allen & Unwin, 1982).

Webb, S. and B.: *Soviet Communism: A New Civilization?* (London: Longmans, Green, 1935).

Wright, A.: *Socialisms: Theories and Practices* (Oxford: Oxford University Press, 1986).

Further reading

Bottomore, T.: *Sociology and Socialism* (Brighton: Harvester Press, 1984).

Crick, B.: *Socialism* (Milton Keynes: Open University Press, 1987).

Dennis, N. and Halsey, A. H.: *English Ethical Socialism* (Oxford: Clarendon Press, 1988).

Harrington, M.: *Socialism Past and Future* (New York: Arcade Publishing, 1989).

Heilbroner, R.: *The Nature and Logic of Capitalism* (New York: W. W. Norton, 1985).

Howe, I., ed.: *Essential Works of Socialism*, 2nd edn (New Haven, Conn.: Yale University Press, 1976).

Lichtheim, G.: *A Short History of Socialism* (London: Weidenfeld & Nicolson, 1970).

Marshall, T. H.: 'Citizenship and social class', in *Sociology at the Crossroads* (London: Heinemann, 1963).

Miller, D.: *Market, State and Community* (Oxford: Clarendon Press, 1989).

Pimlott, B., ed.: *Fabian Essays in Socialist Thought* (London: Heinemann, 1984).

Schumacher, E. F.: *Small is Beautiful* (London: Abacus, 1974).

Schumpteter, J.: *Capitalism, Socialism and Democracy* (1943); 5th edn (London: Allen & Unwin, 1976).

Tawney, R. H.: *Equality* (1935); (London: Allen & Unwin, 1964).

Wright, A.: *Socialisms: Theories and Practices* (Oxford: Oxford University Press, 1986).

PART III
SPECIAL TOPICS

14

Autonomy

GERALD DWORKIN

Introduction

The concept of autonomy has assumed increasing importance in contemporary political philosophy. Philosophers such as Rawls, Wolff, Scanlon, Raz and Hurley have employed the concept to ground principles and illuminate issues such as the choice of principles of justice, the justification of political authority, the limits of free speech, the nature of the liberal state and the justification of democracy.

It is not clear why there has been this increased reliance on the idea of autonomy. Partial explanations include the revival of interest in Kantian moral and political theory, the increased popularity of contractualist theories in general, the search for a fundamental normative notion that would command widespread agreement in societies beset by conflicting ideologies, the popularity of hierarchical analyses of freedom and autonomy in the area of intersection between moral theory and philosophy of mind, the critiques of welfare economics (and utilitarianism more generally) for taking preferences as simply given in light of what we know about how preferences are shaped by society.

But the fact that different theorists may use the same word should not lead one to assume that they are all referring to the same thing. One reason for supposing that they are not is that different political philosophers are worrying about different problems. Perhaps the same concept is useful in thinking about the nature of political obligation and distributive justice, but this cannot be assumed to be the case.

There is also a tendency to use the concept in a very broad fashion. It is sometimes used as equivalent to liberty, sometimes as equivalent to freedom of the will, sometimes identified with rationality or sovereignty. It is applied to very different entities: to actions, to persons, to the will, to desires, to principles, to thoughts.

My own view is that as a term of art, one cannot look to the ordinary uses of the concept. What a theorist must do is construct a concept – given various theoretical purposes and some constraints from normal usage. But the construction of the concept must be relative to a set of problems and questions. Therefore, in looking at the uses of the term in contemporary political philosophers one should do so with the following questions in mind.

First, one wants to know what the set of problems is that the author is confronting. Is she interested in some deep, metaphysical issues about the nature of rationality and freedom as, for example, Kant was? Is she interested in promoting some ideal of human development and fulfilment as Mill was? Is she interested in a practical issue such as Scanlon's concern with principles for freedom of expression? Is she interested in using the concept to ground some broader view of, say, the legitimacy of the state? Is she trying to explain why paternalism is wrong or why the legal enforcement of morality is not a legitimate function of the state?

Second, one wants to know as specifically as possible how the term is actually being used or defined or characterized by a specific author. Of what is the term predicated? Is it of a person? If so is it a term that can apply to a moment of time, a span of time, a life? Is it of his actions? Is it of his beliefs, values, desires? Is it a property that other species could possess or only humans?

Third, one would want to know how the concept is related to other concepts that the author uses. Is autonomy different from liberty? Is it a kind of liberty? Can one be autonomous and unfree? Autonomous and ignorant? Autonomous and irrational? Autonomous and evil? Autonomous and in prison? Autonomous and coerced? Autonomous and a child? Autonomous and a parent? Autonomous and a patient? Autonomous and a law-obeyer?

Fourth, one wants to know how the term is functioning normatively? Is it a good thing to be autonomous? Why? Because autonomous persons are more likely to achieve some other good thing or value? Because autonomy is valuable in and of itself? Is it a good thing to autonomously choose x, where x is a bad thing or a trivial thing? Is it better for people to choose autonomously to do evil things or to do the right thing non-autonomously? Is autonomy supremely important, very important, sometimes important? Does interference with autonomy always call for some kind of justification? Why? Is autonomy a fundamental notion in terms of which other values are explained? Or is its value reducible to other notions?

Finally, one must make an evaluation. Does the concept help with the particular set of problems the author faces? Does it help but lead to other problems? Are the problems created by the use of this concept less serious than those the theorist would face if she used some different notion?

The proper form of criticism of some theorists' use of autonomy is either that the set of problems they are concerned with are uninteresting or confused, or should be replaced by some other set of questions. Or that although the problems are genuine this way of looking at autonomy is not helpful or useful or insightful in thinking about these issues. And that could be for a number of different reasons varying from internal problems with the concept – it is self-contradictory or leads to some kind of regress difficulty or is too vague – to the criticism that while the concept is clear enough and consistent, it runs too many things together or makes distinctions where they are not needed.

For a number of different problems (in particular for thinking about the role of the state in promoting various values, ideals and attitudes) and for considering the limits of legal coercion, I believe the most useful conception of autonomy is the following: autonomy is a second-order capacity of persons to reflect critically upon their first-order preferences, desires, wishes, and so forth, and the capacity to accept or attempt to change these in light of higher-order preferences (Dworkin, 1988, p. 20).

Autonomy and neutrality

I believe that the most important task for which autonomy has been harnessed in contemporary political philosophy is to argue for a certain ideal of the liberal state: that of
neutrality. The idea of neutrality is itself complex and has different formulations. But
the root idea is that the state must recognize and acknowledge the autonomy of persons, i.e. the capacity of persons to stand back from their current ends and ideals, to
question their value, and to attempt to change them if necessary. In order to recognize
this ideal of autonomy the state must not justify its actions on the basis that some ways
of life are intrinsically better than others; the state does not rank various ways of living
and attempt to promote some rather than others. This does not mean that the state is
neutral in any stronger sense. Its policies may differentially favour different conceptions of the good, in that the *consequences* of its policies may promote a more favourable environment for some conception of the good at the expense of others.

The neutral state is opposed to various perfectionist theories, i.e. theories which
believe the state ought to promote certain ways of living and discourage others,
because some ways of living are better, more valuable than others. Theorists of the
neutral state believe perfectionism ought to be resisted, not because they are sceptical
about ranking ways of life, but because they believe that the political sphere must
always honour the capacity of individuals to change their views about what kind of
life is worth living, and that only if we are free to form and revise such ideas can
we be said to be *leading* a good life, as opposed to simply *having* one (Kymlicka,
1990). I would like to trace this theme in three influential political theorists: John
Rawls, Joseph Raz and Ronald Dworkin.

Autonomy and hypothetical consent

As is well known, Rawls believes that the principles of justice are those that would be
chosen by rational and mutually disinterested persons, behind the 'veil of ignorance'.
The veil of ignorance assures, among other things, that the agents do not know what
particular vision of the good life they have. But they do know that they have some
conception of the good, and more importantly, they know that they are motivated
to exercise and realize two moral powers, viz. the capacity for a sense of justice and
'the capacity to form, to revise, and rationally pursue a conception of the good'
(Rawls, 1980, p. 525). It is the last capacity which Rawls calls 'rational autonomy'
which requires the veil of ignorance, for if '[the parties'] ends were restricted in
some specific way, this would appear at the outset as an arbitrary restriction on freedom' (Rawls, 1971, p. 254). This assumption about what motivates the parties in the
'original position' enables Rawls to argue for economic institutions and political liberties which encourage and enhance the capacity of individuals to form and revise their
conception of the good. (What Rawls calls 'full autonomy' is what occurs when persons are motivated to act in accordance with principles that would be chosen by
rationally autonomous persons.)

It looks, then, as if Rawls is building into the foundation of his theory a particular
value, namely, that of autonomy and giving it precedence over other values, such as

being secure from influences that might lead one to change one's ends. In fact I believe he does this, and there is nothing objectionable about it. In political philosophy, as in life, you can't get something from nothing. What is distinctive about a political theorist is the nature of the 'something', and how conscious he is that this is his starting point. For Rawls, his 'something' is a particular ideal of the person, having obvious grounding in Kant.

An obvious objection to the theory is that those who reject this ideal (either completely or at least give it much lower priority among values) will have no reason to follow the further development of the theory. Rawls attempts to soften this objection by arguing that he values autonomy not as part of a 'comprehensive' moral doctrine, but as part of a purely 'political' conception. Justice as fairness does not 'seek to cultivate the distinctive virtues and values of the liberalism of autonomy', i.e. does not attempt to promote autonomy as a general moral value, but only as part of the 'political good of a well ordered society' (Rawls, 1988, p. 270). His hope is that there will be a sufficient consensus among different ideological viewpoints (including those that do not give great value to autonomy considered as a general ideal for persons) that for deriving principles of social justice 'rational' autonomy is a common value. I am less confident that such a consensus is likely, but I do not take the absence of such a consensus as showing that the Rawlsian project is mistaken. For if the theory contains as part of it a non *ad hoc* explanation of why some differing viewpoint does not (cannot?) see the genuine value of autonomy the absence of a consensus only shows that the theory cannot 'convince', not that it is not convincing.

Autonomy and coercion

Joseph Raz uses the concept of autonomy to consider a related problem: the legitimacy of state coercion (Raz, 1986). He wants to derive principles which will determine what kinds of behaviour the state may seek to limit by means of the criminal law. Like Mill, he believes that harm to others (the harm principle) is the only legitimate reason for justifying criminal sanctions. Unlike Mill, he believes a certain amount of paternalism may be justifiable – justified by the harm principle but the harm in question being that to the person who is being restricted.

Unlike Mill, Raz does not seek to derive the harm principle from utilitarian considerations. Instead he believes it is derivable from a principle of autonomy. He defines autonomous persons as 'those who can shape their life and determine its course . . . creators of their own moral world' (Raz, 1986, p. 154). There are certain conditions which are necessary for a person to be autonomous – adequate options, sufficient mental abilities and freedom from coercion and manipulation. Finally, Raz interprets autonomy so that its value is dependent on being directed at good options. A person may be autonomous even if he pursues what is bad, but his autonomy only has value if he chooses the good.

One might think that since autonomy 'supplies no reason to . . . protect worthless let alone bad options' (Raz, 1986, p. 411) this opens the way to the justification of legal moralism, i.e. the view that the state is entitled to interfere with immoral (although harmless) conduct. Raz does not think so. Here is his argument:

[The] harm principle is defensible in the light of the principle of autonomy for one simple reason. The means used, coercive interference, violates the autonomy of its victim. First, it violates the condition of independence and expresses a relation of domination and an attitude of disrespect for the coerced individual. Second, coercion by criminal penalties is a global and indiscriminate invasion of autonomy. Imprisoning a person prevents him from almost all autonomous pursuits . . . there is no practical way of ensuring that coercion will restrict the victim's choice of repugnant options but will not interfere with their other choices. (Raz, 1986, pp. 418–19)

This argument is not convincing. First, coercing a person for some immoral behaviour need not show disrespect for him, merely for his conduct. Second, of course by Raz's definition of autonomy coercion interferes with autonomy. But this is just as true if we coerce people who harm others. Two additional premises are required.

The first is that autonomy may be interfered with only to promote greater autonomy. The second is that when one harms another one interferes with autonomy, but when one does something immoral but not harmful one does not. The first is unsupported by any arguments, and has unacceptable implications. For example, it would not allow the law to restrict conduct which offends others, such as defecation in public.

The second premiss is also implausible. If I stick a pin into you causing pain I would certainly seem to harm you, but if one refers back to the definition of autonomy I see no reason to suppose that I have interfered with your autonomy. On page 414 Raz notes that 'the prevention of severe pain justifies coercion. The explanation of our concern to avoid pain is a fascinating subject which cannot be undertaken in this book.' In addition to this omission in the argument, he seems, by implication, not to consider either less than severe pain or offence as a ground for coercion. Conversely, if pornography is freely available thus making it difficult for some to raise their children with certain ideals of sexuality, it would seem that their ability to 'shape their life . . . create their own moral world' is adversely affected.

Autonomy and moral paternalism

The last use of autonomy I want to examine is that of Ronald Dworkin. In his Tanner Lectures on the 'Foundations of Liberal Equality' he develops an argument against state paternalism which, although he does not use the term autonomy, relies on the idea that the good life for persons is necessarily one that they create for themselves, that is lived from the inside as opposed to led from the outside. He argues for what Kymlicka has called the 'endorsement constraint': 'no component [of a person's life] may even so much as contribute to the value of a person's life without his endorsement . . . no event or achievement can make a person's life better against his opinion that it does not' (Dworkin, 1991, p. 50).

This thesis grounds an objection to moral paternalism, i.e. the state's use of coercion to make people morally better. For it is an essential premiss of that view that some intervention can improve the quality of a person's moral life or character, and as a result her life go better for her. But according to the endorsement thesis if genuine endorsement is not forthcoming then moral paternalism cannot be successful.

363

In principle this argument also applies to ordinary paternalism. If the would-be suicide is prevented from committing suicide, but does not welcome the life he is forced to lead, then on the endorsement view we cannot say that his welfare had been increased. The reason the argument has less interest in this case is that in most cases it is uncontroversial that the actions being interfered with have a description under which they are not counter to endorsed ends of the agent. Few deny that smoking cigarettes is unhealthy, or that cancer is detrimental to their life. They simply insist on their right to engage in unhealthy activities. It should be noted, however, that there is an argument which is parallel to the one we are considering. This is the claim that since autonomy, the ability to determine for oneself what to do, is itself an important component of well-being, one cannot be made better off against one's will.

What makes moral paternalism distinctive is that it is precisely the evaluation of the activity being interfered with that is controversial. Most homosexuals do not think they are engaging in immoral activities. Atheists do not think that they are living a life of sin. Those who watch pornography do not think they are being corrupted. A *fortiori* they do not usually think that a life without these activities is a morally superior life.

It is important to see that even accepting the endorsement view does not rule out moral paternalism on conceptual grounds alone. For even if, say, forced prayers cannot by themselves contribute any value to the person's well-being (on the assumption that a life of religious devotion is a good for a person) it may still be that as a result of praying the person comes to see the value of prayer and its attendant way of life.

There is a second way in which moral paternalism can be effective even assuming the endorsement constraint. Namely, that although there may be some fact about the person that he does not value or endorse, e.g. that he is loved by others or is courageous, this fact may have consequences for other aspects of the person's life that he does endorse. For example, the person who is loved may, in spite of his lack of endorsement, benefit from that fact. He may, for example, be more confident and therefore successful in achieving his goals. And given that he does endorse the idea of success he is benefited by the existence of the fact in question. This is so even if he does not recognize the fact that there is this causal connection.

Still, if the endorsement constraint is correct, it does seem to provide strong grounds for resisting moral paternalism. The interesting issue then becomes whether the constraint is correct. Does autonomy enter crucially as a constraint on what makes a person's life go well? This question goes back at least to Kant, who denied that any natural fact about a person's situation, e.g. that a certain course of action would give him great pleasure, provided a reason for that person to act unless he endorsed pleasure as one of his ends.

So we end our tour having seen how autonomy enters into every part of contemporary political philosophy theory from the theory of justice to the theory of value.

See also I ANALYTICAL PHILOSOPHY; 7 LEGAL STUDIES; 8 ANARCHISM; II LIBERALISM; 16 CONTRACT AND CONSENT; 19 DEMOCRACY; 22 DISTRIBUTIVE JUSTICE; 25 EQUALITY; 28 LEGITIMACY; 29 LIBERTY; 30 POWER; 32 REPUBLICANISM; 33 RIGHTS; 40 VIRTUE; 41 WELFARE

References

Dworkin, G.: The *Theory and Practice of Autonomy* (Cambridge: Cambridge University Press, 1988).

Dworkin, R.: 'Foundations of liberal equality', in *Tanner Lectures on Human Values* (Salt Lake City: University of Utah Press, 1991).

Hurley, S.: *Natural Reasons* (Oxford: Oxford University Press, 1989).

Kymlicka, W.: *Contemporary Political Philosophy* (Oxford: Clarendon Press, 1990).

Rawls, J.: *A Theory of Justice* (Cambridge, Mass.: Harvard University Press, 1971).

————: 'Kantian constructivism in moral theory', *Journal of Philosophy*, 77 (1980), 515–72.

————: 'The priority of right and ideas of the Good', *Philosophy and Public Affairs*, 17 (1988), 251–76.

Raz, J.: *The Morality of Freedom* (Oxford: Oxford University Press, 1986).

Scanlon, T.: 'Freedom of expression and categories of expression', in *Pornography and Censorship* (Buffalo: Prometheus Press, 1983).

Wolff, R. P.: *In Defense of Anarchism* (New York: Harper & Row, 1970).

Further reading

Dworkin, R.: 'Liberal community', *California Law Review*, 77 (1989), 479–504.

Feinberg, J.: *Harmless Wrongdoing* (Oxford: Oxford University Press, 1988).

Haworth, L.: *Autonomy: An Essay in Philosophical Psychology and Ethics* (New Haven, Conn.: Yale University Press, 1986).

Mason, A.: 'Autonomy, liberalism and state neutrality', *Philosophical Quarterly*, 40 (1991), 433–52.

Rawls, J.: 'Justice as fairness: political not metaphysical', *Philosophy and Public Affairs*, 14 (1985), 223–51.

Scanlon, T.: 'The significance of choice', in *Tanner Lectures on Human Values* (Salt Lake City: University of Utah Press, 1988).

Waldron, J.: 'Autonomy and perfectionism in Raz's morality of freedom', *Southern California Law Review*, 62 (1989), 1097–152.

Young, R.: *Personal Autonomy: Beyond Negative and Positive Liberty* (London: Croom Helm, 1986).

15

Community

WILL KYMLICKA

Introduction

The rallying cry of the French Revolution – 'liberté, égalité et fraternité' – lists the three basic ideals of the modern democratic age. The great ideologies of the eighteenth and nineteenth centuries – socialism, conservatism, liberalism, nationalism and republicanism – each offered its own conception of the ideals of liberty, equality and community. The ideal of community took many different forms, from class solidarity or shared citizenship to a common ethnic descent or cultural identity. But for all of these theories, and for the philosophers who helped defend them, community was one of the basic conceptual building blocks to be shaped and defined.

After the Second World War, however, community seemed to drop out of the picture. For example, John Rawls, whose book *A Theory of Justice* (1971) is largely credited with reviving the tradition of normative political philosophy in the Anglo-American world, says that his work is intended to provide an interpretation of the concepts of liberty and equality. It is not that Rawls rejects the value of community. It is rather that he paid little attention to it. Perhaps he thought that community was no longer a subject of ideological dispute, or that recent history had revealed that the ideal of community was too liable to manipulation by fascist, racist or totalitarian regimes.

Rawls is not unique in this regard. Most contemporary liberal philosophers have little to say about the ideal of community. If community is discussed at all, it is often seen as derivative of liberty and equality – i.e. a society lives up to the ideal of community if its members are treated as free and equal persons. Liberal visions of politics do not include any independent principle of community, such as shared nationality, language, culture, religion, history or way of life.

Today, in the 1980s and 1990s, community has resurfaced. An entire school of thought, known as 'communitarianism', has arisen in political philosophy whose central claim is precisely the necessity of attending to community alongside, if not prior to, liberty and equality. Communitarians believe that the value of community is not sufficiently recognized in liberal theories of justice, or in the public culture of liberal societies.

This emphasis on community can be found in Marxism as well, and is of course a defining feature of the communist ideal. However, the kind of communitarianism which has recently come to prominence with the writings of Michael Sandel, Michael Walzer, Alasdair MacIntyre and Charles Taylor is quite different from traditional

Marxism. Marxists see community as something that can only be achieved by a revolutionary change in society, by the overthrow of capitalism and the building of a socialist society. The new communitarians, on the other hand, believe that community already exists, in the form of common social practices, cultural traditions and shared social understandings. Community does not need to be built *de novo*, but rather needs to be respected and protected. To some extent, communitarians see community in the very social practices that Marxists see as exploitative and alienating. As Amy Gutmann put it, whereas the 'old' communitarians looked to Marx, and his desire to remake the world, the 'new' communitarians look to Hegel, and his desire to reconcile people to their world (Gutmann, 1985).

The idea that community can be constructed from the ground up has few defenders today, even on the Left. When contemporary socialists appeal to community, their ideal is often a variation of the liberals' – i.e. membership in a community involves being treated as a free and equal citizen. The major difference is that Rawls says that our sense of equal citizenship (and hence community membership) is based on the possession of civil and political rights, whereas socialists argue that social rights are equally important. For the new communitarians, however, the socialist conception of community in terms of 'social citizenship' (King and Waldron, 1988) still treats community as derivative of freedom and equality, rather than as an independent value or principle. For communitarians, community is something more than, or other than, a society of free and equal citizens.

So the new communitarians are united by the belief that political philosophy must pay more attention to the shared practices and understandings within each society. They also agree that this requires modification of traditional liberal principles of justice and rights. They differ, however, on how these principles should be modified.

We can distinguish three distinct, sometimes conflicting, strands of communitarian thought. Some communitarians believe that community replaces the need for principles of justice. Others see justice and community as perfectly consistent, but think that a proper appreciation of the value of community requires us to modify our conception of what justice is. These latter communitarians fall into two camps. One camp argues that community should be seen as the source of principles of justice (i.e. justice should be based on the shared understandings of society, not on universal and ahistorical principles); the other camp argues that community should play a greater role in the content of principles of justice (i.e. justice should give more weight to the common good, and less weight to individual rights). I will look at these three positions in turn.

Community and the limits of justice

Rawls claims that justice is 'the first virtue of social institutions' (1971, p. 3). Michael Sandel (1982) responds that justice is not the first virtue of social life, to be valued for its own sake, but rather is a 'remedial' virtue, remedying a flaw in social life. Drawing partly on Rawls' own account of the 'circumstances of justice', Sandel argues that justice is only needed where there is an absence of the 'more noble' virtues of benevolence or solidarity. If people responded spontaneously to the needs of others out of love or shared goals, then there would be no need to claim one's rights. Hence an increased concern with justice can, in some circumstances, reflect a worsening of the moral situation, rather than a moral improvement. Sandel suggests that the family is a social institution where justice is not needed, and where a preoccupation with justice may diminish the sense of love, and thereby lead to more conflict (1982, pp. 28–35).

Similar views about the 'limits of justice' can be found among some Marxists and feminists, who see the preoccupation with justice as arising from the need to 'stand up for one's due' in a world full of conflicting interests. On this view, justice helps mediate conflicts, but it also tends to create conflicts and to decrease the natural expression of sociability. Hence justice is a regrettable necessity at present, but a barrier to a higher form of community.

This view about the dichotomy between community and justice is, I believe, mistaken. Justice does not displace love or solidarity, and nothing in the idea of justice precludes people from choosing to forgo their rightful claims in order to help others. Justice simply ensures that these decisions are genuinely voluntary, and that no one can force others to accept a subordinate position. Justice enables loving relationships, but ensures that they are not corrupted by domination or subordination.

Justice and shared meanings

Many communitarians agree with Rawls about the importance of justice. However, they claim that liberals misinterpret justice as an ahistorical and external criterion for criticizing the ways of life of every society. Utilitarians, liberal egalitarians and libertarians may disagree about the content of justice, but they all seem to think that their preferred theory provides a standard that every society should live up to. They do not see it as a decisive objection that their theory may be in conflict with local beliefs.

Indeed, this is sometimes seen by liberals as the point of discussing justice – it provides a standpoint for questioning our beliefs, and for ensuring that they are not merely local prejudices. As Ronald Dworkin (1985, p. 219) puts it, 'In the end, political theory can make no contribution to how we govern ourselves except by struggling, against all the impulses that drag us back into our own culture, towards generality and some reflective basis for deciding which of our traditional distinctions and discriminations are genuine and which spurious.' For Dworkin, justice should be our critic, not our mirror.

Michael Walzer argues that this quest for a universal theory of justice is misguided. There is no such thing as a perspective external to the community, no way to step outside our history and culture. The only way to identify the requirements of justice, he claims, is to see how each particular community understands the value of social goods. A society is just if it acts in accordance with the shared understandings of its members, as embodied in its characteristic practices and institutions. Hence identifying principles of justice is more a matter of cultural interpretation than of philosophical argument.

According to Walzer, the shared understandings in our society require 'complex equality' – i.e. a system of distribution that does not try to equalize all goods, but rather seeks to ensure that inequalities in one 'sphere' (e.g. wealth) do not permeate other spheres (e.g. health care, political power). However, he acknowledges that other societies do not share this understanding of justice, and for some societies (e.g. caste societies) justice may involve virtually unlimited inequality in rights and goods (Walzer, 1983).

Walzer's theory is, of course, a form of cultural relativism, and it is beyond the scope of this paper to discuss that age-old philosophical debate. However, there are two common objections to communitarian attempts to define justice in terms of a community's shared understandings. First, and paradoxically, Walzer's theory violates one of our deepest shared understandings. According to Walzer, slavery is wrong if our society disapproves of it. But that is not how most people understand claims of justice. They put the causal arrow the other way around – i.e. we disapprove of slavery because it is wrong. Its wrongness is a reason for, not the product of, our shared understanding. Second, there may not be many shared understandings about justice, especially if we attend not only to the voices of the vocal and powerful, but also to the weak and marginalized. People disagree about issues such as the proper role of markets (on which Walzer wishes to impose severe limits). In order to resolve these disagreements, we need to assess competing understandings in the light of a more general conception of justice. So even if we start with local understandings, as Walzer suggests, we are driven by the existence of disagreement, and our own critical reflection, towards a more general and less parochial standpoint.

Individual rights and the common good

For many communitarians, the problem with liberalism is not its emphasis on justice, nor its universalism, but rather its 'individualism'. According to this criticism, liberals base their theories on notions of individual rights and personal freedom, but neglect the extent to which individual freedom and well-being is only possible within community. Once we recognize the dependence of human beings on society, then our obligations to sustain the common good of society are as weighty as our rights to individual liberty. Hence, communitarians argue, the liberal 'politics of rights' should be abandoned for a 'politics of the common good'.

This, I believe, is the most important issue raised by the new communitarians. However, we need to put it in perspective. A liberal society does restrict individual liberty, since it demands compliance with the principles of freedom and equality. A liberal state will prevent me from acting in ways that deprive you of your liberty or your fair share of resources. Moreover, a liberal state appeals to a notion of the common good as the basis for its decisions about allocating public resources (e.g. taxing people to fund health care or education). Hence a liberal society often restricts individual liberty to promote the 'common good'.

However, liberals believe that there is an important constraint on the way the state restricts individual liberty – namely, it cannot take a stand on the intrinsic merits of different lifestyles (or 'conceptions of the good'). A liberal state does not deprive people of their rights or resources on the grounds that their lifestyle is worthless. Nor does it reward people with greater liberty or resources on the grounds that their lifestyle has more intrinsic value. Each person's conception of the good is shown equal respect, if consistent with the principles of justice, 'not in the sense that there is an agreed public measure of intrinsic value or satisfaction with respect to which all these conceptions come out equal, but in the sense that they are not evaluated at all from a [public] standpoint' (Rawls, 1982, p. 172). This idea that the state does not rank the intrinsic merit of different conceptions of the good is often called the idea of 'state neutrality'.

Communitarians, on the other hand, conceive of the common good as a substantive conception of the good which defines the community's 'way of life'. This way of life forms the basis for a public ranking of conceptions of the good, and the weight given to an individual's preferences depends on how much she conforms or contributes to this common good. A communitarian state is not, therefore, constrained by the requirement of 'neutrality'. It encourages people to adopt conceptions of the good that conform to the community's way of life, while discouraging conceptions of the good that conflict with it.

Should we prefer this 'politics of the common good' over liberal neutrality? Liberals say that neutrality is required to respect people's autonomy. According to liberal theory, individuals should be free to decide for themselves what sort of life they will lead. In particular, they should be free to question their participation in existing social practices, and opt out of them, should those practices seem no longer worth pursuing. Rawls (1971, p. 560) summarizes this view by saying that 'the self is prior to the ends which are affirmed by it', by which he means that we can always step back from any particular project and question whether we want to continue pursuing it. If people no longer find the community's traditional 'way of life' satisfying, they should be free to seek out more worthwhile alternatives. For liberals, a politics of the common good would preclude or distort this process of evaluating and revising our commitments.

As noted earlier, communitarians believe that the liberal emphasis on autonomy is unbalanced. It ignores the way that individuals are dependent on society. There are many different communitarian objections here, both to the idea of autonomy and to the idea of state neutrality. I will consider four such objections.

The embedded self

According to Michael Sandel and Alasdair MacIntyre, the liberal picture of individuals picking and choosing their conceptions of the good is facile. They argue that Rawls exaggerates our capacity to stand back from and question our social roles, and ignores the fact that the self is 'embedded' in existing social practices. Our social roles and relationships, or at least some of them, must be taken as fixed for the purposes of deciding how to lead our lives. As Sandel puts it, the self is not prior to, but rather constituted by, its ends. Our identity is defined by certain ends that we did not 'choose', but rather 'discovered' by virtue of our being embedded in some shared social context (Sandel, 1982, pp. 52–5, 150; cf. MacIntyre, 1981, pp. 204–5). Deciding how to lead one's life, therefore, is not a matter of choosing one's social roles, but rather of understanding the roles we already find ourselves in. A politics of the common good, by expressing these constitutive ends, enables us to 'know a good in common that we cannot know alone' (Sandel, 1982, p. 183).

I think that communitarians exaggerate our 'embeddedness' in particular roles. It may not be easy to question deeply held beliefs about the good, but the history of the women's movement, for example, shows that people can question and reject even the most deeply entrenched sexual, economic and family roles. We are not trapped by our present attachments, incapable of judging the worth of the goals we inherited or ourselves chose earlier. It is true that we find ourselves in various relationships, often without having consciously chosen them. But we do not always like what we find. No matter how deeply implicated we are in a social practice, we feel capable of questioning whether the practice is worthwhile. The process is often difficult. But it is a defining feature of the modern world that people claim the right, and the responsibility, to decide for themselves whether their inherited roles are worthy of their allegiance.

The social thesis

Many communitarians criticize liberalism, not for its belief in individual autonomy, but for neglecting the social conditions required for the exercise of autonomy. For example, Charles Taylor claims that many liberal theories are based on 'atomism', the view that individuals are not in need of any communal context in order to develop and exercise their capacity for self-determination. Taylor argues instead for the 'social thesis', which says that autonomy can only be developed and exercised in a certain kind of social environment (Taylor, 1985).

Of course, liberals do not literally deny the social thesis. The view that we might acquire autonomy outside of society is absurd. However, Taylor believes that liberals ignore the full implications of the social thesis. The social thesis tells us that the capacity to assess one's conception of the good can only be exercised in a particular sort of community. But, Taylor argues, this sort of autonomy-supporting community can only be sustained by a politics of the common good. I will consider three versions of this claim, focusing respectively on the need to sustain a diverse culture that provides people with meaningful options; the need for shared forums in which to evaluate these options; and the need to sustain political legitimacy.

The need for cultural diversity

The freedom to choose one's way of life is only meaningful if we have options to choose from, and the social thesis tells us that these options come from our culture. Communitarians argue that liberal neutrality is incapable of ensuring the existence of a rich and diverse culture which provides such options. According to liberal theory, a state which intervenes in the cultural market-place to encourage or discourage any particular way of life restricts people's autonomy. But what if the cultural market-place, left on its own, eventually undermines cultural pluralism, leading to a drab and uniform mass culture? Neutrality would then be self-defeating.

This is an important objection. Many liberals are surprisingly silent about the possibility that cultural diversity could falter. As Taylor (1985, p. 206) says, 'it is as though the conditions of a creative, diversifying freedom were given by nature.' One liberal response is to claim that a wide range of good ways of life will in fact sustain themselves in the cultural market-place without state assistance, because people are able to recognize the worth of good ways of fife, and will support them (this is Rawls' response). Another response is to accept that the state must actively protect cultural diversity, but to deny that this requires abandoning state neutrality. For example, the state could ensure an adequate range of options by providing tax credits to people who make culture-supporting contributions in accordance with their personal ideals. The state thereby acts to ensure that there are sufficient options, but the evaluation of these options occurs outside the state, through the choices of private individuals (this is Dworkin's response).

Taylor, on the other hand, suggests that the evaluation of conceptions of the good should be a political question, and that the state should intervene not simply to ensure an adequate range of options, but to promote particular options. The debate, therefore, is not whether an adequate range of options is required, but rather how these options should be evaluated. Communitarians argue that the preferability of different ways of life should be a matter of political advocacy and state action; liberals argue that it should be left to the cultural market-place.

Communitarians might argue that they can improve the quality of people's options, by encouraging the replacement of less valuable options by more valuable ones. But liberals also hope to improve the range of people's options. Freedom of speech and association allows each group to advertise its way of life, and unsatisfying ways of life will have difficulty attracting adherents. Since people are free to choose between competing visions of the good life, valuable options will tend to drive out those that are worthless, without the state having to engage in a public ranking of different ways of life.

The need for shared deliberations

Some communitarians argue that the liberal preference for the cultural market-place over the state as the appropriate arena for evaluating ways of life stems from an atomistic belief that judgements about the good are only 'autonomous' when they are made by isolated individuals who are protected from social pressure. Liberals think that autonomy is promoted when judgements about the good are taken out of the political realm. But in reality individuals require the sharing of experiences and the give and take of collective deliberation. Individual judgements about the good become a matter of subjective and arbitrary whim if they are cut off from collective deliberations. According to some people, this is precisely what has happened to most Americans as a result of the influence of liberal individualism (Bellah et al., 1985).

Communitarianism's politics of the common good, on the other hand, adopts the view that 'men living in a community of shared experiences and language is the only context in which the individual and society can discover and test their values through the essentially political activities of discussion, criticism, example, and emulation' (Crowley, 1987, p. 282). The state is the proper arena in which to formulate our visions of the good, because these visions require shared inquiry. They cannot be pursued, or even known, by solitary individuals.

This misconstrues the sense in which Rawls claims that the evaluation of ways of life should not be a public concern. For Rawls, shared experiences concerning the good are at the heart of the various groups or 'communities of interests' that exist in a liberal society. Freedom of association is important precisely because it enables people to enter into this 'free social union with others' (Rawls, 1971, p. 543). Rawls simply denies that the state is an appropriate forum for those deliberations.

Unfortunately, communitarians rarely distinguish between collective activities and political activities. It is, of course, true that participation in 'a community of shared experiences and language' is what enables individuals to make intelligent decisions about the good life. But why should such participation be organized through the state rather than through the free association of individuals? It is true that we should 'create opportunities for men to give voice to what they have discovered about themselves and the world and to persuade others of its worth' (Crowley, 1987, p. 295). But a liberal society does create such opportunities – freedom of assembly, speech and association are fundamental liberal rights. The opportunities for shared inquiry simply occur within and between groups and associations below the level of the state – friends and family, churches, cultural associations, professional groups, trade unions, universities, the media etc.

A similar problem weakens Habermas' radical critique of liberal neutrality. Habermas wants the evaluation of different ways of life to be a political question, but unlike communitarians, he does not want thereby to promote people's acceptance of the community's 'way of life'. Indeed, he thinks that political deliberation is required precisely because in its absence people will tend to accept existing practices as givens, and thereby perpetuate the false needs which accompany those practices. Only when existing ways of life are 'the objects of discursive will-formation' can people's understanding of the good be free of deception. Liberalism does not demand the scrutiny of these practices, and so fails to recognize people's interest in escaping false needs (Habermas, 1979, pp. 188–9).

But again, why should the evaluation of people's conceptions of the good be done through the state? Groups of various sizes below the level of the state might be more appropriate forums for the sort of 'discursive will-formation' which involves interpreting one's genuine needs.

So liberalism does not neglect the importance of a shared culture for meaningful options, or of the sharing of experiences for meaningful evaluation of those options. Liberalism recognizes these social requirements of individual autonomy, but interprets them in a way that relies on social rather than political processes. Of course, this aspect of liberal theory requires a certain faith in the operation of non-state forums for individual judgement and cultural development, and a distrust of the operation of state forums for evaluating the good. This optimism and distrust may not be warranted. Indeed, just as critics of liberalism have failed to defend their faith in politics, so liberals have failed to defend their faith in non-state forums.

In fact, it seems that each side in this debate has failed to learn the lesson taught by the other side. Despite centuries of liberal insistence on the importance of the distinction between state and society, communitarians still seem to assume that whatever is properly social must become the province of the political. They have not confronted the liberal worry that the all-embracing authority and coercive means which characterize the state make it a particularly inappropriate forum for the sort of genuinely shared deliberation and commitment that they desire. Despite centuries of communitarian insistence on the fragile nature of a tolerant and diverse culture, liberals still tend to take the existence of such a culture for granted, as something which naturally arises and sustains itself. Liberals have not confronted the worry that state neutrality threatens the cultural preconditions of autonomy, either by failing to involve people in a deep enough way in their communal practices (as communitarians fear), or conversely, by failing to detach people in a strong enough way from the expectations of existing practices and ideologies (as Habermas fears). So both sides need to give us a more comprehensive comparison of the opportunities and dangers present in state and nonstate forums for evaluating the good.

While this question remains open, it should be clear that we are not likely to answer it if we continue to see it as a debate between liberal 'atomism' and the communitarian 'social thesis'. Liberals and communitarians do not disagree about the need for communal practices and forums. Rather, they disagree about the need for state involvement in evaluating and protecting those practices. If this is the real issue, then the disagreement is more empirical than philosophical. What is needed is empirical evidence about the extent to which valued social practices require state support, or state restrictions on individual liberty, in order to survive.

The need for political legitimacy

There is another issue raised by the social thesis. Whatever the proper role of the state, it can only fulfil its functions if public institutions are stable, and that in turn requires that they have legitimacy in the eyes of the citizens. Taylor believes that political institutions governed by the principle of neutrality are incapable of sustaining legitimacy, and hence incapable of sustaining the social context required for self-determination.

According to Taylor, the neutral state undermines the sense of community which is required for citizens to accept the sacrifices demanded by the welfare state. Citizens will only identify with the state, and accept its demands as legitimate, when there is a 'common form of life' which 'is seen as a supremely important good, so that its continuance and flourishing matters to the citizen for its own sake and not just instrumentally to their several individual goods or as the sum total of these individual goods' (Taylor, 1986, p. 215). This sense of the common good has been undermined partly because state neutrality means that people are free to choose their goals independently of this 'common form of life', and to trump the pursuit of this common good should it violate their rights. Whereas a communitarian state would foster an identification with the common form of life, the liberal model

goes very well with a more atomist consciousness, where I understand my dignity as that of an individual bearer of rights. Indeed – and here the tension surfaces between the two – I cannot be too willing to trump the collective decision in the name of individual rights if I haven't already moved some distance from the community which makes these decisions. (Taylor, 1986, p. 211)

This 'distancing' from the community's shared form of life means we become unwilling to shoulder the burdens of liberal justice. As a result, liberal democracies are facing a 'legitimation crisis'. Citizens are asked to sacrifice more and more in the name of justice, but they share less and less with those for whom they are making sacrifices. Taylor (1986, p. 225) worries that 'the increasing stress on rights as dominant over collective decisions' will eventually 'undermine the very legitimacy of the democratic order'.

Liberals, on the other hand, believe that citizens will accept the burdens of justice even in their relations with people who have very different conceptions of the good. Conflicting conceptions can be tolerated because the public recognition of principles of justice is sufficient to ensure stability even in the face of such conflicts. People with different lifestyles will respect each other's rights, not because it promotes a shared way of life, but because they accept that each person has an equal claim to consideration. Hence the basis for state legitimacy is a shared sense of justice, not a shared conception of the good.

Why do communitarians think that a shared way of life is required to sustain legitimacy? Communitarians often look to history for examples of societies, such as the democracies of Ancient Greece, or eighteenth-century New England town governments, that were based on a politics of the common good, and that had a high degree of civic participation and loyalty. But these historical examples are misleading. New England town governments may have had great legitimacy among their members, but that is at least partly because women, atheists, Indians and the propertyless were all denied membership. Had these groups been allowed membership, they would not have been impressed by the pursuit of what was often a racist and sexist 'common good'. The way in which legitimacy was ensured among all members was to exclude from membership those groups most likely to reject the community's ideals.

Contemporary communitarians are not advocating that legitimacy be secured by denying membership to those groups in the community who have not historically participated in shaping the 'common form of life'. Sandel and Taylor say that there are shared ends that can serve as the basis for a politics of the common good which will be legitimate to all groups in society. But they give no examples of such ends, perhaps because there are none. They say that these shared ends are to be found in our historical practices, but they do not mention that those practices were defined by a small section of society – propertied white men – to serve the interests of propertied, white men. Attempts to promote these kinds of ends reduce legitimacy and further exclude marginalized groups. This is clearest in the case of various forms of right-wing communitarianism (e.g. the Moral Majority in the United States, based on the Christian, patriarchal family). Many communitarians dislike this view of the common good, but the problem of the exclusion of historically marginalized groups is endemic to the communitarian project (Gutmann, 1985, pp. 318–22). As Hirsch (1986, p. 424) notes, 'any "renewal" or strengthening of community sentiment will accomplish nothing for these groups'. On the contrary, our historical sentiments are 'part of the problem, not part of the solution'.

Political legitimacy may require participation by all groups in society. This is one of the central insights of 'civic republicanism' (Pettit, 1989). But it only makes sense to invite people to participate in politics (or for people to accept that invitation) if they will be treated as equals. And that is incompatible with defining people in terms of roles they did not shape or endorse. If legitimacy is to be earned, it will require empowering the oppressed to define their own aims. It is not surprising, therefore, to find representatives of the 'new social movements' (e.g. women, people with disabilities, immigrants and visible minorities, gays and lesbians) expressing concern about the appeal to 'community' (e.g. Okin, 1989, pp. 41–73; Young, 1990, pp. 227–36). While these groups have objections to liberalism, which they feel has ignored the roots of their oppression, they see communitarianism as even more threatening to their claim for recognition.

What then is the basis for social unity in modern democracies? According to Mill (1962, pp. 122–3), 'the only shape in which the feeling is likely to exist hereafter' is an attachment to 'principles of individual freedom and political and social equality'. Likewise, Rawls says that social unity is grounded in a public acceptance of society as a system of fair co-operation among free and equal persons. In other words, as I noted at the beginning, liberals treat community as derivative of freedom and equality, rather than an independent principle. We can now see that this reduction in the status of community as a political ideal does not reflect indifference to its value, but rather a realistic assessment of modern realities. Any 'thicker' conception of community, liberals argue, is inconsistent with two basic aspects of modern life: the demand for individual autonomy, and the existence of social pluralism. As Rawls (1987, p. 10) puts it, the 'fact of pluralism' means that 'the hope of political community must be abandoned, if by such a community we mean a political society united in affirming a general and comprehensive' conception of the good.

Community and nationalism

Yet there is something wrong with this liberal picture. For one thing, it does not explain why the world is divided into almost 200 separate countries. If principles of freedom and equality are the basis of political legitimacy, why don't all democratic nations become amalgamated into one unified country? In the real world, the opposite is occurring. Everywhere we look, multinational states are disintegrating. Many colonies of multinational empires (e.g. in Africa), and provinces in multinational federations (e.g. Croatia or Quebec), are seeking independence. They do not want to be free and equal citizens within a larger state, they want to be free and equal citizens of their own state. They want the right to be self-governing or the right of national self-determination.

This right of each people to self-determination is accepted in principle under international law. On the other hand, this right is in practice denied to many internal minorities (e.g. the Kurds). A common, if somewhat unstable, response to the presence of national minorities is some form of limited self-government within a larger federation. But which communities have the right to which forms of self-government? This issue is one of the great difficulties facing the emerging democracies in Eastern Europe, the Middle East and the Third World, and continues to afflict some Western democracies (e.g. Canada, Spain). Yet, with few exceptions, one looks in vain to contemporary liberal or communitarian authors for a discussion of this principle of community (Barry, 1983; Miller, 1988).

This is a major gap in the current literature on community. Both communitarians and liberals operate, implicitly or explicitly, with the assumption that all states are 'nation-states' – that everyone in each country shares the same nationality, and so speaks the same language, and can join in a meaningful debate about culture. They debate what role the state should play in promoting 'its culture' and enriching 'its language', but they never ask whose culture and which language. As a result, they never broach the question of the right of self-government.

The real question of community facing many countries today is not the choice of neutrality vs the common good, or autonomy vs constitutive ends. These are questions about how a given political community will govern itself. The more fundamental question, however, is how we draw the boundaries of the political community in the first place. Which communities should have which forms or degrees of self-government? Contrary to contemporary liberal orthodoxy, we cannot answer this question on the basis of principles of equality and liberty, since these are shared across national boundaries. Nor, contrary to the communitarian orthodoxy, can we answer it by appealing to particular conceptions of the good life, since these are not shared within national boundaries. What we need is an entirely different principle of community. Identifying this principle will be one of the challenges facing theorists of community in the 1990s.

See also I ANALYTICAL PHILOSOPHY; 3 HISTORY; 4 SOCIOLOGY; 9 CONSERVATISM; I I LIBERALISM; I 2 MARXISM; I 3 SOCIALISM; I 4 AUTONOMY; I 9 DEMOCRACY; 2 I DISCOURSE; 2 2 DISTRIBUTIVE JUSTICE; 2 7 INTERNATIONAL AFFAIRS; 3 2 REPUBLICANISM; 3 3 RIGHTS; 3 4 SECESSION AND NATIONALISM; 3 5 SOCIO-BIOLOGY; 3 7 TOLERATION AND FUNDAMENTALISM; 3 9 TRUST; 4 I WELFARE

References

Barry, B.: 'Self-government revisited', *The Nature of Political Theory*, ed. D. Miller and L. Siedentop (Oxford: Clarendon Press, 1983), pp. 121–54.

Bellah, R., Madsen, R., Sullivan, W. M., Swidler, A. and Tipton, S. M.: *Habits of the Heart: Individualism and Commitment in American Life* (Berkeley: University of California Press, 1985).

Crowley, B.: *The Self, the Individual and the Community: Liberalism in the Political Thought of F. A. Hayek and Sidney and Beatrice Webb* (Oxford: Oxford University Press, 1987).

Dworkin, R. M.: *A Matter of Principle* (Cambridge, Mass.: Harvard University Press, 1985).

Gutmann, A.: 'Communitarian critics of liberalism', *Philosophy and Public Affairs*, 14 (1985), 308–22.

Habermas, J.: *Communication and the Evolution of Society*, trans. T. McCarthy (Boston: Beacon Press, 1979).

Hirsch, H.: 'The threnody of liberalism: constitutional liberty and the renewal of community', *Political Theory*, 14 (1986), 423–49.

King, D. S. and Waldron, J.: 'Citizenship, social citizenship and the defence of welfare provision', *British Journal of Political Science*, 18 (1988), 415–44.

MacIntyre, A.: *After Virtue: A Study in Moral Theory* (London: Duckworth, 1981).

Mill, J. S.: *Mill on Bentham and Coleridge*, ed. F. Leavis (London: Chatto & Windus, 1962).

Miller, D.: 'The ethical significance of nationality', *Ethics*, 98 (1988), 647–62.

Okin, S. M.: *Justice, Gender and the Family* (New York: Basic Books, 1989).

Pettit, P.: 'The freedom of the city: a republican ideal', *The Good Polity*, ed. A. Hamlin and P. Pettit (Oxford: Blackwell, 1989), pp. 141–68.

Rawls, J.: *A Theory of Justice* (Cambridge, Mass.: Harvard University Press, 1971).

————: 'Social unity and primary goods', *Utilitarianism and Beyond*, ed. A. Sen and B. Williams (Cambridge: Cambridge University Press, 1982), pp. 159–85.

————: 'The idea of an overlapping consensus', *Oxford Journal of Legal Studies*, 7 (1987), 1–25.

Sandel, M.: *Liberalism and the Limits of Justice* (Cambridge: Cambridge University Press, 1982).

Taylor, C.: *Philosophy and the Human Sciences* (Cambridge: Cambridge University Press, 1985).

————: 'Alternative futures: legitimacy, identity and alienation in late twentieth century Canada', *Constitutionalism, Citizenship and Society in Canada*, ed. A. Cairns and C. Williams (Toronto: University of Toronto Press, 1986), pp. 183–229.

Walzer, M.: *Spheres of Justice: A Defence of Pluralism and Equality* (Oxford: Blackwell, 1983).

Young, I. M.: *Justice and the Politics of Difference* (Princeton, NJ: Princeton University Press, 1990).

Further reading

Buchanan, A.: 'Assessing the communitarian critique of liberalism', *Ethics*, 99 (1989), 852–82.

Dworkin, R. M.: 'Liberal community', *California Law Review*, 77 (1989), 479–504.

Friedman, M.: 'Feminism and modern friendship: dislocating the community', *Ethics*, 99 (1989), 275–90.

Galston, W.: 'Community, democracy, philosophy: the political thought of Michael Walzer', *Political Theory*, 17 (1989), 119–30.

Greschner, D.: 'Feminist concerns with the new communitarians', *Law and the Community*, ed. L. Green and A. Hutchinson (Toronto: Carswell, 1989), pp. 119–50.

Kamenka, E., ed.: *Community as a Social Ideal* (London: Edward Arnold, 1982).

Kymlicka, W.: *Liberalism, Community, and Culture* (Oxford: Oxford University Press, 1989).

MacIntyre, A.: *Whose Justice? Which Rationality?* (Notre Dame: University of Notre Dame Press, 1988).

Miller, D.: 'In what sense must socialism be communitarian?', *Social Philosophy and Policy*, 6 (1989), 51–73.

Plant, R.: *Community and Ideology* (London: Routledge & Kegan Paul, 1974).

Taylor, C.: 'Cross-purposes: the liberal–communitarian debate', *Liberalism and the Moral Life*, ed. N. Rosenblum (Cambridge, Mass.: Harvard University Press, 1989), pp. 159–82.

Walzer, M.: 'The communitarian critique of liberalism', *Political Theory*, 18 (1990), 6–23.

16

Contract and consent

JEAN HAMPTON

Since the ancient Greeks, philosophers have often mounted arguments for political or moral conclusions by invoking the idea of a 'social contract', either between the people and the ruler, or among the people themselves, or both. The contractarian form of argument became popular in the seventeenth century, and its popularity continues to this day. Advocates of this approach tell us to resolve answers to moral and political issues by asking what a group of rational persons could all agree to, or alternatively, what such people would be unreasonable to reject.

However, both proponents and opponents of this style of argument have failed to appreciate just how many argumentative uses of the contract idea have appeared over the centuries. Although early uses of the argument were intended to justify and explain the state, later uses of the argument – particularly since the seventies – have aimed to justify certain moral conceptions, especially conceptions of justice. Moreover, even though theorists who call themselves 'contractarians' have all supposedly begun from the same reflective starting point, namely, what rational people could 'agree to', the many differences and disagreements among them show that although they are supposedly in the same philosophical camp, in fact they are united not by a common philosophical theory but by a common *image*. Philosophers hate to admit it, but sometimes they work from pictures rather than ideas. In an attempt to get a handle on both the nature of a justified state and the legitimate moral claims each of us can make on our own behalf against others, the contract imagery has struck many as enormously promising. But how that image has been translated into argument has varied considerably, and philosophers have disagreed about what political or moral issue that image can most profitably illuminate.

This article will attempt to explain the promise behind the image, and clarify the different forms of argument in which that image has been used. First, I will discuss the nature and meaning of the contract device as it has been used to justify states, governments and political societies. Later I will discuss the nature and meaning of the contract device as it has been used to define and defend moral conceptions, and particularly, conceptions of justice. And finally I will suggest ways in which the argument has influenced the development of political societies during the last four centuries. As I do so, I will explore the extent to which this style of argument can be defended against attacks levelled against it by critics over the years.

Contracting to create the state

Traditionally, the idea of a social contract has been used in arguments that attempt to

379

explain and defend the state, while addressing the nature of political obligation and the kind of responsibility that rulers have to their subjects. Philosophers such as Plato, Hobbes, Locke, Rousseau and Kant have argued that human beings would find life in a pre-political 'state of nature' (a state which some of them, e.g. Hobbes, have also argued is pre-societal) so difficult that they would agree – either with one another or with a prospective ruler – to the creation of political institutions that they believe would improve their lot. But how are we to understand the terms of a social contract establishing a state? When the people agree to obey the ruler, do they surrender their own power to him, as the philosopher Thomas Hobbes ([1651] 1990) tried to argue? Or do they merely lend him that power, reserving the right to take it from him if and when they see fit, as John Locke ([1690] 1991) maintained? These questions were first debated by medieval political theorists troubled by a very contractarian passage in Justinian's *Digest* known as the *lex regia*: 'What pleases the prince has the force of law, because by the *lex regia*, which was made concerning his authority, the people confers to him and upon him all its own authority and power' (Morrall, 1971, p. 46). If, when the people 'confer' the power on their prince, they are merely loaning him their own power, rebellion against him could be condoned if he has violated the conditions attached to that loan. But if the people's grant of power is interpreted as a surrender (or alienation) of their own power, there are no such conditions, and the people could never be justified in taking back that power via revolution. Over the centuries, the Lockean answer, which I have called the 'agency' contractarian theory, has struck people as more plausible and defensible than the Hobbesian answer, which I have called the 'alienation' contractarian theory (Hampton, 1986, ch. 5).

Note that if we were to accept the agency contractarian theory, we would be implicitly claiming that the individual members of a state are conceptually prior to the states themselves, in so far as the latter are the creations of the former. Karl Marx and subsequent socialist and communitarian thinkers have argued against conceptualizing an individual's relationship to her political and social community in this way. We would also appear to be claiming that political cohesion in a society is the product of an *actual* agreement between and among individuals and their rulers, which means treating these social contracts as agreements that really took place in any political society we regard as justifiable. On this view, we have contracted for certain things with the ruler, so that the terms of the contract are what bind us to him. Moreover, if certain constraints are built into the contract, these constraints also oblige him to rule in a certain way. So on this reading of the social contract argument, it works by pointing out to us how our explicit consent binds us to political regimes, whose justification is largely a matter of our having consented to them.

But as David Hume points out, virtually none of us remembers making such a contract, or giving such consent!

... were you to ask the far greatest part of the nation, whether they had ever consented to the authority of their rulers, or promised to obey them, they would be inclined to think very strangely of you, and would certainly reply, that the affair depended not on their consent but that they were born to such obedience. (Hume, [1739–40] 1978, III, II, viii, p. 548)

And if we have never made such a contract, and hence have never given our explicit consent to a regime, all talk of a social contract seems to be completely irrelevant to an understanding of political obligation and the justification of the state's rule over us.

Some contractarians through the centuries have confidently responded to Hume by insisting that the contract talk is entirely hypothetical: on this view, the social contract talk is not meant as an historical account of the origin of a justified regime, but rather as a (mere) way of thinking about when, and under what conditions, a regime is authoritative over those whom it rules. However, critics of contractarianism have not been persuaded by this response. For what value do make-believe agreements have as explanations of actual political obligations? It seems that speculating about how various regimes *could have been* the product of the consent of certain people, idealized in a certain way, tells us little about why actual regimes, whose creation had nothing to do with the citizenry's consent, exercise legitimate political control over those subject to them. As Ronald Dworkin puts it, 'A hypothetical contract is not simply a pale form of an actual contract; it is no contract at all' (Dworkin, 1976, pp. 17–18).

Other social contract theorists have tried to defend their argument, not by treating the contract as hypothetical, but by trying to find an attenuated form of a contract implicit in all political societies. For example, some theorists admit that there is almost never an explicit act of agreement in a community, but none the less maintain that such an agreement is implicitly made when members of the society engage in certain acts through which they give their 'tacit' consent to the ruling regime. It has been controversial which actions constitute the giving of tacit consent: philosophers such as Plato and John Locke have argued that the acceptance of benefits is sufficient to give such consent, but others (e.g. Robert Nozick) have argued that it is wrong to feel obliged to those who foist upon us benefits for which we have not asked. (See Plato, *Crito*, 50e–51c (1956, pp. 61–2); Locke, [1690] 1991, pp. 347–9, sections 119–22; Gauthier, 1979, p. 12; Rawls, 1971, p. 118; Hart, 1961, pp. 85ff; Nozick, 1974, pp. 90–5.) It is also unclear how much of an obligation a person can be under if he gives only tacit consent to a regime. For example, Locke recognizes a distinction between the political obligations of those who have explicitly consented to belong to a society, and those who have only tacitly consented to it. He argues that tacit consent, by which Locke means 'submitting to the Laws of any Country, living quietly, and enjoying Privileges and Protection under them', is not sufficient to make someone a full member of a political society:

Nothing can make any Man so, but his actually entering into it by positive Engagement, and express Promise and Compact. This is that, which I think, concerning the beginning of Political Societies, and that *Consent which makes any one a Member* of any Commonwealth. (Locke, [1690] 1991, p. 349, section 122; *my emphasis*)

But Locke has no argument for his contention that this is all tacit consent can secure. Moreover, if hardly anyone has ever given their explicit consent to a regime anyway, and there are controversies about when, if ever, someone has tacitly consented to a regime as well as what they have tacitly consented to, the nature of the political obligation of a full citizen of a state remains obscure, and the justification of the state's rule over us has not been adequately explained or defended.

However, I believe that it is possible to offer an interpretation of how the social contract idea works in these arguments, such that the state, and its rule over us, is both justified and explained. This interpretation recognizes that these arguments have both a descriptive and a hypothetical component to them.

Descriptive and prescriptive forms of the contract argument

I will argue that social contract theorists have intended simultaneously to describe the nature of political societies, and to prescribe a new and more defensible form for such societies.

The contractarians' descriptive project will strike present-day theorists as obvious and unremarkable, yet in its day it was both controversial and highly important. People such as Hobbes and Locke were certainly well aware that the subjects of their state had not explicitly consented to any ruler. None the less, I believe their invocation of a social contract among the people as the source of the state is, in part, an attempt to make one modest factual statement, namely, that authoritative political societies are human creations. This thesis was highly radical in the seventeenth century, because it essentially insists that, as a matter of *fact*, the authority of the state is not something that can be derived from some sort of natural or innate authority possessed by some set of supposedly superior persons over others, nor something that is derived solely from the word of God. Instead, this thesis insists that the authority of the state is the creation of the people who constitute it (albeit perhaps also a human creation that God endorses). The creation of the state is the creation of rules, or authoritative norms, which define the legal system and establish the obligations of those who would serve in it. Only officials who are empowered by this set of norms, are correctly known as 'legal authorities'. Although no contractarian has argued that all authorities are human creations in this sense (Locke maintained that parental authority was natural, and even Hobbes accepted that God's authority was natural and not a human creation), the thrust of their argument is that the authority of a *legal* system is a human invention – and yet one to which we none the less believe we owe great allegiance.

How do the people interact so as to create and sustain a political and legal system? The contractarian's term of 'social contract' is misleading in so far as it suggests that people either tacitly or explicitly exchange promises with one another to create or support certain governmental structures. We do no such thing. But I have suggested elsewhere that an analysis of the details of the contractarians' own arguments suggests that they see government structures as *conventionally* generated (Hampton, 1990; see also Kavka, 1986). Certain institutions, practices and rules become conventionally entrenched (in a variety of ways) in a social system, and in so far as the people continue to support them, these conventions continue to prevail, and thus comprise the political and legal system in the country. Hobbes suggests this analysis when he insists that each of us should appreciate the way in which adherence to the dictates of government is to our advantage, as long as we are in a situation where others are also willing to follow these dictates (Hobbes, [1651] 1990, chs 14 and 15). And David Hume explicitly presents certain political institutions such as the property system as conventionally generated and supported because such institutions are perceived to be mutually advantageous (Hume, [1739–40] 1978, III, II, viii, p. 548).

So a 'conventional' reading of the nature of the 'social agreement' which is supposed to be the foundation of a legal system yields a descriptive account of the nature of the state which is neither implausible nor indefensible. Indeed, such a reading even provides us with a plausible interpretation of the nature of the 'tacit consent' given by citizens to their government: such consent is indicated by activities that, taken together, are supportive of the conventions comprising the political and legal systems of the state. A person bestows such consent when she believes it is in her interest to support these conventions; and she withdraws this consent by failing to support, or else actively undermining, those conventions.

Note that this conception of consent is merely *descriptive*; I have not argued – nor would I wish to suggest – that any contractarian has maintained that when a government receives such consent, it is thereby justified as a legitimate and morally successful regime. All I have said thus far is that social contract arguments for the state can be interpreted so as to provide plausible descriptions of political societies as conventionally-generated human creations – far more plausible, indeed, than rival divine rights arguments or natural subjugation theories.

Contract and consent

Given the weak conception of consent in social contract arguments functioning as descriptive accounts of political societies, how can such arguments have prescriptive force?

The contractarian is, as I have said, committed to the idea that the state is a human-made institution. Contractarians explain the *existence* of morality in society by appealing to the convention-creating activities of human beings. However, they also argue that the *justification* of the state in any human society depends upon how well its (conventionally defined) structure serves individuals, needs and desires. By considering 'what we *could* agree to' if we had the chance to reappraise and redo the co-operative conventions in our society, we are able to determine the extent to which our present conventions are mutually acceptable and so rational for us to accept and act on. Thus, contractarians can be understood to be invoking both actual agreements (or rather, conventions) and hypothetical agreements (which involve considering what conventions would be 'mutually agreeable') at different points in their theory; the former are what they believe our political life in fact consists in; the latter are what they believe our political life *should* consist in – and thus what our state should model. So what we 'could agree to' has prescriptive force for the contractarians not because make-believe promises in hypothetical worlds have any binding force upon us, but because this sort of agreement is a device that (merely) reveals the way in which (what is represented as) the agreed-upon outcome is rational for all of us.

Hence the contractarians' argument is that our tacit consent binds us to a *legitimate* and morally acceptable state only if the conventions which comprise it are the sort of conventions that we could agree to, were we able to impartially and fairly reappraise and recreate those conventions.

383

But exactly how should we reflect upon what we 'could' have agreed to? Contractarians have answered that question in a variety of ways, but they have basically been inspired by two fundamentally different perspectives on how to use the contract image to reveal moral political structures. It is to these two perspectives that I now turn.

Morality and the contract argument

Social contract arguments purport to have prescriptive force when they maintain that we *ought* to do that which human beings – appropriately rational – 'could agree to'. As I have already indicated, this kind of prescriptive use of the argument is generally made by contractarians aiming not merely to describe but also to prescribe the best, or most just, form of political society. But some theorists have suggested that this argument can be used, more generally, to prescribe the moral rules upon which individuals should decide their conduct with respect to one another. There have been a number of attempts to categorize prescriptive social contract arguments. (See for example, Hamlin, 1989; Pettit, 1990. Brian Barry's (1989) categorization is also relevant, although not explicitly about contractarian theories.) However, here I shall isolate two kinds of prescriptive argument which the contract image has spawned (based on Hampton, 1992a), the first having its roots in Hobbes and the second having its roots in Kant.

Hobbesians (a category that includes not only Hobbes but modern theorists such as David Gauthier (1986) and James Buchanan (1975)) start by insisting that what is valuable is what a person desires or prefers, not what he ought to desire or prefer (for no such prescriptively powerful object exists); and rational action is action which achieves or maximizes the satisfaction of desires or preferences. They then go on to insist that moral action is rational for a person to perform if and only if such action advances the satisfaction of his desires or preferences. Finally, they argue that because moral action leads to peaceful and harmonious living conducive to the satisfaction of almost everyone's desires or preferences, moral actions are rational for almost everyone and thus 'mutually agreeable'. But in order to insure that no co-operative person becomes the prey of immoral aggressors, Hobbesians believe that moral actions must be the conventional norms in a community, so that each person can expect that if she behaves co-operatively, others will do so too. These conventions comprise the institution of morality in a society.

So the Hobbesian moral theory almost exactly parallels the structure of social contract arguments with respect to the state. It is committed to the idea that morality is a human-made institution, which is justified only to the extent that it effectively furthers human interests. Hobbesians explain the *existence* of both moral and political institutions in society by appealing to the convention-creating activities of human beings. And they argue that the *justification* of both sorts of institution in a human society depends upon how well these conventions serve individuals' desires or preferences. By considering 'what we *could* agree to' (if we had the chance to reappraise and re-do the co-operative conventions in our society, we are able to determine the extent to which our present conventions are 'mutually agreeable' and so rational for us to accept and act on. Thus, Hobbesians invoke both actual agreements (or rather, conventions) and hypothetical agreements (which involve considering what conventions would be 'mutually agreeable') at different points in their theory; the former are what they believe our moral and political life consist in; the latter are what they believe our moral life and political life *should* consist in – i.e. what our actual moral life should model.

Hence, the notion of the contract does not do justificational work *by itself* in the Hobbesian moral theory: this term is only used metaphorically. What we 'could agree to' has prescriptive force for the Hobbesians, not because make-believe promises in hypothetical worlds have any binding force but because this sort of agreement is a device that (merely) reveals the way in which the agreed-upon outcome is rational for all of us. Hence, thinking about 'what we could all agree to' allows us to construct a deduction of practical reason to determine what policies are mutually advantageous.

Many theorists are attracted to this theory because of its sensible metaphysics: just as it does not base political society on the unseen hand of omnipotent deities or some kind of mysterious natural superiority supposedly possessed by some but not all, it also refuses to base morality on strange, non-natural properties or objects, and it refuses to credit human beings with what Mackie calls 'magical' powers capable of discerning the moral truth 'out there' (Mackie, 1977, ch. 1). Instead, it sees morality as a human invention, which we commend to the extent that it is mutually advantageous for those who would use it.

But such a metaphysical foundation is attractive only if what is built upon it counts as a genuine morality, with genuine prescriptive force. And there are good reasons for complaining that Hobbesian contractarianism yields considerably less than the real thing. When *Leviathan* was originally published, some readers sympathetic to Aristotelian ideas were shocked by the idea that the nature of our ties to others was interest-based, and contended that Hobbes' theory went too far in trying to represent us as radically separate from others. Their worries are also the worries of many twentieth-century critics including feminists, who insist that any adequate moral theory must take into account our emotion-based connections with others, and the fact that we are socially defined beings (e.g. see Pateman, 1988; and even Gauthier, 1977, pp. 13–64).

But I would argue that what disqualifies it at a more fundamental level as an acceptable moral theory is its failure to incorporate the idea that individuals have what I will call 'intrinsic value'. It has not been sufficiently appreciated, I believe, that by answering the 'Why be moral?' question by invoking self-interest in the way that Hobbesians do, one makes not only co-operative action but also the human beings with whom one will co-operate merely of *instrumental value*. That is, if you ask me why I should treat you morally, and I respond by saying that it is in my interest to do so, I am telling you that my regard for you is something that is merely instrumentally valuable to me; I do not give you that regard because there is something about you yourself that merits it, regardless of the usefulness of that regard to me. Now Hobbes is unembarrassed by the fact that on his view, 'The *Value*, or WORTH of a man, is as of all other things, his Price; that is to say, so much as would be given for the use of his Power: and therefore is not absolute; but a thing dependent on the need and judgement of another' (Hobbes, [1651] 1990, p. 63 (chapter 10, paragraph 16)). But this way of viewing people is not something that we, or even some Hobbesians, can take with equanimity. In the final two chapters of his book, *Morals by Agreement*, David Gauthier openly worries about the fact that the reason why we value moral imperatives on this Hobbesian view is that they are instrumentally valuable to us in our pursuit of what we value. But note *why* they are instrumentally valuable: in virtue of our physical and intellectual weaknesses that make it impossible for us to be self-sufficient we need the co-operation of others to prosper. If there were some way that we could remedy our weaknesses and become self-sufficient, e.g. by becoming a superman or superwoman, or by using a Ring of Gyges to make ourselves invisible and so steal from the stores of others with impunity, then it seems we would no longer value or respect moral constraints because they would no longer be useful to us – unless we happened to like the idea. But in this case sentiment, rather than reason, would motivate kind treatment. And without such sentiment, it would be rational for us to take other people as 'prey'.

Even in a world in which we are not self-sufficient, the Hobbesian moral theory gives us no reason outside of contingent emotional sentiment to respect those with whom we have no need of co-operating, or those whom we are strong enough to dominate, such as old people, or the handicapped, or retarded children whom we do not want to rear, or people from other societies with whom we have no interest in trading. And I would argue that this shows that Hobbesian moral contractarianism fails in a very serious way to capture the nature of morality. *Regardless* of whether or not one can engage in beneficial co-operative interactions with another, our moral intuitions push us to assent to the idea that one owes that person respectful treatment simply in virtue of the fact that he or she is a *person*. It seems to be a feature of our moral life that we regard a human being, whether or not she is instrumentally valuable, as always intrinsically valuable. Indeed, note that to the extent the results of a Hobbesian theory are acceptable, this is because one's concern to co-operate with someone whom one cannot dominate leads one to behave in ways that mimic the respect one ought to show her simply in virtue of her worth as a human being.

Kantian contractarian theory

The second kind of prescriptive contractarian theory is derived from the theorizing of Immanuel Kant. In his later writings Kant proposed that the 'idea' of the 'Original Contract' could be used to determine which social policies would be just (e.g. see Kant, 1970). When Kant asks 'What could people agree to?' he is not trying to justify actions or policies by invoking, in any literal sense, the consent of the people. Only the consent of real people can be legitimating, and Kant talks about hypothetical agreements made by hypothetical people. But he does believe these make-believe agreements have moral force for us because the process by which these people reach agreement is morally revealing. By imagining what fully rational people would agree to, each of whom is concerned that he should get his due, and none of whom is affected by prejudice or the distorting powers of passion, Kant believes we can determine political policies that are logically consistent, prudentially sound and properly respectful of each person as an 'end in himself'.

Kant's contracting process has been further developed by subsequent philosophers.

For example, in his classic *A Theory of Justice*, John Rawls concentrates on defining the hypothetical people who are supposed to make this agreement so that their reasoning will not be tarnished by immorality, injustice or prejudice, thus insuring the outcome of their joint deliberations will be morally sound. By subjecting his contractors to a 'veil of ignorance', which removes all specific knowledge of their culturally deter-mined beliefs and political views, along with knowledge of their personal characteris-tics (e.g. race or gender), Rawls hopes to purge people of any immoral prejudices and any tainted perspectives inculcated by an unjust social system, before he asks them to reach agreement on a suitable conception of justice. In this way he hopes to ensure that they will reason about and reach agreement on a conception of justice in a fully moral way (although it is problematic how 'contractarian' Rawls' method is if it incorporates the veil of ignorance, in so far as this veil makes every person in the original position exactly the same (see Hampton, 1980). Some contractarians who disagree with Rawls' conclusions none the less approve of the Kantian use of the social contract as a method of revealing that which is morally acceptable, and use the method to justify different conclusions by defining the contracting parties differently. Others, such as T. M. Scanlon, argue that the method should be used not merely to define the best conception of political justice, but also morality as a whole.

The Kantians' social contract is therefore a *device* used in their theorizing to *reveal* what is just, or what is moral. So like the Hobbesians, their contract talk in their pre-scriptive theories is really just a way of reasoning that allows us to work out concep-tual answers to moral problems. But whereas the Hobbesians' use of contract language expresses the fact that, on their view, morality is a human invention which (if it is well invented) ought to be mutually advantageous, the Kantians' use of the contract language is meant to to show that moral principles and conceptions are pro-vable theorems derived from a morally revealing and authoritative reasoning process or 'moral proof procedure' that makes use of the social contract idea.

Kantian contractarian arguments are frequently more appealing to people than the Hobbesian variety. However, they are highly vulnerable to attack for a different rea-son. People such as Rawls who espouse them argue that when we reflect upon what (suitably defined) people could 'agree to', we are reflecting from an 'Archimedean point', surveying the terrain of morality from an acceptably impartial and morally revealing vantage point. But no Kantian contractarian, including Rawls, has convin-cingly demonstrated that his contractarian theory provides such an Archimedean point, because no contractarian has specified his theory sufficiently such that we can be sure it relies only upon 'morally pure' starting points and not the sort of biased (e.g. sexist or racist) ideas or intuitions that an unjust society would encourage in its citizens.

There are two ways in which these morally suspect intuitions might be intruding into a Kantian's theory. First, they may be covertly motivating the particular con-straints, assumptions or features that are supposed to apply in the contract situa-tion. Feminists are implicitly criticizing Rawls' theory on this basis when they charge that his assumption that parties in the original position are self-interested is motivated by intuitions about what counts as a plausibly 'weak' psychology that actually derive from a discredited Hobbesian view of human nature. According to these critics, this component of Rawls' thinking drives out of his theory both our emotion-based attachments to others' well-being and our other-regarding, duty-based commitments to them, demonstrating the extent to which even this high-minded Kantian appears heavily in the grip of outmoded and distorting individualistic intuitions. Second, suspect intuitions may be illicitly operating *within* the Kantian's reasoning procedure, thereby playing a direct role in the justification of his political conclusions. For example, many critics have charged that Rawls fails to motivate the inclusion of the maximin rule of choice under uncertainty effectively in his argument; but because that rule is essentially what picks out Rawls' own conception of justice as that which is favoured by his contractors, removing the rule from the argument would mean that the selection of that conception could only be based on appeals to vague intuitions about what seems 'best', intuitions which might not withstand sustained moral scrutiny if they were better understood. (For a review of the problems with Rawls' maximin rule, see Harsanyi, 1975, 594–606; and Hubin, 1980, 363–72.)

Although Scanlon does not presume that his contract approach defines an 'Archimedean point', his approach is even more susceptible to the charge that it is covertly relying on ill-defined or ill-defended intuitions (Scanlon, 1982, pp. 103–28). Scanlon, argues that (what he calls) the 'contractualist' account of the nature of moral wrongdoing goes as follows: 'An act is wrong if its performance under the circumstances would be disallowed by any system of rules for the general regulation of behavior which no one could reasonably reject as a basis for informed, unforced general agreement' (ibid., p. 110). This definition is intended as 'a characterization of the kind of property which moral wrongness is' (ibid.). Now in this statement of contractualism, the reader is inevitably drawn to the word 'reasonably', yet Scanlon never explicitly cashes out the term. He claims, for example, that a policy A which would pass an average utilitarian test but which would cause some to fare badly is, *prima facie*, a policy that the 'losers' would be reasonable to reject (ibid., pp. 123-4). However, he goes on to say that ultimately the reasonableness of the losers' objection to A is not established simply by the fact that they are worse off under A than they would be under some alternative policy E in which no one's situation is as bad. Instead, says Scanlon, the complaint against A by the A-losers must be weighed against the complaints made by those who would do worse under E than under A. 'The question to be asked is, is it unreasonable for someone to refuse to put up with the Loser's situation under A in order that someone else should be able to enjoy the benefits which he would have to give up under E?' (Scanlon, 1982, p. 123). But on what grounds, or using what criteria, can we provide the right answer to this question? Scanlon gives us no directions for adjudicating the complaints of the two groups in this situation, and one begins to worry that his appeal to 'reasonableness' as a way of determining the solution is an appeal to inchoate intuitions.

So we do not know what is really doing the work in Scanlon's test, and this generates at least three problems for his theory. First, we cannot be sure that everyone who uses Scanlon's test will rely on the same conception of 'reasonableness' to arrive at the same answer. Second, unless his conception of reasonableness is fully (and acceptably) explicated, we have good reason to worry about what might seem 'reasonable' to people raised in unjust (e.g. sexist or racist) societies. And third, unless this conception is fully explicated, those of us loyal to contractarianism as a distinctive form of moral argument have reason to worry that there is so much reliance on intuition in the operation of Scanlon's test, that his approach ultimately reduces to some other ethical theory. For example, if these intuitions are understood as foundational, his theory would seem to amount to nothing more than a version of ethical intuitionism, or if they are understood to be generated by some other moral theory, such as utilitarianism, the contract method would appear to be merely a way of marshalling ideas generated by that other theory. Thus a utilitarian might argue that 'reasonable rejection', should be understood as rejection on the grounds that what is being proposed is not utility-maximizing for the group. But Scanlon wants to be able to draw upon and generate anti-utilitarian ideas in his contractarian theory via argument rather than via appeal to intuition alone. And although Scanlon is prepared to allow that contractarian reasoning might endorse the utilitarian principle, he insists that it must do so in a 'contractarian way', i.e. a way that was not itself a form of utilitarian reasoning. Hence he needs to give us the structure of this uniquely contractarian way of reasoning. Since neither he nor, for that matter, any Kantian contractarian has given us any sense of what these ideas are, why they are appropriate to rely upon, or how they work together to form a non-intuitionistic moral reasoning procedure, we begin to wonder whether or not this or indeed any Kantian's appeal to 'what we could agree to' is just a way to fabricate a defence for moral or political conceptions that these Kantian theorists happen to like, but for which they cannot provide a valid argument resting on plausible and well-explicated premises.

Thus far, no fully satisfactory prescriptive form of contractarianism has been generated that is immune from any of the problems I have just detailed. However, many theorists – including this author – continue to be attracted to a contractarian way of thinking about morality because of what they take to be its appealing form of individualism. This type of argument assumes that moral and political policies must be justified with respect to, and answer the needs of, individuals rather than large-scale social groups, ethnic nations or other forms of community. Now, precisely for this reason, contractarian theories have been criticized by what are called 'communitarian' philosophers who argue that moral and political policies can and should be decided on the basis of what is best for a community. They are also attacked by utilitarian theorists whose criterion of morality is the maximization of the utility of the community, and not the mutual satisfaction of the needs or preferences of individuals. However, contractarians contend that both sorts of theory fail to take seriously the distinction between, and intrinsic importance of, persons as individuals, whereas contractarian theories make moral and political policies answerable to the legitimate interests and needs of each of us. Hence for this reason, contractarians insist that the individual has to be the starting point of all moral and political theorizing. How successful they will be in persuading sceptics about the advantages of their justificational strategy will depend in part on how successful they are in developing the prescriptive form of their theory so that it is more than just an intuitive appeal to ill-defined and possibly suspect intuitions.

Social contract arguments and democracy

Despite controversies surrounding their interpretation, social contract arguments have been important to the development of modern democratic states. In this section I want to suggest (based on arguments in Hampton, 1992b) how the idea of the government as the creation of the people, which they can and should judge and which they have the right to overthrow if they find it wanting, has contributed to the development of democratic forms of polity in the eighteenth and nineteenth centuries.

In the old days, those theorists, such as Hobbes or Locke, who maintained, *contra* the divine rights theorists, that it was the people, and not God, who established and legitimized political power, also assumed that, as a matter of fact (albeit perhaps not of right), what the people did when they did not like a regime was to stage a revolution, preferably bloodless, in which rulers were overthrown, and if necessary (as in Britain in 1688), the political rules changed. But what if one could design a political system in which 'revolution' was an organized and regular part of the political process? This is the idea which inspired the founders of modern democratic societies (and particularly the founders of the American polity); it is at the heart of the structure of contemporary democratic states.

Defenders of modern democracy self-consciously recognize one of the main descriptive points the contractarians aimed to articulate through their arguments, namely that *political societies are created and maintained by the people that are ruled in them.* And this creation-and-maintenance process involves the creation and maintenance of a set of authoritative norms that define the legal system and the obligations of the officials who work within it. However, *modern democracies operate so that the people have continual control over the process of creating and maintaining the regime.* In modern democracies, the people have created not only the 'legal game', but also another game that defines how to play the 'creation-and-maintainance' game. Let me explain.

Consider the standard coup: Ruler X has power because there is a rule, accepted by the people, that he is authorized to do so. But when some or all of the people no longer accept that rule, they engage in various power-retracting activities, and if enough people (or enough of the people who have most control over the present rulership convention) engage in these activities, Ruler X is gone. (So, for example, in the case of the 1991 Soviet coup, when too many people in powerful positions refused to obey orders – e.g. Russian and Baltic soldiers in the army, political officers in various Soviet states, and various people involved in the economic life of the nation – the coup collapsed.) How such activities can come to be possible, and even co-ordinated despite the opposition of rulers is a fascinating story – communication among opponents of a ruler is critical (and thus some pundits argued that one of the reasons the Soviet regime eventually collapsed was the existence of the FAX machine). In another place I have described this kind of revolutionary activity at length and labelled it 'convention-dissolving', in virtue of the fact that it unravels the convention defining who is to hold power – which is just to say that it destroys the society's rule of recognition (Hampton, 1990).

The experience of England in the seventeenth century was that political convention-dissolving could be difficult, lengthy and even deadly dangerous for those involved in it. This lesson was not lost on the American revolutionaries. But the men who formed the American Constitution essentially asked themselves this: what if the people could get control of convention-dissolving activity – establishing rules that would actually allow it to occur on a periodic basis if the people so decided, and which would regulate it so that the dissolution would be as peaceful and orderly as possible? If there could be a 'system of revolution' that was attached to the legal system, both rules and rulers could be changed quickly with minimal cost and disruption to the people. And the possibility of replacing them peacefully and painlessly would increase the people's control over the shape of their political game and thus allow them to better supervise their leaders (who would know that their being fired was not a particularly costly action for the people, and who would thus be under pressure, if they wanted to retain their jobs, to perform them as the people required). By and large, this 'controlled convention-dissolving activity' involves what is commonly referred to as 'voting', as I shall now explain.

Consider how constitutions for democratic societies tend to work. They not only set up a certain kind of government, with offices that involve distinctive kinds of power and jurisdiction, but also rules for creating and dissolving conventions about who holds these offices. Through these rules various government officials are empowered; but through these rules they can also be peacefully and effectively deprived of power. *Voting is therefore a form of controlled revolutionary activity.* Socialist radicals of the early twentieth century were right when they referred to votes as 'paper stones' (see Przeworski and Sprague, 1986). Elected 'representatives' do not represent the citizenry in any literal sense – as if the citizenry were doing the ruling 'through them'. This is nonsense. They rule and we do not. But it is because those of us in modern democratic societies can easily deprive them of power – depose them, if you will – at certain regular intervals that they have (at least theoretically) the incentive to rule in a way responsive to our interests. Just like any other employee, if they want to keep their jobs they must work to the satisfaction of their employer. They therefore 'represent' us in the way that any agent represents those who authorize her. In modern democratic regimes, representation is actually a form of agency, so that it is a form of political society that explicitly recognizes the relationship between ruler and people which the Lockean contractarian theory set out. This is not unlike Hannah Pitkin's view of the nature of representation in modern democratic societies (see Pitkin, 1967). However Pitkin tends to use the metaphor of trust, and that metaphor is problematic. A trustor does not own that which is used on his behalf by the trustee. Moreover, unlike in an agent/client relationship, the trustee/trustor relationship is one in which the trustor does not have sufficient standing to fire the trustee, and is generally regarded as inferior to or less competent than the trustee, such that he must be subject to the trustee's care. (So children are assigned trustees; and in nineteenth-century England married women could only hold property in trust, in virtue of what was taken to be their inferior reasoning abilities.) The assumptions of the rights and powers of citizens in modern democratic societies are at odds with the presumption of the trustor's incompetence. Those who would rule us are, in a democracy, obliged to respect the citizens who choose them, and are in a continual competition with one another, as they attempt to gather votes which will, each hopes, be sufficient, according to the rules, to hire her as ruler.

So a modern democracy is a government that is by the people, for the people and of the people – except that this last preposition is misleading. Unlike in ancient Athens, most of us are not actually in the government – only a few of us are. What makes this a government of the people is the fact that the overarching rule defining the government not only includes rules that define the operation and structure of the political system, but also rules that grant the people the power to create and dissolve portions of that political system if they choose to do so with relatively little cost. Creating these latter rules is a novel way of extending the activity involved in creating and maintaining government. Such rules allow the people to play their role as definers of their political society in a more effective and controlled way. Those who fashioned modern democracies came to see that not only such activities as criminal punishment and tort litigation but also the very process of adding to or changing the political game itself could be made part of a larger conception of the 'political game'. Or to put it another way, they discovered that revolutionary activity could be an everyday part of the operation of a political society.

Conclusion

It remains to be seen what further effects contractarian arguments will have on moral and political institutions. But the increasing experimentation in the world today with non-traditional but partially consent-based forms of polity, such as the European Community, the remarkable (albeit sometimes stormy) resilience of multi-cultural consent-based regimes, and the astonishing success of contractarian-based modern democratic polities, suggests that the contractarians' insistence that justified and stable regimes are those in which people are consensually bound to one another and to their government for as long as the political society is operating in a morally successful way, will continue to be an extremely promising and important contribution to the political and moral life of people into the next century.

See also 1 ANALYTICAL PHILOSOPHY; 5 ECONOMICS; 8 ANARCHISM; 11 LIBERALISM; 14 AUTONOMY; 17 CONSTITUTIONALISM AND THE RULE OF LAW; 19 DEMOCRACY; 22 DISTRIBUTIVE JUSTICE; 28 LEGITIMACY; 29 LIBERTY; 31 PROPERTY; 33 RIGHTS; 34 SECESSION AND NATIONALISM; 39 TRUST

References

Barry, B.: *Treatise on Social Justice*. Vol. 1: *Theories of Justice* (Berkeley: University of California Press, 1989).

Buchanan, J.: *The Limits of Liberty: Between Anarchy and Leviathan* (Chicago: University of Chicago Press, 1975).

Dworkin, R.: 'The original position', in *Reading Rawls*, ed. N. Daniels (New York: Basic Books, 1976).

Gauthier, D.: 'Social contract as ideology', *Philosophy and Public Affairs*, 6 (1977), 130–64.

———: 'David Hume: contractarian', *Philosophical Review*, 88 (1979), 3–38.

———: *Morals by Agreement* (Oxford: Oxford University Press, 1986).

Hamlin, A.: 'Liberty, contract and the state', in *The Good Polity*, ed. A. Hamlin and P. Pettit (Oxford: Blackwell, 1989).

Hampton, J.: 'Contracts and choices: does Rawls have a social contract theory?', *Journal of Philosophy*, 77 (1980), 315–38.

————: *Hobbes and the Social Contract Tradition* (Cambridge: Cambridge University Press, 1986).

————: 'The contractarian explanation of the state', in *Midwest Studies in Philosophy: The Philosophy of the Human Sciences*, ed. T. Ueling (Minneapolis: University of Minnesota Press, 1990).

————: 'Feminist contractarianism', in *A Mind of Her Own*, ed. L. Antony and C. Witt (Boulder, Colo.: Westview Press, 1992a).

————: 'Democracy and the rule of law', in *Nomos*, ed. I. Shapiro and R. Barnett (New York: New York University Press, 1992b).

Harsanyi, J.: 'Can the maximin principle serve as a basis for morality? A critique of John Rawls' *A Theory of Justice*', *American Political Science Review*, 69 (1975), 594–606.

Hart, H. L. A.: *The Concept of Law* (Oxford: Clarendon Press, 1961).

Hobbes, T.: *Leviathan* (1651), ed. Richard Tuck (Cambridge: Cambridge University Press, 1990).

Hubin, D. C.: 'Minimizing maximin', *Philosophical Studies*, 37 (1979), 363–72.

Hume, D.: *A Treatise of Human Nature* (1739–40), ed. L. A. Selby-Bigge and revised P. H. Nidditch (Oxford: Clarendon Press, 1978).

————: 'The original contract?', *Hume's Ethical Writings*, ed. A. MacIntyre (London: Collier, 1965), pp. 255–73.

Kant, I.: 'On the common saying, "This may be true in theory, but it does not apply in practice"', H. Reiss, ed., *Kant's Political Writings* (Cambridge: Cambridge University Press, 1970), pp. 61–92.

Kavka, G.: *Hobbesian Moral and Political Theory* (Princeton, NJ: Princeton University Press, 1986).

Kukathas, C. and Pettit, P.: *A Theory of Justice and its Critics* (Stanford, Calif.: Stanford University Press, 1990).

Locke, J.: *Two Treatises of Government* (1690); ed. Peter Laslett (Cambridge: Cambridge University Press, 1991).

Mackie, J. L.: *Ethics: Inventing Right and Wrong* (New York: Penguin Books, 1977).

Morrall, J. B.: *Political Thought in Medieval Times* (London: Hutchinson, 1971).

Nozick, R.: *Anarchy, State and Utopia* (New York: Basic Books, 1974).

Pateman, C.: *The Sexual Contract* (Stanford, Calif.: Stanford University Press, 1988).

Pitkin, H.: *The Concept of Representation* (Berkeley: University of California, 1967).

Plato: *Crito*, in *Euthyphro, Apology, Crito*, trans. F. Church (Indianapolis: Bobbs-Merrill, 1956).

Przeworski, A. and Sprague, J.: *Paper Stones: A History of Electoral Socialism* (Chicago: University of Chicago Press, 1986).

Rawls, J.: *A Theory of Justice* (Cambridge, Mass.: Harvard University Press, 1971).

Scanlon, T. M.: 'Contractualism and utilitarianism', in *Utilitarianism and Beyond*, ed. A. Sen and B. Williams (Cambridge: Cambridge University Press, 1982), pp. 103–28.

Further reading

Rousseau, J.-J.: *The Social Contract* and *A Discourse on Inequality* (1762), *The Social Contract and Discourses*, trans. G. D. H. Cole (New York: Dutton, 1950), pp. 1–141; 175–282.

Skinner, Q.: *The Foundations of Modern Political Thought* (Cambridge: Cambridge University Press, 1978).

17

Constitutionalism and the rule of law

C. L. TEN

Constitutionalism and the Rule of Law are related ideas about how the powers of government and of state officials are to be limited. The two ideas are sometimes equated. But constitutionalism usually refers to specific constitutional devices and procedures, such as the separation of powers between the legislature, the executive and the judiciary, the independence of the judiciary, due process or fair hearings for those charged with criminal offences, and respect for individual rights, which are partly constitutive of a liberal democratic system of government. The Rule of Law, on the other hand, embodies certain standards which define the characteristic virtues of a legal system as such. The requirements of constitutionalism are derived from a political morality which seeks to promote individual rights and freedom, and not directly from values that are supposed to be implicit in the very idea of law itself. Of course, even though the principles of constitutionalism have different foundations, they may still help to maintain the Rule of Law.

There is, however, a tendency to expand the notion of the Rule of Law to embrace all the features of a desirable system of government, especially one in which the liberties and rights of individuals are protected from interference by officials. But such a broad conception of the Rule of Law provides no clear legal foundations for the values it embodies. It is more interesting to begin with a narrower conception of the Rule of Law that incorporates values which are not derivable from a comprehensive political theory about the nature of good government, but that is based on values which are inherent in the very notion of law itself. Not all the characteristics of a good system of government can be derived from whatever values are implicit in the idea of a legal system as such. We shall then see how this narrow conception of the Rule of Law can be developed to embrace the requirements of constitutionalism.

Some recent accounts of the Rule of Law may be viewed from this perspective as attempts to develop a conception that rests on specifically legal values. Lon Fuller's exposition of 'the internal morality of law' is perhaps the most original and ambitious attempt (Fuller, 1971).

Fuller begins with a relatively uncontroversial characterization of a legal system as 'a system for subjecting human conduct to the governance of rules' (ibid., p. 46). The enterprise of creating and maintaining such a system can fail in various ways if certain principles are not complied with. These principles constitute the internal morality of law, which define different kinds of legal excellence towards which a system of legal rules should strive. If any of these principles is completely violated, then we do not have a legal system at all, not even a bad legal system. There are eight such principles.

The first is that the law should be general. If there is to be a legal system then there must be rules that lay down general standards of conduct. This requirement contrasts law with another form of social ordering which Fuller calls 'managerial direction' (ibid., p. 207). Managers may choose, as a matter of expediency, to direct the conduct of subordinates by means of standing orders instead of giving step-by-step instructions. But subordinates have no basis for complaint if, on a particular occasion, managers direct them to deviate from those general orders. Unlike law, which is a system of guiding conduct by means of general rules, managerial direction does not require the adoption of general orders, although it may find such general orders convenient in appropriate contexts.

The second demand of the internal morality is that laws should be promulgated or made known to those to whom they apply. This is obvious if laws are to guide their conduct.

Third, laws should be prospective and not retroactive. It is not possible for people's conduct to be guided today by rules which do not as yet exist and will only be enacted tomorrow. However, Fuller points out that there are certain contexts in which a retroactive statute does not violate the internal morality of law. He gives the example of a statute which specifies that a valid marriage should have a stamp on the marriage certificate to be affixed by the person performing the ceremony. But the printing machine breaks down, and the statute is not sufficiently publicized. Marriages take place between persons ignorant of the statute and before ignorant officials. A second statute retrospectively validates these marriages and thereby remedies defects caused by the earlier failure of the law to comply with the internal morality. Fuller also discusses some of the complexities of the notion of retrospective legislation. The requirement that laws should be prospective is obviously breached by a statute that makes criminal an act which was not an offence at the time of its commission. It is also violated by Hitler, for example, when he killed those he regarded as a threat and then passed a retroactive statute to make his killings lawful. But Fuller believes that the internal morality is not breached by a tax law that imposes a tax this year on financial gains made in a previous year when there was no such tax. The requirement that the tax be paid applies prospectively. It is unlike a retrospective statute enacted today requiring that certain taxes should have been paid yesterday.

The fourth principle of the internal morality is that laws should be clear. Unclear laws cannot be understood and therefore will fail to guide conduct. However, Fuller believes that rules which are formulated in terms of standards of what is 'fair' or 'reasonable' are not necessarily vague because we can sometimes rely on shared standards and practices in the relevant areas to define the legal requirements.

Fifth, there should be no contradictions in the laws. By 'contradiction' Fuller does not mean strict logical contradiction. A law is contradictory in his sense if it gives no intelligible guide to conduct. He gives the hypothetical example of a statute with one provision requiring car owners to install new licence plates on New Year's Day, and another provision making it a crime to work on that day.

The sixth principle of the internal morality is that laws should not demand the impossible. Fuller discusses the application of this principle to strict liability rules in which legal liability arises without fault or intent. The internal morality does not condemn strict liability in torts, but it condemns strict criminal liability. For example, a law making people strictly liable for all the harm caused in blasting operations may be construed as imposing a tax or surcharge on such activities. Blasting operators can take account of the special tax in their economic calculations of the costs of carrying out their operations. On the other hand, a rule that makes persons criminally liable, even when they acted with due care and with innocent intent, is 'the most serious infringement of the principle that the laws should not command the impossible' (Fuller, 1971, p. 77). Strict criminal liability makes the task of the prosecutor much easier, and it has sometimes been defended on the ground that in practice it is only selectively enforced, with prosecutions confined to the real villains. But Fuller believes that such selective enforcement undermines respect for law as a system of publicly enacted rules which are applied without the need to make private settlements with law enforcement agencies.

The seventh principle of the internal morality is that laws should not be changed too frequently. Laws which are changed too often are difficult to comply with and thereby fail to direct people's conduct.

Finally, the internal morality requires a congruence between official action and the law. This congruence can be undermined in many ways: 'mistaken interpretation, inaccessibility of the law, lack of insight into what is required to maintain the integrity of the legal system, bribery, prejudice, indifference, stupidity, and the drive toward personal power' (Fuller, 1971, p. 80). Similarly, there are many devices for maintaining it, including the requirements of due process. But the most interesting part of Fuller's discussion is his attempt to develop a theory of statutory interpretation that will best meet the demand of congruence. He rejects the 'atomistic view of intention', according to which a statute directed against 'dangerous weapons' is aimed at particular objects such as pistols and daggers, and will therefore exclude those weapons which had not been thought of by those who drafted the statute. A court that applies the statute to weapons not yet invented at the time the statute was enacted would, in this view, be legislating (ibid., p. 84). Fuller develops his alternative theory of interpretation with an analogy of a son who has to carry out his father's wish to complete an invention of a household device for which the father had left a pencil sketch before he died. To be faithful to the father's intention, the son does not have to determine the intention that the father had actually formed about how to complete the invention. Instead, the son has to decide what purpose the invention was supposed to serve, and how it would remedy defects in existing household devices. The problem would not be essentially different if the incomplete design had been left by someone unknown to the son. For it is important that the son should look at the incomplete design itself to determine the purpose of the invention and its underlying principle. Similarly, in interpreting a statute, judges have to see what its purpose is, and what problem it is supposed to solve.

In an earlier paper, Fuller gives a vivid illustration of his purposive interpretation of the law (Fuller, 1958, p. 64). Suppose a statute makes it a misdemeanour to sleep in any railway station. The statute is directed at tramps who deprive weary passengers of seats. How should a judge decide two cases of alleged violations of the statute? In the first case, a weary passenger was sitting in an upright position at 3 a.m. waiting for a delayed train. However, the arresting officer heard him snoring. In the second case, a man had settled himself down on the railway bench with a blanket and pillow, but was arrested before he actually fell asleep. Fuller suggests that the judge, who decides to fine the second person and release the first, would not have misinterpreted the law. Similarly, a rule, excluding vehicles from a park, is aimed at noisy automobiles which destroy the quiet and risk causing injuries to strollers. It cannot therefore be interpreted as ruling out the mounting on a pedestal in the park of a truck used in World War II (ibid., p. 663). (Presumably the same truck, if parked in a busy street, would violate a rule prohibiting the parking of vehicles when the purpose of that rule is to prevent obstruction to the free flow of traffic.)

Fuller compares the internal morality of law with 'the natural laws of carpentry' which the carpenter has to follow whether his aim is to build a hideout for thieves or an orphanage (Fuller, 1971, pp. 96, 155). The internal morality is to be distinguished from the external morality, or the substantive aims or values that particular legal rules seek to promote. Fuller develops a conception of the Rule of Law, not by appealing to moral values drawn from the external morality, which will of course vary with different legal rules and systems, but by spelling out the values that underlie the concept of law itself.

This general approach has been followed by others. For example, Rawls treats the legal order as a system of public rules addressed to rational persons, and conceives of the Rule of Law as the regular and impartial administration of these public rules (Rawls, 1971, pp. 235–43). The precepts associated with the Rule of Law are 'those that would be followed by any system of rules which perfectly embodied the idea of a legal system' (ibid., p. 236). These precepts include the idea that 'ought implies can', thus ruling out laws that require or forbid actions which people cannot reasonably be expected to do or to avoid. The notion of regulating conduct by rules also implies the precept that 'similar cases be treated similarly', and thereby imposes limitations on the discretion of officials applying the rules. Rules for organizing social behaviour provide a basis for legitimate expectations. Laws should therefore be promulgated, be clear and non-retrospective. There should be no offence without a law. Rawls also believes that the precepts of natural justice form part of the requirements of the Rule of Law because they are needed to ensure that decisions as to whether the law has been broken are properly made, and that the correct penalties are imposed.

This approach to the Rule of Law is instructive. It provides some grounds for evaluating laws and legal systems without challenging the substantive values of their external moralities. But these grounds are limited. Rawls acknowledges this when he points out that although the precepts of the Rule of Law provide 'a more secure basis for liberty and a more effective means for organizing cooperative schemes', they 'guarantee only the impartial and regular administration of rules, whatever these are', and are 'compatible with injustice' (Rawls, 1971, p. 263). However, Fuller thinks that the internal morality of law is richer, and provides a basis for establishing a necessary connection between law and substantive morality. The claim is made in the context of his rejection of legal positivism's separation of law and morality, and has been subjected to searching criticisms by Hart (1965) and Lyons (1970–1). I shall confine my discussion to the related issue of the nature of the values promoted by Fuller's conception of the Rule of Law.

He believes that although the internal morality is neutral over a wide range of substantive moral aims, it rules out the pursuit of some evil aims. For example, laws promoting racial discrimination will run foul of the requirement of clarity because there is no way of making clear racial categories. But what this shows is that substantive aims involving vague notions cannot be pursued without infringements of the internal morality. These substantive aims may be morally good or bad (Hart, 1965, p. 1287). So far there is no reason to believe that the internal morality will necessarily favour good moral aims.

Of course, as Fuller points out, if rules are publicized, then they are open to public criticism. It is easier for a tyrant to pursue wicked ends if he can, like Hitler, pass 'secret laws'. Fuller also believes that the requirement that there be *general*, public rules will force lawmakers to spell out the principles on which they act and thereby make them more responsible for their conduct (Fuller, 1971, p. 159). However, the extent to which these considerations will undermine evil aims depends on the presence of other factors. The known existence of a bad law need not result in significant attempts to repeal it if we live in a society in which freedom of expression is not allowed or encouraged, or in which citizens have been indoctrinated to accept authority uncritically. And there is nothing in Fuller's conception of the Rule of Law which guarantees the existence of social and educational institutions conducive to freedom of expression.

Fuller makes much of the claim that underlying the internal morality of law is a view of persons as responsible, self-determining agents. But this conception of persons is supposed to be implicit in the idea of guiding conduct by means of general rules, and is not derived from a system of rules with a specific content. It must therefore be a conception that is equally compatible with all systems of general rules, including unjust systems. Even those who seek to dominate over others, and make them subservient to their settled wishes, will need to express their plans clearly and take account of the fact that people are capable of following rules. Indeed, the moral thinness of this conception of persons is shown by the fact that it is presupposed not just by moral practices of various kinds, but also by any rule-governed enterprise, including the rules of etiquette, games, social clubs and the rules constitutive of ceremonies and rituals.

Fuller rejects the notion of law as 'a one-way projection of authority' in favour of what he calls 'an interactional' view of law (Fuller, 1971, p. 221). He invests this interactional view with substantive moral content that cannot be derived from the basic idea of regulating the conduct of responsible, self-determining agents by means of public, general rules. He sees law-makers as making a commitment that amounts to a kind of promise. 'By enacting laws government says to the citizen, "These are the rules we wish you to follow. If you will obey them, you have our promise that they are the rules we will apply to your conduct"' (ibid., p. 217). He goes on to argue that obedience to rules is pointless if it is known that those who make the rules will not pay any attention to them. Conversely, the rule-makers will lack any incentive to conform to the Rule of Law if they know that their subjects lack the disposition and capacity to follow the rules. He argues that 'the functioning of a legal system depends upon a co-operative effort – an effective and responsible interaction between lawgiver and subject' (ibid., p. 219).

The argument may have some force if we assume a certain institutional background. For example, in democratic elections when a political party, seeking to form the government, puts up a legislative programme, it may be said to have made a promise to the electorate. But the mere existence of a rule-governed enterprise is not sufficient to establish the making of a promise. Laws exist not just in democracies, but also in systems of government which do not rest on the consent of the governed. If there is a commitment on the part of the law-maker as such, then this is no different from that of the gangster who gives a specific instruction, 'Your money or your life'. We may wish to say that the gangster has made a promise not to take your life if you co-operate and hand over your money, and that he will only have an incentive to keep his promise if he knows that you are a responsible agent capable of, and well-disposed to, following his instruction. But the gangster's conduct is still morally unjustified. Similarly, the existence of law as a system of public rules, with all its implicit commitments, is consistent with these rules being directed toward great evil.

Fuller's discussion of strict liability laws also shows his propensity to clothe the internal morality of law with unwarranted moral content. The requirement that laws should not demand the impossible is supposed to rule out strict criminal liability, but not strict civil liability. However, as Hart has pointed out, strict liability in criminal law can guide conduct by steering people away from those activities to which it applies if they cannot be sure of their ability to comply with the law (Hart, 1965, p. 285). Thus if strict liability attaches to the production of adulterated food, then those fearful of being convicted can avoid working in the relevant food industry. Of course, such an escape is only possible if strict criminal liability does not apply to all the activities of our normal social life. The objection to strict criminal liability rests on the unfairness of *punishing* those who are not at fault and have taken all reasonable precautions to conform to the law (Ten, 1987, pp. 105–10). The unfairness here is a thicker moral notion than Fuller's conception of persons as responsible, self-determining agents.

Raz has argued that the independence of the judiciary is essential for the preservation of the Rule of Law because we need to be sure that judges apply the law free from extraneous pressures (Raz, 1979, p. 217). And Rawls has suggested that, 'while there are variations in these procedures, the rule of law requires some form of due process: that is, a process reasonably designed to ascertain the truth, in ways consistent with the other ends of the legal system, as to whether a violation has taken place and under what circumstances' (Rawls, 1971, p. 239). If they are right, then some of the principles of constitutionalism can be derived from the narrow conception of the Rule of Law. But the prospect of deriving all of them seems remote.

Even some of the requirements of natural justice and due process seem to go beyond what is clearly implicit in that conception. The procedures for determining whether a violation of the criminal law has taken place may be weighted in favour of avoiding the conviction of the innocent as against maximizing the conviction of the guilty. The right balance to be struck in ascertaining the truth in a criminal trial depends on moral values that are external to the requirement of applying, as best we can, a system of general rules. Similarly, the separation of powers between the legislature, the executive, and the judiciary, is not to be justified simply in terms of the narrow conception of the Rule of Law, but also in terms of what will be most effective in checking the powers of government to make bad laws. It is the content of legal rules, and not just the proper application of rules, which is of concern. We need constitutional devices to minimize the danger that rules severely restrictive of liberty will be enacted. The demands of constitutionalism go beyond the requirement that legal rules have certain formal characteristics.

The best-known attempt to develop a conception of the Rule of Law which relies on the formal features of legal rules to defend individual liberty is Hayek's. For him the Rule of Law is a meta-legal or political ideal of what the law ought to be (Hayek, 1960, p. 206). Hayek's conception, although similar to Fuller's in some respects, differs to the extent that Fuller believes the standards embodied in the Rule of Law are not distinct from those which identify the legal system. While a legal system can fail to some degree to conform to the Rule of Law, any major departures from it will, for Fuller, result in the system ceasing to be a legal system.

Hayek conceives of the Rule of Law as the regulation by general, abstract rules equally applicable to all. Law, in this sense, is to be contrasted with a specific command that directs one to perform a particular action. A specific command subjects one to the will of another person, and thereby deprives one of freedom. General rules, on the other hand, are like the laws of nature which provide fixed features of the environment that one can use to plan one's activities. 'There is little difference between the knowledge that if one builds a bonfire on the floor of his living room his house will burn down, and the knowledge that if he sets his neighbour's house on fire he will find himself in jail' (Hayek, 1960, p. 153). In obeying general rules one is using the general knowledge of the obstacles in one's environment to lead a life in accordance with one's own purposes rather than at the direction of another person. Even if some of the obstacles placed by general rules are not avoidable, Hayek believes that the obstacles, being predictable and not being aimed at the particular individuals affected, lose much of the 'evil nature of coercion' (ibid., p. 143).

Now a defence of freedom in terms of conformity to general rules, without reference to the content of these rules, cannot be adequate. General rules may distinguish between classes of persons or of activities in terms of general properties, and if groups are discriminated against on the basis of morally irrelevant properties, then their liberties would be unjustly curtailed. As Hart has argued, justice in the administration of a rule involves applying a general rule 'without prejudice, interest, or caprice', but this is quite compatible with the rule itself being unjust. Thus an unjust law prohibiting coloured persons from entering parks may be justly administered 'in that only persons genuinely guilty of breaking the law were punished under it and then only after a fair trial' (Hart, 1961, p. 157).

Hayek, however, believes that distinctions made in the law are acceptable 'if they are equally recognized as justified by those inside and those outside the group' (Hayek, 1960, p. 154). He also argues that although it is conceivable that even general and abstract rules equally applicable to all will severely restrict freedom, this is in fact very unlikely because conduct prohibited or required by such rules apply without exception to all, including the lawmakers themselves. He immediately qualifies this claim by acknowledging that a fanatical religious group might impose restrictions which are burdensome to others, though not to its own members. However, he believes that most of the religious restrictions imposed on all, such as the Scottish Sabbath, are 'comparatively innocuous, even if irksome' (ibid., p. 155). He is obviously wrong: the prohibitions of certain sexual activities on religious grounds are severe restrictions of freedom. So also are those restrictions on interracial marriage or sexual relations which apply equally to all. The fact that these obstacles are predictable, and even avoidable, does not rule them out as serious infringements of freedom because they undermine the vital interests of those affected. Of course, these restrictions run foul of Hayek's test that the distinctions made in the law should be equally acceptable to both sides. But this test would condemn not just religious and racial discriminations, but also many other laws that are justified on other grounds. For example, if we define the inside and outside groups in the case of the law against burglary as the group of actual and potential burglars as opposed to the group of victims and potential victims, or the rest of the population, then the law will not be equally acceptable to both groups. Even if the test is one of general acceptance by all those affected, this will rule out laws guaranteeing religious and racial toleration if they are opposed by a majority group of religious and racial fanatics for *failing* to make certain discriminations.

It has been suggested that Hayek's conception of the Rule of Law embodies a strong Kantian principle of universalizability that demands the impartial consideration of the interests of all (Gray, 1984, pp. 61–71). But now we have gone beyond the requirement of impartially *applying* a system of general and abstract rules. If we base the Rule of Law simply on such a system of rules, then the virtues of the Rule of Law are more limited than Fuller and Hayek tried to make out. Perhaps we have to agree with Raz that its value is essentially negative (Raz, 1979, p. 224). According to him the Rule of Law is designed to minimize the danger of arbitrary power created by the law itself. It is also designed to prevent infringements of the liberty and dignity of persons caused by laws which are unstable, unclear, or retrospective.

The maintenance of the Rule of Law is not enough to ensure substantive justice, but neither should it be seen as an unnecessary barrier to the promotion of substantive justice. Indeed, in a liberal and democratic political culture, the Rule of Law provides important safeguards against the enthusiasm of those seeking substantive justice. It gives some protection to those who are 'least popular and most despised' (Tribe, 1989, p. 727).

Dworkin has recently expounded a conception of the Rule of Law that rests on a broader notion of the law than that relied on by what he calls the 'rule-book' conception. According to the rule-book conception, the standards to be applied in the legal system must be in accordance with 'rules explicitly set out in a public rule book available to all' (Dworkin, 1985, p. 11). This conception treats the ideal of substantive justice as separate from that of the Rule of Law. Dworkin's alternative is a 'rights' conception of the Rule of Law which assumes that citizens have moral and political rights which should be enforced by the courts. In hard cases, in which no explicit rule applies, the rights conception requires that judges make political judgements, not in the party political sense, but in the sense that they give 'a coherent general interpretation of the legal and political culture of the community' (ibid., p. 2) The political judgements involve moral and political arguments. The approach is therefore different to that of the rule-book conception, which recommends various types of historical enquiries in hard cases to discover the intention or will of the law-makers who have been authorized by the community to decide what rules should apply.

In an easy case where an explicit rule clearly applies, the rights and the rule-book conceptions will support the same decision. However, the rights conception recognizes that the rights of citizens are not exhausted in explicitly enacted or formulated rules to be found in the rule-book. Judges are not free to ignore what is in the rule-book, and in hard cases a coherent interpretation of the law must be compatible with what is in the rule-book. For example, judges who themselves believe in the radical Christian principle that the poor are entitled to the surplus from those who are wealthier, should not apply it to tort or contract cases by refusing damages against a poor defendant. The principle is inconsistent with the explicit rules. But different sets of moral principle may each be compatible with the rules in the rule-book, and judges would have to interpret the law on the basis of what they believe to be the correct moral principles. They will construct the moral and political theory which best explains and justifies the explicit rules of the legal system. Dworkin (1986) has developed and refined his views into a sophisticated and much discussed theory of the law and of adjudication. Without going into the details of the theory, we can note that if Dworkin's rights conception of the Rule of Law is accepted, then the virtues of the Rule of Law would not be entirely negative. A significant element of substantive justice is promoted by the Rule of Law in communities whose moral and political culture takes individual rights seriously.

See also 1 ANALYTICAL PHILOSOPHY; 7 LEGAL STUDIES; 9 CONSERVATISM; 11 LIBERALISM; 14 AUTONOMY; 16 CONTRACT AND CONSENT; 28 LEGITIMACY; 29 LIBERTY; 31 PROPERTY; 33 RIGHTS; 38 TOTALITARIANISM

References

Dworkin, R.: *A Matter of Principle* (Cambridge, Mass.: Harvard University Press, 1985).
————: *Law's Empire* (London: Fontana Press, 1986).
Fuller, L. L.: 'Positivism and fidelity to law – a reply to Professor Hart', *Harvard Law Review*, 71 (1958), 630–72.
————: *The Morality of Law*, revised edn (New Haven, Conn.: Yale University Press, 1971).
Gray, J.: *Hayek on Liberty* (Oxford: Blackwell, 1984).
Hart, H. L. A.: *The Concept of Law* (Oxford: Clarendon Press, 1961).
————: 'Lon L. Fuller: *The Morality of Law*', *Harvard Law Review*, 78 (1965), 1281–96. Reprinted in H. L. A. Hart, *Essays in Jurisprudence* (Oxford: Clarendon Press, 1983).
Hayek, F. A.: *The Constitution of Liberty* (London: Routledge & Kegan Paul, 1960).
Lyons, D.: 'The internal morality of law', *Proceedings of the Aristotelian Society*, 70 (1970–1), 105–19.
Rawls, J.: *A Theory of Justice* (Cambridge, Mass.: Harvard University Press, 1971).

Raz, J.: *The Authority of Law* (Oxford: Clarendon Press, 1979).

Ten, C. L.: *Crime, Guilt, and Punishment* (Oxford: Clarendon Press, 1987).

Tribe, L. H.: 'Revisiting the rule of law', *New York University Law Review*, 64 (1989), 726–31.

Further reading

Dworkin, R.: *Taking Rights Seriously* (London: Duckworth, 1984).

Finnis, J.: *Natural Law and Natural Rights* (Oxford: Clarendon Press, 1980).

Hutchinson, A. C. and Monahan, P., eds: *The Rule of Law: Ideal or Ideology* (Toronto: Carswell, 1987).

Kukathas, C.: *Hayek and Modern Liberalism* (Oxford: Clarendon Press, 1989).

Letwin, S. R.: 'Justice, law and liberty', *Lives, Liberties and the Public Good*, ed. G. Feaver and F. Rosen (London: Macmillan, 1987), pp. 229–49.

Lucas, J. R.: *The Principles of Politics* (Oxford: Clarendon Press, 1966).

Lyons, D.: *Ethics and the Rule of Law* (Cambridge: Cambridge University Press, 1984).

MacCormick, D. N.: 'Spontaneous order and the Rule of Law: some problems', *Ratio Juris*, 2 (1989), 41–54.

Pennock, J. R. and Chapman, J. W., eds: *Constitutionalism* (New York: New York University Press, 1979).

Raz, J.: 'The politics of the rule of law', *Ratio Juris*, 3 (1990), 331–9.

Reynolds, N. B.: 'Grounding the rule of law', *Ratio Juris*, 2 (1989), 1–16.

Waldron, J.: 'The rule of law in contemporary liberal theory', *Ratio Juris*, 2 (1989), 79–96.

————: *The Law* (London: Routledge, 1990).

18

Corporatism and syndicalism

BOB JESSOP

Corporatism and syndicalism have a certain family resemblance as political philosophies and political projects committed to functional representation, but they also differ in other, more fundamental respects. Viewed as forms of economic and political interest intermediation their crucial common feature is their explicit and self-conscious organization in terms of the function performed within the division of labour by those represented through such organizational forms. But such forms of functional representation can be organized in various ways and these in turn enable one to distinguish syndicalism from corporatism and differentiate the variants of each. Whether seen historically or comparatively, syndicalism is a less complex phenomenon than corporatism and is correspondingly easier to define. Essentially it comprises an economic and political movement of the working class which is avowedly both anti-capitalist and anti-statist; its ultimate goal is to abolish capitalism and the state in favour of a loose decentralized federation of worker-owned and worker-managed production units.

Corporatism is a much more heterogeneous phenomenon and thus less amenable to encapsulation in a sentence or two. None the less there would be a broad consensus that most corporatist projects accept the legitimacy (or, at least, the inevitability) of market forces and the state but also seek to limit or modify their activities and effects by linking them to some explicit form of functional representation. Since corporatism is more complex, it will provide the focus for this entry.

The core meaning of corporatism

Corporatism is a word with many meanings. However, although a resurgence of corporatist practices during the 1970s prompted definitions touching on many different fields, a broad consensus has emerged around a core meaning. This can be simply stated: corporatism comprises an ongoing, integrated system of representation, policy-formation and policy implementation, which is organized in terms of the function in the division of labour of those involved. The ideological justification, the political legitimation, the specific functional bases and precise organizational forms of representation, the various levels and sites on which corporatist structures are organized, the actual scope, purposes, and mode of policy-making, the particular forms of implementation, and the place (if any) of corporatism within the state system as a whole: all these features (and many others), however important they might be in practice, should be regarded as contingent. For they depend on the national economy and its place in the world market, the specific political discourses and practices into which corporatism gets articulated, and the changing balance of forces involved in corporatist activities. Such complexities explain why so much of the recent literature on corporatism has developed detailed typologies of corporatism (as opposed to typologies in which corporatism is only one among several types) and/or has referred to a few specific cases and then conceded that further generalization is unwise or impossible. Most analysts now seem to realize that simple dichotomies or crude typologies are unhelpful in grasping the richness of actual historical cases.

Just to illustrate some of the problems: (1) function could refer to income categories (capital, wage-labour, land ownership), fractions of capital, branches of the national economy, role within the division of mental and manual labour, or some combination of these; (2) policies could be determined by corporatist leaders and/or through consultation with members of functional corporations; (3) policy implementation could be direct (through corporations themselves) and/or delegated to other economic or political organs; (4) the state could be an active, passive or silent partner in establishing and operating corporatist arrangements; and (5) corporatism could be separate from or linked to other forms of political representation, such as clientelism, one or more political parties, or a pluralistic pressure group system. These issues have generated much debate in corporatist programmes and scientific studies. It is also worth distinguishing between corporatist policy regimes (institutionalized structures) and corporatist strategies (efforts to establish regularized patterns of corporatist institutions). For there is no necessary link between structures and strategies: corporatist structures could well be 'dignified' rather than 'efficient', corporatist strategies could be pursued on an *ad hoc* basis without established corporatist structures. There is a growing body of research addressed to just these issues.

A periodization of corporatism and corporatist tendencies

Whether as a total ideology or as a core element in a broader ideological ensemble, corporatism has been advocated by an amazing range of theorists, ideologues, and activists as well as for widely divergent motives, interests and reasons (Schmitter, [1974] 1979, p. 9). It has been variously associated with: romantic, organic theories of the state; pre-Marxist, proto-socialists; Social Christians; fascist authoritarianism; secular modernizing nationalism; radical bourgeois solidarism; mystical universalism; internationalist functionalism; reactionary, pseudo-Catholic integralism; communitarian socialism; technocratic, pro-capitalist reformism; anti-capitalist revolutionary syndicalism; and guild socialism (ibid., pp. 9–10). As corporatist ideologies vary so much and their realization is so limited, it would be more fruitful to explore actual existing corporatisms in various periods and conjunctures.

Different types of corporatist discourse and practice correspond to different stages in capitalist development and/or different forms of economic and political crisis. However, in general, there appear to have been three main phases in corporatism's evolution.

It first arose as a politico-ideological critique of liberal capitalism. It reflected oppositional movements among both feudal and traditional petty bourgeois classes (such as artisans and yeoman farmers), Catholic and/or other religious groups and some intellectual circles. They criticized the rampant individualism, social disorder and open class conflict which accompanied the transition to capitalism and its subsequent *laissez-faire* operation; and they called in turn for a restoration of social order through co-operation between professional and vocational associations. Inspired in part by medieval occupational guilds and estate representation and also oriented to a universalistic, harmonistic state and society, such an organic corporativism was both reactionary and utopian. It could not halt the rise of a liberal capitalism that was mediated through anarchic market forces nor of a mass democracy based on individual suffrage.

The second corporatist phase was not so much ideological as practical. The onset of this phase coincided with the rise of monopoly capitalism and growing competition among capitalist economies and it was closely linked with notions such as 'organized capitalism'. In this context the dominant corporatist projects were not so much opposed to capitalism as such but to the threats it had created of economic domination by foreign capital and political revolution by organized labour. Thus corporatist projects called for new forms of interest organization and/or societal regulation to defuse discontent as well as new institutional means and strategies to promote national economic competitiveness. This sort of corporatism was typically promoted by firms and business associations but, especially in periods of acute political crisis, prolonged war or immediate postwar reconstruction, it was often directly advanced by the state itself. In all such cases the extent of labour movement involvement alongside business and the state depended on its own economic and political orientation as well as the changing balance of economic and political forces.

These second-wave corporatist tendencies were reinforced during the crisis-ridden interwar period and took two main forms. Some corporatist structures and strategies were imposed from above by fascist or authoritarian regimes in response to acute economic, political and ideological crises. In other cases they emerged in the form of a societal corporatism promoted from below (often with state sponsorship) to help in economic or political crisis-management in liberal democratic regimes. These tendencies became so common between the wars that one political theorist predicted that the 'twentieth century will be the century of corporatism just as the nineteenth century was the century of liberalism' (Manoilesco, 1936). But it is important to put these tendencies into perspective and assess how far corporatist projects were realized in practice – especially in relation to the more authoritarian regimes of this period.

The third distinctive wave of corporatism emerged in the attempts at economic crisis-management in the 1960s and 1970s. It usually took a tripartite form (involving business, organized labour and the state) and was inserted into liberal democratic political systems. Where successful they have often helped to stabilize societies oriented to economic growth and mass consumption by supporting already existing macro-economic measures with incomes, labour market and industrial policies. In this context corporatism was not intended to replace the market economy or liberal parliamentary democracy. Instead, it was meant to supplement and reinforce them by legitimating new forms of state intervention which went beyond traditional methods of parliamentary and bureaucratic rule and by securing more effective representation for different producer interests than would be possible through a generalized pluralism or catch-all electoral parties. In many cases this third wave of corporatism has been partial and tendential, intermittent and *ad hoc*; nowhere does one find continuous and fully institutionalized corporatist bargaining across all sectors of the economy and state. It was the relative novelty of this form of corporatism and its apparent compatibility with the survival of liberal democratic capitalism that prompted the social scientific interest in 'neo-corporatism' in the 1970s.

The normative bases of corporatism

Corporatism today has no well-articulated social, political and moral philosophy. In part this is because corporatist philosophy was morally condemned through its links with fascism; in part it stems from the seemingly purely technical role of contemporary corporatist arrangements in promoting economic management and class compromise. But the two earlier incarnations of corporatism were associated with clearly expressed philosophical foundations and had quite explicit normative implications. They stressed the need for a hierarchically ordered moral community which would realize the will of God (in Catholic variants) or the national interest (in secular variants). Corporatist theorists opposed both the allegedly amoral liberalism of anarchic free market capitalism, and the egalitarian demands of a godless, unpatriotic socialism. To defeat liberal capitalism and egalitarian socialism alike, corporatists aimed to restore a solidaristic, organic society. This would involve at least three steps: the re-moralization of capitalist private property by tying it to social obligations as well as rights; the reintegration of an alienated and militant proletariat by associating the duty of labour with social rights and dignity; and the organizationally mediated linking of both capital and labour into the wider social community through functionally based corporations which both expressed their economic interdependence and provided a real and continuing basis for political representation. Corporatist organizations would have a key role in all three steps. They would provide moral communities for capital and labour and replace the fictional and sporadic ties between effectively powerless electors and largely self-serving parliamentary deputies. But these organizations were never intended to be the final arbiters of social progress. For, while individual functional corporations would certainly be self-regulating, their activities must still be guided by an overarching concept of Christian duty or a secular national leadership committed to the common good.

Corporatism as seen by social science

Interest among social scientists in corporatism as a novel phenomenon and potential analytical concept grew markedly in the 1970s. While the concept was first used in its modern, 'neo-corporatist' sense to describe patterns in certain Scandinavian societies in 1945, it was a substantial review article by Schmitter in 1974 that promoted the real paradigm shift and set a new research agenda. Other work was also written at this time but Schmitter's work remains the standard reference point. As interest grew, however, the concept acquired ever more connotations and became more unwieldy. Conversely, as scientific interest came to focus on modern liberal democracies, 'corporatism' also lost its pejorative association with fascist and authoritarian regimes. Indeed, almost all contemporary societies have, at some time or other, been adjudged corporatist – either *tout court* or in a qualified sense. Since no article could review all the literature on corporatism (for one recent book-length attempt, see Williamson, 1989), this entry focuses on the main tendencies and research interests.

Schmitter gave the following influential definition:

Corporatism can be defined as a system of interest representation in which the constituent units are organized into a limited number of singular, compulsory, noncompetitive, hierarchically ordered and functionally differentiated categories, recognized or licensed (if not created) by the state and granted a deliberate representational monopoly within their respective categories in exchange for observing certain controls on their selection of leaders and articulation of demands and supports. (Schmitter, [1974] 1979, p. 13)

He also contrasted two basic forms of corporatism according to whether it was imposed from above or emerged through pressures from below. Thus societal corporatism emerges from below as a form of economic crisis management and general economic and social bargaining. It is embedded in political systems with: relatively autonomous, multilayered territorial units; open, competitive electoral processes and party systems; ideologically varied, coalitionally-based governments; and is compatible with a plurality of social cleavages. In contrast, statist corporatism is imposed by the state. It occurs in centralized, bureaucratic systems, with purely plebiscitary or even non-existent elections, weak single-party systems, and inaccessible authorities with a limited recruitment base; and it often suppresses class, ethnic, linguistic and/ or regional differences. Schmitter also suggested that societal corporatism is post-liberal, is well suited to advanced capitalism, and is associated with democratic welfare states; whereas state corporatism is anti-liberal, is usually associated with delayed capitalist development, and forms part of an authoritarian, neo-mercantilist state (Schmitter, 1974).

This definition apart, societal corporatism has also been defined as: a special form of policy intermediation based on organized labour, business associations, and the state; a third species of political economy between capitalism and socialism; a feature of a distinctive type of state; a pattern of industrial relations; a partial structure or strategy linking different societal spheres; a form of trade union incorporation; a system of private interest government; and in other ways besides. There is also an extensive literature on statist or authoritarian forms of corporatism, notably in Spain, Portugal and Latin America (see Collier, 1980; Williamson, 1989).

After this conceptual proliferation, social scientific attention turned to the genesis, specificities and dynamics of different examples of societal or liberal corporatism. It soon became apparent that corporatism could exist on one or more levels of the economy (micro, meso and macro); could be limited to specific sectors or provide the basis for more general concertation; need not be confined to the economy in the narrow sense of the primary or secondary sectors but could also extend into the service sectors and/or welfare, health, education, scientific and other subsystems;

could be linked to local, regional and supranational as well as national states; could be firmly institutionalized or take the form of temporary strategies; and, in almost all its manifold forms, displayed chronic tendencies towards instability. The last of these features has led in turn to increasing concern with the conditions which favour more or less stability in corporatist arrangements. The conditions most often cited as favouring such stability include: strong, centralized industrial unions; strong, centralized employers' organizations, and a state which has the capacities to intervene in economic management but also depends on co-operation from its social partners.

The discussion of the political aspects of corporatism has also become more complex. Studies have shown that corporatism can compensate for parliamentary crisis or instability by reducing governmental overload and/or securing extra support; undermine the legitimacy of parliamentarism by providing alternative channels for interest intermediation and by-passing political parties; or function effectively only through close links to political parties, parliament, and the administration. One broad point of agreement is that political stability and legitimacy is hard to secure through corporatist arrangements alone and that these must be complemented by other political agencies and mechanisms. More generally it has become clear that, as a political form, corporatism has no clear *a priori* consequences for the balance of forces; it is best seen as a structurally and/or strategically selective form of political organization whose effects depend on organizational, strategic and conjunctural factors. There is no substantial evidence for the Marxist claim that corporatism is unambiguously favourable to capitalist interests. Indeed, there is much evidence that corporatism can provide a real basis for securing and consolidating working-class gains within capitalism.

It would also seem that strong corporatist structures helped to stabilize the postwar mode of economic growth (by moderating its tendencies towards stagflation) and to manage the initial reaction to its growing crisis in the 1970s. In this sense corporatism could also be said to favour the interests of capital. Where the preconditions for stable corporatism were absent, however, corporatist strategies failed to secure favourable tradeoffs between growth, jobs and price stability and generated severe conflicts in corporatist associations (especially trade unions). As national economies have become more open and the state's primary economic concerns have shifted from macroeconomic management to supply-side innovation and international competitiveness, however, the old neo-corporatist structures and strategies seem less viable. This explains why the death of corporatism has been demanded by the new right and proclaimed by observers too attached to the third-wave corporatist paradigm.

Syndicalism

As a form of functional representation, syndicalism could be characterized as 'corporatism without capital or the state'. For, in essence, it involves a decentralized system of workers' control based on decentralized, collective ownership of economic units and a loose political federation of self-managing economic organizations. In organizing for such direct and exclusive workers' control, revolutionary syndicalists rejected all forms of institutionalized political participation and any thought of allying with non-proletarian class forces. Instead, syndicalist activities were to be concentrated at the point of production and aimed at improving the position of workers and building class solidarity; such everyday struggles would eventually ensure the success of the ultimate syndicalist weapon – a spontaneous general strike. However, although it enjoyed a certain influence from the 1880s to the First World War, syndicalism was increasingly marginalized by socialism, communism and more orthodox trade unionism. Thereafter it survived both as a political theory and project mainly through anarcho-syndicalist and 'council communist' currents and left-wing think tanks calling for workers' control. Moreover, even during its heyday, its real impact was largely confined to countries such as France, Italy and Spain. These all had strong anarchist traditions, trade unions with a substantial artisan and/or migrant peasant base, and only limited experience of institutionalized collective bargaining. Since the Second World War syndicalism has seen a limited revival with small-scale experiments on the capitalist semi-periphery (such as the relatively successful small-scale experiments in the Mondragon region of Spain or the self-managing kibbutzim of Israel); and the much larger-scale Yugoslavian attempt in the socialist semi-periphery to move stepwise to workers' self-management as an alternative to both the centrally planned economy and capitalism. Even in the later stages of the Yugoslavian experiment, however, overall state guidance of the economy remained. As yet there is precious little evidence to support Schmitter's twenty-year-old prediction that the century of corporatism would be succeeded by that of syndicalism.

See also 4 SOCIOLOGY; 5 ECONOMICS; 6 POLITICAL SCIENCE; 8 ANARCHISM; 9 CONSERVATISM; 13 SOCIAL-ISM; 15 COMMUNITY; 19 DEMOCRACY; 22 DISTRIBUTIVE JUSTICE; 25 EQUALITY; 26 FEDERALISM; 30 POWER; 31 PROPERTY; 41 WELFARE

References

Collier, D., ed.: *The New Authoritarianism in Latin America* (Princeton, NJ: Princeton University Press, 1980).

Manoilesco, M.: *Le Siècle du corporatisme* (Paris: Felix Alcan, 1936).

Schmitter, P. C.: 'Still the century of corporatism?', *Review of Politics*, 36 (1974), 85–121. Reprinted in *Trends toward Corporatist Intermediation*, ed. P. C. Schmitter and G. Lehmbruch (London: Sage, 1979), pp. 7–52.

Williamson, P. J.: *Corporatism in Perspective* (London: Sage, 1989).

19

Democracy

AMY GUTMANN

Although the root meaning of democracy is simple – 'rule by the people' from the fifth-century BC Greek *demokratia* – and democracy is almost universally commended in contemporary politics, the ideal of democracy is complex and contested, as are its justifications and practical implications. Democracy is sometimes identified narrowly with majority rule (Hardin, 1990, p. 185), and other times broadly to encompass all that is humanly good (Macpherson, 1973), but neither view is adequate to an understanding of democracy as a social ideal. Majoritarian decision-making may be a presumptive means of democratic rule, but it cannot be a sufficient democratic standard. Other standards – concerning who rules, by what procedures, over what matters, within what limits and with what degree of deliberation – have from the beginning been implicated in the ideal of democracy as rule by the people, and continue to be entailed by the public aspirations of democratic and democratizing societies.

The contrastingly broad identification of democracy with the complete human good is similarly unhelpful in presuming away increasingly important problems that have long animated advocates of democracy and their critics, for example, whether the people should be permitted to rule on complicated matters even when they lack the knowledge of experts or whether the freedom of a few should be limited for the sake of authorizing the many to shape social policy. A democratic ideal, no matter how inclusive, cannot credibly lay claim to maximizing all the human goods at issue in such political choices.

What does democracy aspire to achieve? Although answers vary according to the types of democracy discussed below, several general justifications for democratic rule can be identified. All types of democracy presume that people who live together in a society need a process for arriving at binding decisions that takes everybody's interests into account. One common justification for democratic rule allies the premiss that people are generally the best judge of their own interests with the argument that equal citizenship rights are necessary to protect those interests. There is no better way to minimize the abuse of political power, democrats claim, than to distribute it equally. Another common, and complementary, justification is that popular rule expresses and encourages the autonomy, or self-determination, of individuals under conditions of social interdependence, where many important matters must be decided collectively (Dahl, 1989, chs 6 and 7).

Many democratic theorists also argue that democracy is instrumental to human development in so far as it encourages people to take responsibility for their political lives. Others argue that democracy represents fair terms of a social contract among people who share a territory but do not agree upon a single conception of the good. On this common contractarian view, democracy consists of a fair moral compromise, although the precise terms of that compromise vary with different democratic conceptions. Democratic theorists argue that even if democracy cannot live up to its aspirations, its promise on each of these counts is greater than that of any non-democratic government. The strongest if not most inspiring justification of democracy, well expressed by Winston Churchill, is that it is the worst form of government except for all the others.

But what form of government is democracy? Is it only a form of government? The six types of democracy considered below, each more complex than majority rule without claiming to be all inclusive, offer theoretically and practically influential answers. After briefly examining Schumpeterian democracy, populist democracy, liberal democracy, participatory democracy, social democracy, and deliberative democracy, we evaluate two famous paradoxes that are said to apply to all forms of democracy, and conclude by discussing an inescapable disharmony of democracy.

Schumpeterian democracy

Among the least inclusive, and least inspiring, conceptions of democracy that have gained currency in contemporary political theory is Joseph Schumpeter's understanding of democracy as 'that institutional arrangement for arriving at political decisions in which individuals acquire the power to decide by means of a competitive struggle for people's vote' (Schumpeter, 1943, p. 269). At the same time as this understanding recognizes the centrality of political competition in democracy, it denies that the democratic process of competing for people's vote has any substantive value. And no wonder, since by Schumpeter's understanding, South Africa in 1993 (with, effectively, an exclusively white electorate) is democratic and Stalinist Russia would have been if only members of the Communist Party had been able to vote.

Insisting on *procedural minimalism* entails forsaking democracy as an ideal. As Robert Dahl points out, Schumpeter's understanding 'leaves us with no particular reason for wanting to know whether a system is "democratic" or not. Indeed, if a demos can be a tiny group that exercises a brutal despotism over a vast subject population, then "democracy" is conceptually, morally, and empirically indistinguishable from autocracy' (Dahl, 1989, pp. 121–2).

It is a small step from Schumpeter's understanding to the conclusion that only a fool or a fanatic would sacrifice any significant values to democracy. But this conclusion says less about the limited value of democracy than about the importance of understanding democracy as more than a mere political procedure. The value of democracy is limited, but its limits can be understood only in light of a more robust and substantive conception than Schumpeter's.

Populist democracy

Many contemporary political theorists who consider democracy first and foremost a political procedure none the less reject Schumpeter's conclusion in favour of the view that there is something valuable about democratic procedures, the value of popular as contrasted with unpopular rule. The inspiration of populist democracy is the idea of the people ruling themselves as free and equal beings rather than being ruled by an external power or by a self-selected minority among themselves. Recognizing the value of popular rule is consistent with, indeed requires, putting some significant constraints on popular will in the name of democracy. The constraints none the less leave a wide range of legitimate decisions open to popular decision-making.

The constraints that are typically built into populist democracy to ensure that democratic decisions reflect the popular will are:

1 free speech, press and association necessary for political freedom;
2 the rule of law, as contrasted to the arbitrary will of public officials;
3 formal voting equality, but not equality of actual influence on outcomes (Barry, 1979, pp. 156–7); and
4 enfranchisement of 'all adult members of the association except transients and persons proved to be mentally defective' (Dahl, 1989, p. 129).

The populist ideal therefore requires certain substantive outcomes – unmanipulated political preferences, the rule of law, formal voting equality, and inclusive citizenship – which can, and sometimes do, conflict with the actual popular will as revealed by any procedure designed for the sake of popular rule.

In cases of conflict, some democrats say that the popular will is not a democratic will, even by populist standards, because it does not either reflect the popular will or uphold the conditions necessary for maintaining a truly popular will over time. In these cases, populist democrats can draw attention to the substantive content of the populist democratic ideal, and they are strictly speaking correct to do so. But this way of speaking may also be misleading. In light of the populist ideal of the people ruling themselves as free and equal beings, any constraints on popular rule are undemocratic even if, all things considered, the constraints are justified. In light of the conflict, democrats must concede either that some degree of unpopular rule, such as judicial review, is justified for the sake of achieving outcomes unsupported by popular will, or that a truly democratic will, i.e. a popular will that supports the outcomes that make it democratic, is unlikely to be fully realized, or both.

Liberal democracy

In partial contrast to populist democracy, liberal democracy denies that popular rule is the ultimate political value. Liberal democrats qualify the value of popular rule by recognizing a set of basic liberties that take priority over popular rule and its conclusions. The basic liberties typically include those that John Rawls in *A Theory of Justice* (1971, p. 61) identifies as basic to the ideal of free and equal human beings: freedoms of thought, speech, press, association and religion, the right to hold personal property, the freedom to vote and hold public office, and freedom from arbitrary arrest and seizure as defined by the concept of the rule of law. By giving priority to these basic liberties over democratic decision-making and thereby qualifying the value of populist democracy, liberal democracy makes more principled room for judicial review, checks and balances, separation of powers, and other means of tempering popular will that are quite common in Western constitutional democracies.

Any institutional constraints on popular will may be used to preserve or further the unjust advantages of entrenched minorities, against the spirit of liberal as well as populist democracy. Some contemporary democrats, following John Stuart Mill, emphasize the possibility of educating public opinion to respect individual liberty, a possibility which if realized would permit democracy to do without any constraints on popular rule (Waldron, 1990, p. 56). But no society has yet succeeded in educating public opinion continually to respect the conditions of liberal democracy, and it is hard to imagine success in the foreseeable future.

To recognize the risks that popular rule poses for personal freedom does not entail recommending institutional constraints on popular will unless the minority in control of the constraining institutions is predictably more reliable than the majority of the people, or their elected representatives. Liberal democrats can consistently support judicial review if but only if the judiciary can predictably be relied upon to protect individual rights better than more majoritarian institutions. The historical record of judicial review in the United States remains open to interpretation in this regard.

The contrast between populist democracy and liberal democracy is greater in principle than in practice. Populist democracy is committed not only to processes that reflect popular will but also to outcomes that secure popular will over time (Walzer, 1981; Ely 1980). Those outcomes – including freedoms of speech, press and association necessary for the formation, expression and aggregation of political preferences – are also among the basic liberties that liberal democracy is committed to protecting against popular rule (Gutmann, 1983).

Populist democracy and liberal democracy diverge only when confronted with a conflict between popular rule and those basic liberties that are not conditions of democracy. A paradigm case is hard-core pornography that intends no political message. The particular liberty at issue is, at least arguably, unnecessary for the formation, expression or aggregation of political preferences. Populist democrats have a principled reason to defend popularly-sanctioned restrictions on hard-core pornography, which liberal democrats have a principled reason to oppose. Populist democrats may oppose such restrictions on the grounds that restrictive legislation gives government an opening to regulate pornographic speech, which is part of political freedom. But the slippery slope argument will not always apply, or suffice as a reason to restrict popular will. In cases where the government can be trusted to respect the democratically mandated line or where the risk of over-reach is small, populist and liberal democrats will be at loggerheads, disputing the value of community standards versus free speech, where community standards are articulated by a democratic decision that finds the speech in question harmful to the interests of members of the community.

In the face of reasonable disagreement over the value of personal freedom relative to other social goods, populist democrats say that majorities rather than minorities should decide for their communities. Liberal democrats wonder why populists place so much value on popular rule when in practice each of us has so little chance of affecting the outcome of any decision. Would reasonable people not choose an expanded realm of personal freedom instead of one mere voice, or vote, among so many in making decisions (Berlin, 1969)? At most, only a small minority of people relish political activity; many people choose not even to vote. In practice, for a majority of people, the democratic choice constitutes a loss of personal freedom with no corresponding gain, indeed perhaps yet another loss in the unwelcome pressure to engage in politics for the sake of protecting one's personal freedom.

Participatory democracy

Participatory democracy challenges the relative emphasis liberal democracy places on protecting personal freedom compared to participating in politics. Participatory democrats argue that political participation is undervalued by democratic citizens today because contemporary democracies offer such limited opportunities for meaningful participation, especially compared to ancient Greek democracy. Were democratic societies to offer citizens greater opportunities to voice their political views, citizens would take advantage of those opportunities to voice their political views and make collective decisions that they now delegate to their representatives (Barber, 1984).

Participatory democrats frequently invoke the more extensive and richer political life of Athenian citizens, and the corresponding ancient Greek disdain for a purely private life, in support of recommendations to reconstruct contemporary democratic life so that it offers greater opportunities for citizens to participate directly in politics, rather than indirectly through periodic elections for representatives. But participatory democrats are not primarily animated by nostalgia for ancient Greek democracy, which they along with other modern democrats criticize for justifying slavery and excluding women and the majority of working people from citizenship and public life. Participatory democracy is better understood as an attempt to respond to the widespread recognition that many representative democracies today face serious problems stemming from inadequate political understanding and information among the electorate, increasingly low levels of voter turnout, corruption and other violations of democratic accountability by public officials, all of which can be attributed to the non-participatory nature of large-scale representative democracies.

To the extent that ordinary citizens are limited in their political interest and understanding, the liberal democratic search for institutional mechanisms to prevent the abuse of power by public officials is also limited in its promise. Participatory democracy holds out the hope that inviting citizens to participate directly in political decision-making will increase their understanding of, and interest in, politics. Participatory democrats count upon citizens to participate in politics instead of pursuing more private pleasures when offered the choice. While Rousseau expected democratic citizens to fly to the political assemblies (*The Social Contract* (1762), Book 3, ch. 15), some contemporary participatory democrats scale down their expectations to popular use of interactive cable television for making informed decisions on political referenda (Barber, 1984). Both sets of expectations may be unrealistic. One might say about participatory democracy what Oscar Wilde is reputed to have said about socialism, that it would take too many evenings.

Participatory democrats offer two arguments, reminiscent of Rousseau, in response to such scepticism. The first is that political participation is a central part of the good life for human beings, and will be recognized as such under the right social conditions. The second is that widespread participation is necessary to prevent the abuse of power by public officials. Participation, on this view, is at the same time a necessary means to a good society, and an essential part of the good life.

Social democracy

Social democracy extends the logic of liberal democracy to realms that traditional liberals considered private and therefore not subject to democratic principles. Economic enterprises and, more recently, the family are the primary realms that social democrats seek to democratize, at least in part. The principled basis for democratization is typically not the intrinsic value of participation but rather avoidance of the tyrannical threat over individual lives that accompanies concentrations of power (Dahl, 1970; Walzer, 1983).

In the case of economic enterprises, the threat takes the form of the unequal power of owners and managers of large corporations to determine workplace conditions as well as the income and even the general welfare of their employees. Although some liberals oppose any mandatory form of economic democracy on grounds that only the owners have a right to govern, most liberal democrats recognize that various principled bases of the right to own personal property, such as securing the conditions for personal autonomy, rule out the more far-ranging right to control large-scale economic enterprises at any cost to the freedom of the employees. Even the Lockean principle that people are entitled to the fruits of their labour does not entail that 'investors are entitled to govern the firms in which they invest' (Dahl, 1989, p. 330). Securing the conditions for autonomy for all members of a society requires some degree of democratic control either *over* or *within* large-scale economic enterprises.

The most common objection to democratizing industry from within is that ordinary workers are not competent to make the range of decisions necessary for profitable and efficient management of an economic enterprise. The same objection can be directed against democratic state control over industry, along with the argument that too much state control threatens state tyranny, which is potentially far worse than the tyranny any economic enterprise can exert over its employees or a democratic state. These objections do not devastate the case for some form and degree of economic democracy, but they challenge social democrats to unpack the bundle of property rights to determine which are best exercised democratically by workers within firms, which by publicly accountable officials over firms, and which best ceded to owners and managers on the basis of competence, efficiency, or the need to secure strong bulwarks against potentially tyrannical state power.

The challenge of democratizing the family is similarly significant and complex, although for different reasons. The relation between parents and children presents the paradigm case for justified paternalism, but the justification does not extend to exclusive parental authority over education, or other powers claimed by parents that interfere with the freedom and equality of future citizens (Gutmann, 1987). Social democracy also highlights the undemocratic consequences of gender inequality. By virtue of unequal economic, social and sexual power, men are able to exert tyrannical power over women. Democrats argue for a range of reforms (such as legislation against sexual harassment and subsidized child care) that respect the rights and equalize the opportunity of women, but they also rightly worry about intrusions of the state into family matters as basic as the internal division of labour over child care or the discretionary use of family income. Yet these traditionally private matters profoundly and differentially influence the personal freedom and political equality of democratic citizens.

Deliberative democracy

Why, a critic might ask, do populists place so much value on popular rule and liberals so much on personal freedom? Deliberative democracy offers an answer that integrates the populist and liberal ideals. Personal freedom and political equality are valuable to the extent that they express or support individual autonomy, the willingness and ability of persons to shape their lives through rational deliberation (Hurley, 1989; Cohen and Rogers, 1983). Deliberative democracy employs popular rule to express and support the autonomy of all persons.

Whereas populist democracy assumes that the expression of popular will is an overriding good, deliberative democracy values popular rule as a means of encouraging public deliberation on issues that are best understood through open, deliberative processes. Accompanying the ideal of autonomous persons is an ideal of politics where people routinely relate to one another not merely by asserting their wills or fighting for their predetermined interests, but by influencing each other through the publicly valued use of reasoned argument, evidence, evaluation and persuasion that enlists reasons in its cause. In a deliberative democracy, people collectively shape their own politics through persuasive argument (Walzer, 1983, p. 304; Fishkin, 1991, pp. 1–13). Deliberative democrats defend persuasion as the most justifiable form of *political* power because it is the most consistent with respecting the autonomy of persons, their capacity for self-government.

Granted that democracy can express popular will and prevent minority tyranny, how can any form of democracy claim to express and support the autonomy of persons? Some critics suspect that calling democracy deliberative is a verbal smokescreen for restricting individual freedom. Democracy limits the opportunity of all of us to live under laws of our own individual choosing. In this sense, democracy seems to undermine rather than express or support autonomy. If autonomy is understood individualistically, as all individuals legislating by themselves for themselves, then democracy's relation to autonomy is at best instrumental. The most limited form of government, one that maximized the number of decisions left to individual choice, might do better.

Deliberative democrats respond that autonomy has a broader, more political dimension that is lost by taking the social context of individual choice for granted, and focusing only on the control individuals have over those life choices that they can make by themselves for themselves, free from interference. Many important life choices are influenced and constrained by social context, over which political authority has the greatest human control. To the extent that individuals are excluded from that authority, they lack autonomy over an important dimension of their lives.

Autonomy requires a distinctive kind of democracy, a system of popular rule that encourages citizens to deliberate over political decisions. Ongoing accountability, not direct political participation, is the key to deliberative democracy. Accountability is a form of active political engagement, but it does not require continual and direct involvement in politics; it is compatible with the division of labour between professional politicians and citizens that is characteristic of representative democracy. Whereas participatory democracy strives for a polity in which all citizens actively participate in making decisions that affect their lives, deliberative democracy takes account of the burden of political action and the advantages of a division of political labour.

Theorists of deliberative democracy believe that institutions of public accountability can encourage deliberation about public issues that affect people's lives. If this belief is false, there may be no prospect that deliberative democracy can make good on its promise of supporting autonomy through democracy. If true, then the ideal of deliberative democracy may be more compelling than that of other forms of democracy.

Two paradoxes of democracy

Whether any form of democracy can be compelling partly depends on an assessment of two paradoxes that are said to be endemic to all forms of democracy. One paradox of democracy was discovered by Richard Wollheim (1962, pp. 153–67), and can be briefly described as follows. A voter believes, and has good reason to believe, that a ban on deer hunting is the right policy, and therefore votes for the ban. The majority votes against the ban. The voter, being a reasonable person and a democrat, must now believe contradictory things: that the ban is justified (by the best reasons) and that it is not justified (because the majority opposed it). The voter is caught in a clear paradox, according to Wollheim's view.

The paradox disappears on a more defensible understanding of the nature of the democrat's beliefs (Honderich, 1973, pp. 221–6; Pennock, 1974, pp. 88–93). I vote against deer hunting because I think a hunting ban is the best policy alternative available, but I accept deer hunting as the policy that should be implemented once a majority chooses it, using legitimate democratic procedures. I still believe that the majority is wrong, but I also believe that they have a right to implement the wrong policy so long as it does not violate the conditions of democracy that are necessary for maintaining popular rule over time. There is no paradox here, just a difference between what a voter believes constitutes a correct policy on its merits, and what she believes constitutes a legitimate one for a democratic community to implement in light of the results of democratic procedures.

A second paradox, first influentially elaborated by Anthony Downs (1957, ch. 14), takes the form of a collective goods problem flowing from the fact that no citizen is excluded from the benefits of election results or from the more general benefits of continuing the democratic system itself. Voting is irrational from the point of view of the cost–benefit calculation of an individual in a large electorate, yet not voting also leads to undesirable results. Because no individual voter can expect to have more than a minuscule effect upon the outcome of a large-scale election, even the smallest costs of voting are likely to outweigh the benefits to the individual voter. It is therefore irrational for any individual citizen to vote. Yet the consequences of our not voting would be disastrous both for a democratic society as a whole and for any individual citizens who want the benefits that democracy has to offer.

If most people are cost–benefit calculators, then democracies are doomed to collapse under the weight of all the rational free riders on the system. If most people are not cost–benefit calculators, by the terms of this analysis, then democracies depend on the irrationality of citizens. In either case, democracy appears to be less defensible than democratic theorists have claimed.

Some rational choice theorists, most notably William Riker and Peter Ordeshook (1968, pp. 36–40), reconcile a utilitarian account of human beings as cost–benefit calculators with the incongruous evidence of widespread voting by assuming that citizens obtain benefits from voting, which can be formally expressed in utiles or informally as a satisfaction gained in living up to the democratic ethic of voting. The satisfaction we gain from living up to our moral duty is then factored into the equation of costs and benefits that determines whether it is rational for us to vote in any given election.

This way of explaining when and why citizens vote is *ad hoc* and misleading. If we vote because we recognize an obligation to do so, then 'we do not simply accord it [the obligation] greater weight in an ordinary decision calculus. Rather, we formally set it apart' (Goodin, 1982, pp. 101, 115–16). The utilitarian account not only fails to provide a satisfactory explanation of why people vote, it also misrepresents the way in which many people treat moral obligations and the way they can rationally understand their electoral choices. Electoral choice need not be just another component of a self-interested calculus, but rather a product of moral understanding and dedication to furthering social justice. To the extent that citizens do not live up to this moral ideal, democratic societies face not a paradox but a challenge, to design institutions that encourage moral deliberation, rather than self-interested calculation. Self-interested calculators create a paradox for democracy. Moral deliberators do not.

The disharmony of democracy

Democracy is not paradoxical, but it is disharmonious. In politics, as in personal life, autonomy requires choice among conflicting and incommensurable values. Even the most thorough deliberation does not guarantee that any single deliberator or a community of deliberators will converge upon a singularly correct resolution to a difficult social problem, especially in cases where there are several attractive alternatives each of which entails the sacrifice of some important value.

Democracy does not offer a calculus of choice. It is compatible with the belief that rational deliberation can, at least in theory, yield uniquely correct answers to all political questions, but it does not presuppose this belief. In practice, under conditions of imperfect information and understanding, public deliberation (like private deliberation) often does not yield knowledge of uniquely correct resolutions to political controversies. Democracy is therefore bound to be disharmonious both because individual citizens face hard political choices without any assurance of finding clear-cut resolutions, and because the conclusions of a community of deliberators are likely to differ when confronted with a difficult issue like abortion. The more political life encourages autonomy, the more agonizing decisions may become. But the level of political acrimony and violence may decrease as citizens learn to respect each other as deliberative, rather than merely willful or self-interested, beings (Gutmann and Thompson, 1990). And greater public deliberation may also lead to more justifiable public policies. These are among the most inspiring prospects democracy has to offer.

See also 5 ECONOMICS; 6 POLITICAL SCIENCE; 11 LIBERALISM; 13 SOCIALISM; 14 AUTONOMY; 16 CON-
TRACT AND CONSENT; 17 CONSTITUTIONALISM AND THE RULE OF LAW; 21 DISCOURSE; 22 DISTRIBUTIVE
JUSTICE; 25 EQUALITY; 28 LEGITIMACY; 30 POWER; 33 RIGHTS; 36 STATE; 37 TOLERATION AND FUN-
DAMENTALISM; 38 TOTALITARIANISM; 39 TRUST

References and Further reading

Barber, B.: *Strong Democracy: Participatory Politics for a New Age* (Berkeley: University of California Press, 1984).

Barry, B.: *Sociologists, Economists, and Democracy* (London: Collier-Macmillan: 1970).

————: 'Is democracy special?', in Peter Laslett and James Fishkin, eds, *Philosophy, Politics, and Society*, 5th Series (New Haven, Conn.: Yale University Press, 1979).

Berlin, I.: 'Two concepts of liberty', in *Four Essays on Liberty* (London: Oxford University Press, 1969), pp. 118–72.

Chapman, J. W. and Wertheimer, A.: *Nomos XXXII: Majorities and Minorities* (New York: New York University Press, 1990).

Cohen, J. and Rogers, J.: *On Democracy: Toward a Transformation of American Society* (New York: Penguin Books, 1983).

Dahl, R. A.: *A Preface to Democratic Theory* (Chicago: University of Chicago Press, 1956).

————: *After the Revolution* (New Haven, Conn.: Yale University Press, 1970).

————: *Democracy and its Critics* (New Haven, Conn.: Yale University Press, 1989).

Downs, A.: *An Economic Theory of Democracy* (New York: Harper & Row, 1957).

Ely, J. H.: *Democracy and Distrust* (Cambridge, Mass.: Harvard University Press, 1980).

Fishkin, J. S.: *Democracy and Deliberation* (New Haven, Conn.: Yale University Press, 1991).

Goodin, R. E.: *Political Theory and Public Policy* (Chicago: University of Chicago Press, 1982).

Gutmann, A.: *Liberal Equality* (Cambridge: Cambridge University Press, 1980).

————: 'How liberal is democracy?', *Liberalism Reconsidered*, ed. D. MacLean and C. Mills (Totowa, NJ: Rowman & Allanheld, 1983), pp. 25–50.

————: *Democratic Education* (Princeton, NJ: Princeton University Press, 1987).

———— and Thompson, D.: 'Moral conflict and political consensus', *Ethics*, 101 (October 1990), 64–88.

Hardin, R.: 'Public choice versus democracy', John W. Chapman and Alan Wertheimer, eds, *Majorities and Minorities* (New York: New York University Press, 1990), pp. 185–203.

Honderich, T.: 'A difficulty with democracy', *Philosophy & Public Affairs*, 3 (Winter 1973), 221–6.

Hurley, S. L.: *Natural Reasons: Personality and Polity* (New York: Oxford University Press, 1989).

Macpherson, C. B.: *Democratic Theory: Essays in Retrieval* (Oxford: Oxford University Press, 1973).

Mill, J. S.: *Considerations on Representative Government*, in *Collected Works*, vol. XIX, ed. J. J. Robson (Toronto: University of Toronto Press, 1977).

————: *On Liberty*, in *Collected Works*, vol. XVIII, ed. J. J. Robson (Toronto: University of Toronto Press, 1977).

Okin, S. M.: *Justice, Gender and the Family* (New York: Basic Books, 1989).

Pennock, J. R.: *Democratic Political Theory* (Princeton, NJ: Princeton University Press, 1979).

————: 'Democracy is not paradoxical: comment', *Political Theory*, 2, 1 (February 1974), 88–93.

Phillips, A.: *Engendering Democracy* (University Park: Pennsylvania State University Press, 1991).

Rawls, J.: *A Theory of Justice* (Cambridge, Mass.: Harvard University Press, 1971).

Riker, W. H. and Ordeshook, P. C.: 'A theory of the calculus of voting', *American Political Science Review*, 62 (1968), 25–42.

Rousseau, J.-J.: *The Social Contract* (1762); (Harmondsworth: Penguin Books, 1968).

Schumpeter, J.: *Capitalism, Socialism, and Democracy* (London: George Allen & Unwin, 1943).

Thompson, D. F.: *The Democratic Citizen: Social Science and Democratic Theory in the Twentieth Century* (Cambridge: Cambridge University Press, 1970).

Waldron, J.: 'Rights and majorities: Rousseau revisited', John W. Chapman and Alan Wertheimer, eds, *Majorities and Minorities* (New York: New York University Press, 1991), pp. 44–75.

Walzer, M.: 'Philosophy and democracy', *Political Theory*, 9, 3 (August 1981), 379–99.

————: *Spheres of Justice* (New York: Basic Books, 1983).

Wollheim, R.: 'A paradox in the theory of democracy', Peter Laslett and W. G. Runciman, eds, *Philosophy, Politics and Society*, 2nd series (Oxford: Blackwell, 1962), pp. 71–87.

20

Dirty hands

C. A. J. COADY

'All kings is mostly rapscallions.'
Mark Twain, *The Adventures of Huckleberry Finn* ·

When Huck Finn embarks upon his hilarious education of the slave Jim in the moral vagaries of the monarchies of Europe, he takes himself to be propounding the merest common sense. He may have thought large-scale villainy restricted to autocracies, but his creator was clearly not so naive. More to the present point, Huck ends his discourse on princely rule with remarks that show he was not merely cataloguing the fact of widespread royal vice, but willing to countenance it as necessary. As he puts it, 'kings is kings, and you got to make allowances. Take them all around, they're a mighty ornery lot.'

Though Machiavelli ([1513] 1984, p. 52) puts the thought at its starkest, with his insistence that the Prince 'must learn how not to be good', the idea that political life essentially involves the transcendence or violation of ordinary morality has shown remarkable resilience. It was a common, though not universal, view in the nine-teenth century, and has seen a revival amongst many contemporary philosophers, who, echoing Sartre, characterize it as the problem of 'dirty hands'. Actually, it is not one thought but several, and they need to be disentangled. In what follows, I shall begin with some clarification of the issue, proceed to examine the claims of role mor-ality, and then lay out the crucial situational factors that tend to produce the chal-lenge of dirty hands. This leads on to a discussion of the complex ways that ideals and moral duties interact with the messy realities characteristic of, but not confined to, politics.

The first clarification required is the obvious one that we are not dealing merely with the claim that politics is an area in which immorality or villainy is common. This is a partly empirical claim from which nothing follows directly about a striking normative thesis like Machiavelli's. If some practice or field of endeavour is corrupt, this calls for condemnation and reform, not accommodation. Nor, to be fair, do those who rail against politicians ('they're all crooks'), usually condone all the crookedness they claim to detect. None the less, if what they say is true, there are normative pro-blems posed by its truth. Consider the parallel with crime itself. Even though there may sometimes be 'honour among thieves' and some criminals are kind to their mothers or dogs, the claim that 'all criminals are mostly rapscallions' can be admitted without raising any qualms about the legitimate reach of ordinary morality. But politics is different: we could happily do without crime, though we do not know how to elimi-nate it, but politics seems an inescapable ingredient in the good life itself.

Aristotle certainly thought as much because, not only did he insist that we humans were essentially political animals, but he made the political process so central to *eudae-monia* as to maintain that the fullest achievement of virtue was available *only* to the political leader (Aristotle, *The Politics*, Book III, ch. iv). We may think Aristotle's exal-tation of the political realm exaggerated; none the less, it is hard to deny that we need politics in a way that we do not need crime. If the anarchist vision is ultimately a mirage, then the political process, in something not too dissimilar to its present form, is needed to deliver so much that seems integral to the good life, e.g. health, comfort, justice, self-respect and education. The claim, therefore, that politicians are corrupt through and through rightly creates acute moral anxiety, since the idea that evil-doing is pretty much universal among the practitioners of politics implies that there is something about the very activity of politics that goes against the demands of morality as ordinarily understood. Furthermore, the anxiety remains even if we allow (as we should) for the considerable exaggeration in the line that 'they're all crooks', because enough morally shocking behaviour still seems typically political to suggest a conflict within the moral order itself: morality requires behaviour that is essentially immoral.

Morality and the political role

One line of response to this alarming conclusion is to distinguish between wrong-doing that is a natural result of the particular temptations of political life, especially those of power, but remains wrong none the less, and other apparent wrong-doing that is more integral to political activity. The latter is then seen as part of a distinctive political ethic even though it conflicts with 'ordinary morality'. The underlying premiss here is that there is something so distinctive about political activity that it requires ethical thinking specific to its distinctiveness. Put like this, the idea is per-suasive. Moral thinking is essentially adaptive to circumstance and context, and it is perfectly clear that different types of role, office or (as used to be said) station will affect the sorts of duty, responsibility, power and permissions that one has and ought to have. There are good reasons for allowing (some) police to carry guns and (most) ordinary citizens not to – though these good reasons do not prevail as widely as they should in the civilized world – and foresters are rightly empowered to cut down trees where ordinary citizens dare not hack. But such duties and rights hardly mark a departure from 'ordinary morality' since it is precisely in terms of 'ordinary morality' (i.e. moral reasoning readily recognizable by non-esoteric thinkers) that they are plausibly defensible. Moreover, what creates these distinctive necessities is something continuous with ordinary life, in that the special powers and duties granted to particular role-bearers, such as firemen, may be assumed by ordinary citizens in emergency situations.

What is also debatable is whether the political vocation is sufficiently distinguish-able as a role for considerations of role morality or professional ethics to take us into exciting, Machiavellian territory. The political role is far more undifferentiated, even amorphous, than such roles as lawyer, doctor or fireman. This is because there are political dimensions to most, if not all, aspects of life. There are political roles in academic life, in the churches, in the law, in the crafts and trades, even (as traditional literature and modern feminism both emphasize) in the family. The point or *telos* of politics is also less clear than that of medicine or policing. We could say that its end is the concern for the common good, but this, though possibly true, raises more problems than it solves. Certainly, these facts make it difficult to read off specific moral injunctions from the phenomena of political life, as we might more easily do, say, with medical life. We may think that the good purpose of treating sickness and promoting health cannot be achieved unless those who practise medicine have certain particular duties, rights and powers, and, although there is considerable room for disagreement as to detail, the broad nature of these is clear enough. In the case of politics, especially in the context of the alleged necessity for 'dirty hands', the situation is far more obscure. This is reflected in the fact that if we determine some imperative to be part of medical ethics, e.g. that a doctor need not consult with parents before prescribing the contraceptive pill to teenage girls older than thirteen, then this determination, if correct, stands as part of ordinary morality, not in opposition to it. Any such opposition must be merely apparent. Nor are we dealing with the sort of moral impasse philosophers have discussed under the label 'moral dilemma' for these are cases where reason yields *no* right answer. For politics, the Machiavellian thought, at least in its most challenging form, is quite different; the idea is that it is sometimes legitimate for political rulers, precisely because they are rulers, to deceive, cheat, betray or even torture and murder, where these acts are clear violations of the moral code that seems to bind us all.

The qualification, 'in its most challenging form', is important. In Machiavelli himself (especially in *The Prince*), it does take this form, though at times his formulations move further in the direction of including the princely imperatives within the scope of ordinary morality. So he says of the prince that 'carefully taking everything into account, he will discover that something which appears to be a virtue, if pursued, will end in his destruction; while some other thing which seems to be a vice, if pursued, will result in his safety and well-being' (Machiavelli, [1513] 1984, p. 53). Here, the reference to appearances make his position a little more accommodating of morality's claim to a dominant position among reasons for acting, even if it is subversive of its normal substance. This wavering among formulations is philosophically interesting, and I have discussed it elsewhere (Coady, 1990, pp. 259–63). Here we need only note that, because we tend to think of morality both as forming a coherent whole and as dominating all other reasons for action, there are at least two different ways of stating the 'dirty hands' thesis. We may state it as the view that political reasons sometimes legitimately override the most serious moral considerations, or as the view that morality is divided against itself, with the virtues required by political life incompatible with what we think of as normal (or 'private') virtues. There is a third option, but it is less a formulation of the dirty hands challenge than a way of sanitizing its confrontation with morality. This is the option of treating the apparent clash between political and ordinary morality as reconciled by some overarching moral principle, such as the principle of utility.

However we state it, two interesting points need settling. Are 'dirty hands' restricted to politicians, and, if they are not, is there something that makes political life a special 'showpiece' for dirty hands? It seems to me clear that the sorts of argument made by those who promote the category of 'dirty hands' are applicable beyond the arena of politics as narrowly, or even broadly, understood. When, for instance, philosophers stress the momentous consequences of political decisions, and argue that the consequences of abiding by normal moral prohibitions are sometimes so disastrous as to require the violation of moral constraints, they tend to ignore the way in which the same can be said of relatively private areas of life like the decisions facing a mother in an impoverished, crime-dominated urban ghetto, or those confronting an inmate of a concentration camp. This is not the place to examine the detail of the different arguments offered, but there are certain themes implicit, and sometimes explicit, in the argumentation, and an examination of these can show both that the dirty hands issue cannot be restricted to politics and why it is so often taken to exemplify it.

The generating of dirty hands

Machiavelli makes it clear that one of the situations generating the need for the ruler to act wickedly is the fact that others with whom one interacts cannot be relied upon to act morally, and hence conformity to morality is foolish and dangerous for survival. We might call this the problem of moral isolation. As befits someone who puts survival at the heart of morality, Thomas Hobbes gives an even clearer account of this than Machiavelli. Hobbes thought that the laws of nature gave us a valid moral code and associated virtues, but that they obliged *in foro interno* and 'not always' *in foro externo*. He meant that we ought to want the laws of nature to be obeyed, but that we would be stupid to practise morality unilaterally. Hobbes did not think the point applied solely to politics; rather, he thought it an important feature of life in a state of nature, but, as Sidgwick noted in a perceptive and neglected essay (Sidgwick, 1898), and as Hobbes would certainly have insisted, rulers often stand in relations to one another that resemble a state of nature. Hence the sphere of international relations is one that naturally lends itself to the dirty hands story. To the extent that morality depends upon the co-operation stressed by Hobbes, then where it is absent, we *may* be licensed to engage in the deception and violence of 'covert operations' against other nations. (It is worth noting, however, that the moral isolation of a state of nature may work to impose more, rather than less, stringent duties upon individuals or states. As Sidgwick (1898, pp. 77–8) saw, promises extracted by wrongful force are not binding in 'an orderly state', but are binding to some degree upon the defeated victims of an unjust war.)

The claims of 'moral isolation' have none the less to be treated with great caution. They are at their strongest in situations where the moral issues are heavily conventional. Where politeness decrees that no one need tell the truth about his feelings on meeting an unwelcome visitor, it might be folly not to lie, indeed it is not even clear that our linguistic intuitions would count as lies such falsehoods as 'I'm pleased to see you'. More interesting are the cases where broad non-compliance by others in the moral enterprise raises large issues of survival and so gives us a dispensation from

425

strict compliance ourselves. Arguably this is so of certain dealings by the police with criminals, as in undercover investigations, and it seems particularly clear during war in activities such as spying on the enemy or providing him with misinformation. It seems reasonable to say that the drug-dealer or hit-man has, by his activities, forfeited any right to complain of such methods. Even so, issues of implicit contract, or even survival, do not exhaust the foundations of morality and there are two reasons for caution about the concessions founded on moral isolation. One concerns the matter of character and the other the possible consequences of the policy of relaxing moral prohibitions.

As to the former, it is not always folly to exercise the virtues of honesty, kindness and justice when others ignore them, since there is a personal and communal value in good character, even in such circumstances. As so many of the better spy novels teach us, the world of the spy is one of paranoia, self-deception and emotional sterility. Immersion in this world not only tends to distort the personalities of the spies, but, as recent history teaches us, it tends to damage the political culture of the wider society to which they belong. Nor are these direct consequences the only ones to be expected. If governments and their agencies are ready to relax moral standards *in extremis*, they cannot expect other groups and agencies within the community not to follow suit. This should give particular pause when we consider some of the supposed extremes in the dirty hands literature licensing serious moral exceptions in such areas as campaign funding (see Walzer, 1973, p. 165).

This problem is sometimes obscured by a certain romantic pomposity about the state, which sees it as the only agency of political thought and activity and as having such a special role and purpose that exemptions granted to it could hardly be extended further. A certain Gustro Rumelin, Chancellor of the University of Tübingen, put the matter splendidly in 1875: 'The state is self-sufficient. Self-regard is its appointed duty; the maintenance and development of its power and well-being – egoism, if you like to call this egoism – is the supreme principle of all politics' (quoted in Sidgwick, 1898, p. 64). But the example of egoism is infectious, and other corporations and groups within the state have not been slow in claiming the same prerogatives, especially where anything remotely connected with survival is at stake – survival of the party, the business, the department, the club, or the individual as indispensable leader of the group. The consequences of this, in turn, include the promotion of widespread cynicism about politicians and public life generally, and this itself makes inroads upon the achievability of the goods that politics is supposed to promote.

Another source of this cynicism resides in the tension that seems inevitable between the supposed requirements of dirty hands and the moral underpinnings of democratic polity. The cultivation of the capacity for judicious vice in the ruler sits oddly with the values of public accountability and relative openness characteristic of genuine democracy. It is significant that Machiavelli urges his prince to keep up a public pretence of virtue while engaging in vicious acts as required, and certainly the success in ruling that Machiavelli so admired frequently requires the necessary wrong-doings to be cloaked in secrecy. But the prevalence of such secrecy, especially with regard to the breach of commonly accepted moral standards, is corrosive of the basic ideals of a democracy, and productive of cynicism about the political process. Witness the effects of the many, decidedly *unnecessary* moral enormities committed, without adequate scrutiny, under the rubric of 'national security' in so many Western democracies in recent years. For the hands to be successfully dirty, it seems they must also be democratically illegitimate. (For further discussion of this see Thompson, 1987, ch. 1.)

Ideals and messy realities

One thing that the discussion of moral isolation suggests is that morality often presents us with certain ideals that may have to be adapted to the messy realities of a world in which the ideals are widely disregarded or face difficulties of implementation. In much of life, we are faced with social realities that exhibit what Rawls (1972, pp. 245–8) has called 'partial compliance' to the conditions and norms of justice and other social virtues. If the champions of politics are often insensitive to the force of moral demands, the champions of morality are sometimes blind to political (and other) realities. There are two situations that need attention here, though it must regrettably be brief, and these are situations of compromise and extrication.

Problems of compromise are endemic to political life and, indeed, to all collaborative activities, for they allow joint enterprises to proceed, in spite of the conflicting goals, values and ideals of the participants. They do this because a compromise is a sort of bargain in which people who see advantages in co-operation for certain ends sacrifice other objectives, temporarily or permanently, in order to gain the ends that they believe are only achievable by co-operation. Compromise is not inherently immoral and it often has little to do with morality, but the losses may have a moral flavour about them, as when someone abandons certain ideals or sacrifices the hope of achieving certain valuable outcomes. To achieve economic stability, a politician may have to abandon much-needed reform of the health services, or a taxation scheme that would achieve more just social results. The moral losses incurred in such compromises are a necessary part of all politics, but they should not be treated lightly since persistent trading of central and cherished ideals can lead to the situation where a politician stands for nothing but personal or the party's survival in office. The problem with pragmatism is that the point of survival is swallowed up by the day-to-day necessities of compromise. Furthermore, beyond ideals, which may be modified, postponed or even legitimately abandoned, there exist basic moral standards and commitments that should be integral to an individual's character. To trade these is not just to compromise but to be compromised, and this is a description that invariably has negative force. When 'dirty hands' requires not just the limiting of moral hopes, and a certain lowering of moral outlook, but the abandonment of principle, it is an altogether more dubious and difficult demand.

Another important source for dirty hands problems are situations in which the agent needs to extricate from a moral mess of her own or others' making. In the political context, the agent may have initiated the immorality herself, or may have acquired responsibility for it, perhaps by inheriting office. Believing an existing war her country is waging to be unjust, for instance, she may, as the new leader of the government, be unable to stop the war at once without being responsible for grave harms and even wrongs, which are bound to follow on an immediate surrender or

427

withdrawal. Gradual disengagement, however, offers good prospects for avoiding such evils, though it means that she must continue to direct an unjust war and the unjust killings it involves. More detail is required for a full discussion of this point, but it seems plausible that the example could be so constructed that the leader is morally responsible for wrong-doing whichever way she acts, but that gradual extrication is less wrong than immediate cessation. It also seems plausible that her responsibility is not the wholesale negative responsibility integral to consequentialist ethics but the responsibility inherent in ordinary moral thinking. Yet it is important to note that these are not simple cases of politics triumphing over morality since the moral verdict on the war remains dominant in showing the way to extrication. (There are fuller discussions of this issue in Coady, 1989; 1990.)

There is an intriguing issue related to the dirty hands debate which is created by the role of bureaucracy in public life. This has been called the problem of 'many hands' (Thompson, 1987, ch. 2) though it might just as well be called the problem of 'no hands'. It arises when, in a complex organization, so many people contribute to an outcome that the question of who is morally responsible for producing it is seriously muddled. Part of the problem is informational and part of it is attitudinal. It is particularly relevant to the role of expert advisers in political or commercial contexts. The informational point is that such advisers sometimes know little about the overall purposes for which their advice will be used; the attitudinal point is that, whether they know it or not, they frequently see themselves as having no moral responsibility for the organizational outcomes of their work. 'I am paid for my expertise', says the lawyer, soldier, accountant, or scientist. 'It is my duty to my client or employer to give them the benefits of that expertise no matter how they might use it.' It is not that the advisers are like Machiavelli's prince in considering that the end justifies the means, but rather that they disclaim any knowledge of, or concern for, the end, and restrict themselves to purely technical consideration of the means. There are many complex problems raised by this phenomenon, but it is easy to see the dangers that such widespread abdication of moral responsibility poses for the relevance of morality to politics and public life generally.

Finally, it is important in considering the problem of 'dirty hands' or 'no hands' not to be trapped into considering the issue in a static way, as though the background circumstances in which hands are likely to get dirty, or empty of moral responsibility, are somehow immutable. Machiavellian thinking has a tendency to obscure the fact that the background to political life is itself a fit subject for moral scrutiny and structural change, especially when it is that background itself that contributes to the alleged need for dirty or empty hands. Talk of the necessity for hands to get dirty often assumes a complacent, even conniving, tone, and tends to stifle the moral imagination, making local necessities seem global and eternal. The Machiavellian outlook also puts morality into too defensive a posture, as though morality could only confront politics as an inhibition and a problem. But, although there are plenty of difficulties with a merely moralistic approach to politics, we must not lose sight of the power of morality as a dynamic for political change. The recent, mostly peaceful, overthrow of entrenched communist tyranny in Eastern Europe, with all its ambiguities, is a timely reminder of this (see O'Neill, 1990).

428

References

Aristotle: *The Politics*, trans. T. A. Sinclair, revised Trevor J. Saunders (Harmondsworth: Penguin Books, 1981).

Coady, C. A. J.: 'Escaping from the bomb: immoral deterrence and the problem of extrication', in *Nuclear Deterrence and Moral Restraint*, ed. Henry Shue (New York: Cambridge University Press, 1989).

————: 'Messy morality and the art of the possible', *Proceedings of the Aristotelian Society*, supplementary, 64 (1990).

Hobbes, T.: *Leviathan* (1651), ed. C. B. Macpherson (Harmondsworth: Penguin Books, 1981).

Machiavelli, N.: *The Prince* (1513), ed. P. Bondanella (Oxford: Oxford University Press, 1984).

————: *The Discourses* (1513), trans. and ed. L. J. Walker (Harmondsworth: Penguin Books, 1950).

O'Neill, O.: 'Messy morality and the art of the possible', *Proceedings of the Aristotelian Society*, supplementary, 64 (1990).

Rawls, J.: *A Theory of Justice* (Oxford: Oxford University Press, 1972).

Sidgwick, H.: 'Public morality', in *Practical Ethics* (London: Swan Sonnenschein & Co., 1898).

Thompson, D. F.: *Political Ethics and Public Office* (Harvard, Mass.: Harvard University Press, 1987).

Walzer, M.: 'Political action: the problem of dirty hands', *Philosophy and Public Affairs*, 2 (1973) 160–80.

Further reading

Acheson, D.: 'Ethics in international relations today', in *The Vietnam Reader*, ed. M. G. Raskin and B. Fall (New York: Random House, 1965).

————: 'Homage to plain dumb luck', in *The Cuban Missile Crisis*, ed. R. A. Divine (Chicago: Quadrangle Books, 1971).

Coady, C. A. J.: 'Politics and the problem of dirty hands', in *A Companion to Ethics*, ed. P. Singer (Oxford: Blackwell, 1991).

Day, J. P.: 'Compromise', *Philosophy*, 64 (1989).

Erasmus, D.: *The Education of a Christian Prince*, trans. and intro. L. K. Born (New York: 1936).

Gaita, R.: 'Ethics and politics', in his *Good and Evil: An Absolute Conception* (London: Macmillan, 1990).

Kavka, G. S.: 'Nuclear coercion', in *Moral Paradoxes of Nuclear Deterrence*, ed. G. S. Kavka (Cambridge: Cambridge University Press, 1987).

Hampshire, S.: 'Morality and pessimism', in *Public and Private Morality*, ed. S. Hampshire (Cambridge: Cambridge University Press, 1978).

Marx, K.: *Writings of the Young Marx on Philosophy and Society*, ed. and trans. L. D. Easton and K. H. Guddat (New York: Anchor, 1967).

Nagel, T.: 'Ruthlessness in public life', in *Public and Private Morality*, ed. S. Hampshire (Cambridge: Cambridge University Press, 1978), pp. 75–92.

Oberdiek, H.: 'Clean and dirty hands in politics', *International Journal of Moral and Social Studies*, 1, 1 (1986).

Plato: *The Republic*, any edition, especially Book 1.

Rousseau, J.-J.: *The First and Second Discourses Together with the Replies to Critics and Essay on the Origin of Languages*, ed. V. Gourevitch (New York: 1986).

Stocker, M.: *Plural and Conflicting Values* (Oxford: Oxford University Press, 1990).

Walzer, M.: *Just and Unjust Wars* (New York: Basic Books, 1977; Harmondsworth: Penguin Books, 1980).

Weber, M.: 'Politics as a vocation' (1919), in *From Max Weber: Essays in Sociology*, ed. H. H. Gerth and C. Wright Mills (New York: 1946).

Williams, B.: 'Politics and moral character', in *Public and Private Morality*, ed. S. Hampshire (Cambridge: Cambridge University Press, 1978), pp. 55–74.

21

Discourse

ERNESTO LACLAU

The notion of 'discourse', as developed in some contemporary approaches to political analysis, has its distant roots in what can be called the transcendental turn in modern philosophy – i.e. a type of analysis primarily addressed not to *facts* but to their *conditions of possibility*. The basic hypothesis of a discursive approach is that the very possibility of perception, thought and action depends on the structuration of a certain meaningful field which pre-exists any factual immediacy. A transcendental enquiry as an investigation of the conditions of possibility of experience started with Kant, for whom space, time and the categories of understanding constitute the *a priori* dimension in the constitution of phenomena. And in the early twentieth century Husserl's phenomenology strictly differentiated an intuition of facts from an intuition of essences, and asserted that the latter is constitutive of all 'givenness'. These classical transcendental approaches differ, however, in two crucial respects from contemporary theories of discourse. The first is that, while in a philosophy like Kant's the '*a priori*' constitutes a basic structure of the mind which transcends all historical variations, contemporary discourse theories are eminently historical and try to study discursive fields which experience temporal variations in spite of their transcendental role – i.e. that the line separating the 'empirical' and the 'transcendental' is an impure one, submitted to continuous displacements. A second differentiating feature is that the concept of 'discursive fields' in contemporary approaches depends on a notion of structure which has received the full impact of Saussurean and post-Saussurean linguistics.

Even within this very general characterization we must differentiate between those theories of discourse that are strongly related to transformations in the field of structural linguistics and those whose links to structural analysis are more distant and do not pass through an internal critique of the Saussurean notion of the sign. The first approach is represented by post-structuralism conceived in a broad sense, the second by the work of Michel Foucault and his school. We will treat successively these two trends and will later deal with the consequences of such developments for the conceptualization of politics.

Theories of discourse

The linguistic theory of Ferdinand de Saussure (1959), originally presented in three courses given in Geneva between 1906 and 1911, turn around the notion of the *sign* conceived as the relation between an acoustic image (the *signifier*) and a concept (the *signified*). According to Saussure there are two basic principles around which structural linguistics is organized. The first is that in language there are no positive terms, only differences. To understand the meaning of the term 'father' I have to understand the meaning of the terms 'mother', 'son', etc. This purely relational and differential character of linguistic identities means that language constitutes a *system* in which no element can be defined independently of the others. The second principle is that language is *form* and not *substance* – that is, that each element of the system is exclusively defined by the rules of its combinations and substitutions with the other elements. To use Saussure's analogy, if I substitute the wooden pieces in a chessboard with marbles or even pieces of paper, I can still play chess as far as the rules governing the movements of the pieces remain the same. In this entirely differential universe, dominated by purely formal rules, there is strict isomorphism: to each stream of sounds constituting a word corresponds one and only one concept. The order of the signifier and the order of the signified strictly overlap.

There were, however, for Saussure, strict limits to the possibility of developing a linguistic theory of discourse. From a Saussurean point of view discourse is any linguistic sequence more extended than the sentence. Now, in a Saussurean perspective a linguistics of discourse is impossible because a succession of sentences is only governed by the whims of the speaker and does not present any structural regularity graspable by a general theory. With this Cartesian assertion of the omnipotence of the subject, the very possibility of a linguistic theory of discourse was ruled out. On top of that, the Saussurean theory of the sign was ultimately inconsistent, for if language is form and not substance, and if there is a strict isomorphism between the order of the signifier and the order of the signified, the two orders become – from a formal point of view – indistinguishable from each other, and the duality of the linguistic sign cannot be maintained. At this point Saussure had to reintroduce surreptitiously the distinction between phonic and conceptual *substances*, with the result of tying even more closely structural analysis to the linguistic sign. Although he had vaguely announced the possibility of a semiology as a general science of signs in society, his dependence on linguistic *substances* made difficult this enlargement of the fields of application of structural principles.

It was only with the *glossematic school* of Copenhagen that these internal inconsistencies of Saussureanism were properly addressed. The result was the formulation of a second model of structural linguistics which clearly advanced in the direction of an increasing formalism. Hjelmslev (1961; 1970) broke with Saussure's isomorphic conception of the relation between signifier and signified by subdividing both orders into units smaller than the sign:

phonologists . . . have brought to light linguistic units smaller than signs: the phonemes . . . (the sign *calf* is made up of the three phonemes k/ae/ and f/). The same method applied to content allows the distinction, in the same sign, of at least three elements . . . or semes . . . bovine/male/young. Now it is clear that the semantic and the phonic units thus located can be distinguished from the formal point of view: the combinatorial laws concerning the phonemes of a language and those applied to the semes cannot be shown to correspond to each other . . . (Ducrot and Todorov, 1980, p. 22)

The consequences of this trend towards formalism were far-reaching as far as a theory of discourse is concerned. The main ones are the following.

1 If the abstract system of formal rules governing the combination and substitution between elements is no longer necessarily attached to any particular substance, *any* signifying system in society – the alimentary code, furniture, fashion, etc. – can be described in terms of that system. This was the direction that semiology took since the 1960s, starting with the pioneering works of Roland Barthes (1967; 1968; 1972; see also Kristeva, 1969). In fact, there was an increasing realization that 'discourse' did not refer to a particular set of objects, but to a viewpoint from which it was possible to redescribe the totality of social life.

2 If formalism strictly applies, this means that the *substantial* differences between the linguistic and the non-linguistic have also to be dropped. In other terms, that the distinction between action and structure becomes a secondary distinction within the wider category of meaningful totalities. This point has been particularly stressed in Laclau and Mouffe (1985), and it brings discourse theory close to the conclusions reached by the work of the later Wittgenstein, i.e. the notion that 'language games' embrace both language and the actions in which it is woven (Wittgenstein, 1983, p. 5).

3 Finally, strict formalism made it also possible to overcome the other obstacle to the formulation of a linguistic theory of discourse: as far as all distinctions had to be considered as merely differential – i.e. as internal to the structure – the subject could no longer be conceived as *the source* of meaning but, instead, as just one more particular location within a meaningful totality. The 'death of the subject' was one of the battle cries of classical structuralism. The way in which the speaker put sentences together could no longer be conceived as the expression of the whims of an entirely autonomous subject but, rather, as largely determined by the way in which institutions are structured, by what is 'sayable' in some contexts, etc. The task of discourse analysis for classical structuralism was to uncover these basic regularities which govern the production of meaning in social life. This programme was carried out, from a technical point of view, by putting together the contributions of various disciplines such as the theory of argumentation, the theory of enunciation, speech-act theory, semantic and syntactic analysis, etc.

In recent years the structuralist tradition has experienced, from various quarters, a series of reformulations which have led to what can properly be called a post-structuralist moment. The common denominator of these revisions has been to put into question the notion of closed totality, which was the cornerstone of classical structuralism. (If identities are only differences within a discursive system, no identity can be fully constituted unless the system is a closed one.) The post-structuralist trend has been to experiment in the logic of subversion of discursive identities which follows from the logical impossibility of constituting a closed system. The main currents within this trend are the following:

1 The reformulation of the logic of meaning in the later work of Roland Barthes (1974). While in his early semiological works Barthes believed in a strict differentiation between denotative and connotative meanings, he realized later that no

strict differentiation between both can be established. This led to the notion of a *plural text*, whose signifiers cannot be permanently attached to particular signifieds.

2 A similar loosening of the relation between signifier and signified takes place in the psychoanalytic current inspired by Jacques Lacan (1977). Freudian theory, through its emphasis on the process of overdetermination (condensation and displacement), which intervenes in the constitution of all psychical formations, had already insisted in the impossibility of fixing meaning through a strict correlation between signifier and signified. This tendency is radicalized by Lacanian theory in what is called the *logic of the signifier*, i.e. the permanent slide of the signified under the signifier (the latter becoming the stable element).

3 Finally, the *deconstructionist* movement, initiated by Jacques Derrida (1976; also Gasché, 1986), attempts to show the elements of radical undecidability to be found in all structural arrangements (in a way not dissimilar to the Gödel's theorem) and how no structure of signification can find in itself the principle of its own closure. The latter requires, consequently, a dimension of force which has to operate from outside the structure.

An entirely different approach to a theory of what he calls 'discursive formations' is to be found in the work of Michel Foucault. While both structuralism and post-structuralism start from the logic of the sign and its subversion once the conditions of total closure do not obtain, Foucault's starting point is a second-level phenomenology trying to isolate the totalities within which any production of meaning takes place. Classical phenomenology had focused on the meaning of statements by bracketing their reference to any external reality. Foucault proceeds to a second bracketing by showing that meaning itself pre-supposes conditions of production which are not themselves reducible to meaning. This 'quasi- transcendental' move leads to the isolation of a stratum of phenomena, which Foucault calls discourse. The central problem in his analysis is to determine what constitutes the unity and principle of coherence of a discursive formation. The minimal unit of any discourse is, for Foucault, the *statement* (*énoncé*). A statement cannot be considered as a proposition because the same proposition can involve two different statements (both I and a doctor can say that somebody has a cancer, but only the latter's proposition can be considered as a medical statement). It cannot be considered as an utterance either, because different utterances can involve the same statement. Finally, statements cannot be identified with speech-acts, given that the former are restricted by Foucault to what he calls 'serious speech-acts' – those that are not ordinary, everyday speech-acts, but are constituted through an authoritative or autonomous activity (like the medical discourse). But this is just to put the same problem in a different way: what constitutes the principle of unity of a particular discursive field or formation? For a while Foucault played with the idea of finding this principle of unity in what he called an *episteme*: a basic outlook which unifies the intellectual production during a certain age. 'By *episteme* we mean ... the total set of relations that unite, at a given period, the discursive practices that give rise to epistemological figures, sciences, and possibly formalized systems' (Foucault, 1972, p. 191). In this sense he tried to isolate the basic *epistemes* of the ages that he conventionally called the Renaissance, the Classical Age and Modernity

(Foucault, 1973). The intellectual operation of uncovering these basic discursive strategies is what he called *archaeology*. But the main trend of his thought led him to the increasing realization that the heterogeneity of a discursive formation cannot be reduced to such a simple principle of unity. So, he concluded that the principle of unity of a discursive formation cannot be found in the reference to the same object, or in a common style in the production of statements, or in the constancy of the concepts, or in the reference to a common theme, but in what he called 'regularity in dispersion' – the constancy in the external relations between elements which do not obey any underlying or essential principle of structuration. However, if regularity in dispersion is the only principle of unity of a discursive formation, what remains open is the question of the frontiers between discursive formations, a question to which Foucault, at this stage, was unable to give any precise answer.

Discourse theory and politics

The main contributions of discourse theory to the field of politics have been linked so far to the conceptualization of power. The same broad division pointed out earlier applies here: we have, on the one hand, analysts whose theoretical roots are to be found in the post-structuralist theory of the sign and, on the other, those which are mainly linked to the reformulation of Foucault's intellectual project in his later work.

The first tendency can be found especially in the work of Laclau and Mouffe (Laclau and Mouffe, 1985; Laclau, 1990). Two aspects of the post-structuralist tradition have been important in their formulation of an approach to political power centred in the category of *hegemony*. The first is the notion of 'discourse' as a meaningful totality which transcends the distinction between the linguistic and the extra-linguistic. As we have seen, the impossibility of a closed totality unties the connection between signifier and signified. In that sense there is a proliferation of 'floating signifiers' in society, and political competition can be seen as attempts by rival political forces to partially fix those signifiers to particular signifying configurations. Discursive struggles about the ways of fixing the meaning of a signifier like 'democracy', for instance, are central to explain the political semantics of our contemporary political world. This partial fixing of the relation between signifier and signified is what in these works is called 'hegemony'. The second aspect in which post-structuralism contributes to a theory of hegemony is closely connected with the first. As we have seen, deconstruction shows that the various possible connections between elements of the structure are, in their own terms, undecidable. As, however, one configuration rather than the other possible ones has been actualized, it follows: (1) that the actually existing configuration is essentially contingent; (2) that it cannot be explained by the structure itself but by a force which has to be partially external to the structure. This is the role of a hegemonic force. 'Hegemony' is a theory of the decisions taken in an undecidable terrain. The conclusion is, as deconstruction shows, that as undecidability operates at the very ground of the social, objectivity and power become indistinguishable. It is in these terms that it has been asserted that power is the trace of contingency within the structure (Laclau, 1990). Laclau and Mouffe present a history of Marxism, from the Second International to Gramsci, as a progressive recognition of the contingent character of social links which had previously been considered as grounded in the necessary laws of History. This is what has extended always further the area of operativity of hegemonic links.

There has recently also been an important attempt by Slavoj Žižek (1989) to extend discourse theory to the field of political analysis through an approach which brings together Lacanian psychoanalysis, Hegelian philosophy and some trends in analytical philosophy, especially Saul Kripke's anti-descriptivism. The central aspect of Žižek's approach is his attempt to reintroduce the category of the subject without any kind of essentialist connotation. His 'subject' is not the substantial *cogito* of the philosophical tradition of modernity, but it is not either the dispersion of *subject positions* that structuralism had postulated. The subject is rather – following Lacan – the place of the *lack*, an empty place that various attempts at identification try to fill. Žižek shows the complexity involved in any process of *identification* (in the psychoanalytic sense) and attempts to explain on that basis the constitution of political identities.

The later work of Foucault (1979; 1980) was an attempt to deal with the difficulties to which his analysis of discursive formations had led. Foucault had defined the realm of discourse as just one object among others. Discourse related to the statement as one object of analysis sharply separated from the others: discursive regularities did not cut across the frontier between the linguistic and the non-linguistic. As a result, the presence of certain discursive configurations had to be explained in terms which for him were extra-discursive. This led to a new kind of approach, which he called *genealogy*. While archaeology *pre-supposed* the unity of a discursive field which could not appeal to any deeper principle of unification, genealogy tried to locate the elements entering a discursive configuration within the framework of a discontinuous history whose elements did not have any principle of teleological unity. The external character of the unifying forces behind the genealogical dispersion of elements is at the basis of the Foucauldian conception of power: power is ubiquitous because elements are discontinuous, and their being linked is nothing that we can explain out of the elements themselves. So, while post-structuralism and genealogy both deal with the question of discontinuity and its production out of unsutured identities, they approach discontinuity from two different angles: in the first case it is a question of extending the category of discourse to the point in which it embraces its radical other – i.e. it is a question of showing the working of a logic of *difference* which cuts across any distinction between the linguistic and the non-linguistic; in the second case it is a question of showing how linguistic regularities depend on putting together elements which can only be conceived in non-discursive terms.

See also 2 CONTINENTAL PHILOSOPHY; 4 SOCIOLOGY; 12 MARXISM; 15 COMMUNITY; 19 DEMOCRACY; 28 LEGITIMACY

References

Barthes, R.: *Elements of Semiology*, trans. A. Lavers and C. Smith (New York: Hill and Wong, 1968).
———: *Mythologies*, trans. A. Lavers (London: Cape, 1972).

————: *S/Z* (London: Jonathan Cape, 1974).

————: *The Fashion System*, trans. M. Ward and R. Howard (New York: Hill and Wang, 1983).

Derrida, J.: *Of Grammatology*, trans. G. C. Spivak (Baltimore, Md: Johns Hopkins University Press, 1976).

Ducrot, O. and Todorov, T.: *Encyclopedic Dictionary of the Sciences of Languages* (Baltimore, Md.: Johns Hopkins University Press, 1979).

Foucault, M.: *The Archaeology of Knowledge*, trans. A. M. Sheridan Smith (London: Tavistock, 1972).

————: *The Order of Things: An Archaeology of the Human Sciences* (New York: Pantheon, 1973).

————: 'Nietzsche, genealogy and history', in *Michel Foucault: Language, Counter-Memory, Practice: Selected Essays and Interviews*, ed. D. F. Bouchard (New York: Vintage Books, 1977).

————: *Discipline and Punish: the Birth of the Prison*, trans. A. Sheridan (New York: Vintage, 1979).

————: *The History of Sexuality*. Vol. I: *An Introduction*, trans. R. Hurley (New York: Pantheon, 1980).

Gasché, R.: *The Tain of the Mirror* (Cambridge, Mass.: Harvard University Press, 1986).

Hjelmslev, L.: *Prolegomena to a Theory of Language*, trans. F. A. Whitfield (Madison: University of Wisconsin Press, 1961).

————: *Language: An Introduction*, trans. F. A. Whitfield (Madison: University of Wisconsin Press, 1970).

Kristeva, J.: *Semeiotike* (Paris: Editions du Seuil, 1969).

Lacan, J.: *Ecrits. A Selection*, trans. A. Sheridan (New York: Norton, 1977).

Laclau, E.: *New Reflections on the Revolution of Our Time* (London: Verso, 1990).

———— and Mouffe, C.: *Hegemony and Soicalist Strategy: Towards a Radical Democratic Politics* (London: Verso, 1985).

Saussure, F. de: *Course in General Linguistics*, trans. C. Bailey and A. Sechehaye (New York: McGraw-Hill, 1959).

Wittgenstein, L.: *Philosophical Investigations* (Oxford: Blackwell, 1983).

Žižek, S.: *The Sublime Object of Ideology* (London: Verso, 1989).

22

Distributive justice

SERGE-CHRISTOPHE KOLM

This chapter explores the central debate in the contemporary theory of distributive justice, deducing the various positions in that debate from basic questions of liberty and equality. Although they are often more important, ideas not central to this specific debate are barely noted. Among them are topics such as needs and misery, altruism and reciprocity, community and history, virtue and education, the self and selflessness, 'social welfare' and 'sums of pleasures', dialogue and communication, methodologies, factual descriptions and innumerable more specific theoretical issues. Even with this restriction, however, the bibliography of writings strictly relevant to distributive justice would alone have exceeded the space allowed in this *Companion* for the topic as a whole.

The nature and operation of distributive justice

Justice is the central ethical judgement regarding the effects of society on the situation of social entities, with respect to each entity's valuation of its own situation for its own purposes. 'Situation' here denotes anything relevant to the entity's purposes. Natural individuals are most often the entities in view. But questions of justice also arise as regards looser groupings, which may or may not be 'reducible' (conceptually or otherwise) to individuals. Included here are nations, families, firms, cities, classes, regions and perhaps even cultures.

When the purposes of several such entities oppose each other, and the issue is how to arbitrate among their competing claims, the question is one of 'distributive justice'. Obviously, the central application of distributive justice is 'economic justice' – the allocation of the goods, resources, services or commodities that are scarce and raise rival desires, directly or indirectly.

For a judgement of justice, there is a set of variables on which the ethical evaluation bears directly, the 'directly ethically relevant variables'. Other variables are evaluated only in an indirect or derivative way by the considered judgement.

A theory of distributive justice is, it shall be argued, completely characterized by the nature of the variables it deems to be directly ethically relevant. As shall further be argued, such theories solve the problem of distributive justice by appeal to directly ethically relevant variables that are either 'non-rival' or, ideally, 'equal'.

Reduction to non-rivalry

Non-rivalry can take either of two forms. In the one case, there might be no rivalry

438

because giving more of the items referred to by these variables to one social entity does not preclude giving more of them to others, as well, up to the point where all entities are satiated. This is, for example, the case of 'basic liberties' or the 'rights of man and of the citizens' – things like a right to worship, speak freely, to apply for positions, to hold property, to compete, to exchange, to vote, not to be arrested arbitrarily, to be judged fairly according to 'due process of law', and so on. Giving one person (or social entity, more generally) more of one of these rights does not imply giving less of any of these rights to anyone else, although others might of course be adversely affected in other ways.

In the second case, the variables that are directly ethically relevant are not even assigned in themselves to the social entities under consideration – although they are related more or less directly to variables concerning those entities. Examples include cases where the variable deemed to be directly ethically relevant is a global social aim (such as national power, social welfare, culture or nature *per se*) or some quality of society.

Equality as non-arbitrariness or rationality

Equality as an end is equality of directly ethically relevant variables. These variables can have various forms: these can, for instance, be equal facts or equal rules (functions). They can also have various natures. This crucially differentiates alternative theories, in ways which will be discussed shortly. First, however, it is essential to explain the basic reason for equality. Far from being an arbitrary ethical stance, equality is, on the contrary, a requirement of non-arbitrariness.

Equality results from putting a moral value on non-arbitrariness, in the sense of requiring a reason (rationality). Suppose the ethic is used for choosing a policy. This is the choice of a unique set of the relevant variables among the alternatives (there may exist other variables, not considered relevant here). Then, if there is no arbitrariness, the ethic should pick out a unique good or just set of those variables. The resulting state includes the considered situations of claimants (or 'justiciables', more generally); and it depends on all relevant parameters, including all the relevant characteristics of the justiciables. If this relation is not arbitrary, it must allow for a permutation of two justiciables, in both their relevant characteristics and their situations. Then if two justiciables with the same relevant characteristics had different just situations, the same reason would also declare 'just' the state resulting from a permutation of their situations between themselves. But this makes two outcomes 'just', whereas the completeness of the reason implies that justice must designate only one. Therefore, justiciables with the same relevant characteristics should have the same just situation. In particular, when no different relevant characteristics are mentioned in a problem of justice, justice is equality.

Considerations of non-arbitrariness also enter into the choice of the variables and, in particular, of what characteristics are the relevant ones. This is what differentiates the various theories of justice and sets them in opposition to one another.

Non-arbitrariness is not, however, the only possible reason for equality. Another may be avoiding the social effects of jealousy, when the propensity to this sentiment cannot be eradicated.

Liberties

Justice concerns social entities with purposes. These entities are therefore also 'agents' which can perform 'actions' and are endowed with a 'will'. A will has 'intentions' and can influence (or 'cause' or 'determine', at least in part) certain acts of the agent. An 'action' of an agent is a set of wilful (or voluntary) acts of the agent aiming at the same objective. An agent's action can be said to be more 'free' when it is more 'caused by that agent's will'. The other causes of an action constitute 'constraints'. They determine the corresponding 'domain of liberty' (or 'of possibilities' or 'of choice'). A 'right', in these terms, is just a socially defined domain of liberty.

The aim of an agent's actions can be either a 'final aim' of the agent, or it can be an 'intermediary aim' that affects the agent's final aims. Examples of final aims of individuals are happiness, need-satisfaction, self-fulfilment, living a well-considered 'good life', and so on.

An agent-oriented social ethic values directly either (or both) the final aims of the relevant agents or the possibilities of the relevant agents. Liberty is valued as a means to the agent's final aims. It can thus also have an indirect value. But that is hardly the end of the story, for as Tocqueville (1843) said 'he who values freedom for anything but for itself does not deserve it and will soon lose it.' Another reason for valuing liberty is that it manifests agency. This is the ontological–existential value of liberty, and touches upon questions of responsibility and dignity. Agents themselves may value their own liberty for either, or both, of these two reasons. (They may also dislike responsibility and the costs and 'anguish' of choice.)

Three dimensions of liberty can be isolated in the following fashion. An 'action' can be seen as a set of 'acts' using 'means' for an 'aim'. The acts, the aim and the relation between them constitute the 'process'.

Since the agent's will can influence the world only through certain capacities of the agent, an action always employs means of some sorts. Means indeed include capacities intrinsic to the agent, as well as tools and other forms of external property. They also include anything giving rise to 'social power', understood as that which gives one agent the capacity to influence the acts of other agents by force or by inducement (i.e. in opposition to their wills, or in accordance with and thanks to them). Pre-eminently among these are income and wealth – which is to say, purchasing power (the power to induce without persuading), which enables the agent to secure voluntary services or transfers from other agents through exchange.

The constraints on an action can bear either: (1) on the availability of the *means* for action; or (2) on the *acts*, given the means; or (3) on the *aim*, given the acts and means, i.e. either on the aim or product itself, or on its relation to the acts or the means that cause it. Reducing constraints of each of these types increases 'means-freedom' (or just 'means'), 'act-freedom' and 'aim-freedom', respectively.

'Liberalism' is defined as a social ethic that advocates liberty, in general. Given these three types of liberty, however, that ethic can be seen to contain 'act-liberalism', 'aim-liberalism', 'process-liberalism' that is both, and 'means-liberalism'.

The field of modern theories of justice

Basic issues and theories

These distinctions structure the field of contemporary theories of distributive justice in the following manner, that will be explained in detail in the following sections:

1 Liberty of acts, aims and hence processes can (a) be at satiety for all agents, and (b) be non-rival among agents, in the sense that any rivalry can be attributed to the allocation of means and managed by it.

2 As a consequence, 'full act-freedom' is a very strong position. It is, for instance, the 1789 Declaration's 'Rights of Man and of the Citizen' or Rawls' (1971) 'basic liberties'.

3 By its very definition, full economic process-freedom dictates solutions to all distributional issues. It allocates the product to its producer; requires unfettered freedom of exchanges; justifies bequest; and, with some qualifications, allocates natural resources. This leaves nothing else to be distributed and precludes any redistribution. Distribution reduces to remuneration and restitution, and distributive justice to this form of compensatory justice. (The basic steps of this theory are made more precise at pp. 451–3 below.) This is the central, founding theory of the modern world. It powerfully says 'this is mine because I made it, because I bought it with well-earned money, or because I was given it.' It is the main ideology of capitalism. It is the 'proprietarianism' of Locke (1690) and Nozick (1974). Paradoxically, it is also the theory of Marx (1867), the difference between them bearing just on the question of whether the supply of wage-labour is free (as it formally is) or is forced (since the worker has no other choice, all his life long). Extended to the public correction of 'market failures' according to implicit 'liberal social contracts', this theory finally leads to a notable role for the public sector and to notable transfers which implement effective full-process freedom (Kolm, 1985).

4 With less than full economic aim-freedom, (re)distribution according to some other criteria becomes possible. These will necessarily be according to criteria either of 'efficient egalitarianism' or of 'social ends'.

5 Social ends provide 'indirect distributive justice', either aggregating or transcending individual ends or means. Aggregation can be either of individual end-fulfilment (leading to 'general utilitarianism') or of individual means (like maximizing global income). In the case of transcendence, the social ends in view might concern the nation or culture or some such.

6 Egalitarian theories are distinguished according to the variables concerning claimants that are deemed to be directly ethically relevant. These can be either 'the fulfilment of agents ends' or means to fulfil them. Hence, these theories are forms either of 'end-egalitarianism' or of 'means-egalitarianism'. These correspond to what are elsewhere (Kolm, 1971) called, respectively, 'justice' and 'equity': the former referring to equality of 'utility', the latter to equality of liberty.

7 Means-egalitarianisms might seek to equalize means at any of three stages of the economic process.

   (a) *Resources* (or, in the economists' term, 'primary resources') (Kolm, 1971; Dworkin, 1981). 'Exploitation' relates to the unequal allocation of 'capital', that is, produced primary resources (Roemer, 1982). Direct redistribution of human capital interferes with act-freedom, however.

(b) *Power* (or, in Rawls' (1971) term, 'primary goods'). This comes either in the form of purchasing power provided by income (flow) or wealth (stock), or in the form of other kinds of power provided by social positions.

(c) *Consumption goods*. 'Specific egalitarianism' shares out equally specific goods (e.g. Tobin, 1970), eventually within broad 'spheres of justice' (Walzer, 1983). Sold resources become income, which buys consumption goods that satisfy individuals' ends.

8 Act-freedom (either for direct ethical reasons, or for decentralized informational efficiency, or for costs of constraints) limits the possible redistributions, since confiscation deters production or exchange. This may render equality inefficient or impossible. Furthermore, differences in inherent consumptive-evaluative capacities may be uncompensatable, which may also prevent or render inefficient any kind of equalization of the satisfaction one derives from life. This leads to forms of 'second-best distributive justice' (of, more particularly, 'second-best efficient egalitarianism') such as 'practical justice' (Kolm, 1971) and Rawls' (1971) 'difference principle'.

9 Criteria could be mixed. We might, for example, want to consider both total income and the inequality in its distribution; and we might, furthermore, want to differentiate these inequalities according to their various different ethical properties.

10 Minimal needs satisfaction may be the most important criterion of justice (see, for instance, Braybrooke, 1987; Doyal and Gough, 1991).

11 Actual justice is 'open dialectical rational moral polyarchy', the method of which is the central question, either through correct dialogue or communication, or by the methodology specific to questions of justice.

Figure 22.1 summarizes the whole modern question of distributive justice. It situates the main theories according to their positions on the basic issues at each point in the socioeconomic process.

Freedom to act: full basic liberties

The crucial distinction between the liberty to act *per se* and the availability of means to do so is emphasized in various ways. Act-freedoms correspond to the 1789 Declaration's 'Rights of Man and of the Citizens' (for a discussion, see Kolm, 1993), to Marx's (1843) 'formal freedoms', to Rawls' (1971) 'basic liberties', and so on. Means – 'primary goods' to Rawls (1971), 'resources' to Dworkin (1981) – must be added in order to obtain Marx's 'real freedom'. The 'right to hold property', mentioned (twice) by the 1789 Declaration of the Rights of Man and by Rawls, is an act-freedom which does not by itself imply any right to hold, as a means, any specific amount of property.

An agent can be 'satiated' in terms of act-freedom but not usually in terms of means-freedom. Indeed, being satiated in respect of some means typically results from some limitation in other, complementary means (including personal capacities to consume or to use).

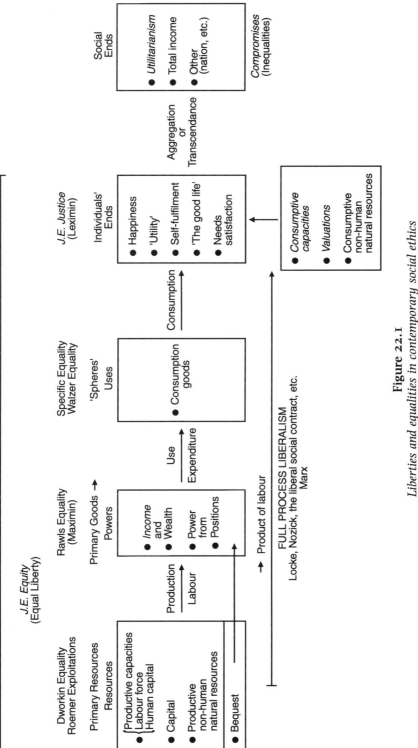

Figure 22.1

Liberties and equalities in contemporary social ethics

443

Corresponding act-freedoms and means-freedoms are 'complementary', in the economists' sense. They are strictly so at the 'zero' level, in the sense that at least some of each must exist for the other to have any actuality: unusable means are of no avail, and an act does not exist without some means. Yet, for any given level of attainment of an aim, there is a rough substitutability between means- and act-freedoms: for instance, having the same income but less access to a market is roughly equivalent to having the same access with less income; and having a reduced right to compete in processes of election or selection can produce the same result as having less talent.

Actions of different agents are 'rival' whenever it is necessarily the case that the more one agent achieves his aim, the less other agents achieve theirs. Distinguishing carefully, however, it turns out that the cause of rivalry can almost always be seen as resting in the means rather than in the realm of act-freedom.

Giving an agent more liberty of either sort enables him to pursue his own aims better. Other agents might be either indifferent to this expansion of his liberty or they might even favour it: a seller, for example, benefits from a buyer's having more income or more rights to buy, and a buyer benefits from a seller's having more rights to sell or more commodities for sale. Or, yet again, expanding the liberty of one might undermine the aims of others, as when a competitor gets more means (or more rights) to compete.

In that case, for an expansion of an act-freedom, many items can be used to compensate others for their losses, without in the end eating up all the gains. Therefore on the whole, and after appropriate transfers, a general increase in act-freedom is likely to enable everyone to fulfil their final aims at least as well or better than under less act-free states. And of course, this increase of liberty might also be valued *per se*, for ontological-existential reasons. Thus, an agent-oriented social ethic should probably advocate full act-freedom, at least in the economic sphere.

Most contemporary theories of justice do just that. Certain theories, such as the 1789 Declaration's arguments for basic rights and Rawls' (1971) arguments for 'basic liberties', say that the set of act-freedoms should be equal and maximal for all individuals. Usually, though – and in the economic sphere, always – the principle can just be that all agents be satiated in act-freedoms. Free exchange, and free collective agreement more generally, are prime examples of rights (rights of veto on the process in view) that are equal for all and, indeed, satiated for all.

Process-freedom and aim-constraints

In the economic sphere, 'full act-freedom' forbids various things. Among them are forced labour of all kinds (from slavery or *corvée* to conscript labour, 'socialist' obligations to work or assignment to jobs); barriers to market entry; discrimination not relevantly based on capacities. It implies the right to hold property, to exchange, sell and buy, and so on (although it does not imply that returns on those processes are not taxed).

'Full process-freedom' implies, in addition, 'full aim-freedom'. Normally, the aim of labour is to benefit from the product; the aim of an exchange is to benefit from what one receives; the aim of a gift is that the receiver benefits from it (in particular, the aim of bequest that the heir benefits from the inheritance). Full process-freedom thus implies, respectively: the classical 'right to the full product of one's labour'; the right to unfettered and untaxed exchange; and the right to full gift and full bequest.

These are the starting points of full process-liberalism, elaborated below pp. 451–3. This theory will indeed end up with certain taxes; but these are designed merely as implementation of this liberty. On this theory, nothing is available for redistribution according to any other criterion.

Backtracking from full aim-freedom, though, some redistribution of some such sort is indeed possible. This creates the room – and indeed the necessity – for some other style theory of distributive justice.

Theories of non-full process-freedom

These other theories of justice consider, as directly ethically relevant, either something that favours agents' own ends or else some global social end. These social ends either aggregate or transcend the items favoured by individuals. The aggregation can be either of agents' fulfilment of their ends (a kind of utilitarianism), or of agents' means (such as global social income). Transcendent aims can refer to groups, nations, cultures, nature, and so on (Sandel, 1982; Kymlicka, 1989).

Making agents' own ends or means as directly ethically relevant necessarily implies equality as an ideal, thus leading to a form of egalitarianism. Egalitarianisms can be distinguished according to the variables they regard as directly ethically relevant. Hence the question, 'equality of what?' There are, *a priori*, two types of answers. The variables could be either the agents' fulfilment of their ends, or the agents' means to fulfil their ends.

The difference between them is that 'ends-justice' takes into account, along with the effects of means, the effects of other items that 'means-justice' regards as irrelevant to the problem of justice. These items fall into two categories. One is the agents' own view of their end – their 'own conception of the good' as Rawls (1971) puts it. The other category includes agents' capacities to consume, to enjoy life or to fulfil their ends. These are means (such as the absence of handicaps, strength, intelligence, beauty, culture, tastes) which are inherent to the agent. They are not transferable and may be only imperfectly compensatable.

Second-best distributive justice

Egalitarianism may settle for less than strict equality of the relevant variables for various reasons: because they compromise with another egalitarianism or some other social end; or because strict equality is impossible; or because strict equality would be inefficient, in the sense that every claimant would prefer some other unequal possible state. For one obvious example, announcing that incomes will be equalized in a large economy where people work freely for income would lead to zero labour and labour income. Or no transfer could compensate people for certain kinds of handicaps in their capacity for enjoying life.

In particular, act-freedom constrains in this manner redistributions made possible by constraints (such as taxes) on aims or on the relation between acts and aims. Act-freedom may be adopted for the direct ethical reason described above; but it can also be for other reasons, not directly ethical, which even illiberal egalitarianisms and 'social-end theories' may have to take into account. One is the informational efficiency of free, decentralized action, whenever the agent has superior information – particularly concerning his own ends and capacities. Another is the costs, difficulties and impossibilities in constraining agents, in monitoring and enforcing constraints, in preventing shirking, and so on.

If we tax away all the products of labour, all the benefits of exchange or all of gifts received, then the act-free reaction may be to abstain from labour, exchange and giving. In that case nothing at all would be extracted by these taxes. Hence, the possibility of redistribution is itself constrained by this 'disincentive effect'.

Furthermore, individuals have both productive capacities and consumptive and evaluative ones. One person's owning the productive capacities of somebody else violates act-freedom (it would permit forced labour), and owning a share in their output produces the disincentive effects noted above. The non-transferability becomes absolute for consumptive and evaluative capacities: these are such that nobody else can use them or benefit from them. Furthermore, the effects of inequalities in these dimensions may not be fully compensatable by transfers of any other items.

Contemporary theorists of justice

Justice and Equity

In *Justice and Equity* (Kolm, 1971), two possible types of equality are considered. 'Justice' refers to the equality of individual end-fulfilment – perhaps of 'satisfaction', 'utility' or 'happiness'. 'Equity' refers to the equality of liberty, for reasons to be elaborated below.

The theory of *'justice'*, thus conceived, faces two problems. One is how to give meaning to interpersonal comparisons of end-fulfilment. The second one concerns questions of 'second-best efficient egalitarianism': what shall we do when some unequal solutions leave everyone better off than all possible equal solutions, or when equality is impossible?

The answer proposed for this second question – called 'practical justice' – is, technically, 'lexical maximin' (or 'leximin'). That is to say, choose the possible state where the least-satisfied individual is the most satisfied; if there is more than one solution of which that is true, then choose the state that best satisfies the next-least-satisfied individual; and so on. 'Practical justice' is equivalent to 'justice' when there exists an equal solution that does not suffer such inefficiencies of the sort discussed in the previous section.

The answer proposed to the question of interpersonal comparison is the concept of 'fundamental preferences' (following Kolm, 1968). Individuals commonly express preferences not only on what they have but also on what they are – and in particular on what makes them value what they have. They often wish they were less sensitive to certain misfortunes, that they were more appreciative of certain things, that they had a certain sort of training, culture, experience or nature. If the observer conceptually extrapolates this remark to its logical extreme – irrespective of any practical informational difficulty for the observed – the resulting preferences would necessarily be the same for all individuals, since what differentiates the individuals has been incorporated in the *objects* of preferences. These identical, common preferences are 'fundamental preferences'. These preferences also result from the fact that we can sometimes say that one person is 'more satisfied' or 'happier' than another (furthermore, when this is difficult to say, we can assume that the reason is a lack of information on how these persons feel). 'Fundamental preferences' provide conceptual meaning to expressions such as that one individual's ends are 'more fulfilled than' (or 'as well fulfilled as') another's, and that one individual is 'more satisfied' or 'happier' than (or 'as satisfied' or 'happy' as) another.

'Equity', in the technical economic sense, means merely that 'no one prefers another's allocation to one's own' (Tinbergen, 1946; Foley, 1964; Kolm, 1971; Baumol, 1986; and others). This property is satisfied, however, if and only if there exists a domain of individual choice such that each individual allocation can be considered as chosen by this individual on this domain, the same domain for all. And that is equivalent to saying that 'equity', thus conceived, characterizes 'equal liberty'.

(The proof of this proposition is straightforward. Identical domains of choice imply this criterion, since then each individual could have chosen an allocation identical to the one chosen by anyone else. Conversely, if it is true that no one prefer's another's allocation to one's own, then there must exist domains of choice such that the individuals' free choice on identical domains yield the overall allocation under consideration, since the set of actual individual allocations is one such.)

This 'equal liberty' could consist in, or include, equality with respect to: the 'rights of man' (Rawls' (1971) 'basic liberties'); resources; income or wealth; power; hence Rawls' (1971) 'primary goods'; opportunity, more-or-less extensively defined (with, in particular, more-or-less personal capacities being included in the definition of 'opportunity'); market possibilities, in the form of equality of tradeable resources and of exchange opportunities; and so on. This latter 'free exchange from equal resources' is of particular interest, in this connection.

Rawls' Theory of Justice

John Rawls' (1971) *Theory of Justice* is the most influential contemporary work on the subject. (For surveys, see Daniels, 1975; Pettit, 1980; Kukathas and Pettit, 1991.) For Rawls, what is directly relevant for social ethics and justice is the individuals' means to pursue their own ends and to live whatever 'good life' they choose for themselves.

These means are 'basic liberties', on the one hand, and 'primary goods', on the other. The former are the act-freedoms in all fields, which also implies non-discrimination. Rawls' 'basic liberties' correspond (with the single exception of their treatment of taxation) to the 'Rights of Man and of the Citizen' of the 1789 Declaration. Rawls' 'primary goods' are essentially social power – either purchasing power derived from flows (income) or stocks (wealth), or other power obtained from positions. To these, Rawls sometimes adds 'opportunities' and the means for promoting 'self-respect'.

Rawls establishes priorities to solve inevitable conflicts among these two criteria. First come basic liberties, then non-discrimination, then primary goods. The set of basic liberties should, first of all, be the same for all and, within that constraint, maximal (or, as Rawls (1982) says elsewhere, 'adequate'). Primary goods should ideally be allocated equally, as well. But seeing that a thoroughly egalitarian allocation of primary goods faces a problem of disincentives in production, of the sort discussed above (pp. 445–6), Rawls falls back on the 'difference principle', according to which the lowest individual endowment is maximized.

On its face, such a theory of justice raises many questions. As with 'primary goods', might not unequal basic liberties none the less provide more basic liberties for everybody? Why not allow one person to have more of one basic liberty, and another more of some other, in order to serve better their own different aims? How do we identify the least well-off individual, when one primary good is the lowest for one person and some other is lowest for another? How can we maximize a multidimensional bundle of primary goods? Could not individual aims be better served by other priorities, or by compromises among Rawls' various principles?

Furthermore, in modern economies there is an artificial separation – which recurs in Rawls' theory – between capacities that individuals use to produce 'income' and capacities that they use in consuming with it (or in directly fulfilling their own ends, more generally). Now, Rawls wants to compensate to the utmost for people's having poor productive capacities; but he does not propose to compensate at all for people's having poor evaluative, appreciative and even productive-like consumptive capacities (strength, intelligence, and so on). Is this consistent? Income transfers or the financing of specific policies can try to compensate for differences in both types of capacities. Indeed, the vast array of public policies in health and education aim in part at improving consumptive capacities among people with poor health, poor home environment and narrow cultural outlooks.

Finally, Rawls asserts that people would agree with his 'principles of justice'. Yet if this were so then producers would share his egalitarian ideal and the most productive people would work voluntarily to realize it, rather than reducing their output in response to redistributive policies. Then there would be no problem of 'second-best efficient egalitarianism' and no need for the 'difference principle' (Narveson, 1976; Barry, 1989).

Now, Rawls' whole construction implicitly answers these criticisms – by logical necessity, or almost so. This has already been seen with respect to 'basic liberties', which can indeed be at satiety for all since they are act-freedoms.

Rawls deduces his principles from a theory of a 'social contract', that is, a hypothetical unanimous agreement. To eliminate the 'arbitrariness' of natural endowments of capacities, his hypothetical contract has individuals choosing general rules for their society 'before' they receive what makes them different from one another. In the 'original position' or 'behind the veil of ignorance', as he puts it, everyone prefers the same rules because everyone is identical with everyone else.

These 'original' (or 'noumenal') individuals are rational in the sense that each has 'a coherent set of preferences between the options open to him'. Each is capable of comparing the overall alternatives, defined by both the state of society and who he will happen to be. These comparisons will be according to a set of preferences which are the same for all individuals in the 'original position', since everyone there is identical. Those identical preferences bear on who one will be, what position one will be in and what one will have: which is to say, they are the 'fundamental preferences' discussed above.

448

Such preferences, when the primary goods are the variables, permit us to determine not only which actual, embodied individual is worst-off but also when that person's situation is the best it possibly can be. Consumptive capacities, notice, are among the distinctive characteristics of individuals, so this maximin rule strives to compensate for the effects of people's differences in respect of them. Finally, if the maximization of the position of the worst endowed does not yield unique, determinate distributions, the same is to be done with the second worst, and so on. This transforms the maximin into 'leximin'. Finally, one obtains 'practical justice' of the sort presented above.

Still, it is surely implausible that all society should be set up so exclusively for the benefit of the least well off. (This is especially so if the least well off are badly off just because they have low enjoyment capacities: this might happen under the 'social contract' here in view, although not with Rawls' 'difference principle' bearing only on the allocation of 'primary goods'.) There are limits to 'practical justice' as a universal and unique criterion, which individuals in Rawls' 'original position' are bound to appreciate. Indeed, the classical theory of 'rational' choice under uncertainty holds that they should choose the rules of society that maximize the *mathematical expectation* of a 'utility function', that can represent the 'fundamental preference ordering' described above.

(Actual individuals, of course, often do not follow these rational prescriptions for choice in situations of uncertainty. Part of the reason has to do with the effects of sentiments concerning the process rather than the result (disappointment, hope, and so on). Part of the reason has to do with the limits on people's time and attention, leading them to focus more than rationally they should on extreme possibilities. Even if for such reasons actual individuals fail to abide by the prescriptions of rational decision-making under uncertainty, one could none the less argue that it is only prudent for them to abide by them.)

The uncertainty in view in Rawls' theory concerns which specific real individual each proto-individual in the 'original position' will actually turn out to be. If the set of individual characteristics to be assigned is known, and if each proto-individual has the same chances of receiving any given set of actual individual characteristics, then rational choice in the original position dictates maximization of the sum of individual utilities (cf. Kolm, 1985). That is to say, the solution is a form of utilitarianism. This is exactly the theory that was presented by John Harsanyi in 1953. The practical consequence with regard to allocation depends on the structure of utility functions and on the feasible set: it may, in the end, turn out not to be far from the implications of 'practical justice', though the utilitarian version will never display the unacceptably extreme characteristics noted above.

However, such an individual 'in the original position' may well unjustly sacrifice an actual individual if this enables another actual individual to have much more, since it may then be worthwhile to take this risk about one's future possible embodiments. Hence, rational self-interest 'behind the veil of ignorance' may be a poor guide to actual justice. Then, the definition of justice has to rely on rational egalitarianism, (possibly a second-best definition), and this may well restore Rawls' solution, albeit with a different justification.

Finally, notice that it might be perfectly rational for the rich both to want justice and, at the same time, to try to evade its requirements. Suppose the most productive individuals, being convinced by the principles of justice, would like to give part of their product to the poorest individuals, without reducing their total output. Yet suppose there are several such productive individuals. Then any one of them might be ready to give only if the others give too. That is simply to say that he might not value the rule of justice over his own interest, to the point of singlehandedly giving (to any great extent), regardless of what the others do independently of his own action. Or at least he may not do so, when they do not give sufficiently. This partly egoistic, partly moral mentality is actually really rather realistic: as Pascal says, 'man is neither angel nor beast'.

In such a case, all these individuals would welcome an institutional or public obligation transferring income from all of them to the poorest. In their own individual behaviour, they would none the less behave egoistically subject to the constraint imposed for this transfer (an income tax, for example); and consequently increasing transfers may actually induce them to reduce output. This gives rise to a problem of 'second-best efficient egalitarianism', in spite of the fact that everyone accepts the general rules of justice.

Technically, this situation is one of 'collective gift-giving', a particular instance of 'the problem of collective action'. The end in view (be it characterized as 'maximizing the income of the poor', or 'promoting the rule of justice' in the abstract) is a 'public good', and that raises the classical problem of 'free-riding'. The free-riding aspect of social rules in general is the basis of all social contract theories that derive a justification for public coercion from a putative voluntary unanimous agreement. Rousseau (1762) is the keenest expositor of this view: recall, in this light, his famous remark that people 'must be forced to be free' (cf. Kolm, 1993a). But the same basic dynamic can also be assumed in Rawls' framework (Pettit, 1986).

Furthermore, the individuals may well have a dual standard, one for their own self interest, and one for the ideal social policy.

In his later writings, Rawls (1985; 1987) has emphasized – in a spirit of pluralism and toleration – that his proposal is 'political, not metaphysical'. The aspiration is to show how various cultural traditions can coexist peacefully within the same polity. Most commonly, though, the poor come disproportionately from certain distinct communities, and making them as well off as possible would require substantial transfers across those communities. Yet the cross-community sense of solidarity that would be politically required to sustain such transfers is conspicuously lacking. In the United States, white communities are not about to do everything they possibly can to raise living standards in the poor black community, which is what the 'difference principle' would require. Similarly, in old countries where the culture is deeply embodied in the historical places, recent immigration leading suddenly to a plurality of cultures raises deep problems of cultural identity and tradition.

Dworkin's resourcism

Suppose, as Rawls asserts, justice is concerned with individuals' means rather than with what they do with them. Then there is no reason to consider income and other primary goods that are produced by individuals. The relevant variables should instead be the unproduced 'primary goods'. We are then led to advocate equal sharing of primary goods, together with their free exchange, justified as being a process-freedom (Kolm, 1971; Dworkin, 1981).

While it is perfectly possible to share out divisible resources of a non-human sort, that is not however possible with the personal capacities embodied in people themselves. One can, of course, imagine sharing rights in the outputs of these capacities. Or one can imagine hypothetical forms of 'fundamental insurance' against having received poor productive capacities at birth or in family upbringing that might give rise to transfers (Dworkin, 1981; Kolm, 1985). The problem, however, is not one of how to generate the rights but rather of how to implement them. If (for any number of reasons) we adopt the principle of act-freedom, and hence we preclude forced labour, then the transfers in view can only be implemented by reallocating the resulting output or income. And that yields the same disincentive effects as Rawls' solution, so once again we face a problem of 'second-best efficient egalitarianism'.

The only difference would be a purely formal one. The inequality here in view would legally take the form of unequal shares in individual capacities, with each one receiving a larger share of himself. But then the equal sharing of non-human resources cannot be maintained, either; and more should be allocated to people with lower skills (Kolm, 1985; Roemer, 1985).

Theories of exploitation

The opposite extreme of inequality in the ownership of capital – namely, the situation where many people do not own any – is both a cause and a consequence of 'exploitation' in the classic Marxian sense. Workers have nothing else to sell but their labour power, and the unconsumed product is accumulated in capital (Marx, 1867). Marx's own theory was marred by the limitations of his 'labour theory of value' (which is to say, of prices). Still, it has been very influential, and 'exploitation' is a powerful and widespread sentiment of injustice.

Several modern theories have attempted to rebuild this theory, using one or the other of the features of Marx's vision. Joan Robinson (1933) focuses on the exploitative potential of a monopoly in the demand for labour. Kolm (1984a) emphasizes the basic 'immorality' of the domination characterizing the wage relationship that Marx considers: renting labour power is akin to buying and selling it (which is to say, slavery). Weizsäcker (1972) concentrates on the inequality in inter-temporal consumption. Finally, Roemer (1982) defines exploitation according to the inequality in capital ownership: this enables him to consider other relevant kinds of exploitation, deriving from the unequal distribution of the human capital formed by socialization and education.

Walzer's specific egalitarianism

Claims of justice often attach to specific allocations or processes, rather than to the overall allocation. We commonly hear demands for equal access to education, health care, housing, culture, and so on. Tobin (1970) advocates general equality. Walzer (1983) argues that actual communities do not consider overall justice but, rather, such 'spheres of justice' with the relevant equality within each sphere.

To economists this seems irrational. It is a waste for people with different tastes to be forced to consume identical quantities of everything. And those inefficiencies are only partially mitigated by lumping items together into large 'spheres'. Indeed, there are only certain very special conditions under which specific egalitarianism can hope to be efficient (Kolm, 1977). Specific support is better based on other rationales such as basic needs or effects on children.

Full process-liberalism

We now present the rational construction of complete full process-liberalism:

1 Full process-liberalism is based on a single principle, that of full process-freedom.

2 The consequent 'right to the full product of one's labour' (discussed above, p. 445) implies that individuals have the 'usufruct of themselves', which is something short of classical 'self-ownership' that has been recently discussed by Cohen (1981; 1986).

3 Full process-freedom implies full freedom to transfer rights: rights to commit oneself, to exchange, to give, to bequeath, to make a collective agreement with any number of other persons. And it implies, *a priori*, that these rights should be without limits, constraints or taxes. Note that the outcome of a collective agreement is completely determined by the participants' resources (be they material resources, rights, information, bargaining skill, intelligence, speed or whatever).

4 The set of rights in society is 'fully liberally legitimate' if and only if: it has always been so in the past; it has never been violated; and full process-freedom has been respected all along the way. Of course, this will rarely prove true of any actual society's history, and rectifications of the effects of actual past violations may be required (Nozick, 1974, ch. 7; Phillips, 1979).

5 The allocation of initial rights to non-produced natural resources is reduced to process-freedom by collective agreement (eventually a putative one; see below). In this there will be a certain scope for the classical rule of 'first occupancy'.

6 Since ethical rights are not defined by the force of the right holder (they are not defined by 'might') they have to be protected by a particular dominant 'public' force. This includes rights born from agreements. That is the role of the minimal, 'nightwatchman' state derived by Locke (1690) from a social contract among owners and by Nozick (1974) through a hypothetical evolutionary process.

7 'Market failures' (or more generally 'agreement failures') result from three sources, which are often interlocked: (a) from difficulties in information and communication; (b) from difficulties in the setting of constraints; and (c) from difficulties due to certain strategic behaviour in the process of co-operation itself. Whenever a liberally legitimate free act, exchange or agreement (that is to say, one respecting the full liberal set of rights) is thus impeded, full process-liberalism requires us to recreate, as well as possible, whatever the outcome would have been. This hypothetical, putative agreement among any number of persons is a 'liberal social contract'. The duty to implement it is one which can be taken up by any person, but since some use of the public force is usually implied the state ordinarily has at least some role to play. What the public sector should do is then indicated by liberal

theory itself, together with theories of bargaining and information revealed by actual exchanges and political processes (Kolm, 1985; 1987a, b).

8 A series of taxes, in particular, will then result. These taxes are both voluntary and forced: each taxpayer prefers the set of taxes and the action it finances to their absence; yet, given what the others do, each would usually prefer not to pay himself. Extracting tax payments is then nothing more than the enforcement of a voluntary contract, albeit an hypothetical, putative one. This applies in particular to financing 'non-excludable public goods' (items that concern several persons who cannot be excluded specifically from the benefit). One particular very important application is the 'collective gift' described above (p. 450), where the public good is the income, or welfare or needs of the least well-off people. Then, the existence of even quite moderate levels of altruism or of a sense of justice leads the full process-liberalism to advocate public (and apparently 'forced') redistributive transfers which can be substantial.

Theories of market failure

Questions of the performance of the market and the corresponding role of the government lie at the heart of most present-day theories of distributive justice. Markets have well-known potentials for promoting liberty and welfare, but they often fail to realize that potential. And correcting those market failures carries clear distributional consequences. (Indeed, the very distribution resulting from markets can be considered either as good or as a failure.)

Theories differ widely, however, according to where they find market failures and according to the accounts they give of motivations, of governments and of ethics.

Locke and Nozick, for example, see no market failure; they praise the distribution resulting from the market; and they advocate only a minimal, rights-protecting state.

The correction of market failures by the public sector is studied by 'public economics'. 'Liberal public economics' studies the implicit agreements and exchanges that result from complete full process-liberalism, described above as 'liberal social contracts'; and it determines the corresponding government actions, taxes and transfers (Kolm, 1985; 1987a, b). By contrast, the much-studied 'welfarist public economics' uses another ethical criterion which aims at maximizing 'social welfare'; it includes many studies concerning aspects of the justice of distributions, such as inequality and poverty (Kolm, 1968–9, secs 6 and 7, and the subsequent literature).

Other influential economists, such as Friedrich Hayek (1976) and Milton Friedman (1962; see also Friedman and Friedman, 1981), advocate an economy that is about 95 per cent market and 5 per cent government. The large market role is for the sake of freedom, the small government role for the sake of welfare. The government's job is to take care of certain feeble market failures (externalities, non-excludable public goods) and to alleviate severe poverty, in addition of course to protecting rights.

Both Hayek and Friedman suppose that giving any larger role to government would necessarily diminish freedom, as well-meaning officials pursue the 'mirage of social justice' (Hayek, 1976). Hayek positively praises the development of a social 'spontaneous order'. Friedman concedes that the existing distribution came by chance anyway, and is therefore always unjust; his point is that to rely on a government to correct it can only be worse. The practical upshot is much the same either way.

David Gauthier's *Morals by Agreement* (1986) extraordinarily speaks only of market failures, 'public goods', externalities and the like, without once mentioning as remedies government, the state, the public sector, politics, voting or elections. Indeed Gauthier considers only one type of market failure, represented by the Prisoners' Dilemma; and he proposes that individuals should solve this problem through an ethic of co-operation (from which everybody gains) that picks out one specific outcome. This outcome is defined as 'the' rational solution to the bargaining problem, from an idealized starting point of non-coercive interaction.

Gauthier's solution – 'equal relative concessions' – is unfortunately meaningless, requiring as it does a concept of cardinal utility. The same problem plagues various other bargaining solutions, including most notably the Nash (1950) bargaining solution, discussed by Braithwaite (1955) and Barry (1989). The only exception is where this Nash solution is derived, as by Binmore and Rubinstein (in Binmore and Dasgupta, 1987), from behaviour under uncertainty: this cardinal utility then is the valid one of Neumann and Morgenstern (1944) for behaviour under uncertainty. 'Cardinal utility' has meaning if and only if one can compare 'differences in happiness or satisfaction'. It is not enough just to be able to say, 'I prefer A over B more than I prefer C over D': one must be able to express the preference of A over B as a meaningful difference in utility levels. That is not warranted by introspection, behavioural observation or reason.

Replacing 'utility' by 'income' would render Gauthier's prescriptions meaningful. Doing so might even be justified by Rawls' view that what is relevant to justice is not individuals' ends but the means to them. But then Gauthier could not deduce justice from bargaining, where it really is 'subjective utility' rather than 'objective pay-offs' that matters. Nash's reason for his solution would similarly disappear with any such substitution.

Self-styled 'libertarians' such as Murray Rothbard (1973) and David Friedman (1978) define liberty as the absence of government. Attaching as they do supreme value to liberty, government then becomes bad or evil, literally by definition. The protection of property is left to self-defence, or perhaps it is entrusted to profit-making protection firms. Logically, though, it is only to be expected that such firms would turn to racketeering and gang warfare.

Individuals could all avert the harm and save the resources used for combat and defence, however, by accepting a truce. This truce would inevitably take the form of following a certain set of rules, owing to the informational difficulties of agreeing all the specifics in advance. These rules, be they explicit or tacit, constitute what James Buchanan (1975) calls a 'constitution'. They serve to specify, most particularly, basic rights and a political process for dealing with market failures.

By Buchanan's definition of a constitution, this political process would have to be voluntary for everybody. Hence it amounts to a set of exchanges – for instance, of government services for votes. The important field of study called 'public choice' sets out to study political processes as free exchanges among exclusively self-interested individuals (power-seeking politicians, and such like). Distribution, and in particular public redistribution, results from this whole process (Buchanan and Tullock, 1962).

This theory can explain any inequality, serfdom or slavery, since, in the end, might makes right in this sort of constitution. The main point is that it is not an ethical theory. When it sounds most like an ethical stance, it is actually advocating rules that would make everybody better off and, hence, is not distributional. Its relevance to distributive justice and to social ethics in general lies basically just in denying the very relevance of their question: if everybody is exclusively self-interested for all relevant purposes, there exists nobody who could implement any social ethical ideals, which are then merely useless and sterile 'noises'.

That view has much realism about it. Yet reflecting carefully upon the motivations of and options before voters, statesmen and public servants, we cannot deny that judgments of social ethics and justice are at least sometimes influential. What Buchanan and the public choice school rightly show is that we should propose only theories for which there exists the motivation (as well as the power and the information) that would be required to implement them.

Utilitarianisms and social choice

This public choice perspective emerged as the third drastic reaction against 'utilitarianism', the social ethic that dominated the thought of both economists and English-speaking philosophers. In one voice, Rawls (1971) said that you *must not* do what utilitarianism prescribes; Buchanan (1975; Buchanan and Tullock, 1962) said that there is *nobody to do it*; and Arrow (1951) said that you *cannot meaningfully* do it.

Utilitarianism advocates maximizing the sum of individuals' pleasures less pains, or 'utilities'. This both determines the distribution and is egalitarian by virtue of the equality of the weights attached to individuals' pleasures or 'utilities' in the sum. It raises both moral and logical problems. The moral problems can be addressed by a number of adjustments that for instance advocate judging rules rather than acts or using modified utilities (Goodin, 1983). This lively debate occupies a vast literature (as an example, see Sen and Williams, 1982).

The logical problem is that the name 'sum' cannot be taken literally since nothing that can meaningfully represent 'pleasure' or 'happiness' can be strictly summed. This prompted economists to replace the 'sum' by a more general 'social welfare function'. Arrow (1953) shows that one cannot define a rule that derives such a function for any possible set of individuals' preferences while at the same time satisfying a few more or less necessary conditions. However, we do not need a solution for any possible preferences of the individuals. Indeed, we do not even need such a function, but only a determination of the social optimum given the actual possibilities. In fact, though, the optimum cannot be defined by the maximization of something which does not depend on the possibilities, in many cases where it has to be an equitable or balanced compromise among the possibilities.

However, if we follow Rawls in thinking that what is relevant for justice are individuals' means rather than their utilities, utilitarianism can be transformed into maximizing the sum of incomes, in particular. The summation then becomes meaningful, and this criterion is indeed widespread. (Judge Posner (1981) is one of its most articulate advocates.)

Yet if individual incomes are considered as directly relevant to inter-individual justice (as Rawls thinks), then non-arbitrariness leads one to advocate equal incomes. But, as we have noted (pp. 445–6), equal incomes are likely to be dominated by higher unequal incomes for all. Furthermore, even in situations where one must have less if another is to have more, should we not accept that someone (whose important needs are, let us assume, amply satisfied) has a *little* less if this permits that millions of others have *much* more? The problem then becomes a compromise between equality in the distribution and the size of the total. That requires us to compare various possible inequalities.

This comparison has given rise to an extensive literature. A natural criterion is that a transfer from a richer to a poorer person (so long as it does not cause those individuals actually to reverse their positions) is seen as decreasing inequality. This criterion, suggested by various people (among them, Pigou, Loria and Dalton), was shown to be mathematically equivalent to a number of other criteria that seem quite meaningful for defining 'more equal'; this led to the proposal of a number of ethically well-founded measures of inequality (Kolm, 1968).

Yet, even this simple criterion is not warranted. Suppose ten people have three units and one has zero. Suppose, now, that we transfer one unit from one of the former people to the latter person. Following this criterion, we would be led to say that inequality has been decreased. Yet one can also say that inequality has been increased, on the grounds that two people now deviate from the crowd whereas previously only one did.

Another problem is the following. It is commonly supposed that inequality remains the same if all incomes vary in the same proportion. But consider the pair of incomes, 0 and 1. Multiply both by 10: the distribution then becomes 0 and 10. Whoever would say that the inequality has remained the same? Most people indeed say that it has increased by 9. Of course, when the incomes are close to equal, varying them by the same proportion or by the same absolute amount comes to nearly the same thing. But that is irrelevant: it is for unequal distributions, not almost equal ones, that measuring inequality matters (Kolm, 1968; 1976; Atkinson, 1970).

Needs theories

When we think it better that an extra dollar should be given to the poor rather than to the rich, the reason we do standardly has less to do with the fact that that attenuates inequality and more to do with the fact that it alleviates poverty. Hence a focus on low incomes. The classical headcount of 'poor' with an income below a certain level was improved by the consideration of the total income deficit by Sen (1976) and others. This makes the measure of poverty an aspect of the logic of inequality just described. Yet all these approaches were strongly criticized for missing or hiding the essence of the problem of poverty, which – it was argued – requires concepts of need and sociological considerations.

Of course, genuine deprivation and wretchedness really do exist. But lower incomes *per se* measure neither inequality nor the level of unsatisfied needs. Indeed, in the real world, those with the lowest incomes often feel that their needs are best satisfied, either because they have philosophical-ethical-religious values leading them to tolerate (or even desire) poverty, or else because they live in stable traditional societies where all the needs they know of are being met. That is merely to say that deprivation and misery arise out of cultural, psychic and physiological situations. Ignoring that fact has led not only to meaningless statistics but also to deeply damaging policies under the banner of 'development'.

These features of needs have given rise to analyses of 'relative deprivation'. Here, 'relative' refers not so much to others' incomes or consumption levels. It points instead to what is considered 'normal' in any given society (Runciman, 1966), to the means of carrying out a good personal and social life as that society understands it (Townsend, 1971). Trying to produce an intrinsic definition of these essential needs is not merely a difficult task; it might even be an impossibly self-defeating task, because the definitional reference is cultural (basic cultural needs being defined as such by the very culture that creates them). By the same token, however, this renders the practical and political definition of these needs rather an easy matter, since there is *ex hypothesi* a rough consensus about them in the society concerned.

Any more extensive use of the concept of needs – an extreme example of which is Marx's (1875) proposal to give 'to each one according to his needs' in a society of men 'rich in needs' – inevitably raises various problems. These range from problems with the meaning and definition of needs to problems of respect of agents' own opinions, interpersonal comparisons and incentive effects of transfers.

Still, the concept of needs is bound to play a central role in the deep analysis of distributive justice, if only because it occupies a particular place at the intersection of the various otherwise incommensurable fields. 'Needs' play the role of a bridging concept. They are both 'is' and 'ought', 'objective' and 'subjective', an 'asset' and a 'liability', an 'existential condition' and a 'desire', satiable and expandable, a constraint even though to satisfy them is an intention (Braybrooke, 1987; Doyal and Gough, 1991).

Dialogue theories and method

It is easy to produce counter-examples showing that everybody rejects any social ethic that claims to answer all specific cases by the application of the same criterion, or the same set of criteria, or even by criteria belonging to a predetermined list. An overall social ethical position can only be a 'moral polyarchy'. This gives a prominent place to notions of method – of how we come to conclusions in social ethics. This question divides in two, one concerning ethical dialogue (argumentation and communication, and so on), the other concerning questions of method *per se*.

Ackerman's (1980) *Social Justice in the Liberal State* explores the rational constraints on arguments in a dialogue between competing claimers, so as to reach and determine a just solution. The 'communicative ethics' of Apel, Habermas and others is more ambitious, but perhaps less practical. (For critical commentaries, see Benhabib and Dallmayr, 1990.) Through exploring the phenomenology of ethics, this approach attempts to derive the just or good from the very conditions that makes mutual understanding possible. What is 'just' would be that which is recognized in an 'ideal speech situation'. This device is fanciful to be sure, but perhaps it is no more so than those of hypothetical social contracts or impartial observers.

The method of justice applies the general method of rational judgment to the specific questions of justice. This includes: the consequences of considering several comparable claimants and the logical structure of ethical equality ('isology'); the analysis of the sentiments of justice and injustice ('thymology'); the iterative induction concerning principles and their consequences (Plato's dialectics or Rawls' 'reflective equilibrium'); the similar comparison of principles; the analysis of the relevant generalizations; the use of introspection, empathy and 'objective subjectivity'; and so on (Kolm, 1993b).

Beyond justice?

When we hear someone making a claim of justice on his own behalf, his claim may sound right, but it does not, on the face of it, sound nice. Such claims may be motivated by needs; but they may also be motivated by greed, egoism, jealousy or envy. Sentiments of justice are second-best morality.

Sufficient altruism can take the conflict out of distributive justice, but it leaves the problem of the actual sharing. There is indeed a whole field of social sentiments and behaviour that mixes justice and altruism; or is intermediary between them; or amounts to altruism or gift-giving motivated by justice; or again, is voluntary actualization of justice. This field constitutes reciprocity, a central phenomenon of social life and an essential cement of societies (Kolm, 1984b; see also 1984c).

Finally, justice is an essential property of communities. It is defined by traditions and by shared culture, meanings and practices. History brings about this idea, maintains it and changes it, as writers such as Walzer (1983) and Taylor (1975) would have emphasized. Yet norms of justice – their origin, maintenance and change – are also something to be explained. These explanations both need the concepts and results of the 'pure theory of justice' and, at the same time, provide the empirical materials that feed it.

See also I ANALYTICAL PHILOSOPHY; 5 ECONOMICS; 6 POLITICAL SCIENCE; II LIBERALISM; I3 SOCIALISM; I4 AUTONOMY; I6 CONTRACT AND CONSENT; I7 CONSTITUTIONALISM AND THE RULE OF LAW; I9 DEMOCRACY; 2I DISCOURSE; 23 EFFICIENCY; 25 EQUALITY; 28 LEGITIMACY; 29 LIBERTY; 30 POWER; 3I PROPERTY; 33 RIGHTS; 4I WELFARE.

References

Ackerman, B. A.: *Social Justice in the Liberal State* (New Haven, Conn.: Yale University Press, 1980).

Arrow, K. J.: *Social Choice and Individual Values* (New Haven, Conn.: 1951); 2nd edn (New Haven, Conn.: Yale University Press, 1963).

Atkinson, A. B.: 'On the measurement of inequality', *Journal of Economic Theory*, 2 (1970), 244–63.

Barry, B.: *Theories of Justice* (Hemel Hempstead: Harvester Wheatsheaf, 1989).

Baumol, W. J.: *Superfairness* (Cambridge, Mass.: MIT Press, 1986).

Benhabib, S. and Dallmayr, F., eds: *The Communicative Ethics Controversy* (Cambridge, Mass.: MIT Press, 1990).

Binmore, K. and Dasgupta, P., eds: *The Economics of Bargaining* (Oxford: Blackwell, 1987).

Braithwaite, R. B.: *The Theory of Games as a Tool for the Moral Philosopher* (Cambridge: Cambridge University Press, 1955).

Braybrooke, D.: *Meeting Needs* (Princeton, NJ: Princeton University Press, 1987).

Buchanan, J. M.: *The Limits of Liberty* (Chicago: University of Chicago Press, 1975).

————— and Tullock, G.: *The Calculus of Consent* (Ann Arbor, Mich.: University of Michigan Press, 1962).

Cohen, G. A: 'Self-ownership, world-ownership and equality', *Justice and Equality Here and Now*, ed. F. S. Lucash (Ithaca, NY: Cornell University Press, 1986), pp. 108–35.

—————: 'Freedom, justice and capitalism', *New Left Review*, 126 (1981), 3–16.

Daniels, N., ed.: *Reading Rawls* (New York: Basic Books, 1975).

Doyal, L. and Gough, I.: *A Theory of Human Need* (London: Macmillan, 1991).

Dreze, J. and Sen, A. K.: *Hunger and Public Action* (Oxford: Clarendon Press, 1989).

Dworkin, R. M.: 'What is equality? Part II: equality of resources', *Philosophy and Public Affairs*, 10 (1981), 283–345.

Foley, D.: 'Resource allocation in the public sector', *Yale Economic Essays*, 7, 1 (1967), 45–98.

Friedman, D.: *The Machinery of Freedom*, 2nd edn (La Salle, Ill.: Open Court Press, 1978).

Friedman, M.: *Capitalism and Freedom* (Chicago: University of Chicago Press, 1962).

————— and Friedman, R.: *Free to Choose* (New York: Avon, 1981).

Gauthier, D.: *Morals by Agreement* (Oxford: Clarendon Press, 1986).

Goodin, R. E.: 'Laundering preferences', in *Foundations of Social Choice Theory*, ed. J. Elster and A. Hylland (Cambridge: Cambridge University Press, 1986).

Harsanyi, J. C.: 'Cardinal welfare in welfare economics and in the theory of risk-taking', *Journal of Political Economy*, 61 (1953), 434–5.

Hayek, F. A.: *Law, Legislation and Liberty* (Chicago: University of Chicago Press, 1976).

Kolm, S.-C.: 'The optimal production of social justice', *Economie Publique*, ed. H. Guitton and J. Margolis (Paris: CNRS, 1968), pp. 109–73; *Public Economics*, ed. H. Guitton and J. Margolis (London: Macmillan, 1969), pp. 145–201.

—————: *Justice et equité* (Paris: CEPREMAP, 1971; reprinted Paris: CNRS, 1972); *Justice and Equality*, trans. H. See (Cambridge, Mass.: MIT Press, 1992).

—————: 'Unequal inequalities', *Journal of Economic Theory*, 12 (1976), 416–42 and 13 (1976), 82–111.

—————: 'Multidimensional egalitarianism', *Quarterly Journal of Economics*, 91 (1977), 1–13.

—————: *Le Libéralisme moderne* (Paris: Presses Universitaires de France, 1984a).

—————: *La Bonne Economie: la réciprocité générale* (Paris: Presses Universiaires de France, 1984b).

—————: 'Altruism and efficiency', *Ethics*, 94 (1984c), 18–65.

—————: *Le Contrat social libéral* (Paris: Presses Universitaires de France, 1985).

—————: 'Public economics', *New Palgrave Dictionary in Economics*, ed. J. Eatwell et al. (London: Macmillan, 1987a), pp. 1047–55.

—————: 'The freedom and consensus normative theory of the state: the liberal social contract', *Individual Liberty and Democratic Decision-Making*, ed. P. Koslowski (Tübingen: Mohr, 1987b), pp. 98–127.

—————: 'The normative economics of unanimity and equality: equity, adequacy and fundamental dominance', *Markets and Welfare*, ed. K. J. Arrow (London: Macmillan, for the International Economics Association, 1991), pp. 243–86.

—————: 'Free and equal in rights: the philosophies of the 1789 Declaration of the Rights of Man and of the Citizen', *Journal of Political Philosophy*, 1 (1993a), forthcoming.

—————: *The General Theory of Justice* (Cambridge, Mass.: MIT Press, 1993b).

Kukathas, C. and Pettit, P.: *Rawls: A Theory of Justice and Its Critics* (Oxford: Polity Press, 1990).

Kymlicka, W.: *Liberalism, Community and Culture* (Oxford: Clarendon Press, 1989).

Locke, J.: *Second Treatise of Government* (1690), ed. P. Laslett (Cambridge: Cambridge University Press, 1960).

Marx, K.: 'Critique of the Gotha Programme' (1875), reprinted in *The Marx–Engels Reader*, ed. R. C. Tucker (New York: Norton 1972), pp. 363–98.

————: 'On the Jewish question' (1844), reprinted in The *Marx–Engels Reader*, ed. R. C. Tucker (New York: Norton, 1972), pp. 24–51.

————: *Das Kapital*, vol. 1 (1867), trans. B. Fowkes (Harmondsworth: Penguin Books, 1976).

Narveson, J.: 'A puzzle about economic justice in Rawls' theory', *Social Theory and Practice*, 4 (1976), 1–27.

Nash, J. F.: 'The bargaining problem', *Econometrica*, 18 (1950), 155–62.

Neumann, J. von and Morgenstern, O.: *Theory of Games and Economic Behavior* (Princeton, NJ: Princeton University Press, 1944).

Nozick, R.: *Anarchy, State and Utopia* (New York: Basic Books, 1974).

Pettit, P.: *Judging Justice* (London: Routledge & Kegan Paul, 1980).

————: 'Free riding and foul dealing', *Journal of Philosophy*, 83 (1986), 361–79.

Phillips, D.: *Equality, Justice and Rectification* (London: Academic Press, 1979).

Posner, R. A.: *The Economics of Justice* (Cambridge, Mass.: Harvard University Press, 1981).

Rawls, J.: *A Theory of Justice* (Cambridge, Mass.: Harvard University Press, 1971).

————: 'The basic liberties and their priority', *The Tanner Lectures on Human Values*, ed. S. MacMurrin (Cambridge: Cambridge University Press, 1982), vol. 3, pp. 1–89.

————: 'Justice as fairness: political not metaphysical', *Philosophy and Public Affairs*, 14 (1985), 223–51.

————: 'The idea of an overlapping consensus', *Oxford Journal of Legal Studies*, 7 (1987), 1–25.

Robinson, J.: *The Economics of Imperfect Competition* (London: Macmillan, 1933).

Roemer, J. E.: *A General Theory of Exploitation and Class* (Cambridge, Mass.: Harvard University Press, 1982).

————: 'Equality of talent', *Economics and Philosophy*, 1 (1985), 151–88.

Rothbard, M.: *For a New Liberty* (New York: Macmillan, 1973).

Rousseau, J.-J.: *Du contrat social* (1762), trans. G. D. H. Cole (London: Dent, 1913).

Runciman, W. G.: *Relative Deprivation and Social Justice* (London: Routledge, 1966).

Sandel, M.: *Liberalism and the Limits of Justice* (Cambridge: Cambridge University Press, 1982).

Sen, A. K.: 'Poverty: an ordinal approach to measurement', *Econometrica*, 44 (1976), 219–31.

———— and Williams, B., eds: *Utilitarianism and Beyond* (Cambridge: Cambridge University Press, 1982).

Taylor, C.: 'The nature and scope of distributive justice', *Philosophical Papers* (Cambridge: Cambridge University Press, 1985), vol. 2, pp. 289–317.

Tinbergen, J.: *Redelijke Inkoensverdeling* (Haarlem: De Gulden Pers, 1946).

Tobin, J.: 'On limiting the domain of inequality', *Journal of Law and Economics*, 13 (1970), 363–78.

Tocqueville, A. de: *Democracy in America* (1843), trans. G. Lawrence, ed. J. P. Meyer and M. Lerner (New York: Harper & Row, 1966).

Townsend, P.: *The Concept of Poverty* (London: Heinemann, 1971).

Walzer, M.: *Spheres of Justice* (Oxford: Blackwell, 1983).

Weizsäcker, C. C.: 'Modern capital theory and the concept of exploitation', *Kyklos*, 26 (1973), 245–81.

Further reading

Campbell, T.: *Justice* (London: Macmillan, 1988).

Feldman, A.: *Welfare Economics and Social Choice Theory* (Boston: Kluwer/Nijhoff, 1980).

Harsanyi, J. C.: 'Cardinal welfare, individualistic ethics and interpersonal comparisons of utility', *Journal of Political Economy*, 63 (1955), 309–21.

Kamenka, E. and Tay, A. E.-S., eds: *Justice* (London: Edward Arnold, 1979).

Macpherson, C. B.: *The Rise and Fall of Economic Justice* (Oxford: Oxford University Press, 1985).

Miller, D.: *Social Justice* (Oxford: Clarendon Press, 1976).

Moulin, H.: *The Strategy of Social Choice* (Amsterdam: North-Holland, 1983).

Paul, J., ed.: *Reading Nozick* (Oxford: Blackwell, 1982).

Rawls, J.: 'Justice as fairness', *Philosophical Review*, 67 (1958), 164–94.

————: 'A well-ordered society', *Philosophy, Politics and Society*, 5th series, ed. P. Laslett and J. Fishkin (Oxford: Blackwell, 1979), pp. 6–20.

————: 'Social unity and primary goods', *Utilitarianism and Beyond*, ed. A. Sen and B. Williams (Cambridge: Cambridge University Press, 1982), pp. 159–85.

————: 'The domain of the political and overlapping consensus', *New York University Law Review*, 64 (1989), 233–55.

Sen, A. K.: *On Economic Inequality* (Oxford: Clarendon Press, 1973).

Sher, G.: *Desert* (Princeton, NJ: Princeton University Press, 1987).

23

Efficiency

RUSSELL HARDIN

Introduction

In the vernacular, 'efficiency' typically concerns means. I can choose efficient rather than inefficient means to accomplish my ends. Or more generally, I can be efficient or inefficient in allocating my limited resources. If we could measure the aggregate utility or welfare of a society, as in Benthamite utilitarianism, we could say that a society is efficient in an analogous sense: it uses effective institutions to achieve the greatest possible welfare. But the normative notion of efficiency commonly in use in social and political theory today is about social choices without aggregative welfare measures. Efficiency is invoked as an alternative to such aggregative measures.

Without interpersonally comparable welfare measures we typically cannot say that one state of society has more welfare and is therefore better than another. But we might be able to say that in one state of society all are individually better off than they are in another state; or, more likely, we might be able to say that some are individually better off while none is worse off. Efficiency in this sense is a restricted form of welfare for contexts in which aggregative measures are impossible or meaningless.

As a welfare criterion, efficiency has taken two rough forms. The first, which we may call static efficiency, is merely the implication of subjective utility at the level of the individual in a market. Given our present holdings, we may be able to trade with each other to make both of us better off. The second form, which we may call dynamic efficiency, takes incentives for being productive into account in assessing the differential productivity of systems of production. Vilfredo Pareto focused on static efficiency. Thomas Hobbes, Ronald Coase, and John Rawls have all been concerned with dynamic efficiency.

Heightened concern with efficiency has come into contemporary moral and political philosophy from standard economic debates over conflict between equity and efficiency and from law and economics, which arguably has become the most articulately developed area of contemporary moral, political, and legal philosophy. The potential conflict between equity and productive efficiency is central to much of the discussion of distributive justice. The experience of communist nations seems to support concern with such conflict, although their recently troubled economic experience may have been grossly overdetermined.

A brief history

We may begin the story of efficiency in moral and political philosophy with Hobbes.

Hobbes supposed that almost everyone would be better off with government than without, and he therefore concluded we should have government. He also supposed we could not know very much about the specific or differential effects of one form of government or another, so that we must be very nearly indifferent about the actual choice. Moreover, he supposed that movements for reform of an actual government must risk descent into civil war and destructive anarchy, so that it is in our interest to keep an extant government rather than attempt to change it (Hardin, 1991). His conclusions from these assumptions presaged the rise of concern with efficiency when, about a century ago, the Benthamite vision of value theory failed. That vision was of additive, cardinal utility whose sum across persons could be maximized.

What we might call Hobbesian efficiency has much in common with and might be seen as a vague form of Pareto efficiency. Both Hobbes and Pareto insisted on grounding their value theoretic accounts in individuals. Pareto (sometimes) forcefully rejected aggregative utility and interpersonal comparisons. The idea of aggregate or summed welfare may never even have occurred to Hobbes, whose natural instincts are individualist and ordinalist. From cardinal, interpersonally comparable welfare measures, we could determine which of several alternative states of affairs is best simply by checking the sum of utilities to find which state has the greatest sum. From ordinal, individual assumptions without interpersonal comparability we cannot do such sums. We can only say that one state is better than another if everyone concerned is better off or, more weakly, if at least one is better off and none is worse off in the first state.

During the nineteenth century, economists and utilitarians typically assumed cardinal, aggregative utility. This seemed to be an advance over earlier visions, such as that of Hobbes, because it allowed easy calculation, at least in principle. Often, the assumption of aggregative utility was coupled with the assumption that utility is objective, that it is a fixed measure of the goodness of an object. Developments in price theory in the latter half of the nineteenth century destroyed the view that utility is objective, external to the enjoying subject. For instance, the notion of the declining marginal utility of the consumption of any particular good implies that the utility is that of the subject, not of the object. But once utility was seen as subjective, it seemed obviously individualist and not aggregative. Eventually, it seemed even that it need not be cardinal for the individual, but merely ordinal. Hence, even though I may be able to tell you how I rank various alternative states of affairs, it might seem unclear what it would mean for me to give cardinal, additive weights to those states.

Cardinality was brought back for the individual's utility function in the analysis of risky choices. Suppose I face a choice between a lottery of a 10 per cent chance of outcome A with an associated 90 per cent chance of outcome B, on one hand, and a sure prospect of outcome C, on the other hand. I may be unable to decide unless I can attach cardinal values to A, B, and C, so that I can evaluate the lottery over A and B and can compare the expected value of that lottery to the value of C. Remarkably, if I can give an ordinal ranking over these possible outcomes and over every probabilistic combination of them, then a cardinal measure of each can be inferred from my ordinal rankings. But this does not yield Benthamite utility

463

measurements for the society without the additional claim that values are interpersonally comparable.

Pareto

If we had a cardinal, interpersonally aggregative value theory, we could speak of
efficiency of a group or society in terms analogous to those we use for an individual. If such a theory is ruled out, we might therefore seem to have no notion of
efficiency. Perhaps we could make no claims of simple utility or welfare to justify
choosing one policy over another. Pareto (1927) proposed a principle that would
give us some purchase on such choices. The principle is the family of what have since
come to be called Pareto efficiency, Pareto superiority and Pareto improvement.

If you and I have some distribution of commodities, it may be possible for us to trade
with each other to make both of us better off. Eventually we may reach a state from
which it is no longer possible to enter trades without making at least one of us worse
off. Each of our trades is a *Pareto improvement*; the result of one of our trades is to produce a state of *Pareto superiority* over the state before the trade; and the end result of a
sequence of trades from which no further trade can produce a Pareto improvement is
Pareto efficient. In figure 23.1, your evaluation of various distributions of all of our
initial holdings is represented on the x-axis and mine is represented on the y-axis. Suppose we start at the distribution at the origin, o. The curve ab is the *Pareto frontier* if it
represents all of the states in which we could possibly achieve Pareto efficiency. If we
trade to reach point p, our Pareto frontier is reduced to the segment RS.

There are three peculiarities of this vision of our interests. First, distribution p is
neither better nor worse than distribution q. To move from one of these to the other
is not a Pareto improvement. The same is true of all of the points on the frontier.
None of them is superior to any other and there is no way to make a Pareto improving
move from one of them to another. Hence, the Pareto principle is often indeterminate
in the sense that it cannot rank certain pairs of outcomes or states. Although individuals may be assumed to have complete ordinal rankings of states of affairs, groups or
societies need not have. (If the range of choices is sufficiently restricted, a society might
have a ranking. For example, we might all prefer not to have a major nuclear war
rather than to have one.) A strong commitment to paretianism, either for epistemological or for conceptual reasons, is a commitment to indeterminacy of social welfare
values.

Second, a point very close to a is Pareto superior to o, just as the point S is. We
started by assuming that the values of the two parties are not interpersonally comparable. But the difference between a and S involves not only differences in your and my
welfare; it also involves objective distributions of goods. I may receive large quantities
of some goods while trading away only small quantities of others. If you started with
very little or none of one of the goods and a lot of the other while I started with substantial quantities of both, you might trade most of your holdings for very little of the
goods you are missing. You might do this independently of which of the two goods you
are missing. If you have an interpersonally comparable value theory, you might think
this a bad result. Hence, the Pareto principle is a meaningful and distinctive principle.

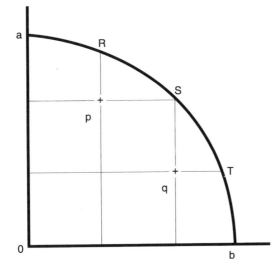

Figure 23.1
Pareto frontier and two interior points, p and q

Third, all of our evaluation here is strictly from the status quo at 0. You may have vast stores of our commodities and have only slight interest in getting more from trade while I have very little. Still, you may do very well in our interaction, so that we end up close to b. Your greater resources and consequent lesser needs may enable you to bargain harder. (This is not a certain claim – I may be a very hard, stoic bargainer and I may wear you down.)

Clearly, a Pareto improvement is not efficient in the simple commonsense meaning of the term. Pareto himself tried to distinguish what is now commonly called Pareto efficiency from efficiency as conceived in notions of efficient production. He spoke of optimality for his principle. Economists have tended to prefer efficiency over optimality because the latter has stronger normative connotations in economic usage while efficiency seems more nearly to be purely descriptive. Nevertheless, the Pareto principle is often invoked as though it were a normative principle, as though to say that what is Pareto superior is therefore in some sense better. For example, in his general impossibility theorem for social choice, Kenneth Arrow (1951) imposes a lesser form of the Pareto principle as a minimal moral constraint on the aggregation of collective from individual preferences.

It is sometimes thought that it would be rational for an individual to agree to any Pareto improvement. But this conclusion does not follow. Even though we might all be better off on the frontier than inside it, I might be especially better off at one point on the frontier while others would be especially better off at other points. Hence, there may be opportunity costs to me of settling on a frontier point that, for me, is inferior to other frontier points. It is therefore not trivially obvious what it would be rational for me to agree to – other than that it would be rational for me to accept a move to a point on the frontier that is at least as good as any other for me. This problem may

465

seem especially acute in many contexts of interest in moral and political choice, in which the issues before us cannot reasonably be seen or approximated as static. They are inherently dynamic. The frontier we face in this moment will provide only the starting point from which we make our next move. If we move to a point that gives you a great gain and me little or no gain, we then face a new future in which you start well ahead in the important causal sense that you have more resources for dealing with me.

Pareto's discussions of his principle exhibit a flaw that is evident in figure 23.1. The discussions are generally about reallocating what we already have. For Pareto, of course, the reallocation is to be accomplished through voluntary exchange. There is no production of what we are to allocate in figure 23.1 or in most discussions of the Pareto principle. In this respect, although his account is more careful and precise, Pareto's concern is less rich than that of Hobbes, who was overwhelmingly concerned with making life better. Sometimes, the paretian reallocation of what we already have is called static efficiency or allocative efficiency, while the problem of jointly enhancing production through reallocation is called dynamic or productive efficiency. However, the vocabulary is not uniform or even generally precise or clear.

Pareto's objection to cardinal, interpersonally comparable utility in economics may have been that it is philosophically meaningless. He typically argued that no one could make sense of the comparison of a supposed unit of my welfare and a unit of yours, although he sometimes supposed this could be done in particular cases. Hence, his objection may primarily have been epistemological rather than conceptual. You and I typically know too little to make comparisons because we cannot know enough about others. His complaint against such comparison was part of his general push for greater realism in economic assumptions, many of which were stretched beyond common sense by the urge to make them complete and to mathematize them.

An oddity of a hard common-sense complaint against interpersonal comparison is that most people seem to labour under the common sense assumption that they *do* know what it means in many contexts. I might immediately grant that the welfare consequences of your major injury or disease are greater than those of my stubbed toe or common cold. It takes a relatively abstruse argument to make this comparison seem meaningless and, once the aura of splendidly refined argument has faded, the comparison regains its psychological hold for all but the most firmly dedicated theorists.

If we reject interpersonal comparison of utilities, we cannot make common sense efficiency claims for a group or an aggregate population. But, Pareto argued, we would not be completely unable to make claims about aggregate welfare. We could still say of one state of affairs that it was better than another if everyone were at least as well off and no one were worse off in it than they would be in the other state. As critics have long noted, this criterion suggests that the state of affairs W in which a great deal of new wealth is created that all goes to the tsar is better than the state X in which the wealth is not created and the tsar is not so much better off than all others. Some of the critics think W is more unfair than X and is therefore not better than X. (It is important not to suppose that the tsar's greater wealth means greater power to abuse or exploit others; if the wealth has such a causal effect, then W is not better than X even by the Pareto criterion.) Resolute paretians seem to think this criticism incoherent or irrational. All that should matter to me is how well off I am, not how relatively well off others are, so long as their greater wealth does not give them harmful influence over my well-being. Psychologically, however, we know that people do care about relative status and that they have strong moral views about it. Neither the paretian nor the relativist psychology is obviously moral.

Coase

In moving from the classical utilitarian view with interpersonally comparable, additive welfare to the view of Pareto we lose the capacity to judge between many outcomes, all of which are Pareto efficient. Although we might be able to say that we should improve our lot collectively by moving from a status quo to the Pareto frontier, we could not say that one point on that frontier would be more attractive than another by the Pareto principle. Hence, again, the Pareto principle might yield no determinate advice on what to do.

Hobbes had already foreseen the problem of choosing from states that might not be preferred in the same order by all of us. In choosing a government, we could establish a monarchy, oligarchy or democracy, and some of us might prefer one of these while others prefer another. Even if we all agree with Hobbes that monarchy is best for our interests, we may still disagree about who should be the monarch. Hobbes resolved this problem with a slight cheat. He supposed we know too little about the effects of any of these governments for us to be able to care substantially about which is established. More realistically, he also noted that our real problem is not construction of a government but maintenance or overthrow of the one we already have. Here, although I may rightly suppose my interests would be better served by a different government, I must recognize that the task of getting to it would be very destructive. Hobbes argued that, in general, the improvements one might expect from a change of government would be outweighed by the costs of making the change, at least for the present generation.

Pareto's claim differs from that of Hobbes in that it is analytic rather than explanatory. He was concerned with evaluating the various prospects in principle. If the paretian evaluations are then to play a role in choice, they must be joined by causal considerations. For example, if the tsar in the example above thought his keeping all the new wealth his society created would lead to revolution, he might conclude that this point on the frontier would be causally excluded.

Even after certain states on the frontier are causally ruled out, however, we might find that we still face a set of many possibilities and that the Pareto principle is indeterminate. Ronald Coase, an economist at the University of Chicago Law School, has proposed a resolution for many such problems (Coase, 1960). That resolution is implicit in what the economist George Stigler dubbed the Coase theorem. This theorem may be loosely characterized as bringing production coherently into the paretian vision, thus making our problem that of dynamic efficiency. We are concerned not merely to reallocate what we already have in some status quo to our mutual benefit. We are also concerned to produce additional goods and services to be allocated to our mutual benefit.

The Coase theorem can best be articulated by example. Suppose a farmer and a rancher operate as neighbours. The rancher's cattle tend to trample the farmer's crops. One might suppose it obvious that the rancher is *prima facie* in the wrong. But, at least since Hume, we are reluctant to read moral conclusions directly off matters of fact. We could as well say the farmer causes harm to the rancher if the rancher's cattle are not free to roam. To resolve such a case legally requires prior legal rules that address the case, or that at least prescribe how to address it through relevant institutions, such as a common law court, if there is no adequately explicit rule in effect. We might similarly suppose that a moral resolution, which might not agree with the legal resolution, would turn on a prior moral theory that we apply to the case. We cannot simply intuit what is the right and what the wrong action. The law, of course, is contingent, and it is conceivable that it could have gone either way (it has gone both ways in various jurisdictions).

The Coase theorem says that, subject to transaction costs, the production from the joint property of the farmer and the rancher will not be affected by how the law assigns the right to use the farmer's property. Suppose the law assigns the right to the farmer, so that the farmer may legally erect a fence to keep the rancher's cattle out. Now, if the rancher can get more profit from running cattle on the land than the farmer loses from having the cattle run, the rancher and the farmer will bargain over sharing that extra profit and the cattle will run over the farmer's crops. Suppose the law assigns the right to the rancher. If the farmer can get more profit from not having the cattle on the land than the rancher can get from having the cattle run free, the farmer and the rancher will similarly bargain over the extra profit and the cattle will be excluded. Hence, the rule on how to use the property will not determine the property's use. Its possibilities for production will.

In this example, we have taken one point on the Pareto frontier and traded it for another point by introducing side payments. We can do this because the case is assumed to be entirely about income in the market. And the beauty of such income is that it is cardinal and it can be added across people. We might then be able to divide the income in a way that makes both parties better off than they could have been at either of the pristine states of affairs that might be supposed to be determined by our legal rule. In principle, we can bargain around any legal rule in such market contexts. Unfortunately, we may in fact sometimes find it impossible to bargain around a rule because bargaining itself can be costly and can eat up the gains in income that might be produced by a successful bargain. But, when transaction costs are not as destructive as this, significantly different legal rules may be relatively neutral in their impact.

In Coase's resolution of our problem of reaching the frontier, we are able to push the frontier out further to where various bargains have been made to enhance productivity, where there is therefore greater total production as valued in the market. Making these bargains depends on the cardinal, additive nature of market income. Here, out of the potentially large range of possible bargained outcomes, we should naturally choose that (or one of those) which maximizes total market income to be divided between us. Hence, we no longer face the entire frontier with indeterminacy. Our only indeterminacy is that of how to allocate between us the excess income over what either of us would have got from bullheadedly following the extant legal rule. This is the universal indeterminacy of all constant sum bargaining games.

With this remarkable move, Coase has gone further than Hobbes. Hobbes reduced the frontier set to a collection of indifferently equally desirable states of affairs by stipulating epistemological barriers to our judgement of any differences between them. Coase actually makes a choice from the somewhat expanded frontier: that state which produces greatest market income. Coase's device may not work for various cases, such as those in which evaluations may in principle be easy enough but bargaining is hard, such as cases involving large groups rather than individual choosers, and those in which what is at stake does not have a market value. These two considerations may be brought destructively together, as in ethnic conflicts over territorial control.

Note, however, that Coase's problem is clearly and fundamentally different from Hobbes'. Hobbes was concerned with the general arrangement of order in society, with a welfarist or self-interest justification of the state. Coase's theorem comes to bear only against the background of such a state and its general legal structures and rules. It is inherently about marginal problems because it assumes a general framework of extant prices. Coase's resolution could not be applied to Hobbes' problem. Hobbes' and Coase's contributions to the analysis of efficiency are essentially complementary, not alternative accounts.

Contemporary political theory

Apart from law and economics, the most influential area in contemporary political philosophy is the debates over distributive justice sparked by John Rawls (1971). Rawls begins with a concern for the apparent conflict between equity and efficiency. The efficiency that bothers him is productive efficiency. He wants to put our resources and incentives into producing the largest possible set of relevant goods for distribution. That is to say, he is concerned with Hobbesian efficiency. Conflict arises if individual productivity depends heavily on incentives, as it will if the way to induce greater production is to let effective producers have larger than average shares of the society's wealth, income or consumption.

Rawls attempts to do something roughly similar to Hobbes and Coase: he narrows the range of possible efficient outcomes that we need consider. One might suppose this is merely a move to overcome the indeterminacy of paretian efficiency. But Rawls' narrowing of the set of outcomes is fundamentally motivated by normative considerations of, most perspicuously, fairness and, especially in his later Kantian mode, such vague concerns as respect for persons and autonomy. Hobbes fell back on epistemological ignorance to reduce the set. Coase uses market values to trade beyond the bare allocations of the law. Rawls uses his criterion of equity, that the worst off do as well as possible, to eliminate many possible political arrangements. His focus is that of Hobbes on the general structure of political-legal order and not that of Coase on the resolution of marginal interactions against the background of an established political-legal order.

Contemporary utilitarian political theory, which seems to be every other theory's chief antagonist, cannot be grounded in a trivially Benthamite value theory. Quite

469

apart from metaphysical objections to making interpersonal comparisons, such as Pareto may have had, there are obvious epistemological difficulties that may be insurmountable. Utilitarians may still accept at least some interpersonal comparisons and some aggregations across persons, as the anti-utilitarian Rawls implicitly does in his account of primary goods. But for many matters in political philosophy, they must settle for either Hobbesian or Coasian efficiency rather than aggregate welfare comparisons. If utilitarians are not happy with Hobbes or Coase, they must attempt to define an alternative notion of dynamic efficiency that can lie at the core of their political theory. And if they do not improve on these, they face the perplexing problem that the Hobbesian foundationalist vision does not coherently connect with the Coasian marginalist vision.

See also 3 HISTORY; 5 ECONOMICS; 6 POLITICAL SCIENCE; 16 CONTRACT AND CONSENT; 22 DISTRIBUTIVE JUSTICE; 25 EQUALITY; 41 WELFARE

References

Arrow, K. J.: *Social Choice and Individual Values* (New York: Wiley, 1951; 2nd edn 1963).
Coase, R. H.: 'The problem of social cost' (1960), *The Firm, the Market and the Law* (Chicago: University of Chicago Press, 1988), pp. 95–156.
Hardin, R.: 'Hobbesian political order', *Political Theory*, 19 (May 1991), 156–80.
Pareto, V.: *Manual of Political Economy* (1927); (New York: Kelley, 1971).
Rawls, J.: *A Theory of Justice* (Cambridge, Mass.: Harvard University Press, 1971).

24

Environmentalism

JOHN PASSMORE

When the Supplement to the *Oxford English Dictionary* went to press in 1971, it still recognized only one sense of 'environmentalism' – as the name of a particular sociological theory holding that the differences between human cultures were to be wholly explained in terms of such factors as soil, climate and food supplies. As for the now cognate term 'ecological', that too had a purely scientific significance. The German zoologist Ernst Haeckel had coined the word 'ecology' in its German form as early as 1870, to signify 'the investigation of the total relations of the animal both to its organic and its inorganic environment'. It was soon extended beyond animals to the study, in these terms, of both plant life and human societies.

Since the early 1970s, however, the 'environmental' or the 'ecological' movement has connoted a socio-political force rather than a specific scientific doctrine or field of study, a change particularly marked in such coinages as 'eco-politics', 'eco-left', 'eco-feminism'. It has sometimes found expression in the formation of 'Green' political parties, sometimes in pressure groups which seek to modify the programmes of already established parties or which, scorning political parties, confine themselves to direct action of a 'grassroots' kind.

There are links between the older and the newer meanings. Sociological environmentalists emphasized that the natural environment was not just a passive 'surrounding', but had a profound effect on social practices. Biological ecologists drew attention to the complex interactions within biological communities and between them and their habitats. Environmentalists often express hostility to science and technology, blaming them for environmental degradation. The fact remains that unlike most traditional political movements, they constantly appeal to evidence from the natural sciences, whether it be to food chains or to greenhouse effects or to ozone layers. Nevertheless, they also, here like other political parties, make use of classical social and political concepts and urge the need for social and political changes, often of a quite radical kind. Indeed, the lengthy Manifesto of the German Greens (Die Grünen, 1983) devotes most of its space (48 pages out of 54) to the proclamation of such 'dissident left' policies as decentralization, non-violence, participatory democracy, egalitarianism, anti-nuclearism, rotary office-holding as being both good in themselves and essential preconditions of fundamental ecological reform – this in opposition to the view that such reform can take place, with the help of technological fixes and such devices as legal penalties and taxes, within a capitalist politico-social framework. The word 'environmentalism' is now sometimes confined to this last type of view; it is then contrasted, unfavourably, with the 'Green' (subdivided into various shades) or with the 'ecological' movement (Porritt, 1984).

The environment

What constitutes 'the environment'? In its now relevant, biological, sense it includes anything that affects the capacity of organisms to survive, to reproduce and to flourish. The environment of any particular organism, or species of organism, will include other organisms. The human being's environment may include mosquitoes; human beings may be part of a mosquito's environment. To the human being mosquitoes are a threat; to mosquitoes human beings are both a threat and a resource.

In the case of human beings we can roughly distinguish three kinds of environment. Every human being is born into a community, or more accurately communities, of human beings bound together by social practices. These together constitute an individual's social environment, even if over time the individual so internalizes these social practices that they largely constitute that person's actions. There is no novelty in the view that a human being's capacity to survive, to reproduce, to flourish can be deeply affected by the nature of these practices. What has only recently been fully recognized is they can affect the capacity of the human species as a whole to survive, to say nothing of the survival of other species. The environmentalist movement springs out of a recognition of the manifest ways in which social practices can give rise to environmental degradation.

Second, every human being has at hand a variety of physical objects which other human beings have deliberately designed in order to satisfy human needs and desires. They constitute the built environment. This includes a great deal more than buildings in the normal sense; it includes, for example, machines, roads, manufactured chemical products. Many built objects were constructed as a response to environmental threats. Nevertheless, environmentalists point to the fact that even then they can themselves constitute an environmental threat, as in the case of insecticides. For some environmentalists almost every built object constitutes a threat; others will agitate for the preservation of certain kinds of built objects, as historically or artistically of peculiar interest.

Finally, there is the natural environment, to which the word 'environment' is now mostly commonly taken to refer. Its distinction from the built environment is not absolute. Although there are still, in some parts of the world, genuine wildernesses containing nothing that has been placed there by human hands, in industrially advanced countries what counts as the natural environment will often have been deliberately modified, socialized. An inner-city dweller will no doubt encounter forms of insect and bird life – flies, cockroaches, starlings, pigeons – which, although they have changed their food habits as a result of contacts with human beings, have not been deliberately modified by them. But the flowers on the window-sill and the trees in a park have not only been deliberately placed where they now stand, but are usually varieties bred to meet the rigours of city life.

The countryside is in a similar position, except that its trees may sometimes have been left standing, although normally now in a different plant and animal community. Its fields have been laid out, its plants and animals genetically transformed. Nevertheless, parks and countryside are normally thought of as forming part of the natural environment, with their preservation fought for as such, just because plants, animals and trees, if man-modified, are not man-made. Even when they have been severely polluted as a result of human intervention, rivers, the seas and the climate fall into this same category. What, in general terms, environmentalists want to do is to preserve remaining wilderness areas, to restore degenerated natural environments to something like their pristine condition, to prevent further degeneration. They all realize that in order to achieve these aims they will have to press for changes in social practices and in the built environment. But they differ notably in their motives, in respect to the degree of change with which they would be satisfied and in the means which they would be prepared to see employed in order to reach that point. Together they constitute a family of movements rather than a single movement, one of those families within which there is considerable internecine hostility.

Varieties of environmentalism

Their opponents, whether industrialists, miners or foresters, tend to divide environmentalists into two groups: 'hard' and 'mainstream'. By 'hard' environmentalists they mean those with whom they find it impossible to negotiate. By distinguishing them from 'mainstream' environmentalists they mean to suggest that the 'hard' constitute a fanatical minority. But these appellations do not draw attention to what intellectually distinguishes the hard group, namely the fact that 'hard' environmentalists are not only indifferent to economic growth (which is all their opponents have to offer) but are totally hostile to it. They entirely reject the concept of sustainable development, as supported in the United Nations report *Our Common Future* (Brundtland, 1987), if this is taken to imply any measure at all of economic growth; as they see it, only by moving in the reverse direction can environmental degradation be prevented.

Within the environmentalist movement itself, a distinction is often drawn, following Arne Naess (1973, pp. 95–100), between 'shallow' and 'deep' environmentalism. These are distinctly value-laden descriptions. No one would care to enrol under the banners of the 'shallow', whereas 'deep' has for many people an irresistible appeal. It will be less question-begging to contrast, in a manner now familiar, 'humanistic' and 'biocentric' environmentalism. 'Anthropocentric' – or in the writings of eco-feminists 'androcentric' – is perhaps in more common use than 'humanistic', but these words suggest a metaphysical view, that the whole of nature exists for the sake of human beings, which no serious humanistic environmentalist could possibly hold.

Humanistic environmentalism sets out to change social practices which have an adverse effect on the environment because, in their judgement, these will eventually give rise to adverse effects on human interests. Biocentric environmentalists take as their final end the preservation of the biosphere in all its complexity. If they foresee that human beings will destroy themselves they might accept that with equanimity, as no novelty over time, but not in so far as their manner of self-destruction carries with it damage to the biosphere as a whole.

Humanistic environmentalism

In its narrowest form, humanistic environmentalism confines itself to the local effects of pollution or environmental degradation. It is sometimes then described as 'not in my backyard' environmentalism; 'local' environmentalism is a more manageable name. It objects, say, to the pollution of a river because the pollution lowers local property values or destroys traditional amenities. Universalistic humanists go beyond this in a number of ways. First, they campaign against environmental degradation at places where they do not themselves live or at times at which they will no longer be alive; second, they stress human interests other than property values and local amenities.

Since, however, local pollution certainly falls within their ambit, universalistic environmentalists may be called upon to help out in local disputes, where indeed information is generally easier to discover, pressure easier to mount. The motto: 'think globally, act locally' has now, in fact, won widespread support among environmentalists of every kind. Such alliances, however, tend to be temporary, the community falling back into its customary environmental complacency unless the local campaign can be used to persuade them that remoter places, distant generations, are also of local concern.

Remoter places

Environmentalism began as local environmentalism, if on a relatively large scale. The triumphs to which it pointed were the dispersal of the more deadly kind of London fog, the return of fish to the Thames. But it was obvious from the beginning that there were rivers like the Rhine, seas like the Baltic, which called upon cooperative action, which could not stop at national boundaries. With the discovery that acid rain could damage the environment of countries as relatively remote from the polluting sources as Norway is from England, it became even more apparent that environmental degradation is no respecter of national boundaries. If atmospheric warming and holes in the ozone layer are indeed the result of industrial pollution as distinct from natural cycles, the human importance of environmental degradation in a particular country on localities everywhere is beyond dispute.

Such facts produce both opportunities and problems for universalistic humanistic environmentalists. The advantage is that Donne's 'no man is an island' can be transposed into 'nowhere is an island', in order to persuade local environmentalists to extend their interests further. Campaigns against, say, the cutting down of rainforests in the Amazon can win wider support by pointing to its effects on the atmosphere than would have been available had the resulting degradation of both the natural and the social environment been purely local. The problems are mainly political. When the source of pollution is in one country, the degradation in another, there will be more than usual pressure on their governments by the industries involved to ignore such effects. When the destruction of rainforests in the Amazon basin is condemned by environmentalists, the local entrepreneurs may argue that this condemnation is a variety of neo-colonialism, preventing the economic development of their country.

This may also happen when environmentalists object to polluting chemical factories being transferred to developing countries.

To the accusation of neo-colonialism the environmentalist may reply that, in fact, it is the overseas entrepreneurs – which is what they generally are – who are the neo-colonialists, degrading the developing country's environment for the sake of short-term profits. But whereas the biocentric environmentalists may argue further that development is in itself a bad thing, humanistic environmentalists cannot close their eyes to the fact that without economic growth the developing countries, with their present (to say nothing of future) populations, may be condemned to unemployment, low life expectancy and violent political instability. Whether in their own country or in other countries, however remote, humanistic environmentalists cannot ignore, as a biocentric environmentalist can, such actual or possible outcomes. That is why industrialists, foresters and miners find them relatively 'soft'; they are not generally prepared to give a zero value to economic development.

It by no means follows, however, that humanistic environmentalists will immediately acquiesce once they are told that there are economic gains for the developing country in transferring to it chemical factories or in cutting down its forests. If they are environmentalists of any sort whatsoever, they will appeal to considerations other than immediate economic losses and gains – to the degradation these activities will bring into being, to the long-term losses they entail, to their effects on ethnic minorities, and so on. They may well conclude that certain forms of economic activity are unsupportable.

At the political level, they may then urge on their own governments the provision of economic and expert aid to developing countries to make possible alternative forms of employment, legislation against the import of rain forest timber and so on. Environmentalists and supporters of foreign aid may be sufficiently powerful to make such pressures on established parties not entirely nugatory. In the developing countries, however, environmentalism is unlikely to be powerful and the political situation may well be very difficult for outsiders to grasp. Environmentalists may find political parties who are prepared to support their environmentalist activities and may think of themselves as using these parties to advance their cause when in fact they are being used by such parties, which have as their real aim the assumption of political power. This, of course, is simply an example of the problems besetting all minority groups who need allies but then come to be identified with their allies. Anti-nuclear groups are another case in point.

Future generations

A concern for future generations is no novelty. It can take a variety of forms, as comes out in testamentary dispositions. These may include legacies to great-grandchildren but also to organizations which the testator expects to carry on certain kinds of activity during future generations. Such concern is, of course, local, but the principles that underlie it can readily be generalized. In the first case, the testator is handing on resources which will, the testator thinks, help the legatees to live the kind of life the testator would like them to live. The resources will for the most part consist of man-made resources – property, money – rather than natural resources, but we can easily generalize this attitude into handing over natural resources to later generations. In the second case, the legacies may go in a more impersonal fashion to institutions, but again on the assumption that these institutions promote ways of life which the testator regards as being important. There can, of course, be deep differences of opinion about what these ways of life are. Biocentric environmentalists are sometimes primitivists, but humanistic environmentalists are generally interested in maintaining and developing some form of liberal democratic society in its rich diversity, nowhere more manifest than in some of its cities, as well as a similarly diverse biosphere. In consequence such environmentalists are particularly concerned about the conservation of natural resources.

That was the theme of the Club of Rome report *The Limits to Growth* (Meadows et al., 1972). The report was attacked by economists and technologists on its first appearance as underestimating the capacity of technology, both as a means of discovering new mineral resources and of providing substitutes for the resources we at present employ. They were right, in so far as the gloomier prognostications of the report have not yet eventuated. Nevertheless, resources are limited, by the nature of the case, and although increases in prices as they became scarcer might ensure that they would not entirely run out, high prices could have a considerable effect on future societies. The environmentalist would also point out that markets can be slow to react to scarcities, as has happened in relation to several species of fish. As for substitutes, these have often turned out to present unexpected problems (as in the disposal of nuclear wastes) or to be considerably more expensive than anticipated or, like nuclear fusion or the production of long-life batteries, to present technological difficulties. It is also true, of course, that they use natural resources, although different ones.

Environmentalists still have to face the general objection that we should concentrate our attention on here-and-now problems, leaving future generations to face their problems as we have had to face our problems. The pace of technological innovation may be invoked to argue that we cannot really tell what they will regard as problems or what tools they will have to deal with them. It is a firm economic principle that we ought to discount the future heavily and never more so than in rapidly changing societies.

Replying to such views, universalistic humanists argue that the fact that human beings live in the future rather than now does not affect our obligations towards them, any more than the fact that they live in a different part of the globe: we are still obliged to take their interests into account. Admittedly, the degree of uncertainty which commonly attaches to the outcomes of our actions is in this case accentuated; we are very likely, trying to do the right thing, actually to do the wrong thing. The information we have at our disposal is more than ordinarily limited.

We have, however, at least this much information: we know that the human beings who succeed us on the earth's surface will need water, food, an atmosphere they can breathe, protection from heat and cold and space to live in. On any but the most localized moral view, the humanistic environmentalist argues, we should not put these perennial human needs at risk by seriously modifying the constitution of the atmosphere, the temperature of the globe, the amount of land that is above sea-level, by cutting down forests, exhausting mineral deposits or allowing the top-soil to degenerate or rivers to be polluted. In many of these cases, of course, environmental reform offers advantages to the present inhabitants of the earth as well as to later generations; in other cases the time-scale involved is relatively short so that at the very least our own great-grandchildren, for whom we might quite naturally make testamentary provision, would be affected. So we are not passing beyond the normal bounds of natural affection.

Here again, then, we have a situation in which a generalised humanistic environmentalism can appeal to localized effects. Its theoretical concern, however, is with future generations as such, whether or not they stand in any closer association with us than that of being fellow human beings. Thus it relates to our everyday concern for the welfare of our immediate descendants much as classical utilitarianism, with its demand that we act so as to produce the greatest happiness for the greatest number, does to our everyday concern for the welfare of those to whom we are bound by special ties of affection or responsibility. The consequentialism espoused by a humanistic environmentalism is not, however, committed to the classical emphasis on pain and pleasure. Its commitment is simply to the view that some ways of living are better than others and that we ought not to act now in such a way that future generations will inevitably live worse lives than they otherwise could. Whether 'better' can simply be equated with 'less painful' or 'happier' is a question we need not consider.

The political problem, of course, arises when in order to ensure that future generations will have some chance of living a good life or satisfying their interests present generations will have to make important sacrifices, especially as these sacrifices are likely to be unequally distributed. There can be considerable debate about what constitutes an important sacrifice. North Americans could considerably reduce their extremely high rate of energy consumption while still having a high rate of consumption by international standards. They have, however, built many of their ways of life around high energy consumption. They would certainly regard themselves as making important sacrifices were they called upon to walk or to use public transport in some instances when they now drive or were obliged to wear heavy clothing inside in winter. Many environmentalists would argue that with lower energy consumption people would actually live better lives but, even in these relatively trivial cases, politicians would be reluctant to impose regulations to secure lower consumption if this is only for the sake of future generations. Once again, then, it may be politically necessary to stress more immediate, local, consequences.

At their least demanding, environmentalists may urge consumers to abandon such practices as throwing away containers, industrialists to produce recyclable containers, and local governments to subsidize their collection – or the collection of used paper – when recycling is otherwise not economically viable. This is partly to conserve natural resources, partly to reduce the size of rubbish heaps. At this level they have been relatively successful. Recycling makes people feel virtuous, in societies where saving is officially regarded as being a virtue; it is relatively painless and it does not involve any radical change in social and political attitudes. In short, it is environmentalism without tears. But it requires the use of industrial processes, takes energy, produces by-products and can help to sustain the illusion that resources are inexhaustible.

In some other cases, the sacrifices called for are uncontroversially serious, as when reductions are urged in the logging of forests and the result is unemployment – not only for loggers but in nearby towns. The environmentalist may point out that in a society which breaks away from totalitarianism many dedicated members of the secret police will similarly be thrown out of work, that this is indeed characteristic of a great many desirable social changes. But in these cases the compensating benefits for present, as well as future, generations are clear. If a similar point can be made about the logging of trees, the political problems can equally be eased; once again to find a way of appealing to local environmentalism increases the chances of securing environmental ends which are not purely localized.

Similar problems arise if the environmentalist speaks in terms of human rights, rather than of interests or kinds of life, and argues that these rights are possessed as much by members of future as by members of present generations. So far as the classical rights are concerned, such as the right to free speech, one can certainly argue in a quite general way that one ought not to act in such a manner as to increase the risk that future generations will be less likely, in consequence, to possess such rights. This is a line of reasoning which is particularly appealing to liberal democrats. The problem is to link it with environmentalism, without having recourse to scenarios which have a science fiction air about them. One is called upon to envisage ways in which environmental degradation would inevitably lead to the setting up of totalitarian (or at least military-authoritarian) governments which would not recognize human rights. Such scenarios are extremely plausible but they are unlikely to look that way to ordinary electors, just because they so closely resemble fictional speculations.

Such an appeal to the classical rights, it should also be observed, does not lie open to all environmentalists. Biocentric environmentalists such as Callicott (1980, pp. 311–38), sometimes describe themselves as 'holists' and regard with equanimity a society in which individual rights are sacrificed to 'the good of the whole'. Indeed, they may even urge that we should now become such a society. It is certainly very difficult to see how environmental degradation can be diminished without a considerable amount of regulation, which will often interfere with established property rights and with the non-classical 'right to work'. But these can in principle be compensated for; in the eyes of a liberal democrat there can be no compensation for the loss of such rights as freedom of speech.

Particular problems centre on control over population, in the interests of future generations. Environmentalists of every kind argue that the world either is, or will in the relatively near future become, over-populated. For humanists this means that as a result in part of environmental degradation human life will come to be, as in places it has already become, 'nasty, brutish and short' once the population goes beyond a not precisely specifiable level. As usual the facts are disputed; there are some who argue that, as a result of technical advances, the world (perhaps by colonizing nearby planets) could adequately support a much greater population than it now does. But, for all that we have recently made such vast gains in agricultural pro ductivity, these claims are generally dismissed by environmentalists. The gains have always been accompanied, they point out, by serious losses in the form, for example, of fertilizer flow-offs into streams.

478

The objection can be raised, however, that it is morally wrong to try to stem population growth. Classical utilitarians sometimes get into difficulties on this point. For if what we ought to do is to maximize total happiness, then on the face of it, as Parfit (1986, pp. 145–64) has pointed out, a large population can be what we ought to try to secure, provided only that each member of that population is marginally happy, rather than a considerably smaller population in which individuals are more than marginally happy. Of course, if it can be shown that the inhabitants of a more populated world are going to live lives of unremitting misery, the calculation comes out very differently, but it is extremely difficult to show convincingly that this is bound to be the case.

Even supposing it can be shown, however, that a more heavily populated future world will contain less total happiness than a society in which growth has been restrained or that it will be a society in which there is no political freedom or in which it is impossible to live certain kinds of good life, moral objections may still be raised to the steps which would have to be taken to restrain population growth.

Some of these objections relate to the fact that population control depends upon the use of contraceptives and abortion. Humanistic environmentalists may be disturbed by this fact, but are not necessarily so provided the use of such devices is voluntary. What is morally disturbing is that such voluntary reductions in family size are not, on a world-wide scale, likely to produce a sharp decline in population growth over any but a long period of time and yet there are good reasons for believing that excess population is a major cause of environmental degradation. This is far from being the only case in which the question, 'How are we to get from here to there?', is a very uncomfortable one for environmentalists. But the population question faces all environmentalists, not only those for whom 'there' is some form of Utopia. So it is not altogether surprising that population control has come largely to be ignored in recent environmental discussions, vital though it would seem to be.

Environmental concerns

The third difference between local and universalistic humanistic environmentalists is the wide range of the interests in the environment which universalists can display. They are not at all committed to the traditional view that human beings ought to think of the natural environment only as a threat or a resource. This is particularly so if 'resource' is understood to mean something which is used as a way of maintaining, or increasing, economic prosperity, whether in the conventional manner of mining or forestry or in the modern manner of a tourist attraction. They will reject, as firmly as does the biocentric environmentalist, the doctrine that human beings stand apart from Nature; indeed, the contrary view has been commonplace since Darwin. But in their defences of environmentalism they still unashamedly appeal only to the losses human beings will experience as a result of environmental degradation, directly or indirectly.

The most politically effective of these defences appeals to broad environmental effects on human health. Here humanists can often join hands with local environmentalists in the places which are affected by the pollution and hence can strengthen their political influence. The opposition, in contrast, will generally come from the places where the pollution is generated, although it will extend to places and persons economically or politically linked with the polluter. The central figures will normally be the farmers, whose insecticides or fertilizers pollute ground-water and streams, and the industrialists, whose factories pollute the atmosphere or water. But they may be joined by workers who fear losing their jobs (particularly but not only when they do not themselves suffer from the pollution), industries which supply the polluting substances and scientists and technologists who have created them. They may win the support of governments, shareholders and others who fear the economic effects of prohibiting polluting practices, charging those who pollute or demanding costly changes to factories. This is especially so in a highly competitive world, where other countries may have no hesitation in accommodating the offending factory or permitting ecologically dangerous farming practices. The situation is even more difficult when, as often happens, the precise damage done by the pollutant is hard to establish and scientists differ about its importance.

Pollution is no respecter of species. Indeed its effects on non-human species may be easier to detect than its effects on human beings. In some such circumstances, there may be clear economic costs, as to fishing industries. And in political debates the humanistic environmentalist may emphasize them. Equally, when the point at issue is the disappearance of species, not only from a particular place but from the face of the earth, humanistic environmentalists will often emphasize the possible loss, with the species, of biological structures which might turn out to be useful as drugs or insecticides.

That is likely to be more effective politically than the considerations which are in fact most influential in the mind of the environmentalist. There is nothing hypocritical in this. Environmentalists may be genuinely concerned about the fate of fishermen or bathers, and may genuinely believe, what is by no means a mere guess, that some threatened species – even if they cannot specify in advance exactly what species – contain unique substances which will turn out over time to be very useful to human beings. But it does mean that the humanistic environmentalists, in a manner which biocentric environmentalists of the purer sort will find intolerable, accommodate their case to what they take to be the political realities.

Two other considerations to which they might appeal are likely to be less effective. (It must be remembered that politically powerful appeals to economic development will be the weapon of their opponents.) The first is that a disappearing species or a disappearing habitat or unique geological formation is a lost opportunity for scientific investigation. The second is more difficult to formulate – it is sometimes described as an appeal to 'aesthetic' considerations. This wrongly suggests, however, that the appeal has to be to the beautiful or the sublime.

In some cases such an appeal to the beautiful or the sublime can be politically effective and it may take shape practically in a temporary alliance with the tourist industry – an alliance surviving only until that industry reveals its plans for development. But the humanistic environmentalist can join hands with the biocentric environmentalist in wanting to preserve species to which adjectives like 'beautiful' and 'sublime' are not ordinarily applied, rejoicing in the sheer diversity of the natural environment, in being able to feel a part of it rather than a spectator, appreciating the interplays within the web of life. These are all of them purely human reactions, no other animal is capable of them; there is no departure from humanism in taking them seriously. But it is at this point, certainly, that the humanist is most likely to be accused of sentimentality, of trying to impose middle-class values or of a lack of realism. So it is not surprising that as a political movement, humanistic environmentalism tends to appeal to more obviously utilitarian considerations or, alternatively, to doctrines of rights.

Extended humanism

Extended humanism falls between humanistic and biocentric environmentalism. It does not take the interests of human beings, however broadly regarded, to be central; on the other side, it does not take the interests of the ecosystem as a whole to be central. One might even refuse to call it 'environmentalism' on the ground that its interest is ordinarily confined to a concern for certain types of animal but it sometimes goes beyond that point, perhaps by recognizing that concern for animals carries with it a concern for their habitat, perhaps by trying to extend to all members of ecosystems concepts which have first been extended from human beings to other animals, whether these be interests, or equality, or rights, or liberation.

Extended humanism commonly begins, as it did for Bentham ([1789] 1970, ch. IV, sec. 7), and for Leopold ([1949] 1966, p. 138) from a belief that human beings have over time made moral advances. (That is one reason why it is unpopular with those biocentric environmentalists for whom the view that human beings have in any way progressed over the last millennia is anathema.) So human beings have abolished slavery, attacked sexism and racism and even, in relation to animals, set up Humane Societies and Societies for the Prevention of Cruelty to Animals. But they are still 'speciesist', to use the term introduced by Richard Ryder (1972, p. 81), they still treat human beings as being superior to other species, in a way which condones treating animals in ways in which it would not be permissible to treat even a human being in the most hopelessly vegetative state. Extended humanism rejects such practices as morally impermissible.

Bentham had said that the crucial question when we are considering how we should treat other species is whether they can suffer, and this is the principal theme in Singer's *Animal Liberation* (1975), a work which has had considerable impact in the political sphere. If it leads him to speak in terms of the 'equality' of all animals, this, he thinks, is in respect to their capacity for suffering; that is the only sense in which, he indeed argues, we can plausibly think of human beings as being equal. One feature of his argument, which also runs through much extended humanism, is that he will not allow us to describe something as being a species characteristic unless it is characteristic of all members of the species. (He uses 'species' as if it simply meant 'class'.) So we are not allowed to say that human beings are peculiarly rational and deserve preference as a species for this reason, seeing that there are decerebrate or vegetative human beings.

That is not our usual practice. We say that dogs are quadrupeds even though some are born with three legs or lose a leg in an accident; we do not regard the existence of

Siamese twins as falsifying generalizations about human anatomy. The individuals to whom animal liberationists refer in order to dispute the view that human beings are peculiarly rational could in principle be cured of their dementia or prevented from developing it by genetic intervention, whereas we cannot by medical intervention turn mice into metaphysicians. A coma resulting from an accident no more demonstrates that human beings are not, as a species, rational than does the occasional amputation of a leg demonstrate that they are not bipeds. Furthermore, it can be an important fact about a species that some members of it have exceptional characteristics, that it contains peculiarly striking varieties. In the case of human beings, these varieties include geniuses. It is not absurd to place a particular value on a species because it sometimes produces individuals of very great value, even if it also produces villains of the deepest dye. But although the humanist environmentalist is not prepared to blur the distinction between the human species and other species, even in respect to the kind of suffering they endure – much human suffering being related to fears about the future, guilt about the past or the sight of suffering in others – that need not prevent them from joining with extended environmentalists in protests against, say, battery farming or unnecessary (or unnecessarily cruel) scientific experimentation.

Singer's reference to suffering is essential to his argument. He does not demand that we give up planting vegetables in rows in order to eat them, as the Greek philosopher Porphyry (*c.* 280) substantially did. But other extended humanists, just because the argument is thus confined to animals which are capable of suffering, prefer to argue in terms of rights.

They cannot, of course, have recourse to the classical rights, as formulated in declarations of the rights of man. For these all relate to the relationships of human beings with one another in a peculiarly human type of society; they are modes of protecting one human being against another. They arise within a judicial system; they generate claims within such systems.

In the animal case, the situation is quite different. The rights are not claimed by one member of an animal species as against other members of that species, as they are in the human case. Looking at a country other than our own, we might protest against the way some members of that society are treated by other members of that society and we might appeal to rights on behalf of what we regard as the oppressed members of that society, even when they are not recognized (whether in theory or, as now more commonly happens, in practice) in that society. It would be quite ridiculous to demand such rights on behalf of worker-ants in an ant heap. Even such non-classical rights as the right to work have no application in this context.

The 'right to life' as ordinarily employed in arguments against abortion and euthanasia also has no application here, in so far as 'the sanctity of life' is taken to mean the sanctity of *human* life. But if we take it, rather, as a general precept against arbitrary killing then it can be used not only in relation to animals but to plants. The disputes are then about what counts as 'arbitrary'. In this case, of course, the tree, for example, cannot of itself claim the right not to be chopped down. But it is sometimes true even in human cases that someone has to speak on behalf of the person whose rights are infringed. So such legal philosophers as Christopher Stone (1974) have sought to describe ways in which damages can be sought on behalf of the fish in a polluted river as distinct from economically affected fishermen, the damages in successful cases being awarded to some form of nature-protection organization.

Political action in this sphere has generally taken the form of legislation to prohibit in particular circumstances the cutting down of trees or the pollution of rivers. So the plaintiff appeals to legislation which in fact takes away rights from human beings rather than granting them to non-human entities. Such legislation is often resisted in precisely these terms as an infringement, not an extension, of rights, and it is often impossible for anybody but a government organization to act as a plaintiff, as it is commonly very reluctant to do. The existence of laws relating to, let us say the emission of gases into the atmosphere or of pollutants into rivers, to the degree that environmental law is now an established specialism (Anderson, Mandelker and Tarlock, 1990), is an indication of how successful environmentalist political pressures have been. The common failure to prosecute and the minuscule fines set down indicate, however, that these successes are often more apparent than real, particularly under conditions of economic recession.

Whatever form it takes, extended humanism is usually egalitarian, except in so far as its utilitarian version makes a distinction between the sentient and the non-sentient. Nevertheless, since the argument commonly begins by stressing continuities between human beings and other animals, it usually emphasizes what human beings think of as being 'higher' animals. So the fate of whales and dolphins is more likely to concern extended humanists than the fate of other sea-dwellers; experiments on chimpanzees, monkeys, cats, perhaps rats, than on fruit-flies. In Regan's large-scale work entitled *The Case for Animal Rights* (1981), his case is in fact made out only for the rights of mammalian animals. Even those who argue that cells should be respected may still suggest that some animals have 'richer experiences' than others (Birch and Cobb, 1981), as, for example, dolphins more than sharks; the death of individual members of these species arouses grief among their fellows, and so our concern for them should be greater. It is easier to win public sympathy for picturesque animals than for the drabber kind.

Biocentric environmentalism

When the critics of environmentalism refer to the environmentalist 'lunatic fringe' this may be a way of concealing the now politically unpopular fact that the critics are actually opposed to every form of environmentalism. Sometimes, too, those whose economic interests are as animal experimenters or battery farmers may categorize every form of extended humanism in these terms. But biocentric environmentalism is most often attacked as lunatic.

We need to draw a distinction, at this point, between biocentric environmentalism considered as a biological thesis with practical environmentalist consequences and the metaphysico-politico-religious views that have been built up around that thesis. As a biological theory it turns attention away from the individual animals, including human beings, who can suffer as a result of social practices (whether pollution or experimentation) and towards the total ecosystem of which they form part, within

483

which individual suffering and individual deaths are of little consequence. (Biocentric environmentalists not uncommonly defend hunting.) What counts is the preservation of the entire system which makes possible the continued existence of living things; it is on the continued health of that system that we should, according to biocentric environmentalism, be concentrating our attention. Its key concept is 'the web of life', now emphasized by biologists who not so long ago were pointing to differences between species rather than to their interrelatedness.

The web of life differs from the older concept of the balance of nature, commonly invoked by earlier environmentalists, in so far as that was taken to be static, often providentially sustained. The web of life, in contrast, recognizes struggles and conflicts; it grants that species can be extinguished, even without human intervention. The most complex version of web of life theory is the Gaia hypothesis. As first presented by Lovelock (1979), this was widely interpreted as being a quasi-religious theory, as its name might suggest. But the later version (Lovelock, 1989) makes plain its character as an elaboration of Darwinism in which species are thought of as modifying the biosphere, through the familiar processes of mutation and natural selection, in a way that assists them to survive.

The practical importance of web-of-life biologies is that they draw attention to the crucial importance for the maintenance of the biosphere of relatively remote, individually minuscule, quite unspectacular, biological processes. Such catch-cries as 'everything is connected to everything else' exaggerate the situation; to pluck a leaf from a eucalypt in Australia will not influence the rate of growth of seaweed in the Sargasso Sea. But it gives expression to the astonishment we feel as totally unexpected connections come to light. They only come to light, however, as the discovery of particular connections; if everything we do influences the constitution of the ozone layer, it would be impossible to pick out the contribution of refrigerants.

Politically, biocentric environmentalism presents special problems. The effects of pollution are often direct and visible, even to those who have no knowledge whatsoever of biology. So are the effects of deforestation on landscapes. Even when they are in remote places, devastated landscapes, landslides, muddy rivers can be shown on television. This is a great assistance to the proponents of environmentalist programmes. In relatively straightforward cases like the connection 'refrigerants – depleted ozone layer – skin cancer' the fear of cancer, too, may win an audience which would not be at all capable of understanding the mechanisms here involved. But in more complicated cases, where the effects of environmental degradation at a particular place are remote and involve complex and often hypothetical connections, it is hard to make a political issue of them.

Even the simpler cases such as pollution reduction, as was earlier said, may involve international co-operation. Similar problems can arise when what is at issue is the preservation of species which do not, at least for their entire life-cycle, belong to any particular country. Whales, fish and migrating birds are examples. In such cases the refusal of a single country to sign (or to keep to the terms of) an international agreement, can lead to the loss of species. Almost all the interactions in which the biocentric environmentalist is interested transcend national borders; they require for their survival the securing of genuine national adherence to international agreements.

There is nothing 'lunatic' about biocentric environmentalism as such. It rests on scientific discoveries, on a network of scientific theories which can only be substantiated or refuted by further investigation. It can be accepted, at this level, by humanists provided only that they abandon certain theses which have often been associated with humanism.

In particular, human beings must not think of themselves as standing in a god-like fashion outside the web of life, able to change, manipulate and govern it as they choose. If segments of what they think of as their natural environment serve as resources for them, this is as true of every other species. In an important sense the traditional concept of *the* environment is dissolved; there are only particular environments (habitats) in a biosphere. Cartesianism therefore has to go, but that does not carry humanism with it. Humanism is quite compatible with the 'process-philosophies' to which many environmentalists now turn, with its starting point Heraclitean, its emphasis on change, activity, interaction and continuous existence through constant interchanges, rather than on fixed substances only externally related to one another.

None of this, however, demonstrates that the human species is 'just one species among others'. The mere existence of environmentalism is enough to demonstrate the contrary. On the one side, it exists only because some members of the human species are unique among living things in their capacity to create environmental devastation, by such means as using medical and agricultural technology to overcome natural population checks. Most other species can safely proceed in the manner advocated by anti-environmentalists, using as a resource anything they can get hold of; those which cannot safely do so neither recognize this fact nor can do anything to avert their fate. On the other side, environmentalism makes sense as a movement only on the assumption that human beings can sometimes be persuaded by informing and preaching to change their ways, to go against their training. Members of some other species can be trained to change their habits, but not by these means. The Hindus created their god Brahma in a human image, with three aspects: human beings can create, preserve and destroy. Even those misanthropists who are so repelled by the third aspect of human beings that they would like to see them wiped off the face of the earth – and it has been said that the degree to which a person is biocentric can be judged by the extent of that person's misanthropy – are displaying their humanity. No other species contains members who are capable of hating their own species. Environmentalists often distrust creating and want to place all the emphasis on preserving. But this is usually taken to involve a return to things as they once were rather than preserving things as they now are – and hence involves destruction. They put their case by creating books and articles in which they call upon their readers to engage in that imaginative thinking which is the essence of creativity.

If in spite of the fact that the conception of the web of life on which biocentrism depends has sound scientific foundations, biocentric environmentalism is so often dismissed as a 'lunatic fringe' doctrine, not only by anti-environmentalists but also by humanistic environmentalists, this is in so far as it has (especially in the United States) come to be associated with attitudes of mind which flourished in the 1960s but have taken new shape under the influence of environmentalism.

That association can come about in a number of ways. The web of life is sometimes interpreted monistically, as if it were the name of an entity which could be thought of as having a specific good of its own. Then biocentrism is taken to bring with it the totalitarian conception of a system to the good of which individual rights and individual happiness ought to be sacrificed.

In some eco-feminist versions, where Lovelock's earlier statement of the Gaia hypothesis caught on, the web of life is identified with an Earth-Mother (as indeed the name 'Gaia' suggests) and such metaphors as 'the rape of nature' are called upon to support the view that environmental degradation is simply a particular manifestation of patriarchal oppression (Merchant, 1980). A *mélange* of ideas from India, China, Japan is appealed to as inculcating proper attitudes to the environment, in spite of the dismal environmental record of the countries where they flourish. Pantheism and pan-psychism are reinstated, along with such doctrines as that every segment of the web of life, including the material environment which living things inhabit, is of equal worth, a doctrine which carries egalitarianism to its most extreme point (Rodman, 1977).

None of these metaphysical speculations, however, is essentially related to the web of life doctrine. This comes out in such a volume as *Green Politics in Australia* (Hutton, 1987), a set of essays by a series of environmental activists. They can by no means be contemptuously dismissed as 'resource environmentalists'; they have fought for the preservation of wildernesses and some of them were closely involved in the formation of the first-ever Green Party in the Australian state of Tasmania, a state rich in wildernesses but relatively poor in other resources. But their political position, like that of most Green parties, stands as far as can be from totalitarianism; they associate environmentalism, rather, with a fully participatory democracy, including industrial democracy. Some of them fought hard to protect urban areas in Sydney against developers; they certainly would not accept any doctrine of equal worth, since they saw Old Sydney as more valuable than what would replace it. One of them recognizes 'eco-fascism' as an outcome particularly to be dreaded (Hutton, 1987, p. 31), in the course of remarking that every political movement has its dark side; a radical eco-feminist Ariel Salleh observes (ibid., p. 87) that a fascination with Indian gurus is in Australia confined to young unemployed women, principally lesbian and generally anti-intellectual. Eco-feminism, indeed, takes a wide variety of very different forms (Plumwood, 1986), some of them insisting upon, others rejecting as a stereotype, the view that women will naturally take a uniquely 'caring' attitude to nature.

There could be no better indication of the fact that, although environmentalists can often join hands on particular issues as in the defence of wildernesses or opposition to the mining and export of uranium, they do not form a coherent political group, even to the extent that, say, Marxists or Roman Catholics do. There is an enormous gap between Plato's Republic and a fully participatory community, or between the Christianity, the Zen Buddhism, the Hinduism and the secularism which different environmentalists may display. In general terms, although with greatly varying emphases, they nevertheless share such objectives as the reduction of population growth, the minimizing of pollution, the economizing of resources, the protection of wild species and their habitats. Very many of them link historically with that variety of perfectibilism which sought salvation in small, self-sustaining communities, if now for ecological as well as personal salvation (Bookchin, 1990). They share the belief that fundamental changes are needed both in the built and the social environment and in the attitudes which have both engendered them and flown from them. But their differences are absolute when it comes to the means of bringing about these changes, about exactly what attitudes need to be engendered, exactly what changes must be made in the built and the social environment. The problem which particularly faces them is how our society could move from its present condition to the ideal 'small is beautiful' society they envisage without using agencies – violence, for example or authoritarian regulation – to which they mostly object (Goodin, 1992). How, too, are big cities to be abolished, even on the assumption that this is desirable, without the effect being that even less empty space is available? It is not surprising that they operate more effectively as pressure groups than as parties, where many of them feel contaminated by the political atmosphere and others find themselves on opposite sides on some of the issues which a parliament has to debate.

See also 1 ANALYTICAL PHILOSOPHY; 8 ANARCHISM; 9 CONSERVATISM; 11 LIBERALISM; 13 SOCIALISM; 14 AUTONOMY; 15 COMMUNITY; 22 DISTRIBUTIVE JUSTICE; 23 EFFICIENCY; 25 EQUALITY; 30 POWER; 31 PROPERTY; 33 RIGHTS; 35 SOCIOBIOLOGY; 38 TOTALITARIANISM; 40 VIRTUE; 41 WELFARE

References

Anderson, F., Mandelker, D. and Tarlock, D., eds: *Environmental Protection: Law and Policy* (Boston: Little, Brown, 2nd edn, 1990).
Bentham, J.: *Introduction to the Principles of Morals and Legislation* (1789), ed. J. H. Burns and H. L. A. Hart (London: Athlone Press, 1970).
Birch, C. and Cobb, J. B.: *The Liberation of Life* (Cambridge: Cambridge University Press, 1981).
Bookchin, M.: *Remaking Society: Pathways to a Green Future* (Boston: South End Press, 1990).
Brundtland, G. H., chair: *Our Common Future* (Oxford: Oxford University Press, 1987).
Callicott, J. B.: 'Animal liberation', *Environmental Ethics*, 2 (1980), 311–38.
Die Grünen: *Das Bundesprogramm* (1983), trans. Hans Fernbach, *The Programme of the German Green Party* (London: Heretic Books, 1983).
Goodin, R. E.: *Green Political Theory* (Oxford: Polity Press, 1992).
Hutton, D.: *Green Politics in Australia* (North Ryde, Sydney: Angus and Robertson, 1987).
Leopold, A.: *A Sand County Almanac* (1949); (New York: Oxford University Press, 1966).
Lovelock, J. E.: *Gaia, A New Look at Life on Earth* (Oxford: Oxford University Press, 1979).
————: *The Ages of Gaia* (Oxford: Oxford University Press, 1989).
Meadows, D. H. et al.: *The Limits of Growth* (Boston: MIT Press, 1972).
Merchant, C.: *The Death of Nature* (San Francisco: Harper & Row 1980).
Naess, A.: 'The shallow and the deep long range environmental movement', *Inquiry*, 16 (1973), 95–100.
Parfit, D.: 'Overpopulation and the quality of life', *Applied Ethics*, ed. Peter Singer (Oxford: Oxford University Press, 1986), pp. 145–64.
Plumwood, V.: 'Ecofeminism: an overview and discussion of positions and arguments: critical review', *Australasian Journal of Philosophy*, Supplement, 64 (1986), 120–38.

Porphyry: *de Abstinentia*, iv, 20.

Porritt, J.: *Seeing Green* (Oxford: Blackwell, 1984).

Regan, T.: *The Case for Animal Rights* (Berkeley: University of California Press, 1981).

Rodman, J.: 'The liberation of nature', *Inquiry*, 20 (1977), 83–145.

Ryder, R.: 'Experiments on animals', *Animals, Men and Morals*, ed. R. Godlovitch and J. Harris (New York: Taplinger, 1972).

Singer, P.: *Animal Liberation* (London: Jonathan Cape, 1975).

Stone, C.: *Should Trees Have Standing?* (Los Altos: Kaufmann, 1974).

Further Reading

For critical bibliographies see Nash (1989, appendix) and Davis (1989).

See also:

Attfield, R.: *The Ethics of Environmental Concern* (Oxford: Blackwell, 1983).

Bramwell, A.: *Ecology in the Twentieth Century* (New Haven, Conn.: Yale University Press, 1989).

Davis, D.: *Ecophilosophy: a Field Guide to the Literature* (San Pedro: R. & E. Miles, 1989).

Devall, B. and Sessions, G.: *Deep Ecology: Living as if Nature Mattered* (Salt Lake City, Utah: Peregrine Smith, 1985).

Dobson, A.: *Green Political Thought* (London: Unwin Hyman, 1990).

Dryzek, J. S.: *Rational Ecology* (Oxford: Blackwell, 1987).

Goodin, R. E.: *Green Political Theory* (Oxford: Polity Press, 1992).

Naess, A.: *Ecology, Community and Lifestyle*, trans. D. Rothenberg (Cambridge: Cambridge University Press, 1989).

Nash, R.: *The Rights of Nature* (Madison: University of Wisconsin Press, 1989; Sydney: Primavera Press, 1990).

Passmore, J.: *Man's Responsibility for Nature* (London: Duckworth; New York: Scribner, 1974; 2nd edn, 1980).

Spretnak, C. and Capra, F.: *Green Politics* (Santa Fe, N.Mex.: Bear, 1986).

Sylvan, R.: 'A critique of deep ecology', *Radical Philosophy*, 40 (1985), 2–12 and 41 (1985), 10–22.

25

Equality

RICHARD J. ARNESON

Introduction

The ideal of equality has led a double existence in modern society. In one guise the ideal has been at least very popular if not uncontroversial and in its other guise the ideal has been attractive to some and repulsive to others. These two aspects of equality are *equality of democratic citizenship* and *equality of condition*.

Equality of democratic citizenship has risen in stature because so many of the twentieth-century regimes that have flouted this ideal have been truly despicable. The ideal demands that each member of society equally should be assured basic rights of freedom of expression, freedom of religion, the right to vote and stand for office in free elections that determine who controls the government, the right not to suffer imprisonment or deprivation at the hands of the state without due process of law, the right to equal protection of the law construed as forbidding laws that assign benefits and burdens in ways that discriminate arbitrarily on the basis of such factors as race, creed, gender, sexual orientation, and ethnicity, and perhaps the right to an education adequate to enable one to fulfil the duties of democratic citizenship. Different theorists conceive the status of equal democratic citizenship somewhat differently; there is no firm consensus as to exactly what rights are essential to democratic citizenship or what should be the reach of these rights (see Chapter 19).

Equality of condition

The notion

Beyond equality of democratic citizenship, the political ideal of egalitarianism encompasses something further. Every nation of the world is divided into haves and have-nots. In industrially advanced market economies, some persons live spectacularly well, some moderately well, some stagnate in poverty. The gap between the life prospects of the best-off and the worst-off individuals, in terms of wealth, income, education, access to medical care, employment and leisure-time options, and any other index of well-being one might care to name, is enormous. If one makes comparisons across rich and poor nations, the gap between best off and worst off is vastly increased. Confronting these disparities, the egalitarian holds that it would be a morally better state of affairs if everyone enjoyed the same level of social and economic benefits. Call this ideal *equality of condition* or *equality of life prospects*.

Equality of condition as I have just characterized it is an amorphous ideal. It cries out for clarification. Exactly what sort of equality of condition is desirable and for what reasons? But before trying to answer that question I want to indicate that egalitarianism in its social and economic dimension has struck many observers as an uninspiring ideal or even as menacingly unattractive or horribly misguided. For the critics, egalitarianism is a dead end, so the exercise of clarifying the notion of equality of condition has been haunted by the worry that the task of clarification will turn out to have been an exercise in futility.

Preliminary doubts

'Equality literally understood is an ideal ripe for betrayal', writes Michael Walzer (1983, p. xi). Equality literally understood requires that everyone should get the same or be treated the same in some specified respect. For example, the regime of *simple equality* according to Walzer is a regime in which everyone has the same amount of money, the same income and wealth, and there are no restrictions on what can be bought and sold. Walzer's objection against simple equality is reminiscent of the distributive justice views of Robert Nozick (1974, pp. 160–4). Since individuals left unrestricted would freely exchange goods and make deals in ways that would swiftly overturn an initially established condition of simple equality, this norm could be upheld over time (if at all) only by continuous exercise of harsh coercion over individuals by the state. But any state capable of carrying out such coercion would become an irresistible target for takeover by a small elite, and the vast inequality in political power among citizens in a society governed by a controlling elite would overshadow the alleged evils of inequality of wealth and income.

This way of putting the point suggests that there might be several forms of literal equality worth seeking, equality of political power among them, and that simple equality of money should not be pursued with singleminded intensity at the expense of other values including the diverse valuable forms of literal equality. The lesson that Walzer wishes to draw from his discussion is quite different, however. According to him the analysis shows the futility of the pursuit of simple equality and by extension the futility of the pursuit of any other sort of literal equality. It is hopeless to try to achieve and sustain any significant literal equality, and the attempt to do so would inevitably steamroller individual liberty and wreak havoc generally. Therefore, we should not seek literal equality, thinks Walzer.

This argument for scrapping the ideal of literal equality proceeds too swiftly. From the stipulated fact that equality conflicts with individual liberty it does not follow that any tradeoff that purchases some progress toward equality at the cost of some loss of individual liberty must be morally unacceptable. And from the stipulated fact that no significant norm of literal equality can be fully achieved and sustained it does not follow that the pursuit of no form of literal equality is worthwhile. For all that has been said so far, movement from a state of great inequality to a state of lesser inequality might be feasible and, from a moral standpoint, highly desirable (Arneson, 1990a). (To clarify this claim, it would be necessary to assert a defensible rule that determines, for any two unequal patterns of distribution, which of the two is the more unequal. For analysis of various measures of inequality, see Sen, 1973.)

A further clue as to what considerations underlie Walzer's position is his suggestion that egalitarians would be well advised to renounce literal equality and seek to promote a non-literal equality ideal which he calls 'complex equality'. The ideal of equality must be complex because there is no one overarching distributional mechanism. Society is divided into distributive spheres, and within each sphere there will arise norms regulating the proper distribution of the good or goods that are unique to that sphere. Such autonomous distribution of each good by the norms of its sphere is threatened by the domination of distribution in one sphere by the outcome of distribution in another sphere, for example, when wealth procures political power or when political power subverts meritocratic job assignment. Walzer stipulates that complex equality obtains in a society when no such domination exists and distribution in all spheres proceeds autonomously according to the norms internal to each sphere.

It is hard to see in what sense complex equality is supposed to be *equality* (Arneson, 1990a; countered by Miller, unpublished). But the ideas – that many different sorts of goods are distributed in a modern society and that the proper way to distribute a good depends on the sort of good that it is – suggest reason to resist the idea that it is morally important to achieve equal distribution of some one good or equal distribution of some measure of all goods among all members of society. The idea that each distributive sphere has its own integrity which should be respected is reason to doubt that society should try to tinker with all distributions in order to achieve some overall measure of equality. There is no reason to expect that some invisible hand would bring it about that the distribution of goods within every sphere according to its own norms would yield an overall pattern of equal distribution, and adjustment by a visible hand would destroy the desired autonomy of the spheres. Or one might think that the various distributional outcomes will not be commensurable on a single scale. But if there is no overall measure of distributional outcomes then the ideal of overall equal distribution is a chimera.

To advance the discussion at this point we need to investigate how *equality of condition* might be defined so as to meet these objections lurking somewhat buried in Walzer's discussion of complex equality.

The resourcist view of equality of condition

Equality of what?

We might start with the thought that people have equal chances to achieve whatever they might seek in life when each person commands equal resources. For the sake of simplicity, imagine that resources can be grouped into three categories: (1) leisure or free time; (2) income (a flow) and wealth (a stock), understood as the opportunity to purchase any of a given array of goods at going prices, up to the limit of one's monetary holdings; and (3) freedom to use whatever goods one possesses in desired ways, within broad limits. One initial difficulty with this resourcist conception of equality of condition is that it does not seem to realize the ideal of equal life chances for all citizens. Consider a simple example (Arneson, 1989). Suppose that Smith and Jones have similar tastes and talents, but Smith is born legless and Jones has two good legs.

Endowed with equal resources (money, leisure time, and freedoms), Smith must spend virtually all his money on crutches whereas Jones is able to use his money to advance his aims in a rich variety of ways. In this example it does not seem as though equality of resources guarantees that Smith and Jones enjoy equality of material condition or equality of life chances in any sense that matters.

The objection against a resourcist measure of equality is that it makes more sense to consider what people are enabled to do and be with their resource shares and measure these opportunities than to fixate on resource shares. Resources are means, and (the objection goes) it is fetishistic to focus on means rather than on what individuals gain with these means (Sen, 1980). People are different, and among the differences among people are differences in individuals' capacities to transform given stocks of resources into satisfaction of their goals. Since resources matter to us in so far as they enable us to achieve goals that matter to us, a proper measure of equal life chances should register variations in people's opportunities to fulfil their goals. This fetishism objection against a resourcist measure of equality suggests two alternative standards: we could measure either (1) to what extent individuals are able to fulfil the goals that they themselves value, or (2) to what extent individuals are able to fulfil goals that are deemed to be objectively valuable or worthwhile. In broad terms, the two options are equality of utility or welfare and equality of valued functionings (Sen, 1985, pp. 185–203).

The advocate of a resourcist conception of equality can try to defend her position with two lines of argument. Responding defensively, the resourcist can suggest that the Smith and Jones example only shows that the domain of resources that should be captured by an equality measure should include internal resources of the person as well as external resources. Healthy legs are a valuable personal resource; so, other things equal, Smith who lacks legs is lacking in resources as compared with Jones who is equipped with a healthy pair of legs. This thought gives rise to the extended resourcist ideal of equality of external resources plus talents broadly construed.

At first glance it is not obvious what might be meant by an ideal of equality of individual talents. External resources such as money can be transferred from one individual to another, so the idea of shifting external resources so as to render people's holdings equal is readily comprehensible. But if talents are non-transferable and we eschew the option of achieving equality by destroying the superior talent of the better endowed, how could we conceive of achieving equality of individual talent endowments? We could implement compensatory education offsetting differences of native endowment, but aside from the evident great inefficiencies that would result from any serious effort in this direction, for many talent differences no amount of training could compensate: no feasible educational regimen would enable me to play piano, run high hurdles, or solve mathematical problems as well as people who are natively gifted at these endeavours.

One ingenious resourcist ploy, introduced by economists and developed for philosophers by Ronald Dworkin, is to interpret equality of internal and external resources as satisfied when persons assigned identical bidding resources bid to an equilibrium in which all external and internal resources are put to auction (Dworkin, 1981; Varian, 1974). When one person bids to purchase a person's internal resources –

her own or another's – in this auction, ownership is interpreted as ownership of hours of time of the person who has the resource, and ownership of time in turn is interpreted as ownership of labour power – the right to demand from the possessor of the resource the highest amount of money that the person could have earned in the labour market working for the length of time that is owned. On this conception any talent an individual possesses that enhances the value of an hour of her labour power is an internal resource that is up for grabs in the imagined auction. In given circumstances the outcome of such an auction would depend on the ensemble of the tastes and talents of the persons assigned equal bidding resources who participate in the auction procedure. In effect equality of resources so conceived gives each individual an equal share of social scarcity. The value of each resource as measured by the auction is (marginally above) the value placed on that resource by the person or persons in society who make the highest bid for it except for the winning bid.

The weakness in this conception of equality of resources as interpreted by the equal auction is that it leads to the 'slavery of the talented'. To see the difficulty, imagine that Smith has a great talent for singing, which commands a very high price in a given society. Other people will then be willing to bid a lot for hours of Smith's labour time in the equal auction. For each hour of her labour time purchased by others in the auction, Smith will have to work at her most lucrative employment for that hour in order to satisfy the legitimate demand for remuneration by the 'owner' of that hour. Smith's free time is a scarce social resource, so in order to obtain genuine free time for herself Smith must bid for hours of her time, on which the auction sets a high price. In contrast, the untalented Jones, whose labour time is not in high demand, can cheaply purchase hours of her free time for her own use. Smith is as it were enslaved by her talent in the equal auction (Roemer, 1985; 1986).

There are various *ad hoc* devices for avoiding this 'slavery of the talented' result. But none can carry conviction, because slavery of the talented is the straightforward result of applying the auction view of resources to personal talents in order to interpret the norm of equality of external and internal resources. It is not a quirk of formulation.

Against the fetishism objection stated at the beginning of this section, the resourcist has both a defensive and an offensive response. The defensive response is the idea of extending the equal auction to talents, which we have just found to be inadequate. Going on the offensive, the resourcist objects that neither the ideal of equality of welfare nor the ideal of equality of capabilities can satisfactorily interpret the intuitive pre-theoretical norm of equality of life chances. Let us take each objection in turn.

Against welfare as the measure

Imagine that we have a stock of goods to distribute to a given group of persons and that our guiding idea is that the distribution should count as equal if and only if it induces the same welfare or desire-satisfaction level for each person in the group. But suppose that Smith has expensive tastes and wants only champagne and fancy sports cars, whereas Jones has cheap tastes and wants only beer and a sturdy bicycle. Other things equal, Smith must be assigned far more resources than Jones if the two are to satisfy their desires to the same extent. But according to the resourcist view, equality of welfare is an inadequate conception of equality of life chances, because individuals should be regarded as capable of taking responsibility for their ends, but equality of welfare takes tastes as given, as though they were beyond the power of individuals to control. Taking tastes to be fixed and dividing resources so that persons with different desires, which put varying pressure on socially scarce resources, end up at the same level of desire satisfaction is unfair to those who have cheap tastes (Rawls, 1982).

This objection initially sounds plausible but is rooted in confusion. In order to defend equality of resources it is urged against the norm of equality of welfare that people should be held responsible for their ends, so it is wrong to adjust resource shares so that whatever ends people select, they ultimately obtain equal welfare. What is being appealed to here is the thought that society should not compensate an individual who reaches one rather than another outcome if it lay within the individual's power to determine which outcome she reached. What lies within the voluntary control of an individual should be deemed to be her responsibility, not the responsibility of society.

That something is awry with this line of thought becomes plain when one reflects that what level of resources an individual succeeds in gaining for herself over the course of her life is to some considerable extent a matter that lies within her voluntary control. The idea that society should not take responsibility for compensating individuals for aspects of their situation that are within their power to control does not support equality of resources rather than equality of welfare.

There are two entirely independent issues that must be distinguished in this context. One issue is whether a norm of equality of condition should measure people's positions (to determine if they are equally or unequally situated) in terms of their resources, welfare, or functionings. A second issue is whether a norm of equality of condition should be concerned to equalize the outcomes that individuals reach or the opportunities they have to reach various outcomes. The responsibility-for-ends objection in effect holds that it would be unfair to compensate an individual in the name of equality for a deficit in the welfare outcome she reaches if it lay within her voluntary control to have reached higher welfare outcomes. The objection then is urging that as egalitarians we should be concerned to render equal the opportunities that people enjoy rather than the outcomes that people reach by voluntary choice among their opportunities. If this is what the responsibility-for-ends objection is driving at, then it is strictly irrelevant to the issue of whether welfare, resources, or functionings would be the best measure for a norm of equality of condition to employ.

This point can be misunderstood. I am not agreeing that individuals should always be deemed fully responsible for their final ends or basic life goals. To some extent these are set for each individual by her genetic endowment and early socialization and education, matters which lie beyond her power to control. Also, even if two persons could voluntarily alter their basic goals from A to B, this task might be extremely difficult or costly for one individual and easy or costless for the second individual. In this case individuals might be deemed responsible to different degrees for their ends (suppose they both adhere to the A goals) even though each of them could have altered her ends by voluntary choice. Third, sometimes even though it is possible for me to alter my ends it would be unreasonable for me to do so. Suppose I now value rock music and I know there is a therapy regimen I could choose to undergo which would alter my tastes, as I suppose, for the worse, so that my taste for rock music would be supplanted by a love of country & western music. It is at least not clear that a norm of equality of condition should refuse to compensate me for any welfare deficit arising from the fact that I prefer rock over country & western music in these circumstances. The point is not that the responsibility-for-ends objection is fully acceptable but rather that to whatever extent the objection is well taken, it has no bearing on the choice of resources versus welfare as the measure.

Against functionings as the measure

Instead of evaluating people's resource holdings by determining what welfare levels they reach by means of these holdings, we could instead list specific things that their resources enable them to do or be. For example, a given allotment of food to a person can be assessed in terms of the nutritional and vigour levels that the food assists that person to attain. Notice, first, that the same pile of food would be transformed by different individuals into different functionings. Notice, second, that just as we can distinguish the actual level of welfare that a person reaches with her resources and the possible welfare levels that she could have reached had she chosen differently, we can distinguish the functionings an individual actually reaches with a given set of resources and the opportunity set of functionings that the individual could have reached with that set of resources. Amartya Sen speaks in this connection of the *functioning capabilities* provided for a particular person by a given set of resources (Sen, 1990). Here then is another conception of equality: arrange distribution so as to render people's functioning capabilities the same.

At this point the resourcist can object that an indexing problem looms. An egalitarian norm has to incorporate a measure such that one can determine whether or not individuals endowed with mixed lots of resources should be deemed equal or not. But given that there are indefinitely many kinds of things that persons can do or become, how are we supposed to sum a person's various capability scores into an overall total? In the absence of such an index, equality of functioning capabilities cannot qualify as a candidate conception of distributive equality. If your resources give you capabilities A, B and C, and mine give me capabilities C, D and E, our capability sets are non-comparable. Only if your set dominates mine, containing everything in mine plus more, is comparison possible. In the general case, comparison will be possible only if we accept a perfectionist standard which ranks the value of all the functionings that an individual's resources enable her to reach. But the resourcist will further object that no single perfectionist scale of value could possibly be an acceptable basis for interpersonal comparisons for the administration of a distributive equality norm in a modern diverse democracy. For example, capabilities could be assessed according to a Roman Catholic standard that gives priority to prospects of salvation, but a norm of equality of condition rooted in this or any other perfectionist dogma would rightly seem merely arbitrary to many citizens. Equality of functioning capabilities thus collapses as an alternative to equality of resources.

We are now in a better position to appreciate Walzer's doubts about equality of money. We can suppose that equality of money stands as a proxy for the more general

495

doctrine of equality of resources. Pluralism defeats this ideal – not so much the pluralism of types of goods cited by Walzer but rather the plurality of reasonable evaluative perspectives that citizens might take toward the goods they have. How can we determine definitively that people's holdings of resources are to be judged equal or unequal when individuals will differ in their evaluations of those resource sets? The indexing problem arises for the equality of resources ideal and so far as I can see proves fatal to it (Arneson, 1990b). Given that there are many sorts of resources or goods that individuals may command, in order to decide whether people's holdings are equal or unequal we need to be able to attach an overall value to the holdings of each person. There are just two possibilities. Either resources are indexed by individuals' subjective evaluation of the contribution their resources can make towards their welfare or they are indexed by some scale of value that is deemed to be objectively valid regardless of people's subjective evaluations. This would be a perfectionist norm. In short, equality of resources must collapse either into a welfarist or a perfectionist view, into equality of welfare or equality of valuable functionings.

Equality of condition: rivals and alternatives

Equality versus the doctrine of sufficiency

Harry Frankfurt has advanced strong objections against the doctrine that it is intrinsically desirable that everyone should have the same income and wealth. Some of his objections apply more broadly than just to this specific target. They reach any form of equality of condition.

With respect to the distribution of income and wealth, the argument goes, what should matter intrinsically to an individual is not how well he does compared to others. What matters is not whether one has more or less money or other resources than other persons but rather whether one has enough, given one's aims and aspirations. This rival to egalitarianism can be labelled the *doctrine of sufficiency*. According to Frankfurt, the amount of resources one possesses is sufficient if a reasonable and well-informed person with one's basic aims would be content with that amount and would not actively seek more. Egalitarian doctrines by contrast tend to focus people's attention on questions of comparison – the size of my resource bundle compared to the amount of resources that other individuals command. By encouraging people to think that these comparisons matter intrinsically, even though on a proper analysis they do not matter intrinsically at all, egalitarianism is alienating. It diverts people's energy, their focus of attention, and their will to critical reflection away from matters of substance and toward matters that do not really intrinsically matter (Frankfurt, 1987).

Once one clearly distinguishes the question of whether one has enough from the question of whether one has more or less than other persons, the examples that some philosophers offer to illustrate the intrinsic importance of equality will be seen to show nothing of the sort. The resource-egalitarian tries to present her favoured principle in an attractive light by considering its application to a situation in which society is divided into income classes that include a very poor and a very rich

496

group. The resource-egalitarian then describes the squalid living conditions of the poor. Their infant mortality rate is high, they lack proper nutrition, clothing and shelter, they are ravaged by diseases that are preventable with the help of medical assistance they cannot afford. The poor are denied access to all but the shabbiest education and degrading, rote, unskilled jobs. They are cruelly afflicted by vulnerability to crime. And so on. In all these respects the rich enjoy vastly more favourable life expectations. The resource-egalitarian then invites us to accept the moral principle that other things equal it is morally desirable that people should have equal money (or, more broadly, equal resources).

The proponent of the doctrine of sufficiency protests that the considerations adduced in the presentation of such examples do not support egalitarianism. For the story the egalitarian tells is one according to which the poor manifestly do not have enough to enable them to lead decently satisfactory lives. The poor are also described as worse off than the rich along the dimension of resource share possession. But is the morally salient feature of the example, prompting the judgement that resources ought to be transferred from the rich to the poor, really the relative disadvantage or rather the insufficiency suffered by the poor?

The sufficiency advocate proposes a way to answer this question. Imagine that all of the members of a society enjoy a very high standard of living, so that everyone can reasonably be presumed to have sufficient resources to support a thoroughly satisfactory life, even though the relative gap between the wealth and income of the rich and poor remains just as large as in the first example described by the resource egalitarian. In comparative terms, the poor are just as badly off in the revised example, in which they enjoy a high level of affluence, as they were in the original example. Resource egalitarianism would then seem to be committed to the judgement that the moral imperative of transferring resources from rich to poor is equally compelling in the two examples. Many will find this judgement unappealing. In contrast, the sufficiency advocate has a ready explanation for the judgement that the case for transfer from rich to poor is strong in the first example and nonexistent in the second example. In the second example it is plausible to suppose that the poor have enough, and how resources are distributed above the line of sufficiency is simply not important from a moral standpoint.

Frankfurt's argument is explicitly directed against the doctrine that upholds equality of money, and some of his comments reflect the thought that it is fetishistic to attach intrinsic significance to resources rather than the extent to which people are enabled by their resource shares to satisfy reasonable goals. So understood, his argument, if successful, would rebut resource egalitarianism not welfare egalitarianism. But the sufficiency advocate is better interpreted as opposing all versions of equality of condition, not just resourcist versions of this doctrine. The problem is not (merely) that the resource egalitarian is focusing on the wrong sort of comparisons. According to the doctrine of sufficiency, the flaw in egalitarianism lies deeper. Any distributive doctrine that ascribes intrinsic significance to comparisons of relative shares – and hence any egalitarian doctrine – is wrong-headed and fetishistic.

The argument of the sufficiency theorist against egalitarianism raises complex issues. I shall respond briefly to three major issues that should be held distinct.

Resource-egalitarianism is fetishistic We care about resources only because either they can do something for us or we can do something with them. Even Silas Marner who wants resources for their own sake likes them because of what one can do with them. And anyway, the Silas Marner syndrome of wanting to have resources but not to use them is uncommon. Since resources virtually by definition are valued as means rather than as ends for their own sake, a theory of distributive justice should at the fundamental level be concerned with what resources enable a person to be or do. This scale could be either subjectivist or perfectionist. The resource holdings of an individual could be measured either by the extent of desire satisfaction they enable her to achieve or by the extent to which they enable her to reach objectively valuable states of affairs. Both the subjectivist and the perfectionist options run into difficulties, but whichever way we go at this juncture, resources drop out of the picture of what fundamentally matters for distributive justice.

Comparisons are alienating The claim is that we should not care about equality of condition because no one should care, except instrumentally, how his condition compares to that of others. I defer consideration of this issue until later.

Sufficiency for all is morally important whereas equality among all is not According to the doctrine of sufficiency, what is morally important is not that everyone should have the same but that as many as possible should have enough. But how much is 'enough'? The examples cited above appeal to the thought that the project of enabling people to rise above dire poverty is a matter of greater moral urgency than the project of enabling everyone to have the same whatever her level of affluence. But a person who has risen above dire poverty could still do much better. As Frankfurt defines *sufficiency*, a person attains this level only when she is content with what she has and would not actively seek more. If there is any level at which it would be reasonable for a person to be content and not seek more, this sufficiency-marking level will surely be high – far above the barely beyond poverty level. But then one cannot appeal to the great moral urgency of lifting people above dire poverty to demonstrate the moral urgency of bringing it about that everyone has enough, for the sufficiency level and the just above poverty level are unlikely to coincide for any individual. If attaining sufficiency is morally important that cannot be because escaping poverty is morally important.

There may also be a problem about continuity for the doctrine of sufficiency. If the doctrine of sufficiency holds that getting people just to the sufficiency level is important but moving them beyond that level is unimportant, that would seem to attach undue weight to a tiny gain from a point just on one side of a line as compared to a tiny gain to a point just past the line. Assume that the level of sufficiency is calculated in welfare terms and that Smith's sufficiency level is judged to be 100. The doctrine of sufficiency would seem to be committed to saying that moving Smith from 99.99 to 100 is a morally weighty matter whereas moving Smith from 100 to 100.01 is a trivial matter. This view seems arbitrary. However, this result could be avoided by a function that weights the moral value of gains so that in the neighbourhood of the sufficiency line (on either side) gains matter more, with the weight gradually tapering off as one moves away from the sufficiency line. So the continuity objection against the doctrine of sufficiency is not decisive.

According to Frankfurt, an individual has enough at the point at which she is content with what she has, and reasonably would not actively seek more. But perhaps a reasonable person would always seek ever more. If so, the doctrine of sufficiency as interpreted by Frankfurt sets no upper bound to reasonable seeking. The doctrine of sufficiency is supposed to be counterposed to a maximizing view of rationality (Slote, 1989). Instead of seeking to maximize one's benefits, a rational person (in so far as she seeks her own self-interest) according to the sufficiency doctrine might seek a moderate amount deemed to be satisfactory and be content with that. But in order to get clear on the difference between a maximizing conception of rationality and a sufficiency conception, one should note that the decision not to seek further gains can be part of a maximizing strategy. The gains might be associated with costs such that there is no net gain from further seeking. Or the reach for gain might also carry a risk of losses, such that one maximizes expected utility by forgoing the reach for gain. A satisficing strategy (seek a satisfactory level of gain and do not search further for more) can be a maximizing strategy in circumstances where any further stretch for more carries a loss of expected utility. Moreover, viewing a policy of moderation as a maximizing strategy solves the problem of how one might non-arbitrarily set the 'satisfactory' or 'sufficiency' level: the level is to be set at a level that maximizes expected gain.

Once we observe the need to distinguish a genuine doctrine of sufficiency or moderation from moderation or satisficing as a means to maximization in certain circumstances, we see that the doctrine of sufficiency is committed to the following. For each individual one can determine a level of benefit such that with her aims, the individual should reasonably be content with this level and not seek more. Even if the individual could certainly secure a large net gain for herself by taking action, the individual would be reasonable to forgo such action on the ground that what she has already suffices. For example, I have been looking for a house that is by the beach, large, and visually attractive, and I have determined that finding a house with any two of these desirable features would suffice. I have located such a house and am satisfied with it, but before I conclude a deal for a sale an agent who knows my tastes perfectly informs me that a house with all three desirable features is available at the same price on the same terms. The first house suffices, the second house is better, and the cost of making a deal and the risk that no deal can be reached are the same for the first house and the second. The doctrine of sufficiency is committed to the claim that in some cases that fit this description the individual would be reasonable to take the first house rather than the second because the first house suffices. On a maximizing view, taking less when one could get more is irrational.

As the doctrine of sufficiency is described, it becomes decreasingly clear why attaining the level of sufficiency should always be a matter of special moral urgency. Suppose that there are three groups of individuals, very poor, poor and well off, and that all individuals within each group happen to have goals such that the level of sufficiency is the same for all of them. Suppose that we could either move the very poor group to the poor level, where none will attain the level of sufficiency, or we could move an equal number of well-off individuals to a level of sufficiency for each of them. I don't see that helping the very poor should have lesser priority than helping the well-off even though only helping the well-off in these circumstances will thin the ranks of those who do not have enough. For example, it is consistent with the terms of the example set so far that more utility is gained overall if the very poor are helped than if the well-off are enabled to gain sufficiency. Consider also a second example. We can choose either to move the very poor group to the poor level or with the same resources we can move the well-off group far past sufficiency to the bliss level, which we may assume to be far past sufficiency on a utility scale. Suppose that in the second example enormously more utility is produced by raising the better-off to bliss than by raising the very poor up the ladder a bit. So in this case, I submit, choosing to help the better-off might well be morally preferable to helping the very poor, given the disparity in the gains each group would get from the help we could give. In neither example does the 'sufficiency' level, even supposing it can be defined coherently and determined non-arbitrarily, provide any special reasons for choosing to help one set of potential beneficiaries rather than another.

I conclude this section by summarizing the discussion: three aspects of Frankfurt's attack on the ideal of equality of condition have been distinguished. The objection that resource-egalitarianism is fetishistic is well taken, but leaves other versions of the equality of condition ideal unscathed. A second objection is that any doctrine of distributive justice that attaches intrinsic importance to comparisons among persons' holdings is alienating. I have set this aside for now. A third objection claims that egalitarianism should be rejected in favour of a superior rival, the doctrine of sufficiency. I have tried to rebut this objection by casting doubt on the adequacy of the doctrine of sufficiency.

Equality versus Pareto

Equality of condition conflicts with the Pareto norm, which many view as a minimally controversial and highly plausible fairness requirement.

Consider the version of equality of condition that holds: everyone should have the same amount of goods (according to the most appropriate measure of 'goods'). Following Joseph Raz (1986, pp. 225–7), we can state the principle in these other words: if anyone is to have some amount of goods, everyone should have the same amount. In a context where lumpy (not continuously divisible) goods are to be distributed, this principle of strict equality dictates wastage or destruction of goods. If there are three exquisite marble statues to be distributed among four persons, the only distribution consistent with equality is that no person gets any statues. As Douglas Rae and his associates (1981, p. 129) comment, reflecting on this implication of equality, 'Equality itself is as well pleased by graveyards as by vineyards.'

Another equally familiar example involves the distribution of goods to persons when the distribution we enforce now will affect people's incentives to behave and thus the distribution that will come about later. In the familiar image, how a pie is distributed now can affect the size of the pie that will be produced later. If society offers superior remuneration for superior performance, those capable of superior performance will be given an incentive to produce it. Remuneration schemes that elicit higher productivity can produce gains for everyone over an extent of time compared to the baseline of equal distribution.

The principle of strict equality holds that the equality it recommends should be upheld (1) even when unequal distribution would render everyone better off, and (2) even when unequal distribution would render someone better off and no one worse off. In the face of these implications, one might temper advocacy of equality by holding that equality should have lesser priority than the Pareto norm. A state of affairs is Pareto optimal when it is not possible to change it by making someone better off without making anyone worse off. A state of affairs is Pareto suboptimal when it is possible to change it by making someone better off without making anyone worse off. The Pareto norm simply holds that principles of distributive justice must not recommend Pareto suboptimal distributions.

The Pareto norm appears to express a minimal and rather uncontroversial notion of fairness: if one can make someone better off without making anyone else worse off, why not do so? Sometimes the idea of Pareto optimality is construed in terms of utility or desire satisfaction: a state of affairs is Pareto optimal when no one's level of desire satisfaction can be increased without decreasing someone else's level of desire satisfaction. When the idea of Pareto optimality is so construed, it can be challenged by imagining cases in which someone's desires are perverse or degraded, and querying why matters are improved when someone's perverse or degraded desires are better satisfied. But this challenge reflects doubt that someone is always better off whenever their level of desire satisfaction is increased, not a challenge to the idea of Pareto optimality or the Pareto norm *per se*.

The Pareto norm as stated at the end of the next-to-last paragraph is ambiguous. When the ambiguity is removed, the Pareto norm takes a less controversial and a more controversial form. First, notice that *Pareto optimality* is defined in terms of what is possible in principle. In practice, the achievement of Pareto-optimal or efficient outcomes may be unfeasible. We can imagine a possible improvement but cannot achieve it. Second, the Pareto norm can be given a weak and a strong formulation. The weak Pareto norm holds that principles of distributive justice should not recommend outcomes from which it is feasible to effect a Pareto-improvement. The strong Pareto norm holds that principles of distributive justice should not recommend outcomes from which it is in principle possible to effect a Pareto improvement, whether or not such improvement is feasible. The weak Pareto norm is less controversial, the strong Pareto norm more so.

To illustrate the difference: suppose that raising the incomes of the poor is a goal of equity and that to achieve this goal an income tax is instituted. The income tax will distort taxpayers' leisure versus income decisions and hence inevitably produces inefficiency. If we do all we can to pick the policy that results in the least efficiency that is compatible with achieving the equity goal, the policy is a constrained Pareto optimum and the weak Pareto norm is satisfied. But the strong Pareto norm tells us not to select any outcome off the Pareto frontier. Restricting the policy choice in this way may not allow any movement at all in the direction of satisfying the equity goal, given that any move toward equity inevitably involves some inefficiency. In general, the strong Pareto norm is a very demanding principle that many will reject. The weak Pareto norm says that other things being equal, achieving Pareto optimality is desirable. The strong Pareto norm says that the goal of achieving Pareto optimality should take absolute priority over all other values.

The principle of strict equality conflicts with the strong, not the weak, Pareto norm. So if one's response to the conflict between Pareto optimality and equality is to give equality no weight at all in conflict with Pareto, my hunch is that the explanation of this response is likely to be that one gives little or no weight to equality *per se* (contrary to what one might initially have supposed). After all, where a fairness or equity requirement that elicits strong allegiance conflicts with the strong Pareto norm, the committed will dig in their heels: 'So much the worse for efficiency.'

A commitment to adherence to the norm of strict equality when it conflicts with the Pareto norm need not involve complete indifference to the level of human welfare or well-being at which equality is sustained. For instance, one might opt for the view that equality should be always sustained at the highest feasible level of welfare for all. This view might be motivated by the background beliefs that (1) people's welfare should be proportional to their personal deservingness, and (2) no one ever really is more deserving than another person because the achievements and dispositions that are cited as evidence of superior deservingness always turn out under examination to be determined by features of inheritance and favourable socialization for which the supposedly deserving individual can take no credit. So everyone's deservingness is always the same as anyone else's and if people are to be rewarded according to their deservingness their rewards should always be exactly equal. But what is odd about these background beliefs is the combination of the thoughts that the conditions of differential deservingness among persons are never met and that deservingness still matters morally a great deal.

Equality versus tilting towards the worse-off

If you give lexical priority to the Pareto norm over the principle of strict equality, my suggestion is that this ranking reveals that equality *per se* matters little or not at all to you. One possibility worth exploring is that the commitment to egalitarianism is not a matter of favouring equality *per se* but a matter of giving priority to the worst-off. Parfit (1990) explores the differences between these and related moral norms.

It is instructive to observe how giving priority to the interests of the worse-off might readily be conflated with valuing equality of condition for its own sake when the task is to distribute a fixed stock of goods. Suppose that we have on hand a fixed stock of the good X, which can be divided as finely as one pleases. X is intrinsically valuable, not merely valuable as a means to further goods, and the morally appropriate distribution of X is thought to be desirable for its own sake and not merely as a means to achieving a distribution of some further good. There are N individuals in society and for each of them, the more of X one has, the better off one is. If the task is to distribute X according to one's moral values, the goal of equal distribution and the goal of doing as well as one can for the worst off both recommend the same choice of distribution: divide X so that each of the N persons has an equal share, a 1/N share. Indeed, not only a strict leximin priority for the worst off recommends equal division. Any rule that assigns even slightly greater weight to the worst off as against everyone else would recommend equal division.

The differences between literal equality and priority to the worst-off only emerge into view when one considers examples in which how one distributes a stock of goods affects aggregate production of the final good whose distribution is the object of moral concern. Consider a simple two-period example in which the pattern of distribution in the first period affects the amount to be distributed as well as the pattern of distribution in the second period. Imagine that society can choose between just two distributions: one which yields an equal distribution of utility for all persons summed across the two periods, and another distribution, which induces able individuals to produce more in the first period by offering a reward of high consumption in the second period for high production in the first period. In the second distribution there is inequality of utility but everyone is better off under this distribution than they would be under the equal distribution rule. In this example the norm of equalizing utility favours the equal distribution choice while the norm of maximizing utility giving priority to the worst-off favours the unequal distribution because the worst-off do better under inequality than under the regime of equality. Equality is only instrumentally valuable from the perspective of the norm of giving priority to the interests of the worst-off.

This tilting conception of egalitarianism is given a specific expression in John Rawls' difference principle, the maximin norm (Rawls, 1971). Thomas Nagel (1979, pp. 117–18) offers this characterization of the general idea: 'The essential feature of an egalitarian priority system is that it counts improvements to the welfare of the worse off as more urgent than improvements to the welfare of the better off.' The idea of giving priority to the worse off is of course independent of the issue of whether one measures individual positions in terms of welfare, resources, functionings or some further alternative, but let that pass. If in pairwise competition one always favours the worse-off, one ultimately favours the worst-off, so Nagel continues: 'What makes a system egalitarian is the priority it gives to the claims of those whose overall life prospects put them at the bottom, irrespective of numbers or of overall utility.' Notice that the last phrase quoted from Nagel introduces a quite new idea: to the proposal to favour the least advantaged is now conjoined the much stronger requirement of lexical priority – a prohibition against tradeoffs between the advantage of the least well-off and the better-off. But in the general case the maximin injunction to give lexical priority to the interests of the worst-off in any conflict with the interests of better-off individuals is implausible. Maximin implies that if one's choices are limited to keeping the status quo or altering it by subtracting a penny from the holdings of the worst-off so as to gain a million dollars for the second worst-off, the status quo should be retained. Few would ratify such an extreme weighting. It would be better to examine Nagel's interpretation of egalitarianism separately from the issue of the appropriateness of lexical priority.

Let us say that a *tilting* conception of egalitarianism is one that assigns greater moral weight (as specified in the next sentence) to achieving same-sized gains or preventing same-sized losses for those persons who rank worse off than others on an ordinal scale. According to a tilting conception, the comparative moral urgency of bringing about a same-sized gain for one person as opposed to another is deter-

503

mined, so far as egalitarianism is concerned, entirely by their ordinal ranking. The worst-off is given priority over the second worst-off, who in turn is given priority over the third worst-off, and so on. The comparative weighting, the degree of tilting towards the interests of the worse-off, is a matter that this definition leaves open: This can vary from the extreme weighting of a maximin principle to a principle that accords just marginally greater urgency to gains for the worse-off (such a principle would be barely distinguishable in its recommendations from a straight aggregate maximizing principle).

Tilting conceptions including Rawlsian maximin regard the moral urgency of achieving a benefit of a given size for a given person as a function solely of the ranking that identifies how well off the person is by comparison with others (so long as the benefit to be conferred does not alter the comparative rankings). What counts is only whether the person is worst-off, second worst-off, and so on. The absolute amount of the gap that separates individuals at these various benefit levels does not have any bearing on the issue of moral urgency. But the information that tilting conceptions bid us ignore in deciding on our course of action is plainly relevant.

To illustrate the problem, consider the issue of the moral value of conferring a very small welfare gain on either the best-off or the worst-off member of society under two conditions, great inequality and approximate equality. Under great inequality the gap between worst-off and best-off is enormous, say 1000 on a welfare scale. Under approximate equality the distribution of welfare has been compressed so that there is only a very slight difference, say two units, between the welfare levels enjoyed by the best-off and the worst-off. Tilting principles will not find these two conditions morally distinguishable. Exactly the same priority will be assigned to aiding the worst-off in the two conditions. But I submit that whether we confer a welfare gain on the best-off or the worst-off is intuitively a matter of grave urgency when the gap between top and bottom is very great and a morally inconsiderable matter when the gap between top and bottom is very small. Moreover, it is not just the absolute value of the gap between top and bottom welfare levels that is decisive for judgements ranking the moral urgency of giving aid to better-off or worse-off, but also the absolute value of the welfare level enjoyed by the worse-off. (An absolute gap of 8 between the welfare levels of top and bottom might qualify as a great gap if the initial welfare level of the worst-off is zero yet would qualify as a small gap if the initial welfare level enjoyed by the worst-off is 1000 on the same scale.)

It is implausible to suppose that only ordinal welfare rankings determine the moral value of conferring a gain of a given size on a person. Consider instead the thought that comparison of any sort is a secondary phenomenon in determining the value of conferring a gain on a person. This is the thought raised by Frankfurt above (p. 498). Consider this principle: the moral value of achieving a welfare gain of a given size (or preventing the loss of a given size) for a person is greater, the lower is that person's cardinal welfare level (Weirich, 1983). This principle is not essentially comparative, as we can see by noting that it has implications for a one-person Robinson Crusoe world. (Suppose that there are two moral principles that should guide Crusoe: respect the natural environment for its own sake, and increase your welfare. The principle we are considering tells Crusoe that the higher his welfare becomes, the more weight he should give to respecting the environment.) But of course, in cases where we have to choose between helping one of several persons, the principle (once rendered determinate in content) would provide a basis for comparison that would determine the moral urgency of helping one rather than another.

Conclusion

One lesson of this chapter is that equality of life prospects is an elusive ideal. Versions of it abound. The indefiniteness of this egalitarian ideal tends to obscure the issue of its attractiveness. My hunch is that for many persons (including myself) who regard themselves as egalitarians, the content of this concern has nothing to do with favouring equality *per se* or even with giving priority to the worse-off. The underlying value that supports equality sometimes and giving priority to the worst-off often is the idea that the moral benefit of conferring a given benefit on a person is greater, the worse off the person is prior to receipt of this benefit. But whether or not one happens to agree with this thought, it should be agreed that the extent to which it is rational to endorse the norm of equality cannot be determined until equality is distinguished from priority to the worse-off and other, different values with which it might be conflated. 'How could it not be an evil that some people's life prospects at birth are radically inferior to others?' Nagel (1991, p. 28) asks. But in fact, Nagel agrees with Rawls that to the extent that these inequalities were found to be maximally productive for those who suffer inferior prospects, the inequalities would not be morally regrettable.

The displacement of equality by other moral ideals can seem disquieting. In the writings of several of the authors canvassed in this survey one can discern in those who reject some versions of equality a tendency to cast about for some sort of equality that can be embraced as intrinsically morally desirable. Rejecting simple equality, Walzer endorses complex equality (whatever that is). Rejecting any ideal of equality of condition prescribing equal distribution of some good to all members of society, Miller (1990) endorses equality of status, which is stipulated as holding just in case every citizen regards herself as fundamentally the equal of every other citizen. (This ideal could be met in a hierarchical feudal or *laissez-faire* capitalist society all of whose members are Christian and regard each other as equally loved by God and so fundamentally equals.)

Even Ronald Dworkin, who at least tentatively appears to endorse equality of resources as a distributive ideal, regards a commitment to equality of resources as flowing from a commitment to a more abstract and more fundamental political ideal of treating all citizens as equals. Government has 'an abstract responsibility to treat each citizen's fate as equally important' (1986, p. 296). According to this abstract conception of equality, 'the interests of each member of the community matter, and matter equally' (Kymlicka, 1990, p. 4). Abstract equality is also said to require the government to treat all citizens with equal concern. In response: these formulations are not equivalent to one another. Different notions are being bandied about under the heading of 'abstract equality'. Roughly, what the ideal of abstract equality appears to come to is non-discrimination or impartiality: a government should not arbitrarily discriminate in its treatment of one citizen versus another, but should impartially treat all citizens in a principled way. The interests of any citizen should weigh the same as any other in government policy, according to whatever function mapping interests to policy is entailed by correct principles. Without further substantive moral premisses this abstract 'equality' does not imply egalitarian treatment of citizens in any substantive sense. If Dworkin ends up endorsing any conception of equality of life prospects, that posture cannot be supported by interpreting abstract equality. No amount of interpretation of a non-egalitarian premiss will imply a substantively egalitarian principle without the addition of substantive moral premisses. The rhetoric of 'interpretation' and of rendering 'abstract' equality more 'concrete' can only serve to obscure exactly what those premisses might be and what reasons might support them.

See also I ANALYTICAL PHILOSOPHY; 3 HISTORY; 5 ECONOMICS; 6 POLITICAL SCIENCE; IO FEMINISM; II LIBERALISM; I3 SOCIALISM; I8 CORPORATISM AND SYNDICALISM; I9 DEMOCRACY; 22 DISTRIBUTIVE JUSTICE; 23 EFFICIENCY; 30 POWER; 3I PROPERTY; 34 SECESSION AND NATIONALISM; 4I WELFARE

References

Arneson, R.: 'Equality and equal opportunity for welfare', *Philosophical Studies*, 56 (1989), 77–93.
————: 'Against "complex equality"', *Public Affairs Quarterly*, 4 (1990a), 99–110.
————: 'Primary goods reconsidered', *Nous*, 24 (1990b), 429–54.
Dworkin, R.: 'What is equality? Part 2: equality of resources', *Philosophy and Public Affairs*, 10 (1981), 283–345.
————: *Law's Empire* (Cambridge, Mass. and London: Harvard University Press, 1986).
Frankfurt, H.: 'Equality as a moral idea', *Ethics*, 98 (1987), 21–43.
Kymlicka, W.: *Contemporary Political Philosophy: An Introduction* (Oxford: Oxford University Press, 1990).
Miller, D.: 'Equality', in *Philosophy and Politics*, ed. G. Hunt (Cambridge: Cambridge University Press, 1990).
————: 'Complex equality', manuscript.
Nagel, T.: 'Equality', in *Moral Questions* (Cambridge: Cambridge University Press, 1979), pp. 106–27.
————: *Equality and Partiality* (Oxford: Oxford University Press, 1991).
Nozick, R.: *Anarchy, State, and Utopia* (New York: Basic Books, 1974).
Parfit, D.: 'On giving priority to the worse off', manuscript, 1990.
Rae, D., Yates, D., Hochschild, J., Morone, J. and Fessler, C.: *Equalities* (Cambridge, Mass.: Harvard University Press, 1981).
Rawls, J.: *A Theory of Justice* (Cambridge, Mass.: Harvard University Press, 1971).
————: 'Social unity and primary goods', *Utilitarianism and Beyond*, ed. A. Sen and B. Williams (Cambridge: Cambridge University Press, 1982), pp. 159–86.
Raz, J.: 'Equality', in *The Morality of Freedom* (Oxford: Oxford University Press, 1986), pp. 217–44.
Roemer, J.: 'Equality of talent', *Economics and Philosophy*, I (1985), 151–86.
————: 'Equality of resources implies equality of welfare', *Quarterly Journal of Economics*, 101 (1986), 751–84.
Sen, A.: 'Equality of what?', *The Tanner Lectures on Human Values*, vol. 1, ed. S. McMurrin (Cambridge: Cambridge University Press, 1980), pp. 195–220.

————: 'Well-being, agency and freedom: the Dewey lectures 1984', *Journal of Philosophy*, 82 (1985), 169–221.

————: 'Justice: means versus freedom', *Philosophy and Public Affairs*, 19 (1990), 111–21.

Slote, M.: *Beyond Optimizing: A Study of Rational Choice* (Cambridge, Mass.: Harvard University Press, 1989).

Walzer, M.: *Spheres of Justice: an Essay on Pluralism and Equality* (New York: Basic Books, 1983).

Varian, H.: 'Equity, envy, and efficiency', *Journal of Economic Theory*, 9 (1974), 63–91.

Weirich, P.: 'Utility tempered with equality', *Nous*, 17 (1983), 423–39.

Further reading

Alexander, L. and Schwarzschild, M.: 'Liberalism, neutrality and equality of welfare vs. equality of resources', *Philosophy and Public Affairs*, 16 (1987), 85–110.

Arneson, R.: 'Liberalism, distributive subjectivism, and equal opportunity for welfare', *Philosophy and Public Affairs*, 19 (1990), 158–94.

Cohen, G. A.: 'On the currency of egalitarian justice', *Ethics*, 99 (1989), 906–44.

————: 'Incentives, inequality, and community', unpublished Tanner Lectures.

Daniels, N.: 'Equality of what? Welfare, resources, or capabilities?', *Philosophy and Phenomenological Research*, 50, supp. (1990), 273–96.

Dworkin, R.: 'What is equality? Part 1: equality of welfare', *Philosophy and Public Affairs*, 10 (1981), 185–246.

Scanlon, T.: 'Preference and urgency', *Journal of Philosophy*, 72 (1976), 655–69.

————: 'The significance of choice', *The Tanner Lectures on Human Values*, vol. 8, ed. S. McMurrin (Salt Lake City: University of Utah Press, 1988), pp. 149–216.

Sen, A.: *On Economic Inequality* (Oxford: Oxford University Press, 1973).

Van Parijs, P.: 'Equal endowments as undominated diversity', *Alternatives to Welfarism: Essays in Honour of Amartya Sen*, a special issue of *Recherches Economiques de Louvain*, 56 (1990), 327–55.

26

Federalism

WILLIAM H. RIKER

In the nineteenth and twentieth centuries, federations became a widely used constitutional form. They were rare before the nineteenth century and it may be that they will become less attractive in the twenty-first century. But for now they are well approved. And this is surprising because this era has also been an era of nationalism when the nation-state, the sovereign political organization of the folk, is also well approved. These two forms are in some ways contradictory: nation-states derive from, justify, and separate out a single ethnic group, while federations may – and often do – bring together political units with different ethnic bases. So a difficult problem for interpreting federalism is to explain the modern approval of this pragmatic, instrumental constitution in an era that embraces simultaneously the emotional and often irrational loyalties of nationalism.

To begin, just what is federalism or the notion of government by federation? One elementary feature is a two-tier government. A set of constituent governments acknowledge that a federal government has authority over all their territory and peoples for those functions covering the whole territory, while they retain for themselves those functions related just to their own territories. But, of course, all governments – except those with tiny populations – are decentralized with at least two tiers. So the number of tiers cannot be the distinguishing feature of federalism.

If we take the word seriously, it must depend on an agreement. Its Latin root *foedus* is an agreement or covenant, but it is a very special kind of agreement because *foedus* is also *fides* or trust. So by its root a federation is a bargain about government, a bargain based, however, not on an enforcement procedure, but on simple trust itself. Ordinary bargains or contracts depend on a judiciary to punish reneging. But the agreement to create a judiciary can hardly depend on what is yet to be created. So the special covenant of a federation is necessarily something continuously advantageous to all parties. When all are known to benefit, then each can reasonably rely on the others to keep the agreement. This is enforcement by rational mutual confidence in each other.

The content of this agreement is the division of functions among tiers. All governments are organized in tiers, but federations embody the arrangement of tiers in a permanent agreement. It ensures that governments at the constituent and central tiers always exist and retain their assigned duties. Governments that are not federations can reorganize the local units at will, destroying old regional units and creating new ones. But in federations the constituent units have agreed with each other that each will retain its identity and its unique functions.

Extreme decentralization			Extreme centralization
Independent	Alliance	Federation	Unitary state or empire
		Peripheralized Centralized	

Figure 26.1
Degrees of centralization

Thus federalism is a constitutionally determined tier-structure. If its constitutional feature is ignored, then it is merely some particular arrangement for decentralization. Unfortunately, in recent years students of policy (especially economists) have so treated it, thereby overlooking the whole point of federalism; namely that the tiered structure cannot be arbitrarily revised.

To visualize this concept of federalism, consider a set of governments each with its own territory. At one extreme they can be totally independent of each other. If they undertake concerted action, however, they at least need institutions to execute it. The simplest such institution is an alliance, where all the decision-making power continues to reside in the independent governments, but where there is also some executive authority to carry out the (usually unanimously) agreed action. Alliances are, however, often fragile and ineffective. So if the independent governments want permanence and efficiency, they may federate and thereby create a central government with independent decision-making authority for some functions. Finally, at the extreme of integration, the independent governments may simply vanish into the imperial centre. So we can set forth the scale of centralization in figure 26.1 and thereby demarcate federation from other forms fairly sharply. For a federation to exist, the central government must have authority to decide on action for at least one function entirely on its own and without reference to the preferences of the constituent governments. (If the central government cannot do this much, then the organization is at best an alliance.) On the other hand, the constituent governments must also have authority to decide on action for at least one function entirely independently of the centre and each other. (If they cannot do this much, then the organization is completely unitary.) Federations thus cover a wide range of divisions of functions. Those close to the alliance end of the scale are called peripheralized, and those close to the unitary end are called centralized.

The complexity of this description and the lack of clarity in the assignments of functions suggest an obvious question: Why on earth would framers of constitutions adopt so difficult a political form? The answer is, of course: so that the rulers of a set of independent states can accomplish some objective that is not feasible independently or in alliance. Of course, the rulers of one state might incorporate other states into their state in order to aggregate resources. Indeed, throughout recorded history this is what has usually happened. Imperial expansion is a far more frequent method of aggregation than is federalism. But imperial expansion is costly, if, that is, the potential victims resist. So occasionally ambitious expansionists federate rather than conquer.

What goals are sufficiently desired to lead to federation? The goal most frequently observed is military, though, of course, that goal is always instrumental. Wars are not usually fought for their own sake, for the pure joy of fighting and dying, but aggressively for the sake of trade, territory, plunder and tribute, or defensively, for the sake of resistance and independence. Success in war depends, however, on resources. So the aggregation of resources for war is the primary, though instrumental, motive for federation. Indeed, the rulers of all successful federations, that is, federations that have lasted more than a few years, have initially displayed some kind of military purpose.

One frequent purpose has been rebellion or civil war. Subordinate units of an empire rebel simultaneously and then federate for better resistance. Thus the Dutch republic facilitated the rebellion of the provinces in the Netherlands against the Spanish dominion; the United States facilitated the rebellion of some American colonies against Great Britain; and the several Spanish American federations (Argentina, Mexico, Venezuela, Gran Columbia, the Central American Federation, the latter two of which were short-lived) facilitated the rebellion against Spain. Another frequent purpose has been to defend against the imperial ambition of neighbours; for example, the Swiss confederation (against Habsburg ambition), the Soviet Union (against a potential Western threat which Lenin preferred to meet by seducing the non-Russian provinces rather than by conquering them, which he probably could not have done anyway), the Canadian confederation (against the threat of invasion from the United States, which had occurred thrice previously and seemed again potential at the end of its civil war), the Australian commonwealth (as against the new – in 1900 – Pacific imperialism of Japan and Germany), etc. Still a third military purpose has been to absorb neighbours in order to prepare for aggressive expansion. Thus Yugoslavia became a federation to further Tito's plans for a middle European empire (but Stalin beat him to the draw). And a fourth military purpose is to absorb neighbours, with less cost than conquest, mollifying them with the appearance of continuing sovereignty. The Delian league of the Athenian empire is an ancient example. Dual monarchies also have this character: the Austro-Hungarian empire in the nineteenth century and perhaps even Britain in the eighteenth. Surely the German empire, which absorbed Bavaria and Württemberg after 1871, is a clear-cut example. And the Indian federation of today proved an excellent way to absorb the princely states. The Malay federation, turned Malaysia, absorbed Singapore and Brunei, and the Nigerian federation enabled the North to subdue the East. Of course, many cases fall in two categories. India seems best placed in the fourth category, but it could just as easily fit in second (in the sense of defending against Pakistan) and Malaysia surely also was defending against an aggressive Indonesia.

This outline of categories of military rationales for federation, within which I have included most well-known federations, makes it clear that at their initiation they all had some military purpose. This observation is strengthened by considering the instances of federations that didn't work; i.e. that were abandoned within a few years, returning to independent states or becoming fully unitary. These failures reflected the lack of any military purpose, defective structures (e.g. one large and dominant unit, as in the USSR or the short-lived Egyptian–Syrian federation or very few units as in New Zealand) or both.

Many of these failed federations were initially established by the British government, which also established some successful ones. After observing the success of the United States, the first federation formed from previous British colonies, and after successfully acquiescing in Canada and Australia, the British government repeatedly urged its newly independent or about-to-be independent colonies to federate. Many did so. Canada, Australia and India remain federations. But New Zealand, South Africa, Pakistan, the West Indies and Rhodesia-Nyasaland all abandoned the federal form. Nigeria is an equivocal case: it has been a federation for two brief periods, otherwise a centralized dictatorship. Two of these governments (Pakistan and Nigeria) had very defective structures (i.e. very few units and one dominant unit) and found they needed a unitary form for civil war. With geographically separated parts, Pakistan broke up into two non-federated independent states. Nigeria, with only three states, had a defective structure, revealed when one unit rebelled and civil war ensued. When again a federation, Nigeria restructured into twenty-one states, though this did not prevent the re-establishment of dictatorship.

The other failed ex-British federations abandoned federalism because there was simply no military reason for them to be federal. There were no enemies on the scene and hence they did not need to worry about maintaining internal order. Non-British federations that were born dead displayed the same range of reasons for failure: the French-sponsored Mali federation in West Africa had no military rationale and hence collapsed into unitary governments; the Javanese immediately rejected the Dutch-sponsored Indonesian federation, thinking it a Dutch trick and preferring to integrate by conquest; and several Spanish-American federations collapsed as militarily unnecessary. In general, the history of failed federations implies about the same point as the history of successful ones: initially, there must be a compelling reason to aggregate resources and this compulsion is invariably military, though sometimes framers prefer imperial to federal institutions to solve the military problems at, perhaps, less cost.

As the previous paragraphs indicate, federations have appeared ever since ancient times: in ancient Greece (and some say in ancient Israel), in medieval Europe (the Swiss, Suabian and north Italian leagues), and in early modern Europe (the Dutch republic). But federalism began to flourish in the nineteenth century with imperial Germany as well as with the spin-offs of Spanish, Portuguese and British empires. The pace accelerated in the twentieth century with the break-up of empires, bringing new African, Asian and European federations.

What accounts for this burst of federalism? One step is the invention of centralized federalism in the United States in the late eighteenth century. The other is the collapse of empires. The invention provided a viable organization that turned out to be useful in partially reassembling the debris of empire. Imperial administrators organize political units appropriate for their purposes and these are typically too small to be militarily effective by themselves. But a centralized federation can aggregate resources and, given its invention and availability, framers of constitutions for ex-imperial units used it frequently. Of course, not all the contemporary federations derive from collapsed empires. But even those that do not have adopted the centralized form. Switzerland reorganized in 1848 and Germany and Austria after the first and second World

Wars on the centralized model. The Soviet Union and Yugoslavia – if their claims to be federations are justifiable – would probably never have adopted a federal structure if the centralized form had not been available. Recent 'federalizing' movements (e.g. Belgium) would probably make no headway without the centralized model. So the invention of centralized federalism is crucial to the contemporary use and approval of federalism and thus therefore deserves explanation.

When the thirteen colonies that formed the United States rebelled against Britain, they initially formed a loose, peripheralized federation. Though the main organ (that is, the Continental Congress) of what became this federation did declare independence (1776), send ambassadors, organize an army and borrow money, it was kept on tight rein by the new state governments which, as it turned out, really controlled taxes and military resources. A peripheralized constitution, the Articles of Confederation, adopted in 1781, embodied the principles of state control so that decisions on national policy were really made in the state capitals. Nationalist leaders, who in fact controlled the federal government from 1781 onwards, were deeply discontented with this state of affairs. They tried several times to amend the Articles modestly, but failed because of the unanimity requirement characteristic of peripheralized federations. Then in a bold move they attempted a complete revision of the constitution, based on a proposal by James Madison for a wholly national government, entirely uninfluenced by the states and fully in control of them. This would have been a government as unitary as any in the world. Madison's proposal was revised to give the states unique functions and an independent juristic identity and also a role in supplying national officials. Thus, by way of a compromise between nationalists and provincials, these nationalists created a new kind of centralized federation, one with almost the governing strength of a unitary government, but also with unique functions and perpetual guarantees for the constituent units. It was this combination of features that rendered centralized federalism so popular in succeeding centuries.

The foregoing discussion suggests that people have welcomed federalism for purely instrumental reasons. In fact, however, many political philosophers have justified the federal form on moral grounds: that it promotes liberty by allowing freedom of action for small groups or units, or, more generally, that it limits big government and thus promotes individual freedom.

There is no question that federalism restricts the ability of the central government to prescribe public policy. The constitution prohibits central government action in functions reserved for the constituent units. Indeed, when the central government ignores these prohibitions, as, for example, in the Soviet Union from a few months after its establishment to its dissolution in 1991, then federalism is itself destroyed. A dictatorship really cannot be a federation. When the central government denies omnipotence and guarantees constituent governments unique functions, then groups that lose nationally have a chance to win locally. With such compensation for national losers, the society as a whole is not zero-sum. In that sense, federalism really does promote individual freedom.

It is possible, however, to exaggerate the freedom-generating effects of federalism. While the foregoing argument is valid in general, nevertheless local freedom of action may not in fact generate true liberty. The United States offers a perverse example. In 1787 one of the constitutional compromises provided that states govern slavery. After a generation, however, the northern, slave-free, more populous region deeply regretted that concession. In the southern, slaveholding, less populous region, federalism came to mean protection of slaveholders' property rights and the absence of freedom for the black-skinned slaves. As a bare majority, the northern region lacked the two-thirds and three-quarters majority for constitutional amendments. Therefore, the only feasible method of eliminating slavery was the civil war from 1861 to 1865. While that war did end slavery, it still left such matters as voting rights in the local jurisdictions. Within a generation after the civil war, southern states had again repressed the former slaves. Again federalism, the supposed protection of minorities, worked out as a device for condoning repression. Only in 1954–65 did the north become sufficiently populous and sympathetic to eliminate that second repression. Thus for well over half its history federalism in the United States actually meant freedom for some southern whites to oppress blacks, hardly the conventional picture of federalism as freedom. Fortunately, in the recent generation, however, federalism in the United States has served as an addition to the separation of powers and has thus, on the whole, served liberty. Taking together all federations in the world at all times, I believe that federalism has been a significant force for limited government and hence for personal freedom.

Owing to the success of federalism both as an instrument to aggregate resources and as a protection for liberty, many political idealists today hope to adopt it to new circumstances, such as a federal world or a federal Europe. If the description in this article of the origin of federations is even remotely correct, a federal world is a chimera. There must be a reason to aggregate resources, some external (or internal) enemy or object of aggression, or else no one would be willing to give up independence for aggregation. But a federal world precludes an enemy or an opportunity for attack and hence also precludes a reason for aggregation. A federal Europe is a more complicated case. So long as the United States and the Soviet Union continued the Cold War, there was reason for Europe to extricate itself from that conflict by federating. Now (1993) the threat has eased, Western Europe need not fear invasion from the East and it is not clear what can be gained by federation, except perhaps a European autarchy that shuts out Asiatic and American trade goods from the European market. This is, however, a perverse goal more harmful to Europeans than anyone else. It is difficult to imagine a long-term self-flagellation by federating. Consequently, it seems to me that the future of a united Europe is as chimerical as a united world. In any event, the success or failure of the move to federalize Europe will be a good test of the validity of this argument about the nature of federalism.

See also: 3 HISTORY; 4 SOCIOLOGY; 5 ECONOMICS; 6 POLITICAL SCIENCE; 7 LEGAL STUDIES; 8 ANARCHISM; 11 LIBERALISM; 14 AUTONOMY; 15 COMMUNITY; 16 CONTRACT AND CONSENT; 17 CONSTITUTIONALISM AND THE RULE OF LAW; 18 CORPORATION AND SYNDICALISM; 19 DEMOCRACY; 23 EFFICIENCY; 25 EQUALITY; 27 INTERNATIONAL AFFAIRS; 30 POWER; 34 SECESSION AND NATIONALISM; 36 STATE; 37 TOLERATION AND FUNDAMENTALISM.

References

Davis, S. R.: *The Federal Principle: A Journey Through Time in Quest of a Meaning* (Berkeley: University of California Press, 1978).

Dye, T. R.: *American Federalism: Competition among Governments* (Lexington, Mass.: Lexington Books, 1990).

Elazar, D. J.: *The American Partnership* (Chicago: University of Chicago Press, 1962).

Riker, W. H.: *Federalism: Origin, Operation, Significance* (Boston: Little, Brown, 1964).

————: 'Federalism', *Handbook of Political Science*, ed. Fred I. Greenstein and Nelson W. Polsby, vol. 5, *Governmental Institutions and Processes* (Reading, Mass.: Addison-Wesley, 1975), pp. 93–172.

Wheare, K. D.: *Federal Government* (London: Oxford University Press, 3rd edn, 1956).

27

International affairs

CHRIS BROWN

Introduction

Barely a generation ago, a chapter on international affairs in a *Companion* to political philosophy would have had little of contemporary interest to report. The medieval and Catholic notion of 'Just War' still attracted attention (Ramsey, 1968), as did the 'international theorists' of the eighteenth and nineteenth centuries (Hinsley, 1963), but *contemporary* political philosophy and *contemporary* international relations seemed to inhabit different worlds. This strange state of affairs partly reflected the unwillingness of philosophers to engage with real ethical issues but was mainly a by-product of the dominance in international relations of 'realist' thinking. Realism (Carr, 1939; Morgenthau, 1948) holds that the state is the only significant actor in international relations, that foreign policy is determined by the national interest, that international outcomes are determined by the power of states, and that a concern with ethical and moral considerations is either, at best, inappropriate in international affairs, or worse, positively harmful if it encourages unrealistic, 'utopian' thinking. Even if a stable peace is the supreme goal of international policy – and the realist perspective is not necessarily hostile to this view – such a peace is obtainable only through a creative response to the realities of power, and not through the pursuit of abstract notions of justice or by virtue of moral obligations assumed to bind diplomats. This is only a very brief and summary account of realism; none the less it will be clear why, from such a perspective, international relations and political philosophy will have little to say to each other.

Realism claims to be an account of how things are and always have been, tracing its origins either to Classical Greece (Thucydides, *Peloponnesian War*) or to Renaissance Italy (Machiavelli, *The Prince*). However, this genealogy is somewhat suspect, and the full realist position outlined above is best seen as a twentieth-century production, perhaps building on Weberian ideas of the state (Smith, 1986) but certainly responding to the mid-century challenge of the dictators. It is not surprising that faced with the horrors of Nazism and Stalinism a great many thinkers came to the conclusion that only power mattered in world politics, and that good intentions and a desire to behave morally were always likely to be exploited by the unscrupulous. Thus the power of realism – and thus the need for changes in the world to take place before the grip of this bleak doctrine can be loosened.

Such changes begin to come about in the 1960s and 1970s, partly as a response to nuclear stalemate, partly because of the conscious adoption of policies designed to lower tension and 'normalize' relations between East and West – in particular the détente policies of the Nixon/Brezhnev era, and the Ostpolitik practised by the (then West) German government. Although at the end of the 1970s some writers were still restating realist positions (Waltz, 1979), a more fruitful reaction saw the revival of the older European notion of an 'anarchical society' (Bull, 1977), which approach offers at least some possibilities for normative international relations theory, albeit of a limited kind. However, more significant than the change in power relations of this period was the increasing salience of cross-border relationships which were not primarily concerned with so-called 'high' politics: the movement towards economic integration in some parts of the world, and, more generally, the growth of transnational relations involving bodies other than the state, particularly economic actors such as the multinational corporation, which created conditions of 'complex interdependence' and, possibly, a 'world society' (Burton, 1972; Keohane and Nye, 1977). These latter developments challenged the notion of the state as a self-contained, autonomous actor – a challenge which posed a greater threat to realism's intellectual dominance than could any change in the actual distribution of world power.

The moral standing of the state

The first writer to recognize the philosophical significance of these changes was Charles Beitz, whose pioneering work demonstrated the inapplicability of Hobbesian analogies to modern international relations (Beitz, 1979). The realist notion that states were to one another as individuals in a state of nature simply could not survive the empirical challenge posed by interdependence; state autonomy is no longer a brute fact – if it ever was – and therefore analysts of international relations who wish to rely on this notion must now defend it normatively. Beitz argues that no such defence is available; although there may be pragmatic reasons why in some circumstances it would be desirable for state autonomy to be accepted, there is no *principled* reason for a norm of non-intervention in international affairs – and hence, no principled reason why differences of nationality or citizenship should be considered to justify different treatment in such matters as human rights. In his book, Beitz reaches this conclusion on the basis of the fact of interdependence; this is not convincing and in later work he revises and generalizes his argument, though not his conclusions, putting stress on Kantian ideas about the capacities of all individuals to act as moral beings rather than on contingent arguments about the non self-sufficiency of states (Beitz, 1983).

Beitz is a major contributor to the debate on international distributive justice, which will be considered below, but first the more general issue he raises concerning the moral basis of state autonomy should be addressed, because this is at the heart of all normative approaches to international relations, whether they concern the new agenda of distributive justice, human rights and environmental protection, or the older agenda based on international society and international law. Do states have a right to be left to their own devices? If so, is this an absolute right, or one conditional on meeting certain standards? If states cannot be said to have a right to be left alone, who has the right to intervene in their affairs? Other states? The world community? Looking at state autonomy from another angle, are there good reasons for giving priority to the interests of one's own fellow citizens as against foreigners when it comes to such matters as the distribution of rights and duties? Realism assumes that these questions simply do not arise. Autonomy is a fact not a moral status, and it therefore does not require a moral defence. Beitz rightly sees that this will not do, and, unable to find a satisfactory defence of state autonomy, he concludes that no such defence exists; he is a 'cosmopolitan' in the sense that he is unprepared to assign moral status to any political entity between the individual and the world community (see also Shue, 1980; Richards, 1982; Pogge, 1989). However, the key question here is whether the failure of realism necessarily leads to cosmopolitanism; a number of authors would deny this, arguing that a positive moral case can be made for the autonomy of states and, thus, a norm of non-intervention.

One of the most influential of arguments along these lines has been that of Michael Walzer, to be found in such works as *Spheres of Justice* (1983) and especially, *Just and Unjust Wars* (1980). This latter text was one of a number of studies stimulated by America's involvement in the Vietnam War (see e.g. the essays in Cohen, Nagel and Scanlon, 1974). In it Walzer sets out what he calls the 'Legalist Paradigm' – the set of principles which, under current understandings of international law, define non-intervention as the norm and aggression as a crime which justifies war as a direct or indirect act of self-defence. He argues that the Legalist Paradigm is not just a summary of current law, it also describes a morally defensible position: political communities as such have moral rights – such as the right to persist over time – and are entitled to defend these rights by whatever means are necessary, including, in 'supreme emergencies' the performance of acts which would otherwise be illegal (Walzer, 1977, ch. 16).

This position is sometimes described as 'communitarian' (Kymlicka, 1989), although Walzer rejects the label, largely it seems on the basis that his account of the rights of communities is grounded in a liberal concern for the rights of individuals, as exemplified by the approach to self-determination of J. S. Mill (Walzer, 1990; Mill, [1861] 1972, p. 361). A more thoroughgoing communitarianism can be found in the neo-Hegelian work of Mervyn Frost (1986), in which it is argued that human individuality is actually constituted by the family, civil society and the state. States need to be left alone, have a right to their autonomy, in order that they should be able to perform this constitutive role. It should be noted that neither Walzer nor Frost put forward arguments for the moral status of autonomy which could be undermined by the facts of interdependence – the issue is the right to make decisions on behalf of a community, not the prudential constraints that always have shaped the actual decisions made.

An argument that *does* present problems for communitarian thinking challenges the lack of 'fit' between political community and the state. Even if one were prepared to allow that communities should have rights, it is by no means clear that communities and states often, usually or, indeed, ever actually coincide; we should beware, in David Luban's evocative phrase, of allowing ourselves to be seduced by the 'romance of the nation-state' into assigning rights to states which blatantly repress the communities they allegedly represent (Beitz et al., 1985, p. 238). Frost's position is relatively unaffected by this point. He believes there to be settled international norms covering both non-intervention and respect for human rights; only properly constituted states which meet the latter norm can claim the protection of the former, and he is prepared to acknowledge that this may only apply in a limited number of cases, if at all. Walzer's ideas are designed to have more general application; his response to the lack of fit between community and state is essentially to make the pragmatic points that these things are always a matter of degree, and that, in any event, the criteria proposed by his critics for accepting the legitimacy of states are so strict as to destroy the moral basis for any norm of non-intervention, with potentially chaotic consequences for the actual conduct of international relations (Beitz et al., 1985, pp. 217–37).

Walzer and Frost justify the moral standing of the norm of non-intervention by reference to actual or potential features of political communities. An alternative position is that of Nardin (1983), who defends state autonomy as an expression of pluralism in the international system. Adapting a distinction made originally by Oakeshott (1975), he describes the international system as a 'practical' association of states based on an ethic of coexistence rather than on the pursuit of any common purpose. Thus, for example, states may voluntarily sign a treaty to create a customs union – a 'purposive' association – but the rules of international law which define what a treaty is in the first place – how it is made and amended, the circumstances under which it is, or is not binding – are the product of practical association. Nardin's position is pluralist: the international system must be designed in such a way as to allow for different ways of life and different conceptions of the good. This is a position of particular value in an increasingly multicultural world, although its effectiveness is dependent on non-Westerners being prepared to discount the Western origin of the rules of practical association.

The works of Beitz, Walzer, Frost and Nardin can stand as examples of modern studies which address the general issue of the moral standing of state autonomy. To repeat a point, the very posing of this issue only became possible after the dominance of realism came to be challenged. However, now that this challenge has been delivered, and with some success, it becomes possible to place the newer work in a much wider context, relating the authors named above to predecessors such as Kant, Hegel, Bentham and Mill (Brown, 1992, chs 2 and 3). In this sense the apparently new discourse of 'normative' international relations theory can be seen as a recovery of an older tradition (or of older traditions). It is realism, and other theories which attempt to understand international relations as though they were an aspect of social and political life, that could be separated out and theorized in isolation from all others, that is innovatory, denying the relevance of the long tradition of thinking about the relationship between our duties as 'men' and as 'citizens' (Linklater, 1990).

Just war

The sense of rediscovering a lost, or at any rate undervalued, past is most evident in modern work on the ethics of force and violence in international relations. Unless one is prepared to be an absolute pacifist or an uncompromisingly amoral realist, such an ethics necessarily involves discriminating between legitimate and illegitimate uses of force, and the idea of the 'Just War' seems to provide a well-established and refined language for making precisely such distinctions – both in terms of just causes of war (*ius ad bellum*) and just means in warfare (*ius in bello*) (Ramsey, 1968; Johnson, 1975; 1981; Brown, 1992, ch. 6). Complex notions such as double effect, proportionality of response, 'right intention' of participants, and immunity for non-combatants are well established in the classical literature, and the various writings inspired by the Vietnam War, problems of nuclear deterrence, international terrorism and, most recently, the 1991 Gulf War have added relatively little in substantive terms (Cohen, Nagel and Scanlon, 1974; Walzer, 1980; Hardin and Mearsheimer, 1985; Frey and Morris, 1991; Elshtain, 1992).

What, on the other hand, has been of considerable interest in this area is not so much the *content* of just war doctrine, as the basis upon which it can be grounded. Whereas writers such as Anscombe (1981) and Finnis, Boyle and Grisez (1987) write explicitly from a Roman Catholic Natural Law viewpoint, the majority of contributors to recent debates on Just War have no such foundations and there is no doubt that this presents difficulties. Nagel (in Beitz et al., 1985), for example, wishes to argue that certain means in warfare ought to be absolutely prohibited, but, faced with the possibility that his moral absolutism could result in the triumph of an evil cause, he can only regret that this is so and that we are left in a 'moral blind alley' (ibid., p. 73). On the other hand, those who, with Walzer (1980, ch. 16), would be prepared to allow supreme emergency to override codes of conduct are, indeed, in danger of letting loose 'utilitarian justifications for large scale murder' (Nagel, in Beitz et al., p. 56). This dilemma is particularly pressing when it comes to assessing the morality of the strategy of nuclear deterrence; consequentialist calculations are so difficult to make that the unrequited desire to find absolutist principles is understandably very strong – although it should be said that one of the best utilitarian contributions to the debate uses precisely the difficulty of calculating utilities as a reason for adopting the absolutist strategy of disarmament, on the grounds that even the smallest risk of total annihilation could not be balanced by any potential gain (Goodin, in Hardin and Mearsheimer, 1985).

What this may suggest is that although traditional Just War thinking does provide a language for looking at these issues, for many of us it is a dead language. It is based on an essentially religious conception of the world in which the consequences of action are necessarily of secondary importance because eventually, in the next world if not in this one, the defeat of evil is guaranteed. In the absence of such a guarantee, the absolutism of some aspects of Just War doctrine is difficult to accept. On the other hand, Nagel's warning of the dangers of utilitarianism cannnot be disregarded either. It is difficult to imagine that a wholly consequentialist alternative to Just War theory could successfully perform the most basic task of distinguishing legitimate from illegitimate uses of force. Perhaps this is simply another example of a situation common to political philosophy generally in the twentieth century, namely that of having to think and live in a world in which the foundations upon which the moral beliefs of the past rested have disappeared without any compelling replacement emerging.

Human rights

Just War can be taken as an example of an area of theorizing where modern work has not in any essential respect taken us much beyond the achievements of the past; indeed, there may actually have been a falling off here, given that the old language of Just War theory seems to have lost some of its power while no new vocabulary has taken its place. However, in other areas progress is discernible. In the area of human rights for example, the international legal tradition provided only limited coverage – some customary law and commentary on the subject of responses to gross violations of human dignity – while the second half of the twentieth century has been marked by a great deal of treaty law establishing individual rights, and by accompanying philosophical studies of a new and higher level of sophistication (for a good overview see Vincent, 1986).

Two aspects of human rights have attracted particular attention in contemporary writings: the relationship between 'political' and 'economic and social' rights and the extent to which human rights, as currently encapsulated in e.g. UN Declarations, are essentially Western in content as well as, obviously, in origin. In both cases, political pressures from the (formerly) socialist countries and the Third World have forced thinkers from within the Western liberal-democratic tradition to rework some of their notions. Shue (1980) and Donnelly (1989) redefine human rights to include economic and social rights, with the difference that Donnelly argues that the evidence suggests that a concern for political rights is actually conducive to economic development, while Shue appears to give priority to his, essentially economic, notion of 'basic rights' It is not entirely clear that the first of these positions is empirically defensible, while the second will be seen by some as undermining the distinctive features of rights within the Western tradition – the notion that individual rights are in Dworkin's phrase 'political trumps' to constrain authorities. While one sympathizes with Shue's point that the starving and destitute find it difficult to exercise rights that are purely political, his apparent willingness to allow such rights to be overridden in the name of others allegedly more basic is questionable – indeed, in the latter case it may stretch the notion 'rights' to breaking point and beyond.

However, in some respects, the more significant challenges to individual human rights come from non-Western perspectives such as that of Islam. The dialogue of the deaf generated by the Salman Rushdie affair (Akhtar, 1989; Ruthven, 1990; Piscatori, 1990) reminds us that the Saudi Arabian abstention on the Universal Declaration of Human Rights as long ago as 1948 was made on a matter of high principle; in fact – something relevant to the Rushdie case – it was Article 18 of the Declaration, which enshrines a right to change religion, which was particularly problematic for the Saudis, then the only explicitly Islamic UN member state. In face of such a long-established position, the cosmopolitan universalism of the more conventional human rights literature seems unconvincing, while the belief of Renteln (1990) that problems of relativism will be overcome by cross-cultural empirical research which will reveal common patterns of belief seems excessively optimistic. None the less, one reason for optimism is the increasing sensitivity of the rights literature to these issues; on the whole it is better not to have a solution to a recognized problem rather than not to recognize the problem as a problem in the first place.

Global distributive justice?

When in 1974 the United Nations General Assembly called for the establishment of a New International Economic Order (NIEO) and a Charter of Economic Rights and Duties of States a political debate was set in train, one product of which was the afore-mentioned attempt to reconcile economic and political rights. This took place within an already established discourse concerning rights but, partly in response to the same political impetus, the late 1970s and 1980s also saw a movement into new territory – the previously almost entirely domestically oriented realm of theories of distributive justice.

Justice is, of course, one of the oldest topics of political philosophy, and such topics as the Just War have an almost equally long history in international relations theory – as have theories of *procedural* justice generally within the international legal tradition. However, a concern for *distributive* justice has no such international past existence. Although from the 1950s onwards arguments for assistance from rich to poor countries were commonplace, they rested, on the whole, on general notions of duty and benevolence rather than on the demands of justice as such (see, for example, Singer's (1973), radical utilitarianism or O'Neill's (1986) Kantianism.) That justice moves centre stage is partly a response to the demand for a NIEO, but also to the revolution brought about by the seminal work of John Rawls (1971) – although Rawls himself did not apply his notion of distributive social justice to international relations. Assuming a 'society' to be a cooperative venture for mutual advantage, he saw this assumption as ruling out anything other than a procedural account of *inter*societal justice. However, this was identified as a weakness by some of his earliest critics (Barry, 1973), and undermining this limitation was one of the goals of the attack on the idea of states as independent actors made in Beitz's (1979) pioneering work referred to above.

Beitz was more royalist than the king, wishing to apply Rawls' ideas in areas where Rawls thought them inappropriate. He argued that the existing resource endowment of states is, to use a Rawlsian phrase, 'morally arbitrary' and thus not something to which state representatives would willingly agree, and, moreover, as we have seen, that interdependence between nations means that the notion of self-contained socie-ties must be abandoned. Distributive justice applies between, as well as within, societies; and the 'difference principle' which Rawls uses to privilege the interests of the poorest should thus also apply internationally – with, of course, very radical results.

Beitz now acknowledges that interdependence cannot be employed in this way, and he makes his case for a radical redistribution on Kantian lines (1983) – although it should be noted that Pogge (1989) still defends the notion of an international differ-ence principle. It clearly is difficult to apply Rawlsian ideas directly to international relations; what is interesting is whether this difficulty tells us more about the special conditions of the latter or about the limitations of the former. Barry argues that the significance of the difficulty of fitting international justice into the Rawlsian schema is that it reveals the weakness of Rawls' attempt to base the requirements of justice on the foundations of mutual advantage (Barry, 1982; 1989). It self-evidently is not to the advantage of rich states to transfer a great part of their wealth to poor states, and it cannot be argued that they should do so because the world forms a single co-operative scheme for mutual advantage, because this is, equally self-evidently, an inaccurate description of rich–poor economic relations. Thus, from a Rawlsian perspective the requirements of justice cannot apply – but, Barry argues, this is simply perverse, since spectacular inequalities exist in the world system, inequalities that could not possibly be regarded as 'just' under any reasonable meaning of the term. The answer is to divorce justice from mutual advantage and see it instead in terms of 'impartiality' – with the implication that internationally this notion will require large-scale transfers from rich to poor.

If the aspiration to create theories of social justice makes sense, and if, in any event, international society is the sort of society that can be the subject of such theories, then Barry's notion of justice as impartiality seems the most fruitful way of proceeding. However, both these conditions can be challenged. Communitarians such as Sandel (1982) reject the Rawlsian view that justice is the first virtue of social institutions, proposing instead the common good of the community. Marxian writers argue that both 'justice' *and* the 'common good' are notions that cover the dominance of one class over another (Nielson, 1983). And, of course, those who value the autonomy of a plurality of states in the international system will resist the suggestion that the obligations that states have towards one another should be extended from those generated by the procedural needs of practical association to the adoption of a common international purpose of eradicating poverty (Nardin, 1983).

This latter point has wide implications. If poor states assert a duty on the part of the rich to come to their aid, do they not thereby legitimate a great deal of external interference in their domestic affairs? Jackson (1990) elaborates the point. The traditional doctrine of sovereignty involved positive and negative factors – negatively, a right to be left to one's own devices, positively, a capacity to govern effectively. One of the features of rapid decolonization has been the creation of many 'quasi-states' who possess the legal rights of negative sovereignty without the political capabilities that make up positive sovereignty – such as the capacity to manage their own economy and avoid starvation. It is difficult to see how international action to correct the latter condition could avoid interfering with the negative side of sovereignty – which is not a problem for cosmopolitans who do not believe in the virtues of this status, but is a problem for communitarians, and modern governments, who do. Jackson's way of posing these issues is precise, although he perhaps overestimates the ability (and willingness) of established state authorities to use the positive attributes of sovereignty for the benefit of their own citizens, and, by a similar token, underestimates the extent to which the 'quasi-states' of the Third World are faced with problems not of their own making. Indeed, the exercise of positive sovereignty by those who have it in the 'North' can easily create problems for the 'South' – as shown, for example, by the economic consequences for debt-burdened Third World countries of US fiscal policies in the early 1980s (see e.g. Lever and Huhne, 1985).

Conclusion

The basic philosophical problem posed by international politics is much the same whether the specific issue under consideration is Just War, human rights, migration (Barry and Goodin, 1992) or social justice in general – namely, whether the independence that much of the time states behave as though they possessed has any moral standing. The issue seems truly intractable. In the face of intense human suffering such as that of the Kurds in Iraq or famine victims in Africa the intuitive reaction of most well-meaning individuals is to think that 'something must be done' – and never mind the consequences for abstract theories of sovereignty. On the other hand, an (almost?) equally strong intuition tells most of us that, on the whole, self-determination is a good thing and that it is not right for even well-intentioned outsiders to interfere in the affairs of others. Which of these powerful intuitions dominates in which circumstances does not seem to be a question for political *philosophy* as much as a matter for political *action*. A clear-cut philosophical answer to the dilemma here can only come from an, undesirable, attempt to suppress one of these two intuitions – undesirable because both rest on valid general positions.

Can this deadlock be broken? Some seek to bypass the dilemma by turning to critical theory or postmodernism (Der Derian and Shapiro, 1989; Linklater, 1990) without as yet showing what this might achieve; but a more compelling resolution of the stalemate may be achieved by changes taking place outside of the realm of discourse. The issue of global environmental change may reshape international political philosophy once and for all by giving new force to the ideal of a global community. The autonomy of any one state has always involved costs for others, but in the past it has been possible to argue that these costs are outweighed by associated benefits, or that they are a necessary price to pay for preserving something in itself good. However, for the first time, states now have the ability and, apparently, in some cases the will, to bring about permanent large-scale damage to the environment, and it is impossible to think of any philosophical argument that could justify their right to behave in this way. But if this point is conceded – and to date no argument worth the name has been made asserting, for example, the right of any state to destroy the ozone layer – then, given the potential scope of environmental issues, a wholesale revaluation of international ethics will be required. Communitarian defenders of the right of self-determination will have to accept strict limits on the autonomy they value, while cosmopolitan universalists will find their case immeasurably strengthened by a notion of the common good based on a genuine environmental interdependence rather than on the contrived economic variety. The challenge for the new international political philosophy that may – certainly should – emerge from this nexus of issues will be to find a way of realizing and expressing the common good that does not privilege the interests of rich and powerful states, and that combines effective action with a proper pluralist respect for the rights of all cultures.

See also 5 ECONOMICS; 8 ANARCHISM; 15 COMMUNITY; 20 DIRTY HANDS; 22 DISTRIBUTIVE JUSTICE; 33 RIGHTS; 34 SECESSION AND NATIONALISM; 36 STATE

References

Akhtar, S.: *Be Careful with Muhammad!* (London: Bellew Publishing, 1989).

Anscombe, G. E. M.: *The Collected Philosophical Papers of G. E. M. Anscombe*. Vol. 3: *Ethics, Religion and Politics* (Oxford: Blackwell, 1981).

Barry, B.: *The Liberal Theory of Justice* (Oxford: Clarendon Press, 1973).

————: 'Humanity and justice in global perspective', *Nomos 24: Ethics, Economics and the Law*, ed. J. R. Pennock and J. W. Chapman (New York: New York University Press, 1982), pp. 219–52.

————: *Theories of Justice* (Hemel Hempstead: Harvester Wheatsheaf, 1989).

———— and Goodin, R. E., eds: *Free Movement* (Hemel Hempstead: Harvester Wheatsheaf, 1992).

Beitz, C. R.: *Political Theory and International Relations* (Princeton, NJ: Princeton University Press, 1979).

————: 'Cosmopolitan ideals and national sentiment', *Journal of Philosophy*, 80 (1983), 591–600.

————, Cohen, M., Scanlon, T. and Simmons, A. J., eds: *International Ethics* (Princeton, NJ: Princeton University Press, 1985).

Brown, C. J.: *International Relations Theory* (Hemel Hempstead: Harvester Wheatsheaf, 1992).

Bull, H.: *The Anarchical Society* (London: Macmillan, 1977).

Burton, J. W.: *World Society* (Cambridge: Cambridge University Press, 1972).

Carr, E. H.: *The Twenty Years Crisis* (London: Macmillan, 1939).

Cohen, M., Nagel, T. and Scanlon, T., eds: *War and Moral Responsibility* (Princeton, NJ: Princeton University Press, 1974).

Der Derian, J. and Shapiro, M. J., eds: *International/Intertextual Relations: Postmodern Readings of World Politics* (Lexington, Mass.: Lexington Books, 1989).

Donnelly, J.: *Universal Human Rights in Theory and Practice* (Ithaca, NY: Cornell University Press, 1989).

Elshtain, J. B., ed.: *Just War Theory* (Oxford: Blackwell, 1992).

Finnis, J., Boyle, J. and Grisez, G.: *Nuclear Deterrence, Morality and Realism* (Oxford: Clarendon Press, 1987).

Frey, R. G. and Morris, C. W., eds: *Violence, Terrorism and Justice* (Cambridge: Cambridge University Press, 1991).

Frost, M.: *Towards a Normative Theory of International Relations* (Cambridge: Cambridge University Press, 1986).

Hardin, R. and Mearsheimer, J. J., eds: 'Special issue on nuclear deterrence and disarmament', *Ethics*, 95 (1985).

Hinsley, F. H.: *Power and the Pursuit of Peace* (Cambridge: Cambridge University Press, 1963).

Jackson, R. H.: *Quasi-States: Sovereignty, International Relations and the Third World* (Cambridge: Cambridge University Press, 1990).

Johnson, J. T.: *Ideology, Reason and the Limitation of War* (Princeton, NJ: Princeton University Press, 1975).

————: *Just War Tradition and the Restraint of War* (Princeton, NJ: Princeton University Press, 1981).

Keohane, R. O. and Nye, J.: *Power and Interdependence* (Boston: Little, Brown, 1977).

Kymlicka, W.: *Liberalism, Community and Culture* (Oxford: Clarendon Press, 1989).

Lever, H. and Huhne, C.: *Debt and Danger: The World Financial Crisis* (Harmondsworth: Penguin Books, 1985).

Linklater, A.: *Men and Citizens in the Theory of International Relations* (London: Macmillan, 1990).

————: *Beyond Realism and Marxism: Critical Theory and International Relations* (London: Macmillan, 1990).

Machiavelli, N.: *The Prince* (1532), trans. Russell Price (Cambridge: Cambridge University Press, 1988).

Mill, J. S.: *Utilitarianism, On Liberty and Representative Government* (1859); (London: Dent, 1972).

Morgenthau, H. J.: *Politics among Nations* (New York: Alfred A. Knopf, 1948).

Nardin, T.: *Law, Morality and the Relations of States* (Princeton, NJ: Princeton University Press, 1983).

Nielson, K.: 'Global justice and the imperatives of capitalism', *Journal of Philosophy*, 80 (1983), 608–10.

Oakeshott, M.: *On Human Conduct* (Oxford: Oxford University Press, 1975).

O'Neill, O.: *Faces of Hunger: An Essay on Poverty, Justice and Development* (London: Allen & Unwin, 1986).

Piscatori, J.: 'The Rushdie affair and the politics of ambiguity', *International Affairs*, 66 (1990), 767–89.

Pogge, T.: *Realising Rawls* (Ithaca, NY: Cornell University Press, 1989).

Ramsey, P.: *The Just War* (New York: Charles Scribner's Sons, 1968).

Rawls, J.: *A Theory of Justice* (Cambridge, Mass.: Harvard University Press, 1971).

Renteln, A. D.: *International Human Rights* (London: Sage, 1990).

Richards, D.: 'International distributive justice', *Nomos 24: Ethics, Economics and the Law*, ed. J. R. Pennock and J. W. Chapman (New York: New York University Press, 1982).

Ruthven, M.: *A Satanic Affair: Salman Rushdie and the Rage of Islam* (London: Chatto and Windus, 1990).

Sandel, M. J.: *Liberalism and the Limits of Justice* (Cambridge: Cambridge University Press, 1982).

Shue, H.: *Basic Rights* (Princeton, NJ: Princeton University Press, 1980).

Singer, P.: *Practical Ethics* (Cambridge: Cambridge University Press, 1979).

Smith, M. J.: *Realist Thought from Weber to Kissinger* (Baton Rouge: Louisiana State University Press, 1986).

Thucydides: *The Peloponnesian War*, trans. Richard Crawley (London: J. M. Dent and Sons, 1910).

Vincent, R. J.: *Human Rights and International Relations* (Cambridge: Cambridge University Press, 1986).

Waltz, K.: *Theory of International Politics* (Reading, Mass.: Addison-Wesley, 1979).

Walzer, M.: *Just and Unjust Wars* (Harmondsworth: Penguin Books, 1980).

————: *Spheres of Justice* (Oxford: Martin Robertson, 1983).

————: 'The communitarian critique of liberalism', *Political Theory*, 18 (1990), 6–23.

Further reading

Beitz, C. R.: *Political Theory and International Relations* (Princeton, NJ: Princeton University Press, 1979).

Brown, C. J.: *International Relations Theory* (Hemel Hempstead: Harvester Wheatsheaf, 1992).

Bull, H.: *The Anarchical Society* (London: Macmillan, 1977).

Elshtain, J. B., ed.: *Just War Theory* (Oxford: Blackwell, 1992).

Frost, M.: *Towards a Normative Theory of International Relations* (Cambridge: Cambridge University Press, 1986).

Jackson, R. H.: *Quasi-States: Sovereignty, International Relations and the Third World* (Cambridge: Cambridge University Press, 1990).

Linklater, A.: *Men and Citizens in the Theory of International Relations* (London: Macmillan, 1990).

Nardin, T.: *Law, Morality and the Relations of States* (Princeton, NJ: Princeton University Press, 1983).

Shue, H.: *Basic Rights* (Princeton, NJ: Princeton University Press, 1980).

Vincent, R. J.: *Human Rights and International Relations* (Cambridge: Cambridge University Press, 1986).

Walzer, M.: *Just and Unjust Wars* (Harmondsworth: Penguin Books, 1980).

28

Legitimacy

RICHARD E. FLATHMAN

Together with its kissing cousins 'authority' and 'obligation', legitimacy is a notion that should arouse apprehension. Governments that are legitimate have the 'right to rule', to demand obedience from their citizens or subjects. It is at least partly correct to say that this authority is independent of the content of the laws or commands issued by those invested with it (Hart, 1961), that the authority of a law or command is a reason for obeying it regardless of its contents or their merits. As widely construed, reasons of this kind are conclusive in that they leave those subject to authority with but two choices; either obey the command or disassociate from the political association of which authority is a constitutive feature. Theories of 'passive' and 'civil' disobedience add the third option of disobedience to commands judged to be unjust but on condition of peaceful submission to the penalty assigned (King, 1964).

To concede the legitimacy of government is to accord to some number of persons a right that we otherwise reserve to ourselves, the right to conduct our own lives and affairs as each of us deems appropriate.

Much past and present political philosophy either subordinates the question of legitimacy or implicitly treats its possibility and desirability as philosophically and politically unproblematic. It is widely assumed that politically organized association in which some persons rule others is the divinely, naturally or ontologically ordained state of human affairs. According to one influential version of this view, there is a good for humankind that can be realized only in a society ruled by those who know what that good is and how to pursue it. Proponents of this understanding also commonly assume that some number of (changing but in principle always identifiable) persons are divinely or naturally fitted for the task of ruling. On these assumptions a *question* about legitimacy can arise only in the sense that rule by the naturally inferior would be illegitimate.

In the form now most familiar, legitimacy as a distinct issue traces to the seventeenth century when the above assumptions were challenged by the view that human beings (some among them) are, by nature or before God, free and equal in at least one respect: no human being has natural or divinely ordained authority to rule them. On this picture, the only unproblematic authority is each person's authority over herself. Government of any kind, certainly government with content-independent authority, demands justification. Because from this period forward human beings have increasingly claimed natural freedom and equality in various further respects, the prospects of legitimate government seem remote. If nature is our standard, and if by nature no person has political authority over any other, the notion of legitimate political authority appears to be on a par with 'square circle'.

Post-seventeenth-century political philosophers have for the most part refused this conclusion. No small number have rejected or narrowly qualified the postulates of natural freedom and equality. Those who profess to accept them have engaged in a spirited but somewhat dispiriting philosophical scuffle over the best way to accord, nevertheless, legitimacy to government.

Those who have accepted these premises but rejected the attractive but probably unachievable ideal of anarchism have argued for legitimacy along one or another version of the following lines. (Some) human beings have authority over themselves. As indicated by esteemed practices such as promising and making agreements, the freedom this authority licenses allows them to transfer some or all of their authority to others, to authorize others to act on their behalf. When a number of people transfer their natural authority to a government the latter thereby acquires the legitimacy of the former.

After flourishing in the seventeenth and eighteenth centuries, theories of this basic type were attacked and rejected by thinkers of the stature and diversity of Burke, Hume, Bentham, Hegel and Marx. Despite their forceful objections, in recent years consent or contractarian theories have been revived and other arguments for legitimacy have been on the defensive. The objections against consent theory are increasingly regarded as tied to positions more problematic than the view their proponents joined in attacking. Whether due to or a cause of consent theory, the notion that government must rest on the consent of the governed has become an article of political faith, a conviction that much contemporary political philosophy labours to secure.

A major version of consent theory was initiated by Hobbes and elements of his formulation are prominent in the recent work of Michael Oakeshott (1975a, b), in thinkers in the tradition of legal positivism (e.g. Kelsen, 1945) and among rational choice theorists (e.g. Gauthier, 1986; Kavka, 1986). Hobbes ([1651] 1962, p. 164) asserts that all human beings have a right of nature to do whatever they judge necessary to their preservation and well-being. Accordingly, there is 'no obligation on any man, which ariseth not from some act of his own'. Because authority entails obligation, authority can only 'arise' from 'some act' of each person in its jurisdiction.

Despite his avowal of these voluntarist and egalitarian axioms, Hobbes adopts the notorious notion of tacit consent, and makes it the basis of government with absolute authority. If other consent theorists have compounded the first difficulty by turning 'consent' into an objective or collective concept, most of them have combated Hobbes' authoritarianism. But the brutal clarity of Hobbes' account of authority assures his continuing relevance and his larger theory has features that merit sympathetic consideration.

Hobbes distinguishes sharply between the authority of a law or command and its wisdom, moral value or other substantive characteristics. His sovereigns are in authority but have no standing as an authority concerning the questions they decide (Friedman, 1973). If human beings could agree on what should and should not be done, there would be no need for government. If they agreed that Jones knows best what should be done, they would do what Jones says for that reason. We are to obey political authority, surrender our judgement (Friedman, 1973; Raz, 1979; 1986) to those who have it, not because we believe or approve what they say but because we have no reliable basis on which to agree concerning questions that must be authoritatively decided.

The distinction between *in* and *an* authority is central to Oakeshott's (1975b) distinction between two types of regime that he styles civil societies and enterprise associations. Enterprise associations cannot abide a separation between the authority and the substantive merits of law. They consist of persons who share some number of substantive purposes such as conquest, distributive justice, material well-being, and the like. When politically organized so that their rules have the standing of laws, those laws are chosen to achieve the agreed objectives and can properly be disobeyed by those convinced that they do not do so. In consequence, such associations are either unstable due to disagreement or become tyrannical teleocracies. By contrast, a civil society postulates and celebrates a diversity of purposes, a variety of incommensurable and often conflicting conceptions and criteria of the good and the right. Its members subscribe to its authority in the hope of maintaining conditions, generically the condition of civility, under which they can pursue whatever purposes they severally happen to have. Authority, 'subscription' to which is the sole constitutive feature of such an association, enforces respect for the 'adverbial considerations' that together comprise the condition of civility. It does so primarily through adjudication, minimally and circumspectly by legislation. Its laws are indifferent to ends and purposes; they do not tell us *what* to do, they tell us *how* we may go about doing whatever we do. In a civil society I have every reason to obey, no pertinent reason to disobey authority.

All known political associations contain fluctuating mixtures of the elements of the 'ideal characters' civil society and enterprise association (Oakeshott, 1975b, essay 3). In so far as one's society is civil no considerations other than the authority of the law are relevant to the decision to obey it. On the other hand, in so far as one's society is an enterprise association, the authority of a law is *a* reason to obey it, is always relevant to the question whether I ought, all things considered, to obey it. Contrary to strict forms of legal positivism, it cannot exclude (Raz, 1979) considerations of other kinds from decisions about obedience. If a law is purposive, I am warranted in asking whether the purpose is acceptable to me and whether the law serves that purpose.

Hobbes does not use the elusive notion of purely adverbial laws, but distinctions analogous to Oakeshott's are prominent in his and numerous contemporary theories of legitimacy. Whether by consent or in some other fashion, we acquire the political status of citizen, a status that carries with it the obligation to obey authority. But this is not our only status, is not the only role we play. We have commitments and purposes that connect with authority, if at all, only in that the latter maintains conditions favourable to enacting and serving them. These further characteristics and concerns (often called 'private') generate reasons for action that can conflict with the reason for obedience provided by our political obligation. Hobbes ([1651] 1962, esp. ch. 21) dramatizes this point by insisting that each of us retains the natural right to do what we judge necessary for our preservation and well-being. (Hobbes attributes consent much too freely, but he is equally liberal in allowing subjects to cancel it or its implications.) Because all authority has content-independent qualities, the reason or warrant for action that this right provides is different in kind from the reason for action that is an obligation. Contrary to utilitarianism, the two cannot be 'measured' on the same scale and neither can outweigh the other. As Hobbes makes clear, they can conflict but cannot cancel one another.

On these versions of consent theory, life in a society with a legitimate government requires its citizens to make an intricate array of quite refined judgements. Neither Hobbes nor Oakeshott is optimistic that these heavy demands can be steadily met, but the prospects are enhanced if we adopt their view that government, while essential, should attempt very few of the activities that governments now routinely undertake.

(These remarks invite comparison with Hannah Arendt's (1958; 1963) anti-contractarian but promise-dependent thinking. The judgements her theory demands are on different dimensions but are no less intricate than those urged by Hobbes and Oakeshott. And she shares their view that legitimate authority and the politics to which it is necessary, while precious, must operate in a carefully delineated domain.)

With the notable exceptions of Rousseau and his contemporary communitarian and collectivist heirs, and of a number of philosophical anarchists who make individual consent a necessary but unsatisfiable condition of political legitimacy (Wolff, 1970; Simmons, 1979; Green, 1988 [with qualifications]), the elements foregrounded above are present in most post-Hobbes consent theories, particularly those of Locke, Kant and contemporary writers such as John Rawls (1971), Joseph Raz (1979; 1986) and Ackerman (1980). The works of these thinkers include: the postulates of freedom and equality; the denial of divine or natural authority and the consequent necessity of some form (however attenuated) of consent; the proposition that there are and should be a diversity of conceptions of good and that authority and obligation are necessary in part because of disagreement concerning ends and purposes; the idea that government and law should be neutral among a wide range of (the actively contested) conceptions of the good and otherwise respect the private dimensions of the lives of its citizens. For these influential theorists the foregoing are among the components of legitimacy.

These and numerous other self-styled liberal thinkers such as Ronald Dworkin (1977) and William Galston (1980), however, make demands upon or have expectations concerning politically organized society that go well beyond those countenanced by Hobbes or Oakeshott. Government is to use its authority to achieve and sustain a substantive conception of justice (Rawls, 1971; Ackerman, 1980), to encourage 'valid conceptions of the good and to discourage evil or empty ones' (Raz, 1986, p. 133), to inculcate the virtues necessary to a liberal society (Galston, 1980), to provide for the welfare of all of its citizens (Dworkin, 1979).

Perhaps in the hope of diminishing the abuses that Oakeshott predicts when authority is used to pursue enterprise association objectives, these thinkers promote institutionalized limitations on authority (constitutionalism, bills of rights, the rule of law) that Hobbes and Oakeshott oppose because reliance upon them underestimates the contingency of human affairs. They also press for political democracy which Hobbes fears on the ground that it generates excessive power and that Oakeshott accepts as an established feature of his political culture but that he (and Arendt) thinks tends to engender conformism and the tyranny of the majority.

In the specific sense of the legitimacy of government, for these thinkers legitimacy depends primarily on these devices, those of the first kind protecting the 'civil' character of rule and democracy serving to sustain and invigorate the consent of the citizenry. These theories nevertheless blur the distinction between the legitimacy of government and the justice or goodness of the society more broadly conceived. It is not enough for government itself to be lawful, just or democratic. If society is disfigured by unjustifiable inequalities or other forms of injustice, and if government does not use its authority to combat them and to pursue the ends and purposes mentioned above, the legitimacy of the politically organized society or 'regime' is called into question. These substantive-purposive criteria do not exclude or supplant the formal-procedural criteria (Flathman, 1980) on which Hobbes, Kant and Oakeshott (Locke is an ambiguous case) rely, but because they are independent of one another the former readily conflict with the latter.

In their most pronounced forms these tendencies in recent consent and liberal theory have the further effect of returning the question of legitimate authority to the subsidiary status it had in most pre-modern political thought and has in much contemporary political philosophy. For utilitarians, neo-Thomists, Marxists, communitarians, neo-Aristotelians and rationalists, individual consent, while valuable as a source of political stability and energy, is no more than a symptom of a society that is just, good or right by criteria that are rational, reasonable or otherwise deserve interpersonal standing. Political societies that satisfy such criteria thereby acquire the right to rule, their members thereby acquire obligations to obey and perhaps sustain allegiance to them. Recent theorists of democracy influenced by Rousseau (e.g. Pateman, 1970; Barber, 1984) appear to sustain the independence of the question of legitimacy and to make consent a necessary and perhaps a sufficient condition of it. As a part of substituting the collective or communal consent of participatory or 'strong' democracy for individualist or liberal versions, however, they also follow Rousseau in attaching substantive and moralistic conditions which must be met for the consent to be genuine and to yield legitimacy.

From a strict conceptual perspective, the success of these programmes would signal the end of authority and authority relations. Laws and commands would be obeyed not because some have authority and others corollary obligations but because they are right or good by the standards the theories provide (Green, 1988). From the Hobbes/Oakeshott perspective this is a dangerous and indeed a repugnant fantasy. It is a fantasy because uncoerced agreement on this range of questions will never be achieved or sustained for long. It is dangerous because it emboldens rulers by adding moral zeal to the lust for power and because it convinces citizens that they ought to submit to requirements and prohibitions for which there is no good reason, burdens dissent and disobedience with guilt and shame. It is repugnant because its effects are invariably to diminish plurality, individuality and freedom.

Analogous but yet more negative assessments of these and earlier ambitious political programmes are provided by thinkers who share the affirmation of individuality and the non-doctrinaire but potent scepticism that pervade the thinking of Hobbes and Oakeshott. Socrates might be mentioned in this connection and early modern opponents of moralistic politics such as Montaigne certainly should be. Friedrich Nietzsche's perspectivalism dramatizes the fantastic character of the notion of a political society harmonized by general, voluntary but rationally warranted acceptance of a common good or right, his genealogies expose the intrusive and coercive character of the regimes that have claimed this kind of legitimacy, and his avid promotion of a pathos of distance from and towards all authority and authorities identifies the political stance he thinks self-esteeming individuals should take toward them (Nietzsche, 1887; 1906).

Contemporary deconstructionists and postmodernists have taken the first of these themes to the point of problematizing the possibility not only of legitimacy (e.g. Lyotard and Thebaud, 1985) but mutual intelligibility (e.g. Derrida, 1982; DeMan, 1986). Recent genealogists have disclosed the ubiquitous role of often deeply gendered or otherwise ascriptively based power in human arrangements (e.g. Foucault, 1979; Butler, 1990). And political thinkers who acquiesce in the possibility and necessity of authority have developed recognizably Nietzschian notions into theories of democratic individuality (Kateb, 1984), contestational democracy (Connolly, 1991) and willful liberalism (Flathman, 1992).

It is not impossible that further development of these and related tendencies of thought will help to realize the best political possibility – anarchism aside – engendered by the postulates of freedom and equality. That would be a political order in which authority is accepted reluctantly, viewed with suspicion if not disdain, used little, disobeyed cheerfully and resisted as necessary.

See also 1 ANALYTICAL PHILOSOPHY; 2 CONTINENTAL PHILOSOPHY; 8 ANARCHISM; 9 CONSERVATISM; 11 LIBERALISM; 13 SOCIALISM; 14 AUTONOMY; 15 COMMUNITY; 16 CONTRACT AND CONSENT; 17 CONSTITUTIONALISM AND THE RULE OF LAW; 19 DEMOCRACY; 25 EQUALITY; 29 LIBERTY; 30 POWER; 33 RIGHTS; 34 SECESSION AND NATIONALISM; 38 TOTALITARIANISM; 39 TRUST; 40 VIRTUE

References

Ackerman, B.: *Social Justice in the Liberal State* (New Haven, Conn.: Yale University Press, 1980).
Arendt, H.: *The Human Condition* (Chicago: University of Chicago Press, 1958).
————: *On Revolution* (New York: Viking Press, 1963).
Barber, B.: *Strong Democracy* (Berkeley: University of California Press, 1984).
Butler, J.: *Gender Troubles* (New York: Routledge, 1990).
Connolly, W.: *Identity/Difference: Democratic Negotiations of Political Paradox* (Ithaca, NY: Cornell University Press, 1991).
DeMan, P.: *The Resistance to Theory* (Minneapolis: University of Minnesota Press, 1986).
Derrida, J.: *Margins of Philosophy* (Chicago: University of Chicago Press, 1982).
Dworkin, R.: *Taking Rights Seriously* (Cambridge, Mass.: Harvard University Press, 1977).
Flathman, R.: *The Practice of Political Authority* (Chicago: University of Chicago Press, 1980).
————: *Willful Liberalism* (Ithaca, NY: Cornell University Press, 1992).
Foucault, M.: *Discipline and Punish* (New York: Vintage Books, 1979).
Friedman, R.: 'On the concept of authority in political philosophy', *Concepts in Social and Political Philosophy*, ed. R. Flathman (New York: Macmillan, 1973).

Galston, W.: *Justice and the Human Good* (Chicago: University of Chicago Press, 1980).

Gauthier, D.: *Morals by Agreement* (Oxford: Clarendon Press, 1986).

Green, L.: *The Authority of the State* (Oxford: Clarendon Press, 1988).

Hart, H. L. A.: *The Concept of Law* (Oxford: Clarendon Press, 1961).

Hobbes, T.: *Leviathan* (1651), ed. M. Oakeshott (New York: Collier Books, 1962).

Kateb, G.: 'Democratic individuality and the claims of politics', *Political Theory*, 12 (1984), 331–60.

Kavka, G.: *Hobbesian Moral and Political Theory* (Princeton, NJ: Princeton University Press, 1986).

Kelsen, H.: *General Theory of Law and State* (Cambridge: Harvard University Press, 1945).

King, M. L., Jr: *Why We Can't Wait* (New York: Signet Books, 1964).

Lyotard, J.-F. and Thebaud, J.-L.: *Just Gaming* (Minneapolis: University of Minnesota Press, 1985).

Nietzsche, F.: *The Genealogy of Morals* (1887), trans. F. Golffing (Garden City: Doubleday Anchor, 1956).

————: *The Will to Power* (1906), trans. W. Kaufmann and R. J. Hollingdale (New York: Vintage Books, 1968).

Oakeshott, M.: *Hobbes on Civil Association* (Oxford: Blackwell, 1975a).

————: *On Human Conduct* (Oxford: Oxford University Press, 1975b).

Pateman, C.: *Participation and Democratic Theory* (Cambridge: Cambridge University Press, 1970).

Rawls, J.: *A Theory of Justice* (Cambridge, Mass.: Harvard University Press, 1971).

Raz, J.: *The Authority of Law* (Oxford: Clarendon Press, 1979).

————: *The Morality of Freedom* (Oxford: Clarendon Press, 1986).

Sandel, M.: *Liberalism and the Limits of Justice* (Cambridge: Cambridge University Press, 1982).

Simmons, A. J.: *Moral Principles and Political Obligations* (Princeton, NJ: Princeton University Press, 1979).

Wolff, R. P.: *In Defence of Anarchism* (New York: Harper Books, 1970).

29

Liberty

CHANDRAN KUKATHAS

Such is the rhetorical appeal of the idea of liberty that a variety of political philosophies claim to honour it. Republicans and Marxists, no less than libertarians and liberals, maintain that they and they alone are the true defenders of freedom. The literature of contemporary political theory is thus replete with rival analyses of the meaning of liberty, and disputes about its measurement, distribution and institutional requirements. Our aim here is to gain some understanding of the meaning and the conditions of liberty by working through the thicket of contemporary argument, though we may have to rest content with a better knowledge of the terrain.

The concept of liberty

Contemporary discussion of the concept of liberty has been most profoundly shaped by the analysis of Isaiah Berlin. In his essay 'Two concepts of liberty', Berlin argues that, in the history of ideas, liberty has had two quite different meanings or senses. In the first, 'negative' sense of the word, a person is free 'to the degree to which no man or body of men interferes' with his activity. 'Political liberty in this sense is simply the area within which a man can act unobstructed by others' (Berlin, 1979a, p. 122). In the second, 'positive' sense of the word, a person is free to the extent that he is his own master, whose life and decisions depend upon himself and not upon external forces of any kind. A person who is autonomous or self-determining – who is 'a thinking, willing, active being, bearing responsibility for [his] own choices and able to explain them by references to [his] own ideas and purposes' – is 'positively' free (Berlin, 1979a, p. 31).

Whether or not such a distinction can properly be drawn might be disputed. In Berlin's analysis, the contrast is more readily seen if we recognize that the positive and negative concepts of liberty are responses to 'logically distinct' questions. If one asks, 'Who governs me?', the answer will reveal the extent of one's positive liberty: someone who can reply, 'I govern myself', is positively free. If, on the other hand, one asks, 'How far do others interfere with me?', the answer will reveal the extent of one's negative liberty: someone who can answer, 'very little', is negatively free. In general, a person enjoys greater negative liberty to the extent that he is unimpeded or unconstrained by other human agents and can act without being interfered with. On this view, a lack of ability does not mean a lack of freedom – I am not unfree because I am unable to understand Hegel. However, if my inability is due to human arrangements which obstruct or interfere with me, then I am negatively unfree.

In drawing the contrast between negative and positive liberty, Berlin thinks he has identified an important conceptual distinction. But it is also a part of his concern to criticize positive conceptions of freedom. His criticisms are worth considering because they open up a number of issues which must be tackled in order to come to terms with the notion of freedom. Berlin presents his criticisms in the form of an account of the historical development of the negative and positive notions of liberty. Positive libertarians begin by invoking the harmless metaphor of self-mastery, maintaining that one is free if one is one's own master and a slave to no man. But they go on to suggest that one might equally be a slave to nature, or to one's own unbridled passions, or indeed to one's lower self. At this point, Berlin maintains, they proceed to develop a distinction between two selves: the dominant self, invariably identified with reason and man's 'higher nature', which is also the 'real' or 'ideal' or the 'autonomous' self – the self 'at its best'; and the 'lower', 'empirical' or 'heteronomous' self, which is the self of irrational impulse and uncontrolled desire, 'swept by every gust of desire and passion, needing to be rigidly disciplined if it is ever to rise to the full height of its 'real nature' (Berlin, 1979a, p. 132). From here it is a short step to claim that the real self may be best understood as something greater than the individual, as a social whole (such as a tribe or a state) of which the individual is only a part. 'This entity is then identified as being the "true" self which, by imposing its collective, or "organic", single will upon its recalcitrant "members", achieves its own, and therefore their, "higher" freedom' (ibid.). This positive libertarian understanding of freedom, according to Berlin, has in this way made it easy to justify coercing people, for the coercion is of the lower self by the higher, and such coercion is deemed not only consistent with but required by freedom.

Berlin is careful enough to concede that even negative libertarians could make such questionable philosophical moves, by maintaining, for example, that only the individual's real or higher self should not be constrained or interfered with. They too might argue that obstructing the individual's actual wishes would better serve his real desires. None the less, Berlin insists, 'the "positive" conception of freedom as self-mastery, with its suggestion of a man divided against himself, has, in fact, and as matter of history, of doctrine and of practice lent itself more easily to this splitting of personality into two' (ibid., p. 134). Indeed, he suggests that 'socialized' forms of the 'positive doctrine of liberation by reason' lie at the heart of many of the nationalist, communist, authoritarian and totalitarian creeds of today (ibid., p. 144).

But these propositions, and Berlin's famous distinction between negative and positive liberty, have not gone unchallenged. Gerald MacCallum, in his almost as famous paper, 'Negative and positive freedom', rejects Berlin's distinction between two concepts of liberty. Freedom, he maintains, is always one and the same triadic relation; 'Whenever the freedom of some agent or agents is in question, it is always freedom from some constraint or restriction on, interference with, or barrier to doing, not doing, becoming, or not becoming something' (MacCallum, 1991, p. 102). Freedom is always *of* something (an agent or agents), *from* something, *to* do or not do, become or not become, something. Any statement about freedom must take the form '*x* is (is not) free from y to do (not do) z', where x ranges over agents, y ranges over constraints, restrictions, interferences or barriers, and z ranges over actions or conditions of character or circumstance.

MacCallum does not deny that there might be uncertainty, or even disagreement, about what counts as an agent or about what counts as a constraint or restriction. But this does not alter his view that there is only a single triadic concept of liberty. Thus he rejects Berlin's distinction between negative or 'freedom from', and positive or 'freedom to' concepts of liberty (Berlin, 1979a, p. 131) on the grounds that any statement about liberty is a statement about the freedom of x *from* y *to* z. Berlin, in a reply to his critics, concedes that the terms 'negative' and 'positive' liberty 'start at no great logical distance from each other', and that the questions 'Who is master?' and 'Over what area am I master?' 'cannot be kept wholly distinct' (Berlin, 1979b, p. xliii). Indeed, MacCallum's understanding of liberty as a single triadic concept has been endorsed by a number of contemporary theorists, including Benn and Weinstein (1971, p. 194), Rawls (1971, p. 202), Feinberg (1980, pp. 3–4) and T. Gray (1990, pp. 11–16).

Nevertheless, others have argued that MacCallum's triadic formula does not capture all there is to the concept of liberty (Gray, J., 1984, pp. 326–7), though there is also disagreement over whether Berlin has in fact distinguished different *concepts* of liberty or merely identified two kinds of *conceptions* of liberty. To some extent the question of whether there are two concepts or one is a matter to be settled by convention. In Berlin's favour it might be said that a distinction between negative and positive liberty has been drawn and widely employed. On the other hand, not all usages of the distinction have conformed to Berlin's original. One common way of drawing the distinction has been as a contrast between the opportunities available to a person (negative liberty) and the capacity or the resources that person has to take advantage of them (positive liberty). As Levin expresses it, 'a man is *positively* free when he is doing what he wants to do, and *negatively* free when no one is interfering with him' (Levin, 1984, p. 85). Rawls (1971, p. 204) suggests that the 'inability to take advantage of one's rights and opportunities as a result of poverty and ignorance, and a lack of means generally' should not be counted as among the constraints definitive of liberty. Instead, he maintains, we should distinguish between liberty and the worth of liberty. But for some proponents of the negative/positive distinction, the correct inference to be drawn from this way of viewing matters is that both opportunities (or negative liberties) and resources (positive liberties) must be viewed as different but equally important dimensions of liberty (Goodin, 1982, p. 152).

Yet while this kind of analysis has been influential, there are other philosophers who have tried to show that a much deeper distinction exists between negative and positive liberty. A particularly influential discussion of the distinction is offered by Charles Taylor, who suggests that negative freedom is usually an 'opportunity concept', while positive freedom is always an 'exercise concept' (Taylor, 1979). In Taylor's analysis, negative liberty is usually an opportunity concept because it suggests that 'being free is a matter of what we can do, of what it is open to us to do, whether or not we do anything to exercise these options'. This is so, he says, with the negative conceptions of freedom employed by Hobbes and Bentham. Positive freedom, however, is an exercise concept because doctrines of positive freedom 'are concerned with a view of freedom which involves essentially the exercising of control over one's life. On this view, one is free only to the extent that one has effectively determined oneself and the shape of one's life' (ibid., p. 176). The key to Taylor's distinction, as he understands it, lies in the fact that the opportunity concept sees only 'external' obstacles to action as obstacles to freedom. By contrast, to recognize freedom as an exercise concept is to accept that the 'internal' obstacles of the mind, which affect our motivations, our self-control and our capacity for moral discrimination, also affect our freedom (ibid., p. 179).

One problem with Taylor's view is that it is not clear why, for the negative libertarian, only external obstacles count. 'Internal' impediments to action may just as easily be regarded as obstacles which affect an individual's freedom. Physical barriers, legal prohibitions and credible threats reduce my negative liberty since they are impediments or constraints upon my action. But my negative liberty is similarly reduced if I am drugged or brainwashed, or if I am manipulated or deceived into taking particular actions: the 'internal' obstacles reducing my liberty are the false beliefs with which I have been inculcated.

Now, Taylor argues that, once it is conceded that 'internal' obstacles restrict freedom, the negative libertarian is no longer using freedom as an opportunity concept but is using it as an exercise concept. This is because to be free of internal obstacles invariably involves actively 'exercising' freedom by removing those internal barriers (ibid., pp. 177–8). This seems to be a mistake. While removing or surmounting internal obstacles, such as fears or anxieties, involves action, the same is also true of the overcoming of external obstacles. Whether or not activity is required to enjoy freedom is irrelevant. Furthermore, as Baldwin tellingly observes, one might agree that overcoming internal obstacles involves one in action, 'but it does not follow that the freedom thereby attained is more than an opportunity to act' (Baldwin, 1984, pp. 131–2).

Negative freedom, then, I would suggest, is always to be understood as an opportunity concept; but the contrast to be drawn is not between negative liberty meaning the mere absence of external obstacles and positive liberty meaning the active overcoming of internal obstacles. Negative liberty is what an agent enjoys when there are no humanly imposed impediments, internal or external, to action.

Conceptions of negative liberty

Among those who conceive of liberty in negative terms there is still disagreement about when an individual can be said to be free. Although all might concur that liberty means an absence of impediments or constraints or interference, there remains the question of what is to count as a constraint which makes us unfree. There are also the questions of who (or what) is the subject of freedom, and what it is that the free subject is free to do. The first of these three questions is undoubtedly the most problematic for an account of liberty, but something should be said about the latter two.

Generally, theories of liberty assume that the subject of freedom is the individual. G. A. Cohen, however, has suggested that there may be good reason to recognize the collective dimensions of freedom and unfreedom: arguing that while members of the proletarian class are held to be free because they are at liberty to leave the proletariat this does not alter the fact of their unfreedom, since they are not free *collectively* or *as a class* to leave the proletariat (Cohen, 1979, pp. 21–5). Under capitalist institutions, even though anyone might rise up from the proletariat, it is not possible for everyone to do so since capitalism requires 'a substantial hired labour force, which would not exist if more than just a few workers rose' (ibid., p. 21). This way of viewing liberty is important for Cohen because it bears upon claims made about freedom under capitalism. The position of the proletariat he holds to be analogous to that of a group of imprisoned individuals who have the opportunity for only one of their number to escape. Since *all* cannot escape, even though *each* has an opportunity to do so, the group is collectively unfree or unfree as a class.

Cohen's paper has been widely discussed, but it is not clear that thinking about the subject of freedom in these collective terms adds a great deal to our understanding of the notion. At the very least, it is odd to think that we are in any significant way unfree to do something simply because we cannot all do it at the same time. We cannot all claim unemployment benefits at the same time, nor can we all become plumbers or professors of political theory, but this does not mean that we are unfree to do or become any of these things (Gray, J., 1986, p. 166).

The second question which needs to be asked is that of what the subject of freedom must be free to do if liberty is to be enjoyed. One might say, for example, that to be free the subject must have the opportunity to exercise traditional liberties, or to do what he desires, or to do anything. At first sight it appears that to be free one must have the opportunity to do what one wants or desires. The difficulty with this position is that it means that liberty can be increased by trimming or reducing desires. Thus the contented slave could be seen as free because he has no desire to escape. This problem was raised in criticism of Berlin's original formulation of the notion of liberty (McFarlane, 1966, pp. 77–81). Berlin's response was to acknowledge that the 'extent of my social or political freedom consists in the absence of obstacles not merely to my actual, but to my potential choices – to my acting in this or that way if I choose to do so' (Berlin, 1979b). On this view, then, an individual enjoys negative liberty if he is not obstructed or interfered with should he seek to perform an action. Generally, this account of the ends of negative liberty meets the relevant objections and its acceptance should not be controversial.

The more difficult problem in accounting for negative liberty is in answering the question of what counts as an obstacle or interference. Here, there is a greater variety of views on offer, and conceptions of liberty generally differ on the basis of their answers to this question. A clear, if uncompromising, answer to the question is offered by Hillel Steiner: 'An individual is unfree if, and only if, his doing of any action is rendered *impossible* by the action of another individual' (Steiner, 1991, p. 123, emphasis added; see also Parent, 1974). If an individual is still able to perform an action, even if someone has made doing so extremely undesirable, the individual remains free. In this regard, threats and penalties do not make anyone unfree to perform an action since they leave open the option of performing the action and incurring its costs. Indeed, these kinds of *threatening* interventions are indistinguishable from *offers,* and neither diminish liberty; in both cases the intervention alters the *desirability* of performing the action, but not the *possibility* of doing so. Steiner's reasons for taking this path are not difficult to discern: if liberty can be reduced by interventions which merely make a course of action less desirable, then a person can be rendered less free if he is subject to any kind of influence by other human agents. I could claim to be made less free in term time because I will not go to restaurants for fear of running into pesky undergraduates. Any departure from the stance that only interference rendering action impossible makes an individual unfree, Steiner maintains, makes freedom dependent upon desire and leads to our misconceiving it as a psychological condition rather than as a physical fact.

If only *prevention* of action and not mere intervention in its course can reduce liberty, however, what exactly does prevention amount to in this account of liberty as a physical fact? In Steiner's theory an agent is prevented from action to the extent that he is rendered unable to make use of a portion of physical space or a number of physical objects: 'the greater the amount of physical space and/or material objects the use of which is blocked to one individual by another, the greater is the extent of the prevention to which the former individual is subject' (Steiner, 1991, p. 137). A person who is imprisoned is thus unfree to the extent that he has use of less space and fewer resources. Furthermore, Steiner maintains, some of the persons who are not imprisoned have now had their freedom expanded, since they can make use of the space and material objects to which the prisoner is denied access. This is because, according to Steiner, freedom has to be seen as a fixed quantity which cannot be expanded or reduced but only redistributed. One person's loss of freedom must involve another's gain: the 'universal quest for greater personal liberty is . . . a zero-sum game' (Steiner, 1983, pp. 88–9). It is thus pointless to talk of maximizing the total amount of freedom; the important normative questions are not about the manufacture but about the *distribution of* freedom.

Steiner's views, I would like to suggest, are mistaken in important ways. Essentially, the idea that freedom has to be understood purely as a physical fact (wholly independently of desire) is, in the end, untenable. To see this, we should consider first the idea that freedom involves the use or control of physical space and resources. Steiner is quite precise: 'to act is, among other things, to occupy particular portions of physical space and to dispose of particular material objects' (1991, p. 137). For an agent to be free to perform an action entails that all the physical components of doing that 'action are (simultaneously) unoccupied and/or disposed of by another' (ibid., p. 138). In other words, the agent must *possess* that physical space or those material objects, and he possesses an object only 'when he enjoys exclusive physical control of it, that is, when what happens to that object – allowing for the operation of the laws of physics – is not subject to the determination of any other agent and is therefore subject only to his own determination'. As Steiner prefers to understand the notion, control only obtains when an agent is able to render it *physically impossible* for another to occupy space or use an object.

Yet it seems clear that this sort of complete physical control Steiner thinks is necessary for freedom cannot be had. For the most part individuals seeking to exercise control over their possessions look to putting in place non-physical impediments to trespass. My freedom to use my house, and to exclude the uninvited, is enjoyed not because I am capable of physically excluding others but because of a range of non-physical circumstances: I have title to my property, property rights are respected and can be be enforced if necessary, and so on. Now it might be maintained that I only have freedom to the extent that others do not in fact physically intrude, and that if they do I do not have (as much) freedom because I do not control as much physical material. But the implication of this strongly physicalist attitude which must be noted is that such things as rights, entitlements, and laws have to be regarded as having no bearing on liberty. This does not appear to be a plausible line of argument. Indeed, if one accepts Steiner's view that we should be concerned primarily about the *distribution* of liberty, then our concerns would most likely be about the rules or laws which affect that distribution, rather than with physical impediments.

The implication which has to be – and generally is – accepted, then, is that liberty can be affected by interventions which affect the desirability of performing particular actions. But we have to deal with the question of which kinds of interventions that affect the desirability of an action are to be regarded as freedom restricting – since we do not want to say that all influences on an action diminish the agent's liberty by making other options less attractive.

One argument, put by F. A. Hayek, is that we only regard as freedom restricting those actions which are *coercive*: ' "freedom" refers solely to a relation of men to other men, and the only infringement on it is coercion by men' (Hayek, 1960, p. 12). What is striking about Hayek's formulation is that he maintains that freedom is restricted only by coercive intervention by *persons*; the law, however, does not restrict freedom. Freedom, for him, is best described as 'independence of the arbitrary will of another' (ibid.). But it is also his contention that 'when we obey laws, in the sense of general abstract rules laid down irrespective of their application to us, we are not subject to another man's will and are therefore free' (ibid., p. 153). There is coercion if a person threatens to inflict harm with the intention of bringing about a change in the conduct of a second person (who regards himself as having been made worse off). But there is no coercion – and so there is liberty – if the law makes a person worse off and 'forces' a change in conduct (ibid., pp. 134–6; and see Kukathas, 1989, pp. 150–1).

Hayek's solution, however, is unsatisfactory on two counts. First, his account of coercion is inadequate because it makes many kinds of competitive action appear liberty restricting. A trader who intends to inflict harm on his competitor by lowering prices, and brings about a change in conduct (by forcing him out of this line of business) would, on Hayek's definition, be infringing liberty. Yet Hayek himself would not want to say that this kind of competitive conduct is coercive or liberty diminishing. Second, his suggestion that law does not restrict liberty because any 'coercion' implicit in its commands and prohibitions is predictable and avoidable is unconvincing: predictable coercion remains coercion. While there is merit in Hayek's attempt to argue that law should be viewed as a condition of, rather than an obstacle to, liberty, the theory of coercion does not really account for this.

A different solution to the question of which kinds of intervention are freedom restricting comes from Robert Nozick. Like Hayek, he thinks that a distinction has to be drawn between threats and offers, and while he does not think it right to 'capsulize freedom as absence of coercion' (Nozick, 1972, p. 101), he also sees liberty as intimately bound up with coercion. Moreover, Nozick's view is in line with Hayek's in that he sees threats, but not offers, as coercive for the reason that 'when a person does something because of threats, the will of another is operating or predominant' (ibid., p. 128). This thought forms the basis of the conception of liberty which is invoked (but not explicitly developed) by Nozick in *Anarchy, State and Utopia*, where it is suggested that interference with individual choice makes for liberty infringement (Nozick, 1974, pp. 160–4). What has to be noted about this account, however, is that only some kinds of intervention count as interference which involves restriction of liberty. For example, it cannot be said that the choices of individuals acting 'within their rights' (ibid., p. 262) interfere with or restrict the liberty of another individual, even if those choices leave that individual with no reasonable options. So if, as a result of others acting within their rights, I am left with the choice of working for Robert Maxwell or starving I cannot claim that I am forced or coerced into involuntary employment. If, however, Mr Maxwell had engineered this situation (say, by stealing from and bankrupting his competitors) I can claim to have been forced.

Nozick's conception of liberty here is one which is dependent upon his conception of justice, which in turn is founded upon a view about what rights individuals have (since any action which does not violate rights is not unjust). Liberty cannot be violated by actions which are just. In some respects this understanding of liberty is consistent with our everyday use of the term. We do not normally say that the gang-member's liberty is lost because the law forbids assault and battery. None the less, the problem with Nozick's conception of liberty is that it is so dependent upon a theory of rights which is never fully expounded. Furthermore, tying liberty so intimately to another substantial moral value risks depriving the notion of liberty of independent force in political argument.

This latter objection lies at the centre of G. A. Cohen's criticisms of Nozick's view of freedom. According to Cohen, because Nozick sees only illegitimate actions as capable of violating liberty he is operating with a 'moralized' notion of freedom. This allows Nozick to ignore many situations in which people are 'forced' by circumstances such as poverty to take or to forgo particular options. Nozick's 'moralized' definition allows him to deny that the indigent are necessarily unfree since the mark of unfreedom is not the absence of options or opportunities but the violation of (a narrow range of) rights (Cohen, 1978). Yet Cohen's critique of Nozick may not be as telling as he suggests. While rejecting 'moralized' conceptions of freedom, Cohen does not deny that we are concerned here with freedom as it relates to interaction between human agents. We are not concerned with those obstacles which are not subject to human influence. Someone whose path has been blocked by a rockslide is not unfree, although unable, to continue on that route – unless someone can be held responsible for the creation of (or failure to remove) that obstacle, in which case we would say the traveller is not merely unable to journey but unfree to do so. The important issue, however, as David Miller makes clear, is that of the basis upon which we determine whether someone can be held responsible, for this will determine whether or not we can regard an obstacle as a constraint on freedom. This is a moral issue, and an answer to it cannot be morally neutral (Miller, 1983, p. 72). Nozick has not provided a morally neutral account of what counts as a constraint on freedom, but neither can one be expected. There is, however, the stronger criticism of Nozick that he does not merely offer a morally non-neutral definition of freedom, but a view that says that morally justified interferences do not restrict liberty; the definition is thus 'moralized'. But this is not quite the case. In Nozick's theory the domain of individual liberty is specified by (rights-based) principles of justice. Morally justifiable interferences with individual liberty (to avoid 'catastrophic moral horror', for example; Nozick, 1974, p. 30) do restrict liberty. However, they restrict liberty not because they are unjustified but because they are *unjust*. Nozick invokes a *justicized* account of liberty, but not a moralized one (Gray, J., 1986, p. 169).

None the less, this does not mean that Nozick's approach to specifying what counts as a constraint on freedom is satisfactory. For Nozick justice can never compete with liberty; justice cannot violate liberty. Yet this seems too strong a demand; there may well be times when liberty must be violated for justice to be done. For example, upholding justice in rectification by transferring property rights may infringe the liberty of those whose justly acquired property is now taken. Specifying what makes for constraints upon liberty may be a more complicated matter than Nozick's theory suggests.

These attempts to specify what counts as a constraint upon individual liberty illustrate the difficulty of developing an uncontroversial conception of liberty. In part, this may simply reflect the 'essential contestability' of the concept. The more important reason, however, is that judgements about freedom cannot be insulated completely from other evaluative questions and from issues in social theory. While it should be recognized that freedom requires the absence of obstruction, and that coercive behaviour (which penalizes or frustrates action) restricts liberty, it is a matter of moral argument what precisely qualifies as an obstruction, or constitutes coercive behaviour. Rawls, for example, suggests that a person is obstructed by others if they fail to uphold the rights or perform the duties which they are obliged to. 'If, for example, we consider liberty of conscience as defined by law, then individuals have this liberty when they are free to pursue their moral, philosophical, or religious interests without legal restrictions requiring them to engage or not to engage in any particular form of religious or other practice, and when other men have a legal duty not to interfere' (Rawls, 1971, pp. 202–3). Yet what is crucial here is the specification of the relevant rights and duties. Whether or not any particular individual is free according to a Rawlsian conception of liberty may be a purely *descriptive* matter in so far as it is necessary only for us to enquire whether or not he is actually obstructed to establish whether he is free. But what counts as an obstruction under that conception is an *evaluative* matter which requires the development of arguments in moral and social theory (Berlin, 1979a; Gray, J., 1984). Thus we should expect to find that different political theories or ideologies, even if they should accept the core understanding of negative liberty as the absence of interference, will embrace quite different conceptions of liberty.

Liberty: liberal and republican

What, then, would make for a free society? One prominent answer in modern thinking about liberty is that a free society is fundamentally a *liberal* society. It is the answer offered by Berlin (1979a), as well as by other contemporary theorists such as John Rawls, F. A. Hayek and James Buchanan (1975). Liberalism has, in recent times, come under severe criticism for a range of alleged inadequacies – for overvaluing justice and for undervaluing community, among other things (Sandel, 1982). But since liberty is often taken to be the core value upheld by liberalism, it is worth examining its claim to being the philosophy of a free society.

The most substantial challenge to liberalism's libertarian credentials has come from Quentin Skinner in a series of papers (1984; 1991) criticizing liberal conceptions of negative liberty and advancing a 'republican' conception of negative liberty. Skinner's primary claim is that there is something unsatisfactory about liberalism's reliance on a particular notion of negative liberty merely as the absence of of interference. His targets are the Hobbesian notions that liberty consists in the absence of external impediments to motion, and that in political society the 'greatest liberty of subjects, dependeth on the silence of the law', since law is an obstacle to liberty (Hobbes, [1651] 1968, II, 21, 143). His criticism of liberalism is largely a criticism of the legal theories of writers like Jeremy Bentham, for whom law itself must be viewed as an invasion of liberty. Skinner himself seeks to uphold a negative conception of liberty; but it is the particular negative conception associated with the notion of law as a fetter on freedom which he associates with liberalism that he seeks to criticize.

To see why Skinner may have a point we might consider again the case of the slave who enjoys a good measure of negative liberty, and yet chooses not to escape. However much negative liberty the slave might enjoy, there is something unsatisfactory about this liberty. The reason, essentially, is that he is not secure in its possession. Whether or not, and for how long, he is able to exercise that liberty is subject to the good will and the good fortune of the master. In Philip Pettit's useful term, his liberty has no 'resilience' (Pettit, 1993). Thus we find, for example, that even the most contented slaves, living under the kindest masters, in *Uncle Tom's Cabin* want manumission for fear that, should their masters die or be forced to sell them, their lives could instantly be transformed for the worse. The point here was well recognized by Edmund Burke in arguing against the Chatham Methodists in 1773. The Methodists objected to a Bill for the relief of Protestant Dissenters on the grounds that Dissenters did in fact enjoy a measure of liberty, and that it would be dangerous to grant it to them as a matter of law. To Burke, however, this was 'liberty under a connivance', which he rejected because 'connivance is a relaxation from slavery, not a definition of liberty. What is connivance, but a state under which all slaves live? If I was to describe slavery, I would say, with those who *hate* it, it is living under will, not under law' (Burke, 1970, p. 77).

Skinner's concern is that liberty exercised in spite of the law, rather than enjoyed under its protection, is insecure – indeed, no more than liberty under a connivance – and will soon be lost. His argument is that what are needed are social institutions which will better assure individuals of their liberty. More specifically, we need institutions which make for active self-government, even to the point of coercing citizens into performing their public duties and so 'upholding a liberty which, left to ourselves, we would have undermined' (Skinner, 1991, p. 186). The target of Skinner's criticism is contemporary liberalism, 'especially in its so-called libertarian form' which, by threatening to sweep 'the public arena bare of any concepts save those of self-interest and individual rights', threatens also our rights and liberties themselves (Skinner, 1991, p. 204).

Skinner's contention that it is the liberty that is enjoyed under the protection of the laws which is the liberty to be sought is entirely persuasive, I would suggest, because the contrast it draws is that between free individuals and slaves. In the moral world, the opposite of liberty is slavery. (See Patterson, 1991, for a discussion of the origin of the ideal of freedom in the experience of slavery.) What is more disputable, however, is whether he is right to say that it is the institutions of self-government, underpinned by the enforcement of republican virtue, which are going to preserve that liberty. Equally contestable is the claim that liberalism, with its emphasis on individual rights, is a threat to that liberty. Indeed, the very idea that liberalism necessarily views law as invasive of liberty is questionable. Hayek, for example, has consistently argued that law is not invasive of liberty but its necessary precondition.

The liberal and republican traditions are not always easy to disentangle. One reason for this is that both attach great value to institutions which check, and attempt to control, political power. Both emphasize the importance of the rule of law, of constitutional government and of the separation of powers for the preservation of a free society. Yet where they might be seen to differ is over the question of how political power is to be checked. Republicans, like Skinner and Pettit (see also Pettit, 1989; and Pettit, 1992), seem to suggest that it is best checked by political institutions which increase public participation and so increase the accountability of the executive power. Liberals, I would suggest, are less impressed by such checks *within* the structure of political institutions because they do not serve sufficiently to disperse power in society. It is not the political separation of powers that is vital but their social separation. While republicans are concerned 'to improve the accountability of our soi-disant representatives' (Skinner, 1991, p. 204), they also look to extending the power of the ('checked and controlled') state both to empower (Pettit, 1992, p. 30) and to coerce its citizens. Liberals, while they might accept that institutional checks are of some value, insist that it is the accumulation of power which is the danger – above all, to liberty.

It is in this context that one should understand the liberal preoccupation with *individual* rights and liberties rather than *public* duties. Asserting such claims on behalf of individuals is intended to deny power to the state by limiting the scope of legitimate public concern. There are at least two reasons for limiting the scope of the public domain, both of which bear upon liberty. The first is one alluded to by J. S. Mill when he wrote:

If the roads, the railways, the banks, the insurance offices, the great joint-stock companies, the universities, and the public charities, were all of them branches of the government; if, in addition, the municipal corporations and local boards, with all that now devolves on them, become departments of the central administration; if the employés of all these different enterprises were appointed and paid by the government, and look to the government for every rise in life; not all the freedom of the press and popular constitution of the legislature would make this or any other country free otherwise than in name. (Mill, [1859] 1985, pp. 244–5)

Mill's fear was partly that such power would convert 'the active and ambitious part of the public' into 'hangers-on' of the government. But the greater danger was that, as the more able were drawn into government office because 'every part of the business of society which required organized concert, or large and comprehensive views' was in the hands of government, there would be fewer people among those outside capable, 'for want of practical experience', of criticizing or checking the government's mode of operation (ibid., p. 245). An extensive public power would weaken public life.

The second reason for diminishing the scope of the public domain is to be found in an argument advanced by Edmund Burke, who maintained that 'the state ought to confine itself to what regards the state', and not embroil itself in the affairs of society. For as rulers 'descend from the state to a province, from a province to a parish, and from a parish to a private house, they go on accelerated in their fall. They *cannot* do the lower duty; and in proportion as they try it, they will certainly fail in the higher. They ought to know the different departments of things, – what belongs to laws, and what manners alone can regulate' (Burke, 1970, p. 31). As the state expands it will perform all its functions less well, and particularly its primary function of upholding the peace and security which is necessary for liberty (ibid., p. 65). Once again, the argument is that expanding the scope of the public domain weakens the public in its capacity to supply a check upon executive rule.

If these points are sound, then what is needed to uphold liberty is a set of institutions which foster individual responsibility and protect certain individual rights – and not institutions which purport to make for public virtue. Whether or not these points are sound, however, is a matter of social theory which cannot be easily resolved here. If questions of liberty are to be answered there must be recourse to social theory. (This is a point made by Berlin; for a discussion see Gray, J., 1984.) The contention which can only be asserted here is that for answers we should turn not to the classical republicans but to the ideas of classical liberalism.

See also 1 ANALYTICAL PHILOSOPHY; 4 SOCIOLOGY; 5 ECONOMICS; 6 POLITICAL SCIENCE; 7 LEGAL STUDIES; 8 ANARCHISM; 9 CONSERVATISM; 11 LIBERALISM; 13 SOCIALISM; 14 AUTONOMY; 15 COMMUNITY; 16 CONTRACT AND CONSENT; 17 CONSTITUTIONALISM AND THE RULE OF LAW; 19 DEMOCRACY; 22 DISTRIBUTIVE JUSTICE; 23 EFFICIENCY; 25 EQUALITY; 26 FEDERALISM; 30 POWER; 31 PROPERTY; 32 REPUBLICANISM; 33 RIGHTS; 34 SECESSION AND NATIONALISM; 35 SOCIOBIOLOGY; 37 TOLERATION AND FUNDAMENTALISM; 38 TOTALITARIANISM; 41 WELFARE

References

Baldwin, T.: 'MacCallum and the two concepts of freedom', *Ratio*, 26 (1984), 125–42.
Benn, S. I. and Weinstein, W. L.: 'Being free to act, and being a free man', *Mind*, 80 (1971), 194–211.
Berlin, I.: 'Two concepts of liberty', *Four Essays on Liberty* (Oxford: Oxford University Press, 1979a), pp. 118–72.
————: 'Introduct]ion', *Four Essays on Liberty* (Oxford: Oxford University Press, 1979b), pp. ix–lxiii.

Buchanan, J. M.: *The Limits of Liberty: Between Anarchy and Leviathan* (Chicago: University of Chicago Press, 1975).

Burke, E.: *The Philosophy of Edmund Burke*, ed. L. I. Bredvold and R. G. Ross (Ann Arbor: University of Michigan Press, 1970).

Cohen, G. A.: 'Robert Nozick and Wilt Chamberlain: how patterns preserve liberty', *Justice and Economic Distribution*, ed. J. Arthur and W. H. Shaw (Englewood Cliffs, NJ: Prentice-Hall, 1978), pp. 246–62.

——————: 'Capitalism, freedom, and the proletariat', *The Idea of Freedom: Essays in Honour of Isaiah Berlin*, ed. A. Ryan (Oxford: Oxford University Press, 1979), pp. 9–26.

Feinberg, J.: *Rights, Justice and the Bounds of Liberty* (Princeton, NJ: Princeton University Press, 1980).

Goodin, R. E.: 'Freedom and the welfare state: theoretical foundations', *Journal of Social Policy*, 11 (1982), 149–76.

Gray, J.: 'On negative and positive liberty', *Conceptions of Liberty in Political Philosophy*, eds J. Gray and Z. Pelczynski (London: Athlone Press, 1984), pp. 321–48.

——————: 'Marxian freedom, individual liberty, and the end of alienation', *Social Philosophy and Policy*, 4 (1986), pp. 160–87.

Gray, T.: *Freedom* (London: Macmillan, 1990).

Hayek, F. A.: *The Constitution of Liberty* (London: Routledge & Kegan Paul, 1960).

Hobbes, T.: *Leviathan* (1651); (Harmondsworth: Penguin, 1968).

Kukathas, C.: *Hayek and Modern Liberalism* (Oxford: Clarendon Press, 1989).

Levin, M.: 'Negative liberty', *Social Philosophy and Policy*, 2 (1984), 84–100.

MacCallum, G.: 'Negative and positive freedom', *Liberty*, ed. D. Miller (Oxford: Oxford University Press, 1991), pp. 100–22.

McFarlane, L. J.: 'On two concepts of liberty', *Political Studies*, 14 (1966), 77–81.

Mill, J. S.: *On Liberty* (1859), in *Utilitarianism, On Liberty, Essay on Bentham*, ed. Mary Warnock (Glasgow: Fontana, 1985).

Miller, D.: 'Constraints on freedom', *Ethics*, 94 (1983), 66–86.

Nozick, R.: 'Coercion', *Philosophy, Politics and Society*, Fourth series, ed. P. Laslett, W. G. Runciman and Q. Skinner (Oxford: Blackwell, 1972), pp. 101–35.

——————: *Anarchy, State and Utopia* (Oxford: Blackwell, 1974).

Parent, W. A.: 'Some recent work on the concept of liberty', *American Philosophical Quarterly*, 11 (1974), 149–67.

Patterson, O.: *Freedom*. Vol. 1: *Freedom in the Making of Western Culture* (New York: Basic Books, 1991).

Pettit, P.: 'The freedom of the city: a republican ideal', *The Good Polity. Normative Analysis of the State*, ed. A. Hamlin and P. Pettit (Oxford: Blackwell, 1989), pp. 141–68.

——————: 'Republican themes', *Legislative Studies*, 6 (1992), 29–30.

——————: *The Common Mind: From Folk Psychology to Social and Political Theory* (Oxford: Clarendon Press, 1993).

Rawls, J.: *A Theory of Justice* (Cambridge, Mass.: Harvard University Press, 1971).

Sandel, M.: *Liberalism and the Limits of Justice* (Cambridge: Cambridge University Press, 1982).

Skinner, Q.: 'The idea of negative liberty: philosophical and historical perspectives', *Philosophy in History*, ed. R. Rorty, J. B. Schneewind and Q. Skinner (Cambridge: Cambridge University Press, 1984), pp. 193–221.

——————: 'The paradoxes of political liberty', *Liberty*, ed. D. Miller (Oxford: Oxford University Press, 1991), pp. 183–205.

Steiner, H.: 'How free: computing personal liberty', *Of Liberty*, ed. A. Phillips Griffiths (Cambridge: Cambridge University Press, 1983), pp. 73–90.

————: 'Individual liberty', *Liberty*, ed. D. Miller (Oxford: Oxford University Press, 1991), pp. 123–40.

Taylor, C.: 'What's wrong with negative liberty', *The Idea of Freedom. Essays in Honour of Isaiah Berlin*, ed. A. Ryan (Oxford: Oxford University Press, 1979), pp. 175–94.

Further reading

Benn, S. I.: *A Theory of Freedom* (Cambridge: Cambridge University Press, 1988).

Cohen, G. A.: 'The structure of proletarian unfreedom', *Philosophy and Public Affairs*, 12 (1983), 3–33.

Cohen, M.: 'Berlin and the liberal tradition', *Philosophical Quarterly*, 10 (1960), 216–27.

Day, J. P.: *Liberty and Justice* (London: Croom Helm, 1987).

Flathman, R. E.: *The Philosophy and Politics of Freedom* (Chicago: Chicago University Press, 1987).

Friedman, M.: *Capitalism and Freedom* (Chicago: Chicago University Press, 1962).

Gray, J.: 'Liberalism and the choice of liberties', *Liberalisms: Essays in Political Philosophy* (London: Routledge, 1989), pp. 140–60.

Green, T. H.: 'Liberal legislation and freedom of contract', *Liberty*, ed. D. Miller (Oxford: Oxford University Press, 1991), pp. 21–32.

Hayek, F. A.: *Law, Legislation and Liberty*, 3 vols (London: Routledge & Kegan Paul, 1982).

Pettit, P.: 'A definition of negative liberty', *Ratio*, NS 2 (1989), 153–68.

Raz, J.: *The Morality of Freedom* (Oxford: Clarendon Press, 1986).

Schauer, F.: *Free Speech. A Philosophical Inquiry* (Cambridge: Cambridge University Press, 1982).

Taylor, M.: *Community, Anarchy and Liberty* (Cambridge: Cambridge University Press, 1982).

Weinstein, W. L.: 'The concept of liberty in 19th century English political thought', *Political Studies*, 13 (1965), 145–62.

30

Power

TERENCE BALL

Power – the word, anyway – is a pervasive part of everyday discourse. It is a word we use often, and mostly without giving it much thought. When we do think about it, however, 'power' proves to be a peculiarly problematic concept. My aim here is to consider a number of difficulties, real or imagined, that arise when we use the term, particularly in *political* contexts or situations, with an eye to clarifying, if not resolving, these difficulties. I begin by canvassing several influential conceptions of power. Despite their apparent diversity, they nevertheless share several common or 'core' features. Next, I look a little more closely at some of the disagreements about the meaning of 'power' that arise despite widespread agreement about what constitutes its essential or core meaning. I then examine the strengths and shortcomings of Steven Lukes' important and influential analysis of 'power', as a prelude to sketching in brief outline a more comprehensive 'communicative' conception of power. And finally, I conclude by examining and criticizing the claim that 'power' is an 'essentially contested' concept.

'Power': essential features

In looking at various views or conceptions of power one is immediately struck by their variety and diversity. For Thomas Hobbes, power is one's 'present means, to obtain some future apparent Good' and life itself is 'a perpetuall and restlesse desire of Power after power that ceaseth only in Death' (Hobbes, [1651] 1991, Book I, ch. 10, p. 62; Book I, ch. 11, p. 70). Two centuries later Alexander Hamilton asked rhetorically, 'What is power, but the ability or faculty of doing a thing?' (Federalist No. 33). Early in the present century Max Weber defined power as 'the probability that one actor in a social relationship will carry out his own will against the resistance of others' (Weber, 1968, vol. I, p. 53). At mid-century Harold Lasswell and Abraham Kaplan construed exercises of power as 'acts . . . affecting or determining other acts' (Lasswell and Kaplan, 1950, p. xiv). Shortly thereafter, Robert Dahl defined power as one actor's ability to make another do something that the latter 'would not otherwise do' (Dahl, 1957, p. 203).

At the same time, however, Hannah Arendt argued that power is not the property of lone agents or actors, but of groups or collectivities acting together. 'Power', she wrote, 'corresponds to the human ability not just to act but to act in concert. Power is never the property of an individual; it belongs to a group and remains in existence

548

only so long as the group keeps together' (Arendt, 1972, p. 143; 1958, pp. 200–5). Rejecting this as an 'interestingly idiosyncratic view of power', Steven Lukes suggests that 'The absolutely basic common core to, or primitive notion lying behind, all talk of power is the notion that A in some way affects B' (Lukes, 1974, pp. 59, 26). Yet, to exercise power, as Peter Morriss notes, is not merely a matter of affecting someone or something; it implies *effecting*, that is, causally affecting someone or something so as to bring about some sort of change (Morriss, 1987, pp. 29–32). Or, as Anthony Giddens puts it, to have power is to be able to act in ways that will 'make a difference' to the way things turn out (Giddens, 1984, p. 14).

Clearly, conceptions of power are diverse and apparently divergent. This degree of diversity has led several modern political theorists to claim that 'power' has, and can have, no single agreed upon meaning, but is an 'essentially contested concept'. For reasons given below (pp. 553ff), I do not believe this to be a valid claim. Without previewing that argument here, we can begin by noting that, despite differences of detail and nuance, various conceptions of power do nevertheless share several core or fundamental features. But before inquiring into what these may be, we might ask an even more fundamental question: Why do we even have the concept of power in our moral and political vocabulary? Or, to pose the question in a slightly different way, what difference does it make that we have the notion of power at our disposal?

To raise this question leads us to consider an obvious, though often overlooked, point about 'power'. It is a word, a term, a concept that political analysts and agents use to *do* things. But what, typically, does one do with the concept of power? Several modern theorists, including Lukes (1974), Connolly (1983) and Isaac (1987), claim that we use ascriptions of power to fix responsibility for actions and their outcomes. Ascriptions of power are ascriptions of responsibility. As Isaac puts it, 'To locate the sources of power in society is to locate the enablements and constraints that operate on all of us . . . To locate power is to fix moral responsibility' (Isaac, 1987, p. 5). Were we to be without the concept of power, our ability to judge actions and actors as blameworthy or creditable would be greatly impaired if not rendered impossible.

But why is this so? Simply because 'power' is an 'ability' or 'capacity' concept (Emmett, 1954, pp. 19–20; Morriss, 1987, pp. 48f). That is, to impute power to someone (or even to some thing) is tantamount to saying that that person (or thing) has the ability or capacity to cause results or outcomes or effects that affect the existence and/or interests of those things or persons. A powerful storm or earthquake, for example, is one that has the capacity for causing widespread destruction. But storms and earthquakes, unlike political agents, cannot form intentions or act according to some purpose or design. And while natural disasters can certainly affect the interests of human beings, we do not hold them morally responsible or culpable for their actions since, strictly speaking, they do not 'act' at all; they just happen. They are causally effective but not morally responsible.

It is, of course, quite a different matter with moral and political agents or agencies. They, unlike storms or earthquakes, have a repertoire of peculiarly human powers or capacities – the power to reason, to reflect, to communicate, to foresee (some) results of their actions and practices, to understand and assess consequences, and to alter their actions or practices in light of those understandings and assessments. It is because of these uniquely human capacities or 'powers' that we have, and make moral and political use of, the concept of power. Before sketching an argument in support of this view of power, I want to take a closer look at Steven Lukes' important and influential, albeit controversial, analysis of power.

Lukes and his critics

Most of Steven Lukes' book, *Power: A Radical View* (1974), is devoted to explicating and criticizing conceptions of power advanced by American social scientists of the 'pluralist' persuasion (the so-called 'one-dimensional' view defended by Dahl, 1957) and their 'non-decisionist' critics (the 'two-dimensional' view defended by Bachrach and Baratz, 1962) as a prelude to advancing and defending his own 'radical' or 'three-dimensional' view (which has proven fruitful in subsequent empirical research: see Gaventa, 1980). Despite their differences, these three views share a common core. 'The absolutely basic common core to, or primitive notion lying behind, all talk of power,' Lukes writes, is the idea that one actor somehow affects another. But presumably not just any sort of affecting can count as an exercise of power. Each of us daily affects others in countless ways, not all of which can be correctly characterized as exercises of power. To exercise power, as Lukes puts it, is to affect another in some morally significant or 'non-trivial' way (Lukes, 1974, p. 26). But by what standard or criterion can we distinguish between trivial and non-trivial actions and effects? Lukes answers that to affect someone in a non-trivial or significant manner – i.e. to exercise power – is to affect their *interests* in some adverse way. He goes on to argue that an exercise of power, properly speaking, involves impeding or impairing their human interest in autonomy.

As Lukes' critics were quick to note, however, his account equates 'exercising power' with 'causing harm' (where 'harm' is further understood as impairing someone's capacity for autonomy). This appears to rule out many instances in which we want to say that someone has the power to persuade or the power to do good – which, as Lukes himself acknowledges, is both odd and troubling (1974, pp. 32–3). Teachers and physicians, for example, exercise certain sorts of power *vis-à-vis* pupils and patients; and yet we would, by Lukes' lights, either have to deny that they have and exercise power *or* that, if they do, they must therefore harm those in their care; if the latter, one would have to concede that the most powerful physicians and teachers would have to be the least competent and caring ones, i.e. those least likely to do good and most likely to cause harm!

If an action is to count as an exercise of power, it must be calculated to cause some other person(s) to do something that they would not otherwise do, and meant to result in some advantage to someone, without necessarily resulting in any disadvantage or harm to anyone. Lukes is surely right to take note of instances in which the exerciser of power benefits, and the recipient is harmed as a result. Slave-owners and exploitative employers do indeed exercise power. But to take these as paradigm cases is to cast our net too narrowly. To return to our earlier examples: imagine a physician remonstrating with her reluctant patient to try to persuade him to stop smoking; or a teacher telling a student to read and ponder the meaning of a particular poem. If successful, each exercises power in that they cause these people to do something that they would not otherwise do, with non-trivial results that each believes to be beneficial. These are no less exercises of power for bringing some sort of benefit to the reluctant recipients.

Now such disagreements might at first sight seem to be grist for the essential contestability mill (see below): Lukes has his view; his critics have theirs; and never the twain shall meet. But several points are worth noting in this connection. Lukes's critics have, for the most part, pointed not to some unbridgeable conceptual chasm yawning between his definition of power and theirs, but to apparent inconsistencies or contradictions within his own account, and to odd or counterintuitive implications that arise when one attempts to apply his conception of power to ordinarily unproblematic situations (see, *inter alia*, Oppenheim, 1981; Gray, 1983; Morriss, 1987). Nor does Lukes claim that the conceptions of power he criticizes were mistaken *simpliciter*, but that they are too narrow and apt to exclude actions and practices that we would ordinarily identify as relations or exercises of power. Far from supporting the thesis of essential contestability, these considerations suggest that disagreements about the meaning(s) of power are rationally debatable and, at least potentially and in principle, resolvable.

One way to begin resolving some of these disputes is to draw a distinction between someone's having 'power to' do something or to affect someone and one's having 'power over' another. Lukes typically takes the latter as his paradigm case, which is why he is reluctant to admit locutions like 'the power to persuade' or 'the power to benefit another' into his analysis of power (Lukes, 1974, pp. 32–3). But since politics is not only (or even mainly) about coercion or domination – i.e. about power *over* – but about people having the power to persuade or dissuade, or to bestow benefits upon others, then Lukes has drawn his conceptual net too tightly and has thereby excluded from his analysis several fundamental or defining features of political life. As Hannah Arendt noted, 'It is only after one ceases to reduce public affairs to the business of dominion [i.e. of "power over"] that the original data in the realm of human affairs will appear, or rather reappear, in their authentic diversity' (Arendt, 1972, pp. 142–3).

Important as it is, 'power *over*' is not paradigmatic of power *per se* nor does it exhaust all political possibilities. Indeed, the idea of 'power over' is parasitic on, or derivative from, 'power to'. A kidnapper, for instance, has power over his victim and her family only in so far as he has (or is believed to have and be prepared to use) the power to kill or injure his victim. Where the victim does not believe the kidnapper to have or be willing to use this ability, the tables are turned and his 'power' disappears, as is made abundantly and hilariously clear in O. Henry's short story, 'The Ransom of Red Chief'. In any event, political analysts are more apt to speak about political actors' power to *do* things than their power *over* someone. Few can doubt, for example, that the American President is a powerful political actor. And yet, as Richard Neustadt observes, 'presidential power' is pre-eminently 'the power to persuade', adding that 'persuasion is a two-way street' and that 'the power to persuade is the power to bargain' (Neustadt, 1964, pp. 41, 44–5).

Power, communication and community

The power to persuade is perhaps the uniquely human aspect or version of a more inclusive power that homo sapiens shares with other species – the power or capacity to communicate via speech, signals, symbols or other signs. And communication, as I shall suggest shortly, is the medium through which communities are created and sustained. An adequate analysis of power would therefore seem to require or presuppose a theory of communication or 'communicative action' (Habermas, 1984). And this is indeed the direction in which most modern analyses of 'power' appear to be headed. Different as they are in other respects, the conceptions of power advanced by certain social scientists and by political philosophers such as Hannah Arendt (1958; 1972), Jürgen Habermas (1984), Michel Foucault (1980) and Anthony Giddens (1984) are alike in emphasizing the 'communicative' aspect of power (see Ball, 1988, ch. 4).

Consider, by way of illustration, that staple of so many analyses of 'power': the relationship between the traffic cop and the motorist (see, e.g., Dahl, 1957). By standing in an intersection and blowing her whistle, gesturing, pointing, etc., the police officer causes the motorist to do what he would not otherwise do – stop, turn left (or right), and so on. The traffic cop has, and exercises, power *vis-à-vis* the motorist. But what makes this exercise of power possible? Simply that both share a language, broadly understood, which enables each to understand the other. This language includes the concepts of 'command' or 'order', 'obedience', etc., as well as a stock of gestures or signs (arm waving, whistle blowing, etc.) for signalling these. The police officer gives, and the motorist (dis)obeys, not a plea or suggestion, but a command or order. As Peter Winch notes, 'An act of obedience itself contains, as an essential element, a recognition of what went before it as an order' (Winch, 1970, pp. 9–10). As Herbert Simon once put, there can be 'no [power or] influence without communication'. 'Of course', Simon added, ' "communication" cannot be taken quite literally as "verbal communication," but the principle remains an important, and probably indispensable, tool for the identification of influence mechanisms' (Simon, 1957, p. 7). Without a common stock of concepts and signs, there would be no ability to communicate, and no power could be exercised.

Now it might be objected that power can be exercised without communication. The police officer could simply shoot the motorist or bludgeon him into submission. It is important to note, however, that this would not be an exercise of power but an act of force or violence, which is quite a different thing. If the communication of a threat to use force or violence results in the threatener getting his way, he has exercised power; but if the recipient of the communication does not think the threat credible, and the threatener actually follows through on his threat, then the latter has in fact failed to exercise power. I can, for instance, exercise power by threatening to use force to get my way; but if the threat fails, and I resort to force, then this is a failure, and not an exercise, of power. This is an important distinction on which analysts as different as Arendt, Habermas, Foucault and Giddens agree (see Ball, 1988, pp. 91–105).

'All political institutions', Arendt maintains, 'are manifestations and materializations of power; they petrify and decay as soon as the living power of the people ceases to uphold them' (Arendt, 1972, p. 140). Thus 'power' is generated when and only when people communicate and act together in some shared or common enterprise. Far from being the 'interestingly idiosyncratic' conception that Lukes believes it to be, Arendt's understanding of power is as ancient as Cicero's *potestas in populo* ('power in the people') and is, moreover, implicit in the actions and practices of modern liberation movements. To refuse individually and en masse to comply or to kowtow to threats of force by presumably powerful forces or figures, thereby leading the latter either to back down or to follow through on their threats, is one of the main ways in which ostensibly powerless people can empower themselves. The presumably powerful part of society – be it the party or the state or the individual dictator – is thereby shown to be, not powerful, but brutal and violent. The presumably powerful are thus shown to be both powerless and illegitimate in the eyes of their subjects.

This insight is by no means new. It is, for example, the moral of Hegel's parable of the master and slave. And it was exemplified in the non-violent strategies employed by Gandhi in India and by Martin Luther King in the American South. This is also what was meant by 'People Power' in the Philippine revolution, which ousted Ferdinand Marcos, and what Vaclav Havel meant by 'the power of the powerless', which was exercised during the 'Velvet Revolution' which ended communist rule in Czechoslovakia (Havel, 1988).

Something very like Arendt's understanding of power is present in contemporary Critical Theory, as espoused by Habermas and others, and exemplified in the writings of many modern feminist theorists, liberation theologians, and other 'emancipatory' thinkers and movements (Leonard, 1990). As Brian Fay summarizes their view,

> power exists not only when a group is controlled but also when a group comes together, becomes energized, and organizes itself, thereby becoming able to achieve something for itself. Here the paradigm case is not one of command but one of enablement in which a disorganized and unfocused group acquires an identity and a resolve to act in light of its new-found sense of purpose. (Fay, 1987, p. 130)

Critical theories of this sort see people 'as creatures actively involved in creating and sustaining all their forms of social life, including their relations of power' (Fay, 1987, p. 130; cf. Wartenberg, 1990). Thus 'power', as Anthony Giddens notes, 'is not inherently oppressive.' Power is simply 'the ability to make a difference' or 'the capacity to achieve outcomes' and 'is not, as such, an obstacle to freedom or emancipation but is their very medium' (Giddens, 1984, p. 257). Having power, then, is the *sine qua non* of being able to act as a morally responsible human being. Thus contemporary thinking or theorizing about power is not confined to any real or imagined ivory tower inhabited only by a few eccentric academics. The concept of power is too central and too important to be ignored or downplayed by anyone.

Conclusion: is 'power' an 'essentially contested' concept?

According to W. B. Gallie (1956) a concept is 'essentially contested' if its meaning and criteria of application are forever open to dispute and disagreement. Such disputes are less apt to arise in the natural sciences than in social and political philosophy, the social sciences, and the humanities. Virtually all the concepts constitutive of ethical, political and aesthetic discourse are 'essentially contested'. Take 'art' for example. We might agree that the term applies to Leonardo's 'Last Supper'; but does it apply to Andy Warhol's paintings of row upon row of identical soup cans and other everyday objects? Or consider 'music'. We may well agree that the concept applies in the case of Beethoven's Ninth Symphony, but disagree over whether it extends so far as to cover a cacophony of car horns and electronic beeps, as some modern composers and critics claim. Such disputes cannot be definitively and finally resolved, Gallie claimed, because there are no commonly shared criteria for deciding definitively what constitutes or counts as 'art' and 'music'.

And what is true of 'art' and 'music' is no less true of 'political' concepts like 'justice', 'equality', 'freedom' – and 'power'. Following Gallie's lead, Lukes (1974) and Connolly (1983) claim that 'power' is an essentially contested concept characterized by unresolved – and indeed unresolvable – disputes over its meaning and proper application. Just as art critics can never agree in all possible cases whether some object is indeed a work of art, so political actors and analysts will never agree in all instances that some particular action is an exercise of power.

As applied to 'power' and other political concepts, the thesis of essential contestability is both bold and provocative. Moreover, the thesis appears to account for the persistence of conceptual disagreements: if competent speakers continue to disagree over the definition and meaning of 'power', that must be because its very 'contestability' is an 'essential' feature of its use or application. The thesis of essential contestability also appears to be admirably even-handed, non-partisan, normatively neutral and non-judgemental, in that it seems to suggest that no one conception of power is superior to any other. You have your understanding of power; I have mine; and never the twain shall meet.

On closer examination, however, the thesis of essential contestability can be seen to suffer from a number of shortcomings and liabilities. For one, if true, then all disputes about 'power' (and other concepts constitutive of political discourse) are unresolvable *a priori* and *in principle*. Anyone attempting to construct a conception of power in hopes that others will agree is on an utterly misguided mission. One cannot even hope to construct a conception of power upon which everyone might conceivably agree, since 'power' belongs to the class of essentially contested concepts. From this it follows that all arguments for and against this or that conception of power are beside the point, if the point is not merely to express one's views but to carry on a meaningful conversation which could conceivably yield some sort of agreement.

Those subscribing to different views of what constitutes or counts as 'power' (or 'freedom', 'justice', etc.) would then appear to be left with only two ways of dealing with each other: coercion or conversion. And presumably those who cannot be converted must be coerced (excluded, silenced, ignored, etc.). As Connolly puts it, 'Disputes about the proper concept and interpretation of power, then, are part of larger ideological debates. To convert others to my idea of power is to implicate them to some degree in my political ideology' (Connolly, 1983, p. 128).

Now to speak of 'converting' others to one's own view may be good theology; but it is dangerous politics, if indeed it is politics at all. For political argument – which is to say, politics itself – is about the public airing of differences, not as an end in itself but in an attempt to resolve those differences through argument and persuasion. And this requires, as a precondition, a shared language or lexicon. As Bertrand de Jouvenel notes,

The elementary political process is the action of mind upon mind through speech. Communication by speech completely depends upon the existence in the memories of both parties of a common stock of words to which they attach much the same meanings. Even as people belong to the same culture by the use of the same language, so they belong to the same society by the understanding of the same moral language. As this common moral language extends, so does society; as it breaks up, so does society. (De Jouvenel, 1957, p. 304)

But if the concepts constitutive of political discourse, and therefore of political life, are indeed *essentially* contested, then of course there can be no common moral language or civic lexicon; hence no communication; hence no community. For, as John Dewey noted,

Society not only continues to exist . . . by communication, but it may be fairly said to exist in . . . communication. There is more than a verbal tie between the words common, community, and communication. Men [sic] live in a community in virtue of the things which they have in common; and communication is the way in which they come to possess things in common. (Dewey, 1916, p. 4)

Now if the thesis of essential contestability were true, then presumably political discourse – and therefore political life itself – would be well-nigh impossible, and for precisely the reasons that civility and the civic life is impossible in Hobbes' imaginary but no less horrifying state of nature: each individual is a monad, radically disconnected from all other individuals in so far as each speaks, as it were, a private language of his own devising. Because the concepts comprising these individual languages cannot be translated or otherwise understood, each speaker is a stranger and an enemy to every other. The result, says Hobbes, 'is a state of warre' in which every life is 'nasty, poore, solitary, brutish, and short'. Hobbes' state of nature is nothing less than a condition in which the thesis of essential contestability is imagined to be true: the inability to communicate is, so to speak, its essential feature.

Clearly, then, claims about the essential contestability of political concepts are not merely assertions about the limits of language and meaning, but about the (very limited) possibility of communication and thus of community. From this it follows that questions about the truth or falsity of the thesis of essential contestability are of more than abstract or academic interest but are, in fact, of profound political importance. We therefore need to ask: does the essential contestability thesis hold true about political concepts generally, and about 'power' in particular? For, if so, the prospects for meaningful communication, and hence community, are very dismal indeed.

Happily, our predicament appears, on closer examination, not to be so grim, after all. I have argued elsewhere (Ball, 1988) that the essential contestability thesis is itself contestable and problematic; and, if not false, then circular and logically vacuous. I readily concede that claims about conceptual contestability are well supported by empirical evidence from a variety of sources. Even granting that, the thesis is circular and commits the fallacy of *post hoc, ergo propter hoc*. That is, the evidence cited in support of the claim that 'power' is an *essentially* contested concept is that some have *in fact* disagreed about its meaning and application (which we have already conceded). But all that can be inferred from an enumeration of instances of disagreement, however long the list, is that there *have been* disagreements, and not that there *must always* continue to be. At most, all that can be concluded is that 'power' is a *contingently contested* concept.

If we look, not at Lukes' and Connolly's pronouncements but at their actual practice, we find that they do not always practise what they preach. Indeed, they proceed to offer criticisms (often very telling ones) of other conceptions of power, and arguments (some of them quite persuasive) in defence of their own alternative accounts. Lukes, for example, contends that his conception of power is 'superior' to rival accounts, and he advances arguments to support his claim that they are of 'less value' than his own (Lukes, 1974, pp. 9, 30). Nor should we be surprised by this gap between preachment and practice. For if one seriously and sincerely believes that political concepts are *essentially* contestable, then one could hardly judge one understanding to be *better* than another, for there would be no grounds upon which to base such a judgement. That judgements are made and arguments advanced suggests that the thesis of essential contestability is both logically and practically self-defeating.

But if claims about the essential contestability of 'power' and other political concepts are circular and self-defeating, they are not necessarily without value. They belong, perhaps, not so much to a vicious circle as (to borrow a phrase from Nelson Goodman) to a virtuous circle, the exploration of which can yield valuable insights. The thesis of essential contestability might best be viewed, not as a valid philosophical thesis about language and meaning, but as a rhetorical stratagem whose value lies in calling attention to a persistent and recurring feature of political discourse – namely, the perpetual possibility of disagreement. This possibility is intermittently actualized, and nowhere more frequently and vehemently than in disputes over 'power'. But it is important to remember that these disagreements cannot be resolved by fiat or by force of arms or ideological conversion but only by power of a peculiarly human kind – the power of reason, of argument and persuasion.

See also 5 ECONOMICS; 6 POLITICAL SCIENCE; 8 ANARCHISM; 14 AUTONOMY; 15 COMMUNITY; 16 CONTRACT AND CONSENT; 19 DEMOCRACY; 21 DISCOURSE; 28 LEGITIMACY; 29 LIBERTY; 31 PROPERTY; 38 TOTALITARIANISM

References

Arendt, H.: *The Human Condition* (Chicago: University of Chicago Press, 1958).
————: 'On violence', *Crises of the Republic* (New York: Harcourt Brace Jovanovich, 1972).
Bachrach, P. and Baratz, M. S.: 'The two faces of power', *American Political Science Review*, 56 (1962), 947–52.
Ball, T.: *Transforming Political Discourse* (Oxford: Blackwell, 1988).

Connolly, W. E.: *The Terms of Political Discourse*, 2nd edn (Princeton, NJ: Princeton University Press, 1983).

Dahl, R.: 'The concept of power', *Behavioral Science*, 2 (1957), 201–15.

De Jouvenel, B.: *Sovereignty*, trans. J. F. Huntington (Chicago: University of Chicago Press, 1957).

Dewey, J.: *Democracy and Education* (New York: Macmillan, 1916).

Emmett, D.: 'The concept of power', *Proceedings of the Aristotelian Society*, 54 (1954), 1–26.

Fay, B.: *Critical Social Science* (Ithaca, NY: Cornell University Press, 1987).

Foucault, M.: *Power/Knowledge*, ed. Colin Gordon (New York: Pantheon, 1980).

Gallie, W.: 'Essentially contested concepts', *Proceedings of the Aristotelian Society*, 56 (1956), 167–98.

Gaventa, J.: *Power and Powerlessness: Quiescence and Rebellion in an Appalachian Valley* (Urbana, Ill.: University of Illinois Press, 1980).

Giddens, A.: *The Constitution of Society* (Berkeley and Los Angeles: University of California Press, 1984).

Gray, J.: 'Political power, social theory, and essential contestability', *The Nature of Political Theory*, ed. David Miller and Larry Siedentop (Oxford: Clarendon Press, 1983), pp. 75–102.

Habermas, J.: *The Theory of Communicative Action*, 2 vols, trans. Thomas McCarthy (Boston: Beacon Press, 1984).

Havel, V. et al.: *The Power of the Powerless: Citizens against the State in Central–Eastern Europe*, ed. Steven Lukes (Armonk, NY: M. E. Sharpe, 1988).

Hobbes, T.: *Leviathan* (1651), ed. Richard Tuck (Cambridge: Cambridge University Press, 1991).

Isaac, J.: *Power and Marxist Theory: A Realist View* (Ithaca, NY: Cornell University Press, 1987).

Lasswell, D. and Kaplan, A.: *Power and Society* (New Haven, Conn.: Yale University Press, 1950).

Leonard, S. T.: *Critical Theory in Political Practice* (Princeton, NJ: Princeton University Press, 1990).

Lukes, S.: *Power: A Radical View* (London: Macmillan, 1974).

Morriss, P.: *Power: A Philosophical Analysis* (New York: St Martin's Press, 1987).

Neustadt, R. E.: *Presidential Power* (New York: Signet Books, 1964).

Oppenheim, F.: *Political Concepts: A Reconstruction* (Oxford: Blackwell, 1981).

Simon, H.: *Models of Man* (New York: Wiley, 1957).

Wartenberg, T. E.: *The Forms of Power: From Domination to Transformation* (Philadelphia, Pa.: Temple University Press, 1990).

Weber, M.: *Economy and Society*, 2 vols, ed. Guenther Roth and Claus Wittich (New York: Bedminster Press, 1968).

Winch, P.: 'The idea of a social science', *Rationality*, ed. Bryan R. Wilson (Oxford: Blackwell, 1970).

Further reading

Foucault. M.: 'The subject and power', Afterword to Hubert L. Dreyfus and Paul Rabinow, *Michel Foucault: Beyond Structuralism and Hermeneutics* (Chicago: University of Chicago Press, 1983).

Wartenberg. T, E., ed.: *Rethinking Power* (Albany, NY: State University of New York Press, 1992).

31

Property

ANDREW REEVE

Property undoubtedly has a central place in arrangements surrounding social life, a place so central that some writers have claimed that it is impossible to imagine anything which could be called a society without some property institution. A moment's thought suggests that property is a key element of an economic system, a major concern of the legal system, and a focus of political dispute. But the longstanding recognition of the importance of property was often coupled with taking many aspects of it for granted, particularly with respect to the possible justification of private property. The development of a specialized literature has been a fairly recent phenomenon. This is not, of course, to say that nothing valuable or important had been said about property in the history of political and social thought: nothing could be further from the truth. But much of the political theory of property has been embedded in works with more comprehensive ambitions in political philosophy: Locke's *Two Treatises of Government* (1689) and Hegel's *Philosophy of Right* (1821) are obvious examples. The coherence of such theories of property is clearly dependent – to an extent which may be disputed – on the wider philosophical framework in which they are embedded. Again, the relevance of such theories to contemporary normative analysis depends – again, to a disputable degree – on the compatibility of the economic and political institutions envisaged by their authors with present-day conditions.

The major problems in political philosophy raised by thinking about property are simply stated. First, what is property? Which rights are property rights, and what is the nature of those rights? What is ownership, and how is it related to property? Second, is there a coherent justification for any property system? This question has been approached both by asking whether any present-day system is defensible and by offering models of defensible arrangements by which to criticize existing practice.

In general terms, contemporary political theorizing about property has two major and closely related characteristics. On the one hand, it has focused on purported justifications for private property, examining the works of writers like Locke and Hegel and subjecting their ideas to critical scrutiny. This scrutiny has usually recognized a distinction between the attempt to recover what an author intended, dissecting the argument thus attributed to him, and using these works as sources of suggestive patterns of argument, often supplying alternative premises to those identified as defective. On the other hand, recent theorizing has tried to produce a more integrated approach to the theory of property. The recognition that there are sociological, psychological, economic, legal and political aspects of property has led to the ambition of putting together a theory which takes proper account of these ramifications. This ambition has required further development of some of the aspects of the analysis to be integrated, and in any case has been flanked by contributions to the debate from within adjacent disciplines like economic theory. It will be helpful to look at the legal, economic and historical approaches to property to explain this further, and to identify some important disputes.

The analysis of 'ownership' as employed by the legal system has been deeply influenced by a classic article provided by A. M. Honoré (1961), although the nature of his enterprise has not always been fully appreciated by those who have adopted some form of his characterization of 'ownership'. Honoré wanted to identify the way in which 'ownership' was understood by mature legal systems. He thought that there were some items of property which were owned in the same way in different mature legal systems, despite whatever other differences there might be between them. But because this notion of ownership was not specified in law, and indeed was often unnecessary to the resolution of legal disputes, the way in which 'ownership' was understood had to be worked out from the practices of the legal system. Honoré identified eleven 'incidents' of ownership in the standard case. He used this terminology because he argued that, for the legal system, there were elements of ownership which were certainly not rights, and that to see ownership merely as a set of rights would be misleading. As we shall see, it is the status of some of the non-right incidents which has sometimes been doubted. It is also important to bear in mind two points Honoré made which are sometimes overlooked. First, he started out from 'the standard case', recognizing that the complexities of the legal treatment of something as varied as property could not always be reduced to that standard specification (1961, pp. 110–11). Second, he distinguished the specification of ownership from the identification of the owner. Since the incidents involved in ownership might be attached to different persons or institutions, it might be difficult to say with confidence who the owner was, or indeed whether there was one at all: but this is consistent with the incidents together constituting ownership (ibid., pp. 142–4).

The rights listed by Honoré were the rights to use and to manage, the right to an income, the right to the capital, the right to possession and the right to security. The further incidents were: transmissibility, absence of term, prohibition of harmful use, residuary character and liability to execution. Some writers who have set out from Honoré's characterisation have been doubtful about the inclusion of liability to execution – the liability to have the property taken away because of the judgement of a court – and the prohibition of harmful use (Carter, 1989, pp. 5–8). Other work has been offered in an attempt to elucidate the incidents further by formulating them in the terms of Hohfeld's (1919) classification of the correlatives and opposites of the 'right' elements. This helps with the analysis of the relationship between 'ownership' and property, as Munzer explains:

For the purposes of this book it is useful to extend Hohfeld and Honoré as follows. The idea of *property* – or, if you prefer, the sophisticated or legal conception of property – involves a constellation of Hohfeldian elements, correlatives, and opposites; a specification of standard incidents of ownership and other related but less powerful interests; and the catalog of 'things' (tangible and intangible) that are the subjects of these incidents. Hohfeld's conceptions are normative modalities. In the more specific form of Honoré's incidents, these are the relations that constitute property. Metaphorically, they are the 'sticks' in the bundle called property. Notice, however, that property also includes less powerful collections of incidents that do not rise to the level of ownership. (Munzer, 1990, p. 23)

The clarity of this exposition should not disguise the difficulties in providing a comprehensive account of the legal treatment of property (whether of an actual or proposed legal system) based upon it. The difficulties arise from the variety of 'things' that are or could be the subject of the standard incidents, and the variety of 'property' that represents a less powerful collection of incidents. One of the important issues connected with these difficulties is the status of self-ownership, or property in oneself. Premises about self-ownership or self-propriety have featured in a variety of arguments about legitimate property arrangements, but the coherence of the notion has been doubted, and the extent to which it is helpful to envisage persons as having property in their own bodies or other attributes is still in dispute (Reeve, 1991, p. 100).

The legal analysis has been developed by refining Honoré's approach through combining it with Hohfeldian categories. The economic approach to property has developed in a different way, by emphasising the gap between 'legal' and 'economic' property rights. The classic contributions to that approach were provided by Coase (1960) and Demsetz (1966). The concern is with the relationship between property rights and efficiency, and it has been noticed before that the tenor of the argument sometimes appears prescriptive (Barzel, 1989, p. 65n; Carter, 1989, pp. 64–75). The definition of property rights affects the extent to which individuals bear the full costs, and reap the full rewards, of their own activity. Efficiency is said to require that individuals do indeed bear those costs and reap those rewards. There is both the idea that individuals will respond to changing structures of incentives by redefining property rights to bring this result about, and the idea that they (or the government) should do so.

Recent work developing this approach has explicitly divorced the legal property from economic property rights, and defined the latter in a way which suggests they will rarely be 'perfectly delineated' (Barzel, 1989, p. 2). The project is then to explain the behaviour brought about by these imperfections, which involves trying to appropriate others' 'property' by free-riding, shirking, overusing, and so on.

Property rights of individuals over assets consist of the rights, or the powers, to consume, obtain income from, and alienate these assets. Obtaining income from and alienating assets require exchange; exchange is the mutual ceding of rights. Legal rights, as a rule, enhance economic rights, but the former are neither necessary nor sufficient for the existence of the latter . . . Economists' past failure to exploit the property rights notion in the analysis of behavior probably stems from their tendency to consider rights as absolute.

The concept of property rights is closely related to that of transaction costs. I define transaction costs as the costs associated with the transfer, capture and protection of rights. If it is assumed that for any asset each of these costs is rising and that both the full protection and the full transfer of rights are prohibitively costly, then it follows that rights are never complete, because people will never find it worthwhile to gain the entire potential of 'their' assets. (Barzel, 1989, p. 2)

This approach no doubt leads to some interesting explanations of behaviour, although it involves some shift in perspective to escape from the conventional terminology. For example, a fire insurance company is conceived to acquire 'ownership over the attribute of fire incidence' by paying the negative price of receiving a premium (Barzel, 1989, p. 49). Of course, the behavioural assumptions underlying this sort of analysis are open to challenge. For example, it may simply not be true that all individuals who enter into a wage contract are restrained from shirking only by supervision rather than by conscientiousness. But since any interesting proposals about a desirable property system will have to exhibit the economic arrangements with which it is consistent, the economic approach to property rights will have to be taken into account, even if only to reject its premises, by any integrated theory.

A specific application of the economic approach has been historical. Here the classic example is provided by North and Thomas, who tried to explain different rates of economic growth in sixteenth- and seventeenth-century Europe by reference to the arrangements governing property in different countries. This application of the economic approach has led to puzzlement among its practitioners, however, for they suggest that property arrangements which are, from the analysts' standpoint, inefficient have also been very common and persistent. This in turn has led to an attempt to provide an economic theory of changes in property rights. Libecap argues that

Regardless of whether observed institutions represent the most efficient responses to particular social and economic problems, both economic theory and history provide reasons for believing that the net social gains from changes in property rights at any time will be quite modest. This is because it is difficult to resolve the distributional conflicts inherent in major changes in ownership arrangements. (Libecap, 1989, pp. 3–4)

In effect, the economic theory becomes a theory of politics, or at least of institutions, a theory about how overall benefits from changes in property rights are to be distributed among particular actors.

The history of political thought about property has (obviously enough) made a considerable contribution to contemporary discussion. The first book to bring together essays on the theories of particular authors tried to cover 'Aristotle to the present' (Parel and Flanagan, 1979). Indeed, some of the theories which have been 'rediscovered' strikingly anticipate contemporary theories, or at least address problems identified by contemporary theories. This seems particularly true of radical thought in the late eighteenth and early nineteenth centuries, which often tried to produce coherent theories of property from natural rights premises (Cunliffe, 1987; 1988; 1990; Reeve, 1987). The contemporary reinstatement of such premises is, of course, largely a product of libertarianism. Dispute between 'libertarian', 'liberal' and 'socialist' perspectives has partly been dispute about the interpretation of the history of the political theory of property. It was the work of C. B. Macpherson, thirty years ago, which first refocused attention on theories of property. In *The Political Theory of Possessive Individualism*, Macpherson (1962) argued that the political theory of the seventeenth century, or at least of some of the 'major' theorists of the seventeenth century, was deeply imbued with possessive assumptions about market society. The assumptions were, of course, largely 'revealed' by examining theories of property. The interpretation of the writers in question turned out to be highly controversial, but because theories of property lay at the heart of the dispute a considerable stimulus was given to the study of the history of ideas about property.

The radical critique of liberalism – that it was flawed by incorporation of possessive individualism – was supplemented by the critique flowing from a libertarian attachment to property rights, remembering that in this perspective all rights are in effect property rights (Ryan, 1987, p. 2). Natural rights libertarianism, with its emphasis on the inviolability of rights, could scarcely be reconciled with Benthamite utilitarianism, despite Bentham's insistence on the importance of security of property, or with J. S. Mill's more pragmatic assessment of the benefits of alternative property arrangments. Bentham, Mill (to some degree) and the new liberals were pictured in one study as deviating from the true path of liberalism, which had a tender regard for private property (Gray, 1987, pp. 28–31, 62–72). At the same time, the developing criticism of the Nozickian theory of property and justice, in particular the relationship between natural rights premises and the apparently welfare-oriented Lockean proviso, has stimulated contemporary debate aiming to show what a coherent natural rights-based theory of property would look like. The problem, clearly enough, is to develop rules of legitimate appropriation (or constraints on legitimate appropriation) such that any two persons, at no matter what time or place, can reasonably be pictured as enjoying the same natural rights. It is here that the radical theories of the early nineteenth century turn out to be so interesting, particularly since they often tried to unite the study of property with the study of (what came to be called) exploitation. A recent study provides a new interpretation of the development of ideas of property from the period studied by Macpherson to the nineteenth century, and will no doubt add further impulsion to these discussions (Horne, 1990). It is especially interesting that this study claims that the liberal tradition always included limitations on exclusive rights in the name of inclusive claims to resources.

If economic theories of history and the history of political thought have contributed to our understanding of the history of property, it might be expected that the legal analysis, so important to the philosophical understanding of the institution, would be flanked by a contribution from legal history. On the whole this expectation has not been realized. Perhaps because of the highly technical nature of legal history, there seems to be little integration between the economic, legal and intellectual histories. For example, Locke makes assertions about the law of inheritance in seventeenth-century England, but it is not clear that he was correct in what he took the law to be. It may well be that a deeper understanding of legal development would enrich our understanding of intellectual history in this field.

A further component of contemporary discussion about property – already mentioned in relation to the history of political thought – is the concern with exploitation. Of course, not all such theories have a primary emphasis on the labour process. It remains a matter of controversy whether exploitation is best approached primarily as a market-related phenomenon, or whether market-related exploitation is simply a special case of a phenomenon which can be identified and analysed in a number of different contexts. Examples of market-related analyses are provided by Marx (about whom more below) and Miller (1987). An example of a more general theory is provided by Goodin (1987), who analyses exploitation as 'taking unfair advantage of the specially vulnerable'. But such an account can still accommodate particular vulnerability which arises from 'economic' features, like poverty. Theories which do focus on the 'economic' – on the labour process in particular, or on market transactions more generally – will naturally address some important issues about property. This is because theories of exploitation typically combine some analysis of power relations with some account of (in)justice. This is not to say, of course, that rival theories of exploitation will share an account of 'power' or 'justice'. Indeed, the distinctiveness of a particular theory will usually be given by the interpretation of these two notions, and the relationship between them, within that theory.

But if, in general, assertions about exploitation rest on particular claims about power and justice, then it is easy to see how property relations will enter the picture. For example, inequalities in the distribution of property, or the nature of the legal definition of property rights, are both potential explanations of the existence of a power relationship between one individual (or group) and another. In so far as a theory of exploitation needs to account for A's capacity to take advantage of B, the empirical distribution of property and the legal definition of property rights will be important considerations. (A further step is to argue for a necessary relationship between forms of property and its distribution – for example, in the claim that capital has a tendency to concentration; or to argue similar connections between the legal definition of property rights and the distribution of property, typically in a concern with the practice of inheritance and the persistence of social inequality.)

Just as property is importantly implicated in the 'power' side of exploitation, so it is plausibly the centre of attention in assertions about the justice – or, in this context, injustice – of states of affairs identified with exploitative acts or situations. For example, inequality in property holdings may be cited as evidence of injustice, particularly of historical injustice in acquisition. Again, there may be a justice-based critique of positive legal property rights.

The many points of contact between a concern with property and property relations, and a theory of exploitation, are best illustrated by reference to some of the disputes surrounding Marx's account of capitalist exploitation (cf. Kymlicka, 1990, pp. 171–83). Marx's theory combines a thesis about power relations – that workers are coerced into work despite the apparent freedom of the wage contract – with an account of the generation and appropriation of surplus value – that the capitalists receive surplus value despite the worker receiving the value of labour as wages. There are important controversies about both the 'power' and 'justice' elements of this. Marx seems to argue that the capitalist class is powerful, even though individual capitalists are not. (In parallel, Cohen (1979) has argued that the proletariat is unfree, even though some proletarians are free to leave the working class.) Is this analysis of the structure of power acceptable? What is the relation between the power of the state – which defines and guarantees property rights – and the power of the capitalist class – which apparently rests on its monopoly ownership of the means of production? Is the theory primarily a political or an economic account of exploitation (Carver, 1987)?

Turning to 'justice', one account holds that the theory of surplus value – even if technically sound, which is often denied – cannot supply any normative grounds to support a charge of injustice. On this view, the theory of surplus value merely describes what happens, but does not condemn it. This is because Marx was not committed to a political programme, or to a philosophical principle, which is derived from overturning the apparent basis of normative criticism of the appropriation of surplus value. The implication would be that the worker is entitled to the full value his labour produces, but Marx criticized socialist programmes which adhered to this. Alternatively, it has been argued that having relativized values to modes of production, Marx was not in a position to use a standard of justice derived from a form of society not yet in existence. This has led to the thought that there might be some (non-relative?) value – perhaps freedom or self-development – which was (or is) violated by the capitalist–labourer relation, or that exploitation should be identified less with the account of surplus value and more with the inequality of property-ownership which is alleged to make its extraction possible.

The convergence of the analysis of property with that of justice is not confined to those trying to explicate Marx's position, or sympathetic to his outlook. The libertarian identifies injustice with rights violation, and the rights (or entitlements) are property rights. Nozick's hyperbolic remark that 'taxation is on a par with forced labour' suggests that both are equally unjust infringements of natural (property) rights. Both Marx's account of exploitation and Nozick's entitlement theory illustrate the way in which property provides a link between legal, economic and political arrangements. But whereas Nozick set out from an entitlement to the product of labour to advocate strong private property rights, others, both in contemporary philosophy and, as we have seen, historically, have doubted whether natural rights are compatible with private property, especially in non-produced resources.

This point may be developed, and will bring us back to the general characterization of present-day theorizing offered earlier. It was suggested that much contemporary work focuses on the analysis of purported justifications for private property, and that it has developed an ambition to produce a more integrated theory. The integration may be thought of in two ways – as integration between possible justifications, within limits set upon what different premises will actually sustain; and as integration between political, economic, legal, psychological and sociological concerns within a general theory. The problem for any 'single-track' justification for private property – for example, that a commitment to general utility justifies the institution, or that a commitment to a particular form of liberty does so – is the distance which has to be travelled between the generality of the value from which the argument sets out, and the details of a particular justified property system which is the destination. If we refer back to Munzer's characterization of the details of the Hohfeld–Honoré analysis, we can see just how difficult it would be to elaborate all the elements of any practical system of property. To explain how, for example, utility justifies all those elements will require reference to a great many disputable arguments on the way. To take a simple case, Bentham himself placed great store by 'security' in his account of the ends of civil law, and he consequently gave it precedence over equality which might be promoted by redistribution. Hence his position was more solicitous of private property than would be the case for another utilitarian who weighted the contribution of 'security' and 'equality' to utility in the other order. It often emerges that a reassessment of one step in the argument, such as this, will lead to quite different conclusions, as Carter (1989) demonstrates for a large number of 'single-track' justifications. Alan Ryan has demonstrated the point in a rather different way in two essays which relate the theory of property to concerns with liberty (1987) and with labour expenditure (1984).

Three works which illustrate the attempt to integrate different bases of justification are those of Becker (1977), Grunebaum (1987) and Munzer (1990). Becker provided the first modern review of the purported justifications of private property, and concluded with a suggested approach to take account of those elements of justification which had survived criticism. Grunebaum similarly argued for the justifiability of 'autonomous ownership' by trying to delineate the proper claims of self-ownership from other more limited claims over natural and produced resources, suggesting the need for a property system flanked by world-wide democracy, clearly something very different from anything that has yet been put into place. Munzer puts forward three justificatory principles and argues for a necessarily pluralist approach:

The picture of property rights that emerges, then, locates their justification in a carefully-constructed pluralist scheme that knits together utilitarian considerations, considerations of justice of a roughly Kantian or Rawlsian kind, and considerations of desert of a thoroughly un-Rawlsian kind. (Munzer, 1990, p. 7)

All this leads Munzer to a system of constrained private property, and here there is a parallel with an important study by Jeremy Waldron. Waldron suggests that the arguments for private property he examines – chiefly Locke's, Nozick's and Hegel's – when passed under critical scrutiny and defects amended yield important distributional implications:

The important conclusion, then, is this. Under serious scrutiny, there is no right-based argument to be found which provides an adequate justification for a society in which some people have lots of property and many have next to none. The slogan that property is a human right can be deployed only disingenuously to legitimize the massive inequality that we find in modern capitalist countries. (Waldron, 1988, p. 5)

This emphasis on the limits of justification, a concern to identify what cannot be justified by particular lines of argument, and perhaps to go on to combine different approaches in the attempt to produce a coherent theory of property, is a welcome development. It illustrates a refusal to take anything for granted, or to be carried along by the broad-brush assertions of single-track justifications. Recent work also goes beyond sceptical negativity to produce constructive proposals for reform, reform which at least some of these theories would suggest is all the more necessary as the market economy extends its sway.

See also 5 ECONOMICS; 6 POLITICAL SCIENCE; 7 LEGAL STUDIES; 11 LIBERALISM; 12 MARXISM; 13 SOCIALISM; 14 AUTONOMY; 18 CORPORATISM AND SYNDICALISM; 19 DEMOCRACY; 22 DISTRIBUTIVE JUSTICE; 24 ENVIRONMENTALISM; 25 EQUALITY; 29 LIBERTY; 30 POWER; 33 RIGHTS; 34 SECESSION AND NATIONALISM; 41 WELFARE

References

Barzel, Y.: *Economic Analysis of Property Rights* (Cambridge: Cambridge University Press, 1989).

Becker, L. C.: *Property Rights – Philosophic Foundations* (London: Routledge & Kegan Paul, 1977).

Carter, A.: *The Philosophical Foundations of Property Rights* (Hemel Hempstead: Harvester Wheatsheaf, 1989).

Carver, T.: 'Marx's political theory of exploitation', *Modern Theories of Exploitation*, ed. A. Reeve (London: Sage, 1987), pp. 68–79.

Coase, R.: 'The problem of social cost', *Journal of Law and Economics*, 3 (1960), 1–44.

Cohen, G. A.: 'Capitalism, freedom and the proletariat', *The Idea of Freedom – Essays Presented to Sir Isaiah Berlin*, ed. A. Ryan (Oxford: Oxford University Press, 1979), pp. 9–25.

————: 'Nozick on appropriation', *New Left Review*, 150 (1985), 89–105.

————: 'Self-ownership, world ownership and equality, part II', *Social Philosophy and Policy*, 3 (1986), 77–96.

Cunliffe, J.: 'A mutualist theory of exploitation?', *Modern Theories of Exploitation*, ed. A Reeve (London: Sage, 1987), pp. 53–67.

————: 'The liberal rationale of "Rational Socialism"', *Political Studies*, 36 (1988), 653–62.

————: 'The neglected background of radical liberalism; P. E. Dove's theory of property', *History of Political Thought*, 11 (1990), 467–90.

Demsetz, H.: 'Some aspects of property rights', *Journal of Law and Economics*, 9 (1966), 61–70.

Goodin, R. E.: 'Exploiting a situation and exploiting a person', *Modern Theories of Exploitation*, ed. A. Reeve (London: Sage, 1987), pp. 166–200.

Gray, J.: *Liberalism* (Milton Keynes: Open University Press, 1986).

Grunebaum, J. O.: *Private Ownership* (London: Routledge & Kegan Paul, 1987).

Hegel, G.: *Hegel's Philosophy of Right* (1821), ed. T. Knox (Oxford: Clarendon Press, 1942).

Hohfeld, W. N.: *Fundamental Legal Conceptions as Applied in Judicial Reasoning* (New Haven, Conn.: Yale University Press, 1919).

Honoré, A. M.: 'Ownership', *Oxford Essays in Jurisprudence*, ed. A. G. Guest (Oxford: Oxford University Press, 1961), pp. 107–47.

Horne, T.: *Property Rights and Poverty – Political Argument in Britain, 1605–1834* (Chapel Hill, NC: University of North Carolina Press, 1990).

Kymlicka, W.: *Contemporary Political Philosophy – An Introduction* (Oxford: Clarendon Press, 1990).

Libecap, D. L.: *Contracting for Property Rights* (Cambridge: Cambridge University Press, 1989).

Locke, J.: *Two Treatises of Government* (1689), ed. P. Laslett (Cambridge: Cambridge University Press, 1988).

Macpherson, C. B.: *The Political Theory of Possessive Individualism* (Oxford: Clarendon Press, 1962).

Miller, D.: 'Exploitation in the market', *Modern Theories of Exploitation*, ed. A. Reeve (London: Sage, 1987), pp. 149–65.

Munzer, S. R.: *A Theory of Property* (Cambridge: Cambridge University Press, 1986).

North, D. C. and Thomas, R. P.: *The Rise of the Western World* (Cambridge: Cambridge University Press, 1973).

Nozick, R.: *Anarchy, State and Utopia* (Oxford, Blackwell, 1974).

Parel, A. and Flanagan T., eds: *Theories of Property. Aristotle to the Present* (Ontario: Wilfrid Laurier University Press, 1979).

Reeve, A.: *Property* (Basingstoke: Macmillan, 1986).

————: 'Thomas Hodgskin and John Bray: free exchange and equal exchange', *Modern Theories of Exploitation*, ed. A. Reeve (London: Sage, 1987), pp. 30–52.

————: 'The theory of property: beyond private *versus* common property', *Political Theory Today*, ed. D. Held (Cambridge: Polity Press, 1991), pp. 91–114.

Ryan, A.: *Property and Political Theory* (Oxford: Blackwell, 1984).

————: *Property* (Milton Keynes: Open University Press, 1987).

Waldron, J.: *The Right to Private Property* (Oxford: Oxford University Press, 1988).

32

Republicanism

KNUD HAAKONSSEN

In the 1960s republic and republicanism hardly figured in political theory. Today they are prominent, if highly contested, topics in political thought in the English-speaking world. While there may be many reasons for this, undoubtedly a particularly important factor was one of the periodic convulsions in the American search for identity. From the late 1960s onwards, American scholars launched a sustained criticism of the assumption that America was founded on the institutionalization of a complex of ideas identified broadly as individualistic liberalism and began a long and fertile search for alternative roots (see especially Bailyn, 1967) which were soon identified as republican (see especially Wood, 1969; cf. Shalhope, 1972; 1982). This endeavour on the part of American historians was quickly supplemented by a magisterial interpretation of the whole of Anglo-American political culture in the early modern period as predominantly a development of the civic humanist republicanism hammered out in Renaissance Italy (Pocock, 1975), a topic that was undergoing its own rapid development (e.g. Baron, 1955; Skinner, 1978, vol. I). The result was a rich historical panorama of the development of republican ideas and practices from the Renaissance to our own time: the Italian cities attempting to avoid princely rule by basing republican government on the virtues of an aristocracy; the Dutch provinces shoring up their independence from Iberian monarchy by developing that entirely new and controversial government, republics based on a commercial, not landed, wealth; the English Commonwealth which, though short-lived, helped to secure the continuing influence of republican ideas and enabled people in the eighteenth century to see Britain's mixed constitution as that apparent paradox, a monarchical republic – and one based on representation; the American Revolution which, by renewing the idea of federation, refuted the traditional republican dogma that a republic could not exist in a large country and, in the process, made republicanism decisively anti-aristocratic; the French Revolution which transformed so much of republican thought into a still continuing debate about democracy.

In view of the overwhelming success of the republican idea in practice, it is perhaps surprising to see it revive as a potent factor in recent political theory, and even more so that the historiography of its success should have inspired and informed this revival (e.g. Skinner, 1983, 1984; Fraser, 1984; Lerner, 1987; Vetterli and Bryner, 1987; Pangle, 1988; Isaac, 1988; Sunstein, 1988; Boyte, 1989; Pettit, 1989a; Bock, Skinner and Viroli, 1990; Braithwaite and Pettit, 1990). A brief consideration of the historical roots of the republican idea will make possible a better appreciation of its transformation.

'Republic' is the Anglicized form of the Latin *res publica*, which originally was contrasted with *res privata*. It was the public realm of affairs that people had in common outside their familial lives, and traditionally has also been identified as the common weal. *Res publica* also meant the institutional structures of public life and can often be translated as 'the commonwealth' or simply, though anachronistically, 'the state'. The idea of *res publica* as the institutionally organized public realm rather than a particular form of organization, or government, may seem far removed from the modern sense of the word 'republic', but it should be remembered that this basic meaning of the Latin was preserved from republican Rome, through the Empire, the Middle Ages and Early Modern times until well into the eighteenth century in nearly every variety of political theory.

The association of 'republic' with a particular organization of the public realm owes much to the course of Roman history. As the traditional constitutional arrangement, with its elements of democracy, aristocracy and 'monarchy', crumbled and eventually became the principate, its defenders represented it as the only way in which the public realm could be properly organized and the common weal secured. *Res publica Romana* thus acquired a normative, ideal-typical reference to the way in which Rome's public realm was supposedly arranged between the expulsion of the Roman monarchs in 510 BC and the first *princeps*, Augustus, in 31 BC. So important was this normative concept that for 300 years the 'emperors' continued to call themselves *principes*, chief men, and generally went to some lengths to maintain the outward forms of republican government.

The crux of the ideal type of the Roman *res publica* was that the people (*populus*, giving the adjective *publicus*) had a decisive say in the organization of the public realm and this understanding linked the idea of an organized public realm in general to that of a specific form, or rather source, of such organization – namely 'the people' – thus creating the basis for modern concepts of 'republic'.

Disregarding its rather subterranean life during the Middle Ages, it was this idea of republic that was revived in the Italian city-states during the Renaissance and let loose on Europe in the spectacular way indicated above. We may express the composite nature of the concept by saying that in a republic, public affairs are looked after by the public, but this word-play should not be extended to suggest that in a commonwealth the common weal is necessarily looked after by the commonalty. The great debates about and experiments with republicanism in post-Renaissance Europe were all centrally concerned with who could and should count as the public from which order and governance in the public realm was to be derived. In them, the extension of the people to include the common people was a late and hard-won achievement. In fact, in most parts of the world, it was only in this century that property qualifications for participation in the political process were abolished.

Traditional republicanism linked citizenship and property because only the propertied man was thought able to sustain the key republican virtues of independence and honour. Private means fostered independence from other men – there was never any public room for women in the republic – in the vote of the assembly; and ownership of

property encouraged honourable self-defence. This strongly individualistic side to traditional republicanism was balanced by a desire, sometimes bordering upon mania, for
designing institutions to ensure that no individual or group should become so independent and imbued with honour as to dominate the rest. Hence the concern with
limiting the influence of wealth – sometimes by limiting wealth itself – by rotating
offices, frequent elections, ballots, separation of powers and functions, general militia
service, and much more.

While the link between property and citizenship was firm, one of the most difficult
points for republican thinkers, especially in the English-speaking world in the eighteenth century, was whether property other than land counted. The growing wealth
of commerce – which eventually became capitalism – seemed too fluid and easily
transferable to give a man any stake in his country, and it immediately proved dis-
tastefully intertwinable with the conduct of government, as Adam Smith spent half
a million words explaining and denouncing in the *Wealth of Nations*. According to
liberal democratic theory this Gordian knot was cut by the democratic revolution,
which supposedly set aside the republican obsession with the link between property
and citizenship. The contemporary revival of republican thought is centrally aimed
at questioning this liberal democratic thesis, pointing out that the formal equality of
citizens in the liberal democratic state is not reflected in the conduct of government,
which instead is determined, not by the common weal, but by the particular, if not
private, weal of interest groups and individuals. In these criticisms republicanism is,
of course, joined by other critics, many of them from within liberal democratic theory
itself. The distinctive feature of the republican argument is that it is set in the context
of an historical thesis, and its current prominence in contemporary political theory
has been triggered by the new historiography of the republican tradition.

The new history of republicanism is an impressive piece of subtle, complex revisionism which may be briefly summarized as follows. Liberal theorists had for long maintained that they inherited a long tradition, stretching back to Hobbes, Locke and
beyond, according to which civil society is a protection society mutually agreed
upon by individuals whose central characteristic is that they each have natural
rights. Republican critics hold that this was historically false, creating a distorted
view of contemporary society and simply ignoring the fact that Anglo-American
politics was dominated by a conceptual apparatus derived from the republican tradition as revived and shaped in the Renaissance. True, the juristic rights-tradition
emphasized by liberalism was present, but it only came to prominence after the democratic revolution, as an ideological smoke-screen for the inadequate outcome of that
revolution. To dispel this we must appreciate that behind it are institutions that
were decisively formed by republican ideas and which will only function adequately
if we recapture republican ways of being citizens.

Republican revisionism has redressed the balance of the historical picture left by the
more simplistic versions of liberal mythology but, in the process, new myths have been
created. It is impossible to see the division between a juristic-liberal and a republican
tradition as fundamental to post-Renaissance political thought. In Locke, Montesquieu, Rousseau, Price, most of the Scottish Enlightenment thinkers and the American founders – to take a wide selection – elements from both traditions go hand in

hand. It is not between natural rights and republican citizenship that the fault-lines lie. An important reason why republican scholars so often think otherwise is that they themselves believe the old liberal tale that ideas of natural rights, where they occur, are deeply individualistic and subjectivist. In fact, there have been very few thinkers of note for whom rights were the primary moral feature of the individual upon which the rest of morality and its institutions had to be built. The pervasive view was that rights were to be understood in relationship to duty and that both were dependent upon a universal, justifying moral order which was commonly thought of in terms of natural law. Natural law theory thus provided the means for understanding the combination of interdependent duties and rights which made up the various roles or stations in life, including the roles of citizen and civic office-bearer (Haakonssen, 1990; 1991; forthcoming). Natural law theory and republican theory may be considered as different genres and of different scope but they are not inherently incompatible. Natural law, though often adapted to suit absolute monarchy, was equally readily adapted by republicans, the most spectacular example being the American founders.

The opposition between liberalism and republicanism, while a source of inspiration for the recent revival of the latter, is more an invention of this revival than ascertainable historical fact. The same may be said of another, closely associated phenomenon, the warm embrace of republican ideas by communitarianism (e.g. Sandel, 1982; 1984a; 1984b; Barber, 1984; Boyte and Schwartz, 1984; Green, 1985; Oldfield, 1990). This rests upon the traditional republican notion of the 'virtue' that is required and generated in the republic, a tradition now commonly known as civic humanism. Such a tradition undoubtedly exists, but it is difficult to see that it delivers anything like that with which the communitarians and other modern moral theorists want to mesh their republicanism. A striking feature of traditional republicanism is that, for all its talk of virtue, it rarely presents anything that can be called a moral theory. At most, there may be an invocation of Aristotle or neo-Stoic ideas to support what is little more than an intuitive and tradition-bound idea of the wholeness of character that is required of the independent citizen. The parts of the whole character are, however, largely determined in terms of the public functions or offices required by the republican constitutional machinery. Of course, respect for republican forms is emphasized and, in that sense, a republican ethos inculcated. But this is a far cry from the ethical way of life detailed by communitarian and other contemporary moralists. The traditional republican tirades against 'corruption' and 'luxury' had little to do with immorality as such, being primarily protests against intermixing one's private life, whether good or bad, with the public realm, especially in economic matters. Thus, republican virtue represented a partial, institutionally circumscribed view of the moral life, and a republic the institutionalization of traditional public duties and the associated rights of the man of independent means.

It has been argued that this view of republicanism shows that it shares the negative ideal of liberty – an absence of interference with one's independence – with modern liberalism (Skinner, 1983; 1984; Pettit, 1989a, 1989b) and, further, that the moralizing notions of civic empowerment or positive liberty found in communitarianism are a misunderstanding of republican liberty (Pettit, forthcoming). Yet an important distinction between the liberal and republican notions of negative liberty remains according to this view; while liberalism is centrally concerned with the absence of interference with people's independence, republicanism extends the ideal to include the absence of the danger of interference. In a republic, not only is one not interfered with but the republican institutions secure one against such interference. One has not only liberty, but 'resilient' liberty.

Republican liberty, so formulated, seems to amount to little more than the old liberal ideal of equal freedom under the law but the suggestion does go further. In the republican conception, it is suggested, danger of interference is only really absent when each individual can obviate such danger. The point of a republic is therefore to put each individual in a position where he or she can live in resilient, self-asserted freedom. The independence that in traditional republics was derived from owning property must in the new republic be derived from simply being a person.

The problem with this idea of republican negative freedom, resilient freedom, is much the same as the problems that have always been perceived in the liberal ideal of negative freedom. As long as the pursuits of individuals are likely to involve them in occasional interference with each other, we need some criterion to decide which aspects of the individual's independence warrant the special protection of the law. The liberal tradition has generally tried to formulate this by means of the concept of rights, and one strand of liberalism has as its ideal a negative concept of rights. The suggested republican idea of negative liberty shifts the problem but does not solve it. The problem is now, which forms of resilience should be backed or instituted by law. The typical case will arise from the inequalities of the market, e.g. the labour market, where one has to ask, how much equality has to be instituted in order for each individual to have resilient freedom? In the traditional republic, resilience was determined by traditional ideas of property-based independence. This was what was called citizenship. The challenge to the new republican theorist is to find a principled replacement for this, suitable for an egalitarian republic. In short, even in its twentieth-century revival, republican theory continues to centre on the problem of what should be the qualifying criteria for membership of the public in its governance of the public realm. Traditional liberalism side-stepped the issue by separating the question of the source of government from the question of the exercise of government, leaving the former to democratic theory. The new republicans still have to find a plausible answer.

See also 3 HISTORY; 11 LIBERALISM; 15 COMMUNITY; 29 LIBERTY; 31 PROPERTY; 39 TRUST; 40 VIRTUE

References

Bailyn, B.: *The Ideological Origins of the American Revolution* (Cambridge, Mass.: Harvard University Press, 1967).

Barber, B.: *Strong Democracy: Participatory Politics in a New Age* (Berkeley: University of California Press, 1984).

Baron, H.: *The Crisis of the Early Italian Renaissance. Civic Humanism and Republican Liberty in an Age of Classicism and Tyranny* (Princeton, NJ: Princeton University Press, 1955; 2nd edn, 1966).

Bock, G., Skinner, Q. and Viroli, M., eds: *Machiavelli and Republicanism* (Cambridge: Cambridge University Press, 1990).

Boyte, H. C.: *Commonwealth: A Return to Citizen Politics* (New York: Free Press, 1989).

———— and Schwartz, J.: 'Communitarianism and the left', *Dissent*, 31 (1984), 475–81.

Braithwaite, J. and Pettit, P.: *Not Just Deserts. A Republican Theory of Criminal Justice* (Oxford: Clarendon Press, 1990).

Fraser, A.: 'Legal amnesia: Modernism versus the republican tradition in American legal theory', *Telos*, 60 (1984), 15–52.

Green, P.: *Retrieving Democracy: In Search of Civic Equality* (Totowa, NJ: Rowman & Littlefield, 1985).

Haakonssen, K.: 'Introduction', Thomas Reid, *Practical Ethics. Being Lectures and Papers on Natural Religion, Self-Government, Natural Jurisprudence and the Law of Nations*, ed. K. Haakonssen (Princeton, NJ: Princeton University Press, 1990), pp. 1–99.

————: 'From natural law to the rights of man: a European perspective on American debates', *A Culture of Rights, The Bill of Rights in Philosophy, Politics and Law – 1791 and 1991*, ed. M. Lacey and K. Haakonssen (Cambridge: Cambridge University Press, 1991), pp. 19–61.

————: 'Natural/divine law theories of ethics', *Cambridge History of Seventeenth-century Philosophy*, ed. M. Ayers and D. Garber (Cambridge: Cambridge University Press, forthcoming).

Isaac, J. C.: 'Republicanism vs. liberalism? A reconsideration', *History of Political Thought*, 9 (1988), 349–77.

Lerner, R.: *The Thinking Revolutionary: Principle and Practice in the New Republic* (Ithaca, NY: Cornell University Press, 1987).

Oldfield, A.: *Citizenship and Community, Civic Republicanism and the Modern World* (London and New York: Routledge, 1990).

Pangle, T. L.: *The Spirit of Modern Republicanism: The Moral Vision of the American Founders and the Philosophy of Locke* (Chicago: University of Chicago Press, 1988).

Pettit, P.: 'The freedom of the city: a republican ideal', *The Good Polity*, ed. A. Hamlin and P. Pettit (Oxford: Blackwell, 1989a), pp. 141–68.

————: 'A definition of negative liberty', *Ratio*, NS 2 (1989b), 153–68.

————: 'Negative liberty: liberal and republican', *European Journal of Philosophy* (forthcoming).

Pocock, J. G. A.: *The Machiavellian Moment: Florentine Political Thought and the Atlantic Republican Tradition* (Princeton, NJ: Princeton University Press, 1975).

Sandel, M.: *Liberalism and the Limits of Justice* (Cambridge: Cambridge University Press, 1982).

———— ed.: *Liberalism and Its Critics* (Oxford: Blackwell, 1984a).

————: 'The procedural republic and the unencumbered self', *Political Theory*, 12 (1984), 81–96.

Shalhope, R. E.: 'Toward a republican synthesis: the emergence of an understanding of republicanism in American historiography', *William and Mary Quarterly*, 3rd ser., 29 (1972), 49–80.

————: 'Republicanism and early American historiography', *William and Mary Quarterly*, 3rd ser., 39 (1982), 334–56.

Skinner, Q.: *The Foundations of Modern Political Thought*, 2 vols. Vol. 1: *The Renaissance* (Cambridge: Cambridge University Press, 1978).

————: 'Machiavelli on the maintenance of liberty', *Politics*, 18 (1983), 3–15.

————: 'The idea of negative liberty', *Philosophy in History*, ed. R. Rorty, J. B. Schneewind and Q. Skinner (Cambridge: Cambridge University Press, 1984), pp. 193–221.

Sunstein, C. R.: 'Beyond the republican revival', *The Yale Law Review*, 97 (1988), 1539–90.

Vetterli, R. and Bryner, G.: *In Search of the Republic: Public Virtue and the Roots of American Government* (Totowa, NJ: Rowman & Littlefield, 1987).

Wood, G. S.: *The Creation of the American Republic 1776–1787* (Chapel Hill, NC: University of North Carolina Press, 1969).

33

Rights

JEREMY WALDRON

That individuals have *rights* and that these rights mark important limits on what may be done to them by the state, or in the name of other moral conceptions – this is now a familiar position in modern political philosophy.

Of course, the idea is familiar in non-philosophical contexts too. Many countries embody a list of rights in their constitution, proclaiming, for example, that the government will not interfere with the free speech of its citizens, or with their freedom of travel, their sexual privacy, their religious liberty, or their equal access to the law. These Bills of Rights also reflect the importance in the international community of the idea of *human* rights – the conviction that there are liberties and interests so basic that *every* society should secure them irrespective of its traditions, history or level of economic development.

The philosophical discussion of rights is largely an exploration of this idea: what are the implications and the presuppositions of such a 'right-based' approach to political morality? But as well as their usual preoccupation with conceptual analysis – what does it *mean* to say 'P has a right to X' – philosophers are participating also in the political debates about what rights we actually have. For example, are there rights to economic assistance as well as to civil liberty (Shue, 1980)? Should feminist claims, or the claims of ethnic minorities, be phrased in terms of rights? Or should these claims be expressed in a more radical political language, or in language that stresses the things that mark them as different from others in their society (Williams, 1991)? The readiness to address these controversies is part of the wider public affairs movement in philosophy over the past two decades. It stems in large part from a realization that issues of analysis and issues of content are interrelated, and that neither can be isolated from a consideration of the deeper theories of justification – Kantianism, utilitarianism, Aristotelianism and contractarianism – that are the province of moral philosophy.

It will be impossible in a chapter of this length to do justice to all the discussions that have taken place in recent years. In what follows, I shall outline a few of the more prominent issues that have emerged: first, in the analysis of rights; then in disputes about their content; and finally in the deeper discussion of their ethical underpinnings.

Analysis

Although the formula 'P has a right to do X' is sometimes used to indicate merely that P has no duty not to do X, its main use is to assert (1) that others have a duty not to

575

prevent P from doing X, (2) that the point of such a duty is to promote or protect some interest of P's, and (3) that although it is a matter of self-interest, P should feel no embarrassment about insisting upon and enforcing this duty. Together these elements capture the sense in which a right is a legitimate claim that one person can make against others.

Some critics (e.g. Glendon, 1991) have argued that rights, conceived in this way, are too egoistic to provide a satisfactory basis for communal morality. They suggest we should place less emphasis on rights and more on responsibilities. This suggestion is misconceived. The analysis I have just provided indicates that rights are *correlative* to duties, so that talking about rights *is* a way of talking about people's responsibilities. Moreover, most rights are conceived in universal terms: if P has a right against Q, then Q will usually have a similar right against P so that Q's own duties are reciprocated by responsibilities that her right in turn imposes on P.

Other have taken exception to the peremptory and querulous tone in which claims of right are often expressed. Critics like Glendon (1991) and Gilligan (1982, pp. 136–8) associate this tone with the dominance of masculine values, and the unhealthy litigiousness of modern society. But while there are certainly abuses, theorists of rights should not feel compelled to withdraw their claims about the moral importance of self-assertion. In social life, it matters not only that people's interests be respected, but that they have sufficient self-respect to stand up for their interests themselves (Hill, 1973). Rights express the idea that respect for a given interest is to be understood from the point of view of the individual whose interest it is. By protecting the interest, we vindicate that point of view, proclaiming that it has as much validity as any other perspective in morality (e.g. the perspective of society or the God's-eye point of view).

It is sometimes said that a humane social policy should focus less on rights and more on needs. I think this too is a misunderstanding, confusing as it does the content of a claim with the normative form in which that claim is couched. (It is like saying we should concentrate less on duties and more on truth-telling!) The language of rights as it is nowadays understood is perfectly accommodating to a concern about human need. To invoke a right is to predicate a duty on some concern for a certain individual interest (Raz, 1986, p. 166), and while the interest in question is often an interest in liberty, it might equally be an interest in some material satisfaction. There used to be a controversy in the analysis of rights about whether the concept itself presupposed an exclusive concern with liberty. But the claim that it did (e.g. Hart, 1955) has now largely been abandoned, and the language of rights is used to refer to any demand that an individual interest should be protected or promoted, made from the individual's own point of view, and accorded decisive moral importance.

(It should, perhaps, be noted that many of these attacks on rights, particularly in the American literature of 'Critical Legal Studies', turn out to be objections, not to the philosophical idea of human rights at all, but to the tactic of using constitutional litigation as a means to social reform. That is an issue of quite limited philosophical interest and I have not tried to address it here.)

There is one controversy of a broadly analytical kind which still remains unresolved. Although rights express the importance of certain interests from the individual's perspective, they posit them also as matters of moral concern. P's right to life, for example, marks not only the importance of P's life to P, but the moral importance (and thus, in some sense, the importance to all of us) of P's not being killed. But philosophers disagree about how this wider moral importance is to be understood. Clearly each of us can say to herself, 'I must not kill P'. Clearly also if Q kills P, then it is incumbent on the rest of us to condemn Q and call for her apprehension and punishment. But suppose R has an opportunity to prevent Q from killing P, but that doing so will involve some considerable cost to herself. Does she have a duty to prevent the killing? And, if so, is that duty as important as her *own* duty not to kill P?

Some philosophers, most prominently Nozick (1974, pp. 28–51) think that the last question at least is to be answered in the negative. The duty that P's right imposes on R, they say, is just the duty *not to kill P*; it is not the duty to do whatever is necessary to secure that P not be killed. The duty, in other words, is 'agent-relative'. It prohibits killing, but it focuses that prohibition peculiarly on the agency of each person who considers it. From Q's perspective, the duty is that Q not kill P; from R's perspective, the duty is that R not kill P. There is no common 'agent-neutral' duty incumbent on both Q and R, that P not be killed. The right does not command Q and R to pursue the common consequentialist goal of P's not being killed (Williams, 1973, pp. 98–118).

No one doubts that the idea of an agent-relative duty is a coherent one. But justifying it is another matter (Scheffler, 1982, pp. 80–115) and, in my opinion, it is quite clear that it cannot be justified on the basis of rights. To justify an agent-relative duty, we would have to show why each agent should be peculiarly concerned with the quality of her own conduct. Now, as Bernard Williams (1981, pp. 40–53) and Thomas Nagel (1986, pp. 164–85) have argued, it sometimes *is* more important to orient moral justification to an agent's own perspective than to attempt to take an impartial point of view. But one of the features of my earlier analysis of rights was that the point of imposing the duty is our concern for the *right-bearer's* point of view, not the point of view of the agent or duty-bearer who is constrained by the right. Barring special cases like matricide, what matters to P is simply *not being killed*, as opposed to not being killed by any agent in particular. If this interest is really the basis of R's duty, R should be as concerned about the threat posed to P by Q's actions as she would be about any threat posed to P by her own.

The advantage of this approach is that it takes seriously the distinction between right-based duties and other duties (Dworkin, 1978, pp. 169–73; Mackie, 1984; and Waldron, 1988, pp. 62–105). By presenting *P's not being killed* as a common goal for Q and R to pursue, it emphasizes that the duties Q and R have are really imposed for P's sake not their own (Sen, 1982). The disadvantage, however, is that it forces us to abandon any sense we might have had that rights express *absolute* moral constraints, any sense that it is their job to prevent the interests of one individual from being traded off against the interests of others. If rights themselves involve the conflict and balancing of competing goals, it seems that there is no getting away from the casuistry and complex moral calculations that were thought to be the hallmark of more blatantly consequentialist theories (Waldron, 1989, pp. 507–9). In the end I do not think this worry is decisive. The world really *is* a complex place and we

577

should not pride ourselves on confronting it with principles whose simplicity represents moral dilemmas as much easier than they actually are.

Content

In international human rights circles, diplomats talk about 'first-', 'second-' and 'third-generation' rights (see Alston, 1987, p. 307). First-generation rights are the traditional liberties and privileges of citizenship: religious toleration, freedom from arbitrary arrest, free speech, the right to vote, and so on. Second-generation rights are socio-economic claims: the right to education, housing, health care, employment and an adequate standard of living. Though these are thought to be more radical claims requiring a more interventionist state, they remain essentially individualistic in their content, inasmuch as it is the material welfare of each man, woman, and child that is supposed to be secured by these provisions. Third-generation rights, by contrast, have to do with communities or whole peoples, rather than individual persons. They include minority language rights, national rights to self-determination and the right to such diffuse goods as peace, environmental integrity and economic development.

Though all these ideas express laudable aspirations, the second- and third-generation claims are very controversial. Many theorists maintain, for substantive philosophical if not analytical reasons, that the new claims represent a degradation of the currency of rights, a hijacking of the concept by ideologues who are very little concerned with its liberal provenance.

I shall begin with some comments about third-generation rights. Briefly, the difficulty here is that they are rights to 'non-individualized' goods – goods enjoyed collectively, rather than by individuals on their own account. The health of the environment, for example, is a public good: if it is secured for one person (in a region) it is necessarily secured for all. This makes it difficult to express the case for environmental integrity in the traditional form of rights analysis, where duties are generated on the basis of respect for an individual's interests (Raz, 1984, pp. 186–90). The problem is even more acute for those goods such as the survival of a language, which seem to be the essential property of a community. But perhaps we can treat groups as right-bearers, and say that the rights of a community, particularly a minority community, have more or less the same logic *vis-à-vis* some larger political entity as individual rights have *vis-à-vis* the community. True, there will sometimes be problems about the identity and definition of the groups in question. But there does not seem to be any logical or ethical difficulty with this approach, provided of course that the rights of the group are always asserted against some larger entity rather than against its own individual members (Waldron, 1987a, pp. 314–20).

What about second-generation rights? Do people have rights to social and economic welfare? There are three lines of argument, which lead to the conclusion that they do. The first argues that recognition of second-generation rights is necessary if we are to be serious in our commitment to any rights at all. No one can fully enjoy or exercise *any* right that she is supposed to have if she lacks the essentials for a healthy and active life. Even if most rights are oriented towards the exercise of agency and freedom, still we know that things like malnutrition and epidemic disease can debilitate and finally destroy all the human faculties that individual autonomy involves (Shue, 1980, pp. 24–5).

Particular versions of this argument can also be developed for specific rights. Many feminists say, for example, that it is not enough for abortion to be a legally secured right, if all that means is that procuring an abortion is not a criminal offence. A poor woman who is unable to take advantage of this liberty because she has no access to clinical services or cannot pay for the procedure is about as badly off as she would be if there were no legal liberty at all (MacKinnon, 1991). In general, if the point of a right is to ensure that a certain choice can be exercised, then actually facilitating the exercise may sometimes be as important as not obstructing it.

The second argument for welfare rights is more direct. Instead of saying that economic security is necessary if *other* rights are to be taken seriously, it states bluntly that socio-economic needs are as important as any other interests, and that a moral theory of individual dignity and well-being is plainly inadequate if it does not take them into account. The advantage of this approach is that it concedes nothing in the way of priority to first-generation rights. Though we may be worried about the proliferation of rights claims, it is by no means clear that demands for welfare should be the ones to give way. Death, disease, malnutrition and exposure are as much matters of concern as any denials of political or civil liberty. Where such predicaments are avoidable, a refusal to address them is an evident insult to human dignity and a failure to take seriously the unconditional worth of each person.

However, arguments along these lines must meet the challenge posed by Robert Nozick: it is all very well to base human rights on material need, but other people may already have property rights over the resources that would have to be used to satisfy these needs. Particular private entitlements might, as he put it, 'fill the space of rights, leaving no room for general rights to be in a certain material condition' (Nozick, 1974, p. 238).

This critique assumes that rights based on need occupy a relatively superficial role in a general theory of economic entitlement – as though we *first* determine who owns what, and *then* determine what to do about the needs that are left unsatisfied. Perhaps needs should play a more fundamental role, governing the initial allocation of property rights themselves. This is the third of the arguments I mentioned. Instead of making socioeconomic rights the basis of a duty of compulsory charity incumbent upon existing property-holders, we use them instead to call existing property arrangements into question. We reverse Nozick's order of priorities, and insist that no system of ownership is justified if it leaves large numbers of people destitute and hungry (Waldron, 1986, pp. 475–82). On this account, welfare provision is seen as a first step towards a complete overhaul of a property distribution whose failure to respect fundamental rights is indicated by the fact that many people continue to be without access to the resources they need in order to live.

This third line of argument can also be used to respond to another common criticism of second-generation claims – that they are impracticable or too expensive. Some critics argue that putative welfare rights violate the logical principle '*Ought implies can*': many states do not have the resources to provide even minimal economic security for masses of their citizens. Moreover, since states differ considerably in this regard, it hardly makes sense to regard economic provision as matter of universal human entitlement (Cranston, 1967, pp. 50–1). However, the alleged impossibility in many of these cases stems from an assumption that the existing distribution of resources (local and global) is to remain largely undisturbed. When a conservative government in the West says, for example, in response to some plea for welfare provision or overseas aid, 'The money simply isn't there', what is usually meant is that it would be impolitic to try to raise it by taxation. The more radical challenge posed to the underlying distribution of wealth is simply ignored. once matters are put in this way, it becomes clear that the *'ought'* of human rights is being frustrated less by the *'can't'* of impracticability, than by the *'won't'* of selfishness and greed.

Still, someone might insist, aren't these rights awfully demanding? At least first-generation rights require only that we and our governments refrain from various acts of tyranny and violence. They are 'negative' rights correlative to duties of omission, whereas socioeconomic rights are correlated with positive duties of assistance. One advantage of negative rights is that they never conflict with one another, for one can perform an infinite number of omissions at any given time. With positive rights, by contrast, we always have to consider the scarcity of the resources and services that are called for (Cranston, 1967, p. 50).

Unfortunately, this correlation of first- and second-generation claims with duties of omission and duties of positive assistance will not stand up. Many first-generation rights (for example, the right to vote) require a considerable effort to establish and maintain political frameworks, and all such rights make costly calls upon scarce police and forensic resources. As for second-generation rights, they may be correlated with duties that are positive or negative, depending on the context. If people are actually starving, their rights make a call on our active assistance. But if they are living satisfactorily in a traditional subsistence economy, all the right may require is that we refrain from economic initiatives that might disturb that situation (Shue, 1980, pp. 35–64).

In general, where resources are scarce relative to human wants, *any* system of rights or entitlements will seem demanding to those who are constrained by it. If an economic system includes provision for welfare assistance, it may seem overly demanding to taxpayers. But if it does not include such provision, then the system of *property rights* in such an economy will seem overly demanding to the poor, requiring as it does that they refrain from making use of resources (belonging to others) that they need in order to survive. As usual, the question is not whether we are to have a system of demanding rights, but how the costs of these demands are to be distributed.

All the same, thinking about scarcity does have the advantage of forcing rights theorists to take seriously the issue of justice. It is an unhappy feature of rights that they express moral claims in a sort of 'line item' way, presenting each individual's case peremptorily as though it brooked no denial or compromise. If we want to say (as I have argued) that people have rights that may conflict, then rights have got to be linked to a theory of social justice that takes seriously the distributive issues that they raise. But once that link is established, we may find it harder than we thought to insist on a determinate content for either property rights or welfare rights (or, for that matter, civil rights). John Rawls' work on social justice suggests that problems of fair distribution are better approached by articulating general principles for the evaluation of social structures than by laying down particular rights which allocate to individuals as a matter of entitlement a certain share of social wealth (Rawls, 1971, pp. 64 and 88–90).

Justification

Since the time of Jeremy Bentham, it has been a common complaint against rights that they are nothing but question-begging assertions. Reasoned social reform, Bentham argued, requires detailed attention to empirical circumstances, and that in turn requires 'strength of mind to weigh, and patience to investigate'. The language of natural rights, by contrast, 'is from beginning to end so much flat assertion: it lays down as a fundamental and inviolable principle whatever is in dispute' (Bentham [1794] 1987, p. 74).

This concern continues to resonate 200 years later. Though rights sound nice, most students of public policy prefer the idiom of utilitarian analysis – calculating the effects of a given reform proposal on the well-being of each individual, and choosing the course of action which will produce the greatest balance of satisfaction over suffering, taking everything into account.

In considering this critique, we must take care that our admiration for the painstaking complexity of policy analysis does not blind us to some of its real moral difficulties. Since utilitarians aggregate all consequences on the same scale, they must figure that any loss to an individual can always be offset by a sufficiently widespread gain to others, even if that gain is just a marginal increment of convenience for each of a large number of people. The maximizing logic of their position requires them to accept with equanimity the neglect or sacrifice of some for the sake of the greater good of others. Often what sounds like 'so much flat assertion', on the part of rights theorists, is simply an adamant insistence that that is not satisfactory as a moral basis for public policy.

Some utilitarians return the favour, responding with a 'flat assertion' of their own that there is nothing wrong with their calculus. But others take a less hard-line approach, suggesting that a sophisticated utilitarianism may itself yield the conclusion that individuals be accorded certain rights. Given our fallibility as calculators, it is possible that human happiness might be better promoted by, for example, an absolute prohibition on torture than by a utilitarian reconsideration of the issue every time a plausible case for torture presents itself. Opinions differ as to whether this sort of 'indirect' utilitarianism can yield genuine rights (compare Hare, 1981, pp. 44–64, 147–68 with Lyons, 1984). But even if it can, the fundamental problem remains: the 'rights' in question are still generated on the assumption that there is nothing intrinsically wrong with sacrificing an important individual interest to a greater sum of lesser interests. That assumption is retained in the foundations of the theory, and it remains a real source of moral concern.

Theorists of rights also have difficulty with the utilitarian assumption that every human preference has a claim to satisfaction. Ronald Dworkin (1978, pp. 232–8;

1984, pp. 155–67) has argued that racist preferences, for example, should not be counted when we are calculating costs and benefits since their content is incompatible with the egalitarian assumption that everyone is entitled to the same concern and respect. Now in practice it is impossible to disentangle such 'external' preferences from people's desires for their own well-being. However, Dworkin suggests that it is the role of rights to correct for the distortions introduced into utilitarian calculations by the entangled presence of external preferences. This explains why rights are to be conceived, in his famous phrase, as 'trumps' over utility (Dworkin, 1978, p. xi) – that is, why rights have moral priority over any cost/benefit calculation in which racist or other inegalitarian preferences may be present.

The details of Dworkin's position remain controversial (see Hart, 1979, pp. 86–97). But the general assumption on which it is predicated – that the idea of rights involves a commitment to equality and that it is profoundly antithetical to racist and sexist conceptions of human value – is now beyond dispute. Much of the recent *foundational* work in rights theory has involved an attempt to elaborate the nature of this underlying egalitarianism.

One account involves a distinction between 'merit' and 'worth' (Vlastos, 1984, pp. 49–60). Though people differ in their virtues and abilities, the idea of rights attaches an unconditional *worth* to the existence of each person, irrespective of her particular value to others. Traditionally, this was given a theological interpretation: since God has invested His creative love in each of us, it behoves us to treat all others in a way that reflects that status (Locke [1689] 1988, pp. 270–1). In a more secular framework, the assumption of unconditional worth is based on the importance of each life to the person whose life it is, irrespective of her wealth, power or social status. People try to make lives for themselves, each on their own terms. A theory of rights maintains that that enterprise is to be respected, equally, in each person, and that all forms of power, organization, authority and exclusion are to be evaluated on the basis of how they serve these individual undertakings.

This explains the antipathy in modern political theory between defenders of rights and those who are called 'communitarians' (Sandel, 1984). For the latter, the cardinal point about human society is that people make lives on terms provided by their culture or the community around them. That each lives a life on her own terms is, on that approach, a myth – and a pernicious myth if it encourages people to neglect or undermine the communal structures that in fact make human life bearable (Taylor, 1985, pp. 187–210). However, it is important not to confuse moral and sociological issues here. From a scientific point of view, perhaps it is possible to give a complete explanation of the life each person is leading in terms of social and cultural frameworks. But the idea of rights is a claim about value: whatever its provenance, the life of a given person is *hers, and it feels important to her*, from the inside as it were. The idea of rights involves a determination to reflect that feeling of importance in the respect we offer to one another as a fundamental basis of our life together.

Earlier I raised the issue of the relation between rights and liberty. I indicated that modern political thought leaves open the possibility that there may be rights to things other than freedom. We see now that individual freedom is nevertheless implicated with rights at a much deeper level. What I have taken as the underlying idea of rights

– an individual leading a life on her own terms – is not simply the idea of an individual's *being alive*. It is of a life's *being led*, and that connotes agency, choice, and a sense of individual responsibility. In a number of recent works, Alan Gewirth (1978; 1982, pp. 41–178) has argued that the idea of agency holds the key to rights: each of us values agency in her own case, and so each is committed, by what Gewirth calls 'the Principle of Generic Consistency', to value agency and facilitate its exercise in everyone's life. It is perhaps unfortunate that Gewirth has entangled these considerations with the messier enterprise of trying to construct a *logical proof* of the moral claims he is making: he wants to show that the person who does not value everyone's agency is reasoning irrationally. It seems wiser to leave that to the specialist enterprise of meta-ethics. But the importance of agency in modern discussions of rights is indisputable: it is because each of us wants a life governed in large part by her own thinking, feeling and decision-making that the idea of individual rights seems so attractive.

Certainly this is the sense that modern theories give to the old Kantian precept that we are to treat humanity in each person as an end in itself, never merely as a means to others' ends (Kant, [1785] 1969, pp. 52–4). Morally the most important fact about our humanity is the ability each of us has to exercise agency in accordance with practical reason. We know that this capacity can be exploited in some people for the benefit of others: slavery and the domestic subordination of women remain the most striking examples of people living lives on others' terms, not their own. In the final analysis, the idea of rights commits its proponent to oppose all such subordination, and in general to do what she can (individually and collectively through the state) to secure the benefits of each person's own rational agency, fully developed, for the life that that person has chosen to lead.

See also 1 ANALYTICAL PHILOSOPHY; 5 ECONOMICS; 6 POLITICAL SCIENCE; 7 LEGAL STUDIES; 11 LIBERALISM; 14 AUTONOMY; 15 COMMUNITY; 16 CONTRACT AND CONSENT; 17 CONSTITUTIONALISM AND THE RULE OF LAW; 22 DISTRIBUTIVE JUSTICE; 25 EQUALITY; 29 LIBERTY; 31 PROPERTY; 34 SECESSION AND NATIONALISM; 37 TOLERATION AND FUNDAMENTALISM; 38 TOTALITARIANISM

References

Alston, P.: 'A third generation of solidarity rights: progressive development or obfuscation of international human rights law?', *Netherlands International Law Review*, 29 (1987), 307–65.
Arendt, H.: *The Origins of Totalitarianism* (New York: Harcourt, Brace and Company, 1951).
Bentham, J.: *Anarchical Fallacies; being an examination of the Declarations of Rights issued during the French Revolution* (1796), excerpted in Waldron (1987a, pp. 46–76).
Cranston, M.: 'Human rights, real and supposed', in *Political Theory and the Rights of Man*, ed. D. D. Raphael (London: Macmillan, 1967).
Dworkin, R.: *Taking Rights Seriously* (London: Duckworth, 1978).
————: 'Rights as trumps', in Waldron (1984), pp. 153–67.
Gewirth, A.: *Reason and Morality* (Chicago: University of Chicago Press, 1978).
————: *Human Rights: Essays on Justification and Applications* (Chicago: University of Chicago Press, 1982).
Gilligan, C.: *In a Different Voice: Psychological Theory and Women's Development* (Cambridge, Mass.: Harvard University Press, 1982).

Glendon, M. A.: *Rights Talk* (New York: Free Press, 1991).

Hare, R. M.: *Moral Thinking* (Oxford: Clarendon Press, 1981).

Hart, H. L. A.: 'Are there any natural rights?', *Philosophical Review*, 64 (1955), 175–91.

————: 'Between utility and rights', in Ryan (1979), pp. 77–98.

Hill, T. E.: 'Servility and self-respect', *The Monist*, 57 (1973), 137–52.

Lyons, D.: 'Utility and rights', in Waldron (1984), pp. 110–36.

Mackie, J. L.: 'Can there be a right-based moral theory?', in Waldron (1984), pp. 168–81.

MacKinnon, C. A.: *Toward a Feminist Theory of the State* (Cambridge, Mass.: Harvard University Press, 1991).

Nagel, T.: *The View from Nowhere* (Oxford: Oxford University Press, 1986).

Nozick, R.: *Anarchy, State and Utopia* (Oxford: Blackwell, 1974).

Rawls, J.: *A Theory of Justice* (Cambridge, Mass.: Harvard University Press, 1971).

Raz, J.: 'Right-based moralities', in Waldron (1984), pp. 182–200.

————: *The Morality of Freedom* (Oxford: Clarendon Press, 1986).

Ryan, A., ed.: *The Idea of Freedom: Essays in Honour of Isaiah Berlin* (Oxford: Oxford University Press, 1979).

Sandel, M., ed.: *Liberalism and its Critics* (Oxford: Blackwell, 1984).

Scheffler, S.: *The Rejection of Consequentialism* (Oxford: Clarendon Press, 1982).

Sen, A.: 'Rights and agency', *Philosophy and Public Affairs*, 11 (1982), 3–39.

Shue, H.: *Basic Rights: Subsistence, Affluence, and U.S. Foreign Policy* (Princeton, NJ: Princeton University Press, 1980).

Taylor, C.: 'Atomism', in C. Taylor, *Philosophy and the Human Sciences: Philosophical Papers 2* (Cambridge: Cambridge University Press, 1985), pp. 87–210.

Vlastos, G.: 'Justice and equality', in Waldron (1984), pp. 41–76.

Waldron, J., ed.: *Theories of Rights* (Oxford: Oxford University Press, 1984).

————: 'Welfare and the images of charity', *Philosophical Quarterly*, 36 (1986), 463–82.

————: *Nonsense Upon Stilts: Bentham, Burke and Marx on the Rights of Man* (London: Methuen, 1987a) .

————: 'Can communal goods be human rights?', *Archives européennes de sociologie*, 27 (1987b), 296–321.

————: *The Right to Private Property* (Oxford: Clarendon Press, 1988).

————: 'Rights in conflict', *Ethics*, 99 (1989), 503–19.

Williams, B.: 'A critique of utilitarianism', in J. J. C. Smart and B. Williams, *Utilitarianism, For and Against* (Cambridge: Cambridge University Press, 1973), pp. 75–150.

————: 'Utilitarianism and moral self-indulgence', in B. Williams, *Moral Luck: Philosophical Papers 1973–1980* (Cambridge: Cambridge University Press, 1981), pp. 40–53.

Williams, P.: *The Alchemy of Race and Rights* (Cambridge, Mass.: Harvard University Press, 1991).

Further reading

Donnelly, J.: *The Concept of Human Rights* (London: Croom Helm, 1985).

Finnis, J.: *Natural Law and Natural Rights* (Oxford: Clarendon Press, 1980).

Held, V.: *Rights and Goods: Justifying Social Action* (Chicago: University of Chicago Press, 1984).

Lyons, D., ed.: *Rights* (Belmont: University of California Press, 1979).

MacCormick, N.: *Legal Right and Social Democracy: Essays in Legal and Political Philosophy* (Oxford: Clarendon Press, 1982).

Nickel, J. W.: *Making Sense of Human Rights: Philosophical Reflections on the Universal Declaration of Human Rights* (Berkeley: University of California Press, 1987).

Scheffler, S., ed.: *Consequentialism and its Critics* (Oxford: Oxford University Press, 1988).

Shapiro, I.: *The Evolution of Rights in Liberal Theory* (Cambridge: Cambridge University Press, 1986).

Thomson, J. J.: *The Realm of Rights* (Cambridge, Mass.: Harvard University Press, 1990).

Tuck, R.: *Natural Rights Theories: Their Origin and Development* (Cambridge: Cambridge University Press, 1979).

Wellman, C.: *A Theory of Rights: Persons Under Laws, Institutions, and Morals* (Totowa, NJ: Rowman & Allenheld, 1985).

34

Secession and nationalism

ALLEN BUCHANAN

Secession, autonomy and the modern state

From Croatia to Azerbaijan to Quebec, secessionist movements are breaking states apart. In some cases, as with Lithuania, a formerly subordinate unit seeks to become and remain a fully sovereign state in its own right. In others, such as Ukraine, one of the first exercises of new-found sovereignty is to forge ties with other units to create new forms of political association – ties which immediately limit the sovereignty of their components. These momentous events call into question not only the legitimacy of particular states and their boundaries, but also the nature of sovereignty and the purposes of political association.

Less publicized and less dramatic movements for greater self-determination of groups within the framework of existing states are also becoming pervasive. The indigenous peoples' rights movement, pursued with vigour in the United Nations and other arenas of international law, embraces Indians in North, Central and South America, Southeast Asian Hill Tribes, the Saami (Lapps) in a number of countries touched by the Arctic Circle, and Native Hawaiians, among others. Self-determination movements among Flemings in Belgium and Scots in the United Kingdom appear to be building as well. In most of these cases the groups in question do not seek full sovereignty, but rather greater autonomy through the achievement of limited rights of self-government as distinct subunits within the state.

The proper analysis of the concept of sovereignty is, of course, a matter of dispute. However, the root idea is that of a supreme authority – one whose powers are unrestricted by those of other entities. It is useful to distinguish between *internal* and *external* sovereignty (McCallum, 1987, pp. 36–45). Internal sovereignty is the state's supremacy with respect to all affairs within its borders. External sovereignty is the state's supremacy with respect to its relations with other political units beyond its borders; in particular, its right to the integrity of its territory, and to control crossings of its borders, as well as the right to enter as an independent party into economic agreements or military alliances or treaties with other states.

No state enjoys literally unrestricted external sovereignty. International law imposes a number of restrictions on every state's dealings with other states, the most fundamental of which is that each is to recognize the others' territorial integrity. In addition, virtually all modern states acknowledge (in principle if not in practice) that their internal sovereignty is limited by *individual rights*, in particular the human rights recognized in international law.

Autonomy movements seek to impose further limitations on internal sovereignty through the recognition of various *group rights*. These include not only so-called minority cultural rights, such as the right to speak one's own language or to wear cultural dress, but also collective property rights for the group, rights of internal self-government, and in some cases rights to participate in joint decision-making concerning the development and exploitation of resources in the area occupied by the group (Quebec, 1991).

Autonomy movements may appear to be less radical than outright bids for secession. After all, what they demand is not the dismemberment of the state into two or more new states, but only a reallocation of certain powers within the state. This appearance, however, is misleading. If a state recognizes substantial powers of self-determination for groups within its borders, it thereby acknowledges limits on its own sovereignty. And if the modern state is defined as a political authority which (credibly) claims full sovereignty over the entire area within its borders, then a state that recognizes rights of self-determination for minorities within its borders thereby transforms itself into something less than a fully sovereign state. (For example, American Indian law in conferring significant powers of self-government upon Indian tribes, uses the term 'Indian Nation', and is increasing regarded as approaching the status of *inter*national law; Williams, 1990, pp. 74–103.)

Thus, secession movements only threaten the myth of the permanence of the state; autonomy movements assault the concept of state sovereignty itself. Successful and frequent secession would certainly shatter the international order; but it would not challenge the basic conceptual framework that has governed international law for over 300 years, since the rise of the modern state. What is fundamental to that framework is the assumption that international law concerns relations among sovereign states. If successful, autonomy movements within existing states may make the case of sovereign states the exception rather than the rule (Hannum, 1990, pp. 14–26, 453–77).

Even though secession is in this sense a phenomenon which the traditional framework of international law and relations can in principle accommodate, it is the most extreme and radical response to the problems of group conflict within the state. For this reason, a consideration of the case for and against secession puts the moral issues of group conflict in bold relief. In what follows, we will explore the morality of secession, while bearing in mind that it is only the most extreme point on a continuum of phenomena involving the struggles of groups within existing political units to gain greater autonomy.

Nationalism and the justification of secession

Some see the spate of secessionist movements now appearing around the globe as the expression of an unpredicted and profoundly disturbing resurgence of *nationalism*, which many rightly regard as one of the most dangerous phenomena of the modern era (Buchanan, 1991, pp. 2, 48–52). And indeed one of the most familiar and stirring justifications offered for secession appeals to *the right of self-determination for 'peoples'*, interpreted such that it is equivalent to what is sometimes called the *normative nationalist principle*. It is also one of the least plausible justifications.

The normative nationalist principle states that every 'people' is entitled to its own state, that is, that political and cultural (or ethnic) boundaries must coincide (Gellner, 1983, pp. 1–3). In other words, according to the normative nationalist principle, the right of self-determination is to be understood in a very strong way, as requiring complete political independence – that is, full sovereignty.

An immediate difficulty, of course, is the meaning of 'peoples'. Presumably a 'people' is a distinct ethnic group, the identifying marks of which are a common language, shared tradition and a common culture. Each of these criteria has its own difficulties. The question of what count as different dialects of the same language, as opposed to two or more distinct languages, raises complex theoretical and metatheoretical issues in linguistics. The histories of many groups exhibit frequent discontinuities, infusion of new cultural elements from outside, and alternating degrees of assimilation to and separation from other groups.

More disturbingly, if 'people' is interpreted broadly enough, then the normative nationalist principle denies the legitimacy of any state containing more than one cultural group (unless all 'peoples' within it freely waive their rights to their own states). Yet cultural pluralism is often taken to be a distinguishing feature of the modern state, or at least of the modern liberal state. Moreover, if the number of ethnic or cultural groups or peoples is not fixed but may increase, then the normative nationalist principle is a recipe for limitless political fragmentation.

Nor is this all. Even aside from the instability and economic costs of the repeated fragmentation which it endorses, there is a more serious objection to the normative nationalist principle, forcefully formulated by Ernest Gellner.

To put it in the simplest terms: there is a very large number of potential nations on earth. Our planet also contains room for a certain number of independent or autonomous political units. On any reasonable calculation, the former number (of potential nations) is probably much, much larger than that of possible viable states. If this argument or calculation is correct, not all nationalisms can be satisfied, at any rate not at the same time. The satisfaction of some spells the frustration of others. This argument is furthered and immeasurably strengthened by the fact that very many of the potential nations of this world live, or until recently have lived, not in compact territorial units but intermixed with each other in complex patterns. It follows that a territorial political unit can only become ethnically homogenous, in such cases if it either kills, or expels, or assimilates all non-nationals. (Gellner, 1983, p. 2)

With arch understatement, Gellner concludes that the unwillingness of people to suffer such fates 'may make the implementation of the nationalist principle difficult'. Thus, to say that the normative nationalist principle must be rejected because it is too *impractical* or *economically costly* would be grossly misleading. It ought to be abandoned because the *moral costs*, of even attempting to implement it would be prohibitive.

It is important to see that this criticism of the principle of self-determination is decisive *only* against the strong version of that principle that makes it equivalent to the normative nationalist principle, which states that each people (or ethnic group) is to have its own fully sovereign state. For the objection focuses on the unacceptable implications of granting a right of self-determination to all 'peoples' *on the assumption that self-determination means complete political independence, that is, full sovereignty.*

However, as we have already suggested, the notion of self-determination is vague or, rather, multiply ambiguous, inasmuch as there are numerous forms and a range of degrees of political independence or autonomy that a group might attain. Instead of asserting an ambiguous *right* to self-determination, it might be better to acknowledge that many if not most groups have a *legitimate interest* in self-determination and that this interest can best be served in different circumstances by a range of more specific rights or combinations of rights, including a number of distinct group rights to varying forms and degrees of political autonomy, with the right to secede being only the most extreme of these.

I have argued elsewhere that there is a moral right to secede, though it is a highly qualified, limited right. It is not a right which all 'peoples' or ethnic or cultural groups have simply by virtue of their being distinct groups. Instead, only those groups whose predicament satisfies the conditions laid out in any of several sound justifications for secession have this right. In this sense the right to secede, as I conceive it, is not a general right of groups, but rather a special or selective right that obtains only under certain conditions (Buchanan, 1991, pp. 151–62).

Among the strongest justifications that can be given for the claim that a group has a right to secede under certain circumstances are (1) the argument from the rectification of past unjust takings; (2) the self-defence argument; and (3) the argument from discriminatory redistribution (Buchanan, 1991, pp. 27–81). Since secession involves the taking of territory, not just the severing of bonds of political obligation, each prosecession argument must be construed as including the establishment of a valid claim to the territory on the part of the seceding group.

Rectifying past unjust takings

This first justification is the simplest and most intuitively appealing argument for secession. It has obvious application to many actual secessionist movements, including some of those which completed the dissolution of the Soviet Union. The claim is that a region has a right to secede if it was unjustly incorporated into the larger unit from which its members seek to separate.

The argument's power stems from the assumption that secession is simply the reappropriation, by the legitimate owner, of stolen property. The right to secede, under these circumstances, is just the right to reclaim what is one's own. This simple interpretation is most plausible, of course, in situations in which the people attempting to secede are literally the same people who held legitimate title to the territory at the time of the unjust annexation, or at least are the indisputable descendants of those people (their legitimate political heirs, so to speak). But matters are considerably more complex if the seceding group is not closely or clearly related to the group whose territory was unjustly taken, or if the group that was wrongly dispossessed did not itself have clear, unambiguous title to it. But at least in the paradigm case, the argument from rectificatory justice is a convincing argument for a moral right to secede. The right of the Baltic Republics to secede from the Soviet Union, which forcibly and unjustly annexed them in 1940, is well supported by this first justification.

It is one thing to say that a group has the right to secede because in so doing they will simply be reclaiming what was unjustly taken from them. The *terms* of secession are another question. In some cases secession will adversely affect individuals who had no part in the unjust acquisition of the territory. Whether, or under what conditions, they are owed compensation or other special consideration is a complex matter (Buchanan, 1991, pp. 87–91).

The self-defence argument

The common law, common-sense morality and the great majority of ethical systems, religious and secular, acknowledge a right of self-defence against an aggressor who threatens lethal force. For good reason this is not thought to be an unlimited right. Among the more obvious restrictions on it are (1) that only that degree of force necessary to avert the threat be used, and (2) that the attack against which one defends oneself not be provoked by one's own actions. If such restrictions are acknowledged, the assertion that there is a right of self-defence is highly plausible. Each of these restrictions is pertinent to the right of groups to defend themselves. There are two quite different types of situations in which a group might invoke the right of self-defence to justify secession.

In the first, a group wishes to secede from a state in order to protect its members from extermination by that state itself. Under such conditions the group may either attempt to overthrow the government, that is, to engage in revolution; or, if strategy requires it, the group may secede in order to organize a defensible territory, forcibly appropriating the needed territory from the aggressor, creating the political and military machinery required for its survival, and seeking recognition and aid from other sovereign states and international bodies. Whatever moral title to the seceding territory the aggressor state previously held is *invalidated* by the gross injustice of its genocidal efforts. Or, at the very least, we can say that whatever legitimate claims to the seceding territory the state had are *outweighed* by the claims of its innocent victims. We may think of the aggressor's right to the territory, in the former case, as dissolving in the acid of his own iniquities, and, in the latter, as being pushed down in the scales of the balance by the greater weight of the victim's right of self-defence. Whether we say that the evil state's right to territory is invalidated (and disappears entirely) or merely is outweighed, it is clear enough that in these circumstances its claim to the territory should not be an insurmountable bar to the victim group's seceding, if this is the only way to avoid its wrongful destruction. Unfortunately, this type of case is far from fanciful. One of the strongest arguments for recognizing an independent Kurdish state, for example, is that only this status, with the control over territory it includes, will ensure the survival of this group in the face of genocidal threats from Turkey, Iran and Iraq.

There is a second situation in which secessionists might invoke the right of self-defence, but in a more controversial manner. They could argue that in order to defend itself against a lethal aggressor a group may secede from a state that is not itself that aggressor. This amounts to the claim that the need to defend itself against genocide can *generate* a claim to territory of sufficient moral weight to override the claims of those who until now held valid title to it and who, unlike the aggressor in the first version of the argument, have not forfeited their claim to it by lethal aggression.

Suppose the year is 1939. Germany has inaugurated a policy of genocide against the Jews. Jewish pleas to the democracies for protection have fallen on deaf ears (in part because the Jews are not regarded as a *nation* – nationhood carrying a strong presumption of territory, which they do not possess). Leaders of Jewish populations in Germany, Eastern Europe and the Soviet Union agree that the only hope for the survival of their people is to create a Jewish state, a sovereign territory to serve as a last refuge for European Jewry. Suppose further that the logical choice for its location – the only choice with the prospect of any success in saving large numbers of Jews – is a portion of Poland. Polish Jews, who are not being protected from the Nazis by the government of Poland, therefore occupy a portion of Poland and invite other Jews to join them there in a Jewish sanctuary state. They do not expel non-Jewish Poles who already reside in that area but, instead, treat them as equal citizens. (From 1941 until 1945 something like this actually occurred on a smaller scale. Jewish partisans, who proved to be heroic and ferocious fighters, occupied and defended an area in the forests of Poland, in effect creating their own mini-state, for purposes of defending themselves and others from annihilation by the Germans.)

The force of this second application of the self-defence argument derives in part from the assumption that the Polish Jews who create the sanctuary state *are not being protected by their own state, Poland*. The idea is that a *state's authority over territory is based at least in part in its providing protection to all its citizens* – and that its retaining that authority is conditional on its continuing to do so. In the circumstances described, the Polish state is not providing protection to its Jewish citizens, and this fact voids the state's title to the territory in question. The Jews may rightly claim the territory, if doing so is necessary for their protection against extermination.

Escaping discriminatory redistribution

The idea here is that a group may secede if this is the only way for them to escape discriminatory redistribution. Discriminatory redistribution, also called regional exploitation and internal colonization, occurs whenever the state implements economic policies that systematically work to the disadvantage of some groups, while benefiting others, in morally arbitrary ways. A clear example of discriminatory redistribution would be the state imposing higher taxes on one group while spending less on it, or placing economic restrictions on one region, without any sound moral justification for this unequal treatment.

Charges of discriminatory redistribution abound in actual secessionist movements. Indeed, it would be hard to find cases in which this charge does not play a central role in justifications for secession, even though other reasons are often given as well. Here are only a few illustrations):

1 American Southerners complained that the federal tariff laws were discriminatory in intent and effect – that they served to foster the growth of infant industries in the North by protecting them from European and especially British competition, at the expense of the South's import-dependent economy. The Southern statesman John C. Calhoun and others argued that the amount of money the South was contributing to the federal government, once the effects of the tariff were taken into account, far exceeded what that region was receiving from it.

2 Basque secessionists have noted that the percentage of total tax revenues in Spain paid by those in their region is more than three times the percentage of state expenditures there (a popular Basque protest song expresses this point vividly, saying that 'the cow of the state has its mouth in the Basque country but its udder elsewhere') (Horowitz, 1985, pp. 249–54).

3 Biafra, which unsuccessfully attempted to become independent from Nigeria in 1967, while containing only 22 per cent of the Nigerian population, contributed 38 per cent of total revenues, and received back from the government only 14 per cent of those revenues (Nwanko and Ifejika, 1970, p. 229).

4 Secessionists in the Baltic Republics and in Soviet Central Asia protested that the government in Moscow for many years implemented economic policies that benefited the rest of the country at the expense of staggering environmental damage in their regions. To support this allegation of discriminatory redistribution, they cited reports of abnormally high rates of birth defects in Estonia, Latvia and Lithuania, apparently due to chemical pollutants from the heavy industry which Soviet economic policy concentrated there, and contamination of ground water in Central Asia due to massive use of pesticides and herbicides at the order of planners in Moscow whose goal it was to make that area a major cotton producer.

An implicit premiss of the argument from discriminatory redistribution is that *failure to satisfy this fundamental condition of non-discrimination voids the state's claim to the territory in which the victims reside*, whereas the fact that they have no other recourse to avoid this fundamental injustice *gives them a valid title to it*. This premiss forges the needed connection between the grounds for seceding (discriminatory redistribution) and the territorial claim that every sound justification for secession must include (since secession involves the taking of territory). One good reason for accepting this premiss is that it explains our intuitions about the justifiability of secession in certain central and relatively uncontroversial cases.

In other words, unless this premiss is acceptable, the argument from discriminatory redistribution is not sound; and unless the argument from discriminatory redistribution is sound, it is hard to see how secession is justifiable in certain cases in which there is widespread agreement that it is justified. Consider, for example, the secession of the thirteen American Colonies from the British Empire. (Strictly speaking this was secession, not revolution. The aim of the American colonists was not to overthrow the British government, but only to remove a part of the North American territory from the Empire.) The chief justification for American independence was discriminatory redistribution: Britain's mercantilist policies systematically worked to the disadvantage of the colonies for the benefit of the mother country. Lacking representation in the British Parliament, the colonists reasonably concluded that this injustice would persist. It seems, then, that if the American 'Revolution' was justified, then there are cases in which the state's persistence in the injustice of discriminatory redistribution, together with the lack of alternatives to secession for remedying it, *generates* a valid claim to territory on the part of the secessionists.

The force of the argument from discriminatory redistribution does not rest solely, however, on brute moral intuitions about particular cases such as that of American independence. We can *explain* our responses to such cases by a simple but powerful principle: the legitimacy of the state – including its rightful jurisdiction over territory – depends upon its providing a framework for co-operation that does not systematically discriminate against any group.

The self-defence argument and the argument from discriminatory redistribution share an underlying assumption, namely, that the justification for a state's control over territory is at least in part *functional*. Generally speaking, what entitles a state to exercise exclusive jurisdiction ('territorial sovereignty') over a territory is the state's provision of a regime that enforces basic rights in a nondiscriminatory way. If the state fails to fulfil these legitimating jurisdictional functions with respect to a group, and if there is no other way for the group to protect itself from the ensuing injustices, then it can rightfully claim the jurisdictional authority for itself.

Attempts to justify secession on grounds of discriminatory redistribution are more complicated than might first appear. The mere fact that there is a net flow of revenue out of one region does not show that discriminatory redistribution is occurring. Instead, the state may simply be implementing policies designed to satisfy the demands of *distributive justice*. (Theories of distributive justice attempt to formulate and defend principles that specify the proper distribution of the burdens and benefits of social co-operation.) The problem is that distributive justice is a highly controversial matter and that different theories will yield different and in some cases directly opposing assessments of distributive patterns across regions of a country. A policy which redistributes wealth from one region to others may be a case of discriminatory redistribution according to one theory of distributive justice, but a case of just redistribution according to another. Even if there is fairly widespread agreement that the better-off owe *something* to the worse-off, there can be and is disagreement as to *how much* is owed. To this extent, the theory of secession is derivative upon the theory of distributive justice and subject to its uncertainties.

Justifications for forcible resistance to secession

An adequate moral theory of secession must consider not only arguments to justify secession but justifications for resisting it as well. Here I will concentrate on only two of the more influential and plausible of the latter (Buchanan, 1991, pp. 87–125).

Avoiding anarchy

From Lincoln to Gorbachev, leaders of states have opposed secession, warning that recognition of a right to secede would result in chaos. The *reductio ad absurdum* of the right to secede is the prospect of the most extreme anarchy: not every man's home his castle; rather, every man's yard his country. Even if political fragmentation stops short of this, recognition of a right to secede is likely to produce more fragmentation than is tolerable.

This argument would be much more plausible if recognizing a right to secede meant recognizing an *unlimited* right to secede. But as we have argued, the right to secede is a special or selective right that exists only when one or more of a limited set of justifying conditions is satisfied; it is not a general right of all peoples. Nor, as we have also seen, can it reasonably be understood to be included in or derivable from an alleged right of all peoples to self-determination. At most, the threat of anarchy could create a rebuttable presumption against secession, so that secessionists would, generally speaking, have to make a case for seceding.

The theory of the right to secede sketched above can be seen as including such a presumption: a sound justification for secession is to include a justification for the secessionists' claim to the territory. In a sense, this requirement constitutes a presumption in favour of the status quo and to that extent addresses the worry about anarchy. And since, as I have also noted, secession involves not only the severing of bonds of political obligation but also the taking of territory, this requirement seems reasonable.

Some might argue that by requiring secessionists to offer grounds for their claim to the territory, the theory proposed here stacks the deck against them (Kymlicka, 1992). Especially from the standpoint of liberal political philosophy, which prizes liberty and self-determination, why should there not be a presumption that secession is justified, or at the very least, why should not secessionists and anti-secessionists start out on level ground in the process of justification?

There are, I believe, two sound reasons for a presumption that secessionists must make a case for taking the territory. First, a moral theory of secession should be viewed as a branch of *institutional ethics.* One relevant consideration for evaluating proposed principles for institutional ethics is the consequences of their general acceptance. So long as it is recognized that the presumption against secession can be rebutted by any of the arguments stated above in favour of a right to secede, such a presumption seems superior to the alternatives. Given the gravity of secession – and the predictable and unpredictable disruptions and violence which it may produce – legitimate interests in the stability of the international order speak in favour of the presumption.

Another consideration in favour of assigning the burden of argument where I have is that such a presumption – which gives some weight to the status quo – is much more likely to contribute to general acceptance of a right to secede in the international community. Other things being equal, a moral theory which is more likely to gain acceptance is to be preferred, especially if it is a theory of how institutions, in this case, the institutions of international law and diplomacy, ought to operate. It is often remarked that the one principle of international law that has gained almost universal acceptance is a strong presumption against violations of the territorial integrity of existing states. Requiring that secessionists be able to justify secession and in such a way as to establish their claim to the territory in question, serves to give appropriate weight to this fundamental principle, while at the same time recognizing that the state's claim to control over its territory is not absolute and can be overridden under certain conditions.

Avoiding strategic bargaining that undermines majority rule

It could be argued that if the right to secede is recognized, then a minority may use the threat of secession to undermine majority rule. In conditions in which the majority views secession a prohibitive cost, a group's threat to secede can function as a veto over the majority's decisions. Consideration of this risk might lead one to conclude that the only adequate way to protect democracy is to refuse to acknowledge a right to secede.

However, as we have seen, there can be compelling justifications for secession under certain conditions. Accordingly, a more appropriate response than denying the right to secede is to devise constitutional mechanisms or processes of international law that give some weight both to legitimate interests in secession and to the equally legitimate interest in preserving the integrity of majority rule (and in political stability). The most obvious way to do this would be to allow secession under certain circumstances, but to minimize the risk of strategic bargaining with the threat of secession by erecting inconvenient but surmountable procedural hurdles to secession. For example a constitution might recognize a right to secede, but require a strong majority – say three-quarters – of those in the potentially seceding area to endorse secession in a referendum. This type of hurdle is the analogue of an obstacle to constitutional amendment which the US Constitution's Amendment Clause itself establishes: any proposed amendment must receive a two-thirds vote in Congress and be ratified by three-quarters of the states.

The purpose of allowing amendment while erecting these two strong (that is, non-simple) majority requirements is to strike an appropriate balance between two legitimate interests: the interest in providing flexibility for needed change and the interest in securing stability. Similarly, the point of erecting inconvenient but surmountable barriers to secession (either in a constitution or in international law) would be not to make secession impossible but to avoid making it too easy. A second approach would be to levy special exit costs, a secession tax (Buchanan, 1991). Once these possibilities are recognized, the objection that acknowledgment of a right to secede necessarily undermines democracy is seen to be less than compelling.

Secession and the problem of group conflict in the modern state

Secession is only the most extreme – and in some cases the least desirable – response to problems of group conflict. A comprehensive moral theory of international relations would include an account of the scope and limits of the right to secede; but it would also formulate and support principles to guide the establishment of a wider range of rights of self-determination. Such a theory, if it gained wide acceptance, would undoubtedly produce fundamental changes in our conceptions of the state, of sovereignty, and of the basic categories of international law.

See also 4 SOCIOLOGY; 5 ECONOMICS; 6 POLITICAL SCIENCE; 7 LEGAL STUDIES; 8 ANARCHISM; 9 CONSERVATISM; 13 SOCIALISM; 14 AUTONOMY; 15 COMMUNITY; 19 DEMOCRACY; 21 DISCOURSE; 22 DISTRIBUTIVE JUSTICE; 26 FEDERALISM; 27 INTERNATIONAL AFFAIRS; 28 LEGITIMACY; 29 LIBERTY; 30 POWER; 31 PROPERTY; 33 RIGHTS; 35 SOCIOBIOLOGY; 36 STATE, 37 TOLERATION AND FUNDAMENTALISM

References

Buchanan, A.: *Secession: The Morality of Political Divorce: From Fort Sumter to Lithuania and Quebec* (Boulder, Colo.: Westview Press, 1991).

Gellner, E.: *Nations and Nationalism* (Oxford: Blackwell, 1983).

Hannum, H.: *Autonomy, Sovereignty, and Self-Determination* (Philadelphia: University of Pennsylvania Press, 1990).

Horowitz, D.: *Ethnic Groups in Conflict* (Berkeley: University of California Press, 1985).

Kymlicka, W.: 'Review of *Secession: The Morality of Political Divorce: From Fort Sumter to Lithuania and Quebec*', *Political Theory*, 20 (1992), 527–32.

McCallum, G. C.: *Political Philosophy* (Englewood Cliffs, NJ: Prentice-Hall, 1987).

Nwanko, A. and Ifejika, S.: *The Making of a Nation: Biafra* (London: C. Hurst and Co., 1970).

Quebec, Province of: *James Bay and Northern Quebec Agreement and Complementary Agreements* (Quebec: Les Publications du Québec, 1991).

Williams, R. A., Jr: *The American Indian in Western Legal Thought: The Discourses of Conquest* (New York: Oxford University Press, 1990).

Further reading

Barry, B.: 'Self-government revisited', *The Nature of Political Theory*, ed. D. Miller and L. Siedentop (Oxford: Clarendon Press, 1983), pp. 121–55.

Buchheit, L. C.: *Secession: The Legitimacy of Self-Determination* (New Haven, Conn.: Yale University Press, 1978).

Cobban, A.: *The Nation State and National Self-Determination* (New York: Thomas Y. Crowell Co., 1970).

Held, V., Morgenbesser, S. and Nagel, T., eds: *Philosophy, Morality and International Affairs* (New York: Oxford University Press, 1974).

Johnson, H. S.: *Self-Determination Within the Community of Nations* (Leyden: A. W. Sijthoff, 1967).

Kamenka, E.: *Nationalism: The Nature and Evolution of an Idea* (Canberra: Australian National University Press, 1973).

Kohn, H.: *The Idea of Nationalism: A Study in Its Origins and Background* (New York: Macmillan, 1944).

Margalit, A. and Raz, J.: 'National self-determination', *Journal of Philosophy*, 87 (1990), 439–63.

Plamenatz, J.: *On Alien Rule and Self-Government* (London: Longman, 1960).

Rigo Sureda, A.: *The Evolution of the Right of Self-Determination* (Leiden: A. W. Sijthoff, 1973).

Ronen, D.: *The Quest for Self-Determination* (New Haven, Conn.: Yale University Press, 1979).

Seton-Watson, H.: *Nations and States: An Enquiry into the Origins of Nations and the Politics of Nationalism* (Boulder, Colo.: Westview Press, 1977).

Tivey, L.: *The Nation-State: The Formation of Modern Politics* (Oxford: Martin Robertson, 1981).

Umozurike, U. O.: *Self-Determination in International Law* (Hamden, Conn.: Archon Book, 1972).

35

Sociobiology

ALLAN GIBBARD

Politics is a part of human life, and biology is the study of life. All political beings are biological organisms. These are truisms, but they might suggest lines of investigation. Sociobiology, the name suggests, means social theory taken as a branch of the life sciences. Human sociobiology, then, would apply biological theory to human society. How might this be done?

Living things appear unmistakably to be designed, with miraculous cunning and intricacy. Darwin explained this appearance away: it results from a long, blind process of heritable variation and natural selection. Natural selection mimics design: it will look as if each organism were crafted to promote the representation of its own genes in distant generations. Fancifully, a person is his genes' way of making more of themselves.

How might this bear on human society and politics? A sociobiologist's picture might be this. Social science is an ecology of micromotives; societies consist in the interactions of individuals, their mutual influences (Schelling, 1978). Social facts emerge much as they do with economists' stories of the invisible hand. Men pursue each their own advantage, go the stories, but the amazing result – in the more cheery models – is that society is led, as if by an invisible hand, to satisfy individual wants with Pareto efficiency. Now economists are right to construct such 'micro-theories', a sociobiologist might say: social facts emerge from individual motivations in interaction, and they may emerge surprisingly. Explanations of a practice in terms, say, of its social function, or of a group's collective interests, will stand in need of underlying mechanisms. Economists are wrong, though, if they believe their models too fully, if they claim that a Hobbesian rational egoism gives the full story of human motivation. Social theory needs a more adequate individual psychology – and Darwin might help us find one.

The job of evolutionary theory in this programme, then, will be to suggest promising psychological hypotheses, by explaining how the human psychic makeup came to be what it is. Just as natural selection shaped our anatomy, it shaped our behaviour. Or to speak a little more exactly: nurture as well as nature affects gross anatomy, and it vastly affects behaviour. What our genes gave us was not behaviours, but native propensities to behaviour – perhaps amazingly complex and layered propensities. That genes matter is obvious: even such a close genetic relative as a chimpanzee, raised as you were, would behave quite differently. Environment matters too, though, and vastly. If you are male, we can tell you this: if you had lived your whole life in certain environments, you not only would be illiterate and have a fine head for proverbs; you would glory in taking human heads as trophies. What our genes might give us is intricate ways for our psychic development to respond to various features of our environments. Genes will code for conditional rules; they may say to develop one way, psychically, if given one set of cues, and other ways if given other cues. Incredibly complex interactions of genes with environment will lead to our feelings, thoughts and actions being what they are.

Human sociobiology has spurred wild controversies. Eminent population geneticists write books with titles like *Not in Our Genes* (Lewontin, Rose and Kamin, 1984), and a major philosopher of science calls his book on the subject *Vaulting Ambition* (Kitcher, 1985). E. O. Wilson, who coined the term with his book *Sociobiology* (1975), was attacked as joining a long line of biological determinists. 'The reason for the survival of these recurrent determinist theories is that they consistently tend to provide a genetic justification of the status quo and of existing privileges for certain groups according to class, race or sex' (Allen et al., 1975).

Attacks on 'sociobiology' as a whole, though, would seem misdirected – at least as I have defined the term. At their broadest, the attacks should be on particular schools or programmes. The term itself may be what misleads us. Many sociobiologists reject it, or use it to apply to whatever they think Wilson did wrong (Wilson, 1975; 1978; cf. Kitcher, 1985, on 'pop sociobiology'). I myself include as sociobiology any treatment of social phenomena that draws crucially on neo-Darwinian theory. With the term used in this way, it is easy to see how to oppose particular instances or kinds of sociobiology, but hard to see why one should oppose human sociobiology in general. Is the human native makeup not a result of genetic evolution? Is good evolutionary thinking about the human psyche beyond our capacity, or too dangerous even to attempt? Social thought is difficult in general and fraught with dangers, and questions of evidential support always need careful scrutiny. Clearly, though, none of this would justify a blanket moratorium on social thought – and as we think, why renounce the Darwinian framework that so richly explains how species get their characteristics?

Altruism

What, then, might evolution tell us of human motivation? Darwin threatens a paradox. We see human beings, at times, constraining their actions by the requirements of morality. Sometimes people act to help others. Whether any but self-interested actions are to be found in us has long been debated, but we do seem to find such actions – not often enough, but at times. Yet if our genes single-mindedly programme us to reproduce them, how would altruism be possible? Will one person's genes help another's reproduce? This is the sociobiological paradox of altruism.

One response is that altruism benefits the species or the group. The current wave of sociobiology started with a vigorous critique of such species and group selectionism (Williams, 1966). A gene that enhances one's group's reproduction at the expense of one's own, goes the critique, will be a loser: as the group gets bigger, the gene will become less and less common within the group. Vigorous modelling and debates over group selection have ensued, but the prevailing view is that group selection could be rare at best. It arises only in extreme conditions – and so we should look elsewhere to explain human altruism.

One prime suspect must be *kin-selection*. Roughly half my genes I share with my full-sister. My genes can reproduce by helping hers to reproduce: genetically speaking, two full nieces are on average worth a daughter. This lore is attributed to J. B. S. Haldane, and Hamilton (1964) worked out a full mathematical model for it. Natural selection promotes not individual fitness but *inclusive* fitness: not just having grandchildren, but also having great nephews and nieces and the like, each weighted by the proportion of one's genes they carry. Dawkins (1976) proposes it is the genes we should think of as selfish – figuratively. Genes could promote their reproduction in close kin by coding for altruistic motivations.

Much apparent altruism, though, is not directed at close kin. One explanation could be that modern conditions are evolutionarily novel, so that now we respond to non-kin as we were designed to respond to kin. This can't be the full story, though. In tribal societies, social co-operation is likely to be organized along kin lines, but co-operating relatives may be fairly distant genetically. Trivers (1971) initiated discussions of 'reciprocal altruism', dispositions, in effect, to trade benefits. Some altruistic propensities may have been selected for because they elicit reciprocal benefits. (See Frank's (1988) treatment of moral emotions.) Trivers has spurred much science, and also speculation by philosophers. Schelling, in his famous game-theoretic treatment of rational bargaining (1960, ch. 2), had stressed that reciprocity – even mutual restraint in hostilities – requires co-ordinated expectations on the terms of trade. Maynard Smith (1974; 1982) applied an evolutionary analogue of game theory to animal conflicts, and developed the concept of an *evolutionarily stable strategy* (or *ESS*). This is roughly an assignment of strategies to organisms such that each, given the strategies of the others, is doing as well reproductively as possible. (An ESS is much like a 'Nash equilibrium' in game theory.) In Schelling's sense, ESS's are co-ordinated. Rawls treats common standards of justice as producing such co-ordination, and suggests that natural selection would favour 'the capacity to follow the principles of justice and natural duty in relations between groups and individuals other than kin' (1971, p. 504). 'The system of the moral feelings', he adds, might evolve 'as stabilizing mechanisms for just schemes'. By 'the principles of justice' Rawls means his own Two Principles, and so he seems to be picturing human standards of justice as 'wired in' as a biological adaptation. Gibbard (1981) speculates that standards of justice might instead emerge in discussion, so that the adaptations involved are propensities to engage in discussion in certain ways and to be motivated by the results. He proposes this (1990) as an account of what is going on with normative judgment in general: we are adapted to attain a special kind of psychic state he calls 'accepting a norm'. Propensities to engage in 'normative discussion' coordinate the norms people accept, and 'normative governance' – a tendency to act on the norms one accepts – leads to coordinated action. These combined propensities constitute an ESS, and thus solve a kind of evolutionary bargaining problem.

In such treatments, it is crucial to distinguish an individual's goals, concerns, and benefits from the the figurative aims of the genes. A person may, for instance, care strongly about not being cheated, and be motivated accordingly. The evolutist's question is then: how did he come to have this concern? Why does he have a genetic makeup such that, given his lifetime environment, he cares strongly about not being cheated? Many kinds of answers are possible, but one might be that this is the work of a biological adaptation. It is a matter of special genetic 'design' to have such motivations in such circumstances. That is to say, extant people are genetically disposed towards having such motivations in such circumstances, because those members of the ancestral population who did tended to be the ones who reproduced. The features of this genetic programme that promoted reproduction then constitute the figurative aims of one's genes: the *biological function* of the feature they code for.

Adaptive contingency plans

Sociobiologists are often accused of genetic determinism. Now if genetic determinism means that genes matter for behaviour, the thesis seems hard to reject. Dogs act differently from humans, and this is not just a matter of different environments. If, on the other hand, genetic determinism means that genes settle behaviour independently of environment, then it is biological nonsense. Genes programme organisms to reproduce, and reproduction will often require being responsive to features of the environment. What we can expect from genes is contingency plans: psychic mechanisms that respond to different environmental histories with different motivations. The sociobiologist's problem is to identify what these adaptive contingency plans are.

Are there genes for behaviour then? The development of a psychic mechanism might be programmed by hundreds of genes, but a genetic programme develops by the selection of a gene at each locus. If a gene is part of the programme because of selection pressures that worked through behaviour, then it follows that in some ancestral environment, the gene made a difference to what organisms did. In this sense, we can well expect that there are genes for behaviour (Tooby and Cosmides, 1990, p. 44).

This in no way means that when people behave differently, it must be because their genes differ. Genes govern not so much behaviour directly, but the ways behaviour will respond to certain features of the environment. Still, geneticists devote great efforts to finding what individual differences are 'heritable' – and it is easy to confuse genetic 'heritability' with adaptation. The two are quite different, it could hardly be overstressed. With human beings, walking erect is an adaptation, but it is not heritable in the geneticist's sense. Adaptation is a matter of history: does the propensity to a behaviour result from genetic programming in response to selection pressures that favoured that very propensity? With walking erect, the answer must be yes – perhaps because of the advantages of having one's hands free. Genetic heritability is a matter of current population: to what extent are observed differences between people in current environments – psychic and behavioural differences, for example – a result of current genetic differences. Bipedal motion is not heritable; crawling doesn't run in the family for adults. Adaptations like walking erect are a result of heritability only in the past: in an ancestral population, different genes made for different tendencies to walk erect – and the genes that made for walking erect did better. Long ago, though, the genes came to fixation. Adaptations are not heritable for long; they win out (Tooby and Cosmides, 1990, pp. 37–9).

The crucial questions, then, are what adaptations all human beings share, and how these adaptations figure in human life and societies. How should these questions be studied? Some researchers seem to hypothesize that people act in general to promote their inclusive fitness. A research programme would follow: to investigate, in a variety of early circumstances, whether striking behaviours indeed do promote agents' inclusive fitness, and how. Dickemann (1979), for instance, wrote of a group of nineteenth-century Brahmins in India who killed all their newborn daughters. This, she argued, promoted their inclusive fitness.

This hypothesis, though, even if true, would not explain Dickemann's fascinating data. Evolution tells us to expect not some general tendency to spread one's genes, but specific adaptive mechanisms: ones that worked to enhance individual reproduction in the circumstances of our proto-human hunting-gathering ancestors (Symons, 1987). Reproduction even in primitive human social circumstances will pose incredibly complex problems. There could be no tractable general way to maximize it. Evolution would have to select for specific psychic stratagems that tended to work on the whole – what computer scientists call 'heuristics' (Nisbett and Ross, 1980). Evolutionists studying the beasts, to be sure, can often postpone asking about mechanisms, if the current environment is relevantly like the ancestral one. Modern human beings, though – even primitive horticulturalists – live in social environments sharply different from those of our distant ancestors. We are adapted to reproduce in hunting-gathering groups, and so human sociobiologists cannot expect that we will always reproduce well in current social circumstances. (Note the low current fitness, or 'reproductive success', of European populations in various parts of the world.)

Human ecology

We should picture psychic mechanisms, then, as rough stratagems that genes found in long ago times for enhancing their reproduction. This leads to a Darwinian human ecology. Human genetic evolution always proceeded in social and cultural settings. Human genes and hunting-gathering cultures coevolved. As a result, we appear intricately – though imperfectly – designed to reproduce in the complex cultural surroundings of our increasingly human ancestors. At the same time, their emerging cultural life was a matter of the interactions and mutual influences of genetic products of this design.

How, though, can we study long-ago cultures that rarely left even fossils? We can look to current hunter-gatherers, but they are peoples who have been pushed to the parts of the earth no one else wanted, and they interact with surrounding horticulturalists. We don't know, then, how much their lives tell us of life when hunter-gatherers had the run of the earth.

We get some hints of the possibilities, though, by constructing simple mathematical models. We can model gene-culture coevolution, and check the results against current human beings. Boyd and Richerson (1985) make a major start on such a programme. They study, among other things, the reproductive advantages of emulating role models. In complex social circumstances, no practicable mechanism could compute directly what modes of life will work best reproductively. Imitation may be the best stratagem. The best way might even be to emulate someone's mode of life indiscriminately, even if some aspects of the target life do not in fact enhance the reproductive prospects of anyone. It may be too hard to fathom which aspects of a way of life do the work of promoting reproductive prospects. Think of such emulation not as a thought out plan, but figuratively as a scheme of the genes.

What sorts of mechanisms could genes code for to enhance reproductive prospects through such emulation? First, mechanisms would have to select whom to emulate. The selection must be astute: adopting the wrong role model can shatter one's reproductive prospects instead of enhancing them. The mechanisms, then, must respond to observable features of candidates for emulation. These should be features that, in ancestral environments, were good proxies for reproductive success. A good role model (from the genes' point of view) has two virtues: good reproductive prospects and successful emulability – relevance, that is, to oneself. Portents of reproductive success might include signs of admiration, or wealth or domination. Indications of successful emulability might include badges of membership in one's own social group: being a family member or family friend, or having the same style of talk, dress, and the like as do family and friends. This picture suggests, then, why we might be equipped to find style of life so crucial.

When people interact, and each is equipped to select others as models for emulation, the emergent social effects can be remarkable. Boyd and Richerson (1985, ch. 8) model 'runaway' cultural processes; these bear analogy to the runaway sexual selection that population geneticists study – the kind that leads to peacocks' tails and the like. Such runaway culture could explain anthropologists' frequent talk of culture as detached from human genes. Taken at face value, such talk must be nonsense: it makes it sound as if human genetic adaptations don't matter for culture. It appeals to a false dichotomy between the genetic and the cultural – whereas genes will code for rules for responding to cultural cues. Taken more charitably, the claim might be that human genes code for one very general mechanism of cultural learning, such as Locke's *tabula rasa*, or an undifferentiated tendency to imitate others, or a broad tendency to do things that have been pleasantly reinforced. On this two things must be said. First, even broad tendencies like these would need far more specification, and specifying them would make it clear that even they require the human psyche to have a native structure. If we imitate others, then what if different people around us do different things? Do we average, or choose someone at random to emulate, or always choose our early nurturers, or what? We choose 'attractive' role models, it might be said – and so what makes us find them attractive? Second, indiscriminate absorption of culture seems a bad evolutionary plan. It has some advantage: if one emulates the living, one emulates a way of life that allowed survival, and if one emulates parents (or one's role models did), one emulates a mode of life that led to reproduction. Still, far better, from the genes' perspective, if one can latch onto cues that have gone – on the whole in ancestral environments – with emulation's leading to high reproduction. Boyd and Richerson's models show that our genes might code for refined propensities to select whom to emulate, and that still, the resulting interactions could lead to a dynamic of runaway culture.

Fallacies

It is pernicious to think that the natural must be good, or that it must be unavoidable. Everything that happens is natural, and much that happens is avoidable. Not all human biological adaptations are good. Man's bellicosity was noted long before Darwin, and it may involve biological adaptations. Warfare might even have been a prime force in the explosion of proto-human intelligence: for small human beings to hunt big game in a group takes intelligence, but enough might be enough: the game don't get smarter as the hunters do. In war, over the millennia, the enemy will get smarter as you do: he is of your species. Military and diplomatic guile could become objects of a genetic arms race (Alexander, 1979, pp. 211–33). Still, if men are adapted, given certain cues, to killing, looting, destruction and rapine, that doesn't make such things good.

Still, this scenario must be chilling: warfare, it suggests, may be very difficult to eliminate, and some rosy stories of what would end it are simplistic. We shouldn't, though, need evolution to see bellicosity as a terrifying problem – and nothing in such a story tells us that war and nuclear holocaust are inevitable. We know that many men go their whole lives without trying to kill. Sometimes too, though, peaceful neighbours quickly fall into murderous enmity, and this we must recognize as a part of our human predicament. It may that sad but true that men – adult males in particular, that is – are adapted to be killers given certain environmental cues (cf. Daly and Wilson, 1988). Our problem is to construct a world where no one receives those cues. Over substantial areas and periods, that has been done from time to time.

What, then, of sociobiology's political motivations? Racists, oppressors and others can travesty any material. We must oppose misuse, but it would be vain to seek a theory that could not be perverted. The bigger problem, though, may not be fanaticism but confusion. Some distortions will stem from political motivations, but a lot may result from the sheer difficulty of the subject.

Sociobiology must be a shaky basis for political thought; at best it is a group of infant research programmes. The alternatives too, though, are shaky. We should reject pseudo-scientific claims of sociobiologists, but not, say, to make way for a dogmatic Marxism, or for a hazy environmentalism. As for good old common sense, it leaves much in social life mysterious. Why do people marry at times, and at other times divorce? Why, in many places, do they now marry less and divorce more? Why do men sometimes support their children and sometimes leave them destitute? Why do some parents abuse their children and others not? Why do teens sometimes make such horrendous choices, and sometimes progress marvellously? Why are social groups sometimes well disposed to each other and sometimes at each others' throats? Common sense has things to say, of course: people marry because they fall in love, and they divorce because they can't stand each other. Why, though, do the same two people fall in love at one time and later find they cannot stand each other? Common sense needs help, and sociobiological considerations may suggest hypotheses. (See Kitcher, 1985, pp. 84–8, for what may be a rosier view of the explanatory powers of folk psychology.)

Sociobiologists have been attacked for the sins of 'adaptationism' and 'Panglossianism': thinking that all important features of organisms are adaptations, and that organisms are somehow designed for the best (Gould and Lewontin, 1979). An adaptation is metaphorically an object of 'special design'; an artifact is a byproduct. Red blood is an artifact; the selection that made blood red was for oxygen transport. Reading is an artifact. Biologists are at pains to distinguish ways in which a feature can be an evolutionary artifact: pleiotropy, linkage and genetic drift, and others (Kitcher, 1985, p. 57). The evolution of the human mind, moreover, has had to work within a mammalian and ape-like *Bauplan* (Gould and Lewontin, 1979). Our species was cobbled together from apes in an evolutionary twinkling, and the job must have been rough.

Still, where we find strong evidence of special design, we should expect adaptation. Fish gotta swim and birds gotta fly, and we don't have to wait to learn if wings are adaptations. The best sociobiological work is at pains to distinguish adaptations from evolutionary artifacts (Williams, 1966; Symons, 1979). Where selection pressures are strong we should expect adaptive shaping. A propensity to rush into battle, say, clearly matters to reproduction, and we must ask why selection pressures did not eliminate any such tendency. Sociobiologists should be cautioned but not cowed. (See Dawkins, 1982, ch. 3.)

Group differences

Sociobiology, I have stressed, should focus on features of genetic design that all people share. Still, human differences figure greatly in our lives and our thoughts, and they need discussion.

'Racial' groups differ in skin colour and hair texture, and individuals differ in height and eye colour. Men and women differ in their genitalia and in voice pitch. We accept that these differences are heritable. Sociobiology has been embraced by some as telling us that genetic group differences extend not only to qualities like these, but to qualities that bear on human worth, or on one's suitability for good jobs, political power and other routes to privilege. Many hope – or fear – that the evidence is plain, and suspect that the facts are being suppressed for fear of social consequences. Claims like these are explosive, as we all know, and it would be worth while trying to say explicitly why group differences threaten us in a way that individual differences do not.

Biological theory and scraps of evidence, though, now suggest that psychically, all ethnic groups are genetically pretty much alike. At times groups do differ hugely in performance, and old attempts to explain these differences have seemed hard to sustain – fuelling suspicion that racists have been on to something. New studies, though, offer a new kind of explanation: they begin to explain even gross differences in group performance as the upshot of adaptations all people share.

Group genetic differences are differences in frequency. No genes are present in what we think of as one racial group and absent in another. Still, where groups have long been separate and in different environments, selection pressures can make for sharp adaptive differences. Skin colour is the prime example: long tropical ancestry selects for genes for dark skin; long northern ancestry for genes for light skin. When groups from far parts of the world settle together, then at first certain heritable characteristics may distinguish them. Talk of 'race' then makes some local sense.

Still, the basic plan for all human beings is the same. There is no race with the heart on the right. Tooby and Cosmides (1990) argue from general biological considerations that the same must hold for the human mind: humanity enjoys a unified psychic design. The mind will be composed of genetically-coded 'organs', each in effect designed to solve a recurrent reproductive problem. Each organ's development will be coded for by hundreds or thousands of genes. Now in sexual reproduction, genes recombine, and if mother's and father's genes did not code for the same organs, the result would be chaos – and no grandchildren. Members of a species can mate to produce reproductive offspring, and so within a species, the design of organs must be universal. This includes psychic organs (Tooby and Cosmides, 1990, pp. 26–30).

There may nevertheless be individual variation in the detailed execution of the design. The genetic variability of individuals is vast: two neighbours will differ in a quarter of their protein codings. This genetic diversity is tied in with sexual reproduction, which reshuffles DNA. Sex has long been a biological puzzle, but a recent hypothesis is standing up well against evidence and modelling: that sex protects us from germs. Our parasites exploit our body chemistry to reproduce, and they reproduce many generations for each one of ours. They can adapt genetically to our body chemistry far more quickly than we can adapt genetically to resist them. If we and our neighbours were alike in our body chemistry, germs fit to infect one of us could easily infect us all. Nature's solution has been sex – or so goes this hypothesis. Sex makes each of us unique in detailed chemistry, even though we must be alike in functional organization. The effect of the pressure to diversify body chemistry is to vary, and even degrade, the execution of the universal human functional design in each individual. This could explain heritable variation among individuals in ethnically homogeneous communities (Tooby and Cosmides, 1990). (Whether heritable variability in important human capacities has been established at all is controversial; see Plomin and Daniels, 1987; Lewontin, Rose and Kamin, 1984, ch. 5.)

What, then, of ethnic groups? In the same population, 85 per cent of human genetic variance is within individuals and only 7 per cent between 'races' (Lewontin, Rose and Kamin, 1984, p. 126). Most genetic variability stems from selection pressures to differ chemically from one's neighbours; one does not often catch diseases from people across the sea. Still, this allows for some group differences, if they are adaptively neutral and adventitious. It allows too for genetically coded group differences that were adaptive for each group in its distinct circumstances. Might some such adaptive differences be psychic? Genes will not code for different functional architectures in different individuals – this we have already said. The highly general theory of Tooby and Cosmides, though, is inconclusive on whether there might be adaptive genetic differences among groups in psychic *parameters*: in matters of more or less that can vary separately, as skin colour does, without debilitation. A prime example might be thresholds for genetically programmed responses (Tooby and Cosmides, 1990, pp. 47–8).

Even group differences like these, however, could arise only in conditions that met strong demands. The environmental differences that make them adaptive must have endured for many generations – probably for scores at least – and there must be a tradeoff: different values of the parameter must have been more adaptive in different circumstances. Take 'native intelligence', if there is such a thing: in no environment will low intelligence be an advantage in itself. What, then, are the tradeoffs supposed to be? What advantages could be incompatible with intelligence, so that intelligence is traded off for them in certain environments? In this case, a good 'just so' story is hard to find.

A more promising genetic strategy would be to programme environmentally triggered 'switches' or contingency plans. These could respond to hints about what behavioural strategies would best work for reproduction in one's particular circumstances. Suffering violence in childhood, for instance, might be a good sign that one is in a social milieu where violence pays. We might, then, be programmed to lower our thresholds for violence if battered as children. Such a mechanism might help account for the finding that child abusers tend themselves to have been abused as children (Tooby and Cosmides, 1990, p. 54).

Reactive heritability

Environmentally triggered switches can make a trait technically 'heritable', even though differences in the trait are not themselves 'in the genes'. We might all be endowed, for instance, with a mechanism that sets one's level of brashness or timidity by assessing one's physical prowess, compared to those around one. Genes that coded for small size, relatively, would thus make for timidity, but indirectly. (The same genotype among pygmies would make for brashness.) Timidity, then, would be genetically 'heritable', but only because genes for size interact with a genetically coded parameter-setting mechanism for brashness/timidity that weaklings and hulks all share. This is called *reactive* heritability (Tooby and Cosmides, 1990, pp. 58–60).

Recent studies suggest that disturbing group psychic differences – the 'underclass' phenomena of low average measured IQ, poor average school performance, terrible rates of criminality, and the like – might stem from a combination of genetically programmed environmental switches and such reactive heritability. The directly heritable features would be skin colour and other salient marks of 'racial' appearance. These may, in special current environments, indirectly trigger switches that we all share, light and dark. Scarr and co-workers (1977) used blood samples from Philadelphia children classified as 'black' to estimate percentages of European and African ancestry. Skin colour varies somewhat independently of this percentage. Measures of intellectual skills, these researchers found, do correlate with skin colour, but not because skin colour correlates with African ancestry. Once they held skin colour constant, they found no correlation between intellectual skills and proportion of African ancestry. Some consequence of mere pigmentation was making the difference – indeed almost as big a difference as the measured socio-economic factors (Scarr et al., 1977, p. 176).

The 'underclass' pattern is found across the world, wherever there are caste-like minority groups (Ogbu, 1986, pp. 31–4). Even with racially similar groups like the Buraku minority and Ippan majority of Japan, minority IQ scores are roughly a standard deviation down from the majority – as with black Americans. The gap disappears among immigrants to America, where majority culture does not distinguish the two Japanese groups.

Claude Steele (1992) proposes a mechanism to explain these things: a *disidentification* with majority roles and values, in response to cues of stigma and group devaluation. We strive powerfully to protect our self-esteem, and self-conception fixes the realms of achievement to which self-esteem responds. When members of a group encounter signs of stigma, they may respond by transforming their self-conception and redirecting their self-esteem. One American study of black and white children in a classroom found this: whereas, on average, the blacks in this class had substantially lower grades than the whites, they had equal overall levels of self-esteem. Black children played down school and played up their skills in peer group relations (Hare and Castenell, 1985). They had rejected majority values and rendered their self-esteem impervious to their disastrous school performance. These are symptoms of disidentification with a majority role: the role of a good student with bright prospects. The tragedy extends to students at major American universities. Among black and white students with equal test scores on entry, black students get sharply lower grades, and drop out in far greater proportions. Indices of disidentification turn out to predict black students' grades better than do measures of ability and preparation. Disidentification is enforced as a group norm, with hard-studying blacks at one top university derided by other black students as 'incognegroes' (Steele, 1992).

What triggers this painful and self-thwarting disidentification? Steele's answer is that tying one's identity to school performance requires 'treatment as a valued person with good prospects'. Identification involves 'holding one's esteem at least partially accountable to achievement. And this requires believing that school achievement can be a promising basis of self-esteem'. Initially, he finds, teachers seem not to respond to 'black' students' academic talents, to demand and then praise intellectual performance. Steele does identify scattered programmes that succeed in treating deprived black students as valued people with good prospects. These programmes have had striking success: they spur achievement and allay any protective disidentification.

Mechanisms like these fit Tooby and Cosmides' talk of environmentally triggered adaptive 'switches', and they show the flip side of Boyd and Richerson's model of wholesale identification with role models. Among our ancestors it might have been adaptive to be extremely sensitive to cues as to which roles are emulable. Perhaps we are programmed to respond specially to cues of stigma: to cues that a role we might aspire to is 'not for the likes of you'. It could be adaptive to focus one's aspirations on models that are realistic for people of one's own group. Self-esteem is a chief spur to maintaining a role and achieving within it, and it could be highly adaptive to focus one's self-esteem on the qualities needed for attainable roles.

Sharp group differences in measured IQ and the like, then, may well be the upshot of biological adaptations we all share: environmentally triggered switches that determine whom one will emulate, and where one's self-esteem will be invested. In many cases, a strong element of reactive heritability is involved: for want of a light skin, say, IQ-test performance and much else may be lost.

Commentary

Most applications of sociobiology run aground on botched understandings, and so I have mostly been expounding the subject, not trying to apply it to political philosophy. Various writers have been searching for philosophical morals to be drawn from human sociobiology (see, for instance, Alexander, 1987; Gibbard, 1990; Murphy, 1982; Singer, 1981), but these attempts are at best newborn and struggling. We can say almost truistically that no *ought* comes from a biological *is* alone, and that we must not automatically celebrate the 'natural'. Truistically too, though, facts do bear on the oughts, and bear crucially. Methodologies like Rawls' (1971) 'wide reflective equilibrium' explicitly steer clear of delimiting in advance the ways they can bear.

Is there any upshot, then, for political philosophy? The most evident philosophical import comes where philosophy merges with political and social advocacy. Social engineering requires knowing one's materials, and the aim of human sociobiology is a good theory of human nature. Still, however secure Darwinism may be as a general account, specific claims – theories about the mechanisms of human motivation, fulfillment, and the like – must be taken with a grain of salt. It may be rash to stake a lot on some particular sociobiological account's being right.

Let me finish, nevertheless, with a capsule of broadly political commentary. The core of modern political theory has been a kind of egalitarianism. Its key drive has been to replace ascriptive status with earned status. High political and social roles are not to depend on group, sex or parentage. Now biology, to be sure, cannot tell us directly what to value, but it can bear heavily on questions of feasibility.

The hopes the new Darwinian psychology can raise for the egalitarian seem mixed at this point. Humanity's unity of design means that no ethnic group is precluded by sheer genetic capacity from rewarding, socially valued roles. As individuals we probably do differ substantially in some of our genetic psychic propensities, and so too, on average, we may as men and women. Still, we no doubt see far more variation than traces in any simple, direct way to differing genes. The most disturbing news for us egalitarians may stem not from genetic differences, but from the complexities of human motivation: from mechanisms such as role-modelling, self-conception, investment of self-esteem, and the like – mechanisms we all share. It may be mechanisms like these that especially frustrate social attempts to channel human strivings for the good. They must be designed by the genes, in effect, to resist various kinds of manipulation, or they could too easily render one a dupe of manipulators around one. That does not mean that we cannot manage better, socially, with a better understanding of these mechanisms. Why should the advertisers have all the good stratagems? Still, mechanisms like these may well guarantee not only that we will differ sharply from each other – 'Vivent les différences!' we can reply – but that some of the consequences will be sad and serious, and difficult or worse to correct.

History, if this is right, will not come to an end. Human talents and aspirations, our attachments and loyalties and enthusiasms will always be manifold. Mechanisms for humiliation, hatred and deprecation will always stand waiting in the background, even if we attain conditions that keep them from being activated. Our prime social challenges will be to cope: in the face of these things to keep the peace, to elicit the varied strivings we require from each other, and to foster dignity, fulfilment and the rewards of intimacy for the widest variety of people.

One hope must be that a better understanding of the human psyche will help us pursue these aims. Humanity is complex enough that straight flights toward social betterment will often crash. We are beginning to see how our psychic complexity might stem from the reproductive challenges of our proto-human ancestors. Imaginative and careful theorizing about humanity may help political theorists understand the pieces that go into our grand political and social puzzles.

See also 4 SOCIOLOGY; 5 ECONOMICS; 9 CONSERVATISM; 10 FEMINISM; 14 AUTONOMY; 15 COMMUNITY; 23 EFFICIENCY; 24 ENVIRONMENTALISM; 25 EQUALITY

References

Alexander, R. D.: *Darwinism and Human Affairs* (London: University of Washington Press, 1979).
————: *The Biology of Moral Systems* (Hawthorne, NY: Aldine de Gruyter, 1987).
Allen, E. et al.: 'Letter to the editors', *The New York Review of Books* (13 November 1975).
Boyd, R. and Richerson, P. J.: *Culture and the Evolutionary Process* (Chicago: University of Chicago Press, 1985).
Buss, D. M.: 'Sex differences in human mate preferences: evolutionary hypotheses tested in 37 cultures', *Behavioral and Brain Sciences*, 12 (1989), 1–49.
Daly, M. and Wilson, M.: *Homicide* (New York: Aldine, 1988).
Dawkins, R.: *The Selfish Gene* (Oxford: Oxford University Press, 1976).
————: *The Extended Phenotype* (San Francisco: W. H. Freeman, 1982).
Dickemann, M.: 'Female infanticide, reproductive strategies, and social stratification: a preliminary model', *Evolutionary Biology and Human Social Behavior: An Anthropological Perspective*, ed. N. A. Chagnon and W. Irons (N. Scituate, Mass.: Duxbury, 1979), pp. 321–67.
Frank, R. H.: *Passions within Reason: The Strategic Role of the Emotions* (London: W. W. Norton, 1988).
Gibbard, A: 'Human evolution and the sense of justice', *Midwest Studies in Philosophy VII: Social and Political Philosophy*, ed. P. A. French, T. E. Uehling and H. K. Wettstein (Minneapolis: University of Minnesota Press, 1981).
————: *Wise Choices, Apt Feelings: A Theory of Normative Judgment* (Oxford: Oxford University Press, 1990).
Gould, S. J. and Lewontin, R. C.: 'The spandrels of San Marco and the Panglossian paradigm: a critique of the adaptationist programme', *Proceedings of the Royal Society of London*, B 205 (1979), 581–98. Reprinted in *Conceptual Issues in Evolutionary Biology*, ed. E. Sober (Cambridge, Mass.: MIT Press, 1984).
Hamilton, W. D.: 'The genetical evolution of social behaviour I', *Journal of Theoretical Biology*, 7 (1964), 1–16.
Hare, B. R. and Castenell, L. A.: 'No place to run, no place to hide: comparative status and future prospects of black boys' *Beginnings: The Social and Affective Development of Black Children*, ed. M. B. Spencer, G. K. Brookins, and W. Allen (Hillsdale, NJ: Erlbaum, 1985).
Kitcher, P.: *Vaulting Ambition: Sociobiology and the Quest for Human Nature* (London: MIT Press, 1985).

Lewontin, R. C., Rose, S. and Kamin, L.: *Not in Our Genes* (New York: Pantheon, 1984).

Maynard Smith, J.: 'The theory of games and the solution of animal conflicts', *Journal of Theoretical Biology*, 47 (1974), 209–21.

————: *Evolution and the Theory of Games* (Cambridge: Cambridge University Press, 1982).

Murphy, J. G.: *Evolution, Morality, and the Meaning of Life* (Totowa, NJ: Rowman and Littlefield, 1982).

Nisbett, R. and Ross, L.: *Human Inference: Strategies and Shortcomings of Social Judgment* (Englewood Cliffs, NJ: Prentice-Hall, 1980).

Ogbu, J. U.: 'The consequences of the American caste system', *The School Achievement of Minority Children*, ed. U. Neisser (London: Lawrence Erlbaum Associates, 1986).

Plomin, R. and Daniels, D.: 'Why are children from the same family so different from each other?', *Behavioral and Brain Sciences*, 10 (1987), 1–16.

Rawls, J.: *A Theory of Justice* (Cambridge, Mass.: Harvard University Press, 1971).

Scarr, S., Pakstis, A. J., Katz, S. H. and Barker, W. B.: 'Absence of a relationship between degree of white ancestry and intellectual skills within a black population', *Human Genetics*, 39 (1977), 69–86. Reprinted in *Race, Social Class, and Individual Differences in I.Q.*, ed. S. Scarr (Hillsdale, NJ: Erlbaum, 1981).

Schelling, T. C.: *The Strategy of Conflict* (Cambridge, Mass.: Harvard University Press, 1960).

————: *Micromotives and Macrobehavior* (New York: Norton, 1978).

Singer, P.: *The Expanding Circle: Ethics and Sociobiology* (New York: Farrar, Straus, and Giroux, 1981).

Steele, C. M.: 'Race and the schooling of black Americans', *Atlantic*, 269, 4 (April 1992), 68–78.

Symons, D.: *The Evolution of Human Sexuality* (Oxford: Oxford University Press, 1979).

————: 'If we're all Darwinians, what's the fuss about?', in *Sociobiology and Psychology: Ideas, Issues, and Applications*, ed. C. B. Crawford, M. F. Smith and D. L. Krebs (Hillsdale, NJ: Erlbaum, 1987).

Tooby, J. and Cosmides, L.: 'On the universality of human nature and the uniqueness of the individual', *Journal of Personality*, 58 (1990), 17–67.

Trivers, R.: 'The evolution of reciprocal altruism', *Quarterly Review of Biology*, 46 (1971), 35–57.

Williams, G. C.: *Adaptation and Natural Selection: A Critique of Some Current Evolutionary Thought* (Princeton, NJ: Princeton University Press, 1966).

Wilson, E. O.: *Sociobiology: The New Synthesis* (Cambridge, Mass.: Harvard University Press, 1975).

————: *On Human Nature* (Cambridge, Mass.: Harvard University Press, 1978).

36

The state

PATRICK DUNLEAVY

Controversies over defining the state

The state is a complex, multi-criteria concept. In the contemporary era it refers to:

1. A set of organized institutions with a level of connectedness or cohesion, justifying short-hand descriptions of their behaviour in 'unitary' terms.
2. Operating in a given spatial territory, inhabited by a substantial population organized as a distinct 'society'.
3. These institutions' 'socially accepted function is to define and enforce collectively binding decisions on the members of [that] society' (Jessop, 1990, p. 341).
4. Their existence creates a 'public' sphere differentiated from the realm of 'private' activity or decision-making.

Each such state (ensemble of institutions) must also:

5. Claim sovereignty over all other social institutions and effectively monopolize the legitimate use of force within the given territory (Weber, 1948, p. 78).
6. Be able to define members and non-members of the society, and control entry to and exit from the territory.
7. Make strong ideological/ethical claims to be advancing the common interests or general will of members of the society.
8. Be accepted as legitimate by significant groups or elements in the society.
9. Command bureaucratic resources (Weber, 1968, pp. 212–26) so as to be able to collect taxation (Schumpeter, 1954) and order governmental affairs effectively, given prevailing transactions costs (Levi, 1988).
10. Substantially regulate societal activities by means of a legal apparatus, and government activities by means of a constitution.
11. Be recognized as a 'state' by other states.

Contemporary nation-states commonly meet all these criteria simultaneously. But historically, this complex governmental form evolved slowly and partially, with particular characteristics developing unevenly in different locales and becoming generalized over long time-periods. The processes of state formation have been strongly influenced by many factors – the transition from feudalism to capitalism, changes in military technology, wars, revolutions, imitative effects, geopolitical situations, the rise of nationalism and of liberal democracy, and the experience of communism, fascism and other forms of 'exceptional regimes' in industrialized countries. Within the defining characteristics set out above, there can be many different state variants, with contrasting institutional arrangements. Circumstances quite often arise where most defining characteristics are present but one or several features are missing or called in question – creating difficult cases where the attribution of statehood becomes problematic.

The multi-criteria nature of concept, the tangled web of historically-specific pathways of state development, and differences in state forms have all contributed to substantial theoretical difficulties in reaching any wide agreement about how to define 'the state'. As Walzer (1985, p. 4) remarked in another context: 'History displays a great variety of arrangements and ideologies. But the first impulse of the philosopher is to resist the displays of history, the world of appearances, and to search for some underlying unity.' There has been a marked tendency for theorists to fasten on to one or a few of the defining characteristics above, and either to ignore or de-emphasize others, downgrading them to the level of associated characteristics or corollaries of statehood. Alternatively, other authors try to identify a small sub-set of features which form the primary root of state power or character.

Rival definitions of the state have proliferated, but they can conveniently be grouped into two views. Philosophical approaches, the juridical literature influenced by Roman law, Marxist 'state theory' and evolutionary/systems theory approaches have generally adopted an 'organic' view of the state. Here the state is construed in terms of some moral purpose, human drive or social function which requires the coming into existence of a specialized sovereign body, operating in the ways characteristic of modern states – for example, separating out the exercise of ultimate political power from the lineage or characteristics of particular individuals (unlike earlier monarchies), and unifying political controls instead of retaining the multiple independent or interleaved centres of political autonomy found in feudal arrangements. All organic approaches try to establish the necessary quality of the (modern) state form, relaying on logical argument. Most work follows some form of 'derivationist' method where the multiple defining characteristics of the state are inferred from its necessary purposes or functions within a wider social theory or philosophical apparatus. Much of this literature, especially in Marxist-influenced work, seems to reify the state, creating a unitary social actor to which massive social influence is assigned, but whose precise identification or inner workings often remain obscure.

The alternative approach is a methodological individualist view of the state as a composite set of public institutions or of public officials, most commonly those at the central or national government levels alone, or alternatively of all designated governing organizations. This view predominates in pluralist political science, mainstream economics and historical sociology. It typically produces definitions of the state closer to 'trait theory' approaches, which seek to encompass or reorganize the tangled empirical corollaries of statehood.

The state has also been paired in numerous dichotomies with equally problematic 'opposite' terms. These contrasts attempt to clarify the fundamental core of stateness, but are usually not exhaustive and hence only exacerbate definitional problems. Typical of such false dichotomies is 'the state' vs 'the individual' contrast, which predominated in Anglo-American liberal thought from the end of the eighteenth century to the 1970s; 'the state' vs 'civil society' contrast in Marx's work, and parallel distinctions in Hegelian-influenced approaches, feeding through into the blanker 'state-centred' vs 'society-centred' explanations of some contemporary neo-elite and 'new institutional' theory; and the 'domestic' or 'welfare' state vs the external or 'power state' contrast which has sustained the postwar split between political science and international relations. Each of these perspectives prioritizes some of the defining features listed above and de-emphasizes others. They point to different core elements of the state – the legal system for liberal approaches, the bureaucracy for neo-elite theory, the realm of 'high politics' for realist theory in international relations.

Finally, there has been acute controversy about whether the modern state form is a set of governmental arrangements generally applicable to industrialized countries, as all forms of liberal theory assert, or whether this state form is particular to the capitalist mode of production, as Marxist theory long claimed. The debate here was partly historical and partly counterfactual. Historically, while all participants can agree on the clear distinction between the modern state form and feudalism, other earlier historic forms of government, especially the Roman empire and Eastern empires, share significant characteristics with the modern form (such as an extended administrative apparatus, tax-raising abilities, use of law and maintenance of a standing army). Counterfactually, the claim of a distinctively capitalist state form rests on the potential existence of an alternative mode of production, socialism. Even within Marxism there was acute controversy about whether such a radically different system ever existed under communist regimes, or whether the state form realized there was distinct from that of Western countries, and if so in what ways. The possibility of an 'Asiatic mode of production', briefly hinted at by Marx and Engels as a way of characterizing some early forms of oriental empires marked by a strong societal guidance by apparently developed state institutions, united historical and counterfactual debates as a possible characterization of communist rule. With the collapse of the Soviet Union and its satellite regimes in Eastern Europe during 1989–92, and the changing form of communist rule in China, the identification of a socialist mode of production has apparently receded into the distant future, and the pathways for achieving such a transition have become almost completely indeterminate even for Western Marxists. The specificity of the modern state to a capitalist mode of production can still be maintained theoretically. But it has become *de facto* the general state form in the world as we know it.

Surveying these manifold disputes, some observers have sought refuge in the idea that 'the state' is an essentially contested concept, in Gallie's (1956) sense of a complex, multi-criteria idea, with a strong appraisive content, whose basic meaning and scope of application are strongly disputed by different schools of thought, in a way likely to prove irresolvable (e.g. Jessop, 1990, p. 340; for other political examples, see Connnolly, 1974, ch. 1). Problems in delineating 'the state' are also bound up closely with equally serious difficulties, such as defining a 'society'. But whether labelling a disputed concept 'essentially contested' is more than a dignified way of confessing deadlock seems unclear.

State and society under liberal democracy

After a prolonged static period, the number of liberal democracies has again risen sharply – generating increased interest in the idea that modern social and economic development contains a logic which converges on this particular state form (Fukuyama, 1989; 1991). Yet the state's role in liberal democratic societies remains the central puzzle in contemporary state theory. Analysing the historical state of pre-democratic eras, or state intervention under contemporary authoritarian regimes, is relatively straightforward. Where political power is concentrated and controlled overtly or observably by other power centres – by wealth or military force or a secret police, for example – acute problems of maintaining legitimacy, of constraints on rulers from transactions costs, of achieving state rationality, etc. may all occur.

Characterizing state action and intervention is much more difficult, much more paradoxical, however, where a system of political decision-making both formally vests ultimate control in the dispersed votes of citizens, and yet creates substantial power centres and institutions with significant degrees of autonomy, inertia, institutionalized dispositional biases, and so on. Similarly the liberal democratic state claims unconstrained sovereignty over the social arrangements within its territory, yet binds itself formally with an apparatus of legalism and constitutionalism. And in practice the politically controlled and putatively sovereign liberal democratic state must interface with a capitalist economy and operate in a culture where money is effectively a 'dominant good', transmutable into political power and social influence (Walzer, 1983, pp. 10–13), not just at national level but increasingly on a global scale.

Rival theories of the state and society have predictably reached different conclusions about how these contradictions are resolved (Alford and Friedland, 1985; Dunleavy and O'Leary, 1987). For classical pluralists the state in liberal democracy self-evidently plays an autonomous role:

> Governments [are] . . . organizations that have a sufficient monopoly of control to enforce an orderly settlement of disputes with other organizations in the [territorial] area . . . Whoever controls government usually has the *last word* on a question; whoever controls government can enforce decisions on other organizations in the area. (Dahl and Lindblom, 1953, p. 42)

> In the real world, governments in fact do almost everything which an organization conceivably can . . . Every government is the locus of ultimate power in its society, i.e. it can coerce all other groups into obeying its decisions, whereas they cannot similarly coerce it . . . Thus . . . the government is a particular and unique social agent. (Downs, 1957, pp. 11–12, 21–3)

Pluralists assert the separateness of the political sphere, and the effectiveness of the constitutionally and electorally enforced 'blocked exchanges' which inhibit the transferability of economic or social power into political influence or administrative control.

More recent neo-pluralist work acknowledges the strength of elite theory and neo-Marxist criticisms about the under-involvement of ordinary citizens and the structurally privileged position of business in liberal democracy (Lindblom, 1977). But it defends the idea of state autonomy in new ways – specifically, arguments about the complexity of modern societies' specialization of labour. In Luhmann's (1979; 1982) 'autopoietic' approach, the political-administrative sub-system (like the legal, the economic or the cultural sub-systems) is radically autonomous and inherently uncontrollable by any external dynamic, although it must constantly interface with other equally autonomous societal sub-systems. This argument restates in an evolutionary/systems theory guise a classical pluralist theme, the separation of elites. Less functionalist neo-pluralists vest state autonomy in interactive policy networks, professional socialization and internalized values, specialized policy scrutiny mechanisms, planning machineries, varied governmental technologies and localized implementation systems – which recreate within the state apparatus the analogues to the decentralized 'discovery systems' of private markets.

The new right by contrast develop a strong theoretical analysis in which pluralist politics emerges as a source of pathology within the capitalist order, with escalating state intervention as the chief symptom. A decade of experience of governments strongly influenced by this pattern of thinking (notably under Thatcher and Reagan) has split the new right into two streams. A fatalist wing accepts that the current scale of government spending and employment are probably irremoveable by political action (Regan, 1986, pp. 424–5), but can none the less keep the faith with the initial theoretical analysis. By contrast, a 'heroic' wing insists that new right policy analysis will yet permit strong-willed leaders to push through a qualitative change in state–society relations (Savas, 1987; Pirie, 1988) implying that there is nothing inherent about state growth in liberal democracies. Exponents of the heroic model junked Hayek's imperative against coercing others, in favour of trying to bounce their societies away from welfare-state 'dependence' – envisaging that state cutbacks could force people to be free. By contrast fatalists admit the political salience of distinctive kinds of vested interests within new right governments, the continuing strength of the political–business cycle, and the bidding up of voters' expectations implied in Laffer-style 'voodoo economics'.

If the experience of seeing their ideas partially implemented has fractured the new right's previously powerful fusion of deductive theory and practical policy analysis, it has apparently only encouraged a stasis in elite theory instrumentalist Marxist accounts. The defensive stances of liberal or social democratic parties in practical politics have been mirrored by the intellectual stagnation of left thinking about the state. American state-centred elite theories have stressed the autonomy of public officials against society-centred explanations, this time vesting the old pluralist separation of elites argument with a (faint) radical tinge (Nordlinger, 1981; Skocpol, 1985). Some European Marxists have redescribed the social and economic forces underlying economic stagnation and political conservatism as the collapse of a postwar Fordist system of mass production and mass consumption. In this view, the state is one among a complex of middle-range 'regulation' arrangements by means of which global capitalist economic imperatives are translated into social action, yet also differentiated across countries in ways which facilitate both social control and decentralized policy learning.

Feminist thinking about the state has generated volumes of criticism of existing approaches, without yet culminating in any distinctive theory of the state. Radical feminist analysis has apparently retreated before the task of producing a gender-based analysis of state institutions and operations into a defensive position – poring over legal judgments for indications of the remaining gender-bias of courts, laws and wel-fare-rules, the continuing reverberations of a historic or ideological 'sexual contract' (Pateman, 1988). The apparent 'neutrality' of the contemporary state then has to be explained away in terms reminiscent of Marxist accounts of why liberal democratic politics is *prima facie* dominated by non-class issues:

Women are oppressed socially, prior to law, without express state acts, often in intimate con-texts. The negative [i.e. liberal] state cannot address their situation in any but an equal society – the one in which it is needed least . . . The Weberian monopoly on the means of legitimate coercion, thought to distinguish the state as an entity, actually describes the power of men over women in the home, in the bedroom, on the job, in the street, throughout social life. It is difficult, actually, to find a place it does not circumscribe and describe. Men are sovereign in the way Austin describes law as sovereign: a person or group whose commands are habi-tually obeyed and who is not in the habit of obeying anyone else. Men are the group that has had the authority to make law, embodying H. L. A. Hart's 'rule of recognition' that, in his conception, makes law authoritative. (MacKinnon, 1989, pp. 165, 169–70)

Reasoning on these lines only dissolves the state as an object of enquiry. This tendency may explain why there is as yet no viable feminist theory of the state – despite the potentially powerful apparatus of concepts assembled by feminist thought (e.g. patri-archalism, exploitation, false consciousness, phallocentrism, public/private spheres, etc.), and despite the strong social, psychological and socio-biological bases for char-acterizing key aspects of state behaviour as gender-specific (e.g. warfare). A rather similar criticism could be made of green political theory, where distinctions between the state and societal influences are similarly blurred (Dobson, 1990).

Underlying the surface dissimilarities of pluralist, neo-pluralist, new right, elite theory and Marxist approaches to the state – indeed perhaps underlying any similar theory of the state – there are three structurally invariant images, which recur in dif-ferent guises across diverse substantive theory (Dunleavy and O'Leary, 1987, ch. 7). The first is the state as a cipher, a mechanism for condensing and transmitting exter-nal influences. What gets communicated ranges from voters' demands and diverse interest group pressures under pluralism, to the dominant pressure of capital under Marxism. In its external affairs with other countries, the cipher state acts directly as a vehicle for domestically dominant social interests.

The second image is the state as guardian, an active autonomous institutional in-fluence, whose interventions always re-weight societal outcomes towards long-run ends, and away from immediate social pressures. In pluralist thought state interven-tion is adjusted by electoral competition towards groups otherwise lacking social clout; in neo-pluralism the guardian state is a partly insulated, professionalized mechanism for delivering citizens' desired outcomes without direct citizen control and in a sustain-able manner; and for some neo-Marxists, state autonomy in policy formation is an indispensable foundation for the long-run functionality of an internally complex capitalist mode of production. In international policy arenas the guardian state pur-sues an autonomously formulated and strongly ideological conception of the national interest. Although domestic public opinion or major social groups are also normally supportive, this congruence primarily reflects state elites' ability to persuade voters or interests to view external affairs as they do, rather than societal interests effectively formulating foreign or defence policies.

The third image is of the state as a partisan actor, not situated above and qualitatively apart from civil society, but intermeshed within it by a complex of relations, of resource interchanges and of bargains. For pluralists taking this view, the state is a broker, able to coerce other social actors if need be, but unable to coerce all or many simultaneously; and staffed by personnel with distinct if still constrained organizational interests. In the Marxist variant, the state is seen as arbiter of a relatively balanced class struggle, able to implement crisis management strategies fostering distinctive state or national interests. In external affairs the partisan state pursues the narrowly sectional interests of key parts of the state apparatus (such as the defence sector, the intelligence community, the diplomatic/foreign service, and politicians anxious to demonstrate symbolic 'strong leadership') in tandem with other social interests (such as defence contractors and their employees, corporations with a stake in different external policies, sections of public opinion with strong commitments on foreign policy issues and the mass media). Foreign and defence policies reflect these shifting interest coalitions, but with intrastate influences always important.

The contemporary state and the international system

All three images of the liberal democratic state explain international policy primarily in terms of domestic imperatives and power structures. Yet in practice the external relations of states with other states are strongly shaped by international system influences, while domestic policies also do not operate in a vacuum. Cross-national policy emulation, cumulative policy learning and the emergence of strong pressures for international policy standardization or joint policy-making are no longer isolated policy constraints – their dynamics lie at the heart of policy change in such core domestic areas as the welfare state, tariff and taxation policies, law and order, environmental regulation and microeconomic development.

Conceptually, the 'sovereign' state operates in a system of states, each sharing the same properties. Empirically, however, there are major variations across countries in the autonomous capabilities of their sets of governing institutions. Large, medium and small states have quite different levels of control over their own military and foreign policy decision-making. Really large states, like the United States for much of the postwar period, have a vastly greater scope for intervention in other countries' affairs. 'Normal' constraints on the ambitions of large state elites can be so reduced that their conception of the national interest expands exponentially, selectively overriding or undermining the recognition of smaller states' autonomy, notwithstanding liberal democracies' constitutional and legal commitments to this ideal (Krasner, 1978, p. 340). Another potent influence undermining constraints on the liberal democratic and authoritarian super-powers was the pattern of official discourse which developed in the United States and the Soviet Union (and to a much lesser degree in Britain and France) during the hottest phases of the Cold War (Rapoport, 1968). By first stressing internal state unity as the condition for 'winning' a nuclear exchange and later the unreasoning external use of unlimited force (entailed by the Mutually Assured

Destruction doctrine), 'neo-Clausewitzian' elite attitudes and defence policies pictured the world not as an international system of states but simply as an arena of super-power action.

At the other end of the scale, small nation-states operate as very weak centres of decision in an international environment of strong influences – especially where their geopolitical situation places them adjacent to larger and stronger neighbours. In past turbulent conditions, such as those prevailing in Europe as recently as 1938–9 (Watt, 1990), small states' existence was completely dependent upon their large neighbours continuing to recognize them as sovereign entities. Small states' abilities to muster internal legitimacy or command a domestic monopoly over the use of force were easily undermined where this recognition was withdrawn. Since 1945, the creation of the United Nations and the freezing of nation-state status within an historically unprecedented international legal framework have both strengthened the position of small countries. But these additional safeguards of statehood easily collapse where internal political strife or civil war emerges, and external states can intervene to back favoured factions; where inter-country disputes involve ethnic minorities in one country wanting to secede to another; or where territorial disputes are blurred by historical or legal complications. So in practice, small states' ability to survive external aggression still rests as much as in the past on their ability to engage allies in their cause – by controlling strategic resources, occupying a pivotal geopolitical position, or commanding strong ideological arguments which sway international opinion.

States which are neither super-powers nor exceptionally small or domestically vulnerable operate in the international system in much the way that legal models suggest. Their dealings with other states are governed both by instrumental motives (such as reciprocity or prudential calculations) and by respect for international law and international treaty obligations. In liberal democracies compliance with international obligations is necessary for government legitimacy as much as it is a prerequisite for maintaining effective external relations.

In the contemporary era the Cold War has ended, curbing super-power abilities to override constraints on their external behaviour. The collapse of the USSR into its component republics (some with continuing internal tensions), the re-emergence of diverse states in Eastern Europe and the messy fragmentation of Yugoslavia have created the first substantial increase in the number of nation-states since the 1960s. And small states' position has been progressively strengthened by several influences – especially the spread of liberal democracy, the re-emergence of the United Nations as a potent force for peace-keeping, and a secular increase in the global legitimacy of international law constraints. As a result the most fundamental challenge to prevailing ideas of statehood is presented by the emergence of new forms of international policy standardization. In addition to the UN's peacekeeping role, the post-war period has seen a rapid accretion of internationally binding policy-making around such increasingly global institutions as GATT, the International Monetary Fund, and the World Bank. A host of single-subject bodies now seek to handle problems of collective action (such as mass starvation crises, or airport security and counter-terrorism) and 'common pool goods' (such as international whaling, or the emission of CFCs and other ozone-depleting chemicals). In addition, subscription to international standards (such as the UN Declaration of Human Rights) has generally increased, and regionally-based mechanisms for ensuring practical compliance with similar schemes have emerged in some parts of the world (as with the European Court on Human Rights).

In Western Europe the uneven development of the European Community over nearly four decades poses perhaps the most fundamental challenge to the nationally-based conception of statehood. The EC has long ceased to be simply a confederation of nation-states, with substantial progress towards a common monetary system, and a common foreign policy (with an emergent defence component handled by the West European Union), coming on top of a single labour market (with joint immigration controls), a complete tariff union (with extended action against all forms of quasi-protection of domestic markets), and substantial standardization of social policy and environmental regulation. Yet neither is the EC a state (or even a proto-state) in the sense defined at the start of this paper. EC decision-making procedures are overtly coalitional and non-unitary, and its central organs have no control over the domestic use of force in any member country. Progress towards greater political union may somewhat qualify these exceptions compared with the current situation, that is, it may make the EC as a whole begin to resemble more closely a form of federal super-state at a regional bloc level. But it is highly unlikely to completely remove the difficulties in analysing the EC.

The EC's development also throws into doubt the status of its component nation-states. Some authors in the Marxist tradition have developed accounts of 'the regional state' or 'the local state', which differ primarily from the initial definition in four respects – their territory includes only a part of a wider 'society' (criterion 2); they do not claim exclusive sovereignty within their territory, nor can they command a monopoly of legitimate force, since the national state's writ also runs there (criterion 5); regional or local 'states' cannot define their membership or (formally) control entry and exit by national citizens into their territory (criterion 6); and the existence of regional or local 'states' depends not on recognition by other states but on a national constitution (criterion 11). The EC member countries similarly may begin to regulate only sections of a wider European 'society' (a trend already pronounced in the area around northern France, northern Germany and the Benelux countries). They will retain a domestic monopoly of force, but no longer claim the sweeping sovereignty of past eras. The EC may in future define citizenship collectively, and what national specification remains may be of declining significance. Finally, member countries' positions are already partly defined by collective EC treaties and institutions, while the EC is already recognized as a 'state' by other non-EC states.

All these trends seem to imply that an important change of state form is in prospect, at least for relatively stable and prosperous liberal democracies. The traditional 'high politics' core of the state remains, with its twin focus on securing order and social coherence internally and on the command of strategic resources externally. But the salience of these policy areas is declining as meaningful levels of collective security become feasible and the system of states solidifies into an apparently permanent form. At the same time the internal and external dynamics which fuelled the expansion of the welfare state in the postwar era have slowed. Yet persistent ethnic tensions, a new emphasis upon 'subsidiarity' principles, and changes in governmental technologies towards decentralization all seem likely to ensure the further development of sub-national governments. The 'steady state' welfare systems now in prospect may generate less partisan controversy and require less distinctively national management than in the past. Finally, there has been and looks certain to continue to be a progressive drift of decision-making authority from national to trans-national institutions, with more globalized policy-making, and with regional blocs becoming the focus of economic and social policy decision-making. Very large nation-states (like the United States and Japan), or land-based empires (like India and China), may operate in this environment on multiple levels, for a time. Many nation-states in still industrializing countries may remain on the fringes of this emergent system, for a time and with progressively more remote claims to be exercising national sovereignty. But these exceptions should not disguise the continuing pressures acting on the nation-state from above, due to the globalization of capital, and from below, due to technological shifts and the continuing salience of ethnicity. The age of the unitary nation-state commanding strategic resources and acting in a realist mode in international relations may yet prove to be a transitory period in human affairs.

See also 4 SOCIOLOGY; 6 POLITICAL SCIENCE; 7 LEGAL STUDIES; 8 ANARCHISM; 10 FEMINISM; 11 LIBERALISM; 12 MARXISM; 13 SOCIALISM; 15 COMMUNITY; 17 CONSTITUTIONALISM AND THE RULE OF LAW; 19 DEMOCRACY; 26 FEDERALISM; 27 INTERNATIONAL AFFAIRS; 29 LIBERTY; 30 POWER; 34 SECES-SION AND NATIONALISM; 38 TOTALITARIANISM

References

Alford, R. and Friedland, R.: *Powers of Theory: Capitalism, the State and Democracy* (Cambridge: Cambridge University Press, 1985).

Connolly, W.: *The Terms of Political Discourse* (Lexington, Mass.: Heath, 1974).

Dahl, R. and Lindblom, C.: *Politics, Economics and Welfare* (New York: Harper, 1953).

Dobson, A.: *Green Political Thought* (London: Unwin Hyman, 1990).

Downs, A.: *Economic Theory of Democracy* (New York: Harper & Row, 1957).

Dunleavy, P. and O'Leary, B.: *Theories of the State: The Politics of Liberal Democracy* (London: Macmillan, 1987).

Fukuyama, F.: 'The end of history?', *The National Interest*, Summer, 1989.

————: 'Liberal democracy as a global phenomenon', *PS: Political Science and Politics*, 24, (1991), 659–64.

Gallie, W.: 'Essentially contested concepts', *Proceedings of the Aristotelian Society*, 56 (1956), 167–93.

Jessop, R.: *The Capitalist State* (Oxford: Martin Robertson, 1982).

————: *State Theory: Putting Capitalist States in Their Place* (Cambridge: Polity, 1990).

Krasner, S.: *Defending the National Interest* (Princeton, NJ: Princeton University Press, 1978).

————: 'Approaches to the state: alternative conceptions and historical dynamics', *Comparative Politics*, 16, 2 (1984), 223–46.

Levi, M.: *Of Rule and Revenue* (Berkeley: University of California Press, 1986).

Lindblom, C. E.: *Politics and Markets: The World's Political Economic Systems* (New York: Basic Books, 1977).

Luhmann, N.: *Trust and Power* (Chichester: Wiley, 1979).

————: *The Differentiation of Society* (New York: Columbia University Press, 1982).

MacKinnon, C.: *Towards a Feminist Theory of the State* (Cambridge, Mass.: Harvard University Press, 1989).

Nordlinger, E.: *The Autonomy of the Democratic State* (Cambridge, Mass.: Harvard University Press, 1981).

O'Leary, B.: *The Asiatic Mode of Production* (Cambridge: Cambridge University Press, 1990).

Pateman, C.: *The Sexual Contract* (Cambridge: Polity, 1988).

Pirie, M.: *Micro-Politics* (London: Wildwood House, 1988).

Rapoport, A.: Introduction to Clausewitz's *On War* (Harmondsworth: Penguin Books, 1968).

Regan, D.: *The Triumph of Politics* (New York: Avon, 1986).

Savas, E.: *Privatization: The Key to Better Government* (Chatham House, NJ: Chatham House, 1987).

Schumpeter, J. L: 'Crisis of the tax state', *International Economic Papers*, 4 (1954), 5–38.

Skocpol, T.: 'Bringing the state back in', in P. Evans, D. Rueschemeyer and T. Skocpol (eds), *Bringing the State Back In* (Cambridge: Cambridge University Press, 1985).

Walzer, M.: *Spheres of Justice: A Defence of Pluralism and Equality* (Oxford: Blackwell, 1985).

Watt, D. C.: *How War Came* (London: Heinemann, 1990).

Weber, M.: 'Politics as a vocation', in M. Weber, *Essays from Max Weber*, trans H. Gerth and C. W. Mills (London: Routlege & Kegan Paul, 1948).

————: *Economy and Society* (New York: Bedminster Press, 1968).

37

Toleration and fundamentalism

STEPHEN MACEDO

Religious toleration would seem an unlikely source of controversy in contemporary political philosophy. Surely, if anything is settled in modern liberal democracies it is the broad principle of toleration for religious diversity. Of course, a few zealots and dogmatists refuse to make their peace with the modern world. In the United States, some Protestant fundamentalists charge that public schooling promotes secularism. They seek to revise textbooks or to require that equal time be given to the teaching of 'creation science' (the view that human life appeared suddenly, which is based, allegedly, on gaps in the fossil record rather than on religious convictions) alongside the theory of evolution. In Great Britain, violent Moslem demonstrations against Salman Rushdie's depiction of Mohammed in *The Satanic Verses* helped provoke the Ayatollah Khomeini into pronouncing a death sentence on the author, who was driven into hiding.

The fact is that such incidents do more than illuminate the outer edges of the reigning political settlement. They reveal problems at the very foundation of the case for liberal democracy. Can the liberal state really claim to be non-partisan on religious questions, or is it not only inhospitable to robust forms of religious faith but ultimately based on dogmatic assertions of its own? The success of the case for liberal toleration is less certain than one might suppose.

It was long thought that social peace required religious uniformity, and that belief persisted after the Reformation shattered the hegemony of Catholicism. It took a good deal of pious killing before toleration gained widespread acceptance in Europe. Battle fatigue presented the state with an opportunity to rise above divisive conflict and focus on the pursuit of shared interests and aims, such as peace, freedom, and material prosperity. But how can religious toleration be defended as a matter of political principle rather than as an unfortunate necessity?

John Locke advanced an early and classic statement of the principled case for religious toleration in his *Letter Concerning Toleration*. The most memorable parts of the *Letter* are impassioned pleas for a separation of sacred and secular concerns, and the confinement of political authority to certain narrowly drawn 'civil interests': the security and property of individuals, goods of the body rather than the soul. The church, Locke insisted, is a thing 'absolutely separate and distinct from the Commonwealth. The Boundaries on both sides are fixed and immovable. He jumbles Heaven and Earth together, the things most remote and opposite, who mixes these two Societies . . . (Locke, [1689] 1985, p. 33). All of this sounds pretty conclusive, and suggests the later ideal of a 'wall of separation' between church and state.

Locke advanced a host of reasons on behalf of toleration. He denied that people would, in forming political societies, consent to delegate authority over religion to governments. He denied that secular rulers had any special expertise in matters of faith and asserted that princes would, in any case, use power over religion for their own ends. Like the contemporary liberal Karl Popper, Locke emphasized the fallibility of our judgements in many religious matters and the importance of correcting our views through peaceful public argument (King, 1976; Popper 1987).

Lockean arguments for toleration are far from airtight (Herzog, 1989; Barry, 1990; Waldron, 1991). Locke insists that persecution is irrational because faith depends on inward assent and cannot be coerced. But while suppression might not persuade particular individuals, it may slow or halt the spread of ideas and so shape the social environment in which individuals learn. Locke also claims that people should not object to living peacefully with those regarded as heretics: one man's salvation is nobody else's business, his damnation is no harm to others. Once again, however, the devout might hold that heresy threatens their ability to raise their children to the true faith. Locke does not really succeed, then, in fashioning arguments capable of convincing those who regard a supportive social and political environment as crucial to salvation.

While the aim of arguments for toleration is to distinguish the concerns of politics and religion, the argument for toleration itself cannot leave religion aside. Indeed, before many people could accept toleration their religious ideas had to change. Locke takes this bull by the horns, announcing, 'I esteem that Toleration to be the chief Characteristical Mark of the True Church', and appealing 'to the Consciences of those that persecute', and otherwise trying to shape Christian doctrine to support toleration (Locke, [1689] 1985, p. 23). Locke repeatedly signals the dependence of his argument on what he takes to be the proper understanding of Christianity.

All of this leads to a grave problem. It appears that the success of arguments for toleration depend upon getting people to think about religion in certain ways (we would need to include arguments for Jews, Moslems and many others). Thus, the case for toleration seems to require the impossible: showing that for each and every religion, a 'liberal' interpretation of its strictures is to be preferred by believers. Locke's problem dogs theorists to this day.

Herzog pointedly suggests that perhaps we should regard Locke's argument for toleration less as philosophical argument than as an effort in social transformation: 'since religion has created political havoc for decades, treat it as if it were politically inconsequential – and it will become inconsequential' (Herzog, 1989, p. 165). As a practical matter that seems right: peaceful coexistence and diversity become possible when people accept that religious uniformity is not essential for civil peace or salvation. The question remains, can we justify toleration as a matter of principle? Neither Herzog nor Locke can fully justify the transformation of religious views on which liberalism seems to depend: Locke's religious arguments remain eminently contestable, and Herzog, like other contemporary liberal theorists, simply leaves religious issues to one side.

623

The importance of this problem becomes apparent when we recognize one central aspiration that contemporary liberals share with Locke. 'Liberals demand', as Jeremy Waldron puts it, 'that the social order should in principle be capable of explaining itself at the tribunal of each person's understanding' (Waldron, 1987, p. 149). Since laws are backed by force, the least we owe to our fellow citizens who are subject to the laws we help shape are reasons and evidence that can be openly presented and publicly examined, secular reasons the recognition of whose force does not depend on adopting a special religious framework or being in a state of grace (Nagel, 1987). Reason-giving manifests our respect for the reasonableness of others, and informs many of the central institutions and practices of liberal society (Macedo, 1990).

One way of handling the problem of toleration is to argue that liberalism is based on a conception of human good as a whole. John Stuart Mill celebrated freedom and diversity because they provoke experimentation, criticism and public argument, which contribute to human happiness and progress, properly understood, in the religious realm as elsewhere. In such an environment human nature can, like a tree, 'grow and develop itself on all sides, according to the tendency of the inward forces which make it a living thing' (Mill, [1861] 1975, p. 56). Joseph Raz, like-wise, has recently defended an autonomy-based liberalism, which demands 'that people should be allowed freely to create their own lives' (Raz, 1988, p. 426).

The toleration that autonomy-based liberalism justifies may, however, turn out to be narrow in scope. Susan Mendus argues that autonomy-based liberalism justifies toleration only toward 'those diverse forms of life which themselves value autonomy and thus makes toleration a pragmatic device' (Mendus, 1989, p. 108). Religious communities that value simplicity and withdrawal from the modern world, such as the old Order Amish, or fundamentalist communities committed to honouring the literal and inerrant truth of the revealed word of God, may fail to win full protection from a toleration guided by the promotion of individual autonomy. Deborah Fitzmaurice accepts this conclusion, arguing that autonomy is more important than neutrality (Fitzmaurice, 1992). Similarly, Raz regards autonomy-rejecting communities as 'inferior to . . . the dominant liberal society', and as harmful to children (Raz, 1988, p. 423). Admittedly, Raz believes that such communities should in most instances be tolerated, so long as they are viable and do not harm others, but his support is luke-warm.

Autonomy-based liberalism has the additional liability of heightening and dramatiz-ing the tension between liberalism and religious fundamentalism. Autonomy is a broad and deeply partisan ideal of life. It is at odds with uncritical forms of devotion or community membership. Basing liberalism on the ideal of autonomy may provoke deep opposition to liberalism (Galston, 1991, part IV).

A number of contemporary liberals try to avoid the obvious partisanship of autonomy-based liberalism by emphasizing that the state should strive to be neutral toward competing conceptions of the good life (Ackerman, 1980; Dworkin, 1985, essay 8; Larmore, 1987; Goodin and Reeve, 1989). Such neutrality allows the state to show equal concern for the freedom of all its citizens, citizens whose status in the political community is independent of their particular religious commitments or views about a good life. One problem for liberal neutrality is that nearly everything the government does will have unequal effects on different conceptions of a good life, or on different religious beliefs. Liberal politics will advantage those wishy-washy forms of belief that 'go with the flow' of a diverse, individualistic social environment. Religions that oppose diversity and critical thinking will have to swim against the current of this society (Macedo, 1990; Galston, 1991). The liberal deck would appear to be stacked against ascetic, totalistic and otherworldly religions.

Larmore addresses the problem of non-neutral effects by insisting that the concern of liberal neutrality is with procedure rather than outcome: 'political neutrality consists in a constraint on what factors can be invoked to justify a political decision.' The liberal state may restrict ways of life for '*extrinsic* reasons, because, for example they threaten the lives of others', but not because of any 'presumed *intrinsic* superiority – that is, because it is a supposedly truer conception' (Larmore, 1987, pp. 44, 43). By avoiding direct judgements about the intrinsic value of different lives the state exhibits equal respect for persons, who have an equal right to pursue different conceptions of a good life.

One might ask, however, just how thoroughgoing can be a liberal's commitment to neutrality: does the ideal of neutrality rests on neutral foundations? Larmore claims that indeed it does: a neutral justification for neutrality can be found in 'a universal norm of rational dialogue' (Larmore, 1987, p. 53). All that neutrality requires, he says, is that people be prepared to keep the conversation going in order to find ground for agreement that neither side can reasonably reject. But is this ultimate mutual deference to the authority of reasonable conversation a neutral standard of authority?

In the end, even Larmore seems to admit that neutrality stands for mutual respect among only those people committed to basic values that are by no means neutral. The conversational or dialogic ideal that underpins liberal neutrality defers to the authority of public reasons and evidence, but 'true believers' may not regard these as reliable or non-partisan. Left out of neutral dialogue are 'fanatics and would-be martyrs' among others, for whom 'civil peace is not so important' (Larmore, 1987, p. 60). But how on earth can liberals really show that civil peace *is* so important? Which is to say, more important than conflicting moral and religious demands? Here again we run into Locke's problem: liberal toleration depends upon a ranking of ultimate values that supports the authority of peace, freedom, and public reasonableness, but that ranking cannot be established through public reason.

Other liberals pursue somewhat different strategies to try and avert Locke's problem. John Rawls argues that liberalism should be 'political not metaphysical', it should avoid 'claims to universal truth', and it should avoid claiming that 'political values are intrinsically more important than other values and that's why the other values are overridden' (Rawls, 1985, p. 223; 1987, p. 17; see also Rawls, 1971, pp. 211–21; 1988; 1989). Political justification seeks only 'to identify the kernel of overlapping consensus' likely to be affirmed by each of the opposing comprehensive moral and religious doctrines in a reasonably just society (Rawls, 1985, p. 246).

What does a Rawlsian liberal say, however, about a range of religious beliefs that includes liberal Protestantism, the Roman Catholicism of Pope Pius IX, and sects that require holy war against non-believers? Rawls insists that there are 'no resources within the political view to judge those conflicting conceptions. They are equally

PART III · SPECIAL TOPICS

permissible provided they respect the limits imposed by the principles of political justice' (Rawls, 1987, p. 9). A good deal is built into that word 'provided': religions not compatible with liberal political requirements will be opposed by the liberal state. Illiberal religions will perhaps be tolerated (so long as they go along with the regime) but prevented from acting on their illiberal beliefs. Thus, the Rawlsian liberal (like other liberals) must implicitly assert the falsehood of religious convictions incompatible with liberalism (see Rawls, 1971, pp. 201–21; Barry, 1973, pp. 121–7).

Rawls' political liberalism must invoke shared values capable of overriding any conflicting values and ideals, including religious ones. Only then can one justify the political settlement. It would seem necessary, then, for liberals to try to maintain, as did Locke, that religious beliefs and other extra-political values are compatible with or actively support the liberal political settlement. That is precisely the kind of excursion that liberals have wanted to avoid all along, for reasons we have seen.

In the face of these and other difficulties it is not surprising that some liberals have retreated from the ideal of a political community based on shared moral principles. Larmore argues that liberalism represents a *modus vivendi*, a means of accommodation among people with deep disagreements – indeed, among people with ultimate and irresolvable disagreements (Larmore, 1987, p. 129). Stephen Holmes contends, likewise, that modern liberal democracies depend on 'gag rules' on especially divisive issues. We do not settle many deep disagreements, rather, we shift them off the political agenda for the sake of co-operation on other matters, and we remain deeply divided (Holmes, 1988).

The *modus vivendi* view of liberal toleration has a number of problems. A *modus vivendi* would seem unstable compared to an agreement on basic principles of political morality. Given the transcendent importance of religion in many people's lives, convergence on a positive principle of religious toleration would appear to be of great practical importance, and well worth trying to justify. It is not clear, in any case, that characterizing liberalism as a *modus vivendi* is really more successful than the other strategies of avoidance that we have seen. In order for religious toleration and political co-operation to be stable, our shared values and aims must be more important than our disagreements. Shared values must, in other words, be of overriding importance, and we must care, as a political matter, that their overriding importance can be justified publicly.

Modus vivendi liberals must show that common values are weighty enough to justify shifting religion off the political agenda permanently: that leads us right back to Locke's problem. The fact is that liberalism must *settle*, rather than *avoid*, the question of religion to a much greater degree than the *modus vivendi* liberals want to admit. At base, liberal citizens must still be people who agree rather than disagree. While autonomy-based liberalism may be too demanding, the *modus vivendi* view (like other strategies of avoidance) is not demanding enough to ground a morally principled and stable liberal settlement.

Other thinkers believe we can avoid deep problems if we treat liberalism as an ongoing tradition which *we* have reason to value but that cannot be universally justified through abstract argument. John Gray urges liberals to drop what he sees as their universalizing tendencies, and to adopt a postmodernist stance which is satisfied with a liberalism grounded only in the particularities of our own culture and the specific ways in which it suits us (Gray, 1989, postscript; Rorty, 1989, esp. essay 9). Liberalism is just the way we do things around here, and it suits us just fine.

The postmodern turn, I believe, rests on a false analysis of our problem. It supposes that philosophers are preoccupied with generating abstract, general principles for their own sake. Dispense with the strange preoccupation and philosophy's contrived problems will go away. But that is wrong. A practical and honourable aspiration lies behind the desire to justify toleration: if we are going to coerce and punish people who break the law, the least we can do is to try to give them good reasons for obeying it. And the fact is that radical disagreement is not only something that we encounter on trips to strange lands: deep diversity is an increasingly prominent feature of the internal life of Western societies.

Pressing practical dilemmas raise questions about the bounds of toleration and demand resolution on the basis of the best reasons we can muster. It is argued, for example, that some of our political rules and practices indirectly discriminate against members of minority religions. It is not accidental, after all, that our weekends are positioned so as to accommodate the religious practices of Christians and Jews. Fairness may require us to make special efforts to accommodate Muslims, for example, whose religious observances fall on Fridays (Jones, 1992).

The controversy surrounding Salman Rushdie raises the issue of whether freedom of speech should ever be limited simply because its exercise is deemed offensive and insulting to believers. Must a society like Britain that has a blasphemy law protecting Christianity extend similar protections to Islam and other religions? It seems hard to believe that sanctions against blasphemy could be justified in a way that would extend only to the dominant religion in a pluralistic society. Can expressions that are offensive in manner be regulated without curtailing substantive criticisms of particular religious beliefs (Jones, 1990; Parekh, 1990)?

As a practical matter, toleration seems well established in liberal democracies, but its contours and limits require ongoing reasoned negotiation. Many actual complaints raised by fundamentalists and other believers do more, however, than provoke exercises at the outer edges of liberalism. Fundamentalism provides an important vantage point from which to critically examine our deepest political commitments: it raises the question of whether, at the end of the day, liberals can do more than simply assert the ultimate values of individuality, liberty and public reasonableness. The challenge of fundamentalism is not easily disposed of. In the final analysis, it would not be too much to say that liberalism depends on a certain configuration of ultimate ends and a certain ordering of the soul, neither of which are entirely within the power of liberal public philosophy to bring about.

See also 4 SOCIOLOGY; 9 CONSERVATISM; I I LIBERALISM; I 3 SOCIALISM; I 4 AUTONOMY; I 5 COMMUNITY; I 9 DEMOCRACY; 28 LEGITIMACY; 33 RIGHTS; 34 SECESSION AND NATIONALISM; 36 STATE; 38 TOTALITARIANISM; 39 TRUST; 40 VIRTUE

References

Ackerman, B.: *Social Justice in the Liberal State* (New Haven. Conn.: Yale University Press, 1980).

Barry, B.: *The Liberal Theory of Justice* (Oxford: Clarendon Press, 1973).

————: 'How not to defend liberalism', *British Journal of Political Science*, 20 (1990), 1–14.

Dworkin, R.: *A Matter of Principle* (Cambridge, Mass.: Harvard University Press, 1985).

Fitzmaurice, D.: 'Autonomy as a good', *The Journal of Political Philosophy*, 1 (1993), 3–19.

Galston, W. A.: *Liberal Purposes: Goods, Virtues, and Diversity in the Liberal State* (Cambridge: Cambridge University Press, 1991).

Goodin, R. E. and Reeve, A., eds: *Liberal Neutrality* (London: Routledge, 1989).

Gray, J.: *Liberalisms: Essays in Political Philosophy* (London: Routledge, 1989).

Herzog, D.: *Happy Slaves: A Critique of Consent Theory* (Chicago: University of Chicago Press, 1989).

Holmes, S.: 'Gag rules or the politics of omission', in *Constitutionalism and Democracy*, ed. J. Elster and R. Slagstad (Cambridge: Cambridge University Press, 1988), pp. 19–58.

Jones, P.: 'Rushdie, race, and religion', *Political Studies*, 38 (1990), 687–94.

————: 'Bearing the consequences of belief', *The Journal of Political Philosophy*, 2 (1994).

King, P.: *Toleration* (London: George Allen & Unwin, 1976).

Larmore, C.: *Patterns of Moral Complexity* (Cambridge: Cambridge University Press, 1987).

Locke, J.: *A Letter Concerning Toleration* (1689), ed. J. H. Tully (Indianapolis: Hackett, 1985).

Macedo, S.: *Liberal Virtues: Citizenship, Virtue, and Community in Liberal Constitutionalism* (Oxford: Clarendon Press, 1990).

Mendus, S.: *Toleration and the Limits of Liberalism* (Atlantic Highlands, NJ: Humanities Press, 1989).

Mill, J. S.: *On Liberty* (1861), ed. D. Spitz (New York: Norton, 1975).

Nagel, T.: 'Moral conflict and political legitimacy', *Philosophy and Public Affairs*, 16 (1987), 215–40.

Parekh, B.: 'The Rushdie affair: research agenda for political philosophy', *Political Studies*, 38 (1990), 695–709.

Popper, K.: 'Toleration and intellectual responsibility', in *On Toleration*, ed. S. Mendus and D. Edwards (Oxford: Clarendon Press, 1987).

Rawls, J.: *A Theory of Justice* (Cambridge. Mass.: Harvard University Press, 1971).

————: 'Justice as fairness: political, not metaphysical', *Philosophy and Public Affairs*, 14 (1985), 223–51.

————: 'The idea of an overlapping consensus', *Oxford Journal of Legal Studies*, 17 (1987), 1–25.

————: 'The priority of right and ideas of the good', *Philosophy and Public Affairs*, 17 (1988), 251–76.

————: 'The domain of the political and overlapping consensus', *New York University Law Review*, 64 (May 1989), 233–55.

Raz, J.: *The Morality of Freedom* (Oxford: Clarendon Press, 1988).

Rorty, R.: *Contingency, Irony, and Solidarity* (Cambridge: Cambridge University Press, 1989).

Waldron, J.: 'Theoretical foundations of liberalism', *Philosophical Quarterly*, 37 (1987), 127–50.

————: 'Locke: toleration and the rationality of persecution', in *Locke and Toleration*, ed. S. Mendus and J. Horton (London: Routledge, 1991).

38

Totalitarianism

EUGENE KAMENKA

History

Totalitarian, totalitarianism are twentieth-century words. They are used to describe states, ideologies, leaders and political parties that aim at total transformation and control of their own societies or, at least, at total control of everything that is actually or potentially politically significant within those societies. More positively, 'totalitarians' may see themselves as promoting a total conception of life and an organically cohesive state and community. They have been accused of aiming, inevitably, at a total transformation of the world. Applied to a whole society, 'totalitarian' is, quixotically, a success word – to call a society totalitarian is to suggest the ruler's control measures up to this programme.

The word *totalitarian* was linked, initially, with Italian fascism and Mussolini's rise to power. It is derived from the Italian *totalitario*, meaning complete, absolute. There is a similar French usage and priority is disputed by philologists. The derivative English *totalitarian* appeared in B. B. Carter's 1926 translation of Sturzo's *Italy and Fascisms*.

Mussolini in a speech on 22 June 1925, attacking the remnants of his political opposition in the Italian Parliament, spoke of *la nostra feroce voluntà totalitaria* (our fierce totalitarian will). The soon-to-be-official philosopher of Italian fascism, Giovanni Gentile, had written of fascism as a 'total conception of life'. Mussolini over the next few years came more and more to describe the system he had created as *'lo stato totalitario'* – the total or totalitarian state.

Critics of authoritarianism, of Mussolini's actual reliance on castor oil and the cosh and of Hitler's National-Socialist terror state, came increasingly to link fascism, Nazism and communism as promoting totalitarian rule and a totalitarian concept of society, fundamentally opposed to the pluralism of democracy. In 1929, *The Times* wrote of 'a reaction against parliamentarism . . . in favour of a "totalitarian" or unitary state, whether Fascist or Communist'. Nazis (especially Hitler himself) used the term sparingly in the early 1930s and hardly at all after that, though their attacks on parliamentarianism and the 'spiritual decay' of democracy were vicious and uncompromising. They preferred the terms 'authoritarian' and 'leadership principle'.

With the Second World War, *totalitarian* came to be a negative, a pejorative description of what an increasing number of politically and sociologically-minded critics, from Franz Borkenau to George Orwell, saw as a dangerous new phenomenon, powerful, ideologically-based and implacably opposed to freedom, creativity and independence, organizing the masses in the interest of evil. Borkenau's *The Totalitarian Enemy* appeared in 1940; Aldous Huxley, by 1944, was accusing the left-wing intellectuals and the Labour Party in the United Kingdom of being 'eager totalitarians'.

Equally influential, if not even more so, was Karl Popper's *The Open Society and Its Enemies*, which linked Plato, Hegel and Marx as propounders of a closed monism, which rejected both actual and methodological individualism, pitting essentialism against pluralism, authoritarianism against freedom. Popper himself did not, at that stage, stress the word totalitarian but his elevation of the open society became an important intellectual slogan in the critique of both fascism and communism.

It was especially after the Second World War, with increasing consciousness of communist methods of statecraft and growing suspicion of Stalin, that totalitarianism came to be an important wider political concept, suggesting that fascism, National Socialism and communism all rejected 'plurality of thinking' and ruthlessly imposed their will on society. In doing so, they not only posed similar threats to democracy but were developing similar types of states, in which the state or the political leadership or the all-embracing ideological party was more powerful than the rest of society put together. Successful internal resistance was impossible.

The late Professor Carl J. Friedrich played a leading role in the conference on *Totalitarianism* held in the American Academy of Art and Sciences in 1953 by seeking to define, or at least characterize, that concept. He published, with Z. K. Brzezinski, their highly influential *Totalitarian Dictatorship and Autocracy* in 1956. Hannah Arendt had completed her *The Origins of Totalitarianism* in autumn 1949 and published the first edition of the book in 1951, emphasizing that anti-Semitism was an outrage to common sense and that Progress and Doom are two sides of the same medal – both articles of superstition, not of faith. Totalitarianism came at the end of a century of rubbish.

Karl A. Wittfogel, in his *Oriental Despotism: A Comparative Study of Total Power* (1957) linked communist totalitarianism with the traditions and realities of an agro-managerial despotism based on what Marx called an 'Asiatic mode of production', rooted in the historical primacy of state-sponsored irrigation and flood control. Here the state was, and is, the chief organizer of the necessary foundations of economic activity and, as some quasi-Marxists have subsequently preferred to stress, the principal appropriator of surplus value. Power, Wittfogel demonstrated *contra* Marx, did not derive from ownership alone; the state was not necessarily the executive committee of an owning class. Power could rest on managerial and organizational functions and be aided by the absence of security in private property. It could therefore be intensified rather than *aufgehoben* ('sublated', i.e. abolished and transcended) in societies in which significant private property had been abolished. Both their technological sophistication and modernization and their more complete control of the economy made twentieth-century totalitarianism in Russia and China more powerful, more pervasive, more successful in controlling society than the totalitarianisms, the agro-managerial despotisms, of the past. Truly fragmented and feudal societies like Japan, however, were not instances of totalitarianism or Oriental despotism, though they lay in the Orient and copied some Chinese imperial pretensions.

In the next ten to twenty years the word 'totalitarianism' entered more and more into popular usage, especially in the English-speaking world. The Marxist Left derided or criticized it as an imprecise or dishonest attempt to link fascism and communism as enemies of democracy, to deflect attention from the class struggle and to promote the Cold War. Others thought it captured the essential thing about Leninist communism: its ruthless use of state power to suppress everything that might challenge such power or the ultimate vision of communism.

With Khrushchev's 1956 secret speech admitting the crimes of Stalin came the rapid disintegration of the comparatively monolithic World Communist Movement, especially after the failure of the 1960 World Communist Conference. Some communists and not only social democrats began to be more openly and sharply critical of the 'Russian model' for communism and to argue that a true socialism required genuine democratic institutions and traditions and not only the abolition of significant private ownership in the means of production, distribution and exchange and the rational organization of the economy. The more academically-minded and the less politically *engagé* worried how totalitarianism was to be defined, what its essential or necessary characteristics were and who, if anybody, was the person, class, group or party whose will shaped the character and policies of a totalitarian society. That discussion took on increasing urgency and scope both within and outside Marxism as Stalinism and then Maoism came to be more widely repudiated. Just as the changes in the communist world and fading of the Cold War into history seemed to be making the concept 'totalitarian' politically and ideologically obsolete, rebellious dissidents and democrats in Eastern Europe, the territories of the then USSR and even in China began in 1990 and 1991 to take up the term once more to express their disgust for a system that strove to smother instead of liberating civil society, individual liberty and human rights and that used unprincipled force and trickery to suppress opposition. Many such anti-totalitarians are now the rulers of their country.

Analysis

Fundamental concepts in social thought, Max Weber reminds us, are not well presented as classificatory concepts, as pigeonholes into which societies, social institutions and social ideologies are to be fitted on an all-or-nothing basis. They are rather 'ideal types', logically interrelated complexes of attitudes, institutions and trends that are mutually supportive within each ideal type and strive to realize themselves in history. Further, many fundamental political concepts, like power, authority, control, are similarly porous, relative, incapable of clear-cut separation, distinction, absoluteness. They are points, often moving points, in a continuum that knows not truly absolute power and control, totally uncontested authority or the complete absence of those phenomena. No one sensitive or informed has any doubt about the difference between Stalin's Soviet Union and the situation that preceded and followed his period of power – yet there are important continuities. It is plausible to say that Stalin's Russia and Stalin's practice and ideology were paradigmatically totalitarian, that Lenin was only an authoritarian with proto-totalitarian tendencies and that Khrushchev and his successors moved the Soviet Union back in fits and starts to an authoritarian society that nevertheless had continuing totalitarian structures and potentials. There is no great profit or interest in seeking to carve up the flux of history into formally separate segments; the important issue is the direction and strength of a development. Even the most fervent proponents of the concept of a totalitarian state do not believe that the dividing lines between the authoritarian and the totalitarian will not be blurred or problematic, a matter of degree, or that authoritarianism in fact knows no plurality of thinking or of action.

The most influential attempt to reduce to order the features which characterize the regimes generally considered totalitarian – the fascist Italian, the Nazi German and the communist model created in the Soviet Union and copied in China and elsewhere – was that made by Carl J. Friedrich in 1954. He strove, in his presentation to the 1953 *Totalitarianism* Conference published in 1954 as 'The Unique Character in Totalitarian Society', to show that totalitarianism was a new and unique form of rule and that its characteristics were common to both the fascist and the communist type of totalitarianism. Friedrich listed five factors that made up or justified the label 'totalitarian':

1 An official ideology focused on a perfect final state of humankind, to which everyone is supposed to adhere.
2 A single mass party usually symbolized by or subordinated to one person; it is hierarchically organized and superior to or intertwined with the state bureaucracy.
3 A technologically advanced, near-complete monopoly of the weapons of armed combat by that party and the bureaucracy subordinated to it.
4 A similar nearly complete monopoly of the means of mass communication.
5 A system of physical or psychological control by terror.

Hannah Arendt, another distinguished student of totalitarianism, has emphasized that totalitarian movements aim at and succeed in organizing masses, not classes, and George Mosse, studying the nationalist *mise-en-scène*, war memorials, rallies and diaries, has brought out the theatrical means by which the Nazis especially welded the masses into a disciplined unity. As a more recent writer has put it, 'The totalitarian society is a single-minded structure. It mobilises all its resources under one authority to achieve one goal' (Walker, 1972, p. 5). Neither the Nazis nor the fascists, however – admittedly in a much shorter period – ever achieved the ubiquity of control over initially independent structures and institutions – the economy, the military – that the communists achieved. There is now some historical argument whether Bolshevik Russia, its rallies and show-trials provided the theatrical and organizational model for the Nazis, or vice versa, but the element of psychological manipulation is now emphasized more strongly than it was in the earlier writing.

Friedrich, by then collaborating with Brzezinski and now increasingly conscious of communism, rather than fascism, in 1956 added a sixth factor to the totalitarian syndrome – central control and direction of the entire economy. (The Nazis, students have noted with surprise, exercised less pervasive and much more haphazard economic control.) Friedrich also extended the monopolies of control he had noted from mass communications and arms to all organizations including economic ones.

The expanded six-point syndrome promulgated by Friedrich and Brzezinski has long dominated the academic discussion of totalitarianism among political scientists and helped to raise a host of problems. It has been argued that a monopoly of weapons is basic to most governments and not confined to those that are totalitarian and that most of the other five factors differ relatively rather than absolutely from the pretensions of many non-totalitarian governments. Some have thought that a theory and a programme of world domination and a need for constant mass mobilization of effort are essential to totalitarianism. The greatest problem, for everyone, has been the description of the ruling group or elite that dominates a totalitarian society. Most attempts to define it in class, educational, ideological, functional or interest group terms have not been conspicuously successful; nor have they reinforced the claim that there is a monolithic totalitarian system, party, bureaucracy or state. The true totalitarian servant, it has been said, is simply he (or she) who will do whatever is necessary to gain and keep favour. The most plausible Soviet 'ruling class' – the *nomenklatura* (Voslensky, 1984) – was defined by the fact that each appointment had to be approved by the highest party level.

More recently, the discussion of totalitarianism has put more emphasis on the absence or presence of those factors in society which are, at least relatively, independent of the state and capable of confronting it on the basis of their own authority. Private enterprise and private property made secure by law are two such factors; a comparatively autonomous legal system, tradition and profession is another; democratic institutions, a multiplicity of parties, a church not created by or subservient to the state constitute others. The upshot of these wide-ranging discussions is not a listing of the essential factors of totalitarianism or the marking off of unambiguous borders between the totalitarian, the authoritarian and the pluralist-democratic.

One of the most distinguished students of the Soviet Union and totalitarianism, Leonard Shapiro, has argued, indeed, that totalitarianism has pillars, such as ideology and the party, but that central to totalitarianism is a single leader, who usually recognizes that he will not have an equally determined and competent successor and who knows instinctively that collective leadership spells the beginning of the end. Shapiro (1972, pp. 124–5) concludes his *Totalitarianism* with perceptive and moving words:

What, then, is the value of 'totalitarianism' as a concept? The evidence that has been adduced suggests that it stands for a distinct and new form of government which first became possible in the age of mass democracy, of modern technology and of twentieth-century nationalism. It can vary in its extent, in its success, in its totality – from the relative failure to erect a system of total power in the cases of Mussolini and Nkrumah, to the relative success of Hitler and Stalin. It is not a fixed and immutable form: it can change and evolve, as well as end in collapse and overthrow. It can develop into something approximating to liberal democracy, as in Yugoslavia or in the short-lived attempt in Czechoslovakia [1968], which required brute force to put it down. It can coexist, at all events for a time, with an independent church, as in Poland; with pluralism of institutions, as in some of the other Communist governments in the Central and East European 'People's Democracies'; and with dissent, incipient pressure groups and some pluralism of institutions in the Soviet Union. These instances of coexistence may well be transitional stages towards a different form of dictatorship, towards some kind of liberal democracy, or towards a return of full and unqualified totalitarian power. All this suggests that totalitarianism is not a final and immutable 'model' of government, but more in the nature of a spectrum, with varying degrees of intensity and totality . . . Perhaps as a concept totalitarianism is elusive, hard to define, liable to abuse by the demagogue, and, if wrongly used, a source of confusion when we are trying to find our way through the maze of the many forms which a polity can assume. Yet, we should be poorer without it, if only because we would lack the reminder that there are stages in the history of nations, perhaps of every nation, when the fanaticism, the arrogance, the ruthlessness, the ambition and the hubris of one individual can plunge millions of men and women into madness, suffering, fear and destruction.

Collapse?

Totalitarianism is a twentieth-century word, but not one without earlier adumbrations or exemplifications. Consider only Aristotle's contrast between the unstable tyrannies among the Greeks and the pervasive, accepted, constitutionalized Oriental despotisms of successive Persian empires in which citizens are reduced to subjects and servility becomes a habit. Most students of totalitarianism believe that modern technology, especially the dramatic improvement in communication and techniques of surveillance, have made possible degrees of control by the centre undreamt of in earlier societies. Nevertheless, a strong sub-current in the literature emphasizes historical conditions and precedents that made possible the twentieth-century totalitarian state. That sub-current has derived inspiration from Marx's half-hearted conception of an Asiatic mode of production based on the state's organization of public works, especially irrigation and flood control, and from Max Weber's studies of bureaucracy, satrapy and rule by officials in Ancient Egypt, the Roman and Byzantine empires, Imperial China and Maurya India. The concept totalitarian has thus been enriched, though also made more complex, by a wealth of historical detail, allusion and controversy. Much of that discussion, too, was initially but not permanently or exclusively organized around an allied and quasi-Marxist response to the rise of Mussolini, Hitler and Stalin, the concept of a bureaucratic or managerial class that owns collectively rather than individually. Such a class, it was now argued, could well use socialism as an ideology for legitimizing its own rule. Such bureaucracies created a society in which everyone who did not derive his power from the state was equally powerless and dependent, whether he lived in the 'Socialist Empire of the Incas', the Egypt of the New Kingdom or the Russia of the Muscovite Tsars. Bruno Rizzi's *La Bureaucratisation du monde*, like Jan Waclaw Machajski's earlier *The Intellectual Worker* and James Burnham's *The Managerial Revolution* helped to inspire this trend, though their somewhat pamphleteering contributions were quickly left behind, even if their anti-managerial sentiments were not.

Max Weber, studying ancient societies and traditional authority, distinguished three different types of traditional authority. *Gerontocracy* was the rule of elders taken to represent the group and to understand its sacred traditions. In *patriarchalism*, authority was exercised by a particular individual, designated by a partial rule of inheritance, but his authority was still pre-eminently on behalf of the group as a whole. *Patrimonialism*, for Weber, was dependent on the development of a purely personal administrative staff and especially of a military force belonging to the ruler himself. Members of the society or group now become 'subjects'. Authority, though still primarily oriented to tradition in its exercise, makes the claim of full personal powers. Patrimonial bureaucracy enables the system to expand through regularized co-ordination of imperatives, through increasingly large staffs. But such authority continues to rest on tradition, and its focus is the personal authority of the ruler, including a large measure of charismatic or routinized charismatic authority. Weber argues that in the ancient world, but also in parts of the non-rational modern, such personal authority rests heavily on the external support of otherwise statusless dependants: slaves, coloni, eunuchs, conscripted subjects, mercenaries, bodyguards and others. Freed from traditional limitations, such patrimonial authority can approach the arbitrary exercise of the ruler's will and can become sultanism. Similar authoritarian tendencies coupled with the promotion of bureaucratization have been discussed by Edward Shils and Shmuel Eisenstadt as part of the political system of empires. In late imperial and imperial feudal societies, central authority rested to an important extent on a cultural and social tradition, created, represented and controlled by the centre, which reconstructed and evaluated social reality, the cosmic and the socio-political order, and the ultimate duties of the peripheries, providing symbols of collective identity and major modes of legitimacy. Such systems were indeed at their most powerful when they were Byzantine or Caesaro-Papist, welding together religious and political authority, ideologizing the work of the centre and its servants. Stalin's Russia and Mao's China have been seen as displaying significant continuity with the traditional empires they displaced.

Bureaucracies and authority can be civil or military or both. The remarkable rise of Russia and of Prussia as great powers in the most adverse circumstances was significantly connected in each case with the militarization of the population and of administration as the basis of expanded and rationalizing central power and with the consequent weakness of non-bureaucratic social classes as independent groups – a situation very different from that which obtained in most of Western Europe and especially in England, France, Italy, the Netherlands, etc. Reflection on these and similar developments led theorists who used the concept of totalitarianism to a sharp distinction between tyranny and totalitarianism or, in its earlier manifestation, between Oriental despotism and the contractually-based pluralist European feudalism in which the king was never more powerful than the rest of society combined. Despotisms, systems of rule that knew only subjects and not citizens, were premissed on and made possible by the underdevelopment of social classes as independent economic or political groups. Whatever the reasons for such underdevelopment, and they might be many and contingent, one had no difficulty in recognizing a society in which no one was great or authoritative unless and until the ruler made him so. Much of this line of approach was premissed on and given heart by the claim that the two great successes of communism – the creation of the Soviet state and the formation of the People's Republic of China - took place in societies that had for much of their history been 'Oriental despotisms' in which a serving class totally dependent on the ruler was strong and respected and in which merchants and the non-official middle classes generally were weak and despised. On all this, of course, the literature is enormous, the dispute never ending and the supply of considerations adduced as relevant inexhaustible. One implication of this way of approaching the rise and initial success of communism – that Bolshevik communism is more at home with the legacy

635

of the Tsars or the Sons of Heaven than with that of Jan Hus, the Polish *szlachta*, the Italian city-states or the Common Law – has again been given vivid plausibility by the collapse of communism in Eastern Europe and the break-up of the Soviet Empire.

Max Weber believed, correctly, that the prebendal authority of traditional bureaucracies produced a constant element of instability in which officials turned their offices into fiefs. This was irremediable until modern times, when a money economy, the development of Roman law and other factors gave rise to the impersonality of rational-legal authority that separated the office and the function from the home and independent social status of the office-holder. Communist totalitarian societies combined both prebendal and rational-legal elements in their structure of authority, using terror as the ultimate safeguard against independence while a strong leader was in charge. Without terror, even the allegedly rational bureaucratic structures extolled by Weber proved to be less 'rational' and more potentially competitive and client-oriented than he admitted. The central issue about totalitarianism is not the absence of competitive and conflicting groups, an absence falsely proclaimed by the official ideology, but their ultimate insecurity while the leader or the centre remains seriously totalitarian. Totalitarianism in our time has collapsed from the top, but it has been seriously undermined by a process of education, rationalization and internationalization of outlooks and behaviour patterns on which much modern economic achievement depends. That process is still not badly described as 'modernization'.

See also 4 SOCIOLOGY; 6 POLITICAL SCIENCE; 8 ANARCHISM; 11 LIBERALISM; 12 MARXISM; 17 CONSTITUTIONALISM AND THE RULE OF LAW; 19 DEMOCRACY; 21 DISCOURSE; 26 FEDERALISM; 28 LEGITIMACY; 30 POWER; 34 SECESSION AND NATIONALISM; 36 STATE; 37 TOLERATION AND FUNDAMENTALISM; 39 TRUST

References

Arendt, H.: *The Origins of Totalitarianism*, 3rd edn (London: Allen & Unwin, 1967; first published as *The Burden of Our Time*, 1951).

Burnham, J.: *The Managerial Revolution* (New York: John Day Co. Inc., 1941).

Eisenstadt, S. N.: *The Political Systems of Empires* (New York: Free Press of Glencoe, 1963).

Friedrich, C. J. and Brzezinski, Z. K.: *Totalitarian Dictatorship and Autocracy* (1956), 2nd edn rev. C. J. Friedrich (Cambridge, Mass.: Harvard University Press, 1965).

Huxley, A. L.: *Letters*, ed. G. Smith (London: Chatto & Windus, 1969).

Kamenka, E.: *Bureaucracy* (Oxford: Blackwell, 1989).

Machajski, J. W., as Volsky, A.: *Umstvennyi rabochii* (1905); trans. as *The Intellectual Worker* (New York: Interlanguage Literary Associates, 1968).

Popper, K. R.: *The Open Society and Its Enemies* (1945); 5th edn, 2 vols (London: Routledge & Kegan Paul, 1966).

Rizzi, B.: *The Bureaucratization of the World*, trans. A. Westoby (New York: Free Press, 1985; originally published as Part 1 of *La Bureaucratisation du monde*, 1939).

Shapiro, L. B.: *Totalitarianism* (London: Pall Mall, 1972).

Shils, E. A.: *Center and Periphery: Essays in Macrosociology* (Chicago: University of Chicago Press, 1975).

Sturzo, L.: *Italy and Fascismo*, trans. B. B. Carter (London: Faber and Gwyer, 1926).

Voslensky, M.: *Nomenklatura: Anatomy of the Soviet Ruling Class*, trans. E. Mosbacher (London: Bodley Head, 1984).

Walker, M.: *The National Front* (London: Fontana, 1972).

Weber, M.: *Economy and Society: An Outline of Interpretive Sociology*, ed. G. Roth and C. Wittich, trans. E. Fischoff and others, 3 vols (New York: Bedminster Press, 1968; from 4th German edn of *Wirtschaft und Gesellschaft*, first published 1922).

————: *From Max Weber: Essays in Sociology*, ed. and trans. H. H. Gerth and C. W. Mills (New York: Oxford University Press, 1946).

Wittfogel, K. A.: *Oriental Despotism: A Comparative Study of Total Power* (New Haven, Conn.: Yale University Press, 1957).

39

Trust

JOHN DUNN

Few modern philosophers are convinced that the nature and availability of trust between human beings really is a central issue in the theoretical understanding of politics. This is in some ways surprising, since the the most prominent recent movement in political philosophy, the largely North American dialogue about the content of social justice inaugurated by John Rawls (1971), has been strongly committed to the theoretical centrality of the idea of a contract: a free, but binding, agreement. The normative force of the standard of uncoerced choice by free and rational agents unites the great seventeenth and eighteenth-century philosophical exponents of natural law and natural rights with modern contractarian critics of the claims of utility to serve as a uniform criterion for political and social decisions. But the two groups of thinkers differ drastically in their estimate of the practical significance of that normative force.

For early modern theorists of natural law (Locke, Rousseau, even Hobbes), there were the closest of ties between voluntary self-commitment, the obligatory force of a contract or promise, and the psychological and social foundations of human collective life. *Fides*, the duty to keep faith and the practical virtue of discharging that duty in a dependable fashion, was the foundation for social life in its entirety (Dunn, 1985, ch. 2), the key practical capacity which made it possible for human beings to live with one another on tolerable terms at all. Modern contractarians agree with their seventeenth-century predecessors on what gives the standard its normative force: the irreducible separateness of human persons – the fact that each human being experiences, values, judges and chooses in the last instance for themselves. It is, above all, this feature of the human condition to which utilitarianism, rightly or wrongly, is held to give insufficient recognition. But unlike their seventeenth-century predecessors, modern contractarians see no apparent connection between the normative force of the idea of free choice and the practical issue of how far and why human beings conceive themselves as bound by their own choices. Which of the two groups is right?

It is easy to lose sight of the importance of this question. The two groups of contractarians plainly differ extensively within their own ranks over a wide range of issues. There is a large measure of unreality in presuming all the members of either group to be discussing essentially the same question; and there are still more obvious and drastic differences between the intellectual and historical assumptions of the two groups taken together and between the very diverse topics with which their members have been severally concerned. But it is not strategically intelligent, either for philosophers or for political theorists, to rest content with noting the historical heterogeneity of assumptions and preoccupations across these rather distant and somewhat arbitrarily composed and juxtaposed groups. From the evident fact that they were discussing widely discrepant issues on the basis of readily distinguishable systems of belief, it does not follow that their views do not imply on some points sharply contradictory judgements. More importantly, if political philosophy is conceived not simply in terms of the lucid analysis of an array of politically current conceptions but also as an understanding of what politics is and what it means, it does not follow that one of these two bodies of human reflection may not and does not offer a far more penetrating and less parochial account of politics than the other (compare Dunn, 1990, chs 2–4). No one today would be surprised by the claim that some aspects of recent political philosophy mark a clear cognitive advance on the intellectual products of the seventeenth century. (It would be discouraging if none did.) But in so far as that judgement makes coherent sense, it must leave open the real possibility that some aspects of recent political philosophy may represent something of a cognitive retreat on the same level of achievement. In the case of the significance of trust for an understanding of what politics is and what it means, there are grounds for supposing that this is indeed the case. (Compare Bernard Williams' arguments for the superior strategic insight furnished by Greek ethics for a post-Christian era: Williams, 1985.)

What are these grounds? The first and most important is the very different relation between morality and politics in the two bodies of thinking: the narrowing of scope and the sharp constriction in the scale of cognitive responsibility assumed in the modern recensions of contractarianism. There has been some apparent shift in Rawls' understanding of the nature of his own theory (Rawls, 1971; 1980; 1985; cf. Barry, 1989); and there is considerable disagreement among subsequent American contributions to the analysis of social justice about the relation between reflective equilibrium within the mind of an individual moral theorist and political argument between such theorists. But despite these real variations in theoretical strategy and intellectual ambition, it is broadly correct to say that no modern political philosophers of any stature attempt to understand both morality and politics through essentially the same set of concepts, while all major political philosophers of the seventeenth century (and many of the eighteenth) attempted precisely that. This was not because all seventeenth-century political philosophers were religiously, morally or culturally credulous, while all late twentieth-century political philosophers are religiously, morally and culturally sceptical. (Compare Hobbes with Rawls, Dworkin, Walzer or Taylor.) But it is a natural consequence of the greater overall pressure of scepticism in the intellectual atmosphere of the late twentieth century than in seventeenth-century Europe.

For seventeenth-century contractarians, to understand political obligation through the idea of a contract had powerful attractions. It could explain why individual subjects of a legitimate government should be obliged to obey its laws by invoking their own acts and the determinations of their own wills (Riley, 1982). The strongest answer that could be given to a political sceptic for why he should regard himself as politically obliged was that he had bound himself by his own acts. (Female sceptics were not yet thought to need an answer: a consideration still tacitly important in late twentieth-century theories of social justice: cf. Kymlicka, 1991.) The clearest example of a free choice binding the future acts of a human agent (or indeed a supra-human agent: Locke, [1690] 1988, II, 195, p. 396: '*Grants, Promises* and *Oaths* are Bonds that hold the *Almighty*') was a promise or compact. To keep a promise, to observe covenants made, was both in itself a rational practice and a moral duty. It was above all the capacity to see the rationality of this duty which enabled human beings to live dependably with one another. It constituted the bond (*vinculum*) of human society. This view was common to thinkers who disagreed as sharply as Hobbes and Locke, both about the circumstances in which human beings could be validly inferred to have chosen to accept the authority of their government, about the degree of political subjection which it was rational for them to accept, and about the measure of mutual security afforded in practice by purely verbal undertakings. ('And Covenants, without the Sword, are but Words, and of no strength to secure a man at all': Hobbes, [1651] 1991, XVII, 117). Hence the overwhelming importance of the question why in the last instance human beings had good reason to keep their word: Locke's estimate of the menace of atheism ('The taking away of God, tho but even in thought dissolves all': Locke, [1689] 1983, 51) and the practical foundations of Hobbes' bleakly minimalist 'laws of nature'. For seventeenth-century contractarians the issue of what human beings had good reason to do (the normative theory of rationality) was in the end inseparable from the question of how they should in practice be expected to behave.

It is the rejection of this connection, the modern epistemic presumption of a categorical disjunction between fact and value, drawn from Locke, Hume and Kant, which has thrust the issue of trust to the margins of modern political philosophy. The question of how human beings can be expected to behave is a matter of fact, consigned to social science. The question of how they should behave is a matter of value, to be decided by free and rational agents, perhaps in the light of the findings of the social sciences (whatever these might be), but in the end in terms of the reflective self-consciousness of an individual moral theorist. Whether human beings should keep their promises is a question of moral theory, with a range of possible answers: usually, sometimes yes, sometimes no. But whether they will do so is a quite separate question of fact, with no intrinsic implications for moral theory. This point of view has deep imaginative and theoretical roots; and it need carry no particularly dismaying implications for morality seen as the assessment by individual human beings of how they have good reason to live their own lives. (The question of how dismaying its implications in fact are is simply a matter for future social scientists.) But it is appreciably more destructive to the attempt to understand the nature and significance of politics.

As it happens, the modern social sciences have not been at their most impressive when it comes to analysing either the conditions in which human beings do or do not trust one another or the consequences of their success or failure in doing so (Gambetta, 1988). Until very recently, indeed, they have been remarkably unsuccessful even in grasping the practical importance virtually throughout human collective life of the extent to which human beings do trust one another on a small or large scale or of the degree to which their mutual confidence or distrust is well-founded (but cf. Luhmann, 1979; 1988). A focus on the significance of trust in human relations has been replaced by an image of the more or less rational pursuit of interest; and any attempt to restore that focus has come to suggest sentimentality or a residually feudal social imagination (Hawthorn, 1988). This is not an unequivocal instance of intellectual progress. The model of rational pursuit of interest is illuminating enough as far as it goes. But it severely underemphasizes the epistemic difficulties which human beings face in identifying their interests in the first place, their modest capacity to pursue them effectively even in their own immediate environment, and the massive further obstacles which confront them in concerting together to pursue such interests in the refractory medium of political and economic competition. For creatures with the properties of human beings the problem of mutual trust today is no closer to the margins of practical life (no more narrowly domestic and personal) than it was in the High Middle Ages. It lies at the centre of all political processes; and it cannot be adequately modelled in terms of rational egoists pursuing clearly conceived individual interests.

Trust is both a passion (an affective condition, linked to expectations of others' future actions) and a policy (a method of dealing with the fact that most important human interests depend profoundly on the future free actions of other human beings). These are probably better seen over time as two ways of conceiving essentially the same reality, not as descriptions of two comprehensively distinguishable phenomena. (You are credulous; but I trust rationally.) The passion, plainly enough, can be disabling as well as enabling. (So too can its antithesis: a more or less acute or compulsive mistrust.) The question of whom to trust and how far is as central a question of political life as it is of personal life. Modern philosophy has essentially given up on this question (not just as a concrete question of existential or political judgement, where seventeenth-century philosophers, no doubt, overestimated the epistemic resources available to them, but as a domain which requires philosophical comprehension precisely because no understanding of politics which did not do justice to it could in principle be coherent and well founded). If it is right in committing itself to this by now rather deeply motivated imaginative option, we can be confident that the political contribution of academic philosophy (as opposed, for example, to that of academic economics) will remain severely marginal (Dunn, 1985, ch. 10; cf. Dunn, 1990). But can the option really be right?

There are several strong reasons for supposing that it is in fact right. In the first place, if human values are essentially human inventions, then even the most elegant and imaginatively attractive theory of human values could at best be only an especially impressive human invention, and one which would be impressive only in so far as other human beings happened to find it so. One reason why some seventeenth-century philosophers saw fidelity as a morally and epistemically decisive foundation for human relations was their confidence in the existence of an effective sanction for that virtue independently of the wills or mental processes of any human beings whatever. The Law of Nature was not merely a set of humanly beneficial precepts. It was also an authoritative, and in the last instance an effectively enforced command of Nature's omniscient and omnipotent Creator. With the effective disappearance of the assumption that Nature was created for a purpose, and with the associated awareness of the variability in human values and social arrangements over time and space, it is hard today to believe that Nature has any Law, and quite hard to believe that human beings, in any politically illuminating sense, share a common nature. The Law of Nature specified a supra-political context for human politics and one within which that politics must *ex hypothesi* be understood (Dunn, 1969). But few contemporary thinkers presume that there is in this sense any supra-political context for human politics, over and above the naturally given universe within which human beings still have to live: a setting to be understood, as best it can be, through the sciences of nature.

In the second place, in so far as trust must be conceived as a passion, its causal incidence must surely be understood (if at all) through the resources of the human sciences, the sciences of man envisaged as a natural creature living in society over time. What causes people to be able (or unable) to trust others is a no doubt complicated matter of fact. We may not yet have learnt much about it. But it can only be the human sciences (individual and social psychology, political science, sociology, anthropology, economics, the theory of games) that could teach us how to understand it.

In the third place, even if trust is viewed firmly as policy, a more or less consciously adopted strategy for dealing with the freedom of other human beings over time, any assessment of how far it is well- or ill-founded would have to distinguish given purposes and preoccupations sharply from available means. It would have, in effect to endorse the values of particular human agents or groups (family, village, tribe, city, class, firm, nation, ideological movement) and ask how these values could be most effectively implemented in a heavily objectified social, economic and political setting, seen as a set of constraints upon and opportunities for the agents in question. Within this framework, values are taken as given (causal products of socialization of varying effectiveness) or as freely chosen; and policies of giving or withholding trust are monitored solely in terms of their strategic or tactical effectiveness. Contemporary philosophers aspire to ask clear and manageable questions and to answer them frankly and with some intellectual economy, passing firmly on to other clearly prescribed intellectual specialists responsibility for answering the parts which their own professional competence cannot reach. It would be silly to deny the cumulative intellectual advantages which have come from determined adoption of this policy. But in relation to politics the tradeoff between these palpable cumulative benefits and the equally apparent cumulative costs of its adoption has been peculiarly unfavourable.

Why should this have proved so? Why, to take a somewhat tendentious example, should central elements in the political arguments of Hobbes and Locke three centuries later not merely have come to serve as leading themes in modern conceptions of political authority across the world but even been firmly incorporated into the practical structures of a large range of modern states (Skinner, 1989; Dunn, 1991; 1992; Fontana, 1993)? Why, by contrast, should the sophisticated modern theorization of social justice, the grounds for allocating the costs and benefits of social membership in a rationally defensible manner (which certainly addresses a central question in contemporary democratic politics), have been so readily brushed aside by the electorates of Western democracies over the last fifteen years when they came to take their sovereign decisions?

There is no reason to suppose that either Hobbes or Locke (or, for that matter, Rousseau or Hegel) succeeded in providing a convincing theory of political obligation: of how far and why individual subjects of particular governments should see themselves as bound by (and not merely menaced by) the laws issued by those governments (Dunn, 1991). It may well be the case that the leading Western political philosophers of the last twenty years have asked clearer and more manageable questions than their great contractarian predecessors, and even that in some cases they have given neater and more convincing answers to these questions. But in contrast with the vividly political and often intuitively compelling efforts of these predecessors, they have been notably ineffectual in the suggestions they contrived to offer their readers for how the latter had good reason to act (Dunn, 1980, ch. 10; Nagel, 1991).

Unsympathetically considered, contemporary theorists of social justice have advanced moral theories about a distinctively political subject matter, and done so within an at least formally democratic space in which their own moral consciousness is, *ex hypothesi*, on a par with that of any of their readers. (It may be far better thought through; but it cannot carry any greater intrinsic authority.) They have advanced their theories, moreover, without attempting to develop an accompanying conception of the place of morality in human life (a modern analogue of the Law of Nature) that might give them some capacity to penetrate and re-order the moral consciousness of their readers (cf. Nagel, 1991). But, more importantly, they have done so, too, without making any real effort to reconceive the nature of the political space within which that offer will be either accepted or rejected. In tacitly (or in some cases explicitly) presupposing a massively objectified and alienated vision of the nature of that space they have offered an apolitical answer to an intensely political question (cf. Unger, 1987; Dunn, 1990).

If they are right in endorsing this massively objectified and alienated vision, their offer is pre-condemned to political futility. If they are wrong, they have been directing their moral and political imaginations on far too narrow a target to give their moral vision any real political chance. Whether they are in fact wrong may seem simply a question for others: in particular, the practitioners of the social sciences. It is clearly under active dispute amongst the latter. But it may well be a question which requires a more philosophical answer: not in the discredited sense of appeals to grandiose metaphysical structures but in the simpler sense of an answer that captures and relates clearly together the key elements in the subject under consideration. If a less alienated and objectified understanding of what politics is is epistemically appropriate, this will in the end be because what politics consists in (at least from a human point of view) is a huge array of free agents coping with each others' freedom over time. In politics so understood the rationality of trust will always be the most fundamental question.

See also 4 SOCIOLOGY; 9 CONSERVATISM; 11 LIBERALISM; 13 SOCIALISM; 15 COMMUNITY; 16 CONTRACT AND CONSENT; 21 DISCOURSE; 25 EQUALITY; 28 LEGITIMACY; 35 SOCIOBIOLOGY; 37 TOLERATION AND FUNDAMENTALISM; 40 VIRTUE

References

Baier, A.: 'Trust and distrust', *Ethics*, 96 (1986), 231–60.

Ball, T., Farr, J. and Hanson, R., eds: *Political Innovation and Conceptual Change* (Cambridge: Cambridge University Press, 1989).

Barry, B.: *Theories of Justice* (Hemel Hempstead: Harvester, 1989).

Dunn, J.: *The Political Thought of John Locke* (Cambridge: Cambridge University Press, 1969).

————: *Political Obligation in its Historical Context* (Cambridge: Cambridge University Press, 1980).

————: *Rethinking Modern Political Theory* (Cambridge: Cambridge University Press, 1985).

————: *Interpreting Political Responsibility* (Cambridge: Polity Press, 1990).

———— ed.: *The Economic Limits to Modern Politics* (Cambridge: Cambridge University Press, 1990).

————: 'Political obligation', in David Held (ed.), *Political Theory Today* (Cambridge: Polity Press, 1991), pp. 23–47.

———— ed.: *Democracy: the Unfinished Journey* (Oxford: Oxford University Press, 1992).

Dworkin, R.: *Taking Rights Seriously* (London: Duckworth, 1977).

Fontanta, B., ed.: *The Invention of the Modern Republic* (Cambridge: Cambridge University Press, 1993).

Gambetta, D.: *Trust: Making and Breaking Cooperative Relations* (Oxford: Blackwell, 1988).

Hawthorn, G.: 'Three ironies in trust', in D. Gambetta, *Trust* (Oxford: Blackwell, 1988), pp. 111–26.

Held, D., ed.: *Political Theory Today* (Cambridge: Polity Press, 1991).

Hobbes, T.: *Leviathan* (1651), ed. Richard Tuck (Cambridge: Cambridge University Press, 1991).

Kymlicka, W.: 'Rethinking the family', *Philosophy and Public Affairs*, 20 (1991), 77–97.

Locke, J.: *A Letter Concerning Toleration* (1689), ed. James Tully (Indianapolis: Hackett, 1983).

————: *Two Treatise of Government* (1690), ed. Peter Laslett (Cambridge: Cambridge University Press, 1988).

Luhmann, N.: *Trust and Power*, trans. H. David, J. Raffan and K. Rooney (Chichester: John Wiley, 1979).

————: 'Familiarity, confidence and trust', in D. Gambetta ed., *Trust* (Oxford: Blackwell, 1988), pp. 94–107.

Nagel, T.: *Equality and Partiality* (New York: Oxford University Press, 1991).

Rawls, J.: *A Theory of Justice* (Cambridge, Mass.: Harvard University Press, 1971).

————: 'Kantian constructivism in moral theory', *Journal of Philosophy*, 77 (1980), 515–72.

————: 'Justice as fairness: political not metaphysical', *Philosophy and Public Affairs*, 14 (1985), 223–51.

Riley, P.: *Will and Political Legitimacy* (Cambridge, Mass.: Harvard University Press, 1982).

Skinner, Q.: 'The state', in T. Ball, J. Farr and R. Hanson (eds), *Political Innovation and Conceptual Change* (Cambridge: Cambridge University Press, 1989), pp. 90–131.

Taylor, C.: *Sources of the Self* (Cambridge, Mass.: Harvard University Press, 1989).

Tuck, R.: *Natural Rights Theories* (Cambridge: Cambridge University Press, 1979).

Unger, R. M.: *False Necessity* (Cambridge: Cambridge University Press, 1987).

Walzer, M.: *Spheres of Justice* (Oxford: Martin Robertson, 1983).

Williams, B.: *Ethics and the Limits of Philosophy* (London: Fontana, 1985).

40

Virtue

MICHAEL SLOTE

There has recently been a revival of interest in virtue and the virtues among ethicists and political philosophers, and it has even been suggested that a focus on virtue can be the basis for a distinctive general approach to the understanding of human values. Without pressing for such a complete reorientation of ethical thinking, some political thinkers (e.g. Dennis Thompson in *Political Ethics and Public Office*) have stressed the need for a better understanding of what is desirable or counts as a virtue in public servants, and others, like Philip Pettit, John Pocock, John Rawls and Quentin Skinner, have described some of the ways in which republican or liberal-democratic virtues in citizens can be essential to the realization of one or another social ideal.

Ethicists like Bernard Williams in *Ethics and the Limits of Philosophy* and Alasdair MacIntyre in *After Virtue, Whose Justice? Which Rationality?* and *Three Rival Versions of Moral Enquiry* have suggested a return to ancient philosophizing about virtue as a basis for our thinking about ethics and politics generally, but their work raises a problem that any virtue-ethical approach must somehow face. The best known and recently influential ancient virtue ethicists are, of course, Plato and Aristotle, and both espoused anti-democratic political ideals. For that reason virtue ethics has a great deal to live down and one may wonder whether, in the light of present-day democratic thinking, ancient models can provide a relevant or plausible basis for our understanding of political values. In what follows, I would like to suggest a way in which such a thing might indeed be possible.

The ancient Stoics were also virtue ethicists, and although one does not find them defending modern views about the rights of citizens, some of them did defend the idea of the brotherhood of all men and of the divine spark or element in all human beings. (On this point see J. M. Rist's *Human Value*, 1992.) Such ideas seem far from Plato and Aristotle, and they move us in the direction of modern egalitarian/liberal views of social justice. But I also believe we can use other well-known ideas of the Stoics to ground our ethical thinking generally and our political ideals in particular.

The Stoics espoused an ideal of self-sufficiency, or *autarkeia*, according to which one should be free of all attachment to worldly pleasures and privileges and care only about what was assumed to be within one's control, namely, one's own virtue and rationality. But we need not take self-sufficiency to such an extreme to recognize it as an attractive human ideal. For example, when we praise people for being moderate in their desires or needs, we are not thinking of them as having to curb certain strong desires in order to insure their long-run well-being – exercising what we can call instrumental moderation. Rather, we imagine them as simply not desiring certain things many of us do want, as not tempted even by things that tempt us, as, in effect, capable of being entirely satisfied or content with what would not be enough to satisfy other people. Those who are not so easily satisfied seem needy and even greedy by comparison with someone whose desires are moderate, and such moderation represents an ideal of self-sufficiency, as opposed to dependency and neediness, that most of us think well of.

But the common idea of self-sufficiency has another facet less stressed by the Stoics, but perhaps more central to the present attempt to ground democratic political norms. Self-reliance is a form of self-sufficiency, and we expect, for example, that a developing individual will want or, at least typically, have to develop self-reliance, learning to live on her own and make her own way in the world. Typical adolescents and young adults do not want to remain forever dependent on their parents: they want self-reliant self-sufficiency, and they and we think less than highly of someone who remains ever parasitic upon his or her parents. Notice, however, that people who grow up in rich families and never have to earn a living in some measure resemble children who never grow into adult self-reliance.

The connection with Hegel's famous discussion, in the *Phenomenology of Spirit*, of master and slave ('Lordship and Bondage') now stares us in the face. Hegel spoke of work as an ideal (he was not, of course, the first to do so) and argued, in effect, that there is something inferior about the status of a master who depends on slaves or servants for all or most of his needs. Hegel does not mention the connection to child-like parasitism vs self-reliance, but it is precisely that connection which allows us to relate modern ideals of social justice to the fundamental idea of self-sufficiency.

Members of a ruling elite will some of them, obviously, rule; but where such an elite exists, many members do not have to work. And a leisure class is parasitic on working members of a society in the way young children depend on their parents. Children, of course, do a great deal for parents, but the dependence is largely one way – a fact that adolescent rebellion, etc., brings home to us. And to the extent, then, that self-reliance, rather than parasitism, is a condition we think well of, think necessary to adult human dignity, we have the beginnings of an argument from the notion of self-sufficiency to a democratic and somewhat egalitarian conception of social justice.

Ancient models may indeed, then, be relevant to the grounding of modern political ideals. Of course, there are well-known other approaches to democratic ideals of social justice relying on ideas from the Kantian, utilitarian or contractarian traditions of ethics, but the latter have, all of them, well-known problems, and it may therefore be welcome if it turns out that virtue ethics is capable of providing us with a general account of morality and with a defence of modern political ideals, in particular. I do not propose to offer the general account of individual morality in this brief space, but let me briefly sketch how the political ideals emerge from a strictly virtue-ethical, agent-based foundation.

Self-sufficiency is plausibly regarded as an admirable inner trait, and I want to argue that the kinds of societies we think of as unjust exhibit a lack of self-sufficiency in a number of different possible ways. A fully agent-based conception will ground

646

judgements of social justice in claims about the personal admirability or deplorability of the individuals in a given society (Plato's attempt in *The Republic* to move from justice writ large in the state to an understanding of individual justice is thus not purely agent-based). And as a first stage in our account, I would propose that where members of some social class live parasitically on the work/labour of others, the society as a whole fails of justice because of the lack of self-sufficiency of some of its members.

Notice that this charge cannot be evaded by claiming that the leisured may well have the ability to support themselves through work if they so chose: parasitism and self-reliance are more a matter of what one does and wants to do, than of what one *could* do. Also, criticism in terms of parasitism is bound to remind us of the Marxian critique of capitalist and other forms of exploitation. Marx (1972, vol. 2, p. 328) regards those who live off rents or merely finance capitalistic enterprises as parasites, but industrial capitalists are, for him, not parasites but exploiters. Our virtue-ethical account makes up the difference, so to speak, between these notions through further appeals to the notion of self-sufficiency of the sort we shall be making in what follows. What we have just said about economic parasitism represents only the beginning of an account of ethically admirable or just social structures.

What about the conceivable case, for example, where there is a ruling class, but no leisure class and thus no parasitism? Surely, Plato's *Republic* depicts just such a situation, and even granting that no actual human ruling elite would ever be as disinterested as Plato's guardians were supposed to be, it is still, at this point, difficult to see how an absence of parasitism can help to justify democratic political ideals. But even if there is no economic parasitism in Plato's ideal republic, another kind of self-reliance we have not yet spoken of is markedly absent, namely, self-reliance in thought and decision-making. The ruled do as they are told to do and are not supposed to think about important matters for themselves (remember the idea of the 'noble lie'), and at this point I think we need to expand our discussion and recognize that a certain amount, at least, of self-reliance in thought and decision is part of what we take to be involved in personal self-sufficiency, so that Plato's republic also fails to count as a just society according to the present conception. (Important discussions of the value of autonomous or self-reliant thought and decision can be found in Rousseau's *Emile* and Kant's essay 'What is Enlightenment?'.) A just society cannot have substantial economic or cognitive/decisional parasitism, and that conclusion clearly moves us in the direction of democratic structures.

If we exclude the Platonic republic and consider the way ruling elites actually work, we recognize that economic parasitism invariably accompanies political privilege. And such leisure and privilege will generally defend itself against democratic political innovations. Where there is demand, e.g. for (the extension of) voting rights, for the right to unionize, or for greater freedom of speech, a ruling class is likely to see a threat to its economic advantages and not just its political hegemony. (I simplify by ignoring the possibilities of dissociation between political power and economic power or wealth.) And when a leisured elite opposes democratic liberties and structures as a more or less conscious means of defending itself against the erosion of its leisured prerogatives and succeeds in its purpose, the absence of such democracy can be regarded as exhibiting, as the expression of, parasitism, of motivation that we can characterize as parasitical, even if the leisure class in question may not want to think of itself in such terms. But for agent-based virtue ethics, what exhibits a deplorable inner trait is itself morally deplorable, and when we extend this idea to the political sphere, we can say that social structures or institutions that exhibit deplorable motivation on the part of certain groups are themselves deplorable or unjust. We can also say that any society where groups of individuals are economically or cognitively/decisionally non-self-reliant is less than ideal from the standpoint of justice (we have some leeway with our metric of evaluation in determining just how much and what kinds of individual/group non-self-reliance are required for a society to count as *unjust overall*). But is this the whole story about social justice even in outline? I think not.

Notice that we have thus far had very little to say about the role of equality in a virtue-ethical ideal of society. To be sure, democratic institutions and the right, e.g. to unionize can act as a brake on socioeconomic inequalities, but still it is possible to imagine a libertarian meritocracy without socioeconomic or cognitive/decisional parasitism where differences in talent and luck led to great inequalities of income and well-being. Does our virtue-ethical ideal of self-sufficiency give us any reason to criticize such an arrangement and defend a more equal distribution of economic benefits as required by its notion of social justice? I think it does, but in order to see how, we must turn from self-reliance back to the kind of self-sufficiency we earlier saw to be exhibited in moderation in one's desires or wants.

A moderate individual feels she has enough and is thoroughly satisfied at a point where many of us would still want more of some presumptive good or enjoyment. Such an individual will thus not seek more *for herself*, but Nietzsche (in *Beyond Good and Evil* and *Joyful Wisdom*) points out that an individual with a sense of superabundance or a sufficiency of things will also naturally feel he has enough to spare for others, so that a certain sort of generosity also exhibits self-sufficiency. However, there is a difference, with regard to degree of self-sufficiency, between a momentary sense of satisfaction and enoughness that is reflected in momentary generosity and a more long-term sense of sufficiency (a sense, e.g., of 'having it made' or being fixed for the indefinite future or for life) that might naturally exhibit itself in a long-range *commitment* to caring or doing for others. What exhibits such greater self-sufficiency is more admirable (or, given adjustments in the metric, less criticizable), and this bears upon the evaluation of libertarian/democratic meritocracy as a social form.

In a meritocracy, if most people who make more are not generous to the less successful, because they are greedy for more and more wealth or benefits, we can virtue-ethically base a claim of social injustice on the lack of self-sufficiency demonstrated by (a class of) individuals. But even if the better off do give to charity, they evince a less long-range and confident sense of having enough if they insist on always keeping the prerogative of charitable giving or not-giving in their own hands and, by contrast, a greater self-sufficiency if they are willing, so to speak, to tie their own hands through legislation that mandates welfare benefits, progressive taxation, and the like. Such a society demonstrates more generosity and self-sufficiency in what it does with its limited abundance than any sort of meritocracy, and the resultant greater equalization of socioeconomic benefits may be taken, on our theory, as a condition of full social justice.

This result is more than a little reminiscent of Rawls' arguments (1971, pp. 105f.) via the largely egalitarian difference principle against meritocracy (the difference principle, roughly, restricts inequalities to those that most benefit the worst-off members of society); and indeed it is not clear that the social evaluations yielded by a virtue ethics emphasizing motivational self-sufficiency would have to diverge in any great way from those to be found in *A Theory of Justice*. But of course the bases of the evaluations are fundamentally different. We have been defending liberal democratic ideals of (greater) socioeconomic equality and of the powers and liberties of citizens through an ethics that treats the virtue of self-sufficiency as fundamental to understanding social justice. Rawls uses Kantian ideas and the device of a social contract to achieve somewhat similar results. But given the criticisms that have been made of Rawls' whole argument, it is good to be able to defend liberalism on a quite different basis, and the near-coincidence with Rawls' view may not only free virtue ethics from the historically justified suspicion that it is anti-democratic and not really viable as an overall approach to ethical/political questions, but also cause us to look at Rawls' theory in a new light – perhaps even with new hopes.

In addition, the present virtue ethics can speak to the issue of human or political rights, though, again, on a different foundation from that usually associated with talk of rights (though remember that utilitarians too can find ways of speaking about and defending rights). Where ruling elites defend their leisure (and power) by preventing or repressing freedom to criticize the government or to organize unions or to have a say in who governs, they act unjustly and the institutions that exist are unjust, according to our account. But there is every reason to tie the notion of rights to the ideal of self-sufficiency in similar fashion and say that one has a right not to be treated in a certain way (e.g. denied freedom of speech) if such treatment exhibits the opposite of admirable self-sufficiency (it will then also count as unjust) and/or if the virtue-ethical ideals of self-sufficiency (and thus also of justice) require institutions to be set up for the prevention of such treatment. This is the merest hint of what the present kind of virtue ethics can do to anchor the notion of rights in its own fundamental categories, and indeed our whole discussion here is but the sketch of a view that needs working out in detail. I have said nothing, for example, about the issues of parasitism that arise in connection with welfare dependency and have not spoken of cases where people do not want or do not seek voting rights or unionization because of a kind of sour grapes attitude to such privileges or because, quite independently of being manipulated by the wealthy, they think they would be worse off under democracy – topics much discussed by Jon Elster (1985, esp. pp. 413–28, 505). Nor have I spoken of the requirements of justice in conditions of extreme scarcity or in preliterate societies.

But it should at least be possible at this point to see that the ancient ideal of self-sufficiency contains depths or aspects not appreciated in the ancient world but revealed to us in and through the ideas of Kant, Rousseau, Hegel and Nietzsche that I have been drawing on in our discussion. Aristotle has been the major influence informing the recent revival of interest in virtue ethics, but it is very difficult to see how to deploy Aristotelian ideas toward the explanation and justification of democratic or liberal/egalitarian values. An approach of the kind sketched here may be better able to accomplish this task and for that reason, if no other, preferable to Aristotelian-like virtue ethics. In any event, we are perhaps only just beginning to see how much virtue ethics has to offer contemporary ethical and political philosophy.

See also I ANALYTICAL PHILOSOPHY; 4 SOCIOLOGY; IO FEMINISM; I3 SOCIALISM; I4 AUTONOMY; I7 CONSTITUTIONALISM AND THE RULE OF LAW; 2O DIRTY HANDS; 32 REPUBLICANISM; 37 TOLERATION AND FUNDAMENTALISM; 39 TRUST

References

Braithwaite, J. and Pettit, P.: *Not Just Deserts: A Republican Theory of Criminal Justice* (Oxford: Oxford University Press, 1990).

Elster, J.: *Making Sense of Marx* (Cambridge: Cambridge University Pess, 1985).

Kant, I.: 'What is enlightenment?', in *Kant Selections*, ed. L. W. Beck (New York: Macmillan, 1988), pp. 462–7.

MacIntyre, A.: *After Virtue: A Study in Moral Theory*, 2nd edn (South Bend: University of Notre Dame Press, 1984).

————: *Whose Justice? Which Rationality?* (South Bend: University of Notre Dame Press, 1988).

————: *Three Rival Versions of Moral Enquiry: Encyclopaedia, Genealogy, & Tradition* (South Bend: University of Notre Dame Press, 1990).

Marx, K.: *Theories of Surplus Value*, 2 vols (London: Lawrence & Wishart, 1972).

Pocock, J. G. A.: *The Machiavellian Moment: Florentine Political Thought & the Atlantic Republican Tradition* (Princeton, N. J.: Princeton, University Press, 1975).

————: *Virtue, Commerce & History, Chiefly in the Eighteeth Century* (Cambridge: Cambridge University Press, 1985).

Rawls, J.: *A Theory of Justice* (Cambridge, Mass.: Harvard University Press, 1971).

Rist, J.: *Human Value: A Study of Ancient Philosophical Ethics* (Leiden: Brill, 1982).

Skinner, Q.: *The Foundations of Modern Political Thought, The Renaissance*, 2 vols (Cambridge: Cambridge University Press, 1978).

Thompson, D.: *Political Ethics and Public Office* (Cambridge Mass.: Harvard University Press, 1987).

Williams, B. A. O.: *Ethics and the Limits of Philosophy* (Cambridge, Mass.: Harvard University Press, 1985).

Welfare

ALAN HAMLIN

The concept of welfare and the structure of the welfare state are central themes of the normative political debate. But the word 'welfare' identifies a particularly contested part of the conceptual landscape that has been much trampled by economists, philosophers and political theorists, as well as a wide variety of more practical politicians, policy analysts and social commentators. Each group might be conceived as engaged on the production of a map which charts the salient features of 'welfare' and places them in relation to other features of the terrain – 'rights', 'needs', 'equality', 'government policy' and so on. Many maps have been produced, but an inspection of these various maps might not convince the observer that all relate to the same landscape. Some of the apparent differences are no more than differences of emphasis or perspective, and might be thought of as differences in cartographic convention. Some result from simple confusions. Others are more foundational and reflect importantly different views of the world.

Even when the concept of welfare is clarified, the nature of the state's appropriate response to claims of welfare raises further problems. A 'welfare state' might be conceived as a state which views the welfare of its citizens as the primary claim on its policy-making, or it might be conceived as a state which enacts particular 'welfare' policies. These two conceptions will not necessarily coincide, depending on the positive model of politics adopted. More generally, the route taken through the theoretical discussion of the concept of welfare will be a major influence on the discussion of the appropriate notion of the welfare state.

In this chapter I shall provide both a discussion of some of the existing maps of welfare, and some discussion of the use of these maps to guide the normative political debate. The essay is organized in three further sections. The first is concerned with the structure and content of the concept of welfare and the issues raised in considering alternative concepts of welfare. The second is concerned with the politics of welfare and explores the use of concepts of welfare in political discussion. The arguments are drawn together in the final section.

The structure of welfare

I begin with a simple sketch of the standard economist's account of welfare, and consider a number of interpretations and criticisms and a variety of alternatives and embellishments. This way of proceeding does not presume that the simple economist's view is especially favoured. Indeed, in the caricature version presented here, it is both implausible and extreme. But it does have the merits of being relatively precisely drawn, and of identifying many of the key issues.

The economist's map of welfare focuses on three essential features: individual welfare, social welfare and the relationship between the two. At the individual level, the standard economist identifies welfare with utility (Broome, 1991b and c; and Sen, 1991, debate the use and meaning of 'utility'), and argues for a preference satisfaction theory of individual welfare. On this narrow account individual welfare (or utility) simply consists in the satisfaction of the individual's actual desires – whatever they may be. Of course, even such a narrow argument depends on interpreting preferences generally, so that we are not restricted to the simple rankings of alternative bundles of consumer goods familiar from introductory economics texts. Preferences must be understood to include preferences over alternative social arrangements, over alternative distributions of income; more generally, over alternative states of the world.

With a preference satisfaction theory of individual welfare on board, our simple economist turns her attention to social welfare. Here she makes two importantly distinct claims. First, that 'social welfare' is the ethical value or 'goodness' of the social state under consideration. And second that social welfare depends only on individual welfares. The first of these claims is simply stipulative. Social welfare, in the standard economist's usage, is intended to identify the overall good of society, all things considered, and not merely an aspect of the good. With this in mind, the second claim is clearly very strong. It says that the good of society depends only on individual welfare. This is the claim labelled 'welfarism' (Sen, 1979). Welfarism together with the preference satisfaction theory of individual welfare define the core of the mainstream economist's account of welfare. Each provides the starting point for further debate.

Individual welfare

Before exploring further, it is important to expose an ambiguity in the relationship between preferences, choices and welfare. On the one hand (as sketched above), preferences may be conceived as being substantively exogenous characteristics of individuals, defined independently of the individual's choices. This then leaves the relationship between preference and choice for separate theorizing – preference may be one among many potential motivators of choice, but there can be no *a priori* guarantee that individual choice will directly reflect preference. In particular, it is meaningful to suggest that an individual might choose to do π when ϕ was available, despite preferring ϕ over π. This is the use of preference that connects directly with desires or wants.

On the other hand, economists sometimes use preference to refer directly to choice, so that a preference function simply represents individual choices, however those choices are motivated. In this usage, preferences are an analytic convenience rather than characteristics of the individual. To use preferences in this sense as the basis for welfare would be to elevate choice itself to normative significance. There may be some reason for such elevation – and I shall return to the point below – but it has no necessary connection with the satisfaction of underlying desires or wants. Throughout the remainder of this essay I shall use preference in the first of these senses.

Two further points of clarification are in order. First, the significance of satisfying preferences is normally taken to be the benefit that is thereby conferred on the individual whose preferences they are. This may seem obvious, but it does point to some potential pitfalls. Preferences may be satisfied in a formal way without benefit to the relevant individual – as when my grandfather's desire for me to marry was satisfied only after his death (or, less morbidly, only after his desires had changed). Alternatively, the benefit associated with the satisfaction of a preference may be achieved by means other than the satisfaction of that preference – as when the object of my desire can be perfectly simulated so that it is as if my desire were satisfied although, in fact, it is not. These pitfalls are of significance in some contexts but I shall not pursue them here (Parfit, 1984).

The second point concerns the aggregation of welfare over time and the possibility of discounting future welfare. Of course, it is accepted that the uncertainty of the future may lead one to discount future benefits relative to present benefits, and that investment opportunities would lead one to discount material goods in the future relative to the present, but the question is whether a pure discount rate that is intended to operate on welfare itself after all uncertainty has been accounted for should be zero or positive. This debate continues and has major implications, but I shall not go into details here (Sen, 1967; Parfit, 1984).

The most obvious question to ask of any theory of individual welfare is whether welfare is intended as a complete description of an individual's good or, if not, how good and welfare are related at the individual level. The plausibility of any particular account of welfare will depend on the answer to this basic question. If welfare is identical with good, the simple preference satisfaction theory of welfare is clearly open to attack from positions which identify aspects of the good claimed to be unrelated to preference satisfaction – 'needs satisfaction', 'freedom', and so on. But if welfare is held to be only one among several aspects of the good, such criticisms are easily avoided, and the real challenges to the preference satisfaction theory of welfare are to justify the attention paid to this particular aspect of individual good, and to discuss the relationship between welfare and other aspects of the good.

One criticism of the standard economist's account sketched above is that it tempts the reader to slip from the narrow usage of welfare as utility to the broad use of welfare as individual good. Although there is nothing in the preference satisfaction theory of welfare that commits one to the view that welfare is identical to good at the individual level, the welfarism that often accompanies the preference satisfaction theory of welfare might suggest that this is, in fact, the view taken. However, an alternative is available, which combines a preference satisfaction theory of individual welfare with welfarism without involving a commitment to the identity of individual welfare and individual good. This possibility might be termed the anti-paternalist position (Dworkin, 1972). The argument is essentially epistemic. While it is accepted that there are aspects of the good outside the satisfaction of preferences, it is argued that it is impossible to know what these aspects of the good require. Preference satisfaction is not the only aspect of the good, but it is the only aspect of the good that is conceptually knowable. Any attempt to impute good to an individual on evidence other than that individual's preferences must be in some sense paternalistic. A possible response to this anti-paternalist position is that some aspects of individual good are objective, and so may be known without reference to particular individuals. We may know that ϕ is good for Anne simply in virtue of Anne being a person, even though we have no insight into Anne's mind or character.

Against this background, we may consider, very briefly, just three of the leading alternatives to the preference satisfaction theory of individual welfare: the informed preference theory, a theory based on needs, and a theory based on autonomy or freedom (Brandt, 1982; Schwartz, 1982, Griffin, 1986).

An informed preference theory holds that actual preferences may be a defective basis for individual welfare just in case the actual preferences are not those which the individual would hold after full consideration and if she was fully informed. Actual preferences may be simply mistaken, as in the case where I prefer brown bread to white bread because of a mistaken belief that their nutritional properties differ. Actual preferences may also be ill-considered, as in the case where I prefer smoking to non-smoking without thinking through all the implications. The basic appeal of an informed preference satisfaction theory of welfare is that it eliminates these mistakes, and so grounds welfare on the true preferences of the individual rather than those she happens to perceive at any given time.

While this appeal is strong, it also provides a target for the anti-paternalist criticism. How are we to know an individual's informed preferences? One way out of this problem is to argue that while informed preferences are the fundamentally appropriate basis for welfare, actual preferences must be used as the only available guide to informed preferences. In this case, actual preferences will be accepted as the best available indicator of welfare, but the possibility of error will be built in to the analysis. A second escape route from the anti-paternalist argument is that at least some informed preferences are, in fact, objective and so are knowable in principle – one possibility here relates to individual needs.

Most modern accounts of needs stress that preferences and needs are categorically distinct. So that, for example, 'The concept of needs differs top and bottom from the concept of preferences' (Braybrooke, 1987, p. 5), or 'Needs are not a sub-class of desires. They are not, say, strong or widespread or central desires' (Griffin, 1986, p. 41; see also Wiggins, 1985). This seems clear provided that we are referring to actual preferences. I might need medical treatment without being aware of this need and so not desire or prefer the relevant treatment. But such examples rely on the gap between actual preferences and informed preferences. Is it plausible to claim that I might need medical treatment even if my informed preferences indicate no directly related desire?

A negative answer suggests that needs are just those objectively identifiable aspects of an individual's informed preferences. If so, the question arises as to the relationship between needs and other informed preferences. Some argue that needs should have priority over mere preferences or desires. But, at the individual level, it is difficult to defend this line of argument against the attack from the anti-paternalist argument, if the preferences and desires involved are informed. If individual A needs medical treatment and recognizes this, but nevertheless prefers (on the basis of full information and full consideration) to forgo that treatment in favour of some alternative, it is difficult to see that insisting that A's need be satisfied (and other informed desires sacrificed) could improve A's welfare overall.

The relationship between welfare and freedom or autonomy raises rather different issues. In the extreme, a freedom-based view might seem to deny the relevance of welfare altogether. What matters, in this view, is the individual's ability to act independently rather than the particular consequences of the actions taken. In more moderate views both freedom and the consequences of action might contribute to the individual good. In either case, what is significant is that freedom is valued intrinsically rather than instrumentally. A key question in this context concerns the appropriate method of conceptualizing freedom.

The standard distinction between positive and negative freedom is helpful here. Negative freedom simply requires the absence of coercion, and so choice or, more generally, voluntary action, is a direct indicator of freedom regardless of what is chosen or how the choice is motivated. The economist's second usage of 'preference' mentioned above connects with this view of the value of freedom. This view also suggests that expanding the range over which choice can be exercised will contribute to the good of the individual concerned regardless of the choices actually made. This is one aspect of the 'resourcist' position discussed by Dworkin (1981) and others, in which the extent of an individual's command over resources counts as an indicator of that persons ability to choose. The positive view of freedom, by contrast, would stress an individual's capabilities (see Sen, 1985a, b). In this context, capabilities indicate what an individual can do or can be, and so include elements that relate to characteristics of the individual – talents and disabilities, for example – and elements that relate to the resources and opportunities available to the individual.

At first sight it seems that any intrinsic evaluation of freedom must lie outside of the preference satisfaction theory of welfare, and this in turn suggests that welfare and freedom should be seen as two distinct aspects of the individual's overall good. But if freedom is valued intrinsically, who values it? Presumably the benefit of freedom is a benefit to the person whose freedom it is, and, if this is the case, we might expect that person's fully informed preferences to reflect this benefit. Again, we could argue that the conceptualization of welfare as the satisfaction of fully informed preferences is capable of accounting for our common intuitions regarding the value of freedom, and maintaining the formal identity of welfare and good at the individual level.

The strategy of the preceding paragraphs should now be clear. If it is plausible to claim that ϕ is good for individual A – where ϕ may be needs satisfaction, freedom, equality or whatever – it is equally plausible to claim that A's fully informed preferences will account for this fact appropriately. Indeed, it is difficult to see what else 'fully informed' could mean in this context. Furthermore, A's informed preferences will also provide the appropriate tradeoff between the various components of the good. In this way, we can argue that the fully informed preference theory of welfare is capable of being extended to a plausible theory of personal good.

Welfarism and social welfare

The credibility of welfarism depends crucially on the interpretation of individual welfare. If individual welfare is read as individual good (whether conceptualized in terms of informed preferences or not), then the claim of welfarism reduces to the claim that social good consists in individual good. That is, all individual good contributes to the social good, and nothing else contributes to the social good. This interpretation of welfarism is non-standard, since the term is used primarily in the context of the economists' narrow interpretation of welfare as utility, based on actual preferences. This non-standard view of welfarism is much closer to the principle of personal good advanced by Broome (1991a), and to other statements of individualistic theories of good (Raz, 1986; Hamlin and Pettit, 1989); but even so it is contentious. This expanded notion of welfarism denies the existence of irreducibly social goods (Taylor, 1990, and related discussion); that is, aspects of the social good that do not derive from the good of individuals.

If the distinction between welfare and good at the individualistic level is maintained, welfarism is clearly still more contentious. In these circumstances welfarism claims that while all social good is reducible to individual good, not all individual good is social good. Only that aspect of individual good that is included in welfare is to count at the social level. One possible defence of this version of welfarism builds once again on the anti-paternalistic argument. If individual welfare is defined in terms of actual preference satisfaction, then one might argue that although this misses some aspects of individual good, it is nevertheless the only solid foundation for the social good. Of course, such an argument may be attacked by claiming that some further aspects of the individual good are objectively knowable, so that these could, and should, be incorporated into the social good.

The move from individual welfare to social welfare also highlights the question of identifying the relevant population. This is of particular concern given the endogeneity of the population when considering policy options – most obviously in the case of health policy and policy on contraception, but also in areas such as environmental policy, safety policy and so on. The questions raised in the discussion of future generations are amongst the most difficult faced by social scientists. In part they relate to the question of discounting the future, in part to the interpersonal comparability of welfare, but most problematically they relate to the question of the significance of personal identity (Broome, 1988; Dasgupta, 1988; Parfit, 1984; Sikora and Barry, 1978).

The politics of welfare

Welfare enters the normative political debate at two distinct levels. The first may be summarized in the question 'Is welfare the business of the state?' Any affirmative answer to this question then opens up the second level of debate concerning the more detailed responses of the state to claims of welfare.

The first of these levels identifies the location of the classic debate between teleological and deontological schools of thought as applied to the state. The standard notion that teleology is concerned with the good, while deontology is concerned with the right, is sufficient to remind us of that while all teleological theories will regard considerations of welfare as a vital ingredient in the normative appraisal of the state, deontological considerations will work in quite a different way. Considerations of this kind would take us too far from the topic of the present essay, and so

I shall simply assume that the answer to the first level question is, 'Yes'. This still leaves a wide range of possibilities at the second level. The simple fact that the state should recognize considerations of welfare, says nothing about the nature of the recognition, or its implications for policy. It is this range of possibilities that forms the subject matter of this section.

The first distinction to be made is that between a political commitment to individual welfare and a political commitment to social welfare. In the former case the state may be conceived as a collective means for the promotion of individual ends, as suggested by Rawls' well-known phrase: 'society is a cooperative venture for mutual advantage'. In the latter case one might conceive the underlying purpose of the state as the maximization of social welfare (Sugden, 1989).

The political significance of this distinction is great, but not simple. At first glance it might seem that a commitment to individual welfare would lead to the politics of unanimity, with each individual able to veto actions which threatened her welfare; while a commitment to social welfare would allow of a greater flexibility in trading off one person's welfare against another's, with a more redistributive and interventionist result. But this would be to confuse the subject of the commitment with the form of the commitment. We might consider a state that is committed to individual welfare in the sense that no social or aggregate measure of welfare is of political relevance, but is committed to, say, guaranteeing that no individual's welfare falls below a certain level (assuming this to be feasible). Such a state may be extremely interventionist and redistributive without being in the least collectivist.

With this in mind, the second set of distinctions to be made concerns the form of the political commitment to welfare. The most obvious thing to do with the good is to maximize it; and it is hardly surprising that maximization plays a crucial role in the debate on the commitment to welfare. But simple maximization is not the only possibility, and it will be useful to focus on three cases: simple maximization, maximization with minimum constraints, and maximization with equality constraints.

Simple maximization is precisely that in the case of a commitment to social welfare; but in the case of a commitment to individual welfare simple maximization may be interpreted as the maximization of each individual's welfare subject to there being no tradeoff between individuals. Thus, in maximizing A's welfare we may not reduce B's. This notion relates directly to the economists' notion of Pareto efficiency (which is more normally discussed in terms of the narrow concept of welfare as utility). All states of the world in which no further improvement in any individuals' welfare can be attained without reducing the welfare of another are Pareto efficient.

The imposition of minimum constraints may be thought of as building an aversion to poverty into the commitment to welfare (Barry, B., 1990; Sen, 1981, 1983). The minimum constraint (which may be defined in absolute or relative terms) identifies the lowest level of individual welfare which will be tolerated, and this constrains the maximization process in either its individualistic or social form. One point should be noticed here. In the broad understanding of welfare as good, we may assume that each individual's welfare already accounts for their own aversion to poverty, so that to impose such minimum constraints on the maximization process might seem to be a breach of the broad principle of welfarism. That is, we might seem to be importing some valuation of poverty into the political calculus over and above those valuations held by individuals. And in one sense this is true, but it does not constitute a breach of welfarism. All that is required by welfarism is that social welfare depend only on individual welfare, it does not specify the form of that dependence. The imposition of a minimum constraint on the process of maximization merely identifies the form of the relationship between individual and social welfare (see Broome, 1991a, for detailed discussion).

The imposition of equality constraints may be thought of as building inequality aversion into the commitment to welfare. The equality constraint identifies the maximal extent of interpersonal inequality that will be tolerated, and this constrains the maximization process in either its individualistic or social form. Of course, one might wish to incorporate both a minimum constraint and an equality constraint, and other forms of constraint may be motivated; the point is simply that such concerns can be incorporated within the general structure of the maximization of either individual or social welfare.

With all this in mind, we come, at last, to the question of the appropriate response of the state to claims of welfare. Clearly any state that responds to claims of welfare might be said to be a 'welfare state', but that title tends to be reserved for states in which the response takes particular forms (contrast the discussions in: Weale, 1983; Plant, 1985; 1991; Goodin, 1988; Barry, N., 1990). We are now in a position to understand how different groups may come to widely different substantive positions on the particular forms of the response to claims of welfare by taking different routes through our discussion of welfare. Two examples will illustrate the point.

Case 1

Accept the broad definition of individual welfare as good, and the conceptualization of welfare as informed preference satisfaction. But also accept the anti-paternalist critique, so that actual preferences are regarded as the only available guides to individual welfare. Furthermore, accept the political commitment to the simple maximization of welfare in the individualistic, Paretian, sense. In this case the appropriate political response to the acknowledged claims of welfare might be argued to be to rely on the market as a means of achieving the desired objective (subject to the standard battery of qualifications concerning monopoly and other institutional market failures) via the standard result that the outcome of a set of competitive markets will be Pareto efficient relative to the preferences actually held by the participating individuals. In this case, then, a particular brand of commitment to welfare produces a political response of a type normally held to be in sharp contrast to the 'welfare state'.

Case 2

Accept the broad definition of welfare as good, and the conceptualization of welfare as informed preference satisfaction. Also accept that certain informed preferences can be known objectively – label these 'needs'. Accept the political commitment to the maximization of social welfare subject to both minimum and equality constraints. In this case the appropriate political response to the acknowledged claims of welfare may involve the state in redistributive activity in response to the constraints on the maximization of social welfare, and in the direct supply of certain goods or services in amounts greater than would be consumed voluntarily so as to satisfy the objectively identified 'needs' for those goods or services. If we include education, health services and housing services among the identified 'needs' we can see that this case roughly approximates the political conception of the 'welfare state' (on the relationship between the specific 'goods' of education and health care and welfare, see Daniels, 1985; Gutmann, 1987).

Clearly, different routes through the conceptual discussion of welfare could lead to a wide range of alternative positions – each of which could legitimately claim to be based on considerations of welfare, but each advocating a distinct approach to policy. At the same time. it is possible to argue that the policies and structures that might be thought as characteristic of the welfare state can be justified in a wide variety of ways, some of which might have little connection with the traditional welfare concerns with needs, equality, and so on. Again, an example may help to underline this point.

Consider the provision of health services via a system involving no fees at the point of service and financed out of income taxation. Such a policy might be justified in welfare terms by reference to an objective need for health care, perhaps combined with some commitment to positive freedoms and capabilities, or some commitment to equality of access. However, it might also be possible to justify an essentially similar policy from a starting point which accepted none of these commitments. It might be argued that the health care market suffered from a particular range of market imperfections and that the policy was a reaction to these market imperfections rather than a reaction to any particular characteristics of health care *per se*. Thus, it is the asymmetry of information as between the demander (the patient) and the supplier (the doctor), or the possible failure in the market for medical insurance, that are at the root of the argument for the policy, rather than any conception of a need for, or positive right to, health care (for related discussion see Culyer, 1989). Or we might base a health policy of the sort described on more deontological considerations which might operate to identify, say, a duty on the relatively rich to support the health of the relatively poor, without any consideration of the welfare implications of such a duty.

We are left with a problem regarding the best way to define a welfare state. Do we categorize states according to the arguments that are taken as valid in considering policies, or do we categorize states according to the policies that are enacted regardless of their origins? Both approaches have their merits, but they should not be confused. Claims of welfare do not necessarily give rise to what are normally regarded as welfare policies, and welfare policies may be derived from other starting points.

In order to make further progress with this problem, we need to set the normative politics of welfare in the context of a more positive political analysis. For example, if we conceive of democratic politics in terms of the interaction of rational individuals within a framework of rules governing collective decision-making procedures, then it is clear that policies are to be explained in terms of the interaction of the preferences of the individuals making up society and the rules of the political game – the constitution. In this framework there is no central decision-maker who must respond to claims of welfare (or claims of any sort); rather the political decisions will emerge from the complex interaction within the political process. In this context, then, what matters are the political outcomes – the state will be a 'welfare state' to the extent that it enacts certain policies since no real sense can be given to the notion of the argument leading to that outcome. There is no single effective argument, just the myriad of particular actions of individuals within the political process.

Two points stand out in this setting. The first is that the actions of individuals within the political process are presumably motivated (at least in part) by their actual preferences over the considered alternatives, rather than any idealized or fully informed preferences; so that the welfare properties of political outcomes might be expected to fall short of the normative ideal to the extent that political choices do not reflect fully informed preferences. The second is that for any set of individuals the outcomes will depend on the design of the constitutional rules. This suggests that it is in the design of the political process itself that we can exert some influence over the extent to which the state displays the character of a welfare state. If politics is to be more sensitive to underlying claims of welfare (in whatever sense) this must be achieved by restructuring the political process in such a way that it can distinguish true claims of welfare from observed political behaviour.

Of course, the discussion of the last two paragraphs has taken place within the context of a particular positive model of politics, and other models are available (such as the deliberative democracy discussed by Cohen and Rogers, 1983; Cohen, 1989). The general point is simply that the factors which contribute to the realization of a welfare state will depend on the particular positive model of politics that is maintained, as well as the underlying conceptualization of welfare.

Final remarks

The concept of welfare and the role it plays in normative political analysis are topics that are hotly debated. I have done no more than hint at some of the points under debate and their significance, and so provide a guide to the various maps of welfare in current use.

Our brief tour of some of the key issues involved in the conceptualization of welfare suggests that the informed preference theory of individual welfare together with the extended notion of welfarism provide the best conceptualization of welfare at the individual and social level. A clear limitation of this position is indicated by the antipaternalistic, epistemic argument. It may well be the case that the informed preference theory provides an appropriate conception of personal welfare as good, but this may be of little practical significance if we do not and cannot know an individual's fully informed preferences.

This problem focuses attention on two alternative proxies for an individual's fully informed preferences – that individual's actual preferences, and arguments concerning the objectively good. Arguments of the second kind are often presented as arguments of need, or arguments of positive rights, or arguments of equality, but the framework sketched here suggests that they may be understood in terms of claims about the content of fully informed preference. Much of the political debate concerning the appropriate response to claims of welfare derives from the tension between these alternative approaches to identifying the content of fully informed preferences.

The political role of considerations of welfare may be approached from either a normative or a positive standpoint. In terms of the normative evaluation of states and their policies it is clear that a variety of positions can be defended depending upon the precise specification of welfare adopted, and that even rather slight differences in this specification can lead to major differences at the level of policy evaluation. In this way the content of the concept of the welfare state may be seen to be very sensitive to the resolution of the debates identified above. At the positive level, the forces which tend to promote a welfare state (of whatever variety) will vary with the positive model of politics that is adopted. Politics may be conceived, *inter alia*, as the aggregation of individual preferences over social outcomes, as bargaining within institutional constraints, or as a process of public debate aimed at consensus. Only when a specific conception of politics is defended, and a specific conception of welfare defended, can the practical realization of a welfare state be debated without ambiguity.

See also I ANALYTICAL PHILOSOPHY; 4 SOCIOLOGY; 5 ECONOMICS; 6 POLITICAL SCIENCE; II LIBERALISM; I3 SOCIALISM; I4 AUTONOMY; I6 CONTRACT AND CONSENT; 22 DISTRIBUTIVE JUSTICE; 23 EFFICIENCY; 24 ENVIRONMENTALISM; 25 EQUALITY; 29 LIBERTY; 30 POWER; 3I PROPERTY; 33 RIGHTS; 35 SOCIOBIOLOGY

References

Barry, B.: 'The welfare state and poverty', *Ethics*, 100 (1990), 503–29.

Barry, N.: *Welfare* (Milton Keynes: Open University Press, 1990).

Brandt, R. B.: 'Two concepts of utility', *The Limits of Utilitarianism*, ed. H. B. Miller and W. H. Williams (Minneapolis: University of Minnesota Press, 1982), pp. 169–85.

Braybrooke, D.: *Meeting Needs* (Princeton, NJ: Princeton University Press, 1987).

Broome, J.: 'Some principles of population', *Economic Growth and Sustainable Environments*, ed. D. Collard, D. Pearce and D. Ulph (London: Macmillan, 1988), pp. 85–96.

————: *Weighing Goods* (Oxford: Blackwell, 1991a).

————: 'Utility', *Economics and Philosophy*, 7 (1991b), 1–12.

————: 'A reply to Sen', *Economics and Philosophy*, 7 (1991c), 285–7.

Cohen, J.: 'Deliberation and democratic legitimacy', *The Good Polity*, ed. A. Hamlin and P. Pettit (Oxford: Blackwell, 1989), pp. 17–34.

———— and Rogers, J.: *On Democracy* (Harmondsworth: Penguin Books, 1983).

Culyer, A. J.: 'The normative economics of health care finance and provision', *Oxford Review of Economic Policy*, 5 (1989), 34–58.

Daniels, N.: *Just Health Care* (Cambridge: Cambridge University Press, 1985).

Dasgupta, P.: 'Lives and well-being', *Social Choice and Welfare*, 5 (1988), 103–26.

Dworkin, G.: 'Paternalism', *The Monist*, 5 (1972), 64–84.

Dworkin, R.: 'What is equality?', *Philosophy and Public Affairs*, 10 (1981), 185–246, 283–345.

Goodin, R. E.: *Reasons for Welfare* (Princeton, NJ: Princeton University Press, 1988).

Griffin, J.: *Well-being: its Meaning, Measurement and Moral Importance* (Oxford: Oxford University Press, 1986).

Gutmann, A.: *Democratic Education* (Princeton, NJ: Princeton University Press, 1987).

Hamlin, A. and Pettit, P.: 'The normative analysis of the state: some preliminaries', *The Good Polity*, ed. A. Hamlin and P. Pettit (Oxford: Blackwell, 1989), pp. 1–13.

Parfit, D.: *Reasons and Persons* (Oxford: Oxford University Press, 1984).

Plant, R.: 'The very idea of a welfare state', *Defence of Welfare*, ed. P. Bean, J. Ferris and D. Whynes (London: Tavistock Publications, 1985), pp. 3–30.

————: *Modern Political Thought* (Oxford: Blackwell, 1991).

Raz, J.: *The Morality of Freedom* (Oxford: Oxford University Press, 1986).

Schwartz, T.: 'Human welfare: what it is not', *The Limits of Utilitarianism*, ed. H. B. Miller and W.H. Williams (Minneapolis: University of Minnesota Press, 1982), pp. 195–208.

Sen, A. K.: 'Isolation, assurance and the social rate of discount', *Quarterly Journal of Economics*, 81 (1967), 112–24.

————: 'Utilitarianism and welfarism', *Journal of Philosophy*, 76 (1979), 463–89.

————: *Poverty and Famines* (Oxford: Clarendon Press, 1981).

————: 'Poor, relatively speaking', *Oxford Economic Papers*, 35 (1983), 153–69.

————: 'Rights and capabilities', *Morality and Objectivity*, ed. T. Honderich (London: Routledge & Kegan Paul, 1985a), pp. 130–48.

————: *Commodities and Capabilities* (Amsterdam: North-Holland, 1985b).

————: 'Utility: ideas and terminology', *Economics and Philosophy*, 7 (1991), 277–84.

Sikora, R. I. and Barry, B., eds: *Obligations to Future Generations* (Philadelphia: Temple University Press, 1978).

Sugden, R.: 'Maximising social welfare: is it the government's business?', *The Good Polity*, ed. A. Hamlin and P. Pettit (Oxford: Blackwell, 1989), pp. 69–86.

Taylor, C.: 'Irreducibly social goods', *Rationality, Individualism and Public Policy*, ed. G. Brennan and C. Walsh (Canberra: Australian National University, 1990), pp. 45–63.

Weale, A.: *Political Theory and Social Policy* (London: Macmillan, 1983).

Wiggins, D.: 'Claims of need', *Morality and Objectivity*, ed. T. Honderich (London: Routledge & Kegan Paul, 1985), pp. 149–203.

INDEX

Index

665